Views and Viewmakers of Urban America

UNIVERSITY OF MISSOURI PRESS, COLUMBIA, 1984

Views and Viewmakers of Urban America

LITHOGRAPHS OF TOWNS AND CITIES IN THE UNITED STATES
AND CANADA, NOTES ON THE ARTISTS AND PUBLISHERS, AND
A UNION CATALOG OF THEIR WORK, 1825–1925

JOHN W. REPS

TO MY WIFE CONSTANCE PECK REPS

Copyright © 1984 by The Curators
of the University of Missouri

University of Missouri Press,
Columbia, Missouri 65211

Printed and bound in the United States
of America.

All rights reserved

All illustrations are reproduced courtesy of the
institutions or individuals indicated in the captions.

The preparation of this volume was made possible
(in part) by a grant from the Program for Research
Tools of the National Endowment for the
Humanities, an independent research agency.

Library of Congress Cataloging in Publication Data

Reps, John William.

Views and viewmakers of Urban America

Bibliography: p.
Includes index.
1. Lithography, American—Union lists. 2. Lithography—19th century—United States—Union lists. 3. Lithography—20th century—United States—Union lists. 4. United States in art—Union lists. 5. Canada in art—Union lists. 6. City and town life—United States—Pictorial works—Union lists. 7. City and town life—Canada—Pictorial works—Union lists. 8. Catalogs, Union—North America. 9. Lithographers—United States—Biography. I. Title.

Z5961.U5R46   1984   [NE2454]   016.769′44′0973   83–6495
ISBN 0-8262-0416-3

Contents

Preface

This volume is an examination and catalog of all separately published lithographic city views of the United States and Canada. Although I began work on this project a number of years ago, the major portion of my research and writing was carried out during the period between June 1979 and August 1982. In those years a grant from the National Endowment for the Humanities to Cornell University allowed me to devote one entire academic year and four summers to the project. During that time I visited dozens of print collections and gathered information by mail and telephone from hundreds of others.

The grant also covered a substantial portion of the cost of converting all catalog entries into computer records and obtaining the large number of printouts that inevitably followed. This computerization facilitated analysis of the work of individual artists or publishers, made it easier to understand the geographic distribution of city views, allowed me to tabulate the production of views for any period of time or any region, and made it possible to search the records for a variety of other purposes.

I have divided the study into three parts. Part I consists of ten chapters of text dealing with how the views were drawn, the methods by which they were printed, the ways agents, artists, and publishers sold them, the purposes to which views were put by those who first bought them, how they were regarded by contemporary critics, their reliability in recording the appearance and character of towns and cities of past generations, and how they can be used today in historical analysis.

Part II presents notes on the urban viewmakers responsible for the bulk of the lithographic city views produced in the nineteenth century and the early years of the twentieth century. These are the artists and artist-publishers who created the original images that lithographers and printers made available in multiple impressions. Few of the names the reader will encounter in this section have found their way into biographical encyclopedias of American artists, and fewer yet have been the subjects of monographic studies or even essays in exhibition catalogs. Nearly all of these artists remain little known despite the efforts of several scholars in recent years to pull back the curtain of anonymity dividing them from us.

In nearly every note there are far more conjectural words and phrases than I would have preferred. Readers who find themselves dissatisfied with such words as *perhaps, possibly, may have,* and so on, can take comfort in knowing that I share their feelings. The truth is, however, that for many viewmakers there is little or no firm biographical information whatsoever and that for nearly all the rest there are long episodes in their careers about which very little or nothing is known except for the lithographs they drew, printed, or

published. I hope, therefore, that the notes will be looked on only as a starting point for further study.

My own modest success in turning Lucien R. Burleigh from a name into a person follows the work of others who have done the same for such figures as Thaddeus M. Fowler, Joseph J. Stoner, and Albert Ruger. Bettina Norton's full-length and informative study of Edwin Whitefield is not likely to be duplicated unless the diaries, scrapbooks, and original sketches of other view artists turn up as did his. Nevertheless, Norton's work demonstrates what a skillful researcher and an alert, imaginative, and perceptive mind can produce.

Part III records in a standardized and what I hope will prove to be a useful form the details of each lithographic city view located during the course of the project. The introductory notes to the catalog presented at the beginning of Part III explain how to interpret the catalog entries and point out possible sources of ambiguity, inconsistency, and error.

Each full entry in the catalog has been assigned a number. As is the case with other catalogs of this type, these numbers will inevitably be used to identify views referred to by scholars, dealers, and collectors. Nothing would please me more than to find a description of a print now unknown to me accompanied by the slightly triumphant or mildly reproachful annotation, "not in Reps." Nothing would please me less than to hear from a museum whose staff ignored my questionnaires asking about their holdings but now reporting that it has long owned some lithograph that I failed to record.

In any case, I would hope to be furnished full information about such views in the form used for the catalog entries. Although the thought of preparing a supplement is almost more than I can bear after the unexpectedly long time the catalog has required to compile, one will doubtless be needed.

While my efforts to locate and record as catalog entries the views of Canadian cities were as extensive as for those of places in the United States, my treatment of them in the text is inadequate. There is a limit to what one person can master, and I have been forced to leave to scholars of Canadiana the pleasure of analyzing the work of viewmakers in that country.

Elsewhere I acknowledge my almost unending obligations to persons who in one way or another contributed to this study. Most of them are curators, collectors, dealers, or catalogers of American historical prints. I hope that this work will prove useful in making their task easier and more enjoyable.

J.W.R.
Ithaca, N.Y., July 1983

The Color Plates

The color illustrations on the following pages provide a visual introduction to the views and viewmakers that are the subject of this book. They are a sample of the thousands of city views issued by the artists, lithographers, printers, and publishers whose work is recorded and discussed in this volume. These color plates suggest the broad range of the pictorial resource offered by lithographs of this type to persons concerned in some way with the study of American towns and cities or to those seeking enjoyment in the examination of old prints.

The views illustrate two approaches used to portray cities. Before the Civil War most artists, like those who drew these views of Montreal, Georgetown, Cincinnati, and San Francisco, preferred to show their subjects as seen from a moderately elevated viewpoint. Although the later lithographs of Pittsburgh and Minneapolis indicate that some artists continued this style, almost all of the views published after 1865 depicted cities from imaginary viewpoints high in the air.

The lithographs of Boston, New York, Charleston, Louisville, Colorado Springs, Cheyenne, and Phoenix are all examples of this heightened perspective. Views like this provide a better understanding of each city by revealing street patterns, locations of buildings, the appearance and character of every neighborhood, the size of the community, relationships between developed and undeveloped areas, the nature of the site occupied by the city, and its surrounding landscape.

Artists varied in their skills. Edwin Whitefield's Montreal and J. W. Hill's Cincinnati exhibit a level of sophistication that contrasts sharply with the much simpler and more direct town portraits by Albert Ruger of Louisville and Augustus Koch of Cheyenne. The latter view has an almost cartographic quality characteristic of so many other post–Civil War bird's-eye views.

Lithographic craftsmen also differed in how they achieved their effects. C. J. Dyer's view of Phoenix came from the San Francisco press of a firm specializing in labels for fruit and vegetable containers. The same vivid colors used for tomatoes, carrots, and beans appear on the lithograph. John Bachmann's high-level view of Boston represents another approach. His printer used many lithographic stones inked with soft tones and carefully blended them to create this unusual and striking print.

Some of these views were the work of local artists who did only a few prints of this kind: Dyer at Phoenix, Otto Krebs at Pittsburgh, and George Ellsbury and Vernon Green at Minneapolis. Others, like Ruger and Koch, traveled throughout the continent for many years literally drawing for their lives.

Another itinerant viewmaker was Henry Wellge. He may have drawn the splendidly conceived and beautifully printed panorama of Colorado Springs and vicinity issued by the company he headed. This view was published as the nineteenth century was drawing to a close and as the vogue for urban views began to wane. Soon aerial photographs would take the place of the pioneer viewmakers whose lithographs not only delight the eye but reveal so much about the character of American cities a century or more ago.

Color Plate 1. Montreal, Quebec, 1855. Detail. Drawn and published in Montreal by Edwin Whitefield,
printed in New York by Endicott & Co. (Amon Carter Museum.) Catalog 3773.

Color Plate 2. Boston, Massachusetts, 1877. Detail. Drawn and lithographed by John Bachmann, published in Boston by
L. Prang & Co. (Geography and Map Division, Library of Congress.) Catalog 1378.

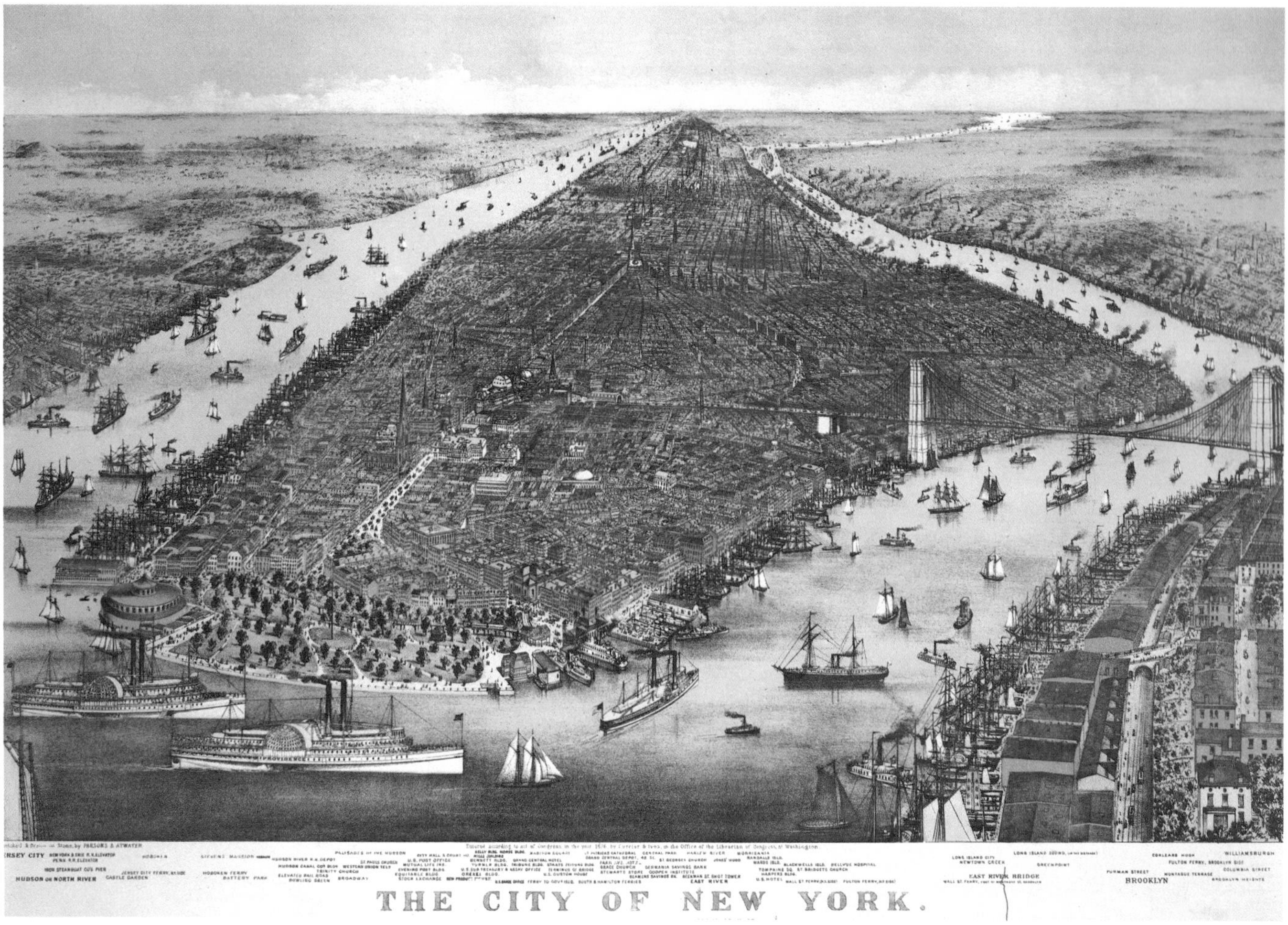

Color Plate 3. New York City, 1876. Drawn and lithographed by Parsons and Atwater, published in New York by Currier & Ives. (New-York Historical Society.) Catalog 2721.

Color Plate 4. Georgetown, Washington, D.C., 1855. Detail. Lithographed, printed, and published in Baltimore by E. Sachse & Co. (Prints and Photographs Division, Library of Congress.) Catalog 671.

Color Plate 5. Charleston, South Carolina, 1872. Drawn, lithographed, and published by C. Drie. (Geography and Map Division, Library of Congress.) Catalog 3901.

Color Plate 6. Pittsburgh, Pennsylvania, 1874. Detail. Lithographed by J. W., printed and published in Pittsburgh by Otto Krebs Lith. (Prints and Photographs Division, Library of Congress.) Catalog 3614.

Color Plate 7. Louisville, Kentucky, 1876. Detail. Drawn by A. Ruger, printed in Chicago by Chas. Shober & Co. (Geography and Map Division, Library of Congress.) Catalog 1135. (Overleaf)

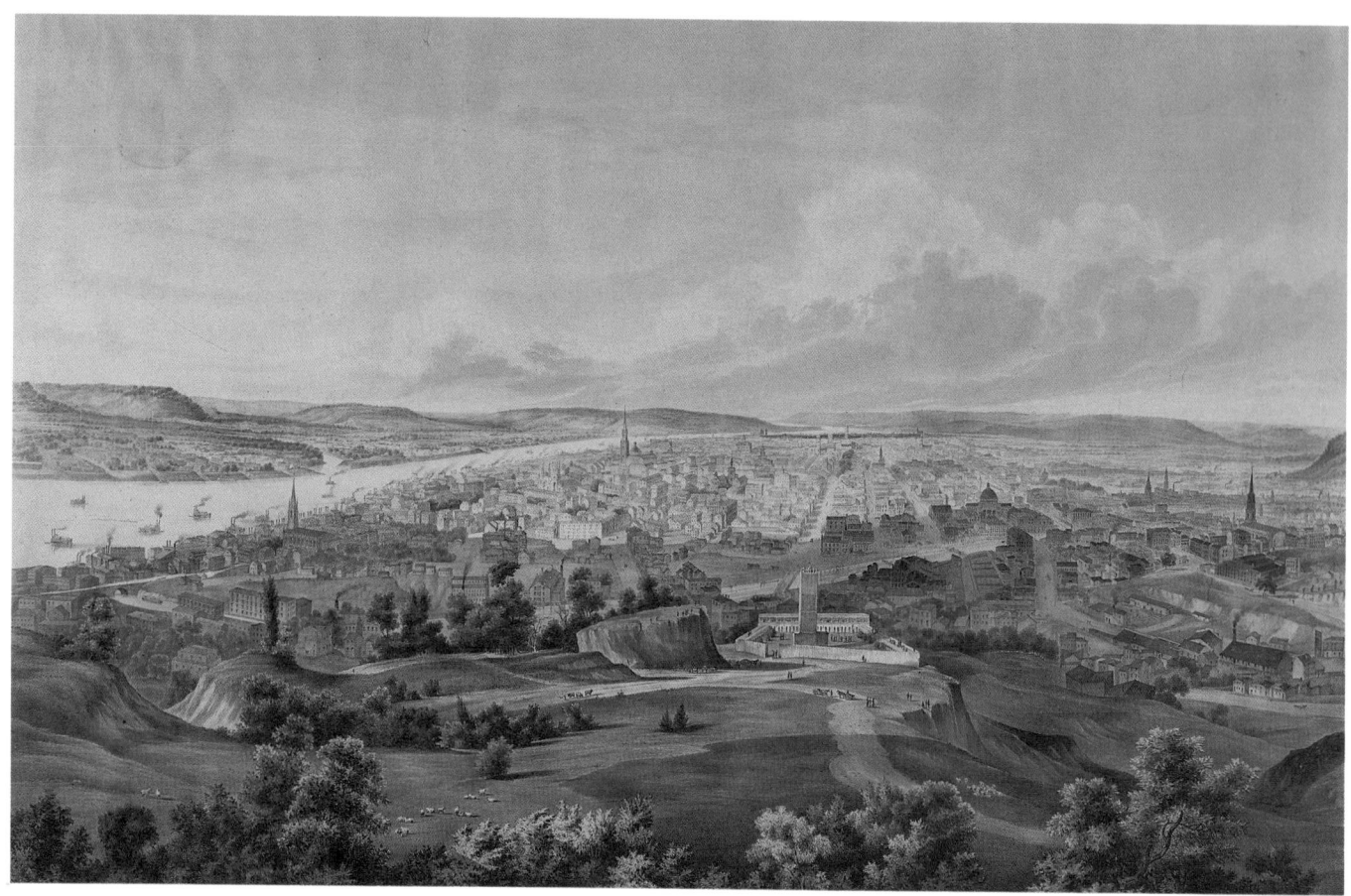

Color Plate 8. Cincinnati, Ohio, 1852. Detail. Drawn by J. W. Hill, printed in New York by F. Michelin and Geo. E. Leefe, published in New York by Smith Brothers & Co. (The Mariners' Museum of Newport News, Virginia.) Catalog 3055.

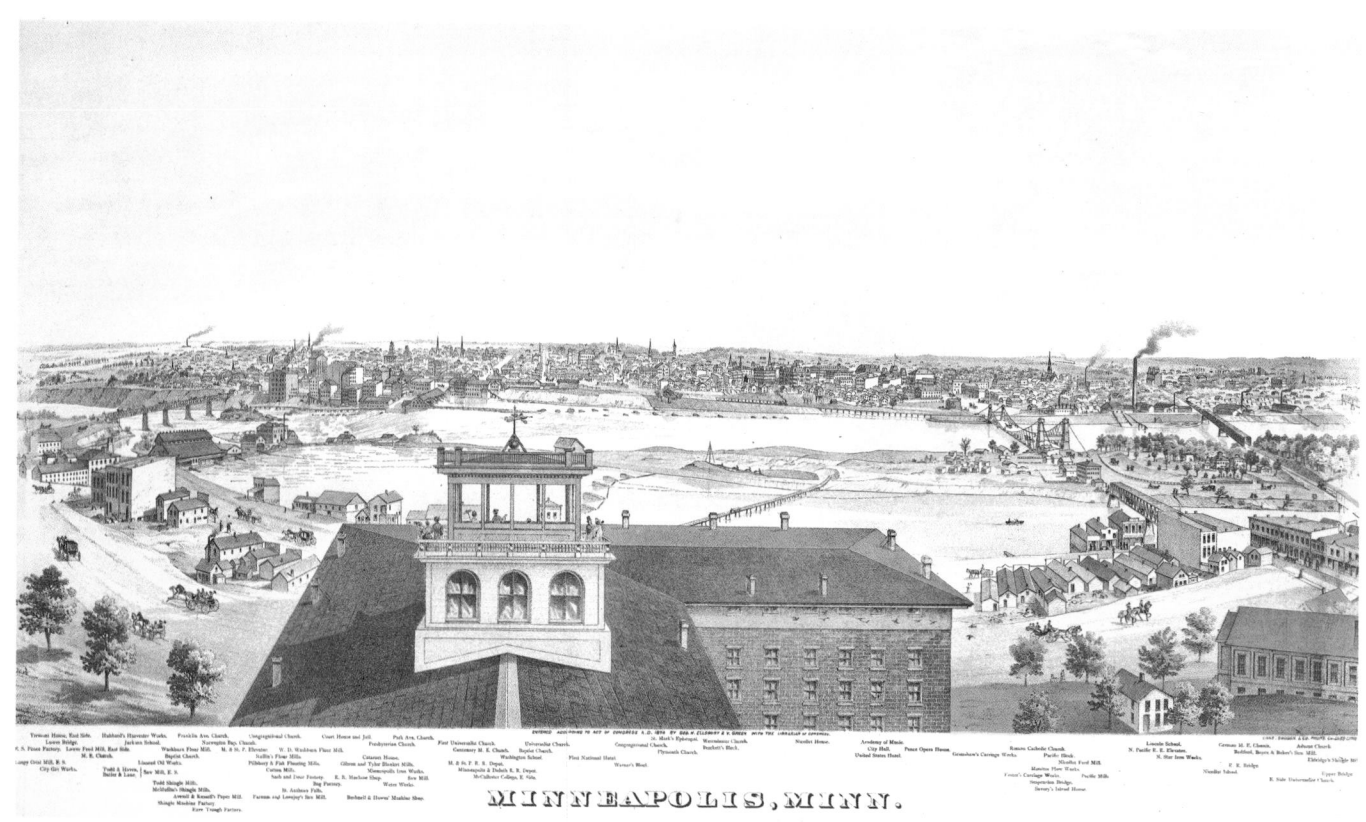

Color Plate 9. Minneapolis, Minnesota, 1874. Lithographed by Hoffman, printed in Chicago by Chas. Shober & Co., published by Geo. H. Ellsbury and V. Green. (John W. Reps.) Catalog 1923.

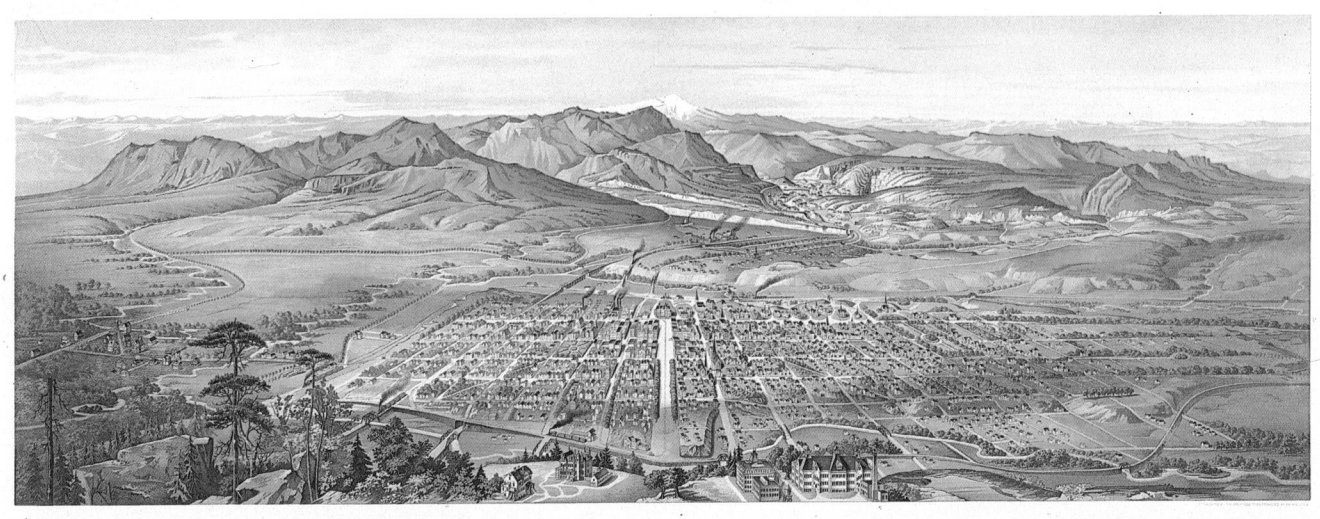

PIKES PEAK PANORAMA.

Color Plate 10. Colorado Springs, Colorado, and vicinity, ca. 1890. Published in Milwaukee
by American Publishing Co. (Amon Carter Museum.) Catalog 474.

BIRD'S EYE VIEW OF
CHEYENNE
LARAMIE COUNTY, WYOMING TERRITORY.

Color Plate 11. Cheyenne, Wyoming, 1870. Drawn by Augustus Koch, printed in Chicago
by Chicago Lithographing Co. (Wyoming State Art Gallery.) Catalog 4478.

Color Plate 12. Phoenix, Arizona, 1885. Drawn and published in Phoenix by C. J. Dyer. Lithographed by W. Byrnes, printed in San Francisco by Schmidt Label & Litho Co. (Geography and Map Division, Library of Congress.) Catalog 20.

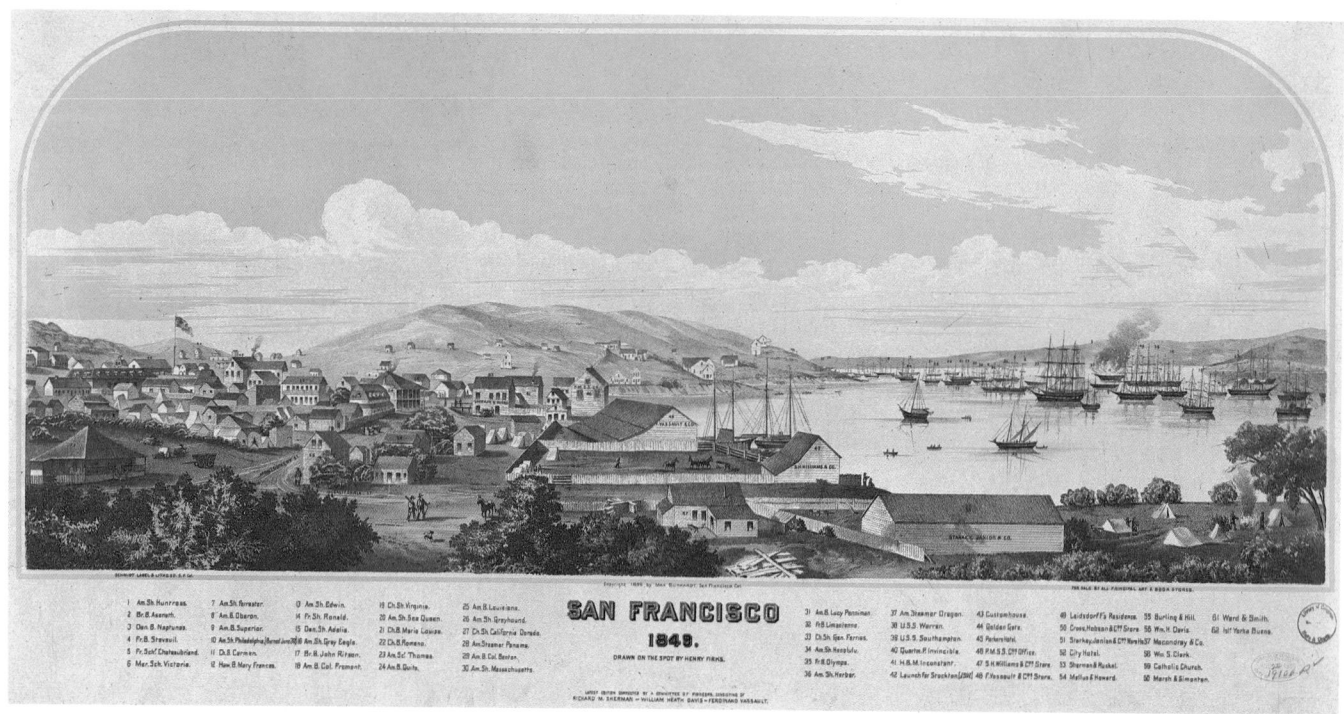

Color Plate 13. San Francisco, California, 1849. Drawn by Henry Firks, printed in San Francisco by Schmidt Label & Litho Co., published in 1886 by Max Burkardt. (Prints and Photographs Division, Library of Congress.) Catalog 344.

Part I

The Making and Selling of Urban Views

1. Urban Viewmaking: Artists and Publishers of the American Scene

Nineteenth-century Americans hungered for images of their country. They bought and displayed in their homes and offices portraits of their leaders; depictions of sailing ships, steamers, river craft, trains, and railroad structures; scenes of sporting events, athletic competitions, and hunting and fishing; pictures of flowers, birds, and animals; sentimental compositions of children and families; patriotic tableaux; prospects of the seas, plains, mountains, and forests; maps of the country, individual states or provinces, and urban areas; representations of naval and military engagements; caricatures and cartoons of politicians, business tycoons, and industrialists; pictures of fires, floods, and other natural disasters; perspectives of churches, factories, colleges, hotels, public buildings, and banks; and, indeed, almost any other aspect of the nation's life whose appearance—real or imagined—could be captured in pictorial form.

Views of towns and cities may have been the single most popular category in this mass of printed images. Before their popularity faded, nearly five thousand separate prints of this type came from printers and publishers located in a dozen or so centers of the trade. Some, like William Wilson's view of Lockport, New York, in 1836 (Plate 1), showed a town as seen from eye level with the buildings appearing against the sky, much as one sees scenery on a stage. Many others displayed their subjects from a slightly elevated position, thus creating a greater illusion of depth and providing some information about the appearance of buildings in the town beyond those visible only from the ground. Edwin Whitefield's lithograph of Toronto in 1854 (Plate 2) offers a good example of this type.

Most city views, including the great majority published after the Civil War, portrayed cities as if seen from an imaginary viewpoint high in the air. The lithograph of Lebanon, New Hampshire, in 1884 by George Norris (Plate 3) typifies these prints, which show every building, street, and open space of the urban community as well as the immediate surroundings. A substantial portion of the views of this type as well as some of the earlier, lower-level panoramas conveyed additional knowledge about the town through numbered legends or keys, passages of descriptive text, and detailed vignettes of individual buildings. A lithograph of Holyoke, Massachusetts, in 1881 drawn by A. F. Poole and published by J. J. Stoner (Plate 4) exhibits these features.

Before the fad for city views like these ended in the early decades of the twentieth century, resident or itinerant artists had produced at least one view each of as many as 2,400 places. More than thirty older or larger cities were the subject of ten or more of these prints each. At least ten metropolitan centers could boast of thirty or more views showing different stages of community growth and change and displaying the city from many vantage points.

As one early authority noted, the demand for these views seemed "to have become a universal hobby—almost a mania," while another mentioned their "immense" volume and commented that he would "hesitate to pick the most remote and unlikely place . . . in the United States and say that there was no lithographed view of it."[1] A few years later another student of American printmaking observed, "Town views form what is by far the largest single classification of lithographs and they are understandably the most popular."[2]

As these statements indicate, most of the viewmakers did use the medium of lithography to transform an artist's drawing into a printed image. Lithographic printing first came into commercial use in the United States early in the 1820s. It proved so cheap and easy compared with the traditional processes of engraving or etching that within another twenty years lithography dominated the market for popular prints. It was a method of printmaking ideally suited to the place and the time. The preparation of high-quality engravings or aquatints required skills that few Americans possessed.[3] These prints took more time and were more expensive. In addition, lithography made it easier to achieve tonal effects, and by the middle of the nineteenth century lithographic printers in America had mastered the art of color printing,

---

1. I. N. Phelps Stokes and Daniel C. Haskell, *American Historical Prints: Early Views of American Cities*, xv; and Harry T. Peters, *America on Stone: The Other Printmakers to the American People . . .*, 39. In my earlier study of views in the American West, I cited these two experts in an early paragraph that concluded with what proved to be an inadequate estimate of the number of views that had been published: "While no complete checklist of these views exists, it is possible to make a rough estimate that at least 2,000 different urban views were published between 1825 and 1900, and the number may well run to 2,500 or even 3,000." See John W. Reps, *Cities on Stone: Nineteenth Century Lithograph Images of the Urban West.*

2. Helen Comstock, *American Lithographs of the Nineteenth Century*, 41.

3. For an engraving, the artist or his engraver incised lines or dots on a metal plate—usually copper—with an engraver's burin and punch. These indentations held the ink that the press transferred to a sheet of paper placed over the inked plate. Aquatints were made by creating a grain on the plate with fine rosin dust and using this to achieve tonal effects. Outlines of images were formed by cutting through an acid-resistant ground with an etching needle. Exposed parts of the plate were then "bitten" with acid to create indentations on the plate where ink could be retained. After the first acid bath, portions of the exposed plate could be "stopped out" with coatings of ground if they were intended to print with less intensity. Successive applications of acid deepened the indentations so the artist could attain variations of intensity of the inked lines. Engraver's tools could also be used on aquatint plates, and in practice most aquatints represent combinations of etching and engraving.

which made it possible to dispense with slower, more expensive, and less uniform hand coloring.

Improvements in lithographic techniques and the growing demand for images showing the changes taking place in older cities in the East and the appearance of new towns on the ever-moving western frontier combined to exert a powerful influence on American graphic art. Donald Karshan put it in these words:

> Some print connoisseurs believe that it was only with the advent of the full-blown city-view lithograph that American print-making reached its first plateau of originality, making a historical contribution to the graphic arts. They cite the differences between the European city-view print and the expansive American version that reflects a new land and a new attitude toward the land.[4]

Those contributions were not primarily in the technical side of printmaking. As Peter Marzio has observed, "Europe remained the source of innovation and expertise for at least seventy-five years. . . . Only three patents for 'improvements in lithography' were granted in America between 1830 and 1860; not one was significant. After the Civil War the patents increased rapidly, but most dealt with methods for using steam power lithographic presses."[5]

Nor were the artistic contributions by Americans to the realm of city views any more original. Even before the discovery of the New World, artists in Europe had begun to depict towns and cities in ground-level panoramas and from wholly imaginary viewpoints looking down obliquely from above. Colonial settlements in America provided subjects for similar views printed in Europe as woodcuts or engravings, and in the eighteenth century some prints of this type came from colonial presses in Philadelphia, New York, and Boston. Most of the artists for the eighteenth-century views and for those produced in the early years of the new republic were European-trained. This tradition continued in the era of lithography, when the field was dominated by artists and craftsmen from England, Switzerland, France, and—above all—Germany who came to the United States for economic, social, or political reasons.

What was distinctively American about nineteenth-century lithographic viewmaking was the sheer number of images drawn, printed, and published and the fact that hundreds of hamlets and towns were recorded along with the small and medium-size cities and the very largest centers of population. The views were thus a democratic art form in that they reflected conditions in urban places of all types throughout the country, ranging from villages with no more than a hundred or so houses to the most populous metropolitan communities.

There is another typically American aspect to the phenomenon of nineteenth-century city views and their production. Most of the persons responsible for producing substantial numbers of these prints began as anonymous assistants to other artists or as their sales and subscription agents and then became artists themselves, publishers, and—in a few cases—owners of printing establishments as well.

The pictures of urban settlements created by these men also helped Americanize and assimilate large numbers of foreign-born immigrants. At a time when the level of education was not high and many of the country's new residents had difficulty with English, these views proved useful. Immigrants recently arrived from Europe might not be able to read easily a promotional booklet or broadside extolling the advantages of living in Minnesota, Nebraska, or the Dakotas, but they could readily grasp the message conveyed by a lithographed city view that urban services, jobs, and markets for their farm produce awaited them in places like St. Paul (Plate 5), Omaha (Plate 6), or Bismarck (Plate 7). Land speculators, townsite promoters, and civic leaders all used urban views to attract people and industry to their communities, often subsidizing the publication of the views to make wider distribution possible.

Because most of these prints reached the market tainted with commercialism of this sort, art critics have generally ignored them as beneath serious attention. That such a major artist as Fitz Hugh Lane and many lesser-known but obviously talented persons—John William Hill, John Caspar Wild, John Bachmann, Lewis Bradley, and George Robertson—drew such views before the Civil War is often overlooked or underemphasized (see Plates 8, 9, and 33). The fact that these prints were, as Joseph Baird, Jr., points out, "intended primarily as commercial ventures," has thus unfortunately prevented many from appreciating "their rich artistic and historic character [as] rewarding byproducts for modern scholars."[6]

The earliest American artists of lithographic city views regarded themselves somewhat more seriously. Such pioneer viewmakers as J. W. Hill, Fitz Hugh Lane, Henry Walton, J. C. Wild, and August Kollner embarked on careers in art that embraced more than topographic printmaking (see Plates 10, 11, and 12). Nevertheless, from time to time they turned to drawing urban portraits as a means of supplementing their meager incomes from doing oil portraits, painting landscapes, or teaching art.

These artists began work in the 1830s. Before these men began their work several lithographic city views had been published as book illustrations, and a very few others had been issued in separate sheets. However, it was these first artists of American urban lithographs who opened the way for many others to follow, developing an approach combining art with commerce that their successors were able to use to good advantage while modifying and expanding its scope.

Table 1 identifies the major American viewmakers and shows the periods in which they created their images of the towns and cities in the United States and Canada.[7] The length of each horizontal bar spans the time between the first and the last years of each artist's viewmaking career. As

4. Donald H. Karshan, "American Printmaking, 1670–1968," 27.
5. Peter C. Marzio, "American Lithographic Technology Before the Civil War," 215–16.

6. Joseph Armstrong Baird, Jr., "Foreword to the Catalogue," in Baird and Edwin Clyve Evans, *Historic Lithographs of San Francisco.*
7. In this and subsequent tables a single view may be counted under more than one name: for example, a view drawn by J. W. Hill and published by the Smiths; or a view drawn jointly by Hill and B. F. Smith; or a view jointly published by Whitefield and Smith. An initial attempt to limit the indications of responsibility only to artists was found to be misleading because drawing and publishing were so closely related and because, especially in the case of the more numerous views after the Civil War, the roles of artist and publisher were frequently exchanged.

Table 1. Years of Activity of Major American Viewmakers

	1840	1850	1860	1870	1880	1890	1900	1910	1920

J. W. Hill
Fitz Hugh Lane
Henry Walton
J. C. Wild

August Kollner
Edwin Whitefield
Smith Brothers
John Bachmann

George H. Baker
Kuchel & Dresel
E. Sachse & Co.
Charles Parsons

George Goddard
J. T. Palmatary
John Bachelder
Henry P. Moore

Grafton T. Brown
C. B. Gifford
A. E. Mathews
George H. Ellsbury

A. Hageboeck
Albert Ruger
Eli S. Glover
Augustus Koch

J. J. Stoner
H. H. Bailey
T. M. Fowler
D. D. Morse

O. H. Bailey
C. N. Drie
Herman Brosius
J. C. Hazen

Henry Steinegger
W. W. Denslow
C. J. Pauli
H. H. Rowley

Henry Wellge
W. W. Elliott
A. E. Downs
C. J. Dyer

T. J. S. Landis
A. F. Poole
W. V. Herancourt
L. R. Burleigh

George E. Norris
E. S. Moore
B. W. Pierce

■■■■■ Years in which views were produced
□□□□□ Years in which no views were produced

the table clearly shows, some of these artists turned to view-making for only a few years: Henry P. Moore, W. W. Denslow, and W. V. Herancourt, for example. Others, like Edwin Whitefield, T. M. Fowler, and O. H. Bailey, made it essentially a lifetime career. As the table also shows, several artists or artist-publishers did not produce printed city views regularly throughout their viewmaking years but often allowed many years to pass between one view and the next. Two Californians, George Baker and George Goddard, among others, fall in this category, as does New Englander A. E. Downs. By contrast, Albert Ruger, Augustus Koch, and George Norris—as well as Fowler and O. H. Bailey—worked steadily at their craft with no substantial intervals interrupting their productive years.

We know that Lane and Walton published their views on a subscription basis after displaying a drawing or painting of a town they felt offered a market for a lithographic print, and this was almost certainly the method used by their contemporaries in the 1830s as well. Only after securing enough orders to make the venture profitable would they go to the additional expense of putting the design on stone and having multiple copies printed for distribution.

Probably these first viewmakers asked editors to print favorable notices of their work in local newspapers. Beginning in 1845 with his lithographs of Albany (Plate 13) and Troy, New York, Edwin Whitefield made this approach a central feature of his subscription and sales efforts. He kept a scrapbook of newspaper clippings concerning his views. The wording of all the notices is so similar that it seems safe to conclude that Whitefield supplied newspapers with publicity releases describing and praising his own work.

Whitefield was the first lithographic viewmaker to travel continually and extensively in search of cities to draw. To help him he recruited sales agents. Two of these agents, B. F. Smith and J. T. Palmatary, soon began to produce their own city views, so it seems likely that Whitefield used his agents to help with drawing as well as selling the views. However, this was probably not regarded as a formal apprenticeship.

By the middle years of the 1850s the leisurely pace of earlier viewmaking accelerated as several new artists joined the ranks of those making a living from producing city views. B. F. Smith and his brothers issued their large and handsome prints of cities from New Orleans north to Halifax and as far west as Milwaukee. J. W. Hill drew many of these, including those regarded by some as the most attractive (see Plates 14 and 77).

A few years earlier Edward Sachse had arrived from Germany and settled in Baltimore to begin producing views of that city (Plate 15), Washington, D.C., and several other places in the region. John Bachmann, probably from Germany also, published his first view in this country in 1849 and a year later began to draw lithographs of such cities as New York (Plate 16), Philadelphia, and Boston. John Bachelder and Henry P. Moore were working in New England at this time, and both produced attractive prints of towns in that area. James T. Palmatary, either alone or with Edward Sachse, started a series of large, occasionally multi-sheet, lithographs of places in West Virginia, Ohio, Indiana (Plate 17), Illinois, and Missouri.

The output of these Eastern viewmakers is best understood and appreciated through an examination of Table 2. This shows the number of views produced by each artist, lithographer, or publisher in every year from 1834 through 1869. Several things can be noted from these yearly records: the slow development of viewmaking through its first decade, the substantial increases in the number of views and the number of persons involved during the 1850s, the depressing effect of the Civil War on this field of art, and the small number of artists active in the early postwar years who had entered the field before the conflict.

This table does not, of course, record all of the views that were being drawn and published, for many came from viewmakers whose output was limited to only a few lithographs. Others were drawn in America but printed and published in Europe to be sold both there and in the United States and Canada. French firms were particularly active in this trade, especially with views of New Orleans (Plate 18) and New York (Plate 19). A Swiss firm with offices in New York City also competed in eastern markets during the period before the Civil War with views of cities such as Philadelphia (Plate 20).

Although eastern and foreign viewmakers controlled the American market in these years and were responsible for nearly all the views done elsewhere in the United States, by the mid-1850s artists and publishers in San Francisco had created a new center of activity. Table 3 shows the names of those responsible for city views in this region, beginning in 1849 with George Baker's two lithographs of San Francisco printed and published in the east, and continuing through 1894, the year of B. W. Pierce's last recorded view.

California viewmaking in this period was dominated by two Europeans, Charles C. Kuchel and Emil Dresel, who settled in San Francisco and began a productive five-year partnership in 1855. In those five years they produced attractive and informative images of dozens of California mining towns and camps in addition to views of such towns as Nevada (Plate 21), Los Angeles (Plate 22), San Jose, and Stockton, California, and Portland, Oregon.

Before the Civil War several artists from the East visited California to draw a few of its towns and cities. After the war the number of easterners moving west and the volume of their work increased and far exceeded the handful of city views produced by resident viewmakers. Then, at the time of the great land boom in Southern California during the 1880s, a new group of local artists and publishers appeared and flourished before their output dropped sharply when depression put an end to the excesses of land speculation. The views drawn by B. W. Pierce (Plate 23) and E. S. Moore (Plate 24) are typical of land-boom lithographs.

Far more is know about the art and business of viewmaking as practiced by a number of persons who began work in the Midwest following the Civil War. Some of them, like T. M. Fowler and O. H. Bailey (Plate 25), began work there and then moved to other regions where they came to dominate viewmaking while occasionally visiting more distant locations to draw and sketch. Others, such as Albert Ruger (Plates 26 and 27), Eli S. Glover (Plate 28), and Augustus Koch (Plate 29), lived an itinerant life and traveled to many

Table 2. Prints by Eastern Viewmakers, 1834–1869
(Figures indicate number of views drawn, printed, lithographed, or published)

	1834	1835	1836	1837	1838	1839	1840	1841	1842	1843	1844	1845	1846	1847	1848	1849	1850	1851	1852	1853	1854	1855	1856	1857	1858	1859	1860	1861	1862	1863	1864	1865	1866	1867	1868	1869
J. W. Hill	4	0	0	0	0	0	0	0	0	0	0	2	0	0	0	0	2	2	4	8	2	3														
F. H. Lane		1	0	1	0	2	1	0	0	0	0	4	0	0	1	1	1	0	0	0	0	1														
H. Walton		2	0	1	1	1	0	0	0	0	0	0	1	0	0	2																				
J. C. Wild				4	2	5	16	0	0	3	0	2																								
A. Kollner									1	0	0	0	0	0	2	1	5	4	0	0	0	1	1													
E. Whitefield												2	9	4	3	6	4	1	5	1	3	6	1	1	3	0	1	5	0	1	0	0	1	0	0	0
The Smiths															1	5	6	2	8	10	5	3														
J. Bachmann																2	8	5	0	0	1	2	2	1	0	7	1	1	1	0	1	3	2	0	3	0
E. Sachse																	1	2	4	1	9	5	4	2	2	5	1	4	7	2	0	3	2	2	1	2
C. Parsons																		1	1	3	3	6	1	0	1	0	0	0	0	0	0	0	0	0	1	0
J. T. Palmatary																				2	6	4	6	1	1											
J. Bachelder																					3	6	18	5	2	0	0	0	0	0	1					
H. P. Moore																						1	2	1	3	2	2	1								

Table 3. Prints by California Viewmakers, 1849–1894
(Figures indicate number of views drawn, printed, lithographed, or published)

	1849	1850	1851	1852	1853	1854	1855	1856	1857	1858	1859	1860	1861	1862	1863	1864	1865	1866	1867	1868	1869	1870	1871	1872	1873	1874	1875	1876	1877	1878	1879	1880	1881	1882	1883	1884	1885	1886	1887	1888	1889	1890	1891	1892	1893	1894
G. Baker	2	2	0	0	0	0	0	0	2	1	0	0	0	0	0	0	0	0	0	0	0	0	0	0	1	0	1	0	0	0	0	0	0	0	0	0	0	0	0	0	0	0	0	0	0	1
C. C. Kuchel	2	0	0	0	0							0	2	1	0	1																														
Kuchel & Dresel							4	16	17	9	4																																			
G. Goddard				3	0	0	0	0	0	0	0	0	0	0	0	0	0	0	0	2	0	0	0	0	0	0	1	1	0	0	0	1														
G. Brown												1	1	2	0	1	1	0	2	1	1	0	2	0	0	0	0	0	0	1	0	0	0	1												
C. B. Gifford												3	0	4	1	1	0	0	0	1	2	1	0	0	0	0	1	0	1																	
H. Steinegger																															1	0	0	0	0	2	0	0	0	0	0	0	1	4		
W. W. Elliott																															1	2	0	0	0	0	2	2	6	7	6	14	5	1	0	0
C. J. Dyer																															1	0	0	0	0	2	0	0	0	0	1					
E. S. Moore																																									1	4	4	3	3	4
B. W. Pierce																																						1	0	1	2	2	1	0	2	1

states or provinces in search of markets for their products. A second generation of midwestern viewmakers who got their start a decade or more later also followed one of two directions in pursuing their careers. Lucien Burleigh, for example, settled in Troy, New York, and established a near monopoly on the market for views in New York State (Plate 30) and Vermont. Henry Wellge, by contrast, roamed the continent to visit twenty-seven states and territories in all parts of the United States and portions of Canada (see Plate 31).

Albert Ruger began the post–Civil War era of midwestern viewmaking in 1866. Table 4 shows his output of views for the first dozen years of his career. In the initial period of 1866–1870 alone his name as artist or artist-publisher appeared on no fewer than 164 views. This table also provides information about the viewmaking achievements of Ruger's most prolific contemporaries. All of these men began work in the upper Midwest, although by the early 1870s T. M. Fowler and the two Baileys had moved eastward and could no longer be regarded as part of this group.

Ruger and his former agent and then partner, Joseph J. Stoner, provided the links connecting these viewmakers. Evidently, Fowler, Glover, and Stoner all began in the field of viewmaking by serving as Ruger's sales and subscription agents. One or both of the Bailey brothers may also have worked for Ruger, but if not they learned all about viewmaking when they and Fowler began their close association in 1870. It would not be surprising to find that Koch or Brosius also worked for Ruger, but in any event these two would have heard about the artist's methods from Stoner, who published many of their views (see Plate 32).

Lithographic printers in Chicago and Milwaukee put on stone the views drawn by all of these artists, although, after they moved East, Fowler and Bailey soon turned to printers closer to their eastern bases. Glover helped found the Mer-

Table 4. Prints by Midwestern Viewmakers, 1866–1877

(Figures indicate number of views drawn, printed, lithographed, or published)

	1866	1867	1868	1869	1870	1871	1872	1873	1874	1875	1876	1877
A. Ruger	10	30	40	62	32	11	3	0	2	0	2	13
E. S. Glover			5	0	4	3	5	6	4	8	8	10
A. Koch			2	2	5	8	2	10	5	5	5	2
H. Bailey					9	22	7	4	6	14	8	2
T. M. Fowler					2	10	5	5	5	1	4	4
D. D. Morse					2	1	0	2	1	3	3	1
O. Bailey						1	2	3	9	15	16	22
H. Brosius						1	9	7	7	15	2	0
C. J. Pauli											6	1

chants Lithographing Company in Chicago and printed there many of the views drawn by Ruger until the fire of 1871 destroyed the enterprise. Clemens J. Pauli, who briefly joined the ranks of view artists in 1876 and 1877, established with Adam Beck the firm of Beck & Pauli in Milwaukee. Hundreds of city views came from their presses, including nearly all of the more than three hundred lithographs of towns and cities in thirty-three states and four provinces published by J. J. Stoner, who maintained his business address in nearby Madison but traveled extensively to promote sales of his views (see Plates 3, 4, 7, 30, and 31).

Although each artist developed certain variations on the basic technique of depicting cities, their common or similar experiences in learning their craft made it almost inevitable that their products all bore a family resemblance. Some of this consistency in appearance also came from the printers where the drawings were put on stone by lithographers. The work of the artist in the field was thus filtered through a process that imposed a certain degree of standardization as house lithographic craftsmen endeavored to maintain a uniform product.

Artists, publishers, and their agents likewise employed nearly uniform methods for promoting and selling views. Viewmakers in all parts of the country used these practices, but it was Ruger, Stoner, and their fellow midwesterners who adapted devices used in prewar years, added new elements, extended the scope of their operations to small towns, and with these revised sales techniques created a mass market.

Viewmakers sought and usually obtained free, continual, and favorable newspaper publicity. They found it easy to persuade editors that the publication of a view of their town would enhance its prestige, advertise its attractions, give pleasure and satisfaction to its residents, and promote its growth and prosperity. Just as in Whitefield's day, the similarity—sometimes the exact duplication of whole sentences—in news accounts in the last third of the century suggests that it was often the artist himself who provided or suggested the wording of newspaper announcements.

The sequence of editorial recognition soon became routine. A first notice announced the arrival in town of an art-ist, often accompanied by his agent and sometimes his publisher if the artist himself did not fill this role. The news account might mention that one or more views had been published or were contemplated of nearby and rival towns and that the visitors were considering such a project in this town. A week or two later a second news story stated that the artist was now at work sketching the buildings of the community and that he would shortly be exhibiting a preliminary drawing and accepting subscriptions for lithographic versions. The newspaper strongly supported this venture and urged citizens and business interests to do likewise and order one or more copies. A third announcement noted the completion of the drawing, referred to it as both appealing and accurate, called for subscribers to come forward in the numbers said by the agent or artist to be the minimum required to justify the expense of printing, and suggested that the eventual lithograph would be a splendid addition to the walls of every drawing room and business office and should be sent to other places in the country to show how attractive and prosperous the town had become.

Several days later, if all went well, the newspaper carried a brief story about the departure of the artist or his agent and reported that arrangements would be made for printing the view. Several months following this, the finished views, usually delivered by the agent, would arrive and be praised as fine examples of the lithographer's craft and even more impressive in appearance than the original drawing. The newspaper would add that subscribers were now being furnished their copies but that the agent had brought with him a few extra impressions that could be purchased by those who acted quickly.

In the early stages of such a sales campaign, the agent would have taken the initiative in seeking subscriptions by visiting residences and calling on businessmen. To the latter he would suggest purchase of multiple copies. With orders for more than a certain number might come a free listing in the legend or business directory at the bottom of the print, or the agent might charge a fee for the privilege of having one's business or profession recognized in this manner. The agent might also visit real estate offices, title companies, or similar enterprises soliciting even larger orders of copies

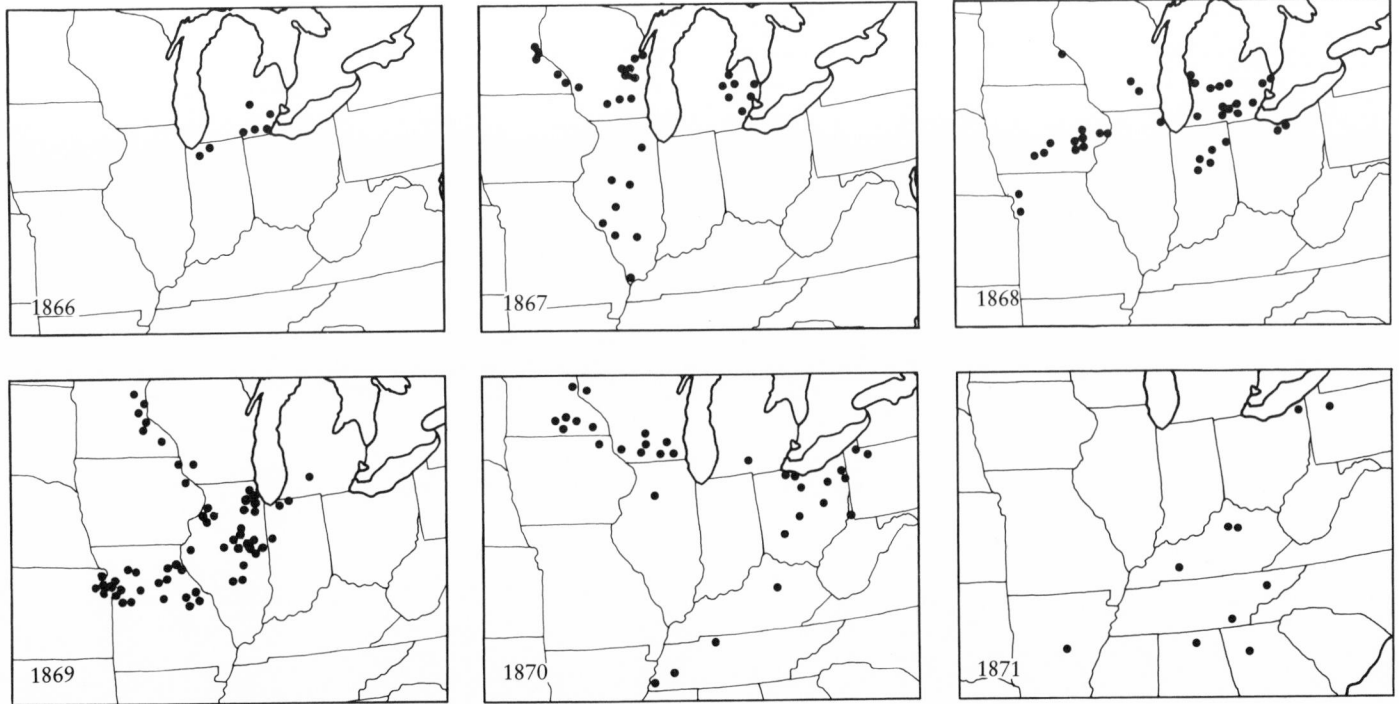

Figure 1. The views of Albert Ruger, 1866–1871.

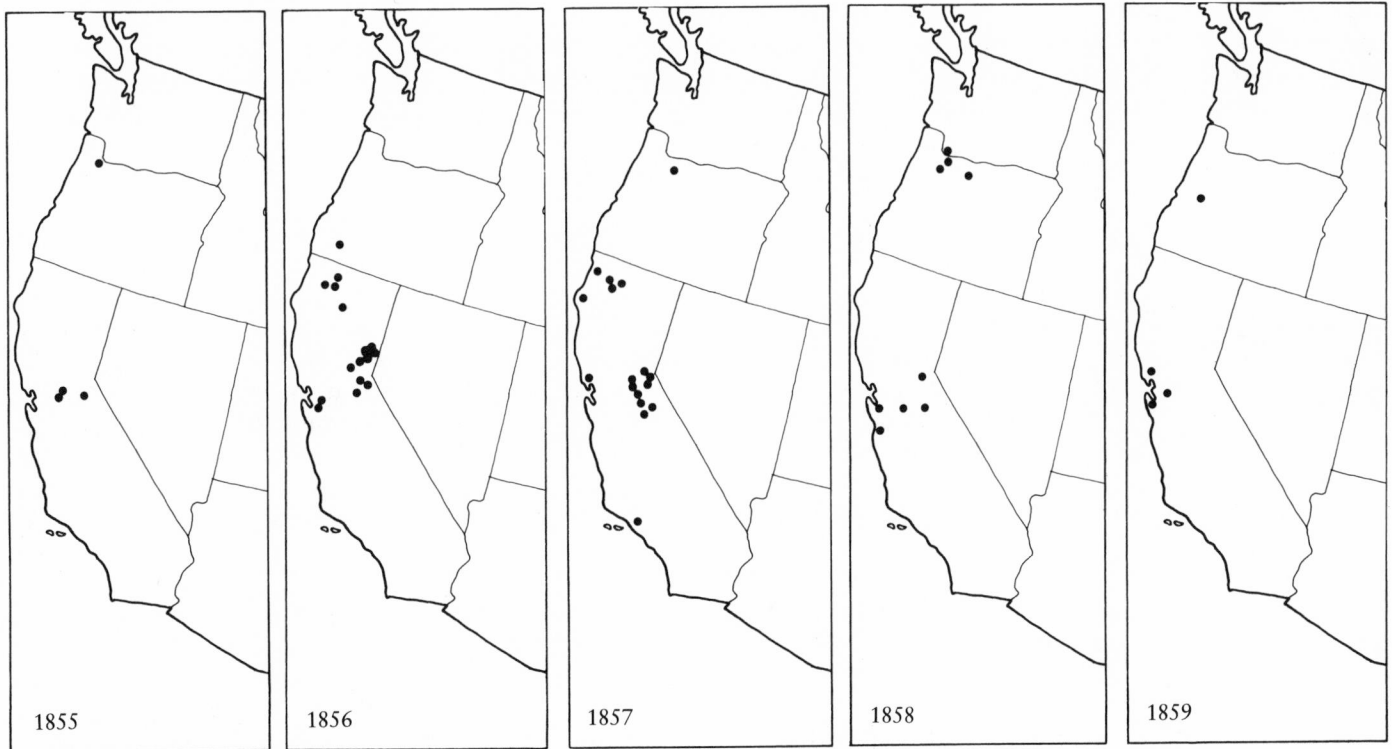

Figure 2. The views of Kuchel & Dresel, 1855–1859.

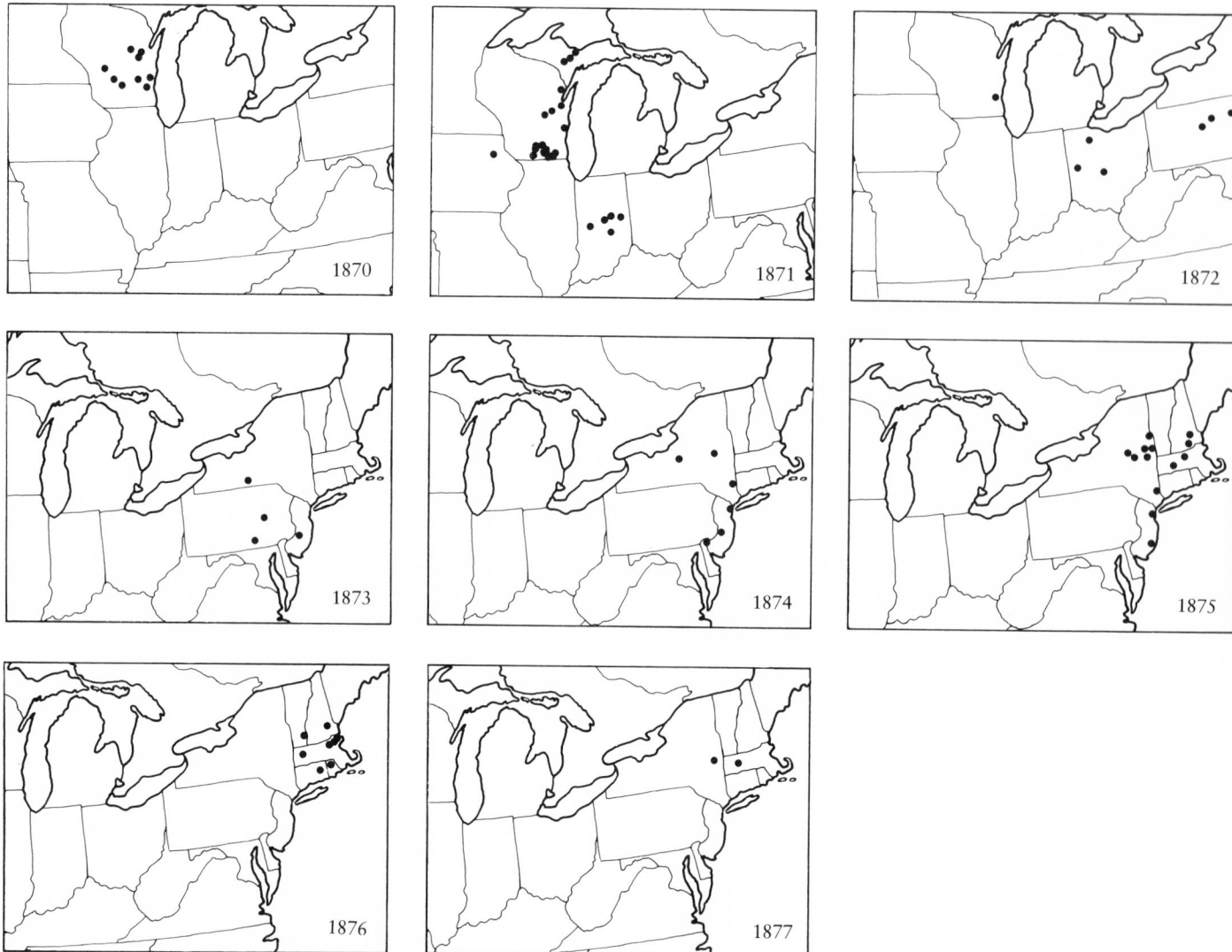

Figure 3. The views of H. H. Bailey, 1870–1877.

with an advertising overprint that could be used for mass distribution by the local entrepreneur. He might seek financial support as well from local governments, attempting to persuade city councils to subscribe for multiple copies to be used in advertising the town in other parts of the country.

For many publishers an important source of income lay in the sale of images that appeared on the sides or top of the lithograph as border vignettes. These smaller scenes showed mansions of the wealthy, churches, principal public buildings, industrial plants, office blocks, and a variety of retail and wholesale business structures. A person wishing his home or business to be given such special prominence was expected to pay a fee or at least to subscribe for many copies of the view. As the agent obtained agreements from owners for such an arrangement, he would notify the artist to prepare a more detailed sketch of the building than had been made for the general view.

The artist, meanwhile, was busy with the arduous task of sketching every building in town. Although he may have used whatever elevated viewpoints existed, in most cases the artist walked the streets and recorded what he saw in his sketchbook. From a town map or, if the place had been plat-

ted in the usual checkerboard pattern, from his own simple measurements and observations, the artist constructed a perspective grid showing the town's streets. On this he redrew the buildings from his sketches, taking care to make each one the correct size. From this rough sketch of the entire town the artist then produced a more finished and attractive drawing. He exhibited this drawing to obtain subscriptions, and if residents called his attention to errors or omissions he made needed corrections. The artist or his agent then sent or brought the drawing to the printer where a lithographer redrew it on stone. The lithographer might be guided in this by written instructions from the artist concerning some features not altogether clear on the drawing.

By that time the artist was in some other community to begin the process again. Some worked with almost unbelievable speed, drawing a dozen or more views a year. Others followed a more leisurely schedule, but most of them must have spent much of their time away from home in the peripatetic life of the itinerant artist. Maps showing the locations of towns and cities depicted each year by representative viewmakers make clear their patterns of work. For example, Figure 1 shows the locales drawn by Albert Ruger in the first years of his viewmaking career from 1866 through 1871. Fowler, Glover, and Stoner served him as agents for varying periods during this time, and they doubtless helped with some of the sketching and drawing as well. Even so, and considering that Ruger may have had other assistants as well, his record is remarkable in the number of views and their wide distribution.

Charles C. Kuchel and Emil Dresel followed a different pattern during the years of their partnership from 1855 through 1859. Operating from their base in San Francisco, they concentrated on the California mining towns, a few other places in that state, and the more important communities in Washington and Oregon. Figure 2 reveals the locations of the subjects they found for their lithographs.

Still another pattern emerges in Figure 3. These maps show the places drawn by H. H. Bailey from 1870, when he began work, through 1877, his last year of viewmaking before his death in 1878. Bailey began producing views in the Midwest, where he was closely associated with his brother, O. H. Bailey, and with T. M. Fowler. All three drew views, published them, and served as sales agents for one another. Similar maps for Fowler and O. H. Bailey show the same movement eastward, with Fowler settling in New

Jersey for a time and the Baileys establishing themselves in Massachusetts.

Figure 4 records the first nine years of Lucien Burleigh's production as a viewmaker, beginning in 1882 with his earliest signed prints. In the next two years Burleigh drew several towns for a publisher in Syracuse, New York, and then went into business for himself as artist-publisher. Sometime in 1886 he established his own printing press in Troy, New York, and used it to print not only his own views but also, increasingly, those drawn by others. Yet during this entire period Burleigh confined himself as artist, publisher, or printer almost entirely to New York State and to New England.

Four other single maps show all the places depicted during their careers by major viewmakers who moved throughout North America. The work of the Smith brothers appears in Figure 5. Alone among pre–Civil War producers of views, this firm achieved national coverage. Most of the views credited here to the Smiths were drawn by others but were issued by the Smiths or, in the case of some early lithographs, published jointly with Edwin Whitefield, their predecessor and one-time employer.

Augustus Koch (Figure 6), Eli S. Glover (Figure 7), and

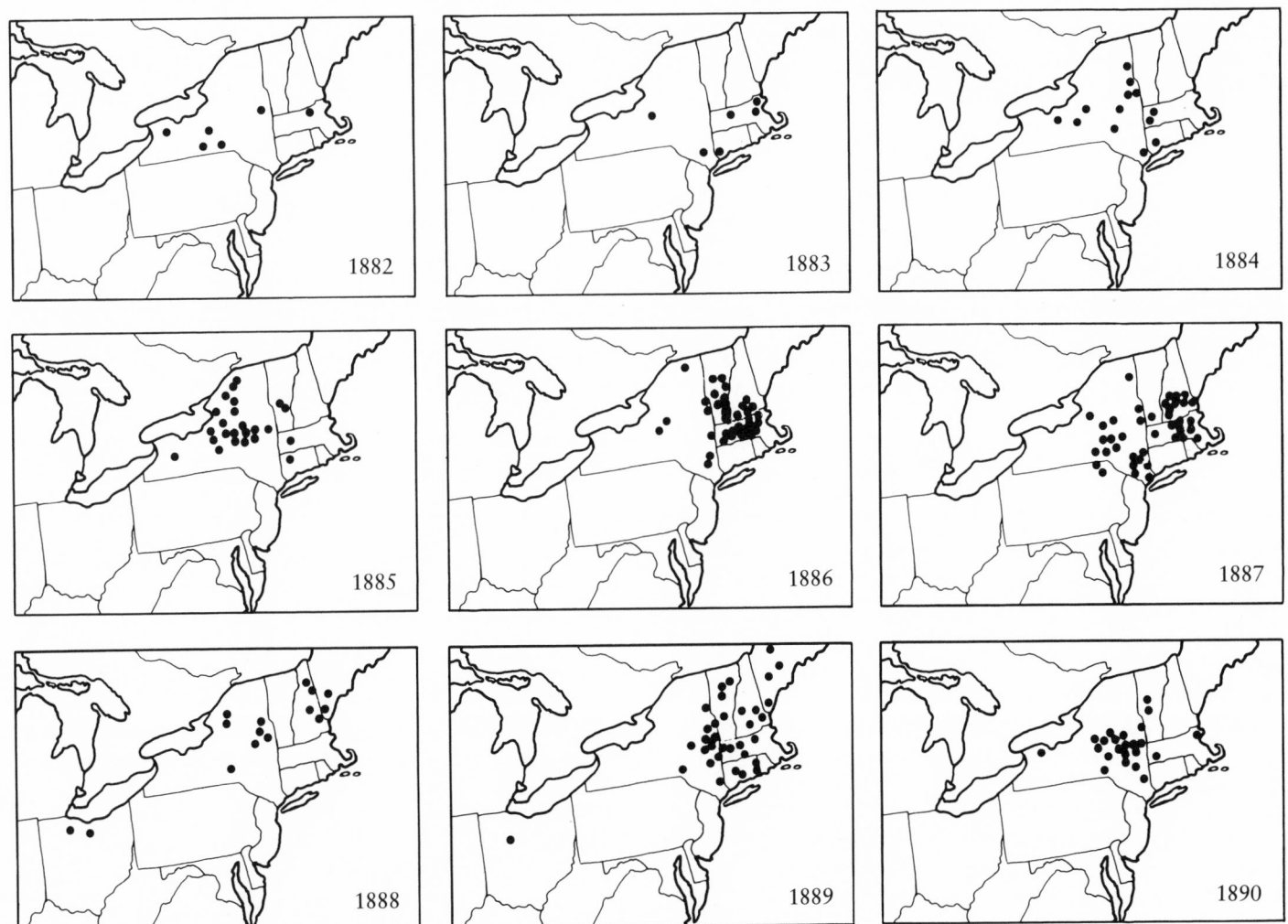

Figure 4. The views of L. R. Burleigh, 1882–1890.

Figure 5. The views of the Smith brothers, 1848–1855.

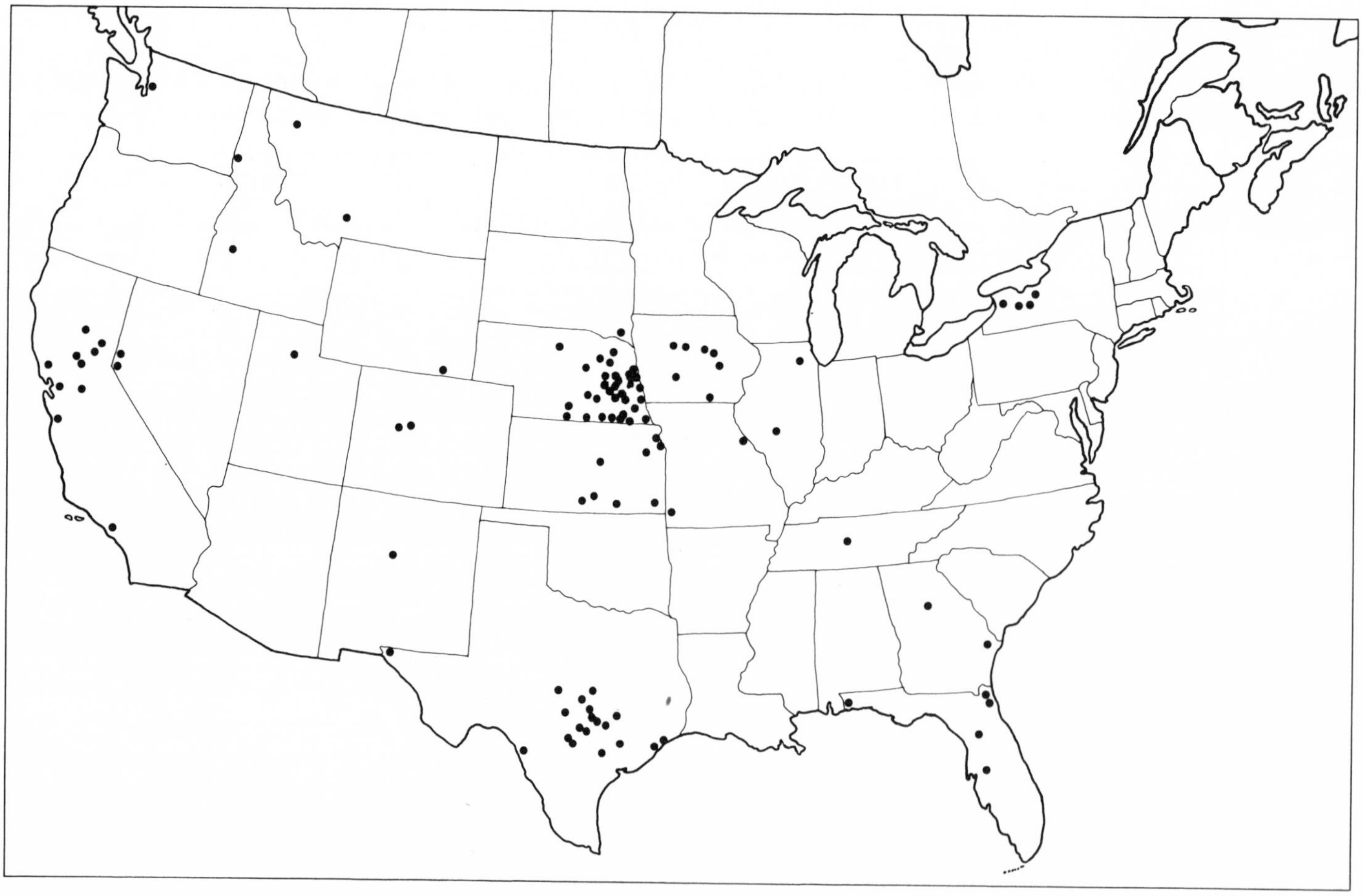

Figure 6. The views of Augustus Koch, 1868–1898.

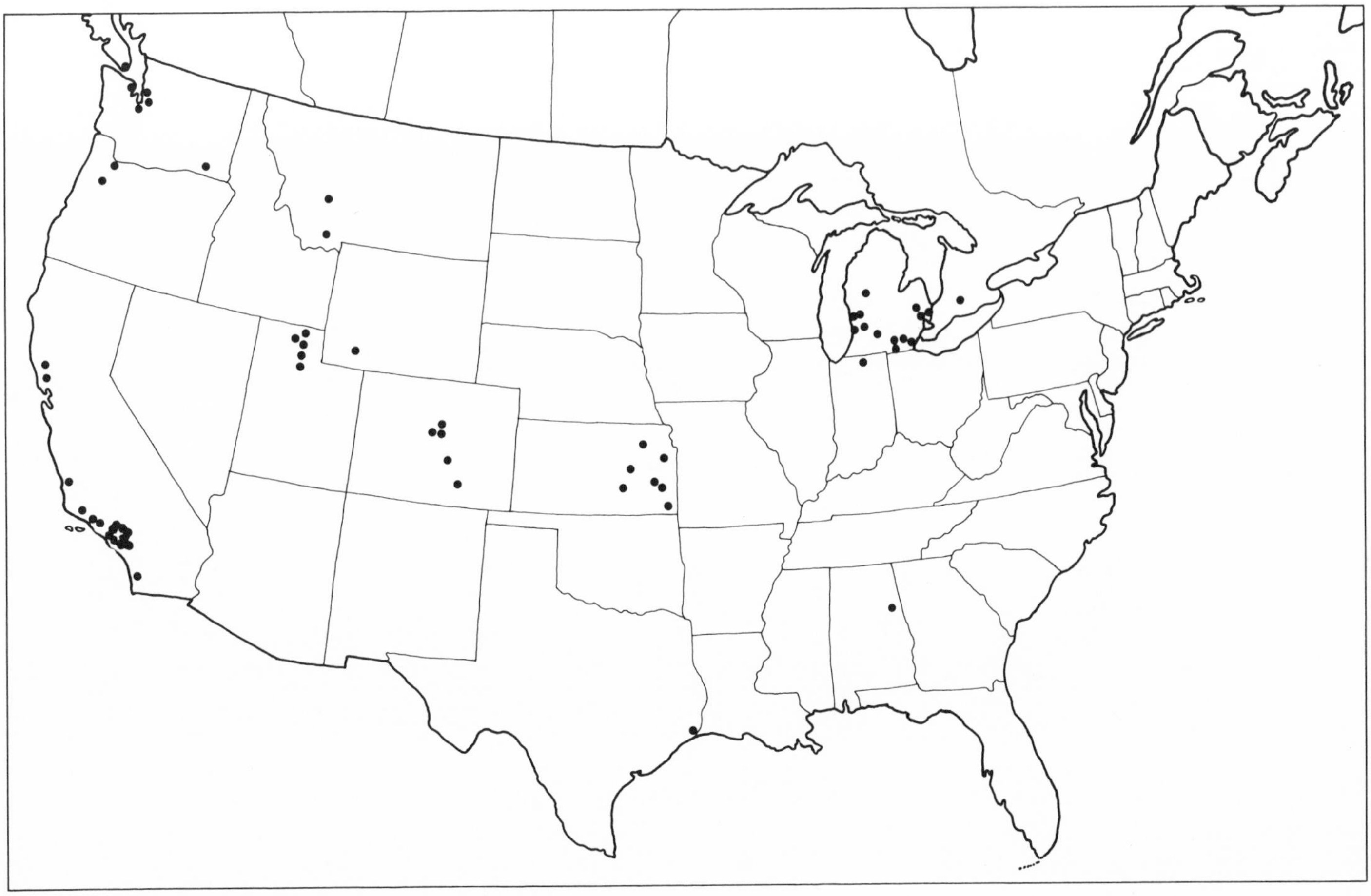

Figure 7. The views of Eli S. Glover, 1868–1912.

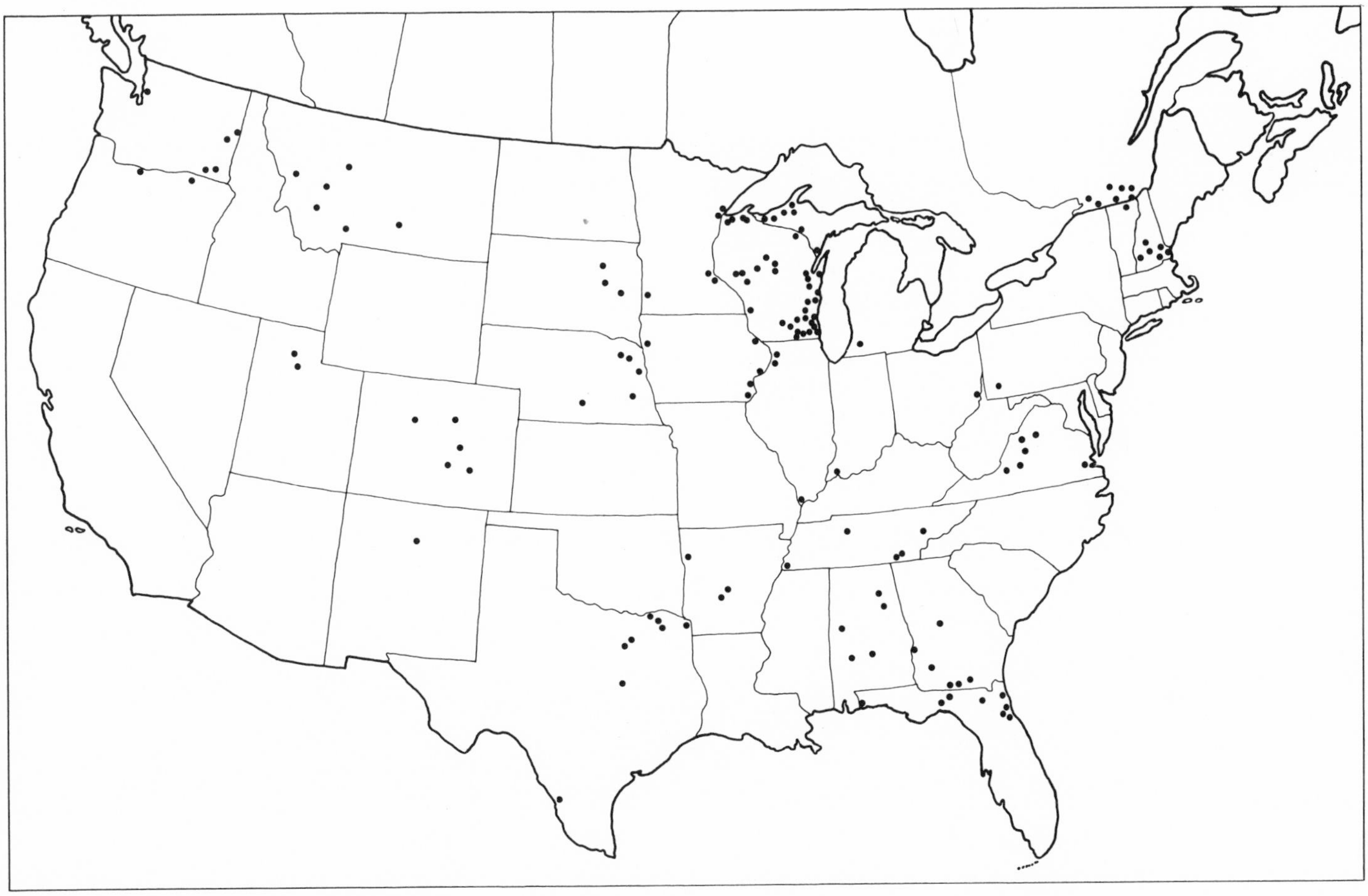

Figure 8. The views of Henry Wellge, 1878–1910.

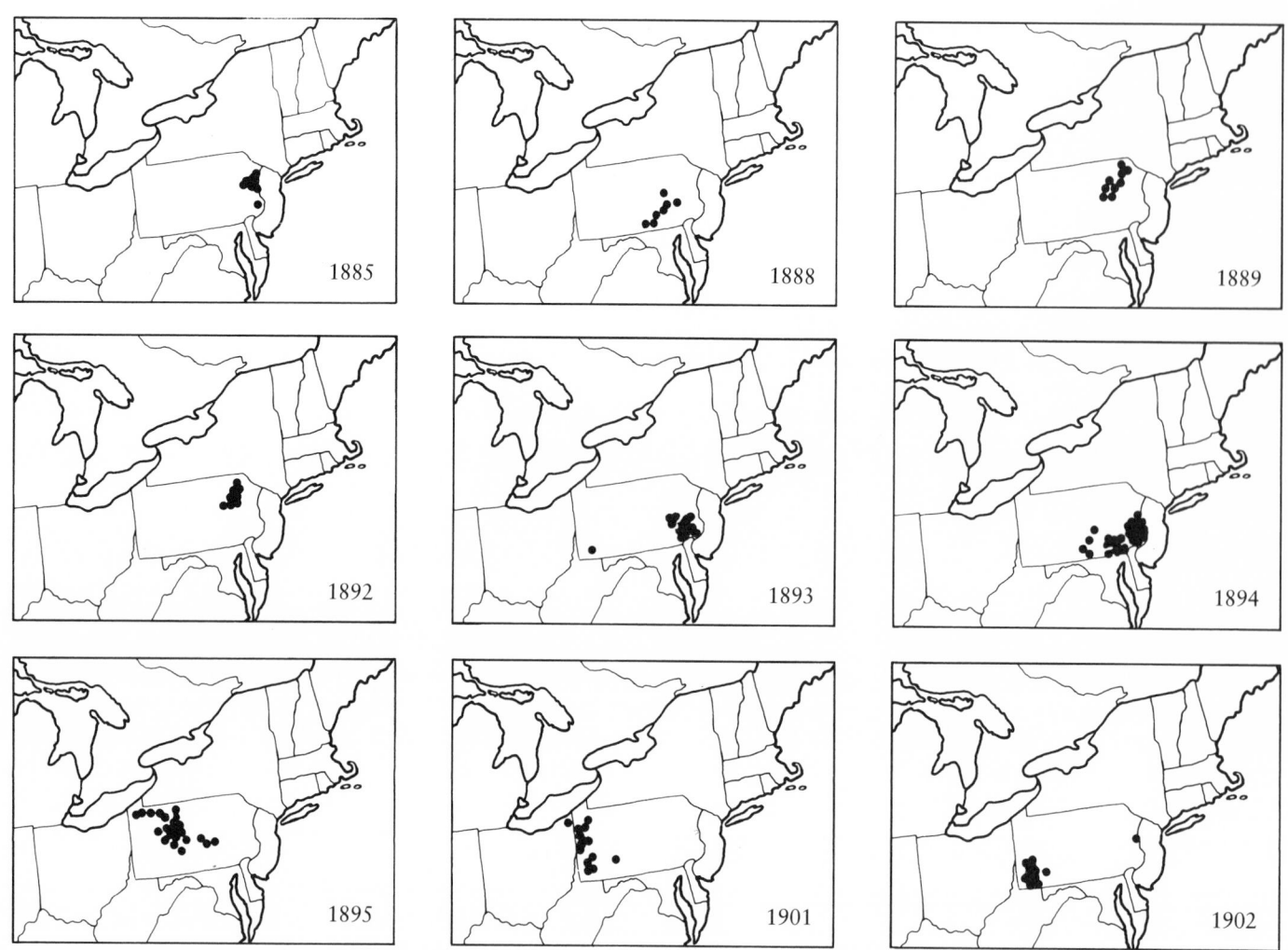

Figure 9. The views of T. M. Fowler for selected years, 1885–1902.

Henry Wellge (Figure 8) also regarded the entire United States and adjoining regions in Canada as offering potential markets for their work. Koch drew all but 18 of his 110 views during the period from 1868 through 1887. Wellge drew all but 6 of his 152 views before 1892, just fourteen years after he began. Glover produced 53 of his 62 views in the first decade of his viewmaking career beginning in 1868. All three, therefore, worked hard and traveled long distances during their most active periods.

Other maps showing the places drawn by T. M. Fowler for selected years (Figure 9) demonstrate how he tried to minimize the amount of travel required by concentrating his efforts in a small region and drawing almost all of the towns offering possibilities for sales. Figure 9 reveals clearly how Fowler systematically focused on one portion of Pennsylvania at a time, although not necessarily in consecutive years. Not only did this reduce his travel time and expenses, but Fowler may also have been able to increase sales by fos-

Table 5. Prints by Selected Viewmakers, 1878–1926

(Figures indicate number of views drawn or published)

	1878	1879	1880	1881	1882	1883	1884	1885	1886	1887	1888	1889	1890	1891	1892	1893	1894	1895	1896	1897	1898	1899	1900	1901
O. H. Bailey	25	26	9	13	17	14	17	22	5	9	16	12	13	17	7	1	1	4	2	5	12	5	2	4
T. M. Fowler	8	10	7	9	1	4	5	8	3	5	7	11	17	13	8	13	25	21	20	22	6	17	21	16
Henry Wellge	1	3	2	11	6	12	18	22	21	13	8	11	5	10	3	0	0	0	0	1	0	0	0	0
A. F. Poole			1	2	5	10	5	8	3	1	2	0	0	1	0	0	1	0	1	0	3	2	0	0
L. R. Burleigh				1	7	5	12	21	34	39	15	35	22	13	16	2	0	1	0	0	0	2		
G. Norris						11	14	22	18	16	6	15	2	1	7	8	3	6	4	1				
C. J. Pauli											2	6	7	7	7	6	4	4	3					

tering community rivalry as he moved from place to place.

Fowler's friend and sometimes associate O. H. Bailey followed much the same practice in exploiting the market for views in Massachusetts. These two veterans continued to produce lithographs of cities until after the First World War. They outlasted other prolific artists and publishers active in the last quarter of the century, including Henry Wellge, Albert F. Poole, Lucien R. Burleigh, George E. Norris, and Clemens J. Pauli.

Table 5 presents the record of this final group of viewmakers. George Norris, who began as a publisher in 1883 before trying his hand at drawing views himself and then acting as his own publisher, was the last major figure to enter the field. Before the end of the nineteenth century he, Pauli, and Burleigh drew their final views and turned to other pursuits. Poole contributed one view in 1905, and five years later Wellge's career ended as well.

Table 6 summarizes the results of a century of lithographic viewmaking. It places in rank order the thirty most productive artists and artist-publishers of city views. Among the ten most prolific, only Edward Sachse began his career prior to the Civil War. Based on numbers alone, viewmaking was primarily a phenomenon that enjoyed its greatest popularity during the quarter-century that began with Albert Ruger's first efforts in 1866.

Fowler died in 1922 at the age of eighty after falling and breaking his leg while sketching for yet another city view. Four years later Bailey retired, bringing to a formal close an era of American popular art that had effectively ended more than two decades before. Almost single-handedly, these long-time practitioners of the craft had kept it alive years after their colleagues had died and the life of the itinerant artist had passed.

No single cause led to the demise of American viewmaking. The depression that began in 1890 certainly must have affected the market at a time when the novelty of city views had begun to pall. Earlier in the century the field had attracted young men who had the energy and, perhaps, the presumption to stimulate sales and promote subscriptions. By the 1890s viewmaking may have seemed no longer a respectable occupation or an attractive way to financial success.

Towns and cities were changing as well, possibly so rapidly that a view drawn by an itinerant artist would be

Table 6. Number of Lithographic City Views by Leading Artists and Publishers

T. M. Fowler	426	C. J. Pauli	53
O. H. Bailey	374	W. W. Elliott	48
J. J. Stoner	314	A. F. Poole	46
Albert Ruger	254	Smith brothers	41
L. R. Burleigh	228	Charles Parsons	39
Henry Wellge	152	A. E. Downs	38
George Norris	135	J. B. Bachelder	36
Augustus Koch	110	Henry Lewis	36
E. Sachse	73	J. C. Wild	32
H. H. Bailey	72	A. E. Mathews	31
Eli Glover	62	D. D. Morse	29
E. Whitefield	59	J. W. Hill	27
H. Brosius	57	J. T. Palmatary	20
C. C. Kuchel	56	T. J. S. Landis	19
J. C. Hazen	55	E. S. Moore	19
J. Bachmann	53	H. H. Rowley	17

rapidly that a view drawn by an itinerant artist would be out-of-date by the time it was printed. In other cases, residents of small towns may have felt less pride in their communities or have been less willing to support the efforts of an artist to draw a place that many of them were leaving for the attractions of large cities. The cities themselves were, by the turn of the century, so large in many cases that accurate views would have taken more time to draw than could have been justified by expected profits. Tastes in decoration had changed as well. The wife of a businessman or professional would no longer regard a printed city view as an appropriate parlor decoration.

With only a few exceptions the views published in the twentieth century were less attractive as prints than earlier efforts. This decline in quality resulted in part from the use of "improved" methods of printing that displaced the lithographic press. Halftone screens may have made it easier to reproduce an artist's original rendering, but the images they created lacked the sharpness of line and crispness of detail that a lithographic stone or zinc plate could produce. This, too, may have led to a reduced demand.

Finally, in an age of flight, the airplane-borne camera made an artist's imaginary viewpoint unnecessary. An Ohio journalist interviewed Oakley H. Bailey in 1930, four years after this venerable viewmaker had produced his last view of a city. Doubtless drawing on Bailey's own wistful words, the

1902	1903	1904	1905	1906	1907	1908	1909	1910	1911	1912	1913	1914	1915	1916	1917	1918	1919	1920	1921	1922	1923	1924	1925	1926
3	0	3	2	2	3	3	3	2	3	1	1	4	2	2	0	4	1	1	1	0	1	1	0	1
14	12	8	12	12	11	5	2	1	5	4	2	2	2	2	3	3	0	2	1	3				
0	0	1	0	0	1	2	0	1																
0	0	0	1																					

reporter noted that while viewmaking had "been practically without competition . . . now the airplane cameras are covering the territory and can put more towns on paper in a day than was possible in months by hand work formerly."[8]

To those with more conventional occupations the lives of viewmakers must have seemed wasted and their works dated and obsolete. For many years the lithographic prints they had produced in such enormous numbers were spurned by most collectors and all but the most perceptive or whimsical of institutional curators. Only in recent years have scholars rediscovered them as useful tools for research in the history of architecture, city planning, transportation, urban geography, printing technology, and other fields.

8. "A 'Young' Old Timer," Sebring, Ohio, *Times*, 21 November 1930.

Historical societies, museums, and libraries vie with one another and with a hoard of private collectors in bidding for city views at auctions or buying them at shops of print dealers. Now old enough to be fashionable, these lithographs once again can be found decorating the walls of professional offices, corporate board rooms, and the modern equivalent of residential parlors and drawing rooms.

Surely no nineteenth-century viewmaker died wealthy, but together the artists and publishers of these prints left a legacy whose full value has yet to be calculated and whose benefits promise to be enduring. How that rich heritage was created is the subject of the chapters to follow, which expand on the background presented in this introduction. In following this narrative the reader will find it helpful from time to time to consult the biographical notes on major viewmakers in Part II of this study.

2. Drawing the Views: The Artist and His Subject

The drawings by the artists provided the focus of sales and promotion activity in the business of viewmaking. An attractive, recognizable, and accurate drawing made easier the agent's task of securing advance subscriptions and collecting fees for advertising, vignettes, and listings in legends. While the agent doubtless displayed lithographs done by his artist of other cities to show how the drawing would ultimately appear, the artist's rendering of a specific community in pencil, ink, watercolor, or oil played a critical role in the process of making a lithograph of that community.

Until about 1850 city views were drawn in the traditional manner of landscape painting. The artist chose a spot from which to depict his subject, set up his easel, and drew what he saw. For a community surrounded by essentially level land, the result was a panorama that showed architectural details only of the parts of the town nearest the artist or of those portions of more distant structures such as church steeples, industrial plants, or multi-story buildings that extended above the skyline.

A true skyline panorama has less pictorial appeal than one showing a city from an elevated viewpoint, and in practice almost all artists of city views drew their subjects as if looking down from a point at least slightly above the horizon. If on flat terrain, the artist used his imagination to render what he could see as if he were in a tower or steeple or ship's mast. An artist with no more than average ability could easily produce such a drawing or painting. At some locations the artist did not need to exercise even this much imagination to portray a city from an elevated perspective, for somewhere in the vicinity of many towns or cities he could find a hill, river bluff, or coastal promontory from which he could look down and see at least some of the buildings of the community beyond its nearest outer limits. Henry Walton's view of Ithaca, New York (Plate 11), is an example of a lithographic view produced in this manner.

By combining some imagination with a hilltop location as an initial viewpoint for the scene before him, the artist could create an urban portrait giving the appearance of being drawn from a much higher elevation. He could enhance this impression by introducing foreground figures or objects drawn as if seen from a point well above their true position. Lewis Bradley's view of Syracuse, New York, in 1852 (Plate 33) is just one of many examples where the artist has, in effect, joined two pictures "taken" from different vertical angles to create an image the eye sees as a single drawing made from a fairly high elevation.

We can characterize the artists responsible for this kind of view as "outsiders." This term is used to indicate only that the person producing such a drawing needed no knowledge of the community whose image he produced other than what he could see as he stood or sat at its outskirts. Fitz Hugh Lane, a native of Gloucester, surely knew every building, street, and footpath of the place, but his lithographs of the city (see Plate 10) would have looked the same if he had never set foot within its boundaries.

Because "outsider" urban lithographs portray cities from familiar viewpoints and in a style of painting pioneered in Europe by widely known and respected artists, they have been more highly regarded by art historians and critics, museum curators, and connoisseurs than the later high-level, bird's-eye views that dominated the market after the Civil War. Generally, too, the earlier, more conventional lithographic townscapes came from versatile artists enjoying reputations achieved through their more numerous watercolors or oil paintings and not from prints alone.

Nineteenth-century critics and their modern counterparts had other reasons for adopting this attitude toward the "outsider" lithographs. These early viewmakers were better trained and, as measured by accepted standards, they produced higher quality work. Frequently they put their own designs on stone and thus exercised full control over the appearance of the resulting print. Moreover, they concerned themselves less with photographic fidelity than with creating effective compositions embodying traditional pictorial values.

The first artists of American city views to depart from this tradition of ground-level or slightly elevated panoramas—men like Edward Sachse and John Bachmann in the 1850s—did not entirely abandon accepted artistic conventions. One need not know or care anything about Boston, for example, to enjoy Bachmann's view of the city in 1850 (Plate 34). However, these viewmakers concentrated as much on conveying detailed and accurate information about their subjects as on producing pleasing compositions.

These views showing cities from high overhead required far greater familiarity with the basic structure of a community and much more information about architectural details than the easel painter needed. Following our previous terminology, we can categorize these bird's-eye views as those done by "insiders." They joined art with elements of cartography to create images that allowed Americans to perceive their cities in new ways.[1]

1. Paradoxically, lithographic "insider" views of American cities first came from the pens of recently arrived foreign artists. In addition, after the Civil War the "insiders" were, in fact, itinerant artists who usually had no longtime knowledge of the communities they drew.

To draw a view showing a town as if seen from a thousand or more feet above ground level, the artist needed detailed information about the street pattern, location and design of open spaces, appearance of every building, topography of the site, and every other observable element of the community's physical fabric. Some of this material—a map of streets, or photographs or printed depictions of major public buildings—would be readily available.[2] For almost everything else, however, the artist had to rely on his own notes and sketches describing and depicting individual buildings in every part of the town.

Before he began to record the facades of buildings in his sketchbook, the artist determined the general orientation of his view. If he decided to show the town as seen from the southwest, he faced from that direction when sketching houses, stores, offices, industries, public buildings, and other structures. He may also have reached a decision as to how elevated his imaginary viewpoint was to be. Within limits, the artist could modify his first decision on direction without being required to make new sketches when the time came to prepare a finished drawing. He had much greater flexibility in his choice of the elevations, for in redrawing sketches of individual buidings he could alter substantially the elevation assumed for the viewpoint so long as he was consistent in his treatment.

For each of the hundreds of lithographic city views published after the Civil War when the bird's-eye style predominated, there once must have been a sketchbook or a stack of separate sheets that the artist used while walking the streets of the community and recording the appearance of its buildings, masses of vegetation, and terrain. However, only Edwin Whitefield seems to have kept some of these drawings, and his sketchbook for a view of Quincy, Massachusetts, in 1877 (Plate 35) helps us understand how he proceeded.

The Quincy lithograph came late in Whitefield's career. All of his earlier work had been in the style of the townscape artists: "outsider" views that presented the subject much like a stage set, although several of his views lifted the observer somewhat above ground level.[3] For his Quincy view he adopted what by then was the more popular and prevailing technique of showing cities as seen from a bird's-eye perspective. Whitefield's surviving sketchbook must have been only one of several that he used in Quincy, for it does not include sketches of all of the town's buildings. Sheets of the book measure about four by ten inches, bound on the longer side, but used horizontally by the artist. He worked in pencil, sometimes using an entire page for major structures like the John Adams and the John Quincy Adams residences and their outbuildings (Plate 36), but often showing all the houses along one side of a block on a single page.

He drew each building in two-point perspective, but as an experienced artist he did this freehand and did not use guidelines to establish vanishing points. His sketches show only a few of the buildings as he saw them from the ground. Instead, he sketched most of them as if he were overhead. Other artists may also have been able to make this imaginary leap into the air, but some doubtless merely drew what they saw and later transformed their ground-level sketches into smaller bird's-eye images when they began work on the preliminary drawing of the entire town.[4]

It was this process that Oakley Hoopes Bailey described for a newspaper reporter in 1930 when the artist and publisher was nearly ninety and long retired. According to this account, Bailey recalled that it "involved a vast amount of painstaking detail hand work, as each job required . . . going along every street and sketching in the buildings, trees and other objects so as to make a complete and accurate view."[5]

Like Whitefield, other artists probably added notes to their sketches to guide them in the next phase of the project. At the edge of one page Whitefield wrote "the R.R. is just beyond this house." Below one street, shown with a gentle curve, he noted a correction to be made: "the street makes an elbow here." He added two inscriptions on the page showing the Charles Francis Adams mansion: "The ground slopes rapidly down on the west side of the house"; "In the hollow west of this house there are many large trees; then another hill and another hollow after that the quarries." Almost every page has similar information accompanying the sketches.

In some cases artists relied on photographs to prepare portions of their drawings or for the border vignettes that they often used. An early example is the lithograph of York, Pennsylvania, published by J. T. Williams in 1852 and stating in the imprint, "From daguerreotype views by Williams."[6] For the typical bird's-eye view, however, which might show hundreds of buildings, or for smaller places that were inadequately documented by photographs, the artist's sketches drawn at ground level as he moved from place to place within the town provided him with the information he required.

He used these sketches and their accompanying notes to prepare a preliminary drawing. Whitefield's drawing for Quincy does not exist, but we can look at Thaddeus M. Fowler's incomplete draft of his view of Sunset, Texas (Plate 37), as a rare example of a preliminary drawing that has been saved. His faint pencil lines are just legible enough to show the tiny images of buildings that Fowler redrew from his individual sketches. In doing so, of course, he saw to it that he placed each building on the proper street and located

2. In almost all towns some kind of street map existed. More detailed and accurate surveys could be found in many larger cities. Maps for property tax or engineering purposes were used in municipal offices. County atlases were also sources of city and village maps. Very few artists acknowledged their cartographic sources. An exception is Herman Brosius's view of Shreveport, Louisiana, in 1872. After the artist's credit line one finds: "according to the Map of O. L. Van Greelen."

3. Whitefield climbed Mount Royal to show Montreal from a point well above the city. His view of Toronto was also from a fairly high level, in this case from an imaginary viewpoint.

4. I am deeply grateful to William Osgood of Boston, owner of the Quincy sketchbook, for allowing me to borrow and photograph it.

5. Sebring, Ohio, *Times*, 21 November 1930. I am indebted to Thomas Beckman for the correct date of this article, which is erroneously dated 1932 in "Introduction" to U.S. Library of Congress, *Panoramic Maps of Anglo-American Cities: A Checklist of Maps in the Collections of the Library of Congress, Geography and Map Division*, 11, n. 1.

6. This is reproduced in color in Judith W. Hansen, comp., *Pennsylvania Prints from the Collection of John C. O'Connor and Ralph M. Yeager: Lithographs, Engravings, Aquatints, and Watercolors from The Tavern Restaurant*, pl. 43.

it correctly with respect to others and to the street line, just as he had observed and drawn it earlier.

Fowler's drawing also shows the parallel streets of Sunset's grid system converging in the distance. This important feature of bird's-eye views can be seen more clearly on his pencil drawing of Quanah (Plate 38), another town in northern Texas that Fowler depicted. This drawing shows the final results of the artist's work before it went to a lithographer to be put on stone and printed. A preliminary drawing, much like that of Sunset, doubtless provided the basis from which Fowler worked to refine the ultimate design.

If lines are drawn down the centers of all of the streets on the Quanah view and are projected beyond its borders, they meet at common points on both the left and right sides. Fowler thus used what is known as a two-point linear perspective to construct his view. He and such contemporaries as Ruger, Glover, Burleigh, Bailey, Brosius, Koch, and Wellge produced hundreds of other lithographic views using this same method to achieve realistic portraits of the communities they visited.

The gridiron plans of most American towns, surveyed into rectangular blocks formed by straight streets intersecting at right angles, made it easy for artists to construct a basic perspective framework over which they could rule street lines to begin their preliminary drawing. Using a street map of the town and rotating it to conform to the angle of view he selected, the artist could then project lines from street intersections on the map to determine their corresponding positions on the perspective grid. This technique was well known in the 1800s; it was explained in countless books on drawing and in encyclopedia articles on perspective and was a fundamental subject taught in all but the most elementary art courses. [7] However, the only statement about derivation of a perspective grid in this manner written by an artist of city views is that appearing in the preface of Camille N. Dry's 110-sheet view of St. Louis of 1875. If Dry himself did not write the following passage, it certainly was based on his analysis of the process he followed, which resulted in "A Topographical Survey Drawn in Perspective," as the subtitle of the publication described the view.

> The preliminary drawings for this work were made early in the spring of 1874. After a careful consideration of the subject, it was determined to locate the point of view so that the city would be seen from the southeast, believing that to be the most advantageous in all respects. Accordingly, the point of sight was established on the Illinois side of the river, looking to the northwest, and at sufficient altitude to overlook the roofs of ordinary houses into the streets. A careful perspective, which required a surface of three hundred square feet, was then erected from a correct survey of the city. . . . Every foot of the vast territory within these limits has been carefully examined and topographically drawn in perspective. [8]

Dry and his publisher obligingly provided an illustration of this procedure. On one of the large folio sheets of the publication they reproduced a map of the city. Above it they placed an outline perspective of the street system. This perspective was divided into numbered rectangles, each corresponding to one of the detailed folio-size sheets, which showed the area outlined at much larger scale and with all buildings in proper place (Plate 39).

Artists must have used many shortcuts in drawing their basic perspective grids. An analysis of the work of any single artist reveals the use of only a small number of combinations of viewpoint and vanishing-point locations. Each artist seemed to have two or three favorite ways of handling perspective and to have used them over and over during his career. Indeed, artists may have prepared a limited number of basic perspective grids, any one of which could be selected as a guide and used under tracing paper in drawing a town's streets. The grid might have lines spaced, say, one hundred feet apart. If the blocks of the town were four hundred by six hundred feet, the artist could trace every fourth line in one direction and every sixth line in the other.

A lithograph of one town might also have been used as a tracing guide for a second if the intervals between streets were identical, as was often the case in the Midwest. Or, if the artist revisited a city that he had drawn in an earlier year, he could use the older lithograph as a base but reverse it to give the appearance of a quite different view. Augustus Koch apparently did just that for a view of Austin, Texas, in 1887, in which the street lines are a mirror image of those in another view he did of the same city in 1873 (Plate 40).

So consistent were most of the artists in working with a limited number of perspective grids that someone familiar with the perspectives can usually identify who drew a print when seeing it from a distance and without looking for the name in the imprint. Both Augustus Koch and Oakley Bailey, for example, almost invariably depicted towns as seen from very high angles (Plates 25, 29, and 40). Eli Glover, on the other hand, usually portrayed the towns he drew from a viewpoint elevated perhaps thirty to forty degrees above the horizontal (Plate 28). In most of Henry Wellge's views, one vanishing point is placed well beyond one margin on the horizon and the other is substantially above the horizon but near where the margin of the view would be if extended upward (Plate 31). [9]

Artists confronted with the task of drawing towns with irregular street patterns, such as many New England communities, or portions of towns not having gridiron streets and square blocks, probably worked from two grids. One would have been a rectangular grid superimposed over a street map. The other would have shown these rectangular lines as if seen in perspective. An experienced artist would

---

7. For an exhaustive examination of pre–Civil War drawing manuals and their use in private and public instruction, see Peter C. Marzio, *The Art Crusade: An Analysis of American Drawing Manuals, 1820–1860.*

8. *Pictorial St. Louis Metropolis of the Mississippi Valley: A Topographical Survey Drawn in Perspective A.D. 1875 by Camille N. Dry, Designed & Edited by Rich. J. Compton* (St. Louis, 1875).

9. I should make it clear that I have no evidence to support my hypothesis that viewmakers used standardized perspective grids, choosing whichever best suited their purposes and provided the most advantageous portrayal of the town. Printed grids of this type are commonly used today as aids in engineering and architectural perspective drawing. I have not been able to locate catalogs or advertisements of the nineteenth century to determine if similar devices could be purchased then. If not, and had I been an artist in 1869 and responsible—even with assistance—for drawing more than sixty city views, I would have prepared two or three basic perspective patterns which, if reversed, would have given me four to six different ways of drawing my subjects. Since the market for views was almost entirely local, it would not have mattered much, if at all, that one town looked very much like another.

have found it easy to locate correctly on his perspective grid any point or object falling within the corresponding rectangle of the grid superimposed on the map. For example, he could draw a curving street by pinpointing several points along the street and then connecting them with a freehand line on his drawing.[10]

While view artists most commonly used a two-point perspective system, they sometimes used a one-point system. Ruger's view of Urbana in 1869 (Plate 41) is one example. Ruger drew this view looking straight down the central thoroughfare of Urbana's regular grid pattern, the center line of which bisected the view. Streets parallel to this thoroughfare on both sides converged to the distant vanishing point on the axis of the main street. Streets intersecting at right angles appear as parallel lines extending across the view. The space separating these streets on the drawing diminished from foreground to background to express their distance from the viewer.[11]

Although viewmakers used the basic principles of linear perspective with almost unvarying consistency in selecting one or two vanishing points toward which lines parallel on the ground were drawn as if converging, most of them introduced one variation that departed from accepted perspective theory. Their reasons can be understood best if one considers the appearance of a city view following all of the requirements of a perspective derived mechanically from a plan or map. George Baker's lithograph of Sacramento, California, in 1857 (Plate 42) can be used as an example. Baker followed the rules of true linear perspective by placing his two vanishing points on the horizon where the ground plane meets that of the sky. The resulting drawing is realistic in that it produces an image approximating what an observer would actually perceive from the point above the ground chosen by Baker as his viewpoint. However, the buildings in the middle and distant background are so small that they can scarcely be distinguished as individual structures. For artists and publishers depending almost entirely on local sales of views to property owners, such a perspective system drastically reduced the potential market. A person residing or having his

place of business in the "back" of a view who could not identify his building through details of roof, fenestration, porch, chimney, or landscape features would be less likely to buy a lithograph no matter how accurate or attractive it might be.

The solution adopted by a majority of the post–Civil War view artists was to locate one or both vanishing points far beyond the horizon. This can be easily verified by extending lines on the view representing parallel streets. If the artist used a vanishing point beyond the horizon, these lines will meet at some point in the sky, and if a horizon line were drawn there it would be miles from the town in the foreground. Since the angles formed by converging parallel lines are much smaller in such a view, buildings and other features at a distance from the observer could be drawn much larger in size and with far more detail, although still giving the impression of distance by being smaller than those in the foreground. Augustus Koch used this method in drawing Carson City, Nevada, in 1875 (Plate 43). He placed one vanishing point in the upper right, well above the true horizon. He located the other more or less on the horizon but even farther away beyond the left border of the scene. The widespread use of this technique explains why so many views look almost like a map drawn on a plane sloping upward to the sky. It is not that the artists were ignorant of the rules of perspective. What they did was to bend the rules in the interests of commerce.

A few artists ignored perspective altogether and used an axonometric projection in which all streets parallel on the ground appear parallel on the drawing rather than as if converging toward points in the distance. Camille N. Dry employed this method for his lithograph of Columbus, Mississippi, in 1871. The next year he modified this approach slightly when he drew Raleigh, North Carolina. In that print (Plate 44), streets in one direction are parallel. Those angled more steeply and leading toward the upper right converge toward a distant vanishing point, but they do so so gradually that the effect is almost the same as in an axonometric projection. The rectangular blocks thus appear as parallelograms. Buildings of equal size in the "front" and the "back" of the town are shown as of equal size in the drawing. The effect is a kind of warped plan-view, almost as if Raleigh were somehow clinging to a vertical surface, and the horizon line is completely artificial. Nevertheless, the effect is not unpleasant, and, considering the ease with which such a "perspective" grid could be constructed, it seems strange that more artists did not employ this system.

Artists did not hesitate to modify the rules of perspective in another way if the viewpoint they selected or the size of the print did not permit showing an important feature of the community. If, for example, a major industry would otherwise fall just beyond a border of the lithograph, the artist could slightly readjust reality and "move" the plant to where it could be seen. Or, as can sometimes be noted, the artist could simply compress the entire view from side to side, allowing him to include more of the city or its surroundings than would be possible if he adhered rigorously to a fixed perspective system.

Once having determined the underlying perspective grid

10. For centuries artists have used two rectangular grids of different sizes to enlarge or reduce drawings in much the same manner. One grid is placed over the drawing, the other is used under tracing paper or ruled lightly on the drawing paper to provide a guide to the artist in reproducing at an appropriate size the lines of the original being copied. In a perspective grid each rectangle becomes a trapezium because all four sides are made up of lines drawn to vanishing points and are therefore not parallel.

11. One-point perspectives were also used for several early lithographic views, among them Henry Walton's first print of Ithaca, New York, in 1836. John William Hill also used a one-point perspective system for several of his views done for the Smith brothers in the 1850s, such as his Albany lithograph of 1853. A later example is the Appleton, Wisconsin, lithograph of 1874 by J. J. Stoner and C. H. Vogt. Some views seem to have been drawn with multiple vanishing points, thus being composites of two views. In Clemens J. Pauli's view of Milwaukee in 1876 the foreground is seen from a different point than the balance of the view. This is noted in Thomas Beckman, *Milwaukee Illustrated: Panoramic and Bird's-Eye Views of a Midwestern Metropolis, 1844–1908*, unpaged, note for exhibit item 28. Beckman also points out that the view of Milwaukee published in 1898 is a 360 degree panorama. What seem to be two rivers, one at the left and one near the right side, are in reality both portions of the Milwaukee River. The artist must, therefore, have used a series of vanishing points. See the long note on this remarkable print in ibid., exhibit item 46. A color reproduction of this view can be found on the title page of John W. Reps, *Cities on Stone: Nineteenth Century Lithograph Images of the Urban West*.

and having used it to draw the street system and major terrain features, the artist turned to his sketchbook to begin filling the drawing with buildings. If he had been careful in identifying the locations of each sketch, it was easy for him to redraw every structure with the appropriate street frontage and in its correct location with respect to others. Although the artist had probably made each sketch at roughly the same scale, the perspective grid provided a guide in redrawing structures at the sizes dictated by their locations in the foreground, middle distance, or background.

Some artists used linear perspective techniques for all or most buildings. Others chose an axonometric approach instead of using converging lines. In a few instances artists used a composite method: parallel horizontal lines for a building's principal façade but converging lines for those portions at right angles to the main elevation. On the Bismarck, North Dakota, view of 1883, unsigned but probably by Henry Wellge, the artist drew the new Dakota territorial capitol in the distance in this manner (Plate 7). A more detailed vignette depicts the structure in conventional two-point perspective, which was the perspective used for the overwhelming majority of vignettes used as borders for views. Although the capitol had only been started at the time this view was drawn and had to be shown as it appeared in architectural renderings, this should not have affected the perspective treatment used by the artist.

For views of very large cities where sketching every structure would have been hopelessly time-consuming or for smaller towns where only limited time was available, artists often found useful the true linear perspective system with its horizon-line vanishing points. In this system, the artists needed to draw only the buildings in the foreground in convincing detail, using progressively stylized rectangles to represent structures in the distance. Several views drawn for Currier and Ives by Charles Parsons of such places as New York, Philadelphia, Chicago, and Washington (Plate 45) provide examples where the intimidating task of showing details of every building in the interests of promoting sales proved insurmountable.

The first version of the artist's drawing of the entire city with its buildings would have been far too cluttered and crude to be exhibited for the purpose of securing subscriptions. Unsophisticated residents of Sunset, Texas—or anywhere else, for that matter—could not have visualized the appearance of a finished lithograph from such an unattractive draft as Fowler's drawing. Using such a draft as a guide, probably by tracing over it, the artist would produce for public display a more finished drawing in pencil or ink. He obviously tried to make this as appealing as possible to help his agent obtain subscriptions and secure fees for vignettes, advertising slogans, and listings in the legend. Fowler's pencil drawing of Honey Grove, Texas, in 1891 (Plate 46) is another example of his work that closely resembles his Quanah drawing referred to earlier in a different context (Plate 38).[12]

Except for the trains, Fowler showed no vehicles in his Honey Grove view, nor did he introduce any human figures. Many artists did, however, include such elements in order to enliven the view and produce an impression of activity and movement in the streets. Some ran into difficulties with perspective in these nonstructural objects. In the view of Salt Lake City in 1867 put on stone by Christian Inger and perhaps sketched by him (Plate 47), the carriage in the foreground is drawn by horses no larger than the sheep grazing in a field the same distance from the point of sight. In the background, on the other hand, a wagon approaching the distant horizon is drawn so large that it would have been almost as high as the Mormon temple.

Another type of exaggeration is encountered more often and is easier to understand. Artists often showed such vertical features as chimneys, spires, towers, and flagpoles as much higher than in reality. Attenuation of vertical elements solved a difficulty created by the bird's-eye viewpoint: these features would appear shortened if drawn to a scale identical to that used for horizontal elements of the composition. Artists also liked the dramatic effects that this use of artistic license created. Lewis Bradley's view of Syracuse, New York, drawn for the Smith brothers in 1852, illustrates a typical result of this approach (Plate 33). Nineteenth-century lithographic artists did not invent this device, for it had been used for centuries.[13]

In the process of exhibiting the drawing to promote advance sales of the proposed lithograph, the artist would have had his attention called to errors or omissions. If these were minor in nature and few in number, he might be able to make corrections on the original. More serious oversights might require an entirely new and revised final drawing. Either at this stage or when the drawing was being put on stone, other effects were often introduced to give the lithograph greater realism and to improve its appearance. Reflections and shadows needed to be added if the artist did not show them in his rendering. In most of the views after the Civil War, this was done rather mechanically on multi-stone lithographs by the use of a tone that uniformly filled the walls of buildings not exposed to sunlight. Cloud shadows rarely can be found, although the views drawn by Parsons and Atwater are exceptions to this generalization. In many views reflections of buildings or foliage in streams, lakes, or ponds are omitted altogether.

Herman Lungkwitz's lithograph of San Antonio, Texas (Plate 48), printed in Germany from a painting executed about 1852, shows how an academically trained artist and skilled lithographer handled these matters. Cloud shadows can be seen in the foreground and on the roof of the first building in the right foreground. Walls not in sunlight are darker in tone than others. Shadows fall on the street from the structures and trees lining its left side, and shading within masses of vegetation adds to the three-dimensional effect. Views by such more commercially oriented view-makers as Albert Ruger, Eli S. Glover, L. R. Burleigh, H. H.

12. I have not been able to locate a lithographic version of the Honey Grove view. Perhaps Fowler did not succeed in obtaining enough subscriptions to make a lithograph commercially feasible.

13. An eighteenth-century American example that would be nearly grotesque were the view not so skillfully done is the large engraving of Boston found in many copies of J. W. Des Barres's *Atlantic Neptune*, issued by the British Navy during the Revolution. The numerous church steeples are shown as far taller than they were.

and O. H. Bailey, and Thaddeus M. Fowler rarely exhibit such sophistication.

Nor do many views make use of what is known as aerial or atmospheric perspective: the portrayal of objects in the background less distinctly and in less vivid colors or lighter shades. This perspective approaches human perceptions in looking at reality, and its use by artists gives three-dimensional character to a drawing, painting, or print constructed of only two-dimensional lines or masses. C. B. Gifford's view of San Francisco in 1864 (Plate 49) is an example of the effective use of atmospheric perspective, although this may not be obvious from the illustration. Not only did Gifford draw the distant background with far less precision than the foreground objects, but the tone stone used to produce sky and shadow effects was prepared and inked so that the intensity of the tones diminishes from the foreground to the distance.

If the artist was his own lithographer, as in the case of Edwin Whitefield, the responsibility for such matters was clearly his. In these cases, differences between the final drawing and the ultimate lithograph obviously resulted only if the artist wished to make changes or add features, not because of some whim by a lithographer or a misunderstanding of what the artist intended.

Whitefield's drawing for his view of Brooklyn, New York, in 1846 was a watercolor on three joined sheets slightly longer than the final print and lacking the rich details of the Manhattan waterfront that make the lithograph so attractive and revealing (Plate 50). Whitefield and David William Moody put the design on stone, doubtless working together at the shop of the printer, Francis Michelin. While the watercolor and lithograph closely resemble each other in broad outlines, the details in the lithograph of the boats in the East River and of virtually every building in Brooklyn differ from the watercolor.

It is clear from this example that the artist's role might continue to be important up to the point where printing began. Even at this stage, Whitefield must have examined proof impressions, and he may have altered the design on the stone if he felt that modifications were essential. Fitz Hugh Lane and Henry Walton, who preceded Whitefield, and such contemporaries as Edward Sachse and John Bachmann also drew on stone, as did such post–Civil War viewmakers as Alfred Mathews and Lucien Burleigh. For them, too, the completion of the final drawing marked the end of only one phase of their work.

However, the great majority of the artists active after 1865 and several before then simply sent or brought their drawings to their printers or publishers to be put on stone by lithographers. Chapter 3 describes how the lithographer and the printer combined to produce a lithographic print from the artist's drawing, but it will be useful here to introduce in summary form some material related to that subject.

Some artists may have submitted their drawings on transfer paper, a special drawing surface that could be placed facedown on a lithographic stone, to which lines of the drawing adhered. The printer could then ink the stone in the normal manner and obtain as many impressions as the pub-lisher ordered. For prints requiring additional stones for tone effects, the lithographer would use the basic design as a guide.

Lithographers might also trace the artist's design directly on the face of a stone. The final drawing would be placed facedown on the stone over a prepared paper whose pigmented surface would be transferred to the stone when the drawing was traced from its back. Perhaps not all lines were traced in this manner, but only those major features providing the basic framework for the view. The lithographer could then fill in the remaining elements by hand.

In many cases, possibly the majority of them, the lithographer actually redrew the artist's design on stone, relying on his skill as an artist to duplicate as closely as possible the details of the view artist's final drawing. Since the lines on the stone had to be a mirror image of those on the drawing, the lithographer needed the ability to do reverse drawing and lettering, or—more likely—he used a mirror to reflect the image of the drawing and used the reflection as his model. [14]

Several final drawings have survived and can be compared to the lithographs derived from them to suggest the technique that may have been used. For example, the drawing (Plate 38) and the print (Plate 51) of Fowler's view of Quanah differ so much in their perspective grid that the lithographic image could not have been produced by tracing. Fowler himself, or some anonymous lithographer, must have put the design on stone freehand, using the final drawing as a general guide. Or a second drawing on transfer paper could have been made in the same manner, and its lines put on stone by the transfer process.

Albert Ruger's view of Wiscasset, Maine (Plate 53), however, seems to have been put on stone with all of the streets exactly as Ruger drew them in his final drawing (Plate 52). This probably indicates that the lithographer traced the main elements of the drawing on stone or, perhaps, made an intermediate enlargement or reduction for this purpose using a pantograph or gridded paper to reproduce precisely the perspective Ruger completed while in Maine.

In comparing Ruger's drawing and the lithograph, one can note innumerable changes in small details of individual buildings, boats, vegetation, and topography. The lithographer introduced some of these modifications in response to instructions Ruger wrote on the back of the drawing. These instructions indicate the important role the lithographer was expected to play in producing the ultimate image that reached the customer:

to lithographer

Wiscassett is on *rough ground*, and you will take Paines with the shading. The counterey is *very rough* and *rocky*, as stone ledges, and Pine timber, get the timber to look *like* Pinewoods and make it look as *rough* and *rocky* as *Possible* in back ground. Print and copies on 18 × 24 paper. Color like North Berwick. . . . The

14. One can find numerous examples of mirror-image letters on lithographs, *S* and *N* being the most frequent. This is an almost certain indication that transfer paper was not used and letters were not traced.

Bridge, *Draw*, must be changed, it does not open, but slides *back* on a rail track. You can make the draw like the one in sketch, but *running back on the Bridge* toward the turn. That Powder house no. 23 is a round Brick and Stands on a mass of rocks on hill, *get the hill* to show and Pine woods back of it is also on a hill or mountain.[15]

The development of photographic techniques for transferring the work of the artist to a printing surface of stone or zinc required final drawings of more finished quality. Lucien Burleigh in 1882 must have furnished his publisher a line rendering of his view of Ithaca (Plate 54) ready to be put on

stone or zinc photographically and requiring little if any hand work.[16]

The gravure process and the use of halftone screens allowed the artist to prepare and submit continuous-tone renderings, like the watercolor of Statesville, North Carolina, produced about 1908 by A. E. Downs and T. M. Fowler (Plate 55). The traditional role of the lithographer as artist thus passed to a new type of technician who produced printing surfaces by photographic means and who needed no drawing skills of his own.

15. Christine Bauer Podmaniczky, "Introduction," in William A. Farnsworth Library and Art Museum, *Through a Bird's Eye: Nineteenth-Century Views of Maine*, 22.

16. In this view, portions of the foreground appear as a dark mass broken by hundreds of tiny white flecks. While these could have been made in white ink over a solid black background on the drawing, it would have been easier to produce this effect by removing minute portions of the stone or zinc printing surface with a sharp instrument, perhaps some version of an engraver's burin.

3. Printing the Views: Lithography and Its Development

The vast majority of separately issued American city views came from lithographic presses. This chapter and the one to follow describe the basic process of lithography, its development in America, changes in technology that occurred in the nineteenth century, and the applications of photography to lithographic printing.

The revolution in the world of printmaking that lithography created began quietly in the waning years of the eighteenth century. A young and unsuccessful Bavarian playwright and actor named Alois Senefelder began to study printing methods in order to publish his own work. He had experimented with making etchings from an incised stone rather than using a copper plate. One day he scribbled a laundry list for his mother on a piece of fine-grained limestone, using a waxy ink to form the letters. It occurred to him that if he used a dilute acid wash he might lower the surface of the unprotected portions of the stone, leaving the letters in relief. The letters could then be inked like a woodcut and used to obtain a printed image on paper. It worked, and Senefelder continued to explore how stone could be used to retain inked lines.

Eventually he realized that he had stumbled on an entirely new method of making prints. When he drew on the stone with a fatty ink and moistened the surface with gum-water, he found that oily printing ink would adhere only to the drawn lines. Paper could then be pressed against the stone and rubbed firmly to transfer the inked image on the stone to the paper. The result was a mirror-image print.[1]

Senefelder called his new printing technique *lithography*. It proved easier, quicker, and cheaper than the traditional methods of engraving, etching, or block cutting, and by 1820 lithographers in Germany, France, and England were busy producing a variety of printed images. In 1818 Senefelder published a long book giving precise and detailed directions on various ways his invention could be used, and a year later an English translation (Figure 10) became available in London. Senefelder's work and the writings of other pioneer lithographers rapidly spread knowledge about this remarkably versatile addition to the graphic arts.[2]

A literate, inquiring, and persistent reader in America could have followed the early development of lithography through notices in general periodicals, scientific journals, and encyclopedia entries during the first third of the nineteenth century. The process was so novel and the results seemed so mysterious that editors and publishers kept their audience aware of emerging applications and improvements in this startling contribution to the technique of printmaking.

Perhaps the first reference to the subject in an American publication was the brief notice carried by the *National Intelligencer and Washington Advertiser* in its 8 January 1808 issue that a "Dr. Mitchell of New York received a lithographic stone and inks from Paris and made some experiments in this new art."[3] The exact nature of this "new art" and how its practitioners followed it were not explained. Nor would our inquiring reader have been enlightened on this matter by consulting a short passage concerning "stone etching" in an artist's handbook that appeared in Philadelphia six years later.[4]

If, however, he had picked up the July 1819 issue of the *Analectic Magazine*, his curiosity would have been satisfied. Nearly six pages of this publication described the process of lithography in surprising detail and presented an example of lithographic printing in the form of a view of an unidentified building drawn and printed by Bass Otis (Figure 11). This article referred knowledgeably to European experience as well as to a few American efforts that seem to have preceded

---

1. Senefelder wrote a long history of his experiments as the first part of his treatise on lithographic printing. German and French editions of this were published in 1818, with an English translation the following year. See Alois Senefelder, *A Complete Course of Lithography: Containing Clear and Explicit Instructions in all the Different Branches and Manners of that Art . . . to which is Prefixed a History of Lithography, from its Origin to the Present Time.* Senefelder summarized the steps he took to secure this first true lithograph, probably in 1798, in these historic words: "My whole process was . . . to wash the polished stone with soap-water, to dry it well, to write or draw upon it with . . . ink of soap and wax, then to etch it with . . . [dilute nitric acid] . . . and, lastly, to prepare it for printing with an infusion of gum-water . . . [which] enters into chemical affinity with the stone, and stops its pores still more effectually against the fat, and opens them to the water" (31–32).

2. The history of Senefelder's contribution to lithography and the development of lithographic printing in Europe before 1850 are thoroughly and clearly explored in Michael L. Twyman's splendid *Lithography, 1800–1850: The Techniques of Drawing on Stone in England and France and Their Application in Works of Topography.* Twyman's classified bibliography should be the starting point for anyone wishing to examine original and secondary sources on the subject. European articles and books on lithography published before 1820 are listed on pp. 257–62. Several of these are in English, and it is likely that they were the main sources of information for the first Americans who attempted lithographic printing.

3. As quoted in John Thomas Carey, "The American Lithograph from Its Inception to 1865 with Biographical Considerations of Twenty Lithographers and a Check List of Their Works," 50. Carey's work is a basic source of information of use to every serious student of the subject despite the advance of scholarship in many of the areas treated in his pioneering work.

4. This publication is identified in ibid., 50, 440, as Jas. Catbush, *The American Artist's Manual or Dictionary of Practical Knowledge in the Application of Philosophy to the Arts and Manufacturers* (Philadelphia, 1814). Carey gives no publisher, and I cannot find the work listed in the National Union Catalog. The entry referred to is in volume 1, a subdivision on Stone Etching under the heading Etching.

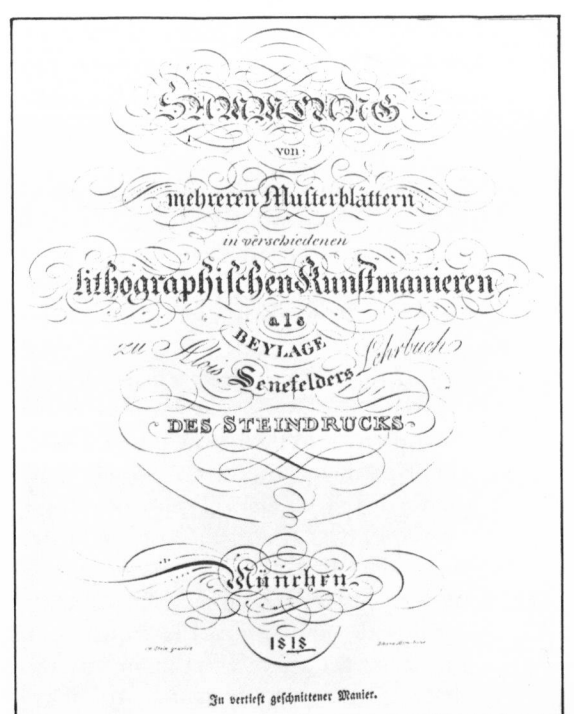

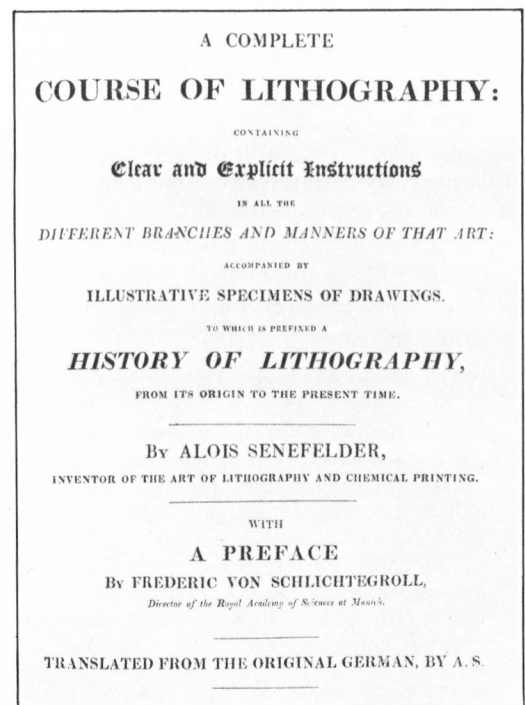

Figure 10. Title pages of German edition in 1818 and English edition in 1819 of Alois Senefelder's treatise on lithography. Facsimiles. (Fine Art Library, Cornell University.)

Figure 11. Unidentified building, 1819. Drawn and lithographed by Bass Otis, published by the *Analectic Magazine*. (American Antiquarian Society.)

those of Otis.[5] Although the English translation of Senefelder's treatise on his invention was published in London in the same year as the *Analectic Magazine*'s article, this journal's account of how to print by lithography would doubtless have been the earliest exposure to the subject for the vast majority of interested Americans. While misleading in some respects, this early description is nonetheless worth quoting at some length because of its historic place in the literature of lithography in the United States.

The author began this part of his article by examining the printing surface:

> The properties required, are, that the stone employed shall bear a tolerably smooth, and perfectly uniform surface; . . . when it has been rubbed down with sand, and then with emery . . . it must have just roughness enough and no more, to catch hold of the crayon, and take the mark of the drawing: hence, although smooth, it must not be polished. Another property is, that when dry, it shall imbibe on its surface a sufficient quantity of water, to become so moist that a greasy or oily substance, will not adhere to the moist part of the stone: . . . the stone from whence Mr. B. Otis took the impression in question, is purely calcareous, dissolving without residuum in marine or muriatic acid. . . .
>
> The stone being thus prepared . . . the proposed design is traced upon it, either by liquid ink, or solid crayon.

The author then provided formulas for making both lithographic ink and crayons. The latter consisted of three parts of "fine white soap," two parts of "purified tallow," one part of "white or yellow wax," melted together with the addition of "sufficient . . . burnt lampblack to give the necessary colour and consistence." With this or an ink of similar properties, the artist was to draw his design on the surface of the stone and let it dry "for 24 to 30 hours."

For a strong impression the author advised "putting a border of wax round the stone" and pouring on the surface "a mixture of one part of nitric acid, mixed with fifty parts . . . of water; or, one part of muriatic acid to forty parts of water, and let it remain for about 6 to 8 minutes." The surface was then to be sponged clean and "moistened by means of a sponge, dipped in pure water, till it refused to imbibe any more."

A leather-covered wooden roller, "charged with very fine engraver's ink, is then passed two or three times over the surface of the stone; the ink adheres to all the lines of the drawing, because, like the ink itself, they are greasy; but it does not adhere to the part of the stone which is moist with water." A sheet of dampened paper was then to be laid over the inked stone in the press, "a smooth board . . . placed above it," and a roller controlled by a winch so as to exert "about a thousand pounds weight . . . passed slowly over the surface of the board." The paper could then be removed, the printer's ink originally put on the stone now being transferred to the paper and producing the print (Figure 12).

The author, in concluding this portion of the article, mentioned that after a time "the stone may begin to be a little blurred." The remedy was to "pass over it a sponge moistened with oil of turpentine; then wash it with pure water. By this treatment, the whole design will be apparently discharged, but it is not so, for on passing the roller charged with ink, over the surface of the stone, every line, even the most delicate, will again become visible, and the printing may be proceeded in, as at first." He explained the reason for this phenomenon: "The drawing is left not merely on the surface of the stone, but the ink and the crayon leave a trace that penetrates to a certain depth." The lampblack in the ink or crayon was added only to enable the artist "to see his drawing as he proceeds."[6]

In the same year that this article appeared, Benjamin Silliman's *American Journal of Science* carried the first of several short notices about lithography, culminating in 1822 with three lithographs from the press of William Armand Barnet and Isaac Doolittle.[7] One of these is a view of an open-face coal mine in France, probably the first view to be printed in America by true lithography.[8] In 1823, Henry Stone, who had announced the establishment of his lithographic press in Washington late in the previous year, printed thirty plates used in a work titled *The Timber Merchant's Guide*.[9]

Following these pioneering efforts came a flood of other notices, articles, and examples. The shop of Peter Maverick, an engraver who used lithography as well, provided several

5. Slightly earlier than the *Analectic Magazine* print, Otis produced a portrait of Rev. Abner Kneeland for use as the frontispiece in a collection of Kneeland's sermons. Most authorities regard this as an example of stone engraving rather than a lithograph. The *Analectic Magazine* print seems to be some combination of stone etching and true lithography. For Otis and these prints, see Joseph Jackson, "Bass Otis, America's First Lithographer"; Harry T. Peters, *America on Stone: The Other Printmakers to the American People, A Chronicle of American Lithography other than that of Currier & Ives*, 303–4; and Carey, "American Lithograph," 32, 52–56. Jackson suggests that the author of the *Analectic Magazine* article, signed only "C," was Judge Cooper. The article mentions that "the art [of lithography] has been successfully tried on specimens of stone from Frankfort, in Kentucky, procured by Judge Cooper." Perhaps it was he who suggested that the editor of the magazine print in its February 1818 issue a short and not very informative article about lithography from the *Edinburgh Magazine*. Thomas Cooper was then professor of applied chemistry and minerology at the University of Pennsylvania. An Englishman who came to America before 1800, Cooper had been involved while a young man with a firm of calico-printers in England. Senefelder's English patent in 1801 was for printing on fabric by lithography, and perhaps Cooper first learned of the process through his former associates.

6. *Analectic Magazine* 14 (July 1819): 66–72.

7. My colleague John Wells called my attention to the notices and provided me with copies. They appeared in this order: 1 (1819): 439; 2 (1820): 341, 346, 348; 3 (1821): 370; 4 (1822): 169–71, 197.

8. The artist was Jacques Milbert, later to produce a series of American views printed in France, including several of urban settlements along the Hudson River. About the same time as those in the *American Journal of Science*, two true lithographs of fish appeared in the *Journal of the Philadelphia Academy of Natural Sciences*. See George H. Eckhardt, "Early Lithography in Philadelphia." Carey, "American Lithograph," 56–57, discusses the matter of priority. Peters, *America on Stone*, 88–90, has an entry on Barnet & Doolittle. Their New York City address was 23 Lumber Street, and there in 1822 they also printed the twenty-one lithographic illustrations for *A Grammar of Botany*, whose publisher added this note: "The publisher feels a becoming gratification in informing the readers of the work that the beautiful and appropriate drawings, which so highly embellish it, are specimens of American Lithography. They are from the pencil of Mr. Stansbury, and were executed at the Lithographic Press of Barnet & Doolittle, of this City." As Peters, from whom this quotation is taken, remarks, "This was the first book illustrated with lithographs in the United States" (Peters, *America on Stone*, 89).

9. For Stone's background and work, together with a list of his works, see Edith A. Wright and Josephine A. McDevitt, "Henry Stone, Lithographer." Carey, "American Lithograph," 63–67, provides additional comments about Stone. See also Peters, *America on Stone*, 376–77.

Figure 12. Lithographer. Published in Boston by L. Prang & Co. (American Antiquarian Society.)

lithographic plates for the *Annals of the Lyceum of Natural History of New York* in 1824 and 1825.[10] The latter year also saw the first examples of lithography produced by John Pendleton in Boston, whose shop under the eventual direction of his brother, William, became the training place of many of the country's early lithographic craftsmen.[11]

In 1826 the *United States Literary Gazette*, a Boston publication, provided its readers with a long and detailed description of the lithographic process. For an American relying only on domestic publications, this would have provided the earliest account of the transfer process, a technique of immeasurable importance in the development of commercial lithography, including the production of city views. Although the anonymous author (possibly William Pendleton) did not reveal the formula for making transfer paper or how an image could be shifted from the paper to a stone, this portion of the article was otherwise admirably informative about the advantages of the process:

> The drawing may be made on prepared paper, and then, by an easy process, be transferred from the paper to the stone. This process is not confined to drawings originally made on paper, but is applicable to impressions already taken from the stone. In this manner, an indefinite number of impressions may be ob-

tained by transferring the copy to several stones, or, when the prints are small, several copies to one large stone, which will greatly diminish the expense of printing; or if a large number of impressions . . . were . . . wanted, several might be thrown off in a few moments, on several stones, and given to be printed in different presses.[12]

12. "Lithography," in *United States Literary Gazette*. The concluding lines of the article suggest Pendleton's authorship or inspiration: "We look upon it as a fortunate circumstance, that a lithographic press has been established in this city by Mr. Pendleton. He has studied the art in the best printing-houses of Paris, and has commenced its practice here, well furnished with knowledge and materials to pursue it to advantage. We hope his skill and enterprise will meet with the encouragement which they so eminently deserve." The transfer process, like virtually all other elements of lithography, had been thoroughly explored and described by Senefelder in his manual of 1818. American readers could have learned of it from the English translation in the following year or from a description by Charles Hullmandel published in 1820 in London. See "Lithography," no. 1 of "Papers in Polite Arts." Hullmandel was a major figure in English lithography and the author of an early treatise that had great influence on his contemporaries both in England and elsewhere, surely including the United States. This was *The Art of Drawing on Stone*. Editions of 1833 and 1835 indicate its popularity. Hullmandel's career figures prominently in Twyman, *Lithography*. Senefelder stated his belief that the transfer technique might prove to be "the principal and most important part of my discovery." Senefelder, *Complete Course*, 256. He provided formulas for preparing transfer paper and for transfer ink. The earliest treatise I have been able to find on transfer paper and transfer techniques is Alexr. Miller, *The Hand-Book of Transfer Lithography*. A copy of this rare work is in the Butler Library, Columbia University. The author provides a formula for preparing transfer paper "made use of by the late Mr. Alexander Forrester, of Edinburgh, so early as 1819 or 1820, whose specimens of transfer-writing and printing have not been surpassed since" (24).

10. Stephen DeWitt Stephens, *The Mavericks: American Engravers*, 65–67; Carey, "American Lithograph," 67–73.

11. For an exemplary account of the Pendleton establishment, see David Tatham, "The Pendleton-Moore Shop—Lithographic Artists in Boston, 1825–1840"; also Carey, "American Lithograph," 77–87.

Lithography and Its Development • 27

One of the major advantages of the transfer process was that a lithographer could draw an unreversed image on transfer paper. If he drew directly on stone he had to produce a mirror image so that the print resulting from placing blank paper facedown on the inked stone would be unreversed when lifted from the surface. Lithographers often used a mirror behind the sketch they were copying on stone and looked at the image in the mirror rather than at the sketch itself.[13] Transfer paper made this unnecessary.

The year 1826 also saw the publication of the first views of American cities printed in this country by lithography. Two views of Buffalo and two of Lockport (Plate 56) appeared with several other lithographs in an elaborate publication issued to commemorate the opening of Erie Canal. These came from the recently established New York press of Anthony Imbert and were drawn by George Catlin. The work was crude, but the images were recognizable. Because of the novelty of the method used to print these illustrations, the compiler of the work provided his readers with a brief description of lithography, including the transfer process.[14]

The *Journal of the Franklin Institute* in Philadelphia helped to spread knowledge of lithographic technology through a series of articles, notices, and announcements of prizes given by the organization for notable examples of lithographic printing.[15] Not long after these began to appear, David Kennedy and William B. Lucas began a lithographic venture in Philadelphia, and a year later, in 1829, John Pendleton came from Boston to join Francis Kearney and Cephas G. Childs in founding a rival firm.[16]

By the end of the 1830s when separately issued lithographic city views began to be published in some numbers,

every major urban center and a number of smaller places could boast of one or more lithographic printers.[17] Knowledge of lithographic printing technology was then widespread, and while individual printers from time to time devised improved techniques, nothing could long remain secret in a trade whose members moved from place to place with such alacrity.[18]

View publishers and customers who wanted colored depictions of cities in the first two decades of American urban lithography had to rely on hand coloring to satisfy their tastes. Perhaps some purchasers of black-and-white lithographs attempted to add their own colors, but most colored prints of this period were supplied by the publisher or the artist. Often the artist acted as his own publisher and offered prospective clients a choice between uncolored and hand-colored impressions.

The development of lithographic color printing made it possible to provide customers with colored prints at far less cost and trouble, although, unfortunately, with results that were often artistically inferior to handwork. Lithographic printing in two or more colors originated in Europe in the 1830s and was brought to America in 1840 by William Sharp, who had worked for the pioneer English color lithographer, Charles Hullmandel.[19] In Boston, Sharp soon went into partnership with Francis Michelin, another former employee of Hullmandel, and it was evidently Michelin who introduced color lithography to New York when he established his own firm in that city, probably in 1844.[20] Edward Weber, the most important early lithographer in Baltimore, used color in 1842 to print a sheet-music cover and an illustration in the *Maryland Medical and Surgical Journal*.[21] By

13. Since many city views contain street names and other lettering, one can look for certain letters that gave lithographers trouble: *N* and *S* in particular. A reversed letter probably indicates that transfer paper was not used.

14. Cadwallader Colden, *Memoir Prepared at the Request of the Committee of the Common Council of the City of New York, and Presented to the Mayor of the City, at the Celebration of the Completion of the New York Canals* (1825). Despite the date on the first title page, there are good reasons to believe that 1826 is the true date of publication. The appendix has a separate title page, with a date of 1826. At the back of the volume are several lithographic facsimiles of letters sent by persons receiving medals commemorating the occasion. The latest is from General Lafayette, written from France and dated 27 June 1826. The year 1826 is also given as the publication date in *Club of Odd Volumes, Notes on an Exhibition of Early American Lithographs, 1819–1859*, 7.

15. Brief quotations from some of these can be found in Eckhardt, "Early Lithography." My search of the early issues of the *Journal of the Franklin Institute* yielded the following: 4 (1827): 57–62, 135–40, 264–68, 334–39, 393–96, 415; 5 (1828): 267–70, 341–44, 403–7; 3, n. s. (1829): 279–83, 302–5; 4, n. s. (1830): 138–39.

16. Carey, "American Lithograph," 87–89; Nicholas B. Wainwright, *Philadelphia in the Romantic Age of Lithography . . .*, 6–29. As in other cities in the early days of American lithography, members of firms changed with great frequency, and new firms came into being as old ones dissolved. In Philadelphia, for example, Pendleton soon withdrew from Pendleton, Kearney, and Childs, and shortly thereafter the firm was terminated, although Childs continued to produce lithographs. Henry Inman joined forces with Childs in 1830. In 1831 Peter Duval arrived from France, worked for Childs and Inman for a time, formed a partnership in 1832 with George Lehman, and the two bought out Childs and Inman (Carey, "American Lithograph," 89–90). For material on other early American lithographic firms, including several already discussed, see Charles Henry Taylor, "Some Notes on Early American Lithography."

17. Peters, *America on Stone*, is the best source on early lithographers. Entries are alphabetical under the names of artists, printers, and publishers. In addition to sources already cited, articles about individual lithographic firms include "Rhea Mansfield Knittle, The Kelloggs, Hartford Lithographers." Maryland printmakers—many of them lithographers—are listed and their firms described in Lois B. McCauley, *Maryland Historical Prints, 1752–1889 . . .*, 227–36. Notes on major American lithographic firms can also be found in John and Katherine Ebert, *Old American Prints for Collectors*, 90–119. Peter C. Marzio, *The Democratic Art: Pictures for a 19th-Century America*, is also a splendid source for material about these early printers. See, for example, his treatment of the Endicott firm, founded in New York in 1828, pp. 42–43.

18. Scientific and technical articles continued to appear also. Those published in England may have had the widest readership in this country, but lithographers from other countries undoubtedly sought out publications in their native languages also. The general reader could have consulted several sources, among them Edward Hazen, *The Panorama of Professions and Trades*, 175–76. Or, both layman and printer alike could have turned to the 1832 American edition of the *Edinburgh Encyclopaedia* for a long and informative entry, David Brewster, ed., 12: 91–95. The modern reader will find this as helpful as any brief technical description of lithography written before the Civil War.

19. Bettina A. Norton, "William Sharp: Accomplished Lithographer"; Sinclair H. Hitchings, "'Fine Art Lithography' in Boston: Craftsmanship in Color," 51–75, 103–25; and Marzio, *The Democratic Art*, 17. I should note that Senefelder in the treatise on his invention describes a method for printing in colors using multiple stones, each inked with the desired color. As he stated in 1818, "Since the year 1809, I have devoted all my leisure to the improvement of Lithography. . . . Such progress has . . . been made in printing in colours, that I produce not only coloured prints, but likewise copies so like oil-paintings, that it is impossible to discover any difference between these copies and the original pictures" (Senefelder, *Complete Course*, 80).

20. Peters, *America on Stone*, 281–84, gives 1844 as the earliest date for Michelin's New York City address.

21. McCauley, *Maryland*, 236.

midcentury or shortly thereafter, Edward Sachse's firm—also in Baltimore—was routinely printing city views in color.

In Philadelphia, Peter Duval added color printing to his services in 1849, and a year later he won a bronze medal for an example of his work at the London world's fair.[22] In 1850 lithographers of two inland cities announced they could print in multiple colors. Hall & Mooney in Buffalo boasted of "Lithographic Printing in Colors, as well done as in the Eastern Cities," while George Gibson and Company of Cincinnati claimed more modestly that they were prepared to do "lithographic Printing in Gold and colors, executed in a superior style."[23] Well before the Civil War, therefore, these and dozens of printers throughout the country had passed through the experimental stage of color printing and were busy producing colored prints, including city views, for their customers.

Each color required the use of a separate stone. A technical encyclopedia of 1872 explains what was involved:

> An outline drawing is made by tracing, and this is transferred to all the stones . . . required to complete the picture; so as to secure exactness in the correlation of all parts on each stone. Within these outlines, and upon these different stones, the artist draws the different tints and colors. The number of stones . . . needed . . . varies of course with the character of the picture to be reproduced. . . .
> . . . The first proof is a light ground-tint, covering nearly all the surface. . . . The next proof, from the second stone, contains all the shades of another color. . . . The number of impressions, however, does not necessarily indicate the number of colors . . . because the colors and tints are greatly multiplied by combinations created in the process of printing one over another.[24]

In printing, therefore, the paper had to be applied successively to each of the stones. Obviously, registration was critical so that the colors could be applied exactly where they should appear without gaps or unplanned overlapping. One manual of lithographic printing devoted an entire chapter to how this could be achieved.[25] The author identified the most used device for securing proper registration as one employing two needles to fit two tiny holes diagonally opposite one another at precisely the same points on each stone. Needle holes made in the sheet for the printing of the first stone could be used to line up the paper exactly on all stones subsequently used. However, accurate registration required more than proper positioning of the paper on each stone. The lithographic artist had to draw the colors accurately on each stone. Often he used a key stone on which the boundaries of the various colors were outlined. He then took an impression on paper and used this to transfer the outlines to the other stones to serve as a guide. Alternatively, he could dust the freshly inked lines on the transfer paper with red chalk, place the paper facedown on the stone for which he wished an outline guide, and thus transfer the chalk to the stone. After drawing on this stone, he could wash away the chalk.

Many—perhaps most—of the city views published after the middle of the nineteenth century were printed with the basic design in black and with a second color added to provide cloud and shadow details. The most common colors were yellow brown or gray green. Many artists and publishers of city views specialized in such toned lithographs, rarely if ever using additional colors.[26]

In the hands of a skilled lithographer, this one color could give the impression of a range of tonal values and even suggest other colors when used by itself, combined with blacks of varying intensity, or omitted altogether to produce highlight effects. To take a ·remarkably effective example, the view of San Jose, California, in 1875 drawn by Charles Gifford and printed in San Francisco by the A. L. Bancroft Company (Plate 57) gives most viewers the impression that parts of the print have been colored green. This is how the eye records the superimposition of gray (actually minute spots of black ink separated from one another by the grain of the stone or zinc plate) and yellow brown—a combination used by the lithographer for areas of grass and trees.

In this print, as on hundreds of others, the tone stone was used to furnish a darkened sky against which appear puffy cumulus clouds created by irregular areas of unprinted white paper. In the lower portion of the print showing the city, the artist applied the tone to the shadowed walls of buildings. To emphasize important structures and perhaps to suggest that they were constructed of light-colored stone, the artist omitted the shadow tone altogether. The effect is like a spotlight and probably was created by scraping the stone to eliminate all traces of tone in those areas. Blacks vary from rich, dark shades to light grays, sometimes used by themselves

22. Duval gives a brief sketch of his firm's experience with color printing in his entry on lithography in J. Luther Ringwalt, ed., *American Encyclopaedia of Printing*, 283. For his color work, see also Marzio, *The Democratic Art*, 23–24; Peters, *America on Stone*, 163–68; and Wainwright, *Philadelphia*, 30–45, 61–74.

23. Peters, *America on Stone*, 203; Marzio, *The Democratic Art*, 131. Marzio gives 1852 as the date of the earliest surviving color lithograph printed in Cincinnati. This was done by Middleton and Wallace, a firm that, with the addition of Hines Strobridge, was to print many city views of Cincinnati and elsewhere in the Midwest for several artists and publishers. Another Cincinnati firm, Ehrgott and Forbriger, also did excellent work in color.

24. Edward H. Knight, comp., *Knight's American Mechanical Dictionary*, 546. For a set of twenty-four plates showing the results of using twelve colors in printing color lithographs of birds in a *Funk & Wagnalls Standard Dictionary*, see Funk & Wagnalls Company, *The Art of Lithography*. The plates were done by the Taber-Prang Art Company of Springfield, Massachusetts. The only copy of this I have seen is in Olin Library, Cornell University.

25. W. D. Richmond, *The Grammar of Lithography, a Practical Guide for the Artist and Printer in Commercial & Artistic Lithography, & Chromo-lithography, Zincography, Photo-lithography, and Lithographic Machine Printing.* The book's chapters evidently appeared in issues of *The Printing Times and Lithographer* before October 1878, the date given in the editor's introduction. I know of no better source of information about the practical aspects of nineteenth-century lithography. It covers all areas of the field and is clearly written and thoroughly detailed. For a full explanation of the methods described, see pp. 144–46.

26. Most nineteenth-century printers seem to have referred to the second stone as a *tint* stone. I prefer to use *tone* for reasons stated by Joseph A. Baird, Jr., in his analysis of the lithographic city views of San Francisco: "A tone in modern color theory is any type of color, of whatever intensity and degree of lightness or darkness. A tint is a tone lighter than normal; a shade is a tone darker than normal. As the 19th century advanced, the degree of chromatic intensity in lithographic 'tints' increased from a tone lighter than normal to normal, or even darker than normal. Therefore it seems preferable to use the general word tone, rather than tint" (Baird, "Introduction" to Joseph Armstrong Baird, Jr., and Edwin Clyve Evans, *Historic Lithographs of San Francisco*). Baird's introduction and notes are invaluable for reviewing lithographic printing and publishing in San Francisco. They are less well known than they deserve to be because of the small size of the edition of this gigantic volume, which includes full-size or nearly full-size facsimiles of the most important lithographic city views of San Francisco.

and other times combined with varying intensities of the tone. Modern reproduction techniques only suggest the subtleties of this and similar lithographic city views.

Not all toned lithographs exhibit such sophistication. Probably in the majority of cases, such as the views produced in the 1850s by Kuchel & Dresel in California or in the 1880s by Lucien Burleigh in New York (see plates 21, 22, and 30), the tone appears with greater uniformity and mainly as a distinctly separate element rather than being combined with the black to give the impression of a derivative color. While these journeyman efforts neither technically nor artistically approach the results achieved by Gifford and Bancroft and a few others, they nevertheless add a pleasing touch of both realism and decoration to the underlying composition.

Nearly as popular as toned lithographic city views were those printed with three stones. Normally, the printer used black, yellow brown, and blue. Overprinting the two colors created green as a derivative. Thus, the blue stone carried ink for the sky, water, and any grass or other vegetation to be green in the finished print. Yellow brown appeared on streets, the shadowed sides of structures, and also in the areas of grass and trees to create green when combined with blue. The lithographer might also use yellow brown for bare earth and unwooded portions of distant hills and mountains.

Such three-stone lithographs apparently came from the press with fairly intense colors. On many impressions today, however, the color is faded and appears less distinct because of general age-toning of the acidic pulp paper on which most were printed. In some cases one or both colors are so badly faded as to be discernible only after careful inspection.

Less common but still numerous are urban lithographs printed from four stones, red being the usual addition to suggest brick or stone building facades but used elsewhere as well where appropriate. While red could also be used with blue to obtain purple, or with yellow to create orange, few prints show this degree of color range. On occasion printers exceeded the normal limit of four colors. One example is a view of Milwaukee printed in 1866 by Louis Lipman. Here at least six stones were used, and all colors were created directly rather than from overprinting. [27]

A far more elaborate piece of color lithography is a very long view of Milwaukee in 1898, printed—probably as a promotional and advertising device—by the Gugler Lithographic Company of that city. Sixteen colors were used in its production. Since each color seems to have been printed from two stones carefully joined, thirty-two stones would have been involved. [28]

Many other examples of skillful or unusual color printing can be found among lithographic city views. Edward Sachse and Co. of Baltimore, John Bachmann of New York, the Strobridge firm and its Middleton and Wallace predecessor

in Cincinnati, the American Publishing Company in Milwaukee, and Britton & Rey of San Francisco were among the printers who did consistently superior work in producing what are sometimes referred to as chromolithographs. [29] Knowledge of the techniques of color lithography spread with the publication of articles and manuals on the subject, and in the post–Civil War years almost any lithographic press could produce acceptable color work if the occasion demanded. [30]

Color printing of city views all but eliminated hand-colored lithographs, although occasionally hand coloring was added to printed color on some views. One can also find views printed in color but with the darker areas coated with hand-applied gum arabic to give these portions of the print greater depth and brilliance. In general, the Civil War years mark the division between the era of the hand-colored lithograph and the time when the colors came from inks applied to multiple stones or zinc plates. In the great majority of cases where post–Civil War lithographs are hand colored, the coloring is likely to be modern. [31]

---

27. This print is illustrated in black and white and described in Thomas Beckman, *Milwaukee Illustrated: Panoramic and Bird's-Eye Views of a Midwestern Metropolis, 1844–1908*, description of exhibit item 15.

28. Ibid., description of item 46, where the view appears in black and white. A color reproduction is used for the title page of John W. Reps, *Cities on Stone: Nineteenth Century Lithograph Images of the Urban West*. The view is remarkable also for another feature: it is a 360-degree panorama.

29. As applied to city views, this term has little meaning. Peter C. Marzio defines "chromolithographs" in part by distinguishing them from "tinted lithographs," which he describes as involving "two or three stones, though seldom more. The image is still printed from just one stone, but one or two tints that flood across the picture surface are printed from second and third stones. The tints thus create atmospheric effects but do not compose the image." According to Marzio, a chromolithograph "is a printed-color lithograph in which the image is composed of at least three colors, each applied to the print from a separate stone. Unlike tinted lithographs, with their second and third colors casting hues across the print, the colors of a chromo make up the picture itself" (Marzio, *The Democratic Art*, 9). Marzio proposed these definitions earlier in "The Democratic Art of Chromolithography in America: An Overview." Marzio is inconsistent in applying his own definition. In *The Democratic Art*, he singles out a view of New Ulm, Minnesota, printed in 1860 by Ehrgott and Forbriger in Cincinnati as "a finely finished chromolithograph." He correctly states,"The New Ulm view contained colors and shades created by the overlapping of four basic inks: red, yellow, blue, and black. The green, for example, was made by printing blue over yellow, while orange was the result of red over yellow, and some of the browns were produced by a mixture of black, yellow, and red." He neglects to note that if the red, yellow, and blue stones had not been used, the image of New Ulm's buildings and topographic features would have clearly appeared from the lines of the stone inked with black. In other words, this is *not* an example where "the colors of a chromo make up the picture itself." It is a conventional lithograph with three colors added. While disagreeing with Marzio on this matter of terminology, I want to express my profound appreciation to him for his research and writing over the years and acknowledge my debt for the help he has extended through his published works and in personal conversation.

30. Encyclopedia articles by Duval in Ringwalt, *Encyclopaedia of Printing*, and in Knight, *Mechanical Dictionary*, probably provided sufficient details for an experienced lithographer to begin color work. Two extensive English manuals, with wide circulation in America, were also available to those who needed every step of the process described at length. In addition to Richmond, *Grammar of Lithography*, with its several chapters on color printing, there was the same author's *Colour and Colour Printing as Applied to Lithography*. In the bibliography of *The Democratic Art*, Marzio cites an edition of 1912, and there were several others during the intervening years. Probably just as important in spreading knowledge about this and other applications of lithography was the constant movement of lithographers from one firm and from one part of the country to another.

31. Most print dealers add color to uncolored or toned lithographic city views in the belief—probably correct—that they will bring higher prices and be easier to sell. Dealers and collectors alike often feel it desirable to treat a badly age-toned, stained, or foxed print by bleaching. Old coloring is usually removed or diminished in intensity by this process. Modern hand coloring then may be justified to restore the view to something like its original appearance. Opinions differ on this matter, with purists preferring to retain the print in the condition in which it came into their hands. I should note that some purchasers of views in the nineteenth century may have

The development of color printing was only one of many technological changes affecting American lithography and

---

added their own color or had the views colored by others. The Amon Carter Museum in Fort Worth has a number of Kuchel & Dresel views of California mining towns, originally issued as toned lithographs, but skillfully and beautifully colored. These once were owned by the Electors of Hannover. My guess is that the coloring was done in Europe rather than California.

thus the printing of city views. Early and crude hand presses gave way to more sophisticated models, which in turn surrendered part of their work to steam-powered presses. Zinc plates came to play an increasingly important role as substitutes for lithographic stones. Innovative photographers and lithographers began to use the camera in creating images on printing surfaces. It is to these developments that we now turn.

4. Changing Technology: Improvements in Lithographic Printing

Although Senefelder experimented with, developed, or anticipated virtually every aspect of lithography, he did not have the time or inclination to perfect every element of his new method of printing. During most of the nineteenth century, others followed in Senefelder's footsteps and changed and improved the process he had invented. Early in the century many persons concentrated on designing and constructing presses that would be more efficient than the pole press Senefelder first developed (Figure 13). His press exerted pressure on the inked stone and the paper laid over its surface by moving a scraper blade across the top of the tympan (a sheet of leather protecting the paper). The printer manipulated a pedal to force the blade against the tympan with sufficient force to make a successful impression.[1] In France, Godefroy Englemann designed a press in which the stone also remained stationary but the pressure came from a cylinder passing over the stone.

Neither Senefelder's nor Englemann's press proved fully satisfactory, and by the time lithography reached America in the early 1820s, most European presses incorporated a stationary scraper bar or blade that could be adjusted for the desired pressure (Figure 13). A movable horizontal frame contained the stone, and the operator caused the stone, paper, and tympan to pass under the scraper by using a crank or turning a wheel with starlike handles projecting beyond the rim.[2]

American lithographic printers depended almost entirely on European manufacturers and suppliers for the materials of their trade. Before the Civil War, most of the presses probably came from England, France, or Germany, although at least one American company advertised presses of its own manufacture.[3] Hand-operated lever or star-wheel presses were slow and inefficient. Peter C. Marzio describes the effort required for their operation:

> The heavy stone had to be fixed to the bed and tightened to prevent any shifting. The scraper had to be adjusted to the proper height so that when the bed was raised just the right amount of pressure was applied. After the stone was inked very carefully and the paper laid across it, the tympan was lowered. Pressure from a lever or pedal was applied, while a handle or star wheel cranked the stone beneath the scraper. When the entire print was made, the pressure was released, the bed drawn back, and the tympan lifted from the stone. The print was then peeled off, and the entire operation repeated.[4]

Development of a self-acting tympan sped the process somewhat. This feature could be found on the presses manufactured in the early 1840s in Scotland by M. McCulloch & Co. The firm advertised that its press could operate up to one-third faster than any others of the time.[5] Even so, lithographic printing remained time-consuming, and the quality of the results remained highly dependent on the skills of the press operator.

An Austrian patented the first commercially successful steam-powered press in 1851 after solving the difficult problems of automatically moistening and inking the stone. An observer for an Edinburgh periodical described the operation of this marvel:

> A boy, standing on a low platform, supplies sheets of damp paper one by one; each sheet is caught by a small piece of apparatus, and is carried under one cylinder and over another, until it presents itself in a printed form near one end of the machine, where a second boy removes it. The machine effects all these movements of the paper by steampower; but it is at the same time actively engaged in preparing the stone for the printing; one cylinder damps it, one roller inks it, and other pieces of apparatus draw it to and fro and press the damped paper down upon it.

The Scottish audience must have appreciated the financial implications of this innovation as analyzed by the author:

> It practically compresses *hours* into *minutes*: it can certainly print thirty times as fast as the hand-press, and in some instances it rises to sixty times. We ourselves have seen a folio shop-bill, with a pictorial heading, printed by the machine at the rate of 800 copies per hour, or 8000 in a day—the day's work at the hand-press amounting usually to only about 150 copies.[6]

1. The development of lithographic presses is the focus of Peter C. Marzio's "American Lithographic Technology Before the Civil War." Figure 6 shows drawings of Senefelder's pole press. See also Michael L. Twyman, "The Lithographic Hand Press 1796–1850." The press is illustrated and described in Senefelder's *A Complete Course of Lithography* . . . , 191–96. The New York reprint of 1977 with an introduction by A. Hyatt Mayor contains supplementary illustrations from the German and French editions of 1818. Several of these illustrate presses of the time. Perhaps it was one of these that Rudolph Ackerman, publisher of the English edition of Senefelder's work, sent to Stephan Elliot of Charleston, South Carolina, in 1822. W. J. Burk, "Rudolph Ackerman, Promoter of the Arts and Sciences."

2. Leather straps were fastened to a cylinder attached to the lever or wheel. The other ends of the straps were fixed on the frame containing the stone. An illustration of an early version of a press of this type can be found in Senefelder, *Complete Course*, opposite p. 198. There a single strap runs from the frame to a drive wheel connected to levers.

3. Marzio, "Lithographic Technology," points out how little is known of American press production. The only American patent issued before 1860 of which records survive is described by Marzio, who on pp. 232–36 reproduces three sheets of the patent application drawings. Marzio's exhaustive search for American press manufacturers turned up only Charles Massey of Philadelphia. There are no records of his product and no surviving example. In fact, as Marzio states, "Not a single press used in America before the Civil War has survived."

4. Ibid., 242.

5. Ibid., 237–39; Twyman, "Lithographic Hand Press," 35.

6. "A New Career for Lithography," 406. The writer of this article makes clear that he is describing the press invented by Sigl of Austria, who is credited by Marzio, "Lithographic Technology," 243, as the patentee on 30 May 1851 of the "first commercially successful steam press." P. S. Duval, the progressive lithographic printer in Philadelphia, on the other hand, states, "The first steam-press was invented in Paris in 1850, by a Frenchman

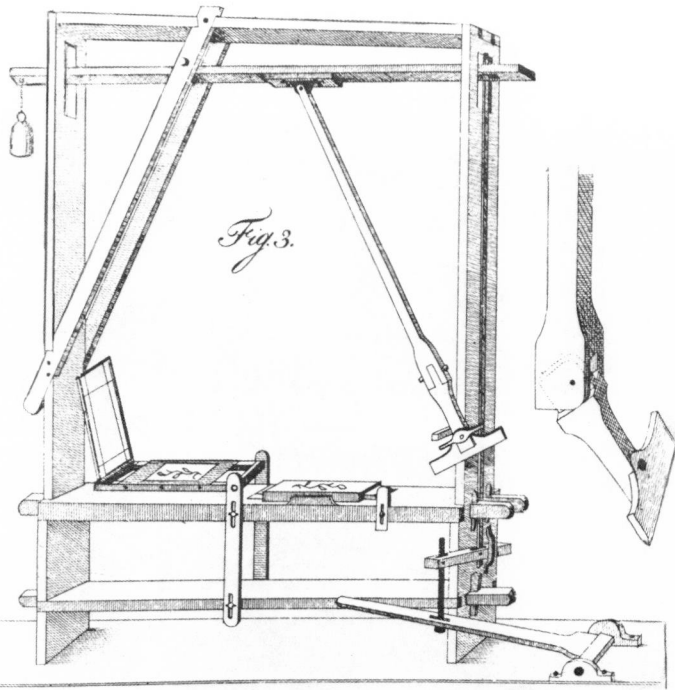

American printers evidently did not immediately acquire presses of this type. Peter Duval, one of the consistently innovative lithographers of America, did begin to use steam power at his Philadelphia shop as early as 1850, but only to the extent of modifying his hand presses slightly to ease the physical labor of cranking the stone under the scraper bar.[7]

Figure 13. Senefelder lithographic press with movable scraper bar (13a). Press depicted in 1836 with fixed scraper bar and movable frame (13b). German press of 1871 (13c). (Olin Library, Cornell University.)

The advantages of higher-speed mechanical presses soon became apparent to American printers. By 1870 many shops had become partly mechanized, although the need for smaller hand presses remained. Doubtless many of these power presses were imported, but Richard Hoe of New York began manufacturing a domestic design, probably as early as 1870 (Figure 14). Illustrations of the R. Hoe & Co. power press were used in Ringwalt's influential *American Encyclopaedia of Printing* of 1871 and *Knight's American Mechanical Dictionary* published two years later. In the latter publication, the operation of the Hoe press was described at length.[8]

Printers of city views owned power presses like this. For example, Henry Seifert of Milwaukee bought his first steam press in 1870, added another two years later, and a third in 1876. Even so, in 1872 Seifert's Milwaukee Lithographing and Engraving Co. operated no fewer than sixteen hand presses alongside its two steam-driven ones.[9] Perhaps only those city views expected to sell in substantial numbers were run on the larger presses—views of places like Boston, New York, Philadelphia, Chicago, and San Francisco—or those

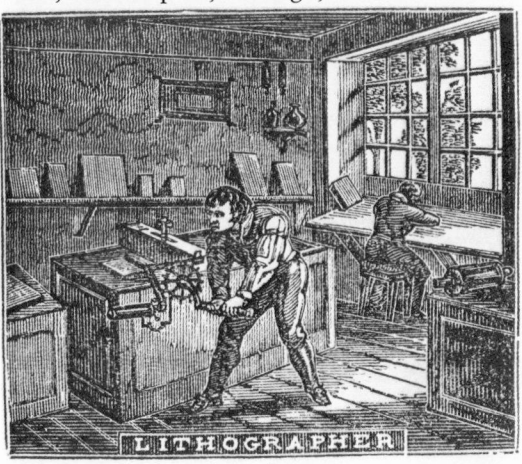

to be given away for advertising or promotional purposes. For the smaller quantities in which the great majority of urban lithographs were printed, the use of a power press may not have been justified.

A variety of hand presses were available to American printers after the Civil War. The popularity of the presses manufactured by Richard Hoe's firm (Figure 15) is suggested by its selection for illustration in the two technical works compiled by Ringwalt and Knight. Both illustrations came from Hoe's catalog, which described a complete line of all types of printing presses and equipment.[10]

Lithographic techniques underwent further substantial changes over the years, and, following the Civil War, American printers speedily responded to refinements in older methods and the introduction of new ways of reproducing images. Two developments, the use of zinc plates instead of

named Eugues. He sold the patent for England to Messrs. Hughes & Kimber, press-builders of London, who made important improvements on the first pattern, and introduced it into the United States in 1866." This appears in Duval's informative entry, "Lithography," in the invaluable *American Encyclopaedia of Printing*, edited by J. Luther Ringwalt, 278.

7. Duval, "Lithography," 279: "In 1850 the writer of this notice, by a simple combination, added the steam-power to his hand-presses, but only so far as to save muscular labor." This seems to dispose of the confusion concerning claims that Duval was using complex, steam-powered presses as early as 1846. On this see Marzio, "Lithographic Technology," 243–44,

where he cites Edward Young's statement about Duval in Young, *Leading Pursuits and Leading Men* (Philadelphia, 1856).

8. See Edward H. Knight, comp., *Knight's American Mechanical Dictionary*, 2:1331–32.

9. Thomas Beckman, *Milwaukee Illustrated: Panoramic and Bird's-Eye Views of a Midwestern Metropolis, 1844–1908*, unpaged introduction and entry for item 51. The latter, a lithographic illustration of a Hoe press dated by Beckman as probably 1870, appears at the conclusion of the introduction.

10. For a description of the operation of the hand press, see Knight, *Mechanical Dictionary*, 2:1331.

Figure 14. Lithographic power press manufactured by R. Hoe & Co. in 1873. (Olin Library, Cornell University.)

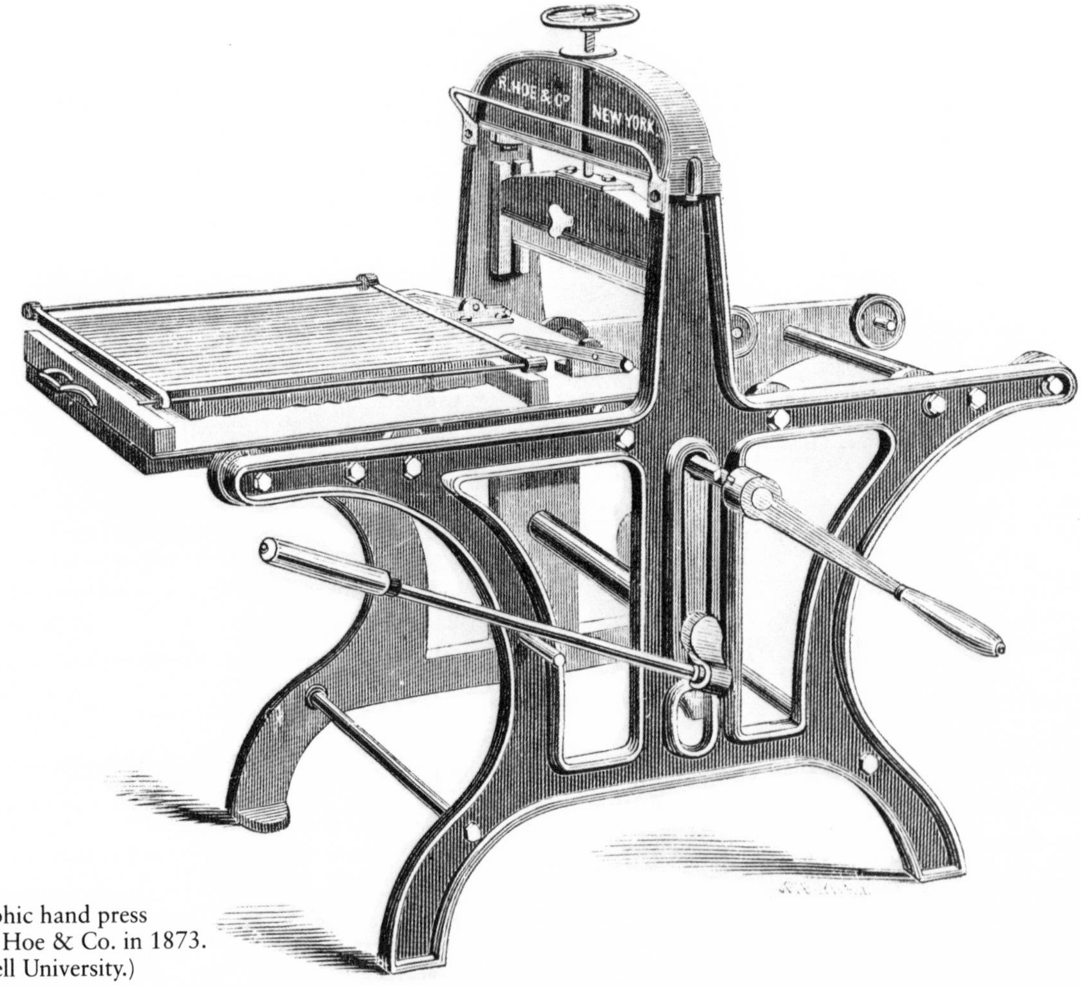

Figure 15. Lithographic hand press
manufactured by R. Hoe & Co. in 1873.
(Olin Library, Cornell University.)

stones and the use of photographic processes to obtain printable images on stones, plates, or transfer paper, deserve further explanation.

European printers discovered soon after the invention of the lithographic process that zinc plates, properly treated to create a suitable surface texture, could be used to obtain results essentially the same as from an inked stone. Frederick Bourquin, a Swiss who supervised P. S. Duval's Philadelphia lithographing establishment, introduced zincography to America in 1849.[11]

Other printers soon began to use zinc instead of or as a supplement to stones. A Philadelphia rival of Duval, L. N. Rosenthal, advertised his firm in 1852 as a "Chromographic and Zincographic Drawing and Printing Establishment."[12] Doubtless the use of zinc plates was widespread well before the publication in 1871 of Luther Ringwalt's *American Encyclopaedia of Printing*, for in the description of zinc plates under the subheading *Zincography* there is no suggestion that this was any kind of novelty or represented any inferior practice.[13] Slightly more than a decade later, the *Inland Printer* stated, "Zinc plates as substitutes for lithographic stones are now in common use."[14]

The celebrated (and self-celebrating) Louis Prang of Boston built an unparalleled reputation in America for his color printing. In discussing their work most lithographers—amateur and expert alike—referred to the use of multiple *stones*. Yet the most authoritative work on Prang informs us that he "had used zinc plates as a substitute for lithographic stones for nearly all his color work since 1873."[15]

A study of a large number of the early city views drawn and published by Lucien Burleigh in upstate New York during the years 1883–1886 yields evidence—circumstantial and inconclusive, it must be admitted—that the artist drew on zinc plates and sent them to be printed in Milwaukee or Cleveland.[16] Burleigh probably needed no instruction in the

use of zinc plates. Certainly they would have been widely used in Milwaukee during the time he worked there as a view artist for a few years following his graduation in 1875 from Worcester Technical Institute. Nevertheless, he and others could have referred to a technical discussion of the process in a highly detailed manual by W. D. Richmond on all aspects of lithographic printing. The discussion first appeared in issues of *The Printing Times and Lithographer of London*, then as a book entitled *The Grammar of Lithography* first published in 1878 and revised two years later.[17]

It therefore seems likely that a great many of the city views published after the early 1870s were drawn on zinc plates. Or, as the *Grammar of Lithography* described in one of its chapters, the images may have been put on the plates by photographic means. Rapid development of photography in the nineteenth century inevitably led to its use in printing. This took many forms; creation of designs on woodblocks for wood engravings; production of relief plates to be used with set type; creation of plates with incised lines to be printed like engravings or etchings; and the transfer of drawn images to light-sensitized lithographic stones, zinc plates, or transfer paper so that lithographic prints could be obtained.

In Philadelphia, Duval experimented with photolithography as early as 1857. A year later, I. Rehn & Co. of the same city exhibited some of its work at the Franklin Institute. In 1860 Duval included on his billhead the statement, "A photographic room is attached to this establishment," and probably he used images created by the camera in his lithographic printing. The Boston firm of L. H. Bradford & Co. advertised in 1858 that it could produce photolithographs.[18]

Inventions, discoveries, and improvements came from many persons in several countries.[19] Publications and patent

11. Nicholas B. Wainwright, *Philadelphia in the Romantic Age of Lithography*, 86, citing the Philadelphia *Public Ledger*, 21 June 1849.

12. R. A. Smith, *Philadelphia as It Is in 1852* (Philadelphia: Lindsay and Blakeston, 1852), 242. I owe this citation to Peter C. Marzio's indispensable work on the technical aspects of nineteenth-century American color lithography, *The Democratic Art: Pictures for a 19th-Century America*, 35. Elsewhere in this book Marzio states, "It was during the 1870s that the American transition from stone to zinc began. It was a gradual shift, not completed by 1880" (69).

13. Ringwalt, *Encyclopaedia of Printing*, 285.

14. The December 1884 issue, as quoted in Marzio, *The Democratic Art*, 69. Zinc plates seem to have been in general use in Britain somewhat earlier than in the United States. Articles on lithography and related printing methods in the winter of 1853–1854 mention zinc plates frequently and in such a way as to suggest that their use was not especially new ("A New Career for Lithography," and "Printing by Magic"). One United States publication declared that, while "zinc plates are used successfully as a substitute for stone, . . . they are by no means so generally useful" (Knight, *Mechanical Dictionary*, 2:1333). This was a general work on industrial technology, however, and may not have accurately reflected recent changes in printing practice. For example, under the heading *Zincography*, rather than discussing planographic printing, the dictionary describes, and only briefly, a method of making relief plates.

15. Katharine Morrison McClinton, *The Chromolithographs of Louis Prang*, 21.

16. Of the twenty-eight views by Burleigh of towns in New York from 1883 through 1885, twenty-seven are known to have been printed in Milwaukee by Beck & Pauli or in Cleveland by C. H. Vogt and Sons. Information is lacking about one, but it is safe to assume that it, too, came from the press of one of these printers, as did three views published in 1886—doubtless before Burleigh established his own press in Troy that year. Several of

these lithographs include Burleigh's signature in the body of the print in addition to the imprint statement that they were drawn by him, which suggests that Burleigh put the drawing on the medium that would be used—directly or indirectly—for printing. I think it doubtful that Burleigh would have risked sending heavy and breakable stones to his midwestern printers or that he would have paid the extra expense of so doing when zinc plates were available. It is almost as improbable that he took his drawings to Milwaukee or Cleveland and drew on the stones in the shops of his printers. He could, of course, have used transfer paper for his designs and sent the sheets to the printers. The alternative remains that Burleigh prepared a drawing that could be put on stone or on a zinc plate photographically, and then he signed his name.

17. The subtitle described its approach: *A Practical Guide for the Artist and Printer*.

18. The information on these pioneer Philadelphia photolithographers is from Wainwright, *Philadelphia*, 73. The Bradford advertisement with its "specimen of Photo-Lithography" is reproduced in C. Koeman, "The Application of Photography to Map Printing and the Transition to Offset Lithography." See also Walter W. Ristow, "Lithography and Maps, 1796–1850." For the early experiments with photography in America and their early applications to printing, see William F. Robinson, *A Certain Slant of Light*. Robinson reproduces the earliest balloon photographs taken in this country showing Providence and Boston in 1860.

19. For a brief summary of the work and processes of the principal contributors to the development of photolithography as seen at a fairly early stage, consult the entry under *Photolithography* in Knight, *Mechanical Dictionary*, 2:1686–87. See also Robert Taft, *Photography and the American Scene: A Social History, 1839–1889*, chap. 21, "Photography and the Pictorial Press," 419–50; Helmut Gernsheim, *The History of Photography from the Camera Obscura to the Beginning of the Modern Era* (New York, 1979), 545–47; Geoffrey Wakeman, *Aspects of Victorian Lithography: Anastatic Printing and Photozincography*, chap. 5, "Photozincography," 43–51; and I. Mumford, "Lithography, Photography and Photozincogra-

Figure 16. Osborne copying camera designed by J. W. Osborne in 1866 for the American Photolithographic Company, Brooklyn, New York. (Olin Library, Cornell University.)

applications spread knowledge rapidly, and, after the Civil War, American lithographic printers made increasing use of the camera in their work. Julius Bien, then superintendent of the New York Lithographic, Engraving and Printing Company, signed one of the firm's broadsides issued in 1868 boasting that "its *Photo-Lithographic* process" was "the best and most reliable in practice, for the almost instantaneous reproduction of all kinds of writing . . . woodcuts, line drawings [and] engravings."[20] A trade card and calendar issued by the firm the following year included a vignette show-

ing a portion of the plant's interior. A camera on a tripod was prominently featured.[21]

As early as 1866, the American Photolithographic Company added a massive and elaborate copy camera (Figure 16) to the equipment at the firm's Brooklyn plant. This camera could accommodate drawings up to forty-eight by sixty inches on its copyboard mounted at one end of a fourteen-foot-long platform. J. W. Osborne designed the camera for the company, but by 1872 it was illustrated in a technical dictionary, and it must have been in general commercial production well before that date. The American Photolithographic Company displayed items printed by lithography from images produced by this camera as part of its exhibit at Photographic Hall in Philadelphia during the Centennial Exposition of 1876.[22]

phy in English Map Production Before 1870." A list of the major contributors to photolithography with the dates of their inventions or discoveries and divided into three categories according to the basic process can be found in Robert Mallet, ed., *The Practical Mechanics' Journal, Scientific Record of the International Exhibition of 1862*, 577–78. Of the fourteen methods listed, two were developed by Americans: Cutting & Bradford (1858) and Austen A. Turner (1860). All three men were from Boston. For Lodowick Bradford's work, see Bettina A. Norton, "Tappan and Bradford: Boston Lithographers with Essex County Associations." Bradford's experiments began as early as 1856, and four years later he listed himself in the Boston city directory as a photolithographer. The firm of Tappan and Bradford printed many city views, but all of them seem to be prior to Bradford's efforts (with James A. Cutting) at photolithography. Cutting, according to Norton, was associated with Austen Turner in producing ambrotypes at premises on Tremont Row in Boston. See also Robinson, *A Certain Slant*.

20. Quoted in Marzio, *The Democratic Art*, 58.

21. An impression of this lithograph is in the author's collection.

22. The illustration of Osborne's camera and a long description of its operation can be found in Knight, *Mechanical Dictionary*, 1681–82. In an article on the photographic exhibits at the Centennial, a technical journal mentioned, "Mr. F. A. Wenderoth . . . shows examples of his photozincographic process" and that nearby one could see "a number of photolithographic prints (Osborne's process,) by the American Photolithographic Company, 103 Fulton Street, New York" (*The Philadelphia Photographer* 13 [August 1876]: 230). Osborne, an Australian, pioneered in developing photolithography by producing images on photosensitized transfer

A few years before the Centennial, Luther Ringwalt introduced the entry on lithography in his invaluable *Encyclopaedia of Printing* with the statement, "Within the past few years this new art has been developed, and there are at the present time establishments in this country and in Europe in full operation." Ringwalt described in some detail the two commercial processes then in use, pointing out, "Photolithographs may be produced in two ways, by taking the impression from the negative direct on stone, and by taking it on prepared paper and transferring it to stone."[23]

It should be noted that only line drawings could be satisfactorily photographed and printed by either of the two methods described by Ringwalt. Successful commercial printing from continuous-tone negatives was not possible until 1886 following the development of the half-tone screen used to break up tonal masses into fine dots of varying sizes. Most of the city views of the period consisted essentially of lines or other discrete marks to be printed in black ink for the basic design. Photographic transfers of these drawings to stone, zinc, or transfer paper thus would have posed no difficulties.

Single tones or multiple colors added to the black image to provide sky, ground, shadow, or building details appear on most views as unscreened washes of colored ink. The camera would have provided no aid in preparing the printing surfaces for such tones, but this could easily have been done by hand in the usual way. The finished lithograph would thus be the result of a composite of methods for obtaining images on the stones or zinc plates.

The extent to which photographic methods were used in producing lithographic city views cannot be determined. We do know that by the end of the 1870s photolithography had clearly ceased to be a novelty and was widely used by printers throughout the country. In 1879 the Cleveland Artotype Company advertised "Photographic Pictures printed on a Lithographic Press." A Boston business directory of 1882 listed four firms under the heading *Photo-lithography*. One of these, George H. Walker, played a major role in printing many city views of New England communities. Walker's place of business was 81 Milk Street in central Boston. Of course Walker did other work; his advertisement in the 1882 directory identifies the firm as "publishers and lithographers" doing "engraving in all its branches, map engraving and photo-lithographing." Walker's establishment also served as a portrait studio, for he advertised "crayon portraits by talented artists. Single copies, original drawing, or lithographed copies."[24]

Other firms printing city views used photographs or photographic methods to create printing surfaces at one time or another. Napoleon Sarony of Sarony, Major & Snapp enjoyed an international reputation as a photographer.[25] The Strobridge Company in Cincinnati used photographs in one of their posters in 1883 and possibly had used a camera earlier when they printed many city views.[26] Louis Kurz, a founding partner of the Chicago Lithographing Company of Chicago, returned to Milwaukee to establish the American Oleograph Co. in 1872 in partnership with a photographer, Hugo Broich. Both these firms included city views among their products.[27]

Thaddeus Mortimer Fowler was the most prolific artist of town views; his lithographs of Pennsylvania communities alone number well over two hundred. After being wounded at Bull Run and receiving his Union discharge, Fowler took up photography and made tintypes of soldiers at army camps. In 1864 he went to Madison, Wisconsin, where he worked in his uncle's photographic studio. A few years later at the age of twenty-six he began his lifelong career publishing and drawing city views.[28] It seems highly likely that Fowler would have used his specialized knowledge of photography to aid in the transfer of his drawn images to either stones or zinc plates.[29]

While the foregoing is mainly speculation, it can be stated with more assurance that several of the early views drawn by Lucien Rinaldo Burleigh in 1882 and 1883 were reproduced through photographic means. Impressions of the views of Binghamton, Ithaca, and Schenectady, New York, for example, all exhibit a common feature: two barely discernible vertical lines dividing each folio print into three roughly equal portions (see Plate 54). Almost certainly these were caused by using three glass-plate negatives on a sensitized stone or plate or by the use of three sheets of transfer paper applied to the printing surface after the photosensitized paper had received the image from photographic negatives.

It was exactly this kind of reproduction that *The Grammar of Lithography* mentioned in its description of a suitable lens for a camera used in photolithography:

> It is necessary to have lenses that will give in the negative straight marginal lines corresponding to . . . similar lines in the original. Suppose, for instance, a very large map is to be copied by this process. It will have to be divided into rectangular portions, each one of which must be suitable for copying to the required size, according to the lens used. It is imperative that the marginal lines of each negative be straight, or they will not join together. A map is a crucial text. . . . We cannot divide it into sections without cutting through portions which would at once show any error when the sections came to be put together.[30]

paper from photographic negatives. His first paper on the subject dates from 1859.

23. For more detailed instructions, see Ringwalt, *Encyclopaedia of Printing*, 285. In both procedures, zinc plates could be substituted for lithographic stones.

24. *The Cleveland Directory for the Year Ending June, 1880* (Cleveland, 1879), 357; *The Boston Business Directory for 1882*. Walker's advertisement can be found on p. 295, immediately below that of J. Mayer & Co., whose business notice ended with the words *Photo-lithography a specialty*. City views printed by Walker include Bar Harbor, Maine, in 1886, Edgartown, Massachusetts, in 1886, and Boston in 1899.

25. For Sarony and the lithographic firms with which he was associated, see Harry T. Peters, *America on Stone: The Other Printmakers to the American People . . .* , 350–57.

26. John W. Merten, "Stone by Stone Along a Hundred Years with the House of Strobridge."

27. Thomas Beckman, *Milwaukee Illustrated*, "Introduction," unpaged, and nn. 48–54.

28. John R. Hébert, "Introduction," in U.S. Library of Congress, *Panoramic Maps of Anglo-American Cities: A Checklist of Maps in the Collections of the Library of Congress, Geography and Map Division*, 5.

29. Very few of Fowler's views contain imprint information identifying the printer. My guess is that Fowler made his own stones or plates (probably the latter) and had them printed at various shops.

30. W. D. Richmond, *The Grammar of Lithography*, 189. The case for the use of photography for the several Burleigh views of 1882 and 1883 does not rest entirely on the evidence of the prints themselves. Several of these, in addition to Burleigh's signature as artist, bear the name J. Lyth,

Applications of photography to lithographic printing were thus well known to American viewmakers even before the publication in 1886 of a comprehensive manual giving precise directions on how to achieve a wide variety of results with the help of the camera. This manual appeared in at least six editions before the end of the nineteenth century, a publishing record attesting to the popularity of the volume and its general use. *Photo-Engraving on Zinc and Copper in Line and Half Tone and Photo-Lithography: A Practical Manual* was the work of an Englishman, W. T. Wilkinson, but its third (and first American) edition was revised and enlarged by Edward L. Wilson, editor of the *Philadelphia Photographer*, an important periodical reporting the latest techniques for professionals in the graphic arts.[31]

Wilkinson and Wilson summarized their recommended approach to photolithography as a process based on the transfer method, rather than on producing a printable image directly on sensitized stone or zinc:

> To gain this end there are three methods: the first by printing upon paper prepared with bichromated gelatine, the tones of which after exposure to light under a direct negative . . . will retain ink, whilst the gelatine protected from light absorbs water, and rejects the ink. The result is a replica of the original in fatty ink, and may be transferred to stone or zinc, and printed from by the usual lithographic method.
>
> In the second method, a print is made upon zinc from a reversed negative . . . in bichromated albumen, which is rolled up in transfer ink, and from that a transfer is pulled on . . . transfer paper, which may then be transferred to stone or zinc, and printed from at a litho. press or machine.
>
> In the third, and by far the best method, the print is made from a reversed negative on zinc, in bitumen, . . . then rolled up in transfer ink, the transfer pulled on . . . transfer paper, then transferred to stone or zinc, and printed from.[32]

Views produced by several artists toward the end of their period of popularity were printed by a photogravure process. They include a number of the late nineteenth-century views of New England communities by Albert F. Poole and some of the twentieth-century views by Thaddeus M. Fowler, such as his Tulsa print of 1918. While these are not proof that the artists or their printers used a photographic process for earlier work, it surely does not indicate any reluctance to turn to the latest mechanical aids in reproducing drawn images. Just as further studies may reveal that most of these city views came from zinc plates and not lithographic stones, so, too, additional research may establish that in many cases photography played an essential role in transferring the artist's composition to the surface used to print the final image on paper.

---

who is identified by the abbreviation *eng.* after his signature. Lyth lived in Syracuse, New York, with a business address in 1882 at 24 Washington St., the same as the publishing house of D. H. Mason & Co., which issued Burleigh's views. The 1882 directory lists Lyth as "artist," in the 1883 directory his occupation is given as "architect" with no business address, and he appears in the 1884 directory as "draughtsman, designer and photo-engraver." The latter directory has a full-page advertisement for "Lyth's Bureau of Engraving" located in the University Block in Syracuse. The advertisement announced Lyth's product as "Photo-Electrotype Engraving, A superior substitute for Wood Cuts." (For a description of this process of engraving, see Knight, *Mechanical Dictionary*, 2:1679–80.) Lyth thus knew about photographic processes. I feel fairly certain that the Burleigh views with Lyth's signature were done by lithography, but it is also possible that they were printed from a zinc relief plate, after the image had been photographed on sensitized lithographic transfer paper, transferred to zinc, and etched so that the lines to be printed stood in relief. A full explanation of this process, as well as the use of photography to produce a planographic zinc plate containing an image to be printed by lithography, can be found in W. T. Wilkinson, *Photo-Engraving, Photo-Etching, and Photo-Lithography in Line and Half-Tone; also, Collotype and Heliotype*. For information concerning Lyth, I am indebted to Richard N. Wright, president of the Onondaga Historical Association, Syracuse, New York.

31. Wilkinson's first and second editions were published in London by England Brothers. The third and subsequent editions as revised by Wilson were published by him in New York. Wilkinson also wrote *Photo-Mechanical Processes: A Practical Guide to Photo-Zincography, Photo-Lithography, and Collotype* (London, 1892), with two subsequent editions.

32. Wilkinson, *Photo-Engraving*, 3d ed., 129. This passage is followed with many pages of technical details, referring also to earlier chapters in the manual providing information on processes used in allied photographic and printing methods common or similar to those used in photolithography. The reader may be curious about how "reversed negatives" were obtained. The explanation appears early in Wilkinson's book, where fig. 1 on p. 10 shows a camera with a diagonal mirror interposed between the lens and the glass plate negative.

5. The Business of Viewmaking: Sales, Promotion, and Advertising

The production of American lithographic city views in the nineteenth century was primarily a commercial venture. Most of the views would never have been printed if they could not have been sold or if their publishers had not had such expectations. This applies equally to the works of those now regarded as important American artists and to the works of the far more numerous illustrators of lesser talent.

Artists and publishers of the 1830s worked out a pattern of promotion and sales that their successors followed in other parts of the country using only variations on the techniques first developed by these pioneering viewmakers. The system combined newspaper publicity with the solicitation of advance subscriptions for one or more copies of the proposed lithograph. One of the earliest such newspaper accounts appeared in a Gloucester newspaper and concerned the work of a native of that Massachusetts seaport:

> VIEW OF GLOUCESTER. It will be recollected that we stated some time since, that it was the intention of Mr. Fitz H. Lane . . . to lithograph a view of Gloucester, provided a sufficient number of copies were subscribed for to warrant the undertaking. The progress of the subscription has been slow, but we are happy to learn it is now large enough to cover the necessary expenses of publication, and that it will be completed and furnished to subscribers as soon as possible. . . . We trust our citizens, and those who have gone from among us to other places, will duly appreciate the labors of Mr. Lane, and render his sketch not only a source of pleasure, but of profit to him. We would not be without a copy of it, when finished, for five times the amount of the subscription price.[1]

Perhaps in some cases the prospective publisher or artist required a formal and legally binding agreement with the would-be purchaser. However, when Lane in 1855 sought out purchasers in Castine, Maine, for his view of that attractive and historic seaport (Plate 58), he evidently asked for nothing more than a signature on a handwritten statement that was either circulated among the townspeople or posted in some frequented place. The single paragraph of text is as straightforward and laconic as a Downeaster's speech:

> It is proposed to have a Lithographic print of Castine struck off, similar to the sketch lately made by Mr. Lane to be executed in the best style in Boston, in plain dark & white, provided 100 copies are subscribed for at $2.00 pr copy. We, the subscribers, agree to take the following number of Copies—Castine, Sept. 13th 1855.

Below this statement appear the names of those who wanted copies with the number desired. Most signators agreed to purchase only one, but A. E. Ives subscribed for three, and ten others wanted two, including one William H. Adams of New York. Other out-of-town subscribers lived in Bangor and Belfast, Maine, and Boston, among other places. In all, 102 impressions were reserved by the eighty-three persons signing the subscription list.[2]

These subscribers got more than they bargained for, unless the price was increased or uncolored impressions were also printed, for Lane's lithograph was printed in several colors from multiple stones. John Wilmerding, the leading authority on Lane, regards this view, Castine from Hospital Island, as this widely acclaimed artist's "most accomplished graphic work."[3]

At the other end of the continent, in the early years of California viewmaking, George H. Baker followed the same practice that Lane used so successfully in the East. Baker relied on newspaper notices and advertisements to call attention to his forthcoming lithograph of Sacramento, published in 1857 (Plate 42). Doubtless prompted by this artist-publisher, at least two newspaper announcements informed potential customers that such a view was in preparation. One read as follows:

> View of Sacramento.—Mr. Geo. H. Baker had completed, in India ink, a beautiful view of Sacramento and surrounding country, which surpasses any other that has yet been published. The view is taken from an elevation in front of the city, and is so perfect that every street and house can be readily recognized. It is to be lithographed as soon as a sufficient number of subscribers are obtained to afford a renumeration [sic] therefor.[4]

Baker followed up with an advertisement giving more details of the project and asking those interested to subscribe for the number of copies desired. He kept a careful record of their names, the number of views they agreed to purchase, and—presumably only after the views were delivered—noted that payments had been received. Only a few subscribers seem to have been "bogus," as two are described.

Although some of the entries are lined through and the entries on one page are confusingly arranged, the record in-

---

1. Gloucester *Telegraph*, 15 August 1835, as quoted in John Wilmerding, *Fitz Hugh Lane*, 22. Unfortunately, we are not told what that price was. Probably it was not more than the one dollar charged for Lane's second view of Gloucester, published a decade later. If the owner wished a more attractive version, he could have it hand-colored for an additional fifty cents. Gloucester *Telegraph*, 25 November 1846, as quoted in ibid., 28.

2. This document, the only one of its type I have encountered, is now in the collection of the Wilson Museum in Castine. Its director, Mrs. Norman Doudiet, was thoughtful enough to provide me with a copy.

3. Wilmerding, *Fitz Hugh Lane*, 30.

4. A clipping of this, with an illegible manuscript identification of the source, is pasted in the manuscript subscription book that Baker maintained for the view. This is now in the collection of the Society of California Pioneers in San Francisco. Other statements and quotations in this portion of the chapter are taken from that document.

dicates that Baker's view must have been a commercial success. Two hundred and twenty-eight names appear in the list for the first edition of the print, and Baker obtained twenty-eight additional customers for the second edition. Many of these ordered multiple copies. Kirk and Co. appear to have received at least eleven; Charles Crocker wanted five, as did Booth & Co. Total orders for the first edition came to just under three hundred, with an additional forty-eight for the second.

Some artist-publishers, like Baker, worked alone. It was not an easy life for such a viewmaker. He had to solicit subscribers, obtain newspaper publicity, exhibit the drawing from which the lithograph was to be made, arrange for the view to be printed, distribute the prints to those who had ordered in advance, and place additional impressions in one or more retail outlets. Baker lived in Sacramento and had his place of business there, but traveling artists needed assistants to do preliminary and follow-up work in the places they visited.

One of the first traveling artists, Edwin Whitefield, employed agents in various cities to handle much of the business side of his enterprise while he busied himself in sketching other cities that were to be the subject of future views. At least eight agents or canvassers served Whitefield in this capacity, including J. T. Palmatary and the four Smith brothers—Benjamin, Francis, David, and George—all of whom eventually went into business for themselves either drawing their own views or employing or associating with artists who prepared the sketches required for such a venture.[5]

For a time, at least, some of Whitefield's agents served him well. Early in 1848 George Smith reported that in Providence he had obtained nearly 1,200 subscribers for the two views of the city that Whitefield had drawn. The number grew to "about 1,260" by the time Whitefield conferred with Smith a few days later, and the artist recorded in his diary that Smith was also attempting to secure subscribers in New York City for the Providence views. Whitefield seemed both elated and surprised at the number of subscribers, for his diary states that Smith "will probably get altogether about 1,300 [subscribers], which will be a much larger number than I anticipated for such a place as Providence." Smith did indeed go on to New York, where he obtained orders for an additional forty-five impressions of the Providence lithographs.[6]

Benjamin Franklin Smith wrote to Whitefield the following year suggesting that a view of Danvers, Massachusetts, might prove successful and advising the artist to make his view of nearby Lynn large in size.[7] It seems likely that other artists received suggestions of this type from agents in the field. A third Smith, Francis, worked on Whitefield's behalf in the Ohio valley. There, in 1846, Whitefield completed his sketches for a view of Cincinnati, although this view was not published until two years later. Perhaps he could not obtain enough subscriptions initially to justify printing the view, but Smith or, possibly, Palmatary must have generated enough sales to convince Whitefield to proceed with the project. By that time—January 1848—Francis Smith had moved on to Louisville and reported to Whitefield that he had obtained "about 300 subscribers" there.[8]

Whitefield never published the Louisville view, although in 1855 a large and handsome lithograph of the city was being sold by J. T. Palmatary, who was evidently no longer acting as Whitefield's agent. It is possible that Palmatary's view was pirated from his former employer or that he was using Whitefield's subscription list to obtain customers for his own print.[9]

Most of the post–Civil War viewmakers used agents; however, except for those who became artists or publishers themselves, we know nothing about these agents but their names as mentioned in contemporary newspaper accounts. H. A. Dorn was the agent in 1882 for D. Mason & Co. of Syracuse when Lucien Burleigh drew Ithaca, New York, for this Syracuse publisher. After Burleigh became an independent artist-publisher, he employed one of his brothers to secure subscriptions and collect payments for his lithograph of Groton, New York, in 1885. A year later Burleigh used B. C. Defendorf as his agent in Middlebury, Vermont, and Defendorf served in a similar capacity for Burleigh's print of Clyde, New York, in 1892. Two of Burleigh's brothers helped sell his views of places in New Hampshire published in 1886 and 1887.[10]

A Capt. H. Coombs worked to obtain subscriptions for Thaddeus M. Fowler when the artist produced his view of Simcoe, Ontario, in 1881. Fowler himself began as Albert

8. Whitefield diaries, 5 January 1848.

9. Palmatary was then active in the Ohio valley, peddling a series of views, some of them unsigned, others signed by Edward Sachse, but several with Palmatary's name as the artist. The Louisville view is known from a unique impression in the collection of the Liberty National Bank & Trust Company. Its publication was preceded by the printing of a proof state, whose appearance the Louisville *Daily Journal* announced on 15 August 1855: "Mr. J. T. Palmatary called yesterday and showed us a lithographic view of Louisville, which he is getting up and which will be ready for delivery to subscribers in six weeks from this time. This picture is taken in perspective, the eye supposed to be elevated above the houses and at some point in the river. The streets, dwelling houses, and public buildings will be distinctly shown in their natural color. It will be the largest view of this kind ever engraved in the United States, being 52 by 40 inches, and will be colored with ten different colors in oil. Persons wishing to subscribe for this splendid picture can do so, by calling on Mr. A. Hagan, No. 99 Third street, where they may see the picture in its plain, uncolored state." Although called an "engraving" in this account, the print was a lithograph, the product of the well-known Cincinnati firm of Middleton, Wallace & Co. The "oil" colors came from multiple stones inked with heavily pigmented inks.

10. Ithaca *Daily Journal*, 18 August 1882; Groton and Lansing *Journal*, 30 April 1885; Middlebury *Register*, 20 November 1885; Clyde *Democratic Herald*, 18 May 1892. The latter newspaper in its issue of 3 August 1892 identified Defendorf as "of Lansingburg." Lansingburg, New York, now part of Troy, was Burleigh's place of residence. J. C. Burleigh's name is mentioned in the Penacook, N. H., *Rays of Light*, 24 June 1886, among other newspaper accounts. Several newspapers also identified W. B. Burleigh as the artist's brother. See, for example, the Hinsdale, N. H., *Valley Record*, 11 December 1885.

5. In addition to the Smiths and Palmatary, Whitefield employed Groves, Holmes, and Foss (first names unknown). This information appears in the definitive study of Whitefield: Bettina A. Norton, *Edwin Whitefield: Nineteenth-Century North American Scenery*, 44–47. Norton's study is a mine of useful material on both the artistic and business aspects of Whitefield's work and draws on his extensive diaries and other papers. They seem to be the most complete records of all those who were involved in drawing and selling city views. Norton's work is a model of scholarship that serves as a challenge to those who might be persuaded to investigate other viewmakers.

6. Entries for 3, 12, and 17 January 1848, Whitefield diaries, Print Room, Boston Public Library.

7. Norton, *Whitefield*, 44.

Ruger's agent in 1868, possibly replacing Eli S. Glover, whom Ruger had employed for these activities in 1866. Herman Brosius in 1873 had a "Mr. Pease" as his agent when doing his Binghamton, New York, view. Charles J. Smith promoted and sold views in Nebraska for Henry Wellge and his American Publishing Company when Wellge drew several Nebraska communities, such as Lincoln (Plate 59), in 1889.[11] The practice was obviously widespread.

Agents must have spent as much time in travel as did the peripatetic artists. Joseph Warner, associated with publisher J. J. Stoner of Madison, Wisconsin, went to distant Nova Scotia in the summer of 1878. A Halifax newspaper described him as "the gentlemanly agent" for a view then being drawn by "Prof." A. Ruger. Warner was then "actively canvassing the city for subscriptions."[12]

For the view of Charlottetown on Prince Edward Island that Ruger drew the same year and that Stoner published, the agent was W. R. Patchen.[13] Stoner was expected to join his agent later to assist him in distributing the views to subscribers. That November a Prince Edward Island newspaper informed its readers that Stoner would arrive with views of Summerside early in December, "or as soon as he gets through delivering the pictures of Pictou and Charlottetown."[14]

Stoner knew what to expect of his agents, for he began his career in city views working in just such a capacity for Albert Ruger as early as February 1868.[15] The two then formed a publishing partnership, but Stoner frequently took to the road to promote their joint business or to publicize the views that Ruger published under his own name. Thus, the Savannah, Georgia, *Morning News* of 19 February 1872 told its readers, "Yesterday we received a call from Mr. J. J. Stoner, General agent for Prof. Ruger, who presented for our inspection a handsomely executed lithograph of Prof. Ruger's sketch of Savannah." A sequence of stories appeared in the Austin and San Antonio, Texas, newspapers in 1873

when this enterprising and successful publisher was actively campaigning in that state with Augustus Koch, another of the major city view artists then associated with Stoner. On 9 January an Austin paper published this item in its "Local Matters" column:

> We have been shown the drawing of a bird's-eye view of the city of Austin, made by Mr. A. Koch, which for accuracy and beauty is remarkable. The supposed elevation from which the view is taken is two thousand feet, a height in which the beholder has the view of the topographical inequalities and enables him to see and recognize many individual houses in the city.
>
> Mr. Stoner, who has already furnished admirable views of this kind for Galveston and Houston, will call upon our citizens and take subscriptions to enable him to have the work lithographed at once. Unless a sufficient number of subscribers are obtained to justify the expense of lithographing, of course the work will fall through.[16]

If an Austin resident had happened to visit San Antonio slightly more than two weeks later, he could have read a similar but somewhat longer account of a Koch-Stoner view in preparation for that city. It mentioned several other Texas cities for which Stoner had published or was contemplating views in addition to Galveston and Houston, the two places listed in the Austin account: Jefferson, Waco, Dallas, Corsicana, Sherman, and Brenham. The story concluded with a description of the publisher's sales techniques:

> Mr. Stoner will call upon our business men, canvassing for this picture. In the Texas cities enumerated above he has the endorsement of their best citizens and business firms manifesting their appreciation of the pictures to be furnished. We wish him every success and feel satisfied that most of our business men, after having seen the drawing and the style upon which it is proposed to complete it will be happy in having an opportunity to subscribe for a copy of the lithograph. It is to be paid for on *delivery*.[17]

In less than fourteen days Stoner evidently succeeded in obtaining at least the 250 subscribers the newspaper had stated were the minimum required. Before leaving for his place of business in Madison, Wisconsin, Stoner, according to the newspaper, "called upon us . . . to say farewell for a short time. He has had no difficulty in making up his subscription list . . . and desires, through us, to extend his thanks to our citizens for the uniform courtesy with which he has been received. He will return . . . in about two months, with his beautiful lithographs completed, which, he does not doubt, will give ample satisfaction to his subscribers."[18]

Two months later almost to the day Stoner returned to San Antonio, having visited Austin a week before to distribute the finished lithographs of that city.[19] His appearance was noted in the local press once again:

> Mr. J. J. Stoner . . . is prepared to deliver his beautiful pictures of our city. . . . The picture comes fully up to the promises made in reference to it, and the drawing exhibited was but a feeble foreshadowing of the striking lithograph now to be furnished. . . . The bird's eye view of our city is highly ornamental and would make a handsome and useful decoration for an office. . . .
>
> Mr. Stoner . . . will have a few copies left after subscribers have been furnished. Those subscribers, therefore, who may

11. Simcoe *British Canadian*, 2 March 1881; Omaha *Daily Herald*, 10 September 1868; Ypsilanti *Commercial*, 15 September 1866; Binghamton *Daily Times*, 1 August 1873; Lincoln *Daily Nebraska State Journal*, 1 June 1889.

12. Halifax *Evening Reporter & Daily & Tri-Weekly Times*, 20 August 1878, p. 3, col. 2. The story began, "Perhaps many of our readers are not aware that we have for some time had a 'chief amang us' takin' a bird's-eye view of our city, in the person of Prof. A. Ruger, an artist of considerable merit."

13. Patchen must have been regularly employed by Stoner, for he is identified as accompanying the publisher on a visit to San Antonio, Texas, in 1873. San Antonio *Daily Herald*, 15 April 1873. References to Patchen as agent for Stoner also can be found in several New Hampshire newspapers, including the Claremont *National Eagle*, 29 September 1877, and the Keene *Sentinel*, 11 October 1877.

14. Prince Edward Island *Farmer*, 20 November 1878. Earlier in the year this paper reported receiving a letter from Stoner, who stated that while not enough subscriptions had been obtained that summer for the Summerside view, he was prepared to "go on and get up the picture" in the hope that he could find "enough purchasers to take up the balance" (Ibid., 20 August 1878). Patchen is named as agent for the Charlottetown view in the Charlottetown *Daily Examiner*, 25 November 1878, which claimed, "The sum of $500 was expended in order to bring this view to its perfect condition." For these Nova Scotia and Prince Edward Island newspaper accounts I am indebted to H. T. Holman, assistant archivist, Public Archives of Prince Edward Island, and Scott Robson, curator, Historic Building and Furnishing, Nova Scotia Museum, Halifax.

15. In its issue of 26 February 1868, the Oberlin, Ohio, *Lorain County News* referred to Stoner as "the agent for Prof. Ruger," who "called upon us today and exhibited the penciled draft of a view of Oberlin."

16. Austin *Daily Democratic Statesman*, 9 January 1873.

17. San Antonio *Daily Herald*, 28 January 1873, p. 3, col. 2.

18. San Antonio *Daily Herald*, 13 February 1873, p. 3, col. 2.

19. Austin *Daily Democratic Statesman*, 9 April 1873, p. 3, col. 1.

wish extra copies to send to friends at a distance, can be accommodated. . . . A glance at the picture will serve to convince any one that it cannot fail to produce a favorable impression of San Antonio. They can also furnish rollers upon which the pictures can be securely rolled, and then covered with a wrapper, and be sent by mail to any post office at home or abroad. The postage on the whole package will only amount to six cents for places in the United States, and twenty-four cents for foreign post offices.[20]

In most cities the artist, the publisher, or their agent was able to secure ample newspaper publicity concerning a forthcoming or delivered view. Local editors looked on the preparation and publication of these lithographs as a form of recognition for their city and appealed to their readers to support attempts to secure sufficient subscriptions. Often, they pointed out that rival communities had met such a challenge to civic pride.

Thus, when Edwin Whitefield in 1847 indicated that he required two hundred subscribers to proceed with publication, the Newark *Eagle*, in a long and laudatory article about the artist's work elsewhere, challenged the citizens of Newark:

Unless two hundred copies can be disposed of in advance, the undertaking will be abandoned. We hope, however, for the credit of our city, that such will not be the case. It would be exceedingly mortifying, if, with a population of 25,000, we could not raise the requisite number of subscribers to secure the publication of a correct and beautiful view of our city.
The same gentleman has published Views of Brooklyn, Newburgh, Troy, &c. If the village of Newburgh, with scarcely one fourth of our population could sustain the publication of such a work, surely Newark can do it. . . .
As the publisher can expect no assistance in such an enterprize out of the city, we hope that as many of our citizens as can afford it will make up their minds and subscribe immediately, that the publication may not be delayed.[21]

In describing the similar promotional efforts used in the 1870s by publishers of county maps, one contemporary observer claimed that the leading midwestern publisher of this allied product "during three years of . . . business . . . paid but two newspapers for advertising his scheme. All other papers were persuaded that the enterprise was one of such public benefit that it was their duty to give free space to all matter he desired inserted." Initial announcements that such a project was under consideration were followed by other statements drafted by the promoters: "The press, by publishing articles as original which were written by map men, tells the people, that it is a disgrace to the county to allow the matter to fall through at that stage of the game, and fairly whips them into support of it. This second dose of free advertising spurs the public on, and the canvassers urge forward the branch of business in their charge."[22]

Publicity and sales agents for viewmakers used the same techniques. From the time Whitefield began work in the mid-1840s to the end of the century, the newspaper accounts of the activities of each artist resemble each other so closely that they must have been based on news releases or other material supplied by agents or publishers. Certain phrases, sometimes complete sentences, appear over and over again.

Charles J. Smith, agent for Henry Wellge's American Publishing Company, succeeded in persuading editors of several Nebraska newspapers in 1889 to use his standardized announcement of forthcoming views with only modest changes or deletions. He must have been delighted with the version used by the Norfolk, Nebraska, *Daily News* on 15 June 1889. Although slightly longer than the others, it is typical of the free advertising that Smith was able to obtain for his employers:

The sketch was made by Capt. Henry Wellge, formerly captain in the engineer corps of the Russian army, who . . . is considered the best artist in the country of perspective drawings of cities and towns. The sketch is taken from one mile elevation . . . and every block, building, streets, residence, parks and etc., are shown. . . . The completed work will be a lithograph . . . , and there will be from ten to twenty thousand copies struck off. . . . This is the best and most handsome thing yet devised for giving a comprehensive idea of our city as it is, and for advertising our city, there could be no better way than to circulate a large number broadcast over the country, so we hope every one will interest themselves in behalf of the scheme to make it a success and a go.[23]

Publishers of county maps—and doubtless those in the business of city views as well—used another technique to stimulate sales:

It is a part of every . . . agent's business to assert the improfitableness of the enterprise. If . . . [prospects] . . . show any hesitation about subscribing, the agents tell them that they have orders to leave the field at once. . . .
When Everts [a major county map and atlas publisher] canvassed Jackson County, Iowa, he got lists fully three times as large as was expected; but all that while he was pleading the expense of getting out so large a number and the likelihood of having to abandon the territory because of non-profit.[24]

Statements about the number of subscribers required vary widely. When he visited Lincoln, Nebraska, in 1880 to do a second view of the city, Augustus Koch stated only that he required "a sufficient number" of advance subscriptions. George Norris and Albert F. Poole in 1883 informed the residents of Plymouth, New Hampshire, that "if seventy-five subscribers can be found [publication] will be secured." Two years later in tiny Groton, New York, Lucien Burleigh claimed, "One hundred subscriptions are necessary to complete the work." Earlier, in 1870 in Lexington, Kentucky, Albert Ruger told a reporter for a local paper that "unless one hundred and fifty subscribers are obtained," he could not afford to have his view of that city lithographed. We have already noted that Stoner in San Antonio stipulated that "two hundred and fifty subscribers [would] ensure . . . publication" of Koch's view.[25]

Subscribers did not always come forward in sufficient

20. San Antonio *Daily Herald*, 15 April 1873, p. 3, col. 2. For these Texas newspaper accounts of Stoner's sales efforts, I am indebted to Margaret S. McClean of the Amon Carter Museum of Western Art, Fort Worth.
21. Newark *Eagle*, 21 August 1846.
22. [Bates Harrington], *How 'Tis Done. A Thorough Ventilation of the Numerous Schemes Conducted by Wandering Canvassers*, 32, 37.

23. Similar accounts, using many identical phrases and passages, appeared in the Lincoln *Daily Nebraska State Journal*, 2 June 1889; and the Fremont *Weekly Herald*, 4 July 1889.
24. Harrington, *How 'Tis Done*.
25. Lincoln *Daily Globe*, 2 August 1880; Ashland, N. H., *Advance*, 22 September 1883; Groton, N.Y., *Groton and Lansing Journal*, 30 April 1885; Lexington, *Kentucky Gazette*, 21 December 1870; San Antonio *Daily Herald*, 28 January 1873.

numbers to justify publication of a view. Edwin Whitefield's failure in this respect at Louisville has already been mentioned. His diary records that in 1855 he spent several days in Galt, Ontario, sketching for what he thought would "make a good view" and attempting to obtain subscribers.[26] While the view may have been good, business was not, and Whitefield did not proceed further with the project.

His experience in Ithaca, New York, two years earlier may have prepared him for this disappointment. An Ithaca newspaper, surely prompted by the artist, carried the usual notice that "he proposes to get up some Views of Ithaca" and asked citizens to "give him that encouragement which an effort of that kind is entitled to." A week later a somewhat longer notice appeared. Whitefield may well have prepared a sketch of the town to display for subscription purposes, but no printed view was ever published. His only lithograph resulting from this trip is of one of the several waterfalls nearby.[27]

It is possible that paid advertisements would have helped Whitefield, but he and other viewmakers seem to have used this way of calling attention to their products only rarely or not at all. One unusual exception was the "specimen page" distributed by Compton and Company of St. Louis to promote a unique 110-sheet view of the city drawn by Camille N. Dry. This specimen reproduced one sheet of the forthcoming view. In the space below, which would be occupied by the legend, the publisher printed three paragraphs of text extolling the value and importance of the view:

> The book will contain about one hundred and fifty pages like this showing collectively an area of nearly seventy square miles upon which all the building and topography of unoccupied property are accurately drawn.
>
> There will also be many pages of printed matter, descriptive of important public and private buildings, and all objects of interest. A fund of statistical information regarding the financial, manufacturing, and general business interests of the city will be introduced; and an exhaustive article on the past, present, and prospective value of real estate in all parts of the city will be a feature of a special value to land owners, investors, all interested in St. Louis property; which, with personal notes and biographical sketches, will make the work a complete compendium of St. Louis in 1875, and the most costly and magnificent publication ever issued in the interests of any city in the world.
>
> Sold only by subscription. Price, elegantly bound in muslin and gilt, $25.00. COMPTON & COMPANY. No. 30, St. Louis Life Insurance Building, Cor. Sixth and Locus Streets.[28]

Eli S. Glover also resorted to an unconventional method of getting one of his views in the public eye. This followed a successful attempt to obtain free publicity of his sectioned lithograph of 1877 showing Los Angeles, Santa Monica, and Wilmington (Plate 60), which was described by the Los Angeles *Daily Star:*

> Mr. E. S. Glover, the artist, who has lately made a very excellent and truthful lithograph picture of this city and its suburbs, received a consignment from Messrs A. L. Bancroft & Co. yesterday. The work is one of great merit, and framed it will ornament either office or parlor. The drawing was executed from a

point which presents a beautiful view of Los Angeles proper and the delightful and growing suburbs of East and West Los Angeles. On the whole, it presents a truthful picture of the city looking south from the hill north of town, with the ocean and intervening objects in clear prospective [*sic*]. The views of Wilmington and Santa Monica are also true to nature, representing the harbors and cities in their exact relations one to another.[29]

Perhaps this free publicity did not stimulate enough sales to satisfy Glover, or possibly he wanted to make clear that the view he had for sale differed from another he had drawn for a land development company that was apparently given away to promote sales of subdivision lots.[30] Whatever his reason, Glover paid for an unusual advertisement in the Los Angeles *Weekly Herald* for 10 March 1877. The ad measured about ten by sixteen inches and featured an outline and reduced illustration of the Los Angeles portion of his view, which occupied the top half of the print. Below the newspaper illustration Glover provided a numbered and lettered key identifying places of interest. Three short columns of text described the city and listed the names and addresses of ten churches.

The advertisement did double duty, since it gave the size and prices of three lithographs. Two were the view illustrated in the advertisement, available in two sizes. The other print contained the large version of Los Angeles and the companion scenes of the nearby port towns of Wilmington and Santa Monica. The advertisement also contained information about sizes and prices.[31]

Like many other viewmakers, Glover thus had to be both artist and businessman. As an artist he needed to think about more than creating a pleasing composition. Decisions concerning what to include or omit in border vignettes were, as has been suggested, often based on financial considerations and not necessarily on which buildings were largest or most important. So, too, in locating vanishing points for his perspective system, the artist needed to reflect on the effect different points would have on the size of the images of houses and business properties owned by possible customers. Even for smaller details, a prudent artist had to keep in

26. His diary entries for this period appear in Norton, *Whitefield,* 20–21.

27. Ithaca *Weekly Chronicle,* 5 and 12 October 1853. Whitefield's "Taghanic Fall" print is reproduced in Norton, *Whitefield,* 100.

28. The only impression of this advertisement I have seen is in the collection of the Missouri Historical Society, St. Louis.

29. 18 January 1877, p. 3. I am indebted to my wife, Constance Peck Reps, for searching for and transcribing this account in the Los Angeles County Museum of Natural History library.

30. Glover's second Los Angeles view of 1877 was published by the Brooklyn Land and Building Co., whose newly subdivided development, Brooklyn Heights (spelled *Hights* on the lithograph) appears prominently featured in the foreground. A search of the newspapers in the library of the Los Angeles County Museum of Natural History for notices of this view proved fruitless. Queries to other collections in Los Angeles holding newspapers not in the County Museum collection were equally unrewarding. My conclusion is that the land promotion view was never placed on sale but distributed free by the company for advertising purposes.

31. The Los Angeles view alone was said to be printed "on heavy paper for framing" and available at $1.00 for the twelve-by-eighteen-inch size or $3.00 for one measuring sixteen by thirty-six inches. The sectioned print showing all three communities was on a sheet twenty-four by thirty-six inches and could be obtained for $5.00 "sent post paid to any address." Glover issued the Santa Monica portion of this sectioned view as a separate print, possibly in 1876. The Wilmington view may also have been available separately, but I have not located any impression. Nor have I been able to find the small version of the Los Angeles view described in the advertisement. The advertisement is in the collection of the Bancroft Library, University of California, Berkeley. In large type in the sky are the letters *Weekly Herald Supplement. Los Angeles, Saturday, March 10th, 1877.* The Bancroft Library has another state of the advertisement without this overprint. Possibly Glover used it as a poster or for distribution to potential customers.

mind who might be among prospective customers. Thus the notation in one of Whitefield's sketchbooks that "J. & R. Ward Tannery must show" may not have been recorded so much in the interests of accuracy and completeness as in the knowledge or hope that the owners of this enterprise were among the likely purchasers for his lithograph.[32]

32. The notation is quoted with a slightly different meaning ascribed to it in Bettina A. Norton, "Sketching America: The New York Public Library's Sketchbook of the Nineteenth-Century American Artist and Traveler Edwin Whitefield," 178.

All these and other matters had to be considered within the framework of how much time could be taken in preparing sketches and the final drawing, the costs of printing, travel, and distribution, the prices for which views could be sold, and the ultimate profits that might be realized. In the two chapters to follow, these and related matters will be explored.

6. The Business of Viewmaking: Time, Costs, Prices, and Volume

How profitable was the business of viewmaking? In this and the following chapter we shall attempt some tentative answers, although the information on which the conclusions are based is incomplete, sometimes conflicting, and far from precise. Nevertheless, enough material has come to light to allow a number of specific conclusions about the time it took artists to prepare views, the costs of preparing the views, the prices for which they sold, and the quantities in which they were printed.

The time required by an artist to sketch individual buildings, establish a perspective grid, redraw each structure at appropriate size and in correct position, and prepare a finished drawing ready to be handed to a lithographer is but one of several poorly documented aspects of the viewmaker's world. From a business standpoint the work undertaken by the artist might have represented the largest element of cost to a publisher, possibly, but not necessarily, exceeded only by expenses for printing and paper. None of the available sources provides more than a rough estimate of the time involved in completing a typical view.

For example, the diaries of Edwin Whitefield, the one view artist whose records have survived, contain little specific information. Whitefield made numerous notes when he was working in various cities, but it is impossible to determine for any given place the amount of time he spent in preparing his first sketches, redrawing them for the final version, putting his design on stone, and arranging to have the view printed. Of his series of four views of Philadelphia issued in 1850 and showing the city as seen from the state house, one of the city's newspapers asserted that Whitefield had "been engaged on the drawings for a year."[1] That may have been so in a general sense, but the artist published ten other views in 1849 and 1850, and he doubtless spent a great deal of time in their final production and, perhaps, in making sketches of other cities for future prints.

Nor, in all probability, did the "four men" employed by the Baltimore firm of E. Sachse & Co. devote all of their days during what was said to be a period of "three years and four months" to the task of "drawing and sketching" even the gigantic twelve-sheet lithograph of the company's home city. These references in a local newspaper were based on statements from the Sachse firm, and the time indicated may well have been exaggerated to whet public interest and to make the results seem even more impressive than they were.[2]

At the other end of the time scale is Albert Ruger's almost incredible record in 1869. Sixty-two city views signed by or attributed to him were published in that year. This works out to just over six days for each town. While his views of this period did not include any very large cities, many of the places he drew were far from insignificant in size, and none of them was a mere village. Probably he did not draw all of them in that year, but in 1868 forty of his views appeared, and he added another thirty-three in 1870. His average annual production for this three-year period, therefore, was about forty-four views. Such a schedule allowed him eight days to complete an average view, with two weeks each year for what anyone would concede to be a well-earned vacation.

We now know that Ruger employed several agents in these years and that two of them—Thaddeus M. Fowler and Eli S. Glover—embarked on artistic and publishing careers of their own. Joseph J. Stoner also served as Ruger's agent at this time, and he, too, knew how to draw, although he made his reputation as a publisher. Augustus Koch, Herman Brosius, and other view artists may also have had their start as Ruger's agents. All this suggests that these agents served as assistant artists as well and that Ruger was most likely not a superhuman artist, capable of finishing a drawing each week before climbing on a train bound for the next community. Our problem remains, however, since we do not know how many agent-assistants Ruger may have employed at any one time or how much of the drawing and sketching each may have carried out.

There are a few newspaper accounts mentioning time spent by single artists. Although they must be used with caution, they do give us some idea of the periods required to produce a finished view. These range from ten days to four months, but it is not known if these longer time spans represented steady work or merely the period between the artist's arrival and the date when he exhibited his finished drawing.

In describing Eli S. Glover's completed sketch of Victoria, British Columbia, in 1878 (Plate 61), a local newspaper referred to the artist as "the gentleman who has for the last four months been studiously engaged taking the view."[3] Glover drew with care and apparent accuracy, and while he produced many views during his career, ten views in a single year represented his largest output, and five or six was a more typical figure. In 1878 he published three other views of places in Washington Territory, so perhaps he spent some of the four months visiting those towns.

1. Philadelphia *Evening Bulletin*, 11 June 1850.
2. Baltimore *Sun*, 22 October 1869, as quoted in Lois B. McCauley, *Maryland Historical Prints, 1752 to 1889*, 26. This news account informed the public that an additional two months would be required to complete the project.

3. Victoria *Colonist*, 8 March 1878, p. 3. A copy of this account was kindly provided me by the library of the University of British Columbia.

A Honolulu newspaper, noting the availability of Paul Emmert's series of six views of the city (Plate 62), asserted that the artist had been "engaged in actual labor" for a period of "three months, with two assistants."[4] Although this multi-sheet lithograph was a panorama and thus involved the delineation of only those buildings that could be seen from a ground-level viewpoint, it did include numerous vignettes of important structures. Nevertheless, with the help of two assistants Emmert would scarcely have needed a full three months of constant sketching and redrawing to complete the project.

Some newspaper accounts contain far less specific indications of the time needed by artists. In 1888 a Chillicothe, Ohio, newspaper announced, "J. W. Smith and Prof. J. R. Buckingham have taken up their residence here and propose making a perspective map of our city. . . . It will take several months of labor to complete the drawings, which will then be submitted to our citizens for inspection."[5] Equally imprecise is the statement by a Denison, Texas, newspaper concerning Thaddeus M. Fowler's tempo of work in 1891. He was said to have required "several weeks" to complete his field sketching and prepare his drawing for exhibit.[6] Fowler published a total of thirteen views that year, so if "several weeks" can be interpreted as four, the news account appears reasonable.

In 1882 Lucien Burleigh drew Ithaca, New York. On 16 June the local paper mentioned that the artist had "been in town some days making a sketch . . . of this village" and that he planned to devote "some weeks yet to filling in details in completion of the sketch." By 18 August his agent had exhibited the final drawing to secure subscriptions for the eventual lithograph. As Burleigh became more proficient or turned his attention to smaller towns, he worked with greater speed. On 9 April he arrived in tiny Groton, New York. By the last day of the month he had completed the drawing.[7]

Even that short period of time would have seemed unnecessarily protracted to Augustus Koch. In 1884 he returned to Fremont, Nebraska, which he had drawn several years earlier when it was much smaller. The newspaper observed that according to Koch's tabulation "there are 1050 buildings in Fremont, residences and business houses," and that it had "at least 5,500 population." The artist spent only "about ten days . . . [and] . . . produced a very large drawing . . . showing all buildings in perspective."[8]

Results of another approach to the question of how long it took an artist to prepare a view appear in Table 7. Artists who produced large numbers of views were selected for comparison. The figures almost surely understate the actual number of views they drew, and the average time required was thus shorter than indicated. This is because the catalog is not complete and because some of the unsigned views published during the periods chosen doubtless were drawn by artists whose names appear in the table.[9] Nor does the average period required to produce a view as indicated in the table take into account the travel time between cities, days or weeks of illness or vacation, or whatever time may have been devoted to business rather than artistic endeavors. Because views dated in one year may have been drawn in the previous year (or even earlier), a three-year average of the most productive three consecutive years of each artist has been used.

Although Ruger had one or more skilled assistants during the years 1868–1870 when his name appeared on 135 views, his impressive rate of production represents a notable achievement. After all, other view artists had assistants as well. J. C. Hazen worked for O. H. Bailey during part of the period of his greatest output, and he may have been H. H. Bailey's assistant in the 1870–1872 period. Virtually all of the Fowler views of 1894–1896 were published by Fowler and James B. Moyer, and Moyer may have been an artistic as well as a business partner in the enterprise.

The speed with which an artist worked clearly depended on many factors, including his natural ability as sharpened by formal or apprenticeship training, his experience in the field, the size and complexity of the community he drew, the perspective system he selected, and his concern for detail and accuracy. Probably the method and amount of payment affected the tempo of his efforts as well. Unfortunately, there does not seem to be any information extant on how artists were paid and how much they received. Such artist-publishers as Edwin Whitefield, Thaddeus Fowler, Alfred Mathews, Eli Glover, and—from time to time—Albert Ruger, did not face this problem of pay directly, although the time they spent in drawing became a cost element in their balance sheets as publishers. Joseph J. Stoner, on the other hand, would have paid salaries or fees to the several artists who at various stages of his career drew the views that this prolific publisher issued from his Madison, Wisconsin, place of business.

As will be suggested later, some of the artists probably received commissions when acting as agents and soliciting subscriptions in the towns whose views they had prepared. Perhaps they also received a flat fee for each view, or their payment may have been based on the time they spent on each project. Some may have been full-time employees receiving a regular salary. Conceivably, they and the publisher may have shared the profits in some agreed-on basis. What-

4. Honolulu *Friend*, 1 November 1854.
5. Chillicothe *Advertiser*, 16 November 1888.
6. Denison *Sunday Gazetteer*, 11 January 1891.
7. Ithaca *Daily Journal*, 16 June and 18 August 1882; New York *Groton and Lansing Journal*, 9 and 30 April 1885. According to the Groton newspaper issued on 20 August 1885, the finished lithographs had arrived in the village. Charles Uhl found and transcribed these notices during his research on the accuracy of the two views and kindly provided me with copies.
8. Fremont *Weekly Herald*, 21 August 1884.
9. The catalog may indicate that some of the views are unsigned only because institutions reporting their holdings to me neglected to include the artist's name in the imprint, or I may have overlooked it in my searches of collections. On the other hand, the O. H. Bailey views with the company name appearing as artist may not have been drawn by Bailey himself. The Kuchel & Dresel views pose special problems. A large number of these views are excluded from the tabulation. These are variant states of otherwise identical views published both with and without border vignettes. While the principal view is the same or virtually so in these cases, the vignettes represent additional work required. Finally, the tabulations do not take into consideration the size of the communities, the numbers of buildings that the artist had to depict, nor the basic town pattern. As to the latter subject, it surely must have been easier to draw a grid town on flat terrain than, say, a New England city with a random street pattern on irregular topography.

Table 7. Rank Order of Selected Artists by Annual Average Views Drawn during Most Productive Consecutive Three-Year Period and Average Days Required per View

	Most Productive Consecutive Three Years	Number Drawn in Period	Average Annual Number of Views	Average Days per View
Albert Ruger	1868–1870	135	45.0	8.1
L. R. Burleigh	1885–1887	94	31.3	11.7
O. H. Bailey	1877–1879	73	24.3	15.0
T. M. Fowler	1894–1896	67	22.3	16.4
Henry Wellge	1884–1886	61	20.3	18.0
Kuchel & Dresel	1856–1858	42	14.0	26.1
H. H. Bailey	1870–1872	38	12.7	28.7
J. B. Bachelder	1855–1857	29	9.7	37.6
Herman Brosius	1873–1875	29	9.7	37.6
Eli S. Glover	1875–1877	26	8.7	42.0
Augustus Koch	1879–1881	23	7.7	47.4
A. F. Poole	1883–1885	23	7.7	47.4
J. C. Wild	1839–1841	23	7.7	47.4
C. J. Pauli	1890–1892	21	7.0	52.1
A. E. Mathews	1865–1867	20	6.7	54.5
J. T. Palmatary	1854–1856	16	5.3	68.9
Edwin Whitefield	1846–1848	16	5.3	68.9
J. W. Hill	1852–1854	14	4.7	77.7
D. D. Morse	1876–1878	14	4.7	77.7
E. S. Moore	1887–1889	11	3.7	98.6

ever the arrangements, nothing exists to reveal their details. In figures to be presented in the following chapter, an arbitrary sum has been selected. It may not be too far from reality, but it should not be regarded as anything more than reasoned speculation.

Other costs of production can be estimated with somewhat more confidence. However, figures appearing in newspapers should be looked at with suspicion. One that appeared in a Honolulu newspaper seems wildly exaggerated and was probably planted by the publisher to stimulate sales. The paper described the six views of the city published in 1854 as involving "an expense exceeding $4,000." [10] More believable is the far more modest statement of a Prince Edward Island newspaper in 1878. The publisher of a view of Charlottetown was said to have spent "the sum of $500 . . . in order to bring" the lithograph "to its perfect condition." [11]

Statements of printer's charges to publishers are far more informative. The earliest is the record of payment to the New York firm of Francis d'Avignon, one of the country's leading lithographic printers. It was here that Thomas Larkin had a handsome pair of views of Monterey (Plate 63) drawn for him in 1842, finally printed in late 1850 or early 1851. Both views were large, and each was printed from two stones. One hundred copies of each were printed on heavy paper, and twenty-five copies of each were printed on lighter stock to be used for a folded version.

D'Avignon's bill dated 11 February 1851 read as follows:

To Lithograph 2 views of Monterey	$300.00
100 copies of each at $25 per hundred	50.00
25 copies of each at $25 per one hundred (thin paper)	12.50

10. Honolulu *Friend*, 1 November 1854.
11. Charlottetown *Daily Examiner*, 25 November 1878.

If the thin-paper copies are disregarded as untypical, this works out to $1.50 each for putting the drawings on stone, preparing the second tone stone, supplying paper, and printing the 200 impressions. It does not include, of course, whatever fee Larkin may have paid the unknown artist nearly a decade earlier, the time and expense involved in getting the drawings or paintings to New York, making the arrangements for their printing, and the costs of distribution, which would have included mailing, collection of payments, and other incidental expenses. [12]

One should note that this was a very small edition of each view. If, say, 250 copies of each had been printed, the unit cost would have been only eighty-five cents. This assumes, of course, that the three-hundred-dollar charge for lithography—presumably representing the work of putting the designs and the tones on the four stones involved—would remain unchanged.

Reflecting the efficiency of modern presses using electric power, photographic methods to transfer the drawing to the printing medium, and metal plates rather than lithographic stones, a bill by the Meriden Gravure Company sent in 1916 to the firm of Hughes and Bailey was much lower. For printing 200 copies of a large view of Lynn, Massachusetts, on twenty-six-by-forty-inch sheets, Meriden charged only $143.90. This included some "Extra Work on Marginal Views" and one "new plate," doubtless required for some last-minute revisions by the publishers. Each print thus cost just under $.72. [13]

12. The printer's bill is from Jeanne Van Nostrand, *A Pictorial and Narrative History of Monterey: Adobe Capital Of California, 1770–1847*, 90–91. What probably is only a partial list of purchasers or those receiving complimentary copies of these views appears in George P. Hammond, ed., *The Larkin Papers*, 3:406.

13. A copy of the bill was kindly provided me by James R. Warren, Jr., the leading expert on the life and work of Thaddeus Fowler.

The most complete and reliable information on nineteenth-century printing costs comes from Edwin Whitefield's diary of 1866, in which he calculated the costs and projected profits for his view of the Boston Commons. Whitefield used a statement of printing charges furnished by J. H. Bufford's establishment for a lithograph measuring eighteen by twenty-five inches. Based on those figures, Whitefield worked out the unit costs for quantities from one hundred to five hundred impressions and also estimated his receipts on the assumption that the view would sell for five dollars.[14]

Lith View of the Common 25 × 18	$150.00
Paper & Printing per 100	35.00
	185.00
2nd. 100	35.00
	220.00
3rd. 100	35.00
	255.00

According to this the lst 100 would cost me each	1.85
If I print 200, each copy will cost	1.10
" 300 "	.85
" 400 "	.72
" 500 "	.65
If I sell 200 I shall make	$780.00
" 300 "	1245.00
" 400 "	1710.00
" 500 "	2185.00

How typical was Whitefield's projected price of five dollars? What did a resident of a city pay in the nineteenth century for a view of his community, and how many did the publisher sell? Many factors determined what a view could be sold for: whether it was black and white, hand-colored, or printed from multiple stones; the general price level of all goods at the time it was published; the number printed; whether the view was purchased through subscription or bought after publication; and the demand existing for such a product.

Other elements were important as well: the skill and energy of the publisher and his agent, sources of income from the view that did not depend entirely on sales volume, subsidies received from governments or business, and how attractive and accurate the view was regarded to be by prospective customers. These and other influences must have differed from one town to another.

Almost all of our information about prices charged comes from newspaper notices printed at the time the view appeared.[15] Table 8 showing a selection of prices draws on this

material and uses several other sources as well. Views are arranged chronologically by date of publication. The size shown is for the printed image. Information on color may not be complete or accurate, although surely this must have been one of the major determinants of price. The table is only a beginning, but it does present the most extensive compilation of such information available.

Two of the views identified in Table 8 were very large, and each was issued in four sheets. These are Palmatary's view of Chicago in 1857 and the Laass lithograph of Syracuse in 1868. Each set sold for $10.00.[16] The enormous twelve-sheet view of Baltimore in 1869, drawn and published by E. Sachse and Company, was advertised to subscribers at $15.00, or a modest $1.25 for each sheet.[17] An even larger view—surely the most heroic effort of its kind—was the lithograph of St. Louis on 110 sheets mentioned above, drawn by Camille N. Dry and sold through subscription by Compton & Company. A person with a wall large enough and possessed of sufficient energy could assemble the view on a space nine by twenty-four feet. The view came "elegantly bound in muslin and gilt" at a price of only $25.00.[18] Each sheet of the view is the size of many single-sheet city lithographs, and the purchaser of the set was thus getting a bargain at less that $.25 a sheet.

Many other views were issued in sets, although individual sheets must also have been available for purchase. The set prices appear low by modern standards, and even the nineteenth-century buyer surely regarded them as bargains. John Caspar Wild and J. B. Chevalier in 1837 announced the forthcoming publication of a series of Philadelphia views, twenty in all, at a price of $2.50 for the set.[19] The views were small, each measuring about five by seven feet, but it is clear that the publishers anticipated that the volume of sales would make the project financially rewarding. They did find

14. This page of the diary is reproduced in Bettina A. Norton, *Edwin Whitefield: Nineteenth-Century North American Scenery*, 48. I have omitted Whitefield's notation just above the last group of calculations: "The weather to-day was very pleasant."

15. It would be tedious to cite each account. Those relating to the Whitefield views come either from the Whitefield scrapbook in the Boston Public Library or from Norton's *Whitefield*. Many of the newspaper accounts used to obtain price data are cited in other contexts elsewhere in this study. For brief discussions of the prices of city views, see Thomas Beckman, *Milwaukee Illustrated: Panoramic and Bird's-Eye Views of a Midwestern Metropolis, 1844–1908*, unpaged introduction; John R. Hébert, "Introduction," U.S. Library of Congress, *Panoramic Maps of Anglo-American Cities: A Checklist of Maps in the Collections of the Library of Congress,*

Geography and Map Division, 4; and John W. Reps, *Cities on Stone: Nineteenth Century Lithograph Images of the Urban West*, 26–27.

16. This was the subscriber's price for the Chicago view. Those who waited until its publication had to pay $12.00.

17. Baltimore *Sun*, 22 October 1869, as quoted in McCauley, *Maryland*, 26.

18. Advertising text appearing at the bottom of a "specimen page" of the view issued by Compton & Company in 1875, an impression of which is in the collection of the Missouri Historical Society, St. Louis. No information about the cost of publication seems to have survived, but it must have been very high if one considers the expenses involved for Dry's drawing, the materials required for lithographic stones, ink, paper, labor needed for printing, press time, and the added expense for covers and binding. While impressions of the view can be found in several public collections—one indication that many copies must have been printed—it is difficult to believe that sales alone would have made such an ambitious project financially successful. Possibly the undertaking received some kind of local subsidy. The date of publication suggests that the view may have been used to advertise St. Louis at the Centennial in Philadelphia the following year. The publisher may also have obtained additional revenues through charges made for identifying commercial and industrial buildings in the body of the view and the legends that appeared at the bottom of each sheet.

19. Philadelphia *Courier*, 2 December 1837, quoted in Martin P. Snyder, "J. C. Wild and His Philadelphia Views," 34. Wild's travels and activities in Philadelphia and Cincinnati have been traced through the efforts of Snyder and John Francis McDermott. See the latter's "J. C. Wild, Western Painter and Lithographer" and "John Caspar Wild: Some New Facts and a Query." In his earlier article McDermott is in error in stating that the four views of Philadelphia from the state house tower were published in 1831 (rather than 1838), and his second article fails to concede this, although Snyder provides the evidence.

Table 8. Place, Date of Publication, Artist, Size, Color, and Price of City Views

Place	Date	Artist	Approximate Size (in inches)	Color	Price
Ithaca, N.Y.	1836	Walton	11 × 17½	hand colored	$1.50
Ithaca, N.Y.	1838	Walton	14 × 16	hand colored	$3.50
Wilmington, Del.	1842	B. Gluck	15 × 27½	unknown	$.75
Albany, N.Y.	1845	Whitefield	15½ × 24	toned	$2.00
Troy, N.Y.	1845	Whitefield	22½ × 39½	toned	$2.00
Gloucester, Mass.	ca. 1845	Lane	15½ × 23½	uncolored	$1.00
				hand colored	$2.00
Harrisburg, Pa.	1846	Whitefield	16½ × 23	toned	$1.00
Newark, N.J.	1846	Whitefield	20 × 35	printed color	$3.00
Baltimore, Md.	1847	Whitefield	17½ × 41	printed color	$5.00
Buffalo, N.Y.	ca. 1848	Whitefield	14¼ × 37	printed color	$3.00
Quebec, Toronto, Montreal, Hamilton, & London, Canada	1852–1854	Whitefield	ca. 22 × 36	toned	one, $5.00; two, $4.00 each; three, $3.67 each; four or more, $3.00 each
Quebec, Toronto, Montreal, Hamilton, & London, Canada	1852–1854	Whitefield	ca. 22 × 36	hand colored	one, $8.00; two, $7.00 each; three, $6.67 each; four or more, $6.00 each
Honolulu, Hawaii	1853	Emmert	20¼ × 27¼	toned	$3.00 each; set of six, $15.00
Frederick, Md.	1854	Sachse	19½ × 31¼	printed color	$5.00
Alexandria, Va.	[1854]	Sachse	20 × 30½	printed color	$5.00
Brantford, Ontario	[1855?]	Whitefield	unknown	[hand?] colored	$15.00
Castine, Maine	1855	Lane	20 × 32½	printed color	$2.00 (price listed in subscription for uncolored print, but issued in printed color)
Galena, Ill.	1855	Whitefield	19½ × 36	unknown	$8.00 (but "discounted" impressions sold for $4.00–5.00)
Sandusky, Ohio	[1855?]	Sachse	20¼ × 33½	printed color	$6.00
Chicago, Ill.	1857	Palmatary	45 × 81½ (in 4 sheets)	printed color	$10.00 to subscribers; $12.00 to others
Sacramento, Calif.	1857	Baker	28½ × 35¼	toned	$5.00
Hartford, Conn.	1864	Weidenman	18 × 23	printed color	$5.00
Adrian, Mich.	1866	Ruger	22 × 34	printed color	$3.00
Boston, Mass.	1866	Whitefield	15¼ × 28½	uncolored	$5.00
Lansing, Mich.	1866	Ruger	23¼ × 30	printed color	$3.00
Milwaukee, Wis.	1866	Lipman	16½ × 30½	printed color	$5.00
Ypsilanti, Mich.	1866	Ruger	20½ × 28	printed color	$3.00
Aurora, Belleville, & Centralia, Ill.; Flint, Mich.; and Winona, Minn.	1867	Ruger	each ca. 20 × 28	printed color	each $3.00
Ionia, Mich.	1868	Ruger	24 × 30	printed color	$3.00
Grand Rapids, Mich.	1868	Ruger	22 × 34	printed color	$5.00
Syracuse, N.Y.	1868	Laass	51½ × 78¼ (in 4 sheets)	printed color	$10.00
Danville, Ill.	1869	Ruger	18¼ × 26	printed color	$4.00
St. Louis, Mich.	1870	unknown	14 × 18	printed color	$2.00
Raleigh, N.C.	1872	Drie	20½ × 28¼	printed color	$5.00
Milwaukee, Wis.	1872	H. H. Bailey	23 × 38	printed color	$3.00
San Diego, Los Angeles, San Bernardino, & Santa Barbara, Calif.	1873	Mathews	each ca. 9 × 16	toned	$1.25 each
Ithaca, N.Y.	1873	O. H. Bailey	20 × 25¼	printed color	$3.00
Austin, Tex.	1873	Koch	20 × 28	printed color	$5.00
Nashua, N.H.	1875	H. H. Bailey	22 × 32½	printed color	$3.00
Farmington, N.H.	1877	Ruger	14 × 17¼	toned	$1.50
Great Falls, N.H.	1877	Ruger	22¼ × 24	toned	$2.80
Keene, N.H.	1877	Ruger	15¼ × 20¼	printed color	one, $3.00; four, $2.50 each
Los Angeles, Calif.	1877	Glover	12 × 18	toned	$1.00
Los Angeles, Calif.	1877	Glover	16 × 36	toned	$3.00
Los Angeles, Calif. (with Santa Monica & Wilmington on same sheet)	1877	Glover	24 × 36	toned	$5.00
Portsmouth, N.H.	1877	Ruger	21¼ × 26½	printed color	$5.00
Portland, Ore.	1879	Glover	24 × 40	toned	$10.00
Canajoharie, N.Y.	1881	Burleigh	18½ × 24½	toned	$3.00

Place	Date	Artist	Approximate Size (in inches)	Color	Price
Ithaca, N.Y.	1882	Burleigh	20 × 29	uncolored	$3.00
Youngstown, Ohio	1882	Ruger	16½ × 28	unknown	$3.00
Hebron, Nebr.	1883	Koch	12 × 22½	unknown	two, $3.00
Laconia, N.H.	1883	Poole	16 × 21	toned	$2.00
Lake Village & Plymouth, N.H.	1883	Poole	each ca. 14 × 16	toned	$2.00 each
Lancaster, Bethlehem, & Littleton, N.H.	1883	Poole	each ca. 16 × 20	uncolored	$2.50 each
Nashua, N.H.	1883	O. H. Bailey	22 × 33	toned	$2.50
Ashland, Ore.	1884	Fred Walpole	14 × 21½	toned	$5.00
Bristol, Lebanon, & Pittsfield, N.H.	1884	Norris	each ca. 16 × 23	toned	$2.00 each
Exeter, Franklin, & Rochester, N.H.	1884	Wellge	each ca. 16 × 20	toned	$2.00 each
Seattle, Wash.	1884	Wellge	16 × 32½	toned	one, $3.00; twelve, $1.66 each; one hundred, $1.00 each
Hinsdale & Peterborough, N.H., and Bellows Falls, Vt.	1886	Burleigh	each ca. 14½ × 24	toned	$3.00 each
Bennington, Derry Depot, Warner, & Winchester, N.H.	1887	Norris	each ca. 14 × 20	toned	$2.00 each
Gorham, N.H.	1888	Norris	20 × 24½	toned	$2.50
Victoria, British Columbia	1889	R. H.	25 × 39½	unknown	$1.00
Henniker & Meredith, N.H.	1889	Norris	each ca. 14 × 21	toned	$2.50
Clyde, N.Y.	1892	Burleigh?	17 × 26½	toned	$2.50
Exeter, N.H.	1896	unsigned	27½ × 32	toned	$1.00
Derry, N.H.	1898	O. H. Bailey	19 × 26½	uncolored	$1.00
Concord, N.H.	1899	Poole	22½ × 28	uncolored	"Prang's Photogravure Print . . . on plate paper 28 × 38 inches, $5.00. Prang's Carbon . . . on heavy plate paper 30 × 40 inches . . . $10.00."

it necessary to raise prices slightly midway through publication, bringing the cost of each group of four views to $.50,[20] and when the entire set was bound it was priced at $3.00.[20]

Four other Wild views of Philadelphia followed in 1838. These were larger, each measuring about six by twelve feet, and showed the city as seen from the steeple of the statehouse looking to the cardinal points of the compass. Wild and Chevalier advertised these at $.25 each, or $1.00 for the entire set. In addition, the twenty earlier views and the four new prints were used by the publishers as a third publication, bound under the title *Panorama and Views of Philadelphia, and its Vicinity*, priced at $5.00.[21] After Wild moved to St. Louis he published a set of eight views of that city, each about ten by fifteen feet. He sold the sets at $4.00 uncolored and $8.00 with hand color added.[22]

Higher in price but containing thirty-six views on twenty-three sheets was the bound set drawn and published by Alfred Mathews in 1866 with the title *Pencil Sketches of Colorado* (Plate 64). He offered this to the public at $30.00. Per-

haps this proved too expensive, for two years later when Mathews published his *Pencil Sketches of Montana* with twenty-seven full-page and four larger folded plates, he set the price at only $17.00.[23]

One additional bit of information concerning prices of city views comes from the probate court inventory of Wild's estate. On his death in August 1846 Wild had in his possession more than two hundred assorted colored and uncolored prints of Galena, Moline, and Bloomington, Illinois; Dubuque, Iowa; and St. Louis, Missouri. The court accepted an appraisal of $1.00 each for the uncolored prints and $2.00 each for those Wild had colored. However, in the estate sale they sold for prices 50 percent higher than these figures.[24]

From all this information we can come to some tentative conclusions about the prices of lithographic city views. Disregarding such atypical items as those issued in sets, bound in volumes, printed in multiple sheets, and so on, the prices of "normal" single-sheet urban prints cluster in the range of

20. Snyder, "J. C. Wild," 40–42, traces the publishing history of these views. The Philadelphia *Courier* used the views as premiums for new subscribers.

21. Snyder, "J. C. Wild," 43–46. Later in 1838, J. T. Bowen acquired the rights to this volume and reissued it with changes only to the title page and the imprint on each sheet. Bowen also brought out the twenty-view set in 1848 without the four others forming the panorama. Prices for these versions are not given by Snyder, who describes the Bowen publications on pp. 47–49.

22. St. Louis *Missouri Republican*, 28 April 1840, quoted in McDermott, "J. C. Wild," 114.

23. Denver *Rocky Mountain News*, 19 October 1866; and Central City *Daily Miners' Register*, 21 July 1868, cited in Robert Taft, *Artists and Illustrators of the Old West, 1850–1900*, 306, n. 14; 308, n. 33. Not all of the plates in these two sets were of cities, although cities make up the bulk of the Colorado views. There were no city views in Mathews's least successful effort, *Gems of Rocky Mountain Scenery*, published in 1869. This had five views of the Rocky Mountain landscape. Its price was $15.00, but it "sold in Denver the same year at $10 'owing to the present hard times'" (Taft, 308, n. 37, quoting the *Rocky Mountain News*, 5 July 1869).

24. McDermott, "J. C. Wild," 124–25. Wild died in Davenport, Iowa. His last few years are described in a biographical sketch by A. H. Sanders in Franc B. Wilkie, *Davenport Past and Present . . .*, 308–10.

Table 9. Number of Subscribers Said To Be Required by Urban Viewmakers

Number	Place	Date	Artist or publisher
25	Hebron, Nebraska	1883	Augustus Koch
75	Plymouth, New Hampshire	1883	George Norris & Albert Poole
100	Alexandria, Virginia	1854	James T. Palmatary
100	Gloucester, Massachusetts	1855	Fitz Hugh Lane
100	Groton, New York	1885	Lucien Burleigh
150	Lexington, Kentucky	1870	Albert Ruger
160	Sandusky, Ohio	1855	James T. Palmatary
200	Newark, New Jersey	1847	Edwin Whitefield
250	San Antonio, Texas	1873	Augustus Koch & J. J. Stoner
500	Milwaukee, Wisconsin	1872	H. H. Bailey

$2.00 to $5.00. Glover's price of $10.00 for his Portland, Oregon, view appears on the print itself, but it may well be that few if any copies actually changed hands at that figure. For the small towns where Ruger did much of his work, $3.00 may have been typical for one of his three-stone lithographs. A larger print of a more populous community might have brought $5.00. Hand coloring or the use of more than three stones would have allowed the publisher to charge somewhat more and still remain within the range that the ordinary purchaser could afford.

Prices and the number of impressions printed were often but not always related. The seemingly very low prices at which Wild and Chevalier sold their small views of Philadelphia were clearly possible only when a mass market existed. Probably they ran off thousands of copies of each view. On the other hand, Whitefield priced his view of Baltimore in 1847 at $5.00, while he sold his view of the same size and also printed in colors showing the much smaller city of Newark, New Jersey, in 1846 for $3.00. Although we do not know how many impressions he had printed, Whitefield certainly would have sold more of his lithographs in Baltimore than in Newark. Here was a case of charging what the market would bear and not setting prices to reflect the unit costs of production.

In the previous chapter we noted Whitefield's surprise when his agent obtained 1,300 subscribers for his two views of Providence. It is not likely that many views enjoyed sales of this magnitude, although we lack information about those of such large cities as New York, Chicago, and San Francisco.[25] At the other end of the scale we have the statement by a firm that printed views early in the twentieth century that only one hundred copies of some views were run off, and that in any event the number printed did not usually exceed two hundred and fifty.[26]

Approximations of the numbers of impressions printed by some viewmakers can be derived from their statements about the number of subscribers needed to proceed from finished sketch to completed lithograph. In the previous chapter a number of these were cited. Table 9 shows these ranked from lowest to highest, with additional figures added from other sources.[27]

While some artists may have overstated for public consumption the number of subscribers they needed, we have already noted that the three hundred subscribers reported to have been received by Whitefield for a projected Louisville view in 1848 were apparently regarded by him as insufficient in number. It is difficult to explain his reluctance in Louisville, given the figure of two hundred that he evidently felt a year earlier would provide him with a suitable profit at Newark.[28]

In addition to information summarized in Table 9, there are several statements about the numbers of views printed that vary from possible exaggerations to wild inflations. Overstating claims for sales of views in rival or nearby towns was a promotional device that publishers doubtless used. One might suspect that this was the case in a news item appearing in a small-town paper not far from Syracuse, where it was said that "the agent has secured six hundred subscribers" for a lithograph of the city.[29]

Henry Wellge drew both Tacoma and Seattle, Washington, in 1884. He must have completed and published the Tacoma lithograph first, for a Seattle newspaper stated that "a bird's eye view of Tacoma has been taken by the same artist, and 1000 copies sold."[30] There can be little doubt both that the quantity came from Wellge and that it far exceeded the true number. Wellge engaged in an even bolder distortion of reality five years later. His firm, the American Publishing Company of Milwaukee, published several views of Nebraska towns drawn by Wellge. His business agent, Charles J. Smith, must have been splendidly persuasive, for

25. Concerning this aspect of San Francisco views the leading scholar of the subject has remarked despairingly, "Original quantities printed and individual or wholesale selling prices are possibly the most troublesome details of the history of San Francisco prints. Few records are available on numbers printed and prices charged in San Francisco" (Joseph Armstrong Baird, Jr., "Introduction" to Baird and Edwin Clyve Evans, Historic Lithographs of San Francisco). In fact, Baird cites no figures at all, pointing out, "The records of the companies that printed and published lithographs . . . were damaged or destroyed in the great earthquake and fire of 1906. Carelessness and disinterest accomplished what 1906 left undone."

26. Letter from Harold Hugo, president of Meriden Gravure Company, Meriden, Connecticut, to John R. Hébert, 1 February 1972, cited in U.S. Library of Congress, Panoramic Maps, 4. This referred to the views published "in the 1910's and 1920's" for Hughes & Bailey and Hughes & Cinquin.

27. Thaddeus Fowler visited Milwaukee in 1872 to secure subscriptions for a view of the city he said would be drawn by O. H. Bailey. At that time he stated that he required five hundred subscribers. Milwaukee Sentinel, 17 January 1872, p. 4, as quoted in Beckman, Milwaukee Illustrated, unpaged introduction. As Beckman points out in his note on the view, it was drawn by H. H. Bailey, O. H. Bailey's older brother. Fowler and the Bailey brothers worked together at this time.

28. Whitefield had about two hundred subscribers for his Albany view of 1845. An undated clipping from the Albany Citizen in Whitefield's scrapbook in the Boston Public Library Print Room notes, "Mr. Whitefield is now furnishing the view to his subscribers, who number about 200."

29. Ithaca Daily Journal, 21 October 1873.

30. Seattle Post Intelligencer, 15 July 1884, p. 2, col. 2.

in otherwise nearly identical news accounts, one local paper stated soberly that "20,000 copies [of the view] are to be struck off and delivered next fall," while another paper more modestly, if no more believably, lowered the number to "ten to twenty thousand."[31]

Probably one must disregard, too, the assertion made when he was a very old man by Oakley H. Bailey, artist and publisher of scores of views. As summarized by John Hébert, Bailey claimed that "he had made sketches of nearly 600 different places and that total reproductions had exceeded a million copies. Simple arithmetic indicates that Bailey's estimate works out to approximately 2,000 copies of each view."[32]

J. C. Hazen's claim that he sold "about 1000" copies of H. H. Bailey's view of Manchester, New Hampshire, of 1876 should also be regarded with some suspicion, but there are a number of other statements about New Hampshire views that seem more reasonable.[33] For example, W. R. Patchen, sales agent for Albert Ruger's view of Rochester, New Hampshire, in 1877, was reported to have made advance sales to "about one hundred subscribers." That same year T. M. Fowler, then also working on Ruger's behalf, reported that he "had secured a few over one hundred subscriptions" for a view of Portsmouth, New Hampshire.[34]

In 1883 Albert F. Poole and George E. Norris produced ten views of places in New Hampshire. Several newspapers reported how many subscribers Norris obtained for the views his partner drew. For Littleton the number reported was 190; at Laconia, 175; and Lakeport (then Lake Village), 130.[35] He had less success at Plymouth, where the local newspaper mentioned that he had delivered "some 70 or more panoramic views" to subscribers. A newspaper in Lit-

tleton reported that in nearby Lisbon an even smaller number of "over 60" copies of the view had been delivered.[36]

When Norris began to draw town views and publish them himself he continued the practice of announcing how many views he had sold. In 1884 he disposed of "220 copies" of his lithograph of Pittsfield, New Hampshire (Plate 65). For his view of Bristol, New Hampshire, that same year he reported "having taken orders for 175 copies."[37]

For the great majority of city views in the nineteenth century it is safe to assume that for small to medium-size places no more than five hundred copies were printed and that two to three hundred was a typical press run. If the publisher's estimate of the market proved too pessimistic and the stones used to print the view had not been reused or a transfer paper impression existed, additional copies could be printed. The later issues of Wild's Philadelphia views are one example. A second printing of Whitefield's view of the Boston Common is another.[38]

It is that view by Whitefield and his diary entry concerning it, already referred to earlier in the chapter, that furnish the most conclusive evidence that five hundred copies can be regarded as a normal upper limit, since this is the highest number Whitefield used in his cost and profit calculations. A view of such an important part of a large and prosperous city would surely have outsold the average lithograph of a small or middle-sized town. By 1866, after years of drawing and selling urban lithographs, Whitefield would have known how many copies were likely to be sold.

We have now looked at the major time and cost elements of the business side of viewmaking and have come to some tentative conclusions about the number of copies printed and the prices at which they sold. In the chapter to follow we will examine additional sources of revenue publishers could obtain and then use all this material together in an effort to estimate the profits to be derived from this distinctive form of nineteenth-century American publishing.

31. Fremont *Weekly Herald*, 4 July 1889; Lincoln *Daily Nebraska State Journal*, 2 June 1889; and—for the lower figure—Norfolk *Daily News*, 15 June 1889.

32. U. S. Library of Congress, *Panoramic Maps*, 4.

33. David Ruell made a thorough search for newspaper accounts of all New Hampshire bird's-eye views, and it is his information that I have drawn on for this section. He cites three Manchester notices concerning the 1876 view, one of which contains the quoted figure of 1,000 copies: Manchester *Daily Union*, 21 August 1875 and 8 February 1876, and Manchester *Mirror and American*, 21 August 1875.

34. Rochester *Courier & Advertiser*, 31 August 1877; Portsmouth *Daily Chronicle*, 24 September 1877.

35. For notices concerning the Littleton view and other numbers mentioned ("about 120 copies" and "nearly two hundred copies"), see the Littleton *White Mountain Republic*, 14 April, 14 and 21 July, 29 September, 13 October, and 8 December 1883. The number of subscribers for the Laconia view appeared in the Bristol *Weekly Enterprise*, 5 June 1884. The Laconia *Democrat*, 13 July 1883, reported the subscribers for the Lakeport view.

36. Plymouth *Republican Star*, 29 December 1883; Littleton *Journal*, 21 December 1883.

37. Dunbarton and Pittsfield *The Analecta*, 31 July 1884; Bristol *Weekly Enterprise*, 22 May 1884.

38. Norton, *Whitefield*, notes for entry 90, observes that an impression of the Whitefield print of 1866 is known on paper with an 1873 watermark. As to reprinting additional copies, I can only repeat what I stated in my *Cities on Stone*: "It seems doubtful that a view would have been in demand more than a few months after it first appeared. Most of the cities were undergoing rapid changes, and a print would be badly out of date before long. It is unlikely, therefore, that more copies were ever printed than the publisher believed would be purchased within a short time after they were first offered for sale" (28).

7. The Business of Viewmaking: Miscellaneous Revenues and Profits

Advance subscriptions and additional sales after the views were published must have accounted for most of the income received by view publishers. Other sources of revenue existed, however, and alert viewmakers surely pursued them all. Receipts derived from other sources not only added to profits directly but, because of the manner in which they were obtained, may also have increased the total number of views that could be sold.

Many views, especially those published after the Civil War, included border vignettes or insets showing details of individual places of business and industry, public buildings, churches, large residences, and other important structures. While artists and publishers in the early days of viewmaking may have used such small border views for decorative purposes and to give their prints broader appeal, it must not have been long before they realized that vignettes offered an opportunity for enhanced profits.

Evidence that viewmakers charged fees to owners for having their buildings given such special prominence is sparse but convincing. The paucity of supporting documentation for such a practice is understandable. View publishers would not have wanted it generally understood that the buildings and business enterprises selected for such special treatment were chosen on anything but an impartial basis. Owners, too, would doubtless have regarded this as a confidential matter.

George Baker's subscription book for his 1857 view of Sacramento provides the most specific information about this practice. In it he recorded payments received for "advertising cards on [the] border of [the] 2nd Edition" of this view. Amounts range from $5.00 to $50.00. Three were for $40.00, two for $30.00, and the thirteen payments came to a total of $335.00. Baker's notes beside some of the payment records suggest that advertisers received one copy of the view for each $5.00 paid.[1]

In a few instances, local newspapers revealed that vignettes were to be included on views if owners of the properties paid suitable fees. When P. F. Castleman visited Walla Walla, Washington, in 1865 to prepare his view of that city, he took a number of photographs of commercial structures. The local paper revealed the use to which these would be put:

> Mr. P. F. Castleman is engaged in taking photographic views of the city and of the principal business houses, with a view of sending them to San Francisco and having them lithographed. The design is to have a view of the city printed on the center of a card 24 × 32 inches, with a view of the garrison, one or two

farms near the city, and the principal business houses in the city in the margin. It is being gotten up by subscription, those who have their places of business or residences printed paying a stipulated sum for the same.[2]

Castleman's efforts succeeded, for the view as printed in 1866 by Grafton T. Brown contained twenty-nine vignettes (Plate 66). If Castleman collected $10.00 for each vignette, his total receipts from this source alone would, in all probability, have paid for Brown's lithographing and printing charges.

In 1882 T. M. Fowler served as O. H. Bailey's sales and subscription agent for the view of Nashua, New Hampshire, that Bailey published the following year (Plate 67). A local newspaper revealed that Fowler was in town "soliciting orders for . . . advertising views of manufacturing and other establishments to be lithographed on the border." The published view had sixteen vignettes, and probably Fowler collected fees from the owners of all the buildings thus given special prominence.[3]

Two Canadian newspapers similarly disclosed that vignettes were for sale. A New Brunswick newspaper printed this announcement in 1881:

> A Bird's Eye View of Chatham is being nicely drawn for publication about the middle of June by A. M. Hubly of Moncton. It is to be lithographed . . . size about 28 × 32 inches. Mr. Hubly is now in Chatham completing his drawings and soliciting subscriptions to the work, which promises to be an accurate and very desirable one. He is also taking a limited number of orders for marginal views of residences, business places, etc., for advertising purposes as well as characterizing the businessmen of the place. This is a commendable feature which should be encouraged.

For another Canadian view showing Port Arthur, Ontario, in 1885, the publisher attempted to secure financial support from the city council. An obviously planted statement in the newspaper urged the council "to purchase a thousand copies to send to the leading newspapers throughout Canada and the U.S." The cautious public officials, however, elected to support the venture only by underwriting "a cut of the new school building," a structure that the artist might have included in any event.[4]

1. George H. Baker, manuscript subscription book, collection of the Society of California Pioneers, San Francisco, unpaged.

2. Walla Walla *Statesman*, 5 May 1865, p. 3, col. 1. A transcription of this important notice was provided by Lawrence L. Dodd, Penrose Memorial Library, Whitman College, Walla Walla.

3. Nashua *Daily Telegraph*, 2 November 1882. David Ruell called my attention to this notice.

4. Miramichi, New Brunswick, *Advance*, 5 May 1881. I am indebted to William R. MacKinnon, Provincial Archives of New Brunswick, for sending me a transcript of this item. The Port Arthur quotations are from that town's *Daily Sentinel*, 14 and 21 April 1885. They appear, with a brief note on the view, in Roy H. Piovesana, "Panoramic Map of Port Arthur, 1885."

Other evidence supporting the conclusion that payments for vignettes was widespread comes from the views themselves. Mr. S. L. Sheldon of Madison, Wisconsin, must have paid a substantial sum to underwrite the publication in 1885 of Norris, Wellge & Co.'s lithograph depicting the city where his agricultural implement business was located (Plate 68). As one authority observed, the print was "framed by 18 pictures of farm machines, including the Gasaday sulky plow, the J. I. Case agitator, Buffalo Pitts coal or wood burning traction engine, and Easterly's twine binding harvester." Sheldon used copies of the view as gifts to his customers with a statement soliciting their "continued patronage."[5]

Two merchants of Hamburg, Pennsylvania, paid Thaddeus Fowler for including vignettes of their shops and products on his print of the city issued in 1889. "One portrays W. William Appel's photographic studio, jewelry store, and residence, with a lithographic reproduction of the owner. The other, an advertisement for W. H. Grim, dealer in musical instruments and sewing machines, includes a view of his shop and representation of a Miller organ, one of Grim's stock items."[6] Apparently other businessmen in Hamburg regarded this as an effective means of advertising. What must be a second state of this view exists, also dated 1889, but with four new vignettes at the top showing two factories, a store, and the public school. At the bottom, Fowler squeezed in another factory view. Rather more puzzling is the replacement of one of the original vignettes of the Miller organ sold at Grim's store by a small view of a church. The exterior view of Mr. Grim's establishment remained unaltered.[7]

In at least one other instance Fowler followed the same practice. The first state of his Shenandoah, Pennsylvania, lithograph of 1889 had only pairs of border views flanking a centered title and legend. A revised version has an additional entire tier of nine vignettes at the bottom of the print. Fowler must have found a number of merchants who wished to advertise their places of business and paid him to add the new group below the first, which, with one exception, showed only churches.[8]

An additional bit of indirect evidence confirming the practice of selling space for border vignettes can be found on several of the Kuchel & Dresel views of California mining towns issued by that enterprising but short-lived firm in the mid-1850s. On their prints of Forrest Hill and St. Louis (Plate 69), among others, the space available for border scenes is not fully used. Instead, small blank rectangles appear. These probably indicate that the publishers could not secure payments from sufficient local merchants or prominent citizens to complete the frieze of small views surrounding the principal scene of the entire town.[9]

Other examples of this exist. Two blank vignettes can be seen on the view of Providence, Pennsylvania, drawn by A. E. Downs in 1892. Four years earlier E. S. Moore also found it impossible to sell all of the space he allocated for vignettes around his lithograph of Bakersfield, California. In 1888, when this view appeared, the great Southern California land boom had ended, and perhaps the hard times that prevailed made merchants cautious about spending advertising funds in this manner.

An unsigned view of Elsinore, California, probably published in 1887, shows a store, similar in appearance to several others featured in border scenes. This one, however, lacks any sign or caption, evidence that perhaps at the last minute the owner withdrew his agreement to subsidize the appearance of his place of business.[10] This example does raise questions about the accuracy of vignettes. It is possible that the artist drew the building as it really appeared, confident of his ability to obtain the fee from its owner. He may, however, have depicted a more or less standardized store in the expectation that at least one merchant with a similar building could be persuaded to subscribe for extra copies of the print or pay a fee for having his business sign lettered above the store windows or on the false front at the second-floor level.

Even if the artist or publisher did not include separate vignettes around the principal view, he might still be able to obtain payments from merchants. On some of the views drawn and published by Alfred Mathews showing street scenes in Nebraska City, Nebraska, and Denver, Colorado, he prominently featured business signs of stores and offices. Several of these are blank, no doubt reflecting his failure to secure payments from their owners for being identified in this manner.[11]

The publishers of the large and detailed four-sheet view of Syracuse in 1868 must have received fees from owners of buildings and proprietors of business places whose premises

5. John R. Hébert, "Introduction," U.S. Library of Congress, *Panoramic Maps of Anglo-American Cities: A Checklist of Maps in the Collections of the Library of Congress, Geography and Map Division*, 4.

6. Ibid.

7. A small reproduction of this state of the Hamburg print can be seen in Leon J. Stout, "Pennsylvania Town Views, 1850–1922: A Union Catalogue," pt. 1, *The Western Pennsylvania Historical Magazine* 58 (July, 1975): opposite p. 422.

8. An illustration of the second state of this view appeared in the sales catalog of a Washington print shop, The Old Print Gallery, *Showcase* 7, no. 3 (May–June 1980). This catalog also described the earlier version, and the proprietors, Mr. and Mrs. James Blakely, kindly furnished me a photograph of it for study. The Blakelys may be correct in identifying this as a proof state, but it has all the characteristics of a finished print. One reason for believing the publisher did not anticipate the additional vignettes is the rather awkward manner in which the border lines of two of them intrude into the title and legend area, extending upward to a point just below the publisher's imprint, which is on both versions.

9. Views of both towns are reproduced in color in John W. Reps, *Cities on Stone: Nineteenth Century Lithograph Images of the Urban West*, pls. 6 and 7. A high proportion of the Kuchel & Dresel views were issued in at least two states. One—probably the earlier—lacked vignettes. The other included vignettes bordering the principal view on two, three, or four sides, sometimes with two rows of them on two or more sides. It is on this second version that one finds a local publisher's name far more often than on those without vignettes. Possibly Kuchel & Dresel relied on a local publisher to solicit subscriptions or collect fees from residents and merchants for having their buildings shown in vignettes. An artist for the firm—Kuchel himself, in all probability—could then have come to the town, prepared the necessary sketches, and returned to San Francisco to add the vignettes on a revised edition that could be sold for additional profits.

10. I noted this curious feature on the impression in the Henry E. Huntington Library. The vignette is the second from the bottom on the left-hand side.

11. This feature of the Mathews views is mentioned in Robert Taft, *Artists and Illustrators of the Old West, 1850–1900*, 78.

the artist identified through signs. This seems a reasonable inference from the delicately worded statement in a local newspaper while the view was in preparation that "every building will be brought upon the paper in exact proportion of its external appearance. Even the sign lettering will appear upon such as the parties may indicate a desire to so have it."[12]

The sale of vignettes or lettering on storefront signs was not the only source of revenues used to supplement payments obtained from subscriptions to the views themselves. A very large number of urban lithographs contained legends or keys, some numbered and others not, usually located at the bottom of each print. These identified not only public buildings but also places of business, industry, professional offices, and—on many views—houses of certain residents. Some legends simply listed public officials and local dignitaries. On other prints, the name of a business or industry appears on the roof of the building. It seems obvious that in many cases, perhaps the majority, view publishers collected fees for including the name of a business or the owner of a building in the legend or in the view itself.

This is a conspicuous feature of the enormous, 110-sheet view of St. Louis in 1875 drawn by Camille N. Dry and published by Compton & Co. While many places of business are identified in this manner, others—as large or larger—are not singled out. A much less obvious but just as revealing example occurs in a view of Little Falls, New York, in 1881, in which of the names and addresses of two dentists appear below the numbered references of the main legend.

Viewmakers also increased their income by providing special issues of their city views overprinted with an advertisement or an announcement like that appearing on some impressions of the American Publishing Company's lithograph of Helena, Montana, in 1890. Below the title one finds this inscription:

Compliments of
KESSLER'S BREWERY,
Nicholas Kessler, Proprietor,
HELENA,—MONTANA

An otherwise identical impression exists with the advertisement of A. M. Thornburg, whose real estate, mortgage loan, and fire insurance business is summarized in seven lines.[13] Possibly other Helena businesses also arranged for quantities to be printed with their advertisements, but obviously the American Publishing Company reached agreements with at least these two local firms to supply multiple copies at a mutually agreeable price.

In some cases publishers and advertisers made certain that a viewer would not overlook the commercial message by placing it in color against the sky. Two of H. H. Bailey's New York views of 1874—Syracuse and Poughkeepsie—are known in such versions.[14] The E. S. Moore view of Berkeley,

California, in 1891 came in at least two versions, one with and one without advertising.[15] Probably the handsome, colored view of Laredo, Texas, in 1892 existed in two states as well, for most subscribers wishing to frame and hang the print in their homes or offices would not have preferred the version with much of the sky occupied by the words "Presented With the Compliments of the Laredo Real Estate & Abstract Co. W. R. Pace, Prest"(Plate 70).[16]

Promoters of new towns or large real estate developments apparently sponsored the publication of city views and thus guaranteed the artist and publisher compensation for their work. One example is a lithograph of Coronado, California, in 1887, another of E. S. Moore's prints (Plate 71). The publisher of this print was the Coronado Beach Company, purchased that year by John D. Spreckels, a sugar-refining tycoon, from the original developers who had platted a large peninsula in San Diego Bay around their huge and luxurious Hotel Del Coronado. Moore's lithograph was clearly intended to be used in publicizing this project, perhaps the largest of all the real estate developments spawned during the land boom of the 1880s in San Diego.[17] Other California views of the 1880s, lithographs of real estate developments in New Jersey, and prints of summer-cottage projects in Massachusetts are among the urban views sponsored and paid for, at least in part, by developers and promoters.[18]

Viewmakers could augment their income in still other ways. They may have printed multiple impressions of the vignettes only and sold them to the owners of the buildings depicted. According to one source, this was a common technique among the publishers of nineteenth-century county wall maps and county atlases, which also featured border vignettes of shops, factories, residences, and farms.[19] At least two publishers also issued their views in folded versions with heavy covers designed to be used as pocket street maps or to make the prints easier to handle for other purposes by

<hr>

N.Y.," while that of Poughkeepsie is worded, "David Lown & Son, Cooperage and Wooden Ware Manufacturers, North Bridge St." An unsigned and undated lithograph of Brockport, New York, has a similar advertisement: "Compliments of D. S. Morgan & Co. Manufacturers Triumph Reapers & Mowers."

15. An impression without the advertising overprint is in the library of the University of California, Berkeley. The version with advertising is known to me from a facsimile of unknown origin made from an unidentified impression.

16. The Amon Carter Museum, Fort Worth, has the version with advertising in its collection. It is reproduced in color as pl. 48 in Reps, *Cities on Stone.*

17. For the initiation of the Coronado Beach project in 1884 by Elisha S. Babcock, see John W. Reps, *Cities of the American West: A History of Frontier Urban Planning,* 278–80, where the view is reproduced as fig. 8.36. The later involvement by Spreckels, who may have commissioned Moore's view, is noted in Rebecca Elizabeth Lytle, "People and Places: Images of Nineteenth-Century San Diego." See also her "People and Places: Images of Nineteenth Century San Diego in Lithographs and Paintings" for a useful treatment of early San Diego views and a reproduction of the Coronado print.

18. Although the figures are undoubtedly inflated, an account in the Norfolk, Nebr., *Daily News,* 15 June 1889, helps to document what must have been a common practice: "The Elkhorn Valley Investment Company have contracted for 1,000 of the handsome perspective views of Norfolk which are to be engraved by the Milwaukee Lithographing company and will use them in advertising Hillside Terrace."

19. [Bates Harrington], *How 'Tis Done. A Thorough Ventilation of the Numerous Schemes Conducted by Wandering Canvassers,* 40–42, 50.

<hr>

12. Syracuse *Standard,* 14 December 1864.

13. I have not found the version with the Thornburg advertisement in any public collection. My knowledge of the print comes from an impression seen at The Old Print Shop in New York City, 8 December 1976.

14. The Syracuse advertisement reads, "H. Spang Manufacturer of all Styles & Sizes of Improved Cabinet Organs No 2 & 3 Noxen St. Syracuse

those who had no interest in using them for framed decorations. Thomas Larkin seems to have started this practice in 1851 with his two views of Monterey, California, and Lucien Burleigh published several of his New York State views of the 1880s in this form. [20]

Some publishers of lithographic city views sold reproduction rights to others or themselves issued the views in smaller sizes and for different purposes. Many of the lithographs of California mining camps, for example, were redrawn and used on illustrated letter sheets. [21] A number of the Smith brothers' views first published in large folio lithographic form also turned up on letter sheets. Some or all of these may have been pirated, but the Smith brothers did receive payment for page-size engravings of several of their views used as illustrations in that genteel magazine of eclectic taste, the *Ladies' Repository* (Plate 72). Each plate carries a credit line indicating the lithographic source from which it was drawn, and in addition to payments for the reproduction rights the Smith brothers may have received some orders for the full-size print. [22]

Small versions of Eli S. Glover's view of San Diego in 1876 have been found mounted on heavy cardboard, with advertisements for several local concerns on the reverse. Whether Glover produced these advertisements himself, sold the rights to others, or was simply the victim of artistic piracy is not known. Glover by that time had acquired substantial experience in business, and it seems likely that he received some payment for this use of his work.

Artists or publishers of large views may also have sold reproduction rights to firms specializing in pictorial souvenir folders. Typically, these were published with stiff, embossed covers, within which could be found an accordian-like sheet of folded views about the size of post cards. The views showed individual buildings, but some folders, those of Galveston and Los Angeles, for example, contained bird's-eye views that closely resemble the prints with which we are concerned. These views, too, may have been pirated, but if not, their use in this manner by permission of the original artist and publisher would have added to their gross receipts and profits. [23]

Finally, some viewmakers probably received subsidies from railroads. A large portion of the early towns in the trans-Mississippi region were created by railroad corporations or by their wholly owned subsidiary land companies. Using land granted them by Congress to support rail construction, these companies selected advantageous sites along their routes for new towns, platted streets and blocks, and vigorously promoted sales of lots throughout America and—through agents abroad—in Europe as well. [24]

An examination of lithographic views of many of the railroad-sponsored towns in Nebraska, the Dakotas, and some other parts of the West reveals that these towns, like Harvard, Nebraska (Plate 73), consisted of so few houses and business places that even the most optimistic view publisher and the most skilled and determined sales agent might have despaired of ever selling enough impressions locally to make such a venture financially worthwhile. [25] Perhaps the Burlington Railroad underwrote all or part of J. J. Stoner's costs for publishing the Harvard view and others like it, just as the Union Pacific a decade earlier had subsidized W. Delavan's panorama of the Union Pacific's route to San Francisco, which included a view of Omaha. An Omaha newspaper claimed that the work would cost about "12,000" but that the Union Pacific "patronizes the enterprise to a large amount in actual cash." [26]

In all these and perhaps other ways as well the nineteenth-century viewmakers sought to add to the income and profits they derived through advance subscriptions and through sales in local stores. The business side of this artistic enterprise may not have completely dominated their thinking, but it must have been uppermost in their minds at all times.

Many of the tentative conclusions that can be drawn from the admittedly fragmentary evidence so far presented are at least partially confirmed by what took place in a closely related publishing effort that flourished during the same period when city views were so popular. This was the county land ownership map business, referred to several times already, which produced hundreds of wall maps mainly in the period between 1850 and 1880. [27]

20. The folded views by both were printed on lighter paper than the normal issues. See the previous chapter for Larkin's printing bill specifying folded copies. Several of the Burleigh folded views are in the collection of the Rensselaer County Historical Society, Troy, New York. They have a separate title on the outside of the wrappers.

21. See Joseph Armstrong Baird, Jr., *California's Pictorial Letter Sheets: 1849–1869* (San Francisco, 1967).

22. The Cincinnati publisher of the *Ladies' Repository* announced in its December 1853 issue, "At great expense Messrs Smith, Brothers & Co., of New York City, have obtained original drawings of most of the large cities of our country, and got up a series of large and splendid lithographic engravings. By the courtesy of these gentlemen we have, upon personal application, obtained permission to use those original drawings for the Repository, and have engaged Mr. Wellstood, one of the best artists in the country, to engrave them in the best style of the art. Albany, New Orleans, Pittsburgh, Portland, Halifax etc., will follow in due time." Reproduced in the issue was the reduced version of J. W. Hill's Buffalo view. Quoted in I. N. Phelps Stokes and Daniel C. Haskell, *American Historical Prints: Early Views of American Cities*, 112, entry under P. 1852—G—43c, which also contains a list of the cities from the Smith brothers' lithographs that appeared in issues from 1853 to 1856.

23. I know of no scholarly examination of the pictorial souvenir folders. Most are printed in two colors, black and sepia, although some are in other colors and less somber in appearance. At first glance one might think them photographs, as an occasional curator has suggested to me. Doubtless many of them were drawn from or traced over photographic images. The Galveston folder is in my own collection. That of Los Angeles is in Olin Library, Cornell University. The Los Angeles view in the folder is a bird's-eye type but does not correspond with any lithographic version I have seen. The Galveston view in the folder appears to be based closely on that drawn by Augustus Koch in 1885, but many foreground details differ.

24. For the activities of railroads as town planners and real estate speculators, see the several chapters dealing with this subject in Reps, *Cities of the American West*, and the sources cited in the notes and bibliography.

25. The view of Harvard shows only about one hundred residential and business structures, and local sales of the lithograph could not have been large. The town had been created a few years earlier by the Eastern Land Association, a company formed by officials of the Burlington Railroad. However, the publisher of the view, J. J. Stoner, apparently sold enough copies of the lithograph he published of Pawnee City, Nebraska, a town not much if any larger than Harvard, through subscriptions paid by residents. The Pawnee City *Republican* of 10 July 1879 reported that Stoner's agent, H. G. Fletcher, "arrived with the drawing . . . and commenced canvassing for the work. He succeeded finely, and the drawing will be ready about the middle of September."

26. Omaha *Weekly Republican*, 5 August 1868.

27. The U.S. Library of Congress, *Land Ownership Maps: A Checklist of Nineteenth Century United States County Maps in the Library of Congress*.

Table 10. Cost and Sales of a County Map Such as Published by Thompson & Everts

Estimate being on an ordinary County of Sixteen townships, with Sales of 1,200 copies, which is an average

Sales

1,200 Maps, at $6 each $7,200	
50 Views, at $40 each 2,000	
	$9,200

Cost

Commissions on Maps, 50 cents each .... $ 600	
Commissions on Views, 10 per cent 200	
Copying Township Plats from Tax Lists, $3.50 each 56	
Making Township Maps from observation and copying, $28 each 448	
Making City and Township Plats 25	
Engraving 16 Townships, $15 each 240	
Engraving Plats 20	
Printing 1,200 140	
Lithographing 50 Views, $5.50 each 275	
Heading and Extras 20	
Sketching Views, 10 per cent 200	
Mounting and Coloring 1,200 Maps, 90 cents each 1,080	
Paper 200	
Freight and incidental expenses 300	
Commissions for collecting on Maps, 40 cts. each 480	
Commissions for collecting Views, 3 per cent .. 60	
	$4,344
Profits	$4,856

Source: Bates Harrington, *How 'Tis Done*

County maps and city views shared several features. Virtually all of the maps included border views of businesses, residences, and farms. Many of them contained some kind of business directory as well. The maps, like the views, were sold by agents and canvassers through subscriptions, and additional sums were collected by charging persons for having their buildings appear as vignettes.

County maps differed from city views in being larger and thus somewhat more expensive to print. Usually they were mounted on cloth and had wooden rollers at top and bottom to facilitate hanging. Probably, too, more copies of the maps were sold, since they encompassed a larger area. Finally, county maps may have been somewhat easier to prepare than the views, since most of them seem to have been based on existing township surveys readily available from official sources. Artists simply redrew these at appropriate scales.

On the other hand, map publishers faced additional expenses involved in acquiring up-to-date information about ownership of farms and other property. They had to examine recent sales records and, where land had recently been divided, to measure these tracts with a wheeled odometer. If adequate surveys did not exist, employees of the map company would tour the entire county with these devices. Questions to landowners about property ownership and size of fields were frequently combined with canvassing for future map sales.

Bates Harrington, author of a curious book published in

1879, described fully the process of compiling, canvassing, drawing, printing, and selling these maps. His title conveys his approach to the subject: *How 'Tis Done. A Thorough Ventilation of the Numerous Schemes Conducted by Wandering Canvassers Together with the Various Advertising Dodges for the Swindling of the Public.*[28] While highly critical of many of the practices of county map publishers, Harrington exhibits a detailed knowledge of their methods and the financial aspects of the business. Perhaps he was once employed by one of the firms specializing in such maps, possibly Thompson & Everts, whose costs and income from a typical map as estimated by Harrington are given in Table 10.

From these figures and the material presented in this and the two preceding chapters, it is possible to arrive at similar estimates for the production of a city view. Several assumptions must be made, and the results must be treated with caution. Some items are sheer guesswork, but an effort has been made to be generous in projecting costs and conservative in estimating income.

The example given in Table 11 assumes that two hundred and fifty views were sold at $3.00 each, with an additional fifty disposed of at $1.00 for advertising pur-

Table 11. Hypothetical Balance Sheet for Publication of a Typical City View

Income

250 views sold at $3.00 each $750.00	
50 views sold at $1.00 each 50.00	
10 vignettes sold at $25.00 each 250.00	
Gross Receipts	$1,050.00

Expenses

Artist's fee $100.00	
Commissions on 250 views at 10 percent 75.00	
Commissions on 50 views at 10 percent ... 5.00	
Commissions for securing vignette fees at 10 percent 25.00	
Lithographing, paper, and printing at $.80 .... 240.00	
Freight 25.00	
Collection fees, 250 views at $.10 .... 25.00	
Miscellaneous, advertising, etc. 25.00	
Total Expenses	$ 520.00
NET PROFITS	$ 530.00

poses. Although many views had no vignettes and some showed only public buildings, others included dozens of these border scenes.[29] The example uses a view with ten vignettes for which the publisher received a fee of $25.00 each.

No evidence exists about what an artist may have been paid. Since many of them seem to have functioned as sales agents as well, commissions received for such work may

---

28. No author's name appears on the title page, but the Library of Congress attributes the work to Bates Harrington, doubtless using copyright entry information.
29. O. H. Bailey's views, for example, included many with thirty or more vignettes.

have been an important part of their income. In the table below, a fee of $100 has been assumed, but the commissions shown are not divided between artist and agent. Agents probably worked on a fee basis, and the example uses a 10 percent commission, somewhat higher than Harrington indicates was paid to county map agents. Estimates for paper, lithographing, and printing are based in part on Harrington's figures. Although large maps and smaller views are not entirely comparable, these costs of production do conform to what we know about printing expenses of lithographic city views.

In the example no income is assumed from advertising overprints; subsidies by railroads, public officials, or local organizations; sale of impressions of individual vignettes, reproduction rights, or fees for including business or professional names in legends or on storefront signs in the view. On the other hand, expenses for freight, collection fees, and advertising are added.

A larger edition would have yielded greater profits, since the basic costs of production represented by the artist's fee and the expenses of putting the drawing on stone and printing it would not change. Paper and press time were relatively cheap, and the unit cost for an edition of five hundred would have been substantially reduced, while the sum derived from sales would have been nearly doubled. Moreover, since some views were priced at $5.00 to $10.00, gross receipts even for an edition of the size used in the example could have been far higher than shown. Even if the view lacked vignettes and produced no revenue from this source, the enterprise could have yielded a nice profit. [30]

If one considers the sixty-two views for which Ruger was responsible in 1869 and multiplies this number by an average profit, exclusive of travel and lodging expenses, the income is impressive. Even a much less ambitious rate of production—say ten views a year—could have brought a net income to the publisher of about $5,000 annually at a time when that figure represented a handsome living.

The business of view publishing obviously depended on volume, a steady flow of drawings to the lithographic printing firms, reliable and energetic agents in the field, and artists who could draw with speed, ease, and passable accuracy. Such publishers as Stoner and artist-publishers as Ruger, Fowler, Bailey, Burleigh, Wellge, Glover, and others developed just such a system. For years they must have enjoyed a comfortable if peripatetic life as they recorded the changing face of urban America.

30. It seems curious that Ruger's views have so few vignettes and that when vignettes do appear they nearly always show public buildings for which it is unlikely that fees could be charged. Possibly Ruger and Stoner found that while additional income might be obtained from the sale of space for a vignette of a store, factory, or mansion, canvassing for this kind of advertising was less profitable than producing a greater number of lithographs each year.

8. Critics and Consumers: Public Reaction and Private Response

Most of the original owners of American lithographic city views acquired them through advance subscription. Artists, agents, and publishers took orders after publicizing their efforts in newspaper announcements and then displaying the drawing from which the lithograph was to be made. Several months later the finished prints were sent or brought to the community and distributed to subscribers.

However, not all copies of views found their way into the hands of consumers through this process. Publishers often had additional impressions printed for retail sale. Or, as George Baker found with his Sacramento view of 1857, some subscribers moved or failed to meet their obligations, leaving the artist with extra copies to dispose of.[1] Edwin Whitefield, for example, seems to have made it a regular practice to print more copies than there were subscribers. In 1854 he consigned a number of views to a Toronto firm to be sold at retail. In addition to his Toronto print, he included views of Quebec, Montreal, Hamilton, and London. Whitefield also authorized the firm to collect amounts due from subscribers.[2]

From the fragmentary evidence appearing in some newspaper notices and advertisements of the time, it appears that bookstores served as the usual place of sale for city views. Albany and Troy newspapers in 1845 announced that Whitefield's views of those cities "can be had . . . at our Bookstores" and that "copies will be placed in the book stores." Whitefield's Rochester print of 1847 could be purchased at "Dewey's News Room," which may also have sold books.[3]

In October 1836, the Ithaca, New York, *Journal & General Advertiser* advised persons interested in obtaining a copy of Henry Walton's view to enter their subscriptions "at the bookstore of Messrs. Mack, Andrus and Woodruff," where they could examine the painting on which the lithograph would be based. The announcement continued with this warning: "As no copies are to be published, except for subscribers, we would recommend for those who wish to procure a copy, to enter their names without delay." Nevertheless, not quite a year later, in an advertisement requesting all subscribers who had not yet received their prints "to call

for them" at their premises, the proprietors added "N.B. A few copies splendidly painted by Walton [are] for sale as above."[4]

Similarly, Fitz Hugh Lane's view of Gloucester, Massachusetts, could be obtained at the bookstore of Charles Smith. The Patch & Lewis bookstore in Bangor, Maine, sold J. W. Hill's view of 1854. In Chillicothe, Ohio, J. R. Whittemore, owner of a book and stationery shop, advertised in 1855 that he had in stock a supply of J. T. Palmatary's view of Chillicothe as well as the same publisher's lithograph of nearby Portsmouth. In a notice issued by the publishers announcing H. H. Bailey's view of Milwaukee in 1872 (Plate 74), potential buyers were advised that it was "for sale by all the Booksellers and Stationers." And Alfred Mathews in 1873 selected Broderick's Bookstore in Los Angeles to sell his four views of Southern California cities.[5]

Other places sold views as well. The six-sheet panorama of Honolulu that Paul Emmert produced in 1854 was available for purchase at "Capt. Snow's Store," perhaps an outlet for general merchandise. The J. H. Flett view of Denver could be seen on display and for sale at the Art Gallery, 323 Sixteenth Street, which Mr. Flett owned with two associates and which had also published the lithograph.[6]

City views were evidently also among the items sold door-to-door by canvassers. The publishers of the 1870 view of St. Louis, Michigan, then a popular spa, not only advertised the publication of the view in the Saginaw *Daily Courier* at a price of $2.00 but added this in conclusion: "The publisher wishes to engage immediately one good active agent in each county for the summer months. This is, an opportunity seldom offered to agents. An immediate application, inclosing $1.50, will secure a sample view, with Key, terms to agents, and the agency of any county not taken."[7]

---

1. Baker's account book in the collection of the Society of California Pioneers, San Francisco, identifies those who failed to pay the previously agreed-on price for this view.

2. The contract between Whitefield and Maclear & Co. is transcribed in Bettina A. Norton, *Edwin Whitefield: Nineteenth-Century North American Scenery*, 47. The terms of this agreement are not entirely clear, but apparently the company was to receive 25 percent of the retail price for selling views from stock and 10 percent for merely collecting money due Whitefield from subscriptions he had already obtained.

3. Undated clippings in the Whitefield scrapbook, Boston Public Library, from the Albany *Microscope* and Troy *Budget*, and the Rochester *Daily American*, 24 November 1847.

4. Issues of 12 October 1836 and 27 September 1837.

5. Gloucester *Telegraph*, 25 November 1846, as quoted in John Wilmerding, *Fitz Hugh Lane*, 28; Bangor *Daily Whig and Courier*, undated clipping of 1854, provided me by The Farnsworth Museum; Chillicothe *Scioto Gazette*, 3 October 1854 and 21 March 1855; notice of prices of the Milwaukee view, quoted in John R. Hébert, "Introduction," U.S. Library of Congress, *Panoramic Maps of Anglo-American Cities . . .* , 4; Los Angeles *Express*, 19 April 1873, as cited in Henry Winfred Splitter, "Art in Los Angeles Before 1900—Part I," 47. Among the bookstores selling the Milwaukee view would certainly have been the book and stationery shop operated by its publishers, Holzapfel & Eskuche, at 443 East Water Street. See note for catalog entry 17 in Thomas Beckman, *Milwaukee Illustrated: Panoramic and Bird's-Eye Views of a Midwestern Metropolis, 1844–1908*.

6. Honolulu *Friend*, 1 November 1854; Denver *Rocky Mountain News*, 9 May 1882.

7. Issue for 16 May 1870, p. 2, col. 5. This was called to my attention by John Cumming, director, Clarke Historical Library, Central Michigan University, Mount Pleasant, who has pursued Michigan city views for years and has collected invaluable information about them, which he has generously shared with me.

Artists also sold their lithographs directly, using their residences, offices, or studios as places where customers might inspect their work. Several of the newspaper notices about Whitefield's city views give his New York address as a place where views could be purchased. Henry Walton, during his stay in Ithaca, New York, in the late 1830s, frequently advertised his services as a "portrait, miniature & Landscape Painter," giving his address as "room at R. P. Clark's, Prospect Hill," just a short walk from the village's business district.[8] Anyone calling to discuss a portrait or a painting of some other type must have had Walton's several urban lithographs called to his attention, and almost certainly purchases of the views resulted.

View publishers sought as well to make direct sales in quantity lots. One target, either through advance subscriptions or after publication, was the local city council. Such sales efforts met with mixed success. Edwin Whitefield disposed of twenty-five copies of his Toronto view of 1854 to the municipality, having them colored by his sons. He may well have given the council a special price, but at his usual figure of five prints for $15.00, plus an additional $3.00 each for coloring, this transaction would have yielded a handsome $150.[9]

While the Toronto transaction must have pleased Whitefield, two years later in Galena, Illinois, he complained to the city council about the method of payment for the ten copies of his view that the municipality had agreed to purchase. Instead of cash, the council sent Whitefield $80 in scrip, which he stated in a firm letter to that body was worth only "about two-thirds of the above sum." He proposed two remedies to what he felt was a breach of good faith: "the first is to pay me in current funds the sum of $80, and the second is to increase your subscription sufficiently to enable me to realize the original amount, say five or six copies extra. In this way you will have a greater number to circulate abroad, and I shall receive as much as I calculated upon."[10]

The council refused to take either course, and all Whitefield received for his efforts was this blunt reply:

> The committee to whom was refered the written communication touching the views of the city with ten copies of said views for the sum of $80—which sum is now drawn in his favor but in consequence of the discount the amt. has not been accepted or the views delivered. They find further that the price of these views from the stores vary from 4 to 5—they would therefore report that the 80—already appropriated is a sufficient sum which he can receive or retain his views.

Records concerning sales to city councils for other views are brief and few. According to one source, Herman Brosius sold 100 copies of his view of Victoria, Texas, to the city for $1.00 each.[11] The mayor and aldermen of Columbus, Mississippi, took a far more conservative position in 1871, agreeing to buy only six copies of C. N. Drie's view at an unspecified price.[12] Although only this meager evidence is now at hand, it seems highly likely that a systematic search of council records and municipal expenditures for other communities would reveal that purchases of city views by local governments were not uncommon.

City officials must have looked on views as a method of stimulating urban growth. Newspapers shared this attitude, seeing lithographs as effective devices to publicize their towns in other parts of the country. The papers urged businessmen and civic leaders to support such projects by subscribing to or purchasing multiple copies for display and distribution. In 1849, for example, the Pittsburgh *Gazette*, after praising Whitefield's view, pointed out, "If it is . . . placed in hotels, and public places of resort, throughout the country, it will do much to give a proper conception of the site and size of this city and environs."[13] Doubtless Whitefield or one of his agents suggested this thought to the editor. Probably it was not the first time this argument for supporting such a project had been advanced. It was certainly not the last, for this theme appeared regularly in similar newspaper accounts throughout much of the nineteenth century as cities vied with one another for publicity.

The newspaper in the little town of Clyde, New York, supported the publication of Lucien Burleigh's lithograph of 1892 on these grounds, stating that the print would have "great commercial value, as any person wishing to locate here, either in business, manufacturing, or as a place of residence, can at a glance take in the lay of the village, the situation of its railroads and canal, the general appearance of the village itself, relative position of the buildings and every other point of interest to strangers."[14] Shorter but more to the point was the assertion of a Chillicothe, Ohio, newspaper in 1888 that "a work of this kind will boom our beautiful city."[15]

In Norfolk, Nebraska, the newspaper urged its readers to subscribe to copies of Henry Wellge's view of 1889 and informed them of a meeting of Wellge's agent, Charles Smith, with a business group to discuss the matter: "This is the best and most handsome thing yet devised for giving a comprehensive idea of our city as it is, and for advertising our city, there could be no better way than to circulate a large number broadcast over the country, so we hope every one will interest themselves in behalf of the scheme to make it a success and a go. The Business Men's association met with Mr. Smith at 4 p.m. to-day, to consider the project and lend their support, and if arrangements can be made it is quite probable the board of trade can use a large quantity of the views."[16]

Wellge's view of Seattle in 1884 (Plate 75) had similarly

8. I have noted these advertisements in the Ithaca *Journal & General Advertiser* for 27 June 1838 and 10 July 1839, and there were doubtless others.

9. Norton, *Whitefield*, 47.

10. Whitefield's long letter and the council's report are transcribed in full in Betty I. Madden, *Art, Crafts, and Architecture in Early Illinois*, 215–16. See also Norton, *Whitefield*, 47, for a brief summary of this event. Neither Madden nor Norton indicates whether the ten views were finally delivered in exchange for the discounted scrip. Whitefield's letter suggests the purpose of the council in agreeing to subscribe to the copies: "so that you might send . . . [them] . . . abroad, and thus let strangers see what you really look like."

11. Leopold Morris, *Pictorial History of Victoria and Victoria County*.

12. Columbus, Mississippi, City Council Minutes, 5 July 1871. Mrs. Douglas Bateman, director of the Lowndes County Library System in Columbus, kindly provided me with a copy of this manuscript record. Although the entry spells Drie's name as *Grie*, it does give his full name as *Camille*. This verifies the identity of C. N. Drie, viewmaker in 1870–1872 in the southeast, as the Camille N. Dry of St. Louis in 1875–1878.

13. In the Whitefield scrapbook, Boston Public Library, this clipping appears with only the date October 1849.

14. Clyde *Democratic Herald*, 18 May 1892.

15. Chillicothe *Advertiser*, 16 November 1888.

16. Norfolk *Daily News*, 15 June 1889.

been supported by that city's leading newspaper, which stated flatly, "It will be a splendid thing to send abroad to advertise the town." Shortly thereafter a Lansing, Michigan, paper echoed this idea in describing Clemens J. Pauli's lithograph of 1890 as "an excellent advertisement of our city." In its highly favorable notice of Thaddeus Fowler's view of 1891, a Denison, Texas, newspaper advised "every person who owns a home in Denison" to buy "at least one copy," adding, "Our real estate and business men would find it profitable, as an advertisement, to purchase many copies for circulating abroad."[17]

Although in this context "abroad" meant only to other cities and regions in the United States, Canadian newspapers added the notion of sending copies of views to England. A Halifax paper in 1878 referred to Albert Ruger's view in this context by stating, "No better means of advertising our city or of showing the good folk 'at home' the sort of place we live in could be devised." That same year at the other end of the continent a British Columbia newspaper commented in a similar vein on Eli Glover's lithograph of Victoria: "For reference, the view will prove invaluable to residents here, whilst for transmission to friends in England and elsewhere who have but a vague idea of the extent and beauty of our city, the picture will be found to be particularly adapted. Indeed, it would take a very lengthy description of the city to convey half as good an idea of Victoria as the view does."[18]

How many copies were used for such purposes is not known. Nor do we have any idea how successful general distribution of views may have been in stimulating urban growth and commercial development. Their effectiveness in accomplishing the goals of community boosters was probably overstated by sales agents and publishers, and experienced business leaders and public officials must have realized that urban growth depended on more than circulation of a handsome civic portrait.

In most cities publishers depended on sales to individuals to make a profit. Why did people buy these views, and how did they use them? Newspaper accounts provide some of the answers. For many, lithographic prints of their city seemed appropriate decorations for the family home. When Henry Walton announced the publication in 1839 of the second of his three views of Ithaca, New York, the village paper urged readers to support the project and stated that the view "should be found to grace the parlor of every citizen of our town."[19]

So many of the reviews of Edwin Whitefield's lithographs repeat this suggestion—often in almost identical phrases—that one can conclude that he incorporated the idea in prepared statements issued to newspapers by him or by his agents. Thus, referring to his Brooklyn print of 1846, one newspaper asserted, "There is hardly a more appropriate ornament for the walls of our dwelling rooms," while another described it as "an ornament to the parlors of our citizens."[20]

Two years later, after Whitefield published his Buffalo view, a paper there urged its purchase as "an ornament, when nicely framed, suitable to grace the parlors of our citizens."[21] The Philadelphia *Courier*, on 10 June 1850, mentioned Whitefield's four views showing the city from atop Independence Hall as "admirably suited for parlor ornaments." Albert Ruger's lithographs received similar endorsements in the late 1870s from papers in such widely separated places as Charlottetown on Prince Edward Island and East Saginaw, Michigan, which referred to them as "a valuable picture for ornament" and as something that "every person . . . will undoubtedly be anxious to secure . . . to adorn their own homes."[22]

The "parlor ornament" theme appears also in descriptions of many of Lucien Burleigh's views. His view of Clyde, New York, according to the local newspaper, was "done in the highest order of art and will be ornamental in every parlor."[23] Persons wishing to ornament their houses but lacking parlors need not have despaired. A Fremont, Nebraska, newspaper in 1889, impressed by Henry Wellge's finished lithograph that had just arrived from Milwaukee, advised residents of the town that the view "will prove an ornament to any house in the city."[24]

Viewmakers, using local papers as their spokesmen, also promoted their products as attractive decorations for the business or professional office. Whitefield's Rochester view of 1847 received editorial endorsement as "an ornament peculiarly worthy of a place in the offices and houses of Rochester Men." A Milwaukee paper claimed that Louis Lipman's 1866 print of the city "will be of great value to our merchants and citizens generally, and will be an ornament to their offices," adding rather unenthusiastically that "it would not disfigure even our best parlor."[25]

This broader appeal of city views was also called to the attention of the readers of a Savannah, Georgia, newspaper when Albert Ruger produced his lithograph of that city in 1872: "This sketch framed would make an admirable and interesting ornament for parlor, library or office, and would prove a most acceptable present to a friend." The versatility of views as decorations for both home and place of business was duly noted when Eli S. Glover's sectioned scene of Los Angeles, Santa Monica, and Wilmington appeared: "The work is one of great merit, and framed it will ornament either office or parlor."[26]

Finally, to complete this chronological sampling, the Victoria, British Columbia, *Colonist*, in announcing the publication of its own view of the city in a front-page story in 1889, claimed almost universal utility for the print: "A copy should adorn the walls of every office, store, and residence in Victoria, while it is invaluable for the purpose of conveying

17. Seattle *Post Intelligencer*, 15 July 1884, p. 2, col. 2; Lansing *State Republican*, 9 June 1890; and Denison *Sunday Gazetteer*, 11 January 1891.

18. Halifax *Evening Reporter & Daily & Tri-Weekly Times*, 20 August 1878, p. 3, col. 2; Victoria *Colonist*, 16 October 1878, p. 3.

19. Ithaca *Journal & General Advertiser*, 13 July 1839.

20. Undated clippings in the Whitefield Scrapbook, Boston Public Library, from the Brooklyn *Daily Eagle* and *Long Island Star*.

21. Buffalo *Morning Express*, undated clipping of 1848 in Whitefield Scrapbook.

22. Charlottetown *Daily Examiner*, 9 August 1878; Saginaw *Daily Courier*, 22 August 1879, p. 2, col. 1.

23. Clyde *Democratic Herald*, 25 May 1892.

24. Fremont *Weekly Herald*, 24 October 1889.

25. Rochester *Daily American*, 24 November 1847; Milwaukee *Daily Sentinel*, 15 November 1866, p. 1, as quoted in Beckman, *Milwaukee Illustrated*, unpaged introduction.

26. Savannah *Morning News*, 19 February 1872, p. 3, col. 4; Los Angeles *Daily Star*, 18 January 1877, p. 3.

to parties at a distance an accurate idea of the Queen City of the West."[27]

The walls of countless homes, banks, hotel lobbies, retail shops, and professional offices thus provided display spaces for the thousands of city views issued in the nineteenth century. Evidence supporting the conclusion that these newspaper suggestions were heeded is provided by many impressions of views still in private ownership or that have found their way to institutional collections through gifts or purchases. A substantial number of these views remain in nineteenth century frames, indicating that their first owners did indeed regard them as worthy of gracing the walls of parlors or offices, or at least chambers of some kind. Many other unframed impressions found in collections bear unmistakable signs of once having been framed, for example, they exhibit the vertical stain lines—usually a brownish discoloration varying in width and darkest at the center—that one so often encounters among unrestored prints. The stains resulted when nitric oxides from gas lighting fixtures entered the cracks between the wide, thin boards that nineteenth-century framers usually employed to back the prints.[28]

Although framing caused many prints to be disfigured in this manner, age-toned through exposure to ultraviolet light, spotted by mold, or waterstained from condensation, the protection afforded by frame and glazing saved many prints that otherwise would have been thrown away when they became torn or creased.[29] A fair number of urban lithographs are known only by unique impressions or exist in numbers of less than half a dozen. Some, documented as having been published, simply cannot be located. Without framing—damaging as it often proved to be—there would doubtless be many more of these lost images. We owe a debt, therefore, to the early owners of these prints who heeded the admonitions of publishers and newspaper writers and hung them on their parlor walls or used them to embellish an office or shop.

Something other than a desire to decorate their homes must have motivated some buyers of city views, however. Contemporary newspaper accounts mention this in words having an appealing ring for modern historians. A Milwaukee writer stated the case in his story on J. T. Palmatary's lithograph of 1856:

> It is not only useful at the present moment as a directory, but will be valuable many years hence, as a record of what Milwaukee was in 1856. . . . with it in hand, a man can find any place in the city, can see the position of every lot, occupied or unoccupied. Every one who can afford it, should have one in his house, not only as a reference, but as a matter of future history.[30]

Nearly every North American community viewed its future in the most optimistic light as promising substantial and sustained population and economic growth. For a city like Los Angeles in 1871, hovering on the edge of its first land boom, Augustus Koch's lithograph offered an opportunity to capture the image of the present for all time. A local newspaper pursued this theme in recommending that its readers purchase the view: "Every household should be provided with one, if for no other purpose, to compare ten years hence the mighty changes and improvements time will have wrought in our fair city."[31]

Following this same line of reasoning, a Prince Edward Island journal pointed out in 1878 how Albert Ruger's view of Charlottetown would become more important with the passing of the years: "It will be a valuable picture for ornament as well as for reference and the changes constantly taking place will make it an interesting relic of today to those that live in the future."[32] A few years later a New Hampshire newspaper noted that Albert Poole's lithographic view of Plymouth would "be looked upon in years to come with the thought that it is a view of Plymouth as seen in 1883."[33]

How many persons purchased views for this purpose is, of course, unknown, although the emphasis placed on the subject by newspapers suggests that many residents acquired views with this in mind. It is exactly for this reason that urban lithographs have begun to attract the attention of modern scholars, and the historical value of the views explains their popularity among private collectors as well as libraries and museums.

Whether such institutions bought the views when they were first published is another aspect of viewmaking about which little knowledge exists. When Whitefield issued his four lithographs of Philadelphia in 1850, one of the city's newspapers, along with the usual comments about their value as home decorations, added a reference to the views as of "marked interest for public institutions." This writer may have meant only that the prints would prove attractive as wall hangings in such places as banks, hotels, and municipal offices, but he may have had in mind their acquisition by museums and galleries. It seems unlikely, however, that many of these institutions would have purchased lithographs created for such obvious commercial purposes. Con-

27. Issue of 27 November 1889, p. 1. For two additional newspaper accounts mentioning home and office as suitable locations for city views, see John W. Reps, *Cities on Stone: Nineteenth Century Lithograph Images of the Urban West*, 30. They refer to Koch's view of San Antonio, Texas, in 1873 and the J. H. Flett lithograph of Denver in 1882.

28. It may be useful to add the text of my comment on this matter in *Cities on Stone*, n. 81: "Many of the views in major collections have been restored by removal of stains and spots through bleaching or washing, often followed by hand coloring. Depending on the condition of the print before such treatment, all or part of the age-toning, discoloration, foxing, and other staining can be removed or made far less noticeable. While restoration may make prints more attractive, it also makes it more difficult to determine whether or not the original color was printed, added by hand, or was some combination of the two." As a clarification, let me note that some people erroneously believe that the backing boards themselves caused the vertical stains referred to in the text. In a few cases this might be so, although discoloration from the boards themselves would cover most of the print and give it a general toned appearance. It is the space between the backing boards that provided entry for compounds in the air that reacted with the vertical strips of exposed paper. Damage could occur in other ways. Nineteenth-century framers did not use mats, and condensation inside the glass thus came directly in contact with the print. This often caused irregular circles of stains. In addition, the paper used on almost all lithographic city views was made from wood pulp and was subject to discoloration, particularly if exposed to light.

29. The wood pulp paper used by printers of the time carried within it the acidic seeds of its own destruction, for with age these sheets became brittle and fragile. Prints kept rolled were especially vulnerable. They crushed easily and tore or creased when handled. When they ceased to be of much interest as curiosities and tears, stains, and flaking surfaces made them unattractive in appearance, they were often simply discarded.

30. *Daily Milwaukee News*, 11 September 1856, p. 4, as quote in Beckman, *Milwaukee Illustrated*, unpaged introduction.

31. Los Angeles *Daily Star*, 28 April 1871, p. 3.

32. Charlottetown *Daily Examiner*, 9 August 1878.

33. Ashland *Advance*, 22 September 1883.

temporary museum directors would have regarded the average lithographic city view as of no more merit than a poster of today's rock or screen star.

Analyses and criticisms of city views as works of art came from newspaper reporters, not art critics. Their attitudes both reflected and formed popular taste, however, and it is useful to examine how the papers treated the views when they first made their appearance on the local scene. Generally, journalists praised the work of viewmakers. Although publishers and their agents furnished editors with statements emphasizing the attractiveness of the lithographs, favorable notices would not have appeared so consistently throughout the country and over such a long period if they had not reflected widespread satisfaction by the great majority of those who bought the viewmakers' products.

Not all editorial reaction followed this pattern, however, and it is instructive first to examine what local critics disliked about certain views. Edwin Whitefield's work drew adverse comments from several newspapers early in his career for what might be regarded as a commercial reason: his selection of unfavorable viewpoints from which to depict his subjects. An Albany writer complained in 1845 that Whitefield's print of the city "scarcely conveys a just idea of . . . [the] . . . magnitude, or rather of the vast number of buildings that bristle the hill and sweep from it below, north and south." Whitefield's Troy lithograph of the same year failed to satisfy a writer in one of the city's papers for the identical reason: "This . . . is not the most favorable point from which to obtain a view of the whole city, and . . . scarcely gives a fair idea of the extent and magnitude of Troy, and especially of the business portion of it."[34]

Both of these accounts balanced their criticisms with words of praise, as did a Buffalo paper reviewing Whitefield's view in 1848: "The harbor, being in the foreground, is more prominent than any other portion of the city. We should have valued it higher if it had been taken from some point that would have spread the city out more before the eye, and showed some of its streets, and the extent of territory which it occupies. But, with these defects, it is a very well executed view."[35]

For the four California lithographs of Alfred E. Mathews in 1873, however, a San Diego newspaper found no redeeming qualities. Mathews, in reading these stinging words, must have felt fortunate that he had used the usual subscription system to obtain purchasers for his prints before he published them:

The perspective in each of these sketches, excepting that of Santa Barbara, is exceedingly defective. The mountain ranges in the background of . . . San Diego, San Bernardino and Los Angeles are represented as in close proximity to the same when in reality they are many miles distant. The Cuyamaca peak, although actually over forty miles distant, is crowding San Diego into the bay. . . . The sketch of this city has also been taken from an unfortunate point of observation, and presents to the view the least populous portion. . . . Had its perspective been less faulty and the point of observation different, the sketch might have been a good one; as it is we believe it will generally be viewed as

an imperfect representation.[36]

Equally devastating, although clearly written tongue-in-cheek, was the "review" appearing in the newspaper of the nearby and rival town of Chillicothe of J. T. Palmatary's view of Portsmouth, Ohio (Plate 76). This review spoofs the lithographic view artist's tendency to show every river (in this case the Scioto) as navigable and filled with steamboats and every factory chimney topped with a plume of black smoke.

Owed to Portsmuth.
ritten on Ceeing a "Vu" in cullers of that Sitty.

butiful sitty, I see the, i behold the,
Thow sitest upon the bank of a river;
i see thy chimlies & the rufs of thy houses;
They hav a fine air of delapedashun.
i behold the smoke of thy iron facturies
I se the blac smoke frum thy terrubal stemers.
it is lovely to behold the, thou sitty by the river!
There i behold a dog, a man & a gun, bewtiful
Sitty? that rock makes a bridge over
the river, U can probably step ovur on it.
It mite fall on sum passin stemur;
i trimbel, i shak, i am afeard
there i se a bridge which has ben
Torne away by the dangerus ciota.
O bewtiful sitty, what du i not O the
for the phellings yu enspire! O
grate city, how long wud it take to
skwirt the watur out of they rivor?
What emoshuns you xsite! i seas,
i kwit, i rite no more![37]

Mockery like this or more straightforward examination of a print's accuracy, favorable viewpoint, excellence in printing, and historical appeal apparently were easier to write than critical analysis of the artistic achievements of viewmakers. Nevertheless, some journalists directed their attention to this aspect of urban lithographs, and more sophisticated consumers must have considered such qualities as composition and color balance in deciding whether or not to make a purchase.

One of the earliest newspaper notices to deal with the aesthetic qualities of a city view called attention in 1835 to a forthcoming print of Gloucester, Massachusetts, by the young and then relatively unknown Fitz Hugh Lane. The writer regarded Lane's work with admiration: "Taking it all in all, the mirror-like surface and graceful bends of the har-

34. Undated clippings from the Albany *Argus* and a Troy newspaper whose name is illegible in my copy of the Whitefield Scrapbook, Boston Public Library.

35. Buffalo *Morning Express*, undated clipping of 1848 in Whitefield Scrapbook.

36. San Diego *Union*, 14 April 1873, p. 3, as quoted in Rebecca Elizabeth Lytle, "People and Places: Images of Nineteenth-Century San Diego," 68. The newspaper stated, "The only point where a truly comprehensive view of the city can be had is on the railroad lands, coming from National City." Mathews viewed San Diego from the water. National City lay inland. This was not the first time Mathews had encountered unfavorable criticism of his work. His *Gems of Rocky Mountain Scenery*, published only a few years earlier and consisting of a few lithographic views of western landscapes, drew this appraisal of his artistic ability in the pages of *Putnam's Magazine*: "Either Mr. Mathews is no artist, or he is no lithographer; or, being both, it is not within the power of lithography to reproduce the larger forms of nature. As a rule there is no distance in the back-grounds of Mr. Mathews, no minuteness in his foregrounds, and nowhere the slightest sign of magnitude. Even in the mere matter of light and shade, his drawings are below mediocrity. Mr. Mathews courageously publishes his own work" (N. S., 4 [August 1869]: 257, 258, as quoted in Robert Taft, *Artists and Illustrators of the Old West, 1850–1900*, 82).

37. John Grabb, archivist of the Ross County Historical Society in Chillicothe, was kind enough to transcribe this choice and perhaps unique item for my use. It appeared in the Chillicothe *Scioto Gazette*, 23 March 1855.

bor, studded here and there with the most exquisitely drawn vessels; the lofty hills which nearly encompass the town, and last, our handsomely situated, and really handsome village, forms the most beautiful picture of the kind we ever saw." [38]

A far longer and much more specific analysis appeared in a review of Henry Walton's view of Ithaca, New York, from South Hill, a print that captured the fancy of an anonymous critic in the summer of 1839. The writer began by calling attention to the way the artist showed "every object . . . to the most minute particular . . . laid down in its proper position, with the strictest adherence to the rules of true perspective and faithful regard to accuracy." [39] Observations like this became common in later years and passed for artistic criticism in most newspapers. In this case, however, the claim for detail and accuracy served only as a preface to an analysis of composition:

> In looking at this masterly production . . . you almost fancy yourself standing upon the spot from which the artist viewed the scene. . . . Directly in front of you . . . you have, in all the rich colorings of nature, the vacant space of ground . . . south of Prospect street. . . . Around this piece of commons, are the buildings, new and old, red, white and wood colored, with their yards, out houses, &c.,—here a workshop and there a dwelling. The embellishments of this foreground are arranged tastefully and pleasingly. A party of some three or four are dashing by in a barouche. . . . A lady and gentleman are standing at a little distance below you, attentively viewing the pleasing prospect before them. [40]

The critic was "struck with the beauty and accuracy of the bold and romantic scenery" that drew his attention to Lake Cayuga extending toward the horizon "until an abrupt bend in the lake interposes to break the view, and the eye wanders with delight among the cultivated fields . . . sloping to the lake in all their rich and rural beauty."

There is more of this lyric analysis of both the view and the handsome landscape Walton chose to include within its borders. A final word on colors closed this long and fascinating examination of the artist's achievement: "The picture is highly colored with the rich and varied tints of the season in which it was taken, which give to it all the soft and glowing charms of an autumnal scene." It must have been something of an anticlimax for readers to learn that they could secure a copy of such a masterwork of lithographic art for "the low sum of $3.50 per copy," a price that the critic felt represented a rare bargain "richly worth twice that sum."

Many of Edwin Whitefield's views impressed contempo-

rary observers as works that deserved to be treated as artistic endeavors. Earlier we noted complaints about his achievements, although these were tempered elsewhere in the story or in another paper by far more favorable comments. Some of these addressed Whitefield's talents in composition. The Albany *Citizen*, for example, praised several features of the lithograph that the rival *Argus* found partly deficient. Whitefield must have found one passage particularly pleasing to him as an artist, and he surely felt added satisfaction in knowing it would stimulate sales of his lithograph:

> This view is taken from an advantageous point . . . and is enriched with a lively fore-ground. The effect of the whole is highly picturesque. . . . the artist . . . successfully avoid[ed] that crowded confusion which has marred all other views of the centre of the city and its public buildings. In this picture the State and City buildings, churches, and other prominent objects, stand separately, and are clearly defined. This is one of the great merits of the work. [41]

Whitefield's lithograph of Pittsburgh also received commendation from one newspaper as a "beautiful view" of the city and "the surrounding country," while another stated that his renderings of "the beauty of the hills in the background and the trees in the fore ground prove that this gentleman's claims to the name of an artist are well merited." [42] Whitefield quoted a number of similar statements in a series of excerpts from press reviews printed at the bottom of a sheet he circulated to advertise his services as a drawing teacher. His use of such comments clearly indicates the value he placed on praise of his artistic talents in addition to the usual laudatory remarks about the accuracy of the views. [43]

The large and attractive views issued by the Smith brothers in the 1850s, like that of Bangor, Maine (Plate 77), received similar recognition as works of art. A Bangor newspaper greeted the publication of a print drawn by the accomplished artist John W. Hill and lithographed for the Smiths by Charles Parsons with these words:

> In the foreground the Penobscot is seen as it comes winding its course from 'neath the extensive Toll Bridge that stretches across its proud waters on the north, filled with countless boats, rafts, logs, &c., besides a large number of vessels that constantly line our docks . . . till it looses itself among the hills on the south. The Kenduskeag, as seen emerging from the deep ravine in the distance dividing the city until its mingling with the waters of the Penobscot presents a most beautiful and pleasing effect. In fact, this picture gives a minute detail and striking likeness of every object that comes within the range of the Artist's eye, and when spread out before you one can hardly realize but that they are beholding nature itself rather than a drawing on paper. [44]

38. Gloucester *Telegraph*, 15 August 1835, as quoted in John Wilmerding, *Fitz Hugh Lane*, 22.

39. This and the quotations to follow are from the notice in the Ithaca *Journal & General Advertiser*, 17 July 1839.

40. In the print the barouche is stationary. The critic must have been describing Walton's painting from which he made the lithograph. There are other differences between painting and print. The writer mentions several uniformed figures in the foreground, pointing out that "by their attitudes, peculiar to themselves, you know their persons" among members of the Ithaca Guards. Their captain, standing to one side, "is an individual with his arms folded across his breast—him you cannot mistake—his military coat was made with folded sleeves, and consequently his arms are always found in that position when in uniform." The captain, according to the account, was "fully and intently absorbed in one of the natural beauties before him—either the landscape, or the fine looking girl who is peeping archly from the window of a house near by." The writer added, just as archly: "The captain was then single." The captain may have been offended by this passage; in any event, Walton's print contained no such figure, nor can one find in the lithograph any girl peeping from a window.

41. Undated clipping of 1846 in Whitefield Scrapbook.

42. Pittsburgh *Gazette*, October [date missing] 1849; and undated clipping of 1849 from the Pittsburgh *Morning Post* in Whitefield Scrapbook.

43. This printed advertisement is reproduced in Norton, *Whitefield*, 19. Among others, Whitefield chose the following reviews:
VIEW OF PITTSBURG.—Mr. E. Whitefield has made the best general view of the city we have ever seen. The effect of the whole is at once imposing and faithful, and is highly creditable to the skill and taste of the artist—*Albany Jour.*
VIEW OF HARTFORD.—We have seen a copy of Mr. Whitefield's view of Hartford, which for accuracy and general beauty will challenge admiration.—*Hart. Daily Cour.*
VIEW OF PROVIDENCE.—Mr. E. Whitefield is certainly deserving of great praise for publishing such beautiful and accurate pictures of Providence.—*Prov. Repub. Herald.*

44. Bangor *Daily Whig and Courier*, 1854 [date unknown], as quoted in Christine Bauer Podmanicsky and Earle G. Shettleworth, Jr., *Through a*

A more elaborate and specific assessment of a city view, combining both aesthetic and utilitarian analysis, guided the readers of a Syracuse, New York, newspaper in understanding and appreciating a lithograph of that city produced by M. de V. Martin in 1859. Although long, this assessment is worth quoting in its entirety as an interesting example of how these prints struck some contemporary eyes.

VIEW OF SYRACUSE.—The well known and accomplished artist, Mr. De V. Martin, has just shown us the proof sheet of a beautiful view of Syracuse on a large scale, suitable for parlor ornaments, hotels, offices and other places. This picture is one of the most perfect we have ever seen, and although the one exhibited is a mere proof impression of the work, it exhibits a taste and skill in its execution that entitles it to rank high as a work of art. The view is a faithful representation of almost the entire city, as seen from the hill just beyond Mr. Longstreet's residence, in the south-east part of the city, extending from the Orphans Asylum on the right, to the Idiot Asylum on the left, embracing also the Onondaga Lake and the Villages of Salina, Liverpool and Geddes in the distance, with the city of Syracuse occupying the entire middle ground where all the public buildings and most of the private residences can be distinctly pointed out. The immediate foreground is occupied by Mr. Longstreet, Baggs and Smith's residences and grounds, which serve admirably for filling up the space, and give great picturesqueness and beauty to the foreground. Several other figures are added which greatly add to the artistic taste and arrangement of the picture, and the whole makes as fine a view as any ever published. The coloring is also very finely done. The view is represented under a morning light, and the lights and shadows are in excellent keeping throughout the entire picture. The great business of our city is fully represented by numerous tall chimneys in active operation, and the cars are seen winding their way on the various lines of railways over the tracks of the N.Y. Central, Oswego and Binghamton Roads. The picture represents the city from as favorable a point as can be found, and the view is one of which Syracuseans may well be proud. The publisher, Mr. De V. Martin, is obtaining subscriptions for the picture among our citizens, and we cheerfully recommend the artist and his beautiful work to the liberal patronage of all Syracuseans. [45]

Whether or not a modern observer agrees with this generous—almost fulsome—praise of the artistic achievements of this view's creator, the description and analysis of the view in this account capture much of the pride and satisfaction with which the publication of a lithograph of a city was greeted by its residents. The print is perceived mainly as a work of art, but art used to bolster commerce and civic pride.

Unless the sample of newspaper notices examined in this study is unrepresentative, claims of aesthetic excellence were made with far less frequency in the years after the Civil War than in the first two decades or so of the views' popularity. One finds, for example, only such modest statements as a Denver reporter used in describing the views of Nebraska cities shown him by Alfred E. Mathews in 1865 when the artist began work on his series of Colorado lithographs.

"Several of his pictures . . . bear the marks of an Artist's hand" strikes one as both suitably ambiguous and distinctly unenthusiastic. [46]

Somewhat more complimentary in his choice of words, a journalist in Lansing, Michigan, proclaimed that Clemens J. Pauli's view of 1890 was "not a stiff-looking affair, such as are often made of American cities, but . . . combines beauty and accuracy in a high degree." [47] Among many similar comments, an assertion that a view of Milwaukee was "a genuine work of art" stands out as an exception during the post–Civil War era. [48] Judgments about the artistic merits of views gave way to comments concerning accuracy or the usefulness of the lithographs in promoting growth and economic development.

This shift in attitudes, at least as expressed in the public press, reflected changes in the way views were drawn, the limited artistic abilities of those responsible for their creation, an increasing emphasis on their commercial value, and a growing specialization in the process of printmaking that diminished the artist's role in determining the appearance and character of the final product. Before the Civil War commerce served art. After the war art became the servant of commerce.

Few American artists of the stature of Fitz Hugh Lane or even of lesser stature such as Wild or Hill concerned themselves with townscape painting or drawing in the second half of the nineteenth century. If the artists of this period moved from portraits or genre scenes to other and larger subjects, it was the marvelously varied landscape of rural or wilderness America that attracted their attention. Serious artists regarded urban scenes as harsh, ugly, and unnatural. Thus, the depiction of towns and cities fell into the hands of artists whose work, with few exceptions, could not be judged by conventional aesthetic standards. Moreover, such men as Ruger, Fowler, Koch, the Bailey brothers, Glover, Burleigh, Wellge, Pauli, and Norris drew cities to make money, not to satisfy their artistic impulses.

The need to sell prints in sufficient numbers to make their efforts financially rewarding led most of these artists to adopt the bird's-eye viewpoint. Only in this manner could they show all the buildings of the town and thus widen the appeal of the lithograph to include all residents, not just those with taste cultivated enough to appreciate the artistic attractions of a conventional low-level panorama. Recognized artists, trained in the tradition of easel painting, doubtless regarded this technique of representing the urban scene as little more than a specialized form of cartography.

Serious artists also came to look on lithography as stigmatized by commercialism and as suitable only for reproducing cheap art prints for the masses and for printing posters, billheads, advertisements, and certificates. Steam-powered presses and the use of photography separated the artist from the final product and reduced his control over the appearance of the print. As Joseph Pennell, an artist and printmaker, sarcastically declared, lithographers "could put everything but art on stone" under a system where a "creative

Bird's Eye: Nineteenth-Century Views of Maine (Rockland, Maine, 1981), 8–12. Podmanicsky's introductory essay to this exhibit catalog is a major contribution to the small but growing literature on city views. I wish to acknowledge my debt to her for the material she has so ably summarized in her essay as well as for other information she has shared with me.

45. Undated transcription of a newspaper account from an unidentified source provided me by the Onondaga Historical Association, Syracuse, New York.

46. Rocky Mountain News, 13 November 1865, p. 4, col. 2.
47. Lansing State Republican, 9 June 1890.
48. Daily Milwaukee News, 17 January 1872, p. 4, as quoted in Beckman, Milwaukee Illustrated, unpaged introduction.

artist . . . had no place in the lithographic establishment."[49]

Modern art historians share the disdain with which nineteenth-century artists and critics regarded lithographic printmaking of the period. Writing of an allied product, the chromolithographic reproductions of paintings that flooded the market during the years from 1840 to 1900, Peter Marzio has noted that until quite recently these prints were "viewed as something of an embarrassment by the keepers of America's printed fine art." Curators of public collections "paid much more attention to 'art prints'—etchings, copper engravings, and the like—than to chromolithographs, and if these institutions admit to having any chromos at all, they keep them out of sight—chromos are the unwanted leftovers of early collection policies."[50]

Even Harry T. Peters, who did so much to rescue nineteenth-century lithography from the scrapheap of American art where establishment critics and historians had consigned it, found little merit in the post–Civil War prints. He believed that artistic quality declined with the development of steam presses and color printing. These and other technical innovations, he said, "separated the artists from the craftsmen." For Peters, the "hey-day" of lithography was "in the thirties, forties and fifties," and the city views that flourished after the war did not interest him.[51] Similarly, Nicholas Wainwright, in his valuable book on lithography in Philadelphia, concluded, "Success and progress bring their penalties . . . , and lithography, in attaining its comparatively modern technology of 1865, had lost the flavor which had distinguished its earlier productions."[52]

City views can be looked at critically in another way, however. That most avid collector of them, Isaac Newton Phelps Stokes, argued the case for this approach in his monumental work, *The Iconography of Manhattan Island*, and repeated it in the introduction to the catalog he compiled of the views he first assembled and then generously gave to the New York Public Library:

> In most of the higher forms of collecting, beauty is the ideal towards which the collector strives, the one essential characteristic which guides his choice. Not so with the collecting of historical prints, which, for the most part, must be judged by a different standard. Few of the prints of American Cities can justly be called beautiful, but many possess other qualities which endear them to the heart of the intelligent collector, who regards them almost with reverence and awe as the frail documents of a by-gone age. . . . In themselves admittedly incomplete and unsatisfying, if judged by the standards of the average picture lover, as contemporary illustrations of successive steps in the physical growth of our great continent, they render more real and vivid our written history, and become at once instructive and intensely interesting.[53]

Tastes change and greater knowledge and understanding create a more tolerant attitude concerning what at one time seemed to be appropriate measures for distinguishing between art and mere illustration. A new generation of Americans can now enjoy without guilt examples of folk art that museum curators earlier in the century would not have allowed even in their discarded trash. The city views of the last four decades of the nineteenth century can also be looked at with pleasure as examples of popular art in America during the Victorian era.

While no one would contend that these post–Civil War views, taken as a whole, represent any notable artistic achievement, among them are prints of far more than routine quality. Some of the large lithographs of Henry Wellge's American Publishing Company fall into this category. Eli Glover's views, too, are handsome compositions, usually with foreground figures that add pictorial interest and with elements of the landscape handled in a convincing manner. Even Albert Ruger, who concentrated more on quantity than on quality, was capable of producing urban scenes of remarkable charm and interest, such as his Hannibal, Missouri, lithograph of 1869.

Beyond that, of course, are the characteristics that Stokes cherished: the prints as graphic evidence of how our cities appeared in the last century and the elements that made up their fabric. In concentrating on this aspect of city views the newspaper critics of the time may have applied the most appropriate standards in judging the output of the nation's viewmakers. They saw accuracy as more important than artistic excellence, and in the next chapter we will examine how well the view artists achieved this objective.

49. Joseph Pennell and Elizabeth Robins Pennell, *Lithography and Lithographers*, 122.

50. Peter C. Marzio, *The Democratic Art: Pictures for a 19th-Century America*, xii.

51. Harry T. Peters, *America on Stone: The Other Printmakers to the American People*, 24, 26.

52. Nicholas B. Wainwright, *Philadelphia in the Romantic Age of Lithography*, 90.

53. I. N. Phelps Stokes, "Introduction," in I. N. Phelps Stokes and Daniel C. Haskell, *American Historical Prints: Early Views of American Cities* . . . , xxii.

9. Lithographic City Views: Reliable Records of the Urban Past

To what extent are city views accurate representations of what our communities were like? Harry Peters, our first real scholar of American lithography, flatly stated, "Views were usually accurate [and] contain a wealth of detail, such as shipping, railways, customs, churches, museums, shops, farms, forests, rivers, mansions, cottages, etc., etc."[1] Two other authorities on historic prints take issue with this position and assert that in "a town view printed for a local urban booster . . . one can expect to find idealized settings and gross exaggerations."[2]

While it is true that some artists did indeed grossly exaggerate, especially in views commissioned by local real estate promoters, and that artists of nearly all views delineated their subjects in a favorable light, the overwhelming number of city views can be regarded as substantially accurate in showing the city as a whole as well as in showing details of individual buildings and their surroundings. In this chapter we will examine the evidence for this conclusion as well as look at ways in which views may be deceptive or misleading.

One measure of the accuracy of the prints is their reception in the community at the time they were drawn or published. Contemporary newspaper accounts provide the basis for judging how faithful the images were to reality. In all but a very few cases, notices in local newspapers were laudatory, although the modern reader should not regard this as conclusive evidence of accuracy. Certainly a lithograph that made a city appear large, prosperous, and attractive would receive more favorable attention than one featuring run-down buildings, vacant lots, false fronts on business establishments, an untidy industrial district, or a harbor empty of ships.

Newspapers reflected the spirit of civic boosterism that prevailed in nineteenth-century America, whether in a long-established eastern community or in a raw, new town on the western frontier. Objective reporting of facts about the pres-

ent often blurred into hopes and expectations for the future. Artists and publishers who wished to sell their views locally certainly understood this attitude. In promoting their lithographs by issuing prepared statements describing their own work, they obviously took pains to emphasize how carefully they had sketched every building and how faithfully they had portrayed every community. At a time when newspapers were understaffed and when, at least in the smaller towns, few editors would have had much familiarity with city views, those responsible for filling the pages of a local daily or weekly publication must have welcomed a well-written handout, even if it was obviously self-serving and not necessarily wholly in accord with the truth.

Nevertheless, one cannot dismiss the mass of favorable reviews as entirely or mainly the results of skilled and successful promotional efforts by publishers, subscription agents, and artists. There is a ring of authenticity, for example, in the story appearing in the Salem *Observer* a week after the paper noted the publication of Edwin Whitefield's view of that Massachusetts city in 1849:

> For the purpose of satisfying ourselves concerning the merits of Mr. Whitefield's view of Salem . . . we recently visited the point on Gallows Hill from which that view was obtained. And as the result of our observations we beg leave to report as a subcommittee to the committee of the whole that we find Mr. Whitefield's picture to be a very satisfactory transcript of the municipal aspect at the point aforesaid. It is indeed a very faithful and correct drawing; and persons who may visit that sightly eminence will perceive that the relative positions of prominent objects in the city are rightly given.[3]

Another Salem newspaper endorsed this appraisal of Whitefield's work. At a time when rival journals in the same city often disagreed on even small issues almost as a matter of policy, this additional support for Whitefield's view takes on added significance: "The artist . . . has been extremely successful in giving a perfect sketch of the town."[4]

The later high-level bird's-eye views that predominated after the Civil War attracted many such favorable notices. Albert Ruger's graphic records of Charlottetown and Halifax (Plate 78), prepared in 1878 when the artist visited the Canadian maritime provinces, impressed local editors with their detail and accuracy. One noted that Ruger "with unwearied patience . . . has drawn every building in outline on a scale small enough to show the whole city; has located every building so exactly that every citizen can pick out his own place. Streets, railways, streams, public and private

1. Harry T. Peters, *America on Stone: The Other Printmakers to the American People*, 39.

2. Peter C. Marzio and Milton Kaplan, "Lithographs as Historical Documents," 674. Elsewhere in this book I have acknowledged my debt to Marzio's work. For many years Kaplan was the specialist in American historical prints at the Division of Prints and Photographs, Library of Congress. Sometime in the mid-1950s he introduced me to lithographic city views at a time when my concern as a city planning historian lay almost exclusively in printed and manuscript maps and plans. I want to record here my gratitude to him for broadening my interests, for his skilled and informed assistance over the years on many visits to the collection over which he presided, and for his advice and suggestions that almost always proved sound and productive. My respect for these two scholars is profound, but, for reasons that will be explained, I think that in this instance they overstated a warning that city views can be misleading. The case that is developed in this chapter is more briefly stated in John W. Reps, *Cities on Stone: Nineteenth Century Lithograph Images of the Urban West*, 34–35.

3. Manuscript transcription, doubtless by Whitefield, of a notice in the 19 May 1849 issue of the Salem *Observer*, Edwin Whitefield Scrapbook, Boston Public Library.

4. Salem *Gazette*, 15 May 1849, in Whitefield Scrapbook.

buildings seem to be quite correct."[5] A Halifax newspaper echoed this favorable judgment a few weeks later: "The picture . . . presents clearly and distinctly every part of the city. Not only the streets but each house can be distinctly pointed out; while the public buildings can be distinguished in a moment. . . . The view of the harbor too, is excellent, as much care being taken to shew each wharf as to outline the public and other buildings."[6] The following year, when Ruger campaigned in Michigan, the Saginaw *Daily Courier* stated, "Prof. Ruger . . . draws . . . in place every building and street in the city with mathematical accuracy. The drawing possesses all the accuracy of a map, with the beauty of a picture."[7]

In reviewing a lithograph drawn by Augustus Koch and published by J. J. Stoner, a San Antonio newspaper advanced a similar claim of cartographic precision: "While not intended to answer the purpose of a map, it gives a fair idea of locations and distances, and is particularly accurate in its delineations of the extent of improvements, and representations of notable buildings as well as private residences."[8]

A newspaper in Lincoln, Nebraska, also praised the fidelity with which Koch had drawn that city:

> Mr. Koch has with him his sketch which shows every street, block, railroad track, switch and turn-table, every bridge, tree and barn, and in fact every object that would strike the eye of a man up a little ways in a balloon from a point a little northwest of the B. & M. depot. The architectural style, dimensions, and position of each building is faithfully preserved in the sketch, and when it shall be printed in colors by the lithographic stone it will make a fine picture that will introduce them immediately to the acquaintance of a stranger and to the recognition of all who have seen it.[9]

The review greeting Thaddeus M. Fowler's view of Denison, Texas, in 1891 (Plate 79) was just as effusive and approving. Only five years before, Henry Wellge had drawn and sold a print of the city, but after inspecting the drawing that Fowler had produced and proposed to publish, the editor found the new version superior for reasons he specified at length:

> The view will be much larger, and take in a good deal more territory, than any view which has been heretofore published of the city, indeed, it is believed to include every residence within the city limits, covering a territory of over three miles square, also showing the cotton factory, exposition building, waterworks and standpipe on the South. Every public school building, all the churches, and every residence is easily recognized. The streets are plainly represented and named, and trains are represented as entering the city on the several railroads. This is certainly the largest, the most perfect view of Denison that has ever been produced.[10]

The same themes appear in notices of views drawn in the Far West. Henry Wellge's lithograph of Seattle (Plate 75)

appeared in 1884, and the leading newspaper of the city praised it because "in the town are shown the streets and houses, fences, gardens and shade trees, with the timber beyond, all beautifully plain, clear and distinct. With but little difficulty every house in town can be picked out."[11] Eli Glover must have been delighted with the review of his lithograph of Victoria, British Columbia (Plate 61). The writer singled out its meticulous attention to detail and the care with which the artist had worked:

> The view is . . . supposed to be taken from a considerable elevation and thus every street, public building, and private residence is depicted with extraordinary accuracy. The picture . . . contains almost photographic representations of more than 2,500 buildings, a fact which will convey an idea, but only a faint one, of the extraordinary trouble the artist has been put to and the unbounded patience he must necessarily have exercised.[12]

Countless other newspaper accounts of the period included similar comments concerning the work of artists in depicting their communities.[13] Only rarely did a local paper find fault with an artist on grounds of accuracy, although, as has been noted in another context, editors sometimes criticized views for not showing their towns from the most advantageous or favorable viewpoints.

Perhaps sharper eyes and less inclination to follow the wording of promotional statements provided by agents and publishers might have produced less laudatory remarks. Certainly a more critical attitude would have saved the editor of the Bellefonte, Pennsylvania, *Democratic Watchman* from an embarrassing about-face in the paper's judgment of W. W. Denslow's view (Plate 80) of that city. The report in mid-July 1878 referred to Denslow as "an artist of rare ability," and the writer stated flatly, "As far as the drawing is completed we cannot see where there could be any improvement." Yet when the finished lithograph arrived some six weeks later the *Watchman* found it necessary to switch its position on the merits of the view for reasons it bluntly pointed out: "In the picture of Bellefonte lately published . . . the entire block or row of buildings on Spring Street from the Presbyterian Church is omitted. And yet some pretend this is a good picture."[14]

Denslow probably made a simple error in his drawing and was not attempting the kind of fantasy for which he later became famous as the illustrator of *The Wizard of Oz*. Far more serious were deliberate deceptions that a few artists

5. Charlottetown *Daily Examiner*, 9 July 1878.
6. Halifax *Evening Reporter & Daily & Tri-Weekly Times*, 20 August 1878, p. 3, col. 2.
7. Issue of 22 August 1879, p. 2, col. 1. The view was of East Saginaw.
8. San Antonio *Daily Herald*, 15 April 1873, p. 3, col. 2.
9. Lincoln *Daily Nebraska State Journal*, 10 April 1874. When the lithograph arrived a few months later the same newspaper in its issue of 10 July 1874 stated, "every house, store, shop, block and stable in the corporate limits is drawn in perfection."
10. Denison *Sunday Gazetteer*, 11 January 1891.
11. Seattle *Post Intelligencer*, 15 July 1884, p. 2, col. 2.
12. Victoria *Colonist*, 8 March 1878, p. 3.
13. See, for example, the following: undated and unidentified clippings in the Whitefield Scrapbook concerning his views of Albany in 1845 and Baltimore in 1847; Ruger's view of Oberlin, Ohio, in 1868, noted in the *Lorain County News*, 13 May 1868; C. J. Pauli's view of Lansing, Michigan, reviewed in the Lansing *State Republican*, 9 June 1890; the Simcoe, Ontario, *British Canadian*'s notice of 2 March 1881 about Fowler's sketch for a lithograph of the city; and the comment on Burleigh's view of Middlebury, Vermont, in the Middlebury *Register*, 20 November 1885. Hundreds of such notices must have been printed, since it would have been a rare newspaper that ignored the publication of a lithograph of its place of publication. My guess is that those quoted in this and other chapters are a fair representation of such news accounts.
14. Issues of 19 July and 29 August 1878, as quoted in Pennsylvania State University, Museum of Art, *Pennsylvania Prints from the Collection of John C. O'Connor and Ralph M. Yeager: Lithographs, Engravings, Aquatints, and Watercolors from The Tavern Restaurant*, notes for pls. 70–73.

engaged in by drawing cities that never existed or by creating imaginary images at the request of unscrupulous publishers.

One early example is a handsome lithograph drawn in 1838 by the well-known architect William Strickland, skillfully put on stone by Alfred Hoffy, and printed in Philadelphia by Peter Duval (Plate 81). This showed Strickland's design for the development of Cairo, Illinois, whose low-lying, frequently flooded, and nearly vacant site was owned by Darius Holbrook, a land speculator and town promoter with limitless ambitions and unburdened by any sense of business ethics. Holbrook's stated intention was to turn Cairo's mud flats into a great rail center and commercial metropolis. With copies of Strickland's view he sailed for England, where he apparently exhibited the lithograph as evidence of what already existed. With its help he succeeded in borrowing more than one million dollars. The loans were to be used to finance further improvements, but Holbrook pocketed most or all of the money, and no part of Strickland's plan for the town was ever carried out.[15]

An even more attractive and compelling lithograph, lacking any artist's identification, was issued about 1857 by an anonymous publisher (Plate 82). It appeared during the great land boom in Kansas following the opening of the territory to settlement three years earlier. Printed in colors by the Cincinnati firm of Middleton, Strobridge & Co., it showed Sumner, Kansas, as a prosperous community with many handsome brick buildings lining a Missouri River steamboat landing, four fine churches, an industrial plant, a domed college building, and the imposing four-story Sumner House standing at the intersection of two of the many wide thoroughfares shown parallel and perpendicular to the river.

Copies of this print were displayed in New England to stimulate settlement. One young and proper Bostonian who was lured to Sumner after seeing the lithograph reported to his father that, although he "was not surprised at not finding a Boston or New York," he was infuriated that there were no churches, no college, and that the main street was "so gullied with rains, so interspersed with rocks and the stumps of trees . . . that a New Hampshire teamster of ordinary temerity would shun the task of traversing it." The industrial building shown in the view turned out to be only "a rickety old blacksmith's shop." The view, he concluded, was a "chromatic triumph of lithographed mendacity."[16]

Artists also erred or practiced deliberate deception in drawing some of the vignettes that can be found around the borders of many views. One would think that these little scenes, each usually identified by a business sign or the name of the owner and often showing even small architectural details, could be relied on with almost as much confidence as a photograph. According to the author of *How 'Tis Done*, that remarkably interesting exposé of the county map business where the sale of vignettes played such an important role in generating income for the publishers, these border scenes could be quite misleading.

He offers several examples. In one passage he presents an imaginary sales pitch of an agent who has approached a farmer regarded by the publishers as a likely prospect for the 'purchase' of a vignette:

Our plan is, to have an artist of acknowledged ability visit you, Mr. Jones—in case you accept—and make the drawings from nature. In this way, any changes or improvements you may contemplate making in the future can be made in the sketch, just as you may dictate, and appear in proper form in the years to come. . . . For instance, you would want that pile of wood near your house left out of the sketch, and the rubbish about the back-yard, which you are about to cart off, should not appear. You had better have a picket fence in front, instead of those rails, as you undoubtedly will have a picket fence there some day. It will only be necessary for you to tell the artist what sort of a picket you prefer, and the thing will be properly done. I would put a pump in that well, and make your barn a little larger. Of course we can make your house look as though it had just been painted, and we can put a grass lawn in front. A few evergreen trees would look well. In fact, just think up what improvements you design having, and we will have the sketch made giving you just such a house and yard as you will probably have three or four years from this time.[17]

Elsewhere in his book the author describes two specific examples. One involved "a two-story-and-half brick" house "covered with grapevines." The owner was out of town when the published map was delivered. His son refused payment when he, "to his astonishment, saw at a glance that the lithographer had left out all the windows in the upper story . . . and had mistaken the grape-vines to represent a stone house."[18]

The second was an even more drastic error, which this critic of the map business recounts with obvious relish:

A man named Ellsworth, living in Maquoketa, Iowa . . . had a desirable lot, on which he intended, some day to erect a fine mansion. He contracted for a view of his residence to be printed on the map of Jackson County. Between himself and the artist, a fine exterior was drawn. . . . When the map did come, the citizens flocked to the spot where the "palace" was reported to be located, but to see only a few piles of stone and an excavation for a cellar. Mr. Ellsworth's finances had failed to connect. . . . the only thing for him to do was to visit some distant relatives until the people got through making sport of his visions of a home.[19]

While it seems inevitable that such things also occurred in the business of publishing city views, gross inaccuracies of this kind were probably not numerous and certainly were not typical. In preparing these vignettes the artist and publisher knew that significant inaccuracies would quickly be noticed. Both they and the owner would be subject to

15. For the early history of Cairo's planning, see John W. Reps, "Great Expectations and Hard Times: The Planning of Cairo, Illinois."

16. Letter from John James Ingalls to his father, 5 October 1858, in Kansas State Historical Society, *Collections* 14 (1915–1918): 99–100; Sheffield Ingalls, *History of Atchison County, Kansas*, 93.

17. [Bates Harrington], *How 'Tis Done. A Thorough Ventilation of the Numerous Schemes Conducted by Wandering Canvassers*, 42–43. A specialist in Canadian county maps has pointed out, "Harrington's account tends to be scurrilous and must be used carefully" ("Introduction" by Joan Winearls, in National Map Collection, Public Archives of Canada, *County Maps: Land Ownership Maps of Canada in the 19th Century*, 7, n. 3). Harrington regarded county maps and county atlases as essentially fraudulent business ventures when in fact they provided much useful and badly needed information for a variety of purposes. His writing indicates he bore a grudge, and it should not be accepted as the impartial analysis he claims it to be.

18. Ibid., 91.

19. Ibid., 87–88.

ridicule if they indulged in too much artistic license. Sales of views depended far more on accurate representations of the town or city than on features that concern a modern art critic: composition, color, and perspective.

A potential subscriber examining the artist's final drawing before deciding whether or not to add his name to a subscription list would have been concerned almost entirely with the faithfulness with which the features of his town and its buildings had been rendered. If he noted several errors or exaggerations, he might conclude that the entire view was faulty and decide not to make a purchase. In particular, he would be concerned with exactly how his house, place of business, or church had been rendered. Artists exhibited their sketches primarily to secure subscriptions, but as a New Hampshire newspaper pointed out, another reason was "for the purpose of correcting any errors that may exist, and of making any additions that are necessary for accuracy."[20]

Nevertheless, one should look at these lithographic images, whether in vignettes or in the body of the view, as flattering, carefully posed, and retouched portraits rather than as completely candid records of reality. Artists emphasized attractive features while softening or omitting altogether less pleasant elements of a building. And just as a portrait artist chooses the most advantageous viewpoint from which to paint or photograph his client, so, too, did the lithographic viewmaker usually select the most impressive facade. It is thus far from accidental that so many of the border vignettes on the early prints of California mining towns appear as front elevations or perspectives taken from only a slight angle to one side (see Plates 21 and 69). Views from wider angles would have revealed the numerous false fronts that gave these buildings the appearance of larger size when seen from the streets on which they faced.[21]

One other feature occasionally encountered in the city views that may mislead the unwary is the tendency of artists when drawing towns in an era of constant change and growth to anticipate the completion of some structure or project under way but not finished at the time of the drawing. Only rarely did the artist or publisher provide a warning that such liberties had been taken. The author of the preface to Camille N. Dry's bound, multi-sheet view of St. Louis was thus unusually candid in stating that Dry had gone beyond

the bounds of fact in a few instances by drawing "important public and private edifices that are not yet finished . . . as they will appear when done."[22]

It was unusual, too, for Augustus Koch to identify in the legend as "proposed" the post office and the union railroad station that he included on his view of Lincoln, Nebraska, in 1874.[23] Koch used no such word in the legend of his Salt Lake City view four years earlier (Plate 83), on which he showed the Mormon temple as if completed, although at the time of his visit construction was still in an early stage, and the temple was not fully finished until 1893. Koch probably used illustrations based on the architect's design in drawing his image on the lithograph, and, although his depiction of this massive building is substantially correct, he turned the clock well ahead to make it so.

Many of the Sachse views of Washington, D.C., show the Washington Monument as if it had been built according to the original design by Robert Mills (Plate 84). In fact, from 1854 to 1879 the monument existed only as an unfinished shaft, and the elaborate colonnaded base Mills proposed was never even begun. Several of these Sachse lithographs also anticipated the completion of new wings and a dome on the Capitol, although in some cases it was many years before the building came to resemble the lithographic image that Sachse had so obligingly furnished.

Railroads proved less difficult for a lithographer to draw than for engineers to construct. George Baker's view of San Diego, undated but probably published between 1870 and 1873, shows the Texas Pacific Railroad, a line that never reached the city. As one student of San Diego views observes, this feature was "added, no doubt, at the request of local promoters of the railroad venture."[24]

Albert Ruger's view of Nebraska City, Nebraska (Plate 85), appeared in 1868. Two years earlier local entrepreneurs organized the Midland Pacific Railway Company to connect their town with Lincoln, and on the print the tracks of the railway lead convincingly from the distant prairie to the depot near the Missouri River steamboat landing. In fact, service on the railroad did not begin until 1871.

Ruger also anticipated the completion of a major structure when he produced his view of St. Charles, Missouri, in 1869. At the bottom center Ruger drew a train chuffing its way south. Behind it one can see a great bridge across the Missouri River and the elevated railroad approaches to the

20. Littleton *White Mountain Republic*, 14 July 1883. In writing this paragraph, my memory took me back to the days early in my career when I frequently served as a city planning consultant in preparing zoning ordinances. The initial phase of such studies always involved the preparation of a land-use map of the municipality that showed in colors how each lot was currently being used. At public hearings the citizens attending invariably located their lots to see if the proper color had been used. Even the smallest mistakes were regarded as casting doubt on the abilities of the consultant, although the zoning districts proposed were based on general patterns of land use rather than on the use of individual lots or buildings. I have no reason to doubt that city view artists who displayed their final drawings for subscription purposes had numerous errors called to their attention.

21. An excellent example of this is the Kuchel & Dresel view of Nevada, California, in 1856 reproduced as Plate 21. See also the Kuchel & Dresel lithograph of Shasta in 1856. Twenty-three vignettes surround the principal view. All but five are front elevations, and one of these, while technically a perspective, shows only the front facade. A color reproduction of this and several other similar Kuchel & Dresel views can be found in Reps, *Cities on Stone*, pls. 6–10. See also the vignettes on Grafton Brown's splendid view of Virginia City, Nevada, in 1861. This is reproduced as fig. 7.25 and pl. 10 (where it is erroneously dated 1875) in John W. Reps, *Cities of the American West: A History of Frontier Urban Planning*.

22. *Pictorial St. Louis Metropolis of the Mississippi Valley: A Topographical Survey Drawn in Perspective A.D. 1875 by Camille N. Dry, Designed & Edited by Rich. J. Compton* (St. Louis, 1875).

23. My attention was called to this unusual designation in notes on a handlist issued for an exhibition of town views at the Sheldon Art Gallery in Lincoln in 1981. The notes are the work of Helen Brooks and Karen Pearson, both of whom have exchanged information on Nebraska lithographic views with me, with much the greater amount of material flowing in my direction. I am particularly grateful to them for locating and transcribing many contemporary newspaper notices about Nebraska views, which have been quoted or cited in several chapters of this book. Henry Wellge labeled one feature on his view of Franklin and Franklin Falls, New Hampshire, of 1884 as "Paper Co.'s Proposed Dam," and George Norris identified one of the thoroughfares on his view of Antrim, New Hampshire, in 1887 as "Proposed St." David Ruell provided me with this information by allowing me use of his manuscript article on New Hampshire town views.

24. Rebecca Elizabeth Lytle, "People and Places: Images of Nineteenth-Century San Diego," 74.

bridge on both sides of the river. A visitor relying on Ruger's print and expecting to enter or leave the town by rail would have been disappointed, for it was not until two years later that the bridge finally opened for traffic.[25]

Of course not all buildings were completed exactly as planned. H. H. Bailey confidently drew the railroad station of the Concord Railroad in his view of Nashua, New Hampshire, in 1875 (Plate 86), although no such building existed. He seems to have relied on information supplied him by officials of the line, for the local newspaper explained to its readers, "We are told that the new Union station shown on the fine lithographic map . . . is not a fancy sketch, but is an actual design furnished by one of the railroad companies. We hope that it will soon represent the real thing." Unfortunately for Bailey's reputation, however, when the station was finally completed five years later it did not resemble the structure appearing on the view.

O. H. Bailey had better luck in another New Hampshire community many years later. He issued a lithograph of Derry in 1898 just one month before construction began on the Odd Fellows Hall (Plate 87). Nevertheless, Bailey showed the building in his view and added a separate border vignette as well. His faith that the members of the lodge would not change their plans proved not to be misplaced, for shortly thereafter the building was finished according to the plans Bailey must have consulted when preparing his drawing.[26]

Erroneous or misleading details can be found in some views because of the artist's mistakes or a decision to forego accuracy in the interests of composition. On the view of St. Louis published about 1865 and printed by E. Sachse & Co. in Baltimore, an imposing structure appears where no such building ever existed (Plate 88). After studying the print for some time, a local authority finally determined that this was intended to be "the building of the Episcopal Sisterhood of the Good Shepherd," which in reality was located some distance away and faced in another direction. It was a "most extreme liberty," for while "the move was a happy one artistically" it was "frustrating historically."[27]

Probably no lithographic view was totally correct in all respects. What is remarkable, however, and what should not be lost sight of notwithstanding the examples of errors reviewed above, is the vast amount of accurate information available in the typical print of this type. This assertion is supported by evidence from many sources.

Scholars and local historians examining individual lithographs of cities about which they have intimate knowledge have been struck by how reliable the artist's image was of the community at the time he drew his view. For example, an exhaustive and painstaking analysis of Henry Walton's three prints of Ithaca, New York, published in 1837–1839 revealed dozens of small details of individual buildings whose accuracy was verified by comparison with other contemporary illustrations, old photographs, or the surviving structures themselves.[28]

The author of a similar study of the Lewis Bradley view of Syracuse, New York, published by the Smith brothers in 1852 (Plate 33), came to similar conclusions. He noted, "In the lithograph, perspective is sacrificed for clarity," and "the view is actually a group of detailed sections, enlarged and placed in approximate relation to each other. Areas of lesser interest are diminished or omitted." Nevertheless, this scholar concluded, "a resident could inspect the scene and feel completely satisfied as he found one building after another clearly shown and true in general form."[29]

Of forty-four major buildings and landscape features studied on Albert Ruger's view of St. Joseph, Missouri, in 1868, an authority on local history of that city was able to find only one error: the mistaken designation of the Odd Fellows Hall as the City Hall.[30] On his view of Beatrice, Nebraska, in 1881, Augustus Koch's lithographer used a darker shade in his tone stone to identify buildings constructed of brick. Modern scholars have compared his depiction with a detailed fire insurance map prepared at the same time as the view and concluded that Koch's print is a completely reliable guide in this respect.[31]

A more detailed and systematic study of the accuracy of city views has recently been carried out by Charles Uhl, who has examined two views of Ithaca, New York, and single prints of Groton, Waterloo, Seneca Falls, and Binghamton, New York, all drawn and published in 1873–1885.[32] Two of these views (Ithaca in 1882 and Groton) were the work of Lucien Burleigh, and two (Ithaca in 1873 and Seneca Falls) were drawn by Oakley Hoopes Bailey. Augustus Koch prepared the Waterloo view, and Herman Brosius was responsi-

25. Ruger's anticipatory details on both of these views are noted under colored reproductions of the lithographs in Editors of Time-Life Books, *The Rivermen*, 194–95, 198–99. For reasons given in this chapter, I feel that despite these misleading elements the author of the general statement introducing these views in *The Rivermen* is overly harsh: "While impressively accurate in many details, the panoramas oftimes indulged in flights of self-serving fancy: steamboats lined levees that had long fallen into disuse; trains sped along nonexistent railbeds and bridges; and smoke belched industriously from vacant factories. The deliberate deceptions, designed to attract new residents and industry, were studiously ignored by the townspeople who prominently displayed the maps on the walls of their homes and offices" (ibid., 194). The text may be by Paul O'Neil, identified on the title page after the phrase *with text by*, but more than thirty other names appear under the headings *editorial staff* or *editorial production* in this typical product of corporate writing and publishing.

26. The quotation concerning H. H. Bailey's Nashua view is from the Nashua *Daily Telegraph*, 13 November 1875. This and the information about the Odd Fellows building in Derry come from a manuscript by David Ruell on New Hampshire town views. He cites the Derry *News* of 18 February, 18 and 26 March 1898 for material about O. H. Bailey's view. One other relevant example has been called to my attention by Professor Clinton Adams. On the unsigned view of Santa Fe, New Mexico, in 1882, probably drawn by Henry Wellge, the artist shows spires on the cathedral. While these were part of the original design, they were never executed.

27. Ruth K. Field, "Some Misconceptions About Lucas Place," 122.

28. John G. Brooks, "Historical Settings of Ithaca Paintings," 11–18.

29. The quotations are from an unpublished analysis of the view prepared by Richard N. Wright, president of the Onondaga Historical Association, Syracuse, New York, who kindly provided me with a copy. Wright's notes provide information about dozens of buildings appearing in the view, and he identifies fifteen major structures erected in 1850 or 1851 to indicate that Bradley's drawing reflected all major changes in the community up to the time the view was sent to the printer.

30. Frederick W. Slater, "St. Joseph as It Looked in 1868."

31. Exhibition handlist note by Helen Brooks and Karen Pearson for item 16, "Nebraska Towns on View."

32. While I suggested the topic to Uhl as a subject for his master's thesis and passed on to him a number of ideas about how he might carry out his research, he went well beyond what I had originally conceived. It is a pioneering study, and we both hope that others will apply elsewhere some or all of the methods of investigation he developed and will devise other means of testing the reliability of these views.

ble for that of Binghamton (Plate 89). Four major view-makers of America were thus represented. Although the purpose of the study was to develop and test methods of investigation rather than to arrive at general conclusions based on a very small sample, the findings that emerged suggest that confidence in the accuracy of these views is not misplaced.

Comparisons of the images on the lithographs with architectural details of surviving buildings indicate that despite some modest errors of omission or exaggerations of the size of certain buildings, the artists drew what existed. Some produced more accurate work than others; Burleigh's depiction of the small village of Groton, for example, was so accurate that no errors could be detected in the way he drew the more than one hundred structures still standing.

Studies were also made comparing the views with information provided by large-scale fire-insurance maps of the same period and with data obtained from city directories listing addresses of every building along each city block. Photographs and other illustrations dating from the period were also used in an effort to visualize the true appearance of each community at the time of the artist's visit.

Although no single view of the six analyzed in these ways was free from error, each lithograph provided a generally accurate image of how the community would have appeared to an observer looking down on it from the viewpoint assumed by the artist. True, Koch exaggerated the size of the churches in Waterloo, O. H. Bailey failed to include some buildings in his Ithaca view of 1873, and Brosius in his lithographic depiction of Binghamton grossly distorted the Court House in one of the two vignettes he prepared. Far more remarkable than the existence of such discrepancies, however, is the presentation of so much that is accurate, useful, and available from no other source.[33]

Probably the most intensive and painstaking study of the accuracy of a single view is the examination of Augustus Koch's lithograph of Salt Lake City in 1870, whose central portion is reproduced in Figure 83.[34] This study was carried out in 1982 and 1983 by staff members of the Historical Department of the Mormon Church. Working on a block-by-block basis over a square mile encompassing most of the area of the city that was developed when Koch prepared his view, this group compared the details on the lithograph with dozens of old photographs.

Steven L. Olsen, the historian in charge of this phase of the study, concluded that, although Koch exaggerated the size of some of the major buildings, "anticipated the completion of . . . the temple and possibly the train station," and eliminated "many, though not all out buildings" and "fences, lightpoles and other smaller items," his study "determined that the view can be relied upon as highly accurate."[35] This was true even for Koch's depiction of vegetation. Several photographs show shade and fruit trees planted in orderly rows within the blocks in patterns closely resembling those appearing on the lithograph.

The view proved a reliable guide to the appearance of buildings and their placement. In one case researchers tentatively concluded that Koch made an error in recording the orientation of a small store because the earliest photographs showed it facing north while Koch drew it with its entrance to the west. However, a clearer print of the early 1880s photograph revealed "the foundations of a smaller building which had recently been demolished and whose materials had been reused in the later structure. The foundations indicate that the earlier structure indeed faced west."[36]

As lithographic city views come to be used by more scholars for a variety of purposes, other tests of their accuracy will surely be carried out. It seems likely that these will confirm or modify only slightly the findings reported in this chapter. If that is so, more attention can be directed to the ways in which the views can enrich our knowledge of the urban scene during the period when they flourished in the nineteenth century and the early years of the present era.

33. A full account of Uhl's studies can be found in Charles Uhl, "'Every Building Is Accurately Represented': An Examination of Five Bird's Eye Views of Upstate New York."

34. For a color reproduction of the entire view, see pl. 13, following p. 192, in Reps, *Cities of the American West.*

35. Memorandum to the author from Steven L. Olsen, 30 March 1983. Mr. Olsen and I discussed this subject in Salt Lake City a few days earlier and at my request he was kind enough to prepare this memorandum and authorize references to it and quotations from it in this book. See Chapter 10 for additional comments on how this study was used.

36. Ibid. Mr. Olsen adds, "I could go on, but you get the point. We have identified a few inaccuracies, although having been caught in error before I hasten to add 'apparent inaccuracies.' Heber C. Kimball's mill on the block northeast of Temple Square appears not to have been exactly as Koch pictured it, and there appears to be a mill wheel on the west side of a building at the end of the ridge of earth . . . (the ridge appears to cover a culvert leading to a mill of some kind and photographs indicate a wheel where Koch has none). I'll grant him minor errors like these for the invaluable contribution he has made to our knowledge of pioneer Salt Lake City."

10. Lithographic Images and Urban Analysis: Using Views to Study Cities

There are a number of ways scholars can use images of North American cities produced during the era of urban lithographic viewmaking. An individual city can be examined in detail to show many aspects of its land use and development. A view can also provide many helpful clues to the architectural character of a community. Views from two or more cities can be compared for a variety of purposes or as sources for images depicting such things as works of municipal engineering or maritime activities.

Museums often use city views for display and exhibit purposes, and the views can serve as guides for the construction of models of communities as they existed in the past. Finally, views may be enjoyed by their present owners for the same reasons as their original purchasers enjoyed them: as wall decorations for home or office or as treasured mementos of towns or cities where they lived. In this chapter we will explore these aspects of lithographic city views, beginning with some suggestions for analyzing a single city.

Plate 90 reproduces Camille N. Dry's view of Columbia, South Carolina, in 1872.[1] The several figures on the following pages show in diagrammatic form some of the major elements of Columbia's urban pattern as Dry recorded them well over a century ago. These drawings are based in part on the legend Dry provided but also on close study of the images of individual buildings on the view.

The simple graphic technique used here focuses attention on a single type of building or on a limited number of related buildings by showing them as black silhouettes against a subdued version of the lithograph. An even more flexible method but one not possible to demonstrate in book form is to draw each set of silhouettes on a sheet of transparent film. This makes it easy to superimpose any combination of these overlays to emphasize the spatial relationships (or the lack of them) between major functional components of the city.

The location of stores and offices and other commercial buildings can be shown in this manner, and the patterns that result tell us something about the character of the city under study. Information from the legend of the Columbia view made it possible to identify the city's hotels. The black silhouettes on Figure 17 represent the visible facades of the buildings as Dry drew them. More conventional mapping methods would have shown these locations by a symbol or by shading of either the foundation lines or the lots occupied by the buildings. The silhouette technique may not be locationally as precise, but it has the advantage of suggesting realistically the bulk of each structure.

1. The view is signed *C. M. Drie*, but the artist later changed the spelling to *Dry*.

The buildings shown in Figure 18 are the other commercial buildings of Columbia that Dry found in its central business district as well as in more isolated locations. These structures were identified solely through examination of details on the view and were those found to have flat roofs or false fronts. The false fronts, masking pitched roofs behind, are difficult to see on the reproduction in Plate 90, but they are quite obvious on the print itself. Almost certainly there are errors, both on Dry's part and in this interpretation of his work, but the general pattern of commercial development shown on the overlay should be substantially accurate.

Columbia clearly possessed a strong central business district. Aside from a group of commercial structures at the entrance to the city in the center background and a few small stores here and there, the only other places of business were located near the two railroad depots. The hotels follow this pattern as well, although the large hotel on the right seems to be in an unusual location. Probably it was related to the Presbyterian Theological Seminary just one block above, and it doubtless also served passengers arriving at the depot in the upper right on the line of the Charlotte, Columbia, and Augusta Railroad.

That and other railroads with their freight and passenger depots appear in Figure 19. This also locates the industries Dry identified in the legend. This overlay helps us understand a bit more about Columbia. It is obviously not a major industrial center, since there are very few industrial buildings. The most important must have been the railroad roundhouse and shops of the Charlotte, Columbia, and Augusta. The alignment of the lines suggests that Columbia was laid out before the era of railroad transportation. Neither line is centrally located, and the Greenville and Columbia line leading off to the left follows a course that runs diagonally through the grid of streets and must therefore have come after the town plan had been determined.

Railroad lines are also a reliable indicator of level land, since locomotives cannot negotiate steep grades. This is a help in studying the city, for Dry's rendering of Columbia's site is inadequate. The Congaree River and the railroad in the lower left tell us that this is the lowest part of the city. The looping route of the railroad at the bottom right provides a kind of contour line of equal elevation and suggests that the land slopes upward toward the center of the city. An elevated site would probably have been chosen for the state capitol, and its location fits the inference of topography based on the railroad right-of-way.

Figure 20 shows the other important element of the transportation system, the city's streets. One of the virtues of an accurately drawn view as compared to an official city map is

Figure 17. Hotels.

Figure 18. Commercial buildings.

Figure 19. Railroads, depots, and industry.

Figure 20. Streets.

that the view shows what streets were actually open for travel as distinguished from those existing merely as surveyed lines on some recorded plat. At the outskirts of the city on the left and right are a few large blocks through which intended streets have not yet been opened. Unfortunately, the view does not distinguish paved from unpaved streets. It is apparent that local travel took place on foot, on horseback, or by wagon, buggy, or carriage. There is no sign of a horse-drawn street railway, a feature that Drie surely would have depicted had one existed. Nor do there seem to be any vessels plying the waters of the Congaree River.

The unaltered view shows the street system with considerable clarity, but the overlay accentuates the prevailing uniformity of straight streets, right-angle intersections, and standardized blocks.[2] The blocks appear to be square, although one would need a street map—either old or new—to be confident about this. Whether square or not, uniform blocks permit a rough scaling of distances if any dimension is known on the ground that can be expressed in a fraction of a block width or length.[3]

As one might expect in a state capital, many of the blocks created by Columbia's grid system are occupied by public buildings of the state of South Carolina. Figure 21 shows these structures: the capitol (to the right and below the center of the view), the governor's residence (above and left of center), the penitentiary (at the far left), and the insane asylum (at upper right), consisting of two large buildings housing separate facilities for men and women. The other cluster of smaller structures at the lower right represents the buildings of the U.S. Army barracks and its drill ground. This was located adjacent to the campus of the University of South Carolina, whose buildings will appear in a subsequent illustration. Except for the capitol, these state and federal properties occupy sites at or near the periphery of the built-up portion of Columbia.

The location pattern for buildings housing functions of local government is quite different. Figure 22 shows that, with the exception of the waterworks at the far left, city and county buildings—city hall, courthouse, market, and jail— are all close to the central business district.[4] The overlay also locates the semicircular city park near the heart of the community, the rectangular boundary of the fairgrounds, and the irregular outline of the cemetery, which extends beyond the border of the view at the upper left. These strongly contrasting patterns reflect a mixture of functional, aesthetic, and psychological motives and decisions. Central locations for municipal buildings were selected to provide residents easy access to political decisionmakers, public records, po-

lice, and courts, among other offices significant in the daily life of a number of citizens.

State legislators also need to be near hotels, restaurants, and other central urban services, and they in turn generate the demand for such activities. The proximity of the capitol to the business district was thus almost inevitable. In addition, almost any city would regard the existence of a large and handsome capitol as a major civic asset and would seek to have it placed where it would be most visible to citizens and visitors alike.[5] The overlay suggests that quite different considerations governed the selection of sites for the state penitentiary and insane asylum. In the nineteenth century cities vied with one another to obtain these institutions because they provided jobs and increased local business. However, few persons regarded criminals or the insane as desirable neighbors. The compromise was to place such facilities at the edge of town and away from the best residential and commercial districts. Their locations in Columbia demonstrate the application of this policy.

Figures 23 and 24 show two other features of Columbia's development pattern: the placement of churches and the locations of educational institutions. Sites used for all but two of the eleven churches fall within a narrow zone running from the lower right to the upper center of the view. Church placement in the nineteenth century is almost always a reliable clue to the location of wealth in neighborhoods, which often lie beyond a fashionable "Church Street" situated on one side of the business district.

School locations provide another clue to types of neighborhoods. Figure 24 shows that three of the four educational institutions of Columbia are on the same side of town as the churches. The quadrangle at the lower right is the University of South Carolina; above it is the Presbyterian Theological Seminary; while beyond that is the building occupied by the Columbia Male Academy. On the other side of the business district is the public school—located across the street from the city jail.

The buildings shown in Figure 25 confirm what the previous two illustrations strongly suggest. This overlay locates all residential structures that appear to be substantially larger in size than the average Columbia house. Houses exceeding two stories in height or having unusually generous horizontal dimensions, or other large residences with such elaborate architectural features as porticoes, mansard roofs, and pediments, were identified for this purpose.[6]

The overlay clearly indicates the "good" residential neighborhoods of Columbia. One was fairly small and lay beyond the city park. The other was much larger and less regular in outline and was located just beyond the belt of churches to the right of the business district and capitol grounds. An overlay of the smallest houses in Columbia would be the

2. It also emphasizes the fact that Drie placed his vanishing points far off to the right and left. The effect is virtually like an axonometric drawing in which lines parallel on the ground do not converge on the drawing.

3. For example, if two streets parallel on the ground are known to be three hundred feet apart, one-third of that distance will equal one hundred feet. For all blocks of that size, one-third of their width will be one hundred feet no matter how large or small their images appear on the lithograph. The measurements of other objects within the block along the axis of known distance can be approximated by this method.

4. The courthouse shared a building with the post office. The other structure appearing on the view just beyond the semicircular park is the city reservoir.

5. Columbia was planned in 1786 as the state capital, and the commissioners responsible for the town plan were conscious of the desirability of locating the capitol on a prominent site. However, they designated only one block for this purpose, and it was not until later that the adjoining block was acquired so that the building could be placed on the axis of Main Street, the thoroughfare forming the spine of the business district.

6. Any two persons would differ somewhat in deciding which residences to distinguish, but the general patterns they would identify would probably not differ appreciably.

Figure 21. State and federal buildings.

Figure 22. Local government.

Figure 23. Churches.

Figure 24. Educational institutions.

Figure 25. Larger-than-average houses.

reverse image of this and would show that the residences of most low-income families could be found on the other side of the business district on land sloping down to the river.

Several other features of Columbia's physical pattern could be analyzed through the use of evidence appearing on the view or derived from further study of it.[7] However, these examples should suffice to demonstrate the usefulness of city views for such purposes and to suggest the range of further possibilities open to imaginative investigators.

What Dry's view reveals about Columbia's architecture also helps one to understand the character of the town.[8] The public buildings of the state give Columbia a strong neoclassical flavor. Those of the university reinforce this character. Its Greek Revival chapel closes the axis of Sumter Street, and its classroom and dormitory buildings are arranged in a formal, U-shaped court. Another major structure, the Presbyterian Theological Seminary, falls into this neoclassic pattern as well. Most of the large residences also exhibit classical motifs. Some are in the more restrained Federal style, while others feature columns and pediments marking them as Greek Revival.

More recent dwellings, almost certainly constructed after the Civil War, are in the Italianate style. They can be identified by their distinctive, low-hipped roofs surmounted by square cupolas. Six other large residences have mansard roofs, an architectural feature coming into fashion when the view was drawn. The city hall also has such a roof, indicating that it, too, was of recent construction.

Indeed, in 1872 the city was only completing the rebuilding begun after much of it was burned in February 1865 during General Sherman's occupation. It is unlikely that anyone could deduce this from the evidence of the view itself. However, a very large building that is either half destroyed or only partly completed can be seen on Gervais Street in the second block toward the river from the railroad tracks. Because the walls and window openings of this structure are standing alone, it is probably of brick or stone. Otherwise, the view does not distinguish between frame and brick or stone construction. However, most of the two- and three-story commercial buildings on Richardson Street are probably of brick, as doubtless are many of the larger mansions in the fashionable residential districts.

The public buildings and almost all of the churches are almost surely of brick or stone. The majority and most imposing of the latter are designed in Gothic fashion, with only the Baptist Church of the major congregations clinging to the older Greek Revival style. The several church spires and the capitol dome dominate the skyline from a distance, and within the town the many large residences and the buildings of university and local government provide additional points of visual interest within almost every block.

To end this brief architectural survey, we can conclude that a visitor at the time probably would have been favorably impressed by what he saw. Certainly residents—at least those of middle income and above—must have regarded Columbia with great satisfaction, both in real life and as Dry depicted it in his handsome lithograph. His view shows a place of harmony with variety, a character achieved through the unifying presence of trees along almost every street, buildings that did not soar beyond the human scale, and the use of a limited range of building materials and textures. Columbia may not have been architecturally the most exciting city in the nation, but it must have been far more attractive than most.

The preceding pages have discussed some of the ways in which a view can be used to examine the physical structure of a single city. Scholars interested in comparative studies of communities should also find these views invaluable. For example, it would be easy to prepare the same kinds of overlays showing major features of several other southern state capitals, such as Raleigh, Tallahassee, and Austin. All of these cities, like Columbia, were new towns planned as capital cities on virgin sites. Would one find similar development patterns? If not, what might explain the differences? What kinds of conclusions could be reached about the architectural styles in each place and what could that analysis reveal about other characteristics of these cities?

Clearly, the possibilities for comparative studies of this kind are legion because of the very large numbers of views of urban places of all types, sizes, ages, and locations. County seats, company towns, mining communities, resorts, college towns, seaports, and railroad towns are only a few of the types of places that might be studied with the aid of city views. For example, Plates 24, 40, and 41 show Berkeley, Austin, and Urbana, the locations of the state universities of California, Texas, and Illinois. Or, one could analyze a group of towns in the same region, such as the New England mill towns of Holyoke, Massachusetts (Plate 4), Pawtucket, Rhode Island (Plate 25), and Nashua, New Hampshire (Plate 67). How and why development patterns in each place differ or are similar should become more apparent through such an analysis, whether city views are used to supplement material from other sources or to provide the primary base of information.

7. For example, one could plot the locations of the very smallest residential structures. Or a rough measure of dwelling density could be obtained by simply counting the number of residential buildings within each block. This has some obvious limitations, since there is no way of knowing how many dwelling units each structure contains. Nevertheless, plotting the blocks with the highest and the lowest densities of residential structures might add to our understanding of Columbia in 1872. It should show that the highest density was in a block at the upper right, adjacent to the railroad shops and roundhouse. The view shows thirty-two small and identical houses there, doubtless a kind of company compound built by the railroad. Another type of graphic analysis that could be prepared is a building coverage or "figure ground" diagram. Foundation lines of each building could be traced and interpolated and the resulting rectangles inked in solidly. Such maps are commonly used by urban designers who feel that they gain from them a deeper understanding of spatial relationships in existing cities. There is no reason these insights could not be applied to communities of the past through the use of city views.

8. In dealing with this subject, I have received invaluable assistance from my departmental colleague Professor Michael Tomlan. At my request he examined the view and prepared an informal memorandum expressing his opinions of the images of buildings. This is dated 25 July 1983. A trained architect and architectural historian, professional photographer, and specialist in historic preservation, Tomlan proved uniquely qualified to help me. As a consultant in preservation planning, he also has used bird's-eye views in preparing inventories of historic buildings and nominating structures for inclusion in the National Register of Historic Places. In the paragraphs that follow I have, with his permission, occasionally quoted briefly or loosely paraphrased portions of his memorandum. I am grateful for his help. Any misinterpretations of what he wrote are, of course, my responsibility and not his.

City views also can be used in comparative studies that concentrate on a single urban function or building type and examine how location patterns vary from place to place. Thus, it would be fairly easy to analyze the placement of churches in, say, twenty towns of a region. Perhaps these towns could be subdivided into several groups based on their functional characteristics, size, date of settlement, or some other distinguishing feature. Would such a study reveal that the pattern found in Columbia was typical? Or would other patterns emerge? If so, would these vary according to the type or size or age of the communities? If the towns were in the South where viewmakers usually identified which churches had black congregations, could one use the locations of these churches to examine patterns of residential segregation?

The kinds of studies discussed so far deal only with those aspects of the community that the viewmaker chose to record or that could be derived from an analysis of his images. Such studies would not provide much information on how the community might have developed over time. Other kinds of research materials would be necessary to broaden the scope of such investigations. Most of these materials are readily available from local libraries, museums, and historical archives. They include census reports and enumeration schedules, city directories, property-line city maps, fire-insurance maps that distinguish between frame and masonry construction, old photographs, and other records familiar to students of urban studies. For example, city directories listing businesses by streets can be used with the images on a city view to construct a fairly precise land-use map of a commercial district. Or information from census schedules can be plotted on an overlay of a city view to provide an analysis of population density as related to dwelling size.

Persons wishing to extend studies over a period of time will often find that for the town or city in which they are interested two, three, or even more views exist. The use of multiple views makes possible more sophisticated studies of the pace and direction of growth and change. Just as time-lapse photography permits a viewer to perceive and understand how a plant grows, so, too, can the analysis of successive city views reveal fundamental trends in community development. An analysis could include the entire city at several times or could focus more sharply on a single component like industry or on an individual neighborhood or the central business district.

City views probably offer the best source of information for comparative studies of urban design. For example, the treatment of waterfronts in such places as Boston, Brooklyn, Chicago, Milwaukee, Omaha, San Francisco, and Seattle might begin with an examination of the views reproduced in Plates 6, 27, 34, 49, 50, 74, and 75 and with others of the same cities published in different years and perhaps from different viewpoints. These lithographs would not only provide an initial orientation but would also offer detailed glimpses of individual buildings and the related spaces that they form and from which they can be seen.

Architectural historians seeking to compare architectural designs for certain types of buildings can find city views of enormous help. They could, for example, investigate both the locations and the styles selected for state capitols in such diverse state seats of government as Bismarck, Albany, Boston, Madison, and—of course—Columbia, as illustrated in Plates 7, 13, 34, 68, and 90. An architectural historian concerned with the appearance of railroad depots and related structures in the nineteenth century could select from hundreds of views of towns and cities in all parts of the country in compiling a visual archive of these buildings. Such lithographs as those reproduced in Plates 29, 43, 45, and 59 illustrate the range of materials he would encounter in studying views of Albuquerque, Carson City, Washington, and Lincoln.

Elevation drawings appearing in the vignettes of such views as those by Kuchel & Dresel of towns in the West also constitute a rich resource for architectural historians (see Plates 21, 22, and 69). On a number of other views lacking vignettes one can still find meticulously rendered details of architectural features for at least the foreground structures. For example, the lithographs of Milwaukee, New Orleans, Baltimore, Sacramento, and Honolulu in Plates 9, 14, 15, 42, and 62 provide invaluable documentation of how certain major buildings in these cities appeared in the 1850s.

Important works of urban engineering are also on display in many views. These include such projects as the multiple canal locks at Lockport in 1826 (Plate 56), the levee on the waterfront of Sacramento in 1857 (Plate 42), the waterworks at Lincoln in 1889 (Plate 59), and—among many others—the bridges over the Rio Grande at Laredo in 1892 (Plate 70). Still other views show street railways, facilities for the "artificial moonlight" system of lighting cities by arc lamps placed on tall towers, breakwaters, wharves and docks, canals, irrigation systems, mine hoists and settling basins, and countless other elements of the urban landscape created by engineers and therefore of possible interest to persons concerned with the history of public works.[9]

For those concerned with methods of water transportation, the views provide what must be nearly a complete iconographic record of all kinds of ocean, lake, and river vessels. They appear in enormous profusion, ranging from oceangoing and coastal sailing ships in views like those showing Castine and Bangor, Maine (Plates 58 and 77); to sailing and steam-powered lake shipping in the views of Toronto (Plate 2) and Chicago (Plate 27); horse-drawn canal boats in the Lockport view of 1836 (Plate 1); Hudson River steamers in the lithograph of Albany (Plate 13); and Mississippi River stern- and side-wheelers in the depictions of St. Paul (Plate 5) and New Orleans (Plate 18).

Local historical societies frequently use city views as display items in their public exhibits or make them available as part of their library resources. However, one rarely finds any accompanying text or expanded legend explaining or elaborating on the images of the city as the viewmaker recorded it. In the absence of such descriptive or interpretive assistance, an uninitiated visitor can find it difficult to relate

9. The unique reports of the 1880 census dealing with urban improvements could be used in conjunction with a city view drawn about that time to produce a fascinating study of development patterns, density, building heights, and so on, as related to the distribution of urban utilities and other engineering improvements.

the modern city to an image of how it appeared many decades ago or can fail to realize how the view could be of assistance in understanding urban life in an earlier era.

Simple graphic aids, such as those used to analyze the view of Columbia, would make these views more understandable and appealing. More elaborate, but still within the means of most history museums, would be a recorded slide presentation using many details from the views to illustrate aspects of local history and trace changes in the community's physical structure. Even better would be to use video techniques to present the material in a more exciting and fluid manner. Both of these audiovisual methods would attract far more attention than even the best display of static graphics.

Views can also be used to prepare what many museum visitors find the most attractive and instructive of all displays: a model of the city as it existed some time in the past. Models have a fascination that even video lacks, for the selection of what to look at and how long to do so is left to the viewer and not the producer of the exhibit. Moreover, a museum docent or curator can use a model for a variety of purposes and for many types of audiences. Recorded narration, music, sound effects, and special lighting can also be used with the model to dramatize events and emphasize selected parts of the city or individual buildings.

Few museums have elected to build such exhibits, but those responsible for such decisions now have an elaborate prototype to follow. This a ten-foot-square model at a scale of one inch to fifty feet showing Salt Lake City in 1870, in the new museum of Mormon history that opened in that city in 1983. This huge and carefully constructed model is based primarily on Augustus Koch's lithograph of 1870, whose central portion is reproduced in Plate 83. In addition to being one of the featured exhibits of the museum, the model will provide realistic images for slide and video presentations. At least one of these will deal with the construction of the model itself. Other photographs of portions of the model will appear in a publication comparing segments of the model with old photographs of the same parts of the city.[10]

Although views can help in urban research, not only scholars can benefit by exposure to them; these lithographic images can be used for the purpose originally intended by the artists and publishers who made them available to their first owners: as decorative objects presenting cities as works of art for the delight and pride of their residents. Whether fortunate enough to own an original lithograph or obliged to rely on a facsimile, a modern owner can find the same satisfactions in city views as did those who first patronized the itinerant viewmakers of urban America who traveled the continent depicting its towns and cities.

10. The tests for historical accuracy of the view were described in Chapter 9. My information about the museum and the uses to which the model will be put are from Steven L. Olsen, Historical Department, Church of Jesus Christ of Latter-Day Saints, Salt Lake City, in a letter dated 11 April 1983.

Bibliography

1. General

"American City Prints." *Chicago History* 7 (Winter 1963–1964): 51–61.

"Bird's-Eye View of America." *Grit*, 15 December 1974, 36.

Carey, John Thomas. "The American Lithograph from Its Inception to 1865 with Biographical Considerations of Twenty Lithographers and a Check List of Their Works." Ph.D. diss., Ohio State University, 1954.

Cobb, Josephine. "Prints, the Camera, and Historical Accuracy." In *American Printmaking before 1876: Fact, Fiction, and Fantasy.* Washington, D.C.: Library of Congress, 1975.

Comstock, Helen. *American Lithographs of the Nineteenth Century.* New York: M. Barrows and Company, 1950.

Deak, Gloria-Gilda. *American Views: Prospects and Vistas.* New York: Viking Press and the New York Public Library, 1976.

Drepperd, Carl W. *Early American Prints.* New York: Century Co., 1930.

"Early Views of Midwestern American Cities." *Bulletin of the Chicago Historical Society* 2d ser., 2 (March 1936): 7–24.

Ebert, John, and Katherine Ebert. *Old American Prints for Collectors.* New York: Charles Scribner's Sons, 1974.

Edgerton, Samuel Y., Jr. *The Renaissance Rediscovery of Linear Perspective.* New York: Basic Books, 1975.

Editors of Time-Life Books. *The Rivermen.* With text by Paul O'Neil. New York: Time-Life Books, 1975.

Freeman, Graydon La Verne. *Historical Prints of American Cities.* Watkins Glen, N.Y.: Century House, 1952.

Holzer, Harold. "Bird's-Eye Maps: Regional Chauvinism in Lithographs." *The Antique Trader* 21 (20 July 1977): 40–44.

Karshan, Donald H. "American Printmaking, 1670–1968." *Art in America* 56 (July 1968): 22–55.

Kerfoot, Glenn. "Super Sleuth of the Bird's-eye Views." *The Antique Trader,* 29 July 1981, 80–83.

Krim, A. J. "Photographic Imagery of the American City, 1840–1860." *Professional Geographer* 25 (1973): 136–39.

Levine, Carol. "Bird's-Eye View Maps." *Americana* 14 (May 1976): 10–14.

Links, J. G. *Townscape Painting and Drawing.* London: B. T. Batsford, 1972.

Lipman, Jean. "American Townscapes." *Antiques* 46 (December 1944): 340–41.

Looney, Robert F. *Philadelphia Printmaking: American Prints before 1860.* West Chester, Pa.: Tinicum Press, 1976.

Mann, Maybelle. "American Landscape Prints." *Art and Antiques* 4 (May–June 1981): 90–98.

Marzio, Peter C., and Milton Kaplan. "Lithographs as Historical Documents." *Antiques* 102 (October 1972): 669–74.

Morse, John D., ed. *Prints in and of America to 1850.* Charlottesville: University Press of Virginia, 1970.

Peters, Harry T. *America on Stone: The Other Printmakers to the American People.* . . . Garden City, N.Y.: Doubleday, Doran and Co., 1931.

Rees, Ronald. "Historical Links between Cartography and Art." *Geographical Review* 70 (January 1980): 60–78.

Reps, John W. *Cities of the American West: A History of Frontier Urban Planning.* Princeton: Princeton University Press, 1979.

———. *Cities on Stone: Nineteenth Century Lithograph Images of the Urban West.* Fort Worth: Amon Carter Museum of Western Art, 1976.

Uhl, Charles. "'Every Building Is Accurately Represented': An Examination of Five Bird's Eye Views of Upstate New York." Master's thesis, Cornell University, 1983.

U.S. Library of Congress. *American Printmaking before 1876: Fact, Fiction, and Fantasy.* Washington, D.C.: Library of Congress, 1975.

Weitenkampf, Frank. "American City Views in American Prints." *Print Connoisseur* 5 (January 1925): 25–47.

———. *American Graphic Art.* New York: Macmillan Co., 1924.

2. Local, State, and Regional Studies

Angle, Paul M. "Views of Chicago 1866–1867." *Antiques* 63 (January 1953): 60–61.

"Art and Artists in Manchester." *Manchester Historic Association Collections* 4 (October–December 1902): 117–18.

"Artists Draw South Dakota: Panoramic Views of Pioneer Towns." *South Dakota History* 8 (Summer 1978): 221–49.

Avery, B. P. "Art Beginnings on the Pacific." *Overland Monthly* 1 (July 1868): 28–34; (August 1868): 113–19.

Baird, Joseph Armstrong, Jr. "Introduction." In *Historic Lithographs of San Francisco,* by Baird and Edwin Clyve Evans. San Francisco: Burger & Evans, 1972.

Bellman, David, ed. "Mount Royal Montreal." Supplement. *Canadian Art Review* 4, no. 2 (1977): S1–S30.

Bilodeau, Francis W., and Mrs. Thomas J. Tobias, comps. and eds. *Art in South Carolina, 1670–1970.* Columbia: South Carolina Tricentennial Commission, 1970.

Brooks, John G. "Historical Settings of Ithaca Paintings." In *Henry Walton: An Early Artist,* by Leigh Rehner. Ithaca, N.Y.: DeWitt Historical Society of Tompkins County, 1969.

Burnet, Mary Q. *Art and Artists of Indiana.* New York: Century Co., 1921.

Butts, Porter. *Art in Wisconsin.* Madison, Wisc.: Madison Art Association, 1936.

Coulter, Edith Margaret. "California Copyrights, 1851–1856, with Notes on Certain Ghost Books." *California Historical Society Quarterly* 22 (March 1943): 27–40.

Eckhardt, George H. "Early Lithography in Philadelphia." *Antiques* 28 (December 1935): 249–52.

Field, Ruth K. "Some Misconceptions about Lucas Place." *Missouri Historical Society Bulletin* 20 (January 1964): 119–23.

"Fowler's 26 W. Va. Towns." *West Virginia Hillbilly,* 2 July 1977, 8–9.

French, H. W. *Art and Artists in Connecticut.* Boston, 1879. Reprint. New York: Kennedy Graphics, 1970.

Graff, Nancy Price. "Flights of Imagination: Panoramas of Vermont." *Vermont Life* 35 (Fall 1980): 19–23.

Hoover, Catherine, and Robert Sawchuck. "'From the Place We Hear About . . .': A Descriptive Checklist of Pictorial Lithographs and Letter Sheets in the CHS Collections." *California Historical Society Quarterly* 56 (Winter 1977/1978): 346–67.

Horton, Loren N. "Through the Eyes of Artists: Iowa Towns in the

19th Century." *Palimpsest* 59 (September–October 1978): 133–47.

Howell, Warren R. "Lithographic Views of San Francisco Before the Gold Rush." Book Club of California, *Quarterly News Letter*, June 1938, 5–9.

———. "Pictorial Californiana." *Antiques* 65 (January 1954): 62–65.

Howell, Warren R., and Laura R. White. "California in Lithographs: Nineteenth Century Prints from the Robert B. Honeyman, Jr. Collection." In *The Westerners Brand Book, Los Angeles Corral*, 98–121. Los Angeles: Los Angeles Corral, [1957].

Kent, Alan E. "Early Commercial Lithography in Wisconsin." *Wisconsin Magazine of History* 36 (Summer 1953): 247–51.

Klein, Benjamin F. *Lithography in Cincinnati*. Cincinnati: Young & Klein, 1956.

Leonard, A. T., Jr. "California Lithographs." *Quarterly of the Society of California Pioneers* 9 (March 1932): 70–72.

Lewis, Henry. "Journal of a Canoe Voyage from the Falls of St. Anthony to St. Louis." *Minnesota History* 17 (June 1936): 150–58; (September 1936): 288–301; (December 1936): 421–36.

———. *The Valley of the Mississippi Illustrated*. Edited by Bertha L. Heilbron. Translated by A. Hermina Poatgieter. St. Paul: Minnesota Historical Society, 1967.

"Library of Congress Lists Fowler W. Va. Towns." *West Virginia Hillbilly*, 25 January 1975, 1, 7–9.

Lytle, Rebecca Elizabeth. "People and Places: Images of Nineteenth-Century San Diego." Master's thesis, San Diego State University, 1978.

———. "People and Places: Images of Nineteenth Century San Diego in Lithographs and Paintings." *Journal of San Diego History* 24 (Spring 1978): 153–71.

McDermott, John Francis. *The Lost Panoramas of the Mississippi*. Chicago: University of Chicago Press, 1958.

Madden, Betty I. *Art, Crafts, and Architecture in Early Illinois*. Urbana: University of Illinois Press, 1974.

Milbert, J. *Picturesque Itinerary of the Hudson River and the Peripheral Parts of North America*. Translated and annotated by Constance D. Sherman. Ridgewood, N.J.: Gregg Press, 1968.

Morris, Leopold. *Pictorial History of Victoria and Victoria County*. [San Antonio?]: N.p., 1953.

Munsell, Joel. *The Annals of Albany*. Vol. 1. Albany: Joel Munsel, 1850.

Peters, Harry T. *California on Stone*. Garden City, N.Y.: Doubleday, Doran & Co., 1935.

Pinckney, Pauline A. *Painting in Texas: The Nineteenth Century*. Ft. Worth: Amon Carter Museum of Western Art, 1967.

Piovesana, Roy H. "Panoramic Map of Port Arthur, 1885." *Thunder Bay Historical Museum Society Papers & Records* 7 (1979): 17–18.

"The River Towns of Henry Lewis." *The Iowan* 5 (February–March 1957): 13–15, 43.

Rutledge, Anna Wells. *Artists in the Life of Charleston Through Colony and State from Restoration to Reconstruction*. Transactions of the American Philosophical Society, n.s. 34, pt. 2. Philadelphia, 1949.

Scharff, Maurice R. "Collecting Views of Natchez." *Antiques* 65 (March 1954): 217–19.

Slater, Frederick W. "St. Joseph as it Looked in 1868." St. Joseph, Missouri, *News-Press*, 4 January 1976, section B, 1.

Sniffen, Harold S. "Southern Views in Prints." *Antiques* 60 (October 1951): 300–302.

Splitter, Henry Winfred. "Art in Los Angeles Before 1900—Part I." *Historical Society of Southern California Quarterly* 41 (March 1959).

Stokes, I. N. Phelps. *Iconography of Manhattan Island, 1498–1909*. 6 vols. New York: R. H. Dodd, 1915–1928.

"Texas In Pictures." *Antiques* 53 (June 1948): 453–59.

Utterback, Martha, comp. *Early Texas Art in the Witte Museum*. San Antonio: Witte Memorial Museum, 1968.

Van Nostrand, Jeanne. *A Pictorial and Narrative History of Monterey: Adobe Capital of California, 1770–1847*. San Francisco: California Historical Society, 1968.

van Ravenswaay, Charles. *The Arts and Architecture of German Settlements in Missouri*. Columbia: University of Missouri Press, 1977.

Van Zandt, Roland, comp. *Chronicles of the Hudson: Three Centuries of Travelers' Accounts*. New Brunswick, N.J.: Rutgers University Press, 1971.

Wainwright, Nicholas B. *Philadelphia in the Romantic Age of Lithography: An Illustrated History of Early Lithography in Philadelphia with a Descriptive List of Philadelphia Scenes made by Philadelphia Lithographers before 1866*. Philadelphia: Historical Society of Pennsylvania, 1958.

Watson, Douglas A. *California in the Fifties: Fifty Views of Cities and Mining Towns in California and the West*. San Francisco: J. Howell, 1936.

Weddell, Alexander Wilbourne. *Richmond Virginia in Old Prints, 1737–1887*. Richmond, Va.: Richmond Academy of Arts, 1932.

"Whitefield's Views of Chicago." *Chicago History* 3 (Fall 1951): 1–7.

Wild, J. C. *The Valley of the Mississippi Illustrated in a Series of Views*. Edited by Lewis Foulk Thomas. St. Louis: Joseph Garner, 1948.

Wilkie, Franc B. *Davenport Past and Present. . . .* Davenport, Iowa: Luse, Lane & Co., 1858.

3. Biographical Dictionaries and Encyclopedias

Bénézit, Emmanuel. *Dictionnaire des Peintres, Sculpteurs, Dessinateurs et Graveurs*. 8 vols. Paris: Librarie Grund, 1951.

Clement, Clara Erskine. *Artists of the Nineteenth Century and Their Works: A Handbook Containing Two Thousand and Fifty Biographical Sketches*. 2 vols. Boston: Houghton, Mifflin and Co., 1883.

Dawdy, Doris Ostrander. *Artists of the American West: A Biographical Dictionary*. Chicago: Sage Books, 1974.

Earle, Helen L. *Biographical Sketches of American Artists*. Lansing: Michigan State Library, 1915.

Fielding, Mantle. *Dictionary of American Painters, Sculptors and Engravers*. New York: James F. Carr, 1965.

French, H. W. *Art and Artists in Connecticut*. Boston and New York, 1879. Reprint. New York: Kennedy Graphics, Da Capo Press, 1970.

Groce, George C., and David H. Wallace. *The New-York Historical Society's Dictionary of Artists in America, 1564–1860*. New Haven: Yale University Press, 1957.

Johnson, Allen, ed. *Dictionary of American Biography*. 20 vols. New York: Charles Scribner's Sons, 1929–1936.

Mallett, Daniel Trowbridge. *Mallett's Index of Artists*. New York: P. Smith, 1948.

Moure, Nancy Dustin Wall. *Dictionary of Art and Artists in Southern California before 1930*. Los Angeles: Privately printed, 1975.

Samuels, Peggy, and Harold Samuels. *The Illustrated Biographical Encyclopedia of Artists of the American West*. Garden City, N.Y.: Doubleday & Co., 1976.

Smith, Ralph Clifton. *A Biographical Index of American Artists*. Baltimore: Williams & Wilkins Co., 1930.

Taft, Robert. *Artists and Illustrators of the Old West, 1850–1900*. New York: Charles Scribner's Sons, 1953.

Waters, Clara Erskine Clement, and Laurence Hutton. *Artists of the Nineteenth Century and Their Works*. Boston: Houghton, Mifflin and Co., 1894.

Young, William. *A Dictionary of American Artists, Sculptors and Engravers*. Cambridge, Mass.: William Young and Co., 1968.

4. Individual Artists, Lithographers, Printers, and Publishers

Alderfer, William K. "The Artist Gustav Pfau." *Journal of the Illinois State Historical Society* 60 (Winter 1967): 383–90.

Beckman, Thomas. "Louis Kurz: Early Years." *Imprint* 7 (Spring 1982): 14–25.

Bosqui, Edward. *Memoirs of Edward Bosqui*. Oakland: Holmes Book Co., 1952.

Burk, W. J. "Rudolph Ackerman, Promoter of the Arts and Sciences." *New York Public Library Bulletin* 38 (October 1934): 807–26; (November 1934): 939–53.

Burleigh, Lucien R. Obituary. *Journal of the Worcester Polytechnic Institute* 27 (November 1923): 29–30.

Burleigh, William H. *Poems by William H. Burleigh. With a Sketch of His Life by Celia Burleigh.* New York: Hurd and Houghton, 1871.

Burns, Susan. "Biographical Information: Grafton T. Brown, Black Artist and Lithographer." Unpublished biographical note. The Oakland Museum, Oakland, Calif., 1971.

Cochran, Carl Malcolm. "James Queen, Philadelphia Lithographer." *Pennsylvania Magazine of History and Biography* 82 (April 1958): 139–75.

Cumming, John. "Albert Ruger and His Views." Unpublished essay. Clarke Historical Library, Central Michigan University, Mount Pleasant.

Draper, Benjamin P. "John Mix Stanley, Pioneer Painter." *Antiques* 41 (March 1942): 180–82.

[Eddy, Elford]. *The Log of a Cabin Boy.* San Francisco: N.p., 1922.

William A. Farnsworth Library and Art Museum. *Fitz Hugh Lane, 1804–1865.* Rockland, Maine: William A. Farnsworth Library and Art Museum, 1974.

Fox, Michael J. "Joseph John Stoner, 1829–1918?" *Mapline: A Quarterly Newsletter,* Hermon Dunlap Smith Center for the History of Cartography at the Newberry Library, no. 9 (March 1978): unpaged.

Freeman, Larry. *Louis Prang: Color Lithographer, Giant of a Man.* Watkins Glen, N.Y.: Century House, 1971.

Gardner, John. "The Trouble Was Money—Too Much of It." *New York News,* 5 July 1953, 50.

Gideon, Samuel E. "Two Pioneer Artists in Texas." *American Magazine of Art* 9 (September 1918): 452–56.

Greene, Douglas G., and Michael Patrick Hearn. *W. W. Denslow.* [Mount Pleasant]: Clarke Historical Library, Central Michigan University, 1976.

Hammond, George P., ed. *The Larkin Papers: Personal, Business, and Official Correspondence of Thomas Oliver Larkin, Merchant and United States Consul in California,* 2: ix–x, 19–21; 8: 406–7. Berkeley: University of California Press, 1952.

Hartford, William J. *Benjamin Franklin Smith: A Biography of One of Maine's Successful Americans.* New York: Writers Press Association, 1925.

Havens, George R. *Frederick J. Waugh, American Marine Painter.* Orono: University of Maine Press, 1969.

Heffernan, John Paul. "A Maine Family of Smiths." *Down East: The Magazine of Maine* 21 (April 1975): 36–41, 66–70.

Heilbron, Bertha L. "Edwin Whitefield: Settlers' Artist." *Minnesota History* 40 (Summer 1966): 62–77.

———. "Making a Motion Picture in 1848: Henry Lewis on the Upper Mississippi," *Minnesota History* 17 (June 1936): 131–49.

Jackson, Joseph. "Bass Otis, America's First Lithographer." *Pennsylvania Magazine of History and Biography* 37, no. 4 (1913): 385–94.

Johnson, Bruce L. "Labels, Lithography, and Max Schmidt." *The Kemble Occasional,* no. 22 (Autumn 1979): 1–4.

Johnson, Lila M. "Found (and Purchased): Seth Eastman Water Colors." *Minnesota History* 42 (Fall 1971): 258–67.

Keith, Kent. "Sankt Antonius: Germans in the Alamo City in the 1850's." *Southwestern Historical Quarterly* 76 (October 1972): 183–202.

Knittle, Rhea Mansfield. "The Kelloggs, Hartford Lithographers." *Antiques* 10 (July 1926): 42–46.

Koke, Richard J. "John Hill, Master of Aquatint 1770–1850." *New-York Historical Society Quarterly* 43 (January 1959): 51–117.

Krohn, Ernst C., ed. "The Autobiography of William Robyn." *Bulletin of the Missouri Historical Society* 9 (January 1953): 141–54; (April 1953): 230–54.

Lipman, Jean. "Joseph H. Hidley (1830–1872), His New York Townscapes." *American Collector* 16 (June 1947): 10–11.

McCauley, Lois B. *A. Hoen on Stone: Lithographs of E. Weber & Co. and A. Hoen & Co., Baltimore, 1835–1869.* Baltimore: Maryland Historical Society, 1969.

McClinton, Katharine Morrison. *The Chromolithographs of Louis Prang.* New York: Clarkson N. Potter, 1973.

McDermott, John Francis. "J. C. Wild, Western Painter and Lithographer." *Ohio State Archaeological and Historical Quarterly* 60 (April 1951): 111–25.

———. "John Caspar Wild: Some New Facts and A Query." *Pennsylvania Magazine of History and Biography* 83 (October 1959): 452–55.

Mann, Maybelle. "Augustus Kollner." *Imprint* 6 (Spring 1981): 19–22.

Martin, Elizabeth R. "The Civil War Lithographs of Alfred E. Mathews." *Ohio History* 72 (July 1963): 231–42.

———. "Collections and Exhibits." *Ohio History* 72 (July 1963): 230–42.

Marzio, Peter C. *Mr. Audubon and Mr. Bien: An Early Phase in the History of American Chromolithography.* Washington, D.C.: Smithsonian Institution, National Museum of History and Technology, Hall of Printing and Graphic Arts, 1975.

Men of California. San Francisco: Pacific Art Co., 1901.

Merten, John W. "Stone by Stone Along a Hundred Years with the House of Strobridge." *Bulletin of the Historical and Philosophical Society of Ohio* 8 (January 1950): 3–48.

Nama, George A. *William Gillespie Armor, 1834–1924.* Pittsburgh: Historical Society of Western Pennsylvania, 1974.

[Newman, Harry Shaw?] "Kollner's Views of American Cities." *The Old Print Shop Portfolio* 3 (May 1944): 194–203.

———. "Rediscovery of a Distinguished Name." *The Old Print Shop Portfolio* 11 (January 1952): 119.

———. "The Magnificent Smiths." *The Old Print Shop Portfolio* 13 (January 1954): 99–102.

Norton, Bettina A. *Edwin Whitefield: Nineteenth-Century North American Scenery.* Barre, Mass.: Barre Publishing, 1977.

———. "Edwin Whitefield, 1816–1892." *Antiques* 102 (August 1972): 232–43.

———. "Sketching America: The New York Public Library's Sketchbook of the Nineteenth-Century American Artist and Traveler Edwin Whitefield." *Bulletin of Research in the Humanities* 81 (Summer 1978): 169–78.

———. "Tappan and Bradford: Boston Lithographers with Essex County Associations." *Essex Institute Historical Collections* 114 (July 1978): 149–60.

———. "William Sharp: Accomplished Lithographer." In *Art & Commerce: American Prints of the Nineteenth Century,* 51–75. Boston: Boston Museum of Fine Arts, 1978.

Phipps, Frances. "Connecticut's Printmakers: The Kelloggs of Hartford." *The Connecticut Antiquarian* 21 (June 1969): 19–26.

Pierce, Sally, and Temple D. Smith. *Citizens in Conflict: Prints and Photographs of the American Civil War.* Boston: Boston Athenaeum, 1981.

Powell, Mary M. "Three Artists of the Frontier." *Missouri Historical Society Bulletin* 5 (October 1948): 34–43.

Rehner, Leigh. *Henry Walton: 19th Century American Artist.* Ithaca, N.Y.: Ithaca College Museum of Art, 1968.

———. *Henry Walton: An Early Artist.* Ithaca, N.Y.: DeWitt Historical Society of Tompkins County, 1969.

Remarks on Remarkable Men. Doctor Bennett Monroe Pratt's Great Blackboard Lecture, Delivered in Stevens & Duncklee's New Opera House Block, Concord, N.H., April 1, 1886. Concord, N.H.: Printed by the Republican Press Association, 1886.

Rourke, Constance. "Voltaire Combe." In *The Roots of American Culture,* 251–61. New York: Harcourt Brace & Co., 1942.

Rusco, Elmer R. *"Good Time Coming?": Black Nevadans in the Nineteenth Century.* Westport, Conn.: Greenwood Press, 1975.

"S. St. J. Morgan Collection of Kellogg Prints." *Connecticut Historical Society Bulletin* 13 (October 1948): 25–32.

Shumate, Albert. *The Life of George Henry Goddard: Artist, Architect, Surveyor, and Map Maker.* Berkeley: Friends of the Bancroft Library, University of California, 1969.

Snyder, Martin P. "J. C. Wild and His Philadelphia Views." *Penn-*

sylvania Magazine of History and Biography 77 (January 1953): 32–75.

Stauffer, D. McN. "Lithographic Portraits of Albert Newsam." Pennsylvania Magazine of History and Biography 24 (1900): 267–89, 430–52.

Stephens, Stephen DeWitt. The Mavericks: American Engravers. New Brunswick, N.J.: Rutgers University Press, 1950.

Swanson, Evadene. "Early Fort Collins Artist a Mystery." Fort Collins, Colorado, Triangle Review, 6 May 1978, 7.

Tatham, David. "John Henry Bufford: American Lithographer," Proceedings of the American Antiquarian Society 86 (April 1976): 47–73.

———. "The Pendleton-Moore Shop—Lithographic Artists in Boston, 1825–1840." Old-Time New England 62 (Fall 1971): 29–46.

"Theodor Schrader, St. Louis Lithographer." Missouri Historical Society Bulletin 4 (January 1948).

Wagner, Henry R. "Albert Little Bancroft." California Historical Society Quarterly 24 (June 1950): 97–128; (September 1950): 217–27; (December 1950): 357–67.

Wainwright, Nicholas B. "Augustus Kollner, Artist." Pennsylvania Magazine of History and Biography 84 (July 1960): 325–51.

Waite, Emma F. "Pioneer Color Printer: F. Quarre." American Collector 11 (December 1946): 12–13, 20.

Warren, James Raymond, Sr. "Thaddeus Mortimer Fowler, Bird's-eye-view Artist." Special Libraries Association, Geography and Map Division, Bulletin, no. 120 (June 1980): 27–35.

Warren, James Raymond, Sr., and Donald A. Wise. "Two Birds-Eye-View Artists: The Bailey Brothers." Special Libraries Association, Geography and Map Division, Bulletin, no. 124 (June 1981): 20–30.

Wilmerding, John. Fitz Hugh Lane, 1804–1865: American Marine Painter. Gloucester, Mass.: Peter Smith, 1967.

———. Fitz Hugh Lane. New York: Praeger Publishers, 1971.

Winkworth, Peter. Scenes in Canada: C. Krieghoff Lithograph Drawings after His Paintings of Canadian Scenery, 1848–1862. Montreal: McCord Museum, 1962.

Wright, Edith A., and Josephine A. McDevitt. "Henry Stone, Lithographer." Antiques 34 (July 1938): 16–19.

Wright, Lewis R. "Edward Beyer and the Album of Virginia." Virginia Cavalcade 22 (April 1973): 36–44.

5. Nineteenth- and Early Twentieth-Century Works on Lithography

[Bankes, Henry.] Lithography; or, The Art of Taking Impressions from Drawings and Writing Made on Stone. 2d ed. London: Longman, Hurst, Rees, Orme, & Brown, 1816, in Henry Bankes's Treatise on Lithography, reprinted from the 1813 and 1816 editions with an introduction and notes by Michael Twyman. London: Printing Historical Society, 1976.

Colden, Cadwallader. Memoir Prepared at the Request of the Committee of the Common Council of the City of New York, and Presented to the Mayor of the City, at the Celebration of the Completion of the New York Canals. [New York]: Printed by Order of the Corporation of New York, 1825.

Freedley, Edwin Troxell, ed. Leading Pursuits and Leading Men. Philadelphia: E. Young, 1856.

Funk & Wagnalls Company. The Art of Lithography. [New York?]: Funk & Wagnalls Co., n.d.

Hansard, T. C. Typographia: An Historical Sketch of the Origin and Progress of the Art of Printing. . . . London: Baldwin, Cradock, and Joy, 1825.

Hazen, Edward. The Panorama of Professions and Trades. Philadelphia: Uriah Hunt, 1836.

Hullmandel, Charles. The Art of Drawing on Stone, Giving a Full Explanation of the Various Styles, of the Different Methods to be Employed to Ensure Success, and of the Modes of Correcting, as well as of the Several Causes of Failure. London: C. Hullmandel, 1824.

———. "Lithography." No. 1 of "Papers in Polite Arts" in Transactions of the Society for the Encouragement of Arts, Manufacturers and Commerce, London, 37 (1820): 53–57.

Knight, Edward H., comp. Knight's American Mechanical Dictionary. Boston: Houghton, Mifflin & Co., 1872.

"Lithography." American Supplement to Encyclopaedia Britannica (Ninth Edition), 3: 621–22. Philadelphia: Hubbard Brothers, 1889.

"Lithography." The Analectic Magazine 14 (July 1819): 66–72.

"Lithography." Appleton's Dictionary of Machines, Mechanics Engine-Work and Engineering, vol. 2. New York: Appleton, 1851.

"Lithography." The Edinburgh Encyclopaedia . . . First American Edition. . . , 12: 91–95. Philadelphia: Joseph and Edward Parker, 1832.

"Lithography." United States Literary Gazette 4 (15 June 1826): 224–27.

Mallet, Robert, ed. The Practical Mechanics' Journal, Scientific Record of the International Exhibition of 1862. . . . London: Longman, Green, Longman, and Roberts, 1862.

Miller, Alexr. The Hand-Book of Transfer Lithography. Liverpool: Evans, Chegwin & Hall, 1840.

"The New Art of Lithotint." Miss Leslie's Magazine, April 1843, 113–14.

"A New Career for Lithography." Chambers' Edinburgh Journal, n.s. 20, no. 521 (24 December 1853): 404–6.

Pennell, Joseph, and Elizabeth Robins Pennell. Lithography and Lithographers. London: T. Fisher Unwin, 1898.

The Philadelphia Photographer 13 (August 1876).

"Printing by Magic." Chambers's Journal of Popular Literature, Science, and Arts 1, no. 5 (4 February 1854): 68–70.

Richmond, W. D. Colour and Colour Printing as Applied to Lithography. . . . London: Wyman & Sons, [1885].

———. The Grammar of Lithography, a Practical Guide for the Artist and Printer in Commercial & Artistic Lithography, & Chromo-lithography, Zincography, Photo-lithography, and Lithographic Machine Printing. 2d ed. London: Wyman & Sons, 1880.

Ringwalt, J. Luther, ed. American Encyclopaedia of Printing. Philadelphia: Menamin & Ringwalt and J. B. Lippincott & Co., 1871.

Scott, A. De C. On Photo-Zincography and Other Photographic Processes Employed at the Ordinance Survey Office, Southampton. 2d ed. London: Longman, Green, Longman, Roberts, & Green, 1863.

Senefelder, Alois. A Complete Course of Lithography: Containing Clear and Explicit Instructions in all the Different Branches and Manners of that Art . . . to which is Prefixed a History of Lithography, from its Origin to the Present Time. London: R. Ackermann, 1819. Reprinted, with an Introduction by A. Hyatt Mayor, New York: Da Capo Press, 1977.

Seymour, Alfred. Practical Lithography. London: Scott, Greenwood & Son, 1903.

Wilkinson, W. T. Photo-Engraving, Photo-Etching, and Photo-Lithography in Line and Half-Tone; also, Collotype and Heliotype. Revised and enlarged by Edward L. Wilson. 3d ed. New York: Edward L. Wilson, 1888.

6. History and Techniques of Lithographic Printing

Antreasian, Garo Z., and Clinton Adams. The Tamarind Book of Lithography: Art and Techniques. New York: Harry N. Abrams, 1971.

Brunner, Felix. A Handbook of Graphic Reproduction Processes. 2d ed. Teufen, Switzerland: Arthur Niggli, 1964.

Gardner, Robert. Review of The Technique of Fine Lithography by Michael Knigin and Murray Similes (New York: Van Nostrand Reinhold Company, 1970). The Print Collector's Newsletter 1 (September–October 1970): 92–93.

Hitchings, Sinclair H. "'Fine Art Lithography' in Boston: Craftsmanship in Color, 1840–1900." In Art & Commerce: American Prints of the Nineteenth Century, 103–25. Boston: Museum of Fine Arts, 1978.

Koeman, C. "The Application of Photography to Map Printing and the Transition to Offset Lithography." In *Five Centuries of Map Printing*, edited by David Woodward, 137–55. Chicago: University of Chicago Press, 1975.

Langstroth, T. A. *The History of Lithography Mainly in Cincinnati (March, 1958)*. Scrapbook with typed text. Art and Music Division, Cincinnati, Ohio, Public Library.

Latimer, H. C. "History of the Lithographic Industry." In *75 Years of Lithography*, edited by Patricia Donnelly, 5–23. N.p.: Amalgamated Lithographers of America, 1957.

Marzio, Peter C. "American Lithographic Technology before the Civil War." In *Prints in and of America to 1850*, edited by John D. Morse, 215–56. Winterthur Conference Report. Charlottesville: University Press of Virginia, 1970.

———. "The Democratic Art of Chromolithography in America: An Overview." In *Art & Commerce: American Prints of the Nineteenth Century*, 77–102. Boston: Boston Museum of Fine Arts, 1978.

———. *The Democratic Art: Pictures for a 19th-Century America*. Boston: David R. Godine, in association with the Amon Carter Museum of Western Art, Fort Worth, 1979.

Mumford, I. "Lithography, Photography and Photozincography in English Map Production Before 1870." *Cartographic Journal* 9 (1972): 30–35.

Ristow, Walter W. "Lithography and Maps, 1796–1850." In *Five Centuries of Map Printing*, edited by David Woodward, 77–112. Chicago: University of Chicago Press, 1975.

Robinson, William F. *A Certain Slant of Light*. Boston: New York Graphic Society, 1980.

Saff, Donald, and Deli Sacilotto. *Printmaking: History and Process*. New York: Holt, Rinehart and Winston, 1978.

Taft, Robert. *Photography and the American Scene: A Social History, 1839–1889*. 1938. Reprint. New York: Dover Publications, 1964.

Taylor, Charles Henry. "Some Notes on Early American Lithography." American Antiquarian Society, *Proceedings*, n.s. 32 (April 1922): 68–80.

Twyman, Michael L. "The Lithographic Hand Press 1796–1850." *Journal of the Printing Historical Society*, no. 3 (1967): 3–50.

———. *Lithography, 1800–1850: The Techniques of Drawing on Stone in England and France and Their Application in Works of Topography*. London: Oxford University Press, 1970.

Wakeman, Geoffrey. *Aspects of Victorian Lithography: Anastatic Printing and Photozincography*. Wymondham, England: Brewhouse Press, 1970.

Weber, Wilhelm. *A History of Lithography*. London: Thames and Hudson, 1966.

Weitenkampf, Frank. "Lithographs." In *The Concise Encyclopedia of American Antiques*, edited by Helen Comstock, 2: 371–75. 2 vols. New York: Hawthorn Books, 1958.

7. Catalogs of Institutional Collections Containing Lithographic City Views

Amon Carter Museum of Western Art. *Catalogue of the Collection, 1972*. Fort Worth: Amon Carter Museum of Western Art, 1973.

Canada. Public Archives. National Map Collection. *Catalogue of the National Map Collection, Public Archives of Canada*. 16 vols. Boston: G. K. Hall, 1976.

———. *County Maps: Land Ownership Maps of Canada in the 19th Century*. Compiled by Heather Maddick. Ottawa: Public Archives of Canada, 1976.

Hemenway, Alice. "Lithographs in the Collections of the New York State Historical Association." Master's thesis, State University of New York, Oneonta, 1976.

Jefferys, Charles W. W., comp. *A Catalogue of the Sigmund Samuel Collection Canadiana and Americana*. Toronto: Ryerson Press, 1948.

Mariners Museum. *Catalog of Marine Prints and Paints, Mariners Museum Library, Newport News, Virginia*. 3 vols. Boston: G. K. Hall & Co., 1964.

"Panoramic Views of Connecticut." *Connecticut Historical Society Bulletin* 20 (April 1955): 52–61.

Simonetti, Martha L., comp. *Descriptive List of the Map Collection in the Pennsylvania State Archives*. Harrisburg: Pennsylvania Historical and Museum Commission, 1976.

Society of California Pioneers. *Annual Publication of the Society for the Year 1955*, 14–21. Catalog of Topographic Prints, Drawings, and Paintings, compiled by Elliot A. P. Evans, assisted by Helen S. Giffen.

Stokes, I. N. Phelps, and Daniel C. Haskell. *American Historical Prints: Early Views of American Cities, etc. From the Phelps Stokes and Other Collections*. New York: New York Public Library, 1932.

Texas State Library, Austin. Archives Division. *The Map Collection of the Texas State Archives, 1527–1900*. Compiled by James M. Day and Ann B. Dunlap. Austin: Texas State Library, 1962.

Toronto Public Libraries. *Landmarks of Canada: A Guide to the J. Ross Robertson Canadian Historical Collection in the Toronto Public Library*. 3 vols. Toronto: [Toronto Public Library?], 1917–1921 (vol. 1 & 2); Baxter Publ. Co., 1964 (vol. 3). Reprinted in one vol., 1967.

U.S. Library of Congress. *Land Ownership Maps: A Checklist of Nineteenth Century United States County Maps in the Library of Congress*. Compiled by Richard W. Stephenson. Washington, D.C.: Library of Congress, 1967.

———. *Panoramic Maps of Anglo-American Cities: A Checklist of Maps in the Collections of the Library of Congress, Geography and Map Division*. Compiled by John R. Hébert. Washington, D.C.: Library of Congress, 1974.

———. *Panoramic Maps of Cities in the United States and Canada: A Checklist of Maps in the Collections of the Library of Congress, Geography and Map Division*. John R. Hébert and Patrick E. Dempsey, comps. Washington, D.C.: Library of Congress, 1984.

———. Division of Maps. *List of Maps and Views of Washington and District of Columbia in the Library of Congress*. Compiled by Phillip Lee Philips. Washington, D.C.: Government Printing Office, 1900.

———. Prints and Photographic Division. *Pictorial Americana*. Compiled by Milton Kaplan. 2d ed. Washington, D.C.: Library of Congress, 1955.

Weitenkampf, Frank, ed. *The Eno Collection of New York City Views*. New York: New York Public Library, 1925. Reprint. Ann Arbor, Mich.: Gryphon Books, 1971.

8. Exhibition Catalogs, Checklists, and Pictorial Records

Allodi, Mary. *Printmaking in Canada: The Earliest Views and Portraits*. Toronto: Royal Ontario Museum, 1980.

Baird, Joseph Armstrong, Jr., and Edwin Clyve Evans. *Historic Lithographs of San Francisco*. San Francisco: Burger & Evans, 1972.

Beckman, Thomas. *Milwaukee Illustrated: Panoramic and Bird's-Eye Views of a Midwestern Metropolis, 1844–1908*. Milwaukee: Milwaukee Art Center, 1978.

Bland, Jane Cooper. *Currier and Ives: A Manual for Collectors*. Garden City, N.Y., 1931.

Brooks, Helen, and Karen Pearson. "Nebraska Towns on View." Exhibition handlist. Sheldon Art Gallery, Lincoln, Nebr., 1981.

Canada. Public Archives. *Bird's-Eye Views of Canadian Cities: An Exhibition of Panoramic Maps (1865–1905) . . . July to November 1976*. Exhibition handlist reproduced from typewritten copy. Ottawa: Public Archives of Canada, 1976.

Cantor, Jay E. *The Landscape of Change: Views of New England, 1790–1865*. Sturbridge, Mass.: Old Sturbridge Village, 1976.

Club of Odd Volumes. *Notes on an Exhibition of Early American Lithographs, 1819–1859. . . .* Boston: Club of Odd Volumes, 1924.

Cobb, David A. *New Hampshire Maps to 1900: An Annotated Checklist*. Concord: New Hampshire Historical Society, 1981.

Conningham, Frederic A. *Currier & Ives Prints: An Illustrated Check List.* Updated by Colin Simkin. New York: Crown Publishers, 1970.

Cumming, John. *A Preliminary Checklist of 19th Century Lithographs of Michigan Cities and Towns.* Mount Pleasant: Clarke Historical Library, Central Michigan University, 1969.

deVolpi, Charles P. *The Niagara Peninsula, A Pictorial Record: Historical Prints and Illustrations of the Niagara Peninsula Province of Ontario, 1697–1880.* Montreal: Dev-Sco Publications, 1966.

———. *Newfoundland: A Pictorial Record: Historical Prints and Illustrations of the Province of Newfoundland, Canada, 1497–1887.* Don Mills, Ontario: Longman Canada, 1972.

———. *Nova Scotia, A Pictorial Record: Historical Prints and Illustrations of the Province of Nova Scotia Canada, 1605–1878.* N.p.: Longman Canada, 1974.

———. *Ottawa, A Pictorial Record: Historical Prints and Illustrations of the City of Ottawa, Province of Ontario, Canada, 1807–1882.* Montreal: Dev-Sco Publications, 1964.

———. *Quebec, A Pictorial Record: Historical Prints and Illustrations of the City of Quebec, Province of Quebec, Canada, 1608–1875.* N.p.: Longman Canada, 1971.

———. *Toronto, A Pictorial Record: Historical Prints and Illustrations of the City of Toronto, Province of Ontario, Canada, 1813–1882.* Montreal: Dev-Sco Publications, [1965].

deVolpi, Charles P., and P. H. Scowen. *The Eastern Townships: A Pictorial Record, Historical Prints and Illustrations of the Eastern Townships of the Province of Quebec Canada.* Montreal: Dev-Sco Publications, 1962.

deVolpi, Charles P., and Peter S. Winkworth. *Montreal, A Pictorial Record.* 2 vols. Montreal: Dev-Sco Publications, 1963.

William A. Farnsworth Library and Art Museum. *Through a Bird's Eye: Nineteenth-Century Views of Maine.* Compiled by Christine Bauer Podmaniczky. Rockland, Maine: William A. Farnsworth Library and Art Museum, 1981.

Goldsmith, Henry. *The Notable Henry Goldsmith Collection: Historical Maps, Views, Original Drawings, China Relating to New York City.* Catalog Descriptions by Robert Fridenberg. New York: American Art Association, [1926].

Hufeland, Otto. *A Check List of Books, Maps, Pictures and other Printed Matter Relating to the Counties of Westchester and Bronx.* White Plains, N.Y.: Westchester County Historical Society, 1929.

McCauley, Lois B. *Maryland Historical Prints, 1752 to 1889: A Selection from the Robert G. Merrick Collection, Maryland Historical Society and other Maryland Collections.* Baltimore: Maryland Historical Society, 1975.

McClintock, Gilbert Stuart. *Valley Views of Northeastern Pennsylvania. . . .* Wilkes-Barre, Pa.: Wyoming Historical and Geological Society, 1948.

Maule, Elizabeth Singer, comp. *Bird's Eye Views of Wisconsin Communities: A Preliminary Checklist.* Madison: State Historical Society of Wisconsin, 1977.

Merrimack Valley Textile Museum. *New City on the Merrimack: Prints of Lawrence, 1845–1876.* North Andover, Mass.: Merrimack Valley Textile Museum, 1974.

Moffat, Riley Moore. *Printed Maps of Utah to 1900.* Occasional Paper no. 8. N.p.: Western Association of Map Libraries, 1981.

Munsing, Stefanie A. *Made in America: Printmaking 1760–1860.* Philadelphia: Library Company of Philadelphia, 1973.

Munson-Williams-Proctor Institute. *Made in Utica.* Utica, N.Y.: Munson-Williams-Proctor Institute, 1976.

Old Dartmouth Historical Society. *New Bedford and Old Dartmouth: A Portrait of a Region's Past.* New Bedford, Mass., 1975.

Pasadena Art Institute. *Early Prints of California from the Robert B. Honeyman Collection.* Pasadena, Calif.: Pasadena Art Institute, 1952.

Pennsylvania State University. Museum of Art. *Pennsylvania Prints from the Collection of John C. O'Connor and Ralph M. Yeager: Lithographs, Engravings, Aquatints, and Watercolors from The Tavern Restaurant.* Compiled by Judith W. Hansen. Entry information from notes by John C. O'Connor and Ralph M. Yeager. University Park: Museum of Art, Pennsylvania State University, 1980.

Peters, Harry T. *Currier & Ives: Printmakers to the American People.* 2 vols. Garden City, N.Y.: Doubleday, Doran & Co., 1929–1931.

Philadelphia Museum of Art. *Philadelphia: Three Centuries of American Art.* Philadelphia: Philadelphia Museum of Art, 1975.

Pyne, Percy R. *Illustrated Catalogue of the Notable Collection of Views of New York and Other American Cities . . . Formed by Mr. Percy R. Pyne 2d.* Catalog descriptions by Robert Fridenberg. New York: American Art Association, 1917.

Rathbone, Perry T., ed. *Westward the Way: The Character and Development of the Louisiana Territory as Seen by Artists and Writers of the Nineteenth Century.* St. Louis: City Art Museum of St. Louis, 1954.

Ristow, Walter W. *Maps for an Emerging Nation: Commercial Cartography in Nineteenth-Century America, an Exhibition at the Library of Congress.* Washington, D.C.: Library of Congress, 1977.

Rochester University. Memorial Art Gallery. *The Genessee Country.* Essay by Henry W. Clune. Introduction and catalog by Howard S. Merritt. Rochester, N.Y.: Memorial Art Gallery of the University of Rochester, 1975.

Rose, Roger G. *Hawai'i: The Royal Isles.* Special Publication no. 67. Honolulu: Bishop Museum Press, 1980.

Schurre, Jacques. *Currier & Ives Prints: A Checklist of Unrecorded Prints Produced by Currier & Ives, N. Currier and C. Currier.* [New York?]: Jacques Schurre, 1970.

Spendlove, F. St. George. *The Face of Early Canada: Pictures of Canada Which Have Helped to Make History.* Toronto: Ryerson Press, 1958.

Stokes, Anson Phelps. *Historical Prints of New Haven, Connecticut. . . .* New Haven, Conn.: N.p., 1910.

Stout, Leon J. "Pennsylvania Towns Views, 1850–1922; A Union Catalogue." *The Western Pennsylvania Historical Magazine* 18 (July 1975): 409–28; (October 1975): 546–71; 59 (January 1976): 88–109.

Thomas, Samuel W., ed. *Views of Louisville Since 1766.* Louisville, Ky.: N.p., 1971.

Views of Lowell, 1825–1976. Catalog of Exhibit Sponsored by the Lowell Historical Society, April 4–April 25, 1976. Lowell, Mass.: Lowell Historical Society, 1976.

9. Newspapers

Akron, Ohio, *Beacon Journal.* 13 November 1899.

Albany, New York, *Microscope.* [Date unknown] 1845.

Albion, Michigan, *Recorder.* 21 June 1890.

Alexandria, Virginia, *Alexandria Gazette and Virginia Advertiser.* 24 August 1853 and 2 January 1854.

Asheville, North Carolina, *Daily Citizen.* 15 December 1890 and 15 January and 12 May 1891.

Ashland, New Hampshire, *Advance.* 22 September 1883.

Aurora, Illinois, *Beacon.* 31 October 1867.

Austin, Texas, *Daily Democratic Statesman.* 9 January and 9 April 1873.

Baltimore, Maryland, *American & Commercial Advertiser.* 1 July 1853.

Baltimore, Maryland, *Sun.* 22 October 1869.

Bangor, Maine, *Daily Whig and Courier.* [Date unknown] 1854.

Beatrice, Nebraska, *Express.* 26 February and 16 July 1874.

Belknap, New Hampshire, *Toscin.* 27 September 1883.

Bellefonte, Pennsylvania, *Democratic Watchman.* 19 July and 29 August 1878.

Bellefonte, Pennsylvania, *Republican.* 28 June and 17 and 24 July 1878.

Belleville, Illinois, *Advocate*. 21 June 1867.

Bellows Falls, Vermont, *Times*. 27 May 1886.

Bethlehem, New Hampshire, *White Mountain Echo*. 4 August 1883.

Binghamton, New York, *Daily Democrat*. 31 July 1873.

Binghamton, New York, *Daily Times*. 1 August 1873.

Bristol, New Hampshire, *Weekly Enterprise*. 22 May and 5 June 1884.

Brockton, Massachusetts, *Enterprise*. 18 August 1926.

Brockton, Massachusetts, *Times*. 18 August 1926.

Brooklyn, New York, *Daily Eagle*. [Date unknown] 1846.

Buffalo, New York, *Morning Express*. [Date unknown] 1848.

Canajoharie, New York, *Radii*. 20 January 1881.

Central City, Colorado, *Daily Miners' Register*. 21 July 1868.

Centralia, Illinois, *Centinel*. 25 July 1867.

Charlottetown, Prince Edward Island, *Daily Examiner*. 9 July, 22 August, and 25 November 1878.

Chicago, Illinois, *Daily Democratic Press*. 20 March 1856.

Chillicothe, Ohio, *Advertiser*. 16 November 1888 and 11 January 1889.

Chillicothe, Ohio, *The Scioto Gazette*. 8 May and 3 October 1854 and 21 and 23 March and 22 October 1855.

Claremont, New Hampshire, *National Eagle*. 16 June and 22 and 29 September 1877.

Claremont, New Hampshire, *Northern Advocate*. 19 June and 3 July 1877.

Clyde, New York, *Democratic Herald*. 18 and 25 May 1892.

Concord, New Hampshire, *Christian Science Sentinel*. 7 December 1899.

Concord, New Hampshire, *Daily Monitor*. 25 September 1875 and 3 June 1982.

Danville, Illinois, *Commercial*. 29 July 1869.

Denison, Texas, *Sunday Gazetteer*. 11 January 1891.

Denver, Colorado, *Rocky Mountain News*. 13 November 1865, 19 October 1866, 5 July 1869, 4 November 1874, 2 October 1881, and 9 May 1882.

Derry, New Hampshire, *News*. 6 May 1887, 18 February and 18 and 26 March 1898.

Des Moines, Iowa, *Daily State Register*. 14 July 1868.

Detroit, Michigan, *Daily Union*. 18 January 1872.

Detroit, Michigan, *Free Press*. 22 February 1871.

Dunbarton and Pittsfield, New Hampshire, *The Analecta*. 31 July 1884.

Exeter, New Hampshire, *Gazette*. 24 October 1884 and 22 May 1896.

Franklin, New Hampshire, *Merrimack Journal*. 21 November 1884.

Fremont, Nebraska, *Weekly Herald*. 21 and 28 August and 6 November 1884, 4 and 18 July and 24 October 1889.

Fremont, Nebraska, *Weekly Tribune*. 20 August 1884 and 25 July 1889.

Friendville, Nebraska, *Telegraph*. 12 September 1879.

Gloucester, Massachusetts, *Telegraph*. 16 March 1836 and 25 November 1846.

Gorham, New Hampshire, *Mountaineer*. 6 January 1888.

Grand Rapids, Michigan, *Daily Eagle*. 18 March 1868.

Great Falls, New Hampshire, *Free Press*. 31 August 1877.

Groton, New York, *Groton and Lansing Journal*. 30 April and 20 August 1885.

Halifax, Nova Scotia, *Evening Reporter*. 20 August 1878.

Hastings, Nebraska, *Journal*. 17 July 1879.

Hebron, Nebraska, *Journal*. 11 October and 29 November 1883.

Henniker, New Hampshire, *Courier*. 3 October 1889.

Hinsdale, New Hampshire, *Valley Record*. 11 December 1885, 21 and 28 May, and 4 June 1886.

Honolulu, Hawaii, *The Friend*. 1 November 1854.

Hudson, Ohio, *Independent*. 17 November 1899.

Indianapolis, Indiana, *Journal*. 5 January 1855.

Ionia, Michigan, *County Sentinel*. 1 May 1868.

Ithaca, New York, *Weekly Chronicle*. 11 March and 17 April 1840 and 5 and 12 October 1853.

Ithaca, New York, *Daily Journal*. 9 August, 21 October, and 4 December 1873, 16 June and 18 August 1882, and 29 January 1883.

Ithaca, New York, *Democrat*. 23 May 1838, 9 August 1873, and 15 June and 24 August 1882.

Ithaca, New York, *Journal & General Advertiser*. 15 August 1835, 12 October 1836, 2 August 1837, 23 May, 27 June, and 1 August 1838, 10, 13, and 17 July and 4 December 1839.

Jefferson, New York, *Jeffersonian*. 25 December 1847.

Kalamazoo, Michigan, *Gazette*. 7 August 1874.

Kearney, Nebraska, *Daily Hub*. 8 October 1889.

Keene, New Hampshire, *Cheshire Republican*. 21 July 1877.

Keene, New Hampshire, *Sentinel*. 11 October 1877.

Laconia, New Hampshire, *Democrat*. 13 July 1883 and 12 April 1889.

Lancaster, New Hampshire, *Gazette*. 17 August 1883.

Lansing, Michigan, *State Republican*. 9 June 1890.

Lawrence, Kansas, *Kansas Daily Tribune*. 6 January 1869.

Leavenworth, Kansas, *Bulletin*. 8 September 1865.

Lebanon, New Hampshire, *Granite State Free Press*. 15 August 1884.

Lexington, Kentucky, *Kentucky Gazette*. 21 December 1870.

Lincoln, Illinois, *Herald*. 10 June 1869.

Lincoln, Nebraska, *Daily Globe*. 2 August 1880.

Lincoln, Nebraska, *Daily Nebraska State Journal*. 10 April and 10 July 1874, 24 May 1885, and 1 and 2 June 1889.

Littleton, New Hampshire, *Journal*. 21 December 1883.

Littleton, New Hampshire, *White Mountain Republic*. 4 April, 14 and 21 July, 29 September, 13 October, and 8 December 1883.

Los Angeles, California, *Daily Star*. 27 and 28 April 1871, and 18 January 1877.

Los Angeles, California, *Express*. 11 January and 19 April 1873.

Los Angeles, California, *Herald*. 9 June 1876 and 15 July 1887.

Louisville, Kentucky, *Daily Journal*. 15 August 1855.

Louisville, Kentucky, *Morning Courier*. [Date unknown] 1848.

McGregor, Iowa, *North Iowa Times*. 22 September 1869.

Manchester, New Hampshire, *Daily Union*. 21 August 1875 and 8 February 1876.

Manchester, New Hampshire, *Mirror and American*. 21 August 1875.

Mankato, Minnesota, *Record*. 5 March 1870.

Marshalltown, Iowa, *Marshall County Times*. 15 August 1868.

Middlebury, Vermont, *Register*. 20 November 1885 and 16 April 1886.

Milwaukee, Wisconsin, *Daily News*. 11 September 1856, 15 November 1866, and 17 January 1872.

Milwaukee, Wisconsin, *Sentinel*. November 1866, 17 January 1872, and 22 February 1876.

Miramichi, New Brunswick, *Advance*. 5 May 1881.

Monroe, Michigan, *Commercial*. 11 June 1866.

Montana [now Boone], Iowa, *Boone County Democrat*. 19 August 1868.

Nashua, New Hampshire, *Daily Gazette*. 11 April 1883.

Nashua, New Hampshire, *Daily Telegraph*. 25 June, 10 and 13 November 1875, 11 October and 2 November 1882, and 8 April 1883.

Nebraska City, Nebraska, *Nebraska News*. 17 October 1868.

Newark, New Jersey, *Eagle*. 21 August 1846.

Newcastle, New Brunswick, *Union Advocate*. 6 April 1881.

Newport, New Hampshire, *Argus & Spectator*. 29 June, 10 and 24 August, 28 September, and 5 October 1877.

Norfolk, Nebraska, *Daily News*. 15 and 24 June, 23 September 1889, 4 January 1890.

Oberlin, Ohio, *Lorain County News*. 26 February and 13 May 1868.

Omaha, Nebraska, *Daily Herald*. 10 September 1868.

Omaha, Nebraska, *Weekly Republican*. 5 August 1868.

Pawnee City, Nebraska, *Republican*. 10 July 1879.

Penacook, New Hampshire, *Rays of Light.* 24 June 1886.

Peterboro, New Hampshire, *Transcript.* 11 February 1886 and 21 April 1887.

Philadelphia, Pennsylvania, *Enquirer and Courier.* 10 June 1850.

Philadelphia, Pennsylvania, *Evening Bulletin.* 11 June 1850.

Philadelphia, Pennsylvania, *Saturday Courier.* 1 August 1835 and 2 December 1837.

Pittsburgh, Pennsylvania, *Gazette.* [Date unknown] October 1849.

Plymouth, New Hampshire, *Republican Star.* 22 September and 29 December 1883.

Port Arthur, Ontario, *Daily Sentinel.* 14 and 21 April 1885.

Portsmouth, New Hampshire, *Daily Chronicle.* 24 September 1877.

Portsmouth, New Hampshire, *Weekly.* 15 December 1877.

Prince Edward Island *Farmer.* 25 November 1878.

Raleigh, North Carolina, *Daily Sentinel.* 4 September 1872.

Rochester, New Hampshire, *Courier & Advertiser.* 31 August and 2 November 1877 and 28 November 1884.

Rochester, New York, *Daily American.* 24 November 1847.

Rockland, Maine, *Gazette.* 21 April 1854.

Saginaw, Michigan, *Daily Courier.* 16 May 1870 and 22 August 1879.

St. Louis, Missouri, *Daily Evening Gazette.* 29 April 1839.

St. Louis, Missouri, *Republican.* 28 April 1840.

Salem, Massachusetts, *Gazette.* 15 May 1849.

Salem, Massachusetts, *Observer.* 19 May 1849.

San Antonio, Texas, *Daily Herald.* 28 January, 13 February, and 15 April 1873.

San Diego, California, *Union.* 22 December 1872 and 14 April 1873.

Sandusky, Ohio, *Ohio Daily Commercial Register.* 21 and 27 October and 29 November 1854.

Savannah, Georgia, *Morning News.* 19 February 1872.

Seattle, Washington, *Post Intelligencer.* 15 July 1884.

Seneca Falls, New York, *Reveille.* 27 August 1873.

Simcoe, Ontario, *British Canadian.* 2 March 1881.

Syracuse, New York, *Journal.* 30 November 1864, 28 April 1865, and 1 April 1867.

Syracuse, New York, *Standard.* 25 June 1851, 12 December 1852, and 14 December 1864.

Troy, New York, *Argus.* [Date unknown] 1845.

Troy, New York, *Budget.* [Date unknown] 1845.

Victoria, British Columbia, *Colonist.* 8 March and 16 October 1878, 26 June 1883, and 26 and 27 November 1889.

Walla Walla, Washington, *Statesman.* 5 May 1865.

Warner, New Hampshire, *Independent & Times.* 25 March 1887.

Waterloo, New York, *Observer.* 10 September 1873.

Webster City, Iowa, *Hamilton Freeman.* 5 May 1869.

Winchester, New Hampshire, *New Hampshire Sentinel.*

Winona, Minnesota, *Republican.* 25 December 1867.

Ypsilanti, Michigan, *Commercial.* 10 September 1856 and 15 September 1866.

10. Miscellaneous and Manuscript Materials

Andreas, A. T. *An Illustrated Historical Atlas of the State of Minnesota.* Chicago: A. T. Andreas, 1874.

Baker, George H. Account Book. Manuscript. Society of California Pioneers, San Francisco, Calif.

Baker, George H. Subscription Book. Manuscript. Society of California Pioneers, San Francisco, Calif.

The Boston Business Directory for 1882. . . . Boston: W. A. Greenough & Co., 1882.

Burleigh, L. R. Letter to Professor C. O. Thompson, 4 January 1881. Worcester Polytechnic Institute Library, Worcester, Mass.

Mary Cleveland v. *Eli S. Glover.* 13 Wash. 131 (November 1895). Washington Supreme Court.

Embury, Emma C. *American Wildflowers in Their Native Haunts.* Philadelphia: G. S. Appleton, 1845.

Glover, Eli Sheldon. "The Diary of Eli Sheldon Glover, October-December, 1875." Transcribed from the original by The Oregon Historical Records Survey Project, Division of Professional and Service Projects, Work Projects Administration, Sponsored by the University of Oregon. Portland, Oregon: The Oregon Historical Records Survey Project, Official Project No. 65–1–94–25, February 1940.

[Glover, Eli Sheldon?]. *The Illustrated Directory of Oakland California Comprising Views of Business Blocks, with Reference to Owners, Occupants, Professions and Trades, and Brief History of the City.* Oakland, Calif.: Illustrated Directory Company, 1896.

Glover, Sheldon L. "The Glover Family [of] Michigan: William Glover, Charles S. Glover, Eli Sheldon Glover." Transcribed from originals loaned to the Bancroft Library, May 1954. [Berkeley]: The Bancroft Library, University of California, Berkeley.

Great Register of the County of Alameda, 1884. Oakland, Calif.: Times Publishing Company, [1884?].

[Harrington, Bates.] *How 'Tis Done. A Thorough Ventilation of the Numerous Schemes Conducted by Wandering Canvassers Together with the Various Advertising Dodges for the Swindling of the Public.* Chicago: Fidelity Publishing Co., 1879.

Ingalls, Sheffield. *History of Atchison County, Kansas.* Lawrence, Kans.: Standard Publishing Company, 1916.

Los Angeles City and County Directory 1886–7. Los Angeles: A. A. Bynon & Co., 1887.

Los Angeles City Directory 1888. Los Angeles: W. H. L. Corran, 1888.

Los Angeles County. *Register of Voters . . . Los Angeles County.* 1896.

Marzio, Peter C. "American Drawing Books, 1820–1860." In *Philadelphia Printmaking: American Prints Before 1860*, edited by Robert F. Looney. West Chester, Pa.: Tinicum Press, 1976.

———. *The Art Crusade: An Analysis of American Drawing Manuals, 1820–1860.* Washington, D.C.: Smithsonian Institution Press, 1976.

Maxwell's Los Angeles City Directory 1895. [Los Angeles?]: James Milliken, 1895.

Milliken's Los Angeles County Directory. [Los Angeles?]: James Milliken, 1894.

Reps, John W. "Great Expectations and Hard Times: The Planning of Cairo, Illinois." *Journal of the Society of Architectural Historians* 16 (December 1957): 14–21.

The Troy Directory for the Year 1886. Troy, N.Y.: Samson, Murdock & Co., 1886.

Tymeson, Mildred McClary. *Two Towers: The Story of Worcester Tech, 1865–1965.* Worcester, Mass.: Worcester Polytechnic Institute, 1965.

Whitefield, Edwin. Diaries. Manuscript. Boston Public Library Print Room, Boston.

Plate 1. Lockport, New York, 1836. Detail. Drawn and copyrighted by W. Wilson, printed in New York
by Bufford's Lith. (Prints and Photographs Division, Library of Congress.) Catalog 2594.

Plate 2. Toronto, Ontario, 1854. Detail. Drawn and published by E. Whitefield,
printed in New York by Endicott & Co. (The Mariners' Museum of Newport News, Virginia.) Catalog 3239.

Published by GEO. E. NORRIS Brockton, Mass

BECK & PAULI. Litho Milwaukee, Wis.

1 Congregational Church.
2 Methodist. "
3 Catholic. "
4 Baptist "
5 Unitarian "
6 Town Hall and Post Office.
7 Memorial Building.
8 Schools.
9 Depot, Northern Division, Lowell R. R.
10 Sayre's Hotel and Livery.
11 Chiton Spring House.
12 National and Savings Banks
13 { Granite State Free Press Office.
{ Free Press Job Office, Freeman & Richardson
14 Mead Mason & Co., Mfrs. Furniture and Builder's Materials.
15 Mascoma Flannel Co.
16 { Kendrick & Davis, Watch Key Mfg.
{ The Union Cabinet & Paper Co.
17 Lebanon Woolen Co.
18 { C. M. Baxter, Mfg. Wood Working Machinery.
{ The Concord Paint Co.
19 S. Cole & Son, Foundry & Machine Shop.
20 Mascoma Edge Tool Co., Mfrs. Scythes.
21 G. W. & M. L. Stearns, Mfrs. Scythes, Snaths, Sleds and Hammock Chairs.
22 E. F. Emerson, Mfg. Wagon Fellows.
23 G. A. Elliott, Carriage Shop
24 { Joseph Mace, Flour and Grist Mill.
{ A. W. Rix, Mfr. Patent Wood-Working Machinery
{ Machines & Whipple, Contractors and Builders.
25 { N. B. Marston, Rake Mfg.
{ L. N. Miner, Furniture and General Repair Shop.

26 C. E. Marston, Mfr. Coffins and Caskets.
27 H. G. Billings, Marble Works and Livery.
28 H. W. Carter, { Mfr. Overalls, Coats, Vests, Pants etc.
{ Wholesale Jobber, Small Wares and Cigars.
79 Carter & Churchill, { Overall & Shirt Mfrs.
{ Wholesale Jobbers, Small wares
30 { G. C. Whipple, Dry Goods & Clothing, Whipple Block.
{ J. N. Perley, M. D., Drugs and Fancy Goods, Whipple Block.
{ Frank C. Sturtevant, Insurance, " "
{ F. Davis Architect, " "
{ W. S. Hough, Dentist, " "
31 Pulsifer Bros., Groceries and Crockery.
32 O. W. Baldwin, Groceries and Crockery.
33 J. E. Lincoln, Dry Goods and Clothing
34 G. Bennett, Groceries.
35 Brown Bros., Hardware and Agricultural Tools.
36 C. M. Hildreth & Son, Hardware, Iron and Steel.
37 { Simmons Bros., Groceries and Crockery.
{ G. H. Stearns, Meat Market.
38 J. L. Spring, Attorney.
39 { T. A. Morgan, Jeweler.
{ C. E. Lewis, Photographer.
{ Cragin & Sturtevant, Boots and Shoes.
{ G. S. Joslin, Boots and Shoes,
40 { C. J. Dow, Jeweler.
{ F. E. Bugbee, Hair Dressing Rooms,
{ E. Ticknor, Harness Shop.
{ Currie & Clough, Dentists.
41 G. W. Houghton, Dry Goods and Variety Store

LEBANON
GRAFTON COUNTY.
1884 N. H. 1884

Plate 3. Lebanon, New Hampshire, 1884. Drawn and published by George E. Norris, printed in Milwaukee by Beck & Pauli. (Amon Carter Museum.) Catalog 2237.

Plate 4. Holyoke, Massachusetts, 1881. Drawn by A. F. Poole, printed in Milwaukee by Beck & Pauli, published in Madison, Wisconsin, by J. J. Stoner. (Geography and Map Division, Library of Congress.) Catalog 1478.

Plate 5. St. Paul, Minnesota, 1874. Detail. Drawn by Geo. H. Ellsbury, lithographed by Hoffman, printed in Chicago by Chas Shober & Co. (John W. Reps.) Catalog 1951.

97

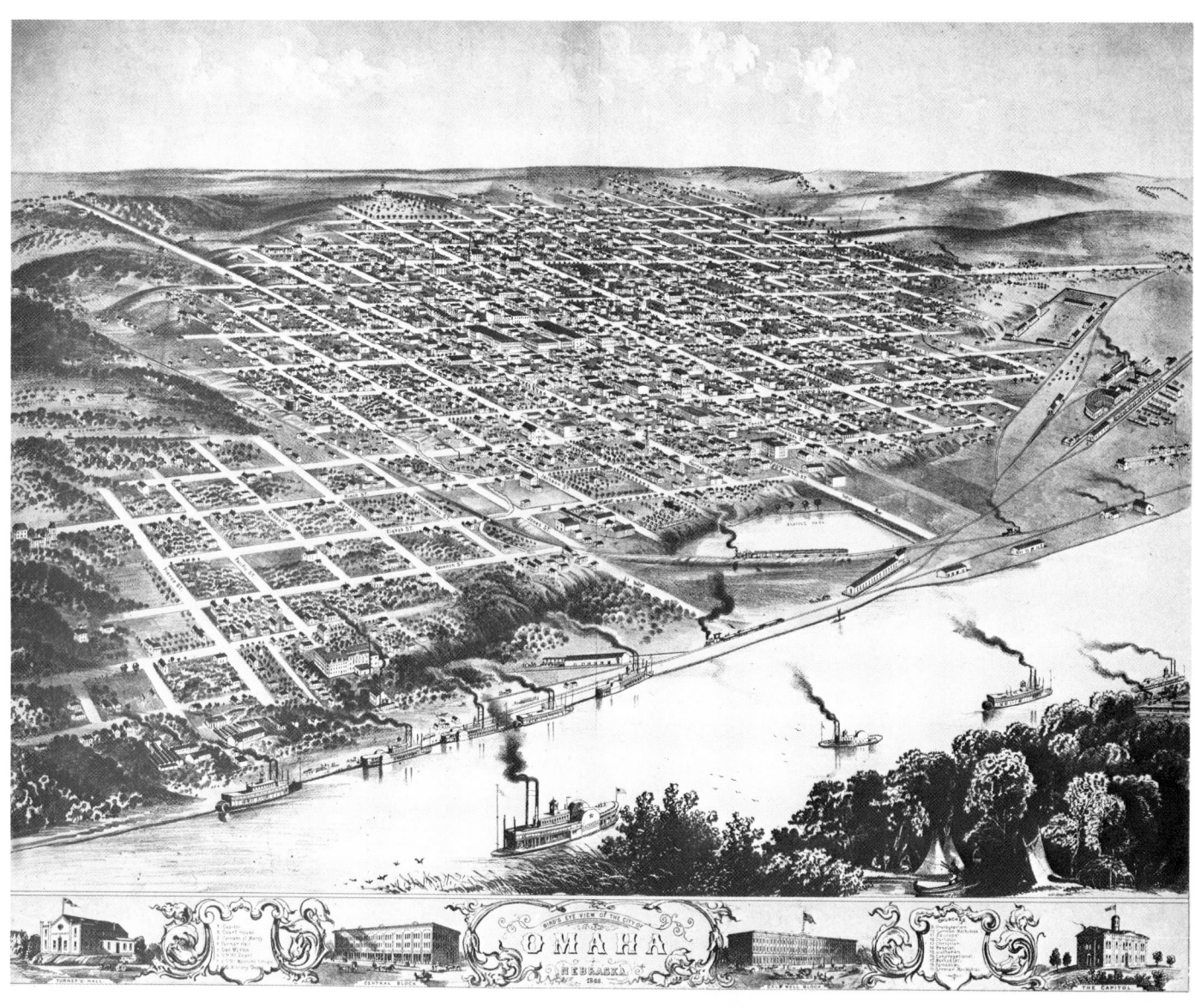

Plate 6. Omaha, Nebraska, 1868. Drawn by A. Ruger, printed in Chicago by the Chicago Lithographing Co. (Geography and Map Division, Library of Congress.) Catalog 2141.

Plate 7. Bismarck, North Dakota, 1883. Unsigned view printed in Milwaukee by Beck & Pauli, published in Madison, Wisconsin, by J. J. Stoner. (Geography and Map Division, Library of Congress.) Catalog 2983.

Plate 8. St. Louis, Missouri, 1840. Drawn by J. C. Wild, printed in St. Louis at the *Missouri Republican* office. (Missouri Historical Society.) Catalog 2027.

MILWAUKEE, WISCONSIN.

Plate 9. Milwaukee, Wisconsin, 1854. Drawn by Geo. J. Robertson, lithographed by D. W.
Moody, printed in New York by Endicott & Co., published in New York by Smith Brothers
& Co. (Prints and Photographs Division, Library of Congress.) Catalog 4377.

VIEW OF THE TOWN OF GLOUCESTER, MASS.

Plate 10. Gloucester, Massachusetts, ca. 1835. Drawn and lithographed by F. H. Lane, printed in Boston by Pendleton's Lithography. (The Mariners' Museum of Newport News, Virginia.) Catalog 1449.

Plate 11. Ithaca, New York, 1836. Detail. Drawn and lithographed by H. Walton, printed in New York by Bufford's Lithography. (Prints and Photographs Division, Library of Congress.) Catalog 2566.

Plate 12. Quebec and Montreal, Quebec, 1851. Drawn by Aug. Kollner, lithographed by Deroy, printed by Jacomme & Co., published in New York and Paris by Goupil & Co. (Picture Division, Public Archives of Canada, C–13444, C–13448.) Catalog 3769, 3816.

VIEW OF ALBANY N. Y.

Plate 13. Albany, New York, ca. 1845. Drawn by E. Whitefield, printed and published in New York by Lewis & Brown. (The Mariners' Museum of Newport News, Virginia.) Catalog 2424.

104

Plate 14. New Orleans, Louisiana, 1852. Detail. Drawn by J. W. Hill & Smith, lithographed by B. F. Smith, Jr., printed in New York by F. Michelin & Geo. E. Leefe, published in New York by Smith Brothers & Co. (Prints and Photographs Division, Library of Congress.) Catalog 1157.

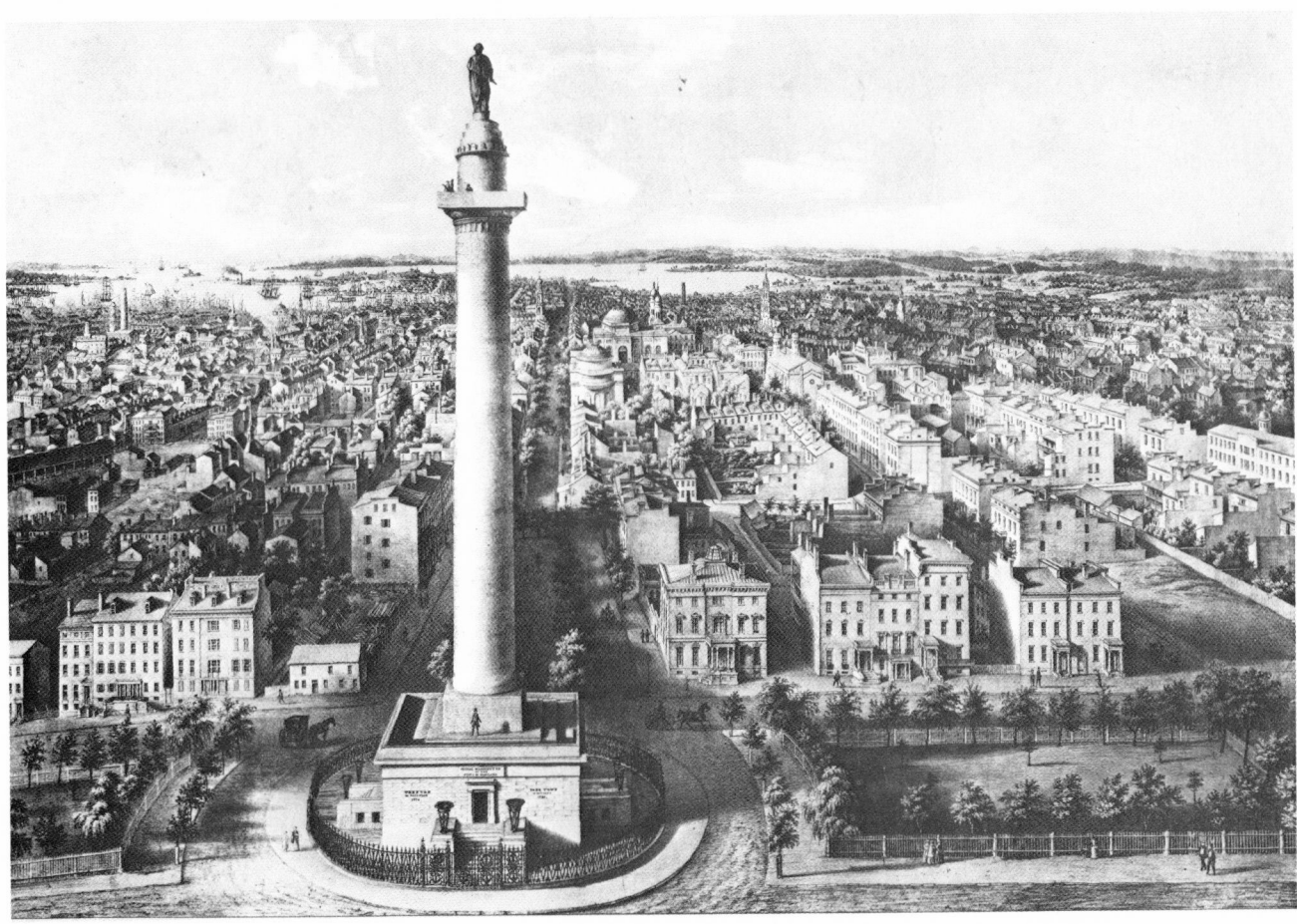

Plate 15. Baltimore, Maryland, 1850. Detail. Drawn by E. Sachse, lithographed and printed in Baltimore by E. Sachse & Co., copyrighted in the District of Columbia by Casimir Bohn. (The Peale Museum.) Catalog 1286.

Plate 16. New York City, 1849. Detail. Drawn and lithographed by C. Bachman, printed in New York by Sarony & Major, published in New York by John Bachmann. (Prints and Photographs Division, Library of Congress.) Catalog 2645.

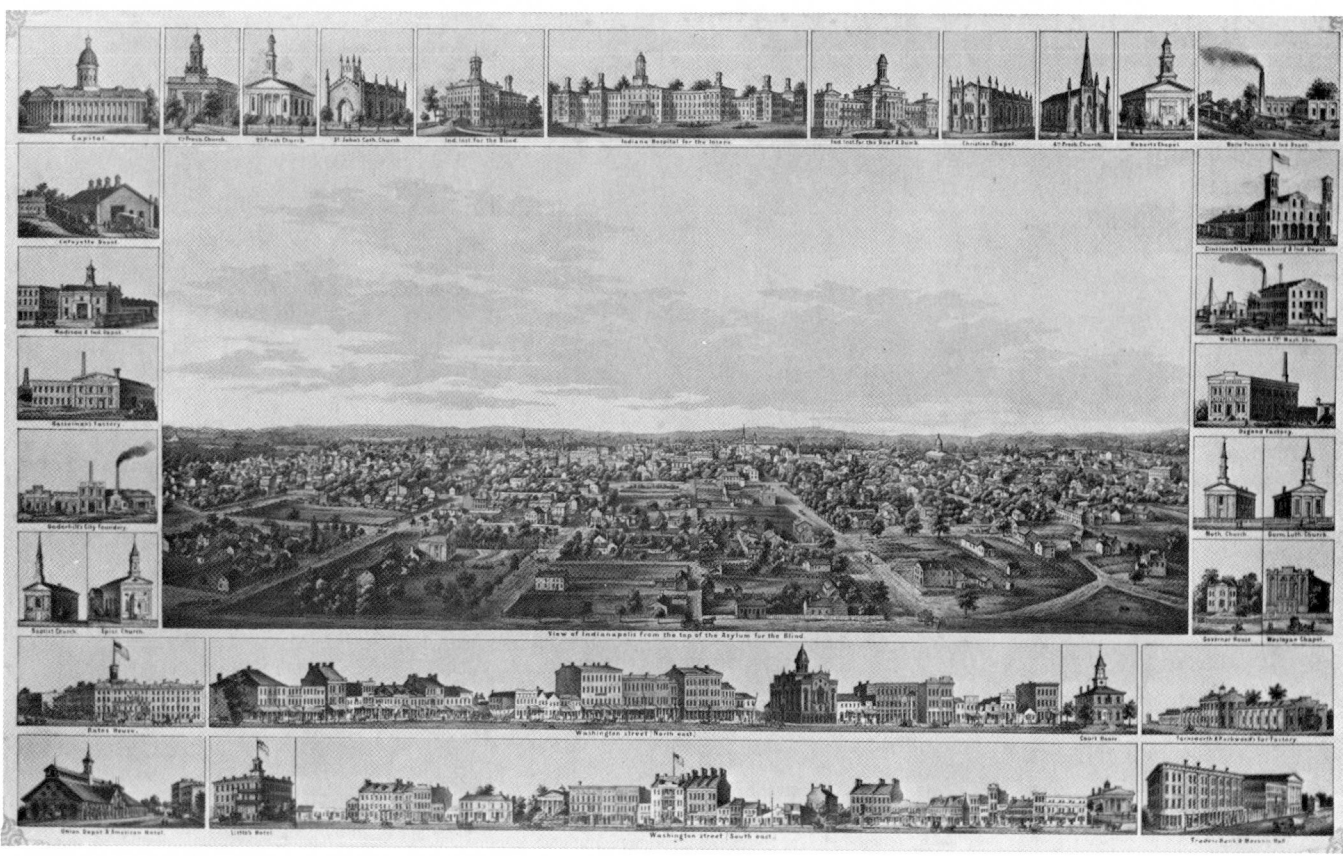

Plate 17. Indianapolis, Indiana, 1854. Detail. Drawn by E. Sachse, printed in Baltimore by E. Sachse & Co., published by J. T. Palmatary. (Yale University Art Gallery, Mabel Brady Garvan Collection.) Catalog 967.

Plate 18. New Orleans, Louisiana, 1850–1859. Detail. Drawn and lithographed by
Th. Muller. (The Mariners' Museum of Newport News, Virginia.) Catalog 1160.

Plate 19. New York City, ca. 1855. Detail. Drawn by Simpson, lithographed by Th. Muller. (Prints and Photographs Division, Library of Congress.) Catalog 2676.

Plate 20. Philadelphia, Pennsylvania, ca. 1850. Detail. Lithographed by G. Matter, printd by I. Schaerer, published in Switzerland by J. U. Locher and in New York by J. H. Locher. (Amon Carter Museum.) Catalog 3585.

108

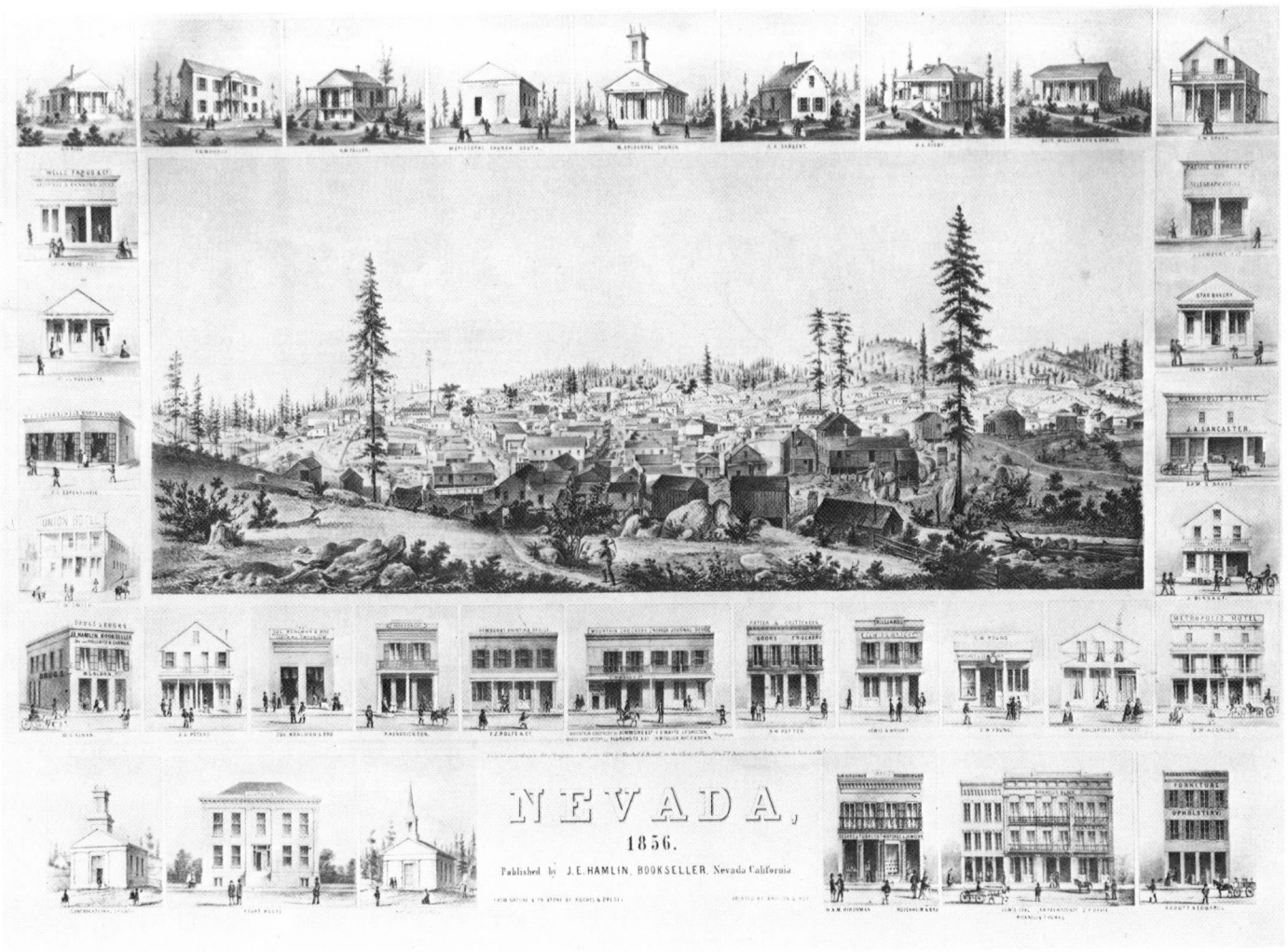

Plate 21. Nevada City, California, 1856. Drawn and lithographed by Kuchel & Dresel, printed in San Francisco, by Britton & Rey, published in Nevada City by J. E. Hamlin. (California State Library.) Catalog 163.

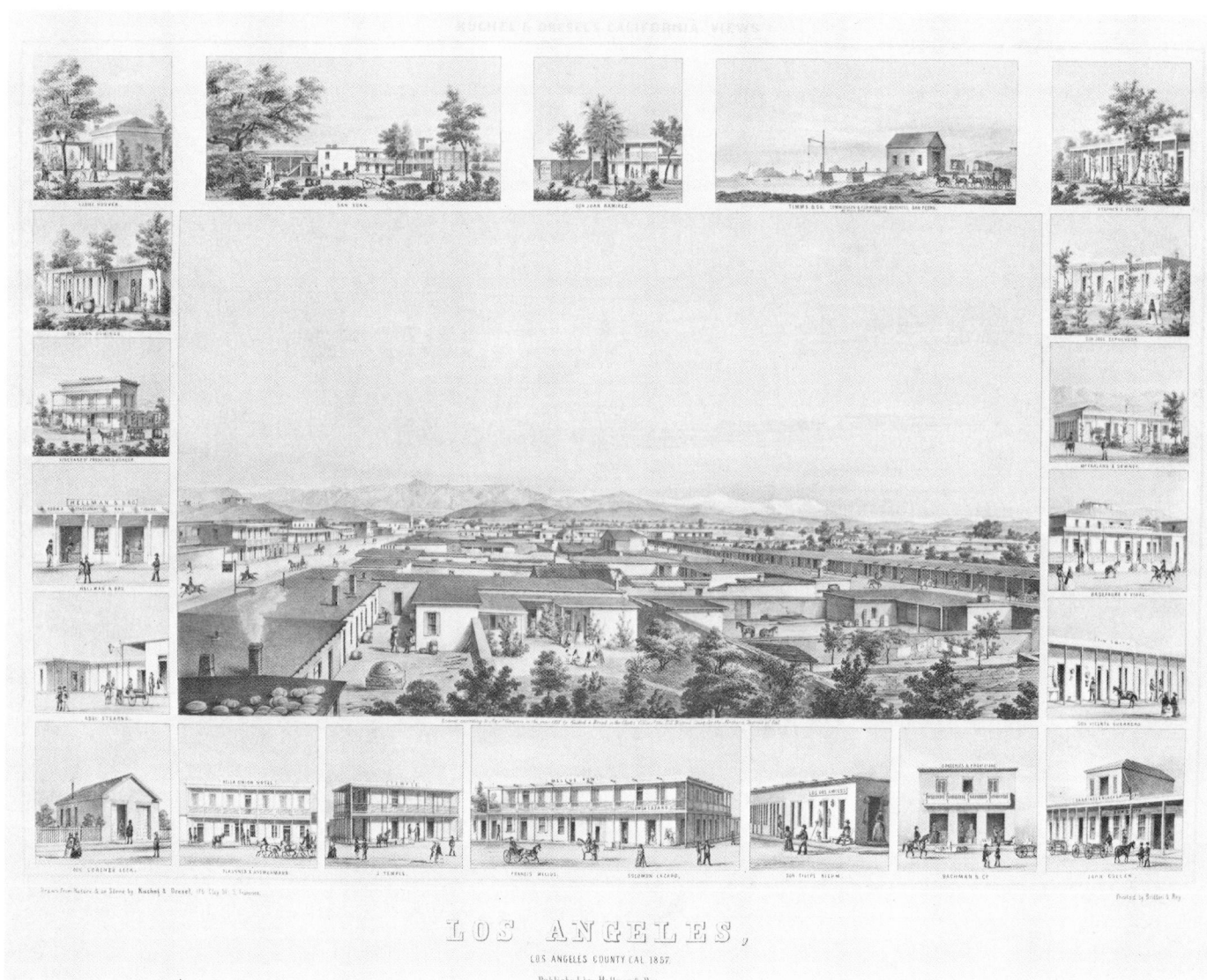

Plate 22. Los Angeles, California, 1857. Drawn and lithographed by Kuchel & Dresel, printed in San Francisco by Britton & Rey, published by Hellman & Bro. (Amon Carter Museum.) Catalog 121.

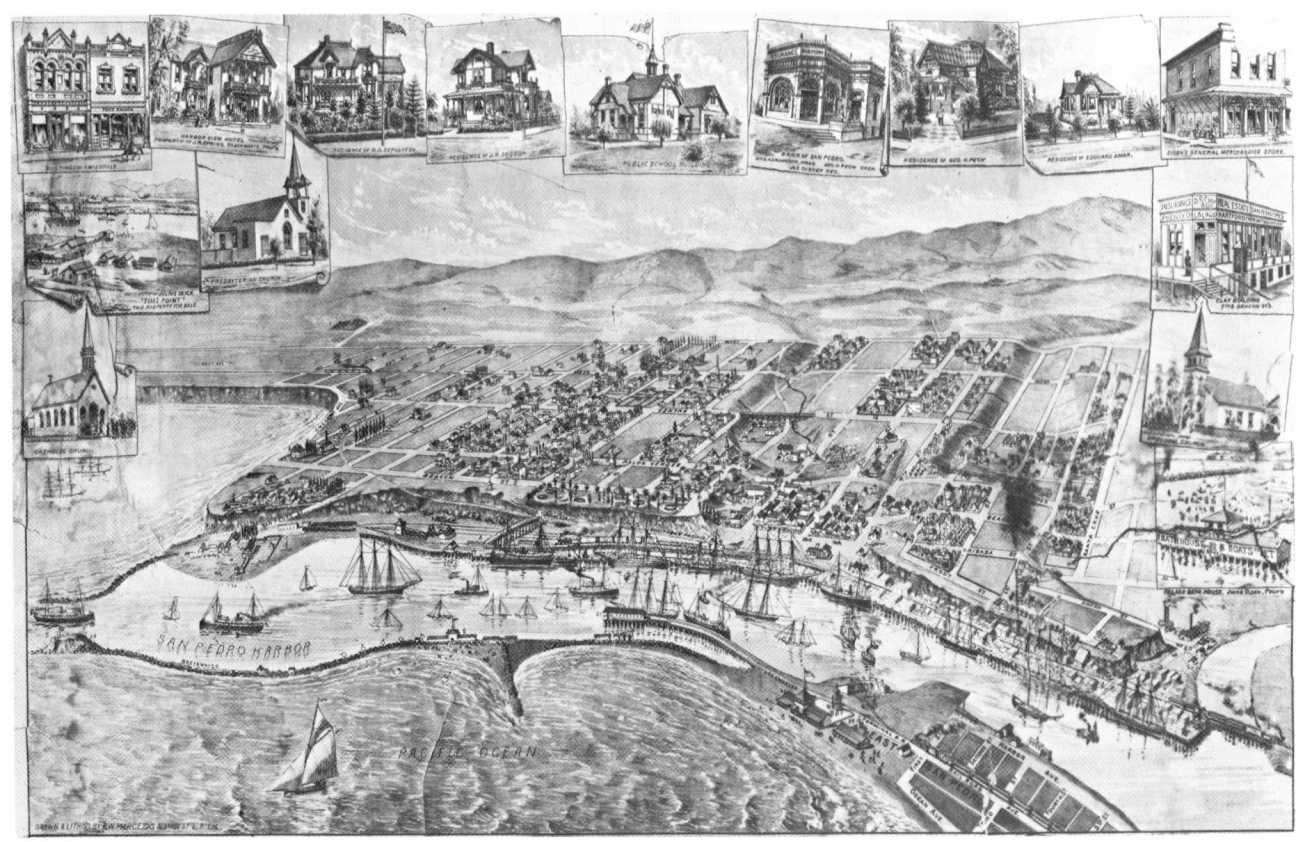

Plate 23. San Pedro, California, 1893. Drawn and published in Los
Angeles by B. W. Pierce. (Amon Carter Musuem.) Catalog 383.

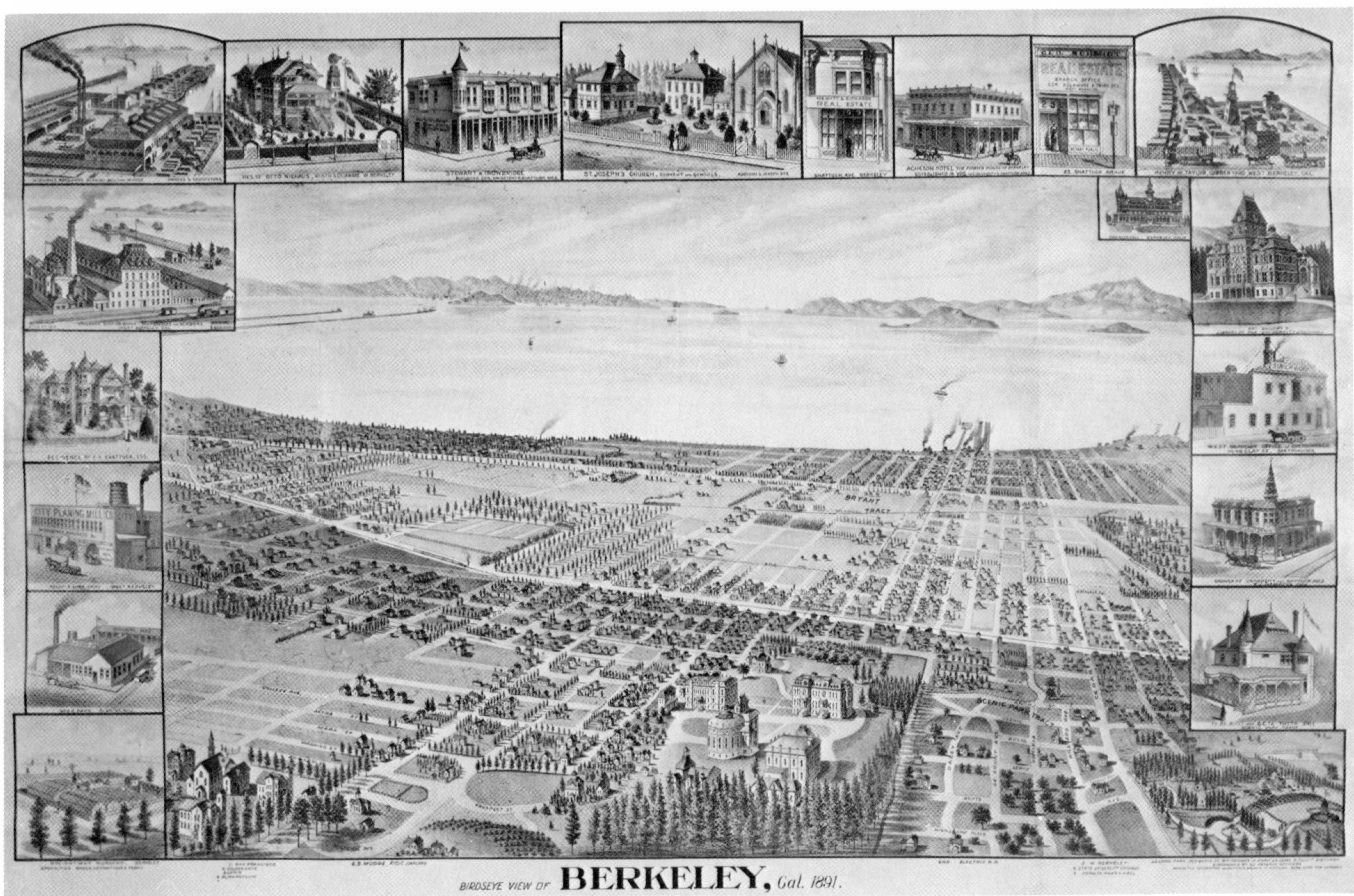

Plate 24. Berkeley, California, 1891. Drawn by E. S. Moore.
(California Historical Society, San Francisco.) Catalog 63.

Plate 25. Pawtucket, Rhode Island, 1877. Drawn and published by O. H. Bailey & J. C. Hazen, lithographed by C. H. Vogt, printed by J. Knauber & Co. (Geography and Map Division, Library of Congress.) Catalog 3868.

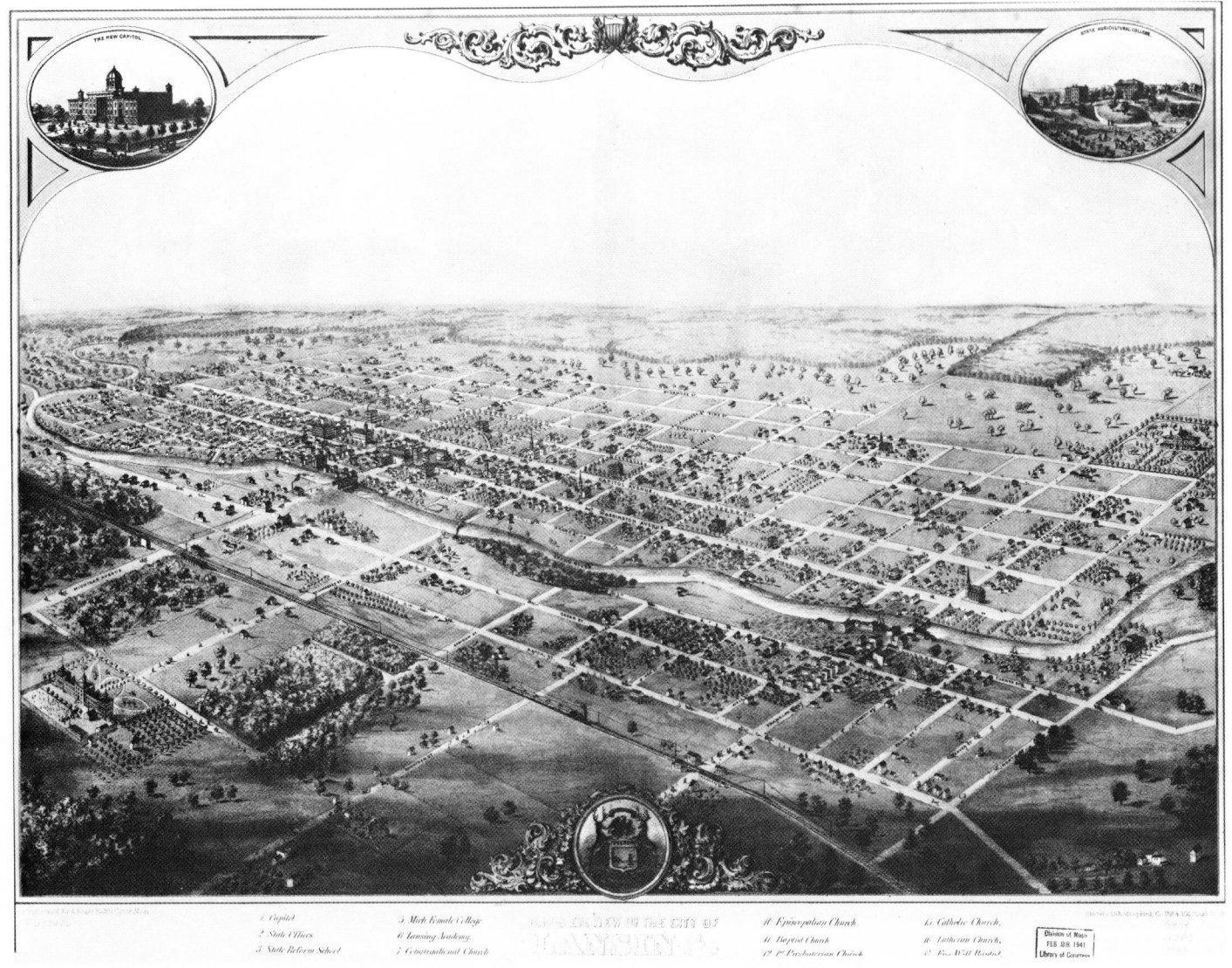

Plate 26. Lansing, Michigan, 1866. Drawn and published by A. Ruger, printed in Chicago by the Chicago Lithographing Co. (Geography and Map Division, Library of Congress.) Catalog 1809.

Plate 27. Chicago, Illinois, 1868. Drawn by A. Ruger, printed in Chicago by the Chicago Lithographing Co. (Geography and Map Division, Library of Congress.) Catalog 843.

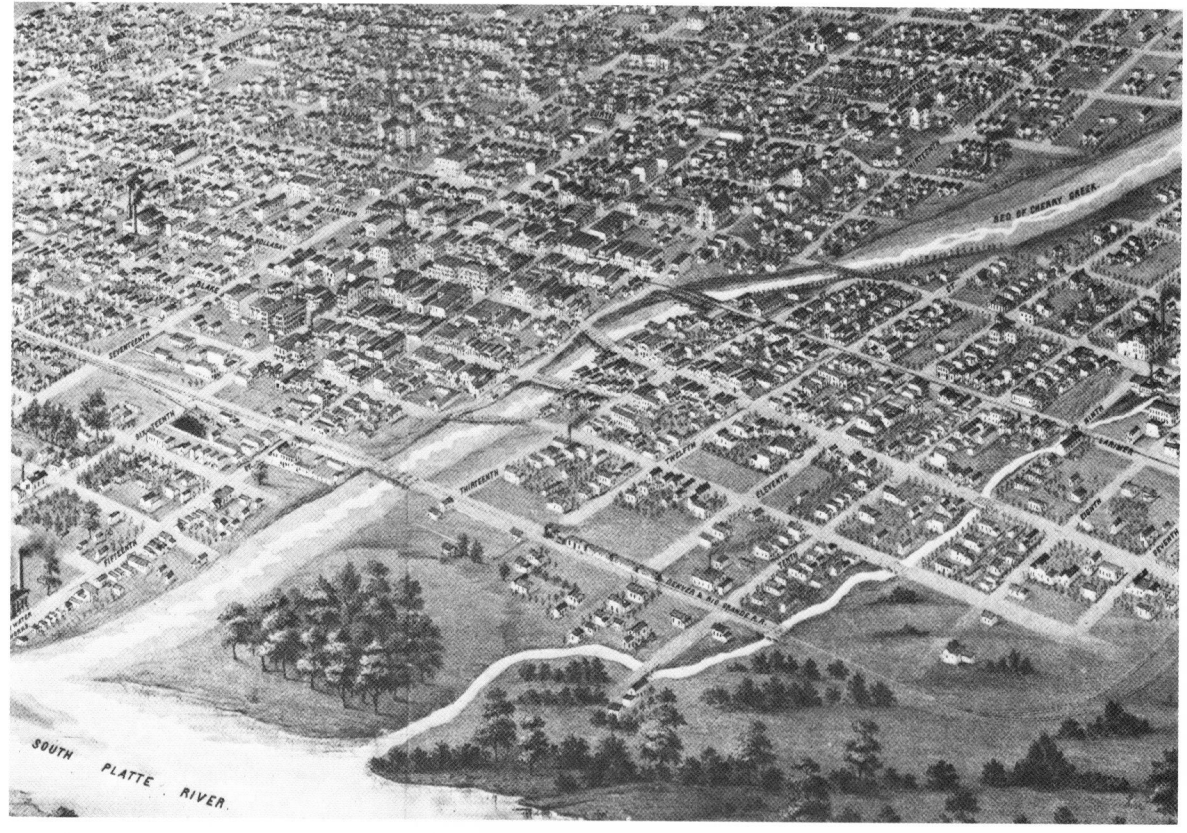

Plate 28. Denver, Colorado, 1874. Detail. Drawn by E. S. Glover, printed in Cincinnati by Strobridge & Co. (Colorado State Historical Society.) Catalog 485.

Plate 29. Albuquerque, New Mexico, 1886. Drawn by Augustus Koch.
(Bancroft Library, University of California, Berkeley.) Catalog 2416.

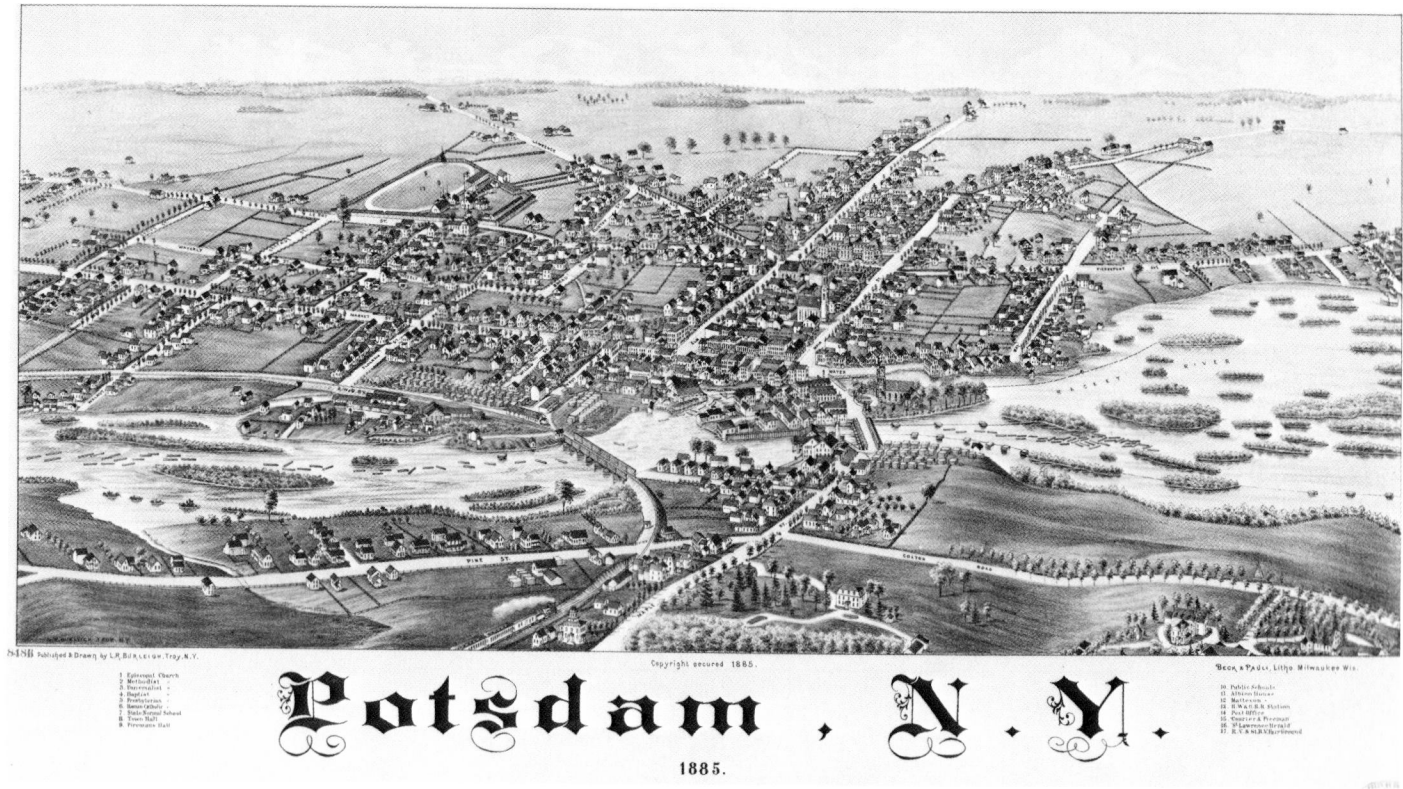

Plate 30. Potsdam, New York, 1885. Drawn and published in Troy, New York, by L. R. Burleigh, printed in Milwaukee by Beck & Pauli. (Geography and Map Division, Library of Congress.) Catalog 2845.

Plate 31. Butte, Montana, 1884. Drawn by H. Wellge, printed in Milwaukee by Beck & Pauli, published in Madison, Wisconsin, by J. J. Stoner. (Geography and Map Division, Library of Congress.) Catalog 2081.

Plate 32. Kingston, Ontario, 1875. Drawn by H. Brosius, printed in Chicago by Chas Shober & Co., published in Madison, Wisconsin, by J. J. Stoner. (Picture Division, Public Archives of Canada, C–16941.) Catalog 3199.

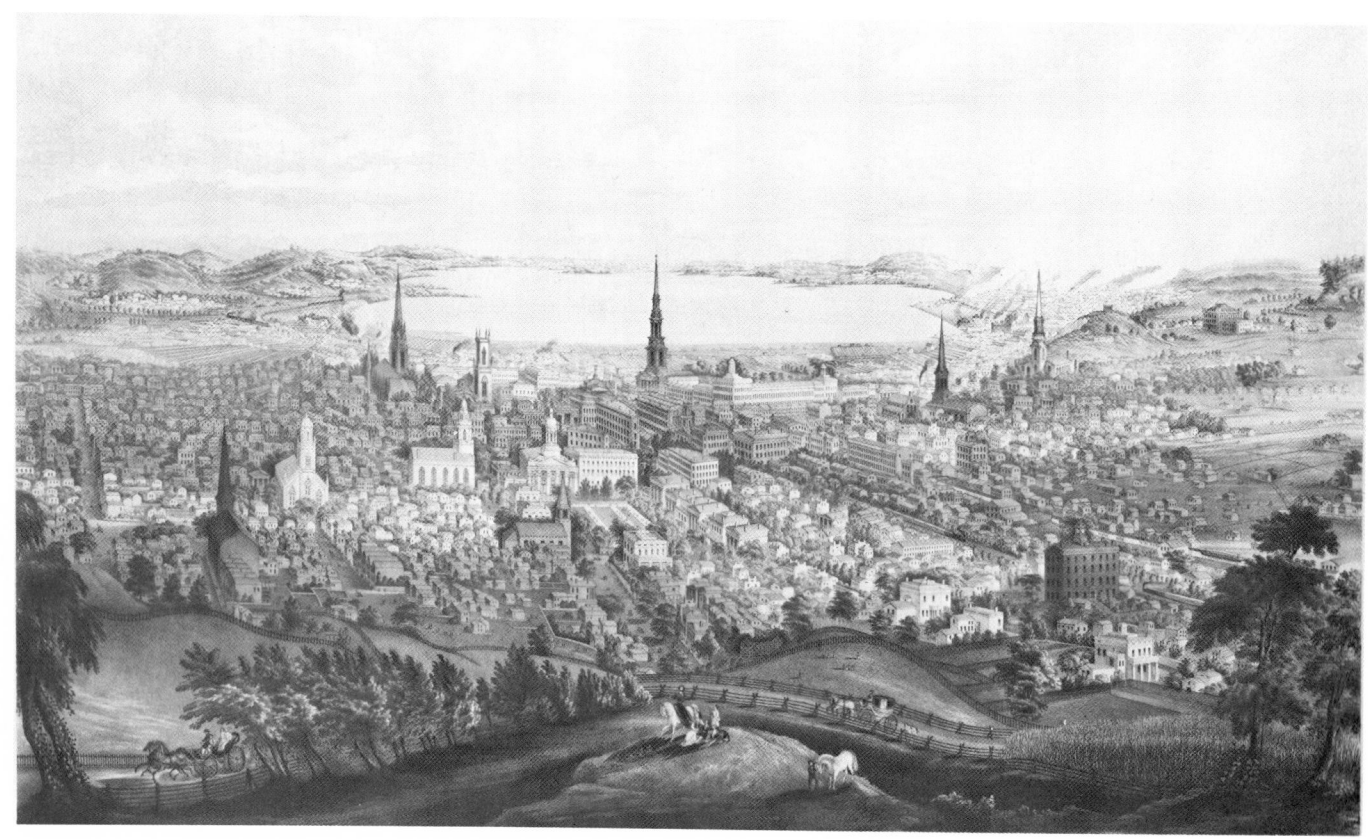

Plate 33. Syracuse, New York, 1852. Detail. Drawn by Lewis Bradley, lithographed by D. W. Moody, printed by F. Michelin, published in New York by Smith Bros. & Co. (Chicago Historical Society.) Catalog 2908.

Plate 34. Boston, Massachusetts, 1850. Detail. Drawn, lithographed, and published in New York by John Bachmann, printed in New York by Sarony & Major. (Prints and Photographs Division, Library of Congress.) Catalog 1366.

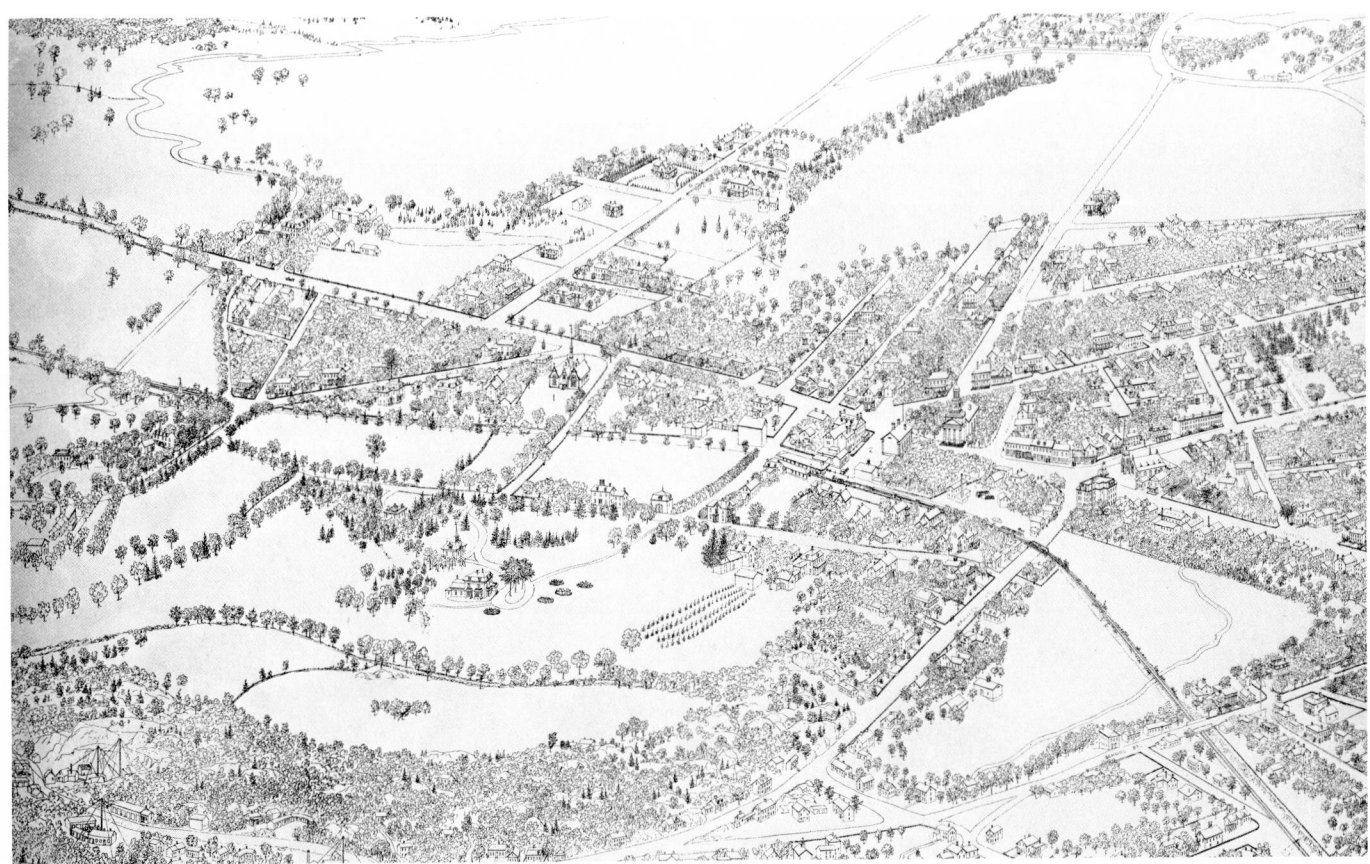

Plate 35. Quincy, Massachusetts, 1877. Detail. Drawn and published by E. Whitefield. (Geography and Map Division, Library of Congress.) Catalog 1610.

Plate 36. Quincy, Massachusetts, 1877. Sketches drawn by E. Whitefield. (Private Collection.)

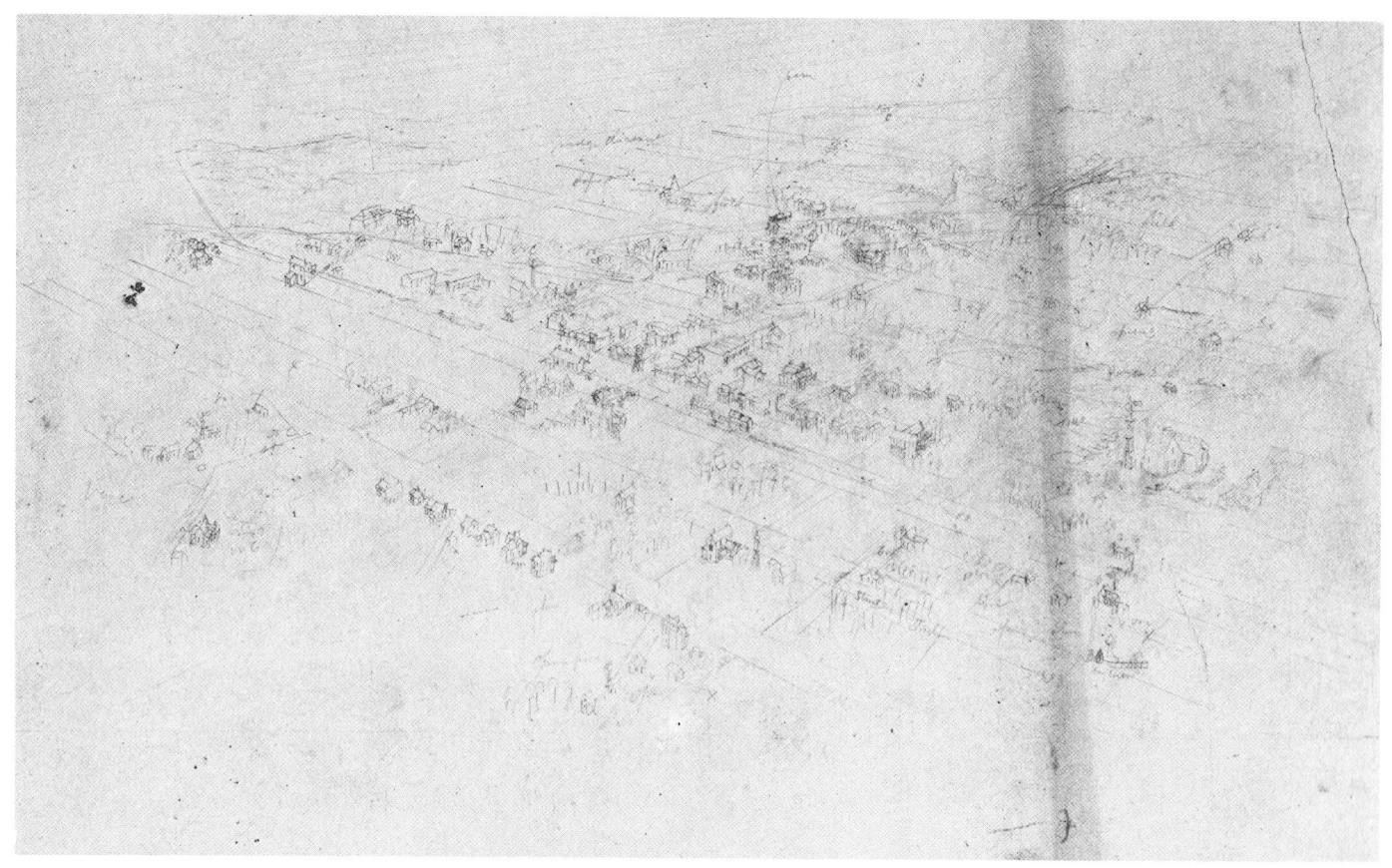

Plate 37. Sunset, Texas, 1890. Sketch drawn by T. M. Fowler. (Amon Carter Museum.)

VIEW OF
QUANAH TEXAS.
HARDEMAN COUNTY
OCTOBER 1890.

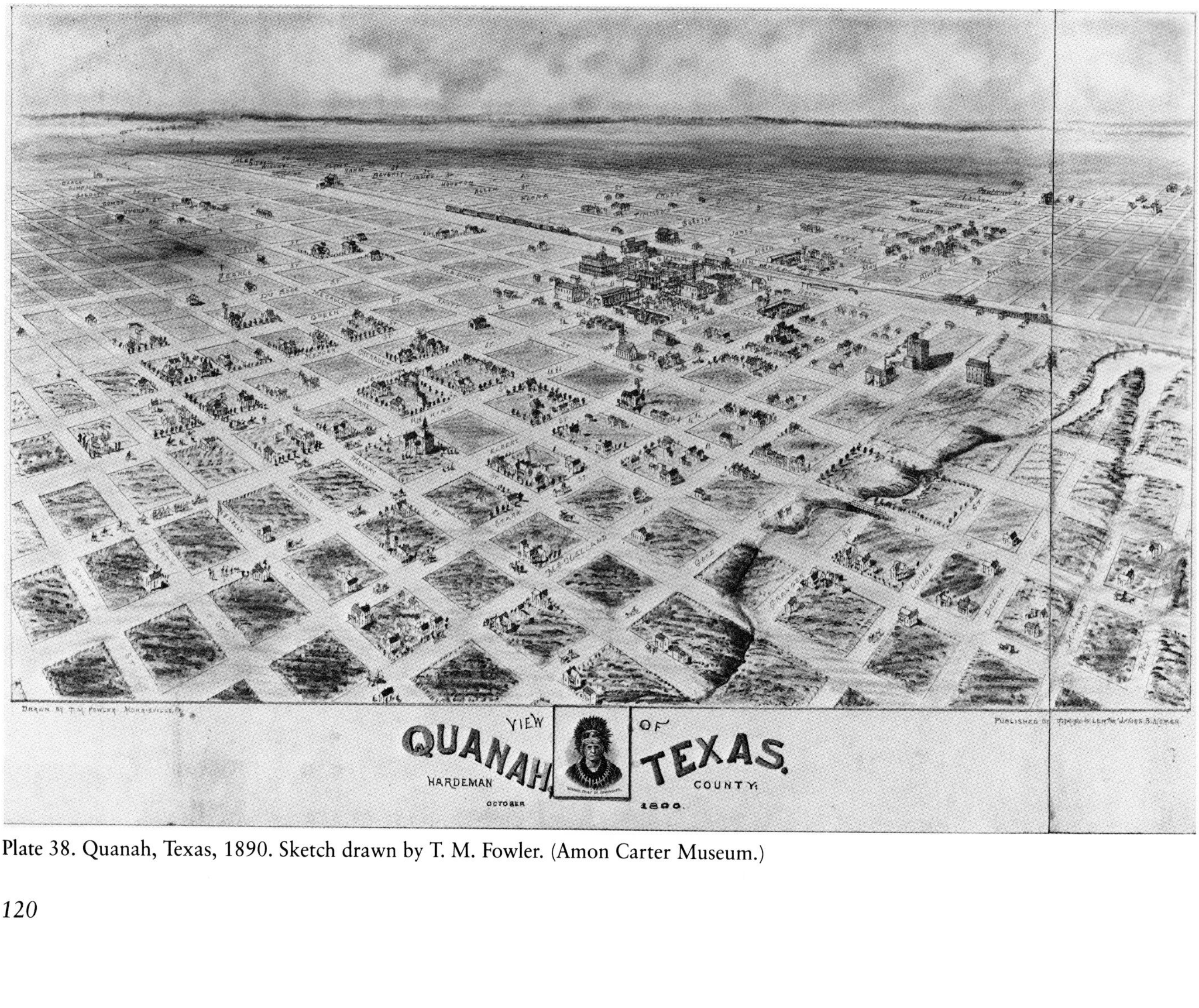

Plate 38. Quanah, Texas, 1890. Sketch drawn by T. M. Fowler. (Amon Carter Museum.)

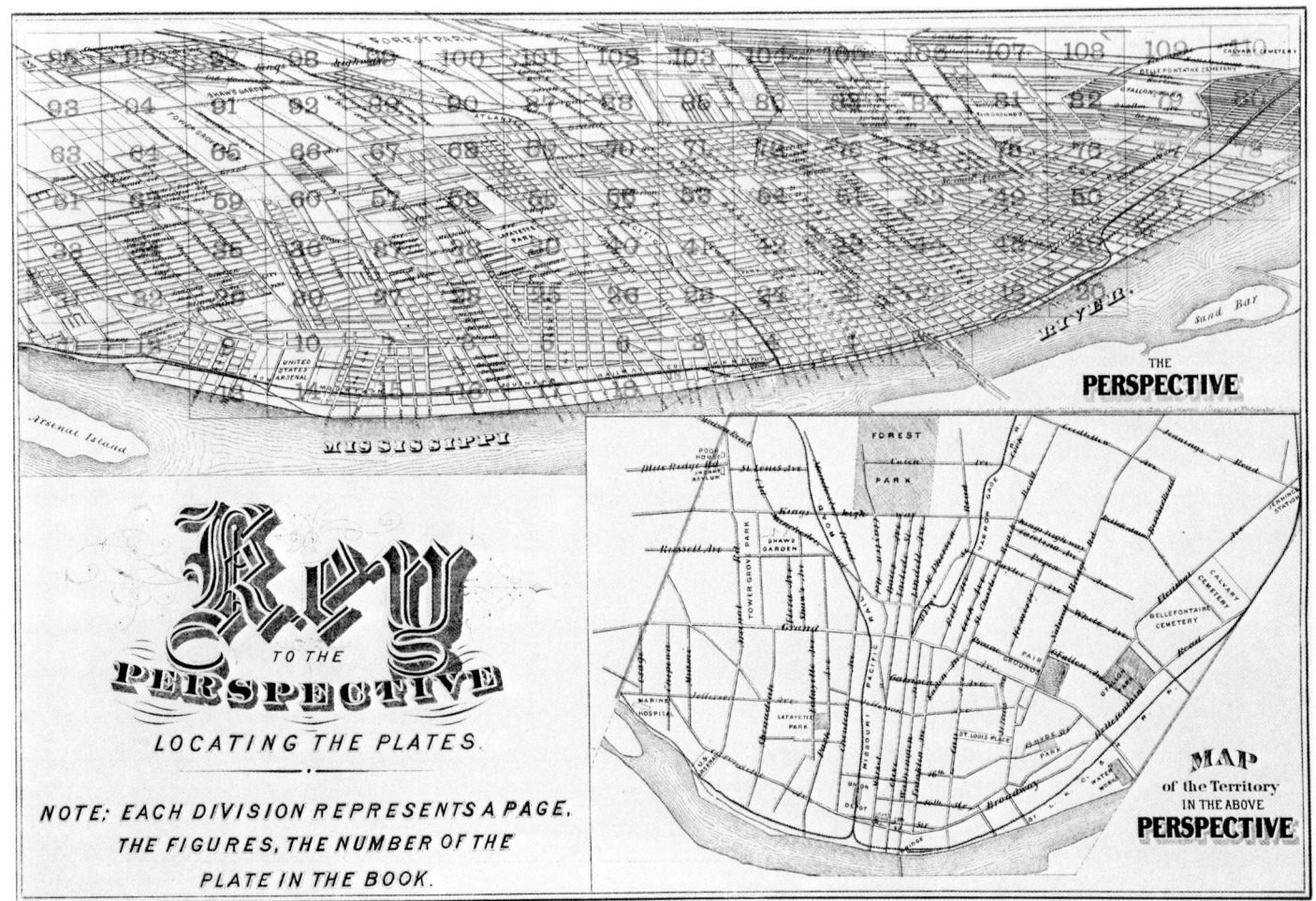

Plate 39. St. Louis, Missouri, 1875. Drawn by Camille N. Dry, printed in St. Louis
by the St. Louis Globe-Democrat Job Printing Co., published in St. Louis by
Compton & Co. (Geography and Map Division, Library of Congress.) Catalog 2057.

COLORADO RIVER

122

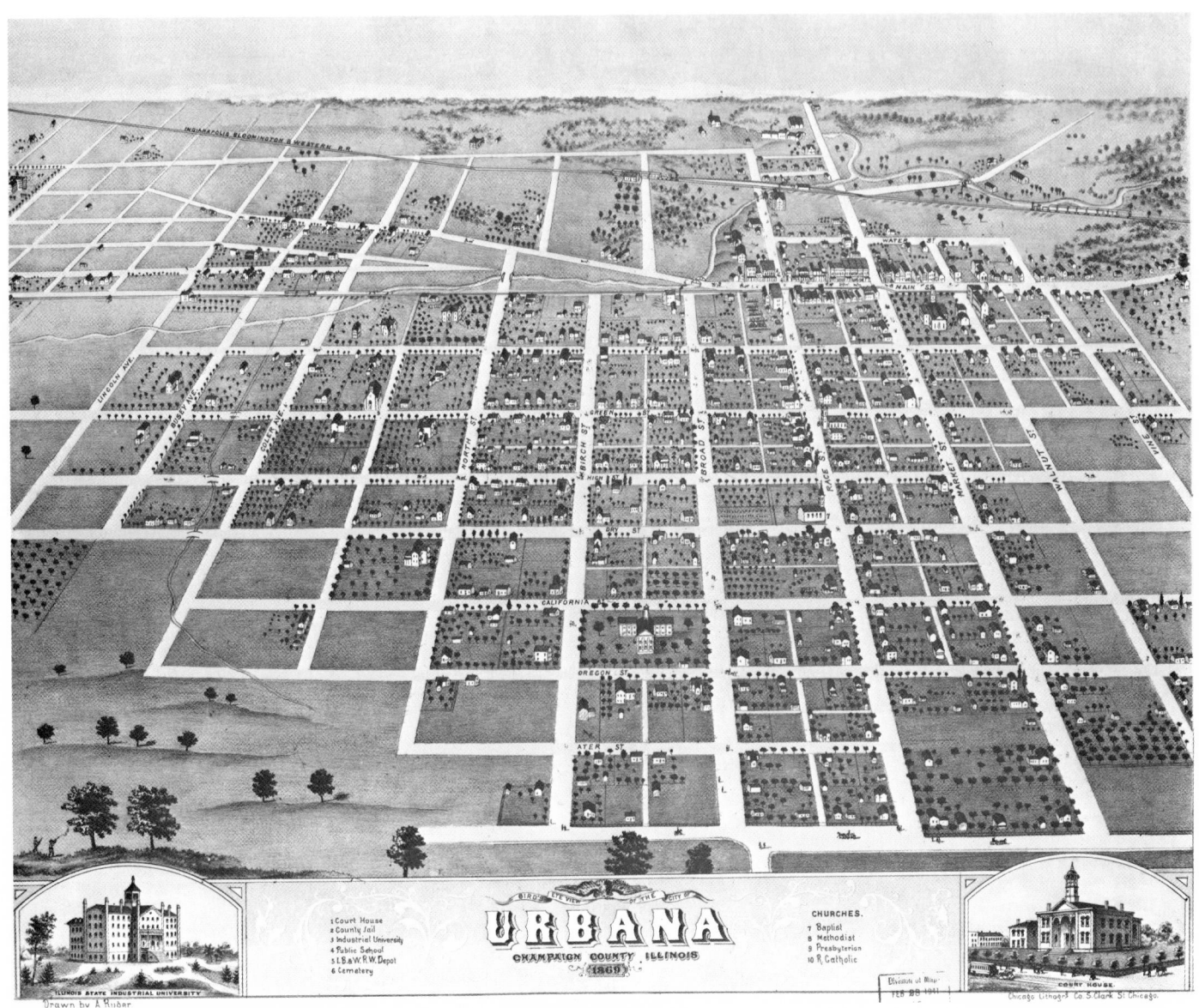

Plate 41. Urbana, Illinois, 1869. Drawn by A. Ruger, printed in Chicago by the
Chicago Lithographing Co. (Geography and Map Division, Library of Congress.) Catalog 947.

Plate 40. Austin, Texas, 1873 and 1887. Details. Drawn by Augustus Koch, the 1873 view
published in Madison, Wisconsin, by J. J. Stoner. (Austin Public Library.) Catalog 3946, 3947.

Plate 42. Sacramento, California, 1857. Drawn and published in Sacramento by George H. Baker, printed in San Francisco by Britton & Rey. (Bancroft Library, University of California, Berkeley.) Catalog 209.

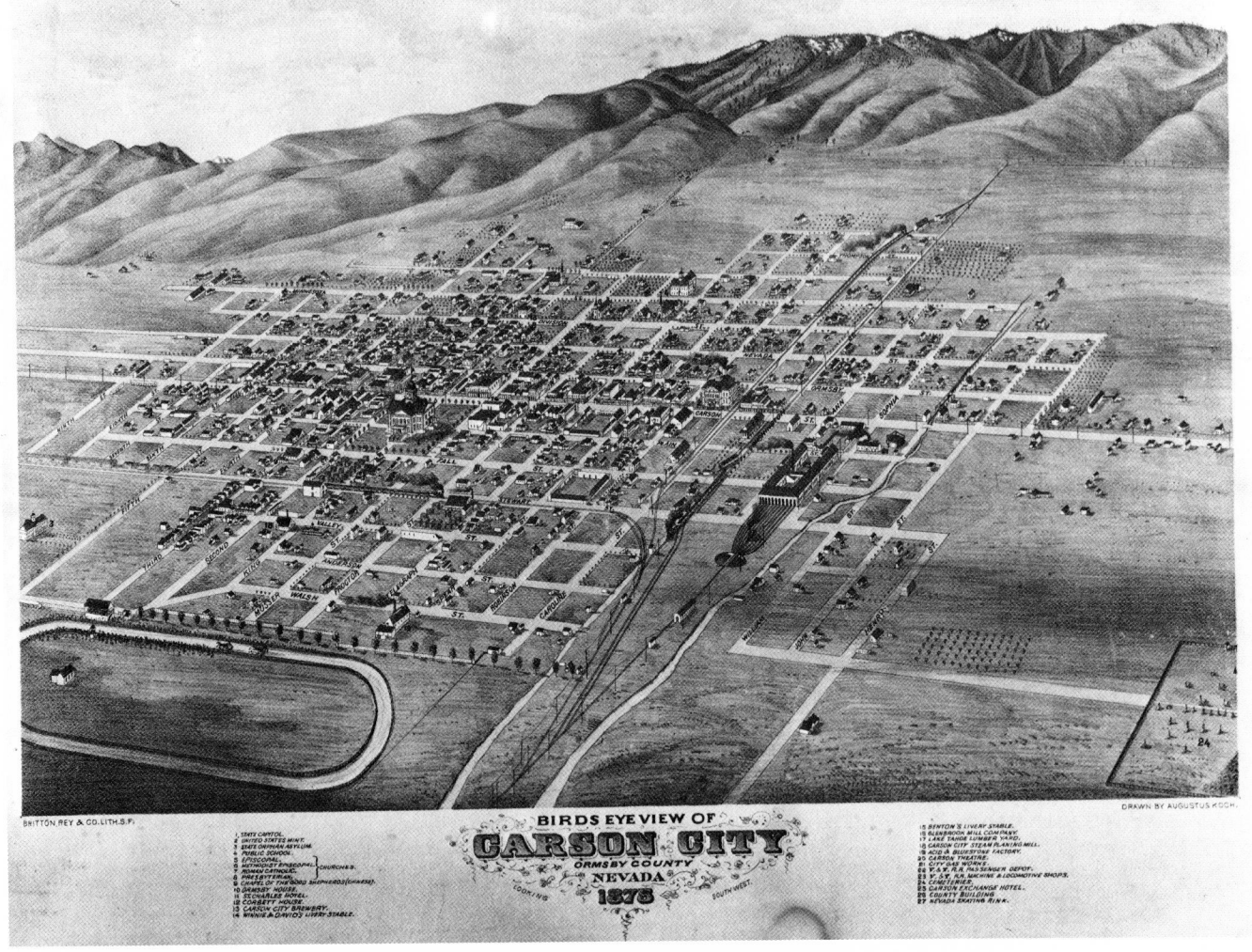

BIRDS EYE VIEW OF

CARSON CITY

ORMSBY COUNTY
NEVADA
1875

LOOKING   SOUTH WEST.

DRAWN BY AUGUSTUS KOCH.

1 STATE CAPITOL.
2 UNITED STATES MINT.
3 STATE ORPHAN ASYLUM.
4 PUBLIC SCHOOL.
5 EPISCOPAL.
6 METHODIST EPISCOPAL. CHURCHES.
7 ROMAN CATHOLIC.
8 PRESBYTERIAN.
9 CHAPEL OF THE GOOD SHEPHERDS (CHINESE).
10 ORMSBY HOUSE.
11 ST. CHARLES HOTEL.
12 CORBETT HOUSE.
13 CARSON CITY BREWERY.
14 WINNIE & DAVIS'S LIVERY STABLE.

15 BENTON'S LIVERY STABLE.
16 GLENBROOK MILL COMPANY.
17 LAKE TAHOE LUMBER YARD.
18 CARSON CITY STEAM PLANING MILL.
19 ACID & BLUESTONE FACTORY.
20 CARSON THEATRE.
21 CITY GAS WORKS.
22 V. & T. R.R. PASSENGER DEPOT.
23 V. & T. R.R. MACHINE & LOCOMOTIVE SHOPS.
24 CEMETERIES.
25 CARSON EXCHANGE HOTEL.
26 COUNTY BUILDING.
27 NEVADA SKATING RINK.

Plate 43. Carson City, Nevada, 1875. Drawn by Augustus Koch, printed in San Francisco by Britton, Rey & Co. (Bancroft Library, University of California, Berkeley.) Catalog 2153.

125

Plate 44. Raleigh, North Carolina, 1872. Drawn and published by C. Drie.
(Geography and Map Division, Library of Congress.) Catalog 2977.

Plate 45. Washington, D.C., 1880. Drawn by C. R. Parsons, published in New York by
Currier & Ives. (Prints and Photographs Division, Library of Congress.) Catalog 687.

126

Plate 46. Honey Grove, Texas, ca. 1890. Sketch drawn by T. M. Fowler. (Amon Carter Museum.)

Plate 47. Salt Lake City, Utah, 1867. Detail. Drawn by C. Inger, lithographed and printed in Philadelphia by H. J. Toudy & Co., published in Walla Walla, Washington, by Philip Ritz. (Amon Carter Museum.) Catalog 4019.

Main Plaza.   Alameda.   Alamo (1850.)   Mission de la Concepcion

SAN ANTONIO DE BEXAR.

Mission San José   The New Bridge.   San Pedro Spring   Mission San Juan.

Plate 48. San Antonio, Texas, ca. 1860. Drawn by Hermann Lungkwitz, lithographed by L. Briedrich, printed in Dresden by Rau & Son. (Amon Carter Museum.) Catalog 3995.

Plate 49. San Francisco, California, 1864. Drawn and lithographed by C. B. Gifford, printed in San Francisco by L. Nagel, published in San Francisco by Robinson & Snow. (Prints and Photographs Division, Library of Congress.) Catalog 297.

VIEW OF BROOKLYN. L. I.

FROM U. S. HOTEL, NEW YORK.

Plate 50. Brooklyn, New York, 1846. Watercolor (top) and lithograph view drawn, lithographed, and published by
E. W. Whitefield, printed in New York by F. Michelin. (Watercolor: New-York Historical Society; lithograph:
The Mariners' Museum of Newport News, Virginia.) Catalog 2451.

QUANAH,
TEXAS.
1890.

Plate 51. Quanah, Texas, 1890. Drawn by T. M. Fowler, published by T. M. Fowler & James B. Moyer. (Amon Carter Museum.) Catalog 3994.

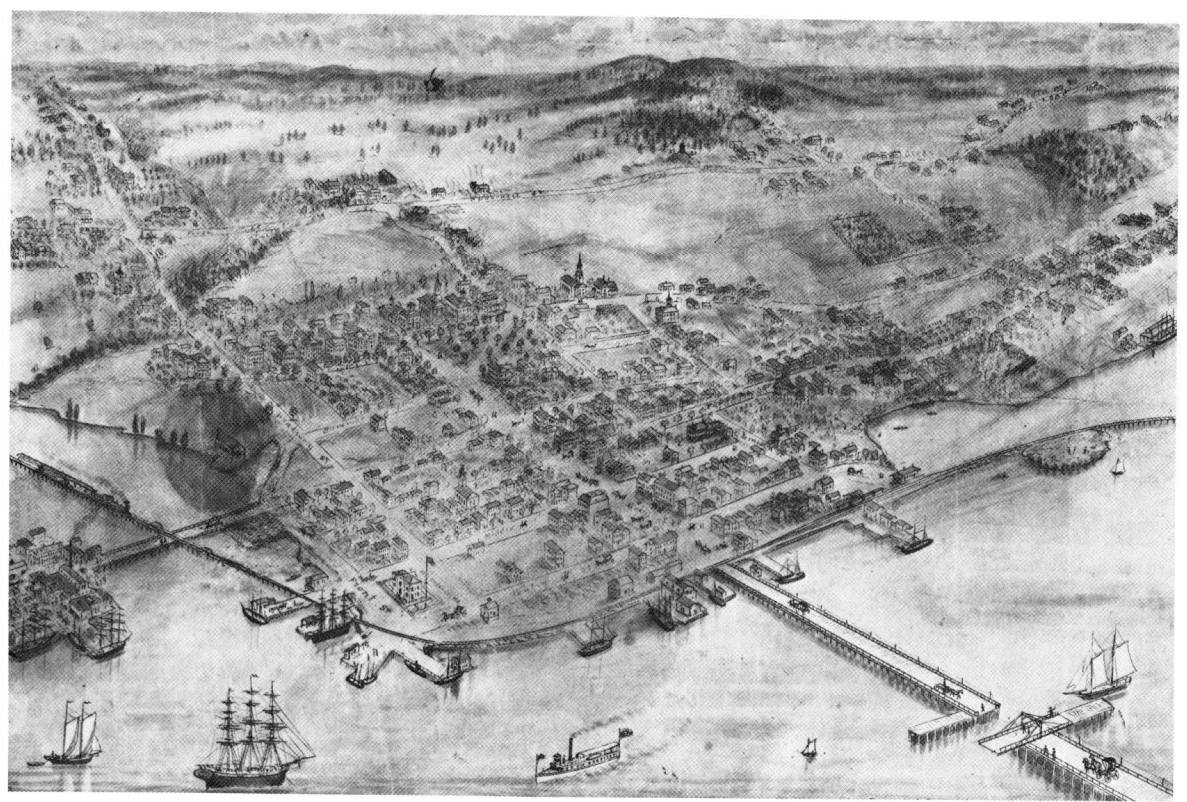

Plate 52. Wiscasset, Maine, 1878. Sketch by Albert Ruger. (Wiscasset, Maine, Public Library Association.)

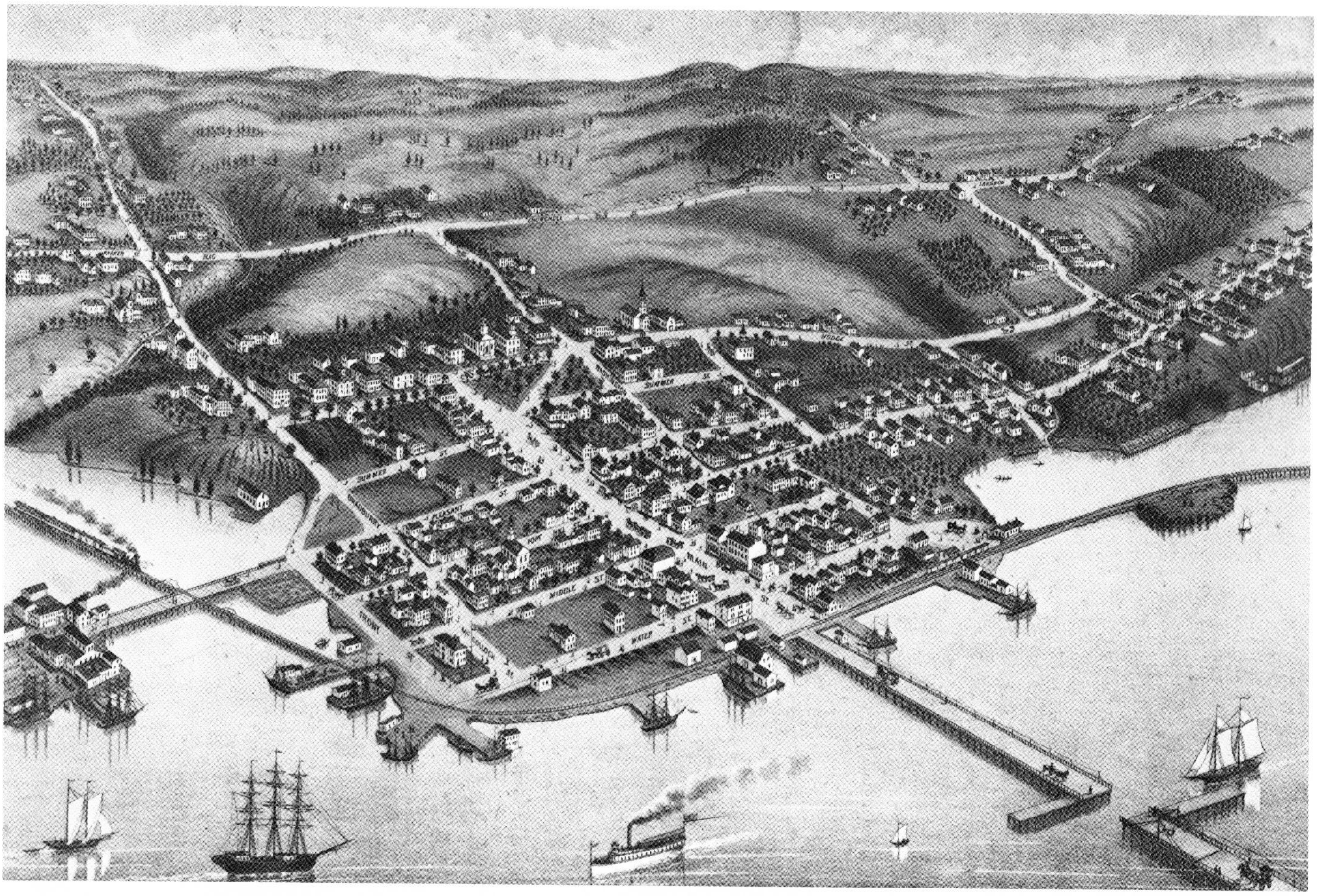

Plate 53. Wiscasset, Maine, 1878. Drawn by A. Ruger, published in Madison, Wisconsin, by J. J. Stoner. (Castle Tucker House Museum, Wiscasset, Maine.) Catalog 1260.

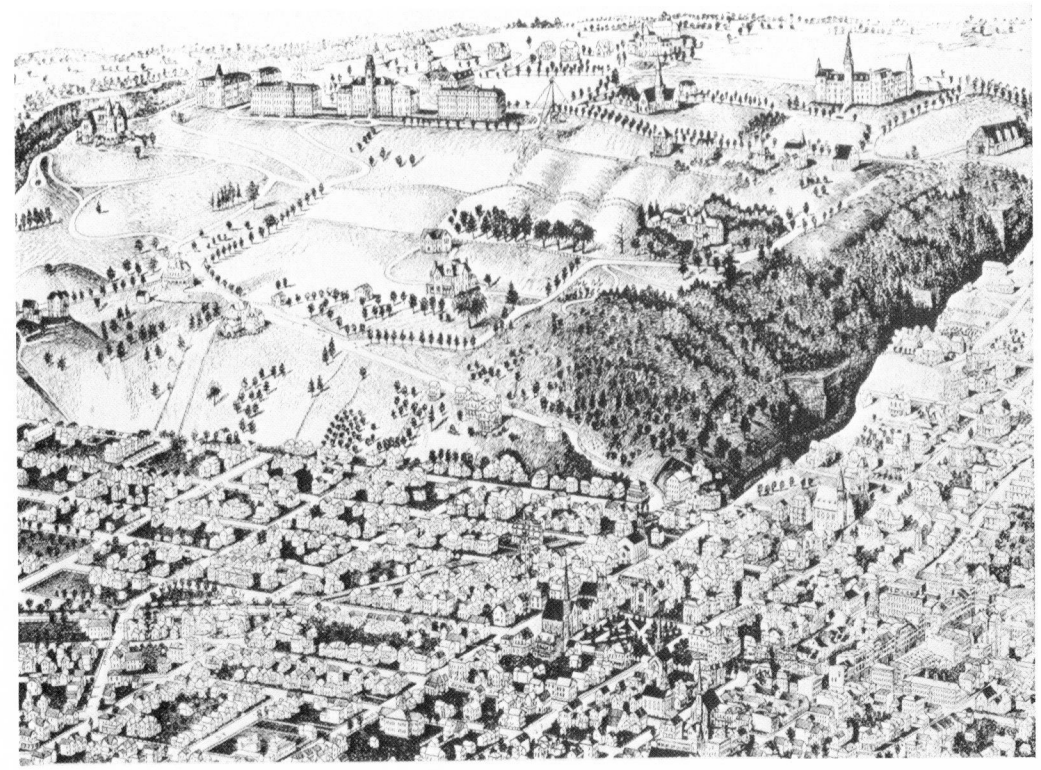

Plate 54. Ithaca, New York, 1882. Detail. Drawn by L. R. Burleigh, lithographed by
J. Lyth. (Tompkins County Trust Company, Ithaca, New York.) Catalog 2571.

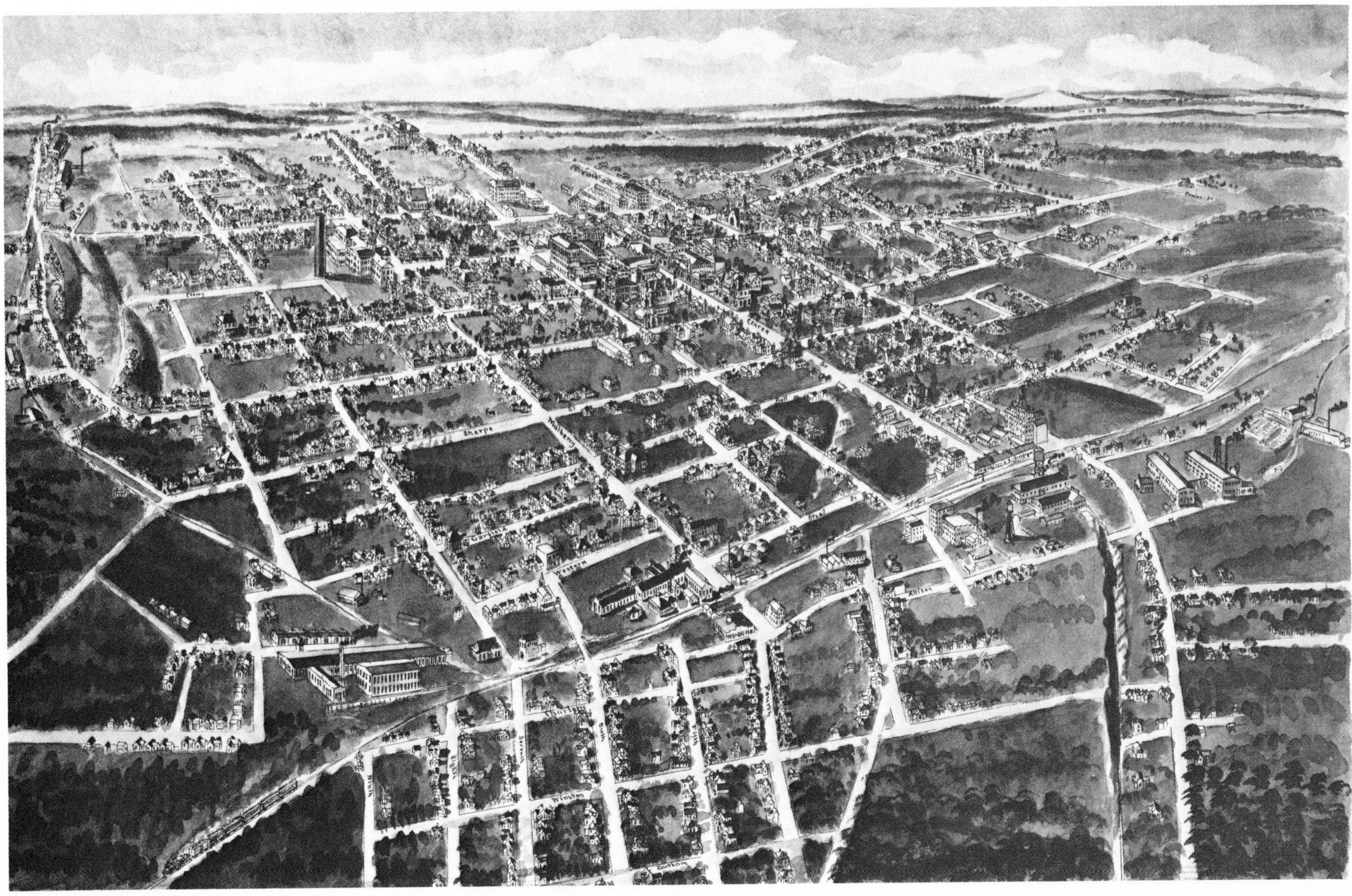

Plate 55. Statesville, North Carolina, ca. 1908. Watercolor by T. M. Fowler
and A. E. Downs. (Geography and Map Division, Library of Congress.)

Plate 56. Lockport, New York, ca. 1826. Drawn by Catlin. (Olin Library, Cornell University.)

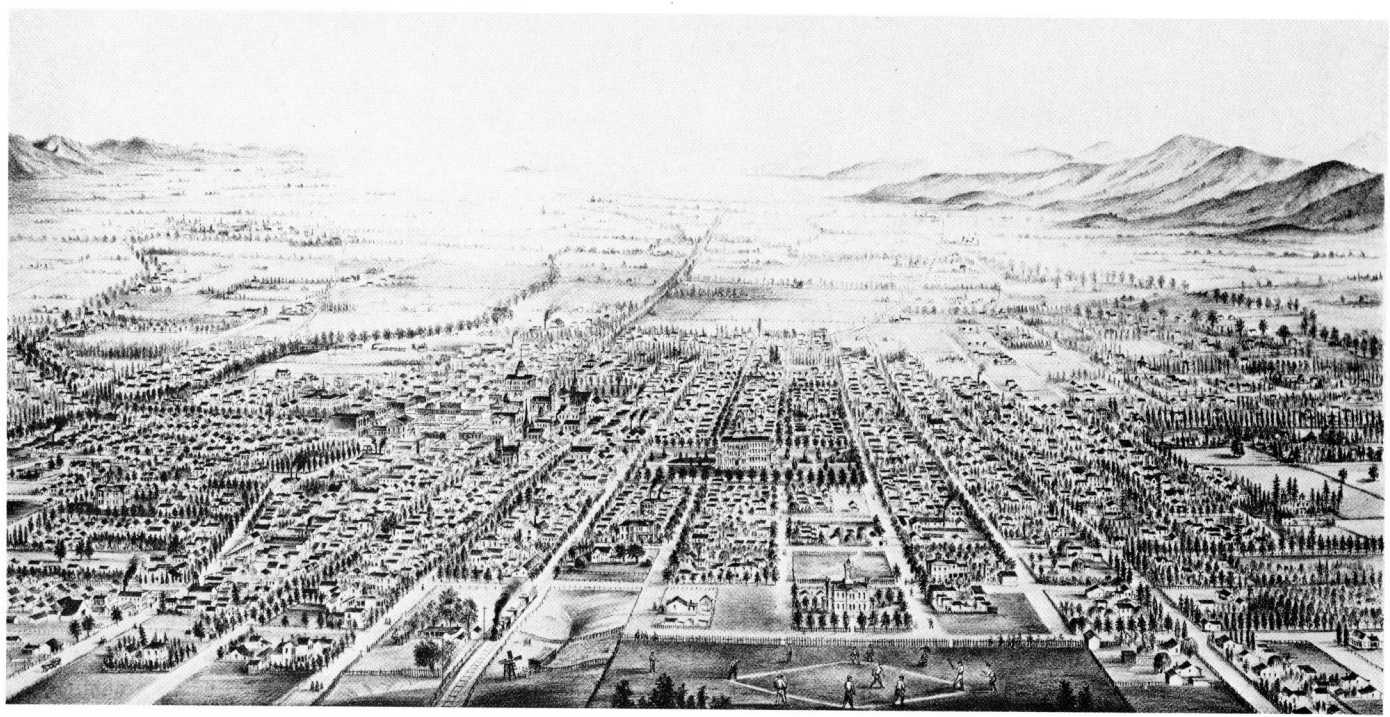

Plate 57. San Jose, California, 1875. Detail. Drawn by C. B. Gifford, printed in San Francisco by A. L. Bancroft
& Co., published in San Jose by W. C. Gifford. (Geography and Map Division, Library of Congress.) Catalog 375.

134

Plate 58. Castine, Maine, 1855. Detail. Drawn by F. H. Lane, printed in Boston by L. H. Bradford & Co., published by Joseph L. Stevens, Jr. (The Mariners' Museum of Newport News, Virginia.) Catalog 1197.

Plate 59. Lincoln, Nebraska, 1889. Drawn by H. Wellge, published in Milwaukee by the American Publishing Co. (Geography and Map Division, Library of Congress.) Catalog 2127.

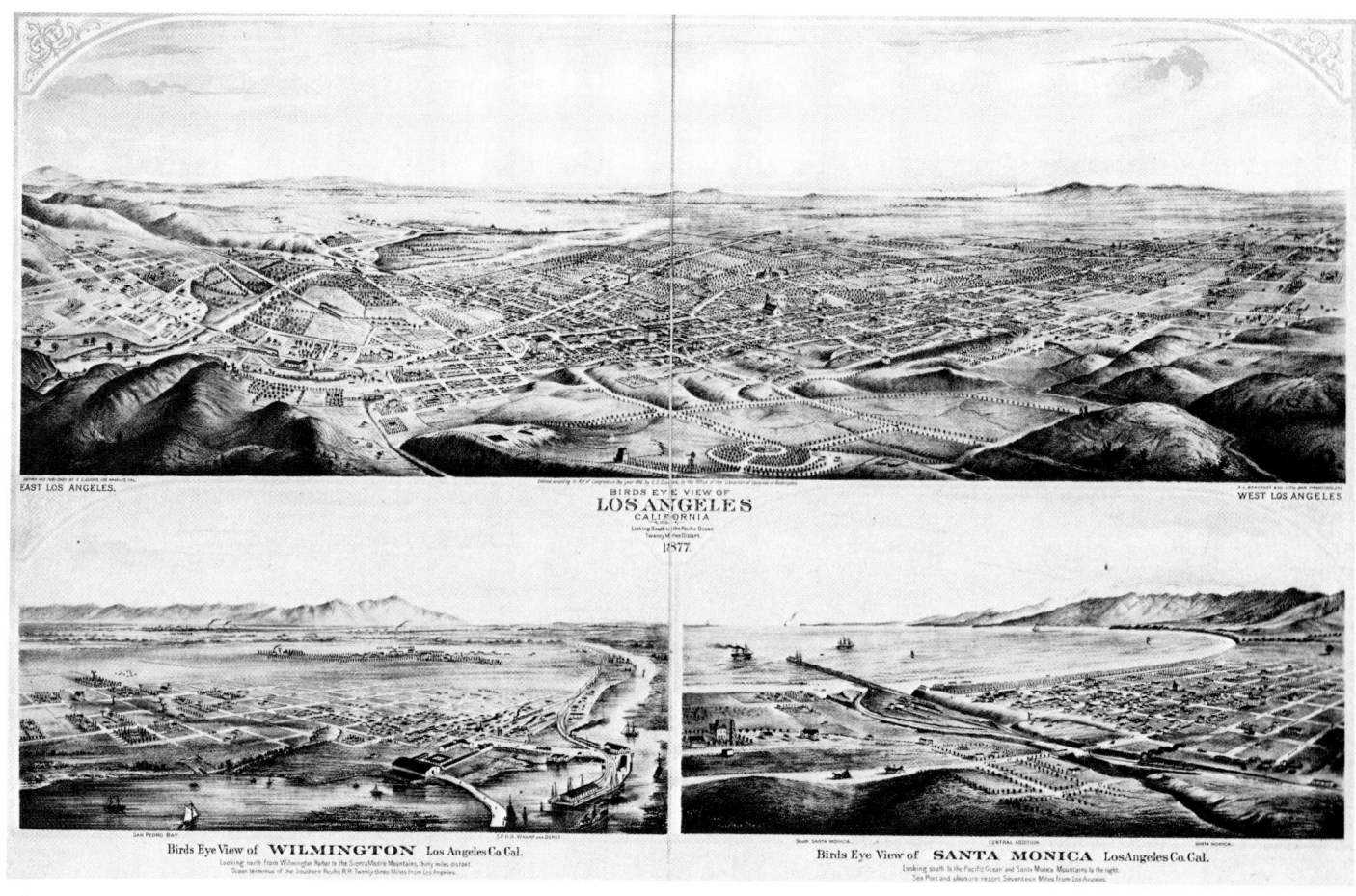

EAST LOS ANGELES.

BIRDS EYE VIEW OF
LOS ANGELES
CALIFORNIA
Looking South to the Pacific Ocean
Twenty Miles Distant.
1877.

WEST LOS ANGELES

SAN PEDRO BAY.

Birds Eye View of **WILMINGTON** Los Angeles Co. Cal.
Looking north from Wilmington Harbor to the Sierra Madre Mountains, thirty miles distant.
Ocean terminus of the Southern Pacific R.R. Twenty-three Miles from Los Angeles.

Birds Eye View of **SANTA MONICA** Los Angeles Co. Cal.
Looking south to the Pacific Ocean and Santa Monica Mountains to the right.
Sea Port and pleasure resort. Seventeen Miles from Los Angeles.

Plate 60. Los Angeles, Wilmington, and Santa Monica, California, 1877. Drawn
and published in Los Angeles by E. S. Glover, printed in San Francisco by A. L.
Bancroft & Co. (Geography and Map Division, Library of Congress.) Catalog 126.

136

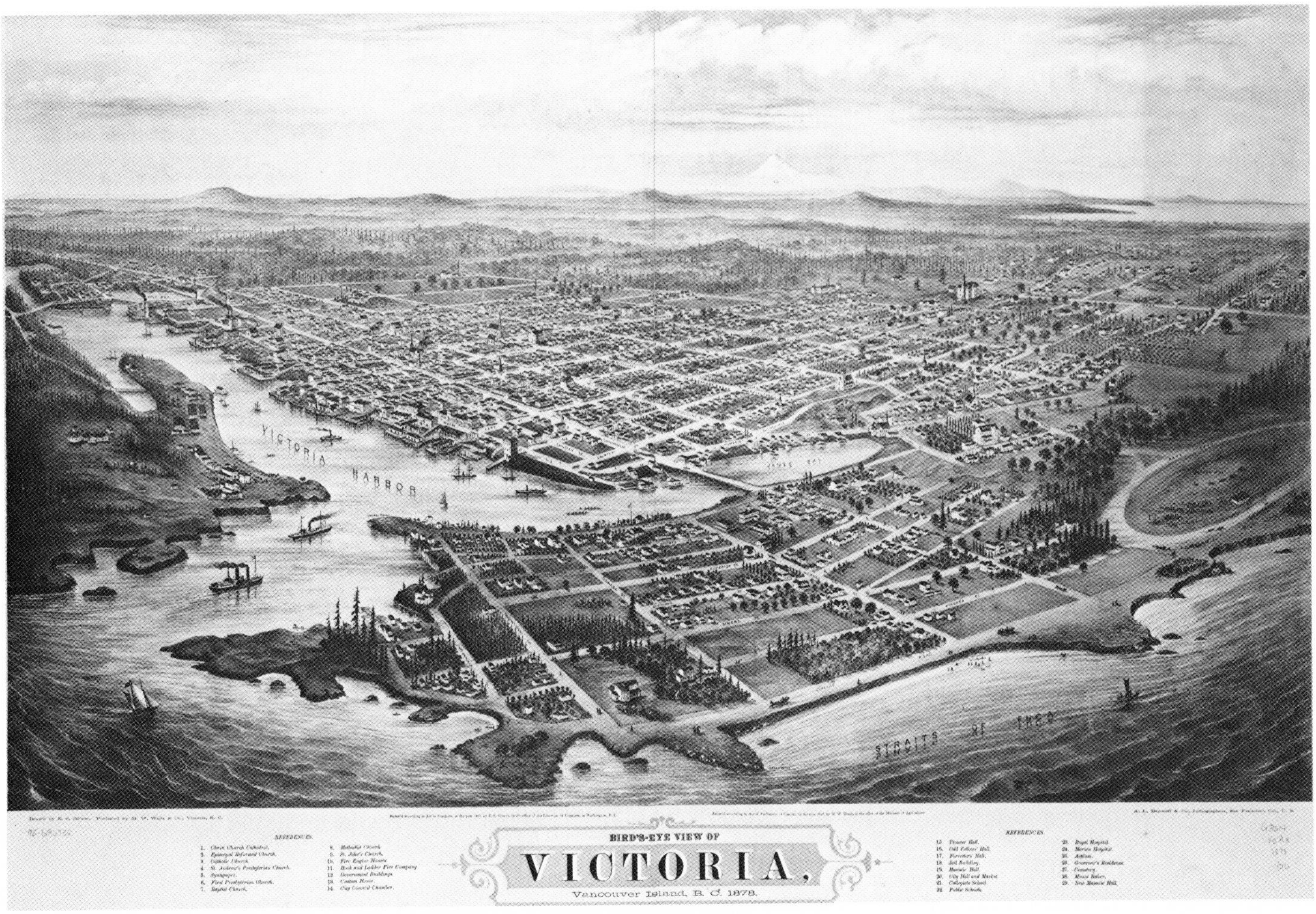

Plate 61. Victoria, British Columbia, 1878. Drawn by E. S. Glover, printed
in San Francisco by A. L. Bancroft & Co., published in Victoria by M. W.
Waitt & Co. (Geography and Map Division, Library of Congress.) Catalog 36.

Plate 62. Honolulu, Hawaii, 1854. Detail. Drawn, lithographed, and copyrighted by Paul
Emmert, printed in San Francisco by Britton & Rey. (Amon Carter Museum.) Catalog 751.

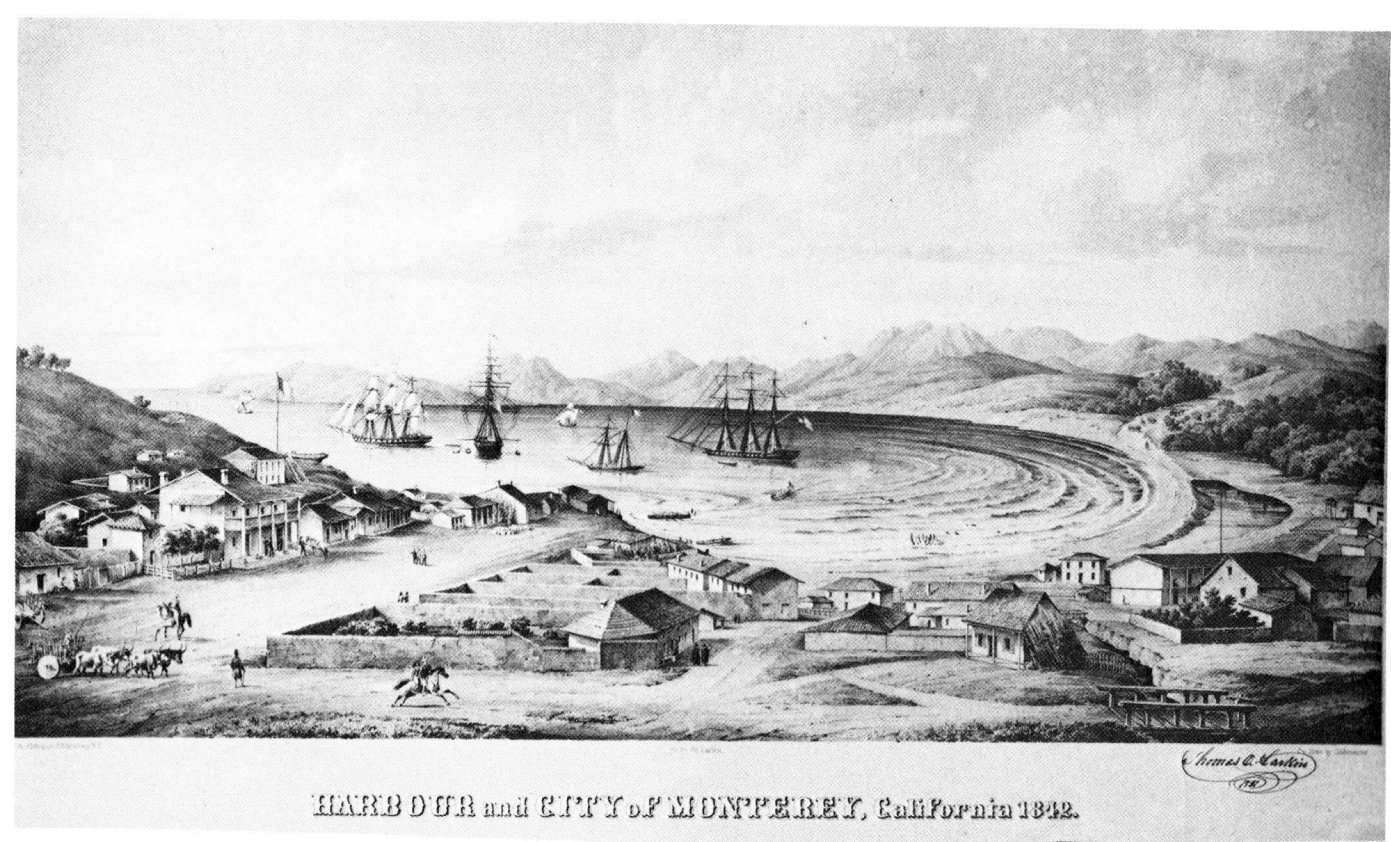

HARBOUR and CITY of MONTEREY, California 1842.

The CITY of MONTEREY, California 1842.

Plate 63. Monterey, California, 1851. Views drawn in 1842 by an unidentified artist, lithographed by Gildemeister, printed in New York by D'Avignon, published by Thomas Larkin. (The Oakland Museum.) Catalog 155.

CENTRAL CITY;

FROM THE SIDE OF MAMMOTH HILL LOOKING UP GREGORY AND EUREKA GULCHES.

Plate 64. Central City, Colorado, 1866. Drawn and copyrighted by A. E. Mathews, printed in New York by J. Bien. (Prints and Photographs Division, Library of Congress.) Catalog 465.

Plate 65. Pittsfield, New Hampshire, 1884. Drawn and published in Brockton, Massachusetts, by George E. Norris, printed in Milwaukee by Beck & Pauli. (Geography and Map Division, Library of Congress.) Catalog 2261.

Plate 66. Walla Walla, Washington, 1866. Drawn from photographs by P. F. Castleman, printed in San Francisco by Grafton T. Brown & Co. (Penrose Memorial Library, Whitman College.) Catalog 4199.

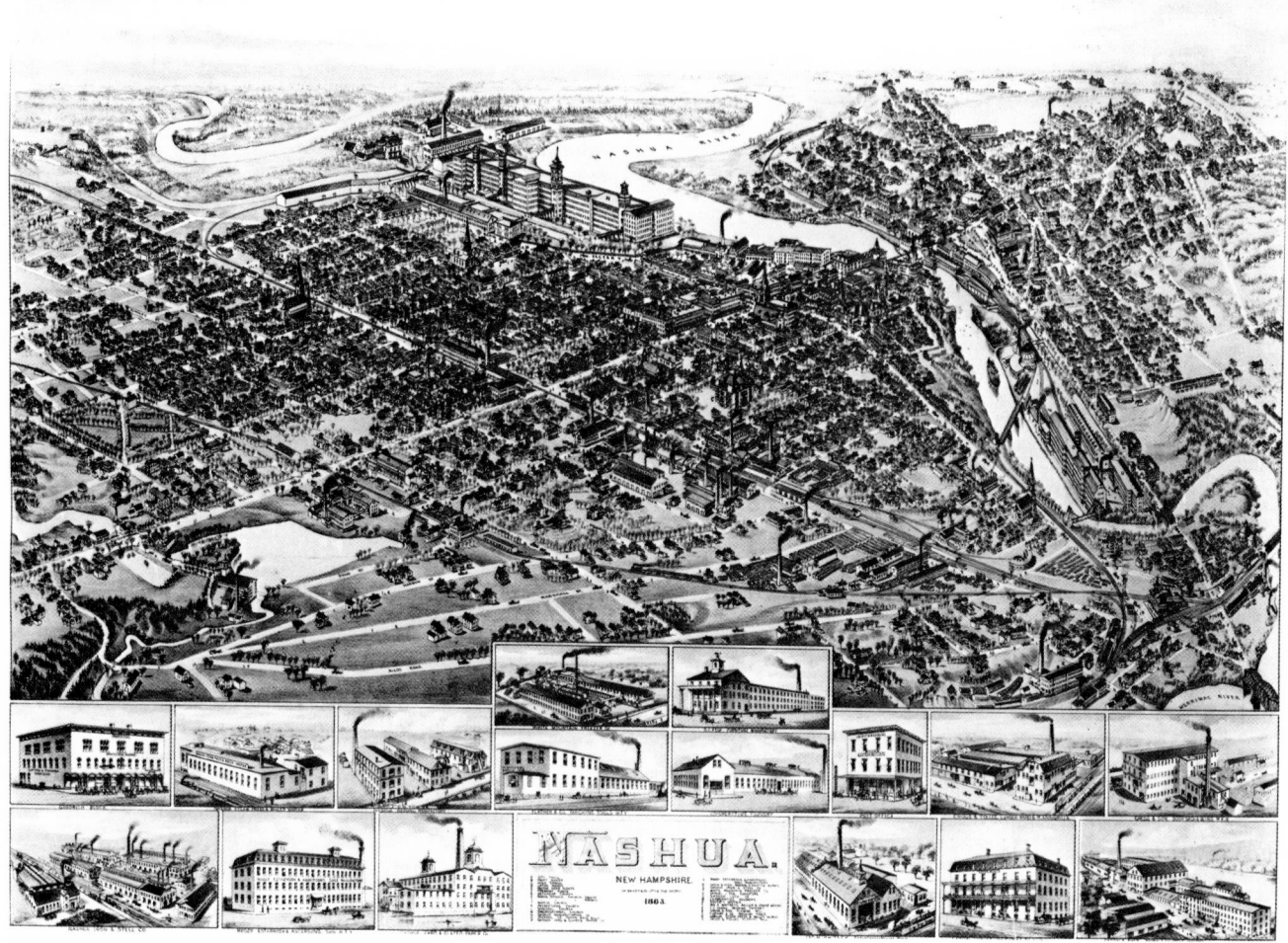

Plate 67. Nashua, New Hampshire, 1883. Printed and published in Boston by O. H. Bailey & Co. (Geography and Map Division, Library of Congress.) Catalog 2253.

Plate 68. Madison, Wisconsin, 1885. Detail. Drawn by H. Wellge, published in Milwaukee by Norris, Wellge, & Co. (Geography and Map Division, Library of Congress.) Catalog 4354.

Plate 70. Laredo, Texas, 1892. Published in Milwaukee by the American Publishing
Co. (Geography and Map Division, Library of Congress.) Catalog 3985.

Plate 69. Forrest Hill, California, 1857. Drawn, lithographed, and published in San Francisco
by Kuchel & Dresel, printed in San Francisco by Britton & Rey. St. Louis, California, 1856.
Drawn and lithographed in San Francisco by Kuchel & Dresel, printed in San Francisco by Britton
& Rey, published by Everts, Wilson & Co. (Amon Carter Museum.) Catalog 91, 220.

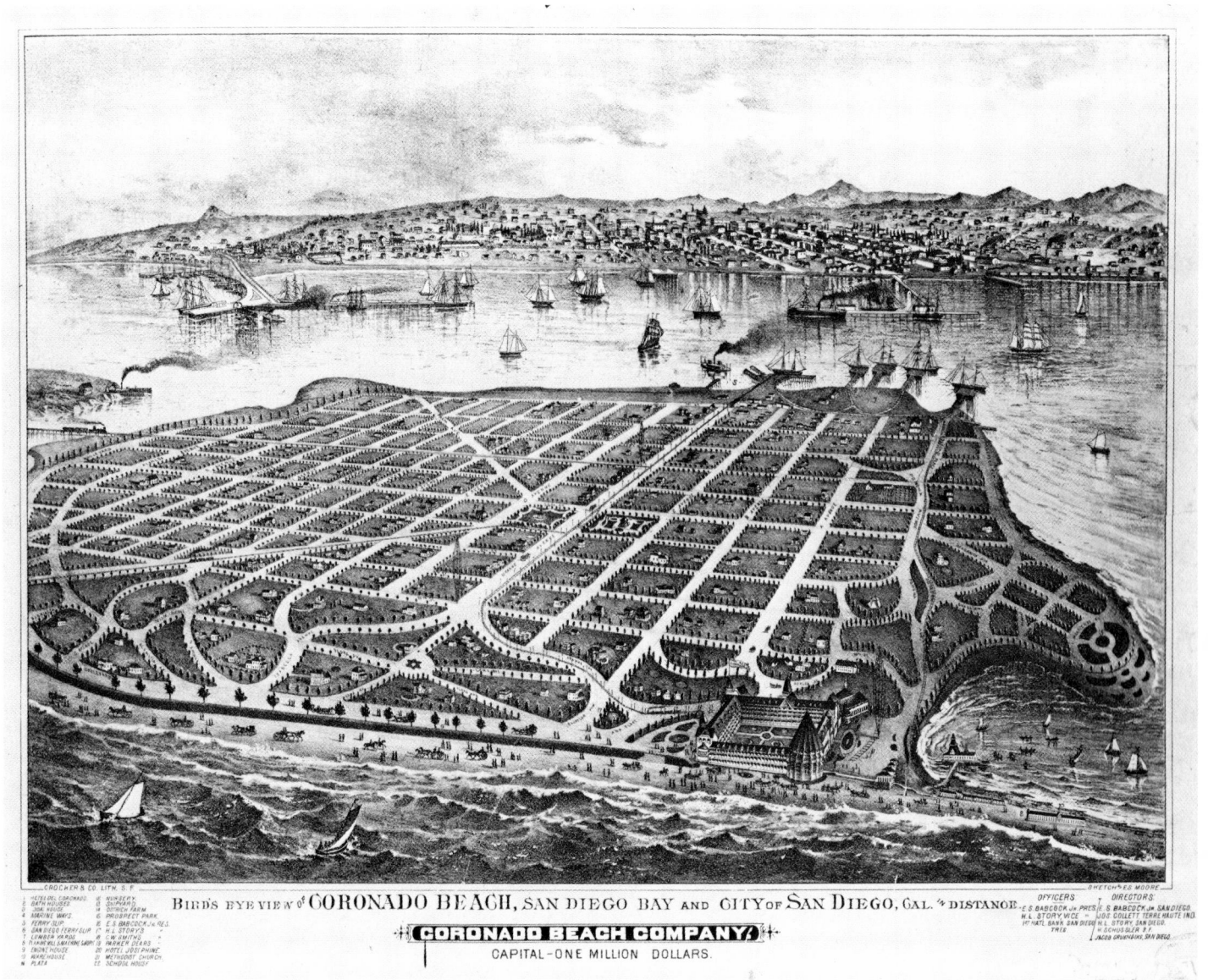

BIRD'S EYE VIEW of CORONADO BEACH, SAN DIEGO BAY and CITY of SAN DIEGO, CAL. ½ DISTANCE

CORONADO BEACH COMPANY.
CAPITAL—ONE MILLION DOLLARS.

Plate 71. Coronado Beach, California, ca. 1887. Drawn by E. S. Moore, printed in San Francisco by Crocker & Co., published by the Coronado Beach Company. (Junipero Serra Museum.) Catalog 80.

CHICAGO, ILL.

Plate 72. Chicago, Illinois, 1856. Steel engraving by W. Wellstood published by *The Ladies'*
Repository from the lithograph of 1853 drawn by Geo. J. Robertson, lithographed by D. W. Moody,
printed in New York by Endicott & Co., published by Smith Brothers & Co. (Private Collection.)

Plate 73. Harvard, Nebraska, 1879. Detail. Drawn by T. M. Fowler, published in Madison, Wisconsin, by J. J. Stoner. (Nebraska State Historical Society.) Catalog 2118.

Plate 74. Milwaukee, Wisconsin, 1872. Detail. Drawn by H. H. Bailey, printed in Milwaukee by the Milwaukee Lithographing & Engraving Co., published in Milwaukee by Holzapfel & Eskuche. (Geography and Map Division, Library of Congress.) Catalog 4382.

Plate 75. Seattle, Washington, 1884. Detail. Drawn by H. Wellge, printed
in Milwaukee by Beck & Pauli, published in Madison, Wisconsin, by J. J.
Stoner. (Geography and Map Division, Library of Congress.) Catalog 4171.

Plate 76. Portsmouth, Ohio, ca. 1855. Drawn and published by J. T. Palmatary, lithographed and printed in Cincinnati by Klauprech & Menzel. (Western Reserve Historical Society.) Catalog 3131.

VIEW OF PORTSMOUTH, O.
FROM THE KENTUCKY HILLS.

Plate 77. Bangor, Maine, 1854. Detail. Drawn by J. W. Hill, lithographed by Charles Parsons, printed in New York by Endicott & Co., published in New York by Smith Brothers & Co. (Chicago Historical Society.) Catalog 1177.

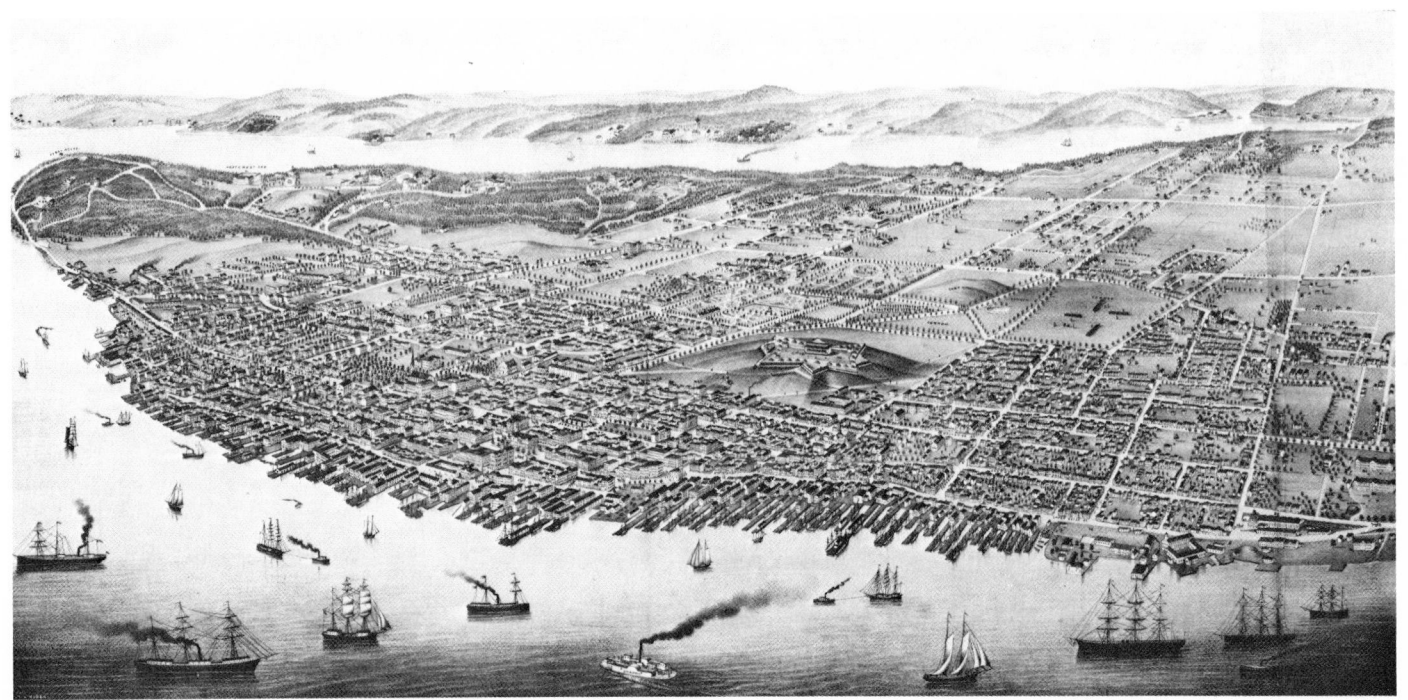

Plate 78. Halifax, Nova Scotia, 1879. Detail. Drawn by A. Ruger.
(Geography and Map Division, Library of Congress.) Catalog 3003.

Plate 79. Denison, Texas, 1891. Drawn by T. M. Fowler, published by
T. M. Fowler & James B. Moyer. (Amon Carter Museum.) Catalog 3961.

BELLEFONTE, PA., 1878.
VIEWED FROM HALF MOON HILL.
PUBLISHED BY C. J. CORBIN & CO.

Plate 80. Bellefonte, Pennsylvania, 1878. Drawn by W. W. Denslow, lithographed by Traubel, printed in Philadelphia by Thos. Hunter, Lith., published in Philadelphia by C. J. Corbin & Co. (Pennsylvania Historical Collections, Pennsylvania State University Library.) Catalog 3324.

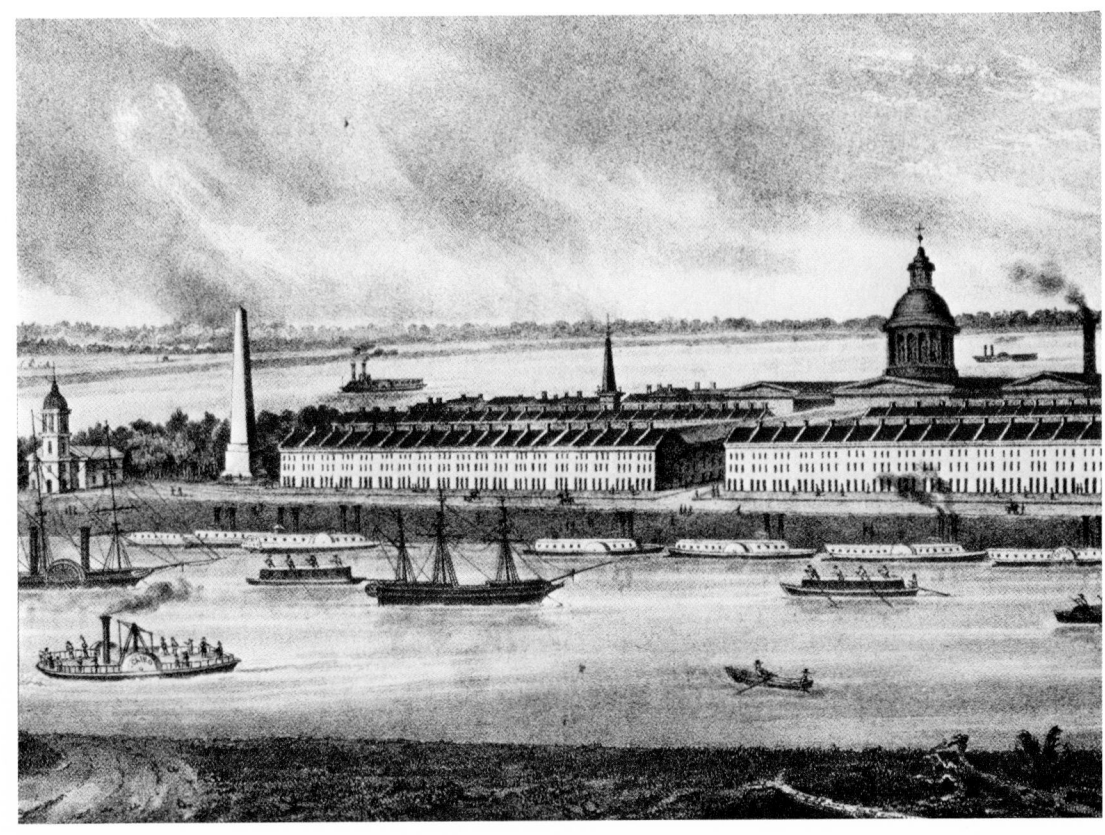

Plate 81. Cairo, Illinois, 1838. Detail. Drawn by Wm. Strickland, lithographed by A. Hoffy, printed in Philadelphia by P. S. Duval. (Amon Carter Museum.) Catalog 786.

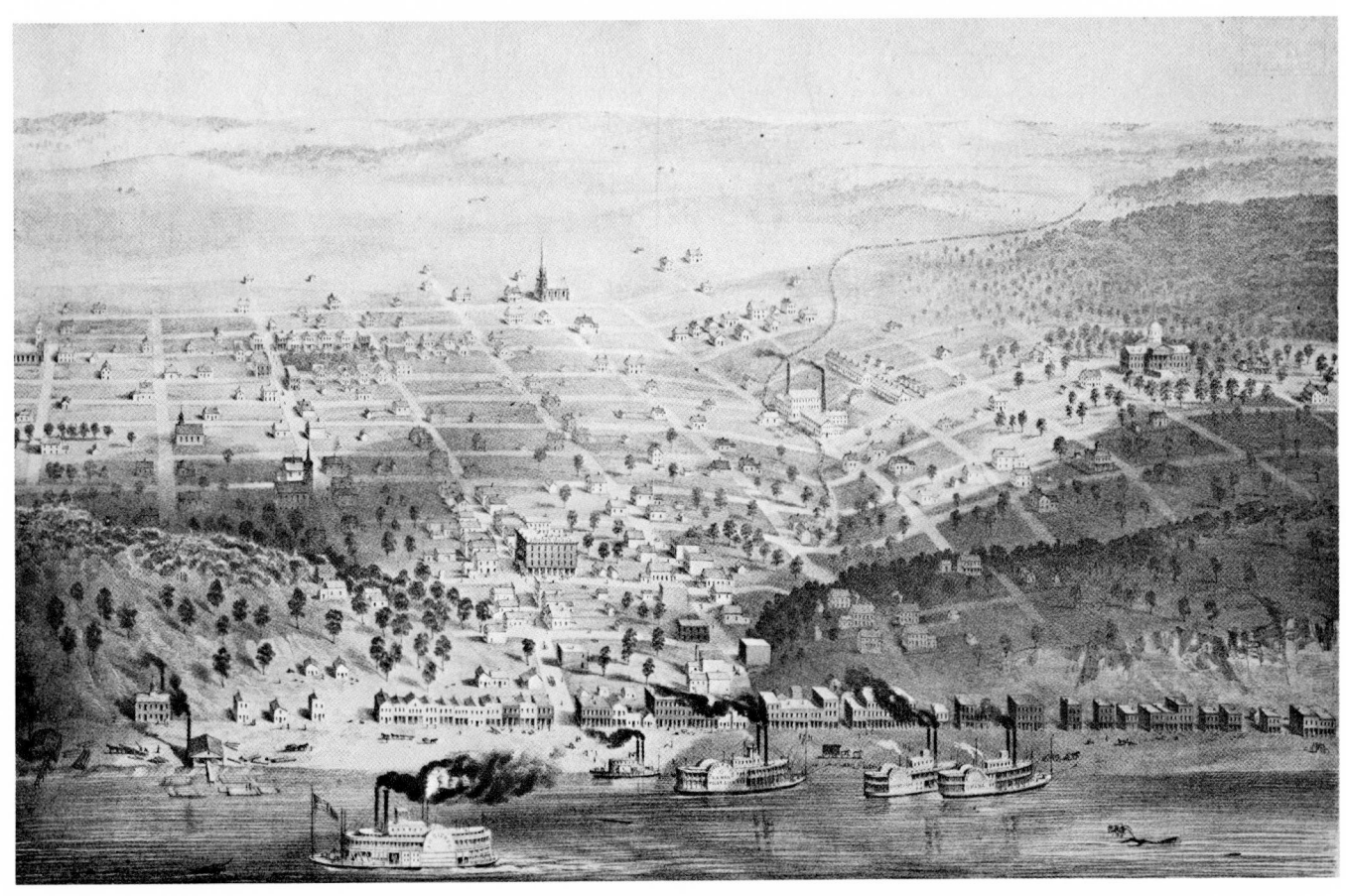

Plate 82. Sumner, Kansas, ca. 1857. Detail. Printed and published in Cincinnati by Middleton-Strobridge & Co. (Kansas State Historical Society.) Catalog 1115.

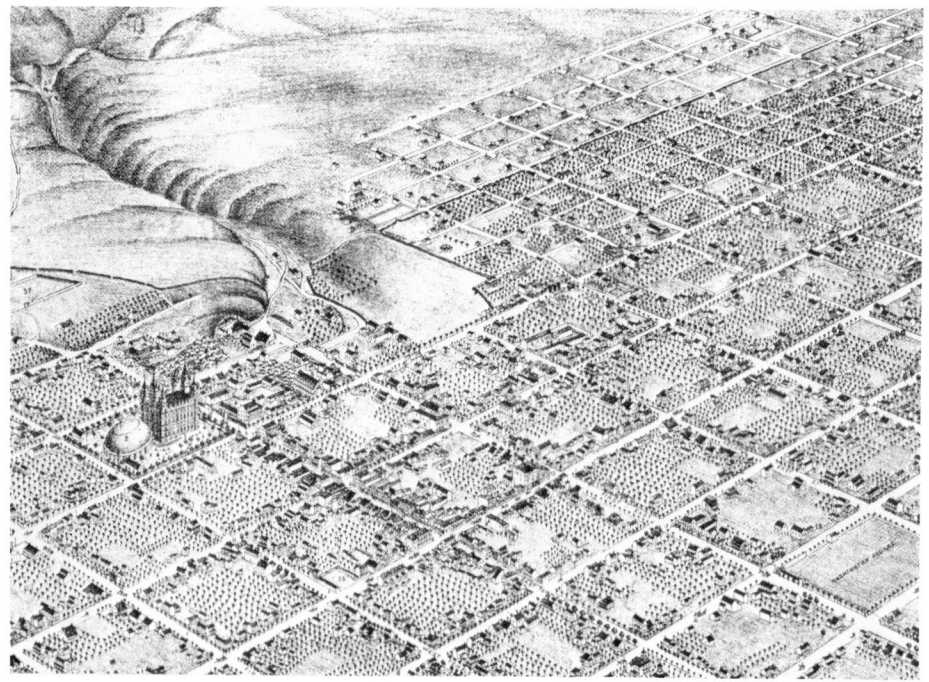

Plate 83. Salt Lake City, Utah, 1870. Detail. Drawn by Augustus Koch, printed in Chicago by the Chicago Lithographing Co. (Geography and Map Division, Library of Congress.) Catalog 4021.

Plate 84. Washington, D.C., 1852. Detail. Drawn and lithographed by E. Sachse, printed in Baltimore and copyrighted by E. Sachse & Co. (Prints and Photographs Division, Library of Congress.) Catalog 669.

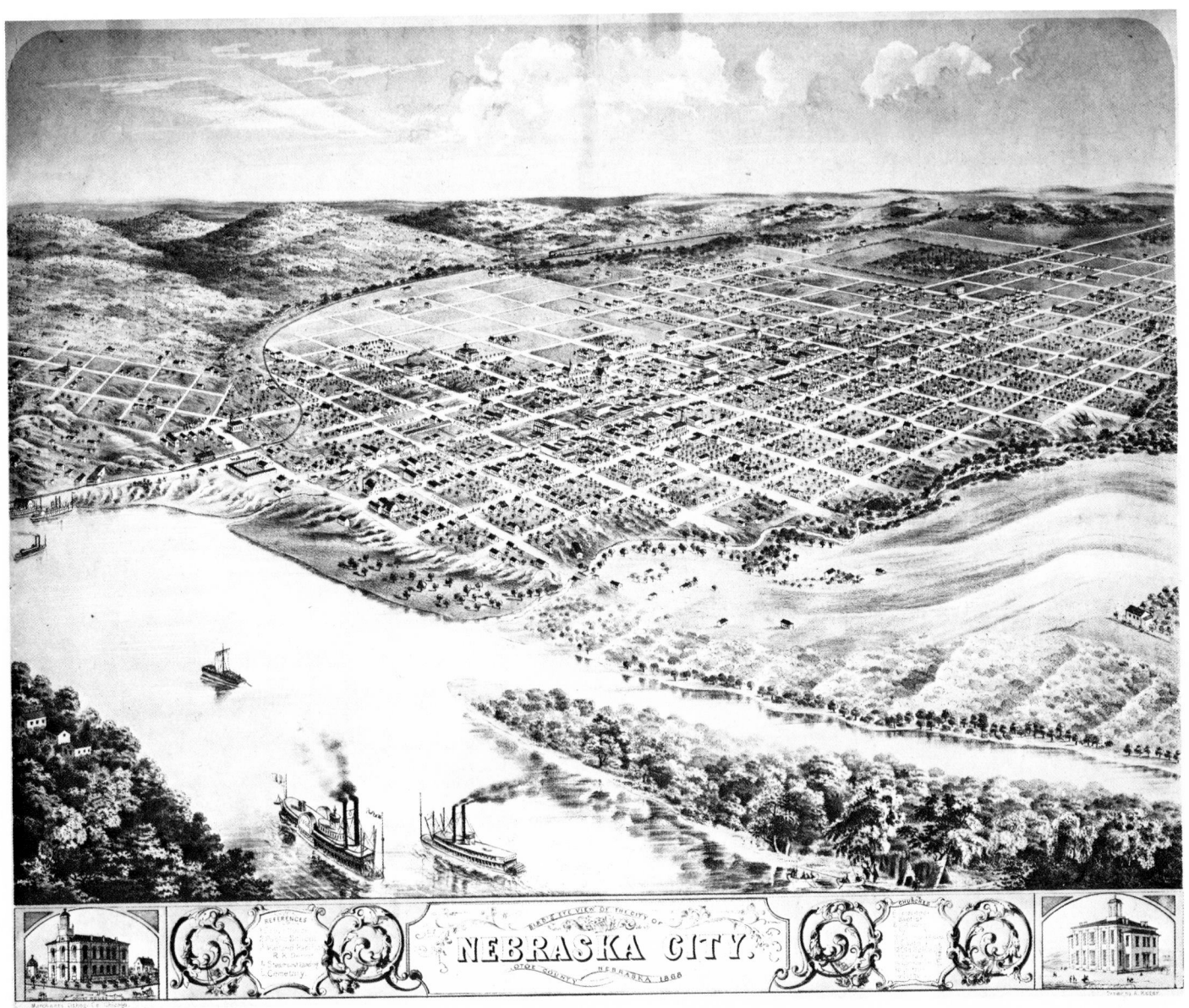

Plate 85. Nebraska City, Nebraska, 1868. Drawn by A. Ruger, printed in Chicago by the Merchants Lithographing Co. (Geography and Map Division, Library of Congress.) Catalog 2134.

NASHUA, N.H.
1875.

Plate 86. Nashua, New Hampshire, 1875. Drawn and published in Boston by H. H. Bailey & Co., lithographed by C. H. Vogt, printed by J. Knauber & Co. (New Hampshire Historical Society.) Catalog 2252.

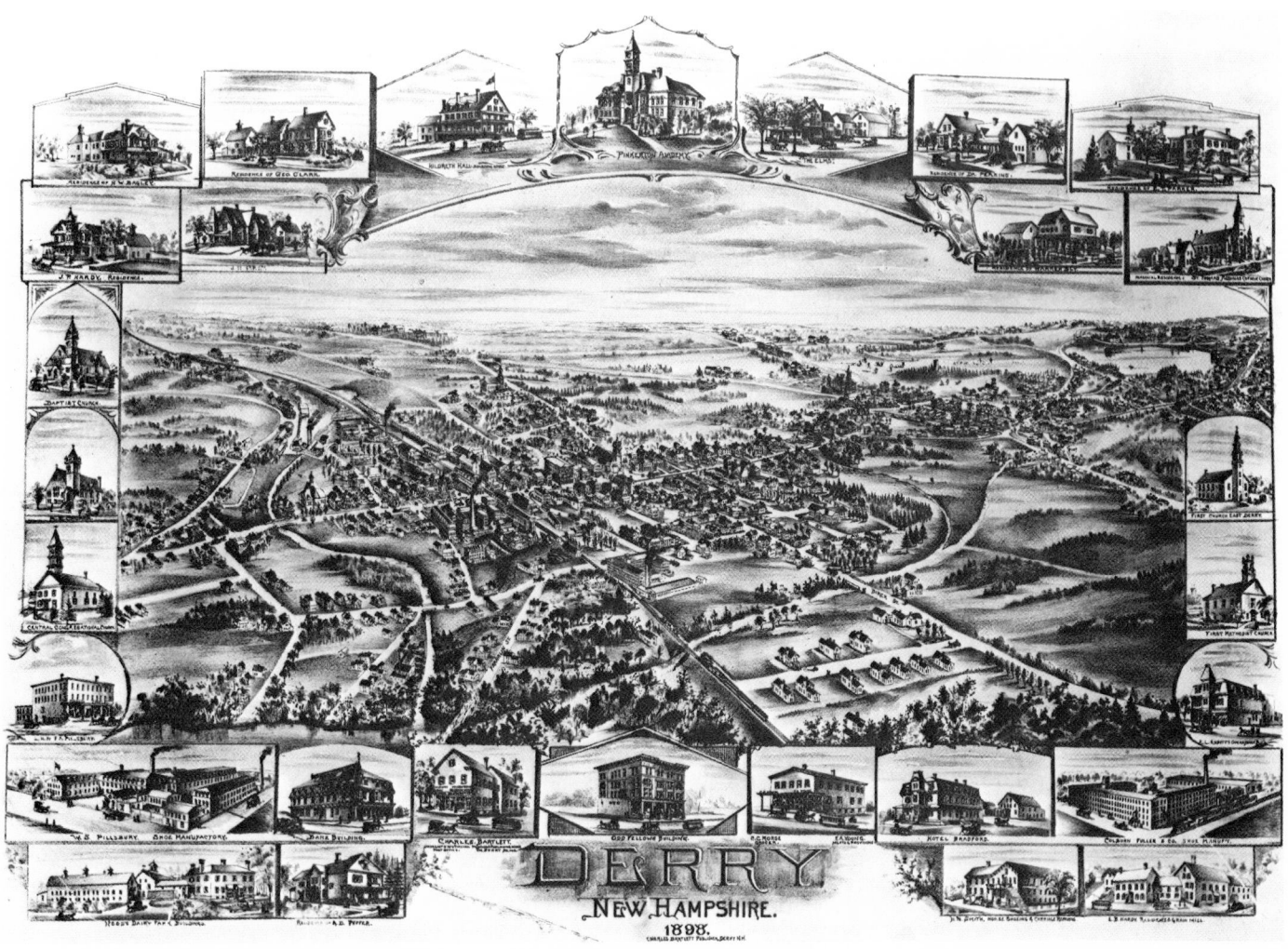

Plate 87. Derry, New Hampshire, 1898. Drawn by O. H. Bailey, published in
Derry by Charles Bartlett. (New Hampshire Historical Society.) Catalog 2213.

VIEW OF ST. LOUIS,
FROM LUCAS PLACE

Plate 88. St. Louis, Missouri, 1865. Printed in Baltimore by E. Sachse & Co., published in
St. Louis by Edw. Buehler. (The Mariners' Museum of Newport News, Virginia.) Catalog 2050.

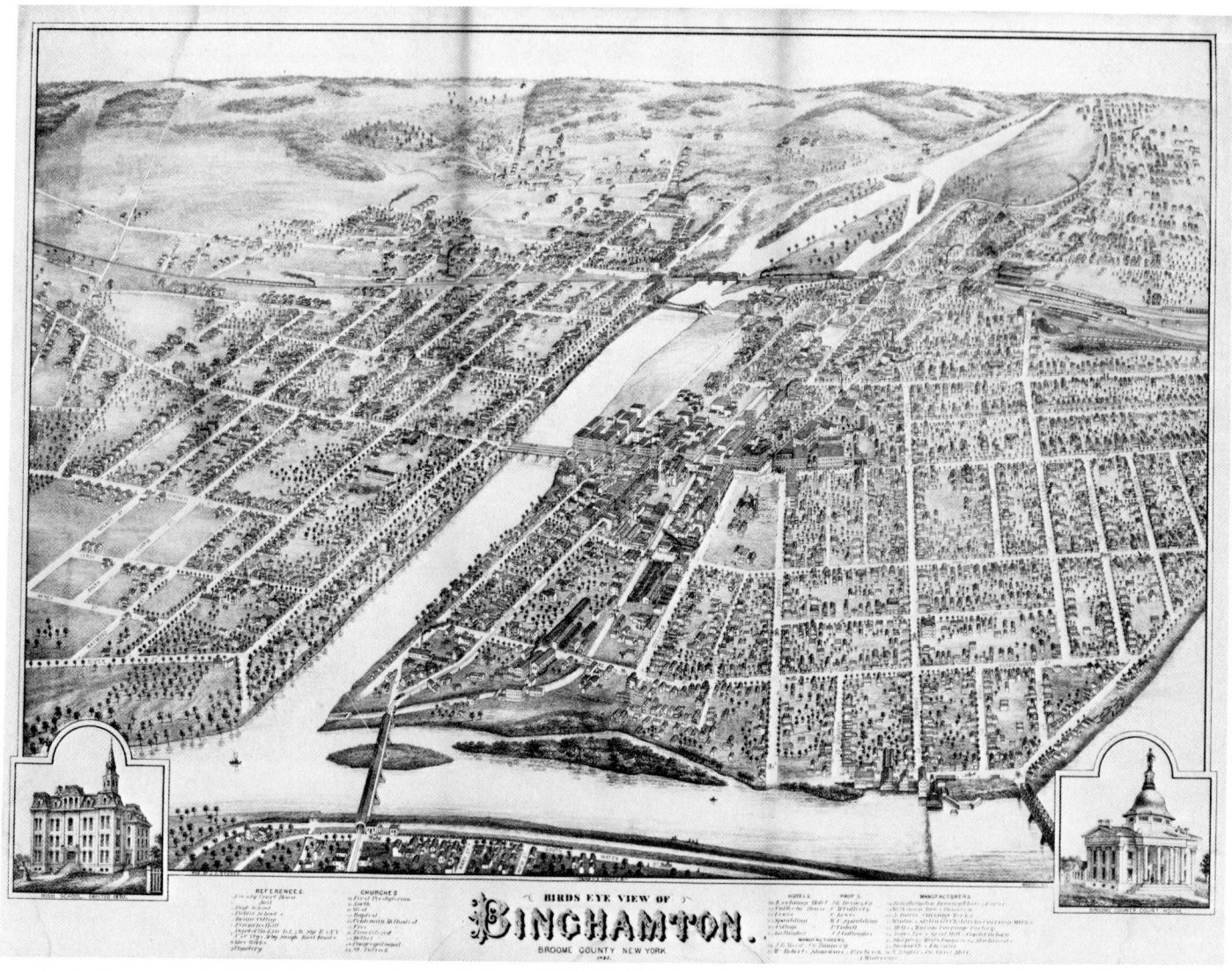

Plate 89. Binghamton, New York, 1873. Drawn by H. Brosius, published in Madison, Wisconsin, by J. J. Stoner. (Broome County Historical Society, Binghamton, New York.) Catalog 2445.

Plate 90. Columbia, South Carolina, 1872. Drawn, lithographed, and published by C. Drie. (Geography and Map Division, Library of Congress.) Catalog 3902.

Part II

The Viewmakers

Introduction

These notes present what is known about the artists and artist-publishers responsible for creating the bulk of the lithographic views of American cities. Excluded are those printers, publishers, or lithographers who did not create images by drawing cities themselves. With a few exceptions, notes appear only for those responsible for producing or participating in the publication of ten or more views.

Footnotes placed immediately after each biographical sketch identify sources of information. Full citations for these sources appear in the bibliography. Statements concerning numbers of views are derived from tabulations of catalog entries. This material is summarized for each person in a chart showing, for every year and by state or province, the number of views drawn, printed, or published.

1. John Badger Bachelder (1825–1894)

John Badger Bachelder, born in Gilmanton, New Hampshire, in 1825, produced thirty-five known city views and took the photograph from which yet another was drawn. All but four of his prints portray his native New England, with twenty of them showing places in Massachusetts and eight places in New Hampshire. Four of his lithographs, including the first three that he did, are of towns in Pennsylvania. The fourth town in Pennsylvania, Bachelder's last dated view, is Gettysburg, whose battlefield and place in military history obsessed Bachelder and about which he wrote extensively.[1]

Two of the three Pennsylvania views of 1854 were printed in Philadelphia by Duval and by Wagner & McGuigan.[2] Bachelder took the other to Endicott and Co. of New York, and in the next few years this firm printed twenty-eight more of his views. William and Francis Endicott were then the company's proprietors, and their advertisements in city directories and elsewhere specifically listing city views as among their major products could have been worded with the business brought to them by Edwin Whitefield, the Smith Brothers, and Bachelder in mind.[3]

The Endicotts served Bachelder well. Since none of the prints shows the artist's signature signed in the stone, it must have been one of the craftsmen in the Endicott plant who skillfully put Bachelder's drawings on the surface to be used for printing. Perhaps more than one helped with this work in 1856, for that date appears on no fewer than eighteen lithographs. Bachelder had drawn six the previous year, and he did five more in 1857. The economic depression that began in the latter year may have cut short what the artist intended as an even more extensive series.

Bachelder acted as his own publisher, but on almost all of the prints his address appears as 59 Beekman St., New York—the address of the Endicott printing establishment. Probably some employee in the firm took care of the artist's business correspondence, for during most of the period from 1854 through 1856 he maintained a studio in Manchester, New Hampshire. He traveled from there to paint or draw the places he selected for his lithographs.

Bachelder, like Fitz Hugh Lane, Henry Walton, and Edwin Whitefield, drew his subjects as he looked at them from a distance and from nonimaginary viewpoints. We thus see his thriving New England industrial communities or ports as they might have appeared to an arriving stranger on the road to town catching his first glimpse of houses, factories, and churches extending across the horizon.

While only two of his views—Chicopee Falls, Massachusetts, and Claremont, New Hampshire (both published in 1857)—make explicit that Bachelder drew them from photographic images, most of his urban scenes possess this kind of documentary character. One finds this quality reflected in titles of great specificity: *Providence, R. I. Harbor View. Taken from the Grounds of Geo. W. Rhodes, Esq.*; *South Danvers, Mass. From Buxton's Hill*; *Lowell, Mass. Sketched from the Residence of Thomas L. Tuxbury Esqu. (Dracut Heights.)* It is not surprising to learn that Bachelder was himself a photographer. An otherwise unsigned view of Worcester, Massachusetts, in 1864 states that it is from photographs by "Black & Batchelder."

John Badger Bachelder

	Mass.	Maine	N.H.	Pa.	R.I.	Vt.	Total
1854				3			3
1855	1	1	4				6
1856	13	1	3			1	18
1857	4		1				5
1858	1				1		2
1859–							
1863				1			1
1864	1						1
Total	20	2	8	4	1	1	36

The final city view drawn by Bachelder and published in 1863 shows Gettysburg, Pennsylvania. It is only one of several lithographs he did related to the Civil War. After the end of that conflict he devoted much of his time to drawing diagrams and views of the Gettysburg battlefield and to writing battle guides and histories. He died at Hyde Park, New York, in 1894, and his viewmaking years of 1854–1863 thus occupied only a short period of his life.

1. Bachelder is another artist-publisher whose life and work need further study. I have based my note mainly on a five-paragraph passage in "Art and Artists in Manchester" and on the material in Harry T. Peters, *America on Stone: The Other Printmakers to the American People . . .*, 82, where a few of the Bachelder prints other than city views are listed.

2. Bachelder's 1854 views of Lock Haven, Williamsport, and Jersey Shore, Pennsylvania, are reproduced as pls. 45, 47, and 48 in Pennsylvania State University, Museum of Art, *Pennsylvania Prints from the Collection of John C. O'Connor and Ralph M. Yeager. . . .*

3. Peters, *America on Stone*, in his long note on the Endicott firm, quotes on p. 176 this excerpt from directory advertisements listing the company's products that began in 1856 and ran for several years: "Hotels, steamers, manufactures, machinery, views of towns, portraits, book illustrations, maps, music titles &c., and every description of show card, plain or in colors, lithographed by Endicott & Co., at their old and well-known establishment, No. 59 Beekman St., N.Y."

2. John Bachmann (—   )

No finer artist of city views worked in America than John Bachmann.[1] Unfortunately, there is no artist about whom less is known, for information concerning his life appears to be nonexistent.[2] His name and its first appearance on a city view in 1849 strongly suggest that he was German and one of the many artists who came to America from that country in the middle and late 1840s as a result of political disturbances in their homeland.

Bachmann brought with him fully developed artistic, lithographic, and printing skills, for his earliest prints reveal a high level of competence and complete command of the lithographic medium. He began his American career, however, as a publisher of a splendid view of New York City as seen from a point high above Union Square looking south to the Battery and the harbor (Plate 16). There are two states of this lithograph: one identifies Bachmann as the publisher; the other has a publisher's imprint of William & Stevens, 353 Broadway, but with Bachmann as the copyright claimant. Both states bear the signature of C. Bachman as artist and lithographer. C. Bachman's relationship to John remains unclear, and his name makes no further appearance on any recorded city view except for reissues in 1850 and 1854 of the original print.[3]

Such variant issues can be found in Bachmann's later work and can make cataloging of his prints both difficult and misleading. If all of those prints naming him in some capacity are counted, the number exceeds fifty. A closer analysis would reveal that the actual number of images he created as artist, lithographer, or publisher would be about thirty-five or so. His associations with other printers and publishers were so numerous and fleeting that a complete narrative of them would be needlessly tedious.

The first views drawn by Bachmann appeared in 1850. For that of New York he was not only the artist and publisher but the lithographer and printer as well. He drew, lithographed, and published a Boston view of that year, and he drew and put on stone a Philadelphia view that Williams and Stevens published. Sarony & Major printed both of the latter lithographs.

Bachmann concentrated his attention on a few large cities, but he also did a view of Superior, Wisconsin, and two of Hoboken, New Jersey. The earliest of the two Hoboken prints, drawn and published by Bachmann in 1860, gives a street address in that city as his place of business.[4]

It was on New York City that he focused his efforts, producing views in 1849, 1850, 1851, 1858, 1861, 1865, 1866, 1868, 1870, 1874, 1877, 1878, 1879, and 1885. While a few of these represent variant states, most of them were new images and thus provide a graphic chronicle of the growth and change in the metropolis over a period of more than thirty years as seen through the eyes of a single artist.

Bachmann chose to portray New York and his other subjects as if seen from imaginary viewpoints far above even the loftiest office building or church steeple. Indeed, his superb Boston lithograph of 1850 (Plate 34) may have been the earliest to use in its title the words *bird's eye* to describe this pictorial approach. Bachmann may not have been the first

John Bachmann
(Includes variant states)

	N.Y.	Mass.	Pa.	La.	Md.	Kans.	Wisc.	N.J.	D.C.	Conn.	Total
1849	2										2
1850	4	1	2	1							8
1851	3			2							5
1852–											
1854	1										1
1855	2										2
1856					1		1				2
1857						1					1
1858											
1859	4			3							7
1860								1			1
1861	1										1
1862									1		1
1863											
1864										1	1
1865	3										3
1866	2										2
1867											
1868	2		1								3
1869											
1870	1										1
1871–											
1874	1							1			2
1875			1								1
1876											
1877	1	1									2
1878	1										1
1879	2										2
1880–											
1885	2										2
n.d.	1			1							2
Total	33	2	4	7	1	1	1	2	1	1	53

artist to apply in America this method, long used in Europe, of depicting cities, but his consistent use of the technique must have helped popularize it as a way of revealing the whole city in some detail, not merely the portion visible from the artist's easel.

Several Bachmann views of New York and New Orleans were published in Paris by a publisher named Wild, who also issued European and other American city views. Wild may have been related to John Caspar Wild of Philadelphia and St. Louis. Bachmann might have known Wild; Auguste Bry and Lemercier, the Paris printers who did his work; or Asselineau, who put most of these lithographs on stone. Wild included Bachmann's name as artist, so presumably the views were not simply pirated. Probably Bachmann and Wild worked together to bring out versions of Bachmann's views to sell on the European market.

While Bachmann printed several of his own views, he relied on others for most of this work. In addition to Sarony & Major, Bachmann turned to Peter S. Duval of Philadelphia, Julius Bien in New York, and a few other New York printers. Probably Louis Prang of Boston printed Bachmann's view of

Boston in 1877 (Color Plate 2), although Prang's name appears on the print only as publisher.

Taken together, Bachmann's views offer a rich sample of lithographic achievement in this country and in France during the third quarter of the last century. Those he executed during the decade of the 1850s are particularly outstanding and are justifiably regarded by collectors and curators as among the finest American views to be found.

---

1. The name appears on prints both as Bachman and as Bachmann, the latter being used more often.

2. I suspect that hard work would produce results. My inquiries directed to print curators at the Museum of the City of New York, the New-York Historical Society, and the New York Public Library—all places with Bachmann views—proved unrewarding. I had hoped that during the course of my research I would find the time and opportunity to pursue other avenues of information about him. This proved impossible. Peters, *America on Stone*, 82–84, provides only a partial list of his prints and the New York City addresses appearing on them. Peters concluded his note, "While the amount of work recorded is not large it is important and of excellent quality."

3. The 1850 and 1854 states appear to be from the same stone but with changed copyright dates.

4. The address is 9 Irving Place. The second Hoboken view of 1874 shows Bachmann's name only as artist, and the publisher is identified as F. Luthin, 197 Washington St., Hoboken.

3. Howard Heston Bailey (1836–1878)

Born in 1836 in Beloit, Ohio, H. H. Bailey taught penmanship, worked for a time in a photographic business, and, in 1865 and 1866, sold illustrated advertisements showing business premises in such cities as Leavenworth, Kansas, Des Moines, Iowa, and Omaha, Nebraska. A Leavenworth newspaper described Bailey's products in these words:

> *Fine Pen Drawing.* As good a specimen of Calligraphy as we have seen for a long time, came under our notice yesterday. It was a collection of the business cards of many of our principal merchants, artists, &c., executed with pen and india ink, by H. H. Baily of Ohio, Professor of Penmanship and Bookkeeping.—Mr. Baily intends making a business of getting up these cards, for which purpose he will visit the principal cities in this part of the country.[1]

Bailey obviously moved from place to place in his attempts to sell his poster-directories. In Omaha in 1866 he would have been too early to find Albert Ruger at work in that city, for that pioneering post-Civil War artist was still producing his first views in Michigan and Indiana, visiting Illinois, Wisconsin, and Minnesota the following year. But if Bailey traveled in this part of the Midwest, he may have seen Ruger's lithographs, perhaps met the artist himself, and it is conceivable that he worked as agent or artist's assistant for Ruger, as did Eli S. Glover in 1866 and T. M. Fowler in 1868 and 1869.

It is said in the Fowler family that young Thaddeus Fowler met H. H. Bailey in Madison, Wisconsin, at the photographic studio of Fowler's uncle. If this was in 1868 when Fowler was acting as Ruger's agent, perhaps it was Fowler who suggested that Bailey turn his artistic talents to city views. Or, if Bailey had been working for Ruger, possibly Bailey recruited Fowler to this line of work. The latter sequence of events would not be incompatible with the assertion by Fowler's daughter that it was H. H. Bailey who "taught her father how to draw" city views.[2]

Whether influenced by Fowler or by someone else, Bailey decided to become an artist of city views. He made an impressive entrance into the world of viewmaking in 1870 with nine lithographs, all of which showed places in central and southern Wisconsin. A publisher's name appears on only one: the print of Oconomowoc with the publisher and his address given as "T. M. Fowler & Co., Box 668, Madison, Wis."

Bailey evidently drew with great speed, for in 1871 twenty-two city views with his name as artist or publisher reached the market. Bailey drew seventeen of these alone, and three of them were published by Fowler. Five others show Fowler and Bailey as publishers, artists, or both. Seven of the twenty-two towns were in Indiana, one in Iowa, three in Michigan, and the remaining eleven in Wisconsin. Fourteen of these views do not identify a publisher, who may have been Bailey himself, Fowler, or the two acting jointly.

While it must have taken much of Bailey's time in 1872 to do the sketching and final drawings for his Milwaukee view of that year (Plate 74), he also sketched three other towns, drew one other with Fowler that they jointly published, collaborated with his brother, O. H. Bailey, on a view of Columbus, Ohio, and was probably involved in the views of Altoona and Wilkes-Barre, Pennsylvania, produced under the name of Fowler & Bailey.

The *Fowler & Bailey* title, sometimes used to designate the artists or—on unsigned prints—the publishers, makes it impossible to know who did the drawing. It could have been either of the Baileys, the two working together, Fowler working alone, or Fowler working with either or both of his two associates. All three came to New York State in 1873. O. H. Bailey drew Ithaca, and Fowler acted as his subscription agent.[3] "Fowler & Bailey" drew and published a lithograph of Cortland. O. H. Bailey drew Seneca Falls for a print lacking a publisher's imprint. H. H. Bailey drew Elmira. The four towns are close to one another, and the three men must have agreed on how to allocate their artistic and sales resources.

H. H. Bailey was also busy in Pennsylvania that year with views of Bloomsburg and York, and he may have been the Bailey of "Fowler & Bailey" who prepared the lithographs of Catasauqua and Easton. The three viewmakers added several other New York views in 1874. H. H. Bailey did those of Syracuse, Poughkeepsie, and Johnstown, two lithographs of towns in New Jersey, and a view of Wilmington, Delaware.

Bailey published his Poughkeepsie lithograph with J. C. Hazen, who in the previous fall had acted as Bailey's subscription and sales agent in Syracuse.[4] James Compton Hazen in 1874 was twenty-two, and for four years beginning in 1874 his name can often be found bracketed with H. H. Bailey's. He was both artist and publisher while associated with Bailey and was doubtless trained by Bailey, just as Fowler and Glover—and perhaps Bailey himself—had learned viewmaking by working for Ruger.

By 1875 H. H. Bailey seems to have terminated his busi-

	Wisc.	Mich.	Ind.	Iowa	Pa.	Ohio	N.Y.	N.J.	Del.	Mass.	N.H.	Conn.	R.I.	Vt.	Total
1870	9														9
1871	13	3	5	1											22
1872	1				3	3									7
1873				2			1	1							4
1874							3	2	1						6
1875							7	2		2	2		1		14
1876										4	1	1	1	1	8
1877							1			1					2
Total	23	3	5	1	5	3	12	5	1	7	3	1	2	1	72

ness relationship with Fowler. In that year and thereafter he published under the name of H. H. Bailey & Co. or H. H. Bailey & J. C. Hazen. He produced fourteen views in 1875: seven in New York, two each of towns in Massachusetts, New Hampshire (see Plate 86), and New Jersey, and one in Rhode Island. The following year he added eight more views, all in New England. Finally, in the year before he died, Bailey drew and published views of Holyoke, Massachusetts, and Troy, New York.

In the eight years of his career as a view artist Bailey left a substantial record of the appearance of towns and cities in the Midwest, the central Atlantic states, and New England. His views number an impressive seventy-two in all, and this total does not include any of the "Fowler & Bailey" prints, on some of which he surely worked. H. H. Bailey used a distinctive high-level perspective that makes his lithographs instantly recognizable by those familiar with his style. This method of depicting the urban scene clearly reveals the patterns of streets, open spaces, public sites, and neighborhoods in the cities portrayed.

No viewmaker surpassed H. H. Bailey in his careful representations of industrial and business districts. Civic leaders must have admired his prints of such places as Syracuse, Troy, Lowell, Holyoke, Lawrence, Woonsocket, and Paterson for their detailed representations of the mill and manufacturing complexes dominating the urban scene in these industrial communities. Most businessmen could find their enterprises identified in the long and detailed legends that Bailey provided, each entry keyed to a number on the view. These men must have been his best customers, and while he lived Bailey probably enjoyed a substantial income from his sales in places of this character.

1. Leavenworth, Kansas, *Bulletin*, 8 September 1865. This notice appears on an advertisement printed by Bailey, probably in 1866. It includes three other newspaper notices under a heading reading, in part, "To Business Men! H. H. Baily of Ohio prepares Business Directories, Does all the work with a Pen, sketches Views of Stores, Interior and Exterior, &c., &c." James Raymond Warren kindly provided me with a copy of this advertisement, printed before Bailey changed the spelling of his name. Warren was responsible for most of what is known about H. H. Bailey and his brother, Oakley Hoopes Bailey. His studies are summarized at length in James Raymond Warren, Sr., and Donald A. Wise, "Two Birds-Eye-View Artists: The Bailey Brothers," 20–23. This includes a checklist of views on which the name *Bailey* appears as artist or publisher. However, the checklist is far from complete; I have recorded nearly one hundred additional views in this category. It is also misleading in attributing to O. H. Bailey & Co. fifteen or

so prints published in the early twentieth century by the firm of Hughes and Bailey.
2. Warren and Wise, "The Bailey Brothers," 20.
3. The Ithaca view lacks any imprint, but a local newspaper account identifies O. H. Bailey as the artist and Fowler as the agent. Ithaca *Daily Journal*, 9 August 1873.
4. The Ithaca *Daily Journal*, 21 October 1873, mentioned Hazen's activities in Syracuse in connection with H. H. Bailey's view.

4. Oakley Hoopes Bailey (1843–1947)

During a career that spanned fifty-six years, Oakley Hoopes Bailey produced about 375 recorded city views, an achievement surpassed only by his longtime friend and sometime associate, Thaddeus M. Fowler. Bailey began drawing cities in 1871 and 1872 in the Midwest. During the next two years he sketched towns and cities in New York, Pennsylvania, and New Jersey. In 1875 he produced his first lithographs of New England, and shortly thereafter he settled in Cambridge, Massachusetts. From that base he concentrated on drawing towns in Connecticut, Rhode Island, and Massachusetts. About two-thirds of his prints are of towns in these states, and more than 130 show Massachusetts communities.

Bailey was born in Beloit, Ohio. He entered Mount Union College in 1864, left for four months of service in the Ohio Volunteer Infantry during the Civil War, and returned to graduate in 1866. After teaching school for a time, he joined his older brother, Howard Heston Bailey, who sold illustrated business directories in Kansas, Iowa, Nebraska, Ohio, Illinois, Indiana, and Minnesota.[1]

He probably helped his brother when Howard began drawing city views in 1870. It was then he would have met T. M. Fowler, who published some of the elder Bailey's views. In 1871 Oakley Bailey did his first view, sketching Marinette and Menekaune, Wisconsin, and Menominee, Michigan, for a lithograph titled *Bird's Eye View of the Towns at the Mouth of the Menominee River*.[2]

Bailey evidently worked closely with his brother and Fowler in his first years as a viewmaker. Most of the views that H. H. Bailey drew in 1871 and 1872 in Wisconsin—several of which Fowler published alone or jointly with the artist—were of cities north of Milwaukee. Peshtigo and

Oconto, for example, were only a few miles away from Marinette. In 1872 Fowler solicited subscriptions for a lithograph of Milwaukee (Plate 74) to be drawn by O. H. Bailey, but when the print appeared later that year, H. H. Bailey was identified as the artist.

All three names appear on one view. This lithograph of Columbus, Ohio, in 1872 lists H. H. & O. H. Bailey as artists and identifies the publisher as Fowler & Bailey. This ambiguous use of the Bailey name can be found on several other prints at this time, as a designation for the artists, for the publishers, or both. In those cases when it is used to designate the publishers one can find examples of either H. H. Bailey or O. H. Bailey as artist.[3]

The most reasonable interpretation of these interactions is that during their early years the three men shared responsibilities, expenses, and profits, and only after the mid-1870s did they establish separate business enterprises. Possibly they cared very little about credit for their work as reflected in imprint information. The lithograph of Ithaca, New York, in 1873, for example, omits imprint identification altogether. Newspaper accounts, however, reveal that O. H. Bailey drew it and that Fowler acted as his subscription agent.[4]

O. H. Bailey drew several other New York views at this time: Seneca Falls in 1873 and Waverly, Port Jervis, Oneida, Penn Yan, and Goshen the year after. On his Port Jervis print Bailey gave his address as Boston. The parents of his wife, whom he married in 1872, lived in Cambridge, Massachusetts, and it was there that Bailey established his home.[5] Although the Boston city directories do not list him as doing business in that city, Bailey's lithographs for many years gave Boston as the location of his firm.[6]

Beginning in 1874 and continuing to 1877, Bailey's name appears on the prints, with only a few exceptions, as both artist and publisher. In 1877 he began his association with J. C. Hazen, formerly his brother's collaborator (see Plate 25). Their association continued through 1879, when Hazen was married and the two terminated their joint publishing venture. During the period from 1874 to 1877, Bailey also continued to draw and publish under his own name.

By the end of 1879 Bailey had produced by himself or with others about one hundred city views. This record by itself would have been impressive enough, but Bailey had only begun. Although he would never again equal the annual output of the Hazen years when by himself or with his associate he was responsible for 25 views both in 1878 and in 1879, by the end of the 1880s he had added another 150 views to his total (see Plate 67). During the 1890s he produced an additional 65 lithographs (see Plate 87).

Bailey may not have drawn all of these views. A substantial number of the lithographs published by him do not identify the artist. One authority on Pennsylvania views has attributed to T. M. Fowler sixteen or so unsigned views of that state published by Bailey in the mid-1880s. The Essex, Connecticut, and Malden, Massachusetts, prints of 1881 are signed *A.E.D.*, and A. E. Downs may have drawn other views for Bailey without even his initials to indicate his participation.

The initials *J. M.* appear on Bailey's Walpole, Massachusetts, lithograph of 1882. Possibly this is James B. Moyer, copublisher with Fowler of dozens of views and whose name can be found on five Pennsylvania views identified as published by Bailey & Moyer in 1898. In 1904 Bailey entered into a publishing arrangement with Thomas J. Hughes, and the imprint of Hughes & Bailey as publishers can be found on about forty lithographs.

Bailey's old friend T. M. Fowler drew several of those published by Hughes & Bailey during the years 1914 to 1918. The earliest and the majority of the Hughes & Bailey views list New York as the business address. Bailey moved there from Cambridge some time after his wife died in 1901. Hughes & Bailey prints can also be found addressed Boston, New York and Boston, or Brooklyn.

The last city view to come from this firm and the final one with Bailey's name in the imprint appeared in 1926. Its title, *Aero View of Hammonton, New Jersey*, used a phrase that Bailey apparently coined. Then eighty-three, Bailey decided to retire, but this already venerable old man still had more than twenty years to live until his death at the age of 104 on 13 August 1947.

The 374 or so views he left as his artistic legacy are no masterworks, but nearly all of them are carefully drawn, and their long and detailed legends are packed with information. The majority of them include numerous vignettes. Indeed, a few of Bailey's views incorporate so many of these border scenes that the depiction of the city as a whole seems almost incidental. Although such features detract from the compositional qualities of the prints, they offer a wealth of architectural and business information for modern urban scholars.

The majority of Bailey's views were printed in black and white with a single tone added. Where they were printed is a mystery. The Bailey imprint is often ambiguous, although many of these views state that the lithograph was printed by O. H. Bailey & Co. On other views one finds the words *lithographed* or *lith.*, which could mean that Bailey only drew on stone or zinc and had someone else do the presswork. Possibly this someone else was Armstrong & Co., whose Riverside Press in Cambridge is listed as the printer for the large and attractive lithograph of Boston in 1879.

In concentrating on the towns of New England, Bailey encountered and mastered problems that rarely troubled such artists as Ruger, Koch, Glover, and others who worked mainly in the rectilinear towns of the Midwest and West. For them it was easy to construct perspective grids of the checkerboard towns they depicted. In attempting to delineate the far less regular patterns of older Massachusetts or Connecticut communities, Bailey's task must have been far more difficult and time-consuming. His remarkably productive career is thus all the more noteworthy.

---

1. Biographical information on O. H. Bailey comes from Warren and Wise, "The Bailey Brothers." This incorporates Warren's genealogical research on the Baily Family. Like his brother, O. H. Bailey added an *e* to his name after the Civil War.

2. There is no date on the print, but its year of publication has been established by the Marinette County Historical Society.

3. "Fowler & Bailey" published lithographs of Burlington and New Brunswick, New Jersey, in 1874. O. H. Bailey drew the New Brunswick view, while H. H. Bailey was the artist for the Burlington print.

	Wisc.	Ind.	Ohio	N.Y.	Pa.	N.J.	Conn.	Mass.	N.H.	R.I.	Vt.	N.B.	Mich.	Del.	N.S.	Total
1871	1															1
1872		1	1													2
1873				2	1											3
1874				7		2										9
1875				5			7	3								15
1876					1		5	7	1	1	1					16
1877					1		9	8		4						22
1878							12	13								25
1879					1		8	16		1						26
1880							6	3								9
1881						1	7	3				2				13
1882					1		4	9		1		2				17
1883					1	4	8		1							14
1884		3	1	8				1					4			17
1885			1		10	2							2	7		22
1886			1		2	3										6
1887								9								9
1888								11		5						16
1889								3		7	1				1	12
1890								8		4					1	13
1891								15		1						16
1892						2		5								7
1893								1								1
1894						1										1
1895				1			1			2						4
1896						1		1								2
1897								5								5
1898					5	1		5	1							12
1899				1		1		3								5
1900				1	1											2
1901				2				2								4
1902				3												3
1903																
1904				1		1	1									3
1905				1			1									2
1906							2									2
1907							3									3
1908							3									3
1909				1		1	1									3
1910						2										2
1911				1			1			1						3
1912							1									1
1913							1									1
1914							2	2								4
1915							1	1								2
1916					1		1									2
1917																
1918					1		2	1								4
1919							1									1
1920							1									1
1921							1									1
1922																
1923				1												1
1924				1												1
1925																
1926						1										1
n.d.				2	1	1										4
Total	1	4	4	33	36	28	80	137	3	27	1	5	6	7	2	374

4. Ithaca, New York, *Daily Journal*, 9 August 1873.

5. Warren and Wise give 1875 as the date when the Baileys moved to Boston, but it may have been a year earlier if the Port Jervis view can be relied on. Bailey lived at 83 Inman Street. He is first listed in the Cambridge city directory in 1877, when he was identified as an artist. After 1879 the directories designate his occupation as "Map publishers" or "maps."

6. On the view of Boston in 1879 published by O. H. Bailey and J. C. Hazen, the imprint shows their address as "Corner Milk & Congress Sts. Boston, Mass. New England Mutual Life Building."

5. George Holbrook Baker (1827–1906)

In May 1849, George H. Baker arrived in San Francisco as a member of a party organized in Boston to find gold. He was then twenty-two and a former student at the National Academy of Design, where he had gone to study art after completing a three-year apprenticeship with a New York City commercial artist.[1] Possibly before leaving for California, Baker made arrangements with the New York *Tribune* to draw what he saw, for his first lithographic city view was published by the newspaper that August. It showed San Francisco as the artist saw it on 1 June. Another of his views of the city was published in New Haven, probably also in 1849.

Baker mined for gold, operated various merchandising businesses, ran an express service, edited and published two periodicals, and drew a series of woodcuts of California scenes. In Sacramento he drew and published several versions of an enormous and very detailed lithograph of that city, which first appeared in 1857 (Plate 42). His account book listing subscribers and charges made by him for advertisements on the view is one of the very few such records to have survived.[2]

About 1862 he moved to San Francisco to establish his own lithographing and publishing firm. Most of his work consisted of posters, advertising cards, views of individual buildings, membership certificates, scenes of western natural wonders, stock certificates, and maps. In the early 1870s, however, Baker produced a view of San Diego, and, about 1875, he drew a lithograph of Fort Yuma, California.[3] His

George Holbrook Baker

	Calif.	Ariz.	Total
1849	2		2
1850–			
1857	2		2
1858	1		1
1859–			
1873	1		1
1874			
1875	1		1
1876–			
1893	1		1
n.d.		1	1
Total	8	1	9

last recorded city view came in 1893. This was based on the drawing or painting done by John J. Vioget and depicted San Francisco in 1837 when it was known as Yerba Buena.

1. Baker was born in East Medway, Massachusetts. He lived in Dedham and Boston, Massachusetts, during his youth, going to New York at an early age to begin his apprenticeship with a man named Smith. According to Harry T. Peters, *California on Stone*, 47, at the end of his apprenticeship "Smith put him to drawing maps so exclusively that Baker got bored with his work and left. He then became a student at the National Academy of Design. . . . While there he won many prizes for his work." The biographical note in Peters, pp. 47–54, is my source of information about the artist. Peters obviously used material he obtained from Baker's family, although he does not cite exact sources.

2. This manuscript is in the collection of the Society of California Pioneers, San Francisco. I have drawn on it for my treatment elsewhere in this study of the business aspects of viewmaking.

3. His San Diego view is described and dated in Rebecca Elizabeth Lytle, "People and Places: Images of Nineteenth-Century San Diego," 73–74.

6. Herman Brosius (–   )

Like so many other city view artists after the Civil War, Herman Brosius in 1871 began with a lithograph of an upper Midwest community, Darlington, Wisconsin. His elder brother, Fred, was associated for many years with Henry Seifert's printing firm in Milwaukee (known from about 1872 as the Milwaukee Lithographing & Engraving Co.), which by 1870 had fourteen presses and thirty-five employees.[1] Herman may have been among them.

In 1872 eight views were published with Brosius's name as artist. They showed places in Wisconsin, Texas, Illinois, Louisiana, and Ontario—places so widely separated that he may have visited and drawn some of them in the previous year. Only one, a lithograph of Peoria, Illinois, which J. J. Stoner entered as the copyright claimant, has the name of a publisher. During the next decade Stoner published many of Brosius's views, including one in 1873 of Highspire, Pennsylvania, Stoner's birthplace.

The artist's most productive year was 1875, when fifteen of his views were published. Six of them showed towns in Ontario (see Plate 32), which Brosius visited during the years 1872–1876, producing a total of fifteen lithographs of towns in this Canadian province. There are no recorded Brosius views of 1877 and 1878, only two in 1876, and one in 1879. He must have had another job during this time, perhaps as a lithographer or printer or—possibly—helping another city view artist.

In the years 1880–1884 he produced another fifteen views, bringing his total known urban lithographs to fifty-seven, showing places in ten states and one province. Quite possibly he was involved with many other views, perhaps working anonymously for Henry Wellge. There is a view of St. Paul, Minnesota, in 1883 drawn by Wellge and published by J. J. Stoner but with the notation that the eighteen vignettes surrounding Wellge's principal scene were drawn by Brosius.

Many of Brosius's views, like that of Utica, New York, in 1873, show cities as seen from a very high angle and with

	Wisc.	Tex.	Ill.	La.	Ont.	Ky.	N.Y.	Pa.	Mich.	Minn.	S.D.	Total
1871	1											1
1872	2	3	1	1	2							9
1873		1	1		1	1	2	1				7
1874	1				4				2			7
1875	9				6							15
1876					2							2
1877–1879									1			1
1880	1								3			4
1881			1									1
1882	1		1				3					5
1883	1									1	2	4
1884	1											1
Total	17	4	4	1	15	1	5	1	6	1	2	57

the street pattern displayed almost like a map. Both H. H. and O. H. Bailey used this same kind of perspective, and it is conceivable that Brosius and the Baileys were associated in some manner at one time.

Herman Brosius drew generally accurate views, if the results of a detailed analysis of his Binghamton, New York, lithograph of 1873 (Plate 89) revealed characteristics typical of his work. Individual buildings stand out distinctly, the business district is particularly well rendered, and the architectural style of each structure can be easily determined. Brosius had less success with topography, and the high-level viewpoint he selected tended to level out the hills and valley walls of Binghamton's site.[2]

1. Seifert and James Lawton maintained a partnership from 1866 through 1871. Fred Brosius became president of the Milwaukee Lithographing & Engraving Co. when Seifert retired in 1898. See Thomas Beckman, *Milwaukee Illustrated: Panoramic and Bird's-Eye Views of a Midwestern Metropolis, 1844–1908*, unpaged introduction. Beckman provides a summary of the company's development and states that Fred Brosius was a "long-time employee."

2. See Charles Uhl, "'Every Building Is Accurately Represented': An Examination of Five Bird's Eye Views of Upstate New York," chap. 4. Uhl also points out that Brosius provided more detailed outbuildings than any of the other artists (Koch, Burleigh, and O. H. Bailey) whose work he examined.

7. Grafton Tyler Brown (1841–1918)

Born in Harrisburg, Pennsylvania, Grafton T. Brown made his way to San Francisco before he was twenty.[1] He began work for Charles C. Kuchel no later than 1861, two years after Kuchel had ceased doing business with Emil Dresel under the name *Kuchel & Dresel*. That year Brown drew and published a view of Virginia City, Nevada, which Kuchel put on stone and Britton & Co. printed in San Francisco.

Brown may have been associated with Kuchel and his partner, Dresel, somewhat earlier than this, for an undated view of Santa Rosa, California, that Brown drew was put on stone by Kuchel & Dresel and printed by Britton & Co. This may have been in 1859, the year Kuchel and Dresel seem to have dissolved their partnership and the first year Britton & Co. did business under that name. It is possible, therefore, that Brown learned viewmaking by working on some of the later Kuchel & Dresel views of California mining camps and West Coast cities in 1858 or 1859.[2]

His association with Kuchel remains unclear, but it was Kuchel who put on stone two other Brown drawings in 1861 and 1864. The latter, Brown's second rendering of Virginia City, is one of the most attractive and fascinating American city views. Britton & Co. printed it in several colors, and Brown surrounded his principal view of Nevada's most important silver mining town with thirty vivid vignettes showing the details of various business structures. Perhaps the most interesting depicts the office of the *Territorial Enterprise* as it looked when the young Samuel Clemens first worked there as a cub reporter.

When Kuchel died in 1865 his business address was 543 Clay Street, an address that Brown retained, first under his name alone and then, after 1867, as G. T. Brown & Co.[3] Possibly it was then that he acquired full interest in the business from Kuchel's widow.

Brown was well equipped to draw, lithograph, print, publish, and sell his work (see Plate 66, printed by Brown). In addition to his training as an artist associated with the older and more experienced Kuchel, he had made a living in Nevada, which he described in an advertisement for the Virginia City *Mercantile Guide and Directory* of 1864: "Traveling Artist in Nevada Territory, views of mills, mines, business houses, residences etc. drawn in the finest style."

His business in San Francisco prospered, and about 1870 Brown moved to larger quarters on Clay Street. It was there that Max Schmidt, later to establish his own printing firm, worked for a few months not long after his arrival from Germany in 1871. Schmidt's biographer describes this brief association: "There was a colored man who had a lithograph establishment at 520 Clay Street. He did business un-

	Calif.	Nev.	Ore.	Wash.	Idaho	Total
1859	1					1
1860	1					1
1861		1	1			2
1862–						
1864		1				1
1865						
1866				1	1	2
1867	1					1
1868	1					1
1869						
1870			2			2
1871–						
1877	1					1
1878–						
1881		1				1
n.d.		1				1
Total	5	4	3	1	1	14

der the name of G. T. Brown & Co. Otto Schoening was his lithographer. . . . After three months with the colored man Max went to work for Korbel Bros."[4]

Of the fourteen city views on which his name appears, Brown drew only seven. On only two is he identified as publisher, but he may have been responsible for one or more of the six lacking any publisher's imprint. City views thus were a relatively unimportant part of his business, which included maps, views of mines, hotels, and residences, illustrations for a history of San Mateo County, membership and stock certificates, posters, sheet music, and the like.

In 1879 Brown sold his business to an associate, W. T. Galloway. He is known to have been in Victoria, British Columbia, in 1882 as a member of a geological survey party. The next year he held an exhibition of twenty-two of his oil paintings in Victoria.[5] He then moved to Portland, Oregon, where he probably lived until at least 1889. Toward the end of this period he traveled to the Yellowstone, producing two paintings of that stream and its falls.

By the latter part of 1892 he was in St. Paul, Minnesota, where he worked for at least five years as a draftsman with the U.S. Engineers. When he died in St. Paul in 1918, a local newspaper stated that he had been "for years a draftsman in the City Civil Engineering department." He was then seventy-seven. No prints or paintings from the time he lived in St. Paul have been discovered. He is the only known black to have been an American viewmaker.

1. Curators at The Oakland Museum, Oakland, California, have been gathering biographical material about Brown for several years. I have relied mainly on notes they compiled in 1972 for a museum exhibit: "Grafton Tyler Brown: Black Artist in the West."

2. In 1858 Kuchel & Dresel first published views with names other than their own identifying the artists: Eugene Camerer's view of Stockton and Levi Goodrich's of San Jose. I think that these artists or others must have helped with many of the earlier Kuchel & Dresel views. Perhaps Brown did, too, or served as an assistant to someone else.

3. Joseph A. Baird, Jr., states that Kuchel's business address at the time of his death was 622 Clay Street, San Francisco. See his "Introduction" to Joseph Armstrong Baird, Jr., and Edwin Clyve Evans, *Historic Lithographs*

of San Francisco, n. 27. He agrees with the Oakland Museum notes that Kuchel's address became Brown's thereafter.

4. [Elford Eddy], *The Log of a Cabin Boy*, 15. The Schmidt Label & Lithographing Company printed a few city views, notably those of Prescott and Phoenix, Arizona, drawn by C. J. Dyer. The successor to the Schmidt firm, Stecher-Traung-Schmidt Corporation, is still in business in downtown San Francisco.

5. Victoria *Colonist*, 26 June 1883.

8. Lucien Rinaldo Burleigh (1853–1923)

Most American artists of city views either worked for publishers or—like Edwin Whitefield, Thaddeus M. Fowler, and Henry Wellge—were publishers as well as artists themselves. Of the artists responsible for large numbers of views, only Lucien R. Burleigh, O. H. Bailey, Edward Sachse, and C. J. Pauli operated their own lithographic printing establishments.[1]

Burleigh drew and published a great many of the city views that came from his press, but he also printed dozens of the lithographs drawn and published by George Norris of towns in New England. Other views of the early 1890s showing towns in New York are unsigned but were printed and published by Burleigh. Christian Fausel may have been the artist of many or all of these.

In one capacity or another, Burleigh's name appears on 228 lithographic city views. Of these, he is known to have drawn about 120. Several other unsigned views may have been his work as well. A substantial number of the Burleigh views contain his signature within the body of the print in addition to his identification elsewhere as the artist. In all probability, this indicates that he put his own design on stone or zinc. In these cases, Burleigh thus exercised full control over every essential element of the final product.[2]

Burleigh may have been the best educated of the American-born viewmakers. He was born and grew up in Plainfield, Connecticut. He was named for his father, Lucien, and for his grandfather, Rinaldo Burleigh, a Yale graduate and principal of Plainfield Academy, where Lucien Rinaldo received his early education.[3] In 1875, at the age of twenty-two, Burleigh graduated with a B.S. in civil engineering from the Worcester County Free Institute of Industrial Science. This Massachusetts school of technology—now Worcester Polytechnic Institute—had begun its existence only a decade earlier, but it already enjoyed a high reputation by the time Burleigh enrolled after graduating from Plainfield Academy.

Particularly well known was one of Burleigh's instructors, Professor George E. Gladwin. The Institute made Gladwin's classes in studio and field sketching a required course, and, as a modern historian of the institution has stated, "Educators came from far and near to see the class in session."[4] Burleigh became one of Gladwin's best pupils, and it was he who some years later helped Burleigh obtain a position with a Hartford firm that published city views.[5]

When Burleigh graduated in 1875 the country had not yet recovered from the severe business depression that had be-

	Mass.	N.Y.	Conn.	Vt.	N.H.	Pa.	Maine	Ohio	N.C.	Ga.	Tenn.	Total
1882	1	6										7
1883	3	2	1									6
1884	2	9	1									12
1885	1	18		2								21
1886	13	8		9	4							34
1887	9	18		1	9	2						39
1888		7			4		2	2				15
1889	5	12	4	5	5		4	1				36
1890	2	19		2								23
1891		9		1					3			13
1892		13			1		1			1	1	17
1893		2										2
1894												
1895		1										1
1896–												
1899		2										2
Total	36	126	6	20	23	2	7	3	3	1	1	228

gun two years earlier. It may have been a lack of employment opportunities in civil engineering that caused Burleigh to look for other ways to earn a living, and "he secured employment with a Milwaukee lithographing company, for whom he made bird's eye view pencil sketches of villages and the smaller cities, to be copied on stone and printed."[6] Probably he arrived in Milwaukee in the summer or fall of 1875, and he may have remained there until the fall of 1878, when he taught school in his hometown of Plainfield through the following spring.

In Milwaukee, Burleigh could have worked for any of several persons or firms. The absence of his name from the Milwaukee city directories of the period suggests that he may have spent most of his time sketching in the field. Perhaps his employer was the American Oleograph Company, founded in 1872 by Louis Kurz, who printed many city views drawn by several itinerant artists. Burleigh's decision to return to Plainfield in 1878 might have been caused by Kurz's decision that year to move his firm to Chicago.

Burleigh might also have worked in Milwaukee for Adam Beck, Clemens J. Pauli, or Charles H. Vogt. Beck arrived in Milwaukee in 1873. Pauli probably moved to that city in 1875. They formed their printing firm in 1878, probably too late for Burleigh to have been an employee. Pauli's first recorded city view was of Milwaukee, and he completed it in February 1876. Burleigh could have served as his assistant then or for some of Pauli's views drawn in 1877 when Pauli worked for C. H. Vogt. It is equally likely that Vogt employed Burleigh. Vogt moved to Milwaukee in 1870, and he printed city views in addition to issuing them as a publisher. Vogt moved his business to Cleveland in 1879, and Burleigh's return to Plainfield could have been in anticipation of that event.

One thing is clear: Burleigh knew all of these persons. When he published his first view in 1882—probably late in that year—he had it printed by Vogt in Cleveland. In 1883

he began to use Beck & Pauli's services as well. Even before Burleigh began to publish views, he probably dealt with both Vogt and Beck & Pauli, for it was to these two firms that the H. H. Rowley Company of Hartford, Connecticut, sent its drawings to be printed in 1879–1881. Burleigh began his employment for Rowley in the summer of 1879.[7]

The identity and background of H. H. Rowley remain a mystery: the Hartford city directories of the time list neither his name nor his business. Early in 1881 Burleigh gave the firm's address as 554 Main Street, and on the lithographs published by Rowley, Hartford, Connecticut, is stated as the place of business in the imprints of all the prints bearing the company's name issued from 1878 through 1885.[8] Virtually all of the seventeen signed views published by this firm bear some version of an imprint reading "drawn and published by H. H. Rowley & Co." Burleigh probably had no responsibility for the publishing side of the business, but his involvement as artist for one of the views—Canajoharie, New York, in 1881—is now established.[9]

The order in which the Rowley lithographs of New York appeared probably indicates Burleigh's whereabouts during these years: 1879, Albany and Fort Plain; 1880, Fulton, Lyons, Palmyra, and Rochester; 1881, Amsterdam, Canajoharie, Ilion, Little Falls, and Valatie. Another view published in 1881 showing Troy lacks any publisher's imprint, but it so closely resembles other Rowley views that it probably came from this firm. Burleigh's role as artist or assistant for this view cannot yet be documented, but he moved to Troy as early as 1880, although the city directory does not list his name until the following year.[10]

In 1882 Burleigh began drawing city views for the firm of D. Mason & Co. of Syracuse.[11] All of these views include Burleigh's name as artist. The 1882 views are of the New York communities of Batavia, Binghamton, Elmira, Ithaca (Plate 54), and Schenectady. Two views dated 1883 show Salem and Woburn, Massachusetts. It seems likely that Burleigh completed his drawings for these two the year before they were published, for in 1882 he issued the first city view with his name as both artist and publisher. It showed Fitchburg, Massachusetts, and Burleigh had it printed in Cleveland by C. H. Vogt. In 1883 Burleigh drew and published several other views, which he had printed by the Beck & Pauli firm in Milwaukee.

In 1884 and 1885 Burleigh continued to have his views printed by either Beck & Pauli or Vogt. He issued twelve in 1884 and twenty-one in 1885, all but six of these thirty-three being of communities in New York State (see Plate 30). In 1886 Burleigh established his own printing plant in Troy at 86 Congress Street. In that year he published a total of thirty-four new city views. Only eleven of these came from his Milwaukee or Cleveland printers, so his own press must have been in operation by late spring. [12]

By this time Burleigh had evidently abandoned whatever hopes he had for a career in engineering. From 1881 through 1884 he listed himself in the city directories as "civil engineer"; he changed this in 1885 to "view publisher"; and in 1886—reflecting his added occupation as a printer—to "lithographer and view publisher." His advertisement in the city directory for 1886 stated that he could do "fine color work in all branches" of "engraving and printing" with "views of buildings and villages a specialty." [13]

In 1887–1889 Burleigh drew, printed, and published virtually all of the thirty-seven city views of New York State that bear his name, along with another twelve of places in Maine, Massachusetts, New Hampshire, Pennsylvania, Connecticut, and Vermont. He also printed more than thirty views drawn and published by George E. Norris of towns in several of the New England states, adding four others by Norris in 1890 and 1892.

Sometime in 1890 Burleigh seems to have given up his role as traveling artist, for only six of the twenty-two views with his name in the imprint identify him as the artist. Fourteen New York views of that year are unsigned. Of the remaining thirteen views published by Burleigh through 1892, only one shows him as the artist. George Norris drew one; the others are unsigned.

Some of these unsigned lithographs may have been the work of Christian Fausel. Fausel is first listed in the Troy directories in 1886, the year that Burleigh established his press. His name as artist also appears on a view of Graniteville, Massachusetts, printed and published that year by Burleigh. Fausel's name or initials can also be found on a few other, later views that came from Burleigh's press. Probably Burleigh recruited Fausel to help him with his city views and his new printing venture. [14]

Although Burleigh continued his printing business well into the twentieth century, no city views with his name on them appeared after 1899. In fact, of the 228 views that Burleigh signed as artist, printer, or publisher, only 5 are dated after 1892. His period of concentrated activity as a viewmaker, therefore, lasted only a dozen years. In that time he achieved an almost total monopoly in upstate New York and Vermont, for few others ventured into this region, which Burleigh had established as his domain.

Aside from his work for Norris, Burleigh printed very few views for other artists or artist-publishers. Three—possibly five—appeared in 1891. Two veteran viewmakers, Albert Ruger and Joseph Stoner—reunited after a long period of inactivity—sent or brought to Troy for Burleigh to print their drawings of Asheville, Durham, and Greensboro, North Carolina. Their lithographs of Spartanburg, South Carolina, and Winston-Salem, while not so identified, doubtless came from the Burleigh press as well.

Burleigh concentrated on small cities and towns for the subjects of the views published by his firm. No Burleigh views exist of Troy, Albany, Rochester, Syracuse, Utica, or Buffalo, except for the Rowley prints of the first three to which Burleigh may have contributed his talents. [15] With this exception, his views provide an immensely valuable record of the urban scene in upstate New York, Vermont, and elsewhere in New England. Because of the brevity of the time in which Burleigh worked, his views make it possible to compare one community with another during the same period.

Burleigh had an excellent eye for architectural and engineering detail, but his towns eerily lack people or animals and appear almost deserted. Burleigh did not experiment with new or different effects either as an artist or as a publisher. He drew each place from about the same imaginary viewpoint, and he invariably printed the views with a single tone added to the basic design. Nevertheless, while unexciting as art, his views document the appearance and pattern of small-town New York and New England with a clarity and thoroughness unsurpassed by any other viewmaker.

1. Eli S. Glover, another artist-publisher, founded and ran the Merchants Lithographing Company in Chicago from 1868 until its destruction by fire in 1871. However, he drew only two of the views printed by his firm: Lowell and Charlotte, Michigan, both dated 1870. His later midwestern, Rocky Mountain, and far western views were printed by Cincinnati and San Francisco firms in which he apparently had no financial interest.

2. Several of the views with Burleigh's name signed in the stone (or plate) were printed in Cleveland or Milwaukee before Burleigh established his own press in Troy, New York.

3. The Burleighs were talented and energetic. Rinaldo Burleigh married Lydia Bradford, a descendant of William Bradford, governor of Plymouth Colony. They had five sons: Charles Calistus, William Henry, George Shepard, Cyrus, and Lucien (Lucien Rinaldo's father). The first three achieved recognition for their activities as journalists and abolitionists. George and William were also poets. One of Lucien's cousins, C. C. Burleigh, Jr., became a painter of landscapes and portraits. He also produced at least one lithographic town view, of Florence, Connecticut. Allen Johnson, ed., *Dictionary of American Biography*, 3:284–86; William H. Burleigh, *Poems by William H. Burleigh. With a Sketch of his Life by Celia Burleigh*; "C. C. Burleigh, Jr.," in H. W. French, *Art and Artists in Connecticut*, 157–58.

4. Mildred McClary Tymeson, *Two Towers: The Story of Worcester Tech, 1865–1965*, 51. Perhaps observers heard Gladwin's vigorous advice to his students in what must have been a session in perspective: "Converge! Converge! Make those lines converge!" (Ibid).

5. Burleigh's obituary in the *Journal of the Worcester Polytechnic Institute* states that he "developed a talent for drawing and while at the Tech he made some excellent sketches in and about Worcester on his tramping tours with the Free Hand Drawing Class, under instruction from Prof. George E. Gladwin." In a letter to the head of Worcester Tech in 1880, Burleigh described his position with the H. H. Rowley Co. of Hartford as one for which he was indebted "to yourself and Prof. Gladwin" (Burleigh to C. O. Thompson, 28 December 1880). I am grateful to Lora Brueck, archivist, Gordon Library, Worcester Polytechnic Institute, and Georgia B. Bumgardner, curator of Graphic Arts, American Antiquarian Society, for locating and transmitting this and other important data about Burleigh to me after an earlier request to another part of that academic forest had been ignored.

6. Burleigh's obituary, *Worcester Polytechnic Institute*, 30.

7. For Beck, Pauli, and the firm they established, see Beckman, *Milwaukee Illustrated*, last page of unpaged introduction and descriptions of

exhibit items 28 and 43. Beckman speculates that Pauli worked for the American Oleograph Company. In 1877 two newspapers in Monroe, Wisconsin, referred to Pauli as "of the firm of" and "representing" C. H. Vogt. Letter to the author from Thomas Beckman, 19 March 1981. Beckman has informed me that Burleigh's name cannot be found in any of the Milwaukee city directories of 1875–1878.

8. I have searched Hartford directories for 1879–1881 without success. Neither the Wadsworth Atheneum nor the Connecticut State Library could provide any information about Rowley. The street address appears in a letter from Burleigh to Professor C. O. Thompson, head of Worcester Tech, dated 4 January 1881. The 1878–1879 issue of the annual directory of alumni of Worcester Tech lists Burleigh as a teacher in Plainfield. The 1879–1880 issue identifies him as a map and view draftsman for H. H. Rowley. Burleigh probably began to work for Rowley after the end of the school year in the spring of 1879, although he may have done some part-time sketching for the firm while still teaching school.

9. The Canajoharie view does not bear the Rowley imprint. A contemporary newspaper account identifies it as drawn by L. R. Burleigh and mentions that his drawing was to be published "by the Hartford, Conn., Art Publishers." In his letter of 4 January 1881, Burleigh stated that he was "still at work for H. H. Rowley the Art publisher," so there can be little doubt that Rowley published the Canajoharie lithograph. Canajoharie *Radii*, 20 January 1881. I am indebted to Susan D. Plank, curator, Historical Collections, Canajoharie Library and Art Gallery, for supplying me with a transcript of this newspaper notice.

10. It was from Troy on 28 December 1880 that Burleigh wrote to the head of Worcester Tech to report that he was "married and keeping house" in the city. Burleigh to Professor C. O. Thompson, Gordon Library, Worcester Polytechnic Institute, Worcester, Massachusetts.

11. Daniel Mason is first listed in Syracuse city directories in 1878 as "publisher." His address in 1882 was 24 E. Washington Street, a building also occupied by the Syracuse *Journal* and perhaps by other printers as well. Mason published many histories of counties in New York and elsewhere, but he is never listed in the Syracuse directories as a printer. The Burleigh views published by Mason were probably put on stone or zinc by some kind of photographic process, a topic discussed elsewhere in this work with specific reference to the Burleigh prints of these years. Information on Mason was kindly provided by Richard N. Wright, president of the Onondaga Historical Association, Syracuse, New York.

12. The 1886 view of Haydenville, Massachusetts, identifies the printer as "Northern Lith Co. Troy, N.Y.," perhaps the name first selected by Burleigh for his company, which became the Burleigh Lithographing Company. *The Troy Directory for the Year 1886* lists his firm in that form on p. 66 and in Burleigh's advertisement on p. 558.

13. Ibid.

14. Fausel was in Cleveland in 1883 when he published a lithograph titled *Vatican & St. Peter's Church, Rome*. This is undated, but the Library of Congress copyright entry is 1883. His name also appears on this print as "Lithographer," with an address as 147 St. Clair, Cleveland. The only other pre-1886 print of his I have located is a view of the Lakeside Campground in Ohio. An impression is in the Geography and Map Division, Library of Congress. On it he is identified as the printer. My guess is that Fausel may have done some work for Vogt in Cleveland and that Burleigh met him there. Just as Burleigh may have drawn many or most of the Rowley views but went unrecognized in their imprints, so Fausel may have served Burleigh first as an assistant in the field and then with full responsibility for doing sketches that Burleigh printed and published. Fausel drew and published a view of West Chazy, New York, in 1899, the last record I can find of his work.

15. No views published by Burleigh of towns in New York duplicated those issued by the Rowley Company except for that of Fort Plain. Nor did he publish more than one view of any community, although he did print for another publisher a second view of Ticonderoga, New York. Perhaps Burleigh felt that having done a city once—either for Rowley or on his own account—there was no need to repeat the effort, even though the place may have undergone substantial change or offered new opportunities for further sales.

9. William Wallace Denslow (1856–1915)

W. W. Denslow, as he almost always signed his name, began a brief period as an artist of city views shortly after studying drawing in New York from 1870 to 1875 at the Cooper Institute and the National Academy of Design. His years as a viewmaker proved only an interlude in his long and active life as an author and as an illustrator for newspapers and books.

His most famous illustrations are those he prepared for *The Wizard of Oz*. He also illustrated several volumes he compiled for children and the eighteen-volume *Denslow's Picture Books for Children*. Denslow designed both costumes and scenery for plays, and he was associated for a time with Elbert Hubbard and his Roycroft group at East Aurora, New York. [1]

Denslow's training and talents are obvious even in his first view, published by Peter Fritts in 1876. It shows Easton, Pennsylvania, as the artist saw it from a hill rising from the New Jersey bank of the Susquehanna River. The town appears set within a wholly convincing landscape, two foreground figures provide momentary visual interest, and the strong diagonal line of a railroad bridge connecting the two sides of the river leads the eye toward the town.

Denslow probably did not put this drawing on stone himself, but the anonymous craftsman who did served the artist well by providing smooth and delicate tonal ranges that decrease in intensity from the strong foreground to the range of hills in the distance. Perhaps C. J. Corbin of Philadelphia had something to do with this print, or he may have seen and admired it, for he published at least nine of Denslow's twelve subsequent city views. Nearly all of these lithographs were printed at the Philadelphia press of Thomas Hunter, who had succeeded the well-known P. S. Duval. Morris Traubel, another respected and longtime Philadelphia lithographer, put most of Denslow's drawings on stone at the Hunter shop. [2]

William Wallace Denslow

	Pa.	Md.	N.Y.	Total
1876	1			1
1877	2			2
1878	5	1	2	8
1879			1	1
1880–				
1882	1			1
Total	9	1	3	13

All but one of Denslow's thirteen city views were done during 1876–1879. Three are of towns in southern New York, one shows Frederick, Maryland, and the other eight depict small communities in Pennsylvania. In 1882 Denslow added a final view of Susquehanna, Pennsylvania. This was published by the Philadelphia Publishing House, which Corbin then managed. Denslow was only one of the artists who worked for Corbin, but his pictorial abilities exceeded those of his associates, and his urban lithographs deserve to be better known. [3]

1. For Denslow's life as a cartoonist, illustrator of books and newspapers, author, compiler, and so on, see Douglas G. Greene and Michael Patrick Hearm, *W. W. Denslow*. His work as a city view artist is summarized on pp. 10–11, and a few of his views are identified on p. 205 in a list of his prints and posters.

2. Traubel and Hunter are mentioned in passing in Nicholas B. Wainwright, *Philadelphia in the Romantic Age of Lithography* . . . , 74, 85, 90. Traubel's business addresses at an earlier period can be found in Peters, *America on Stone*, 389. For some reason, Corbin sent Denslow's Hornell, New York, view of 1878 to be printed at the Krebs Lithographing Company in Cincinnati.

3. A brief note about Corbin, reproductions of three of Denslow's views, and a color plate of another view published by Corbin are in Pennsylvania State University, Museum of Art, *Pennsylvania Prints*, pls. 68, 70, 71, and 73 and n. on pls. 70–73.

10. Albert E. Downs (–   )

The person who signed himself *A D* on an otherwise imprintless view of Fort Atkinson, Wisconsin, of 1880 is probably the *A.E.D.* on prints of Essex, Connecticut, and Malden, Massachusetts, published by O. H. Bailey & Co. in 1881. This artist (or possibly lithographer) emerged from these initials to become *Albert Downs* on a third Bailey lithograph in 1884 showing Richmond, Indiana. Downs may have spent the intervening years working as an assistant either for Bailey or for T. M. Fowler. It is on several of the latter's city views that Downs's name appears from 1886 on as "A. E. Downs Lith. Boston."

It is by no means clear that this signature indicates he printed the views. Instead, he may have been responsible only for putting them on stone. His association with Fowler extended beyond these lithographic activities, for a few prints show the names of Fowler and Downs joined as co-artists and joint publishers. A Wilkes-Barre, Pennsylvania, view of 1889 lists Fowler, Downs, and Moyer as artists and publishers, and a Scranton, Pennsylvania, lithograph of 1890 is signed by Fowler and Downs and published by Fowler and Moyer.

In 1892 Downs began to draw views as sole artist. Some of these he published with Fowler, others with Moyer, and one—a very large print of Boston in 1899—he issued under his own name. Several of his twentieth-century views, like that of Athens, Georgia, in 1909, were printed in a gravure process. This would normally have involved a photograph of the artist's rendering, so it is puzzling to find his signature on the print as "A. E. Dows," although the imprint below the neat line correctly spells his name in stating that the view was published by "Fowler & Downs Morrisville, Pa." His last recorded city view was a collaboration with Fowler to draw Haverhill, Massachusetts, for a print published in 1914 by Hughes & Bailey.

11. Emil Dresel (–   )

See Kuchel & Dresel

Albert E. Downs

	Wisc.	Conn.	Mass.	Ind.	N.J.	Pa.	Okla.	Tex.	Maine	W.V.	Ohio	Ga.	Total
1880	1												1
1881		2	1										3
1882–													
1884				1									1
1885													
1886				2									2
1887													
1888						2							2
1889						3							3
1890						5	1						6
1891						1	1						2
1892						7							7
1893–													
1895									1				1
1896–													
1898										1			1
1899			1							1	2		4
1900–													
1908												1	1
1909			1									1	2
1910–													
1914			1										1
1915													
1916			1										1
Total	1	2	5	1	2	17	2	1	1	2	2	2	38

12. Camille N. Drie [Dry] (–   )

There can be little doubt that the C. Drie whose name appears on lithographs of Vicksburg, Mississippi, and Galveston, Texas, dated 1871 and on a handful of views of other southern cities dated the next year is the Camille N. Dry who drew the most ambitious of all American city views. This is the 110-sheet view of St. Louis, Missouri, published by Compton & Co. in 1875. Perhaps this heroic task exhausted the artist, for subsequently his name—now signed C. N. Dry—appears only on a 1903 print showing Anniston, Alabama, and a view of the business district of Birmingham, Alabama, published by Dry the following year.

Drie's early work exhibits only the most primitive notions of perspective. His Columbus, Mississippi, lithograph, probably published in 1871, has no vanishing points. Instead, Drie used an axonometric projection. This suggests that he may have had some training in mechanical drawing but no experience with rendering townscapes. This same characteristic can be observed in his depictions of the two capitals of the Carolinas, Columbia (Plate 90) and Raleigh (Plate 44). However, both of these prints of 1872 show that the artist took great care in drawing individual buildings.

His Charleston view, also dated 1872 (Color Plate 5), looks down on the city from a high elevation, and uncertainties in perspective are not as evident in this attractive and effective lithograph. Perhaps by the time Drie drew these towns J. J. Stoner or Albert Ruger had offered some suggestions about how he might improve his technique. Stoner published Drie's view of Augusta, Georgia, in 1872, and Ruger published Drie's view of Macon, Georgia, in the same year. How all three met is uncertain, but Stoner visited Savannah that February to promote sales for Ruger's view of the city, and Ruger and Stoner may have encountered Drie when they arrived at Macon or Augusta and arranged to collaborate with him rather than compete. It is also possible, of course, that Drie might have been another of Ruger's several assistants.

Drie's single view of 1873 shows Norfolk, Virginia. Shortly thereafter he must have begun the arduous task of drawing his St. Louis view. We know from the preface of the bound version that "the preliminary drawings for this work were made early in the spring of 1874." The title itself includes a reference to a type of delineation that Drie had not heretofore used, at least in any consistent manner: *Pictorial St. Louis Metropolis of the Mississippi Valley: A Topographical Survey Drawn in Perspective A.D. 1875 by Camille N. Dry, Designed & Edited by Rich. J. Compton.*

Dry (as he was then called) and Compton, his publisher, obligingly provided an illustration of what this meant. On one of the large folio sheets they reproduced a map of the city at small scale (Plate 39). Above it they placed a small perspective of the entire city, dividing it into numbered rectangles to serve as a guide to the plate numbers of the individual perspective sections.

This publication is a tour de force. The detail is minute. Drawing the hundreds of structures in the business district alone at this scale and with such apparent accuracy would have been an accomplishment beyond any reasonable expectation. On many tall buildings one can even note small structural or functional elements extending above the roofs that could not ordinarily be seen from ground level. These must have been drawn from vantage points atop other buildings.

Dry certainly would have required the help of a team of assistants, but there is no record of how many there were or how they were organized. It must have required the full-time efforts of at least one person just to compile and place on the proper sheets the 1,999 names and titles of buildings and places of business that are identified and to put their numbers on the corresponding images of the lithographed plates. Some circumstantial evidence suggests that Albert Ruger was involved in this project, but there is no factual support for this theory.[1]

The only information about the person who accomplished this formidable view are a few business and residential addresses in St. Louis for the years 1875–1878. These are from the city directories of the period, in which Dry is listed merely as a "draughtsman."[2]

---

1. See the biographical note on Ruger in this section.
2. I am grateful to Susan A. Riggs of the Missouri Historical Society in St. Louis for supplying me with the following information on Dry appearing in *Goulds City Directory for St. Louis*:
1875   room 48, 414 Olive, r. 715 Locust
1876   Locust, nw cor. 6th, r. 1021 Gratton
1877   45 McLean's bldg. 4th cor. Market, r. 1232 Clark Av.
1878   4 N. 4th, r. 1019 St. Ange Av.

Camille N. Drie [Dry]
(includes 110-sheet view of St. Louis in 1875)

	Miss.	Tex.	Ga.	S.C.	N.C.	Va.	Mo.	Ala.	Total
1871	2	1							3
1872			2	2	1				5
1873						1			1
1874									
1875							1		1
1876–									
1903								1	1
1904								1	1
Total	2	1	2	2	1	1	1	2	12

13. C. J. Dyer (–   )

Two extremely rare, attractive, and brilliantly printed city views were drawn by this artist in 1885. His Phoenix, Arizona, lithograph (Color Plate 12) identifies the printer as the Schmidt Label & Litho Company of San Francisco, and almost certainly the second view, an undated view of Prescott, then still the capital of Arizona Territory, was printed by the same firm.[1]

The composition of the Phoenix print is both unusual and effective. The principal view of the entire city is surrounded by an oval border of trimmed saplings. Dyer also used this as the rectangular outer border, to create four circular vignettes, and to divide one of the corners—all of which con-

C. J. Dyer

	Calif.	Ariz.	Total
1880	1	·	1
1881–			
1885		2	2
1886–			
1890		1	1
Total	1	3	4

tain additional vignettes—into three compartments. A legend at the bottom left balances a description of Phoenix on the other side of the title, which appears against a background of desert and agricultural vegetation.

Perhaps the W. Byrnes who put Dyer's drawing on stone contributed to this design. Even if he did not, he deserves to be recognized for creating a multiple-stone colored lithograph of glowing quality whose hot tones convey the intensity of the Arizona sunshine.

Dyer gave his Prescott view a more conventional rectangular format, using the corners for vignettes and a legend. He placed three other vignettes above the title as insets and rather awkwardly hung two sets of vignettes below the heavy ruled border on either side of the title. The printer—probably the Schmidt firm—used inks of slightly more subdued colors than those chosen for the Phoenix lithograph.

Five years before these views appeared, Dyer produced a lithograph of Napa, California, and it is possible that he gained his experience in that state working for a more mature artist. He also drew another print showing Novato Rancho in California.[2] No other work of his of this type is known except for a later view of Phoenix showing the city in 1890. Dyer's name is to be found on a map of irrigated land in Arizona, but no biographical information about him has yet come to light.[3]

1. For the Schmidt firm, see the note on Max Schmidt in Peters, *California on Stone*, 187–88, and [Eddy], *The Log of a Cabin Boy*.

2. The Novato Rancho view is not of an urban place. It is undated and printed by Smith & Elliott. An impression is in the collection of the Henry E. Huntington Library at San Marino, California.

3. Neither the Arizona Department of Library, Archives and Public Records nor the Arizona Historical Society could provide me with any additional information on Dyer.

14. William Wallace Elliott (1842–   )

As artist, printer, or publisher, W. W. Elliott of San Francisco was involved in nearly fifty city views over a twenty-year period beginning about 1879. Of these views, thirty-eight date from the years 1887 through 1891. Only fifteen of the lithographs with Elliott's name on them were of communities outside California: seven each in Oregon and Washington and one in British Columbia.

Probably no other viewmaker signed his name on prints

in so many ways. Elliott's signatures include: W. W. Elliott, Elliott Publishing Co., The Elliott Litho. Co., Elliott Litho & Pub. Co., Elliott & Co., and W. W. Elliott & Co. In addition, minor variations on these basic styles can be found, and in some years he used several signatures. He also gave both Oakland and San Francisco as business addresses, although the latter predominates after 1887. Possibly he had a press in one city and a business office in the other.

Little is known of Elliott's life aside from the information appearing in records of voter registrations. He was born in New York in 1842. He registered as a voter in Alameda County, California, in 1876, and in 1884 he lived in the first ward of Oakland.[1]

Elliott printed or lithographed the five views on which his name appears through 1885. In 1886 he drew and printed a view of Pomona, California; he drew Wildomar, California, the following year; and in 1888 he drew and printed views of Fresno, Modesto, and San Jose, California. Except for two views of 1890 with artist credit lines of "The Elliot [*sic*] litho Co.," and "Elliott Pub. Co.," the prints of 1888 are the last with W. W. Elliott identified as the artist. The relationship to him, if any, of the H. B. Elliott who drew the lithographs of Auburn and Los Angeles, California, that the Elliott Publishing Company printed in 1891 is unknown.[2]

As a printer and publisher, Elliott produced some of the views drawn and signed by Bruce Wellington Pierce, either his son-in-law or a nephew by marriage.[3] It is possible that Pierce also drew some of the unsigned lithographs that Elliott issued or that he helped his relative while learning the business. Still other views were signed only with initials (*R.H.*, *T.S.*, and *F.W.*), but these may represent the names of lithographers and not artists. Therefore, all or most of the unsigned prints may be Elliott's own work.

Local newspapers in California published at least twelve views that Elliott printed. They showed such places as Santa Barbara, Sacramento, Ventura, San Francisco, Marysville, Riverside, Eureka, San Jose, Placerville, Fresno, Pomona, and Alameda.[4] The newspapers evidently used these views as premiums to secure subscriptions. In two other places—

William Wallace Elliott

	Calif.	Ore.	Wash.	Br. Col.	Total
1879	1				1
1880	2				2
1881–					
1885	2				2
1886	2				2
1887	6				6
1888	7				7
1889	1	1	4		6
1890	6	5	2	1	14
1891	3	1	1		5
1892	1				1
1893–					
1900	1				1
n.d.	1				1
Total	33	7	7	1	48

Antioch, California, and Albany, Oregon—Elliott succeeded in getting local boards of trade to publish his views.

Probably both his publishing clients and the eventual owners of the views were satisfied with his products. Elliott and those who drew for him were competent artists, and the large format he used for his prints made it possible to show every residential, business, religious, and civic structure in considerable detail. Two dozen or more vignettes surrounding the principal view provided additional information about the appearance of the community. Elliott usually included a panel of text at the bottom of the print describing the community in the most laudatory language.

Perhaps the most interesting of Elliott's lithographs are those showing such Gold Rush mining towns as Auburn, Sonora, and Placerville thirty to forty years after the tumultuous events that created them almost literally overnight. Valuable, too, are the Elliott views of places like Fresno and Modesto in 1888, not long after they began their existence as new towns created by the railroad pushing south from San Francisco.

Elliott printed most of his views in black and white without even the customary tone stone used for clouds and shadows. He was capable of color work as well, however. For Clohessy & Strengele of Portland, Oregon, Elliott in 1890 printed B. W. Pierce's fine view of that city in strong, vivid colors. He used similar inks for the Los Angeles view of 1891 drawn by H. B. Elliott.

1. *Great Register of the County of Alameda, 1884.*
2. H. B. Elliott's only other recorded city view is of Golden Gate Park in San Francisco, a print that includes adjacent portions of the city. It was printed by the Bosqui firm in San Francisco and published in 1892 by A. M. Freeman & Co., also of San Francisco.
3. Pierce's grandson, Lee P. Morris, who provided me some information about Pierce, is uncertain whether Clara Elliott Pierce was W. W. Elliott's daughter or niece. See the biographical note on Pierce.
4. The Vancouver, British Columbia, print of 1890 was published by the Vancouver Daily and Weekly World Publishing Co.

15. George H. Ellsbury (—   )

Ellsbury probably came from Minnesota, for five of his seven views are of places in that state. He began work in 1866 with a lithograph of Winona on which he is identified as the artist. Two years later he drew Rochester, Minnesota. Charles Shober of Chicago printed both views, and doubtless Ellsbury acted as his own publisher.

His last views, appearing in 1874, are four handsome lithographs of Milwaukee, Wisconsin, and Minneapolis (Color Plate 9), St. Paul (Plate 5), and Winona, Minnesota. He published two of these with Vernon Green, and, although no artist's name can be found on the Minneapolis and Winona prints, Ellsbury almost certainly drew all four.

Ellsbury did not use the bird's-eye view perspective so popular with his contemporaries. Instead, he portrayed his cities as seen from the ground or from a slight elevation and some distance. He filled the foregrounds of these long panoramas with interesting and pictorially effective details: waves, projecting breakwaters, and boats in his Milwaukee port scene; a dramatically placed building in the Min-

George H. Ellsbury

	Minn.	Wisc.	Total
1866	1		1
1867			
1868	1		1
1869–			
1873		1	1
1874	3	1	4
Total	5	2	7

neapolis print; and carriages, cattle, and riverbanks as foils for the skyline of St. Paul.

The latter two lithographs are unusual for this type of print and for the time in that they give the name of the lithographer—Hoffman—who put Ellsbury's fine drawings on stone. Probably Hoffman worked for the printer—again, Shober of Chicago—although Hoffman's name does not appear on the Winona print, which came from the same press. [1]

1. I can find no biographical information about the artist, nor could Thomas Beckman, who, in his *Milwaukee Illustrated*, note for exhibit item 25, states, "Little is known of George H. Ellsbury."

16. Thaddeus Mortimer Fowler (1842–1922)

The most prolific of all American city viewmakers, as artist, publisher, co-artist, or joint publisher of more than four hundred views, Thaddeus M. Fowler probably began his career in this field as a sales and subscription agent for Albert Ruger. His association with Ruger may have started earlier, but the first documented date is 14 July 1868, when a Des Moines, Iowa, newspaper announced, "Mr. T. M. Fowler, the agent of A. Ruger, a Chicago artist, has shown us a handsome pencil sketch view of Des Moines, which will be lithographed and on sale very shortly, provided sufficient patronage should be extended to the work." [1]

Fowler worked for Ruger elsewhere in Iowa, as well as in Nebraska, that summer and fall. [2] He continued to serve as Ruger's canvassing and subscription agent through September 1869, when Fowler was selling Ruger's view of McGregor, Iowa. [3] There can be little doubt that Fowler's duties included helping the artist with his drawings. In 1868 Ruger produced more than forty views, while in 1869 his output exceeded sixty, and no single artist could have achieved this record unassisted; it would have been possible only with the help of Fowler and perhaps other as yet unidentified assistants. It is not unlikely that toward the end of his apprenticeship Fowler was given responsibility for much of the initial sketching of buildings and streets or for preparing the final drawings of the views for the lithographer.

Like Ruger, Fowler served in the Civil War, volunteering in 1861. Wounded at the Second Battle of Bull Run, he received a discharge in February 1863. For a time he made a living by visiting army camps and making tintypes of soldiers. In 1864 he moved to the Midwest to work for his uncle, John Mortimer Fowler, a photographer in Madison, Wisconsin.[4]

Ruger probably met Fowler in 1867 when the artist visited Madison to sketch the city for his lithograph issued later that year. Ruger's first assistant, Eli S. Glover, founded a printing business at Chicago in 1868, and, although Glover published a few Ruger views that year, he obviously did not have the time to serve as field agent for the artist. Ruger must have been looking for a replacement, and Fowler probably began work early in 1868, although further research may show that his association with Ruger started at an even earlier date.

After two years with Ruger, Fowler was ready to strike out on his own. In 1870 he published two views of towns in Wisconsin: Oconomowoc and Omro, using a Madison post office box as his business address. Fowler may have drawn the first view, but the Omro lithograph is signed by H. H. Bailey, who is reported to have met Fowler when he visited the Madison studio of Fowler's uncle.[5]

Fowler and Bailey produced nine views in 1871, using firms in Milwaukee, Chicago, and Detroit to print their views of cities in Wisconsin, Indiana, and Michigan. The names *Bailey* and *Fowler* appear on these lithographs in the following rather bewildering combinations:

Co-artists, with no publisher indicated
Co-artists and joint publishers
Joint publishers with no artist identified
Joint publishers with H. H. Bailey as artist
H. H. Bailey as artist and T. M. Fowler as publisher

Howard Heston Bailey's younger brother, Oakley Hoopes Bailey, began work with them in 1872. All three names can be found on a lithograph of Columbus, Ohio, which identifies H. H. and O. H. Bailey as co-artists, while naming the publishers as "Fowler & Bailey."[6] The ambiguity of this imprint, found on many views from 1872 to 1875, prevents us from knowing exactly which Bailey was associated with Fowler or whether both of the brothers were partners in a business operated by all three.

Another lithograph of 1872 showing Altoona, Pennsylvania—the first of more than 240 views of that state that Fowler drew or published—illustrates the problem. The imprint gives both artist and publisher as "Fowler & Bailey." Other and later prints use this designation for the publisher only, while identifying either H. H. or O. H. Bailey as the artist.[7]

At least one other view—that of Ithaca, New York, in 1873—has no imprint showing either artist or publisher. A contemporary newspaper account, however, identifies O. H. Bailey as the artist and T. M. Fowler as the sales agent.[8] Further combinations of artists and publishers in this period of Fowler's career as recorded on prints bearing his name illustrate how roles were interchanged.[9] However, of the twenty-seven views through 1875 on which Fowler's name appears in some capacity, a lithograph of Trenton, New Jersey, in 1874 is the only one to identify him as the sole artist.

In was in 1874 that Fowler and the Baileys parted company for a time. Although H. H. Bailey died in 1878, Fowler and O. H. Bailey collaborated on several views in later years, and they remained close friends. The two surely exchanged opinions and information on the viewmaking business as each developed his separate enterprise, Bailey concentrating on New England and Fowler on the Middle Atlantic states.

Fowler's years as a traveling agent, artist's helper, fledgling artist, and business partner in association with Ruger and the Baileys provided him with the experience to conduct his own publishing firm, which he also served as principal artist. Beginning in 1876 it was his name alone—with less than a dozen exceptions—that appeared as artist on the hundreds of signed lithographs he published himself, issued jointly with one of his associates, or had brought out by other publishers such as J. J. Stoner or O. H. Bailey.

Although Fowler began his independent viewmaking career in 1876 with two views of New Jersey communities and two of towns not far away on Long Island, he resumed his more peripatetic life during 1877–1880 with sketching trips to New Hampshire, Nova Scotia, Ontario, Kansas, Nebraska, North Dakota, and Manitoba.[10] J. J. Stoner, a resident of Madison and publisher of many of Ruger's views, published Fowler's Maine and Nebraska views as well as later lithographs of Fargo, North Dakota, and Winnipeg, Manitoba, in 1880.

Fowler and O. H. Bailey resumed their association in 1879 with the publication of two Pennsylvania town views, one drawn by Bailey alone and the other signed by both. Fowler also drew South Manchester, Connecticut, for Bailey in 1880, and the two published a view of Hackettstown, New Jersey, in 1883. Only one Fowler view of 1882 has been recorded, but Bailey published sixteen, many of them unsigned. Fowler may have been the artist for some or all of these, most of which show New England communities. He did serve as subscription and sales agent for Bailey's view of Nashua, New Hampshire, in 1882 (Plate 67), and in the spring of the following year Fowler delivered the completed lithographs to the Nashua subscribers.[11]

This renewed collaboration with Bailey provides the basis for attributing to Fowler many unsigned lithographs of Pennsylvania towns published by O. H. Bailey in the period 1883–1885.[12] Thereafter, however, almost all of Fowler's views show him not only as artist but also as publisher, either alone or with some associates.[13]

Beginning in 1887 Fowler concentrated on Pennsylvania. Over a twenty-year period ending in 1906 he produced more than 200 lithographs of towns in that state. The great majority identify the publishers as T. M. Fowler and James B. Moyer. This partnership existed from 1888 to 1902. During this peak period of viewmaking Fowler also found time in 1890 and 1891 to visit and draw seventeen towns in Texas (see Plates 51 and 79) and Oklahoma; to draw twenty-five West Virginia communities; and to produce six of the series of ten Maryland views that he completed in 1907. Together with a few other lithographs of places in Michigan, Ohio, Missouri, and New Jersey, his recorded output from 1887 through 1906 came to more than 280 prints.

Another thirty-six views came from this prolific, almost compulsive, viewmaker during the decade 1907–1916, and

	Wisc.	Ind.	Mich.	Ohio	Pa.	N.Y.	N.J.	Conn.	N.H.	Maine	N.S.	Ont.	Kans.	Nebr.	Mont.	Minn.	N.D.	Okla.	Tex.	Mo.	W.V.	Md.	N.C.	Va.	Ga.	Mass.	Total
1870	2																										2
1871	5	4	1																								10
1872				2	2		1																				5
1873					3	1																					4
1874					2	3																					5
1875								1																			1
1876						2	2																				4
1877							3		1																		4
1878							1			2	3	1															7
1879					2						1		1	6													10
1880						1									2	1	2										6
1881							4					3		3													10
1882						1																					1
1883					3	1																					4
1884					5																						5
1885					8																						8
1886						3																					3
1887					4	2																					6
1888					7																						7
1889					11																						11
1890					9													1	7								17
1891					3													3	6	2							14
1892					8																						8
1893					13																						13
1894					25																						25
1895					22																						22
1896			1	2	16																1						20
1897					17																5						22
1898					3																4						7
1899				7	1																10						18
1900					19																2						21
1901					15																						15
1902					14																						14
1903					9		3																				12
1904					8																						8
1905					6																3	3					12
1906					9																	3					12
1907					2																	4	2	3			11
1908																							2		3		5
1909							1																	1			2
1910							1																				1
1911						1																3		1			5
1912																							3	1			4
1913																							2				2
1914																										2	2
1915								1																		1	2
1916					1																					1	2
1917								1												2							3
1918					1			1												1							3
1919																											
1920						1		1																			2
1921						1																					1
1922					1	2																					3
n.d.						1	2	1	1																		5
Total	7	4	2	11	248	13	27	6	1	2	4	4	1	6	5	1	2	7	13	2	18	10	9	5	4	4	426

a final twelve made their appearance through the year of Fowler's death in 1922, when, at the age of eighty, he slipped on an icy street in Middletown, New York, and died a week later on 17 March. Doubtless he had come to Middletown to promote the revised version of a view of that city first published in 1921 and reissued with additional vignettes by Hughes and Fowler the following year.[14]

In addition to Thomas J. Hughes, Fowler joined with A. E. Downs and with a Kelly, whose first name is unknown, in jointly publishing many of the views of his later years. Hughes and Bailey also published several views drawn by Fowler during this period.[15] Downs was an old associate; he had put on stone or printed (perhaps both) several Fowler-drawn lithographs from 1888 through 1891.

In addition to the views on which Downs is identified as lithographer or printer, the names of other printers appear on some of the Fowler lithographs: O. H. Bailey, Beck & Pauli, and a variety of Chicago and Milwaukee firms on the views of the 1870s. It is also known that the Meriden Gravure Company printed some of Fowler's later lithographs.

Most Fowler views, however, omit the name of any printer. It does not seem likely merely because of the total absence of any such information in an imprint that Fowler or Fowler and Moyer did their own presswork, but the identity of the printer is unknown. Nor is it known whether or not Fowler put his drawings on stone or zinc, or if instead his prints were made from finished drawings on transfer paper. Several of his later views, such as that of Tulsa, Oklahoma, in 1918, were printed with the aid of photography to make a gravure plate. It is possible that Fowler, as a former photographer himself, used negatives or film positives to transfer to photosensitized stones or zinc plates the line drawings of his earlier views.

Certainly his spare, mechanical style of rendering the buildings and streets of the cities he depicted would have lent itself well to this method of reproduction. Most of the Fowler views look very much alike, for his style changed little if at all over the more than fifty years he was involved in representing small-town America. In this respect, of course, Fowler differed hardly at all from his fellow delineators of the urban scene.

Fowler's clients probably asked for nothing more than a clear and accurate portrait of the towns in which they lived. Fowler, like Burleigh in New York and his old friend and associate, Bailey, in New England, satisfied this demand with a minimum of artistic frills. Probably they, too, felt the "unadulterated joy" in drawing the towns and cities of their regions that Fowler expressed near the end of his life.[16]

1. Des Moines Daily State Register, p. 1, col. 1. For this account as well as for many others concerning Ruger, Fowler, and Brosius in Iowa, Michigan, and Illinois, I am indebted to Ron Rayman, University Library, Western Illinois University, Macomb, Illinois.

2. Montana, Iowa, Boone County Democrat, 19 August 1868, p. 3, col. 2; Omaha, Nebraska, Daily Herald, 10 September 1868; Nebraska City, Nebraska News, 17 October 1868.

3. McGregor, Iowa, North Iowa Times, 22 September 1869, p. 3, col. 2.

4. James Raymond Warren, Sr., was responsible for assembling virtually all biographical material about Fowler, and he was generous in sharing information with others. Warren, however, was not aware of Fowler's association with Ruger in 1868 and 1869. Warren's most recent findings appear in Warren, "Thaddeus Mortimer Fowler, Bird's-eye-view Artist." The accompanying checklist of Fowler views compiled by Warren includes thir-

teen that I believe were not drawn or published by him and omits about seventy others that I have recorded.

5. The visit to the studio is mentioned in Warren, ibid., 27; and Warren and Wise, "The Bailey Brothers," 20. In the latter article the authors record that "Miss Martha Fowler, a daughter of T. M. Fowler, has stated in an interview that Howard H. Bailey taught her father how to draw birds-eye-views of communities." It is possible that Howard Bailey also worked for Ruger during the time of Fowler's employment and may indeed have helped Fowler learn to draw urban views.

6. Warren and Wise, "The Bailey Brothers," 21, 22, mention the Columbus view as "perhaps [O. H. Bailey's] earliest view." They further state, "The record does not indicate that Howard H. and Oakley H. Bailey ever produced a birds-eye-view together."

7. H. H. Bailey drew Burlington, New Jersey, in 1874, while O. H. Bailey in the same year drew New Brunswick, New Jersey. "Fowler & Bailey" published both.

8. Ithaca Daily Journal, 9 August 1873.

9. T. M. Fowler and H. H. Bailey are identified as co-artists and joint publishers of the Fostoria, Ohio, print of 1872. The Penn Yan, New York, lithograph of 1874 shows O. H. Bailey as the artist and T. M. Fowler & Co. as publisher. The Trenton, New Jersey, view published in 1874 shows T. M. Fowler as artist and Fowler & Bailey as publishers.

10. Several of the early New Jersey and Long Island views were published by Fowler & Evans. The later view of Westfield, New Jersey, in 1878 gives a business address of Box 208, Asbury Park, New Jersey. Fowler settled there for a time with his wife, whom he married in 1875 in Madison. Warren, "Thaddeus Mortimer Fowler," states that the Fowlers' first eastern home was in Orange, New Jersey. After Asbury Park the Fowlers moved to Lewisburg, Pennsylvania, in 1884, then to Trenton, and finally to Morrisville, Pennsylvania, in 1885. Fowler remained there until his wife died in 1910. Thereafter he lived in New Jersey, his last address being in Passaic.

11. Nashua Daily Telegraph, 11 October and 2 November 1882, and 8 April 1883; Nashua Daily Gazette, 11 April 1883.

12. See Leon J. Stout, "Pennsylvania Town Views, 1850–1922: A Union Catalogue." Stout states, "Upon moving east Fowler went to work for O. H. Bailey & Co. Some twenty Pennsylvania views produced from 1883 to 1885 by this company probably stem from the pencil of T. M. Fowler, including Lewisburgh, 1884, where one of his children was born" (p. 411). Stout's list includes fifteen entries for 1883–1885 in which he has inserted [T. M. Fowler] as artist. Stout may well be correct in his assertion that Fowler drew all of these. However, if his catalog had not been published and in wide use, my own entries would have shown the artist's category as blank. Instead, I have used the form [T. M. Fowler?]. For the record, these are the cities and the publication dates of the Pennsylvania views that are in question on this point: Lehighton, 1883; Milton, 1883; Berwick, 1884; Hazelton, 1884; Mifflinburg, 1884; Mount Carmel, 1884; Plymouth, 1884; Bangor, 1885; Bath, 1885; Chapman's Quarries, 1885; East Stroudsburg, 1885; Lansdale, 1885; Nazareth, 1885; Pen Argyl, 1885; and Portland, 1885. Research in local newspapers of the time would help to resolve this issue.

13. Beginning in 1878 Fowler's name can be found coupled with Evans as Fowler & Evans. Fowler & Rhines appears in 1880. Fowler & Tidey and Fowler & Coombs, each on single prints of Ontario towns in 1881, probably indicate local promoters. There is even an inversion of the usual Fowler & Bailey: Bailey & Fowler with a Boston address is used on a view of 1883. I think this is further evidence that Fowler worked as Bailey's artist in 1882 and possibly the year before or after.

14. Warren and Wise, "The Bailey Brothers," give Middletown as the place of the accident. An earlier version of this incident, based on information furnished by Warren to John Hébert, states that Fowler fell while sketching Port Jervis, New York. See Hébert's introduction to U.S. Library of Congress, Panoramic Maps of Anglo-American Cities: A Checklist of Maps in the Collections of the Library of Congress, Geography and Map Division, 7.

15. Hughes worked not only with Fowler and Bailey but also with Rene Cinquin, T. J. S. Landis, and others on a number of views.

16. Letter from Fowler to his granddaughter in 1920, written when he was working on the view of Middletown, New York, as quoted in U.S. Library of Congress, Panoramic Maps, 6.

17. Charles B. Gifford (1830–   )

Gifford was thirty when he began drawing views of California towns, starting in 1860 with a lithograph showing the village that had grown up around Mission Dolores in

San Francisco. Prints of Vallejo and Santa Clara are undated but probably were published the same year. Only the Mission Dolores print identifies a publisher. This was Louis Nagel, who printed several of Gifford's later views.[1]

Gifford's finest and most ambitious view was a sweeping panorama of San Francisco as seen from Russian Hill. This was printed on five sheets and was first issued in 1862 by A. Rosenfield of San Francisco. Gifford put his own drawing on stone, and it was carefully printed by Nagel. Rosenfield made at least three versions available to his customers: one printed on thin paper and mounted on cloth as a single sheet folded in an album, the second with single sheets printed on heavier paper, and the third mounted on cloth and fastened to wooden rollers. A second state of the view appeared in 1863, but the only change was the date.[2]

Charles B. Gifford

	Calif.	Wash.	Total
1860	3		3
1861			
1862	2	2	4
1863	1		1
1864	1		1
1865–			
1868	1		1
1869	2		2
1870	1		1
1871–			
1875	1		1
1876			
1877	1		1
Total	13	2	15

Gifford drew several other fine views of San Francisco printed on single large sheets. He began with one in 1864 showing the city as seen looking west from an imaginary point in the air (Plate 49). Many other artists adopted this same viewpoint in later years. In 1868 and 1869 Gifford collaborated with W. Vallance Gray in drawing and publishing handsome views of San Francisco and San Jose, the former print being reissued several times in later years with slight changes in the image or the legend.

Views of Santa Cruz about 1870, a second San Jose lithograph of 1875, and a final depiction of San Francisco in 1877 are his last recorded views. Gifford drew well, and he was fortunate in having his work printed by such competent lithographers as Nagel, the A. L. Bancroft Company, and Grafton T. Brown.

The San Jose view of 1875 printed by Bancroft (Plate 57) stands as one of the finest examples of two-stone or toned lithographic city views done in America. Variations of intensity in both the black and the buff tones, overprinting of the two, and elimination of the buff tone in places to produce highlight effects all combine to give the viewer an impression of several colors.

1. For a long note on Nagel, active first in New York City and then in San Francisco, see Peters, *California on Stone*, 165–72.

2. An analysis of the various states of this print can be found in Baird and Evans, *Historic Lithographs*, catalog notes by Joseph Baird, Jr., for entry no. 38.

18. Eli Sheldon Glover (1844–1920)

In 1866, the first year of Albert Ruger's career as a city view artist, he employed as his subscription agent a young man of twenty-two named Eli Sheldon Glover. Glover may have worked for Ruger earlier in the year, but our first trace of him is in mid-September in Ypsilanti, Michigan, where he was showing Ruger's original drawing and "canvassing the city to see if the requisite number of . . . [subscriptions] . . . can be secured and to make any improvements that may be suggested."[1]

The wording of this announcement implies that Glover himself might have been capable of making the "improvements," and it thus seems highly likely that in addition to his sales activities he assisted Ruger in drawing and sketching the town. Glover was only the first of several such agents whose services Ruger employed and who learned the business of viewmaking from Ruger well enough to strike out on their own. Thaddeus M. Fowler, Joseph J. Stoner, and Joseph Warner later helped Ruger in what was almost surely the same dual capacity of business agent and artist's assistant before beginning their own ventures.

Glover knew Ypsilanti well, for he had studied at the teacher's college there for two terms after working for a time in a Battle Creek, Michigan, printing firm specializing in religious publications. After the teacher's college he had a job teaching school, and then lived in Detroit, where he pursued a commercial course and a short period of instruction in drawing and painting.[2]

With his practical knowledge of printing and his training in both business and art, Glover must have seemed like the ideal apprentice to Ruger. Ruger not only drew but also published his seven views of 1866, and several of the thirty he did the following year have his name on them as publisher as well as an artist. He needed help, and he probably recruited Glover to act as sales agent and also to assist him in sketching the views.

In 1868 Glover became both a printer and publisher in his own right when he founded in Chicago the Merchants Lithographing Company. His name appears as publisher on only five of the forty Ruger views of that year, but his company is identified as printer on many more, and it appears highly likely that Glover published as well as printed these Ruger views. Curiously, only one of the five on which Glover's name is given as publisher came from his own press. Probably the other views were ready for printing early in the year before Glover's own press was available and he had to send them to the Chicago Lithographing Company, which had printed most of Ruger's earlier views.[3]

Glover's printing business seems to have absorbed all of his attention during 1869, for his name does not appear as publisher on any of the sixty-two views drawn by Ruger that

	Mich.	Ind.	Kans.	Ont.	Colo.	Mont.	Utah	Wyo.	Calif.	Wash.	Ore.	Br. Col.	Ala.	Tex.	Total
1868	5														5
1869															
1870	4														4
1871		1	2												3
1872	2		2	1											5
1873	1		4		1										6
1874					4										4
1875						2	5	1							8
1876									6	1	1				8
1877									10						10
1878										3		1			4
1879										1	1				2
1880–															
1888													1		1
1889	1														1
1890–															
1912														1	1
Total	13	1	8	1	5	2	5	1	16	5	2	1	1	1	62

year. Glover did succeed, however, in obtaining the printing contracts for at least twenty-one of these lithographs, and it is possible he served as publisher for some or even all of them.[4] In 1870 his firm printed at least fifteen views by Ruger.

In 1870 Glover began his own career as a view artist, drawing and printing (and surely publishing as well, although the lithographs do not so indicate) urban scenes of Lowell, Hastings, Big Rapids, and Charlotte, Michigan. In 1871 Glover added three others to his list, but only one came from his own press, and this was the last to do so, for the fire that ravaged Chicago that October destroyed the Merchants Lithographing Company, and Glover's career as a printer came to an end.[5]

To make his living Glover began to travel as a full-time artist of America's cities. In 1872 he drew (and doubtless published) prints of five communities in Ontario, Michigan, and Kansas. The next year he produced another Michigan view, four more of Kansas, and the first of his Colorado views. In 1874 he added four other Colorado towns, including a large lithograph of Denver (Plate 28) and one of Colorado Springs, where he and a partner operated a hotel that spring and summer.

In the fall of 1874 Glover and his wife of two years moved to Salt Lake City, and from there Glover visited and drew Helena and Virginia City, Montana; Green River, Wyoming; and Logan, Ogden, Corinne, and Brigham City, Utah, as well as Salt Lake City itself. Glover sent virtually all of his drawings to Cincinnati for printing by the Strobridge firm, a company well known for quality work.

In the fall of 1875 Glover set out on horseback from Helena, Montana, bound for Washington and Oregon. Late in October he reached Walla Walla, where he stayed for just under three weeks. It was evidently during that period that

he drew the little community of about twenty-five hundred persons for a lithograph dated 1876.

The diary of his trip contains not a word about this artistic endeavor, nor is there anything about his similar activities at Salem, Oregon, where he spent only one full day and the morning of another on a side trip from Portland. It seems scarcely possible that he could have drawn the city in so short a visit. A possible explanation is furnished in the artist's imprint: "Drawn by E. S. Glover from F. A. Smith's Photograph. . . ." Smith, who published the view, must have provided Glover with more than a single photograph, for there is no elevation from which the camera could have recorded with such detail the appearance of the Oregon capital.[6]

From Portland, Glover sailed to San Francisco, where his wife awaited him. They remained there from mid-December 1875 until the following spring, when they moved to Los Angeles. While in San Francisco, Glover probably worked out arrangements with Albert Little Bancroft to print his view of Helena, Montana—finished before Glover set out for Washington—as well as those of Walla Walla and Salem. He probably discussed with Bancroft his plans for a series of California urban views, and it is likely that he completed his lithographs of Santa Rosa and Healdsburg, both located north of San Francisco, before leaving for Southern California.[7]

The Glovers remained in Los Angeles for about a year and a half, but Mrs. Glover must have lived a lonely life. While her husband did produce several views of Los Angeles and nearby Santa Monica and Wilmington (Plate 60), he also visited and drew more distant places, including San Diego in 1876 and Santa Barbara, San Luis Obispo, Ventura, and Anaheim in 1877.

In the fall of 1877 the Glovers moved once again, this time

to Portland, Oregon, which Glover used as a base from which to produce views of Seattle, Port Townsend, Tacoma, and Olympia in Washington, and Victoria, British Columbia (Plate 61), as well as Portland itself—all in 1878 and 1879. The Glover-Bancroft collaboration brought together a skilled topographic artist and high-quality lithographic craftsmanship. The large folio views that resulted are consistent in their style, format, attractive appearance, and use of a single tone stone to provide pleasing and often dramatic cloud and sky effects.

Eli Glover and his wife returned to Michigan in the autumn of 1879. The next year, at Battle Creek, Glover began a business manufacturing loose-leaf books, binders, and metal-backed albums. This proved to be a profitable enterprise, and in the next decade he traveled to Europe to arrange the manufacture of his product under foreign patents, opened a New York City office for his firm, and lived for a short time on Long Island before moving, first to Battle Creek again and then, in 1890, to Tacoma, Washington. While in Michigan briefly, Glover apparently could not resist the temptation to resume his artistic career. In 1888 he drew and published a view of Anniston, Alabama, and in 1889 one of the city of Muskegon, Michigan.

In Tacoma he turned to land development, but this proved a disaster. In the panic of 1893 he lost his money and once again resumed making views. He produced two interesting and highly detailed books containing elevation views of the buildings in the business districts of San Francisco and Oakland.[8] In 1896 he prepared his last California views: a lithograph of San Francisco published by the H. S. Crocker Company and a view of all of Southern California for the Southern Pacific Railroad.

Glover then designed and began to manufacture a prospector's drill for use in the Alaska goldfields. Finally, in 1898 he returned to the Midwest to become an agent and associate editor for historical and biographical works published by the Century Publishing and Engraving Company, becoming one of the proprietors of the Century Publishing Company six years later.

He died in Seattle in 1920, but not before completing one final city view showing Port Arthur, Texas, in 1912. This view was published by the Port Arthur Board of Trade. What took him to Port Arthur and what persuaded him to resume momentarily at the age of sixty-eight a career long since abandoned can only be a matter for speculation. Perhaps he felt that despite his success as an industrialist and publisher, his true calling was as a delineator of cities. In this odd profession he succeeded admirably, leaving a legacy of more than sixty well-drawn views of towns and cities in fourteen states and Canadian provinces.

---

1. Ypsilanti *Commercial*, 15 September 1866, p. 3. In the Division of Geography and Maps, Library of Congress, this undated view has been assigned a conjectural date of 1868. It probably was published no later than 1867, and it might have been printed and distributed before the end of 1866.

2. Most of my information about Glover's background comes from a biographical sketch written by the youngest of Glover's four children, Sheldon L. Glover, "The Glover Family [of] Michigan: William Glover, Charles S. Glover, Eli Sheldon Glover. I am grateful to Warren Howell of San Francisco for calling my attention to this material. Howell drew on it for his article, written with Laura R. White, "California in Lithographs:

Nineteenth Century Prints from the Robert B. Honeyman, Jr. Collection." Additional (and occasionally contradictory) material on Glover can be found in the preface by A. L. Korn to the typescript "The Diary of Eli Sheldon Glover, October-December, 1975." The Oregon Historical Society kindly provided a copy of this document. Relying on the recollections of Glover's daughter, Mrs. R. Hobart Ellsworth, Korn states that Glover "pursued a course of study at the Art league in New York." Korn also asserts that land in Tacoma, Washington, "had been turned over to Glover by the city . . . in exchange for a series of Glover's 'bird's-eye-views,'" and that "the property became involved in a dispute over the title" that was finally settled by a decision in favor of Glover by the Washington Supreme Court. I do not have access to the trial record, but the Supreme Court opinion in the case of *Mary Cleveland* v. *S. Glover*, 13 Wash. 131 (November 1895) refers only to property purchased by the plaintiff's husband acting as Glover's agent.

3. The Chicago Lithographing Company, founded in 1864 by Louis Kurz, Otto Knirsch, and Edward Carqueville, was in business until the fire of 1871 and printed dozens of city views, including many of those by Ruger. Thomas Beckman, "Louis Kurz: Early Years."

4. Many of the Ruger views of these and other years lack either a printer's or a publisher's imprint, sometimes both. In 1869 Ruger entered into a publishing partnership with Joseph J. Stoner of Madison, Wisconsin, and about forty of the Ruger views of 1869 and 1870 bear their name.

5. One of the 1871 prints—Elkhart, Indiana—was printed at the Calvert Lithographing Company in Detroit. The other—Chetopa, Kansas—has the name of the "Union Lith. Co.," Chicago, Ill." I do not know the firm, but its name suggests that it may have been hastily formed by several fire-destroyed companies to use whatever equipment they could muster. The fact that only one of Glover's 1871 city views was printed by him may indicate that his firm was in financial difficulties. That year Ruger brought only one of his views to Glover for printing. Three went to the Chicago Lithographing Company, three others to printers in other cities, while the places of printing of the remaining four do not appear on the prints. Since the fire did not begin until 8 October, Glover would have had ample time to print views that year if the demand had been present. Glover had his Virginia City view printed in Chicago by Charles Shober & Co., the successor to the Chicago Lithographing Company. The A. L. Bancroft Company of San Francisco printed the Helena view. This was the first of many that Bancroft produced from Glover's drawings. For the Strobridge firm, see John W. Merten, "Stone by Stone Along a Hundred Years with the House of Strobridge."

6. Glover's diary records that he arrived in Salem by river steamer "a little before dark" on 25 November 1875. By the evening of 27 November he was back in Portland, this time traveling by rail. It is conceivable that Glover returned to Salem from San Francisco to do further work on the view, but this seems unlikely from what is known of his movements during this period.

7. The Helena view is dated 1875, and it is possible that Glover sent it to Bancroft before leaving Montana for Walla Walla. I think it more likely that Glover would have wanted to meet Bancroft before contracting with him for printing services. In the only detailed treatment of Bancroft that I have found there is no mention of his connection with city views, and the account books for 1876 and 1877 are not among the surviving records of this important printing and publishing firm. See Henry R. Wagner, "Albert Little Bancroft." Bancroft's portrait is reproduced opposite p. 97. See also Peters, *California on Stone*, 54–55.

8. I have seen only the Oakland book, shown to me by Warren Howell. The title page reads: "*The Illustrated Directory of Oakland California Comprising Views of Business Blocks, with Reference to Owners, Occupants, Professions and Trades, and Brief History of the City.* Published by The Illustrated Directory Company Oakland, California. E. S. Glover, Manager. August, 1896. Press of the Oakland Enquirer Publishing Co." The San Francisco book was published a year earlier.

19. George Henry Goddard (1817–1906)

Goddard came to California in the fall of 1850 at the age of thirty-three. Born in England and educated at Oxford, he worked in London as an architect and civil engineer and exhibited paintings at the Royal Academy in 1837 and 1850. He was also a town planner, having designed for Lord Holland a portion of the Notting Hill Division of the Holland Park Estate in the rapidly growing West End of London.[1]

In the goldfields Goddard had no luck as a miner and at first could not find work as a surveyor. Early in January 1852 he wrote his brother from the mining town of Columbia that he and an Irish doctor had formed a partnership in a "General and Drug store." Goddard sketched his new home of Columbia, then a thriving mining camp, as well as the nearby towns of Sonora and Springfield, which also owed their existence to rich gold strikes. All three views appeared in lithographic form in 1852 as printed in San Francisco by Britton & Pollard and Britton & Rey in the first business year of what came to be a well-known and respected printing firm.

Goddard found viewmaking an unprofitable enterprise. He complained to his brother, "My views have done me little good. You are aware that in publishing them the stones remained security to the lithographers for the bill of expenses and as they are sold very slowly, the latter seize the stones and published [sic] a great lot of copies in lettersheets and selling them at a cheap price have made a good deal of money by it." [2]

He soon secured more rewarding employment as a surveyor, architect, and engineer. He worked for the state of California, for real estate developers in San Francisco, where he designed a residential area known as South Park, and for a water company on a variety of projects. He became well known for his cartographic work, and his map of California published in 1857 received recognition as an outstanding accomplishment.

George Henry Goddard
(Excludes variant states)

	Calif.	Total
1852	3	3
1853–		
1868	2	2
1869–		
1875	1	1
1876	1	1
1877–		
1880	1	1
Total	8	8

About 1866 Goddard moved to San Francisco from Sacramento, and two years later his stunning view of San Francisco and its surroundings was ready for publication by Snow & Roos after being printed by Britton & Rey. Goddard's large lithograph showed the city for the first time as seen from the west far above the Pacific Ocean. It encompassed the entire San Francisco Bay area, although to do this Goddard distorted the southern portion of the bay so that its borders appeared within the right margin of the sheet.

Although other errors of less consequence can be found in Goddard's view, his knowledge of topography and his skills in rendering make this one of the most convincing and accurate of the many portraits of San Francisco. It must have impressed the city's residents, for several states of the view exist with minor changes in imprint that indicate its original press run did not satisfy customer demand. Redrawn versions published in 1875, 1876, and 1880 testify to the continued popularity of Goddard's unusual and appealing print.

In April 1906, Goddard's vast collection of maps, books, sketches, prints, rock specimens, and the paintings he continued to produce throughout his years in California were all destroyed in the earthquake and fire that ravaged San Francisco. Copies of his ten lithographic city views were surely among this material, which perhaps also included the original drawings on which the views were based. Eight months later at the age of eighty-nine Goddard died, a death, his family asserted, "brought on as a result of grief over his heavy losses in the . . . disaster." [3]

1. All my information about Goddard's life comes from Albert Shumate's splendid study, *The Life of George Henry Goddard: Artist, Architect, Surveyor, and Map Maker.*
2. Goddard to Augustus Goddard, August 1852, as quoted in ibid., 3.
3. Quoted from an unidentified source in ibid., 9.

20. Augustus Hageboeck (—   )

Augustus Hageboeck drew, printed, and published ten city views between 1866 and 1886. Four of them show Davenport, Iowa, where he lived and where he and his brother, John, operated a lithographic printing establishment. [1] Hageboeck also produced views that he and his brother surely printed of Rock Island and Moline, Illinois; Cedar Falls, Iowa; St. Paul and Minneapolis, Minnesota; and St. Louis, Missouri. While his last lithographic city view is dated 1881, he is known to have prepared the plate from which he printed and published in 1886 an engraved view of Minneapolis. This view shows his address in that city.

At least two persons who played central roles in printing lithographic city views lived for a time in or near Davenport. Clemens J. Pauli appears in the Davenport directories in 1867 and 1868 and in nearby Rock Island in 1873. [2] Pauli moved to Milwaukee about 1875 to begin drawing cities and then to found the printing firm of Beck & Pauli. C. H. Vogt was in Davenport in 1864 to draw a view of the Rock

Augustus Hageboeck

	Iowa	Ill.	Minn.	Mo.	Total
1866	1				1
1867–					
1872	2				2
1873		1	2		3
1874		1		1	2
1875–					
1880	1				1
1881	1				1
Total	5	2	2	1	10

Island Barracks, and he may have lived and worked there before moving to Milwaukee in 1870 where he, too, began to draw views before he established a printing business.

Possibly one or both may have gained some experience with Hageboeck. Both Pauli and Vogt were born in Germany, and Hageboeck probably was German as well. If Hageboeck was their mentor, they had an experienced teacher. His first view, a depiction of Davenport from the east side of the Mississippi, is the work of someone with substantial training in art who not only could render the buildings of the city rising from the water's edge but who also possessed an easy facility for handling people and animals as well as steamboats, other river craft, and a railroad train in the foreground. [3]

1. Thomas Beckman has provided me with a copy of the firm's advertisement in the Davenport directory for 1861. A listing on the following page gives the home address of both brothers as Brown Street between Fourth and Fifth. The advertisement for "Hageboeck & Bro." includes "Maps, Plans, [and] Views" among the items they were prepared to print. The Putnam Museum in Davenport is unable to provide any information about Hageboeck other than his description (from an unidentified source) as "a little man wearing a tall silk hat" (letter from Carol Hunt, Registrar, Putnam Museum, to the author, 3 September 1981).

2. Thomas Beckman has provided me with this information, showing Pauli's listing as draftsman in 1868 and as "U.S. Engineer" in 1873. His occupation in 1867 is not specified. According to Beckman, Pauli's daughter, Clara, was born in 1871 in Rock Island.

3. Hageboeck's Davenport view of 1866 is reproduced in color but his work is not otherwise recognized in Loren N. Horton's "Through the Eyes of Artists: Iowa Towns in the 19th Century."

21. James Compton Hazen (1852–1908)

In his early years of drawing and publishing views, James Compton Hazen was associated with H. H. Bailey. In the fall of 1873 he was in Syracuse to solicit subscriptions for a Bailey view that was published the following year, and he may have been working for Bailey at an even earlier time as an agent or artist's assistant. [1] His name and H. H. Bailey's are found on a number of views from 1874 through 1877 identifying them as joint publishers or co-artists (see Plate 25). It was Hazen, however, who seems to have continued to handle the business side of the venture, since it was he who sold subscriptions or delivered completed lithographs in several New Hampshire communities in 1875 and 1876. [2]

Not all of the H. H. Bailey views on which Hazen worked identify his contribution. Many of the impressions of views in the collection of the Boston Public Library with Bailey's printed name on them have Hazen's name added in manuscript. These include such prints as those of Johnstown, New York, in 1874 and Glens Falls, Amsterdam, Newburgh, and Schenectady, New York, in 1875. If, as seems possible, these inked additions are by Hazen himself, it is an interesting example of pride in workmanship and an attempt to secure recognition for an otherwise anonymous contribution to the achievements of his mentor. [3]

In 1877 Hazen began to draw and publish views with O. H. Bailey, and this association continued through 1880. In that year Hazen's name appears with that of E. H. Bigelow of Framingham, Massachusetts, as joint publisher of a

James Compton Hazen, Bailey & Hazen, etc.

	N.J.	N.Y.	Conn.	Mass.	N.H.	R.I.	Vt.	Total
1874	2	1						3
1875		5						5
1876			1	4	1	1	1	8
1877		1		4		4		9
1878			2	10				12
1879			2	10		1		13
1880				2				2
1881								
1882				2				2
1883–								
1904				1				1
Total	2	7	5	33	1	6	1	55

view of Newburyport, Massachusetts, and in 1882 they collaborated in drawing and publishing two additional Massachusetts views. [4] Hazen's final view was in 1904, a lithograph of Lynn Woods in Lynn, Massachusetts, that brought him together for a final time with O. H. Bailey, whose name appears on this print as co-artist.

1. Ithaca, New York, *Daily Journal*, 21 October 1873.

2. Nashua, New Hampshire, *Daily Telegraph*, 25 June 1875; Concord, New Hampshire, *Daily Monitor*, 25 September 1875; Manchester, New Hampshire, *Daily Union*, 21 August 1875, 8 February 1876.

3. I should add, however, that the annotations may have been placed on the prints by someone else aware of other lithographs on which the names of H. H. Bailey and J. C. Hazen appear in the imprint and on the assumption that Hazen was involved with all the H. H. Bailey city views. This issue is not likely to be resolved.

4. Bigelow published unsigned views of Gardner, Uxbridge, and Westborough, Massachusetts, in 1880, and all three could have been Hazen's work either alone or with Bigelow.

22. William Valentine Herancourt (–)

William Valentine Herancourt was responsible for drawing ten city views during the years 1881–1885. Except for one of Cedar Falls, Iowa, done in his first year as a viewmaker, and his last known work of this type—a print of Minneapolis—all of the towns he depicted were located in South Dakota. Herancourt's eight views of places there supplement nicely those published by J. J. Stoner at about the same time, a few of which are signed by Henry Wellge. Together, Herancourt's views and those by Stoner provide a remarkably fine record of conditions in communites whose growth was then being stimulated by railroad building across the prairies and by the mining boom in the Black Hills.

On one of his early views, that of Chamberlain, South Dakota, in 1882, the address of Dubuque, Iowa, follows the name of the artist. Perhaps that is where he lived while doing his separately issued city views. By the end of the 1880s he had traveled to Oklahoma, where he helped record the extraordinary chaos accompanying the opening of Oklahoma

	Iowa	S.D.	Minn.	Total
1881	1			1
1882		1		1
1883		4		4
1884		3		3
1885			1	1
Total	1	8	1	10

to white settlement. *Harper's Weekly* used several of his drawings to illustrate their articles about this event.[1] However, so far as is known, he did not then produce views other than those used to illustrate periodical articles.[2]

1. See, for example, the issue for 29 April 1889.
2. The Amon Carter Museum classifies its Herancourt views of Deadwood and Lead as wood engravings. I now believe them to be lithographs, quite possibly done with the aid of photography. They resemble in many respects the early views of Lucien R. Burleigh printed in Syracuse in 1882 and 1883. On both the Lead and Deadwood prints the signature of the artist is written in a manner I believe to be inconsistent with a wood engraving. In most wood engravings the signatures are normally much more angular and far less free-flowing.

23. John William Hill (1812–1897)

John William Hill, born in 1812, came to America in 1816 with his father, the well-known English aquatint artist. The family first settled in Philadelphia and then, in 1822, moved to New York, where the younger Hill received his training in art from his father.[1] As a young man he worked for the New York State Geological Survey, and in 1850 at the age of thirty-eight he began an association with the Smith brothers that lasted five years and resulted in some of America's most attractive urban lithographs.

Hill had drawn only a few city views before this time: four in 1834 and two in 1845, all printed by the Endicott firm in New York City. While modest in size, each measuring about nine by thirteen inches, these views showed that Hill possessed his father's abilities as an artist and could delineate with equal skill the buildings of a town and the landscape features within and around the community.

For the Smiths, Hill worked at first with one of the brothers, almost certainly Benjamin Franklin Smith, although on the two views of Philadelphia in 1850 the artists are identified only as "J. W. Hill & Smith." That combination appears also on the firm's two views of New Orleans in 1852 (see Plate 14) and the lithograph of St. Louis the same year. Those prints followed views by Hill alone of St. John, New Brunswick, in 1851 and the often-reproduced lithograph of Charleston, on which the artist's imprint is "Smith & Smith after John William Hill."

In the years 1852–1855 Hill drew many other views for the Smith brothers: two of Cincinnati, Ohio (see Color Plate 8); two of Brooklyn; and one each of Albany, Buffalo, and Rochester, New York; Cleveland, Ohio; Richmond, Virginia; Bangor (Plate 77) and Portland, Maine; Salem, Massachusetts; and Halifax, Nova Scotia. Hill's view of Savannah, Georgia, in 1855, although lacking a publisher's imprint, probably was issued by the Smith brothers as well.[2]

Hill's original drawings or paintings of the cities he depicted for the Smiths do not seem to have survived. No doubt they were done well, for Hill was already recognized as an accomplished artist. Nevertheless, at least some of the splendid quality of the Hill lithographs comes from the skill with which several lithographic artists put his work on stone. They included D. W. Moody, Charles Parsons, J. H. Colen, and Napoleon Sarony. Important, too, were the contributions of the printers used by the Smiths for Hill's lithographs: Francis Michelin, Sarony & Major, and, primarily, the Endicott firm. Artist, lithographers, and printers thus joined to produce extremely handsome lithographs.

Hill used a slightly elevated panoramic style for many of his views, such as those of Richmond and Bangor and the Philadelphia print showing the city as seen from the east side of the Delaware River. For other places, including Albany, Rochester, and Buffalo, the artist imagined himself at a higher elevation from which he could peer into the city to trace its pattern of streets and to depict building facades within the interior of the community.

John William Hill

	N.J.	N.Y.	Pa.	N.B.	S.C.	La.	Mo.	Ohio	Va.	Maine	Mass.	Ga.	N.S.	Total
1834	1	3												4
1835–														
1845	1	1												2
1846–														
1850			2											2
1851				1	1									2
1852						2	1	1						4
1853		5						2	1					8
1854										1	1			2
1855										1		1	1	3
Total	2	9	2	1	1	2	1	3	1	2	1	1	1	27

The generous size of these lithographs, with a horizontal dimension that averaged about forty inches, offered opportunities for Hill to introduce into the foreground little details that add to the delight of the viewer as well as provide knowledge about some elements of the urban scene of the time. Thus, Hill shows us in his Portland, Maine, view a ship being constructed on the waterfront and in his Rochester lithograph provides us fascinating vignettes of the Erie Canal, life along its towpath, and the appearance of the boats traversing its waters.

Altogether Hill's name appears on twenty-seven city views done in the medium of lithography. They are among the most striking of American historical prints and are invaluable records of the appearance of some of the nation's most important cities in the decade before the Civil War.

1. John Hill, the father, did the plates for a series of aquatint views—including several cities—after paintings by William Guy Wall. He also drew several of the city views that William James Bennett superbly etched in aquatint in the mid-1830s. For John Hill (1770–1850), see Richard J. Koke, "John Hill, Master of Aquatint 1770–1850." A brief note on the elder Hill's work and other references can be found in Philadelphia Museum of Art, *Philadelphia: Three Centuries of American Art*, 249–51.
2. Like other Smith brothers lithographs of 1854 and 1855, the Savannah view was printed by Endicott & Co. in New York, and, as in the case of three of the others, Charles Parsons put the drawing on stone.

24. Augustus Koch (1840–?)

Although he produced fewer urban lithographs than such prolific artist-publishers as Albert Ruger, Thaddeus Fowler, and Lucien Burleigh, no American viewmaker traveled more widely in search of subjects than Augustus Koch. He may have started his career somewhat earlier as an assistant to another artist, but his first signed lithographs date from 1868 with the appearance of views of Cedar Falls, Vinton, and Waterloo, Iowa.[1]

In 1869 Koch drew four additional Iowa towns before setting out the following year to depict places in Wyoming, Utah, and California. In 1871 he produced eight views of California towns. From 1872 through 1875 he visited and prepared views of cities in Tennessee, Illinois, Texas, New York, Nebraska, Nevada, South Dakota, and Maine. Toward the end of his career, in the 1890s, his travels took him to Virginia, Washington, Georgia, Florida, Missouri, Colorado, and Montana. Altogether, he was responsible for at least 110 views of towns in nearly every region of the country.

Like many of his fellow view artists, Koch came to this country from Germany. He was born on 15 October 1840 in Birnbaum, a small town in the province of Posen in the Kingdom of Prussia.[2] Perhaps that is where he was "thoroughly educated and went through a good school," as his superior officer described his training in recommending Koch for a commission during the Civil War. It is also possible, of course, that Koch obtained his education in the United States, since it is not known when he immigrated.

In September 1861, just over a month before his twenty-first birthday, Koch enlisted for three years as a private in company B, 9th Regiment, Wisconsin Infantry. Probably his home was then in Manitowoc, Wisconsin, for he applied for a furlough two years later to visit his parents there.[3]

In 1863 Koch was stationed in St. Louis, where his duties were described as "clerk and draughtsman in the Engineers Office" of the Union army. It was from that post that Koch applied for an officer's commission. The examining officers may have had some difficulty understanding him, for in one of his two letters of recommendation the writer asked the colonel heading the examining board "as a particular favor . . . [to] . . . assist him in his examination, if it is in your power, he, not speaking the English language, as it ought to be spoken could make a better examination in German."[4]

Koch won a commission and received an assignment as an engineering officer with one of the black regiments serving in the lower Mississippi valley. He drew a map of Vicksburg, and he also visited Baton Rouge and Mobile, where he probably prepared other drawings. It was doubtless in this region that he contracted what must have been malaria, an ailment described by the Manitowoc physician's statement accompanying Koch's application for release from service as consisting of "intermitant [*sic*] fever & night-sweats." On 16 November 1865 Koch secured his discharge.

After this date Koch's life can be followed only by the trail of lithographs he left behind him. How he came to be an artist of city views is, of course, unknown. Perhaps he sought employment as a skilled draftsman in Milwaukee or Chicago, the two largest cities nearest his home. The latter city seems more likely, since in 1869 a Webster City, Iowa, newspaper referred to him as "Augustus Koch, of Chicago," and a year later the artist gave Chicago as his address on a view he published of Salt Lake City.[5] Possibly in Chicago he met and was hired by Eli S. Glover, who in 1868 started his Merchants Lithographing Co., where Koch's first two city views were printed.

Koch may have been associated with Albert Ruger, whom Glover served in 1866 as assistant and then in 1868 as publisher. Both Ruger and Koch were active in Iowa in 1868, and views by both were printed at Glover's press. These views lack a publisher's name, and it would be no surprise to find that Glover acted in this capacity as well as printer and that all three men were thus involved in the same enterprise.[6]

It may have been Ruger who introduced Koch to Joseph J. Stoner of Madison, who at this time was publishing some of Ruger's views either alone or as copublisher with the artist. After Koch's first trip to the Far West he began to draw cities that Stoner published from his headquarters in Maidson, Wisconsin.[7] The two probably traveled together much of the time. In January 1873, for example, Stoner joined Koch in San Antonio and Austin (Plate 40, top), Texas, to drum up trade for views Koch had sketched. In these towns Stoner worked to get favorable publicity in the local newspapers and then took subscriptions for the lithographic versions of Koch's drawings. Later that year when Koch visited upstate New York to draw towns in the western part of the region Stoner may also have come along to promote the two Koch views of Waterloo and Canandaigua that Stoner published.

Koch's work for Stoner ceased after 1873. Although only four of the seventy-nine lithographs drawn by Koch in the

	Iowa	Utah	Wyo.	Calif.	Tenn.	Ill.	Ala.	N.Y.	Tex.	Nebr.	Nev.	S.D.	Maine	Fla.	Mo.	Kans.	Colo.	N.M.	Idaho	Ga.	Wash.	Va.	Mont.	Total
1868	2																							2
1869	4																							4
1870		1	1	3																				5
1871				8																				8
1872					1	1																		2
1873						1	1	4	4															10
1874	1									4														5
1875				1							2	1	1											5
1876										3				1	1									5
1877														1		1								2
1878																								
1879																1	1							2
1880									1	6						2								9
1881									5	7														12
1882																								
1883									1							1								2
1884									1	7														8
1885									2	1														3
1886									1							1		1						3
1887									3					1					1					5
1888–																								
1890														1					1					2
1891																				1	1	1		3
1892															2						1			3
1893														1			1							2
1894																								
1895																1								1
1896														1										1
1897																							1	1
1898																							1	1
n.d.	1								2	1														4
Total	8	1	1	12	1	2	1	4	19	30	2	1	1	6	3	7	2	1	2	2	1	1	2	110

years 1874–1898 name him as both artist and publisher, it seems likely that he did publish nearly all of his own views.[8] Koch thus followed the pattern of many other viewmakers: first serving (probably) as assistant to an artist, then becoming an artist himself whose work was published by others, and finally assuming the role of artist-publisher—a status offering potentially higher profits and personal satisfactions although involving greater responsibilities.

Koch drew his cities with considerable care, consistently depicting his subjects as if seen from very high viewpoints. The horizon lines appear close to the tops of the images, and the body of each print is thus full of urban detail. Koch also used a distinctive format, making his horizontal dimension not much greater than the vertical. Characteristic views of his include those of Cheyenne (Color Plate 11) and Salt Lake City (Plate 83) in 1870; Los Angeles, California, in 1871; Austin, Texas, in 1873; Virginia City and Carson City (Plate 43), Nevada, in 1875; and the rare Albuquerque, New Mexico, lithograph of 1886 (Plate 29).

Koch revisited and redrew several cities. These sets of views are particularly useful for determining the urban development taking place between the dates of the two views.

The places he recorded in this manner are Austin, Texas (1873 and 1887 [Plate 40]); Lincoln, Nebraska (1874, 1880, and 1885); Brenham, Texas (1873 and 1881); Kingman, Kansas (1883 and 1886); Jacksonville, Florida (1876 and 1893); and San Antonio, Texas (1873 and 1886).

He seems to have drawn with substantial accuracy. A detailed examination of his 1873 view of Waterloo, New York, included a building-by-building comparison with those shown on an engineering survey of the village published just two years before Koch's visit. The two match almost exactly, and one is led to believe that Koch used the map in preparing his lithograph, as he must have done in other cities. On the other hand, a number of smaller buildings appear in only a stylized manner, while Koch exaggerated the size of several larger structures.[9]

In this view as well as in his print of Salt Lake City in 1870, Koch included as if completed two church structures that had only been started. His St. Mary's Catholic church in Waterloo has a steeple that was indeed part of the original design, from which Koch evidently worked. However, this steeple was abandoned in favor of one of different style, which was not completed until nearly thirty years after the lithograph was published. A period of almost equal length intervened between Koch's depiction of the Salt Lake City Temple and its completion. In this case, however, his delineation turned out to be essentially accurate.

Koch in 1874 did call attention in the first of his three portraits of Lincoln, Nebraska, that the Post Office and the Union Depot as he showed them were "proposed," thus providing an implied warning that the appearance of the finished buildings might depart from his drawings. He included this information in the view's legend, a feature that Koch normally supplied and that at least one study found to be both helpful and reliable.[10]

Another of Koch's Nebraska urban views has been studied in a different way. In this print of Beatrice in 1881 Koch used a darker shade in his tone stone to identify buildings constructed of brick. Recently, two scholars have compared his depiction with a detailed fire insurance map prepared at the same time as the view and have concluded that in this respect the artist provided a completely reliable guide.[11]

Koch's pursuit of subjects took him to twenty-three states during a career that began in 1868 and did not end until 1898. Although his views show thirty towns in Nebraska, nineteen places in Texas, and twelve California communities, he sketched at least one view in such widely separated states as Maine, Florida, New Mexico, and Washington. During the long period he was active he failed to draw views only in 1878, 1882, 1888, 1889, and 1894. His recorded output of 110 views was exceeded by only a few other viewmakers.

1. The Vinton view is apparently undated, but I have assigned a date of 1868 based on the close proximity of the three towns.

2. These and other biographical details come entirely from Koch's Civil War records in the National Archives. I found them in two folders. One contains material relating to his service as a private in Company B, 9th Wisconsin Infantry; the other provides information about his activities as 2d Lt., 51st U.S. Colored Infantry. Evidently he never applied for a pension. Requests for additional biographical information were sent to many local and state historical societies, but they produced no results.

3. Neither the Manitowoc County Historical Society nor the Manitowoc Public Library could provide any biographical material on Koch or his parents. Letter from Rosemary Young Singh, Adult Services, Manitowoc Public Library to the author, 23 April 1981.

4. The writer, James R. Gibson, identified Koch as "my friend Koch," who at the time of writing—5 February 1864—was "on detached duty, as Clerk to Capt. Haelcke[?], Topographical Engineer of this Dept." Gibson's rank is illegible. His letter also stated that Koch had two brothers in military service, one a captain, the other a first lieutenant. This suggests a family background of some education and, perhaps, of more than modest means. The reference to Koch's difficulties with English may indicate that the young man was a recent arrival in America. I should add, however, that several documents in Koch's military records written (apparently) in his own hand are in flawless English. They are also executed in elegant calligraphy.

5. Webster City, *Hamilton: Freeman*, 5 May 1869. The paper added that Koch "has been taking a pencil sketch of Webster City, which gives a very correct view of the town and its suburban surroundings. He is preparing to have it lithographed. Many of our citizens have subscribed for one or more copies of the view."

6. Both Koch views of 1868 were printed by the Merchants Lithographing Co. Four of Ruger's Iowa views of 1868 were done there: Clinton, Council Bluffs, Lyons, and Marion.

7. All of Koch's California prints of 1871 were printed in San Francisco by Britton & Rey, and several were published by Snow & Roos. Others bear no publisher's imprint and may have been published by Koch himself.

8. Four other views among the seventy-nine identify other publishers. Probably all were firms located in the places depicted. Seventy-one omit any publisher's imprint.

9. Uhl, "'Every building is Accurately Represented,'" chap. 5.

10. Ibid.

11. Helen Brooks and Karen Pearson, "Nebraska Towns on View," notes to item 16.

25. Augustus Theodore Frederick Adam Kollner (1812–1906)

Augustus Kollner learned to draw when very young, and at sixteen he found employment as an engraver in Stuttgart, capital of Württemberg where he was born in 1812. A few years later he moved to Paris to continue his career as an engraver and etcher, and it may have been there that he acquired his knowledge of lithography. He brought all of these skills to America when he sailed from Europe in 1839.[1]

He found his first job at the lithographic firm of Philip Haas in Washington, D.C., but by the fall of 1840 he had established his own business in Philadelphia. Kollner found he could not earn a living as a portrait painter, and he began to do lithographs for some of Philadelphia's best printers, including Peter S. Duval, Thomas Sinclair, and Frederick Kuhl. It was Kuhl who printed and published Kollner's first city view in 1842, a lithograph of Philadelphia and Camden seen from the New Jersey shore of the Delaware River.

Kollner's next venture was far more ambitious. Beginning in 1848 and continuing through 1851, he sketched scenes in a number of American and Canadian cities for the New York and Paris firm of Goupil, Vibert & Co. His drawings went to Paris, where most of them were put on stone by Deroy and printed by either Cattier or Jacomme & Co. They included many lithographs of individual buildings or streets, but among them were at least eleven that showed all or major portions of such cities as Baltimore, Philadelphia, New York, Albany, Toronto, Montreal, and Quebec (Plate 12).[2]

These city views were issued with attractive hand coloring and measured about nine by twelve inches. All of them are handsomely done, showing their subjects from a distance as seen against more detailed foreground treatment of vegetation, human figures, or the horses that Kollner so loved to draw and that had been the subject of two series of prints he had sketched and published in Europe and Philadelphia.[3]

August Kollner

	Pa.	Md.	Ill.	N.Y.	Ont.	Total
1842	1					1
1843–						
1848	1	1				2
1849			1			1
1850				5		5
1851					4	4
1852–						
1855	1					1
1856	1					1
Total	4	1	1	5	4	15

Kollner did only two other city views. Both were far larger and more detailed than his previous work. One showed Pottsville, Pennsylvania, which he printed and presumably drew and lithographed as well. This appeared about 1855 and was printed in colors from multiple stones.[4] In 1856, for his final lithographic city view, Kollner again drew Philadelphia from Camden, New Jersey, using a large folio format that suggests the size of the city where he made his home.

---

1. Kollner's life and work are the subject of Nicholas B. Wainwright, "Augustus Kollner, Artist." Wainwright's study is summarized in Philadelphia Museum of Art, *Three Centuries of American Art*, 332–33. Wainwright notes that the artist's name appears in many versions: Köllner, Koellner, and Kollner.

2. A Kollner lithograph of ca. 1849, *View of Chicago as Seen from the Top of St. Mary's College*, was put on stone but not drawn by him and does not belong to this Paris series. The Albany print and several of the partial views are illustrated in a brief essay on Kollner's work titled "Kollner's Views of American Cities" in *The Old Print Shop Portfolio*, doubtless written by the shop's proprietor, Harry Shaw Newman.

3. One of Kollner's horse prints is reproduced as pl. 43 in Harry T. Peters, *America on Stone*.

4. The print is rare. It is reproduced in Pennsylvania State University, Museum of Art, *Pennsylvania Prints*, no. 53.

26. Kuchel & Dresel (active, 1855–1859)
Charles C. Kuchel (1820–1866)
Emil Dresel (–)

Charles C. Kuchel and Emil Dresel formed a short-lived but highly productive partnership that resulted in the publication of fifty city views during the period 1855–1859. Except for seven of Oregon towns and single views of places in Washington and Nevada, all of these lithographs showed communities in California. The majority of these were mining camps and towns. These lithographs captured images of the Gold Rush settlements only a few years after their creation, and they provide incomparable records of their urban and architectural character.

Concerning Emil Dresel, little is known. He may have handled most of the business side of the firm's activities, since Kuchel is known to have been an artist before the two came together and continued to do some work of this kind after the partnership terminated. Nevertheless, almost all of the prints include some version of the phrase *drawn from nature and on stone by Kuchel & Dresel*, and it is therefore possible that Dresel, too, participated in drawing and putting on stone the many views the two men produced.

Kuchel was born in Zweibrucken in 1820. As early as 1840 he was in Philadelphia working for P. S. Duval, and he remained with that firm until 1852.[1] While with Duval, Kuchel drew and put on stone a view of San Francisco published in 1850 so misleading in its topographic details that Kuchel could not possibly have had any firsthand knowledge of the city. Perhaps he reached California by 1854, for in the following year the first four of the Kuchel & Dresel city views appeared.[2]

These first views of Portland, Oregon, and Columbia, Mokelumne Hill, and Stockton, California, were printed—like all but a handful of the Kuchel & Dresel urban lithographs—at the San Francisco press of Britton & Rey. It is at least a possibility that Kuchel worked briefly for this company sometime after its founding in 1852 and before the beginning of his partnership with Dresel. In any event, the association between the two partnerships was extremely close, and the prints that reached the market as a result reflect an ideal match of artistic ability and printing skills.[3]

The next two years must have been extremely busy ones for the two partners, who drew and published sixteen views in 1856, followed by seventeen more in 1857. Their output dropped in 1858 to nine, possibly reflecting the economic conditions of the first full year of a national depression. Perhaps the declining market led to their decision to dissolve the partnership after publishing four views in 1859. Kuchel continued his interest in lithography, putting on stone three of Grafton T. Brown's drawings in 1861 and 1864, and—as a member of the short-lived firm of Nagel, Fishbourne & Kuchel—printing another city lithograph in 1862.

Charles C. Kuchel, Kuchel & Dresel
(Excludes variant states differing only in vignettes)

	Calif.	Ore.	Wash.	Nev.	Total
1850	2				2
1851–					
1855	3	1			4
1856	15	1			16
1857	16	1			17
1858	5	3	1		9
1859	3	1			4
1860					
1861		1		1	2
1862	1				1
1863					
1864				1	1
Total	45	8	1	2	56

If one counts the towns and cities depicted in separate images, Kuchel's views total fifty-six. Fifty of these were published during the years of the Kuchel & Dresel partnership, and of these forty-two show places in California (see Plates 21 and 69). These numbers, however, are misleading in that they do not include the many variant issues of views of individual towns. Because of their existence, no catalog or checklist is likely to be either complete or accurate. While not unique to this firm's output, the problem in this case is more complex and requires further explanation.

Kuchel & Dresel followed a practice of issuing views with and without border vignettes. For many of their lithographs, then, there are two distinct prints, but the principal view always seems to have come from the same stone. In many of the views without vignettes the upper corners of the view are rounded, although this is not invariably the case. Further complicating recording and identification are minor variations in imprints. Usually this involves the name of the publisher. Apparently Kuchel & Dresel often issued a print with no publisher identified. Perhaps they then offered this for sale and subsequently sold the publication rights. The name of the publisher—almost always a local businessman—would then be added to the imprint and additional copies printed.

The presence or absence of vignettes and the addition of a publisher's name could therefore produce four principal states of a print. Thus, the view of Angel's Camp, California, published in 1857 can be found in four principal states:

1. No publisher and no vignettes
2. C. G. Lake of Angel's Camp as publisher and no vignettes
3. No publisher and nineteen vignettes
4. C. G. Lake as publisher and nineteen vignettes

There is still another variation on this theme: an impression of the Angel's Camp view lacking the name of Kuchel & Dresel as artists and lithographers (found on all of the above) but with their name as the copyright holder. This impression lacks vignettes. Perhaps there is still another print with the characteristics just described but with vignettes.[4]

There is a possibility that the firm printed a few of their later views. The lithographs of Oregon cities in 1858 and 1859 do not have the familiar inscription indicating they were printed by Britton & Rey. Moreover, Kuchel & Dresel changed the style of their own imprint. For example, their view of The Dalles, Oregon, in 1858 has two inscriptions: "Drawn from nature and lith by Kuchel & Dresel" and "Kuchel & Dresel lithographers, 176 Clay St. S. Francisco." The ambiguous word *lithographer* used in the second inscription may indicate that they were responsible for printing the view as well as drawing it from nature and on stone.[5]

The lithograph images themselves present no such mysteries or ambiguities. Instead, they offer straightforward impressions of California mining towns, although spruced up as if sitting for a formal portrait. Almost always one sees the towns from some distance and from a viewpoint only slightly elevated above the horizon.

For the student of urban structure, therefore, they are less helpful than the bird's-eye views that would shortly dominate viewmaking in California. What makes the Kuchel & Dresel prints so useful and fascinating, however, are the vignettes surrounding the principal views. On some lithographs, like that of Shasta in 1856, these are carefully drawn elevations of major business structures. On others the buildings appear in perspective. In both cases the detailing is clear and convincing. Taken in the aggregate, these border scenes of a variety of buildings constitute a comprehensive catalog of mining town architecture drawn when the earliest permanent structures had scarcely been completed.[6]

1. Peters, in *America on Stone*, 258, mentions a view of the Battle of Princeton signed by C. Kuchel and dated 1840. In *Philadelphia in the Romantic Age of Lithography*, 62, Wainwright states that Kuchel and others in the Duval shop prepared the lithographs of "alligators, lizards, snakes, frogs and salamanders" used as plates in the five-volume study by John Edward Holbrook, *North American Herpetology*, published in 1836–1843. Wainwright also records two Duval lithographs of 1852 signed "C. K." in the stone. See his entries for no. 78, p. 120, and no. 254, p. 174.
2. Peters, in *California on Stone*, 142, states that the partnership began in 1853. However, the firm is not listed in San Francisco directories until

1856, according to Baird in his "Introduction" to Baird and Evans, *Historic Lithographs*.
3. Biographical material and a discussion of the output of Britton & Rey (and successor firms) can be found in the long note in Peters, *California on Stone*, 62–89. Joseph Britton, an Englishman, came to America in 1835 at the age of ten. He worked in New York City as a lithographer and set out for California in 1849. In 1852 he and C. J. Pollard issued a few lithographs in San Francisco before Britton began his association with Rey. Jacques Joseph Rey was a native of Alsace who reached California about 1850 at the age of thirty. Three years after setting up in business with Britton, Rey married his partner's sister. Both men possessed artistic skills, and Britton drew several lettersheet city views for the firm of Cooke & Le Count.
4. My original intention was to assign state numbers to the Kuchel & Dresel lithographs as part of their catalog entries. I decided that this step might be premature. Although my search of the major print collections in California and of those elsewhere known to me to have substantial California holdings was reasonably thorough, there are doubtless many variant impressions of Kuchel & Dresel views yet to be recorded. A study concentrating only on these views and intended to be definitive would be as rewarding as it would be arduous.
5. The year 1858 was the date that Rey withdrew from his company. This somehow may have prompted Kuchel & Dresel to acquire a press. Or, they may simply have arranged to have their Oregon views printed elsewhere and decided to omit the name of the printer.
6. While one encounters many of these views in both institutional and private collections with hand coloring added, most or all of them came from the Britton & Rey press only in black and white with a single buff tone stone to accentuate ground shadows and provide cloud effects. I have not seen any that were printed in color, although a number of the Kuchel & Dresel prints are known to me only through photographs.

27. T. J. Shepherd Landis (–   )
Landis & Hughes
Landis & Alsop

Landis published one view each in 1880, 1883, and 1895. All three were of communities in New Jersey and may have

T. J. Shepherd Landis
Landis & Hughes
Landis & Alsop

	N.J.	N.Y.	Conn.	Pa.	Total
1880	1				1
1881–					
1883	1				1
1884–					
1895	1				1
1896					
1897	1				1
1898	1	1			2
1899	2	1	3		6
1900	1			1	2
1901		2		1	3
1902		1			1
1903–					
1916	1				1
Total	9	5	3	2	19

been drawn by Landis, who signed an 1883 lithograph of Cape May as artist. The Landis address is given as Philadelphia in the first two prints and Newark in the third. These widely spaced dates indicate that Landis made his living in some other occupation, perhaps as a publisher of other materials.

In 1897 he began an association with Thomas J. Hughes, who later was to work with both O. H. Bailey and T. J. Fowler. In three years Landis and Hughes produced eight views of places in New Jersey, New York, and Connecticut. In 1900 Landis started a three-year partnership with one Alsop, whose first name is not known. This firm specialized in very large, four-sheet depictions of cities with dozens of references and many vignettes of important buildings. Those of Binghamton, Elmira, and Buffalo are typical of the seven prints to come from this company through 1902.

All of the Landis & Alsop prints give Newark as the business address. The Landis and Hughes prints, on the other hand, exhibit a variety of addresses: New York; 134 Mulberry St. N.Y.; 294 Roseville Ave., Newark; and 138 Mulberry St., New York. The last city view with the Landis name was published by him alone in 1916 and shows Newark, N.J., as his place of business.

28. Fitz Hugh Lane (1804–1865)

Of the nineteenth-century American artists now generally regarded as of the first rank, only Fitz Hugh Lane produced a substantial body of lithographic city views. It might be more accurate to describe Lane's urban prints as those in which towns appear almost as incidental parts of the landscape. Lane did not draw cities so much as he drew their surroundings, the sky above them, and the water at whose edge they invariably sat. The communites he depicted provided titles for his prints, added variety to the compositions, and furnished forms that contrasted with Lane's images of nature.

Born in Gloucester, Massachusetts, in 1804, Lane lost the use of his legs as an infant and throughout his life could move only with great difficulty by the aid of canes and crutches. He began to draw as a boy, but he probably received no formal training until he began an apprenticeship in Boston at the firm of William S. Pendleton in the early 1830s.[1]

Pendleton was one of the pioneers of American lithography, and there was no better place in the country for Lane to learn this craft. Lane's earliest lithographs included trade cards, music covers, and other commercial work that required no great artistic skill, but after four years of this he was ready for a more ambitious undertaking. He drew and put on stone his first city view, a lithograph of his native city of Gloucester (Plate 10). He published this in 1835 or early 1836 after obtaining a number of subscriptions by displaying his drawing for that purpose the previous summer.

Lane's print drew praise from a local newspaper, which found it "most admirably executed; and so far as we are acquainted with the art, there is a softness and beauty in the design, which we do not always find in the works of older and more distinguished artists. . . . We venture to predict that he will one day become distinguished in his art. Subscribers and others may obtain the print at the store of Isaac A. Smith."[2]

Pendleton printed this first lithograph issued by his former apprentice. Later city views drawn from nature and on stone or put on stone by Lane from drawings by others came from other printers: Thomas Moore, to whom Pendleton sold his business in 1836; Marshall M. Tidd and L. H. Bradford, both of Boston; and Lane's own press, which he operated for a time with John W. A. Scott under the name of "Lane and Scott's Lithography, Boston." Two of his views—Norwich, Connecticut, in 1849 and Baltimore, Maryland, in 1850—went to the New York firm of Sarony and Major.

Fitz Hugh Lane

	Mass.	D.C.	N.B.	R.I.	Conn.	Md.	Maine	Total
1835	1							1
1836								
1837	1							1
1838								
1839		1	1					2
1840	1							1
1841–								
1845	4							4
1846–								
1848			1					1
1849					1			1
1850						1		1
1851–								
1855							1	1
Total	7	1	1	1	1	1	1	13

Aside from the Baltimore lithograph and one showing the destruction by fire of St. John, New Brunswick, the only other view of a city outside of New England on which Lane's name appears is a very large and rare depiction of Washington, D.C., in 1838 showing the capital as seen from Arlington, Virginia. In this case, Lane put on stone the original drawing by P. Anderson.

In addition to his Gloucester view of 1846, Lane put on stone two other views of that year drawn and published by A. Conant.[3] These showed New Bedford and Newburyport, two Massachusetts port communities. Not quite a decade later Lane produced his last two city views, drawing from nature and on stone what are acknowledged to be his two finest prints: *View of Gloucester, Mass.* and *Castine from Hospital Island* (Plate 58).[4]

By this time, Lane's preoccupation with light and shadow had shifted the focus of his prints and paintings from finite elements in the landscape to broader compositional issues. As splendid as are most of Lane's prints, including his city views, and as helpful as they are in suggesting the general atmosphere of the towns and their environs, they tell us rather less about individual buildings and neighborhoods than lesser artists customarily conveyed. [5]

1. No modern book on nineteenth-century American art fails to deal with Lane. I have relied chiefly on the study by John Wilmerding, *Fitz Hugh Lane*. More narrowly focused on his lithographic work is the section on Lane in John Thomas Carey, "The American Lithograph from Its Inception to 1865 with Biographical Considerations of Twenty Lithographers and a Check List of Their Work," 315–29. See also Wilmerding, *Fitz Hugh Lane, 1804–1865: American Marine Painter*, and William A. Farnsworth Library and Art Museum, *Fitz Hugh Lane, 1804–1865*.
2. Gloucester *Telegraph*, 16 March 1836, as quoted in Wilmerding, *Fitz Hugh Lane*, 23.
3. Conant published the Baltimore, Maryland, lithograph of 1850, on which Lane is identified as artist.
4. Another lithographic view of Gloucester of ca. 1853 is in the collection of the Boston Atheneum. Printed by M. M. Tidd of Boston, it is believed to have been drawn by Lane.
5. Calling the Castine view "Lane's most accomplished graphic work," Wilmerding, in *Fitz Hugh Lane*, describes it as "by far the most poetic and sophisticated of all his lithographs. . . . here the sky fills nearly two-thirds of the composition, and the clouds have an animated pattern of their own that keeps that area of the print from becoming visually inert or monotonous. The lower portion of the design is equally open and spacious. Even less is going on in the foreground, fewer vessels fill the harbor, and the landmarks of the town beyond are sparsely defined. This deemphasis of topographical detail and anecdotal subject matter is an important clue to the poetic evocation of his later paintings" (pp. 30–31).

29. Henry Lewis (1819–1904)

In 1829 Henry Lewis came to America at the age of ten from his native Shropshire in England. In Boston, where he and his father settled, young Lewis was apprenticed to a carpenter, but after the two moved to St. Louis in 1836 he decided to become an artist. In the mid-1840s he conceived the idea of a vast panorama of the entire Mississippi valley, and in 1846–1848 he traveled extensively above St. Louis sketching and drawing towns, river scenes, and Indian encampments. He acquired some drawings from Seth Eastman; those of towns on the lower Mississippi were made by an associate named Rogers; and Lewis drew most of the others from a platform mounted on two canoes. [1]

Lewis completed his painting in 1849. It was 12 feet high and 1,300 feet long and was mounted on rollers so that it could be displayed in a large frame while the artist described the images passing before the eyes of his audience. Lewis took this to the East and Canada, and in 1851 he brought it to England. He began a tour of the Continent the following year, and when he reached Düsseldorf, an important center of the arts, he decided to stay.

It was there during the years 1854 to 1857 that Lewis drew and had printed a series of lithographic views of the Mississippi. These appeared in parts, each with accompanying passages of text written by the artist. Eventually they were collected and bound with the title *Das Illustrirte Mississippithal*. An English translation was begun but never completed, although two variant title pages are known on which the title *Valley of the Mississippi* appears. [2]

This venture proved to be a financial disaster. The publishers went out of business, and a local antiquarian book and art dealer acquired the remaining stock. He sold most of the pages of text for scrap and sold or gave away the illustra-

Henry Lewis

	Ill.	Iowa	La.	Minn.	Miss.	Mo.	Tenn.	Wisc.	Total
1854–1857	9	8	3	4	2	7	1	2	36
Total	9	8	3	4	2	7	1	2	36

tions to his customers. Probably no more than three hundred copies of the complete volume ever reached the market, most of them being sent to New York and Philadelphia.

Lewis continued to live in Düsseldorf and to enjoy happier times, although as an artist he never enjoyed the success of many of his companions. He even served for a time as consular agent in the city for the United States government. He returned only once to the Mississippi, visiting family and friends in Iowa and St. Louis in 1881. In the thirty-five years that had passed since his first sketching expedition for the panorama, the character of the towns he then depicted had changed almost beyond recognition, but Lewis had little time and possibly no interest in recording their altered appearance.

This was no great loss, since by that time many others were drawing and publishing views of the river towns. When Lewis first set to work, however, only a handful of other viewmakers were similarly engaged. Much of what we know about the character of these raw, new communities of the frontier comes from the images Lewis created.

Lewis may have had his financial problems with the Düsseldorf firm of Arnz & Co., but these skilled lithographers produced prints of excellent quality whose colors from multiple stones were precisely registered. Together, artist and lithographer created portraits of urban life on the Mississippi unsurpassed in pictorial interest and antiquarian value.

1. Lewis has been the subject of several studies. The most important is the introduction by Bertha L. Heilbron to a translation by A. Hermina Poatgieter of Lewis's *The Valley of the Mississippi Illustrated*. See also John Francis McDermott, *The Lost Panoramas of the Mississippi*; Heilbron, "Making a Motion Picture in 1848: Henry Lewis on the Upper Mississippi"; Henry Lewis, "Journal of a Canoe Voyage from the Falls of St. Anthony to St. Louis"; and Lila M. Johnson, "Found (and Purchased): Seth Eastman Water Colors."
2. In her introduction to the modern translation, Heilbron notes that one of these title pages has the following publisher's imprint: "Published and lithographed by Arnz & Comp. at Dusseldorf. Philadelphia Weik & Wieck." This was John Weik, who in 1857 published John Bachmann's large view of Philadelphia, among other urban lithographs. He and Charles Wieck are listed in the Philadelphia city directory for 1853 as publishers and importers, according to Heilbron, p. 13, n. 22. While Lewis is the nominal author of the text, large portions are quoted from other sources, not all of which Lewis identified.

30. Alfred E. Mathews (1831–1874)

Born in England in 1831, Mathews came to America as an infant and grew up in Rochester, Ohio. He learned typesetting at his brother's newspaper shop, but by the time he was twenty-five he was earning his living as an itinerant book agent. He supplemented his income by selling drawings of the places he visited. [1]

At the outbreak of the Civil War, Mathews left his job teaching school in Alabama and made his way north to enlist in the Union army. His artistic skills matured during his military service, when he drew at least thirty-eight scenes of battles or military camps that were lithographed. His four prints of the siege of Vicksburg received commendation from no less a person than Major General U. S. Grant, who wrote to Private Mathews that after examining the prints he did not "hesitate to pronounce them among the most accurate and true to life I have ever seen." [2]

After his discharge from military service in 1864, Mathews prepared a large painted panorama showing Civil War battle scenes. A year later he was in Nebraska City, Nebraska, where he did a series of four lithographic views. This Missouri River port was then the depot for the great overland freighting firm of Russell, Majors and Waddell, and its streets throbbed with activity. The Mathews views provide an important graphic record of what was then the major jumping-off point for the West. [3]

Late in 1865, Mathews arrived in Denver, Colorado, and almost immediately embarked on an ambitious project to produce a uniform series of views of Denver and the major mining communities in the Colorado Rockies. In March 1866, he distributed the first four prints: a general view of Denver and three street scenes of the city. Four others arrived several weeks later from his New York City printer, Julius Bien.

Alfred E. Mathews

	Miss.	Nebr.	Colo.	Mont.	Calif.	Total
1862	1					1
1863–						
1865		4				4
1866			16			16
1867						
1868				4		4
1869						
1870			1			1
1871–						
1873					4	4
n.d.				1		1
Total	1	4	17	4	5	31

All of these must have been sold as separate prints, but in October they and others became available in bound form with twelve pages of text describing the thirty-six lithographs. Some of these were arranged two to a page. Sixteen can properly be regarded as urban views. [4]

Mathews drew with almost mechanical regularity, and in examining his work one is always aware of looking at lines on paper rather than at the scene itself (see Plate 64). Nevertheless, although far from great as art, the views provide valuable documentation of the appearance of Colorado communities less than a decade after they sprang into existence following the first gold discoveries in 1859.

Mining activity in Montana offered new subjects for Mathews, and in 1867 he toured parts of the territory sketching for a similar series of lithographs. They appeared as *Pencil Sketches of Montana* in 1868, a reprise of his earlier title, *Pencil Sketches of Colorado*. Four of these showed Montana communities: Helena, Virginia City, Union City, and Unionville.

Mathews went to New York in the winter of 1867–1868 to put his own drawings on stone because he was dissatisfied with how his Colorado prints had turned out. It is difficult to see that his presence made any difference, since the standard of lithography of the two series is so similar.

In 1868 Mathews completed another panorama—apparently a continuous painting of western scenery—which he used for lectures and exhibits. He sold this in 1869, the year in which he issued yet another pictorial work, *Gems of Rocky Mountain Scenery*. That fall he purchased land near Canon City, Colorado, and began to promote settlement in the area, but his efforts proved unsuccessful.

Eventually he turned once again to city views, spending the winter of 1872–1873 sketching in Southern California. Five lithographs came from this trip, one of an unidentified "Golden City" and the other four—all printed and published in San Francisco by the A. L. Bancroft firm—showing Los Angeles, San Diego, San Bernardino, and Santa Barbara.

While the lithographs are well printed, the views themselves are undistinguished. A San Diego newspaper criticized them severely when they appeared in April 1873, and the small number of the impressions that are known to exist suggests that residents of the cities Mathews drew agreed with the editorial opinion that "the perspective in each of these sketches . . . is exceedingly defective." [5]

Mathews did no more city views. He lived for a time in Denver and then at a home in the mountains near Longmont. He died there at the end of October 1874. A Denver newspaper, noting his death, referred to him as "an artist of no ordinary merit . . . [who] . . . had sketched more of our Rocky Mountain scenery than any of his contemporaries." [6]

1. See the letter to his aunt, 6 May 1856, quoted in full on pp. 73–74 in the source from which I have drawn most of the material for this note: Robert Taft, *Artists and Illustrators of the Old West, 1850–1900*, 72–85.

2. Grant to Mathews, 9 August 1863, Vicksburg, Mississippi, as quoted in ibid., 75. For further information on the Civil War drawings and prints by Mathews, see also Elizabeth R. Martin, "Collections and Exhibits."

3. No publisher is identified in the imprints, but it must have been Mathews. Three of them show the printer to have been "Donaldson & Elmes, 22 Court St., Cincinnati, O." Peters, in *America on Stone*, 159, notes that the firm published at least two of the Mathews Civil War lithographs.

4. Taft, *Artists and Illustrators*, 305–6, n. 13, provides titles of the complete set. He notes that while the title page has a date of May 1866, the book did not reach Denver until October.

5. San Diego *Union*, 14 April 1873, p. 3, as quoted in Lytle, "People and Places," 68.

6. *Rocky Mountain News*, 4 November 1874, as quoted in Taft, *Artists and Illustrators*, 85.

31. E. S. Moore (—   )

The drawing and selling of city views and the preparation and promotion of county and state atlases in the nineteenth century are such similar activities that it is surprising not to find many names of artists and publishers common to both enterprises. E. S. Moore is one of the very few persons who can be identified in this way.

For Alfred T. Andreas, a major figure in the atlas trade, Moore drew a view of Preston, Minnesota, that appeared in *An Illustrated Historical Atlas of the State of Minnesota*.[1] Probably this is the same E. S. Moore who made an appearance about 1886 as artist and publisher of a view of San Jacinto, California. In the next five years Moore drew eighteen other views, all but three showing towns and cities in California. On only one other city view does his name appear as publisher: an undated lithograph of San Rafael, California, printed by Britton, Rey & Co. in San Francisco and published by Moore & De Pew, also of San Francisco.[2]

Most of Moore's California views show the new towns that speculators created or vastly expanded during the Southern California land boom of the 1880s: San Jacinto, Azusa, Elsinore, Coronado Beach (Plate 71), Monrovia, Glendora, Alosta, Redlands, and Alhambra.[3] His lithographs, therefore, help to document a fascinating period in the region's development. At least two of his views in this category were published by the land companies responsible for the existence of the communities they depicted.[4]

E. S. Moore

	Calif.	Ore.	Total
1886	1		1
1887	4		4
1888	4		4
1889	3		3
1890		3	3
1891	4		4
Total	16	3	19

Moore lived in Los Angeles at this time; at least his name appears in the city directory for 1888 with an address at 11 Schumacher Blk.[5] Either he moved or traveled extensively, for in 1888 he drew views of Bakersfield and Merced and, in the following year, Grass Valley. His three Oregon views, of Ashland, Salem, and Grants Pass, are either dated 1890 or can be assigned to that year.[6]

In 1891 he must have returned to California. His three views of that year show towns in or near the San Francisco Bay area—Berkeley (Plate 24), Redwood, and Vallejo—and the Berkeley view gives Moore's address as Oakland. The undated lithograph of San Rafael, located in this same region, probably belongs to this last year of his recorded work.

Moore's view of Berkeley, interesting because of its focus on the handful of university buildings in the foreground, is typical of his work. It is unconvincing in its handling of topography, and it is mechanical in execution.

1. Chicago, 1874, p. 188. For a review of the county atlas business see Norman J. W. Thrower, "The County Atlas of the United States," *Surveying and Mapping* 21 (September 1961): 365–73.
2. According to Peters in his *California on Stone*, 62, the printing firm operated under that name during 1867–1880. This may indicate that Moore came to California sometime between 1874, when he worked for Andreas, and 1880. However, even Peters can be misleading on such matters. A view of Monrovia, California, drawn by Moore about 1887, has a printer's imprint of *Britton & Rey*. According to Peters, this style for the name of the business was last used in 1858. The name *Britton, Rey & Company* was generally used after 1867, when Henry Steinegger operated the firm. Steinegger is named on Moore's Monrovia view as the lithographer.
3. Moore evidently also began a large view of the Antelope Valley in the Mojave Desert to "be 2½ by 3 feet, embracing a territory thirty miles square, showing the artesian wells, water courses, ditches, towns, and other developments" (Los Angeles, California, *Herald*, 15 July 1887, p. 3, col. 1, as quoted in Henry Winfred Splitter, "Art in Los Angeles Before 1900— Part I," 56).
4. The Coronado Beach Company and the Glendora Land Company are listed as publishers of these views.
5. Nancy Dustin Wall Moure, *Dictionary of Art and Artists in Southern California Before 1930*, 55.
6. There is a variant state of the Salem view, but the differences are only in the imprint, not in the image.

32. Henry P. Moore (—   )

Henry P. Moore is a name and little else. He lived in Concord, New Hampshire, from 1853 to 1902, but nothing is known about his place or date of birth or when and where he died. Beginning in 1862 he took a remarkable series of photographs of New Hampshire soldiers in the Union army, and in the 1870s he operated a photographic copying business in Concord using the "silvertype process" that he invented and patented.[1]

His brief career as a viewmaker preceded this period of his life. It began in 1854 with the publication of his lithograph depicting Burlington, Vermont. The remaining eleven of his recorded views all appeared by 1860. Seven of these show towns in Vermont, and four are of New Hampshire. The single non-New England lithograph is a particularly handsome print of Ogdensburg, New York, but all of Moore's views are skillfully drawn.

Moore took his drawings to the best craftsmen of the time to have them put on stone and printed: Endicott & Co. in New York and two Boston lithographers, J. H. Bufford and L. H. Bradford. Bradford was one of the pioneers in American photography, and it may have been in his shop that Moore learned the profession or trade that apparently occupied most of his time thereafter.

A character sketch of Moore can be found in the published version of a lecture delivered in 1886 in Concord. The date suggests that the sketch might not have been altogether serious, and this is reinforced by the title: *Remarks on Remarkable Men. Doctor Bennett Monore Pratt's Great Blackboard Lecture, Delivered in Stevens & Duncklee's New Opera House Block, Concord, N.H., April 1, 1886*.[2] Each person described is illustrated by a line drawing. Under that of Moore appears the following:

	Vt.	N.H.	N.Y.	Total
1854	1			1
1855	1	1		2
1856		1		1
1857	1	1	1	3
1858	2			2
1859	2			2
1860		1		1
Total	7	4	1	12

Here is a genius. His head presents large constructiveness and large imitation, with large ideality and mirthfulness, together with a very noticeable development of all those faculties which go to constitute a superior artist. His fertile brain will never leave him to go hungry. He is an inventor. In a sleepless hour of the night he might conceive something in mechanism that would startle the world with its originality. With an unexpected impulse he might paint a picture worthy of a great master, and in another moment his love of fun would have reduced it from sublimity to ridiculousness, from high tragedy to trail in the dust of low comedy, from romance to every-day life. To him, that does not know him, he might at times seem somewhat of an enigma, but those who know him best find him a royal good fellow. He greatly loves a good time, and is true to a friend. Only few men have made more money, and only few have spent more than he has; yet his lucrative vocation never fails of rich harvests, and he has means, and to spare. He is regarded as an indispensable member of the Penacook Boat Club, and of the community in which he lives, and is indeed *a very remarkable man.*[3]

1. Notes on Moore prepared 1 June 1982 by Kathryn Grover, New Hampshire Historical Society, deal almost entirely with Moore's career as a photographer. These appeared in the Concord, New Hampshire, *Daily Monitor*, 3 June 1982, with reproductions of some of Moore's Civil War photographs. The photographs are also described in Temple D. Smith, "The Frontier of American War Photography," in Sally Pierce and Temple D. Smith, *Citizens in Conflict: Prints and Photographs of the American Civil War* (Boston, 1981).
2. The New Hampshire Historical Society indicates that the author was Henry Robinson.
3. P. 3. The italicized phrase concludes each sketch in this publication.

33. D. D. Morse (–   )

The first views with Morse's name in the imprint show him as the publisher of two lithographs of Benton Harbor and St. Joseph, Michigan, in 1870 and one of Mishawaka, Indiana, in 1871. The locations and dates suggest that he may have been connected in some way with Ruger, Stoner, Fowler, or Glover, all of whom were involved as artists or publishers in this area by or before 1870. All three views were printed at Glover's Merchants Lithographing Co. in Chicago, and Morse's view of Golden, Colorado, in 1873 came from the Strobridge press in Cincinnati, the same company then used by Glover for his own several prints of towns in Colorado.

On the Golden view, Morse's name appears as artist, and all but two of the later views with his name identify him in

	Mich.	Ind.	Colo.	Tex.	Kans.	Calif.	Total
1870	2						2
1871		1					1
1872							
1873	1		1				2
1874	1						1
1875	4						4
1876				3			3
1877	1						1
1878					10		10
1879					1		1
1880					1		1
1881–							
1892						1	1
n.d.	1				1		2
Total	10	1	1	3	13	1	29

this capacity. With one exception, his name is not given as the publisher, but it seems likely that he was both artist and publisher for virtually all of his twenty-nine recorded lithographs. From 1876 through 1880, Chicago printers did all of his work, with the firm of Lott & Zeuch being responsible for the great majority.

Morse's Fort Worth, Texas, view of 1876 is typical of his work: simple, straightforward, rather mechanical, and probably of reasonable accuracy. Two years after this was published Morse produced ten views of Kansas. This was his total output for that year and was by far the greatest number of views he produced in any one season.

In most years he drew only one or two views, and this volume of work surely could not have provided him with a living. He may have assisted other view artists in the states he visited, or he may have had another occupation. The last view to appear with his name attached was of San Gabriel, California. It was published about 1892, long after his consecutive years as a viewmaker in 1870–1880 had ended. Perhaps Morse lived in or near San Gabriel in retirement.

34. George E. Norris (1855–1926)

George Norris began his viewmaking years in 1883 when he joined with Albert F. Poole to publish ten views of New Hampshire towns drawn by Poole. Poole was then thirty and Norris twenty-eight. Evidently both were residents of Brockton, Massachusetts, where in 1882 Poole lived in a house owned by Norris's mother. Poole seems to have drawn all of these views, but Norris may have helped on some of them in addition to acting as business agent.

In 1884 Norris published some of Poole's views as well as his own. He also began an association with Henry Wellge that, through 1886, produced about fifty views in seven states. While Wellge signed most of these and may have

George E. Norris, Poole & Norris, Norris & Wellge, Norris, Wellge & Co.

	N.H.	Vt.	Ala.	Fla.	Ga.	Tex.	Wisc.	Mich.	Tenn.	Mass.	Maine	Conn.	N.Y.	Total
1883	11													11
1884	9	5												14
1885			1	6	4	1	10							22
1886						5	7	4	2					18
1887	9			1						6				16
1888	4								1		1			6
1889	4	3								2	4	2		15
1890										1		1		2
1891		1												1
1892		2			1				1		1		2	7
1893										3	5			8
1894		1									2			3
1895	1										5			6
1896	1										3			4
1897	1													1
n.d.											1			1
Total	40	12	1	7	5	6	17	4	4	12	22	3	2	135

drawn them all, Norris probably was responsible for at least a few of them. The two did business in Brockton under the name *Norris & Wellge* and then in Milwaukee as *Norris, Wellge & Co.*

By 1887 Norris was ready to launch an independent career, drawing and publishing under his name alone. He began with an impressive number of lithographs: Nine of New Hampshire towns (see Plates 3 and 65) and six of places in Massachusetts. As his printer, Norris selected the Burleigh Litho. Establishment of Troy, N.Y., where Lucien Burleigh had set up his press the year before. Five additional views in 1888 and fifteen in 1889 all show Norris as artist and publisher. Burleigh printed these, too, as well as all other Norris views through 1892. During these years Norris extended his geographic range, depicting towns in Connecticut and Maine in addition to those in New Hampshire and Massachusetts.

His pace slackened momentarily, with single views in 1890 and 1891, but in 1892 he issued a further seven lithographs. This time Norris broke out of New England to draw towns in New York, Tennessee, and Georgia as well as two places in Vermont and one town in Maine. Thereafter he confined himself to Maine, Vermont, and New Hampshire as he rounded out his life as a view artist and publisher with eight lithographs in 1893, three in 1894, six in 1895, four in 1896, and two in 1897.

Norris could look back on more than 135 city views in thirteen states as he entered an entirely new occupation as hotel manager in 1897 when he opened the Hotel Norris in Brockton. In 1912 he acquired the Hotel Grayson in Brockton, which he operated until his death of a cerebral hemorrhage in 1926.[1]

1. Some details of Norris's life appear in William A. Farnsworth Library and Art Museum, *Through a Bird's Eye: Nineteenth-Century Views of Maine*, 17. His portrait is reproduced on p. 21. Christine Bauer Podmaniczky was responsible for much of the research for this publication. David Ruell has provided additional information in a manuscript on New Hampshire city views he has generously allowed me to use. Ruell cites obituaries of Norris in the Brockton *Enterprise*, and the Brockton *Times*, 18 August 1926, and points out that neither newspaper mentioned his earlier career as an artist and publisher of city views.

35. James T. Palmatary (–   )

The roster of nineteenth-century American viewmakers includes many persons about whom little is known except for the prints they drew, printed, or published. James T. Palmatary remains just such a shadowy figure, and only by his views, a few newspaper notices, and some city directory listings is it possible to trace his whereabouts and the bare outlines of his career.

Palmatary may have received his introduction to viewmaking from Edwin Whitefield; he served as that artist's business and subscription agent for more than two years, beginning on 25 April 1850.[1] He may also have helped Whitefield with some of the field sketching for the latter's views; at least Palmatary claimed some of the credit for the Whitefield views of Jersey City, Wilmington, Montreal, and Quebec.[2]

The earliest dated lithograph with Palmatary's name in the imprint is a view drawn by Charles Parsons showing Lancaster, Pennsylvania. This was printed by Endicott & Co. of New York and published by Palmatary in 1853. This is also the only view that gives his first name (although abbreviated) or indicates an address: "Jas. T. Palmatary, N.Y." The New York address may only have reflected the location of the Endicott firm, but it is possible that Palmatary lived there, and it would not be surprising to learn that he worked for Endicott, possibly assisting Parsons, who worked on many of the firm's most impressive lithographs.

Palmatary also drew an important city view in 1853, although his name does not appear on the print. This is a large and attractive lithograph of Baltimore printed in several colors from multiple stones and published by the Baltimore firm of E. Sachse & Co. That portion of the imprint identifying the artist reads "Drawn from Nature, Lith & Printed in Colors by E. Sachse & Co." A contemporary newspaper account, however, reveals Palmatary's role in this view and suggests indirectly that some or all of the views giving the artist as "E. Sachse & Co." were Palmatary's work:

NEW VIEW OF BALTIMORE.—We announced some months ago that Mr. James T. Palmatary was preparing a new view of the City of Baltimore, taken from Fairmount. We now have the pleasure of stating that the work has been completed and will be delivered at once to the subscribers. This is the largest and best view ever taken of our city. . . . The size of the plate is thirty by fifty inches, and is not more remarkable for the attractiveness of its general appearance than for the correctness of its details. . . . We are glad to be able to state that the whole work was executed in this city, being printed by the process lately introduced of printing in oil colors, by Messrs, Sachse & Co. No less than thirteen tints are used, and the picture has much the appearance of a delicate oil painting. We hope this work will be extensively patronized.[3]

Two months after this notice was published, an Alexandria, Virginia, newspaper informed its readers, "Mr. J. T. Palmatary, a professor in drawing, is now on a visit to our city, with the intention of getting up a view of it." On the printed view, however, "E. Sachse & Co." appears as the artist, while Palmatary is identified as the publisher.[4]

Eight other views of towns in the Old West have similar imprints, but contemporary newspaper accounts reveal that Palmatary drew those of Chillicothe, Ohio, and Indianapolis, Indiana (Plate 17), very probably those of Zanesville, Dayton, and Columbus, Ohio, and that he did at least the initial work on a lithograph showing Sandusky, Ohio. It is not unlikely that Palmatary drew the views of Wheeling, West Virginia, and Madison, Indiana, as well. Indeed, Sandusky is the only place among these towns where the local newspaper mentioned the presence of Sachse.[5]

James T. Palmatary

	Md.	Pa.	Ohio	Ind.	Va.	W.Va.	Ky.	Wisc.	Ill.	Mo.	Total
1853	1	1									2
1854			3	2	1						6
1855			2			1	1				4
1856			3	1			1	1			6
1857									1		1
1858										1	1
Total	1	1	8	3	1	1	2	1	1	1	20

Sometime after 1855 Sachse and Palmatary apparently parted company. Palmatary remained in the Midwest, sending his work to lithographic printers in Cincinnati. The firm of Klauprecht & Menzel did his Portsmouth, Ohio, lithograph, but for eight other views through 1858 Palmatary relied on the services of Middleton, Wallace & Co. He used one other printer: Herline & Hensel of Philadelphia. This firm executed the mutlisheet view of Chicago that Palmatary issued in 1857. These printers, along with Sachse, were among the earliest in the United States to explore color lithography, and by the mid 1850s they could produce excellent work. Many of the prints were done in heavily pigmented inks that resembled oil paints, and the effect is striking.[6]

On one occasion, in 1855, Palmatary was apparently not satisfied with the work done by Middleton, Wallace & Co. and had his view of Sandusky, Ohio, printed a second time by Sachse. Evidently he took the opportunity also of changing the drawing so that it included more of the city.[7] Impressions of both of these issues are rare, as are several of the other Palmatary lithographs. The Louisville view, for example, is known by only a single impression.

Only a few of the twenty lithographs on which Palmatary's name appears—Portsmouth, Ohio (Plate 76); St. Louis, Missouri; and Chicago, Illinois—identify him as the artist. In addition to those previously mentioned as having been drawn by him, he also is known to have done the view of Milwaukee in 1856.[8] Except for the misleading use of Sachse's name on many of the prints, no other artist's name can be found. It is thus likely that it was Palmatary himself who did the drawings.

Palmatary followed Whitefield's practice in using local newspapers as sources of advertising and free publicity. The announcement of his view of Louisville, Kentucky, in 1855 provides an example of Palmatary's success in his promotional efforts:

Mr. J. T. Palmatary called yesterday and showed us a lithographic view of Louisville, which he is getting up and which will be ready for delivery to subscribers in six weeks from this time. This picture is taken in perspective, the eye supposed to be elevated above the houses and at some point in the river. The streets, dwelling houses, and public buildings will be distinctly shown in their natural color. It will be the largest view of this kind ever engraved in the United States, being 52 by 40 inches, and will be colored with ten different colors in oil. Persons wishing to subscribe for this splendid picture can do so, by calling on Mr. A. Hagen, No. 99, Third Street, where they may see the picture in its plain, uncolored state.[9]

Although the completed lithograph of Louisville was not quite the size specified in the newspaper, it and most other Palmatary views were very large. At least two required more than one sheet. His Chicago print measured almost four by six and one-half feet. Palmatary's St. Louis view was even larger, being four and one-half by nearly eight feet in size. Lithographs of such heroic dimensions were expensive to print, and the price must have been correspondingly high. The small number of surviving impressions suggests that either few were sold or that such enormous prints proved so difficult to store that they were easily damaged and eventually discarded.

Palmatary's last recorded involvement with city view-making was in 1864.[10] It was then that he visited Syracuse to sketch buildings for a view he proposed to publish at a subscription price of $10.00. The print did not make its appearance until 1868, and when it did Palmatary's name did not appear.[11] By that time he was living in Baltimore. In 1867 the city directory lists him as an employee of E. Sachse &

Co., while in 1868 and 1869 he is named as an artist without a specific business affiliation.[12] It is a reasonable assumption that he was involved in the preparation of the twelve-sheet view of Baltimore printed and published by the Sachse firm in 1869.

When Palmatary visited Milwaukee, Wisconsin, to prepare his view of that city published in 1856, he claimed to have drawn or published fifty-one other views.[13] Less than half that number have been recorded. Palmatary's boast may have been fictitious and made for promotional purposes, but possibly he included in this number many views done anonymously for or with Whitefield, Sachse, Parsons, or some other artist while he learned the viewmaker's business as an agent and artist's assistant.

1. In her *Edwin Whitefield: Nineteenth-Century North American Scenery*, Bettina A. Norton mentions Palmatary's association with Whitefield. Mrs. Norton kindly provided me with copies of her notes made when she examined Whitefield's manuscript diary in the collection of the Boston Public Library. Whitefield records hiring Palmatary in the entry for 25 April 1850. Palmatary is last mentioned in an entry for 24 May 1852.

2. See the Alexandria, Virginia, *Alexandria Gazette and Virginia Advertiser* for 24 August for these and other views that Palmatary showed the author of this newspaper account, apparently representing them as his own work. They included views of Washington and Baltimore (doubtless those signed by Edward Sachse) and the one mentioned below of Lancaster, Pennsylvania, published by Palmatary but identified as drawn by Charles Parsons.

3. Baltimore *American & Commercial Advertiser*, 1 July 1853, p. 2, col. 4. My request to Laurie A. Baty at the Maryland Historical Society in Baltimore for any information she might be able to find on Palmatary was answered with this transcription and other information in a letter to me dated 3 August 1982. As already noted, the print referred to is illustrated in Lois B. McCauley, *Maryland Historical Prints, 1752 to 1889*, 16, and is described under the entry numbered V 18. McCauley's statement about this undated lithograph that it "shows the city . . . about 1852" is thus modified only slightly by the newspaper account. Ms. Baty reported that Baltimore city directories for the years 1849–1866 do not list Palmatary.

4. *Alexandria Gazette*, 24 August. Palmatary's association with Sachse may have begun earlier. At Alexandria, Palmatary exhibited a view of Washington as his own. In all probability this was the view dated 1852 that Sachse published. Doubtless this was the same view that Palmatary claimed credit for in Indianapolis in 1854. See Mary Q. Burnet, *Art and Artists of Indiana*, 65.

5. Indianapolis, Indiana, *Journal*, 5 January 1855; Sandusky, Ohio, *Ohio Daily Commercial Register*, 21 and 27 October and 29 November 1854; Chillicothe, Ohio, *Scioto Gazette*, 8 May 1854. The latter announcement mentioned that "Prof. Palmatary is now in Columbus delivering his 'views' of that city," while the Sandusky newspaper stated that the writer had "inspected some of Mr. P's specimens, viz; views of Columbus, Dayton, Chil[l]icothe, &c."

6. These include the Madison, Indiana, view printed by Sachse; the Chicago view by Herline & Hensel; and the St. Louis view by Middleton, Wallace & Co.

7. Neither of the Sandusky lithographs is dated. The Follett House Museum in Sandusky has assigned 1854 as the date of publication of its view with the imprint "Drawn from nature and printed in colors by E. Sachse & Co. Sun Iron Building, Balto. Md." However, this address was not used by Sachse until 1856, according to McCauley, *Maryland Prints*. The Sandusky print at the State Historical Society of Wisconsin has this imprint: "Drawn on Stone & Printed in Oil Colors by Middleton, Wallace & Co. Lithos. 115 Walnut St. Cincinnati, O." The firm did not move to 115 Walnut St. until 1855, and a newspaper account indicates the view was on sale in that year. Image sizes differ substantially. Helen M. Hansen, Curator of the Follett House Museum, in an undated note to the author in July 1981, stated, "Palmatary was dissatisfied with [the] first views [of Sandusky] he produced and made a second edition with more of [the] east end of town." I have not been able to examine either print, and neither institution is able to provide me with photographs.

8. Beckman, *Milwaukee Illustrated*, notes for exhibit item 7, citing the Chicago, Illinois, *Daily Democratic Press*, 20 March 1856, p. 3.

9. Louisville *Daily Journal*, 15 August 1855.

10. I. N. Phelps Stokes and Daniel C. Haskell, in *American Historical Prints*, 129 (Entry C. 1865—G-77), assign a date of ca. 1867 to a view of

Columbus, Ohio, published by Palmatary and printed by Sachse. The Ohio Historical Society in Columbus dates its impression at 1860 but cannot justify the date. The *Daily Scioto Gazette*, mentioned on 8 May 1854 that Palmatary was then in Columbus delivering his views of that city. This would seem to fix the date of publication in 1854.

11. Newspapers announced Palmatary's visit to Syracuse and that the view would be published by the firm of Anthony Webb & Co. Five months later Palmatary and J. C. Lass, a Syracuse engineer, announced they had acquired Webb's interest in the project and were receiving subscriptions for the view. The four-sheet view published in 1868 identifies the artists as Lass and his son. See Syracuse *Journal*, 30 November 1864, 28 April 1865, and 1 April 1867, and Syracuse *Standard*, 14 December 1864. Apparently only two sets of this lithograph exist. The impression in the Library of Congress is printed from two stones. A fully colored set is in Syracuse, although in divided ownership. The two upper sheets are in the collection of the Onondaga Historical Association, while the two lower sheets are owned by a local bank. The four were briefly on exhibit at the Canal Museum in Syracuse in the spring and summer of 1981.

12. Laurie Baty was kind enough to furnish me the directory listings, which can be found in *Houston's New, Improved and Enlarged Baltimore City Directory* (1867); *and Wood's Baltimore City Directory* (1867–1868 and 1868–1869).

13. Beckman, *Milwaukee Illustrated*.

36. Charles Parsons (1821–1910)
Charles R. Parsons (—   )
Parsons and Atwater

Charles Parsons came to America from England at the age of nine. Three years later he began an apprenticeship with George Endicott and learned his skills as an artist and lithographer under that experienced New York City printer. Parsons put on stone several of the city views printed by the Endicott firm beginning about the middle of the century. The earliest city view with a firm date on which his name appears is one of Rome, New York, in 1851, drawn by F. N. Otis.[1]

Parsons also drew the view of Lancaster, Pennsylvania, published by James T. Palmatary in 1853, and he was both artist and lithographer for the handsome, large view of Portsmouth, New Hampshire, published by the Smith brothers a year later. For three other Smith brothers views printed by Endicott, Parsons put on stone drawings by J. W. Hill showing Bangor (Plate 77) and Portland, Maine, and Halifax, Nova Scotia. Parsons also prepared the lithographic stones for yet another impressive Smith brothers publication, their Detroit lithograph of about 1855 drawn by George Robertson.[2]

First for Nathaniel Currier and then—after James Ives became Currier's partner—for Currier & Ives, Parsons drew and put on stone views of New York City in 1855, 1856, 1858, and probably the two undated later lithographs of ca. 1868 and 1870.[3] Both of the latter prints identify the artist as "C. Parsons," but by this time Charles R. Parsons, son of Charles Parsons, was also doing work for Currier & Ives, while the senior Parsons in 1863 had become head of the art department of the Harpers publishing firm.[4]

The father continued to do occasional work for Currier & Ives. However, it was the son, associated with Lyman W. Atwater, who contributed all or most of the city views the

Charles Parsons, Charles R. Parsons, Parsons and Atwater
(Includes reissues of earlier views)

	N.Y.	Pa.	Maine	N.H.	Calif.	Ga.	Mich.	N.S.	Mass.	Ill.	Mo.	N.J.	D.C.	Md.	Total
1851	1														1
1852	1														1
1853		1													1
1854	1		1	1											3
1855	1		1		1	1	1	1							6
1856	1														1
1857															
1858	1														1
1859– 1868	1														1
1869															
1870	1														1
1871															
1872	1														1
1873	1								1						2
1874	1									1	1	1			4
1875	1	1													2
1876	1														1
1877	2														2
1878	1				2										3
1879	1														1
1880													1	1	2
1881– 1886	1														1
1887– 1889	1														1
1890– 1892	2									1					3
Total	21	2	2	1	3	1	1	1	1	2	1	1	1	1	39

firm published in the years after the Civil War. Many large folio views were drawn by Parsons and Atwater, notably depictions of Boston, Chicago, St. Louis, and Philadelphia in the years 1873–1875 and several New York City views (see Color Plate 3) during the period from 1872 through 1892. Parsons and Atwater also drew and published a similar portrait of Newark in 1874 and put on stone an O. H. Bailey lithograph of Seneca Falls, New York, in 1873.

Charles R. Parsons also drew views without the assistance of Atwater that belong to this Currier & Ives series: San Francisco in 1878 (reissued in 1889 with his name in the imprint), Brooklyn in 1879, and Washington (Plate 45) and Baltimore in 1880.[5] A later and revised version of the Washington view issued in 1892 omits the artist's name, but the view is clearly from the same stone. The evidence can be found in the reflection of the Washington Monument in the waters of the Potomac. In 1880 the monument was still incomplete, and the Parsons view of that year accurately shows its reflection. When Currier & Ives revised and reissued the view they added the top one-third of the monument but neglected to have their lithographer extend the image of the reflection.[6]

Currier & Ives also brought out many revisions of the views Parsons did with Atwater but with their names eliminated in the later issues. These include a second state in 1892 of the Chicago view and a bewildering number of the New York City prints. Some of the latter seem to be changed only in their dates, while others represent either reworked images on the original stones or redrawn prints closely following the Parsons and Atwater designs.[7]

Charles Parsons, his son, and Lyman Atwater all made important contributions to the iconography of American cities. Their prints reveal the appearance of most of the nation's largest urban centers and their surrounding suburbs from points high in the air. They thus capture the images of entire metropolitan regions at a time of vigorous and rapid expansion.

In views of this scope, despite the generous size of the sheets, the artists inevitably sacrificed much background detail. In all of these lithographs, buildings beyond the immediate foreground appear conventionalized, and such depictions cannot be relied on for accurate information. Foreground detail is far more reliable, although harbors are always shown as impossibly crowded.

These views were printed in color for Currier & Ives. They thus differ from most of that firm's work, which was hand colored on the premises or farmed out to colorists paid on a piecework basis. The colors used by the unidentified printer or printers surely attracted the nineteenth-century viewer with their vivid tones and contrasts. They strike some modern eyes as perhaps too harsh and artificial, while others relish their strong hues as typical of the period when they were published and as symbolizing the optimism and energy of civic leaders as cities came to dominate the American scene.

1. Fessenden Nott Otis is the subject of a brief note in *The Old Print Shop Portfolio* 11 (January 1953): 119.

2. Another Hill drawing printed by Endicott in 1855 was put on stone by Parsons. This view of Savannah lacks a publisher's imprint, but it resembles the other Smith brothers views in size and character. Also in 1855 Parsons prepared the lithographic stones for another Otis view showing San Francisco, California.

3. On the latter view, Parsons's name may be in the imprint only as artist. I have not examined the view and know of it only through a description and small illustration in *The Old Print Shop Portfolio* 26 (November 1966): 51.

4. Peters, *America on Stone*, 308, gives the date of Parsons's association with Harpers as 1863. Information on Charles R. Parsons has eluded me. Peters, 308–9, identifies him as the "son of Charles Parsons [who] became associated with Lyman W. Atwater in 1863." Atwater remains a similar biographical mystery. Charles Parsons married at twenty-one in 1842. He had seven children. If one assumes that Charles R. Parsons was the eldest and was born in 1843, he would have been twenty in 1863, an age compatible with Peters's assertion. Parsons and Atwater did one of the famous Four Seasons series for Currier & Ives in 1868 and *Summer Scenes in New York Harbor* a year later. Peters, *Currier & Ives: Printmakers to the American People*, 1: 169–70, 2: 72.

5. Peters, in *California on Stone*, 176, states that it was the senior Parsons who drew the 1878 view of San Francisco, "possibly during his visit . . . with Britton and Rey." Peters notes that Parsons "and Joseph Britton were close friends as young men." I think it more likely that it was his son who was the artist. All of the city views done for Currier & Ives when the senior Parsons was with the firm are signed *C. Parsons*. After the son began to do views for Currier & Ives, and when his name is not bracketed with Atwater's, the signature reads *C. R. Parsons*. This is how the name appears on the San Francisco print.

6. I am indebted to Kenneth Nebenzahl for pointing out to me this amusing lithographic oversight.

7. At one time I hoped that for this study I would be able to provide a detailed analysis of these New York and Brooklyn lithographs. This task proved to be far more complicated and time-consuming than anticipated. Whoever undertakes it should be warned that no single collection comes close to having all of these prints so that they can be easily compared.

37. Clemens J. Pauli (1835?–1896)

Adam Beck and Clemens J. Pauli printed hundreds of lithographs at their Milwaukee press for such publishers of city views as Joseph J. Stoner, Lucien R. Burleigh, and Henry Wellge. Their partnership lasted from 1878 to 1886. In the latter year the business was incorporated with Beck as president. Pauli severed his relationship with the firm and two years later began work as an independent view artist and publisher.[1]

Pauli brought to this venture a wealth of experience. He had a thorough knowledge of printing techniques. Probably he put on stone or zinc plates many of the drawings sent to Beck & Pauli by artists and publishers throughout the country. Moreover, he had been a view artist himself, drawing seven views of towns in Iowa and Wisconsin in 1876 and 1877 before joining Beck to form their printing firm. One of

these early prints identifies Pauli as the publisher, and, since it is likely that he published all of them, he certainly knew the problems and opportunities inherent in the business side of viewmaking.[2]

His Milwaukee view of 1876 shows that Pauli was no stranger to topographic rendering, a skill he must have developed while working as a draftsman in Davenport, Iowa, for the United States Engineer Corps. He had arrived there by 1867 after giving up his studies in agriculture, a field he pursued after leaving the University of Jena, where he studied for two years before departing for America in 1863.[3]

In addition to his training as a topographic draftsman, he may have been exposed to the city views of Davenport drawn and printed by Augustus Hageboeck, a local printer. Pauli probably also knew C. H. Vogt in Davenport, and he eventually followed Vogt to Milwaukee and worked for him briefly before joining forces with Beck. Pauli may well have drawn several city views for Vogt, although he did not receive credit for them in the imprints.

In the reprise that began in 1888 of his earlier, brief career as an artist, Pauli drew forty-six additional prints through 1896. All but a handful also identify him as publisher. He concentrated his efforts on Wisconsin towns, as he had earlier; twenty-eight of these later views show places in that state. One of these was his second depiction of Milwaukee and the only print among the many done of the city to show it as seen by a viewer looking south. It thus adds valuable information about the appearance of the northerly portions of that expanding city.

Clemens J. Pauli
(Excluding views printed by Beck & Pauli)

	Iowa	Wisc.	Ind.	Mich.	Minn.	Ala.	Miss.	Ill.	Total
1876	1	5							6
1877		1							1
1878–									
1888					1			1	2
1889	1		1	3	1				6
1890		1	1	5					7
1891		4		1		1	1		7
1892		6		1					7
1893		6							6
1894				4					4
1895		2		1				1	4
1896		3							3
Total	2	28	2	15	2	1	1	2	53

Pauli traveled through Michigan as well, drawing and publishing views of fifteen of its towns and cities. He went south in 1891 to do views of Mobile, Alabama, and Vicksburg, Mississippi. The latter lithograph is typical of his work at this time in its large size and apparently meticulous attention to details of buildings and landscape. Other Pauli views of this period are of places in Iowa, Indiana, Minnesota, and Illinois.

One of these later lithographs was printed by the Marr & Richards firm in Milwaukee. Three others list Pauli as the printer with an address at 726 Central Avenue, Milwaukee. The others do not identify a printer, but it seems likely that Pauli did them himself, possibly arranging with one or more of his old friends in the industry for the use of a press from time to time.

Pauli drew three views that were published in 1896, the year of his death. Apparently viewmaking had not proved a profitable occupation or, if it had, he had neglected to save anything, for his estate was virtually nonexistent. His only legacy, therefore, was his series of fine, workmanlike views that have survived to enlighten and inform us about conditions in the upper Midwest shortly before the end of the last century.

1. Thomas Beckman is responsible for finding and assembling such details of Pauli's life as are known. Some material on the Beck & Pauli partnership appears in his *Milwaukee Illustrated*, notes for exhibit items 28, 32, and 43. Much additional information is incorporated in a forthcoming article whose preliminary text Beckman has generously allowed me to see.

2. On Pauli's Burlington, Wisconsin, lithograph of 1876 his name is given as publisher with an address of 234 22nd St., Milwaukee. His Milwaukee view of the same year shows Pauli as the copyright claimant. On the three other views of this period for which I have complete information, no publisher is identified.

3. Beckman has provided me with information indicating that Pauli was born in Lubeck in northern Germany in 1835 or 1837 and that his father was a "Supreme Court judge."

38. Bruce Wellington Pierce (1859–1947)

B. W. Pierce, as he usually signed his name, drew his first recorded city view in 1886. It showed the appearance of Red Bluff, California, a town about 125 miles north of Sacramento. Pierce had moved to San Francisco two years earlier at the age of twenty-five shortly after his marriage in Binghamton, New York, to Clara Elliott. Clara Elliott Pierce was either the daughter or niece of William Wallace Elliott, a lithographic printer and publisher who had come to the San Francisco Bay area as early as 1876. Elliott may have suggested that Pierce join him, but all that is known is that Pierce and his wife arrived in San Francisco in 1884, so Pierce may have learned the techniques of viewmaking from some other source. [1]

In 1886 or 1887 Pierce moved to Los Angeles, where he lived for the rest of his life. It was that city he chose for his second view. When he depicted Los Angeles in 1888 at the end of the great land boom, he identified himself to the compilers of the city directory as a draftsman, a title he used, with a single exception, through 1897. In 1894, the year he drew and lithographed his last known view, his name appears in a classified directory of Los Angeles County under the heading *Artists*, a distinction he doubtless appreciated. [2]

Pierce's ten views show some ability, especially his later lithographs of Portland, Oregon, in 1890; Pasadena, California, in 1893; and Los Angeles in 1894. All are large, detailed, bordered by many vignettes of major structures, and show these cities from high elevations. The Los Angeles lithograph is unusual in being divided horizontally into two sections so that the city could be seen as if one were looking in two directions from a central point.

Bruce Wellington Pierce

	Calif.	Wash.	Ore.	Total
1886	1			1
1887				
1888	1			1
1889		2		2
1890			2	2
1891		1		1
1892				
1893	2			2
1894	1			1
Total	5	3	2	10

Pierce apparently published only one of his own views, his San Pedro, California, lithograph with an attributed date of 1893 (Plate 23). W. W. Elliott's printing and publishing company of San Francisco printed and published two of his views and printed two additional Pierce views published by others. The colorful Los Angeles view of 1894 was the work of the Los Angeles Lithographic Company, a rare example of an urban view printed in that city. [3]

1. A grandson of Pierce, Lee P. Morris of Medford, Oregon, brought to my attention the Elliott-Pierce relationship in an undated letter written in May 1983. In 1982 Morris prepared a brief note about his grandfather for the California Historical Society and the Special Collections Division of the University of Washington Libraries. That states that Elliott was Mrs. Pierce's uncle. In his letter to me, Morris indicates that he now believes Elliott was Clara Pierce's father. According to Morris, the Pierces moved to San Francisco in 1884 (the note previously mentioned gives this date as 1885).

2. The *Los Angeles City and County Directory 1886–7* gives an erroneous initial in listing "Pierce E W., elite gallery, Temple blk." The *Los Angeles City Directory 1888* and the corresponding issue of 1890 list him as "Pierce, Bruce W. draftsman." In 1888 his business address was 23 North Spring, and he resided at 301 Montreal. In 1890 only his home address in West Los Angeles was used: the north side of Clinton between Thornton and Vermont avenues. The 1894 *Milliken's Los Angeles County Directory* lists him under the classified heading *Artists* with an address at 230 North Maine. *Maxwell's Los Angeles City Directory 1895* provides an address at 121 West 3rd St. The 1897 issue gives his residence as the north side of West 25th St. in the third house west of Thornton Avenue. This also identifies him more precisely as a "draughtsman L. A. Ry. Co." This was a street railway or trolley company. At the library of the Los Angeles County Museum of Natural History I found him in the *Register of Voters . . . Los Angeles County*, 1896, precinct 72. He then lived at 1321 Clinton Avenue, and it is in this record that his middle name is given. He was then thirty-seven. The balance of the entry reads: "Light complexion. Brown eyes. Light hair. Scar over right eye. Draughtsman." Mr. Morris states that Pierce established the "Pierce Drafting and Art Company in the late 19th or early 20th century" and that his daughter "worked with him in his art shop until shortly before she married my Father in 1909." About that time Pierce took a position with the City of Los Angeles, retiring finally in 1939.

3. In 1894, according to the *Los Angeles Street and Business Directory, 1894*, the company was located at 558–60 Banning. Its president was Theo A. Schmidt, possibly related to the owners of the Schmidt Label and Litho. Company in San Francisco. This firm specialized in labels, but it also printed several city views.

39. Albert F. Poole (1853–1934)

Poole was a native of Brockton, Massachusetts, where he worked as a clerk and then as a school principal. By 1880 he had decided on an artistic career, and the Brockton city directory of that year identified him as an artist.[1] His first city view appeared in 1880, a lithograph of Bar Harbor, Maine, published by J. J. Stoner of Madison, Wisconsin. The following year he did two other views for Stoner (see Plate 4), both showing towns in Massachusetts, and in 1882 he drew four others, including one of Brockton.[2]

That year the city directory shows that he was living at the home of Mrs. Almira Norris, and it was with her son, George E. Norris, that Poole formed a partnership in 1883. During that year they produced ten views of towns in New Hampshire before terminating their association. Newspaper sources indicate that Norris served as the business agent while Poole prepared the sketches and finished drawings. They sent or took most of their work to Milwaukee to be printed by Beck & Pauli, the company used by Stoner to print Poole's earlier views.

In 1884 Poole published some of his own views of Massachusetts, while George Norris published at least two views of Vermont towns that Poole drew. With one or two exceptions thereafter, Poole published his own work, some of the later views just before the turn of the century having the imprint *The Bert Poole Co., Boston.* Virtually all of his nearly fifty views were of New England communities: twenty-two in Massachusetts, twelve in New Hampshire, seven in Maine, and two in Vermont.

"Bert" Poole, as he sometimes signed his name, had a distinctive and original style. Like W. W. Denslow, Poole was a professional illustrator, and he obviously drew with ease and confidence. He used attractively designed titles, decorative borders, and vignettes to enhance the character of his prints.

For several of his later views Poole used a gravure process that made it possible for him to achieve graduated tonal effects that make these prints particularly effective. He maintained a studio on Monhegan Island, where in 1914 eighteen painters working on the island that summer held an exhibition. Among those showing their work were Frederick Waugh and George Bellows.[3] Poole was proud of his work as a viewmaker, and from 1905 through 1919 he identified his calling to the publishers of Boston city directories as "bird's eye view specialist."[4]

1. For many of the details of Poole's life I have relied on information provided by David Ruell, who allowed me to read his manuscript of an article on the city views of New Hampshire and who sent me additional material giving Poole's city directory listings in Brockton and Boston and his obituaries in two Milton, Massachusetts, newspapers.
2. Poole also joined with Henry Wellge in drawing a view of Lake Geneva, Wisconsin, in 1882. This, too, was published by J. J. Stoner, and it was probably Stoner who brought them together for this purpose.
3. David Ruell has called my attention to this event, which is recorded in George R. Havens, *Frederick J. Waugh, American Marine Painter.*
4. Poole's career is summarized in an obituary appearing on 17 November 1934 in the Milton, Massachusetts, *Record:*

> Albert Francis Poole . . . , better known among artists and newspapermen as Bert Poole, died suddenly at his home Friday morning of last week. . . . Mr. Poole was well known as a commercial and newspaper artist and was one of the few to do bird's eye views by hand in pen or pencil, rather than by photography. He did cartoon work on several Boston papers and during the war was engaged as a camoufleur at the Great Lakes. He had been retired from active work for about two years.

40. Eduard Robyn (1820–   )

Eduard Robyn, a native of Emmerich, Westphalia, where he was born 7 December 1820, arrived in St. Louis, Missouri, with his brother, Charles, in 1846. The two went to Philadelphia a year later, both, apparently, to work in the graphic arts.[1] They returned to St. Louis about 1851 to establish their own lithographic printing firm. Two years later Eduard drew, prepared the lithographic stone, and jointly printed and published with Charles a large view of St. Louis.

Eduard's name does not appear on the view of Cape Girardeau, Missouri, of 1858. This was drawn by A. Bottger, and only Charles is identified as the printer. Eduard drew four other views about 1860. Two are known to have been printed by Theodore Schrader (who bought the Robyn firm), and probably he did the other two as well.[2] Those of Washington and Hermann are fine, distant panoramas of these two Missouri River towns. Each lithograph is surrounded by a series of vignettes of churches, business build-

Albert F. Poole, Poole & Norris, etc.

	Maine	Mass.	Wisc.	N.H.	Vt.	Mich.	Ill.	Total
1880	1							1
1881		2						2
1882		4	1					5
1883				10				10
1884		3			2			5
1885	2	6						8
1886	2	1						3
1887		1						1
1888	1			1				2
1889–								
1891						1		1
1892–								
1894		1						1
1895								
1896	1							1
1897								
1898		2					1	3
1899		1		1				2
1900–								
1905		1						1
Total	7	22	1	12	2	1	1	46

Eduard Robyn

	Mo.	Total
1853	1	1
1854–		
1858	1	1
1859	1	1
1860	3	3
Total	6	6

ings, and residences. The other two are of Jefferson City, the state capital on the Missouri River, and Carondelet, just below St. Louis on the Mississippi.

Robyn was an artist of considerable skill, and it is unfortunate that he did not draw more city views. Perhaps he exhausted himself preparing with Ferdinand Welcker, another St. Louis artist, an enormous panorama, *An Artist's Travels in the Eastern Hemisphere*. This was painted on a strip of canvas 8 feet high and 350 feet long and was designed to be unrolled past a stationary frame while a narrator read a description of each scene to the audience.

---

1. Eduard is the artist of a view, *New Oddfellows Hall Philada*, printed by William Hart ca. 1847. Wainwright, *Philadelphia in the Romantic Age of Lithography*, 173. A brief biographical sketch of Robyn can be found in Charles van Ravensway, *The Arts and Architecture of German Settlements in Missouri*, 491. Robyn's arrival in St. Louis is recorded by an older brother who had left Germany earlier. See Ernst C. Krohn, ed., "The Autobiography of William Robyn," 254.

2. Schrader came to St. Louis from Prussia and went to work for the Robyns. After purchasing the firm from the brothers, he continued the business until his death in 1897. See "Theodor Schrader, St. Louis Lithographer," 103. This note by an anonymous author gives 1857 as the date of purchase. Either this is in error and the date of 1858 is incorrect on the Cape Girardeau view, where "Chas. Robyn & Co. Lith, 51 Chestnut St. cor. of 3d. St. Louis, Mo." appears in the imprint, or—more likely—Schrader did not change the name of the business for a time after he acquired it.

41. H. H. Rowley (–   )

From 1878 through 1881 the H. H. Rowley company published fourteen well-drawn and attractively printed lithographs of towns in Massachusetts and New York. All of these give Hartford, Connecticut, as the address of the firm. Two views of Pennsylvania towns in 1885 give Rowley's address as Utica, N.Y., and a final lithograph of 1898 showing Edinboro, Pennsylvania, lists Erie, Pennsylvania, as the publisher's place of business.

Lucien R. Burleigh, then employed by the company, stated in 1881 that the Rowley office in Hartford was at 554 Main Street.[1] No H. H. Rowley appears in the Hartford directories of 1878–1881, nor do the directories list the company under appropriate business headings.[2] Rowley, whoever he may have been, left only a graphic trail devoid of biographical clues.

Four of the Rowley views lack information about who printed them, and a fifth—the 1898 view of Edinboro, appearing long after the others—identifies the printer as a company in nearby Erie, Pennsylvania. The other twelve lithographs came from the presses of either Beck & Pauli in Milwaukee or C. H. Vogt in Cleveland. Since Vogt did not move to Cleveland from Milwaukee until 1879, Rowley may have had some prior connection in Milwaukee as an artist or lithographer for one of those firms or with one of the other companies or artists there who produced city views.

Several of the Rowley views are very large. Those exceeding twenty-four by thirty-six inches include Albany, Boston, and Rochester. Also belonging with this group is the view of Troy, New York, in 1881, printed by Beck & Pauli but lacking any publisher's imprint. Its size, style, location, and date make its attribution to Rowley almost certain.[3]

H. H. Rowley & Co.

	Mass.	N.Y.	Pa.	Total
1878	1			1
1879		3		3
1880	1	4		5
1881	1	4		5
1882–				
1885			2	2
1886–				
1898			1	1
Total	3	11	3	17

All of Rowley's views are extremely detailed, even those of such large cities as Boston and Rochester. The Canajoharie print of 1881 is known to be the work of Lucien R. Burleigh, and Burleigh may have drawn or assisted in preparing many or all of the others.[4] Most of the Rowley views were printed from two stones or zinc plates, a yellow brown or gray green tone being used for clouds and shadows.

---

1. Letter, L. R. Burleigh to Professor C. O. Thompson, 4 January 1881, Worcester Polytechnic Institute Library.

2. I have checked the Hartford directories with no results. Queries to the Connecticut State Library, the Connecticut Historical Society, and the Wadsworth Atheneum were equally unproductive.

3. A preliminary search of the Troy newspapers for 1881 done at the Rensselaer County Historical Society has failed to uncover any newspaper notice of the view's publication that might identify the artist or publisher.

4. Canajoharie *Radii*, 20 January 1881. See the biographical note for Burleigh, above, for additional information concerning this print.

42. Albert Ruger (1828–1899)

Albert Ruger began drawing city views in 1866, and he remained active in the profession for twenty-five years. In that period he produced by himself or with others slightly more than 250 urban lithographs, visiting twenty-four states east of the Rocky Mountains and three Canadian provinces in the Maritimes. In his first five years as an itinerant artist and publisher he completed at least 175 views, or an incredible average for the period of thirty-five a year. For his peak year—1869—sixty-two views can be identified as his work.[1]

Ruger is an important figure for several reasons. His numerous views of midwestern cities provide us with clear and useful images of towns and cities of that region in the first decade after the Civil War. He also prepared views of several communities in the South and in the border states of Kentucky and Tennessee—areas of the country not visited and drawn by many other viewmakers. His views are well drawn and from a sufficiently high perspective to display fully the street patterns and other major elements of the places depicted. Virtually all of his views include a legend identifying important structures and places.

Moreover, unlike other peripatetic artists, such as Fowler, Koch, and Burleigh, who rarely drew larger cities, Ruger drew views of such major urban centers as Chicago

(Plate 27), Cleveland, Omaha (Plate 6), Minneapolis, Memphis, Louisville (Color Plate 7), and Atlanta. Finally, Ruger—often identified with unconscious accuracy in contemporary newspaper accounts as "Professor" Ruger—trained several assistants who became view artists or publishers themselves: Thaddeus M. Fowler, Eli S. Glover, Joseph J. Stoner, Joseph Warner, and (possibly) Augustus Koch, Herman Brosius, and Camille N. Drie.[2]

Very little is known about Ruger's background; indeed almost nothing about him as a person is available. He was born in September 1828 in Prussia, coming to America sometime before 1850 to settle in or near Akron, Ohio, where he completed an apprenticeship as a stone mason, a trade he pursued for fifteen years. He must have been at least moderately successful, for in 1860 he employed a journeyman mason and an apprentice.[3]

At the age of thirty-six and nearly at the end of the Civil War, Ruger enlisted as a Union soldier and served about four months in Company E, 196th Ohio Infantry. While briefly in military service, he prepared drawings of campsites of the Union army, including Camp Chase in Ohio and Stephenson's Depot in Virginia. It seems highly improbable that he developed his artistic skills in this short time, so he must have had some previous artistic training or—more likely—experience as an amateur artist or in designing structures where his skills as a stone mason were required.

In the spring of 1865, apparently while stationed at Camp Chase near Columbus, Ruger drew and had lithographed a bird's-eye view of the scene at the Ohio capitol when Lincoln's body passed by the multitude of mourners. It was a composition considered good enough to be reproduced in pirated versions by at least two other artists.

The following year Ruger moved to Battle Creek, Michigan, and started to draw the towns in the area. Eight of these views were of Michigan communities: Adrian, Ann Arbor, Battle Creek, Hillsdale, Lansing (Plate 26), Marshall, and Monroe. Two others were of La Porte and South Bend, Indiana, located nearby, just south of the Michigan-Indiana state line. An undated view of Ypsilanti may belong to this initial year of Ruger's career, for his subscription agent, Eli S. Glover, was exhibiting the artist's drawing that fall to obtain subscriptions for the finished lithograph.

Ruger acted as his own publisher, identifying himself in this capacity on all of the views of 1866 and on many of the thirty he produced the next year. In visiting and drawing this many towns in Michigan, Minnesota, Wisconsin, and Illinois, Ruger must have had second thoughts about continuing his dual role as artist and publisher. He and Glover obviously worked out some kind of agreement, for Glover's name appears as publisher on five of Ruger's forty views from 1868, and he probably published many of those lacking any publisher's imprint.[4]

Ruger might have desired to expand this association, but Glover's involvement with the Merchants Lithographing Company in Chicago apparently required most of his energies. The two must have parted amicably, for more than twenty of the sixty-two Ruger city views of 1869 came from Glover's press.

In that year and probably for the one before, Ruger had the services of Thaddeus M. Fowler as canvasser and sub-

Albert Ruger

	Ind.	Mich.	Ill.	Minn.	Wisc.	Iowa	Mo.	Nebr.	Ohio	Kans.	Pa.	Ky.	Tenn.	W.Va.	Ala.	Ark.	Ga.	Maine	N.H.	N.Y.	Vt.	N.S.	P.E.I.	Nfd.	Wash.	N.C.	S.C.	Total
1866	2	8																										10
1867		7	8	5	10																							30
1868	5	12	1	1	2	13	2	2	2																			40
1869	3		25	6	1	2	19			5	1																	62
1870		1	1	6	8	1			9		2	1	3	1														33
1871									1		1	3	2		1	1	2											11
1872															1		2											3
1873																												
1874	1				1																							2
1875																												
1876									1		1																	2
1877									1									3	7	1	1							13
1878					1													11				2	2					16
1879		1		1														2				2		1				7
1880		1										1																2
1881		2																										2
1882									7																			7
1883		1							2																			3
1884									1																1			2
1885									1																			1
1886									1		2																	3
1887–1890																												
1891																										4	1	5
Total	11	33	35	19	23	16	21	2	26	5	7	5	5	1	2	1	4	16	7	1	1	4	2	1	1	4	1	254

scription agent.[5] Since both Glover and Fowler embarked on viewmaking enterprises shortly after their association with Ruger, it is reasonable to believe that their activities with Ruger involved more than promoting the artist's work and soliciting subscriptions. Both probably helped Ruger with his field sketching and perhaps in preparing final drawings and in this way began to develop their own artistic skills.

With the help of Glover and Fowler, Ruger was able to complete thirty lithographs in 1867, forty in 1868, and sixty-two in 1869. Ruger's output of thirty-three in 1870 suggests that in that year, too, he had one or more persons assisting him with his drawings. It would be no surprise to discover that Augustus Koch, D. D. Morse, or Herman Brosius—all of whom began their own ventures at about this time and in the Midwest—worked with or for Ruger at one time or another.

Ruger did have another business agent as early as 1868. This was Joseph J. Stoner, who in late February of that year was in Oberlin, Ohio, promoting Ruger's view of the town.[6] Far better known as a publisher, Stoner apparently could draw as well, and he, too, may have helped Ruger in his artistic endeavors. Ruger and Stoner established some kind of partnership in 1869. Their names appear in that capacity on more than a dozen of the Minnesota, Iowa, Missouri, and Illinois views that Ruger drew that year. No other publisher is shown in any of the imprints on the approximately fifty other Ruger prints of 1869. No doubt Ruger and Stoner jointly published many, such as the one lithograph of that year (and one of a very few recorded) to have Ruger & Stoner identified on the print as co-artists. It does seem strange, however, that the partners would have omitted their names as publishers on so many of these views. Glover printed twenty-one of them, and perhaps he published at least some of these as well.[7]

The Ruger-Stoner partnership (if that is what it was) did not last long. Of Ruger's thirty-two views from 1870 showing towns in Minnesota, Kentucky, Ohio, Illinois, Iowa, Pennsylvania, Wisconsin, West Virginia, and Tennessee, Ruger and Stoner published all but seven. However, only one of the ten Ruger views of 1871 bears the firm's imprint, and none of those of 1872, when Ruger produced only three views, do so. There are no Ruger views dated 1873, only two from 1874, and none from 1875.[8]

Although the partnership ended, Ruger and Stoner's association did not. Stoner served as Ruger's business agent for the view of Savannah in 1871.[9] Beginning in 1874 Stoner began to publish under his name alone some of Ruger's city views. For five of the views done in 1871 and 1872, however, Ruger acted as his own publisher, giving his address as St. Louis. He also published one view by C. Drie in 1872.

The Drie view shows Macon, Georgia. Ruger had drawn Savannah and Atlanta in 1871 and Columbus the following year. Possibly Drie helped Ruger on one or more of these Georgia communities.[10] In any event, the two obviously knew each other. This association of Drie and Ruger, the very small number of views with Ruger's name issued in 1873–1875, and the use by Ruger of St. Louis as a business address suggest that Ruger may have been involved with the enormous 110-sheet view of St. Louis published in 1875,

which identifies Drie (now spelling his name Dry) on the title page as the artist.[11]

That project obviously took several years to complete, and it is doubtful if Dry could have done the work unassisted. Moreover, the earlier views signed or known to have been done by Drie all exhibit the most casual knowledge of perspective drawing. The St. Louis view, by contrast, not only follows the rules of linear perspective but also includes two illustrations showing the perspective grid used in its preparation. Unlike Drie, Ruger consistently used a modified perspective system in his views.[12] Circumstantial evidence provides a strong case for Ruger's involvement in this major undertaking, but as yet this cannot be documented.[13]

In 1876 Ruger returned to Akron, Ohio, and resumed viewmaking with prints of Toledo, Ohio, and Louisville, Kentucky (Color Plate 7).[14] The years 1877 and 1878 found him in New England, Nova Scotia (see Plate 78), and Prince Edward Island producing a total of twenty-nine lithographs. Eleven more views followed in the years 1879–1881, including additional New England and Maritime Province views, four in Michigan, and one each in Wisconsin and Minnesota. The great majority were published by J. J. Stoner, who is known to have visited New England and the Canadian towns in efforts to secure subscriptions and obtain newspaper publicity.

From 1882 to 1886 Ruger produced views of towns in the immediate vicinity of Akron or located short distances away in Ohio or in western Pennsylvania. Several of these bear the old publisher's imprint of Ruger & Stoner. The two collaborated for the last time in 1891 when they prepared lithographic views of four cities in North Carolina (Asheville, Durham, Greensboro, and Winston-Salem) and a fifth print showing Spartanburg, South Carolina. Ruger probably drew all of these views, although none of them shows an artist's name. Ruger and Stoner had their views printed by Lucien R. Burleigh of Troy, New York, by that time himself a veteran viewmaker and owner of his own press.[15]

What role Ruger played in the technical aspects of printing will probably never be known. Most of his work appeared in the form of three-stone lithographs, printed in black, yellow brown, and blue. Green was obtained by overprinting brown and blue. It was an effective and economical approach, and Ruger was well served by his printers, especially those in Chicago who did the majority of his lithographs.

We do know that in at least one case Ruger relied heavily on some anonymous lithographer, probably at the Beck & Pauli shop in Milwaukee. To him in 1877 Ruger sent his final drawing (Plate 52) of a view of Wiscasset, Maine, used to produce a lithograph (Plate 53) published the following year by Stoner. On the reverse of the sheet Ruger wrote a long note headed "to lithographer" giving instructions about changes he wanted to have made as his drawing was put on stone.

Ruger produced workmanlike views, more distinguished for their detail and clarity than for any outstanding artistic merit. As the earliest artist of this type after the Civil War, Ruger probably set a standard that others tried to achieve. Certainly the views of Glover, Koch, Fowler, and Wellge, for example, share many of the features that Ruger did so much to popularize.

During the years when he drew and published so many views he must have received a handsome income. Perhaps his success led others to enter the market. The result of his and their efforts is a magnificent legacy of urban portraits—particularly of the Midwest—affording us glimpses of city and town life that are attractive to regard and rewarding to study.

1. This number includes the views with his name in the imprint as well as unsigned lithographs owned by him at his death and attributed to him by the Geography and Map Division, U.S. Library of Congress. Research by Ron Rayman using contemporary newspapers has revealed that the Kalamazoo and Muskegon, Michigan, views of 1874 were drawn by Herman Brosius. This raises questions about the true number of views done by Ruger. On the other hand, Rayman has confirmed that some of the unsigned views attributed by the Library of Congress to Ruger were, in fact, his work. These are of Marshalltown, Iowa; Lawrence, Kansas; Mankato, Minnesota; and Lincoln, Illinois. For material on Ruger I have relied mainly on two sources: the introduction by John Hébert to U.S. Library of Congress, *Panoramic Maps*, and an unpublished biographical note by John Cumming, "Albert Ruger and His Views," which the author kindly sent me. Cumming includes some of this information in the introduction to his *A Preliminary Checklist of 19th Century Lithographs of Michigan Cities and Towns*. Cumming also found and sent me copies of Ruger's brief obituaries in two Ohio newspapers.

2. My findings and conclusions on this point are partly incorporated in this biographical sketch of Ruger but will be found more fully developed in those of Fowler and Glover. Much more research in newspaper accounts will be needed to establish additional connections and more exact dates of association.

3. For the dates of his early years in Akron and the employment information, I am indebted to Thomas Beckman, Registrar, Milwaukee Art Center.

4. Glover also served Ruger as a printer, for in 1868 Glover founded the Merchants Lithographing Company in Chicago. Many of the Ruger views show this imprint.

5. Des Moines, Iowa, *Daily State Register*, 14 July 1868; Montana, Iowa, *Boone County Democrat*, 19 August 1868; Omaha, Nebraska, *Daily Herald*, 10 September 1868; Nebraska City, Nebraska, *Nebraska News*, 17 October 1868; McGregor, Iowa, *North Iowa Times*, 22 September 1869.

6. Oberlin *Lorain County News*, 26 February 1868.

7. Both Stoner and Fowler came to Madison, Wisconsin, to live in 1864. Three years later Ruger visited the town to work on his view. Probably he met one or the other—possibly both—at that time. Stoner already was a traveling salesman in the book trade, associated with Ephraim T. Kellogg of Madison as early as 1864, first in Cincinnati and then in Madison.

8. The single Ruger and Stoner view of 1871 is of Painesville, Ohio. The previous year Ruger did views of nine Ohio towns. I believe that the Painesville view probably had been drawn in 1870 but was not ready to be delivered until 1871 and was given that date. If this is so, The Ruger-Stoner partnership in its first phase thus ended after only two years.

9. Savannah, Georgia, *Morning News*, 19 February 1872. Although dated 1871, the view apparently was not delivered until early the following year.

10. Stoner was also involved with Drie, serving as the publisher for his lithograph of Augusta in 1872.

11. Only two views during 1873–1875 are credited to Ruger. Both are dated 1874. His name does not appear on either of these prints showing South Bend, Indiana, and Reedsburg, Wisconsin. They are among those attributed to Ruger by the Geography and Map Division of the Library of Congress. I have already noted that two other city views of 1874, similarly assigned to Ruger, are now known to have been drawn by Herman Brosius.

12. As is explained elsewhere, most artists—Ruger not excepted—usually "violated" accepted rules of perspective by placing one or both of their vanishing points well beyond the horizon.

13. Ruger's name does not appear in the St. Louis City directories for the years in question, but he may have lived outside the city or across the Mississippi in East St. Louis, Illinois.

14. One of two Ruger obituaries, published in 1899, states that Ruger "had lived in Akron 23 years." Hudson, Ohio, *Independent*, 17 November 1899. His name appeared in the Akron city directory as early as the issue of 1879–1880, when he listed his occupation as "landscape artist," residing at 534 W. Market Street. His name appeared regularly in the Akron directories during 1880–1899. Letter from Warren Skidmore, Akron Public Library, to John Cumming, Central Michigan University, 25 July 1969.

15. The Winston-Salem view has no Burleigh imprint, nor does that of Spartanburg, but they are so similar to the others that they can be attributed to him. Unlike an artist's attribution, however, there is no way to verify this by newspaper accounts. The Spartanburg print has no imprint for publisher or printer, but it clearly belongs to the same series, and a contemporary newspaper account in North Carolina mentions that Stoner was on his way to Spartanburg. See the Asheville *Daily Citizen*, 15 January 1891.

43. Edward Sachse (1804–1873)
E. Sachse & Co. (active 1850–1877)
A. Sachse & Co. (active 1877–1887)

Many distinguished city views, impressive both artistically and technically, came from the Baltimore, Maryland, firm of E. Sachse & Co. During the years of Edward Sachse's viewmaking career through 1873 the firm produced more than sixty lithographic city views, not counting variant states of some of these prints. About half of the firm's views were of two cities: Baltimore and Washington, D.C. Sachse also did several views of other towns in Maryland and Virginia. Eleven of his views published before the Civil War show places in Pennsylvania, West Virginia, Ohio, and Indiana.

Sachse probably came to the United States shortly before his family is known to have arrived from Germany in 1848. For several years prior to that date Sachse operated a small printing and publishing establishment in his native city of Görlitz in Silesia. There he issued a number of small lithographic and engraved views—some of them of towns and others of individual buildings or street scenes.[1]

In Baltimore, Sachse found a position with E. Weber & Co., the city's oldest and most important lithographer. He soon established his own company and in 1850 drew, put on stone, and printed a striking lithograph of Baltimore (Plate 15) handsomely colored through the use of multiple stones. Three states of this print have been recorded. What is probably the first lacks a publisher's imprint but is copyrighted by Casimir Bohn. Bohn's name appears as publisher of many other views printed by Sachse, all before 1868 and all showing Washington or towns in Virginia. These include views of Richmond and Norfolk, both published in 1851.

The following year Sachse issued the first of his many views of Washington, D.C. (Plate 84). He proudly called attention to his ability as a lithographic printer with the inscription "Lith and print. in colors by E. Sachse & Comp." Another inscription states that the view was "Drawn from nature and on stone by E. Sachse." This style of identifying the artist appeared on a few other prints, but far more often the artist is listed as "E. Sachse & Co.," the form used on undated views published by Sachse of Baltimore in 1853 and Alexandria, Virginia, in 1854.

What this form conceals is that both views were drawn by James T. Palmatary, who may also have been responsible in whole or in part for the Washington lithograph of 1852.[2] On the Alexandria lithograph, Palmatary's name does appear, but as publisher rather than as artist. It is this combined imprint showing "E. Sachse & Co." as artist and J. T.

Edward Sachse, E. Sachse & Co., etc.
(Excluding variant states)

	Md.	Va.	D.C.	Pa.	Ohio	Ind.	W.Va.	Del.	Mo.	N.Y.	Total
1850	1										1
1851		2									2
1852	1	1	1	1							4
1853	1										1
1854	2	2			3	2					9
1855			1	1	2		1				5
1856		2	1		1						4
1857		1	1								2
1858	2										2
1859	4		1								5
1860	1										1
1861	3		1								4
1862	3	2	2								7
1863	1						1				2
1864											
1865		1						1	1		3
1866		2									2
1867			2								2
1868										1	1
1869	1		1								2
1870	1		1					1			3
1871			1								1
1872	2										2
1873											
1874	1	1									2
1875–											
1880	2										2
1881–											
1883			1								1
1884			1								1
n.d.		1	1								2
Total	26	15	16	2	6	2	2	2	1	1	73

Palmatary as publisher that the two used for eight views of midwestern towns either dated 1854 or 1855 or known or believed to have been published in those years. The exact nature of their business relationship is unclear, but it seems likely that Sachse employed Palmatary to do the field sketching for the views while Sachse put the drawings on stone in Baltimore. He carried out this task with great skill, for these large and attractive views are splendid examples of color lithography.

Other than a view of St. Louis that Sachse printed in 1865 (Plate 88), he limited his work of this type after the mid-1850s to places within easy reach of Baltimore. He (or Palmatary or other artists) drew such places in Maryland as Ellicotts Mills and Frederick in 1854, Hagerstown at probably about the same time, and Georgetown (Color Plate 4) in the District of Columbia in 1850. In 1856 and 1857 Sachse added the Virginia towns of Fredericksburg, Charlottesville, and Lexington to his list.

His Baltimore views provide a fine record of the city's appearance from several vantage points and over a period of many years. Sachse reissued his 1850 view several times, and in 1858 his company published the first bird's-eye portrait of the entire city as seen from a point high above the harbor.

While Sachse continued to draw, print, and publish views of Baltimore, he also recorded the changing appearance of the nation's capital. He began this series in 1852. All but one of these interesting and appealing lithographs are drawn as if from a position in the air east of the Capitol looking westward down the Mall and Pennsylvania Avenue to the Potomac River and the White House.

All of his prints taken from this viewpoint include a curiously inaccurate feature: a completed Washington Monument drawn as if built according to the original design prepared by Robert Mills, who proposed an elaborate colonnaded base for the obelisk whose shaft was not finished until many years after Sachse's prints appeared (see Plate 84). In his 1852 view Sachse also anticipated the completion of the new wings for the Capitol that had only recently been authorized, and in some of his later views he showed the present lofty dome over the center of the Capitol as if it, too, were finished instead of still under construction.

Theodore Sachse, Edward's brother, joined the firm some time in the mid-1850s. His name can be found as lithographer on a Baltimore view published in 1859, and he may have put on stone some or all of the city views that the firm printed thereafter. He was active at least until 1880, the year when two Baltimore views were published identifying him as lithographer. By that time the firm was operated by Adolph Sachse, probably Theodore's son.

Four years before Edward Sachse's death in 1873 the company drew, put on stone, printed, and published an enormous bird's-eye view of Baltimore. This lithograph of 1869 came in twelve sheets. When assembled as a single image, it measured a generous four by ten feet and included dozens of vignettes showing important buildings in even greater detail than could be seen on the principal view.

The Sachse firm claimed that "four men have been engaged in drawing and sketching on this work for three years and four months."[3] No doubt Edward himself supervised their activities. At only $15.00 for the twelve-sheet set this view must have seemed an attractive purchase by many residents of Baltimore, yet only a few impressions have survived. Possibly Sachse looked on this project as a way of advertising the company's work more than as a source of direct income.

A year earlier the company printed another multiple-sheet city view. This four-sheet lithograph of Syracuse, New York, had originally been promoted by J. T. Palmatary as early as 1864. By the time it appeared in 1868, however, Palmatary had disposed to Syracuse publishers whatever interest he had in the project. The Syracuse view was executed in several colors, while the Baltimore view was done with only two tone stones in addition to the basic black ink of the underlying design.

The Sachse firm produced consistently excellent prints. City views constituted only one part of their business, which included "labels, show and business cards, maps, bills, visiting cards, drawings of steamboats and machinery, portaits, landscapes, and 'drawings taken from Nature or Daguerreotypes, executed like steel engravings.'"[4] During the Civil

War they added scenes of hospitals and military camps to their output of prints.

Adolph Sachse continued the company's tradition of city views, drawing and printing two lithographs of Washington in the 1880s. One of these required four sheets because of its immense size. Although the firm continued in operation after that under various names, these were the last urban prints to come from a company distinguished for superior quality in printing and having a rare record of city view publication bridging the periods before and after the Civil War.

1. Information about Sachse's career in Görlitz comes to me from a letter dated 21 January 1983 from Dr. habil. Ernst-Heinz Lemper of the Görlitz Stadische Kunstammlungen. Genealogical material concerning Sachse was compiled by Lois McCauley, formerly curator of graphics of the Maryland Historical Society. Copies of this and additional information were supplied me by Ms. Laurie A. Baty, assistant librarian, prints & photographs, of the society.

2. Baltimore, Maryland, *American & Commercial Advertiser*, 1 July 1853, p. 2, col. 4; Alexandria, Virginia, *Alexandria Gazette and Virginia Advertiser*, 24 August 1853, p. 2, col. 1, and 2 January 1854. The August account of Palmatary's presence in Alexandria mentions that he represented a view of Washington as his own work. Since at that time he had some association with Sachse it seems unlikely he would have made this claim without some justification.

3. Baltimore, Maryland, *Sun*, 22 October 1869, as quoted in McCauley, *Maryland Historical Prints*, 26. McCauley's work has been of great help in recording the Sachse lithographs. I have also drawn on her biographical note on Sachse and the firm, pp. 232–34.

4. Ibid., 233, quoting from a notice in an 1852 city directory of Baltimore.

44. Francis Smith (1823–1908)
George Warren Smith (1825–1922)
David Clifford Smith (1827–1911)
Benjamin Franklin Smith (1830–1927)
The Smith Brothers

During an eight-year period beginning in 1848, the four Smith brothers issued a remarkably fine series of large folio city views. A few of these were engraved, but about forty others were lithographed by highly skilled printers in Boston and New York. Geographically, their views extended from New Orleans to Halifax and St. John and as far west as Chicago.[1] Probably the Smiths intended to include all of the important urban communities of the nation in their list of urban prints. While the results fell short of this ambitious goal, their efforts produced views of cities from throughout the eastern half of the country.

Biographical information on the Smith brothers is brief, and that on their publishing careers is uninformative.[2] The artist of the family was the youngest brother, Benjamin Franklin Smith. He drew six of the views, collaborated with J. W. Hill on six others (see Plate 14), and undoubtedly was one of the artists of a view signed only by "Smith & Smith." He also put on stone two of his own drawings, two drawn by Hill, one that he had drawn with Hill, and a view of Louisville, Kentucky, that may have been published by the Smiths. On the prints his name as artist almost always reads *B. F. Smith, Jr.*

The name of Francis Smith appears on two views as pub-

lisher, as does that of George Warren Smith on another. David Clifford Smith and B. F. Smith published the Pittsburgh view of 1849. Other lithographs give the firm name as *Smith Brothers & Co.*, but it is probably safe to conclude that all four Smiths were involved in the production, sale, and distribution of most of the prints having any of the Smiths' names attached to them.[3]

The Smith brothers came from South Freedom, Maine, where they worked on their father's farm and received enough formal education to permit each to teach school. While convalescing from an illness at his uncle's home in Albany, New York, George Smith decided to become a subscription agent and salesman. In 1846 he was working for Edwin Whitefield promoting that artist's view of Newburgh, New York, in the second year of Whitefield's career as an artist of American cities.[4] Francis Smith also served as Whitefield's agent in 1846 in Cincinnati, Rochester, and Wheeling and—early in 1848—in Louisville.[5]

Benjamin Franklin Smith began his artistic career in 1846 at the age of sixteen when he put on stone a view of the Albany Exchange and Museum. His first city view came a year later when he drew Albany as seen from the eastern bank of the Hudson. This was engraved and used as the frontispiece of a book on the city's history.[6]

Benjamin soon joined his brothers in working for Whitefield. In 1849 he wrote to the artist from Salem, Massachusetts, suggesting that there was a market for a view of Danvers, and he advised the artist also to make his forthcoming print of Lynn fairly large.[7] It is possible that Whitefield had Benjamin help him in drawing some of his city views. If so, the career of the youngest Smith would be the earliest known example of what came to be the usual way of entering the field of American viewmaking: starting as an artistic assistant or apprentice, helping with publicity and sales, and progressing to the status of artist-publisher.

The names of Whitefield and Smith appear as publishers on Whitefield's 1848 view of Boston, on the two views of Providence that Whitefield drew in 1849, and on a lithograph of Portland, Maine, that is undated but was also issued in 1849. The Whitefield-Smith association thus extended for four years, but over some business or personal disagreement the Smiths and Whitefield broke relations. The artist's diaries only hint at the reasons, and there are no records of the Smith brothers that can be located.[8]

The breach probably resulted from a decision by the Smiths to begin an independent publishing firm and compete with Whitefield in the growing market for city views. In 1849 the Smiths published views of Pittsburgh and New Haven. That same year Whitefield visited Pittsburgh to draw and solicit subscriptions for his own view, which probably was not printed until the following year.[9]

In 1850 the Smiths issued two splendid lithographs of Philadelphia showing the city from different vantage points. These must have competed directly with Whitefield's four smaller views of the city taken from atop the State House and published the same year. While the modern collector or scholar finds the six prints complementary, Whitefield surely looked on the work of his former associates as unwelcome and, possibly, unfair.

	Mass.	Conn.	Maine	Pa.	R.I.	Ky.	N.Y.	N.B.	S.C.	La.	Mo.	Ohio	N.J.	D.C.	Va.	Ill.	N.H.	Wisc.	N.S.	Mich.	Total
1848	1																				1
1849		1	1	1	2																5
1850	1			3		1	1														6
1851								1	1												2
1852	1						1			2	1	1	1	1							8
1853							5					2			1	2					10
1854	1		1				1										1	1			5
1855		1																	1	1	3
1856–																					
1862							1														1
Total	4	1	3	4	2	1	9	1	1	2	1	3	1	1	1	2	1	1	1	1	41

He must have felt the pressure of competition all the keener because the two Smith brothers views drawn by the talented J. W. Hill with B. F. Smith were skillfully done and superbly lithographed by two of the best firms of New York.[10] B. F. Smith put both drawings on stone, and it is obvious from these prints that he possessed artistic skills of a very high order, clearly surpassing those of Whitefield. It may well have been the youngest Smith's confidence in his talents (and his brothers' recognition of them) that brought about the separation from Whitefield.

The year 1850 also saw the publication of the Smith brothers' view of Louisville. This view is unsigned, and no publisher's name appears, but it was put on stone by B. F. Smith, Jr., and printed by Peter S. Duval of Philadelphia, another skilled and experienced lithographic printing firm. Two years earlier during the Smith and Whitefield association Francis Smith wrote to the artist reporting that he had secured "about 300 subscribers" for a lithograph of Louisville to be done by Whitefield.[11] Newspaper announcements in the city identified Smith as the prospective joint publisher with Whitefield, but no such view is known to have been published.[12] Possibly the Smith brothers simply pirated Whitefield's view or regarded it as their property as much as his. This event certainly would have ended their relationship, but it is a step that might also have been taken as a consequence of a break in the association arising from another cause.[13]

Between 1850 and 1855 the firm published nearly thirty large and handsomely executed lithographic city views in addition to those previously mentioned. Benjamin Franklin Smith drew three of these alone and an equal number with John William Hill, with whom he had collaborated on the Philadelphia views. Hill, the subject of a separate biographical note, drew fourteen of the Smith brothers' views, all of them splendid examples of American viewmaking.

The Smiths employed other talented artists. Lewis Bradley drew three cities in upstate New York. Bradley lived and worked in Utica where he painted and taught art. He exhibited still lifes and landscapes at the National Academy of Design, and he must have seemed the logical candidate when the Smith brothers sought out someone to depict Utica.

Bradley also did the drawings for the Smith brothers' prints of Oswego and Syracuse.[14]

For their views of Chicago, Milwaukee (Plate 9), and Detroit the Smith brothers also located a trained artist residing and working in the region. He was George James Robertson, a native of Edinburgh, a student at the Royal Academy in London, and an intermittent resident of Milwaukee after 1847, the year of his thirty-seventh birthday.[15] The Smiths also commissioned Charles Parsons to draw their view of Portsmouth, New Hampshire. Parsons put his own drawing on stone, a task he had carried out for Robertson's Milwaukee and Detroit views and three of Hill's drawings for the Smith brothers.[16]

The brothers evidently found that they had undertaken projects requiring more time than they had anticipated and that they could not deliver lithographs to their subscribers when promised. In 1850 they obtained subscriptions for their view of Syracuse, but in June of the following year a local newspaper announced that the project had been "delayed on account of the illness of Mr. Smith, the Artist."[17]

B. F. Smith may indeed have fallen ill, but he had also fallen behind schedule. Perhaps at this time the Smiths engaged Lewis Bradley to do the Syracuse view (Plate 33). More than a year later, however, the Smiths still had not delivered their lithograph to what must have been very impatient subscribers. In August 1852, they sent a printed notice to Syracuse subscribers stating that they hoped "to have it finished ready for delivery some time this fall."[18] Since the notice did not mention Syracuse by name—using instead the phrase *your city*—it must have been used to mollify disgruntled subscribers in other cities as well. Not until mid-December 1852 were the Smiths finally able to deliver Bradley's fine depiction of Syracuse.[19] Subscribers elsewhere probably encountered similar delays.

Nevertheless, the prints without exception were worth waiting for. Large and imposing in size, splendidly drawn from vantage points carefully selected to show each city to best advantage, skillfully lithographed and printed by some of the best craftsmen of the industry, the Smith brothers' views achieved a standard that equalled or surpassed the best work of its kind.

For reasons that remain obscure and will probably always be so, the firm ceased issuing city views after 1855. Perhaps the Smiths accurately forecast the depression that would begin in 1857, or they may looked toward more conventional and rewarding ways of making a fortune. Francis Smith moved to Omaha in 1858 to establish a bank. After the discovery of gold in Colorado the following year he sent for Benjamin to join him in what proved to be an enormously profitable operation in providing supplies to the mining communities. They bought a mine that yielded even greater wealth, and soon all the brothers were involved with an enterprise that had Colorado and New York offices.

Selling their company for a fortune, they invested first in railroads, then in Omaha real estate, and finally in stockyards. In the 1880s they returned to Maine to construct at Rockport an estate of 500 acres with sumptuous living quarters for each family. The four brothers agreed that as each died his fortune would go to the survivors. The last to die was Benjamin Franklin in 1927, reputed then to be the richest man in Maine. His B. F. Smith Trust, administered by the Guaranty Trust Company of New York, provided generously for the surviving members of the family.[20]

B. F. Smith also left behind a small mystery. Long after the brothers had abandoned their viewmaking activities a lithograph of Elmira, New York, was published in 1862. It is unsigned, but the names of both the lithographer and the publisher appear in the imprint as "B. F. Smith, Jr. & Co., Albany, N.Y."[21] It is hard to believe that this is a mere coincidence of names, but it is just as difficult to determine what took Smith to Elmira or what persuaded him for one last time to draw a city and arrange for its lithographic image to be published.

---

1. The Smith brothers also published a view of Havanna, Cuba, in 1851.

2. See William J. Hartford's brief *Benjamin Franklin Smith: A Biography of One of Maine's Successful Americans*; [Harry Shaw Newman?], "The Magnificent Smiths"; John Paul Heffernan, "A Maine Family of Smiths"; John Gardner, "The Trouble Was Money—Too Much of It"; and Norton, *Edwin Whitefield*, 44–46.

3. Other variations of publisher's imprints occur. Smith & Jenkins appear on lithographs of Fall River, Massachusetts, in 1852 and Washington, D.C., probably in the same year. Jenkins joined with the Smiths in 1853 to issue a large lithograph of a statue of Andrew Jackson. See Peters, *America on Stone*, 370. The Newark, New Jersey, view (undated but 1852) identifies the publishers as Smith, Fern & Co.

4. The view has a copyright date of 1846. An undated clipping from an unidentified newspaper in the Whitefield Scrapbook, Boston Public Library Print Room, contains the statement, "Mr. G. W. Smith, has submitted to our inspection a very fine Lithographic view of our village . . . drawn by Mr. E. Whitefield." George also sought subscribers for Whitefield's print of Baltimore, copyrighted in 1847. See an undated news clipping from the Baltimore *American* in the Whitefield Scrapbook.

5. Norton, *Edwin Whitefield*, 45–46.

6. Joel Munsell, *The Annals of Albany*. The Cornell University copy of this volume is closely bound, and no title or imprint on the view can be seen. However, in the 1869 reprint of volume 1 by Munsell, B. F. Smith's name as artist appears to the left of the copyright entry with a date of 1847.

7. Norton, *Edwin Whitefield*, 44.

8. The episode is treated in ibid., 46–47, but what happened is far from clear. As Norton points out, the information available to her was limited in extent and confusing in nature.

9. Pittsburgh *Gazette*, a clipping dated only October 1849 in Whitefield Scrapbook: "We have had the pleasure of examining a View of Pittsburgh, taken within the last few weeks, by Mr. E. Whitefield . . . [who] . . . is about to take up subscriptions, to justify him in the publication of his . . . view." This lithograph is excessively rare, suggesting that its sale must have been limited. Norton was able to locate an impression only in a private

collection, and my own queries have failed to find any institution holding this print.

10. Francis Michelin, who had printed several of the earlier Whitefield lithographs, did "Philadelphia, From Girard College," while the Sarony firm printed "Philadelphia. From Camden."

11. Edwin Whitefield Diaries, Boston Public Library Print Room, entry for 6 January 1848.

12. Two undated clippings from Louisville newspapers, no doubt printed in 1848, are in the Whitefield Scrapbook. The one from the *Morning Courier* begins: "Messrs. Whitefield and Smith propose publishing an elegant engraving of this city."

13. There is only one other unsigned view published by the Smith brothers. This is of Springfield, Massachusetts, and is undated although believed to be ca. 1851. It is conceivable that Whitefield drew it or commissioned B. F. Smith to do so but that the Smith brothers used it as their own.

14. For Bradley, see Munson-Williams-Proctor Institute, *Made in Utica*, 36; and George C. Groce and David H. Wallace, eds., *The New-York Historical Society's Dictionary of Artists in America, 1564–1860*, 75.

15. Porter Butts, *Art in Wisconsin*, 80. For a note on Robertson's Milwaukee view, see Beckman, *Milwaukee Illustrated*, note for exhibit item 3.

16. Almost certainly this was the senior Charles Parsons, then associated with the Endicott firm, printer of all of the views mentioned. Whether the Smiths sought out Parsons or Endicott assigned him to the job cannot be determined. Other lithographers working for or with Endicott who put drawings on stone for the Smiths were J. H. Colon and D. W. Moody.

17. Syracuse *Standard*, 25 June 1851. This and other material about the Smith brothers view of Syracuse was provided by Richard Wright, president of the Onondaga Historical Association.

18. From a copy in the Onondaga Historical Association, Syracuse, New York. The text is also given in full in Beckman, *Milwaukee Illustrated*, unpaged introduction.

19. Syracuse *Standard*, 12 December 1852.

20. "The trust weathered the stock market crash of 1929 and the Great Depression so well that it was adopted for use in courses at the Harvard Business School as an example of how a family trust should be drawn." Heffernan, "Family of Smiths," 70.

21. The printers were George Lewis and Thomas Goodwin, who had offices in New York City and Albany. Lewis printed Whitefield's three earliest views: Albany and Troy in 1845 and Harrisburg, Pennsylvania, in 1846.

45. Robert Auchmuty Sproule (1799–1845)

Sproule was born in Ireland and attended Trinity College, Dublin. He came to Canada about 1826 and settled in Montreal. Late in 1829 he published the following notice advising the residents of the city of his intention to produce a series of views that would be issued as engravings:

VIEWS OF MONTREAL. ROBERT A. SPROULE proposes publishing a set of SIX VIEWS, comprising some of the principal Streets, Public Buildings and Squares in Montreal, with a general VIEW of the CITY—to be executed in a style fit for colouring, and superior to any thing of the kind yet got up in the Province. An Engraver of the first rate talent shall be employed, and from the Prints being made large enough for framing it is expected that they will become an object of interest to all.

To be delivered to Subscribers at 10s per set, plain or 15s coloured. One or two of the original drawings will be ready for exhibition in a few days, until which time there will be a few small drawings in India-Ink, to be seen at Mr. Cunningham's Bookstore, and at Mr. Hoisington's, where a Prospectus will be ready.[1]

Although only one of the six prints showed the entire city—a distant view from St. Helen's Island—the other five provide splendid documentation of the appearance of important sections of Montreal and together add immeasurably to our knowledge about the appearance of the city. These

	Queb.	Total
1832	4	4
1833–		
1871	6[1]	6
1872–		
1874	4[2]	4
Total	14	14

1. From engravings published in 1830.
2. From engravings published in 1832.

	Nev.	Idaho	Calif.	Total
1875	1			1
1876–				
1880		2		2
1881–				
1887			1	1
1888			4	4
Total	1	2	5	8

engravings were reissued as lithographs in 1871 by Adolphus Bourne of Montreal, and thus they qualify for inclusion in this study.

Bourne also brought out in lithographic form in 1874 several views of Quebec, including four by Sproule first issued as engravings in 1832.[2] Bourne published other views by Sproule in the early 1830s that Bourne took to London to be printed at the famous Hullmandel press. Bourne returned to Montreal with his own lithographic press and used it to print many views, maps, trade cards, and so on, as well as continuing his trade as an engraver and a china and glass merchant.[3]

1. As quoted in Mary Allodi, *Printmaking in Canada: The Earliest Views and Portraits*, 64. There is also a very brief note about Sproule in Charles W. W. Jefferys, comp., *A Catalogue of the Sigmund Samuel Collection Canadiana and Americana*, 74.
2. Titles of some of these are listed in Jefferys, *Sigmund Samuel Collection*, 74, 135.
3. Allodi, *Printmaking in Canada*, 86.

46. Henry Steinegger (1831?–1893?)

A lithographer with Britton & Rey in San Francisco in 1856–1859, Henry Steinegger was made a member of the firm when it was renamed Britton & Company in 1859. In 1867 he became its head under the new name of Britton, Rey & Company. During these years he moved frequently, living at various addresses in Oakland and San Francisco.[1]

Beginning in 1875 Steinegger drew or put on stone several attractive views of communities in Nevada, California, and Idaho, all of which his firm printed. In his first year as an artist he recorded the appearance of Virginia City, Nevada, and its surroundings when silver mining at the Comstock Lode was still in full operation. Five years later he drew two Idaho mining towns, Quartzburg and Rocky Bar, the latter with an E. Green.[2]

The land boom of the 1880s in Southern California brought Steinegger to the region to draw several of the communities affected or to put on stone the work of other artists. On the way or returning he paused long enough to prepare an interesting oval-shaped lithograph of Santa Cruz. He used this same format, which included a decorated frame

for the oval composition, when he put on stone the drawing of Los Angeles in 1888 by S. F. Cook. It is likely that Steinegger collaborated with Cook to produce a similar lithograph of Santa Barbara.[3]

It was probably at this time that Steinegger also drew an undated view with many border vignettes of Sierra Madre, not far from Los Angeles in the San Gabriel valley. He also did the lithography for E. S. Moore's view of Monrovia, one of the new boom towns in the region. His name appears on his prints in a variety of forms: Hy. Steinegger, H. Stggr., H. Steinegger, Stggr., and Steinegger.[4]

1. Peters, *California on Stone*, 62, 194, and notes from San Francisco and Oakland city directories provided me by the California Historical Society, San Francisco. Peters assigns the date of 1856 as the beginning of Steinegger's known association with Britton & Rey. The city directory first lists him with the company in 1858. The directory identifies him in 1891 as a "capitalist" and in 1893, the last listing, as an "artist." In my folder on Steinegger, I have a note "Born in Switzerland ca. 1831," but I cannot recall where this information came from.
2. The dates of both Idaho views are conjectural but are judged to be ca. 1880 by the Idaho Historical Society.
3. The name given on the print is E. F. Cook.
4. The Sierra Madre view is reproduced in Warren R. Howell and Laura R. White, "California in Lithographs: Nineteenth Century Prints from the Robert B. Honeyman, Jr. Collection."

47. Joseph John Stoner (1829–1917)

Nearly all of the artists and publishers who dominated American viewmaking from the end of the Civil War until the turn of the century got their start in southern Wisconsin or soon found themselves doing business there or in nearby Chicago. Many persons who began their careers here eventually established their own enterprises in New England, New York, or Pennsylvania. O. H. Bailey in Boston, L. R. Burleigh in Troy, and T. M. Fowler in Morrisville were the most prolific. Others, like Herman Brosius and Henry Wellge, continued to live in the region while traveling throughout the country drawing towns and cities.

J. J. Stoner was part of this Wisconsin group. A native of Highspire, Pennsylvania, where he was born in 1829, he learned the trade of chair-ornamenting during a four-year apprenticeship in Harrisburg before moving west to work as a book agent. The Cincinnati city directory for 1864 lists him as a map and book agent. His partner was Ephriam T.

	Ill.	Iowa	Minn.	Mo.	Wisc.	Ohio	Pa.	Tenn.	W.Va.	Ala.	Ga.	Ont.	N.Y.	Tex.	Ind.	Mich.	Maine	N.H.
1869	6	2	3	1	1	1												
1870	1	1	5		8	8	2	1	1									
1871						1												
1872	1	1								1	1	1						
1873	1					1							3	3				
1874					6							1			1	2		
1875					6								5				1	
1876					2							1					1	
1877					1							1					2	6
1878																	15	
1879			5		6											3	3	
1880	1				8										1	23	1	
1881					4	2										21		
1882	1				3	7						4						
1883			5		9	4	2									2		
1884					1	1												
1885					1													
1886					2												1	
1887–1891																		
Total	11	4	18	1	52	27	7	1	1	1	1	8	8	3	2	51	24	6

Kellogg, a resident of Madison, Wisconsin, in whose house Stoner married a Madison woman, Harriet Louise Daggett, in September 1864. Kellogg also sold books in Madison, and it was probably in connection with this business that Stoner and his wife moved for a short time to New Orleans.[1]

The Stoners returned to Madison in 1865, purchasing a house in November of that year. Probably Stoner still maintained his association with Kellogg, and the Madison directory of 1868—doubtless compiled the previous year—identifies him as a "traveling agent." As early as February 1868, however, he was serving as a sales agent for Albert Ruger, who had begun his career as an artist of city views two years before.[2]

Ruger had previously employed Eli S. Glover as his agent, but in 1868 Glover founded a printing firm in Chicago and could no longer serve in that capacity. How and when Ruger recruited Stoner is not known, but the two probably met when Ruger visited Madison in 1867 to draw his view of that city. Whether Ruger sought out Stoner or Stoner pursued an opportunity to enter a new line of business, the two obviously reached some kind of agreement early in 1868 and conceivably many months before.[3]

This relationship of artist and agent changed, probably early in 1869, when the two agreed to do business under the name of Ruger & Stoner and to use Madison as the address of the enterprise. In their first year their names appeared as publishers on only eleven of the sixty-two views produced by the energetic Ruger, but they probably issued all or most of the fifty others of that year lacking any publisher's imprint.

One print identifies "Ruger & Stoner" as the artists, a signature that can also be found on one of the views of 1870. Stoner probably could draw, but it was his role as a publisher rather than as an artist that makes him important in

American viewmaking.[4] More than three hundred lithographs have his name in this capacity, but this does not include the numerous views without a publisher's imprint during the Ruger and Stoner years, nor many others that Stoner probably issued as well.

In 1872 the Ruger and Stoner firm was terminated for a time, and Stoner began to publish under his own name alone. Ruger drew some of these views, and, curiously, Stoner also served as Ruger's sales agent for a lithograph of Savannah, Georgia, that Ruger published himself.[5]

Herman Brosius drew his first lithograph for Stoner in 1872 and in the next twelve years produced some thirty views (see Plate 32) that identify Stoner as the publisher. Many more signed by Brosius as the artist have no publisher's imprint, and it is safe to conclude that Stoner was responsible for publishing a number of them. One of the Brosius views of 1873 on which Stoner's name does appear depicts Highspire, Pennsylvania, the publisher's birthplace.

Probably Stoner visited Highspire to promote this view, for at that time in his career he apparently traveled with the artists who did his work. Early in 1873, for example, Stoner went to Texas to obtain subscriptions and otherwise promote sales for the views of San Antonio and Austin that Augustus Koch had drawn and that Stoner subsequently published.[6] Stoner doubtless continued to spend much of his time away from Madison. In 1878, after Ruger had drawn a view of Charlottetown on distant Prince Edward Island and it had been printed in the Midwest, Stoner himself delivered the finished lithographs, as he did those of Summerside and Pictou.[7]

In addition to views by Ruger, Brosius, and Koch, Stoner published the work of several other artists. Thaddeus M. Fowler had already established himself as an artist-publisher,

N.M.	Vt.	N.S.	P.E.I.	Kans.	Nebr.	Mant.	Mass.	N.D.	Queb.	Colo.	Wyo.	Mont.	S.D.	Fla.	Ore.	Wash.	N.C.	S.C.	Total
																			13
																			27
																			1
																			5
																			8
																			10
																			12
																			4
1	2																		13
		1	2																18
				2	7														26
						3	1	1											39
	3						1		5										36
2				1			5			14	1								38
								3				4	5						34
												4		6	2	7			21
																			1
																			3
																	4	1	5
3	5	1	2	3	7	3	7	4	5	14	1	8	5	6	2	7	4	1	314

but beginning in 1878 he did a dozen or so views that Stoner published. These included depictions of places in New England, Nebraska (see Plate 73), North Dakota, and Manitoba. Stoner must have sold his rights to Fowler's Winnipeg view of 1880, for the next year another publisher reissued it without change except for a new date in the title.

From 1880 through 1886 Albert F. Poole drew at least eight New England communities (see Plate 4) for lithographs published by Stoner. Poole also joined Henry Wellge in 1882 and 1883 to draw two midwestern towns whose lithographs were added to the number issued by Stoner. Wellge had begun to draw for Stoner in 1880, and he did at least forty drawings for the Madison publisher. Many of these are of the West, including places in Colorado, Montana (see Plate 31), New Mexico, Oregon, and Washington (see Plate 75). Stoner's name as publisher appears on many other unsigned views of the same region, and Wellge probably did many of them.

Stoner also brought out the work of other artists. One was Joseph Warner, who drew two views that Stoner published in 1876 and 1880. In between those dates Warner acted as an agent for Albert Ruger.[8] Stoner also issued Camille N. Drie's view of Augusta, Georgia, in 1872.

In 1885 Stoner bought a farm near Madison and virtually retired from the business of viewmaking. In 1891, however, he once again joined his old associate, Albert Ruger, to publish four views of towns in North Carolina. Ruger probably did the drawings for these lithographs of Asheville, Durham, Greensboro, and Winston-Salem. Almost surely Ruger and Stoner were responsible as well for a view of Spartanburg, South Carolina, that same year.[9]

This final collaboration between former partners and longtime associates and friends must have been the occasion for much conversation between the two as they recalled the boom years of the city view business after the Civil War when they helped record the face of urban America for all to see. Stoner lived in or near Madison until 1902. He moved in that year to Hayward, California, and later to Berkeley, where he died in 1917.

1. For biographical material on Stoner I am relying on Michael J. Fox, "Joseph John Stoner, 1829–1918?," and Beckman, *Milwaukee Illustrated*, notes for exhibit item 32. Beckman has also provided me with a draft of a forthcoming article in which he mentions the Cincinnati city directory listing of 1864.

2. An Oberlin, Ohio, newspaper referred to Stoner as "the agent for Prof. Ruger" who "called upon us today and exhibited the penciled draft of a view of Oberlin" (*Lorain County News*, 26 February 1868).

3. By the summer of 1868 another Madison resident, Thaddeus M. Fowler, was also helping Ruger sell his views in Iowa, as is mentioned in the Des Moines *Daily State Register*, 14 July 1868. Fowler continued his work for Ruger at least through September of the following year. See the McGregor, Iowa, *North Iowa Times*, 22 September 1869. There are other newspaper accounts of Fowler's activities on behalf of Ruger in Nebraska during the fall of 1868. My biographical note on Fowler suggests that he may also have met Ruger in 1867.

4. The only other view I have recorded naming Stoner as an artist is one of Appleton, Wisconsin, in 1874 drawn and published by "Stoner & Vogt." Vogt was a lithographer and printer, first in Milwaukee and then in Cleveland.

5. "Yesterday we received a call from Mr. J. J. Stoner, General agent for Prof. Ruger, who presented for our inspection a handsomely executed lithograph of Prof. Ruger's sketch of Savannah" (Savannah *Morning News*, 19 February 1872). Ruger published this with a St. Louis address. Ruger also drew and published with the same address views of Atlanta, Georgia, in 1871 and Columbus, Georgia, in 1872. Stoner may have been his sales agent in these places as well.

6. Austin *Daily Democratic Statesman*, 9 January and 9 April 1873; San Antonio *Daily Herald*, 28 January and 13 February 1873.

7. *Prince Edward Island Farmer*, 20 November 1878. A year earlier both Ruger and Stoner were in New Hampshire, as was Thaddeus M. Fowler. Views by both artists were published by Ruger and Stoner, then once again associated. Stoner canvassed for subscriptions, promoted newspaper publicity, and handled other business matters for the enterprise. See, for example, Claremont *National Eagle*, 16 June, 22 and 29 September 1877; Clare-

mont *Northern Advocate*, 19 June and 3 July 1877; and Newport, New Hampshire, *Argus & Spectator*, 29 June, 10 and 24 August, 28 September, and 5 October 1877. Other newspaper accounts that mentioned Stoner's activities are cited in a forthcoming article by David Ruell on the bird's-eye lithographic views of New Hampshire.

8. I have recorded only three views by Warner: Portland, Maine, in 1876; Fenton, Michigan, in 1880; and Zeeland, Michigan, in 1907. In 1878, when Ruger was drawing Halifax, Nova Scotia, for a lithograph issued the next year, a local newspaper referred to "Mr. Joseph Warner, the gentlemanly agent for the work." Halifax *Evening Reporter*, 20 August 1878. In 1879 the Saginaw, Michigan, *Daily Courier* in its 22 August issue announced, "Mr. Joseph Warner is in the city canvassing for subscribers for a bird's eye view of East Saginaw. The artist [is] Prof. Ruger."

9. Ruger and Stoner had these views printed at Lucien Burleigh's press in Troy, New York, apparently the only time these three viewmakers combined forces. The Winston-Salem print does not have the Burleigh name on it, but it is so similar in style that its printing can be attributed to Burleigh with almost complete confidence.

Henry Walton

	N.Y.	Total
1836	2	2
1837		
1838	1	1
1839	1	1
1840	1	1
1841–		
1847	1	1
1848–		
1850	2	2
Total	8	8

48. Henry Walton (1804?–1865)

During the time that Fitz Hugh Lane produced his lithographs of New England seaports, his contemporary and possible onetime associate, Henry Walton, recorded on stone several of the small inland towns of the Finger Lakes region in upstate New York. The two men were the same age, and both learned their skills in lithography while working for the firm of William Pendleton in Boston. While Walton's paintings can scarcely bear comparison with those of Lane, the lithographic city views that each produced have much in common.

Virtually nothing is known of Walton's early life. He probably grew up in or near Saratoga Springs, New York, and as early as 1829 was drawing on stone or in the field for Pendleton.[1] He sharpened his skills as a topographic artist by doing a series of small lithographs showing street scenes and buildings in Saratoga Springs, Philadelphia, New York, and elsewhere.[2]

Whether apprenticed to Pendleton, as seems likely, or associated with the firm as a free-lance artist, Walton would doubtless have known the many artists who worked there in the early 1830s. They included Nathaniel Currier, Fitz Hugh Lane, Rembrandt Peale, David Claypoole Johnston, and John H. Bufford.[3]

It was to Bufford in 1836 that Walton took his first city view to be printed at the New York shop Bufford had established a year earlier.[4] As to Walton's whereabouts and activities from 1832, the year after his last signed work for Pendleton, to July 1836, when he drew Geneva, New York, we can only speculate.

The Geneva lithograph was Walton's only city view put on stone by another person: Eliphalet Brown, Jr., whose premises at 126 Nassau Street were only a few doors away from the Bufford press.[5] It was also the only one of his views that Walton did not publish himself. Probably he was simply paid a fee by the local booksellers who are recorded as the publishers.

In selling his first view of Ithaca (Plate 11), which he drew in 1836 but may not have distributed until the following year, Walton introduced to upstate New York a sales technique that virtually all other city view artists and publishers

followed. This involved the display of the artist's drawing or painting in some convenient place and the solicitation of subscriptions for impressions of the lithograph when they became available. Local editors normally publicized such ventures by praising the projects in their newspapers. They were prompted to do so, surely, by those responsible for the view. Implied, and many times made explicit, was the message that if a sufficient number of subscribers failed to come forward the artist would abandon the enterprise.

Walton did not invent this approach, but he must have been pleased with the favorable reception accorded his first efforts to publicize his work in this manner. Readers of an Ithaca newspaper learned of Walton's plan for a lithograph of their community when the following announcement appeared in the fall of 1836:

> VIEW OF ITHACA.—At the Bookstore of Messrs. Mack, Andrus and Woodruff, of this village, may be seen a most splendid view of Ithaca, taken by Mr. Henry Walton, a young artist of much promise, from a site selected on the east hill. . . . The view is most graphick, superbly painted, and is to be lithographed in the best manner, coloured to correspond with the original, and furnished to subscribers for $1.50 per copy. The original may be seen at the above Bookstore, where subscriptions will be received. As no copies are to be published, except for subscribers, we would recommend for those who wish to procure a copy, to enter their names without delay.[6]

Two other Ithaca views followed, the first drawn late in 1838 and published the next year after Bufford printed it, and the second done at the New York City press of Daniel S. Jenkins and made available for distribution to purchasers in 1840.[7] Walton, like a number of other artist-publishers, moved from one press to another. In addition to Bufford and Jenkins, he had views printed at the G. & W. Endicott firm and the press operated by Napoleon Sarony.

All of these printers worked in New York City. While Walton may have shipped the stones there for printing, he probably took his drawings to New York, where he put them on stone in the shop. This was the case for his Watkins Glen view of 1847. An issue of the local newspaper announced the return of the artist from New York with copies of the lithograph and stated that it "was first drawn from nature by Mr. W., who . . . retired to the city for the purpose of drawing the same on stone."[8]

Walton established a studio in Ithaca in 1838, but after his third view of the town appeared in 1840 he may have moved elsewhere. All of his subsequent city views are of places not far away in the south-central part of New York: Elmira (probably 1840), Watkins Glen (1847), Addison (probably 1850), and Painted Post (probably 1850). The substantial periods of time between views reflect the nature of his artistic career, for his paintings—chiefly portraits—far outnumber his prints.

In his depictions of towns Walton relied on what he could see from vantage points on nearby elevations. Because the region where he worked is hilly, his views resemble the later views of others who selected imaginary viewpoints and showed their subjects as if seen from the air. Walton probably did make close-up sketches of prominent buildings so that he could render their details accurately in smaller size, but he was essentially an easel artist. The images he produced would thus have been familiar to the residents of each town or city.

Sometime after completing his view of Painted Post in 1850, Walton left for California, but practically nothing is known of his life there except that he arrived in San Francisco on 18 September 1851 aboard the *Oregon*. His portrait of a miner painted in the town of Rough and Ready, California, is dated 1853. He finished his last known work of art in 1857. This is a large and attractive watercolor view of Grass Valley, California. It has a carefully lettered title and artist's name, and Walton doubtless expected it would be lithographed, but no printed version has yet been discovered.[9]

Walton died in 1865 while living in Cassopolis, Michigan. It was the year before Albert Ruger began his career by drawing several towns in the immediate vicinity and thus ushered in the great post–Civil War era of bird's-eye views. Walton would have been pleased to see the tradition he helped to establish in America thus carried on.

1. Such scraps of biographical information as exist have been gathered in Leigh Rehner, *Henry Walton: 19th Century American Artist*. Rehner follows the suggestion of Rockwell Gardiner that Walton's father was Judge Henry Walton, a major property owner in Ballston Spa and Saratoga Springs. Her exhibition catalog essay has been reprinted with some notes by John G. Brooks on Walton's Ithaca scenes in Rehner, *Henry Walton, An Early Artist*. Additional material on Walton, including statements that subsequent research indicates are erroneous or misleading, can be found in Carey, "The American Lithograph," 374–87.
2. Several of these are reproduced in Rehner's exhibit catalog, 15–21. One series is dated 1831. Another is undated but presumed to be a year earlier, and one is dated by Rehner as "ca. 1820's."
3. For Pendleton's shop and its distinguished "alumni," see David Tatham, "The Pendleton-Moore Shop—Lithographic Artists in Boston, 1825–1840," and the long note on the shop in Peters, *America on Stone*, 312–23.
4. Bufford's career is reviewed in David Tatham, "John Henry Bufford: American Lithographer."
5. Brown's address is on the lithograph. In Peters, *America on Stone*, the earliest date given for Brown is 1843–1844 when his address was 4 John Street. Bufford's address in 1836—although not appearing on the Geneva print—was 114 Nassau Street.
6. Ithaca *Journal & General Advertiser*, 12 October 1836.
7. Jenkins is the subject of a brief note in Peters, *America on Stone*, 236, where his New York address in 1840 appears as 134 Nassau Street. On the Walton view the address is printed "136 Nassau Street Cor. Beekman, N.Y."
8. Jefferson [now Watkins Glen] *Jeffersonian*, 25 December 1847.
9. The Grass Valley view is in the collection of the Society of California Pioneers in San Francisco. The portrait of the miner, William D. Peck, can be found in the Oakland Museum, Oakland, California.

49. Henry Wellge (1850–1917)

Henry Wellge ranks with the most prolific of the city view artists of America, but he remains something of an enigma biographically. He was born in Germany in 1850. The Milwaukee city directory lists him first in 1878, so if he accompanied his brother, William, to the United States seven years earlier he probably lived in some other city. The Milwaukee directories for the decade following 1878 identify him as lithographer, artist, architect, draftsman, or publisher.[1] It seems unlikely that he was "formerly captain in the engineer corps of the Russian Army," as three Nebraska newspapers described him in 1889.[2]

Whether a military figure or not, Wellge could mobilize his resources and use them to best advantage. In a viewmaking career that spanned more than three decades, he drew or published (sometimes both) more than 150 views of towns and cities in twenty-six states and the Province of Quebec. Always well drawn and printed—sometimes brilliantly so—his views of midwestern and southern cities in the decade of the 1880s provide particularly valuable records of urban conditions at a time when many other post-Civil War viewmakers had stopped work or had reduced their output.

Wellge began work in 1878, when he drew and published a view of Chilton, Wisconsin. He was then associated as co-artist and joint publisher with one J. Bach, about whom nothing is known. Wellge and Bach published views of three other Wisconsin cities the following year, beginning a series of thirty-eight lithographs of towns in that state bearing Wellge's name in one capacity or another. At least two of these early views (and probably all four) came from the newly founded printing firm of Beck & Pauli, a Milwaukee company that Wellge used almost exclusively—as did Joseph J. Stoner and many others—for printing the views he published.

In 1880 Wellge began an association with Stoner, who through 1884 published about forty of the artist's views (see Plates 31 and 75). A number of other unsigned views during these years when the two were working together can be informally attributed to Wellge on the basis of their appearance and location, publication by Stoner, and the printer's imprint of Beck & Pauli (see Plate 7). However, there are also several views with Wellge's name only signed in the stone or on the zinc plate. It is possible that some other artist drew these in the field and Wellge redrew them on the printing surface at the Beck & Pauli establishment.

Wellge apparently anticipated Stoner's retirement from view publishing after 1884. Five of the views signed by him with that date were published by the new firm of Norris & Wellge of Brockton, Massachusetts. George E. Norris lived in Brockton and a year earlier had served as the business agent and partner of Albert F. Poole, doing business as Poole & Norris in New Hampshire.[3] When the two decided to part, Wellge took Poole's place as the artist member of the new company.[4]

After Wellge and Norris had published a number of views in 1884 using Brockton, Massachusetts, as their address, Wellge evidently persuaded Norris that Milwaukee would be a better base for them. In 1885 the publisher's imprint of

	Wisc.	Queb.	Vt.	Colo.	N.M.	N.Y.	Ohio	Mich.	Minn.	Pa.	S.D.	Fla.	Mont.	N.H.	Ore.	Wash.	Ala.	Ga.	Tex.	Tenn.	Ark.	Ill.	Ind.	Iowa	Nebr.	Utah	Va.	Total
1878	1																											1
1879	3																											3
1880	2																											2
1881	3	7	1																									11
1882	1			2	1	1	1																					6
1883	2							1	4	2	3																	12
1884												1	3	6	2	6												18
1885	10											6					1	4	1									22
1886	8							5										1	5	2								21
1887	3								1			1					5	1		1	1							13
1888																			1	1	2	1	1	2				8
1889				1																		2		3	5			11
1890	1			2									1													1		5
1891													2						1							1	6	10
1892									1										1								1	3
1893–																												
1897																				1								1
1898–																												
1904													1															1
1905–																												
1907	1																											1
1908	2																											2
1909																												
1910	1																											1
Total	38	7	1	5	1	1	1	6	6	2	3	8	7	6	2	6	6	6	9	5	3	3	1	5	5	2	7	152

Norris & Wellge became Norris, Wellge & Co. of Milwaukee at 107 Wells Street.[5] That year they produced more than twenty views (see Plate 68), almost all of them signed by Wellge. They published almost as many the next year; at least two-thirds of these also bear Wellge's signature. The artist must have spent little time in Milwaukee, for communities depicted during this two-year period were located in Florida, Georgia, Alabama, Texas, Tennessee, and Michigan, as well as in Wisconsin.[6]

In 1887 Norris returned to New England, leaving Wellge in full control of the firm of Henry Wellge & Co. In that year he produced thirteen views of places in Wisconsin, Minnesota, Florida, Alabama, Georgia, Tennessee, and Arkansas. Eight views followed in 1888, including the first with the imprint of his new company established that July: The American Publishing Company.[7] Wellge's new company doubtless continued to use Beck & Pauli as its printer, for the addresses of the two firms were identical. These later Wellge lithographs, always attractively drawn and—like virtually all of Beck & Pauli's work—printed with admirable skill, became even more impressive examples of the viewmakers' art in the years after this most recent change of business names.

He issued almost all of them in a very large folio size that emphasized the horizontal dimension. They had dignified and unembellished titles and a simple ruled border. Many of these handsome lithographs were printed in multiple colors. A few, like that of Colorado Springs (Color Plate 10), were done in dramatic tones of ink that resembled oil colors. Of the thirty or so views published by Wellge under this imprint, seventeen are signed by him as artist, but he was probably responsible for several others.[8]

Except for a view of Denver, the views published in the first two years of this series all showed towns in the Midwest. Eventually, thirteen midwestern towns (see Plate 59) were depicted, together with eight communities in the mountain states of Colorado, Utah, and Montana; two cities in Texas (see Plate 70); and seven places in Virginia. It was a splendid set of prints that did much to keep alive the interest in bird's-eye city views.

Wellge produced only a few later lithographs, none of them under the imprint of his own company, although it remained in business until 1902. For the American Art Co. of Milwaukee he drew Chattanooga, Tennessee, in 1897.[9] In 1904 he drew and published a view of Billings, Montana; he added Chippewa Falls, Wisconsin, in 1907 to the long list of communities in that state he had depicted; and he did the same for Madison in 1908. Other publishers brought out his last two recorded views: Milwaukee in 1908 and the twin ports of Superior, Wisconsin, and Duluth, Minnesota, in 1910.

1. For the scraps of information about Wellge as a person I am relying entirely on Beckman, *Milwaukee Illustrated*, notes for exhibit item 48, and some additional material in the manuscript of a conference paper by Beckman.

2. Lincoln *Daily Nebraska State Journal*, 2 June 1889; Norfolk *Daily*

News, 15 June 1889; and Fremont *Weekly Herald,* 4 July 1889. All of these accounts contain wild exaggerations, no doubt originated for publicity purposes by Wellge's American Publishing Company's agent, Charles J. Smith, who let his imagination soar for the benefit of the frontier press. The Fremont paper, for example, stated, "Some 20,000 copies [of the view] are to be struck off and delivered next fall." The Lincoln paper gave the same number, while the Norfolk paper more conservatively stated that the edition would "be from ten to twenty thousand." A fictional rank and glamorous military background ascribed to the artist and company head may have been part of Smith's sales promotion campaign. However, Wellge had unmistakable artistic abilities, and it is at least conceivable that he learned his trade while in military service. It is also possible that Smith or the newspapers may have mistakenly used *Russian* instead of *Prussian.* If Wellge did indeed have a military background, it seems doubtful that it would have been acquired while in the service of the Czar.

3. There are several New Hampshire newspaper accounts from 1883 similar to the following from the Ashland *Advance,* 22 September 1883: "Mr. George E. Norris, of the firm of Poole & Norris, publishers of artistic bird's eye views of cities, towns and buildings . . . of Brockton, Mass., has been in town securing subscribers for a bird's eye view of Plymouth."

4. Wellge and Poole knew each other, for their names appear as co-artists on views of Lake Geneva, Wisconsin, in 1882 and Kalamazoo, Michigan, in 1883, both published by J. J. Stoner.

5. In their second year in Milwaukee the firm moved to 205 2d Street.

6. One of the views of 1885—St. Augustine, Florida—has the publisher's name as Norris, Wellge, & Swift, Brockton, Mass.

7. Beckman, *Milwaukee Illustrated,* states, "In addition to Henry Wellge, incorporators of the American Publishing Co. were his brother William and, as secretary and treasurer, Alfred E. von Cotzhausen. Wellge's business address since 1886 had been that of the Beck & Pauli Lithographing Co., of which von Cotzhausen was also secretary and treasurer."

8. The unsigned views issued by the American Publishing Company are all dated 1890 or later: Pueblo and Colorado Springs, Colorado; Ogden, Utah; Duluth, Minnesota; Helena, Great Falls, and Missoula, Montana; Beloit, Wisconsin; Laredo, Texas; and Buena Vista, Newport News, Roanoke, Staunton, and Waynesboro, Virginia. There is also a large, unsigned view of Houston, Texas, in 1891 that lacks a publisher's imprint. In size and style it closely resembles the American Publishing Company's lithographs of Ft. Worth in 1891 and Laredo in 1892.

9. The American Fine Art Co. was headed by Alfred E. von Cotzhausen, secretary and treasurer of both Wellge's company and Beck & Pauli. Its address was also the same as the other two.

50. Edwin Whitefield (1816–1892)

Whitefield came to the United States from England about 1837. Information about his early years in this country is fragmentary. He evidently worked as an agent for *Godey's Lady's Book* in 1838, and that year and the next he was in Troy, New York, and Baltimore, Maryland. His first diary entry in January 1842 records that he was spending "most of the time in teaching, and occasionally practicing a little at lithography." [1]

For several years Whitefield supplemented his income from teaching by drawing and painting flowers, estates, and other Hudson River scenes. Some of his watercolors of flowers provided the basis for lithographic illustrations in *American Wildflowers in Their Native Haunts,* a book by Emma C. Embury published in 1845. It was that year that Whitefield issued his first city views, drawing and publishing two large lithographic prints of Albany (Plate 13) and Troy. Lewis & Brown of New York City printed both, and the Albany drawing may have been put on stone by one of the firm's lithographers. On the Troy view, however, Whitefield signed his name on the stone, and on almost all of the later prints one can find some variety of the imprint line from his Newburgh, New York, view of 1846: "From Nature & on Stone by E. Whitefield."

Whitefield energetically promoted sales of his lithographs by obtaining favorable newspaper reviews of his drawings when he displayed them in each town to secure subscriptions for prints that would be delivered later. He also employed agents to help him with the business side of viewmaking. They included the Smith brothers and James T. Palmatary, who soon learned enough from this experience to launch their own enterprises and become rival artists and publishers.

Whitefield established himself as the first American lithographic viewmaker who saw his potential market as being national rather than local. By 1852 he had drawn and published thirty-four views of places in New York (see Plate 50), Pennsylvania, New Jersey, Maryland, Massachusetts, Rhode Island, Maine, Connecticut, Ohio, and Quebec. He moved on to Canada, doing additional views of towns in the provinces of Quebec (see Color Plate 1) and Ontario (see Plate 2). A view of Galena, Illinois, six prints of Chicago, and four of places in Minnesota, where he settled for a time, rounded out his pre–Civil War years as an artist of cities.

After the war he returned to the East to settle in Massachusetts. Toward the end of his life he drew several city views, but only two appeared as lithographs. Sepia photographs of the others exist, and apparently Whitefield sold these photographs instead of printed versions. He also did the illustrations for his *Homes of Our Forefathers*—a volume showing old and important buildings in New England—and he continued to draw and paint. By the end of his life he had produced just under sixty lithographed views of towns and cities in twelve states and territories and two Canadian provinces.

In nearly all of these urban scenes Whitefield followed the traditions of landscape painting, displaying his cities as seen from some advantageous viewpoint atop a hill or, like the four of Philadelphia, from the steeple of Independence Hall. The quality of his work improved with time and experience. His earliest views, like those of Albany, Troy, and Buffalo, are flat and unconvincing. The Canadian views done in 1852–1854 show far greater skill in both the mechanics of linear perspective and the manner in which Whitefield used his artistic skills to create effective compositions.

In the 1870s Whitefield adopted the prevailing technique of delineating cities by using a bird's-eye or high-level perspective for his lithographs of Dedham and Quincy, Massachusetts (Plate 35). These are curiously spare, linear prints that have an almost maplike quality. His sketchbook for the Quincy view has survived (Plate 36), and from this it is possible to understand how city view artists assembled the material used in preparing their drawings. His diaries—even with their mysterious gaps and excisions—also provide rare insights into the problems and the life of an itinerant artist.

Some critics find his views lacking in appeal. One early student of historic American lithographs summarized Whitefield's contributions in these unflattering words:

> In general, all that can be said of his lithographs is that they are technically proficient, factually rendered, making them the examples of truthfulness of the period. This factual documenting of a spot, a street, or a town sometimes utterly devoid of humans or human habitation and therefore lacking in a sense of scale, are at times as cold as yesterday's potatoes. [2]

	N.Y.	Ohio	Pa.	N.J.	Md.	Mass.	R.I.	Maine	Conn.	Del.	Queb.	Ont.	Ill.	Minn.	Total
1845	2														2
1846	6	1	2												9
1847	2			1	1										4
1848		1				2									3
1849						2	2	1	1						6
1850	1		2			1									4
1851				1											1
1852	2									1	2				5
1853				1											1
1854											1	2			3
1855											2	4			6
1856													1		1
1857														1	1
1858														3	3
1859															
1860													1		1
1861													5		5
1862															
1863													1		1
1864–															
1866						1									1
1867–															
1876						1									1
1877						1									1
Total	13	2	4	3	1	8'	2	1	1	1	5	6	8	4	59

This appraisal seems too harsh, although few, if any, would argue that Whitefield's artistic abilities exceeded mere competence. Historians, however, place a greater emphasis on the capacity to document than do art critics, and in this respect Whitefield's contributions are not inconsiderable.

Many of the cities he drew were also depicted only a few years later by his former agents, the Smith brothers, or by artists retained by them. Most of these later urban portraits showed their subjects from a higher angle of view. Taken together, these pairs of lithographs created by Whitefield and by those who came after him provide revealing glimpses of the major centers of urban America before the Civil War and rapid industrialization changed their appearance so substantially.

1. This quotation and most of my information about Whitefield, his career, and accomplishments come from Norton, *Edwin Whitefield*. The diary entry is on p. 16. See also two other works by Norton: "Edwin Whitefield, 1816–1892" and "Sketching America: The New York Public Library's Sketchbook of the Nineteenth-Century American Artist and Traveler Edwin Whitefield." I have also examined Whitefield's scrapbook of newspaper clippings and notes in the Boston Public Library and, from a private collection, Whitefield's sketchbook for his view of Quincy, Massachusetts, in 1877.

2. Carey, "The American Lithograph," 399.

51. John Caspar Wild (–1846)

Wild was born in or near Zurich, Switzerland. He came to France as a young man, became an artist, and lived in Paris for fifteen years. He specialized in townscapes and painted panoramas of both Venice and Paris. Friedrich Salathe used the latter painting for his aquatint view of the city. For some reason Wild decided to leave Europe and about 1831 arrived in Philadelphia, where he was described by the editor of the *Saturday Courier*, Andrew M'Makin, as "an artist whose skill in sketching, drawing upon stone, and particularly his great proficiency in coloring, attracted considerable attention." [1]

In 1835 Wild went to Cincinnati, where he began work on a series of paintings that he intended to have lithographed. He abandoned this project and returned to Philadelphia in 1837 to carry out his plans for a set of views of that city, where he had already painted several scenes. Wild joined forces with J. B. Chevalier and, with the help and publicity provided by the *Saturday Courier*, they issued the first of twenty projected lithographs showing individual structures or streets of Philadelphia. Wild drew from nature and also put his drawings on lithographic stones. Customers could purchase these prints in groups of four as they appeared or, after all had been published, bound in book form.

In August 1838, Wild published what can be regarded as his first complete city view. This consisted of four prints showing Philadelphia as seen from the steeple of the statehouse looking north, east, south, and west. Then, for reasons that probably never will be known, Wild abruptly left Philadelphia. He disposed of the stones for his four-sheet panorama to J. T. Bowen, who promptly reissued them before the end of the year.

By that time or shortly thereafter Wild may have arrived

in St. Louis, for the following spring a newspaper there announced the publication of "a very neatly colored lithographic drawing of St. Louis, as seen from the opposite shore. The lithographic work was executed by Mr. Dupre's well known establishment; where the sketch was drawn and colored by Mr. J. C. Wild."[2]

By the fall of 1840 Wild had completed a series of eight St. Louis lithographs (see Plate 8), four of which can be classified as city views, although one is an extended street vista rather than a depiction of the city as a whole. Wild printed a title page for the set, but doubtless he sold individual prints. Probably, too, he hand colored each print, a task he accomplished with great skill and taste.[3]

John Caspar Wild

	Pa.	Ill.	Mo.	Iowa	Total
1838	4				4
1839	1		1		2
1840		1	4		5
1841		6	10		16
1842–					
1844				3	3
1845					
1846			2		2
Total	5	7	17	3	32

Still obsessed by the idea of illustrations bound in sets, Wild set to work on a new project: views of the major towns along the Mississippi River. He began publication of these views in July 1841, with the first set of lithographs accompanied by letterpress descriptive text. By May 1842 he had issued all nine parts.[4]

These views provide extremely valuable graphic records of several communities whose appearance we would know little about except for Wild's lithographs. They include Alton, Cahokia, Kaskaskia, Cairo, and East St. Louis, Illinois; and Carondelet, St. Charles, and Selma, Missouri. Because they are all so obviously unflattering, it seems likely that Wild drew these little towns with as much accuracy as he was capable.

The year 1841 also saw the publication of a panorama of St. Louis by Wild that closely resembled in style his earlier set of four Philadelphia views. This four-sheet view provides a detailed record of conditions in the metropolis of the mid-Mississippi valley, and it widens our understanding of the character of this outpost of urban culture just before the Mexican War, the California Gold Rush, and the opening of territories beyond the Missouri River substantially changed its appearance.

In 1844 and 1845 Wild traveled north of St. Louis to draw and paint several other smaller but important river ports. Four large and attractively printed and colored lithographs resulted of Galena, Illinois; Dubuque and Muscatine, Iowa; and one including Fort Armstrong on Rock Island, Davenport, Iowa, and Rock Island and Moline, Illinois. The Muscatine print, titled *Bloomington, Iowa*, is outstanding. It displays the town as it would have been seen by someone arriving on a river steamer, with the buidings of the town silhouetted against the sky.[5]

Wild lived an unhappy life. A companion in his last year described him as a person who "had neither humor of his own, nor an appreciation of humor in others. He looked tragedy, thought tragedy, and his conversation outside of business and art, was never much more cheerful than tragedy." He looked the part: "He was a tall spare man of about forty years, with long raven black hair, whiskers and moustache, and restless brown eyes. He had, at times a worn and haggard look, the result, doubtless, of ill health, and a life-long battle with the world for the bare means of subsistence." Wild never won that battle, but in Davenport, Iowa, in 1846, as this sympathetic and admiring observer described the end of the artist's fatal illness, "kind hands softened the last shadowy pencilings of his life, and laid him gently among the Summer flowers."[6]

1. Philadelphia *Saturday Courier*, 1 August 1835, as quoted in John Francis McDermott, "John Caspar Wild: Some New Facts and a Query." I have drawn on this article, on an earlier and longer one by McDermott, "J. C. Wild, Western Painter and Lithographer," and on Martin P. Snyder, "J. C. Wild and His Philadelphia Views." Snyder provides full entries for Wild's Philadelphia prints and cites sources for Wild's European years. Biographical and personal descriptions of Wild appear in [A. H. Sanders], "Artistic," in Franc B. Wilkie, *Davenport Past and Present*, 307–10. There is a brief description of Wild's Illinois prints in Betty I. Madden, *Art, Crafts, and Architecture in Early Illinois*, 213–15. Wild may have been related to the Wild whose name appears as publisher of several lithographs issued about 1850 in Paris showing such American cities as New York, San Francisco, Sacramento, and New Orleans. At least two addresses for the Wild publishing firm appear on these prints: 15 rue de la Banque, Place de la Bourse; and 36 passage du Saumon.

2. St. Louis *Daily Evening Gazette*, 29 April 1839, as quote in McDermott, "J. C. Wild," 113.

3. I have looked at the bound set in the Missouri Historical Society, St. Louis. Each view is exquisitely colored, some of them dramatically so. McDermott, in "J. C. Wild," mentions what must be an equally handsome set owned in 1951 by Stratford Lee Morton of St. Louis.

4. McDermott, "J. C. Wild," 117–20, provides the dates when each part appeared. The complete set has been reproduced in facsimile with editorial comments. See J. C. Wild, *The Valley of the Mississippi Illustrated in a Series of Views*.

5. An impression at the Yale University Art Gallery is superbly colored, probably by Wild.

6. [Sanders], "Artistic," 308–10.

Part III

The Catalog

Introduction to the Catalog

The entries in this catalog record the significant features of separately issued lithographs showing all or major parts of towns and cities in the United States and Canada. Entries also list one or more institutions where views can be found and provide cross-references to other catalogs or checklists identifying the same view. The views include ground-level and moderately elevated panoramas as well as the more numerous bird's-eye perspectives. The catalog thus excludes wood engravings, etchings, aquatints, and metal-plate engravings; scenes of individual buildings or streets; and book, magazine, and atlas illustrations.

There are some borderline cases included in the catalog that do not fall clearly within the broadly stated criteria just described. Some views, otherwise clearly meeting these guidelines, originally appeared within paper covers accompanied by one or more pages of text following a title page. Other lithographs were separately printed, issued in a series over a period of several months, and, although only groups of buildings or street scenes appear on each print, as a whole they convey as much information about the place depicted as a single citywide bird's-eye view or panorama. Also included in the catalog are a small number of views drawn by artists who in their early years used lithography for their work but turned to the gravure process for some or all of their later prints.[1]

Every full entry in the catalog consists of twelve headings, although not every entry contains information under every heading. Entries appear in the following form:

Number
Place
Date
Title
Size
Artist
Lithographer
Printer

Publisher
Key/Vignettes/Misc
Locations
Catalogs/Checklists

Shorter cross-reference entries are also used for purposes described below.

The arrangement of the entries is alphabetical by name of U.S. states and Canadian provinces, with Washington, D.C., alphabetized as District of Columbia. Within these main groups, the entries appear in alphabetical order by name of the place depicted. Names are alphabetized to the first mark of punctuation or the first word break, so that Hudson would precede Hudson Falls, South Manchester would precede Southington, and New York would precede Newburgh. City names beginning with *Mac* or *Mc* are alphabetized as spelled, so that Macalester would precede Mansfield, while McAlester would follow it. When there are two or more views of one place, the entries are in chronological order beginning with the earliest recorded view and ending with undated views.

In most cases the information found after each of the entry headings is self-explanatory. However, the following full description of the guidelines used in preparing entries should be read by those with more than a casual interest in the prints herein recorded.

No catalog of materials so varied as these views can be entirely free from inconsistencies, ambiguities, or errors. These can arise from a variety of causes, which are summarized and discussed in footnotes attached to the descriptions of how each entry heading was prepared.

Number. Each full entry is assigned a number reflecting its position in the alphabetical order of the catalog.[2]

Place. Under this heading is given the modern name of the place depicted. Usually this is the same as the place identified in the title. If more than one name appears in the title, a full entry is given only for the place named first. Other places named in the title are given as cross-reference entries. A cross-reference entry is also used for the principal name in the title if it is no longer current.[3]

Date. This is the date of publication. It is not necessarily

---

1. Not all partial views issued as part of a series are recorded herein. Excluded are such prints showing only single buildings within the community in question or landscape features outside it. Most of the gravure prints were the work of A. F. Poole. T. M. Fowler also drew and published a few in this medium. Their inclusion in the catalog cannot be defended very strongly on logical grounds, and there may well be entries for other views printed in some medium other than lithography. The ability to distinguish one type of print from another is not a characteristic often found among those charged with the responsibilities for print collections in the hundreds of small historical societies and libraries responding to questionnaires sent by the cataloger. A few wood engravings, aquatints, line etchings, or engravings thus may have been reported in the belief they were lithographs. In the nineteenth century, a dozen or more now-abandoned methods of printmaking enjoyed momentary popularity. Some shared one or more features in common with lithographic printing, and it would not be surprising if the catalog entries included a few examples of heliotypes, ambrotypes, albertypes, electrotypes, or one of the other "types" promoted by ingenious printers and inventors.

2. Because a large number of the prints recorded in the catalog represent multiple images of cities, the date of publication determines the order of these entries and their sequence in the numbering system. As will be discussed below, the dating of many prints is conjectural, while for others no date whatsoever has been determined. Subsequent research, therefore, will doubtless reveal inconsistencies in the assigned numbers.

3. Obviously, not all obsolete place names have been identified. Other inconsistencies may exist because some communities depicted in views were later annexed to adjoining municipalities. In these cases full entries may appear under that subsequent name. Cross-reference entries to the older place name will lead to the desired entry.

the date of depiction, although in most cases the two dates are not more than one year apart. On many prints the date appears either in the title or as part of the copyright. If the date does not appear on the print but is known from other sources, it is shown in brackets.

Approximate dates are preceded by *Ca.* A print lacking a date and without enough information to assign one is designated *N.D.* Periods in which an undated print must have been published appear within brackets. Probable but not certain periods are followed by a question mark. In some cases, a probable decade is given. A question mark by itself indicates that the print may or may not have a date but that this is unknown to the cataloger. Finally, for some undated prints it has been possible to assign either the earliest or the latest date when it could have been published. This designation is also placed within square brackets.

Many views exist in more than one state—that is, impressions printed from the same stone or plate but differing because of additions, deletions, or changes made to the printing surface by the artist or lithographer. Variant states, where they have been identified, are distinguished by the word *State* under the date, followed by a Roman numeral. [4]

Title. After this heading appears the full title exactly as spelled and punctuated on the print. No attempt has been made to reproduce precisely the use of upper- and lower-case letters as they may have appeared on the lithograph. Because many titles were lettered in two or more lines, commas and periods were often omitted. This explains apparently erroneous or awkward transcriptions of titles showing two or more words in sequence that normally would be separated by punctuation marks. A few very long titles have been terminated by ellipses. [5]

Size. Vertical dimensions are shown first, followed by horizontal. They are given to the nearest sixteenth of an inch, followed by (in parentheses) the metric equivalent in centimeters. Since the information comes from a variety of sources and prints themselves are subject to shrinkage and expansion, the exact size of any single impression may vary from those indicated.

Much greater apparent variation may result from the manner in which prints are measured. Measurements made for this catalog are of the entire printed surface, including decorative borders, vignettes, titles, imprint information, and any other inked images made by the press. Some of the dimensions, however, are taken from older catalogs or were reported by curators using a system of measurement excluding all printed matter beyond the inner neat line of the principal view.

The parenthetical designations *cropped, matted,* or *framed* sometimes appear after one dimension or the entire entry. These indicate that the impression measured had some portion of its image concealed or missing; the size shown therefore indicates only the minimum dimensions of what could be a larger image. The designations *photo* or *facsimile* following the dimensions indicate that the dimensions were measured not from an original impression but from a derivative image. The sizes shown in such cases may vary substantially from those of the originals. [6]

Artist. The name of the artist is recorded as it appears on the print. If the print is unsigned but the identity of the artist has been established, the name appears within brackets. A probable but not certain identity is indicated by a question mark following a bracketed name. Brackets are also used to set off supplied letters to complete an unfamiliar name when only initials or a last name appear on the print. The absence of any information under this heading normally means that the print is unsigned, but, as is true for other headings in an entry, it may also indicate lack of information. [7]

Lithographer. The lithographer is the person who put the artist's drawing on stone or zinc. His name is given as it appears on the print. For many lithographs published before the Civil War, the artist served as lithographer. This is indicated by some version of the phrase *From Nature and on Stone by* preceding the name of the artist-lithographer.

It is important to note that in the nineteenth century the words *Lith of* or *Lith by,* followed by the name of a person or (more commonly) a company, usually indicated that this person or firm had printed the view. The person or firm thus indicated might also have served as the lithographer, but in

4. Unless there is evidence to the contrary, the date appearing in the title of the print has been accepted as the date of publication except where the copyright date (if present) differs. Firm dates of publication assigned to undated prints come mainly from contemporary newspaper notices or (less commonly) from newspaper advertisements. Many of the approximate dates were assigned by local historical societies and reported to the cataloger. Others have been assigned by the cataloger on the basis of imprint addresses of printers and publishers and known dates when these addresses were used. A number of dates with question marks are derived from a study of maps showing for each year the locations of the towns depicted by individual viewmakers. In identifying variant states and assigning numbers to them, the cataloger has generally followed the designations used in previous catalogs. Additional states have been designated only where there is no doubt that the same stone or plate was used for all states with only minor variations. In the case of the Kuchel & Dresel views of California, the cataloger felt it was premature to assign state numbers, although many variant states have been otherwise identified by details appearing in the entries.

5. Although every effort was made to reproduce titles as originally spelled, abbreviated, and punctuated, this catalog reflects the inability of many print curators to refrain from correcting spelling, completing abbreviations, and adding modern punctuation when recording print titles and reporting them as thus altered to others. Users of this catalog finding that titles given herein do not correspond exactly with a known print should not, therefore, assume that variant impressions exist, although this may be so. Some prints were issued as part of a series with a series title usually placed above and centered on the view. In almost all cases this has been omitted unless essential to distinguish the print from another that is otherwise identical.

6. Because most prints were produced in horizontal formats with titles at the bottom, measurements taken only of the view itself will be substantially smaller in their vertical dimensions than those made of the entire printed surface. Horizontal dimensions taken in the two ways described are more likely to correspond. There are several prints known only through their listing in Harry T. Peters, *California on Stone.* Peters did not give exact dimensions, and this catalog uses his size classifications of *small, medium,* or *large* for entries derived only from his book. A few other dimensions are preceded by *Ca.* These approximate sizes come from reports compiled by those unable for one reason or another to supply more precise information, or they were used by the cataloger for one or more other prints of a series when dimensions of at least one in the series were known.

7. Corporate or partnership names appear on many prints, including those stated to have been drawn by "O. H. Bailey & Co.," "E. Sachse & Co.," "Kuchel & Dresel," and "H. H. Rowley & Co." The address of the artist is not given even if it appears on the print. The majority of the city views were drawn by itinerant artists. Their addresses appeared rarely and when they did were frequently only the name of the city depicted.

this catalog the name is entered after the printer heading unless another printer is clearly identified on the lithograph. [8]

Printer. This heading is followed by the name of the printer as it appears on the lithograph, followed by any address that may be present. Abbreviations of cities and states (or provinces) are used as shown on the print. Because some of these are unclear, material within brackets has been added where necessary. Where no address is given on the print but the city and state or province of the printer is known, this information has been added within brackets. [9]

Publisher. The entry records the name of the publisher as it appears on the lithograph, followed by any address that may be present. The same rules stated above for printers apply. An entry under *publisher* followed by *(copyright)* indicates that no other person or firm is identified as publisher and that the person or firm identified entered the copyright claim for the print as indicated on its imprint. [10]

Key/Vignettes/Misc. This heading encompasses several features common to many prints and a variety of less standardized elements found on others. *Key* refers to any legend, identification system, or list of community officials, professionals, places of business or manufacture, public buildings, churches, topographic features, or other aspects of the place or its residents. If these keys are designated by numbers or letters, this feature is identified through the use of the abbreviation *Refs.,* followed by the first and last numbers or letters of any series or by individual numbers or letters if the references are not arranged serially.

A typical entry under this heading might appear as *Refs. 1–22, A–H, J–N, P.* If the print has a numbered or lettered key but the numbers or letters used are not known, only the abbreviation *Refs.* appears. If the number of references is known, however, it is given before the abbreviation *Refs.* For many legends or keys the designation *Unnumbered business directory* is used where appropriate. Other entries in this field referring to similar features on lithographs should be self-explanatory. [11]

Vignettes refers to any border or inset view appearing on the sheet with the principal view. Where known, the number of these separate and smaller images appears before the word *vignettes.* The use of the word by itself indicates that the lithograph has one or more vignettes but the number is not known. [12]

Finally, under this heading will appear any miscellaneous feature that cannot appropriately be entered anywhere else. The word *description* is perhaps the most commonly used and refers to any descriptive text, real or fanciful, and of any length. *Advertisements* refers to any commercial announcements about products sold or services offered that may appear on the lithograph. Usually these are located around the borders of the print. Other entries used should be self-explanatory.

Locations. Institutions holding one or more impressions of the print represented by the entry are identified here. Institutions holding three or more different lithographic city views in their collections are identified by a lettered code. A list of the codes and the names and locations of the corresponding institutions appears following this introduction. Institutions reporting only one or two views are identified with full name and location.

The entry *Private Collection* is used for views for which no institutional holding can be verified but which are known to be in at least one private collection. The entry *Unknown* indicates that no original impression has been located in either a private or an institutional collection. These views are known from their listing in sales or auction catalogs, their descriptions in reference works, or their presence in the sales rooms of print shops. *Unknown* is usually followed by a brief note indicating the source of the information about the print's existence and its features. Almost always, the absence of a note indicates that the source of information is the catalog or checklist cited in the heading immediately following.

The use of *(photo)* or *(facsimile)* following a location indicates that the institution does not have an original impression in its collection but rather a photographic or printed copy. Not all such derivative images have been recorded. However, in all cases where the Library of Congress or the Public Archives of Canada holds no original impression but does have a photographic or facsimile copy, an appropriate parenthetical entry appears. [13]

8. Far fewer prints provide the name of the lithographer than they do the names of the artists, printers, or publishers. This is particularly true of the mass of city views issued after the Civil War. With few exceptions, the artists then apparently did not put their own designs on stone or zinc. The major printing firms specializing in city views, such as Beck & Pauli in Milwaukee, employed lithographers for this purpose. Occasionally one can find the lithographer's initials in the body of the print, but usually not even these appear. Apparently, this task was regarded as a mechanical one and as inappropriate for recognition on the lithograph. As with corporate or partnership designations of artists, joint or corporate names for lithographers can also be found.

9. Entries under this heading and the one to follow showing the publisher may be misleading because of erroneous, incomplete, or edited information reported to the cataloger. The propensity of many curators to spell out material found abbreviated on the prints is as frustrating as it is understandable. A user of this catalog should jump to no conclusions about finding a hitherto unrecorded variant state of a view because the catalog gives the printer's address as *Milwaukee, Wisc.* while the print in hand reads *Milwaukee, Wis.*

10. The copyright claimant was not necessarily the publisher, for there are a number of prints identifying the publisher but with a different person named as having entered the copyright.

11. Artists and publishers often tried to avoid confusion by omitting numbers or letters with similar appearance that could be mistaken for one another in the body of the print. Thus, if the number *1* was used, an upper case *I* might not be. Such omissions may not have been noted by everyone reporting this feature to the cataloger. For many of the large folio Currier &

Ives city views and some others as well, the entry might include a designation such as *86 refs. on 9 lines.* In a few cases this is virtually the only way in which one state of a view can be distinguished from another.

12. The presence or absence of vignettes and—where present—their number often distinguish one state of a view from another. The counting of vignettes, like the measurement of a view or the recording of its legend, is subject to normal human error. Moreover, those reporting information for this catalog might have been uncertain about counting such decorative items as portraits, seals, crests, tables of statistics, and other nontypical features appearing on some lithographs.

13. In some instances a date, or dimension, or some other feature of a print as reported to the cataloger by an institution differs significantly from information obtained from other sources concerning what otherwise seems to be the identical print. The anomalous feature has been noted within parentheses following the institutional code. The majority of the prints for which no institutional holding has been verified are known through their appearance in the catalogs or the sales rooms of The Old Print Shop, New York, New York. Information about titles, other imprint material, legends, and vignettes for many of those prints appearing in shop catalogs has been

Catalogs/Checklists. A code, the name of the author, or the name of the author and a brief title are used to identify collection or exhibition catalogs, checklists, exhibition handlists, reference works, or other printed sources listing, describing, or noting the existence of the print represented by the catalog entry. This is followed by the appropriate number or a page reference indicating where the view is illustrated or described. The absence of a number indicates an unnumbered or an unpaged publication. Full bibliographic citations are given for these codes or short titles at the end of this introduction.[14]

obtained through examination of the negatives made for catalog illustration purposes.

14. Occasional departures in these catalog/checklist entries from dimensions or other features as recorded herein have been noted in parentheses where the discrepancies are judged to be significant enough to suggest the existence of a possible variant state.

Abbreviations of Locations

AAS-W	American Antiquarian Society, Worcester, Massachusetts
ACMW-FW	Amon Carter Museum of Western Art, Fort Worth, Texas
AHM-A	Aurora Historical Museum, Aurora, Illinois
AHS-A	Androscoggin Historical Society, Auburn, Maine
AIHA-A	Albany Institute of History and Art, Albany, New York
AO-T	Archives of Ontario, Toronto, Ontario
BA	Boston Athenaeum, Boston, Massachusetts
BAPL-B	Bangor Public Library, Bangor, Maine
BCHS-B	Broome County Historical Society, Binghamton, New York
BDPL-D	Burton Collection, Detroit Public Library, Detroit, Michigan
BECH-B	Buffalo and Erie County Historical Society, Buffalo, New York
BHSP-T	Bureau of Historic Sites and Properties, Division of Archives, History and Records Management, Department of State, Tallahassee, Florida
BMFA	Boston Museum of Fine Arts, Boston, Massachusetts
BML-H	Bishop Museum Library, Honolulu, Hawaii
BM-NY	The Brooklyn Museum, Brooklyn, New York
BPL-P	Print Department, Boston Public Library, Boston, Massachusetts
BPL-R	Rare Book Department, Boston Public Library, Boston, Massachusetts
BS-B	Bostonian Society, Boston, Masachusetts
BYU-P	Lee Library, Brigham Young University, Provo, Utah
CAA-C	Carolina Art Association, Charleston, South Carolina
CAM-C	Cincinnati Art Museum, Cincinnati, Ohio
CCHM-P	Clinton County Historical Museum, Plattsburgh, New York
CCHS-C	Camden County Historical Society, Camden, New Jersey
CCHS-CO	Cortland County Historical Society, Cortland, New York
CCHS-E	Chemung County Historical Society, Elmira, New York
CCHS-S	Clark County Historical Society, Springfield, Ohio
CHS-C	Chicago Historical Society, Chicago, Illinois
CHS-H	Connecticut Historical Society, Hartford, Connecticut
CHS-SF	California Historical Society, San Francisco, California
CLP-P	Carnegie Library of Pittsburgh, Pennsylvania Division, Pittsburgh, Pennsylvania
CM-C	The Charleston Museum, Charleston, South Carolina
CM-S	The Canal Museum, Syracuse, New York
CMU-MP	Clarke Historical Library, Central Michigan University, Mount Pleasant, Michigan
COHS	Cincinnati Historical Society, Cincinnati, Ohio
CPL-AM	Art and Music Division, Cincinnati, Ohio, Public Library
CPL-C	Chicago Public Library, Special Collections, Cultural Center, Chicago, Illinois
CPL-R	Cincinnati Public Library, Rare Books Division, Cincinnati, Ohio
CSHS-D	Colorado State Historical Society, Denver, Colorado
CSL-H	Connecticut State Library, Hartford, Connecticut
CSL-S	California State Library, Sacramento, California
CSNY-S	Canal Society of New York State, Syracuse, New York
CVM-EC	Chippewa Valley Museum, Eau Claire, Wisconsin
DCL-H	Dartmouth College Library, Hanover, New Hampshire
DHM-D	Dartmouth Heritage Museum, Dartmouth, Nova Scotia
DHR-D	Delaware Hall of Records, Dover, Delaware
DRT-SA	Library, Daughters of the Republic of Texas, San Antonio
DSFM-D	Danbury Scott-Fanton Museum and Historical Society, Inc., Danbury, Connecticut
DU-H	Dalhousie University, Halifax, Nova Scotia
DWHS-I	DeWitt Historical Society of Tompkins County, Inc., Ithaca, New York
EHS-E	Enfield Historical Society, Inc., Enfield, Connecticut
EI-S	Essex Institute, Salem, Massachusetts
EPL-B	Enoch Pratt Free Library, Baltimore, Maryland
EWHS-S	Eastern Washington State Historical Society, Spokane, Washington
FAM-R	William A. Farnsworth Library and Art Museum, Rockland, Maine
FC-L	Filson Club, Louisville, Kentucky
FL-P	Free Library of Philadelphia, Philadelphia, Pennsylvania
FSU-T	Robert Manning Strozier Library, Florida State University, Tallahassee, Florida
GCHS-W	Gloucester County Historical Society Library, Woodbury, New Jersey
GHS-S	Georgia Historical Society, Savannah, Georgia
GRPM-GR	Grand Rapids Public Museum, Grand Rapids, Michigan
HCHS-H	Herkimer County Historical Society, Herkimer, New York
HCHS-LL	Houghton County Historical Society, Lake Linden, Michigan
HEHL	Henry E. Huntington Library, San Marino, California
HHM-FA	Hoard Historical Museum, Fort Atkinson, Wisconsin
HHS-H	Hawaiian Historical Society, Honolulu, Hawaii
HLDS-SL	Historical Department, Church of Jesus Christ of Latter-Day Saints, Salt Lake City, Utah
HNM-B	Homestead National Monument, Beatrice, Nebraska
HNOC-NO	The Historic New Orleans Collection, New Orleans, Louisiana
HSD-W	Historical Society of Delaware, Wilmington, Delaware
HSL-H	Hawaii State Library, Honolulu, Hawaii
HSMW-M	Historical Society of Middletown and the Wallkill Precinct, Inc., Middletown, New York
HSP-P	Historical Society of Pennsylvania, Philadelphia, Pennsylvania
HSQA-Q	Historical Socity of Quincy and Adams County, Quincy, Illinois
HSWP-P	Historical Society of Western Pennsylvania, Pittsburgh, Pennsylvania
HSYC-Y	Historical Society of York County, York, Pennsylvania
IHS-I	Indiana Historical Society, Indianapolis, Indiana

ISHL-S	Illinois State Historical Library, Springfield, Illinois
ISHS-B	Idaho State Historical Society, Boise, Idaho
ISHS-I	Iowa State Historical Society, Iowa City, Iowa
ISL-I	Indiana State Library, Indianapolis, Indiana
JWGL-B	John Work Garrett Library of The Johns Hopkins University, Baltimore, Maryland
KC-G	Knox College, Galesburg, Illinois
KCPL-KC	Kansas City Public Library, Kansas City, Missouri
KSHS-T	Kansas State Historical Society, Topeka, Kansas
KUL-L	Kansas University Library, Lawrence, Kansas
LAHS-L	Lansingburgh Historical Society, Lansingburgh, New York
LCHM-L	La Porte County Historical Museum, La Porte, Indiana
LCHS-L	Lebanon County Historical Society, Lebanon, Pennsylvania
LC-M	Geography and Map Division, Library of Congress, Washington, D.C.
LCM-E	Lane County Museum, Eugene, Oregon
LCO-P	The Library Company of Philadelphia, Philadelphia, Pennsylvania
LC-P	Division of Prints and Photographs, Library of Congress, Washington, D.C.
LC-R	Division of Rare Books, Library of Congress, Washington, D.C.
LHS-L	Lowell Historical Society, Lowell, Massachusetts
LIHS-B	Long Island Historical Society, Brooklyn, New York
LPL-L	Lincoln, Nebraska, Public Library, Lincoln, Nebraska
LSM-NO	Louisiana State Museum, New Orleans, Louisiana
LYHS-L	Lynn Historical Society, Lynn, Massachusetts
MAHS-B	Massachusetts Historical Society, Boston, Massachusetts
MARH-M	Marquette County Historical Society, Marquette, Michigan
MCDH-F	Montgomery County Department of History and Archives, Fonda, New York
MCHA-F	Monmouth County Historical Association, Freehold, New Jersey
MCHM-M	Marinette County Historical Museum, Marinette, Wisconsin
MCHS-M	Milwaukee County Historical Society, Milwaukee, Wisconsin
MCHS-W	Marathon County Historical Society, Wausau, Wisconsin
MCM-M	McCord Museum, McGill University, Montreal, Quebec
MCNY	The Museum of the City of New York, New York, New York
MGUR-M	McGill University Library, Department of Rare Books and Special Collections, Montreal, Canada
MHC	Michigan Historical Commission, Ann Arbor, Michigan
MHC-AA	Michigan Historical Collections, Bentley Historical Library, Ann Arbor, Michigan
MHdeY	M. H. de Young Memorial Museum, San Francisco, California
MHS	Michigan Historical Society, Ann Arbor, Michigan
MHSA-L	Michigan History Division, State Archives, Department of State, Lansing, Michigan
MHS-B	Maryland Historical Society, Baltimore, Maryland
MHS-H	Montana Historical Society, Helena, Montana
MHS-P	Maine Historical Society, Portland, Maine
MHS-SL	Missouri Historical Society, St. Louis, Missouri
MHS-SP	Minnesota Historical Society, St. Paul, Minnesota
MMM-B	Maine Maritime Museum, Bath, Maine
MM-NN	Mariners' Museum, Newport News, Virginia
MNM-SF	Museum of New Mexico, Santa Fe, New Mexico
MPL-M	Milwaukee Public Library, Milwaukee, Wisconsin

MPM-M	Milwaukee Public Museum, Milwaukee, Wisconsin
MRL-R	Morrisson-Reeves Library, Richmond, Indiana
MSL-B	Massachusetts State Library, Boston, Massachusetts
MSM-A	Maine State Museum, Augusta, Maine
MTLB-T	Metropolitan Toronto Library Board, Toronto, Ontario
MVTM-NA	Merrimack Valley Textile Museum, North Andover, Massachusetts
NBPL-NB	New Britain Public Library, New Britain, Connecticut
NCM-EM	Nassau County Museum Reference Library, East Meadow, New York
NHHS-C	New Hampshire Historical Society, Concord, New Hampshire
NHM-LA	Natural History Museum, Los Angeles County
NHS-R	Nevada State Historical Society, Reno, Nevada
NJHS-N	New Jersey Historical Society, Newark, New Jersey
NL-C	The Newberry Library, Chicago, Illinois
NM-N	Newark Museum, Newark, New Jersey
NSHS-L	Nebraska State Historical Society, Lincoln, Nebraska
NSM-H	Nova Scotia Museum, Halifax, Nova Scotia
NYH-NY	The New-York Historical Society, New York, New York
NYP-E	Eno Collection, New York Public Library, New York, New York
NYP-P	Print Room, New York Public Library, New York, New York
NYP-S	Stokes Collection, New York Public Library, New York, New York
NYSH-C	New York State Historical Association, Cooperstown, New York
NYSL-A	New York State Library, Albany, New York
NYSM-A	New York State Museum, Albany, New York
OCHS-O	Oswego County Historical Society, Oswego, New York
OCHS-R	Olmsted County Historical Society, Rochester, Minnesota
ODHS-NB	Old Dartmouth Historical Society, New Bedford, Massachusetts
OHA-S	Onondaga Historical Association, Syracuse, New York
OHS-C	Ohio Historical Society, Columbus, Ohio
OHS-P	Oregon Historical Society, Portland, Oregon
OHS-U	Oneida Historical Society, Utica, New York
OM-O	Oakland Museum, Oakland, California
OUL-E	University of Oregon Library, Eugene, Oregon
PABC-V	Provincial Archives of British Columbia, Victoria, British Columbia
PAC	Map Division, Public Archives of Canada, Ottawa, Ontario
PAC-P	Picture Division, Public Archives of Canada, Ottawa, Ontario
PANB-F	Provincial Archives of New Brunswick, Fredericton, New Brunswick
PANS-H	Public Archives of Nova Scotia, Halifax, Nova Scotia
PCHS-R	Portage County Historical Society, Ravenna, Ohio
PHMC-H	Pennsylvania Historical and Museum Commission, Bureau of Archives and History, Division of History, Harrisburg, Pennsylvania
PHS-P	Peoria Historical Society, John C. Flanagan House, Peoria, Illinois
PKY-G	P. K. Yonge Library of Florida History, University of Florida, Gainesville, Florida
PLW-WW	Penrose Memorial Library, Whitman College, Walla Walla, Washington
PM-B	The Peale Museum, Baltimore, Maryland
PM-D	Putnam Museum, Davenport, Iowa
PM-S	Peabody Museum, Salem, Massachusetts

PSU	Pennsylvania State University Libraries, Pennsylvania Historical Collections and Labor Archives, University Park, Pennsylvania
PUL-P	Princeton University Library, Princeton, New Jersey
RCHS-J	Rock County Historical Society, Janesville, Wisconsin
RCHS-T	Rensselaer County Historical Society, Troy, New York
RIHS-P	Rhode Island Historical Society, Providence, Rhode Island
RL-G	Rosenberg Library, Galveston, Texas
RMSC-R	Rochester Museum and Science Center, Rochester, New York
ROM	Royal Ontario Museum, Canadiana Department Collection, Toronto, Ontario
RU-NB	Special Collections Department, Alexander Library, Rutgers University, New Brunswick, New Jersey
SAM-M	Sheldon Art Museum, Middlebury, Vermont
SAM-SL	St. Louis Art Museum, St. Louis, Missouri
SBHS-SB	Santa Barbara Historical Society, Santa Barbara, California
SCHS-B	St. Clair County Historical Society, Belleville, Illinois
SCHS-C	South Carolina Historical Society, Charleston, South Carolina
SCHS-S	Saginaw County Historical Society Museum, Saginaw, Michigan
SCL-C	South Caroliniana Library, University of South Carolina, Columbia, South Carolina
SCP	Society of California Pioneers, San Francisco, California
SDHS-P	South Dakota Historical Society, Pierre, South Dakota
SFPL	San Francisco Public Library, San Francisco, California
SHSM-C	State Historical Society of Missouri, Columbia, Missouri
SHS-S	Seattle Historial Society, Seattle, Washington
SI	The Smithsonian Institution, Washington, D.C.
SIHS-R	Staten Island Historical Society, Richmondtown, Staten Island, New York
SLG-C	Sherman Library and Gardens, Corona del Mar, California
SM-VT	Shelburne Museum, Shelburne, Vermont
SOHS-J	Southern Oregon Historical Society, Jacksonville, Oregon
SSBT-B	State Street Bank and Trust Company, Boston, Massachusetts
SU-SC	Stanford University Library, Special Collections, Palo Alto, California
SWM-LA	Southwest Museum, Los Angeles, California
TCM-S	Tuolumne County Museum, Sonora, California
TUL-NO	Special Collections Division, Tulane University Library, New Orleans, Louisiana
UC-B	University Libraries, University of Colorado at Boulder, Western Historical Collections, Boulder, Colorado
UCBL-B	Bancroft Library, University of California, Berkeley, California
UCLA-SC	Special Collections Division, University Library, University of California at Los Angeles, Los Angeles, California
UG-A	University of Georgia Library, Athens, Georgia
UHS-SL	Utah State Historical Society, Salt Lake City, Utah
UML-AA	University of Michigan, Ann Arbor, Michigan
UML-M	University of Montana Library, Missoula, Montana
UN-R	University of Nevada Library, Reno, Nevada
UPDL-P	Darlington Memorial Library, University of Pittsburgh, Pittsburgh, Pennsylvania
UTB-A	University of Texas, Eugene C. Barker Texas History Center, Austin, Texas
UTR-T	University of Toronto, Thomas Fisher Rare Book Library, Toronto, Ontario
UU-SL	Marriott Library, University of Utah, Salt Lake City, Utah
UVT-B	The University of Vermont, Guy W. Bailey Library, Special Collections, Burlington, Vermont
UWL-S	Special Collections, University of Washington Libraries, Seattle, Washington
VHS-M	Vermont Historical Society, Montpelier, Vermont
VHS-R	Virginia Historical Society, Richmond, Virginia
VM-R	Valentine Museum, Richmond, Virginia
VSL-R	Virginia State Library, Richmond, Virginia
WCM-W	Waukesha County Museum, Waukesha, Wisconsin
WHPL-D	Western History Department, Denver Public Library, Denver, Colorado
WHS-M	Wisconsin Historical Society, Madison, Wisconsin
WIUL-M	Western Illinois University Map Library, Macomb, Illinois
WM-C	Wilson Museum, Castine, Maine
WML-M	Washington Memorial Library, Macon, Georgia
WMM-SA	Witte Memorial Museum, San Antonio, Texas
WRHS-C	Western Reserve Historical Society, Cleveland, Ohio
WSHS-T	Washington State Historical Society, Tacoma, Washington
WU-M	Wesleyan University Library, Middletown, Connecticut
WVAD-C	Archives and History Division, Department of Culture and History, State of West Virginia, Charleston, West Virginia
YO	Ralph M. Yeager-John C. O'Connor Collection, University Park, Pennsylvania
YUAG-NH	Yale University Art Gallery, New Haven, Connecticut

Abbreviations of Catalogs and Checklists

ACMW–FW — Amon Carter Museum of Western Art. *Catalogue of the Collection, 1972*. Fort Worth: Amon Carter Museum of Western Art, 1973.

Allodi, Printmaking in Canada — Allodi, Mary. *Printmaking in Canada: The Earliest Views and Portraits*. Toronto: Royal Ontario Museum, 1980.

Anson Stokes — Stokes, Anson Phelps. *Historical Prints of New Haven, Connecticut with Special Reference to Yale College and The Green*. New Haven, Conn.: n.p., 1910.

Baird & Evans — Baird, Joseph Armstrong, and Edwin Clyve Evans. *Historic Lithographs of San Francisco*. San Francisco: Burger & Evans, 1972.

Beckman — Beckman, Thomas. *Milwaukee Illustrated: Panoramic and Bird's Eye Views of a Midwestern Metropolis, 1844–1908*. Milwaukee: Milwaukee Art Center, 1978.

Bellman — Bellman, David, ed. "Mount Royal Montreal," Supplement, *Canadian Art Review* 4, no. 2 (1977): S1–S30.

Bilodeau, Art in South Carolina — Bilodeau, Francis W., & Mrs. Thomas J. Tobias, comps. & eds. *Art in South Carolina, 1670–1970*. Columbia: South Carolina Tricentennial Commission, 1970.

CHS–H — "Panoramic Views of Connecticut." *Connecticut Historical Society Bulletin* 20 (April 1955): 52–61.

Cobb, New Hampshire Maps — Cobb, David A. *New Hampshire Maps to 1900: An Annotated Checklist*. Concord: New Hampshire Historical Society, 1981.

Conningham — Conningham, Frederic A. *Currier & Ives Prints: An Illustrated Check List*. Updated by Colin Simkin. New York: Crown Publishers, 1970.

Cumming — Cumming, John. *A Preliminary Checklist of 19th Century Lithographs of Michigan Cities and Towns*. Mount Pleasant: Clark Historical Library, Central Michigan University, 1969.

deVolpi, Montreal — deVolpi, Charles P., and Peter S. Winkworth. *Montreal, A Pictorial Record*. 2 vols. Montreal: Dev-Sco Publications, 1963.

deVolpi, Newfoundland — deVolpi, Charles P. *Newfoundland, A Pictorial Record: Historical Prints and Illustrations of the Province of Newfoundland, Canada, 1497–1887*. Don Mills, Ontario: Longman Canada, 1972.

deVolpi, Niagara Peninsula — deVolpi, Charles P. *The Niagara Peninsula, A Pictorial Record: Historical Prints and Illustrations of The Niagara Peninsula Province of Ontario, 1697–1880*. Montreal: Dev-Sco Publications, 1966.

deVolpi, Nova Scotia — deVolpi, Charles P. *Nova Scotia, A Pictorial Record: Historical Prints and Illustrations of the Province of Nova Scotia Canada, 1605–1878*. n.p.: Longman Canada, 1974.

deVolpi, Ottawa — deVolpi, Charles P. *Ottawa, A Pictorial Record: Historical Prints and Illustrations of the City of Ottawa, Province of Ontario, Canada, 1807–1882*. Montreal: Dev-Sco Publications, 1964.

deVolpi, Quebec — deVolpi, Charles P. *Quebec, A Pictorial Record: Historical Prints and Illustrations of the City of Quebec, Province of Quebec, Canada, 1608–1875*. n.p.: Longman Canada, 1971.

deVolpi, Toronto — deVolpi, Charles P. *Toronto, A Pictorial Record: Historical Prints and Illustrations of the City of Toronto, Province of Ontario, 1813–1882*. Montreal: Dev-Sco Publications, 1965.

deVolpi & Scowen, Eastern Townships — deVolpi, Charles P., and P. H. Scowen. *The Eastern Townships: A Pictorial Record: Historical Prints and Illustrations of the Eastern Townships of the Province of Quebec Canada*. Montreal: Dev-Sco Publications, 1962.

Eno — Weitenkampf, Frank. *The Eno Collection of New York City Views*. New York, 1925. Reprinted: Ann Arbor: Gryphon Books, 1971.

Farnsworth — William A. Farnsworth Library and Art Museum. *Through a Bird's Eye: Nineteenth-Century Views of Maine*. Christine Bauer Podmaniczky, comp. Rockland, Maine: William A. Farnsworth Library and Art Museum, 1981.

Freeman, Historical Prints — Freeman, Graydon La Verne. *Historical Prints of American Cities*. Watkins Glen, N.Y.: Century House, 1952.

Genesee Country — Rochester, N.Y., University, Memorial Art Gallery. *The Genesee Country*. Essay by Henry W. Clune. Introduction and Catalogue by Howard S. Merritt. Rochester: Memorial Art Gallery of the University of Rochester, 1975.

Goldsmith — *The Notable Henry Goldsmith Collection: Historical Maps, Views, Original Drawings, China Relating to New York City*. Catalog descriptions by Robert Fridenberg. New York: American Art Association, 1926.

Hemenway — Hemenway, Alice. "Lithographs in the Collections of the New York State Historical Association." Master's thesis, State University of New York, Oneonta, 1976.

Hufeland — Hufeland, Otto. *A Check List of Books, Maps, Pictures and other Printed Matter Relating to the Counties of Westchester and Bronx*. White Plains, N.Y.: Westchester County Historical Society, 1929.

Kaplan, Pictorial Americana — U.S. Library of Congress, Prints and Photographic Division. *Pictorial Americana*. Compiled by Milton Kaplan. 2d ed. Washington, D.C.: Library of Congress, 1955.

LC–M — U.S. Library of Congress. *Panoramic Maps of Cities in the United States and Canada: A Checklist of Maps in the Collections of the Library of Congress, Geography and Map Division*. John R. Hébert and Patrick E. Dempsey, comps. Washington, D.C.: Library of Congress, 1983.

LHS–L, Views of Lowell — *Views of Lowell, 1825–1976*. Catalog of Exhibit Sponsored by the Lowell Historical Society, April 4–April 25, 1976, Whistler House/Parker Gallery, Lowell, Mass. Lowell: Lowell Historical Society, 1976.

McClintock — McClintock, Gilbert Stuart. *Valley Views of Northeastern Pennsylvania.* . . . Wilkes Barre, Pa.: Wyoming Historical and Geological Society, 1948.

McCauley — McCauley, Lois B. *Maryland Historical Prints, 1752–1889*. Baltimore: Maryland Historical Society, 1975.

Maule — Maule, Elizabeth Singer, comp. *Bird's Eye Views of Wisconsin Communities: A Preliminary Checklist*. Madison: The State Historical Society of Wisconsin, 1977.

MM–NN — Mariners' Museum. *Catalog of Marine Prints and Paintings, Mariners' Museum Library, Newport News, Virginia*. 3 vols. Boston: G. K. Hall & Co., 1964.

Moffat — Moffat, Riley Moore. *Printed Maps of Utah to 1900*.

n.p.: Western Association of Map Libraries, Occasional Paper No. 8, 1981.

MVTM, Lawrence — Merrimack Valley Textile Museum. *New City on the Merrimack: Prints of Lawrence, 1845–1876.* North Andover, Mass.: Merrimack Valley Textile Museum, 1974.

Norton, "Whitefield" — Norton, Bettina A. "Edwin Whitefield, 1816–1892." *Antiques* 102 (August 1972): 232–43.

Norton, Whitefield — Norton, Bettina A. *Edwin Whitefield: Nineteenth-Century North American Scenery.* Barre, Mass.: Barre Publishing, 1977.

PAC — Public Archives of Canada, National Map Collection. *Catalogue of the National Map Collection, Public Archives of Canada.* 15 vols. Boston: G. K. Hall, 1976.

PAC (1976) — Public Archives of Canada. "Bird's-Eye Views of Canadian Cities: An Exhibition of Panoramic Maps (1865–1905). . . ." Exhibition handlist reproduced from typewritten copy. Ottawa: Public Archives of Canada, 1976.

PAI — Pasadena Art Institute. *Early Prints of California from the Robert B. Honeyman Collection.* Pasadena: Pasadena Art Institute, 1952.

Peters, C & I — Peters, Harry T. *Currier & Ives: Printmakers to the American People.* 2 vols. New York: Doubleday, Doran and Co., 1929–1931.

Peters, COS — Peters, Harry T. *California on Stone.* Garden City, N.Y.: Doubleday, Doran & Co., 1935.

Philips, Washington — U.S. Library of Congress, Division of Maps. *List of Maps and Views of Washington and District of Columbia in the Library of Congress.* Compiled by Phillip Lee Philips. Washington, D.C.: Government Printing Office, 1900.

PP — Pennsylvania State University, Museum of Art. *Pennsylvania Prints from the Collection of John C. O'Connor and Ralph M. Yeager: Lithographs, Engravings, Aquatints, and Watercolors from the Tavern Restaurant.* Compiled by Judith W. Hansen. University Park: Museum of Art, The Pennsylvania State University, 1980.

Pyne — *Illustrated Catalogue of the Notable Collection of Views of New York and Other American Cities . . . Formed by Mr. Percy R. Pyne 2d.* Catalogue Descriptions Written by Mr Robert Fridenberg. New York: The American Art Association, 1917.

Rathbone, Westward the Way — Rathbone, Perry T., ed. *Westward the Way: The Character and Development of the Louisiana Territory as Seen by Artists and Writers of the Nineteenth Century.* St. Louis: City Art Museum of St. Louis, 1954.

Rehner, Walton — Rehner, Leigh. *Henry Walton: 19th Century American Artist.* Ithaca, N.Y.: Ithaca College Museum of Art, 1968.

Reps, Cities on Stone — Reps, John W. *Cities on Stone: Nineteenth Century Lithograph Images of the Urban West.* Fort Worth: Amon Carter Museum of Western Art, 1976.

Robertson — Toronto Public Libraries. *Landmarks of Canada: A Guide to the J. Ross Robertson Canadian Historical Collection in the Toronto Public Library.* 3 vols. Toronto: Toronto Public Library, 1917–1964.

Rose, Hawai'i — Rose, Roger G. *Hawai'i: The Royal Isles.* Honolulu: Bishop Museum Press, 1980.

Samuel — Jefferys, Charles W., comp. *A Catalogue of the Sigmund Samuel Collection of Canadiana and Americana.* Toronto: Ryerson, 1948.

Schurre, Currier & Ives Prints — Schurre, Jacques. *Currier & Ives Prints: A Checklist of Unrecorded Prints Produced by Currier & Ives, N. Currier and C. Currier.* [New York?]: Jacques Schurre, 1970.

SCP — Society of California Pioneers. "Catalog of Topographic Prints, Drawings, and Paintings." Compiled by Elliot A. P. Evans, assisted by Helen S. Giffen. *Annual Publication of the Society for the Year 1955,* pp. 14–21.

SDH VIII–3 — "Artists Draw South Dakota: Panoramic Views of Pioneer Towns." *South Dakota History* 8 (Summer 1978): 221–49.

Spendlove, Face of Early Canada — Spendlove, F. St. George. *The Face of Early Canada. . . .* Toronto: Ryerson, [1958?].

Stokes — Stokes, I. N. Phelps, and Daniel C. Haskell. *American Historical Prints: Early Views of American Cities, etc. From the Phelps Stokes and Other Collections.* New York: New York Public Library, 1932.

Stokes, Icon. — Stokes, I. N. Phelps, *Iconography of Manhattan Island, 1498–1909.* 6 vols. New York: R. H. Dodd, 1915–1928.

Stout — Stout, Leon J. "Pennsylvania Town Views, 1850–1922: A Union Catalogue." *The Western Pennsylvania Historical Magazine* 58 (July 1975): 409–28; (October 1975): 546–71; 59 (January 1976): 88–109.

Taft — Taft, Robert. *Artists and Illustrators of the Old West, 1850–1900.* New York: Scribner, 1953.

TSA–A — Texas State Library, Archives Division. *The Map Collection of the Texas State Archives, 1527–1900.* Compiled by James M. Day and Ann B. Dunlap. Austin: Texas State Library, 1962.

Van Zandt, Chronicles of the Hudson — Van Zandt, Roland, comp. *Chronicles of the Hudson: Three Centuries of Travelers' Accounts.* New Brunswick, N.J.: Rutgers University Press, 1971.

Wainwright — Wainwright, Nicholas B. *Philadelphia in the Romantic Age of Lithography.* Philadelphia: The Historical Society of Pennsylvania, 1958.

Warren — Warren, James Raymond, Sr. "Thaddeus Mortimer Fowler, Bird's-eye-view Artist." Special Libraries Association, Geography and Map Division, *Bulletin,* no. 120 (June 1980): 27–35.

Warren & Wise — Warren, James Raymond, Sr., and Donald A. Wise. "Two Birds-Eye-View Artists: The Bailey Brothers." Special Libraries Association, Geography and Map Division, *Bulletin,* no. 124 (June 1981): 20–30.

Weddell — Weddell, Alexander Wilbourne. *Richmond, Virginia in Old Prints, 1737–1887.* Richmond: Richmond Academy of Arts, 1932.

Wilmerding — Wilmerding, John. *Fitz Hugh Lane, 1804–1865: American Marine Painter.* Gloucester, Mass.: Peter Smith, 1967.

1
Place: Anniston, Alabama
Date: 1887
Title: Anniston, Ala. 1887.
Size: 13⅜ × 24⅜ in. (34 × 62 cm.)
Artist: H. Wellge
Lithographer:
Printer: Beck & Pauli Lith. Co., Milwaukee
Publisher: Henry Wellge & Co., Milwaukee
Key/Vignettes/Misc: Refs. 1–10, A–H; 5 vignettes; unnumbered business directory
Locations: LC–M
Catalogs/Checklists: LC–M, 1

2
Place: Anniston, Alabama
Date: 1888
Title: Bird's Eye View of Anniston, Ala. 1888
Size: 21 × 31 in. (53.4 × 79 cm.)
Artist: E. S. Glover
Lithographer:
Printer: Shober & Carqueville Litho. Co., Chicago
Publisher: E. S. Glover
Key/Vignettes/Misc: Refs. 1–17, 19–37
Locations: LC–M
Catalogs/Checklists: LC–M, 2

3
Place: Anniston, Alabama
Date: Ca. 1903
Title: Bird's Eye View Looking Northwest, City of Anniston, Calhoun County, Alabama.
Size: 22¾ × 34³⁄₁₆ in. (58 × 87 cm.)
Artist: C. N. Dry
Lithographer:
Printer: Chas. Hart, lith., New York
Publisher:
Key/Vignettes/Misc: Refs. 1–17, 21–61; unnumbered newspaper directory
Locations: LC–M
Catalogs/Checklists: LC–M, 3

4
Place: Birmingham, Alabama
Date: 1885
Title: Birmingham, Alabama.
Size: 23¼ × 32⅝ in. (58.6 × 83 cm.)
Artist: H. Wellge
Lithographer:
Printer: Beck & Pauli, litho., Milwaukee, Wis.
Publisher: Norris, Wellge, & Co. No. 107 Wells St. Milwaukee, Wis.
Key/Vignettes/Misc: Refs. A–J, 2–35; 16 vignettes; unnumbered business directory
Locations: LC–M; LC–P
Catalogs/Checklists: LC–M, 4

5
Place: Birmingham, Alabama
Date: 1904
Title: Business Section of the City of Birmingham, Alabama. Drawn in 1903 by C. N. Dry.
Size: 5⅞ × 9⁷⁄₁₆ in. (15 × 24 cm.) (photo)
Artist: C. N. Dry.
Lithographer:

Printer:
Publisher: C. N. Dry
Key/Vignettes/Misc:
Locations: LC–M (photo)
Catalogs/Checklists: LC–M, 5

6
Place: Gadsden, Alabama
Date: 1887
Title: Perspective Map of the City of Gadsden, Ala. County Seat of Etowah County 1887.
Size: 15¼ × 20½ in. (38.8 × 52.2 cm.)
Artist: H. Wel[l]ge
Lithographer:
Printer: Beck & Pauli Lith. Co., Milwaukee
Publisher: Henry Wellge & Co., Cor. Wells & Second St., Milwaukee, Wis.
Key/Vignettes/Misc: Refs. 1–17, A–K; 4 vignettes
Locations: LC–M; Gadsden, Alabama, Public Library; Duke University Library, Durham, North Carolina
Catalogs/Checklists:

7
Place: Huntsville, Alabama
Date: 1871
Title: Bird's Eye View of the City of Huntsville, Madison County, Alabama 1871.
Size: 21⅝ × 24⅜ in. (55 × 62 cm.)
Artist: [A. Ruger]
Lithographer:
Printer: Ehrgott & Krebs Lith., Cincinnati
Publisher:
Key/Vignettes/Misc: Refs. 1–12; 2 vignettes
Locations: LC–M
Catalogs/Checklists: LC–M, 7

8
Place: Mobile, Alabama
Date: 1873
Title: Bird's Eye View of the City of Mobile, Alabama, 1873
Size: 25¼ × 33¾ in. (64.2 × 85.9 cm.)
Artist: Augustus Koch
Lithographer:
Printer: Ehrgott & Krebs Steam Lth. Printers, Cincinnati
Publisher: Ehrgott & Krebs Steam Lth., Cincinnati, Ohio
Key/Vignettes/Misc: Refs. 1–40
Locations: Museum of the City of Mobile, Mobile, Alabama
Catalogs/Checklists:

9
Place: Mobile, Alabama
Date: 1891
Title: Mobile, Ala. 1891. Looking North West, Population 40,000
Size: 8 × 11 in. (20.4 × 28 cm.) (photo)
Artist: C. J. Pauli
Lithographer: C. J. Pauli
Printer: C. J. Pauli, 726 Central Ave., Milwaukee, Wis.
Publisher: C. J. Pauli, 726 Central Ave., Milwaukee, Wis.
Key/Vignettes/Misc: Refs. 1–76

Locations: Museum of the City of Mobile, Mobile, Alabama
Catalogs/Checklists:

10
Place: Montgomery, Alabama
Date: 1872
Title: Montgomery, Ala. 1872
Size:
Artist:
Lithographer:
Printer:
Publisher: Ruger & Stoner
Key/Vignettes/Misc:
Locations: Alabama Dept. of Archives & History, Montgomery, Alabama (photo)
Catalogs/Checklists:

11
Place: Montgomery, Alabama
Date: 1887
Title: Perspective Map of Montgomery, State Capital of Alabama.
Size: 22 × 36⅛ in. (56 × 92 cm.)
Artist: H. Wellge
Lithographer:
Printer: Beck & Pauli Lith. Co., Milwaukee
Publisher: Henry Wellge & Co., Milwaukee
Key/Vignettes/Misc: Refs. 1–65; 21 vignettes
Locations: LC–M
Catalogs/Checklists: LC–M, 8

12
Place: Montgomery, Alabama
Date: 1912
Title: Montgomery, Alabama, Business Directory
Size: 28 × 44¼ in. (71.2 × 112.6 cm.) (framed)
Artist:
Lithographer:
Printer:
Publisher: S. O. Engraving Co., Akron, Ohio (copyright)
Key/Vignettes/Misc:
Locations: Private collection
Catalogs/Checklists:

13
Place: Selma, Alabama
Date: 1887
Title: Perspective Map of Selma, Ala. County Seat of Dallas County 1887.
Size: 16½ × 33⅜ in. (42 × 85 cm.)
Artist: H. Wellge
Lithographer:
Printer: Beck & Pauli Lith. Co., Milwaukee
Publisher: Henry Wellge & Co., Milwaukee
Key/Vignettes/Misc: Refs. 1–36, A–T; 9 vignettes
Locations: LC–M
Catalogs/Checklists: LC–M, 9

14
Place: Tuskaloosa, Alabama
Date: 1887
Title: Perspective Map of Tuskaloosa, Ala.

County Seat of Tuskaloosa, Co., 1887.
Size: 16½ × 25⅛ in. (42 × 64 cm.)
Artist: H. Wellge
Lithographer:
Printer: Beck & Pauli Lith. Co.,
Milwaukee
Publisher: Henry Wellge & Co.,
Milwaukee
Key/Vignettes/Misc: Refs. 1–20, A–L; 4
vignettes
Locations: LC–M
Catalogs/Checklists: LC–M, 10

15
Place: New Archangel, Alaska
Date: 1851
Title: Novo Arckhangelsk. . .Ameriki
1851
Size: 7⅜ × 13¼ in. (18.7 × 33.7 cm.)
Artist:
Lithographer:
Printer:
Publisher:
Key/Vignettes/Misc:
Locations: UCBL–B
Catalogs/Checklists:

16
Place: New Archangel, Alaska
Date: N.D.
Title: Establissement de
Novo–Arkhangelsk (Ile Sitkha)
Size: 8⁹⁄₁₆ × 10³⁄₁₆ in. (21.8 × 25.9 cm.)
Artist: Kittlitz
Lithographer:
Printer: Hostein
Publisher: Thierry Freres
Key/Vignettes/Misc:
Locations: University of Alaska,
Fairbanks, Alaska
Catalogs/Checklists:

17
Place: Sitka, Alaska
Date: N.D.
Title: [View of Sitka—title in Russian]
Size: 8¼ × 16⁵⁄₁₆ in. (21 × 41.5 cm.)
Artist:
Lithographer:
Printer:
Publisher: [Publishing information in
Russian]
Key/Vignettes/Misc:
Locations: UCBL–B
Catalogs/Checklists:

18
Place: Camp Mohave, Arizona
Date: N.D.
Title: Camp Mohave, Arizona
Size: 10½ × 15¾ in. (26.7 × 40.1 cm.)
Artist:
Lithographer:
Printer: Lith. Geo H. Baker, San Francisco
Publisher:
Key/Vignettes/Misc:
Locations: SWM–LA
Catalogs/Checklists:

19
Place: Flagstaff, Arizona
Date: 1892
Title: Flagstaff, Ariz. and The San

Francisco Peaks on the Atlantic & Pacific
R.R. . . .[Inset view on] The Grand
Canyon of the Colorado River Arizona.
Size: 9 × 11½ in. (22.9 × 29.2 cm.)
Artist: Jules Baumann
Lithographer:
Printer:
Publisher:
Key/Vignettes/Misc:
Locations: ACMW–FW; LC–P
Catalogs/Checklists: LC–M, 10.1

20
Place: Phoenix, Arizona
Date: 1885
Title: Bird's Eye View of Phoenix,
Maricopa Co., Arizona. View Looking
North–East.
Size: 20⅝ × 32½ in. (52.6 × 82.6 cm.)
Artist: C. J. Dyer
Lithographer: W. Byrnes
Printer: Schmidt Label & Litho Co. Print.
S. F.
Publisher: C. J. Dyer, Phoenix, Arizona
(copyright)
Key/Vignettes/Misc: Refs. 1–29; 11
vignettes; description
Locations: LC–M; LC–P
Catalogs/Checklists: LC–M, 11; Reps,
Cities on Stone, p. 95

21
Place: Phoenix, Arizona
Date: 1890
Title: Phoenix Arizona in the Salt River
Valley. View looking northeast.
Size: 30 × 41½ in. (76.3 × 105.5 cm.)
Artist: C. J. Dyer
Lithographer:
Printer: Schmidt, L. & L., S. F., Cal.
Publisher: C. J. Dyer (copyright)
Key/Vignettes/Misc: Refs. 1–33; 12
vignettes; description
Locations: Arizona Department of Library,
Archives and Public Records, Phoenix,
Arizona
Catalogs/Checklists:

22
Place: Prescott, Arizona
Date: Ca. 1885
Title: Bird's–Eye View of Prescott, A. T.
Looking North East.
Size: 19⅛ × 29½ in. (48.5 × 74.9 cm.)
Artist: C. J. Dyer
Lithographer:
Printer:
Publisher:
Key/Vignettes/Misc: Refs. 1–18; 12
vignettes; description
Locations: ACMW–FW; LC–M
(facsimile)
Catalogs/Checklists: ACMW–FW 1058;
Reps, Cities on Stone, p. 96; LC–M, 11.2

23
Place: Prescott, Arizona
Date: 1891
Title: Prescott, Arizona
Size: 28¼ × 40 in. (71.9 × 101.8 cm.)
Artist: Jules Baumann
Lithographer:

Printer: Schmidt Label & Lith. Co., S. F.
Publisher:
Key/Vignettes/Misc: 32 vignettes;
description
Locations: Arizona Department of Library,
Archives and Public Records, Phoenix,
Arizona
Catalogs/Checklists:

24
Place: Hot Springs, Arkansas
Date: 1888
Title: Bird's Eye View of Hot Springs, Ark.
Size: 13³⁄₁₆ × 26¹⁄₁₆ in. (33.5 × 66 cm.)
Artist: H. Wellge
Lithographer:
Printer: Beck & Pauli Lith Co. Milwaukee
Publisher: Henry Wellge & Co., Cor. Wells
& Second St. Milwaukee
Key/Vignettes/Misc: Refs. 1–33, A–M
Locations: ACMW–FW; LC–M
Catalogs/Checklists: ACMW–FW 1927;
LC–M, 12

25
Place: Little Rock, Arkansas
Date: 1871
Title: Bird's Eye View of the City of Little
Rock the Capitol of Arkansas. 1871
Size: 23 × 34 in. (58.4 × 86.4 cm.)
Artist: A. Ruger
Lithographer:
Printer:
Publisher: A. Ruger
Key/Vignettes/Misc: Refs. 1–22; 4
vignettes
Locations: LC–M; Arkansas Historical
Association, Fayetteville, Arkansas
Catalogs/Checklists: LC–M, 13

26
Place: Little Rock, Arkansas
Date: 1887
Title: Perspective Map of the City of Little
Rock, Ark., State Capital of Arkansas,
County Seat of Pulaski County. 1887.
Size: 18⅛ × 30⁵⁄₁₆ in. (46 × 77 cm.)
Artist:
Lithographer:
Printer: Beck & Pauli Lith. Co.,
Milwaukee
Publisher: Henry Wellge & Co.,
Milwaukee
Key/Vignettes/Misc: Refs. A–Y, 1–14; 1
vignette
Locations: LC–M; Arkansas Historical
Association, Fayetteville, Arkansas
Catalogs/Checklists: LC–M, 14

Place: Texarkana, Arkansas
Date: 1888
See Texarkana, Texas, 1888.

27
Place: Van Buren, Arkansas
Date: 1888
Title: Perspective Map of Van Buren, Ark.
County Seat of Crawford County 1888.
Size: 16¾ × 24¹³⁄₁₆ in. (42.7 × 63.2 cm.)
Artist: H. Wellge
Lithographer:
Printer: Beck & Pauli Lith. Co.,
Milwaukee

Publisher: Henry Wellge & Co.,
Milwaukee
Key/Vignettes/Misc: Refs. A–G, 1–32
Locations: LC–M
Catalogs/Checklists: LC–M, 16

28
Place: New Westminster, British Columbia
Date: 1890
Title: New Westminster, B. C. 1890
Size:
Artist:
Lithographer:
Printer:
Publisher:
Key/Vignettes/Misc: Refs.; 30 vignettes
Locations: University of British Columbia
Library, Vancouver, British Columbia
(photo)
Catalogs/Checklists:

29
Place: North Vancouver, British Columbia
Date: 1907
Title: Bird's Eye View of the City of North
Vancouver, B. C. From the
Harbour. . .1907.
Size: 14¹⁵⁄₁₆ × 17¹³⁄₁₆ in. (38 × 45.4 cm.)
Artist: C. H. Rawson
Lithographer:
Printer:
Publisher: Irwin & Billings Co. Ltd.
Key/Vignettes/Misc: 1 blank vignette
Locations: PAC
Catalogs/Checklists: PAC H3/640–North
Vancouver–1907

30
Place: Vancouver, British Columbia
Date: 1890
Title: Vancouver, B. C. 1890.
Size: 24¹⁄₁₆ × 37⁵⁄₁₆ in. (61.2 × 95 cm.)
Artist:
Lithographer: F. W.
Printer: Elliott Pub. Co. 120 Sutter St., S.
F.
Publisher: Vancouver Daily and Weekly
World Publishing Co.
Key/Vignettes/Misc: Refs. 1–71; 41
vignettes
Locations: PAC; PABC–V
Catalogs/Checklists: PAC (1976); PAC
H2/640–Vancouver–1890

31
Place: Vancouver, British Columbia
Date: 1898
Title: Panoramic View of the City of
Vancouver, British Columbia 1898.
Size: 27⅞ × 40⅛ in. (71 × 102 cm.)
Artist: J.[ohn] C.[ampbell] McLagan
Lithographer:
Printer: Toronto Lithographing Co., Ltd.
Publisher: Vancouver World Printing &
Publishing Company
Key/Vignettes/Misc: 160 refs.; 1 vignette
Locations: PAC; PABC–V; LC–M
(facsimile)
Catalogs/Checklists: PAC (1976); PAC
H1/640–Vancouver–1898; LC–M,
1074.4

32
Place: Vancouver, British Columbia
Date: 1907
Title: Birds Eye View of Vancouver B. C.
Size: 15⁵⁄₁₆ × 21¼ in. (39 × 54 cm.)
Artist: C. H. Rawson
Lithographer:
Printer: Angell Eng. Co.
Publisher: Morden & Thornton
(copyright)
Key/Vignettes/Misc:
Locations: PAC
Catalogs/Checklists: PAC
H12/640–Vancouver–1907

33
Place: Vancouver, British Columbia
Date: 1908
Title: City of Vancouver B. C. Canada.
1908.
Size: 12⅜ × 23⅛ in. (31.5 × 59 cm.)
Artist: C. M. Arndt
Lithographer:
Printer: Dominion–Ill Co., Ltd, Vancouver
Publisher: Vancouver Tourist Association
Key/Vignettes/Misc:
Locations: PAC; PABC–V
Catalogs/Checklists: PAC
H12/640–Vancouver–1908

34
Place: Victoria, British Columbia
Date: 1860
Title: View of Victoria, Vancouver Island
Size: 9⅞ × 34⁵⁄₁₆ in. (25.1 × 87.2 cm.)
Artist: H. O. Tiedemann
Lithographer: T. Picken
Printer: Day & Son
Publisher: Day & Son, London
Key/Vignettes/Misc: 14 unnumbered refs.
below places identified
Locations: UCBL–B; LC–M; PAC;
PABC–V; ROM; NYP–S; MTLB–T;
Univ. of British Columbia Library,
Vancouver, British Columbia; PAC–P
Catalogs/Checklists: LC–M, 1075; PAC
H3/640–Victoria–1860; Robertson, no.
5; Stokes P. 1859—H–31

35
Place: Victoria, British Columbia
Date: [1860?]
Title: View of Victoria.
Size: 4¼ × 7⅛ in. (10.7 × 18.2 cm.)
Artist:
Lithographer:
Printer: Clayton & Co., Lith. 17, Bouverie
St.
Publisher:
Key/Vignettes/Misc:
Locations: PAC–P
Catalogs/Checklists:

36
Place: Victoria, British Columbia
Date: 1878
Title: Bird's–Eye View of Victoria,
Vancouver Island, B. C. 1878.
Size: 21⅛ × 32⁵⁄₁₆ in. (53.6 × 82.2 cm.)
Artist: E. S. Glover
Lithographer:

Printer: A. L. Bancroft & Co., San
Francisco
Publisher: M. W. Waitt & Co., Victoria, B.
C.
Key/Vignettes/Misc: Refs. 1–29
Locations: LC–M; UCBL–B; PAC;
PABC–V; MTLB–T; PAC–P
Catalogs/Checklists: LC–M, 1076; PAC
(1976); PAC V1/640–Victoria–1878;
Robertson, no. 25

37
Place: Victoria, British Columbia
Date: 1884
Title: Victoria, B. C. and Vicinity 1884.
Size: 22¾ × 31¹³⁄₁₆ in. (58 × 81 cm.)
Artist: L. Samuel
Lithographer:
Printer: The West Shore
Publisher: J. B. Ferguson & Co., Victoria
Key/Vignettes/Misc: 9 views on sheet
Locations: LC–M; PABC–V
Catalogs/Checklists: LC–M, 1076.1

38
Place: Victoria, British Columbia
Date: 1889
Title: Victoria, B. C. 1889.
Size: 25 × 39⁷⁄₁₆ in. (63.6 × 100.3 cm.)
Artist: R. H.
Lithographer:
Printer:
Publisher: Ellis & Co., Victoria, B. C.
Key/Vignettes/Misc: Refs. 1–63
Locations: LC–M; UCBL–B;
ACMW–FW; UWL–S; PABC–V;
MTLB–T; Victoria, B. C., City Archives;
PAC–P
Catalogs/Checklists: LC–M, 1077;
ACMW–FW 1867; PAC (1976); PAC
H3/640–Victoria–1889

39
Place: Alameda, California
Date: Ca. 1880
Title: Alameda, Cal.
Size: 19⅜ × 35⅞ in. (49.3 × 91.2 cm.)
Artist:
Lithographer:
Printer: W. W. Elliott, S. F.
Publisher: Alameda Semi–Weekly Argus
[Alameda]
Key/Vignettes/Misc: Refs. 1–38; 31
vignettes
Locations: SCP; UCBL–B
Catalogs/Checklists: SCP, p. 19 (1123)

40
Place: Alhambra, California
Date: [188–]
Title: Birds Eye View of Alhambra. Los
Angeles Co. Cal.
Size: 22⅜ × 25⅞ in. (57 × 65.9 cm.)
(photo)
Artist: E. S. Moore
Lithographer:
Printer:
Publisher:
Key/Vignettes/Misc: Refs. 1–10; 9
vignettes
Locations: HEHL; Alhambra, California,

Public Library (photo)
Catalogs/Checklists:

Place: Alsota, California
Date: 1888
See Glendora, California, 1888.

41

Place: Anaheim, California
Date: Ca. 1877
Title: Bird's Eye View of Anaheim, Los Angeles Co., Cal. Looking North to the Sierra Madre Mountains.
Size: 11¼ × 16¼ in. (28.6 × 41.4 cm.)
Artist: E. S. Glover
Lithographer:
Printer: A. L. Bancroft & Co., Lith., San Francisco
Publisher:
Key/Vignettes/Misc: Refs. 1–12, A–D
Locations: UCBL–B; LC–M (photo)
Catalogs/Checklists: LC–M, 16.1

42

Place: Angel's Camp, California
Date: 1857
Title: Angel's Calaveras County Cal. 1857
Size: 14¹⁵⁄₁₆ × 22¼ in. (38 × 56.5 cm.)
Artist: Kuchel & Dresel
Lithographer: Kuchel & Dresel
Printer: Britton & Rey [San Francisco]
Publisher: C. G. Lake, Angels Camp
Key/Vignettes/Misc: 19 vignettes
Locations: SCP
Catalogs/Checklists: SCP, p. 19 (858); Peters, COS, p. 142

43

Place: Angel's Camp, California
Date: 1857
Title: Angel's Calaveras County, Cal.
Size: 14¹⁵⁄₁₆ × 22¼ in. (37.9 × 56.5 cm.)
Artist: Kuchel and Dresel
Lithographer: Kuchel & Dresel
Printer: Britton & Rey [San Francisco]
Publisher: [n.p.]
Key/Vignettes/Misc: 19 vignettes
Locations: ACMW–FW; CHS–C
Catalogs/Checklists: ACMW–FW 1248

44

Place: Angel's Camp, California
Date: 1857
Title: Angel's, Calaveras County, Cal.
Size: 11¼ × 16³⁄₁₆ in. (28.7 × 41.6 cm.)
Artist:
Lithographer:
Printer: Britton & Rey [San Francisco]
Publisher: Kuchel & Dresel (copyright)
Key/Vignettes/Misc: [no vignettes]
Locations: Unknown. Alta California Book Store, 2/9/80
Catalogs/Checklists:

45

Place: Angel's Camp, California
Date: 1857
Title: Angel's, Calaveras County, Cal. 1857.
Size: 11⅜ × 16³⁄₁₆ in. (29 × 41.2 cm.)
Artist: Kuchel & Dresel
Lithographer: Kuchel & Dresel

Printer: Britton & Rey [San Francisco]
Publisher: [n.p.]
Key/Vignettes/Misc: [no vignettes]
Locations: Unknown. Old Print Shop, 1/21/79
Catalogs/Checklists:

46

Place: Angel's Camp, California
Date: 1857
Title: Angel's, Calaveras County, Cal. 1857.
Size: 9 × 16¼ in. (22.9 × 41.4 cm.)
Artist: Kuchel & Dresel
Lithographer: Kuchel & Dresel
Printer: Britton & Rey [San Francisco]
Publisher: C. G. Lake, Angels.
Key/Vignettes/Misc: [no vignettes]
Locations: UCBL–B; CHS–SF
Catalogs/Checklists:

47

Place: Antioch, California
Date: N.D.
Title: Bird's–Eye View, Looking South, of Antioch, Cal.
Size: 19³⁄₁₆ × 26⅝ in. (48.8 × 67.8 cm.)
Artist:
Lithographer:
Printer: Elliott Pub. Co., San Francisco
Publisher: Antioch Board of Trade
Key/Vignettes/Misc: Refs. 1–24; 17 vignettes
Locations: UCBL–B
Catalogs/Checklists:

48

Place: Arcadia, California
Date: [188–?]
Title: Birdseye View of Arcadia and Santa Anita Tract San Gabriel Valley Los Angeles County, California.
Size: 26 × 37¾ in. (66.2 × 96.1 cm.)
Artist:
Lithographer:
Printer: H. S. Crocker & Co. Lith. S. F.
Publisher:
Key/Vignettes/Misc: Refs. 1–7, W
Locations: HEHL; UCLA–SC
Catalogs/Checklists:

49

Place: Arcata, California
Date: 1857
Title: Union, On Humboldt Bay, Humboldt Co. Cal. 1857.
Size: 11½ × 15¼ in. (29.2 × 38.8 cm.)
Artist: Kuchel & Dresel
Lithographer: Kuchel & Dresel
Printer: Britton & Rey [San Francisco]
Publisher:
Key/Vignettes/Misc: [no vignettes]
Locations: CHS–SF
Catalogs/Checklists:

50

Place: Arcata, California
Date: 1857
Title: Union, On Humboldt Bay, Humboldt Co. Cal. 1857.
Size: 14³⁄₁₆ × 20¹³⁄₁₆ in. (36 × 52.8 cm.)

Artist: Kuchel & Dresel
Lithographer: Kuchel & Dresel
Printer: Britton & Rey [San Francisco]
Publisher: B. Henry Wyman, Union
Key/Vignettes/Misc: 14 vignettes
Locations: ACMW–FW; SCP; UCBL–B
Catalogs/Checklists: ACMW–FW 1275; Peters, COS, p. 145; SCP, p. 21 (863); Reps, Cities on Stone, p. 98

51

Place: Auburn, California
Date: 1857
Title: Auburn Placer County, California, 1857
Size: 16⅜ × 23⅛ in. (41.7 × 58.8 cm.)
Artist: Kuchel & Dresel
Lithographer: Kuchel & Dresel
Printer: Britton & Rey [San Francisco]
Publisher: W. K. Parkinson, Auburn
Key/Vignettes/Misc: 24 vignettes
Locations: SCP; UCBL–B; Wells Fargo Bank Historical Collection, San Francisco, California
Catalogs/Checklists: SCP, p. 19 (862); Peters, COS, p. 142

52

Place: Auburn, California
Date: 1857
Title: Auburn, Placer County, Cal. 1857
Size: 10⁵⁄₁₆ × 17³⁄₁₆ in. (26.2 × 43.7 cm.)
Artist: [Kuchel & Dresel]
Lithographer: Kuchel & Dresel
Printer: Britton & Rey [San Francisco]
Publisher: W. K Parkinson
Key/Vignettes/Misc: [no vignettes]
Locations: ACMW–FW; UCBL–B; CHS–SF; LC–M (facsimile)
Catalogs/Checklists: ACMW–FW 1249

53

Place: Auburn, California
Date: Ca. 1879
Title: Auburn, Cal.
Size: 20⅜ × 27¾ in. (51.8 × 70.5 cm.)
Artist: C. P. Cook
Lithographer:
Printer: W. W. Elliott
Publisher: W. B. Lardner & Co.
Key/Vignettes/Misc: Refs. 1–19; 22 vignettes
Locations: ACMW–FW; SCP; UCBL–B
Catalogs/Checklists: ACMW–FW 1029; SCP, p. 19 (1135)

54

Place: Auburn, California
Date: 1891
Title: Birds Eye View of Auburn Placer County, Cal. 1891.
Size: 21⅛ × 31½ in. (53.8 × 80.1 cm.)
Artist: H. B. Elliott
Lithographer:
Printer: Elliott Pub. Co., 120 Sutter St., S. F.
Publisher:
Key/Vignettes/Misc: Refs. 1–28; 22 vignettes; description
Locations: UCBL–B; HEHL; CSL–S
Catalogs/Checklists:

55
Place: Auburn, California
Date: [189–?]
Title: Auburn Placer County California
Size: 26 × 34½ in. (66.2 × 87.8 cm.)
Artist: Carl Dahlgren
Lithographer:
Printer: A. Eckstein, chromolithografische Kunstanstalt, Stuttgart
Publisher:
Key/Vignettes/Misc: 32 vignettes; decorative border of fruits and plants
Locations: CSL–S
Catalogs/Checklists:

56
Place: Avalon, California
Date: [188–?]
Title: Avalon, Santa Catalina Island, Cal.
Size: 17 × 23 in. (43.2 × 58.6 cm.)
Artist:
Lithographer:
Printer:
Publisher: [Kurz & Allison]
Key/Vignettes/Misc:
Locations: UCBL–B; MM–NN; ACMW–FW; CHS–SF
Catalogs/Checklists: MM–NN, LP 4357; PAI 42; ACMW–FW 1250; Peters, COS, p. 41

57
Place: Azusa, California
Date: 1887
Title: Birds Eye View of Azusa Los Angeles Co. Cal. 1887.
Size: 19¼ × 25¼ in. (49 × 64.3 cm.)
Artist: E. S. Moore
Lithographer:
Printer:
Publisher:
Key/Vignettes/Misc: 2 vignettes
Locations: UCBL–B; HEHL; NHM–LA; UCLA–SC; LC–M (photo)
Catalogs/Checklists: PAI 37; LC–M, 16.2

58
Place: Bakersfield, California
Date: 1888
Title: Birds Eye View of Bakersfield, Kern Co. Cal. Looking East. 1888
Size: 20½ × 31¾ in. (52.2 × 80.8 cm.)
Artist: E. S. Moore
Lithographer:
Printer:
Publisher:
Key/Vignettes/Misc: 12 vignettes
Locations: CHS–C
Catalogs/Checklists:

59
Place: Bakersfield, California
Date: 1901
Title: Bakersfield, Kern County, California. 1901
Size: 25⅛ × 37 in. (63.9 × 94.2 cm.)
Artist: Vignettes from photographs by Ashton
Lithographer:
Printer: Britton & Rey, S. F.
Publisher: N. J. Stone Co., San Francisco, Cal.

Key/Vignettes/Misc: 24 vignettes
Locations: LC–M; CSL–S
Catalogs/Checklists: LC–M, 17

Place: Ballona Harbor, California
Date: 1887
See Los Angeles, California, 1887.

60
Place: Belvedere, California
Date: Ca. 1893
Title: Beautiful Belvedere
Size: 19½ × 26 in. (49 × 66.2 cm.)
Artist:
Lithographer:
Printer: Britton & Rey [San Francisco]
Publisher:
Key/Vignettes/Misc:
Locations: Unknown. Sold in 1980 by John Howell Books, San Francisco, California
Catalogs/Checklists:

61
Place: Benicia, California
Date: 1854
Title: Benecia and Mont Diablo from Straits of Carquinez
Size:
Artist: Thomas A. Ayres
Lithographer:
Printer:
Publisher:
Key/Vignettes/Misc:
Locations: MHdeY
Catalogs/Checklists: Peters, COS, p. 45

62
Place: Benicia, California
Date: 1885
Title: Benicia. Solano County, Cal. 1885
Size: 18⅞ × 27 in. (48 × 68.7 cm.)
Artist:
Lithographer:
Printer: W. W. Elliott, Lith. 921 B'dway, Oakland, Cal.
Publisher:
Key/Vignettes/Misc: Refs. 1–40; 23 vignettes
Locations: CSL–S; CHS–SF
Catalogs/Checklists:

Place: Benicia, California
Date: N.D.
See Martinez, California, n.d.

63
Place: Berkeley, California
Date: 1891
Title: Birdseye View of Berkeley, Cal. 1891.
Size: 20⅛ × 33¾ in. (51.2 × 85.8 cm.)
Artist: E. S. Moore
Lithographer:
Printer:
Publisher:
Key/Vignettes/Misc: Refs. 1–7; 18 vignettes
Locations: SCP; UCBL–B; CHS–SF; LC–M (facsimile)
Catalogs/Checklists: SCP, p. 19 (1133); LC–M, 17.1

64
Place: Berkeley, California
Date: [1909?]
Title: Berkeley, Cal.
Size: 12½ × 28½ in. (31.8 × 72.4 cm.)
Artist: Charles Green
Lithographer:
Printer:
Publisher:
Key/Vignettes/Misc:
Locations: LC–M
Catalogs/Checklists: LC–M, 18

65
Place: Berkeley, California
Date: 1926
Title: View of Lorin, South Berkeley, Cal. Looking West San Francisco in Distance
Size: 16 × 23 in. (40.7 × 58.6 cm.)
Artist:
Lithographer:
Printer:
Publisher:
Key/Vignettes/Misc: 6 refs.; 2 vignettes
Locations: CHS–SF
Catalogs/Checklists:

66
Place: Big Bar, California
Date: N.D.
Title: Big Bar—Middle Fork.
Size: 9½ × 12¹³⁄₁₆ in. (24.1 × 32.6 cm.)
Artist: Edwin Glover
Lithographer:
Printer: Justh, Quirot & Co., San Francisco
Publisher: Edwin Glover
Key/Vignettes/Misc:
Locations: UCBL–B
Catalogs/Checklists:

67
Place: Big Oak Flat, California
Date: 1858
Title: Big Oak Flat Tuolumne County California
Size: 8¼ × 12 in. (21 × 30.5 cm.)
Artist:
Lithographer:
Printer: J. Haehnlen's Lith. Phila[delphia]
Publisher: A. A. Mack, California
Key/Vignettes/Misc:
Locations: UCBL–B; SCP
Catalogs/Checklists: SCP, p. 19 (1162)

Place: Cahuenga, California
Date: 1887
See Hollywood, California, 1887.

68
Place: Calistoga, California
Date: Ca. 1870
Title: The Wonderful Calistoga Hot Sulphur Springs Napa Co. California.
Size: 21¹⁵⁄₁₆ × 27¹⁵⁄₁₆ in. (55.9 × 70.9 cm.)
Artist:
Lithographer:
Printer: Britton & Rey, San Francisco
Publisher:
Key/Vignettes/Misc:
Locations: SU–SC; CHS–SF
Catalogs/Checklists: Peters, COS, p. 86

69
Place: Calistoga, California
Date: 1871
Title: Calistoga Springs 1871.
Size: 10½ × 20¼ in. (26.8 × 51.6 cm.)
Artist:
Lithographer:
Printer: Britton & Rey, S. F.
Publisher:
Key/Vignettes/Misc:
Locations: UCBL–B; HEHL
Catalogs/Checklists:

70
Place: Chico, California
Date: 1871
Title: Birds Eye View of Chico Butte
County, Cal. 1871
Size: 18¾ × 24 in. (cropped) (47.7 × 61.1
cm.)
Artist: [Augustus Koch]
Lithographer:
Printer: Britton & Rey, S. F.
Publisher:
Key/Vignettes/Misc: Refs. 1–15
Locations: UCBL–B
Catalogs/Checklists:

71
Place: Chinese Camp, California
Date: 1858
Title: Chinese, Tuolumne County,
Southern Mines, California
Size: 9¾ × 15¾ in. (24.7 × 40 cm.)
Artist: Kuchel & Dresel
Lithographer: Kuchel & Dresel
Printer: Britton & Rey [San Francisco]
Publisher:
Key/Vignettes/Misc: 12 vignettes
Locations: ACMW–FW; SCP
Catalogs/Checklists: ACMW–FW 1251;
SCP, p. 19 (7); Peters, COS, p. 142

72
Place: Clear Lake, California
Date: [1890–91]
Title: Birds–Eye View of Clear Lake and
Surroundings Lake Co., Cal.
Size: 26⅜ × 40 in. (67.2 × 101.7 cm.)
Artist:
Lithographer:
Printer: Elliott Pub. Co. 120 Sutter St. S. F.
Publisher: Gerald S. Hertslet, Lower Lake,
Cal.
Key/Vignettes/Misc: Refs. 1–15; 17
vignettes; description
Locations: UCBL–B
Catalogs/Checklists:

73
Place: Coloma, California
Date: 1850
Title: A View of Sutter's Mill & Culloma
Valley. On the South Fork of the American
Line, Alta California
Size: 20¼ × 24⅞ in. (51.5 × 63.3 cm.)
Artist:
Lithographer:
Printer: Sarony & Major, New York
Publisher: John T. Little
Key/Vignettes/Misc:
Locations: ACMW–FW; CHS–SF;

HEHL; SCP; UCBL–B; YUAG–NH;
NYH–NY
Catalogs/Checklists: SCP, p. 19 (876);
Reps, Cities on Stone, p. 98; Peters, COS,
p. 186

74
Place: Coloma, California
Date: 1857
Title: Coloma, 1857. El Dorado County
California.
Size: 11¼ × 17⅝ in. (28.6 × 44.8 cm.)
Artist: Kuchel & Dresel
Lithographer: Kuchel & Dresel
Printer: Britton & Rey [San Francisco]
Publisher: George Searle, Coloma
Key/Vignettes/Misc: 20 vignettes
Locations: SCP; UCBL–B; CHS–SF
Catalogs/Checklists: SCP, p. 19 (865);
Peters, COS, pp. 86, 142–43

75
Place: Coloma, California
Date: 1857
Title: Coloma, 1857. El Dorado County,
California.
Size: 10½ × 14⅝ in. (26.7 × 37.2 cm.)
Artist: [Kuchel & Dresel]
Lithographer: [Kuchel & Dresel]
Printer:
Publisher: Kuchel & Dresel (copyright)
Key/Vignettes/Misc: Description
Locations: ACMW–FW; HEHL; LC–M
(facsimile)
Catalogs/Checklists: ACMW–FW 1254;
LC–M, 18.1

76
Place: Columbia, California
Date: 1852
Title: Columbia January, 1852.
Size: 10⁹⁄₁₆ × 16¹⁄₁₆ in. (26.9 × 40.9 cm.)
Artist: G. H. Goddard
Lithographer:
Printer: Pollard & Britton's Lith. Merchant
St. SF
Publisher: G. H. Goddard (copyright)
Key/Vignettes/Misc:
Locations: ACMW–FW; SCP; CHS–SF;
AAS–W; UCBL–B; LC–M (facsimile)
Catalogs/Checklists: ACMW–FW 1132;
Peters, COS, p. 124; Reps, Cities on Stone,
p. 92; SCP, p. 19 (1170)

77
Place: Columbia, California
Date: 1855
Title: Columbia, Southern Mines,
California.
Size: 17¾ × 24¹⁄₁₆ in. (45.2 × 61.3 cm.)
Artist: Kuchel & Dresel
Lithographer: Kuchel & Dresel
Printer: Britton & Rey [San Francisco]
Publisher: Towle & Leavitt, Columbia,
Tuolmne County, Cal.
Key/Vignettes/Misc: 20 vignettes
Locations: UCBL–B
Catalogs/Checklists:

78
Place: Columbia, California
Date: Ca. 1855
Title: Columbia, Tuolumne County

Size: ["medium"]
Artist: Kuchel & Dresel
Lithographer: Kuchel & Dresel
Printer: Britton & Rey
Publisher:
Key/Vignettes/Misc: [no vignettes]
Locations: Unknown
Catalogs/Checklists: Peters, COS, p. 143

79
Place: Columbia, California
Date: 1856
Title: Columbia, Southern Mines
(Tuolmne County), California (1856)
Size:
Artist: Kuchel & Dresel
Lithographer: Kuchel & Dresel
Printer: Britton & Rey [San Francisco]
Publisher: Kuchel & Dresel (copyright,
1855)
Key/Vignettes/Misc: 20 vignettes
Locations: Private collection
Catalogs/Checklists: PAI 31

80
Place: Coronado Beach, California
Date: Ca. 1887
Title: Bird's eye view of Coranado Beach,
San Diego Bay and City of San Diego, Cal.
in Distance.
Size: 19⅝ × 25¼ in. (47.4 × 64.2 cm.)
Artist: E. S. Moore
Lithographer:
Printer: Crocker & Co., Lith. S. F.
Publisher: Coronado Beach Company
Key/Vignettes/Misc: Refs. 1–22
Locations: MM–NN; San Diego
Historical Society; Junipero Serra
Museum, San Diego, California;
UCBL–B; EI–S; CHS–SF; UCLA–SC;
SLG–C; LC–M (photo)
Catalogs/Checklists: MM–NN, LP 2052;
Reps, Cities on Stone, p. 92; LC–M, 19.1

81
Place: Crescent City, California
Date: 1857
Title: Crescent City
Size: 9½ × 17⅞ in. (24.1 × 45.3 cm.)
Artist: Kuchel & Dresel
Lithographer: Kuchel & Dresel
Printer: Britton & Rey [San Francisco]
Publisher: Kuchel & Dresel (copyright)
Key/Vignettes/Misc:
Locations: ACMW–FW (lacks imprint);
CHS–SF
Catalogs/Checklists: ACMW–FW 1255;
Peters, COS, p. 143

82
Place: Crescent City, California
Date: 1857
Title: Crescent City, Klamath County, Cal.
1857.
Size: 16 × 24 in. (40.7 × 61 cm.)
Artist: Kuchel & Dresel
Lithographer: Kuchel & Dresel
Printer: Britton & Rey, San Francisco
Publisher:
Key/Vignettes/Misc: 23 vignettes
Locations: UCBL–B
Catalogs/Checklists:

83
Place: Downieville, California
Date: 1851
Title: View of Downieville, Forks of the North Yuba River (1851)
Size: 9¼ × 13¾ in. (23.5 × 35 cm.)
Artist: Wm. H. Grady
Lithographer:
Printer: Justh, Quirot & Co., California St. . ., San Fran.
Publisher: Samuel M. Langton, Downieville
Key/Vignettes/Misc:
Locations: Unknown
Catalogs/Checklists: Peters, COS, pp. 156, 175

84
Place: Downieville, California
Date: 1854
Title: Downieville—California.
Size: 10¹⁵⁄₁₆ × 13¹⁄₁₆ in. (27.8 × 33.2 cm.)
Artist: H. Eastman
Lithographer:
Printer: Britton & Rey, S. F.
Publisher: Downieville Book Store
Key/Vignettes/Misc:
Locations: UCBL–B
Catalogs/Checklists:

85
Place: Downieville, California
Date: 1856
Title: Downieville, 1856. Sierra County, California
Size: 16⅛ × 23⅝ in. (41 × 60 cm.)
Artist: Kuchel & Dresel
Lithographer: Kuchel & Dresel
Printer: Britton & Rey [San Francisco]
Publisher: A. T. Langton
Key/Vignettes/Misc: 24 vignettes
Locations: ACMW–FW; SCP; CHS–SF; UCBL–B; CHS–C; UCLA–SC; NYH–NY
Catalogs/Checklists: ACMW–FW 1257; SCP, p. 19 (821)

86
Place: Downieville, California
Date: 1856
Title: Downieville, Sierra County
Size: 12⅝ × 17½ in. (32.1 × 44.5 cm.)
Artist: Kuchel & Dresel
Lithographer: Kuchel & Dresel
Printer: Britton & Rey [San Francisco]
Publisher: Kuchel & Dresel (copyright)
Key/Vignettes/Misc: [no vignettes]
Locations: Unknown. Alta California Book Store, 2/9/80
Catalogs/Checklists: Peters, COS, p. 143

Place: East Los Angeles, California
Date: Ca. 1876
See Los Angeles, California, ca. 1876.

Place: East Los Angeles, California
Date: 1888
See Los Angeles, California, 1888.

87
Place: El Moro, California
Date: 1894
Title: Bird's Eye View of Moro Bay and Town of El Moro.

Size: 12⁹⁄₁₆ × 26⅞ in. (31 × 68.5 cm.)
Artist:
Lithographer:
Printer: Britton & Rey, S. F.
Publisher:
Key/Vignettes/Misc: Unnumbered refs. below places identified
Locations: HEHL
Catalogs/Checklists:

88
Place: Elsinore, California
Date: [1887]
Title: Elsinore, San Diego Co. Cal.
Size: 17⁵⁄₁₆ × 21¹⁵⁄₁₆ in. (44.1 × 55.9 cm.)
Artist: [E. S. Moore?]
Lithographer:
Printer:
Publisher: Wm. Varcoe & Co., Elsinore
Key/Vignettes/Misc: Refs. 1–26; 26 vignettes
Locations: UCBL–B; HEHL; UCLA–SC; SLG–C
Catalogs/Checklists:

89
Place: Eureka, California
Date: 1888
Title: Birdseye View of Eureka Humboldt County, California.
Size: 20 × 36⅛ in. (50.8 × 91.9 cm.)
Artist:
Lithographer:
Printer: W. W. Elliott
Publisher: Humboldt Times
Key/Vignettes/Misc: 28 vignettes
Locations: SCP; CHS–SF
Catalogs/Checklists: SCP, p. 19 (1113)

90
Place: Eureka, California
Date: 1902
Title: Compliments of Belcher & Crane Company, 531 Third Street, Eureka, Cal.
Size: 26½ × 38 in. (67.4 × 96.6 cm.)
Artist: From photographs by Miller
Lithographer:
Printer: Britton & Rey, San Francisco
Publisher: A. C. Noe & G. R. Georgeson
Key/Vignettes/Misc: 28 vignettes
Locations: LC–M; UCBL–B
Catalogs/Checklists: LC–M, 20

91
Place: Forest Hill, California
Date: 1857
Title: Forrest Hill Placer County 1857.
Size: 17½ × 20⅜ in. (44.6 × 51.9 cm.)
Artist: Kuchel & Dresel
Lithographer: Kuchel & Dresel
Printer: Britton & Rey [San Francisco]
Publisher: Kuchel & Dresel, 176 Clay St., San Francisco
Key/Vignettes/Misc: 10 vignettes
Locations: ACMW–FW; SCP; UCBL–B; HEHL
Catalogs/Checklists: ACMW–FW 1259; SCP, p. 19 (860); Reps, Cities on Stone, p. 93; Peters, COS, p. 143

92
Place: Forest Hill, California
Date: N.D.
Title: Forrest Hill, Placer County

Size: ["small"]
Artist:
Lithographer:
Printer: Britton & Rey
Publisher:
Key/Vignettes/Misc:
Locations: Unknown
Catalogs/Checklists: Peters, COS, p. 82

93
Place: Fort Yuma, California
Date: Ca. 1875
Title: Fort Yuma Colorado Rivr. Cala.
Size: 10 × 14⅞ in. (25.4 × 37.8 cm.)
Artist: [Geo. H. Baker ?]
Lithographer:
Printer: Geo. H. Baker, San Francisco
Publisher:
Key/Vignettes/Misc:
Locations: SCP; MHdeY (on loan to CHS–SF); CHS–C (dates ca. 1868)
Catalogs/Checklists: SCP, p. 19 (1315); Peters, COS, p. 52

Place: French Bar, California
Date: 1856
See Scotts Bar, California, 1856.

94
Place: French Bar, California
Date: 1857
Title: French Bar, Siskiyou Co.
Size: 11 × 10¹¹⁄₁₆ in. (28 × 27.2 cm.)
Artist: [Kuchel & Dresel]
Lithographer: [Kuchel & Dresel]
Printer: [Britton & Rey, San Francisco]
Publisher:
Key/Vignettes/Misc:
Locations: UCBL–B; CHS–SF
Catalogs/Checklists: Peters, COS, p. 143; PAI 22

95
Place: Fresno, California
Date: 1888
Title: Fresno, California
Size: 21¼ × 29¾ in. (54 × 75.6 cm.)
Artist: W. W. Elliott
Lithographer:
Printer: W. W. Elliott
Publisher: Fresno Daily Evening Expositor
Key/Vignettes/Misc: 22 vignettes
Locations: SCP
Catalogs/Checklists: SCP, p. 19 (1134)

96
Place: Fresno, California
Date: 1901
Title: Fresno California
Size: 25½ × 42 in. (64.7 × 106.6 cm.)
Artist: Lawrence
Lithographer:
Printer: Britton & Rey, S. F.
Publisher: L. W. Klein (copyright)
Key/Vignettes/Misc: 33 vignettes
Locations: LC–M
Catalogs/Checklists: Reps, Cities on Stone, p. 93; LC–M, 20.1

97
Place: Glendora, California
Date: 1888
Title: Bird's Eye View of Alosta, Los Angeles Co. Cal. Jan. 1888

Size: 20½ × 26 in. (52.2 × 66.2 cm.)
Artist: E. S. Moore
Lithographer:
Printer:
Publisher:
Key/Vignettes/Misc: Refs. A, 1–7; 8 vignettes
Locations: HEHL; UCBL–B; UCLA–SC
Catalogs/Checklists:

98

Place: Glendora, California
Date: [188–?]
Title: Glendora Los Angeles County California 25 Miles East from Los Angeles–on the Cal. Central R. R. . . .
Size: 16½ (cropped) × 24¾ in. (42 × 63 cm.)
Artist: [E. S. Moore?]
Lithographer:
Printer: Crocker & Company
Publisher: Glendora Land Company [Glendora]
Key/Vignettes/Misc: 21 vignettes; description
Locations: UCBL–B; HEHL (cropped)
Catalogs/Checklists: PAI 35

99

Place: Golden City, California
Date: N.D.
Title: California Golden City, Looking East.
Size: ["small"]
Artist: A. E. Mathews
Lithographer:
Printer:
Publisher:
Key/Vignettes/Misc:
Locations: Unknown
Catalogs/Checklists: Peters, COS, p. 162

100

Place: Goodyears Bar, California
Date: N.D.
Title: View of Goodyears Bar & Goodyears Creek. Sierra Co. Cala. With Monte–Cristo In The Distance.
Size: ["small"]
Artist: Wm. B. Monmonier
Lithographer:
Printer: Britton & Rey
Publisher: Wm. B. Monmonier, Goodyears Bar
Key/Vignettes/Misc:
Locations: Unknown
Catalogs/Checklists: Peters, COS, pp. 86, 164

101

Place: Grand Gulf City, California
Date: Ca. 1860
Title: Grand Gulf City, California
Size: ["medium"]
Artist: Baldwin
Lithographer:
Printer:
Publisher:
Key/Vignettes/Misc:
Locations: Unknown
Catalogs/Checklists: Peters, COS, p. 54

102

Place: Grass Valley, California
Date: 1852
Title: Grass Valley, Nevada County. California.
Size: 24 × 32½ in. (61.1 × 82.7 cm.)
Artist: R. E. Ogilby
Lithographer:
Printer: J. J. Le Count, San Francisco
Publisher:
Key/Vignettes/Misc:
Locations: CHS–SF
Catalogs/Checklists:

103

Place: Grass Valley, California
Date: 1852
Title: Grass Valley, Nevada County. California.
Size: 16¹⁵⁄₁₆ × 25½ in. (43.1 × 64.9 cm.)
Artist: R. E. Ogilby
Lithographer:
Printer: J. J. Le Count, San Francisco
Publisher:
Key/Vignettes/Misc:
Locations: SCP; UCBL–B; YUAG–NH
Catalogs/Checklists: SCP, p. 19 (834); Peters, COS, pp. 103, 175

104

Place: Grass Valley, California
Date: 1858
Title: Grass Valley, Nevada County, California, 1858.
Size: 18⁹⁄₁₆ × 30³⁄₁₆ in. (47.2 × 76.8 cm.)
Artist: Kuchel & Dresel
Lithographer: Kuchel & Dresel
Printer: Britton & Rey, Print [San Francisco]
Publisher: W. K. Spencer, Bookseller and Stationer
Key/Vignettes/Misc: 35 vignettes
Locations: SCP; ACMW–FW; CHS–SF; HEHL (cropped)
Catalogs/Checklists: PAI 28; SCP, p. 19 (908); Peters, COS, p. 143

105

Place: Grass Valley, California
Date: 1858
Title: Grass Valley, Nevada County, California, 1858.
Size: 19¼ × 31 in. (49 × 78.9 cm.)
Artist: Kuchel & Dresel
Lithographer: Kuchel & Dresel
Printer: Britton & Rey, Print [San Francisco]
Publisher: [n.p.]
Key/Vignettes/Misc: 35 vignettes
Locations: UCBL–B
Catalogs/Checklists:

106

Place: Grass Valley, California
Date: 1871
Title: Birds Eye View of Grass Valley, Nevada County, Cal. 1871.
Size: 21½ × 26⅜ in. (54.8 × 67.2 cm.)
Artist: Augustus Koch
Lithographer:
Printer: Britton & Rey, S. F.
Publisher:

Key/Vignettes/Misc: Refs. 1–37; 2 vignettes
Locations: CHS–SF; CSL–S; UCBL–B; ACMW–FW
Catalogs/Checklists:

107

Place: Grass Valley, California
Date: 1889
Title: Grass Valley, Cal. Looking West. 1889.
Size: 20½ × 26½ in. (52.2 × 67.4 cm.)
Artist: E. S. Moore
Lithographer:
Printer:
Publisher: Nevada Co. N. G. R. R. Co.
Key/Vignettes/Misc: 20 vignettes
Locations: CHS–SF; CSL–S; UCBL–B
Catalogs/Checklists:

108

Place: Grass Valley, California
Date: N.D.
Title: View of Grass Valley. Drawn Expressly for and Respectfully Dedicated to General Winchester. . . .
Size: 17⅝ × 26 in. (44.8 × 66.1 cm.)
Artist: R. E. Ogilby
Lithographer:
Printer: Sarony & Major, New York
Publisher:
Key/Vignettes/Misc:
Locations: UCBL–B
Catalogs/Checklists:

109

Place: Hayward, California
Date: Ca. 1890
Title: Birdseye View of Haywards
Size: 12 × 24 in. (30.6 × 61.1 cm.)
Artist: Cook
Lithographer:
Printer: Elliott Pub. Co. 120 Sutter St. S. F.
Publisher: Geo. A. Oakes
Key/Vignettes/Misc: 21 vignettes
Locations: UCBL–B
Catalogs/Checklists:

110

Place: Healdsburg, California
Date: Ca. 1876
Title: Bird's Eye View of Healdsburg, Cal.
Size: 16¹⁵⁄₁₆ × 23¾ in. (43.1 × 60.4 cm.)
Artist: E. S. Glover
Lithographer:
Printer: A. L. Bancroft & Co., Lith., S. F.
Publisher: Jordan Bros.
Key/Vignettes/Misc: 5 vignettes
Locations: LC–M; ACMW–FW; CHS–SF; CSL–S
Catalogs/Checklists: Peters, COS, p. 54; LC–M, 21

111

Place: Hollister, California
Date: Ca. 1884
Title: Hollister, San Benito County, Cal.
Size: 19 × 28¾ in. (48.3 × 73.2 cm.)
Artist: SBL (?)
Lithographer:
Printer: H. S. Crocker & Co.
Publisher: Hollister Free Lance

Key/Vignettes/Misc: Refs. 1–28; 17 vignettes
Locations: UCBL–B
Catalogs/Checklists:

112
Place: Hollywood, California
Date: 1887
Title: Birdeye View of Cahuenga
Size:
Artist:
Lithographer:
Printer:
Publisher: Cahuenga Land and Water Co.
Key/Vignettes/Misc:
Locations: Unknown. Negative in Historical Collection, Security Pacific National Bank, Los Angeles, California, Public Library
Catalogs/Checklists:

113
Place: Hollywood, California
Date: Ca. 1887
Title: Map of Hollywood
Size: 25⅝ × 39⅛ in. (65.3 × 99.6 cm.)
Artist:
Lithographer:
Printer: Los Angeles Litho. Co.
Publisher: H. H. Wilcox & Co. 34 N. Spring St., [Los Angeles?]
Key/Vignettes/Misc: Refs. 1–11; 1 vignette
Locations: HEHL
Catalogs/Checklists:

114
Place: Jackson, California
Date: 1857
Title: Jackson, Amador County, Cal. 1857
Size: 8¹/₁₆ × 14⁷/₁₆ in. (20.5 × 36.7 cm.)
Artist:
Lithographer:
Printer: Britton & Rey [San Francisco]
Publisher: Wesley Jackson
Key/Vignettes/Misc: [no vignettes]
Locations: CHS–SF; UCBL–B
Catalogs/Checklists:

115
Place: Jackson, California
Date: 1857
Title: Jackson, Amador County, Cal. 1857.
Size: 17¼ × 21¼ in. (43.9 × 54.1 cm.)
Artist: Kuchel & Dresel
Lithographer: Kuchel & Dresel
Printer: Britton & Rey [San Francisco]
Publisher: Wesley Jackson
Key/Vignettes/Misc: 16 vignettes
Locations: SCP; UCBL–B
Catalogs/Checklists: SCP, p. 19 (859); Peters, COS, p. 143

116
Place: Lakeport, California
Date: Ca. 1888
Title: Lakeport, Lake County, California, the Switzerland of America
Size: 18½ × 25½ in. (47.1 × 64.8 cm.)
Artist: Stanley Inchbold
Lithographer:

Printer: Britton & Rey, San Francisco
Publisher:
Key/Vignettes/Misc: 13 vignettes; 1 map
Locations: LC–M
Catalogs/Checklists: LC–M, 22

117
Place: Livermore, California
Date: 1889
Title: Livermore & Livermore Valley 1889
Size: 19 × 27 in. (48.4 × 68.7 cm.)
Artist: W. P. Bartlett
Lithographer:
Printer: Schmidt Label and Lithograph Co., S. F.
Publisher: W. W. Elliott
Key/Vignettes/Misc:
Locations: LC–M (photo)
Catalogs/Checklists: LC–M, 22.1

118
Place: Long Beach, California
Date: [1888?]
Title: Long Beach, California
Size: ["large oval"]
Artist: [Henry Steinegger?]
Lithographer:
Printer: Britton & Rey
Publisher:
Key/Vignettes/Misc:
Locations: Unknown
Catalogs/Checklists: Peters, COS, p. 83

119
Place: Los Angeles, California
Date: 1857
Title: Los Angeles, Los Angeles County, Cal. 1857
Size: 11⅞ × 17¾ in. (30.2 × 45.2 cm.)
Artist: Kuchel & Dresel
Lithographer: Kuchel & Dresel
Printer: Britton & Rey [San Francisco]
Publisher: [n.p.]
Key/Vignettes/Misc: [no vignettes]
Locations: ACMW–FW; CHS–SF; LC–M (facsimile); LC–P
Catalogs/Checklists: LC–M, 23

120
Place: Los Angeles, California
Date: 1857
Title: Los Angeles, Los Angeles County, Cal. 1857.
Size: 12⅜ × 17¼ in. (31.5 × 43.9 cm.)
Artist: Kuchel & Dresel
Lithographer: Kuchel & Dresel
Printer: Britton & Rey [San Francisco]
Publisher: Kuchel & Dresel (copyright)
Key/Vignettes/Misc: [no vignettes]
Locations: Unknown. Alta California Bookstore, 2/9/80
Catalogs/Checklists:

121
Place: Los Angeles, California
Date: 1857
Title: Los Angeles, Los Angeles County, Cal. 1857.
Size: 15¾ × 23⅛ in. (40 × 58.7 cm.)
Artist: Kuchel & Dresel
Lithographer: Kuchel & Dresel

Printer: Britton & Rey [San Francisco]
Publisher: Hellman & Bro.
Key/Vignettes/Misc: 20 vignettes
Locations: ACMW–FW; SCP; UCBL–B; HEHL
Catalogs/Checklists: SCP, p. 20 (779); Peters, COS, pp. 86, 143; ACMW–FW 1262; Reps, Cities on Stone, p. 94; PAI 39

122
Place: Los Angeles, California
Date: 1857
Title: Los Angeles, Los Angeles County, Cal. 1857.
Size: 15¾ × 23⅛ in. (40 × 58.7 cm.)
Artist: Kuchel & Dresel
Lithographer: Kuchel & Dresel
Printer: Britton & Rey [San Francisco]
Publisher: [n.p.]
Key/Vignettes/Misc: 20 vignettes
Locations: Wells Fargo Bank Historical Collection, San Francisco, California
Catalogs/Checklists:

123
Place: Los Angeles, California
Date: 1871
Title: City of Los Angeles Los Angeles County, Cal. 1871.
Size: 25 × 30¼ in. (63.5 × 76.9 cm.)
Artist: Augs. Koch
Lithographer:
Printer: Britton & Rey [San Francisco]
Publisher:
Key/Vignettes/Misc: Refs. 1–33; 11 vignettes
Locations: UCLA–SC; UCBL–B
Catalogs/Checklists: Peters, COS, pp. 80, 140

124
Place: Los Angeles, California
Date: 1873
Title: Los Angeles, Cal, 1873.
Size: 9 × 15¼ in. (22.9 × 38.8 cm.)
Artist: A. E. Mathews
Lithographer:
Printer: A. L. Bancroft & Co. Lith. . . .San Francisco
Publisher: A. L. Bancroft & Company, 721 Market Street, San Francisco, Cal.
Key/Vignettes/Misc: Description
Locations: NHS–R; WHPL–D; CHS–C; NHM–LA; LC–M (facsimile); UCBL–B
Catalogs/Checklists: LC–M, 24

125
Place: Los Angeles, California
Date: Ca. 1876
Title: View of East Los Angeles, California. From Brooklyn Hights, looking North to the Sierra Madre Mountains.
Size:
Artist: E. S. Glover
Lithographer:
Printer: A. L. Bancroft & Co., Lith. San Francisco
Publisher:
Key/Vignettes/Misc: Refs. 1–10
Locations: UCBL–B; UCLA–SC
Catalogs/Checklists:

126
Place: Los Angeles, California
Date: 1877
Title: Birds Eye View of Los Angeles California. Birds Eye View of Wilmington Los Angeles Co. Cal. Birds Eye View of Santa Monica Los Angeles Co. Cal.
Size: 20¹³⁄₁₆ × 33¼ in. (53 × 84.6 cm.)
Artist: E. S. Glover
Lithographer:
Printer: A. L. Bancroft & Co. Lith, San Francisco, Cal.
Publisher: E. S. Glover, Los Angeles, Cal.
Key/Vignettes/Misc: 5 unnumbered refs. below places identified
Locations: LC–M; UCBL–B; UCLA–SC
Catalogs/Checklists: LC–M, 26; Reps, Cities on Stone, p. 94; Peters, COS, p. 54

127
Place: Los Angeles, California
Date: 1877
Title: Birds Eye View of Los Angeles, Ca. 1877. Looking South to the Pacific Ocean. Twenty Miles Distant. East Los Angeles. West Los Angeles.
Size: 11⅜ × 33¼ in. (29 × 84.6 cm.)
Artist: E. S. Glover
Lithographer:
Printer: A. L. Bancroft & Co., San Francisco
Publisher: E. S. Glover, Los Angeles
Key/Vignettes/Misc:
Locations: UCBL–B
Catalogs/Checklists:

128
Place: Los Angeles, California
Date: 1877
Title: Key to the City of Los Angeles, Cal. Bird's Eye View, Looking South to the Pacific Ocean. 1877
Size: 9⅜ × 15¹¹⁄₁₆ in. (23.9 × 39.9 cm.)
Artist: E. S. Glover
Lithographer:
Printer: [Los Angeles Weekly Herald]
Publisher: Los Angeles Weekly Herald
Key/Vignettes/Misc: Refs. 1–77, 100–101, A–Z; Unnumbered church directory; description
Locations: UCBL–B
Catalogs/Checklists:

129
Place: Los Angeles, California
Date: 1877
Title: View of Los Angeles from the East. Brooklyn Hights in the foreground. Pacific Ocean and Santa Monica Mountains in the Background.
Size: 9¹³⁄₁₆ × 23½ in. (24.9 × 59.8 cm.)
Artist: E. S. Glover
Lithographer:
Printer: A. L. Bancroft & Co., Lith, S. F.
Publisher: Brooklyn Land and Building Co., Los Angeles, Cal.
Key/Vignettes/Misc: Refs. 1–20
Locations: NYP–S; LC–M; CHS–C; HEHL; ACMW–FW; UCBL–B; CSL–S; SWM–LA; YUAG–NH

Catalogs/Checklists: Stokes P. 1876— G–89; LC–M, 25; Peters, COS, pp. 55, 124

130
Place: Los Angeles, California
Date: 1877
Title: Weekly Herald Supplement. Los Angeles, Saturday, March 10th, 1877. Key to the City of Los Angeles, Cal. Bird's Eye View, Looking South to the Pacific Ocean. 1877
Size: 9¹⁵⁄₁₆ × 15⅝ in. (25.3 × 39.8 cm.)
Artist: E. S. Glover
Lithographer:
Printer: [Los Angeles Weekly Herald]
Publisher: Los Angeles Weekly Herald
Key/Vignettes/Misc: Refs. 1–77, 100–101, A–Z; unnumbered church directory; prices
Locations: UCBL–B
Catalogs/Checklists:

131
Place: Los Angeles, California
Date: 1887
Title: "The Palms" and Birds Eye View of Ballona Harbor (proposed) and Pacific Ocean 5 Miles to the Southwest as Seen from Reservoir Hill September 1887
Size: 39 × 26½ in. (99.3 × 67.5 cm.)
Artist:
Lithographer:
Printer: Los Angeles Lithographic Co. [Los Angeles]
Publisher: [Curtis & Sweetser, Los Angeles?]
Key/Vignettes/Misc: 3 vignettes; 1 map
Locations: SLG–C
Catalogs/Checklists:

132
Place: Los Angeles, California
Date: 1887
Title: Los Angeles, Cal. Looking Southwest to the Pacific Ocean, 1887
Size: 23⁷⁄₁₆ × 35¹¹⁄₁₆ in. (59.7 × 90.8 cm.)
Artist:
Lithographer:
Printer: W. W. Elliott, Lith Oakland, Cal.
Publisher:
Key/Vignettes/Misc: Refs. 1–62 (NHM–LA cropped)
Locations: SCP; NHM–LA; HEHL
Catalogs/Checklists: SCP, p. 20 (1112)

133
Place: Los Angeles, California
Date: 1888
Title: East Los Angeles, Los Angeles County, California. 1888
Size: 22½ × 36 in. (57.3 × 91.6 cm.)
Artist: B. W. Pierce
Lithographer:
Printer: H. S. Crocker & Co. S. F.
Publisher:
Key/Vignettes/Misc: Refs. 1–32; 34 vignettes
Locations: UCBL–B; HEHL; NHM–LA
Catalogs/Checklists:

134
Place: Los Angeles, California
Date: [1888]
Title: Los Angeles, Cal.
Size: 18 × 33⅞ in. (45.8 × 86.2 cm.)
Artist: S. F. Cook
Lithographer: H. Stggr. [H. Steinegger]
Printer: Britton & Rey, S F
Publisher: A. J. Hatch & Co. San Francisco (copyright)
Key/Vignettes/Misc:
Locations: SCP; LC–P; HEHL
Catalogs/Checklists: SCP, p. 20 (1163); Peters, COS, pp. 83, 99; LC–M, 26.1

135
Place: Los Angeles, California
Date: 1891
Title: Los Angeles. Cal. Population of City and Environs 65,000.
Size: 30⅝ × 43¼ in. (77.9 × 110 cm.)
Artist: H. B. Elliott
Lithographer:
Printer: Elliott Pub. Co., 120 Sutter St. San Francisco
Publisher: Southern California Land Co. [Los Angeles]
Key/Vignettes/Misc: Refs. 1–83; 29 vignettes
Locations: LC–M; NHM–LA
Catalogs/Checklists: LC–M, 24

136
Place: Los Angeles, California
Date: [1893?]
Title: Bird–Eye–View of Los Angeles
Size: 8¼ × 19⅝ in. (21 × 50 cm.) (photo)
Artist:
Lithographer:
Printer:
Publisher:
Key/Vignettes/Misc:
Locations: LC–M (photo)
Catalogs/Checklists: LC–M, 27.1

137
Place: Los Angeles, California
Date: 1894
Title: Los Angeles, California, 1894
Size: 29³⁄₁₆ × 43¾ in. (74.1 × 111 cm.)
Artist: B. W. Pierce
Lithographer: B. W. Pierce
Printer: L. A. Litho. Co.
Publisher: Semi–Tropic Homestead Co. Stimpson Block [Los Angeles]
Key/Vignettes/Misc: Refs. upper view, 1–126, lower view, 1–40; 9 vignettes; description
Locations: ACMW–FW; NHM–LA; LC–M
Catalogs/Checklists: Reps, Cities on Stone, p. 94; LC–M, 28

138
Place: Los Angeles, California
Date: 1909
Title: Los Angeles 1909
Size: 39 × 56¾ in. (99.3 × 144.4 cm.)
Artist:
Lithographer:

Printer:
Publisher: Birdseye View Publishing Co.,
L. A.
Key/Vignettes/Misc: Ca. 955 refs.
Locations: HEHL
Catalogs/Checklists:

139
Place: Los Angeles, California
Date: 1909
Title: Los Angeles 1909.
Size: 22½ × 36 in. (57.2 × 91.5 cm.)
Artist: Worthington Gates
Lithographer:
Printer: Western Lith. Co., Los Angeles
Publisher: Bird's Eye View Publishing Co.,
Grosse Bldg. Los Angeles, Cal.
Key/Vignettes/Misc: Numbers and letters
on margin for use with separately
published key
Locations: LC–M
Catalogs/Checklists: LC–M, 29

140
Place: Los Angeles, California
Date: 1913
Title: Business Property Map of Los
Angeles
Size: 17⁷⁄₁₆ × 46⁷⁄₁₆ in. (44.3 × 118 cm.)
Artist:
Lithographer:
Printer:
Publisher: Robert Marsh & Co.
Marsh–Strong Bldg., Los Angeles
Key/Vignettes/Misc:
Locations: UCLA–SC
Catalogs/Checklists:

141
Place: Martinez, California
Date: N.D.
Title: View of Martines and Benicia,
California.
Size: 10¼ × 17½ in. (26.1 × 44.5 cm.)
Artist: Pendergraft
Lithographer: K. Gildemeister
Printer: Nagle & Weingartner, N. Y.
Publisher:
Key/Vignettes/Misc:
Locations: NYH–NY
Catalogs/Checklists:

142
Place: Marysville, California
Date: 1856
Title: Marysville
Size: 21¹⁄₁₆ × 29³⁄₈ in. (53.6 × 74.8 cm.)
Artist: Kuchel & Dresel
Lithographer: Kuchel & Dresel
Printer: Britton & Rey [San Francisco]
Publisher: G. & O. Amy, Music &
Booksellers Marysville
Key/Vignettes/Misc: 32 vignettes
Locations: UCBL–B; CHS–SF
Catalogs/Checklists: Peters, COS, p. 144

143
Place: Marysville, California
Date: Ca. 1888
Title: Bird's Eye View of Marysville and
Yuba City, Cal. and Surrounding Country.
Size: 19½ × 29¼ in. (49.7 × 74.5 cm.)

Artist: C. P. Cook
Lithographer:
Printer: W. W. Elliott, S. F.
Publisher: Daily and Weekly Democrat,
Marysville
Key/Vignettes/Misc: Refs. 1–56, A–C; 18
vignettes; description
Locations: CSL–S
Catalogs/Checklists:

144
Place: Merced, California
Date: 1888
Title: View of Merced Cal. 1888.
Size: 19³⁄₈ × 26¹⁄₈ in. (49.4 × 66.5 cm.)
Artist: E. S. Moore
Lithographer:
Printer:
Publisher: M. S. Huffman
Key/Vignettes/Misc: 8 vignettes
Locations: UCBL–B
Catalogs/Checklists:

145
Place: Minnesota, California
Date: 1858
Title: View of Minnesota with Orleans
Flat in the Distance, Taken from the Hill in
the Rear of The Spring House.
Size: ["small"]
Artist: Wm. B. Monmonier
Lithographer:
Printer: Britton & Rey
Publisher: Wm. B. Monmonier,
Downieville, Cal.
Key/Vignettes/Misc:
Locations: Unknown
Catalogs/Checklists: Peters, COS, pp. 86,
164

Place: Mission Dolores, California
Date: 1860
See San Francisco, 1860.

146
Place: Modesto, California
Date: 1888
Title: Birds Eye View of Modesto
Stanislaus County, Cal. 1888 (Looking
East.)
Size: 14½ × 21¼ in. (36.9 × 54 cm.)
Artist: W. W. Elliott
Lithographer:
Printer: W. W. Elliott, San Francisco
Publisher:
Key/Vignettes/Misc: Refs. 0–35; 22
vignettes; description
Locations: CSL–S
Catalogs/Checklists:

147
Place: Mokelumne Hill, California
Date: 1855
Title: Mokelumne Hill, Calaveras County
Size: 16³⁄₈ × 24 in. (41.7 × 61.1 cm.)
Artist: Kuchel & Dresel
Lithographer: Kuchel & Dresel
Printer: Britton & Rey [San Francisco]
Publisher: A. Rosenfield, Bookseller &
Stationer, Mokelumne Hill
Key/Vignettes/Misc: 22 vignettes
Locations: UCBL–B; CHS–SF; CHS–C
Catalogs/Checklists:

148
Place: Mokelumne Hill, California
Date: Ca. 1855
Title: Mokelumne Hill, Calaveras County
Size: ["medium"]
Artist: Kuchel & Dresel
Lithographer: Kuchel & Dresel
Printer: Britton & Rey
Publisher:
Key/Vignettes/Misc: [no vignettes]
Locations: Unknown
Catalogs/Checklists: Peters, COS, p. 144

149
Place: Mokelumne Hill, California
Date: N.D.
Title: Mokelumne Hill
Size: 8¹⁵⁄₁₆ × 17⁵⁄₈ in. (22.7 × 44.8 cm.)
Artist:
Lithographer:
Printer:
Publisher:
Key/Vignettes/Misc:
Locations: ACMW–FW
Catalogs/Checklists: ACMW–FW 1810

150
Place: Mokelumne Hill, California
Date: N.D.
Title: View of Mokelumne Hill.
Size: ["small"]
Artist: Borthwick
Lithographer:
Printer: Quirot & Company
Publisher:
Key/Vignettes/Misc:
Locations: Unknown
Catalogs/Checklists: Peters, COS, p. 138

151
Place: Mokelumne Hill, California
Date: ?
Title: Mokelumne Hill
Size:
Artist: G. H. Burgess
Lithographer:
Printer: Britton & Rey
Publisher:
Key/Vignettes/Misc:
Locations: Unknown
Catalogs/Checklists: Peters, COS, p. 86

152
Place: Monrovia, California
Date: 1887
Title: The Town of Monrovia, Los Angeles
Co., Cal. 16 Months Old, Oct. 17, 1887.
Population 1500 Also Showing the Map
and Location of the Pacific View Tract.
Size: 21¼ × 29½ in. (54.1 × 75.1 cm.)
Artist:
Lithographer:
Printer: H. S. Crocker & Co., S. F.
Publisher:
Key/Vignettes/Misc: 1 vignette
Locations: NHM–LA
Catalogs/Checklists:

153
Place: Monrovia, California
Date: Ca. 1887
Title: Monrovia.

Size: 17¾ × 26³⁄₁₆ in. (45.2 × 66.7 cm.)
Artist: E. S. Moore
Lithographer: H. Steinegger
Printer: Britton & Rey, S. F.
Publisher:
Key/Vignettes/Misc: 13 vignettes; description
Locations: NHM–LA
Catalogs/Checklists:

154
Place: Monterey, California
Date: [1851]
Title: Harbour and City of Monterey, California 1842.
Size: 15 × 29³⁄₁₆ in. (38.1 × 74.1 cm.)
Artist:
Lithographer: Gildemeister
Printer: D'Avignon
Publisher: [Thomas Larkin]
Key/Vignettes/Misc:
Locations: ACMW–FW; OM–O; SCP; UCBL–B; CHS–C; MMM–B; LC–M (facsimile); NYH–NY
Catalogs/Checklists: Reps, Cities on Stone, p. 94; LC–M, 29.1

155
Place: Monterey, California
Date: [1851]
Title: The City of Monterey, California 1842.
Size: 14½ × 29 in. (36.9 × 73.7 cm.)
Artist:
Lithographer: Gildemeister
Printer: D'Avignon, 323 Broadway, N. Y.
Publisher: [Thomas Larkin]
Key/Vignettes/Misc:
Locations: OM–O; SCP; HEHL; UCBL–B; CSL–S; NYH–NY
Catalogs/Checklists: Peters, COS, p. 111

156
Place: Monterey, California
Date: N.D.
Title: Monterey Capital of California
Size: ["small"]
Artist:
Lithographer:
Printer: William Endicott & Company
Publisher:
Key/Vignettes/Misc:
Locations: Unknown
Catalogs/Checklists: Peters, COS, p. 118

157
Place: Monterey, California
Date: N.D.
Title: View and Map of Oak Grove Addition, Monterey, Calif.
Size:
Artist:
Lithographer:
Printer: H. S. Crocker Co.
Publisher:
Key/Vignettes/Misc:
Locations: UCBL–B
Catalogs/Checklists:

158
Place: Murphys, California
Date: 1857
Title: Murphys Calaveras County, Cal. 1857

Size: 8⅛ × 14⅛ in. (20.7 × 35.9 cm.)
Artist: Kuchel & Dresel
Lithographer: Kuchel & Dresel
Printer: Britton & Rey [San Francisco]
Publisher: Wm. W. Lapham
Key/Vignettes/Misc: [no vignettes]
Locations: UCBL–B; CHS–SF
Catalogs/Checklists:

159
Place: Murphys, California
Date: 1857
Title: Murphys Calaveras County, Cal. 1857
Size: 17⅛ × 21¼ in. (43.6 × 54.1 cm.)
Artist: Kuchel & Dresel
Lithographer: Kuchel & Dresel
Printer: Britton & Rey [San Francisco]
Publisher: Wm. W. Lapham
Key/Vignettes/Misc: 17 vignettes
Locations: SCP
Catalogs/Checklists: SCP, p. 20 (866); Peters, COS, p. 144

160
Place: Murphys, California
Date: 1857
Title: Murphys, Calaveras County, Cal. 1857
Size: 10⅝ × 14½ in. (27 × 36.9 cm.)
Artist: Kuchel & Dresel
Lithographer: Kuchel & Dresel
Printer: Britton & Rey [San Francisco]
Publisher: Kuchel & Dresel (copyright)
Key/Vignettes/Misc: [no vignettes]
Locations: Unknown. Alta California Bookstore, 2/9/80
Catalogs/Checklists:

161
Place: Napa, California
Date: [1880]
Title: Birdseye View of Napa City California. Looking West.
Size: 19⅛ × 29 in. (48.7 × 73.8 cm.)
Artist: C. J. Dyer
Lithographer:
Printer:
Publisher: David L. Haas, Bookseller, Stationer & Lithographer, Napa, Cala.
Key/Vignettes/Misc: Refs. 1–28; 4 vignettes
Locations: UCBL–B; SCP
Catalogs/Checklists: SCP, p. 20 (291)

162
Place: Napa, California
Date: 1889
Title: Napa City 1889
Size: 23½ × 34 in. (59.8 × 86.5 cm.)
Artist:
Lithographer:
Printer:
Publisher:
Key/Vignettes/Misc: 37 vignettes
Locations: CHS–SF
Catalogs/Checklists:

163
Place: Nevada City, California
Date: 1856
Title: Nevada. 1856.
Size: 20⅝ × 30 in. (52.5 × 76.3 cm.)
Artist: Kuchel & Dresel

Lithographer: Kuchel & Dresel
Printer: Britton & Rey [San Francisco]
Publisher: J. E. Hamlin, Bookseller, Nevada, California.
Key/Vignettes/Misc: 34 vignettes
Locations: CHS–C; CSL–S; UCBL–B
Catalogs/Checklists:

164
Place: Nevada City, California
Date: 1856
Title: Nevada, 1856.
Size: 9⅞ × 21¹¹⁄₁₆ in. (25 × 55.1 cm.)
Artist: Kuchel & Dresel
Lithographer: Kuchel & Dresel
Printer: Britton & Rey [San Francisco]
Publisher:
Key/Vignettes/Misc: [no vignettes]
Locations: SCP; ACMW–FW (without letters); UCBL–B; CHS–SF
Catalogs/Checklists: SCP, p. 20 (718); Peters, COS, p. 144; ACMW–FW 1813; Reps, Cities on Stone, p. 94

165
Place: Nevada City, California
Date: 1871
Title: Birdseye View of the City of Nevada Nevada County, Cal. 1871
Size: 19 × 26 in. (48.4 × 66.1 cm.)
Artist: Augustus Koch
Lithographer:
Printer: Britton & Rey, S. F.
Publisher:
Key/Vignettes/Misc: Refs. 1–23; 1 vignette
Locations: SCP; UCBL–B; CHS–SF
Catalogs/Checklists: SCP, p. 20 (100); Peters, COS, pp. 81, 140

166
Place: Nevada City, California
Date: 1883
Title: Birdseye View of Nevada City Nevada County, Cal.
Size: 21¼ × 35 in. (54 × 89 cm.)
Artist:
Lithographer:
Printer: Britton & Rey [San Francisco]
Publisher: A. S. Chase
Key/Vignettes/Misc: Refs. 1–48; 7 vignettes
Locations: SCP; UCBL–B; CHS–SF
Catalogs/Checklists: SCP, p. 20 (1120); Peters, COS, p. 80

167
Place: Nevada City, California
Date: N.D.
Title: View of Nevada.
Size: 7⁷⁄₁₆ × 13³⁄₁₆ in. (18.9 × 33.5 cm.)
Artist: From daguerreotype by Kilbourn
Lithographer:
Printer: Britton & Rey. . .S.F.
Publisher: A. W. Potter, Miners Book Store, Main St.
Key/Vignettes/Misc:
Locations: UCBL–B; NYH–NY
Catalogs/Checklists:

168
Place: North Elsinore, California
Date: Ca. 1887
Title: North Elsinore

Size: 21¼ × 27½ n. (54 × 70 cm.)
Artist:
Lithographer:
Printer: Los Angeles Lithographic Co., Los Angeles
Publisher:
Key/Vignettes/Misc:
Locations: NHM–LA
Catalogs/Checklists:

169
Place: North San Juan, California
Date: 1858
Title: North San Juan, Nevada County, California
Size: 14⅜ × 19⅞ in. (36.5 × 50.5 cm.)
Artist: Kuchel & Dresel
Lithographer: Kuchel & Dresel
Printer: Britton & Rey [San Francisco]
Publisher: Theodore Green
Key/Vignettes/Misc: 16 vignettes
Locations: ACMW–FW; SCP; UCBL–B; CHS–SF; CHS–C; CSL–S
Catalogs/Checklists: ACMW–FW 1263; Peters, COS, p. 144; SCP, p. 20 (830)

170
Place: Oakland, California
Date: Ca. 1870
Title: City of Oakland and Vicinity
Size: 29⅜ × 32¾ in. (74.7 × 83.2 cm.)
Artist: Augustus Koch
Lithographer:
Printer: Britton & Rey [San Francisco]
Publisher: Snow & Roos [San Francisco]
Key/Vignettes/Misc: Refs. 1–55
Locations: SCP; CHS–C
Catalogs/Checklists: SCP, p. 20 (1109); Peters, COS, pp. 81, 140

171
Place: Oakland, California
Date: [1880?]
Title: Oakland, Cal. From Academy Hill on the North.
Size: 19¾ × 33⅛ in. (50.3 × 84.3 cm.)
Artist:
Lithographer:
Printer: Strobridge & Co. Lith. Cin.O.
Publisher: L. K. Mihills, Oakland
Key/Vignettes/Misc: 7 vignettes; advertisement; description
Locations: UCBL–B; CHS–SF
Catalogs/Checklists:

172
Place: Oakland, California
Date: 1881
Title: Bird's Eye View of the City of Oakland, Cal. From the North.
Size: 24³⁄₁₆ × 35⁹⁄₁₆ in. (61.6 × 90.5 cm.)
Artist:
Lithographer:
Printer:
Publisher: Times Pub'g Co. [Oakland?]
Key/Vignettes/Misc: 4 vignettes; table of statistics
Locations: UCBL–B; CHS–SF
Catalogs/Checklists:

173
Place: Oakland, California
Date: [1887]
Title: Bird's Eye View of Oakland &

Vicinity, Alameda Co., California.
Size: 20¹⁄₁₆ × 30⅛ in. (51 × 76.7 cm.)
Artist:
Lithographer:
Printer: Britton & Rey, S. F.
Publisher: The Oakland Tribune [Oakland]
Key/Vignettes/Misc:
Locations: WHS–M; UCBL–B; LC–M (photo)
Catalogs/Checklists: LC–M, 29.2

174
Place: Oakland, California
Date: 1900
Title: Oakland California 1900
Size: 26¹³⁄₁₆ × 43⅛ in. (68 × 109.4 cm.)
Artist: F. L.
Lithographer:
Printer: Mutual L. & Lith. Co. S. F.
Publisher: F. & H. Soderberg
Key/Vignettes/Misc: 32 vignettes
Locations: ACMW–FW; LC–M
Catalogs/Checklists: Reps, Cities on Stone, p. 95; LC–M, 30

175
Place: Oceanside, California
Date: [188–]
Title: Oceanside, San Diego County, California.
Size: 23¼ × 32 in. (59.2 × 81.4 cm.)
Artist:
Lithographer:
Printer:
Publisher: Los Angeles Lith. Co. 48 Banning St. Los Angeles Cal.
Key/Vignettes/Misc: 3 vignettes; description; table of distances to other cities
Locations: HEHL
Catalogs/Checklists:

176
Place: Ontario, California
Date: N.D.
Title: A View Northward from the Town of Ontario, Cal. With San Antonio Heights and, Sierra Madre Mts. Six Miles Distant.
Size: 18 × 25¼ in. (45.8 × 64.3 cm.)
Artist:
Lithographer:
Printer: H. S. Crocker & Co. Lith. S. Fr.
Publisher: Ontario Land and Improvement Co.
Key/Vignettes/Misc:
Locations: UCBL–B; HEHL
Catalogs/Checklists: PAI 38

177
Place: Palo Alto, California
Date: 1888
Title: Palo Alto and the Leland Stanford Junior University Map of Palo Alto, the Town of the Leland Stanford Junior University.
Size: 36 × 26¼ in. (91.6 × 66.8 cm.)
Artist:
Lithographer:
Printer: Dakin Pub. Co., San Francisco
Publisher:
Key/Vignettes/Misc:

Locations: CHS–SF
Catalogs/Checklists:

178
Place: Palo Alto, California
Date: 1889
Title: Birds–Eye View of Mayfield, Leland Stanford, Jr. University and Palo Alto, the University Town.
Size: 20¾ × 31¹⁄₁₆ in. (52.8 × 79.1 cm.)
Artist:
Lithographer:
Printer: Dakin Pub. Co. Lith. 320 Sansome St. S. F.
Publisher: Carnall–Fitzhugh–Hopkins Co. 624 Market St. S. F.
Key/Vignettes/Misc: Refs. 1–7; 12 vignettes
Locations: UCBL–B
Catalogs/Checklists:

179
Place: Pasadena, California
Date: [188–?]
Title: Pasadena, Los Angeles County, Cal.
Size: 21½ × 31 in. (54.8 × 78.9 cm.)
Artist:
Lithographer: C. D.
Printer: Elliott Lith., Oakland, Cal.
Publisher:
Key/Vignettes/Misc: Refs. 1–33, A–C; 22 vignettes
Locations: CHS–SF; HEHL; UCBL–B; UCLA–SC; Pasadena Historical Society, Pasadena, California
Catalogs/Checklists:

180
Place: Pasadena, California
Date: 1893
Title: Pasadena California, 1893
Size: 25³⁄₁₆ × 40⅛ in. (64 × 101.9 cm.)
Artist: B. W. Pierce
Lithographer: B. W. Pierce
Printer:
Publisher: Wood & Church No. 52 E. Colorado St. [Pasadena]
Key/Vignettes/Misc: Refs. 1–60; 19 vignettes
Locations: ACMW–FW; UCBL–B; CHS–SF; Pasadena Historical Society, Pasadena, California; LC–M (facsimile)
Catalogs/Checklists: ACMW–FW 1593; Reps, Cities on Stone, p. 95; LC–M, 30.1

181
Place: Pasadena, California
Date: [1903?]
Title: Bird's Eye View of Pasadena and Vicinity
Size: 17⁵⁄₁₆ × 28⁵⁄₁₆ in. (44 × 72 cm.)
Artist:
Lithographer:
Printer:
Publisher: Wm. R. Staats Co.
Key/Vignettes/Misc:
Locations: LC–M
Catalogs/Checklists: LC–M, 30.2

182
Place: Petaluma, California
Date: 1857
Title: Petaluma Sonoma County, Cal. 1857.

Size: 13⅞ × 20⁹⁄₁₆ in. (35.3 × 52.3 cm.)
Artist: Kuchel & Dresel
Lithographer: Kuchel & Dresel
Printer: Britton & Rey [San Francisco]
Publisher: S. C. Haydon, Petaluma
Key/Vignettes/Misc: 14 vignettes
Locations: SCP; CHS–SF
Catalogs/Checklists: SCP, p. 20 (864);
Peters, COS, p. 144

183

Place: Petaluma, California
Date: 1857
Title: Petaluma, Sonoma County, Cal.
1857.
Size: ca. 10 × 14½ in. (ca. 25.5 × 36.9
cm.)
Artist: Kuchel & Dresel
Lithographer: Kuchel & Dresel
Printer: Britton & Rey [San Francisco]
Publisher: Kuchel & Dresel (copyright)
Key/Vignettes/Misc: [no vignettes]
Locations: UCBL–B (lacks letters except
for copyright); Alta California Book
Store, 3/9/80
Catalogs/Checklists:

184

Place: Petaluma, California
Date: 1871
Title: Birdseye View of the City of
Petaluma Sonoma County, California
1871.
Size: 20⅛ × 26³⁄₁₆ in. (51.1 × 66.6 cm.)
Artist: Augustus Koch
Lithographer:
Printer: Britton & Rey [San Francisco]
Publisher:
Key/Vignettes/Misc:
Locations: SCP
Catalogs/Checklists: SCP, p. 20 (1117);
Peters, COS, pp. 81, 140

185

Place: Petaluma, California
Date: Ca. 1892
Title: Petaluma, Sonoma Co., Calif
Size: 18 × 24½ in. (45.8 × 62.3 cm.)
Artist:
Lithographer:
Printer: Elliott Pub. Co.
Publisher: Geo. C. Codding
Key/Vignettes/Misc: 11 vignettes
Locations: UCBL–B
Catalogs/Checklists:

186

Place: Placerville, California
Date: 1851
Title: Placerville (Hangtown) El Dorado
Co. Cal
Size: 6½ × 8¾ in. (16.5 × 22.2 cm.)
Artist: John Whitford
Lithographer:
Printer: Justh & Co. Montgomery St. 253
[San Francisco]
Publisher: Albert W. Bee, Placerville
Key/Vignettes/Misc:
Locations: CHS–C
Catalogs/Checklists: Peters, COS, p. 133

187

Place: Placerville, California
Date: 1856
Title: Placerville, El Dorado County
Size: 18¹⁄₁₆ × 26⁷⁄₁₆ in. (45.9 × 67.1 cm.)
Artist: Kuchel & Dresel
Lithographer: Kuchel & Dresel
Printer: Britton & Rey [San Francisco]
Publisher: Davis & Roy, Booksellers &
Stationers, Placerville
Key/Vignettes/Misc: 26 vignettes
Locations: ACMW–FW
Catalogs/Checklists: ACMW–FW 1265

188

Place: Placerville, California
Date: 1856
Title: Placerville, El Dorado County.
Size: 13½ × 20½ in. (34.4 × 52.2 cm.)
Artist: Kuchel & Dresel
Lithographer: Kuchel & Dresel
Printer: Britton & Rey [San Francisco]
Publisher:
Key/Vignettes/Misc: [no vignettes]
Locations: CHS–SF
Catalogs/Checklists: Peters, COS, p. 145

189

Place: Placerville, California
Date: 1888
Title: Birdseye View Placerville, Cal.
Size: 18½ × 28⅝ in. (47.1 × 72.8 cm.)
Artist: L. Roethe
Lithographer: R. H.
Printer: W. W. Elliott lith S F
Publisher: Placerville Weekly Observer,
Placerville
Key/Vignettes/Misc: Refs. 1–30; 24
vignettes; description
Locations: SCP; UCBL–B; CHS–C;
HEHL; CHS–SF; UCLA–SC; CSL–S;
LC–M (facsimile)
Catalogs/Checklists: SCP, p. 20 (1108);
LC–M, 31

190

Place: Pomona, California
Date: 1886
Title: Pomona, Cal.
Size: 17⅞ × 25 in. (45.5 × 63.6 cm.)
Artist: W. W. Elliott & Co.
Lithographer:
Printer: W. W. Elliott & Co. Oakland, Cal.
Publisher: Pomona Progress and Telegram,
Pomona
Key/Vignettes/Misc: Refs. 1–30; 12
vignettes; description
Locations: NHM–LA; HEHL (photo);
Chamber of Commerce, Pomona,
California
Catalogs/Checklists:

191

Place: Poplar City, California
Date: Ca. 1880
Title: "Poplar City" Connecting the Cities
of San Jose and Santa Clara, Cal. Owned
by Moses Davis and W. S. Chapman. . . .
Size: 16¼ × 26¼ in. (41.3 × 66.8 cm.)
Artist:
Lithographer:
Printer:

Publisher: Moses Davis and W. S.
Chapman
Key/Vignettes/Misc: 1 vignette
Locations: HEHL; OM–O
Catalogs/Checklists:

192

Place: Rabbit Creek, California
Date: 1856
Title: Rabbit Creek, Sierra Co. Cal.
Size: 8⅝ × 14¾ in. (21.9 × 37.5 cm.)
Artist: Kuchel & Dresel
Lithographer: Kuchel & Dresel
Printer: Britton & Rey, S. F.
Publisher:
Key/Vignettes/Misc:
Locations: ACMW–FW; CHS–C
Catalogs/Checklists: ACMW–FW 1267

193

Place: Rabbit Creek, California
Date: 1856
Title: Rabbit Creek, 1856 Sierra County,
Cala.
Size: 14³⁄₁₆ × 30¾ in. (36.1 × 78.2 cm.)
Artist: Kuchel & Dresel
Lithographer: Kuchel & Dresel
Printer: Britton & Rey [San Francisco]
Publisher: Everts, Wilson & Co.
Key/Vignettes/Misc: 14 vignettes
Locations: SCP
Catalogs/Checklists: SCP, p. 20 (861);
Peters, COS, p. 145

194

Place: Rabbit Creek, California
Date: 1856
Title: Rabbit Creek, 1856. Sierra County,
Cala.
Size: 11¼ × 18¼ in. (28.6 × 46.4 cm.)
Artist: Kuchel & Dresel
Lithographer: Kuchel & Dresel
Printer: Britton & Rey [San Francisco]
Publisher: Everts, Wilson & Co.
Key/Vignettes/Misc: [no vignettes]
Locations: UCBL–B; CHS–SF
Catalogs/Checklists:

195

Place: Red Bluff, California
Date: 1886
Title: Red Bluff Tehama County,
California, 1886.
Size: 19⁵⁄₁₆ × 24 in. (49.1 × 61 cm.)
Artist: B. W. Pierce
Lithographer:
Printer:
Publisher: W. B. H. Dodson, Red Bluff
Key/Vignettes/Misc: 21 vignettes
Locations: SCP
Catalogs/Checklists: SCP, p. 20 (1116)

196

Place: Redding, California
Date: Ca. 1888
Title: Birds Eye View of Redding, Shasta
County,–California. 226 Miles North of
San Francisco, on S. P. R. R. to Oregon.
Size: 21½ × 30½ in. (54.8 × 77.6 cm.)
Artist:
Lithographer: R. H.
Printer: W. W. Elliott, Litho. S. F.

Publisher: D. N. Honn, Yuba Street [Redding]
Key/Vignettes/Misc: Refs. 1–44; 23 vignettes; description
Locations: UCBL–B; HEHL; CSL–S
Catalogs/Checklists:

197

Place: Redlands, California
Date: 1888
Title: Birdseye View of Redlands. San Bernardino Co. Cal. June 1888. Looking South East.
Size: 21¼ × 32 in. (54.1 × 81.4 cm.)
Artist: E. S. Moore
Lithographer:
Printer:
Publisher:
Key/Vignettes/Misc: Refs. 1–10; 14 vignettes
Locations: UCBL–B
Catalogs/Checklists:

198

Place: Redwood City, California
Date: 1891
Title: Birdseye View of Redwood City, Cal. 1891
Size: 19½ × 23¾ in. (49.6 × 63 cm.)
Artist: E. S. Moore
Lithographer:
Printer:
Publisher:
Key/Vignettes/Misc: Refs. 1–7; 6 vignettes
Locations: Unknown
Catalogs/Checklists:

199

Place: Riverside, California
Date: 1877
Title: Bird's Eye View of River Side, San Bernardino Co., Cal. Looking North to the San Bernardino Mountains.
Size: 9⅛ × 16¾ in. (23.2 × 42.6 cm.)
Artist: E. S. Glover
Lithographer:
Printer: A. L. Bancroft & Co., San Francisco
Publisher:
Key/Vignettes/Misc:
Locations: UCBL–B
Catalogs/Checklists:

200

Place: Riverside, California
Date: Ca. 1890
Title: Riverside. San Bernardino Co. California.
Size: 17¾ × 23⅝ in. (45.1 × 60.1 cm.)
Artist:
Lithographer:
Printer: W. W. Elliott, Oakland, Cal.
Publisher: The Press and Horticulturist
Key/Vignettes/Misc: Refs. 1–22; 9 vignettes
Locations: UCBL–B; EI–S
Catalogs/Checklists:

201

Place: Sacramento, California
Date: 1850
Title: Sacramento City Ca. From the Foot

of J. Street, Showing I. J. & K. Sts. with the Sierra Nevada in the Distance.
Size: 15³⁄₁₆ × 23³⁄₁₆ in. (38.5 × 58.8 cm.)
Artist: G. V. Cooper
Lithographer:
Printer: Wm. Endicott & Co., New York
Publisher: Stringer & Townsend 222 Broadway, N. York
Key/Vignettes/Misc: Refs. A–X
Locations: ACMW–FW; MM–NN; NYP–S; UCBL–B; CHS–C; CHS–SF; LC–P; SCP; YUAG–NH; NYH–NY
Catalogs/Checklists: Stokes 1849—F–69; Reps, Cities on Stone, p. 96; ACMW–FW 1034; MM–NN, LP 54; SCP, p. 20 (833); LC–M, 31.2

202

Place: Sacramento, California
Date: 1850
Title: View of Sacramento City. As it appeared during the Great Innundation in January 1850.
Size: 24½ × 36⅝ in. (62.4 × 93.1 cm.)
Artist: Geo. W. Casilear & Henry Bainbridge
Lithographer:
Printer: Sarony, New York
Publisher: Casilear & Bainbridge (copyright)
Key/Vignettes/Misc: description
Locations: MM–NN; SCP; ACMW–FW; UCBL–B; CHS–SF; CHS–C; CSL–S; LC–P
Catalogs/Checklists: ACMW–FW 956; MM–NN, LP [illeg.]; SCP, p. 20 (370); Peters, COS, pp. 46, 97, 184; LC–M, 31.1

203

Place: Sacramento, California
Date: 1851
Title: Ville de Sacramento (Californie)
Size: 12¾ × 19 in. (32.4 × 48.3 cm.)
Artist: L. Le Breton
Lithographer: L. Le Breton
Printer: Auguste Bry, 142, r. du Bac., Paris
Publisher: E. Savary et Cie edit. 10 Place du Louvre [Paris], Gambart et Co., 25 Berniers St. Oxford St., London
Key/Vignettes/Misc:
Locations: MM–NN; UCBL–B (1881); CHS–C
Catalogs/Checklists: MM–NN, LP 296; Peters, COS, p. 157

204

Place: Sacramento, California
Date: Ca. 1851
Title: Ville de Sacramento (Californie) December 1849
Size: 14¼ × 18⅞ in. (36.3 × 48.1 cm.)
Artist: L. Le Breton
Lithographer: L. Le Breton
Printer: Auguste Bry, 142, r. du Bac., Paris
Publisher: Wild, Editeur, 15 rue de la Banque, Place de la Bourse [Paris]
Key/Vignettes/Misc:
Locations: CSL–S
Catalogs/Checklists:

205

Place: Sacramento, California
Date: Ca. 1851
Title: Ville De Sacramento (Californie)

Size: 13⅝ × 19¹⁵⁄₁₆ in. (34.6 × 50.5 cm.)
Artist: L. Le Breton
Lithographer: L. Le Breton
Printer: F. Appel, Paris
Publisher:
Key/Vignettes/Misc:
Locations: ACMW–FW
Catalogs/Checklists: ACMW–FW 1287

206

Place: Sacramento, California
Date: 1852
Title: Sacramento City
Size: 7⅝ × 14⅞ in. (19.4 × 37.8 cm.)
Artist: J. Britton
Lithographer: Cooke & Le Count
Printer: Cooke & Le Count
Publisher:
Key/Vignettes/Misc:
Locations: SCP
Catalogs/Checklists: SCP, p. 20 (1161); Peters, COS, pp. 65, 102

207

Place: Sacramento, California
Date: Ca. 1855
Title: Sacramento City
Size: 21 × 35¾ in. (53.4 × 90.9 cm.)
Artist: Thomas Boyd
Lithographer: Victor Hoffman
Printer: Britton & Rey, San Francisco
Publisher:
Key/Vignettes/Misc:
Locations: MM–NN
Catalogs/Checklists: MM–NN, LP 3810

208

Place: Sacramento, California
Date: [1855–56]
Title: Sacramento City. Water Front with Contemplated Improvements.
Size: 21 × 35¹³⁄₁₆ in. (53.3 × 90.9 cm.)
Artist: Thomas Boyd
Lithographer: V. Hoffman
Printer: Britton & Rey, S. F.
Publisher: J. B. M. Crooks & Co. (?)
Key/Vignettes/Misc:
Locations: ACMW–FW; UCBL–B; CHS–SF; CSL–S
Catalogs/Checklists:

209

Place: Sacramento, California
Date: 1857
Title: A Birds–Eye View of Sacramento "The City of the Plain."
Size: 28¾ × 35⁵⁄₁₆ in. (73.2 × 89.9 cm.)
Artist: George H. Baker
Lithographer:
Printer: Britton & Rey, San Francisco
Publisher: Geo. H. Baker, Sac[ramento]
Key/Vignettes/Misc: 31 vignettes
Locations: UCBL–B; CHS–SF; CSL–S; SCP
Catalogs/Checklists: Peters, COS, p. 51; SCP, p. 20 (91)

210

Place: Sacramento, California
Date: 1857
Title: A Birds–Eye View of Sacramento Capital of the State of California
Size: 27⁵⁄₁₆ × 33¾ in. (69.3 × 85.7 cm.)

Artist: G. H. Baker
Lithographer:
Printer: Britton & Rey, San Francisco
Publisher: G. H. Baker
Key/Vignettes/Misc: 36 vignettes
Locations: ACMW−FW; CSL−S
Catalogs/Checklists: ACMW−FW 810;
Reps, Cities on Stone, p. 96

211
Place: Sacramento, California
Date: 1858
Title: A Birds−Eye View of Sacramento
Capitol of the State of California 1858.
Size: 27 × 33½ in. (68.7 × 85.2 cm.)
Artist:
Lithographer:
Printer:
Publisher:
Key/Vignettes/Misc: 34 vignettes; 1 crest
Locations: Unknown. See Old Print Shop
Portfolio, XXI, p. 85, No. 22
Catalogs/Checklists:

212
Place: Sacramento, California
Date: 1858
Title: Fire Department of the City of
Sacramento A Bird's−Eye View of
Sacramento Capitol of the State of
California
Size: 27⅛ × 33⅝ in. (69 × 85.6 cm.)
Artist: G. H. Baker
Lithographer:
Printer: Britton & Rey, San Francisco
Publisher: G. H. Baker
Key/Vignettes/Misc: 36 vignettes
Locations: CHS−SF; CSL−S
Catalogs/Checklists:

213
Place: Sacramento, California
Date: 1870 State I
Title: Birds Eye View of the City of
Sacramento State Capital of California
1870
Size: 27⁵⁄₁₆ × 33¼ in. (69.3 × 84.4 cm.)
Artist: Augustus Koch
Lithographer:
Printer: Britton & Rey, S. F.
Publisher: [n.p.]
Key/Vignettes/Misc: Refs. 1−78
Locations: ACMW−FW; UCBL−B;
CSL−S
Catalogs/Checklists: ACMW−FW 1232;
Reps, Cities on Stone, p. 96

214
Place: Sacramento, California
Date: 1870 State II
Title: Birds Eye View of the City of
Sacramento State Capital of California
Size: 29¾ × 33½ in. (75.6 × 85.2 cm.)
Artist: Augustus Koch
Lithographer:
Printer: Britton & Rey, S. F.
Publisher: Snow & Roos, San Francisco
Key/Vignettes/Misc: Refs. 1−78
Locations: CSL−S
Catalogs/Checklists:

215
Place: Sacramento, California
Date: 1890
Title: Sacramento, Bird's Eye View
Published by the Daily Record—Union &
Weekly Union
Size: 24 × 36 in. (61 × 91.5 cm.)
Artist:
Lithographer: R. H.
Printer:
Publisher: W. W. Elliott
Key/Vignettes/Misc: 32 vignettes;
description
Locations: LC−M; LC−P
Catalogs/Checklists: LC−M, 32

216
Place: Sacramento, California
Date: [189−?]
Title: Sacramento, Bird's Eye View
Published by the Daily Record—Union &
Weekly Union
Size: 22⁵⁄₁₆ × 35⅛ in. (56.8 × 89.5 cm.)
Artist:
Lithographer: R. H.
Printer: W. W. Elliott Lith. S. F.
Publisher: The Daily Record−Union and
The Weekly Union [Sacramento]
Key/Vignettes/Misc: Refs. 1−40, A−B; 28
vignettes; description
Locations: LC−P
Catalogs/Checklists:

217
Place: Sacramento, California
Date: N.D.
Title: Sacramento in Californien Des
Auswanderers Hoffnung
Size: 9³⁄₁₆ × 14¼ in. (23.4 × 36.3 cm.)
Artist:
Lithographer:
Printer: [J. Hesse] in Berlin
Publisher: Magazin in Berlin, Alte Jacobs
str. 71
Key/Vignettes/Misc:
Locations: UCBL−B
Catalogs/Checklists:

218
Place: Sacramento, California
Date: N.D.
Title: Sacramento in Californien Des
Auswanderers Hoffnung
Size: 9⁵⁄₁₆ × 14⅜ in. (23.7 × 36.6 cm.)
Artist:
Lithographer:
Printer: J. Hesse, Berlin
Publisher: [n.p.]
Key/Vignettes/Misc:
Locations: MM−NN; UCBL−B; CSL−S;
OM−O
Catalogs/Checklists: MM−NN, LP 581

219
Place: Sacramento, California
Date: N.D.
Title: Sacramento in Californien. Des
Auswanderers Hoffnung.
Size: 9 × 14¼ in. (22.9 × 36.3 cm.)
Artist:
Lithographer:
Printer:

Publisher: A. Felchner, Berlin
Key/Vignettes/Misc:
Locations: Unknown. See Walter Reuben,
Catalogue 36, no. 82
Catalogs/Checklists:

220
Place: Saint Louis, California
Date: 1856
Title: City of St. Louis, 1856. Sierra
County, Cal.
Size: 14³⁄₁₆ × 20¾ in. (36 × 52.7 cm.)
Artist: Kuchel & Dresel
Lithographer: Kuchel & Dresel
Printer: Britton & Rey [San Francisco]
Publisher: Everts, Wilson & Co.
Key/Vignettes/Misc: 12 vignettes
Locations: ACMW−FW
Catalogs/Checklists: ACMW−FW 1253;
Reps, Cities on Stone, p. 96

221
Place: Saint Louis, California
Date: [1856]
Title: St. Louis, Sierra Co., Cal.
Size: 8 × 14⅝ in. (20.3 × 37.2 cm.)
Artist: Kuchel & Dresel
Lithographer: Kuchel & Dresel
Printer: Britton & Rey, San Francisco
Publisher:
Key/Vignettes/Misc:
Locations: CHS−SF; UCBL−B (no title)
Catalogs/Checklists: Peters, COS, p. 145

222
Place: Salinas City, California
Date: 1875
Title: Birds Eye View of Salinas City
Monterey County Cal. 1875.
Size: 16½ × 22³⁄₁₆ in. (41.9 × 56.3 cm.)
Artist: Augustus Koch
Lithographer:
Printer: Britton & Rey, Co. Lith [San
Francisco]
Publisher:
Key/Vignettes/Misc: Refs. 1−20
Locations: ACMW−FW; SCP
Catalogs/Checklists: ACMW−FW 1231

223
Place: San Bernardino, California
Date: 1873
Title: San Bernardino, Cal., 1873
Size: 9 × 16⁹⁄₁₆ in. (22.9 × 42.1 cm.)
Artist: A. E. Mathews
Lithographer:
Printer: A. L. Bancroft & Co., San
Francisco
Publisher: A. L. Bancroft & Co., San
Francisco
Key/Vignettes/Misc: Description
Locations: HEHL; ACMW−FW; CHS−C
Catalogs/Checklists:

224
Place: San Bernardino, California
Date: Ca. 1886
Title: San Bernardino. Cal.
Size: 20½ × 29½ in. (52.2 × 75.1 cm.)
Artist:
Lithographer:
Printer: W. W. Elliott, Oak.[land]

Publisher: W. H. Syme & CO.
Key/Vignettes/Misc: Refs. 1–35; 26 vignettes
Locations: UCBL–B; NHM–LA; LC–M (photo)
Catalogs/Checklists: LC–M, 32.1

Place: San Buenaventura, California
Date: 1877
See Ventura, California, 1877.

Place: San Buenaventura, California
Date: [1884–90]
See Ventura, California, [1884–90].

225
Place: San Diego, California
Date: 1871
Title: View of the City and Harbor of San Diego, Southern California, 1871.
Size: 7¼ × 37⅞ in. (18.5 × 81.1 cm.)
Artist:
Lithographer:
Printer: Chicago Lithographing Co. [Chicago]
Publisher: H. M. Higgins, Chicago
Key/Vignettes/Misc: Description
Locations: NYP–S
Catalogs/Checklists:

226
Place: San Diego, California
Date: 1873
Title: San Diego, California. Terminus of the Texas Pacific Railway. From the Peninsula looking east across the Bay, 1873.
Size: 8¹⁵⁄₁₆ × 16⁹⁄₁₆ in. (22.7 × 42.1 cm.)
Artist: A. E. Mathews
Lithographer:
Printer: A. L. Bancroft & Company
Publisher: A. L. Bancroft & Company, Publishers, 721 Market Street, San Francisco, Cal.
Key/Vignettes/Misc: Description
Locations: MM–NN; NHS–R; HEHL; ACMW–FW; CHS–C; LC–M (facsimile); UCBL–B
Catalogs/Checklists: MM–NN, LP 2011; LC–M, 32.3

227
Place: San Diego, California
Date: [1870–73]
Title: San Diego, Cal.
Size: 16⅛ × 18⅛ in. (41 × 46.1 cm.)
Artist:
Lithographer: Geo. H. Baker
Printer:
Publisher:
Key/Vignettes/Misc: 2 vignettes
Locations: SCP
Catalogs/Checklists: SCP, p. 20 (811); Peters, COS, p. 53

228
Place: San Diego, California
Date: 1876
Title: Bird's Eye View of San Diego, California 1876. From the North–East, Looking South–West.
Size: 18⅛ × 25¾ in. (46.1 x 65.5 cm.)

Artist: E. S. Glover
Lithographer:
Printer: A. L. Bancroft & Co., Lithographers, San Francisco, Cal.
Publisher: Schneider & Kueppers, San Diego
Key/Vignettes/Misc: Refs. 1–24; description
Locations: ACMW–FW; LC–M; UCBL–B; CHS–C
Catalogs/Checklists: LC–M, 33; Reps, Cities on Stone, p. 97; Peters, COS, p. 54

229
Place: San Diego, California
Date: 1887
Title:
Size: 14⁹⁄₁₆ × 24¾ in. (37 × 63 cm.)
Artist:
Lithographer:
Printer: W. W. Elliott, San Francisco
Publisher:
Key/Vignettes/Misc:
Locations: WHS–M; CSL–S
Catalogs/Checklists:

230
Place: San Diego, California
Date: 1887
Title: Bird's–Eye View of San Diego Bay Region. . .from Point Loma, Nine Miles West of the City.
Size: 4 × 31 in. (10.1 × 78.9 cm.)
Artist: W. O. Andrew
Lithographer:
Printer:
Publisher: John R. Berry (copyright)
Key/Vignettes/Misc: Refs. 1–20
Locations: UCBL–B
Catalogs/Checklists:

231
Place: San Diego, California
Date: 1887
Title: Pensketch of San Diego Harbor
Size: 4 × 16½ in. (10.1 × 41.9 cm.)
Artist: W. O. Andrew
Lithographer:
Printer:
Publisher:
Key/Vignettes/Misc:
Locations: UCBL–B
Catalogs/Checklists:

232
Place: San Diego, California
Date: 1914
Title:
Size: 7½ × 21¼ in. (19 × 54 cm.)
Artist:
Lithographer:
Printer:
Publisher:
Key/Vignettes/Misc:
Locations: WHS–M
Catalogs/Checklists:

233
Place: San Diego, California
Date: N.D.
Title: San Diego, 1850.
Size: 9½ × 14 in. (24.1 × 35.6 cm.)

Artist: C. G. Conts [C. J. Couts]
Lithographer:
Printer: Britton & Rey, San Francisco
Publisher:
Key/Vignettes/Misc:
Locations: UCBL–B
Catalogs/Checklists:

234
Place: San Francisco, California
Date: 1849
Title: San Francisco Upper California in January 1849
Size: 9 × 16⅜ in. (22.9 × 41.6 cm.)
Artist: Victor Prevost
Lithographer: V. Prevost
Printer: Sarony & Major, New York
Publisher: Robert Wells (copyright)
Key/Vignettes/Misc:
Locations: CHS–SF; NYP–S
Catalogs/Checklists: Baird & Evans, no. 4ci; Peters, COS, p. 185

235
Place: San Francisco, California
Date: 1849
Title: San Francisco Upper California in January 1849.
Size: 9 × 16⅜ in. (22.9 × 41.6 cm.)
Artist: Victor Prevost
Lithographer: V. Prevost
Printer: Sarony & Major 117 Fulton St. N. York
Publisher: Goupil Vibert & Co. 289 Broadway, New York
Key/Vignettes/Misc:
Locations: MHdeY (on loan to SCP)
Catalogs/Checklists: Baird & Evans, no. 4c; Peters, COS, pp. 125, 185

236
Place: San Francisco, California
Date: 1849
Title: San Francisco Upper California in 1847.
Size: 6 × 13⅛ in. (15.2 × 33.4 cm.)
Artist:
Lithographer: V. Prevost
Printer: Sarony & Major 117 Fulton St. N. Y.
Publisher: Robert Wells, New York (copyright)
Key/Vignettes/Misc:
Locations: UCBL–B; CHS–SF
Catalogs/Checklists: Baird & Evans, no. 4b

237
Place: San Francisco, California
Date: 1849
Title: San Francisco Upper California in 1847. Plan of the City of San Francisco. Upper California.
Size: 12½ × 13³⁄₁₆ in. (31.8 × 33.6 cm.)
Artist:
Lithographer: V. Prevost
Printer: Sarony & Major 117 Fulton St. N. Y.
Publisher: Robert Wells New York (copyright)
Key/Vignettes/Misc:

Locations: SCP
Catalogs/Checklists:

238
Place: San Francisco, California
Date: 1849
Title: San Francisco Upper California in 1847. Plan of the City of San Francisco. Upper California. San Francisco Upper California in January 1849.
Size: 6 × 13⅛ in. (15.3 × 33.4 cm.), 5¼ × 7¼ in. (13.4 × 18.4 cm.), & 9 × 16 ⅜ in. (22.9 × 41.7 cm.)
Artist:
Lithographer: V. Prevost
Printer: Sarony & Major 117 Fulton St. N. Y.
Publisher: Goupil Vibert & Co. 289 Broadway, New York
Key/Vignettes/Misc:
Locations: CHS–C; NYH–NY
Catalogs/Checklists: Baird & Evans, no. 4a

239
Place: San Francisco, California
Date: 1849
Title: The Port of San Francisco June 1st. 1849
Size: 10 × 15 in. (25.4 × 38.1 cm.)
Artist: Geo. H. Baker
Lithographer:
Printer:
Publisher: New York Tribune
Key/Vignettes/Misc: Description
Locations: CHS–SF; SFPL; SCP
Catalogs/Checklists: Baird & Evans, no. 6; Peters, COS, p. 53

240
Place: San Francisco, California
Date: 1849 State I
Title: San–Francisco 1849.
Size: 13½ × 32¾ in. (34.4 × 83.2 cm.)
Artist: Henry Firks
Lithographer: Ibbotson
Printer: T. Sinclairs Lith. 101 Ches[t]nut St. Phila.
Publisher: W. H. Jones, San Francisco
Key/Vignettes/Misc: Refs. 1–45
Locations: NYP–S; UCBL–B; LC–P; SCP; EI–S; NYH–NY
Catalogs/Checklists: Stokes 1849—F–64; PAI 3; Baird & Evans, no. 8a; Peters, COS, pp. 120, 130, 191

241
Place: San Francisco, California
Date: 1849 State II
Title: San–Francisco 1849.
Size: 12¾ × 31⅝ in. (32.4 × 80.4 cm.)
Artist: Henry Firks
Lithographer:
Printer: Endicott & Co., N. Y.
Publisher: W. H. Jones, San Francisco
Key/Vignettes/Misc: Refs. 1–46
Locations: MHdeY (on loan to SCP); SFPL; NYH–NY
Catalogs/Checklists: Baird & Evans, no. 8b; Peters, COS, pp. 117, 120, 130

242
Place: San Francisco, California
Date: 1849 State III
Title: San–Francisco 1849 Drawn on the Spot by Henry Firks, for W. H. Jones Esq of San–Francisco U. C.
Size: 16 × 32 in. (40.7 × 81.3 cm.)
Artist: Henry Firks
Lithographer:
Printer: Fishbourne's Lithog. San Francisco, Cal.
Publisher: W. H. Jones, San Francisco
Key/Vignettes/Misc: Refs. 1–51
Locations: LC–P; CHS–SF; NYH–NY; SU–SC
Catalogs/Checklists: Baird & Evans, no. 8c

243
Place: San Francisco, California
Date: [1849?]
Title: A View of the Town, and Harbour of San Francisco.
Size: 8¹¹⁄₁₆ × 12⁹⁄₁₆ in. (22.1 × 31.9 cm.)
Artist: Geo. H. Baker
Lithographer:
Printer:
Publisher: H. Mansfield, New Haven, Conn.
Key/Vignettes/Misc:
Locations: UCBL–B; MHdeY (on loan to CSH–SF); YUAG–NH; SCP
Catalogs/Checklists: Baird & Evans, no. 7; Peters, COS, pp. 53, 160

244
Place: San Francisco, California
Date: [1849?]
Title: San Francisco, California
Size: 8⅜ × 17¼ in. (21.3 × 43.9 cm.)
Artist:
Lithographer:
Printer: C. Hutchins, Lithographer, Liverpool
Publisher:
Key/Vignettes/Misc:
Locations: SCP
Catalogs/Checklists: Baird & Evans, no. 12; SCP, p. 14 (433)

245
Place: San Francisco, California
Date: [1849?]
Title: San Francisco, California From the Bay.
Size: 8½ × 17¼ in. (21.6 × 43.9 cm.)
Artist:
Lithographer:
Printer: C. Hutchins, Lithographer, Liverpool
Publisher:
Key/Vignettes/Misc:
Locations: SCP
Catalogs/Checklists: Baird & Evans, no. 13; Peters, COS, p. 130; SCP, p. 14 (1181)

246
Place: San Francisco, California
Date: 1850
Title: San Francisco. 1850.

Size: 8¾ × 12⁷⁄₁₆ in. (22.3 × 31.6 cm.)
Artist:
Lithographer:
Printer: P. S. Duval's Steam Lith. Press, Philada.
Publisher: Henry Bill No. 81 Cliff St. New York
Key/Vignettes/Misc:
Locations: CHS–SF; HEHL; LC–P; SCP
Catalogs/Checklists: Baird & Evans, no. 18b

247
Place: San Francisco, California
Date: 1850
Title: San Francisco. 1850.
Size: 8¾ × 12⁷⁄₁₆ (22.3 × 31.6 cm.)
Artist:
Lithographer:
Printer:
Publisher: Henry Bill No. 81 Cliff St. New York
Key/Vignettes/Misc:
Locations: Private collection
Catalogs/Checklists: Baird & Evans, no. 18bi

248
Place: San Francisco, California
Date: 1850
Title: View of San Francisco. Taken from the Hill at the Head of California Street
Size: 13⅛ × 21¾ in. (33.4 × 55.3 cm.)
Artist: J. F. Schulthess
Lithographer:
Printer:
Publisher: Corson & Armstrong, Stationers, N. Orleans
Key/Vignettes/Misc: Refs. 1–17; 4 vignettes
Locations: UCBL–B; HEHL; SBHS–SB
Catalogs/Checklists: Baird & Evans, no. 16

249
Place: San Francisco, California
Date: 1850
Title: View of San Francisco. 1850
Size: 8⅜ × 12⅝ in. (21.3 × 32.1 cm.)
Artist: Kuchel
Lithographer: Kuchel
Printer: P. S. Duval, Philad.
Publisher:
Key/Vignettes/Misc:
Locations: Private collection
Catalogs/Checklists: Baird & Evans, no. 17

250
Place: San Francisco, California
Date: 1850
Title: View of San Francisco. 1850. Taken from a High Point on the South Side
Size: 9¹⁄₁₆ × 12⅝ in. (48.5 × 32.1 cm.)
Artist: Kuchel
Lithographer: Kuchel
Printer: P. S. Duval, Phila.
Publisher: Henry Bill. No. 81 Cliff St. New York
Key/Vignettes/Misc:
Locations: AAS–W; UCBL–B; CHS–SF;

CSL–S; NYP–P; SFPL; SCP; SI;
YUAG–NH; LC–P
Catalogs/Checklists: Baird & Evans, no.
18a; Peters, COS, pp. 115, 147

251
Place: San Francisco, California
Date: 1850 State I
Title: View of San Francisco. Taken from
the Telegraph Hill.
Size: 16¼ × 25¼ in. (41.3 × 64.2 cm.)
Artist: J. F. Schultess [Schulthess]
Lithographer:
Printer: G. Haywood's Lith. 180 Fulton St.
New York
Publisher: Corson & Armstrong,
Stationers, N. Orleans
Key/Vignettes/Misc:
Locations: UCBL–B
Catalogs/Checklists: Baird & Evans, no.
15a

252
Place: San Francisco, California
Date: 1850 State II
Title: View of San Francisco. Taken from
the Telegraph Hill.
Size: 16¼ × 25¼ in. (41.3 × 64.2 cm.)
Artist: J. F. Schultess [Schulthess]
Lithographer:
Printer: [n.p.]
Publisher: Corson & Armstrong,
Stationers, N. Orleans
Key/Vignettes/Misc: Refs.; 4 vignettes
Locations: CHS–SF
Catalogs/Checklists: Baird & Evans, no.
15b

253
Place: San Francisco, California
Date: Ca. 1850
Title: Vue de San Francisco
Size: 13 × 18⅛ in. (33.1 × 46.1 cm.)
Artist: Leon Fleury
Lithographer: L. Sabatier
Printer: Lith de Cattier, rue de Lancry, 12
[Paris]
Publisher: la Cie. L'Aurifere, [Paris]
Key/Vignettes/Misc:
Locations: CHS–SF
Catalogs/Checklists: Baird & Evans, no.
75

254
Place: San Francisco, California
Date: Ca. 1850 State I
Title: San Francisco, Vue prise d'un pont
eleve du cote Sud. 45.
Size: 12½ × 19 in. (31.8 × 48.3 cm.)
Artist: L. Le Breton
Lithographer: L. Le Breton
Printer: Auguste Bry, 149, r du Bac. Paris
Publisher: E. Savary et Cie., Paris and E.
Gambart and Co., London
Key/Vignettes/Misc:Locations:
YUAG–NH
Catalogs/Checklists: Baird & Evans, no.
74a

255
Place: San Francisco, California
Date: Ca. 1850 State II
Title: San–Francisco, Vue prise d'un point

eleve du cote Sud. (Californie) 45.
Size: 12⅝ × 19⅛ in. (32.1 × 48.6 cm.)
Artist: L. Le Breton
Lithographer: L. Le Breton
Printer: Auguste Bry, 149, r. du Bac. Paris
Publisher: E. Savary et Cie., Paris and E.
Gambart and Co., London
Key/Vignettes/Misc:
Locations: UCBL–B; SU–SC
Catalogs/Checklists: Baird & Evans, no.
74b; Peters, COS, p. 157; PAI 6

256
Place: San Francisco, California
Date: Ca. 1850 State III
Title: San–Francisco, Vue prise d'un point
eleve du cote Sud. (Californie)
Size: 12⅝ × 19⅛ in. (32.1 × 48.6 cm.)
Artist: L. Le Breton
Lithographer: L. Le Breton
Printer: Auguste Bry, 114,r. du Bac, Paris
Publisher: Wild, Editeur, 15, rue de la
Banque Place de la Bourse, Paris
Key/Vignettes/Misc:
Locations: YUAG–NH
Catalogs/Checklists: Baird & Evans, no.
74c

257
Place: San Francisco, California
Date: Ca. 1850 State IV
Title: San–Francisco, Vue prise d'un point
eleve du cote Sud (Californie)
Size: 13⅜ × 19¹⁵⁄₁₆ in. (33.9 × 50.6 cm.)
Artist: L. Le Breton
Lithographer: L. Le Breton
Printer: F. Appel, 12, rue de Delta, Paris
Publisher:
Key/Vignettes/Misc:
Locations: ACMW–FW
Catalogs/Checklists: Baird & Evans, no.
74d

258
Place: San Francisco, California
Date: 1851
Title: San Francisco.
Size: 16½ × 25⁷⁄₁₆ in. (41.9 × 64.5 cm.)
Artist: S. F. Marryat
Lithographer:
Printer: M. & N. Hanhart, Chromo Lith.
Impt. London
Publisher: Henry Squire & Compy. . . .23
Cockspur Street, [London]
Key/Vignettes/Misc:
Locations: ACMW–FW; UCBL–B;
CHS–SF; CHS–C; NYH–NY; NYP–S;
MM–NN; YUAG–NH; LC–P; MHdeY
(on loan to SCP)
Catalogs/Checklists: Baird & Evans, no.
72; Reps, Cities on Stone, p. 97; PAI 4;
ACMW–FW 1382; MM–NN, LP 1866;
Peters, COS, p. 127

259
Place: San Francisco, California
Date: 1851
Title: View of the Town and Harbour of
San Francisco, California From the Signal
Hill.
Size: 13⅝ × 28⅛ in. (34.7 × 71.6 cm.)
Artist: Captn. Collinson
Lithographer: W. Boosey

Printer: M. & N. Hanhart Lith Printers,
[London]
Publisher: Ackerman & Co., 96 Strand
London
Key/Vignettes/Misc: 11 unnumbered refs.
below places identified
Locations: ACMW–FW; CHS–C; LC–P;
UCBL–B; ROM
Catalogs/Checklists: PAI 8; Baird &
Evans, no. 73; Peters, COS, pp. 59, 98,
127; Samuel, no. 428

260
Place: San Francisco, California
Date: 1851
Title: View of San Francisco, Taken from
the Western Hill at the Foot of Telegraph
Hill, Looking Toward Rincon Point and
Mission Valley.
Size: 20¾ × 34½ in. (52.8 × 87.8 cm.)
Artist: Henry Bainbridge & Geo. W.
Casilear
Lithographer:
Printer: Sarony & Major, 117 Fulton St.
New York
Publisher: Geo. W. Casilear, New York
City and Atwill, San Francisco, California
Key/Vignettes/Misc: Refs. 1–22;
description
Locations: CHS–SF; LC–P; SCP;
UCBL–B
Catalogs/Checklists: Baird & Evans, no.
20; Peters, COS, pp. 46, 97, 185–86;
LC–M, 34.1

261
Place: San Francisco, California
Date: 1851 State I
Title: San Francisco. 1851.
Size: 9¹¹⁄₁₆ × 15⅞ in. (24.6 × 40.4 cm.)
Artist:
Lithographer:
Printer: T. Sinclair's Lith. Phila.
Publisher: Henry Bill, New York
Key/Vignettes/Misc: Refs. 1–25
Locations: UCBL–B; SU–SC
Catalogs/Checklists: Baird & Evans, no.
19a; PAI 9; Peters, COS, p. 191

262
Place: San Francisco, California
Date: 1851 State I
Title: San Francisco. 1852.
Size: 7½ × 15⅝ in. (19 × 39.8 cm.)
Artist:
Lithographer:
Printer: T. Sinclair's Lith., [Philadelphia]
Publisher: Henry Bill New York
(copyright, 1851)
Key/Vignettes/Misc: Refs. 1–13
Locations: SU–SC
Catalogs/Checklists: Baird & Evans, no.
26a

263
Place: San Francisco, California
Date: 1851 State I
Title: View of San Francisco, California.
Taken From Telegraph Hill, April
1850. . . .
Size: 14¹³⁄₁₆ × 29⅞ in. (37.7 × 76 cm.)
Artist: Wm. B. McMurtrie

Lithographer: F. Palmer
Printer: N. Currier, 152 Nassau St Cor. of Spruce N. Y.
Publisher: N. Currier, N. Y.—Wm. B. McMurtrie, San Francisco
Key/Vignettes/Misc: 9 unnumbered refs. below places identified
Locations: UCBL–B; SCP
Catalogs/Checklists: Baird & Evans, no. 14a; PAI 5; Peters, COS, pp. 108, 163, 176; Peters, C & I, 3881

264
Place: San Francisco, California
Date: 1851 State II
Title: San Francisco. 1851
Size: $9^{13}/_{16} \times 15^{15}/_{16}$ in. (25 × 40.5 cm.)
Artist:
Lithographer:
Printer: T. Sinclair's Lith. Phila.
Publisher: Henry Bill, New York
Key/Vignettes/Misc: Refs. 1–25
Locations: AAS–W; CHS–SF; SFPL; SCP
Catalogs/Checklists: Baird & Evans, no. 19b

265
Place: San Francisco, California
Date: 1851 State II
Title: View of San Francisco, California. Taken from Telegraph Hill, April 1850. . . .
Size: $14^{13}/_{16} \times 29^{7}/_{8}$ in. (37.7 × 76 cm.)
Artist: Wm. B McMurtrie
Lithographer: F. Palmer
Printer: N. Currier, 152 Nassau St. . . N. Y.
Publisher: N. Currier, N. Y.
Key/Vignettes/Misc: 9 unnumbered refs. below places identified
Locations: LC–P
Catalogs/Checklists: Baird & Evans, no. 14b

266
Place: San Francisco, California
Date: 1852
Title: Bird's Eye View of San Francisco Drawn from Mariam's Model & Nature July 1852.
Size: $9^{13}/_{16} \times 17^{7}/_{16}$ in. (25 × 44.3 cm.)
Artist: J. Britton
Lithographer:
Printer: Cooke & Le Count. . .[San Francisco]
Publisher: Cook & Le Count Book & Stationers Ware House Montgomery St. between Clay & Commercial. [San Francisco]
Key/Vignettes/Misc:
Locations: SCP
Catalogs/Checklists: Baird & Evans, no. 24; Peters, COS, pp. 65, 102; SCP, p. 14 (1158)

267
Place: San Francisco, California
Date: 1852
Title: City of San Francisco, Cala. . .
Size: $17^{7}/_{16} \times 30$ in. (44.3 × 76.3 cm.)
Artist: From daguerreotypes
Lithographer: F. Michelin, New York

Printer: F. Michelin, 225 Fulton St., N. Y.
Publisher: Marvin & Hitchcock, Booksellers & Stationers, San Francisco
Key/Vignettes/Misc:
Locations: UCBL–B; NYH–NY; SCP; MHdeY (on loan to SCP)
Catalogs/Checklists: Baird &Evans, no. 25; Peters, COS, p. 163; PAI 13

268
Place: San Francisco, California
Date: 1852
Title: San Francisco January 1852.
Size: $9^{5}/_{16} \times 22^{3}/_{4}$ in. (23.7 × 57.9 cm.)
Artist: H. Eastman
Lithographer: J. Britton
Printer: Pollard & Britton Lith. San Francisco
Publisher:
Key/Vignettes/Misc:
Locations: UCBL–B
Catalogs/Checklists: Baird & Evans, no. 23; Peters, COS, pp. 115, 180; PAI 10

269
Place: San Francisco, California
Date: 1852 State II
Title: San Francisco. 1852.
Size: $7^{1}/_{2} \times 15^{5}/_{8}$ in. (19 × 39.7 cm.)
Artist:
Lithographer:
Printer: T. Sinclair's Lith., [Philadelphia]
Publisher: Henry Bill, New York (copyright, 1852 in ms.)
Key/Vignettes/Misc: Refs. 1–13
Locations: ACMW–FW; CHS–SF; CSL–S; OM–O; SCP
Catalogs/Checklists: ACMW–FW 1840; Baird & Evans, no. 26b

270
Place: San Francisco, California
Date: Ca. 1852
Title: San Francisco
Size: $15^{5}/_{16} \times 23^{1}/_{8}$ in. (39 × 58.8 cm.)
Artist: From a daguerreotype
Lithographer: L. Sabatier
Printer: Lemercier, Paris
Publisher: Bulla Freres et Jouy, Paris. . .and Emile Seitz, 413 Broadway, New York
Key/Vignettes/Misc:
Locations: UCBL–B; CHS–SF; YUAG–NH
Catalogs/Checklists: Baird & Evans, no. 76

271
Place: San Francisco, California
Date: 1853 State I
Title: San Francisco. From California Street.
Size: $9^{3}/_{8} \times 34$ in. (23.8 × 86.5 cm.)
Artist: From a daguerreotype
Lithographer:
Printer: Lemercier, Paris
Publisher: M. Knoedler, New York (copyright)
Key/Vignettes/Misc:
Locations: CHS–SF; LC–P; SCP
Catalogs/Checklists: Baird & Evans, no. 31

272
Place: San Francisco, California
Date: 1854
Title: San Francisco. 1854.
Size: $7^{1}/_{2} \times 15^{5}/_{8}$ in. (19 × 39.8 cm.)
Artist:
Lithographer:
Printer: T. Sinclair's Lith., [Philadelphia]
Publisher: Henry Bill, New York
Key/Vignettes/Misc: Refs. 1–13
Locations: AAS–W; UCBL–B; CHS–SF; CSL–S; CHS–C; SCP; LC–P
Catalogs/Checklists: Baird & Evans, no. 27

273
Place: San Francisco, California
Date: 1854
Title: View of the City & Harbour of San Francisco. From the Cor. of Fremont & Harrison Sts.
Size: $12^{1}/_{2} \times 26^{1}/_{16}$ in. (31.8 × 66.4 cm.)
Artist: From a daguerreotype by G. H. Johnson
Lithographer: G. H.Burgess
Printer: Britton & Rey [San Francisco]
Publisher: Britton & Rey [San Francisco]
Key/Vignettes/Misc:
Locations: SCP; MHdeY (on loan to CHS–SF)
Catalogs/Checklists: Baird & Evans, no. 32; Peters, COS, p. 92

274
Place: San Francisco, California
Date: 1855
Title: City of San Francisco from Rincon Point.
Size: $21^{7}/_{8} \times 40^{7}/_{8}$ in. (55.7 × 104 cm.)
Artist: F. N. Otis [Fessenden Nott Otis]
Lithographer: C. Parsons
Printer: Endicott & Co. NY
Publisher: F. N. Otis (copyright)
Key/Vignettes/Misc:
Locations: ACMW–FW; CHS–SF; CSL–S; SCP
Catalogs/Checklists: Baird & Evans, no. 33; ACMW–FW 1503; Peters, COS, p. 119

275
Place: San Francisco, California
Date: 1855
Title: San Francisco. 1855.
Size: $7^{1}/_{2} \times 15^{5}/_{8}$ in. (19 × 39.8 cm.)
Artist:
Lithographer:
Printer: T. Sinclair's Lith., [Philadelphia]
Publisher: Henry Bill
Key/Vignettes/Misc: Refs. 1–13
Locations: CSL–S; HEHL; SCP; WHPL–D; CHS–SF
Catalogs/Checklists: Baird & Evans, no. 28

276
Place: San Francisco, California
Date: 1855 State II
Title: San Francisco. From Californiaa Street.
Size: $9^{3}/_{8} \times 34$ in. (23.8 × 86.5 cm.)
Artist: From a daguerreotype

Lithographer:
Printer: Lemercier, Paris
Publisher: M. Knoedler, New York (copyright)
Key/Vignettes/Misc:
Locations: YUAG–NH
Catalogs/Checklists: Peters, COS, p. 158

277
Place: San Francisco, California
Date: [1850–55?]
Title: Vista de San Francisco de California
Size: 16⅜ × 24¼ in. (41.7 × 61.7 cm.)
Artist:
Lithographer:
Printer: Michaud Thomas [Julio Michaud y Thomas, Mexico City]
Publisher:
Key/Vignettes/Misc:
Locations: Private collection
Catalogs/Checklists: Baird & Evans, no. 81

278
Place: San Francisco, California
Date: 1856
Title: San Francisco. 1856.
Size: 7½ × 15⅝ in. (19 × 39.8 cm.)
Artist:
Lithographer:
Printer: T. Sinclair's Lith., [Philadelphia]
Publisher: Henry Bill
Key/Vignettes/Misc: Refs. 1–13
Locations: CSL–S; SCP; WHPL–D; CHS–SF; SWM–LA (lacks printer's imprint); NYH–NY
Catalogs/Checklists: Baird & Evans, no. 29

279
Place: San Francisco, California
Date: 1857
Title: San Francisco. 1857.
Size: 7½ × 15⅝ in. (19 × 39.8 cm.)
Artist:
Lithographer:
Printer: T. Sinclair's Lith., [Philadelphia]
Publisher: Henry Bill
Key/Vignettes/Misc: Refs. 1–13
Locations: SCP
Catalogs/Checklists: Baird & Evans, no. 30

280
Place: San Francisco, California
Date: 1859
Title: View of that Portion of the City of San Francisco Seen from the Residence of N. Larco Esqre. Green St. Telegraph Hill Looking South 1859.
Size: 19⅝ × 34½ in. (49.8 × 87.5 cm.)
Artist: E.[ugene] Camerer
Lithographer: Kuchel & Dresel
Printer: L. Nagel [San Francisco]
Publisher: F. R. Reynolds, [San Francisco]
Key/Vignettes/Misc:
Locations: ACMW–FW; CHS–SF; SCP; OM–O
Catalogs/Checklists: ACMW–FW 946; Baird & Evans, no. 34; Peters, COS, p. 147

281
Place: San Francisco, California
Date: 1860
Title: Mission Dolores San Francisco—1860 From the Potrero Neuvo
Size: 14¹¹⁄₁₆ × 21¾ in. (37.4 × 55.4 cm.)
Artist: C. B. Gifford
Lithographer: Nahl Brothers
Printer: L. Nagel, 151 Clay St, S. F.
Publisher: L. Nagel, 151 Clay St, S. F.
Key/Vignettes/Misc:
Locations: UCBL–B
Catalogs/Checklists:

282
Place: San Francisco, California
Date: 1860
Title: San Francisco, 1860
Size: 27⅞ × 39½ in. (65.9 × 100.4 cm.)
Artist:
Lithographer:
Printer: L. Nagel, S. F.
Publisher: Hutchings & Rosenfield
Key/Vignettes/Misc: 39 vignettes
Locations: UCBL–B; LC–P; NYP–P; OM–O
Catalogs/Checklists: Baird & Evans, no. 35

283
Place: San Francisco, California
Date: 1860
Title: View of San Francisco in 1860.
Size: 5¼ × 18¹⁵⁄₁₆ in. (13.3 × 48.2 cm.)
Artist:
Lithographer:
Printer:
Publisher: Henry Payot 184 Washington Street
Key/Vignettes/Misc:
Locations: SCP
Catalogs/Checklists: Baird & Evans, no. 36

284
Place: San Francisco, California
Date: 1860
Title: Vue de San Francisco en 1860 View of San Francisco in 1860
Size: 12 × 18¼ in. (30.5 × 46.4 cm.)
Artist:
Lithographer:
Printer: Gosselin, 71, r. St. Jacques, Paris
Publisher: Henry Payot, 184, Washington Street
Key/Vignettes/Misc:
Locations: Private collection
Catalogs/Checklists: Baird & Evans, no. 37

285
Place: San Francisco, California
Date: [1860?]
Title: San Francisco
Size:
Artist:
Lithographer:
Printer: Geo. F. Nesbitt N.Y.
Publisher: Marvin Hitchcock Pioneer Book Store San Francisco
Key/Vignettes/Misc:

Locations: Unknown
Catalogs/Checklists: Peters, COS, p. 174

286
Place: San Francisco, California
Date: Ca. 1860 State I
Title: Vue de San–Francisco 64 Vista de San–Francisco
Size: 12⅜ × 18⅞ in. (31.4 × 48 cm.)
Artist: Deroy
Lithographer: Deroy
Printer:
Publisher:
Key/Vignettes/Misc:
Locations: SCP; YUAG–NH; LC–P
Catalogs/Checklists: LC–M, 33.1

287
Place: San Francisco, California
Date: Ca. 1860 State II
Title: Vue de San–Francisco 64 Vista de San–Francisco
Size: 12⅜ × 18⅞ in. (31.4 × 48 cm.)
Artist: Deroy
Lithographer: Deroy
Printer: L. Turgis Jne., r. des Ecoles, 60, Paris
Publisher: L. Turgis Jne., r. des Ecoles, 60, Paris–Maison a New York
Key/Vignettes/Misc:
Locations: CHS–SF; CHS–C; NYP–P; SFPL
Catalogs/Checklists: Peters, COS, p. 112; Baird & Evans, no. 77; PAI 11

288
Place: San Francisco, California
Date: 1861
Title: View of the City & Harbor of San Francisco, California. Oct. 31, 1849.
Size: 10¹¹⁄₁₆ × 15¼ in. (27.2 × 38.8 cm.)
Artist: Thos. Armstrong
Lithographer:
Printer:
Publisher: A. Rosenfield, California
Key/Vignettes/Misc:
Locations: UCBL–B; CHS–SF; SCP
Catalogs/Checklists: Baird & Evans, no. 11

289
Place: San Francisco, California
Date: 1862
Title: North Beach, San–Francisco. From Russian Hill.
Size: 12¾ × 21⅝ in. (32.4 × 55 cm.)
Artist: C. Gifford
Lithographer: C. Gifford
Printer: L. Nagel
Publisher: Thomas W. Hackett
Key/Vignettes/Misc:
Locations: UCBL–B; CHS–SF; LC–P; MHdeY (on loan to SCP); MM–NN
Catalogs/Checklists: Baird & Evans, no. 38c; MM–NN, LP 2801; Peters, COS, p. 123

290
Place: San Francisco, California
Date: 1862
Title: Panoramic View of San Francisco [This title appears on various versions of

the following five views mounted as one, each separately titled]
Size: 14⁵⁄₁₆ × 106³⁄₈ in. (36.4 × 270.7 cm.)
Artist: C. B. Gifford
Lithographer: C. B. Gifford
Printer: L. Nagel, S. F.
Publisher:
Key/Vignettes/Misc: Refs. 1–100 & 1–21
Locations: AAS–W; CSL–S; HEHL; NYP–S; SCP; UCBL–B; LC–P
Catalogs/Checklists: Baird & Evans, no. 38a; Peters, COS, p. 167; Stokes 1862—G–82; LC–M, 34.2

291
Place: San Francisco, California
Date: 1862
Title: San Francisco, 1862. From Russian Hill. Secn. 1. Looking West
Size: 14¹⁄₁₆ × 20⁹⁄₁₆ in. (35.8 × 52.4 cm.)
Artist: C. B. Gifford
Lithographer: C. B. Gifford
Printer: L. Nagel, S. F.
Publisher: A. Rosenfield, S. F.
Key/Vignettes/Misc: Refs. 1–20
Locations: AAS–W; CSL–S; HEHL; NYP–S; SCP; UCBL–B
Catalogs/Checklists: Baird & Evans, no. 38a; Peters, COS, p. 167; Stokes 1862—G–82

292
Place: San Francisco, California
Date: 1862
Title: San Francisco, 1862. From Russian Hill. Secn. 2. Looking North
Size: 14³⁄₁₆ × 21½ in. (36.1 × 54.8 cm.)
Artist: C. B. Gifford
Lithographer: C. B. Gifford
Printer: L. Nagel, S. F.
Publisher: A. Rosenfield, S. F.
Key/Vignettes/Misc: Refs. 21–40
Locations: AAS–W; CSL–S; HEHL; NYP–S; SCP; UCBL–B; NYH–NY
Catalogs/Checklists: Baird & Evans, no. 38a; Peters, COS, p. 167; Stokes 1862—G–82

293
Place: San Francisco, California
Date: 1862
Title: San Francisco, 1862. From Russian Hill. Secn. 3. Looking East
Size: 13¹⁵⁄₁₆ × 21⁵⁄₈ in. (35.5 × 55.1 cm.)
Artist: C. B. Gifford
Lithographer: C. B. Gifford
Printer: L. Nagel, S. F.
Publisher: A. Rosenfield, S. F.
Key/Vignettes/Misc: Refs. 41–60
Locations: NYH–NY; AAS–W; CSL–S; HEHL; NYP–S; SCP; UCBL–B
Catalogs/Checklists: Baird & Evans, no. 38a; Peters, COS, p. 167; Stokes 1862—G–82

294
Place: San Francisco, California
Date: 1862
Title: San Francisco, 1862. From Russian Hill. Secn. 4. Looking East & South
Size: 14¼ × 20½ in. (36.3 × 52.2 cm.)
Artist: C. B. Gifford

Lithographer: C. B. Gifford
Printer: L. Nagel, S. F.
Publisher: A. Rosenfield, S. F.
Key/Vignettes/Misc: Refs. 61–100
Locations: AAS–W; CSL–S; HEHL; NYP–S; SCP; UCBL–B; NYH–NY
Catalogs/Checklists: Baird & Evans, no. 38a; Peters, COS, p. 167; Stokes 1862—G–82

295
Place: San Francisco, California
Date: 1862
Title: San Francisco, 1862. From Russian Hill. Secn. 5. Looking South & West
Size: 14⁵⁄₁₆ × 21³⁄₈ in. (36.4 × 54.4 cm.)
Artist: C. B. Gifford
Lithographer: C. B. Gifford
Printer: L. Nagel, S. F.
Publisher: A. Rosenfield, S. F.
Key/Vignettes/Misc: Refs. 1–21
Locations: AAS–W; CSL–S; HEHL; NYP–S; SCP; UCBL–B; NYH–NY
Catalogs/Checklists: Baird & Evans, no. 38a; Peters, COS, p. 167; Stokes 1862—G–82

296
Place: San Francisco, California
Date: 1863
Title: San Francisco, 1863, From Russian Hill; [Issued in 5 sections with titles: Looking West, Looking North, Looking East, Looking East & South, Looking South & West]
Size: Each ca. 12½ × 21⁵⁄₈ in. (ca. 31.8 × 55.1 cm.)
Artist: C. B. Gifford
Lithographer: C. B. Gifford
Printer: L. Nagel, San Francisco
Publisher: A. Rosenfield, San Francisco
Key/Vignettes/Misc: Refs. 1–121
Locations: AAS–W; CSL–S
Catalogs/Checklists: Baird & Evans, no. 38b

297
Place: San Francisco, California
Date: 1864 State I
Title: San Francisco. Bird's Eye View.
Size: 25½ × 40 in. (64.9 × 101.7 cm.)
Artist: C. B. Gifford
Lithographer: C. B. Gifford
Printer: L. Nagel, S. F.
Publisher: Robinson & Snow, Washington & Sansome Sts. S. F.
Key/Vignettes/Misc: Refs. 1–78, A–Z, AA–EE (?)
Locations: UCBL–B; CHS–SF; CHS–C; SCP; LC–P; NYH–NY
Catalogs/Checklists: Baird & Evans, no. 39a; Peters, COS, pp. 167, 192; LC–M, 34.3

298
Place: San Francisco, California
Date: 1864 State II
Title: San Francisco. Bird's Eye View.
Size: 25⁵⁄₈ × 40 in. (65.2 × 101.7 cm.)
Artist: C. B. Gifford
Lithographer: C. B. Gifford
Printer: L. Nagel, S. F.

Publisher: Snow & Roos, San Francisco
Key/Vignettes/Misc: Refs. 1–78, A–Z, AA–EE (?)
Locations: Private collection
Catalogs/Checklists: Baird & Evans, no. 39b; Peters, COS, p. 192

299
Place: San Francisco, California
Date: [1860–65?]
Title: Bay von San Francisco
Size: 9⁵⁄₈ × 14¾ in. (24.4 × 37.6 cm.)
Artist: E. Hildebrandt
Lithographer:
Printer:
Publisher:
Key/Vignettes/Misc:
Locations: UCBL–B; SFPL
Catalogs/Checklists: Baird & Evans, no. 80

300
Place: San Francisco, California
Date: [1860–65?] State I
Title: San Francisco
Size: 10¾ × 16⁷⁄₈ in. (27.4 × 42.9 cm.)
Artist: E. Hildebrandt
Lithographer:
Printer:
Publisher: R. Wagner, Berlin, Zimmerstrasse No. ⁹²⁄₉₃
Key/Vignettes/Misc:
Locations: CHS–SF
Catalogs/Checklists: Baird & Evans, no. 79a; Peters, COS, p. 128

301
Place: San Francisco, California
Date: [1860–65?] State II
Title: San Francisco
Size: 10¾ × 16⁷⁄₈ in. (27.4 × 42.9 cm.)
Artist: E. Hildebrandt
Lithographer:
Printer:
Publisher: R. Wagner, Berlin, Mauerstrasse 36
Key/Vignettes/Misc:
Locations: UCBL–B
Catalogs/Checklists: Baird & Evans, no. 79b

302
Place: San Francisco, California
Date: 1867
Title: The Guide Annual Supplement. 1867
Size: 11⁵⁄₈ × 14 in. (29.6 × 35.6 cm.)
Artist:
Lithographer:
Printer: G. T. Brown & Co. 543 Clay St. S. F.
Publisher: Bishop & Co., Publishers
Key/Vignettes/Misc: 96 numbered and 32 lettered refs.; 2 vignettes
Locations: SCP
Catalogs/Checklists: Baird & Evans, no. 40

303
Place: San Francisco, California
Date: 1867
Title: Yerba Buena (Now San Francisco) in

the Spring of 1837.
Size: 14¾ × 20⅝ in. (37.6 × 52.5 cm.)
Artist: John J. Vioget
Lithographer:
Printer: Britton & Rey, S. F.
Publisher: J. J. Du Prat (copyright)
Key/Vignettes/Misc:
Locations: SCP
Catalogs/Checklists: Baird & Evans, no. 1;
Peters, COS, p. 86

304
Place: San Francisco, California
Date: [before 1868] State IV
Title: San−Francisco 1849.
Size: 13¾ × 31¾ in. (35 × 80.8 cm.)
Artist: Henry Firks
Lithographer:
Printer:
Publisher: W. H. Jones, San Francisco
Key/Vignettes/Misc: Refs. 1−51
Locations: CHS−C; YUAG−NH
Catalogs/Checklists: Baird & Evans, no. 8d

305
Place: San Francisco, California
Date: 1868
Title: Birds Eye View of San Francisco, 1868
Size:
Artist: G. H. Goddard
Lithographer:
Printer: Britton & Rey
Publisher:
Key/Vignettes/Misc:
Locations: Unknown
Catalogs/Checklists: Peters, COS, p. 124

306
Place: San Francisco, California
Date: 1868
Title: Birds Eye View of the City of San Francisco
Size: 17⅜ × 25¾ in (45.5 × 65.5 cm.)
Artist:
Lithographer:
Printer: Britton & Rey, S. F.
Publisher: Snow & Roos, San Francisco
Key/Vignettes/Misc:
Locations: UCBL−B; MHdeY (on loan to CHS−SF); HEHL; LC−P
Catalogs/Checklists: Baird & Evans, no. 41

307
Place: San Francisco, California
Date: 1868
Title: Key to View of San Francisco, 1868
Size: 9³⁄₁₆ × 13¹¹⁄₁₆ in. (23.4 × 34.9 cm.)
Artist:
Lithographer:
Printer:
Publisher: A. L. Bancroft & Co., 721 Market St. [San Francisco]
Key/Vignettes/Misc: Refs. 1−124, A−K
Locations: Unknown
Catalogs/Checklists:

308
Place: San Francisco, California
Date: 1868 State I
Title: Bird's Eye View of the City &

County of San Francisco, 1868.
Size: 16⅛ × 27⁹⁄₁₆ in. (41 × 70.1 cm.)
Artist: W. Vallance Gray & C. B. Gifford
Lithographer: W. Vallance Gray & C. B. Gifford
Printer:
Publisher: W. Vallance Gray & C. B. Gifford, 645 Market St., S. F.
Key/Vignettes/Misc:
Locations: UCBL−B; SCP; LC−M (facsimile)
Catalogs/Checklists: Baird & Evans, no. 42a; PAI 15; LC−M, 35.1

309
Place: San Francisco, California
Date: 1868 State I
Title: Birds Eye View of the City of San Francisco and Surrounding Country.
Size: 27¼ × 40¼ in. (69.4 × 102.4 cm.)
Artist: George H. Goddard
Lithographer:
Printer: Britton & Rey, S. F.
Publisher: Snow & Roos, 21 Kearny St. Near Market., [San Francisco]
Key/Vignettes/Misc:
Locations: AAS−W; UCBL−B; CHS−SF; CSL−S
Catalogs/Checklists: Baird & Evans, no. 52a; Peters, COS, p. 81

310
Place: San Francisco, California
Date: 1868 State II
Title: Bird's Eye View of the City & County of San Francisco, 1868.
Size: 16⅛ × 27⅜ in. (41 × 69.6 cm.)
Artist: W. V. Gray & C. B. Gifford
Lithographer: W. V. Gray & C. B. Gifford
Printer: A. L. Bancroft & Co. Print. SF.
Publisher: A. L. Bancroft & Company 721 Market St, San Francisco
Key/Vignettes/Misc:
Locations: Private collection
Catalogs/Checklists: Baird & Evans, no. 42b; Peters, COS, p. 126

311
Place: San Francisco, California
Date: 1868 State II
Title: Birds Eye View of the City of San Francisco and Surrounding Country
Size: 27¼ × 40¼ in. (69.4 × 102.4 cm.)
Artist: George H. Goddard
Lithographer:
Printer: Britton & Rey, S. F.
Publisher: Snow & Roos, San Francisco
Key/Vignettes/Misc:
Locations: SCP; NYH−NY
Catalogs/Checklists: Baird & Evans, no. 52b

312
Place: San Francisco, California
Date: 1868 State III
Title: Birds Eye View of the City of San Francisco and Surrounding Country.
Size: 26¾ × 40½ in. (68.1 × 103.1 cm.)
Artist: George H. Goddard
Lithographer:
Printer: Britton & Rey, S. F.
Publisher: Snow & May, San Francisco
Key/Vignettes/Misc:

Locations: LC−M; NYP−P
Catalogs/Checklists: Baird & Evans, no. 52c; LC−M, 35

313
Place: San Francisco, California
Date: 1868 State IV
Title: Birds Eye View of the City of San Francisco and Surrounding Country
Size: 27⁵⁄₁₆ × 40⅜ in. (69.3 × 102.5 cm.)
Artist: George H. Goddard
Lithographer:
Printer: Britton & Rey, S. F.
Publisher: Snow & Roos (copyright)
Key/Vignettes/Misc:
Locations: ACMW−FW; LC−M (photo)
Catalogs/Checklists: ACMW−FW 1131; Reps, Cities on Stone, p. 97; LC−M, 35.2

314
Place: San Francisco, California
Date: 1868 State V
Title: San−Francisco 1849
Size: 13⅞ × 31¾ in. (35.3 × 80.8 cm.)
Artist: Henry Firks
Lithographer:
Printer: G. T. Brown & Co., 540 Clay St., S. F.
Publisher: W. H. Jones
Key/Vignettes/Misc: Refs. 1−51
Locations: MM−NN; UCBL−B; CHS−SF; OM−O; SCP; MHdeY (on loan to SCP)
Catalogs/Checklists: Reps, Cities on Stone, p. 97; Baird & Evans, no. 8e; Peters, COS, pp. 90, 120

315
Place: San Francisco, California
Date: 1868 State VI
Title: San−Francisco 1849.
Size: 13⅞ × 31¾ in. (35.3 × 80.8 cm.)
Artist: Henry Firks
Lithographer:
Printer: G. T. Brown & Co., 543 Clay St., S. F.
Publisher: W. H. Jones, San Francisco
Key/Vignettes/Misc: Refs. 1−51
Locations: CSL−S
Catalogs/Checklists: Baird & Evans, no. 8ei

316
Place: San Francisco, California
Date: 1869
Title: Bird's Eye View of the Bay of San Francisco and Adjacent Country.
Size: 15⅞ × 28⅜ in. (40.4 × 72.2 cm.)
Artist: W. Vallance Gray & C. B. Gifford
Lithographer:
Printer: W. Vallance Gray & C. B. Gifford, S. F.
Publisher: W. Vallance Gray & C. B. Gifford, S. F.
Key/Vignettes/Misc: Refs. 1−80
Locations: UCBL−B; CHS−SF
Catalogs/Checklists: Baird & Evans, no. 53; Peters, COS, p. 126

317
Place: San Francisco, California .
Date: 1869
Title: Key to View of San Francisco, 1869.

Size: 9³⁄₁₆ × 13¹¹⁄₁₆ in. (23.4 × 34.9 cm.)
Artist:
Lithographer:
Printer:
Publisher: A. L. Bancroft & Co. 721
Market St. [San Francisco]
Key/Vignettes/Misc: Refs. 1–124, A–K
Locations: Unknown
Catalogs/Checklists:

318

Place: San Francisco, California
Date: 1869 State III
Title: Bird's Eye View of the City &
County of San Francisco, 1869
Size: 16⅛ × 27⁹⁄₁₆ in. (41 × 70.1 cm.)
Artist: W. Vallance Gray & C. B. Gifford
Lithographer: W. Vallance Gray & C. B.
Gifford
Printer:
Publisher: W. Vallance Gray & C. B.
Gifford, 645 Market St. S. F.
Key/Vignettes/Misc:
Locations: NYP–P
Catalogs/Checklists: Baird & Evans, no.
43

319

Place: San Francisco, California
Date: 1872
Title: Key to View of San Francisco, 1872.
Size: 9³⁄₁₆ × 13¹¹⁄₁₆ in. (23.4 × 34.9 cm.)
Artist:
Lithographer:
Printer:
Publisher: A. L. Bancroft & Co. 721
Market St. [San Francisco]
Key/Vignettes/Misc: Refs. 1–124, A–K
Locations: UCBL–B
Catalogs/Checklists:

320

Place: San Francisco, California
Date: 1872 State IV
Title: Bird's Eye View of the City &
County of San Francisco, 1872.
Size: 16⅛ × 27⁹⁄₁₆ in. (41 × 70.1 cm.)
Artist: W. V. Gray & C. B. Gifford
Lithographer: W. V. Gray & C. B. Gifford
Printer: A. L. Bancroft & Co. Print. S.F.
Publisher: A. L. Bancroft & Company 721
Market St, San Francisco
Key/Vignettes/Misc:
Locations: CHS–SF
Catalogs/Checklists: Baird & Evans, no.
44

321

Place: San Francisco, California
Date: 1873 State V
Title: Bird's Eye View of the City &
County of San Francisco, 1873.
Size: 16⅛ × 27⁹⁄₁₆ in. (41 × 70.1 cm.)
Artist: W. V. Gray & C. B. Gifford
Lithographer: W. V. Gray & C. B. Gifford
Printer: A. L. Bancroft & Co., San
Francisco
Publisher: A. L. Bancroft & Company, 721
Market St., San Francisco
Key/Vignettes/Misc:
Locations: UCBL–B; CHS–C; SFPL
Catalogs/Checklists: Baird & Evans, no.
45

322

Place: San Francisco, California
Date: 1874
Title: San Francisco, California
Size: 10¾ × 24½ in. (27.4 × 62.4 cm.)
Artist:
Lithographer:
Printer:
Publisher: Frederick Hess
Key/Vignettes/Misc: 22 vignettes
Locations: LC–P; OM–O
Catalogs/Checklists:

323

Place: San Francisco, California
Date: [1870–74?]
Title: Ansicht von San Francisco.
Size: 11¾ × 27⁷⁄₁₆ in. (29.9 × 69.9 cm.)
Artist:
Lithographer:
Printer:
Publisher:
Key/Vignettes/Misc: Advertisements
Locations: UCBL–B
Catalogs/Checklists: Baird & Evans, no.
46

324

Place: San Francisco, California
Date: 1875
Title: Birdseye View of San Francisco and
Surrounding Country.
Size: 29 × 46 in. (73.8 × 117.1 cm.)
Artist: G. H. Goddard
Lithographer:
Printer: Britton Rey & Co. S. F.
Publisher: Snow & May. 21 Kearney St. S.
F.
Key/Vignettes/Misc:
Locations: SCP; MM–NN; CHS–SF;
UCLA–SC
Catalogs/Checklists: Baird & Evans, no.
54; Peters, COS, p. 81; MM–NN, LP
4379

325

Place: San Francisco, California
Date: 1875
Title: Key to Snow & May's
View. . .Looking East. Embracing a View
of the Sierra Nevada Mountains, of 500
Miles in Extent.
Size:
Artist:
Lithographer:
Printer:
Publisher:
Key/Vignettes/Misc: Refs. 1–155, A–Z,
a–h
Locations: UCLA–SC
Catalogs/Checklists:

326

Place: San Francisco, California
Date: 1875
Title: San Francisco News Letter
California Advertiser. Graphic Chart of
the City and County of San Francisco. . . .
Size: 20 × 30 in. (50.9 × 76.3 cm.)
Artist: L. R. Townsend, E. Wyneken & J.
Mendenhall
Lithographer:

Printer: Britton, Rey & Co., S. F.
Publisher: F. Marriott (copyright)
Key/Vignettes/Misc: 188 refs.; 2 vignettes
Locations: UCBL–B; CHS–SF; SFPL;
SCP; LC–M; HEHL (Refs. 1–186 & size
16 ¾ × 30 ½ in.)
Catalogs/Checklists: Baird & Evans, no.
47; LC–M, 36

327

Place: San Francisco, California
Date: 1876
Title: Birdseye View of San Francisco and
Surrounding Country.
Size: 33 × 47 in. (83.9 × 120 cm.)
Artist: G. H. Goddard
Lithographer:
Printer: Britton, Rey & Co., San Francisco
Publisher: Snow & May [San Francisco]
Key/Vignettes/Misc:
Locations: LC–M
Catalogs/Checklists: LC–M, 37

328

Place: San Francisco, California
Date: 1876
Title: San Francisco News Letter
California Advertiser. Graphic Chart of
the City and County of San Francisco. . . .
Revised March 1876
Size: 20 × 30 in. (50.9 × 76.3 cm.)
Artist: L. R. Townsend, E. Wyneken & J.
Mendenhall
Lithographer:
Printer: Britton, Rey & Co. S. F.
Publisher: F. Marriott (copyright)
Key/Vignettes/Misc: 188 refs.; 2 vignettes
Locations: CHS–SF
Catalogs/Checklists: Baird & Evans, no.
48

329

Place: San Francisco, California
Date: 1877
Title: Ansicht von San Francisco 1877.
Size: 11⅞ × 25⅝ in. (30.2 × 65.2 cm.)
Artist:
Lithographer:
Printer:
Publisher: Philo Jacoby's "California State
Almanac"
Key/Vignettes/Misc: 6 advertisements
Locations: UCBL–B
Catalogs/Checklists: Baird & Evans, no.
49

330

Place: San Francisco, California
Date: 1877
Title: San Francisco. Looking South from
North Point.
Size: 19³⁄₁₆ × 30⁷⁄₁₆ in. (48.9 × 77.5 cm.)
Artist: C. B. Gifford
Lithographer:
Printer: G. T. Brown & Co. S. F.
Publisher: G. T. Brown & Co.
Lithographers, 540 Clay St. S. F. Cal.
Key/Vignettes/Misc:
Locations: CHS–SF; UCBL–B; OM–O;
SCP; NYP–P
Catalogs/Checklists: Baird & Evans, no.
56; Peters, COS, pp. 90, 123

331
Place: San Francisco, California
Date: 1877
Title: The City of San Francisco.
Size: 8⅜ × 13⁵/₁₆ in. (21.3 × 33.9 cm.)
Artist:
Lithographer:
Printer:
Publisher: Currier & Ives, 115 Nassau St. New York
Key/Vignettes/Misc: 23 unnumbered refs.
Locations: CHS–SF; LC–P; SFPL; SCP
Catalogs/Checklists: Baird & Evans, no. 57; Peters, COS, p. 109; Peters, C & I, 3882A; PAI 45

332
Place: San Francisco, California
Date: 1878
Title: San Francisco News Letter California Advertiser. Graphic Chart of the City and County of San Francisco. . .Revised March 1878
Size: 11⅞ × 28⅝ in. (30.2 × 72.9 cm.)
Artist:
Lithographer:
Printer: Britton, Rey & Co., S. F.
Publisher: F. Marriott (copyright)
Key/Vignettes/Misc: Refs. 1–188
Locations: CHS–SF; HEHL; SCP
Catalogs/Checklists: Baird & Evans, no. 50

333
Place: San Francisco, California
Date: 1878 State I
Title: The City of San Francisco. Birds Eye View from the Bay Looking South–West.
Size: 21 × 32⅞ in. (53.4 × 83.6 cm.)
Artist: C. R. Parsons
Lithographer:
Printer:
Publisher: Currier & Ives, 115 Nassau St. New York
Key/Vignettes/Misc: Unnumbered refs. below places identified
Locations: MM–NN; NYH–NY; UCBL–B; CHS–C; SCP; HEHL; CHS–SF; YUAG–NH; LC–M (facsimile); LC–P
Catalogs/Checklists: Baird & Evans, no. 58a; Reps, Cities on Stone, p. 97; Peters, COS, p. 109; Peters, C & I, 3882; LC–M, 38

334
Place: San Francisco, California
Date: 1878 State II
Title: The City of San Francisco. Birds Eye View From the Bay Looking South–West. San Francisco—B. McQuilllan. . .Agent for the Pacific Coast
Size: 21 × 32⅞ in. (53.4 × 83.6 cm.)
Artist: C. R. Parsons
Lithographer:
Printer:
Publisher: Currier & Ives, 115 Nassau St., New York
Key/Vignettes/Misc: Unnumbered refs. below places identified
Locations: CHS–SF; LC–M

Catalogs/Checklists: Baird & Evans, no. 58b; LC–M, 37.1

335
Place: San Francisco, California
Date: [1878?]
Title: Veduta de San Francisco, Cal.
Size: 11⅞ × 28⅝ in. (30.2 × 72.9 cm.)
Artist:
Lithographer:
Printer:
Publisher: J. F. Fugazi, Montgomery Avenue No. 5 San Francisco, California
Key/Vignettes/Misc: Refs.
Locations: Private collection
Catalogs/Checklists: Baird & Evans, no. 51

336
Place: San Francisco, California
Date: 1879
Title: San Francisco June 1849
Size: 11⅛ × 19⅜ in. (28.3 × 49.3 cm.)
Artist: [Henry Firks]
Lithographer:
Printer: Buehler & Byrnes Lith. S. F.
Publisher: Illustrated Weekly Telephone, [San Francisco]
Key/Vignettes/Misc: Refs. 1–46
Locations: SFPL
Catalogs/Checklists: Baird & Evans, no. 9

337
Place: San Francisco, California
Date: 1880
Title: Birdseye View of San Francisco and Surrounding Country.
Size: 29 × 46 in. (73.8 × 117 cm.)
Artist: G. H. Goddard
Lithographer:
Printer: Britton Rey & Co. S. F.
Publisher: Snow & May. . .S. F. Re–published in 1880 by Snow & Co. 20 Post Street S. F.
Key/Vignettes/Misc:
Locations: CHS–SF; CSL–S
Catalogs/Checklists: Baird & Evans, no. 55; Peters, COS, pp. 81, 193

338
Place: San Francisco, California
Date: 1880
Title: Key to Snow & May's View. . .Looking East. Embracing a View of the Sierra Nevada Mountains, of 500 Miles in Extent.
Size:
Artist:
Lithographer:
Printer:
Publisher:
Key/Vignettes/Misc: Refs. 1–155, A–Z, a–h
Locations: Unknown
Catalogs/Checklists:

339
Place: San Francisco, California
Date: Ca. 1880
Title: Bird's Eye View of California
Size: 21 × 29 in. (53.4 × 73.8 cm.)
Artist:

Lithographer:
Printer:
Publisher: [Smith & Company?]
Key/Vignettes/Misc:
Locations: Private collection
Catalogs/Checklists: Baird & Evans, no. 60

340
Place: San Francisco, California
Date: [1880–] State VII
Title: San–Francisco 1849.
Size: 12¾ × 31⅝ in. (32.4 × 80.4 cm.)
Artist: [Henry Firks]
Lithographer:
Printer:
Publisher: Snow & Co., 20 Post Street, [San Francisco]
Key/Vignettes/Misc: Refs. 1–52
Locations: UCBL–B; CHS–SF; OM–O; MHdeY (on loan to SCP); YUAG–NH
Catalogs/Checklists: Baird & Evans, no. 8f

341
Place: San Francisco, California
Date: 1883?
Title: San Francisco.
Size: 20 × 30½ in. (50.9 × 77.6 cm.)
Artist:
Lithographer:
Printer:
Publisher:
Key/Vignettes/Misc:
Locations: CHS–SF
Catalogs/Checklists: Baird & Evans, no. 59

342
Place: San Francisco, California
Date: [1883–84?] State I
Title: View of San Francisco, Formerly Yerba Buena, in 1846–47 Before the Discovery of Gold.
Size: 17 × 20½ in. (43.1 × 52 cm.)
Artist: Capt. W. F. Swasey [William F. Swasey]
Lithographer:
Printer: Bosqui Eng. & Print. Co. [San Francisco]
Publisher: Capt. W. F. Swasey
Key/Vignettes/Misc: Refs. 1–35, A–E
Locations: NYP–S; MM–NN; AAS–W; UCBL–B; CHS–SF; CHS–C; CSL–S; OM–O; UCLA–SC; SFPL; SCP; LC–M (facsimile)
Catalogs/Checklists: Stokes Addenda 1846–47—Views; Baird & Evans, no. 3a; PAI 2; LC–M, 34

343
Place: San Francisco, California
Date: 1884 State II
Title: View of San Francisco, Formerly Yerba Buena, in 1846–47 Before the Discovery of Gold.
Size: 16¹³/₁₆ × 21½ in. (42.8 × 54.8 cm.)
Artist: Capt. W. F. Swasey [William F. Swasey]
Lithographer:
Printer: Bosqui Eng. & Print. Co.
Publisher: Capt. W. F. Swasey (copyright, 1884)

Key/Vignettes/Misc: Refs. 1–35, A–E
Locations: CSL–S; LC–M; LC–P
Catalogs/Checklists: Baird & Evans, no. 3b; Peters, COS, pp. 61, 195; LC–M, 33.2

344
Place: San Francisco, California
Date: 1886 State IX
Title: San Francisco 1849, Drawn on the Spot by Henry Firks. Latest Edition Corrected by a Committee of Pioneers. . . .
Size: 12⅞ × 31¾ in. (32.8 × 80.8 cm.)
Artist: Henry Firks
Lithographer:
Printer: Schmidt Label & Litho Co. S. F. Cal.
Publisher: Max Burkardt (copyright)
Key/Vignettes/Misc: Refs. 1–62
Locations: LC–P; CHS–C; CSL–S; SCP; SU–SC; MHdeY (on loan to CHS–SF)
Catalogs/Checklists: Baird & Evans, no. 8h; Peters, COS, pp. 120, 188

345
Place: San Francisco, California
Date: 1888
Title: San Francisco in 1888
Size: 12⅞ × 28¾ in. (32.7 × 73.2 cm.)
Artist:
Lithographer:
Printer:
Publisher: Philo Jacoby's California State Almanac
Key/Vignettes/Misc: Advertisements
Locations: UCBL–B
Catalogs/Checklists: Baird & Evans, no. 62

346
Place: San Francisco, California
Date: 1889 State II
Title: The City of San Francisco. Bird's Eye View from the Bay, Looking South–West.
Size: 21 × 32⅝ in. (53.4 × 83 cm.)
Artist: C. R. Parsons
Lithographer:
Printer:
Publisher: Currier & Ives. 115 Nassau St. New York
Key/Vignettes/Misc:
Locations: Private collection
Catalogs/Checklists: Conningham 1119

347
Place: San Francisco, California
Date: [188–]
Title: Bird Eye View of San Francisco
Size: 8⅛ × 16⅛ in. (20.6 × 41 cm.)
Artist:
Lithographer:
Printer: Bancroft Lith. S. F.
Publisher:
Key/Vignettes/Misc:
Locations: Private collection
Catalogs/Checklists: Baird & Evans, no. 61

348
Place: San Francisco, California
Date: [188–?] State VIII
Title: San–Francisco 1849.
Size: 12¾ × 31¾ in. (32.4 × 80.8 cm.)

Artist: [Henry Firks]
Lithographer:
Printer:
Publisher: [n.p.]
Key/Vignettes/Misc: Refs. 1–52
Locations: ACMW–FW
Catalogs/Checklists: Baird & Evans, no. 8g

349
Place: San Francisco, California
Date: 1890
Title: San Francisco, Cal. 1890. The San Francisco Examiner
Size: ca. 29 × 44 in. (73.8 × 111.9 cm.)
Artist: The Elliot Litho. Co.
Lithographer:
Printer: The Elliot Litho. Co. 120 Sutter St., S. F.
Publisher: San Francisco Examiner (copyright)
Key/Vignettes/Misc: Refs. 1–89; 16 vignettes
Locations: SCP; Arizona Historical Society, Tuscon, Arizona
Catalogs/Checklists: Baird & Evans, no. 65

350
Place: San Francisco, California
Date: 1892
Title: Bird's–Eye View of Golden Gate Park San Francisco, 1892
Size: 17⅛ × 24⅞ in. (43.5 × 63.3 cm.)
Artist: H. B. Elliott
Lithographer:
Printer: Bosqui Eng. Co. S. F.
Publisher: A. M. Freeman & Co. S. F.
Key/Vignettes/Misc: Refs. 1–58; 8 vignettes
Locations: UCBL–B; SCP
Catalogs/Checklists: Baird & Evans, no. 93

351
Place: San Francisco, California
Date: 1892
Title: Birds Eye View of the Eastern Portion of San Francisco Cal. Showing the Potrero District North of Nevada Street and East of Potrero Avenue.
Size: 21⁵⁄₁₆ × 28½ in. (54.2 × 72.5 cm.)
Artist:
Lithographer:
Printer: H. S. Crocker Company S. F.
Publisher: Baldwin & Hammond Real Estate Agents 10 Montgomery St. [San Francisco]
Key/Vignettes/Misc:
Locations: UCBL–B
Catalogs/Checklists: Baird & Evans, no. 66

352
Place: San Francisco, California
Date: 1893
Title: San Francisco in 1893
Size: 12⅛ × 28¼ in. (30.8 × 71.9 cm.)
Artist:
Lithographer:
Printer:
Publisher: Philo Jacoby's California State Almanac

Key/Vignettes/Misc: Advertisements
Locations: CHS–SF
Catalogs/Checklists: Baird & Evans, no. 63

353
Place: San Francisco, California
Date: 1893
Title: Yerba Buena (Now San Francisco) in the Spring of 1837.
Size: 12⅛ × 20¾ in. (30.8 × 52.9 cm.)
Artist: John J. Vioget
Lithographer: Geo. H. Baker
Printer:
Publisher:
Key/Vignettes/Misc: 4 unnumbered refs. below places and ships identified
Locations: UCBL–B; CHS–SF; SCP
Catalogs/Checklists: Baird & Evans, no. 2; SCP, p. 14 (767); Peters, COS, pp. 54, 198; PAI 1

354
Place: San Francisco, California
Date: 1894 State I
Title: San Francisco in 1849. San Francisco in July 1849. From Present Site of S. F. Stock Exchange
Size: 14⅛ × 35⅛ in. (35.9 × 89.4 cm.)
Artist: Geo. H. Burgess
Lithographer:
Printer: H. S. Crocker Company, S. F.
Publisher:
Key/Vignettes/Misc:
Locations: AAS–W; UCBL–B; CHS–SF; HEHL; SFPL; SCP; SU–SC; SBHS–SB
Catalogs/Checklists: Baird & Evans, no. 10a

355
Place: San Francisco, California
Date: 1894 State II
Title: San Francisco in July 1849. From Present Site of S. F. Stock Exchange
Size: 14⅛ × 35⅛ in. (35.9 × 89.4 cm.)
Artist: Geo. H. Burgess
Lithographer:
Printer: H. S. Crocker Company, S.F.
Publisher:
Key/Vignettes/Misc:
Locations: Private collection
Catalogs/Checklists: Baird & Evans, no. 10b

356
Place: San Francisco, California
Date: 1894 State III
Title: San Francisco in July 1849. From Present Site of S. F. Stock Exchange
Size: 14⅛ × 35⅛ in. (35.9 × 89.4 cm.)
Artist: Geo. H. Burgess
Lithographer:
Printer: H. S. Crocker Company S. F. Lith.
Publisher: Elisha Cook (copyright)
Key/Vignettes/Misc:
Locations: EI–S; LC–P
Catalogs/Checklists: Baird & Evans, no. 10c

357
Place: San Francisco, California
Date: 1895
Title: San Francisco, California.

Size: 18⅜ × 24³⁄₁₆ in. (46.7 × 61.6 cm.)
Artist: Edw. Lange
Lithographer:
Printer: Louis Roesch Co. S. F.
Publisher: W. T. Hess (copyright)
Key/Vignettes/Misc: 3 views on a single sheet
Locations: CHS–SF; SFPL; SCP; MHdeY (on loan to SCP)
Catalogs/Checklists: Baird & Evans, no. 67

358
Place: San Francisco, California
Date: 1896
Title: San Francisco in 1896
Size: 12⅛ × 28¼ in. (30.8 × 71.9 cm.)
Artist:
Lithographer:
Printer:
Publisher: Philo Jacoby's California State Almanac
Key/Vignettes/Misc: Advertisements
Locations: SFPL
Catalogs/Checklists: Baird & Evans, no. 64

359
Place: San Francisco, California
Date: Ca. 1900
Title: San Francisco and Surroundings—Looking East Showing the Bay and Great Interior Valleys of California
Size: 23⅛ × 37¾ in. (58.9 × 96 cm.)
Artist:
Lithographer:
Printer:
Publisher: Elliott Pub. Co. S. F.
Key/Vignettes/Misc:
Locations: UCBL–B
Catalogs/Checklists: Baird & Evans, no. 68

360
Place: San Francisco, California
Date: 1904
Title: San Francisco in 1904
Size: 12⅛ × 28¼ in. (30.8 × 71.9 cm.)
Artist:
Lithographer:
Printer:
Publisher: Philo Jacoby's California State Almanac
Key/Vignettes/Misc: Advertisements
Locations: SFPL
Catalogs/Checklists: Baird & Evans, no. 70

361
Place: San Francisco, California
Date: 1904
Title: San Francisco View from the Bay
Size: 7 × 16 in. (17.8 × 40.7 cm.)
Artist:
Lithographer:
Printer:
Publisher: Mutual Label & Litho. Co. [San Francisco]
Key/Vignettes/Misc:
Locations: CHS–SF
Catalogs/Checklists: Baird & Evans, no. 69

362
Place: San Francisco, California
Date: 1906
Title: "The Burning of San Francisco" April 18, 19, 20, 1906. The Greatest Conflagration in the History of the World. . . .
Size: 22¼ × 33⅜ in. (56.6 × 84.9 cm.)
Artist: C. A. Beck
Lithographer:
Printer: Schmidt Lithograph Co. S. F.
Publisher:
Key/Vignettes/Misc:
Locations: UCBL–B; CSL–S; SCP; OM–O
Catalogs/Checklists: Baird & Evans, no. 95

363
Place: San Francisco, California
Date: 1906
Title: Destruction of San Francisco by Earthquake & Fire
Size: 20³⁄₁₆ × 26⁷⁄₁₆ in. (51.3 × 67 cm.)
Artist:
Lithographer:
Printer:
Publisher: Kurz & Allison, Chicago
Key/Vignettes/Misc: 18 vignettes
Locations: ACMW–FW; LC–P
Catalogs/Checklists:

364
Place: San Francisco, California
Date: 1907
Title: [Untitled view of San Francisco Fire of 1906]
Size: 20⅜ × 12⅜ in. (51.8 × 31.4 cm.)
Artist:
Lithographer:
Printer: Britton & Rey S. F.
Publisher: California Insurance Co. (copyright)
Key/Vignettes/Misc:
Locations: Private collection
Catalogs/Checklists: Baird & Evans, no. 119

365
Place: San Francisco, California
Date: 1907
Title: [Untitled View of San Francisco Fire of 1906]
Size: 11½ × 18½ in. (29.2 × 47.1 cm.)
Artist: T. [J.?] Reichard
Lithographer:
Printer:
Publisher: [obliterated]
Key/Vignettes/Misc:
Locations: CHS–SF
Catalogs/Checklists: Baird & Evans, no. 118

366
Place: San Francisco, California
Date: Ca. 1914
Title: The Exposition City San Francisco
Size: 28¼ × 42⅜ in. (71.9 × 107.8 cm.)
Artist:
Lithographer:
Printer: Pingree–Traung Co. Lith. S. F.
Publisher: North American Press Ass'n (copyright)

Key/Vignettes/Misc:
Locations: UCBL–B; SFPL; SCP; SU–SC; WHS–M; OHS–P
Catalogs/Checklists: Baird & Evans, no. 71

367
Place: San Francisco, California
Date: N.D.
Title: Bai San Francisco und Vereinigung des Sacramento mit dem San Joaquin
Size: 8¼ × 10⅜ in. (21 × 26.4 cm.)
Artist:
Lithographer:
Printer: L. Kraatz, Berlin
Publisher: George Westermann, Braunschweig
Key/Vignettes/Misc:
Locations: Private collection
Catalogs/Checklists: Baird & Evans, no. 78

368
Place: San Francisco, California
Date: N.D.
Title: View of San Francisco
Size: ["large"]
Artist: Lopez
Lithographer:
Printer: Jannin
Publisher: Galle, Paris
Key/Vignettes/Misc:
Locations: Unknown
Catalogs/Checklists: Peters, COS, p. 130

369
Place: San Gabriel, California
Date: Ca. 1892
Title: View of San Gabriel, Cal.
Size: 14 × 20½ in. (35.5 × 52 cm.)
Artist:
Lithographer:
Printer:
Publisher: D. D. Morse (copyright)
Key/Vignettes/Misc: Refs. 1–40; 1 vignette
Locations: LC–M; HEHL
Catalogs/Checklists: LC–M, 39; Reps, Cities on Stone, p. 97

370
Place: San Jacinto, California
Date: [1886?]
Title: The Town of San Jacinto is in Great San Jacinto Valley, San Diego Co., Cal., Twelve Miles South of Beaumont (formerly San Gorgonio). . . .
Size: 18 × 25⅜ in. (45.8 × 64.6 cm.)
Artist: E. S. Moore
Lithographer:
Printer:
Publisher: E. S. Moore
Key/Vignettes/Misc: 17 vignettes; description
Locations: LC–M; HEHL; NHM–LA
Catalogs/Checklists: LC–M, 39.2

371
Place: San Jose, California
Date: 1856
Title: San Jose, 1856 County of Santa Clara, Cala.
Size: 9⅛ × 19⅝ in. (23.2 × 49.9 cm.)

Artist: Kuchel & Dresel
Lithographer: Kuchel & Dresel
Printer: Britton & Rey, S. F.
Publisher: Kuchel & Dresel 176 Clay St.,
San Francisco
Key/Vignettes/Misc:
Locations: SCP
Catalogs/Checklists: SCP, p. 20 (425)

372
Place: San Jose, California
Date: 1856
Title: San Jose, 1856. County of Santa
Clara, Cala.
Size: 20⅞ × 26⅜ in. (53.2 × 67.2 cm.)
Artist:
Lithographer:
Printer: Britton & Rey, S. F.
Publisher: Kuchel & Dresel, 176 Clay St.
San Francisco
Key/Vignettes/Misc: 24 vignettes;
description
Locations: ACMW–FW; SCP; CHS–SF
Catalogs/Checklists: ACMW–FW 1269;
Peters, COS, p. 145 (23 vignettes); SCP, p.
20 (629); Reps, Cities on Stone, p. 97

373
Place: San Jose, California
Date: 1858
Title: San Jose, From City Hall. 1858.
Size: 12¼ × 19⅝ in. (31.1 × 49.9 cm.)
Artist: Levi Goodrich
Lithographer: Kuchel & Dresel
Printer: Britton & Rey Print [San
Francisco]
Publisher: Levi Goodrich, San Jose
Key/Vignettes/Misc:
Locations: CHS–SF; UCBL–B
Catalogs/Checklists: Peters, COS, pp. 124,
145

374
Place: San Jose, California
Date: 1869
Title: Bird's Eye View of the City of San
Jose Cal.
Size: 19 × 28 in. (48.3 × 71.2 cm.)
Artist: W. Vallance Gray and C. B. Gifford
Lithographer: W. Vallance Gray and C. B.
Gifford
Printer: L. Nagel, S. F.
Publisher: Geo. H. Hare, Bookseller &
Stationer, First Street [San Jose]
Key/Vignettes/Misc:
Locations: CHS–SF; LC–M; UCBL–B
Catalogs/Checklists: LC–M, 40; Peters,
COS, pp. 126, 16

375
Place: San Jose, California
Date: 1875
Title: City of San Jose, Cal. 1875. From an
Elevation of 500 ft. Looking North.
Size: 17¹³⁄₁₆ × 26¼ in. (45.3 × 66.8 cm.)
Artist: C. B. Gifford
Lithographer:
Printer: A. L. Bancroft & Co. Lith. S. F.
Publisher: W. C. Gifford. . .355 First
Street, S.[an] J.[ose]
Key/Vignettes/Misc:
Locations: UCBL–B; SCP; LC–M;
ACMW–FW; HEHL

Catalogs/Checklists: SCP, p. 20 (351);
LC–M, 41

376
Place: San Jose, California
Date: 1888
Title: San Jose, Santa Clara County,
California.
Size: 22⅛ × 35⅝ in. (56.3 × 90.7 cm.)
Artist: Elliott & Co.
Lithographer:
Printer: Elliott & Co., S. F.
Publisher: San Jose Daily Herald
Key/Vignettes/Misc: Refs. 1–58; 24
vignettes; description
Locations: HEHL
Catalogs/Checklists:

377
Place: San Jose, California
Date: Ca. 1901
Title: San Jose, California
Size: 28½ × 42 in. (72.4 × 107 cm.)
Artist: F. L.
Lithographer:
Printer: Britton & Rey, San Francisco
Publisher: N. J. Stone Company, San
Francisco, Cal.
Key/Vignettes/Misc: 26 vignettes
Locations: LC–M; LC–P
Catalogs/Checklists: LC–M, 42

378
Place: San Juan By The Sea, California
Date: Ca. 1888
Title: San Juan by–the–Sea with Dana's
Point; Mentone. . . .
Size:
Artist:
Lithographer:
Printer: Los Angeles Lithographic Co. [Los
Angeles]
Publisher:
Key/Vignettes/Misc:
Locations: UCBL–B
Catalogs/Checklists:

379
Place: San Juan Del Norte, California
Date: N.D.
Title: San Juan del Norte or Greytown
Size:
Artist:
Lithographer:
Printer: Nagel & Schwartz Lithographers,
58 Montgomery St. Sn Franco.
Publisher:
Key/Vignettes/Misc:
Locations: Unknown
Catalogs/Checklists: Peters, COS, p. 172

380
Place: San Luis Obispo, California
Date: 1877
Title: Bird's Eye View of San Luis Obispo,
Cal. 1877.
Size: 12½ × 23⅞ in. (31.7 × 60.5 cm.)
Artist: E. S. Glover
Lithographer:
Printer: A. L. Bancroft & Co., Lith. San
Francisco
Publisher: E. S. Glover

Key/Vignettes/Misc: Refs. 1–21
Locations: ACMW–FW; UCBL–B;
CSL–S; Mission San Luis Obispo
Museum, San Luis Obispo, California; San
Luis Obispo County Historical Museum,
San Luis Obispo, California; LC–M
(facsimile)
Catalogs/Checklists: ACMW–FW 1125;
Reps, Cities on Stone, p. 97; LC–M, 42.1

381
Place: San Mateo, California
Date: 1931
Title: Aero–View–Map of San Mateo,
San Mateo Co., California
Size: 12½ × 24 in. (31.8 × 61 cm.)
Artist: Aug. Chevalier
Lithographer:
Printer:
Publisher: Aug. Chevalier
Key/Vignettes/Misc:
Locations: LC–M
Catalogs/Checklists: LC–M, 43

382
Place: San Mateo Park, California
Date: 1905
Title: [Untitled view of San Mateo Park]
Size: 8⅝ × 7⅛ in. (22 × 18 cm.)
Artist: W.[illiam] H. Bull
Lithographer:
Printer:
Publisher: Baldwin & Howell
Key/Vignettes/Misc:
Locations: LC–M
Catalogs/Checklists: LC–M, 44

383
Place: San Pedro, California
Date: [1893]
Title: San Pedro, Los Angeles Co.,
California
Size: 21½ × 31⅜ in. (54.6 × 79.8 cm.)
Artist: B. W. Pierce
Lithographer:
Printer:
Publisher: B. W. Pierce, 230 N. Main St L.
A. Cal.
Key/Vignettes/Misc: Refs. 1–24; 19
vignettes
Locations: ACMW–FW; NHM–LA;
HEHL; UCBL–B; WHS–M; UCLA–SC
(cropped); LC–M (photo)
Catalogs/Checklists: ACMW–FW 1594;
LC–M, 44.1

384
Place: San Pedro, California
Date: [1897]
Title: Birds Eye View of Town and Water
Front of San Pedro California. Showing
the Existing Inner and the Proposed Outer
Harbor.
Size: 14⅞ × 21¹³⁄₁₆ in. (37.8 × 55.6 cm.)
Artist:
Lithographer:
Printer: H. S. Crocker & Company, Los
Angeles, S. F. & Sac.
Publisher: Los Angeles Times, Los Angeles
Key/Vignettes/Misc:
Locations: UCBL–B; NHM–LA; CSL–S
Catalogs/Checklists:

385
Place: San Rafael, California
Date: [1891?]
Title: San Rafael. Marin Co. California
Size: 17 × 20 in. (43.2 × 50.8 cm.)
Artist: E. S. Moore
Lithographer:
Printer: Britton, Rey & Co., S. F.
Publisher: Moore & De Pew, San Francisco
Key/Vignettes/Misc: 19 vignettes
Locations: UCBL−B
Catalogs/Checklists:

386
Place: Santa Ana, California
Date: Ca. 1876
Title: Bird's Eye View of Santa Ana, Los Angeles Co., Cal. From the South−West Looking North−East.
Size: 9⁷⁄₁₆ × 16⁵⁄₁₆ in. (24 × 41.5 cm.)
Artist: E. S. Glover
Lithographer:
Printer: A. L. Bancroft & Co., San Francisco
Publisher:
Key/Vignettes/Misc: Refs. 1−10, A−D
Locations: UCBL−B
Catalogs/Checklists:

387
Place: Santa Barbara, California
Date: 1873
Title: Santa Barbara, Cal, 1873.
Size: 9 × 16⁹⁄₁₆ in. (22.9 × 42.1 cm.)
Artist: A. E. Mathews
Lithographer:
Printer: A.·L. Bancroft & Co. Lith. [San Francisco]
Publisher: A. L. Bancroft & Co. 721 Market Street, San Francisco, Cal.
Key/Vignettes/Misc: Description
Locations: MM−NN; UCBL−B; HEHL; SBHS−SB
Catalogs/Checklists: MM−NN, LP 2012; PAI 41

388
Place: Santa Barbara, California
Date: 1877
Title: Bird's Eye View of Santa Barbara, California, 1877. Looking North to the Santa Barbara Mountains.
Size: 17³⁄₁₆ × 30¹⁄₁₆ in. (43.7 × 74.3 cm.)
Artist: E. S. Glover
Lithographer:
Printer: A. L. Bancroft & Co., Lithographers, S. F.
Publisher: E. S. Glover
Key/Vignettes/Misc: Refs. 1−27
Locations: ACMW−FW; LC−M; UCBL−B; HEHL; CSL−S; SBHS−SB; OM−O
Catalogs/Checklists: ACMW−FW 1126; LC−M, 45; PAI 40; Reps, Cities on Stone, p. 97

389
Place: Santa Barbara, California
Date: [1877]
Title: Santa Barbara
Size: 21½ × 35 in. (54.8 × 89.1 cm.)

Artist:
Lithographer: R. H.
Printer: W. W. Elliott, Litho, S. F.
Publisher: The Independent [Santa Barbara]
Key/Vignettes/Misc: Refs. 1−35; 29 vignettes
Locations: SBHS−SB
Catalogs/Checklists:

390
Place: Santa Barbara, California
Date: [1887]
Title: Santa Barbara
Size: 21½ × 35 in. (54.8 × 89.1 cm.)
Artist:
Lithographer: R. H.
Printer: W. W. Elliott Lith. S. F.
Publisher: S. W. Backus & Co., Santa Barbara
Key/Vignettes/Misc: Refs. 1−35; 29 vignettes; description
Locations: CSL−S
Catalogs/Checklists:

391
Place: Santa Barbara, California
Date: [1888?]
Title: Santa Barbara, California
Size: 15³⁄₈ × 31½ in. (39.1 × 80.1 cm.)
Artist: Steinegger & E. F. Cook
Lithographer:
Printer: Britton & Rey [San Francisco]
Publisher:
Key/Vignettes/Misc:
Locations: SCP; SBHS−SB
Catalogs/Checklists: SCP, p. 20 (1111); Peters, COS, pp. 85, 99

392
Place: Santa Barbara, California
Date: 1896
Title: Santa Barbara, California
Size: 5⅛ × 7½ in. (13 × 19 cm.)
Artist:
Lithographer:
Printer:
Publisher:
Key/Vignettes/Misc:
Locations: LC−M
Catalogs/Checklists: LC−M, 46

393
Place: Santa Barbara, California
Date: 1898
Title: Santa Barbara, California 1893 El Pueblo de las Rosas
Size: 25 × 36½ in. (63.5 × 92.8 cm.)
Artist:
Lithographer:
Printer: Los Angeles Lithographic Co. [Los Angeles]
Publisher: P. E. Gifford (copyright)
Key/Vignettes/Misc: 21 vignettes
Locations: LC−M; SBHS−SB
Catalogs/Checklists: LC−M, 47

394
Place: Santa Clara, California
Date: 1856
Title: Santa Clara, 1856
Size: 16⁷⁄₈ × 24⁷⁄₈ in. (42.9 × 63.3 cm.)

Artist: Kuchel & Dresel
Lithographer: Kuchel & Dresel
Printer: Britton & Rey, S. F.
Publisher: Kuchel & Dresel, 176 Clay St., San Francisco
Key/Vignettes/Misc: 14 vignettes; description
Locations: CHS−SF
Catalogs/Checklists: Peters, COS, p. 145 (13 vignettes)

395
Place: Santa Clara, California
Date: 1856
Title: Santa Clara, 1856.
Size: 9⁷⁄₈ × 17⁵⁄₈ in. (25.1 × 44.8 cm.)
Artist: Kuchel & Dresel
Lithographer: Kuchel & Dresel
Printer: Britton & Rey, S. F.
Publisher: Kuchel & Dresel, 176. Clay St. San Francisco
Key/Vignettes/Misc:
Locations: UCBL−B; ACMW−FW; CHS−SF; LC−M (facsimile)
Catalogs/Checklists: ACMW−FW 1270; Reps, Cities on Stone, p. 97

396
Place: Santa Clara, California
Date: Ca. 1860
Title: Bird's Eye View of Santa Clara, Calif.
Size: 15 × 26 in. (38.1 × 66.2 cm.)
Artist: C. B. Gifford
Lithographer: C. B. Gifford
Printer: G. T. Brown & Co.
Publisher:
Key/Vignettes/Misc: Refs. 1−19
Locations: UCBL−B; CHS−SF
Catalogs/Checklists:

397
Place: Santa Cruz, California
Date: Ca. 1870
Title: Bird's Eye View of Santa Cruz, Cal.
Size: 18⅛ × 26¹⁵⁄₁₆ in. (46.1 × 66.1 cm.)
Artist: C. B. Gifford
Lithographer:
Printer: A. L. Bancroft & Co. Lith. S. F.
Publisher:
Key/Vignettes/Misc: Refs. 1−26
Locations: CHS−C; CHS−SF; CSL−S; UCBL−B
Catalogs/Checklists: PAI 32

398
Place: Santa Cruz, California
Date: Ca. 1888
Title: Santa Cruz, Cal.
Size: 19 × 31⅜ in. (48.4 × 79.8 cm.)
Artist: Hy [Henry] Steinegger
Lithographer:
Printer: Britton & Rey, S. F.
Publisher: A. J. Hatch & Co., Publishers, San Francisco
Key/Vignettes/Misc:
Locations: SCP; NYP−P (lacks letters)
Catalogs/Checklists: SCP, p.20 (373)

399
Place: Santa Cruz, California
Date: N.D.
Title: Bird's−Eye View of the City of Santa Cruz

Size: 23 × 37¾ in. (58.6 × 96.1 cm.)
Artist:
Lithographer:
Printer: Britton & Rey, S. F.
Publisher: F. W. Swanton (copyright)
Key/Vignettes/Misc: Refs. 1–24
Locations: CSL–S
Catalogs/Checklists:

400
Place: Santa Cruz, California
Date: N.D.
Title: Santa Cruz. Cal.
Size: 21½ × 35½ in. (54.7 × 90.3 cm.)
Artist:
Lithographer:
Printer: Britton & Rey, S. F.
Publisher: A. H. Hatch & Co., San
Francisco
Key/Vignettes/Misc:
Locations: UCBL–B; CHS–SF
Catalogs/Checklists:

401
Place: Santa Monica, California
Date: Ca. 1876
Title: Birds Eye View of Santa Monica Los
Angeles Co. Cal. Looking South to the
Pacific Ocean and Santa Monica
Mountains to the Right. . . .
Size: 9¹³⁄₁₆ × 16⅝ in. (24.9 × 42.3 cm.)
Artist: E. S. Glover
Lithographer:
Printer: A. L. Bancroft
Publisher:
Key/Vignettes/Misc:
Locations: CHS–C
Catalogs/Checklists: Peters, COS, pp. 54,
124

402
Place: Santa Monica, California
Date: Ca. 1887
Title: Santa Monica Los Angeles County,
California.
Size: 18½ × 22⅝ in. (47.1 × 57.6 cm.)
Artist:
Lithographer:
Printer: Elliott Lith, S. F. & Los Angeles
Publisher:
Key/Vignettes/Misc: Refs. 1–20, A–C; 19
vignettes
Locations: NHM–LA
Catalogs/Checklists:

403
Place: Santa Rosa, California
Date: [1859?]
Title: View of Santa Rosa
Size: 14¾ × 19⅛ in. (37.5 × 48.6 cm.)
Artist: Grafton T. Brown
Lithographer: Kuchel & Dresel
Printer: Britton & Co. [San Francisco]
Publisher:
Key/Vignettes/Misc: 15 vignettes
Locations: SCP; UCBL–B
Catalogs/Checklists: SCP, p. 20 (903);
Peters, COS, pp. 90, 146

404
Place: Santa Rosa, California
Date: 1876
Title: Bird's Eye View of Santa Rosa,

Sonoma County, Cal., 1876. From the
South–East, Looking North–West.
Size: 16¾ × 25 in. (42.6 × 63.5 cm.)
Artist: E. S. Glover
Lithographer:
Printer: A. L. Bancroft & Co.,
Lithographers, San Francisco
Publisher: Wm. M. Evans
Key/Vignettes/Misc: Refs. 1–20; 2
unnumbered refs.; description
Locations: LC–M; ACMW–FW
Catalogs/Checklists: LC–M, 48

405
Place: Santa Rosa, California
Date: 1885
Title: Santa Rosa. Sonoma County.
California. 1885
Size: 20⅜ × 26¹⁄₁₆ in. (51.7 × 66.2 cm.)
Artist:
Lithographer:
Printer: Elliott & Co., Lith, Oakland,
Cala.
Publisher: Guy E. Grosse
Key/Vignettes/Misc: Refs. 1–52; 18
vignettes
Locations: ACMW–FW; SCP; HEHL;
LC–M (facsimile)
Catalogs/Checklists: ACMW–FW 1841;
SCP, p. 20 (322); LC–M, 48.1

406
Place: Scott's Bar, California
Date: 1856
Title: Scotts Bar and French Bar, On Scotts
River, Siskiyou County, California. 1856
Size: 15¹⁵⁄₁₆ × 27⁹⁄₁₆ in. (40.5 × 69.9 cm.)
Artist: Kuchel & Dresel
Lithographer: Kuchel & Dresel
Printer: Britton & Rey [San Francisco]
Publisher: J. M. C. Jones
Key/Vignettes/Misc: 25 vignettes
Locations: ACMW–FW; CHS–SF;
OM–O
Catalogs/Checklists: ACMW–FW 1271;
Peters, COS, pp. 86, 145

407
Place: Scott's Bar, California
Date: Ca. 1856
Title: Scott's Bar, Trinity County
Size: ["medium"]
Artist: Kuchel & Dresel
Lithographer: Kuchel & Dresel
Printer: Britton & Rey
Publisher:
Key/Vignettes/Misc: [no vignettes]
Locations: Unknown
Catalogs/Checklists: Peters, COS, p. 145

408
Place: Scott's Bar, California
Date: 1857
Title: Scott's Bar, Siskiyou County. 1857.
Size: 9⅞ × 10¾ in. (25.1 × 27.4 cm.)
Artist: Kuchel & Dresel
Lithographer:
Printer: Britton & Rey [San Francisco]
Publisher:
Key/Vignettes/Misc: [no vignettes]
Locations: UCBL–B
Catalogs/Checklists:

409
Place: Scott's Bar, California
Date: [1856–57?]
Title: Scotts Bar
Size: 9 × 10⅝ in. (22.9 × 27 cm.)
Artist: [unsigned]
Lithographer:
Printer: [n.p.]
Publisher:
Key/Vignettes/Misc:
Locations: Unknown. Alta California
Bookstore, 2/9/80
Catalogs/Checklists:

410
Place: Shasta, California
Date: [1851–52]
Title: View of Shasta City.
Size:
Artist: Healy
Lithographer:
Printer: Quirot & Co. corner of Montg. &
Califa Sts S Francis[co]
Publisher: Geo. W. King, Shasta
Key/Vignettes/Misc:
Locations: Unknown
Catalogs/Checklists: Peters, COS, pp. 128,
138, Plate 95

411
Place: Shasta, California
Date: 1856
Title: Shasta, Shasta County, Cal.
Size: 12⅜ × 18½ in. (31.4 × 47 cm.)
Artist: Kuchel & Dresel
Lithographer:
Printer: Britton & Rey [San Francisco]
Publisher: A. Roman (copyright)
Key/Vignettes/Misc: [no vignettes]
Locations: ACMW–FW; LC–P
Catalogs/Checklists: Peters, COS, p. 145;
LC–M, 48.2

412
Place: Shasta, California
Date: 1856
Title: Shasta, 1856. Shasta County,
California.
Size: 16⁷⁄₁₆ × 24 in. (41.7 × 60.8 cm.)
Artist: Kuchel & Dresel
Lithographer: Kuchel & Dresel
Printer: Britton & Rey [San Francisco]
Publisher: A. Roman
Key/Vignettes/Misc: 23 vignettes
Locations: ACMW–FW; UCBL–B
Catalogs/Checklists: ACMW–FW 1272;
Reps, Cities on Stone, p. 98

413
Place: Shasta, California
Date: [1856]
Title: Shasta Shasta County, Cal.
Size: 10¼ × 17¹³⁄₁₆ in. (26.1 × 45.3 cm.)
Artist: Kuchel & Dresel
Lithographer: Kuchel & Dresel
Printer: Britton & Rey [San Francisco]
Publisher:
Key/Vignettes/Misc: [no vignettes]
Locations: SCP; CHS–SF
Catalogs/Checklists: SCP, p. 21 (717)

414
Place: Shasta Butte, California
Date: Ca. 1856
Title: Shasta Butte & Shasta Valley. Siskiyou County Cala.
Size: 8 5/16 × 12 3/8 in. (21.2 × 31.5 cm.)
Artist: E. Camerer
Lithographer: Kuchel & Dresel's Lith.
Printer: L. Nagel [San Francisco]
Publisher:
Key/Vignettes/Misc:
Locations: UCBL–B; CHS–SF
Catalogs/Checklists: Peters, COS, p. 169

415
Place: Sierra Madre, California
Date: [1888?]
Title: Birdseye View of Sierra Madre San Gabriel Valley, Los Angeles County, Cal. Elevation from 1400 to 1800 F.
Size: 21 1/2 × 29 5/8 in. (54.7 × 75.4 cm.)
Artist: Stggr [Henry Steinegger]
Lithographer:
Printer: Britton & Rey, San Francisco, Cal.
Publisher:
Key/Vignettes/Misc: 19 vignettes
Locations: HEHL; UCBL–B
Catalogs/Checklists:

416
Place: Silver Creek, California
Date: N.D.
Title: Silver Creek—California
Size: 8 7/16 × 12 7/16 in. (21.4 × 31.6 cm.)
Artist:
Lithographer:
Printer:
Publisher: Currier & Ives [New York]
Key/Vignettes/Misc:
Locations: UCBL–B; HEHL
Catalogs/Checklists:

417
Place: Sonora, California
Date: 1852
Title: Sonora January, 1852
Size: 10 1/2 × 15 3/8 in. (26.7 × 39.1 cm.)
Artist: G. H. Goddard
Lithographer:
Printer: Pollard & Brittons Lith Merchants St. S. F.
Publisher: G. H. Goddard (copyright)
Key/Vignettes/Misc:
Locations: SCP; UCBL–B; CSL–S; LC–M (photo); NYH–NY
Catalogs/Checklists: SCP, p. 21 (1160); LC–M, 49; Peters, COS, p. 124

418
Place: Sonora, California
Date: 1853
Title: Sonora, Jany. 1853.
Size: 7 1/8 × 9 3/4 in. (18.1 × 24.8 cm.)
Artist:
Lithographer:
Printer: Britton & Rey, San Francisco
Publisher: B. R. Sweetland
Key/Vignettes/Misc:
Locations: UCBL–B; HEHL (lacks publisher's imprint)
Catalogs/Checklists:

419
Place: Sonora, California
Date: Ca. 1857
Title: Sonora Tuolumne County, Southern Mines, California
Size: 15 3/4 × 23 5/8 in. (40.1 × 60.1 cm.)
Artist: Kuchel & Dresel
Lithographer: Kuchel & Dresel
Printer: Britton & Rey [San Francisco]
Publisher:
Key/Vignettes/Misc: 21 vignettes
Locations: UCBL–B; SCP; CHS–C; TCM–S
Catalogs/Checklists: SCP, p. 21 (895); Peters, COS, p. 145

420
Place: Sonora, California
Date: Ca. 1857
Title: Sonora Tuolumne County, Southern Mines, California
Size: 21 3/4 × 27 13/16 in. (55.3 × 70.8 cm.)
Artist: Kuchel & Dresel
Lithographer: Kuchel & Dresel
Printer: Britton & Rey [San Francisco]
Publisher:
Key/Vignettes/Misc: 14 vignettes
Locations: UCBL–B; ACMW–FW
Catalogs/Checklists:

421
Place: Sonora, California
Date: Ca. 1880
Title: Sonora, Tuolumne Co. Cal.
Size: 18 5/8 × 26 3/8 in. (47.4 × 67.2 cm.)
Artist: From a photograph by Rehm
Lithographer:
Printer: Elliott Publishing Co., S. F.
Publisher: Elliott Publishing Co. S. F. (copyright)
Key/Vignettes/Misc: Refs. 1–12; 14 vignettes; advertisements
Locations: UCBL–B; TCM–S
Catalogs/Checklists:

422
Place: South Cucamonga, California
Date: [188–?]
Title: Map of South Cucamonga Town Site
Size: 39 1/2 × 26 7/26 in. (100.2 × 67.3 cm.)
Artist:
Lithographer:
Printer: Los Angeles Lithographic Co. 43 to 52 Banning St. [Los Angeles]
Publisher:
Key/Vignettes/Misc:
Locations: UCLA–SC
Catalogs/Checklists:

423
Place: Springfield, California
Date: Ca. 1852
Title: Springfield, Tuolumne County
Size: 8 × 11 in. (20.3 × 28 cm.)
Artist: G. H. Goddard
Lithographer:
Printer: Britton & Rey, San Francisco
Publisher: G. S. Wells, Sonora, Ca.
Key/Vignettes/Misc:
Locations: TCM–S
Catalogs/Checklists:

424
Place: Stockton, California
Date: 1852
Title: Stockton, June 1, 1852
Size: 8 1/8 × 14 3/4 in. (20.6 × 37.5 cm.)
Artist: J. Britton
Lithographer:
Printer: Cooke & LeCount
Publisher: Cooke & LeCount
Key/Vignettes/Misc:
Locations: SCP
Catalogs/Checklists: SCP, p. 21 (1159); Peters, COS, pp. 65, 102, 175

425
Place: Stockton, California
Date: 1855
Title: Stockton.
Size: 10 7/16 × 18 1/8 in. (26.4 × 46 cm.)
Artist: Kuchel & Dresel
Lithographer: Kuchel & Dresel
Printer: Britton & Rey [San Francisco]
Publisher: Kuchel & Dresel (copyright)
Key/Vignettes/Misc:
Locations: ACMW–FW; SCP; CHS–SF
Catalogs/Checklists: ACMW–FW 1273; SCP, p. 21 (748); Peters, COS, p. 145

426
Place: Stockton, California
Date: 1858
Title: Stockton, Cal. 1858
Size: 16 15/16 × 24 3/4 in. (43.1 × 62.9 cm.)
Artist: E.[ugene] Camerer
Lithographer: Kuchel & Dresel
Printer: Britton & Rey [San Francisco]
Publisher: Rosenbaum & Van Allen Booksellers
Key/Vignettes/Misc: 12 vignettes
Locations: UCBL–B
Catalogs/Checklists: Peters, COS, pp. 96, 145

427
Place: Stockton, California
Date: Ca. 1859
Title: Stockton, Cal.
Size: 15 7/8 × 23 3/4 in. (40.2 × 60.3 cm.)
Artist: E.[ugene] Camerer
Lithographer: Kuchel & Dresel
Printer: Britton & Rey [San Francisco]
Publisher: Rosenbaum & Van Allen Booksellers
Key/Vignettes/Misc: 14 vignettes
Locations: ACMW–FW; SCP; Pioneer Museum & Haggin Galleries, Stockton, California
Catalogs/Checklists: ACMW–FW 948; SCP, p. 21 (831); PAI 30

428
Place: Stockton, California
Date: 1870
Title: Birds Eye View of the City of Stockton San Joaquin County California. 1870.
Size: 23 × 28 in. (58.5 × 71.2 cm.)
Artist: Augustus Koch
Lithographer:
Printer: Britton & Rey [San Francisco]
Publisher: Snow & Roos, San Francisco

Key/Vignettes/Misc: Refs. 1–46; 1
vignette
Locations: CHS–C; UCBL–B
Catalogs/Checklists:

429
Place: Stockton, California
Date: 1870
Title: Birds Eye View of the City of
Stockton San Joaquin County. California.
1870.
Size: 22⅝ × 28 in. (57.5 × 71.1 cm.)
Artist: Augustus Koch
Lithographer:
Printer: Britton & Rey, S. F.
Publisher: [n.p.]
Key/Vignettes/Misc: Refs. 1–46; 1
vignette
Locations: ACMW–FW; CHS–SF;
UCBL–B
Catalogs/Checklists: ACMW–FW 1233;
Reps, Cities on Stone, p. 98

430
Place: Stockton, California
Date: 1890
Title: Stockton Looking East San Joaquin
County, Cal. 1890
Size: 21¼ × 35 in. (54 × 89 cm.)
Artist: C. P. Cook
Lithographer: W. W. Elliott
Printer: W. W. Elliott, San Francisco
Publisher: E. A. Crennan & Co., Stockton
Calif.
Key/Vignettes/Misc: 27 vignettes
Locations: WHS–M; Pioneer Museum &
Haggin Galleries, Stockton, California
(photo); LC–M (photo)
Catalogs/Checklists: LC–M, 49.1

431
Place: Stockton, California
Date: Ca. 1895
Title: The City of Stockton, San Joaquin
County, Cal. 1895.
Size: 25⅛ × 36⁹⁄₁₆ in. (64 × 93 cm.)
Artist:
Lithographer:
Printer:
Publisher: Dakin Publishing Co., San
Francisco
Key/Vignettes/Misc:
Locations: LC–M
Catalogs/Checklists: LC–M, 53

432
Place: Stockton, California
Date: Ca. 1895
Title: View of the City of Stockton, the
Manufacturing City of California Showing
the Location of Northern Stockton
Size: 25¹¹⁄₁₆ × 39⅜ in. (66 × 101 cm.)
Artist:
Lithographer:
Printer:
Publisher: Dakin Publishing Co. San
Francisco
Key/Vignettes/Misc: 9 vignettes
Locations: LC–M; UCBL–B
Catalogs/Checklists: LC–M, 51

433
Place: Stockton, California
Date: Ca. 1895
Title: View of the City of Stockton, the
Manufacturing City of California.
Showing the Location of East Stockton
Addition.
Size: 22 × 33 in. (56 × 84 cm.)
Artist:
Lithographer:
Printer:
Publisher: Dakin Publishing Co. S. F.
Key/Vignettes/Misc:
Locations: LC–M
Catalogs/Checklists: LC–M, 50

434
Place: Stockton, California
Date: Ca. 1895
Title: View of City of Stockton, the
Manufacturing City of California
Size: 25¹¹⁄₁₆ × 39⅜ in. (66 × 101 cm.)
Artist:
Lithographer:
Printer:
Publisher: Dakin Publishing Co. San
Francisco
Key/Vignettes/Misc: 9 vignettes
Locations: LC–M
Catalogs/Checklists: LC–M, 52

Place: The Palms, California
Date: 1887
See Los Angeles, California, 1887.

435
Place: Timbuctoo, California
Date: 1862
Title: Timbuctoo, Yuba County,
California, 1862.
Size: 7¹¹⁄₁₆ × 11¾ in. (19.6 × 29.9 cm.)
Artist: C. Barrington
Lithographer:
Printer: Nagel, Fishbourne & Kuchel's
Lithog. San Francisco
Publisher: Wessells, Timbuctoo
Key/Vignettes/Misc:
Locations: UCBL–B; CHS–SF; OM–O
Catalogs/Checklists:

436
Place: Todds Valley, California
Date: 1857
Title: Todds Valley, Placer County,
California. 1857.
Size: 8 × 14 in. (20.3 × 35.6 cm.)
Artist: [Kuchel & Dresel?]
Lithographer: [Kuchel & Dresel?]
Printer: Britton & Rey [San Francisco]
Publisher: Read & Hall
Key/Vignettes/Misc: [no vignettes]
Locations: CHS–SF
Catalogs/Checklists:

437
Place: Todds Valley, California
Date: 1857
Title: Todds Valley, Placer County,
California. 1857.
Size: 17³⁄₁₆ × 21⁷⁄₁₆ in. (43.7 × 54.6 cm.)
Artist: [Kuchel & Dresel?]

Lithographer: [Kuchel & Dresel?]
Printer: Britton & Rey [San Francisco]
Publisher: Read & Hall
Key/Vignettes/Misc: 15 vignettes
Locations: ACMW–FW; SCP; UCBL–B;
EI–S
Catalogs/Checklists: ACMW–FW 1274;
Peters, COS, p. 145; SCP, p. 21 (857);
Reps, Cities on Stone, p. 98

Place: Union, California
Date: 1857
See Arcata, California, 1857.

438
Place: Vallejo, California
Date: Ca. 1860
Title: U. S. Navy–Yard Mare Island, and
City of Vallejo. Solano Co. Cal.
Size: 15½ × 23¾ in. (39.4 × 60.4 cm.)
Artist: C. B. Gifford
Lithographer: C. B. Gifford
Printer: L. Nagel, S. F.
Publisher:
Key/Vignettes/Misc:
Locations: CHS–SF; SCP; UCBL–B
Catalogs/Checklists: SCP, p. 21 (298);
Peters, COS, p. 169

439
Place: Vallejo, California
Date: 1871
Title: Birds Eye View of the City of Vallejo
and U. S. Navy Yard, Mare Island Solano
County, California. 1871.
Size: 23¼ × 27³⁄₁₆ in. (59.1 × 69.2 cm.)
Artist: Augustus Koch
Lithographer:
Printer: Britton & Rey, S. F.
Publisher: Snow & Roos [San Francisco]
Key/Vignettes/Misc: Refs. 1–65
Locations: CHS–C; UCBL–B; CHS–SF
(15 ¾ × 24 in.)
Catalogs/Checklists: Reps, Cities on Stone,
p. 98

440
Place: Vallejo, California
Date: 1891
Title: Birdseye View of Vallejo. From Mare
Island. Navy Yard, Cal. 1891.
Size: 20⅝ × 26¹⁵⁄₁₆ in. (52.5 × 68.6 cm.)
Artist: E. S. Moore
Lithographer:
Printer:
Publisher:
Key/Vignettes/Misc: Refs. 1–9; 13
vignettes
Locations: UCBL–B
Catalogs/Checklists:

441
Place: Ventura, California
Date: 1877
Title: Birds Eye View of San Buenaventura,
Cal. 1877. From the Bay, Looking North.
Size: 13¾ × 23¾ in. (35 × 60.4 cm.)
Artist: E. S. Glover
Lithographer:
Printer: A. L. Bancroft & Co., Lith., San
Francisco

Publisher: E. S. Glover
Key/Vignettes/Misc: Refs. A–P
Locations: UCBL–B; SCP; CHS–SF;
Ventura County Historical Museum,
Ventura, California; LC–M (photo)
Catalogs/Checklists: SCP, p. 21 (790);
LC–M, 32.2

442
Place: Ventura, California
Date: [1884–90]
Title: San Buena Ventura
Size: 19 × 25¹⁵⁄₁₆ in. (48.4 × 66 cm.)
Artist:
Lithographer: T. S.
Printer: W. W. Elliott Lith. S. F.
Publisher: Ventura Daily Free Press
[Ventura]
Key/Vignettes/Misc: Refs. 1–24; 16
vignettes
Locations: Ventura County Historical
Museum, Ventura, California
Catalogs/Checklists:

443
Place: Weaverville, California
Date: 1856
Title: Weaverville, 1856. Trinity County,
California
Size: 12 × 20¼ in. (30.5 × 51.5 cm.)
Artist: Kuchel & Dresel
Lithographer: Kuchel & Dresel
Printer: Britton & Rey [San Francisco]
Publisher: [n.p.]
Key/Vignettes/Misc: [no vignettes]
Locations: UCBL–B; CHS–SF
Catalogs/Checklists:

444
Place: Weaverville, California
Date: 1856
Title: Weaverville, 1856. Trinity County,
California
Size: 18³⁄₁₆ × 26⁷⁄₁₆ in. (45.2 × 67.4 cm.)
Artist: Kuchel
Lithographer: Kuchel
Printer: Britton & Rey [San Francisco]
Publisher: Fagg & Feast (copyright)
Key/Vignettes/Misc: vignettes
Locations: ACMW–FW
Catalogs/Checklists: ACMW–FW 1277

445
Place: Weaverville, California
Date: 1856
Title: Weaverville, 1856. Trinity County,
California.
Size: 18⅝ × 27¼ in. (47.4 × 69.4 cm.)
Artist: Kuchel & Dresel
Lithographer: Kuchel & Dresel
Printer: Britton & Rey [San Francisco]
Publisher: Fagg & Feast
Key/Vignettes/Misc: 28 vignettes
Locations: UCBL–B
Catalogs/Checklists: PAI 33

446
Place: Weaverville, California
Date: 1856
Title: Weaverville, 1856. Trinity County,
California.
Size: ["medium"]

Artist: Kuchel & Dresel
Lithographer: Kuchel & Dresel
Printer: Britton & Rey
Publisher: Fagg & Feast
Key/Vignettes/Misc: [no vignettes]
Locations: Unknown
Catalogs/Checklists: Peters, COS, p. 146

447
Place: Weaverville, California
Date: [1856–57?]
Title: Weaverville
Size: 11¼ × 16 in. (28.7 × 40.8 cm.)
Artist: [unsigned]
Lithographer:
Printer: [n.p.]
Publisher: [n.p.]
Key/Vignettes/Misc: [no vignettes]
Locations: Unknown. Alta California
Book Store, 2/9/80
Catalogs/Checklists:

448
Place: Wildomar, California
Date: [1887]
Title: Wildomar, Cal. in the Lake Colony,
San Diego Co., 22 Miles from the Sea
Coast. Elevation About 1240 Feet.
Size: 16⁵⁄₁₆ × 21¹⁄₁₆ in. (41.5 × 53.6 cm.)
Artist: W. W. Elliott
Lithographer:
Printer:
Publisher:
Key/Vignettes/Misc: Refs. 1–16; 9
vignettes; description
Locations: UCBL–B; HEHL; SLG–C
Catalogs/Checklists:

449
Place: Wilmington, California
Date: [1877?]
Title: Birds Eye View of Wilmington Los
Angeles Co. Cal.
Size: 9¾ × 16½ in. (24.8 × 42 cm.)
Artist:
Lithographer:
Printer: A. L. Bancroft & Co., S. F.
Publisher:
Key/Vignettes/Misc: Description
Locations: HEHL
Catalogs/Checklists:

450
Place: Woodland, California
Date: 1871
Title: Birdseye View of Woodland, Yolo
County. 1871.
Size: 15⅛ × 22 in. (38.4 × 55.9 cm.)
Artist: Augustus Koch
Lithographer:
Printer: Britton & Rey, San Francisco
Publisher:
Key/Vignettes/Misc: Refs. 1–21
Locations: SCP; UCBL–B
Catalogs/Checklists: SCP, p. 21 (323);
Peters, COS, pp. 81, 140

451
Place: Yankee Jim's, California
Date: 1857
Title: Yankee Jim's, Placer County,
California. 1857.

Size: 14⁴⁄₈ × 20⁷⁄₈ in. (37.2 × 53.1 cm.)
Artist: Kuchel & Dresel
Lithographer: Kuchel & Dresel
Printer: Britton & Rey [San Francisco]
Publisher: Scott & Brother
Key/Vignettes/Misc: 12 vignettes
Locations: HEHL; UCBL–B
Catalogs/Checklists:

452
Place: Yankee Jim's, California
Date: 1857
Title: Yankee Jims; Placer County,
California 1857.
Size: 8 × 14½ in. (20.3 × 36.7 cm.)
Artist: Kuchel & Dresel
Lithographer: Kuchel & Dresel
Printer: Britton and Rey [San Francisco]
Publisher:
Key/Vignettes/Misc: [no vignettes]
Locations: ACMW–FW; CHS–SF
Catalogs/Checklists: ACMW–FW 1278;
Peters, COS, p. 146

453
Place: Yreka, California
Date: [1853]
Title: Yreka, Siskayou Cy. A View from
the Humbug Trail with Shasta Bute in the
Distance
Size: 6½ × 8½ in. (16.5 × 21.6 cm.)
Artist:
Lithographer:
Printer: Britton & Rey San Francisco Cala
Publisher:
Key/Vignettes/Misc:
Locations: OM–O
Catalogs/Checklists: Peters, COS, p. 86

454
Place: Yreka, California
Date: 1856
Title: Yreka, Siskiyou County, California,
1856
Size: 9¹⁵⁄₁₆ × 20¾ in. (25.2 × 52.7 cm.)
Artist:
Lithographer: Kuchel & Dresel
Printer: Britton & Rey [San Francisco]
Publisher: A. Roman & Brother
Key/Vignettes/Misc: [no vignettes]
Locations: ACMW–FW; UCBL–B;
CHS–SF (10 ¾ × 14 ⅛)
Catalogs/Checklists: ACMW–FW 1279;
Peters, COS, p. 146

455
Place: Yreka, California
Date: 1857
Title: Yreka, Siskiyou County, California,
1857
Size: 12⅜ × 20⅝ in. (31.5 × 52.5 cm.)
Artist:
Lithographer: Kuchel & Dresel
Printer: Britton & Rey, Print. [San
Francisco]
Publisher: Roman & Brother
Key/Vignettes/Misc: [no vignettes]
Locations: Unknown. Alta California
Book Store, 2/9/80
Catalogs/Checklists:

456
Place: Yreka, California
Date: 1884
Title: Yreka & Mt. Shasta, Siskiyou
County Cal. Looking Southeast 1884
Size: 16⅞ × 21¹³⁄₁₆ in. (43 × 55.6 cm.)
Artist: Fred A. Walpole
Lithographer: Fred. A. Walpole
Printer: Beck & Pauli Lith. Milwaukee
Wis.
Publisher: Fred. A. Walpole
Key/Vignettes/Misc: Refs. 1–14
Locations: LC–P; LC–M
Catalogs/Checklists: LC–M, 53.1

Place: Yuba City, California
Date: Ca. 1888
See Marysville, California, ca. 1888.

457
Place: Aspen, Colorado
Date: 1893
Title: Bird's Eye View of Aspen, Pitkin
Co., Colo. 1893.
Size: 22 × 31¹⁄₁₆ in. (56 × 79 cm.)
Artist: Augustus Koch
Lithographer:
Printer:
Publisher: Aspen Times
Key/Vignettes/Misc: Refs.
Locations: LC–M; UC–B
Catalogs/Checklists: LC–M, 53.2

458
Place: Black Hawk, Colorado
Date: 1863
Title: View of "Black Hawk Point."
Size: 30 × 40 in. (76.3 × 101.7 cm.)
Artist: J.[ohn] E. Dillingham
Lithographer:
Printer: Chas Shober, Chicago
Publisher:
Key/Vignettes/Misc: 1 vignette
Locations: WHPL–D
Catalogs/Checklists:

459
Place: Black Hawk, Colorado
Date: 1866
Title: Black Hawk, Looking up Gregory
and Chase's Gulches
Size: 8¾ × 16 in. (22.2 × 40.7 cm.)
Artist: A. E. Mathews
Lithographer:
Printer: J. Bien, N.Y.
Publisher: A. E. Mathews (copyright)
Key/Vignettes/Misc:
Locations: WHPL–D; CSHS–D
Catalogs/Checklists: Taft, p. 305 No. 7

460
Place: Black Hawk, Colorado
Date: [1866?]
Title: Chase's Gulch, Black Hawk,
Colorado
Size: 9 × 16 in. (22.8 × 40.6 cm.)
Artist: A. E. Mathews
Lithographer:
Printer: J. Bien, Lith., N. Y.
Publisher:
Key/Vignettes/Misc:

Locations: ACMW–FW
Catalogs/Checklists:

Place: Black Hawk, Colorado
Date: 1873
See Central City, Colorado, 1873.

461
Place: Black Hawk, Colorado
Date: 1882
Title: Black Hawk, Colo. 1882. Looking
South East
Size: 8 × 19 in. (20.3 × 48.3 cm.)
Artist:
Lithographer:
Printer: Beck & Pauli, Lithographers
Milwaukee, Wis.
Publisher: J. J. Stoner, Madison, Wis.
Key/Vignettes/Misc: Refs. 1–19; 2
vignettes; unnumbered business directory
Locations: LC–M; LC–P
Catalogs/Checklists: LC–M, 54

462
Place: Buena Vista, Colorado
Date: 1882
Title: Bird's Eye View of Buena Vista, Colo
County Seat of Chaffee County. 1882.
Size: 10 × 14 in. (25.4 × 35.6 cm.)
Artist:
Lithographer:
Printer: Beck & Pauli, Milwaukee
Publisher: J. J. Stoner, Madison, Wisconsin
Key/Vignettes/Misc: Refs. 1–12, A–H,
K–M; 1 vignette
Locations: LC–M; LC–P
Catalogs/Checklists: LC–M, 55

463
Place: Canon City, Colorado
Date: 1882
Title: Bird's Eye View of Canon City,
Colo. County Seat of Fremont County
1882.
Size: 10 × 16½ in. (25.4 × 41.9 cm.)
Artist: H. Wellge
Lithographer:
Printer: Beck & Pauli, Milwaukee, Wis.
Publisher: J. J. Stoner, Madison, Wis.
Key/Vignettes/Misc: Refs. 1–14, A–H,
K–M, O–P; R–T; 2 vignettes
Locations: LC–M; ACMW–FW
Catalogs/Checklists: LC–M, 56

464
Place: Central City, Colorado
Date: 1866
Title: Central City. Looking Up Spring
Gulch.
Size: 9⅛ × 16 in. (23.2 × 40.7 cm.)
Artist: Alfred E. Mathews
Lithographer:
Printer: J. Bien
Publisher:
Key/Vignettes/Misc:
Locations: WHPL–D; CSHS–D
Catalogs/Checklists: Taft, p. 305 No. 9

465
Place: Central City, Colorado
Date: 1866
Title: Central City; From the Side of

Mammoth Hill Looking up Gregory and
Eureka Gulches.
Size: 9⅛ × 16 in. (23.1 × 40.6 cm.)
Artist: A. E. Mathews
Lithographer:
Printer: J. Bien, N. Y.
Publisher: A. E. Mathews (copyright)
Key/Vignettes/Misc:
Locations: WHPL–D; CSHS–D
Catalogs/Checklists: Reps, Cities on Stone,
p. 91; Taft, p. 305 No. 8

466
Place: Central City, Colorado
Date: 1866
Title: Central City, Colorado
Size: 8¾ × 20 in. (22.2 × 50.8 cm.)
Artist: Charles W. Morse
Lithographer:
Printer: Calvin Smith
Publisher:
Key/Vignettes/Misc:
Locations: WHPL–D
Catalogs/Checklists:

467
Place: Central City, Colorado
Date: 1867
Title: Central City, Colorado.
Size: 8⅝ × 19⅞ in. (21.8 × 50.6 cm.)
Artist: C. W. Morse
Lithographer:
Printer: Rae Smith, 120 Nassau St., N. Y.
Publisher:
Key/Vignettes/Misc:
Locations: ACMW–FW
Catalogs/Checklists: ACMW–FW 1458

468
Place: Central City, Colorado
Date: 1873
Title: Central City and Blackhawk,
Colorado, 1873.
Size: 16⅞ × 22¼ in. (42.8 × 56.4 cm.)
Artist: E. S. Glover
Lithographer:
Printer: Strobridge & Co., Cincinnati, O.
Publisher:
Key/Vignettes/Misc: Refs., Central City,
1–9, Blackhawk, 1–8; 5 vignettes
Locations: ACMW–FW; CSHS–D;
WHPL–D; UC–B; LC–M (facsimile)
Catalogs/Checklists: ACMW–FW 1128;
Reps, Cities on Stone, p. 91; LC–M, 56.1

469
Place: Central City, Colorado
Date: N.D.
Title: Central City, Colorado Territory
Size: 8 × 16½ in. (20.4 × 42 cm.)
Artist: [J. E.] Dillingham
Lithographer:
Printer: W. H. Rease & Co., Philadelphia
Publisher:
Key/Vignettes/Misc:
Locations: CSHS–D
Catalogs/Checklists:

470
Place: Colorado City, Colorado
Date: 1866
Title: Pike's Peak and Colorado City.

Size: 9 × 15¾ in. (23 × 40 cm.)
Artist: A. E. Mathews
Lithographer:
Printer: J. Bien, N. Y.
Publisher: A. E. Mathews (copyright)
Key/Vignettes/Misc:
Locations: WHPL−D; CSHS−D; CHS−C
Catalogs/Checklists: Reps, Cities on Stone, p. 92; Taft, p. 306 No. 22; Rathbone, Westward the Way, no. 204

Place: Colorado City, Colorado
Date: 1882
See Colorado Springs, Colorado, 1882.

471
Place: Colorado Springs, Colorado
Date: 1874
Title: Colorado Springs, Colorado City and Manatou El Paso Co. Colorado. January 1874
Size: 16⅞ × 22½ in. (42.9 × 57.2 cm.)
Artist: E. S. Glover
Lithographer:
Printer: Strobridge & Co., Lith. Cin. O.
Publisher:
Key/Vignettes/Misc: Refs. Colorado Springs, 1−7, A−G, Colorado City, 8−11; 3 vignettes; names of springs in Manatou
Locations: WHPL−D; CSHS−D; ACMW−FW
Catalogs/Checklists: ACMW−FW 1129; Reps, Cities on Stone, p. 92

472
Place: Colorado Springs, Colorado
Date: 1882
Title: Panoramic Bird's Eye View of Colorado Springs, Colorado City and Manitou, Colo. 1882.
Size: 15 × 23 in. (38.1 × 58.5 cm.)
Artist:
Lithographer:
Printer: Beck & Pauli, Lithographers, Milwaukee, Wis.
Publisher: J. J. Stoner, Madison, Wis.
Key/Vignettes/Misc:
Locations: LC−M; WHPL−D; ACMW−FW; UC−B
Catalogs/Checklists: LC−M, 58

473
Place: Colorado Springs, Colorado
Date: 1888
Title: Colorado Springs, Colorado
Size: 15¾ × 32⅝ in. (40 × 83 cm.)
Artist: S. N. Francis
Lithographer:
Printer:
Publisher: S. N. Francis
Key/Vignettes/Misc:
Locations: WHPL−D
Catalogs/Checklists:

474
Place: Colorado Springs, Colorado
Date: Ca. 1890
Title: Pikes Peak Panorama
Size: 15³⁄₁₆ × 41¹³⁄₁₆ in. (38.6 × 106.2 cm.)
Artist:
Lithographer:
Printer:

Publisher: American Publishing Co., Milwaukee
Key/Vignettes/Misc:
Locations: WHPL−D; LC−M; ACMW−FW (no publisher's imprint); NYH−NY
Catalogs/Checklists: ACMW−FW 1826; Reps, Cities on Stone, p. 95; LC−M, 58.2

475
Place: Colorado Springs, Colorado
Date: 1909
Title: Bird's−Eye−View of Colorado Springs, Colorado.
Size: 13 × 18½ in. (33 × 47 cm.)
Artist:
Lithographer:
Printer:
Publisher: Benford−Bryan Publishing Co., Denver
Key/Vignettes/Misc:
Locations: LC−M
Catalogs/Checklists: LC−M, 59

476
Place: Cripple Creek, Colorado
Date: 1894
Title: Cripple Creek Mining District, the Gold Fields of Colorado.
Size: 20½ × 33¼ in. (50.1 × 84.4 cm.)
Artist:
Lithographer:
Printer: The Denver Lith Co., Denver
Publisher: Colorado Springs Gazette
Key/Vignettes/Misc: 2 vignettes
Locations: ACMW−FW
Catalogs/Checklists: ACMW−FW 1764

477
Place: Cripple Creek, Colorado
Date: 1895
Title: Cripple Creek Mining District. The Great Gold Camp of Colorado.
Size: 39¹⁵⁄₁₆ × 28¹⁄₁₆ in. (101.6 × 71.3 cm.)
Artist: C. H. Amerine
Lithographer:
Printer: The Denver Lith. Co., Denver, Colo.
Publisher: Cripple Creek Sunday Herald
Key/Vignettes/Misc:
Locations: ACMW−FW; LC−M
Catalogs/Checklists: LC−M, 59.1

478
Place: Cripple Creek, Colorado
Date: 1896
Title: Cripple Creek. Victor.
Size: 27⅛ × 36⅝ in. (68.9 × 93.0 cm.)
Artist:
Lithographer:
Printer: Western Litho. Co.
Publisher:
Key/Vignettes/Misc: 21 vignettes; list of principal mines and owners; description
Locations: ACMW−FW; LC−M
Catalogs/Checklists: ACMW−FW 1763; LC−M, 60; Reps, Cities on Stone, p. 92

479
Place: Del Norte, Colorado
Date: 1882
Title: Del Norte, Colo. 1882

Size: 6⅜ × 13 in. (16.2 × 33 cm.)
Artist:
Lithographer:
Printer:
Publisher: J. J. Stoner, Madison, Wis. (copyright)
Key/Vignettes/Misc: Refs. 1−10
Locations: ACMW−FW
Catalogs/Checklists: ACMW−FW 1768

480
Place: Denver, Colorado
Date: 1862
Title: Denver City Col. Ter.
Size: 11½ × 31½ in. (29.2 × 80 cm.)
Artist: J. E. Dillingham
Lithographer:
Printer:
Publisher:
Key/Vignettes/Misc:
Locations: WHPL−D
Catalogs/Checklists:

481
Place: Denver, Colorado
Date: 1866
Title: Blake Street, Denver Colorado.
Size: 9⅛ × 15⅞ in. (23.2 × 40.4 cm.)
Artist: A. E. Mathews
Lithographer:
Printer: J. Bien, N. Y.
Publisher: A. E. Mathews (copyright)
Key/Vignettes/Misc:
Locations: WHPL−D; CSHS−D
Catalogs/Checklists: Taft, p. 305 No. 4

482
Place: Denver, Colorado
Date: 1866
Title: Denver, City of the Plains.
Size: 8⅛ × 15⅞ in. (20.6 × 40.3 cm.)
Artist: A. E. Mathews
Lithographer:
Printer: J. Bien, N. Y.
Publisher: A. E. Mathews (copyright)
Key/Vignettes/Misc:
Locations: NYP−S; WHPL−D; CSHS−D; YUAG−NH
Catalogs/Checklists: Taft, p. 305 No. 2; Stokes P. 1865—G−71; Reps, Cities on Stone, p. 92

483
Place: Denver, Colorado
Date: 1866
Title: F Street, Denver
Size: 9 × 16 in. (22.9 × 40.7 cm.)
Artist: A. E. Mathews
Lithographer:
Printer: J. Bien, N. Y.
Publisher: A. E. Mathews (copyright)
Key/Vignettes/Misc:
Locations: WHPL−D
Catalogs/Checklists: Taft, p. 305 No. 3

484
Place: Denver, Colorado
Date: 1866
Title: Laramie Street, Denver
Size: 9 × 16 in. (22.8 × 40.7 cm.)
Artist: A. E. Mathews
Lithographer:
Printer: J. Bien, N. Y.

Publisher: A. E. Mathews (copyright)
Key/Vignettes/Misc:
Locations: WHPL–D
Catalogs/Checklists: Taft, p. 305 No. 5

485
Place: Denver, Colorado
Date: 1874
Title: Denver Colorado, 1874
Size: 21¹¹⁄₁₆ × 34¼ in. (55.1 × 87.1 cm.)
Artist: E. S. Glover
Lithographer:
Printer: Strobridge & Co. Lith. Cin. O.
Publisher:
Key/Vignettes/Misc: Unnumbered refs.; 17
vignettes; description
Locations: NYP–S; UC–B; CSHS–D;
WHPL–D; LC–M (facsimile)
Catalogs/Checklists: Stokes 1874—G–94;
LC–M, 61

486
Place: Denver, Colorado
Date: [187–]
Title: Birds Eye View of the City of Denver
Arapahoe County Colorado
Size:
Artist:
Lithographer:
Printer: Chicago Lith. Co. Chicago
Publisher:
Key/Vignettes/Misc: Refs.
Locations: CSHS–D (photo)
Catalogs/Checklists:

487
Place: Denver, Colorado
Date: 1882
Title: Bird's Eye View of the City of
Denver, Colorado.
Size: 27¹⁵⁄₁₆ × 39¾ in. (71 × 101 cm.)
Artist: J. H. Flett
Lithographer:
Printer: Strobridge Lith. Co. Cincinnati,
O.
Publisher:
Key/Vignettes/Misc: 16 vignettes
Locations: WHPL–D; CHS–C; CSHS–D;
LC–M (photo)
Catalogs/Checklists: LC–M, 63 (dated
1881)

488
Place: Denver, Colorado
Date: 1887
Title: Bird's–Eye View of Denver, 1887
Size: 19 × 24 in. (48.3 × 61 cm.)
Artist:
Lithographer:
Printer: Mills Eng. Co., Denver
Publisher: Rocky Mountain News, Denver
Key/Vignettes/Misc:
Locations: LC–M
Catalogs/Checklists: LC–M, 64

489
Place: Denver, Colorado
Date: 1889
Title: Perspective Map of the City of
Denver, Colo.
Size: 27½ × 42½ in. (69.8 × 107.9 cm.)
Artist: H. Wellge

Lithographer:
Printer:
Publisher: American Publishing Co., 205
Second Str. Milwaukee, Wis.
Key/Vignettes/Misc: 23 vignettes;
description
Locations: LC–M; CSHS–D
Catalogs/Checklists: LC–M, 65; Reps,
Cities on Stone, p. 92

490
Place: Denver, Colorado
Date: Ca. 1891
Title: Denver. 1859
Size: 18½ × 23¼ in. (47 × 59.8 cm.)
Artist:
Lithographer:
Printer: Collier & Cleveland.
Publisher:
Key/Vignettes/Misc:
Locations: WHPL–D; Denver Art
Museum, Denver, Colorado
Catalogs/Checklists:

491
Place: Denver, Colorado
Date: 1892
Title: Perspective Map of the City of
Denver, Colorado 1892
Size: 26¾ × 37¾ in. (68 × 96 cm.)
Artist:
Lithographer:
Printer: Denver Lithograph Company,
Denver, Colorado
Publisher: W. A. Barbot, Room 208,
Charles Block, Denver, Colorado
Key/Vignettes/Misc:
Locations: CSHS–D
Catalogs/Checklists:

492
Place: Denver, Colorado
Date: Ca.1907
Title: Birdseye View from South
Broadway. . .Showing Harlem, Jacksons
Broadway Heights & City of Denver.
Size: 19½ × 25 in. (49.6 × 63.5 cm.)
Artist: A. E. Mitchell
Lithographer:
Printer: Denver Engraving Co.
Publisher: A. F. Haraszthey & W. J. Voit,
Colorado Land Headquarters, Denver.
Key/Vignettes/Misc:
Locations: LC–M
Catalogs/Checklists: LC–M, 65.1

493
Place: Denver, Colorado
Date: 1908
Title: Birdseye View of Denver, Colorado,
1908, Looking South from the
Twenty–third Street Viaduct.
Size: 32¼ × 70 in. (82 × 178 cm.)
Artist:
Lithographer:
Printer:
Publisher: Birdseye View Publishing
Company, Denver
Key/Vignettes/Misc: 38 vignettes;
unnumbered directory of 437 residences,
public buildings and businesses

Locations: WHPL–D; LC–M
Catalogs/Checklists: LC–M, 66

494
Place: Elizabethtown, Colorado
Date: 1866
Title: Elizabethtown, Clear Creek County.
From the Griffith Tunnel
Size: 7½ × 10¾ in. (19 × 27.3 cm.)
Artist: Alfred E. Mathews
Lithographer:
Printer: J. Bien
Publisher:
Key/Vignettes/Misc:
Locations: WHPL–D
Catalogs/Checklists: Taft, p. 306 No. 18

495
Place: Empire City, Colorado
Date: 1866
Title: Empire City, Clear Creek County
Size: 7⅛ × 10⅝ in. (18.1 × 27 cm.)
Artist: Alfred E. Mathews
Lithographer:
Printer: J. Bien
Publisher:
Key/Vignettes/Misc:
Locations: WHPL–D
Catalogs/Checklists: Taft, p. 306 No. 17

496
Place: Fall River, Colorado
Date: 1866
Title: Fall River, Clear Creek County
Size: 7¼ × 10½ in. (18.4 × 26.7 cm.)
Artist: Alfred E. Mathews
Lithographer:
Printer: J. Bien
Publisher:
Key/Vignettes/Misc:
Locations: WHPL–D
Catalogs/Checklists: Taft, p. 305 No. 14

497
Place: Fort Collins, Colorado
Date: 1884
Title: Bird's Eye View of Fort Collins
Colorado 1884
Size: 14¼ × 19¼ in. (36.2 × 49 cm.)
Artist: P.[ierre] Dastarac
Lithographer:
Printer:
Publisher:
Key/Vignettes/Misc: Refs. 1–15; 18
vignettes
Locations: Colorado State University
Library, Fort Collins, Colorado
Catalogs/Checklists:

498
Place: Fort Collins, Colorado
Date: 1899
Title: [Fort Collins, Colorado]
Size: 7 × 13 in. (17.8 × 33 cm.) (photo)
Artist: M.[erritt] D.[ana] Houghton
Lithographer:
Printer:
Publisher:
Key/Vignettes/Misc:
Locations: LC–M (photo)
Catalogs/Checklists: LC–M, 67

499
Place: Georgetown, Colorado
Date: 1874
Title: View of Georgetown Colorado, 1874
Size: 15½ × 20 in. (39.3 × 50.7 cm.)
Artist: E. S. Glover
Lithographer:
Printer: Strobridge & Co., Cincinnati
Publisher:
Key/Vignettes/Misc: Refs. 1–19, A–E
Locations: ACMW–FW; WHPL–D; CSHS–D; LC–M (facsimile)
Catalogs/Checklists: ACMW–FW 1130; Reps, Cities on Stone, p. 93; LC–M, 67.1

500
Place: Golden, Colorado
Date: 1866
Title: Golden City
Size: 9½ × 15¾ in. (24.2 × 40.1 cm.)
Artist: Alfred E. Mathews
Lithographer:
Printer: J. Bien
Publisher: A. E. Mathews (copyright)
Key/Vignettes/Misc:
Locations: WHPL–D; CSHS–D; UCBL–B
Catalogs/Checklists: Taft, p. 305 No. 6

501
Place: Golden, Colorado
Date: [1870?]
Title: Golden City, C.T.—Looking West.
Size: 9½ × 14⅞ in. (24.1 × 37.8 cm.)
Artist: A. E. Mathews
Lithographer:
Printer:
Publisher:
Key/Vignettes/Misc:
Locations: LC–M
Catalogs/Checklists:

502
Place: Golden, Colorado
Date: 1873
Title: Birds–Eye View of Golden, Colorado, 1873. Taken From Castle Rock.
Size: 15¼ × 18½ in. (38.8 × 47.1 cm.)
Artist: D. D. Morse
Lithographer:
Printer: Strobridge & Co. Lith. Cin. O.
Publisher:
Key/Vignettes/Misc: Refs. 1–14
Locations: WHPL–D
Catalogs/Checklists:

503
Place: Golden, Colorado
Date: 1882
Title: Bird's Eye View of Golden, Colo. Co. Seat of Jefferson County. 1882.
Size: 14¹/₁₆ × 28⅛ in. (35.8 × 71.5 cm.)
Artist:
Lithographer:
Printer: Beck & Pauli, Lithographers, Milwaukee, Wis.
Publisher: J. J. Stoner, Madison, Wis.
Key/Vignettes/Misc: Refs. 2–35; 3 vignettes
Locations: ACMW–FW; LC–M
Catalogs/Checklists: LC–M, 68

504
Place: Greeley, Colorado
Date: 1882
Title: Bird's Eye View of Greeley, Colo. County Seat of Wild Co. 1882.
Size: 15 × 23 in. (38.2 × 58.5 cm.)
Artist:
Lithographer:
Printer: Beck & Pauli, Milwaukee, Wis.
Publisher: J. J. Stoner, Madison, Wis.
Key/Vignettes/Misc: Refs. A–H, J–P; R–V; 1 vignette; unnumbered busines directory
Locations: LC–M; WHPL–D; ACMW–FW
Catalogs/Checklists: LC–M, 69

505
Place: Gunnison, Colorado
Date: 1882
Title: Bird's Eye View of Gunnison, Colo. County Seat of Gunnison County Population 4500 1882
Size: 9⁷/₁₆ × 20¹¹/₁₆ in. (24 × 52.5 cm.)
Artist:
Lithographer:
Printer: Beck & Pauli, Milwaukee, Wis.
Publisher: J. J. Stoner, Madison, Wis.
Key/Vignettes/Misc: Refs. 1–18, A–F; 1 unnumbered ref.; 4 vignettes
Locations: ACMW–FW; LC–M; WHPL–D
Catalogs/Checklists: ACMW–FW 1726; LC–M, 70

506
Place: Idaho Springs, Colorado
Date: 1866
Title: Idaho, Clear Creek County
Size: 7¼ × 10⅝ in. (18.4 × 27 cm.)
Artist: Alfred E. Mathews
Lithographer:
Printer: J. Bien
Publisher:
Key/Vignettes/Misc:
Locations: WHPL–D
Catalogs/Checklists: Taft, p. 305 No. 13

507
Place: Idaho Springs, Colorado
Date: 1882
Title: Bird's Eye View of Idaho Springs, Colo. 1882. Looking North–West.
Size: 9 × 21 in. (22.9 × 53.4 cm.)
Artist:
Lithographer:
Printer:
Publisher: J. J. Stoner, Madison, Wis.
Key/Vignettes/Misc: Refs. A–C, 2–17; 1 vignette
Locations: WHPL–D
Catalogs/Checklists:

508
Place: Las Animas, Colorado
Date: 1888
Title: Bird's Eye View of Las Animas, Bent County, Colorado.
Size: 13¾ × 20¹/₁₆ in. (35 × 51 cm.)
Artist:
Lithographer:
Printer:

Publisher: Bent County Democrat, Las Animas
Key/Vignettes/Misc: 22 vignettes
Locations: WHPL–D
Catalogs/Checklists:

509
Place: Leadville, Colorado
Date: 1879
Title: Bird's Eye View of Leadville, Lake County, Colo. 1879
Size: 23 × 33½ in. (58.5 × 85.2 cm.)
Artist: Augustus Koch
Lithographer:
Printer: Ramsey, Millet & Hudson, Kansas City, Mo.
Publisher: Augustus Koch
Key/Vignettes/Misc: Refs. 1–26
Locations: LC–M
Catalogs/Checklists: LC–M, 71

510
Place: Leadville, Colorado
Date: 1882
Title: Bird's Eye View of Leadville, Colo. 1882.
Size: 19 × 26½ in. (48.2 × 67.3 cm.)
Artist: H. Wellge
Lithographer:
Printer: Beck & Pauli, Milwaukee, Wis.
Publisher: J. J. Stoner, Madison, Wis.
Key/Vignettes/Misc: Refs. 1–36, A–H, K; 9 vignettes
Locations: LC–M
Catalogs/Checklists: LC–M, 72; Reps, Cities on Stone, p. 94

511
Place: Leadville, Colorado
Date: N.D.
Title: Leadville, Colorado
Size: 20 × 25 in. (50.8 × 63.5 cm.)
Artist: J. Fitz Brind, Dr. Wm. T. Keller
Lithographer:
Printer: St. Joseph Steam Print'g Co., St. Joseph, Mo.
Publisher:
Key/Vignettes/Misc: 16 vignettes
Locations: WHPL–D; UCBL–B
Catalogs/Checklists:

Place: Manitou, Colorado
Date: 1882
See Colorado Springs, Colorado, 1882.

512
Place: Maysville, Colorado
Date: 1882
Title: Bird's Eye View of Maysville, Colo, Chaffee County 1882.
Size: 7 × 15 in. (17.8 × 38.1 cm.)
Artist:
Lithographer:
Printer: Beck & Pauli, Milwaukee, Wis.
Publisher: J. J. Stoner, Madison, Wis.
Key/Vignettes/Misc: Refs. 1–5, A–E; 1 vignette
Locations: LC–M; WHPL–D; LC–P
Catalogs/Checklists: LC–M, 73

513
Place: Montgomery, Colorado
Date: 1866
Title: Mount Lincoln. The Town of

Montgomery is Seen at its Base
Size: 11¼ × 15¾ in. (28.7 × 40.1 cm.)
Artist: Alfred E. Mathews
Lithographer:
Printer: J. Bien
Publisher: A. E. Mathews (copyright)
Key/Vignettes/Misc:
Locations: WHPL–D
Catalogs/Checklists: Taft, p. 306 No. 20

514
Place: Nevada, Colorado
Date: 1866
Title: Nevada, Colorado
Size: 9¼ × 16¼ in. (23.5 × 41.3 cm.)
Artist: A. E. Mathews
Lithographer:
Printer: J. Bien, N. Y.
Publisher: A. E. Mathews (copyright)
Key/Vignettes/Misc:
Locations: WHPL–D; CSHS–D
Catalogs/Checklists: Taft, p. 305 No. 10

515
Place: Poncho, Colorado
Date: 1882
Title: Bird's Eye View of Poncho, Colo.
1882. 6900 Ft. Above Sea Level.
Size: 5⁹⁄₁₆ × 13⁹⁄₁₆ in. (14.1 × 34.4 cm.)
Artist:
Lithographer:
Printer: Beck and Pauli, Lithographers,
Milwaukee, Wis.
Publisher: J. J. Stoner, Madison, Wis.
Key/Vignettes/Misc: Refs. 1–5, A–F; 2
vignettes
Locations: ACMW–FW; LC–P
Catalogs/Checklists: ACMW–FW 1728

516
Place: Pueblo, Colorado
Date: 1874
Title: Birds–Eye View of Pueblo,
Colorado, 1874 South Pueblo. From the
North–East. Looking South–West.
Size: 23¼ × 26¹³⁄₁₆ in. (59 × 68 cm.)
Artist: E. S. Glover
Lithographer:
Printer: Strobridge & Co. Lith. Cin. O.
Publisher:
Key/Vignettes/Misc: Refs. 1–21, A–D; 2
vignettes; table of distances to other cities;
description
Locations: WHPL–D
Catalogs/Checklists: Reps, Cities on Stone,
p. 96

517
Place: Pueblo, Colorado
Date: 1890
Title: Pueblo, Colo. Looking North from
West & 15 Sts. [upper view] Looking
South from West & 15 Sts. [lower view]
1890 Population 30,000
Size: 36 × 26 in. (91.4 × 66 cm.)
Artist:
Lithographer:
Printer:
Publisher: American Publishing Co.,
Milwaukee, Wis.
Key/Vignettes/Misc: 10 vignettes;
unnumbered business directory
Locations: LC–M; ACMW–FW

Catalogs/Checklists: LC–M, 74; Reps,
Cities on Stone, p. 96

518
Place: Russell Gulch, Colorado
Date: 1866
Title: Russell Gulch, Gilpin County
Size: 7¾ × 10½ in. (19.7 × 26.7 cm.)
Artist: Alfred E. Mathews
Lithographer:
Printer: J. Bien
Publisher:
Key/Vignettes/Misc:
Locations: WHPL–D
Catalogs/Checklists: Taft, p. 305 No. 11

519
Place: Salida, Colorado
Date: 1882
Title: Bird's Eye View of Salida. Chaffee
County Colorado. 1882.
Size: 7 × 14½ in. (17.7 × 36.8 cm.)
Artist:
Lithographer:
Printer: Beck & Pauli, Lithographers,
Milwaukee
Publisher: J. J. Stoner, Madison, Wis.
Key/Vignettes/Misc: Refs. 1–15, A–F
Locations: ACMW–FW; LC–M
Catalogs/Checklists: ACMW–FW 1730;
LC–M, 75

520
Place: Silver Cliff, Colorado
Date: Ca. 1880
Title: Silver Cliff, Colorado.
Size: 16⁷⁄₁₆ × 21½ in. (41.7 × 54.6 cm.)
Artist: I. Brind
Lithographer:
Printer: St. Joseph Steam Print'g Co. Lith.
Publisher:
Key/Vignettes/Misc: 12 vignettes
Locations: ACMW–FW
Catalogs/Checklists: ACMW–FW 926

521
Place: Trinidad, Colorado
Date: 1882
Title: Trinidad, Colo. 1882. County Seat
of Las Animas County Population 3500.
Size: 16¹⁄₁₆ × 20¹⁄₁₆ in. (41 × 51 cm.)
Artist:
Lithographer:
Printer: Beck & Pauli, Lithographers,
Milwaukee, Wis.
Publisher: J. J. Stoner, Madison, Wis.
Key/Vignettes/Misc: Refs. 1–17, X, A–H,
K–P; unnumbered refs.; 2 vignettes
Locations: ACMW–FW; LC–M;
WHPL–D
Catalogs/Checklists: LC–M, 76

Place: Victor, Colorado
Date: 1896
See Cripple Creek, Colorado, 1896.

Place: Almyville, Connecticut
Date: 1889
See Moosup, Connecticut, 1889.

522
Place: Ansonia, Connecticut
Date: 1875
Title: View of Ansonia, Conn. 1875

Size: 15¾ × 21⅝ in. (40 × 55 cm.)
Artist: O. H. Bailey & Co.
Lithographer: C. H. Vogt
Printer: J. Knauber & Co.
Publisher: O..H. Bailey & Co., [Boston]
Key/Vignettes/Misc: Refs. 1–20
Locations: BPL–R; LC–M (photo);
CSL–H
Catalogs/Checklists: LC–M, 76.1

523
Place: Ansonia, Connecticut
Date: 1921
Title: Aero View of Ansonia, Connecticut
1921
Size: 22½ x 32½ in. (38 × 82 cm.)
Artist:
Lithographer:
Printer: [Meriden Gravure Co., Meriden,
Conn.]
Publisher: Hughes & Bailey, Waterbury,
Conn.
Key/Vignettes/Misc: Refs. A–E; 21
vignettes; unnumbered business directory;
directory of city officials
Locations: LC–M
Catalogs/Checklists: LC–M, 77

524
Place: Bethel, Connecticut
Date: 1879
Title: View of Bethel, Conn. 1879
Size: 17¼ × 22 in. (43.8 × 55.9 cm.)
Artist:
Lithographer:
Printer:
Publisher: O. H. Bailey & Co., Boston
Key/Vignettes/Misc: Refs. 1–28; list of
public officials
Locations: BPL–R; CSL–H; LC–M
(photo); NYH–NY
Catalogs/Checklists: LC–M, 77.1

525
Place: Birmingham, Connecticut
Date: 1876
Title: Birmingham, Conn. 1876
Size: 19½ × 23½ in. (49.6 × 59.9 cm.)
Artist: O. H. Bailey & Co.
Lithographer: C. H. Vogt
Printer:
Publisher: O. H. Bailey & Co., Boston
Key/Vignettes/Misc: Refs. 1–20; 3
vignettes
Locations: BPL–R; LC–M
Catalogs/Checklists: LC–M, 77.2

526
Place: Bridgeport, Connecticut
Date: 1857
Title: Bridgeport, Conn. and Environs,
from Old Mill Hill.
Size: 17⅝ × 27½ in. (44.9 × 69.9 cm.)
Artist: W. Staengel
Lithographer: W. Staengel
Printer: A. Weingartner, 87 Fulton St., N.
Y.
Publisher: John Cornwall (copyright)
Key/Vignettes/Misc:
Locations: MM–NN
Catalogs/Checklists: MM–NN, LP 2010

527

Place: Bridgeport, Connecticut
Date: 1875
Title: View of Bridgeport, Ct., 1875
Size: 25⅞ × 34⅜ in. (65.9 × 87.5 cm.)
Artist: O. H. Bailey & Co.
Lithographer:
Printer: American Oleograph Co., Milwaukee, Wisc.
Publisher: O.H. Bailey & Co.
Key/Vignettes/Misc: Refs. 1–50, A–M; 3 vignettes
Locations: LC–M
Catalogs/Checklists: LC–M, 77.3

528

Place: Bridgeport, Connecticut
Date: 1882
Title: Bridgeport, Conn. U.S.A. 1882, Bridgeport Brass Co.
Size: 10 × 32¼ in. (25.4 × 82 cm.)
Artist: Wils Porter
Lithographer:
Printer: Charles Hart, Lith. 36 Vesey St. N. Y.
Publisher: W. O. Laughna Art Publishing Co. [New York]
Key/Vignettes/Misc: 1 vignette
Locations: MM–NN; NYH–NY; CHS–H
Catalogs/Checklists: MM–NN, LP 2802; CHS–H, 1

529

Place: Bridgeport, Connecticut
Date: 1882
Title: Bridgeport, Conn. 1882. From 'Old Mill Hill'.
Size: 17¼ × 32³/₁₆ in. (44 × 82.2 cm.)
Artist:
Lithographer:
Printer: Charles Hart Lith. 36 Vesey St., N. Y.
Publisher: W. O. Laughna, Art Publishing Co., N. Y.
Key/Vignettes/Misc:
Locations: LC–P; NYH–NY
Catalogs/Checklists:

530

Place: Bristol, Connecticut
Date: 1878
Title: View of Bristol, Conn.
Size: 21¼ × 25⅝ in. (54.1 × 65.2 cm.)
Artist:
Lithographer:
Printer: Beck & Pauli
Publisher: O. H. Bailey & Co., Boston
Key/Vignettes/Misc: Refs. 1–30; 14 vignettes
Locations: BPL–R; LC–M (photo); CSL–H
Catalogs/Checklists: LC–M, 77.4

531

Place: Bristol, Connecticut
Date: 1889
Title: Bristol, Conn. Looking North–East
Size: 17⅝ × 30⅝ in. (44.8 × 77.9 cm.)
Artist: Geo. E. Norris

Lithographer:
Printer: The Burleigh Lith. Est., Troy, N. Y.
Publisher: Geo. E. Norris, Brockton, Mass.
Key/Vignettes/Misc: Refs. 1–63, A–Z, a–h, *, k
Locations: BPL–R; LC–M
Catalogs/Checklists: LC–M, 78

532

Place: Bristol, Connecticut
Date: 1907
Title: Bird's Eye View of Bristol, Conn. 1907
Size: 31 × 35 in. (78.9 × 89 cm.)
Artist:
Lithographer:
Printer:
Publisher: Hughes & Bailey, New York
Key/Vignettes/Misc: 46 vignettes; unnumbered business directory; unnumbered list of public buildings
Locations: LC–M
Catalogs/Checklists: LC–M, 79

533

Place: Broad Brook, Connecticut
Date: [187–]
Title: Broad Brook, Conn.
Size: 16⅛ × 25⅛ in. (41 × 64 cm.)
Artist:
Lithographer:
Printer:
Publisher: O. H. Bailey, Boston
Key/Vignettes/Misc:
Locations: CSL–H; LC–M (photo)
Catalogs/Checklists: LC–M, 79.1

Place: Centerbrook, Connecticut
Date: 1881
See Essex, Connecticut, 1881.

534

Place: Cheshire, Connecticut
Date: 1882
Title: View of Cheshire, Connecticut. 1882
Size: 19½ × 22½ in. (49.6 × 57.3 cm.)
Artist:
Lithographer:
Printer:
Publisher: O. H. Bailey & Co., Boston
Key/Vignettes/Misc: Refs. A–H, J–A; 6 vignettes
Locations: BPL–R; LC–M
Catalogs/Checklists: LC–M, 79.2

535

Place: Chester, Connecticut
Date: 1881
Title: View of Chester. Connecticut. 1881
Size: 19¾ × 24⅝ in. (50.3 × 62.7 cm.)
Artist:
Lithographer:
Printer:
Publisher: O. H. Bailey & Co., Boston
Key/Vignettes/Misc: Refs. 1–43; 8 vignettes
Locations: BPL–R; CSL–H; LC–M (photo)
Catalogs/Checklists: LC–M, 79.3

536

Place: Clinton, Connecticut
Date: 1881
Title: View of Clinton. Connecticut. 1881
Size: 18⅜ × 24¼ in. (46.7 × 61.7 cm.)
Artist:
Lithographer:
Printer:
Publisher: O. H. Bailey & Co., Boston
Key/Vignettes/Misc: Refs. 1–18; 2 vignettes; list of school and public officials
Locations: BPL–R; LC–M; LC–P; CHS–H
Catalogs/Checklists: LC–M, 79.4; CHS–H, 2

537

Place: Collinsville, Connecticut
Date: 1878
Title: View of Collinsville, Conn. 1878
Size: 16⅜ × 20⅞ in. (41.6 × 53.1 cm.)
Artist:
Lithographer:
Printer: Beck & Pauli
Publisher: O. H. Bailey & Co., Boston
Key/Vignettes/Misc: Refs. 1–126; 4 vignettes
Locations: BPL–R; NYH–NY
Catalogs/Checklists:

538

Place: Danbury, Connecticut
Date: Ca. 1858
Title: Danbury, Ct. Taken from Hayes' Hill
Size: 12¾ × 21¼ in. (32.4 × 54.1 cm.)
Artist: G. Hayward
Lithographer:
Printer: Geo Hayward, 120 Water St., N. Y.
Publisher: E. C. Smith & Van Zandt, New York
Key/Vignettes/Misc: Refs. 1–25
Locations: DSFM–D
Catalogs/Checklists:

539

Place: Danbury, Connecticut
Date: 1875
Title: View of Danbury, Conn. 1875.
Size: 20 × 26 in. (50.8 × 66.1 cm.)
Artist: O. H. Bailey
Lithographer: C. H. Vogt
Printer: J. Knauber & Co.
Publisher: Fowler & Bailey
Key/Vignettes/Misc: Refs. 1–39
Locations: BPL–R; LC–M; DSFM–D; CHS–H
Catalogs/Checklists: LC–M, 79.5; CHS–H, 3

540

Place: Danbury, Connecticut
Date: Ca. 1884
Title: Danbury, Conn.
Size: 18¼ × 36 in. (46.4 × 91.5 cm.)
Artist: L. R. Burleigh
Lithographer:
Printer: Beck & Pauli, Milwaukee, Wis.
Publisher: L. R. Burleigh, Troy, N. Y.

Key/Vignettes/Misc: Refs. 1–59
Locations: BPL–R; DSFM–D; NYH–NY
Catalogs/Checklists:

541
Place: Danielson, Connecticut
Date: 1877
Title: Danielsonville, Conn.
Size: 20 × 24¾ in. (50.8 × 63 cm.)
Artist: O. H. Bailey
Lithographer:
Printer: Bremner & Co., 138 Spring St., Milwaukee, Wis.
Publisher: M. P. Dowe, Danielsonville, Conn.
Key/Vignettes/Misc: Refs. 1–16; 1 vignette
Locations: CSL–H; LC–M (photo)
Catalogs/Checklists: LC–M, 79.6

542
Place: Derby, Connecticut
Date: 1920
Title: City of Derby, Connecticut
Size: 8¼ × 10⅝ in. (21x 27 cm.)
Artist: [T. M. Fowler]
Lithographer:
Printer:
Publisher: Hughes & Bailey, New York
Key/Vignettes/Misc:
Locations: LC–M
Catalogs/Checklists: LC–M, 79.7

543
Place: East Haddam, Connecticut
Date: 1880
Title: View of East Haddam. Connecticut. And Goodspeeds Landing. 1880.
Size: 20 × 26 in. (50.9 × 66.2 cm.)
Artist:
Lithographer:
Printer:
Publisher: O. H. Bailey & Co. Boston
Key/Vignettes/Misc: Refs. 1–20, A–Q; 9 vignettes
Locations: NYH–NY
Catalogs/Checklists:

544
Place: East Hampton, Connecticut
Date: 1880
Title: East Hampton, Connecticut
Size: 19⅞ × 21¾ in. (50.6 × 55.4 cm.)
Artist: O. H. Bailey
Lithographer:
Printer:
Publisher: O. H. Bailey & Co., Boston
Key/Vignettes/Misc:
Locations: CSL–H; LC–M (photo)
Catalogs/Checklists: LC–M, 80.1

Place: East Norwalk, Connecticut
Date: Ca. 1899
See Norwalk, Connecticut, ca. 1899.

545
Place: Essex, Connecticut
Date: 1881
Title: View of Essex. Centerbrook & Ivoryton Conn. 1881.
Size: 20⅜ × 25½ in. (51.8 × 64.8 cm.)
Artist: A. E. D.

Lithographer:
Printer:
Publisher: O. H. Bailey & Co., Boston
Key/Vignettes/Misc: Refs. 1–47; 12 vignettes
Locations: BPL–R; LC–M
Catalogs/Checklists: LC–M, 80.2

546
Place: Farmington, Connecticut
Date: N.D.
Title: Farmington and the Valley of the Tunxis. From the South East.
Size: 15 × 22 in. (38.2 × 56 cm.)
Artist:
Lithographer:
Printer: E. B. & E. C. Kellogg, Hartford, Conn.
Publisher:
Key/Vignettes/Misc:
Locations: CHS–H
Catalogs/Checklists: CHS–H, 4

547
Place: Florence, Connecticut
Date: Ca. 1855
Title: Florence North West View
Size: 9¼ × 13¼ in. (23.5 × 33.7 cm.)
Artist: C. C. Burleigh
Lithographer:
Printer: E. B. & E. C. Kellogg, Hartford, Ct.
Publisher:
Key/Vignettes/Misc: 14 vignettes
Locations: Unknown. See Old Print Shop Portfolio, XXXIV, p. 103, No. 12
Catalogs/Checklists:

548
Place: Forestville, Connecticut
Date: 1880
Title: View of Forestville, Conn.
Size: 18⅝ × 23¼ in. (47.4 × 59.1 cm.)
Artist:
Lithographer:
Printer:
Publisher: O. H. Bailey & Co., Boston
Key/Vignettes/Misc:
Locations: BPL–R
Catalogs/Checklists:

Place: Goodspeeds Landing, Connecticut
Date: 1880
See East Haddam, Connecticut, 1880.

Place: Greenville, Connecticut
Date: N.D.
See Norwich, Connecticut, n.d.

549
Place: Guilford, Connecticut
Date: 1881
Title: View of Guilford. Connecticut. 1881
Size: 19 × 24⅜ in. (48.4 × 62 cm.)
Artist:
Lithographer:
Printer:
Publisher: O. H. Bailey & Co., Boston
Key/Vignettes/Misc: Refs. 1–30; 4 vignettes
Locations: BPL–R
Catalogs/Checklists:

550
Place: Hartford, Connecticut
Date: 1849
Title: View of Hartford, Ct. From the Deaf and Dumb Asylum.
Size: 18 × 35⅛ in. (45.8 × 89.3 cm.)
Artist: E. Whitefield
Lithographer: E. Whitefield
Printer: F. Michelin, 111, Nassau St., N. Y.
Publisher: E. Whitefield
Key/Vignettes/Misc: 4 vignettes
Locations: CHS–H
Catalogs/Checklists: Norton, Whitefield, no. 43; CHS–H, 7

551
Place: Hartford, Connecticut
Date: 1864
Title: City of Hartford, Conn.
Size: 18 × 23 in. (45.8 × 58.6 cm.)
Artist: [Jacob Weidenmann]
Lithographer: John Bachmann
Printer: F. Heppenheimer, 22 & 24 N. W. M. St., N. Y.
Publisher: J. Weidenmann, Hartford, Conn.
Key/Vignettes/Misc:
Locations: LC–M (photo); CSL–H; YUAG–NH; NYH–NY; CHS–H
Catalogs/Checklists: LC–M, 80.3; CHS–H, 9

552
Place: Hartford, Connecticut
Date: 1869
Title: View of Hartford, Conn.
Size: 24¾ × 34 in. (63 × 86.5 cm.)
Artist: J. Bachman
Lithographer: J. Bachman
Printer: P. S. Duval Son & Co, Phil.
Publisher: John Weik, 605 Sansom Str. Philad.
Key/Vignettes/Misc:
Locations: CHS–H
Catalogs/Checklists: CHS–H, 11

553
Place: Hartford, Connecticut
Date: 1877
Title: City of Hartford, Connecticut. 1877.
Size: 23 × 25 in. (58.5 × 63.6 cm.)
Artist: O. H. Bailey & Co.
Lithographer:
Printer:
Publisher: O. H. Bailey & Co., Boston
Key/Vignettes/Misc: Refs.; [no vignettes]
Locations: CHS–H
Catalogs/Checklists: CHS–H, 12

554
Place: Hartford, Connecticut
Date: 1877
Title: The City of Hartford Connecticut. 1877.
Size: 26⅞ × 33 in. (68.4 × 83.9 cm.)
Artist:
Lithographer:
Printer:
Publisher: O. H. Bailey & Co., Boston
Key/Vignettes/Misc: Refs. 1–112; 9 vignettes

Locations: BPL–R; CHS–C; LC–M
(photo); CSL–H; CHS–H
Catalogs/Checklists: LC–M, 80.4;
CHS–H, 13

555
Place: Hartford, Connecticut
Date: [189–?]
Title: "Bluefields" Hartford's High Class
Subdivision
Size: 14 × 21 in. (35.6 × 53.4 cm.)
(photo)
Artist:
Lithographer:
Printer:
Publisher:
Key/Vignettes/Misc: 5 vignettes
Locations: LC–M
Catalogs/Checklists: LC–M, 80.5

556
Place: Hazardville, Connecticut
Date: 1880
Title: View of Hazardville, Connecticut.
1880.
Size: 19⅜ × 22¾ in. (49.3 × 57.9 cm.)
Artist:
Lithographer:
Printer:
Publisher: O. H. Bailey & Co., Boston
Key/Vignettes/Misc: Refs. A–T
Locations: BPL–R; CSL–H; LC–M
(photo); EHS–E
Catalogs/Checklists: LC–M, 80.6

557
Place: Higganum, Connecticut
Date: 1881
Title: View of Higganum, Connecticut
1881
Size: 19⅜ × 21⅝ in. (49.3 × 55.1 cm.)
Artist: A. E. D.
Lithographer:
Printer:
Publisher: O. H. Bailey & Co., Boston
Key/Vignettes/Misc: Refs. 1–17; 9
vignettes
Locations: BPL–R; LC–M
Catalogs/Checklists: LC–M, 80.7

Place: Hotchkissville, Connecticut
Date: Ca. 1840
See Woodbury, Connecticut, ca. 1840.

Place: Ivoryton, Connecticut
Date: 1881
See Essex, Connecticut, 1881.

558
Place: Jewett City, Connecticut
Date: 1889
Title: Jewett City, Conn.
Size: 13¾ × 24 in. (35 × 61.1 cm.)
Artist: L. R. Burleigh
Lithographer:
Printer: The Burleigh Lith. Est., Troy, N. Y.
Publisher: L. R. Burleigh, Troy, N. Y.
Key/Vignettes/Misc: Refs. 1–25
Locations: BPL–R; LC–M; Slater Library,
Jewett City, Connecticut
Catalogs/Checklists: LC–M, 81

559
Place: Jewett City, Connecticut
Date: 1913
Title: Jewett City, Conn.
Size: 13 × 24 in. (33.1 × 61.1 cm.)
Artist: Charles Hart
Lithographer:
Printer:
Publisher: Bailey and Rathburn, Norwich,
Connecticut
Key/Vignettes/Misc: 5 vignettes
Locations: Town Hall, Jewett City,
Connecticut
Catalogs/Checklists:

560
Place: Madison, Connecticut
Date: 1881
Title: View of Madison, Conn. 1881
Size: 16 × 24 in. (40.7 × 61.1 cm.)
Artist:
Lithographer:
Printer:
Publisher: O. H. Bailey & Co., Boston
Key/Vignettes/Misc: Refs. 1–15
Locations: LC–M; BPL–R
Catalogs/Checklists: LC–M, 81.1

561
Place: Manchester, Connecticut
Date: 1914
Title: Aero View of Manchester,
Connecticut 1914
Size: 27 × 36½ in. (40 × 92 cm.)
Artist:
Lithographer:
Printer: [Franklin Engraving Co.]
Publisher: Hughes & Bailey, 39–43 Gold
St. New York
Key/Vignettes/Misc: 35 vignettes;
unnumbered business directory
Locations: LC–M; CHS–H
Catalogs/Checklists: LC–M, 82; CHS–H,
16

562
Place: Meriden, Connecticut
Date: 1875
Title: City of Meriden, Conn. 1875.
Size: 21⅜ × 26⅞ in. (54.4 × 68.4 cm.)
Artist: O. H. Bailey & Co.
Lithographer: C. H. Vogt
Printer: J. Knauber & Co., Milwaukee
Publisher: O. H. Bailey & Co., Boston
Key/Vignettes/Misc: Refs. 1–58; 3
vignettes
Locations: BPL–R; CSL–H; LC–M
(photo); NYH–NY; CHS–H
Catalogs/Checklists: LC–M, 82.1;
CHS–H, 17

563
Place: Meriden, Connecticut
Date: 1881
Title: Meriden, Conn. 1881. From Summit
Heights.
Size: 24 × 28½ in. (61.1 × 72.5 cm.)
Artist: Wils Porter
Lithographer:
Printer:
Publisher: S. B. Farrow, Pattenburg, N. J.

Key/Vignettes/Misc: 25 vignettes
Locations: NYH–NY
Catalogs/Checklists:

564
Place: Meriden, Connecticut
Date: 1918
Title: Aero View of Meriden, Connecticut
1918.
Size: 25 × 35½ in. (63.6 × 90.3 cm.)
Artist: T. M. Fowler
Lithographer:
Printer: [Meriden Gravure Co., Meriden,
Conn.]
Publisher: Hughes & Bailey, New York &
Boston
Key/Vignettes/Misc:
Locations: LC–M
Catalogs/Checklists: LC–M, 83

565
Place: Middletown, Connecticut
Date: [1830–39]
Title: [Untitled]
Size: 18 × 25½ in. (45.8 × 64.9 cm.)
Artist: T. B. Thorp
Lithographer: A. Fleetwood
Printer:
Publisher:
Key/Vignettes/Misc:
Locations: WU–M
Catalogs/Checklists:

566
Place: Middletown, Connecticut
Date: [1824–43]
Title: Middletown. From High Street.
Size: 8¾ × 11¾ in. (22.3 × 29.9 cm.)
Artist:
Lithographer:
Printer: D. W. Kellogg & Co., Hartford,
Conn.
Publisher: E. Hunt & Co. M[iddletown]
Key/Vignettes/Misc:
Locations: WU–M
Catalogs/Checklists:

567
Place: Middletown, Connecticut
Date: [1856–57]
Title: Middletown, Conn.
Size: 20⅛ × 27½ in. (51.2 × 70 cm.)
Artist: Fr. Meyer
Lithographer:
Printer: Dumcke & Keil, 12 Frankfort St.
N.Y.
Publisher: S. N. Gaston, New York
Key/Vignettes/Misc:
Locations: WU–M; NYH–NY; CHS–H
Catalogs/Checklists: CHS–H, 18

568
Place: Middletown, Connecticut
Date: 1877 State I
Title: Middletown, Conn., 1877
Size: 23 × 28 in. (58.6 × 71.2 cm.)
Artist:
Lithographer:
Printer:
Publisher: O. H. Bailey & Co.
Key/Vignettes/Misc: 6 vignettes

Locations: LC−M
Catalogs/Checklists: LC−M, 84

569
Place: Middletown, Connecticut
Date: 1877 State II
Title: Middletown, Conn. 1877. Revised Edition.
Size: 23⅝ × 27⅞ in. (60.2 × 70.9 cm.)
Artist:
Lithographer:
Printer:
Publisher: O. H. Bailey & Co. (copyright)
Key/Vignettes/Misc: Refs. 1−44; 6 vignettes; lists of government officials for 1784 and 1876
Locations: WU−M; CHS−H
Catalogs/Checklists: CHS−H, 19

570
Place: Middletown, Connecticut
Date: 1881
Title: Middletown, Conn. 1881. The "Forest City" Population 11,731
Size: 16¾ × 25 in. (42.6 × 63.6 cm.)
Artist: Wils. Porter
Lithographer:
Printer: M. Bracher, lith., Philada
Publisher: B. S. Farrow, Pattenburg, N. J.
Key/Vignettes/Misc: 10 vignettes
Locations: WU−M
Catalogs/Checklists:

571
Place: Middletown, Connecticut
Date: 1915
Title: Aero View of Middletown Connecticut 1915
Size: 25 × 35½ in. (63.5 × 90.2 cm.)
Artist: T. M. Fowler
Lithographer:
Printer: [Meriden Gravure Co., Meriden, Conn. . . .]
Publisher: Hughes & Bailey, 39−43 Gold Street, New York
Key/Vignettes/Misc: 33 vignettes; unnumbered business directory; list of city and town officials
Locations: WU−M; LC−M; CHS−H
Catalogs/Checklists: LC−M, 85; CHS−H, 20

572
Place: Milford, Connecticut
Date: 1882
Title: View of Milford, Conn. 1882.
Size: 17⅞ × 25¼ in. (45.5 × 64.2 cm.)
Artist:
Lithographer:
Printer:
Publisher: O. H. Bailey and Company, Boston
Key/Vignettes/Misc: Refs. 1−18; 4 vignettes
Locations: BPL−R
Catalogs/Checklists:

573
Place: Moosup, Connecticut
Date: 1889
Title: Moosup, Conn., Uniondale and Almyville

Size: 15 × 27¼ in. (38.2 × 69.3 cm.)
Artist: L. R. Burleigh
Lithographer:
Printer: The Burleigh Lith. Est. Troy, N.Y.
Publisher: L. R. Burleigh, Troy, N.Y.
Key/Vignettes/Misc: Refs. 1−17
Locations: BPL−R; CSL−H; LC−M (photo)
Catalogs/Checklists: LC−M, 85.2

574
Place: Mystic, Connecticut
Date: 1879
Title: View of Mystic River & Mystic Bridge, Conn. 1879
Size: 19¾ × 25¼ in. (47.7 × 64.2 cm.)
Artist: O. H. Bailey & J. C. Hazen
Lithographer:
Printer:
Publisher: O. H. Bailey & J. C. Hazen, Boston
Key/Vignettes/Misc: Refs. A−P R−T;
Locations: BPL−R; LC−M
Catalogs/Checklists: LC−M, 85.3

575
Place: Naugatuck, Connecticut
Date: 1877
Title: View of Naugatuck, Conn., 1877
Size: 18¼ × 24¾ in. (46.5 × 62.9 cm.)
Artist: O. H. Bailey & Co.
Lithographer: C. H. Vogt
Printer:
Publisher: O. H. Bailey & Co., Boston
Key/Vignettes/Misc: Refs. 1−15; 3 vignettes
Locations: LC−M; BPL−R
Catalogs/Checklists: LC−M, 85.4

576
Place: Naugatuck, Connecticut
Date: 1906
Title: Bird's−Eye View of Naugatuck, Connecticut 1906
Size: 27 × 34 in. (68.7 × 86.5 cm.)
Artist:
Lithographer:
Printer:
Publisher: Hughes & Bailey, 39−43 Gold St. New York
Key/Vignettes/Misc: 36 vignettes; unnumbered business directory
Locations: LC−M; NYH−NY
Catalogs/Checklists: LC−M, 86

577
Place: New Britain, Connecticut
Date: Ca. 1860
Title: View of New Britain, Conn.
Size: 17 × 24½ in. (43.3 × 62.4 cm.)
Artist: H. Knecht
Lithographer: H. Knecht
Printer: J. Rau, 381 Pearl St. N.Y.
Publisher:
Key/Vignettes/Misc: 10 vignettes
Locations: NBPL−NB; CHS−H
Catalogs/Checklists: CHS−H, 21

578
Place: New Britain, Connecticut
Date: 1875
Title: View of New Britain, Conn. 1875

Size: 20 × 25⅝ in. (50.8 × 65.2 cm.)
Artist: O. H. Bailey & Co.
Lithographer: C. H. Vogt
Printer: J. Knauber & Co.
Publisher: O. H. Bailey & Co., Boston
Key/Vignettes/Misc: Refs. 1−26; 2 vignettes
Locations: LC−M; BPL−R; NBPL−NB; CHS−H
Catalogs/Checklists: LC−M, 86.1; CHS−H, 22

579
Place: New Britain, Connecticut
Date: 1899
Title: New Britain, Conn.
Size: 31 × 48⅜ in. (79 × 123 cm.)
Artist:
Lithographer:
Printer:
Publisher: Landis & Hughes, 294 Roseville Ave., Newark, N.J.
Key/Vignettes/Misc: 13 vignettes; unnumbered business directory
Locations: CSL−H; NBPL−NB; LC−M (photo)
Catalogs/Checklists: LC−M, 86.2

580
Place: New Canaan, Connecticut
Date: 1878
Title: View of New Canaan, Conn. 1878.
Size: 18 × 23 in. (45.8 × 58.5 cm.)
Artist:
Lithographer: C. H. Vogt
Printer:
Publisher: O. H. Bailey & Co., Boston
Key/Vignettes/Misc: Refs. 1−53; 2 vignettes
Locations: BPL−R; LC−M (photo); NYH−NY; CSL−H
Catalogs/Checklists: LC−M, 86.3

581
Place: New Hartford, Connecticut
Date: 1878
Title: New Hartford, Conn.
Size: 19⅜ × 24¼ in. (49.3 × 61.7 cm.)
Artist: O. H. Bailey & Co.
Lithographer:
Printer:
Publisher: O. H. Bailey & Co., Boston
Key/Vignettes/Misc: Refs. 1−36; 1 vignette
Locations: BPL−R; NYH−NY
Catalogs/Checklists:

582
Place: New Haven, Connecticut
Date: 1849
Title: New Haven, Conn. From Ferry Hill.
Size: 17¾ × 35¾ in. (45.2 × 90.9 cm.)
Artist: B. F. Smith, Jr.
Lithographer:
Printer: Tappan & Bradford, Boston
Publisher: D. C. & B. F. Smith, Jr.
Key/Vignettes/Misc:
Locations: MM−NN; NYP−S; NYH−NY; CHS−H
Catalogs/Checklists: MM−NN, LP 242; Stokes P. 1848—F−70; Anson Stokes, no. 47; CHS−H, 23

583
Place: New Haven, Connecticut
Date: Ca. 1850
Title: [Unknown; proof before letters]
Size: ["large folio"]
Artist:
Lithographer:
Printer:
Publisher:
Key/Vignettes/Misc: 8 vignettes
Locations: Unknown. See Old Print Shop Portfolio, XXIII, p. 87, No. 22
Catalogs/Checklists:

584
Place: New Haven, Connecticut
Date: 1853
Title: New Haven, from East Rock, 1853.
Size: 14 × 21⅞ in. (35.5 × 55.7 cm.)
Artist: T. H. Darrow
Lithographer:
Printer: E. C. Kellogg, Hartford, Conn.
Publisher: T. H. Darrow (copyright)
Key/Vignettes/Misc:
Locations: MM–NN; NYP–S; New Haven Colony Historical Society, New Haven, Connecticut; YUAG–NH; CHS–H
Catalogs/Checklists: MM–NN, LP 3278; Anson Stokes, no. 53

585
Place: New Haven, Connecticut
Date: Ca. 1862
Title: New Haven, Conn.
Size: 18½ × 34 in. (47.1 × 86.5 cm.)
Artist:
Lithographer:
Printer:
Publisher:
Key/Vignettes/Misc:
Locations: YUAG–NH
Catalogs/Checklists: Anson Stokes, no. 61

586
Place: New Haven, Connecticut
Date: Ca. 1862
Title: New Haven, Conn. View from East Rock.
Size: 14½ × 20¾ in. (36.9 × 52.8 cm.)
Artist: L. Schierholz
Lithographer: L. Schierholz
Printer: Punderson & Crisand, N.[ew] H.[aven]
Publisher:
Key/Vignettes/Misc:
Locations: CHS–H
Catalogs/Checklists: CHS–H, 24

587
Place: New Haven, Connecticut
Date: 1876
Title: City of New Haven Connecticut 1776 1876
Size: 8 × 10 in. (20.3 × 25.4 cm.)
Artist: W. Brotherhead
Lithographer:
Printer: H. J. Toudy & Co Steam Lith.
Publisher:
Key/Vignettes/Misc:
Locations:
Catalogs/Checklists: Anson Stokes, no. 66

588
Place: New Haven, Connecticut
Date: 1879
Title: The City of New Haven, Conn. 1879.
Size: 28½ × 34¼ in. (72.5 × 87.1 cm.)
Artist: O. H. Bailey & J. C. Hazen
Lithographer:
Printer:
Publisher: O. H. Bailey & J. C. Hazen, Boston
Key/Vignettes/Misc: Refs. 1–51
Locations: BPL–R; LC–M; New Haven Colony Historical Society, New Haven, Connecticut; CHS–H
Catalogs/Checklists: LC–M, 87; Anson Stokes, no. 68; CHS–H, 28

589
Place: New Haven, Connecticut
Date: N.D.
Title: New Haven From The S. E.
Size: 9¾ × 12¼ in. (24.8 × 31.2 cm.)
Artist: T. K. Wharton
Lithographer: T. K. Wharton
Printer: Thos. Moore's Lithography, Boston
Publisher:
Key/Vignettes/Misc:
Locations: LC–P
Catalogs/Checklists:

590
Place: New London, Connecticut
Date: Ca. 1854
Title: View of New London from Fort Griswold.
Size: 18¼ × 35⅞ in. (46.4 × 91.2 cm.)
Artist: J. Ropes
Lithographer:
Printer: E. C. Kellogg, Hartford, Conn.
Publisher: Holmes & Co.
Key/Vignettes/Misc:
Locations: MM–NN; CHS–H
Catalogs/Checklists: MM–NN, LP 924; CHS–H, 30

591
Place: New London, Connecticut
Date: 1876
Title: New London, Conn. 1876.
Size: 22⅛ × 27⅛ in. (56.3 × 69.1 cm.)
Artist: O. H. Bailey & Co.
Lithographer: C. H. Vogt
Printer:
Publisher: O. H. Bailey & Co. Boston
Key/Vignettes/Misc: Refs. 1–54; 5 vignettes
Locations: BPL–R; CHS–C; CHS–H
Catalogs/Checklists: CHS–H, 31

592
Place: New London, Connecticut
Date: 1911
Title: Aero View of New London, Connecticut 1911
Size: 32 × 39½ in. (81.4 × 100.5 cm.)
Artist:
Lithographer:
Printer:
Publisher: Hughes & Bailey, New York
Key/Vignettes/Misc: 46 vignettes; unnumbered business directory
Locations: LC–M
Catalogs/Checklists: LC–M, 88

593
Place: New Milford, Connecticut
Date: 1882
Title: View of New Milford, Connecticut. 1882
Size: 18⅞ × 24½ in. (48 × 62.3 cm.)
Artist:
Lithographer:
Printer:
Publisher: O. H. Bailey & Co., Boston
Key/Vignettes/Misc: Refs. 1–40
Locations: BPL–R
Catalogs/Checklists:

594
Place: New Milford, Connecticut
Date: 1906
Title: Bird's–Eye–View of New Milford, Connecticut 1906
Size: 27 × 30 in. (68.7 × 76.4 cm.)
Artist:
Lithographer:
Printer:
Publisher: Hughes & Bailey, New York
Key/Vignettes/Misc: Refs. 1–33, A–N; 20 vignettes; unnumbered business directory
Locations: LC–M
Catalogs/Checklists: LC–M, 89

595
Place: North Manchester, Connecticut
Date: 1880
Title: View of North Manchester, Connecticut. 1880.
Size: 18 × 23 in. (45.8 × 58.6 cm.)
Artist:
Lithographer:
Printer:
Publisher: O. H. Bailey & Co.,Boston
Key/Vignettes/Misc: Refs. A–Z, 2–4
Locations: BPL–R
Catalogs/Checklists:

Place: Norwalk, Connecticut
Date: 1875
See South Norwalk, Connecticut, 1875.

596
Place: Norwalk, Connecticut
Date: Ca. 1899
Title: Norwalk, South Norwalk, and East Norwalk, Conn.
Size: 32½ × 44¼ in. (82.7 × 113.2 cm.)
Artist:
Lithographer:
Printer:
Publisher: Landis & Hughes, N. Y.
Key/Vignettes/Misc: 22 vignettes; unnumbered business directory
Locations: LC–M
Catalogs/Checklists: LC–M, 90

597
Place: Norwich, Connecticut
Date: 1849
Title: View of Norwich, From the West Side of the River
Size: 13½ × 16⅝ in. (34.4 × 42.3 cm.)
Artist: [Fitz Hugh] Lane

Lithographer:
Printer: Sarony and Major, 117 Fulton St.,
N. Y.
Publisher: A. Conant
Key/Vignettes/Misc:
Locations: Leffingwell Inn Museum,
Norwich, Connecticut; BM–NY; BA;
CHS–H
Catalogs/Checklists: Wilmerding 154;
Pyne, no. 455; CHS–H, 33

598
Place: Norwich, Connecticut
Date: 1853
Title: View of Norwich, From the South.
1853.
Size: 22¹¹⁄₁₆ × 30⁷⁄₁₆ in. (57.8 × 77.5 cm.)
Artist: J. D. Crocker
Lithographer:
Printer: E. C. Kellogg [Philadelphia]
Publisher: Holmes & Co.
Key/Vignettes/Misc: 3 vignettes
Locations: BA; MM–NN; NYP–S;
YUAG–NH; LC–P; NYH–NY; CHS–H
Catalogs/Checklists: Stokes 1853—G–28;
MM–NN, LP 241; CHS–H, 34

599
Place: Norwich, Connecticut
Date: Ca. 1870
Title: Norwich, Conn.
Size: 18½ × 30½ in. (47 × 77.5 cm.)
Artist: H. Knecht
Lithographer: H. Knecht
Printer: J. Rau, 381 Pearl St., New York
Publisher:
Key/Vignettes/Misc: 3 vignettes
Locations: MM–NN; LC–P;
YUAG–NH; NYH–NY
Catalogs/Checklists: MM–NN, LP 2056

600
Place: Norwich, Connecticut
Date: 1876
Title: City of Norwich Conn. 1876.
Size: 21⅝ × 34 in. (55 × 86.5 cm.)
Artist: O. H. Bailey & Co.
Lithographer: C. H. Vogt
Printer: J. Knauber & Co.
Publisher: O. H. Bailey & Co. [Boston]
Key/Vignettes/Misc: Refs. 1–71; 4
vignettes; list of public officials
Locations: BPL–R; LC–M; MM–NN;
NYH–NY; CHS–H
Catalogs/Checklists: LC–M, 91;
MM–NN, LP 2528; CHS–H, 36

601
Place: Norwich, Connecticut
Date: 1912
Title: Aero View of Norwich, Connecticut
1912
Size: 33 × 39½ in. (84 × 100.5 cm.)
Artist:
Lithographer:
Printer: [Hughes & Bailey, New York]
Publisher: Hughes & Bailey, New York
Key/Vignettes/Misc: Refs. 1–12, 14–15;
50 vignettes
Locations: LC–M
Catalogs/Checklists: LC–M, 92

602
Place: Norwich, Connecticut
Date: N.D.
Title: Norwich, Conn. Norwich Falls.
Norwich Town. Greenville (Norwich).
Size: 17½ × 30½ in. (44.5 × 77.6 cm.)
Artist: H. Knecht
Lithographer: H. Knecht
Printer: J. Rau, 381 Pearl St. New York
Publisher:
Key/Vignettes/Misc:
Locations: CHS–H
Catalogs/Checklists: CHS–H, 35

Place: Norwich Falls, Connecticut
Date: N.D.
See Norwich, Connecticut, N. D.

Place: Norwich Town, Connecticut
Date: N.D.
See Norwich, Connecticut, n.d.

Place: Pequabuck, Connecticut
Date: Ca. 1890
See Terryville, Connecticut, CA. 1890.

603
Place: Plainville, Connecticut
Date: Ca. 1853
Title: Plainville, Conn. From the South
West
Size: 13½ × 21¾ in. (34.4 × 55.4 cm.)
Artist: T. H. Darrow
Lithographer:
Printer: E. B. & E. C. Kellogg, Hartford,
Conn.
Publisher:
Key/Vignettes/Misc:
Locations: Unknown. See Old Print Shop
Portfolio, XXXIV, p. 103, No. 11
Catalogs/Checklists:

604
Place: Plainville, Connecticut
Date: 1878
Title: Plainville, Connecticut 1878
Size: 16¾ × 23⅞ in. (42.6 × 60.8 cm.)
Artist: O. H. Bailey & J. C. Hazen
Lithographer: C. H. Vogt
Printer:
Publisher: O. H. Bailey & J. C. Hazen,
Boston
Key/Vignettes/Misc: Refs. A–G
Locations: BPL–R; LC–M; Plainville
Historic Center, Plainville, Connecticut
Catalogs/Checklists: LC–M, 93

605
Place: Plainville, Connecticut
Date: 1907
Title: Bird's Eye View of Plainville,
Connecticut 1907
Size: 19 × 29 in. (48.4 × 73.8 cm.)
Artist: O. H. Bailey
Lithographer:
Printer:
Publisher: Hughes & Bailey, 39–43 Gold
St. N. Y.
Key/Vignettes/Misc: 12 vignettes;
unnumbered business directory
Locations: LC–M; Plainville Historic

Center, Plainville, Connecticut
Catalogs/Checklists: LC–M, 94

606
Place: Plymouth Hollow, Connecticut
Date: 1852
Title: View of Plymouth Hollow, 1852
(Connecticut)
Size: 11 × 18½ in. (28 × 47.1 cm.)
Artist: T. H. Darrow
Lithographer:
Printer: E. C. Kellogg, Hartford, Conn.
Publisher:
Key/Vignettes/Misc:
Locations: CHS–H
Catalogs/Checklists: CHS–H, 37

607
Place: Putnam, Connecticut
Date: 1877
Title: View of Putnam, Conn., 1877.
Size: 18⅞ × 25 in. (48 × 63.6 cm.)
Artist: O. H. Bailey & Co.
Lithographer:
Printer: J. Knauber & Co.
Publisher: O. H. Bailey & Co., Boston
Key/Vignettes/Misc: Refs. 1–19
Locations: LC–M; BPL–R; CHS–S
Catalogs/Checklists: LC–M, 94.1;
CHS–H, 38

608
Place: Rockville, Connecticut
Date: 1877
Title: View of Rockville, Conn. 1877
Size: 21¾ × 26 in. (55.3 × 66.2 cm.)
Artist:
Lithographer: J. Knauber & Co.
Printer: J. Knauber & Co., Milwaukee
Publisher: O. H. Bailey & Co.
Key/Vignettes/Misc: Refs. 1–51; 7
vignettes
Locations: LC–M; BPL–R; NYH–NY;
CHS–H
Catalogs/Checklists: LC–M, 94.2;
CHS–H, 39

609
Place: Rockville, Connecticut
Date: 1895
Title: Rockville Connecticut. 1895.
Size: 22⅝ × 31¼ in. (57.6 × 79.5 cm.)
Artist:
Lithographer:
Printer: O. H. Bailey & Co., Boston
Publisher: O. H. Bailey & Co. Boston
Key/Vignettes/Misc: Refs. A, 3–98; 55
vignettes
Locations: CHS–H
Catalogs/Checklists: CHS–H, 40

610
Place: Seymour, Connecticut
Date: 1879
Title: View of Seymour, Conn. 1879
Size: 19½ × 24 in. (49.6 × 61.1 cm.)
Artist: O. H. Bailey & Co.
Lithographer:
Printer:
Publisher: O. H. Bailey & Co., Boston
Key/Vignettes/Misc: Refs. 1–40; 6
vignettes

Locations: BPL−R; LC−M
Catalogs/Checklists: LC−M, 94.3

611

Place: Shelton, Connecticut
Date: 1919
Title: Aero View of Shelton, Connecticut 1919
Size: 20 × 31 in. (50.9 × 78.9 cm.)
Artist:
Lithographer:
Printer: [Meriden Gravure Co., Meriden, Conn.]
Publisher: Hughes & Bailey, Boston
Key/Vignettes/Misc: 19 vignettes; unnumbered list of residences; unnumbered lists of public officials
Locations: LC−M
Catalogs/Checklists: LC−M, 95

612

Place: South Coventry, Connecticut
Date: 1878
Title: View of South Coventry, Conn. 1878
Size: 18¼ × 25¼ in. (46.4 × 64.2 cm.)
Artist:
Lithographer:
Printer:
Publisher: O. H. Bailey & Co., Boston
Key/Vignettes/Misc: Refs. 1−25; 4 vignettes
Locations: BPL−R; CSL−H; LC−M (photo); NYH−NY
Catalogs/Checklists: LC−M, 95.1

613

Place: South Manchester, Connecticut
Date: 1880
Title: View of South Manchester, Conn. 1880
Size: 18½ × 24½ in. (47 × 62.3 cm.)
Artist:
Lithographer:
Printer:
Publisher: O. H. Bailey & Co., Boston
Key/Vignettes/Misc: Refs. A−W; 2 vignettes
Locations: LC−M; South Manchester, Connecticut, Public Library
Catalogs/Checklists: LC−M, 97

614

Place: South Norwalk, Connecticut
Date: 1875
Title: South Norwalk and Norwalk, Conn.
Size: 21¼ × 32⅝ in. (54.1 × 83 cm.)
Artist: O. H. Bailey & Co.
Lithographer: C. H. Vogt
Printer: J. Knauber & Co.
Publisher: O. H. Bailey & Co., Boston
Key/Vignettes/Misc: Refs., South Norwalk, 1−15, Norwalk, 1−19
Locations: BPL−R
Catalogs/Checklists:

Place: South Norwalk, Connecticut
Date: Ca. 1899
See Norwalk, Connecticut, ca. 1899.

615

Place: Southington, Connecticut
Date: 1878
Title: Southington, Conn.

Size: 20¼ × 25⅜ in. (51.6 × 64.6 cm.)
Artist:
Lithographer:
Printer:
Publisher: O. H. Bailey & J. C. Hazen, Boston
Key/Vignettes/Misc: Refs. A−H, J−K, 2−8; 8 vignettes
Locations: BPL−R
Catalogs/Checklists:

616

Place: Southington, Connecticut
Date: 1914
Title: Aero View of Southington, Connecticut 1914
Size: 28 × 36 in. (71.2 × 91.6 cm.)
Artist:
Lithographer:
Printer: [Consolidated Engraving Co. & Federal Engraving Co., Boston]
Publisher: Hughes & Bailey
Key/Vignettes/Misc: 27 vignettes; unnumbered business and industrial directory; unnumbered list of city officials
Locations: LC−M
Catalogs/Checklists: LC−M, 96

617

Place: Stafford Springs, Connecticut
Date: 1878
Title: View of Stafford Springs, Conn. 1878.
Size: 20¼ × 23 in. (51.6 × 58.5 cm.)
Artist:
Lithographer:
Printer:
Publisher: O. H. Bailey & Co., Boston
Key/Vignettes/Misc: Refs. 1−40; 7 vignettes
Locations: BPL−R; LC−M; NYH−NY; CHS−H
Catalogs/Checklists: LC−M, 97.1; CHS−H, 42

618

Place: Stamford, Connecticut
Date: 1875
Title: View of Stamford, Conn. 1875.
Size: 20¼ × 25⅝ in. (51.6 × 65.2 cm.)
Artist: O. H. Bailey & Co.
Lithographer: C. H. Vogt
Printer: J. Knauber
Publisher: O. H. Bailey & Co. [Boston]
Key/Vignettes/Misc: Refs. 1−21; 2 vignettes
Locations: BPL−R
Catalogs/Checklists:

619

Place: Stamford, Connecticut
Date: 1883
Title: Stamford, Conn.
Size: 19½ × 34¹⁄₁₆ in. (49.6 × 86.7 cm.)
Artist: L. R. Burleigh
Lithographer:
Printer: Beck & Pauli Lith. Milwaukee, Wis.
Publisher:
Key/Vignettes/Misc: Refs. 1−35
Locations: BPL−R; LC−M
Catalogs/Checklists:

620

Place: Stonington, Connecticut
Date: 1879
Title: View of Stonington, Conn. 1879
Size: 19⅝ × 24¾ in. (49.9 × 63 cm.)
Artist:
Lithographer:
Printer:
Publisher: O. H. Bailey & Co., Boston
Key/Vignettes/Misc: Refs. 1−37
Locations: BPL−R; NYH−NY; LC−M (photo); CSL−H; CHS−H
Catalogs/Checklists: LC−M, 97.3; CHS−H, 43

621

Place: Stonington, Connecticut
Date: N.D.
Title: Stonington, Connecticut
Size: 26¼ × 35½ in. (66.8 × 90.3 cm.)
Artist:
Lithographer:
Printer:
Publisher: National View Co., 36 Columbus Ave, Boston
Key/Vignettes/Misc:
Locations: CHS−H
Catalogs/Checklists: CHS−H, 44

622

Place: Stratford, Connecticut
Date: 1882
Title: Stratford, Conn. 1882
Size: 21⅞ × 24¼ in. (55.7 × 61.7 cm.)
Artist:
Lithographer:
Printer:
Publisher: O. H. Bailey & Co., Boston
Key/Vignettes/Misc: Refs. 1−11; 2 vignettes; plan of Stratford in 1824
Locations: BPL−R
Catalogs/Checklists:

623

Place: Terryville, Connecticut
Date: Ca. 1890
Title: Terryville, Ct. Litchfield Co. Pequabuck or Terryville Station
Size: 15 × 22 in. (38.1 × 56 cm.)
Artist:
Lithographer:
Printer:
Publisher: Geo E. Norris, Brockton, Mass.
Key/Vignettes/Misc:
Locations: CHS−H
Catalogs/Checklists: CHS−H, 45

Place: Terryville Station, Connecticut
Date: Ca. 1890
See Terryville, Connecticut, ca. 1890.

624

Place: Thermos, Connecticut
Date: ?
Title:
Size:
Artist: T. M. Fowler
Lithographer:
Printer:
Publisher:
Key/Vignettes/Misc:
Locations:
Catalogs/Checklists: Warren

625
Place: Thomaston, Connecticut
Date: 1879
Title: View of Thomaston, Conn. 1879
Size: 16⅞ × 24¾ in. (43 × 63 cm.)
Artist:
Lithographer:
Printer:
Publisher: O. H. Bailey & Co., Boston
Key/Vignettes/Misc: Refs. 1–37;
unnumbered business, public building, and
residential directory
Locations: LC–M; NYH–NY
Catalogs/Checklists: LC–M, 97.4

626
Place: Thomaston, Connecticut
Date: 1908
Title: Bird's Eye View of Thomaston,
Connecticut.
Size: 28¼ × 34 in. (71.9 × 86.5 cm.)
Artist:
Lithographer:
Printer:
Publisher: Hughes & Bailey, N. Y.
Key/Vignettes/Misc:
Locations: CHS–H
Catalogs/Checklists: CHS–H, 46

627
Place: Thompsonville, Connecticut
Date: 1878
Title: View of Thompsonville, Conn.
1878.
Size: 19¾ × 24⅞ in. (50.3 × 63.3 cm.)
Artist:
Lithographer:
Printer: Beck & Pauli [Milwaukee]
Publisher: O. H. Bailey & Co., Boston
Key/Vignettes/Misc: Refs. 1–16
Locations: BPL–R; EHS–E
Catalogs/Checklists:

628
Place: Thompsonville, Connecticut
Date: 1908
Title: Bird's Eye View of Thompsonville
Connecticut 1908
Size: 21⅜ × 27⅛ in. (54.3 × 69 cm.)
Artist:
Lithographer:
Printer:
Publisher: Hughes & Bailey, Publishers,
39–43 Gold Street, New York
Key/Vignettes/Misc: Refs. 1–10, A–C,
E–H, J–K, M–N, P; 13 vignettes
Locations: EHS–E
Catalogs/Checklists:

629
Place: Torrington, Connecticut
Date: 1889
Title: Torrington, Conn. 1889.
Size: 17 × 30 in. (43.2 × 76.3 cm.)
Artist: Geo. E. Norris
Lithographer:
Printer: The Burleigh Lith. Est. Troy, N. Y.
Publisher: Geo. E. Norris, Brockton, Mass.
Key/Vignettes/Misc: Refs. 1–57
Locations: BPL–R; LC–M (photo);
CSL–H; CHS–H
Catalogs/Checklists: LC–M, 97.5;
CHS–H, 47

630
Place: Torrington, Connecticut
Date: 1907
Title: Bird's Eye View of Torrington,
Connecticut 1907
Size: 29 × 36 in. (73.8 × 91.6 cm.)
Artist: O. H. Bailey
Lithographer:
Printer:
Publisher: Hughes & Bailey, New York
Key/Vignettes/Misc: 49 vignettes;
unnumbered city official, business, and
public building directories
Locations: LC–M
Catalogs/Checklists: LC–M, 98

Place: Uniondale, Connecticut
Date: 1889
See Moosup, Connecticut, 1889.

631
Place: Unionville, Connecticut
Date: 1878
Title: View of Unionville, Conn. 1878
Size: 19 × 21¼ in. (48.3 × 54.1 cm.)
Artist:
Lithographer:
Printer: Beck & Pauli [Milwaukee]
Publisher: O. H. Bailey & Co., Boston
Key/Vignettes/Misc: Refs. 1–33; 6
vignettes
Locations: BPL–R; CSL–H; NYH–NY;
LC–M (photo)
Catalogs/Checklists: LC–M, 98.1

632
Place: Wallingford, Connecticut
Date: 1881
Title: View of Wallingford, Connecticut.
1881
Size: 18½ × 25¼ in. (47.1 × 64.2 cm.)
Artist:
Lithographer:
Printer:
Publisher: O. H. Bailey & Co., Boston
Key/Vignettes/Misc: Refs. A, 2–29; 7
vignettes
Locations: BPL–R; LC–M (photo);
CSL–H
Catalogs/Checklists: LC–M, 98.2

633
Place: Wallingford, Connecticut
Date: Ca. 1905
Title: Bird's Eye View of Wallingford,
Connecticut
Size: 26 × 34 in. (66.1 × 86.5 cm.)
Artist:
Lithographer:
Printer:
Publisher: Hughes & Bailey, New York
Key/Vignettes/Misc: Refs. 1–33, 33A,
34–44, 44A, 45–49; 25 vignettes
Locations: LC–M
Catalogs/Checklists: LC–M, 99

634
Place: Waterbury, Connecticut
Date: 1876
Title: View of the City of Waterbury,
Conn. 1876.
Size: 22 × 27⅞ in. (56 × 70.9 cm.)
Artist: O. H. Bailey & Co.

Lithographer: C. H. Vogt
Printer: J. Knauber & Co.
Publisher: O. H. Bailey & Co., [Boston]
Key/Vignettes/Misc: Refs. 1–48; 5
vignettes
Locations: BPL–R
Catalogs/Checklists:

635
Place: Waterbury, Connecticut
Date: 1899
Title: Waterbury, Conn. 1899
Size: 35⅝ × 44¼ in. (90.7 × 112.4 cm.)
Artist:
Lithographer:
Printer:
Publisher: Landis & Hughes, 138
Mulberry St., New York
Key/Vignettes/Misc: 26 vignettes;
unnumbered business directory
Locations: LC–M
Catalogs/Checklists: LC–M, 100

636
Place: Waterbury, Connecticut
Date: 1917
Title: Aero View of Waterbury
Connecticut 1917
Size: 23 × 32 in. (58.5 × 81.4 cm.)
Artist: T. M. Fowler
Lithographer:
Printer: [Meriden Gravure Co., Meriden,
Conn. & Tudor Press, Boston]
Publisher:
Key/Vignettes/Misc: 9 vignettes;
unnumbered business directory
Locations: LC–M
Catalogs/Checklists: LC–M, 101

637
Place: Watertown, Connecticut
Date: 1879
Title:
Size:
Artist:
Lithographer:
Printer:
Publisher: O. H. Bailey & Co., Boston
Key/Vignettes/Misc:
Locations: Unknown
Catalogs/Checklists: Warren & Wise

638
Place: Watertown, Connecticut
Date: 1918
Title: Aero View of Watertown,
Connecticut 1918
Size: 22½ × 34½ in. (57.3 × 87.8 cm.)
Artist:
Lithographer:
Printer: [Meriden Gravure Co., Meriden,
Conn.]
Publisher: Hughes & Bailey, Boston
Key/Vignettes/Misc: Refs. A–Y; 15
vignettes; unnumbered list of public
officials
Locations: LC–M
Catalogs/Checklists: LC–M, 102

639
Place: Westport, Connecticut
Date: 1878
Title: View of Westport, Conn. 1878.

Size: 18⅝ × 21 in. (47.4 × 53.4 cm.)
Artist:
Lithographer:
Printer:
Publisher: O. H. Bailey & Co., Boston
Key/Vignettes/Misc: Refs. 1–51
Locations: LC–M (photo); CSL–H; BPL–R; NYH–NY
Catalogs/Checklists: LC–M, 102.1

640
Place: Willimantic, Connecticut
Date: 1876
Title: Bird's Eye View of Willimantic, Conn.
Size: 21⅝ × 27⅞ in. (55 × 71 cm.)
Artist: H. H. Bailey & J. C. Hazen
Lithographer:
Printer:
Publisher: H. H. Bailey & J. C. Hazen, [Boston]
Key/Vignettes/Misc: Refs. A–M
Locations: CSL–H; LC–M (photo)
Catalogs/Checklists: LC–M, 102.2

641
Place: Willimantic, Connecticut
Date: 1882
Title: Willimantic, Conn., 1882. From Blake Mountain.
Size: 24 × 32¼ in. (61.1 × 82 cm.)
Artist: Wils Porter
Lithographer:
Printer: Charles Hart Lith. 36 Vesey St. N. Y.
Publisher: W. O. Laughna, Art Publishing Co. N. Y.
Key/Vignettes/Misc: 20 vignettes
Locations: LC–P; CHS–H
Catalogs/Checklists: LC–M, 102.3; CHS–H, 48

642
Place: Willimantic, Connecticut
Date: 1909
Title: Aero View of Willimantic, Connecticut 1909
Size: 29 × 33 in. (73.8 × 84 cm.)
Artist:
Lithographer:
Printer:
Publisher: Bailey and Hughes, New York
Key/Vignettes/Misc: Refs. 1–22; 33 vignettes; unnumbered business and public building directory
Locations: LC–M
Catalogs/Checklists: LC–M, 103

643
Place: Windham, Connecticut
Date: N.D.
Title: View of Windham, Conn. in 1815. (from the east)
Size: 14¼ × 19½ in.
Artist:
Lithographer:
Printer: E. B. & E. C. Kellogg, Hartford, Conn.
Publisher:
Key/Vignettes/Misc:
Locations: NYH–NY; CHS–H
Catalogs/Checklists: CHS–H, 49

644
Place: Windsor Locks, Connecticut
Date: 1877
Title: View of Windsor Locks, Conn., 1877
Size: 16⅛ × 26⁵⁄₁₆ in. (41 × 67 cm.)
Artist:
Lithographer: J. Knauber & Co.
Printer: J. Knauber & Co., Milwaukee, Wis.
Publisher: O. H. Bailey & Co., Boston
Key/Vignettes/Misc: Refs. 1–24
Locations: LC–M
Catalogs/Checklists: LC–M, 103.1

645
Place: Winsted, Connecticut
Date: 1877
Title: View of Winsted, Conn. 1877.
Size: 21½ × 27½ in. (54.7 × 69.9 cm.)
Artist: O. H. Bailey & Co.
Lithographer: C. H. Vogt & Co.
Printer:
Publisher: O. H. Bailey & Co., Boston
Key/Vignettes/Misc: Refs. 1–39; 9 vignettes
Locations: BPL–R; LC–M (photo); CSL–H; CHS–H
Catalogs/Checklists: LC–M, 103.2; CHS–H, 50

646
Place: Winsted, Connecticut
Date: 1908
Title: Bird's Eye View of Winsted, Connecticut 1908
Size: 32 × 34 in. (81.4 × 86.5 cm.)
Artist:
Lithographer:
Printer:
Publisher: O. H. Bailey, New York
Key/Vignettes/Misc: Refs. 1–9A, 10–11A, 12–30; 46 vignettes; unnumbered business directory
Locations: LC–M; CHS–H
Catalogs/Checklists: LC–M, 104; CHS–H, 51

647
Place: Wolcottville, Connecticut
Date: [1875–78]
Title: Wolcottville, Conn.
Size: 16⅛ × 24⅜ in. (41 × 62 cm.)
Artist:
Lithographer:
Printer: D. Bremner & Co., Milwaukee
Publisher: O. H. Bailey & Co., Boston
Key/Vignettes/Misc: Refs. 1–19; 5 vignettes
Locations: LC–M; NYH–NY
Catalogs/Checklists: LC–M, 104.1

648
Place: Woodbury, Connecticut
Date: Ca. 1840
Title: Southwest View of Hotchkissville (Woodbury) Conn. From the Rocks
Size: 14¹¹⁄₁₆ × 19¹⁄₁₆ in. (37.4 × 48.5 cm.)
Artist:
Lithographer:
Printer: Case & Green Lith. Hartford, Conn.

Publisher:
Key/Vignettes/Misc:
Locations: YUAG–NH; Old Woodbury Historical Society, Woodbury, Connecticut
Catalogs/Checklists:

649
Place: Woodbury, Connecticut
Date: Ca. 1840
Title: View of Woodbury, Connecticut. From Castle Rock.
Size: 13½ × 19 in. (34.3 × 48.3 cm.)
Artist:
Lithographer:
Printer: Case & Green Lith. Hartford, Conn.
Publisher:
Key/Vignettes/Misc:
Locations: Old Woodbury Historical Society, Woodbury, Connecticut; YUAG–NH
Catalogs/Checklists:

650
Place: Clayton, Delaware
Date: 1885
Title: Clayton, Delaware 1885.
Size: 16¼ × 17¾ in. (41.3 × 45.1 cm.)
Artist:
Lithographer:
Printer: O. H. Bailey & Co., Boston
Publisher: O. H. Bailey & Co., Boston
Key/Vignettes/Misc: Refs. 1–24; 2 vignettes
Locations: BPL–R; LC–M (photo); DHR–D (photo)
Catalogs/Checklists: LC–M, 105

651
Place: Dover, Delaware
Date: 1885
Title: Dover, Delaware 1885
Size: 21 × 29 in. (53.4 × 73.7 cm.)
Artist:
Lithographer:
Printer: O. H. Bailey & Co., New York
Publisher: O. H. Bailey & Co., New York
Key/Vignettes/Misc: Refs. 1–93; 17 vignettes
Locations: BPL–R; DHR–D
Catalogs/Checklists:

652
Place: Dover, Delaware
Date: N.D.
Title: Views in Dover Delaware
Size: 14 × 18¾ in. (35.6 × 47.8 cm.)
Artist:
Lithographer:
Printer:
Publisher:
Key/Vignettes/Misc: Refs. 1–13; 13 views on sectioned sheet
Locations: DHR–D (photo)
Catalogs/Checklists:

653
Place: Georgetown, Delaware
Date: 1885
Title: Georgetown. Delaware. 1885
Size: 16⅞ × 23¼ in. (42.9 × 59.2 cm.)
Artist:

Lithographer:
Printer: O. H. Bailey & Co., Boston
Publisher: O. H. Bailey & Co., Boston
Key/Vignettes/Misc: Refs. 1–50; 8 vignettes
Locations: BPL–R; DHR–D (photo)
Catalogs/Checklists:

654
Place: Harrington, Delaware
Date: 1885
Title: Harrington. Delaware. 1885
Size: 11½ × 22¼ in. (29.3 × 56.6 cm.)
Artist:
Lithographer:
Printer: O. H. Bailey & Co., Boston
Publisher: O. H. Bailey & Co., Boston
Key/Vignettes/Misc: Refs. 1–32; 3 vignettes
Locations: BPL–R; DHR–D (photo)
Catalogs/Checklists:

655
Place: Middletown, Delaware
Date: 1885
Title: Middletown Delaware. 1885
Size: 17¼ × 24³⁄₁₆ in. (43.9 × 61.6 cm.)
Artist:
Lithographer:
Printer: O. H. Bailey & Co., New York
Publisher: O. H. Bailey & Co., New York
Key/Vignettes/Misc: Refs. 1–36; 7 vignettes
Locations: BPL–R; DHR–D (facsimile)
Catalogs/Checklists:

656
Place: Milford, Delaware
Date: 1885
Title: Milford. Delaware. 1885
Size: 16⅝ × 24½ in. (42.3 × 62.3 cm.)
Artist:
Lithographer:
Printer: O. H. Bailey & Co., Boston
Publisher: O. H. Bailey & Co., Boston
Key/Vignettes/Misc: Refs. 1–54; 2 vignettes
Locations: BPL–R; DHR–D (photo)
Catalogs/Checklists:

657
Place: Smyrna, Delaware
Date: 1885
Title: Smyrna. Delaware. 1885.
Size: 17½ × 23⅛ in. (44.5 × 58.8 cm.)
Artist:
Lithographer:
Printer: O. H. Bailey & Co. Boston
Publisher: O. H. Bailey & Co., Boston
Key/Vignettes/Misc: Refs. 1–36; 7 vignettes
Locations: BPL–R; DHR–D (photo)
Catalogs/Checklists:

658
Place: Wilmington, Delaware
Date: 1841
Title: City of Wilmington, Del. from the Southeast
Size: 14 × 33½ in. (35.6 × 85.2 cm.)
Artist: B. Gluck
Lithographer:

Printer: T. Sinclair, Philadelphia
Publisher:
Key/Vignettes/Misc: 1 vignette
Locations: HSD–W; NYP–S
Catalogs/Checklists: Freeman, p. 40; Stokes 1841—F–65

659
Place: Wilmington, Delaware
Date: Ca. 1850
Title: Wilmington From Beyond the Christiana River
Size: 14 × 25 in. (35.6 × 63.6 cm.)
Artist: J. H. Sherwin
Lithographer:
Printer: L. N. Rosenthals' Lithographic Press
Publisher:
Key/Vignettes/Misc:
Locations: HSD–W
Catalogs/Checklists:

660
Place: Wilmington, Delaware
Date: 1852
Title: View of Wilmington, Del. From the Newport Road.
Size: 16 × 32½ in. (40.8 × 82.7 cm.)
Artist: E. Whitefield
Lithographer: E. Whitefield
Printer: Endicott & Co., New York
Publisher:
Key/Vignettes/Misc:
Locations: HSD–W
Catalogs/Checklists: Norton, Whitefield, no. 53

661
Place: Wilmington, Delaware
Date: 1865
Title: A Bird's Eye View of the City of Wilmington
Size: 18¾ × 31¾ in. (47.7 × 80.8 cm.)
Artist: Edward Sachse
Lithographer: E. Sachse
Printer: Sachse & Co., Baltimore
Publisher:
Key/Vignettes/Misc:
Locations: HSD–W
Catalogs/Checklists:

662
Place: Wilmington, Delaware
Date: Ca. 1870
Title: Birdseye View of the City of Wilmington, Del.
Size: 18⁹⁄₁₆ × 31⅞ in. (47.3 × 81.1 cm.)
Artist: E. Sachse
Lithographer: E. Sachse
Printer: E. Sachse & Co., Baltimore
Publisher: Julius Krauspe, No. 500 Shipley St., Wilmington, Del.
Key/Vignettes/Misc: 19 places identified by numbered key in margins
Locations: CHS–C; HSD–W
Catalogs/Checklists:

663
Place: Wilmington, Delaware
Date: 1874
Title: Wilmington, Del. 1874.
Size: 17½ × 38⅛ in. (44.5 × 97 cm.)

Artist: H. H. Bailey & Co.
Lithographer:
Printer: G. W. Lewis, Lith., Albany, New York
Publisher: J. C. Harkness (copyright)
Key/Vignettes/Misc: Refs. 1–90; 1 vignette
Locations: BPL–R; LC–M; DHR–D; HSD–W
Catalogs/Checklists: LC–M, 106

664
Place: Washington, District Of Columbia
Date: 1838
Title: View of the City of Washington The Metropolis of the United States of America. Taken from Arlington House, the Residence of George Washington P. Custis Esq.
Size: 18⁷⁄₁₆ × 36³⁄₁₆ in. (46.9 × 92.1 cm.)
Artist: P.[eter] Anderson
Lithographer: F. H. Lane
Printer: T. Moore's Lithography, Boston
Publisher: T. Moore, Boston & P. Anderson, Boston (copyright)
Key/Vignettes/Misc:
Locations: NYP–S; MM–NN; EI–S; LC–P
Catalogs/Checklists: Stokes P. 1837—F–52; Philips, Washington, p. 36; MM–NN, LP 1103; Wilmerding, no. 148

665
Place: Washington, District Of Columbia
Date: 1848
Title: Washington, From the Presidents House Vue de Washington, Prise de la Maison du President Washington von Hause des Prasidenten Gesehn
Size: 8⅝ × 12⁹⁄₁₆ in. (21.9 × 32 cm.)
Artist:
Lithographer:
Printer: N. Currier 152 Nassau St. Cor. of Spruce N. Y.
Publisher: N. Currier 152 Nassau St. Cor. of Spruce N. Y.
Key/Vignettes/Misc:
Locations: YUAG–NH
Catalogs/Checklists:

666
Place: Washington, District Of Columbia
Date: 1849
Title: View of Washington City and Georgetown
Size: 19½ × 27 in. (49.7 × 68.7 cm.)
Artist:
Lithographer:
Printer: E. Weber & Co., Baltimore
Publisher: Casimir Bohn, Washington, D. C.
Key/Vignettes/Misc: 20 vignettes
Locations: NYP–S; CHS–C; LC–P
Catalogs/Checklists: Stokes P. 1848—F–53

667
Place: Washington, District Of Columbia
Date: 1850
Title: View of Washington
Size: 19 × 29¼ in. (48.4 × 74.6 cm.)
Artist: Robert P. Smith

Lithographer:
Printer:
Publisher: Robert P. Smith
Key/Vignettes/Misc:
Locations: LC–P
Catalogs/Checklists:

668
Place: Washington, District Of Columbia
Date: 1852 State I
Title: View of Washington
Size: 18¼ × 27½ in. (46.4 × 70 cm.)
Artist: E. Sachse
Lithographer: E. Sachse & Co.
Printer: E. Sachse & Co., Baltimore
Publisher: Casimir Bohn, Washington, D. C.
Key/Vignettes/Misc:
Locations: HEHL
Catalogs/Checklists:

669
Place: Washington, District Of Columbia
Date: 1852 State II
Title: View of Washington
Size: 20 × 27⅜ in. (50.8 × 69.7 cm.)
Artist: E. Sachse
Lithographer: E. Sachse
Printer: E. Sachse & Co., Baltimore
Publisher: E. Sachse & Co., 3 North Liberty St., Baltimore
Key/Vignettes/Misc:
Locations: NYP–S; LC–P; CHS–C; ROM; LC–M (facsimile)
Catalogs/Checklists: Stokes P. 1851—G–5; Philips, Washington, p. 40; Samuel, no. 431; LC–M, 106.2

670
Place: Washington, District Of Columbia
Date: Ca. 1852 State I
Title: Washington, D. C. With Projected Improvements. . . .
Size: 24⅝ × 42¹⁵⁄₁₆ in. (62.6 × 109.2 cm.)
Artist: B. F. Smith, Jr.
Lithographer: B. F. Smith, Jr.
Printer: F. Michelin, New York
Publisher: Smith & Jenkins, New York, 1852
Key/Vignettes/Misc:
Locations: NYP–S; LC–P; CHS–C
Catalogs/Checklists: Stokes P. 1851—G–16

671
Place: Washington, District Of Columbia
Date: [1855]
Title: View of Georgetown D. C.
Size: 18⁹⁄₁₆ × 26¾ in. (47.2 × 68 cm.)
Artist:
Lithographer: E. Sachse & Co.
Printer: E. Sachse & Co.
Publisher: E. Sachse & Co., N. 3 N Liberty St. Baltimore
Key/Vignettes/Misc:
Locations: LC–P; LC–M (facsimile)
Catalogs/Checklists:

672
Place: Washington, District Of Columbia
Date: 1856
Title: Panoramic View of Washington City.

From the New Dome of the Capitol, Looking West.
Size: 19¹³⁄₁₆ × 32⁷⁄₁₆ in. (50.5 × 82.5 cm.)
Artist: Edwd. Sachse
Lithographer:
Printer:
Publisher: E. Sachse & Co. Sun Iron Building, Baltimore, Md.
Key/Vignettes/Misc:
Locations: LC–P
Catalogs/Checklists:

673
Place: Washington, District Of Columbia
Date: 1857
Title: Panoramic View of Washington City From the Dome of the Capitol, Looking East.
Size: 20¹⁄₁₆ × 32⁵⁄₁₆ in. (51 × 82.3 cm.)
Artist: E. Sachse & Co.
Lithographer:
Printer: E. Sachse & Co.
Publisher: Casimir Bohn, Washington, D. C.
Key/Vignettes/Misc:
Locations: LC–P
Catalogs/Checklists:

674
Place: Washington, District Of Columbia
Date: 1859
Title: View of Washington City.
Size: 19½ × 27 in. (49.6 × 68.7 cm.)
Artist:
Lithographer: E. Sachse & Co.
Printer: E. Sachse & Co.
Publisher: E. Sachse & Co., Baltimore, Md.
Key/Vignettes/Misc: Unnumbered refs.
Locations: LC–P
Catalogs/Checklists:

675
Place: Washington, District Of Columbia
Date: 1861
Title: Panoramic View of the U. S. Camps Around Washington City in 1861, East. Taken From the Top of the Capitol
Size: 12 × 16½ in. (30.6 × 42 cm.)
Artist:
Lithographer:
Printer: E. Sachse & Co., Baltimore, Md.
Publisher: C. Bohn, Washington, D. C.
Key/Vignettes/Misc:
Locations: ISHL–S
Catalogs/Checklists:

676
Place: Washington, District Of Columbia
Date: 1862
Title: [Untitled View of Washington, D. C.]
Size: 4⅛ × 38¹⁄₁₆ in. (10.6 × 96.9 cm.)
Artist:
Lithographer:
Printer:
Publisher:
Key/Vignettes/Misc: Unnumbered refs.
Locations: LC–P
Catalogs/Checklists:

677
Place: Washington, District Of Columbia
Date: 1862
Title: Birds Eye View of the City of Washington, D. C. and the Seat of War in Virginia.
Size: 22¾ × 33⅜ in. (57.9 × 84.9 cm.)
Artist: John Bachmann
Lithographer: John Bachmann
Printer:
Publisher: John Bachmann
Key/Vignettes/Misc: Refs. 1–44
Locations: CHS–C
Catalogs/Checklists:

678
Place: Washington, District Of Columbia
Date: 1862
Title: View of Washington City, D. C.
Size: 9⅛ × 16½ in. (23 × 42 cm.)
Artist:
Lithographer:
Printer: E. Sachse & Co. 104 S. Charles St. Baltimore
Publisher: C. Bohn 268 Penn. Av. Washington, D. C. (Republished by Charles Magnus, Frankfort St., N. Y.)
Key/Vignettes/Misc: Refs. 1–16
Locations: LC–P
Catalogs/Checklists:

679
Place: Washington, District Of Columbia
Date: 1862
Title: View of Washington City, D. C.
Size: 9¾ × 16⅝ in. (24.8 × 42.3 cm.)
Artist:
Lithographer:
Printer: E. Sachse & Co., 104 S. Charles St., Baltimore
Publisher: E. Sachse & Co. (copyright)
Key/Vignettes/Misc:
Locations: MHS–B; LC–M (facsimile); LC–P
Catalogs/Checklists: LC–M, 106.3

680
Place: Washington, District Of Columbia
Date: 1865
Title: Birds–Eye View of Washington, D. C. and Environs, 1865
Size: 11½ × 17½ in. (29.3 × 44.5 cm.)
Artist: J. Bachmann
Lithographer:
Printer: Kimmel & Forster, 254 & 256 Canal St. N. Y.
Publisher: Kimmel & Forster, 254 & 256 Canal St. N. Y.
Key/Vignettes/Misc:
Locations: NYH–NY
Catalogs/Checklists:

681
Place: Washington, District Of Columbia
Date: 1867
Title: View of Washington City
Size: 18¼ × 27 in. (45.8 × 68.7 cm.)
Artist:
Lithographer: E. Sachse & Co.
Printer: E. Sachse & Co., Baltimore, Md.
Publisher: B. W. Field, New York

Key/Vignettes/Misc:
Locations: Unknown. See Old Print Shop Portfolio, XXVIII, p. 199, No. 12
Catalogs/Checklists:

682
Place: Washington, District Of Columbia
Date: 1867
Title: View of Washington City, D. C. West Front of the U. S. Capitol.
Size: 9⅛ × 16⅝ in. (23 × 42.2 cm.)
Artist:
Lithographer:
Printer: E. Sachse & Co. 104 S. Charles St. Baltimore
Publisher: C. Bohn 268 Penn. Av. Washington D. C.
Key/Vignettes/Misc:
Locations: LC–P
Catalogs/Checklists:

683
Place: Washington, District Of Columbia
Date: 1869
Title: View of Washington City.
Size: 19⅛ × 26¹¹⁄₁₆ in. (48.8 × 68 cm.)
Artist:
Lithographer: E. Sachse & Co.
Printer: E. Sachse & Co., Baltimore
Publisher: J. F. Walker
Key/Vignettes/Misc:
Locations: LC–P
Catalogs/Checklists:

684
Place: Washington, District Of Columbia
Date: 1870
Title: View of Washington City
Size: 17¾ × 26¾ in. (45.2 × 68.1 cm.)
Artist:
Lithographer:
Printer: E. Sachse & Co. No. 5 No. Liberty St. Balto
Publisher:
Key/Vignettes/Misc:
Locations: LC–P
Catalogs/Checklists: Philips, Washington, p. 49

685
Place: Washington, District Of Columbia
Date: 1871
Title: View of Washington City.
Size: 19 × 26¾ in. (48.4 × 68.1 cm.)
Artist:
Lithographer:
Printer: E. Sachse & Co. No. 5 N. Liberty St. Balto.
Publisher: E. Sachse & Co., Baltimore (copyright)
Key/Vignettes/Misc:
Locations: LC–P; CHS–C; LC–M (facsimile)
Catalogs/Checklists: Philips, Washington, p. 49; LC–M, 106.5

686
Place: Washington, District Of Columbia
Date: Ca. 1872
Title: Bird's–Eye–View of Washington City, D. C.
Size: 14½ × 22⅜ in. (37 × 57 cm.)

Artist: Geo. A. Morrison
Lithographer:
Printer:
Publisher: W. H. & O. H. Morrison
Key/Vignettes/Misc:
Locations: LC–M
Catalogs/Checklists: LC–M, 107

687
Place: Washington, District Of Columbia
Date: 1880
Title: The City of Washington. Bird's–Eye View from the Potomac—Looking North.
Size: 20½ × 33⅛ in. (52.2 × 84.3 cm.)
Artist: C. R. Parsons
Lithographer:
Printer:
Publisher: Currier & Ives, New York
Key/Vignettes/Misc: Unnumbered refs. below places identified
Locations: LC–P; CHS–C
Catalogs/Checklists: Philips, Washington, p. 54; Peters, C & I, 3908; Conningham 1122; LC–M, 107.1

688
Place: Washington, District Of Columbia
Date: [1883?]
Title: The National Capital Washington City, D. C.
Size: 39⅝ × 33¹³⁄₁₆ in. (108 × 86 cm.)
Artist:
Lithographer:
Printer:
Publisher: Sachse & Co., Baltimore
Key/Vignettes/Misc:
Locations: LC–M
Catalogs/Checklists: LC–M, 109

689
Place: Washington, District Of Columbia
Date: 1884
Title: The National Capital, Washington, D. C. Sketched from Nature. . .1883–1884.
Size: 39⅝ × 64⅞ in. (108 × 165 cm.)
Artist: Adolph Sachse
Lithographer:
Printer: A. Sachse & Co., Balti[more]
Publisher: A. Sachse & Co., Balti[more]
Key/Vignettes/Misc: 18 vignettes; advertisements; description
Locations: LC–M
Catalogs/Checklists: LC–M, 110

690
Place: Washington, District Of Columbia
Date: 1888
Title: Birdseye View of the National Capital Including the Site of the Proposed World's Exposition of 1892 and Permanent Exposition of the Three Americas.
Size: 23⅝ × 34⅝ in. (60 × 88 cm.)
Artist:
Lithographer:
Printer: A. Hoen & Co., Baltimore
Publisher: E. Kurtz Johnson [copyright]
Key/Vignettes/Misc: Unnumbered refs. below places identified
Locations: WHS–M; HEHL
Catalogs/Checklists: Philips, Washington, p. 62

691
Place: Washington, District Of Columbia
Date: 1892
Title: The Altograph of Washington City, or Strangers Guide. An Isometric View of the National Capital, Showing the Public Buildings. . . .
Size: 25 × 35 in. (63.6 × 89.1 cm.)
Artist: James T. Du Bois
Lithographer:
Printer:
Publisher: The Norris Peters Co., Washington
Key/Vignettes/Misc: Description
Locations: LC–M
Catalogs/Checklists: Philips, Washington, p. 62

692
Place: Washington, District Of Columbia
Date: 1892
Title: The City of Washington—Bird's eye view from the Potomac—looking North.
Size: 22¾ × 33 in. (57.9 × 83.9 cm.)
Artist:
Lithographer:
Printer:
Publisher: Currier & Ives, 115 Nassau St. New York
Key/Vignettes/Misc: 60 unnumbered refs. below places identified
Locations: MM–NN; LC–P; MGUR–M; YUAG–NH; LC–M (facsimile)
Catalogs/Checklists: Philips, Washington, p. 63; MM–NN, LP 43; LC–M, 111

693
Place: Washington, District Of Columbia
Date: [1895]
Title: Birds Eye View of Barnes & Weaver's Addition to Brookland
Size: 17½ × 22 in. (44.5 × 56 cm.)
Artist: Gedney & Roberts
Lithographer:
Printer: Barnes & Weaver, Washington, D. C.
Publisher:
Key/Vignettes/Misc:
Locations: LC–M
Catalogs/Checklists: LC–M, 111.1

694
Place: Washington, District Of Columbia
Date: 1921
Title: Washington: The Beautiful Capital of the Nation.
Size: 28¹¹⁄₁₆ × 44⁷⁄₁₆ in. (73 × 113 cm.)
Artist: William Olsen
Lithographer:
Printer:
Publisher: A. B. Graham Co., Washington, D. C.
Key/Vignettes/Misc:
Locations: LC–M
Catalogs/Checklists: LC–M, 111.2

695
Place: Washington, District Of Columbia
Date: 1922
Title: Washington, the Beautiful Capital of the Nation.
Size: 28¹¹⁄₁₆ × 44⁷⁄₁₆ in. (73 × 113 cm.)

Artist: William Olsen
Lithographer:
Printer:
Publisher: Columbia Planograph
Company, Washington, D. C.
Key/Vignettes/Misc:
Locations: LC–M
Catalogs/Checklists: LC–M, 111.3

696
Place: Washington, District Of Columbia
Date: Ca. 1923
Title: Washington, the Beautiful Capital of
the Nation
Size: 19¼ × 29½ in. (49 × 75 cm.)
Artist:
Lithographer:
Printer:
Publisher:
Key/Vignettes/Misc:
Locations: LC–M
Catalogs/Checklists: 111.4

697
Place: Washington, District Of Columbia
Date: N.D.
Title: Birds Eye View of the City of
Washington From the Dome of the U. S.
Capitol
Size: 18⁹⁄₁₆ × 32 in. (47.3 × 81.5 cm.)
Artist: A. Sachse & Co.
Lithographer: A. Sachse & Co.
Printer: A. Sachse & Co. Baltimore &
Eutaw Sts. Balto. Md.
Publisher:
Key/Vignettes/Misc: 18 vignettes
Locations: LC–P
Catalogs/Checklists:

698
Place: Washington, District Of Columbia
Date: N.D.
Title: Washington, D. C.
Size: [View in oval border, ca. 28 in.
across]
Artist:
Lithographer:
Printer:
Publisher:
Key/Vignettes/Misc: [in circle at lower left:
"Compliments of Walter A. Wood Mowing
& Repairing Machine Company Hoosick
Falls N. Y. U. S. A." In Circle at lower
right: "For sale by Enoch Bridges Wilton
Me."]
Locations: Private collection
Catalogs/Checklists:

699
Place: Apalachicola, Florida
Date: 1837
Title: City of Apalachicola
Size: 13 × 21¾ in. (33.1 × 55.4 cm.)
Artist: H. A. Norris
Lithographer:
Printer: N. Calyo, N. York
Publisher: P. A. Mesier and Company Lith
28 Wall Street, New York
Key/Vignettes/Misc:
Locations: BHSP–T; NYH–NY
Catalogs/Checklists:

700
Place: Cedar Keys, Florida
Date: 1884
Title: Bird's Eye View of Cedar–Key, Fla.,
Levy Co. 1884
Size: 9½ × 21⅝ in. (24 × 55 cm.)
Artist:
Lithographer:
Printer: Beck & Pauli, Milwaukee
Publisher: J. J. Stoner, Madison, Wisconsin
Key/Vignettes/Misc: Refs. 1–33
Locations: LC–M; FSU–T
Catalogs/Checklists: LC–M, 111.5

701
Place: Fernandina, Florida
Date: 1884
Title: Bird's Eye View of Fernandina, Fla.,
Amelia Island, County Seat of Nassau
County, 1884
Size: 14½ × 27⅞ in. (37 × 71 cm.)
(facsimile)
Artist:
Lithographer:
Printer: Beck & Pauli, Milwaukee, Wis.
Publisher: J. J. Stoner, Madison, Wis.
Key/Vignettes/Misc: Refs. 2–8, A–H, K;
3 vignettes
Locations: LC–M (facsimile)
Catalogs/Checklists: LC–M, 111.7

702
Place: Gainesville, Florida
Date: 1884
Title: Gainesville. County Seat of Alachua
County Florida. 1884.
Size: 18¹⁵⁄₁₆ × 24 in. (48.2 × 61.1 cm.)
Artist:
Lithographer:
Printer: Beck & Pauli, Litho. Milwaukee,
Wis.
Publisher: J. J. Stoner, Madison, Wis.
Key/Vignettes/Misc: Refs. 1–18, A–G;
unnumbered business directory
Locations: PKY–G; FSU–T; BHSP–T
Catalogs/Checklists:

703
Place: Green Cove Springs, Florida
Date: 1885
Title: Green Cove Springs. County Seat of
Clay County. Florida. 1885.
Size: 18¼ × 27 in. (46.4 × 68.6 cm.)
Artist:
Lithographer:
Printer: Beck & Pauli, Milwaukee
Publisher: Norris, Wellge & Co.,
Milwaukee
Key/Vignettes/Misc: Refs. 1–39;
description
Locations: LC–M; FSU–T; University of
South Florida Library, Tampa, Florida
Catalogs/Checklists: LC–M, 112

704
Place: Jacksonville, Florida
Date: 1876
Title: Birds Eye View of Jacksonville, Fla.
Size: 25 × 30½ in. (63.6 × 77.6 cm.)
Artist: Augustus Koch
Lithographer:

Printer:
Publisher: Alvord, Kellog & Campbell
Key/Vignettes/Misc: Refs. 1–40
Locations: LC–M; FSU–T; LC–P
Catalogs/Checklists: LC–M, 113

705
Place: Jacksonville, Florida
Date: 1893
Title: Jacksonville, Florida
Size: 26¾ × 37½ in. (68 × 95.3 cm.)
Artist: Augustus Koch
Lithographer:
Printer: Hudson–Kimberly Publishing
Co., [Kansas City] Mo.
Publisher: Augustus Koch
Key/Vignettes/Misc: Refs. 1–90
Locations: MM–NN; LC–M; FSU–T
Catalogs/Checklists: MM–NN, LP 4371;
LC–M, 114

706
Place: Jacksonville, Florida
Date: N.D.
Title: Jacksonville, Florida
Size: 24 × 32¼ in. (61.1 × 82.1 cm.)
Artist:
Lithographer:
Printer: Cowford Blueprinting, Inc.
Publisher:
Key/Vignettes/Misc: Refs. 1–108, A–G
Locations: BHSP–T
Catalogs/Checklists:

707
Place: Key West, Florida
Date: Ca. 1855
Title: City of Keywest (Florida)
Size: 12½ × 18¾ in. (31.9 × 47.7 cm.)
Artist: James C. Clapp
Lithographer: Provost
Printer: Lemercier, Paris
Publisher: Goupil & Co, New York
Key/Vignettes/Misc:
Locations: MM–NN; WRHS–C;
NYH–NY
Catalogs/Checklists: MM–NN, LP 1689

708
Place: Key West, Florida
Date: Ca. 1855
Title: Key West
Size: 10 × 20¼ in. (25.5 × 51.6 cm.)
Artist: J. C. Clapp
Lithographer: L. Grozelier
Printer: Chandler & Co. succr. to Thayer
& Co., Boston
Publisher:
Key/Vignettes/Misc:
Locations: MM–NN; NYP–S;
YUAG–NH; LC–M (facsimile)
Catalogs/Checklists: Stokes C. 1855—
G–38; MM–NN, LP 1050; LC–M,
114.1

709
Place: Key West, Florida
Date: 1884
Title: Bird's Eye View of Key West, Fla.
Key West Island. C. S. of Monroe Co 1884
Size: 13 × 25½ in. (33.1 × 64.9 cm.)
Artist: [Henry] Wellge

Lithographer:
Printer: Beck & Pauli, Litho. Milwaukee, Wis.
Publisher: J. J. Stoner, Madison, Wis.
Key/Vignettes/Misc: Refs. 1–78
Locations: Monroe County Public Library, Key West, Florida
Catalogs/Checklists:

710
Place: Lake City, Florida
Date: 1885
Title: Panoramic–View of Lake City, Fla. County Seat of Columbia Cty. 1885.
Size: 10¼ × 22⅜ in. (26 × 57 cm.)
Artist: H. Wellge
Lithographer:
Printer: Beck & Pauli, Milwaukee, Wis.
Publisher: Norris, Wellge & Co.
Key/Vignettes/Misc: Refs. 1–49
Locations: LC–M; FSU–T
Catalogs/Checklists: LC–M, 115

711
Place: Longwood, Florida
Date: 1885
Title: Birds Eye View of Longwood, Florida. Orange County 1885
Size: 22 × 34 in. (56 × 86.5 cm.)
Artist: G. A. Miller
Lithographer:
Printer: Forbes Co. Photo–lith
Publisher: P. A. Demens & Co.
Key/Vignettes/Misc: 6 vignettes
Locations: LC–M; FSU–T
Catalogs/Checklists: LC–M, 116

712
Place: Monticello, Florida
Date: 1885
Title: View of Monticello, Fla. County–Seat of Jefferson Cy. 1885.
Size: 11⁷⁄₁₆ × 17⅜ in. (29.1 × 44.3 cm.)
Artist: H. Wellge
Lithographer:
Printer: Beck & Pauli, Milwaukee, Wis.
Publisher: Norris, Wellge & Co., No. 107 Wells St., Milwaukee, Wis.
Key/Vignettes/Misc: Refs. 1–23
Locations: LC–P; FSU–T (photo)
Catalogs/Checklists:

713
Place: Ocala, Florida
Date: 1892
Title: Bird's Eye View of Ocala Marion County Fla. 1892
Size: ca. 22 × 35 in. (56 × 89.1 cm.)
Artist: Augustus Koch
Lithographer:
Printer: Hudson–Kimberly Pub. Co., Kansas City, Mo.
Publisher:
Key/Vignettes/Misc:
Locations: Central Florida Regional Library, Ocala, Florida
Catalogs/Checklists:

714
Place: Orlando, Florida
Date: 1884
Title: Bird's Eye View of Orlando, Florida.

County Seat of Orange Co. 1884
Size: 11½ × 19¾ in. (29.3 × 50.3 cm.)
Artist:
Lithographer:
Printer: Beck & Pauli, Litho., Milwaukee, Wis.
Publisher: J. J. Stoner
Key/Vignettes/Misc: Refs. 2–10, 12–21, A–D; 1 vignette
Locations: FSU–T (photo); Orange County Historical Museum, Orlando, Florida
Catalogs/Checklists:

715
Place: Palatka, Florida
Date: 1884
Title: Bird's Eye View of Palatka, Fla. C. S. of Putnam County 1884
Size: 13¾ × 22⅜ in. (35 × 57 cm.)
Artist:
Lithographer:
Printer: Beck & Pauli, Milwaukee
Publisher: J. J. Stoner, Madison, Wis.
Key/Vignettes/Misc:
Locations: PKY–G; LC–M (facsimile)
Catalogs/Checklists: LC–M, 116.1

716
Place: Pensacola, Florida
Date: 1885
Title: Pensacola, Fla. County Seat of Escambia County 1885.
Size: 16½ × 25⅞ in. (42 × 66 cm.)
Artist: H. Wellge
Lithographer:
Printer: Beck & Pauli, Milwaukee, Wis.
Publisher: Norris, Wellge, & Co., Milwaukee, Wis.
Key/Vignettes/Misc: Refs. A–H, 2–26; 3 vignettes; unnumbered business directory
Locations: LC–M; PKY–G; FSU–T; Pensacola Historical Society, Pensacola, Florida
Catalogs/Checklists: LC–M, 117

717
Place: Pensacola, Florida
Date: 1896
Title: Bird's Eye View of Pensacola, County Seat of Escambia County, Florida, the Only Natural Deep Water Harbor on the Gulf.
Size: 29½ × 41½ in. (75.1 × 105.5 cm.)
Artist: Augustus Koch
Lithographer:
Printer: Clinton Lith. Co., Chicago
Publisher: Thos. C. Watson & Co., Pensacola
Key/Vignettes/Misc: Refs. 1–70; 2 vignettes
Locations: PKY–G (facsimile); Thomas C. Watson, Mutual Federal Savings & Loan Associaton, Pensacola, Florida; LC–M (facsimile)
Catalogs/Checklists: LC–M, 117.3

718
Place: Saint Augustine, Florida
Date: 1885
Title: View of the City of St. Augustine,

Fla. The Oldest Town in the United States. . .1885.
Size: 13¼ × 20⅛ in. (33.8 × 51.2 cm.)
Artist: H. Wellge
Lithographer:
Printer:
Publisher: Norris, Wellge, & Swift, Brockton, Mass.
Key/Vignettes/Misc: Refs. 1–54
Locations: BPL–R
Catalogs/Checklists:

719
Place: Saint Augustine, Florida
Date: [1887]
Title: Birds Eye View of St. Augustine, Florida
Size: 15⅜ × 24½ in. (39.1 × 62.4 cm.)
Artist: Augustus Koch
Lithographer:
Printer: Matthews–Northrup Co., Buffalo
Publisher: H. J. Ritchie, St. Augustine (copyright)
Key/Vignettes/Misc:
Locations: Library, Castillo San Marcos National Monument, St. Augustine, Florida
Catalogs/Checklists:

720
Place: Saint Augustine, Florida
Date: N.D.
Title: View of St. Augustine, East Florida.
Size: 4⁹⁄₁₆ × 55⅝ in. (11.5 × 141.2 cm.)
Artist: John Horton
Lithographer: John Horton
Printer:
Publisher:
Key/Vignettes/Misc: Refs. 1–23
Locations: LC–P
Catalogs/Checklists:

721
Place: Tallahassee, Florida
Date: 1885
Title: View of the City of Tallahassee. State Capital of Florida, County Seat of Leon County 1885.
Size: 17 × 23½ in. (43.3 × 59.8 cm.)
Artist: H. Wellge
Lithographer:
Printer: Beck & Pauli, Milwaukee, Wis.
Publisher: Norris, Wellge & Co., North 107 Wells Street, Milwaukee, Wisconsin
Key/Vignettes/Misc: Refs. 1–49; 2 vignettes
Locations: LC–M; FSU–T; BHSP–T
Catalogs/Checklists: LC–M, 118

722
Place: Tallahassee, Florida
Date: 1926
Title: Aero–View of Tallahassee, 1926
Size: 19 × 15 in. (48.3 × 38.1 cm.)
Artist:
Lithographer:
Printer:
Publisher: James Wynne
Key/Vignettes/Misc:
Locations: LC–M; FSU–T
Catalogs/Checklists: LC–M, 119

723
Place: Tampa, Florida
Date: 1892
Title: Bird's Eye View of the City of Tampa Hillsborough County Florida 1892
Size: 24 × 36 in. (61.1 × 91.6 cm.)
Artist: Aug. Koch
Lithographer:
Printer: Hudson Kimberly Pub. Co., Kansas City, Mo.
Publisher:
Key/Vignettes/Misc: Refs. 1–41; 1 vignette
Locations: Private collection
Catalogs/Checklists:

724
Place: Albany, Georgia
Date: 1885
Title: View of the City of Albany, Ga. (the Artesian City) County–Seat of Dougherty–County. 1885.
Size: 10⅝ × 23⅛ in. (27 × 59 cm.)
Artist:
Lithographer:
Printer: Beck & Pauli, Milwaukee, Wis.
Publisher: Norris, Wellge & Co., Milwaukee
Key/Vignettes/Misc: Refs. 1–51; 1 vignette
Locations: LC–M
Catalogs/Checklists: LC–M, 120

725
Place: Americus, Georgia
Date: 1883
Title:
Size:
Artist:
Lithographer:
Printer:
Publisher:
Key/Vignettes/Misc:
Locations: Lake Blackshear Regional Library, Americus, Georgia
Catalogs/Checklists:

726
Place: Americus, Georgia
Date: 1896
Title:
Size:
Artist:
Lithographer:
Printer:
Publisher:
Key/Vignettes/Misc:
Locations: Lake Blackshear Regional Library, Americus, Georgia
Catalogs/Checklists:

727
Place: Athens, Georgia
Date: 1909
Title: Birds Eye View of Athens, Georgia 1909
Size: 20⅜ × 29⅜ (51.9 × 74.8 cm.)
Artist: A. E. Dow[n]s
Lithographer:
Printer:
Publisher: Fowler & Downs, Morrisville, Pa.

Key/Vignettes/Misc: 6 vignettes
Locations: UG–A
Catalogs/Checklists:

728
Place: Atlanta, Georgia
Date: 1871
Title: Birds Eye View of the City of Atlanta The Capitol of Georgia 1871. Looking North East.
Size: 20½ × 27¾ in. (52.1 × 70.5 cm.)
Artist: A. Ruger
Lithographer:
Printer:
Publisher: A. Ruger, St. Louis
Key/Vignettes/Misc: Refs. 1–23, A–O; 1 vignette
Locations: LC–M
Catalogs/Checklists: LC–M, 121

729
Place: Atlanta, Georgia
Date: Ca. 1892
Title: Bird's Eye View of Atlanta, Fulton Co., State Capital, Georgia. 1892.
Size: 33½ × 52 in. (85.3 × 132.3 cm.)
Artist: Augustus Koch
Lithographer:
Printer: Hughes Litho. Co., Chicago
Publisher: H. G. Saunders & W. L. Kline
Key/Vignettes/Misc: Refs. 1–58
Locations: LC–M
Catalogs/Checklists: LC–M, 122

730
Place: Atlanta, Georgia
Date: 1919
Title: Atlanta.
Size: 18 × 30 in. (45.8 × 76.3 cm.)
Artist:
Lithographer:
Printer:
Publisher: Foote & Davies Co. (copyright)
Key/Vignettes/Misc:
Locations: LC–M
Catalogs/Checklists: LC–M, 123

731
Place: Augusta, Georgia
Date: 1872
Title: Bird's Eye View of Augusta Georgia 1872
Size: 18 × 23¼ in. (45.8 × 59.2 cm.)
Artist: C. Drie
Lithographer:
Printer:
Publisher: J. J. Stoner
Key/Vignettes/Misc: Refs. 1–67; 2 vignettes
Locations: Augusta–Richmond County Museum, Augusta, Georgia
Catalogs/Checklists:

732
Place: Columbus, Georgia
Date: 1872
Title: Bird's Eye View of the City of Columbus Muscogee Co., Georgia. Looking North East 1872
Size: 24½ × 32 in. (62.3 × 81.4 cm.) (facsimile)
Artist:

Lithographer:
Printer:
Publisher: A. Ruger, St. Louis, Missouri
Key/Vignettes/Misc: Refs. 1–26; description
Locations: Historic Columbus Foundation, Columbus, Georgia (facsimile); private collection
Catalogs/Checklists:

733
Place: Columbus, Georgia
Date: 1886
Title: Perspective Map of Columbus, Ga. County Seat of Muscogee County, 1886. Population: 22,000.
Size: 24½ × 36 in. (62.3 × 91.6 cm.)
Artist: H. Wellge
Lithographer:
Printer: Beck & Pauli Lith. Co., Milwaukee, Wis.
Publisher: Henry Wellge & Co., Milwaukee, Wis.
Key/Vignettes/Misc: Refs. A–Z, 1–60; 20 vignettes
Locations: LC–M
Catalogs/Checklists: LC–M, 124

734
Place: Cordele, Georgia
Date: 1908
Title: Birds Eye View Cordele, Georgia 1908.
Size: 18½ × 29 in. (47 × 73.7 cm.)
Artist: A. E. Downs
Lithographer:
Printer:
Publisher: T. M. Fowler & A. E. Downs, Morrisville, Pa.
Key/Vignettes/Misc:
Locations: LC–M
Catalogs/Checklists: LC–M, 125

735
Place: Fitzgerald, Georgia
Date: 1908
Title: Bird's Eye View of Fitzgerald, Georgia 1908.
Size: 23 × 29 in. (58.6 × 73.8 cm.)
Artist: T. M. Fowler
Lithographer:
Printer:
Publisher: T. M. Fowler, Morrisville, Pa.
Key/Vignettes/Misc: 17 vignettes
Locations: LC–M
Catalogs/Checklists: LC–M, 126

736
Place: Macon, Georgia
Date: 1872
Title: Bird's Eye View of Macon, Georgia 1872
Size: 17½ × 20 in. (44.5 × 50.9 cm.)
Artist: C. Drie
Lithographer:
Printer:
Publisher: A. Ruger
Key/Vignettes/Misc: Refs. 1–37; 2 vignettes
Locations: WML–M
Catalogs/Checklists:

737
Place: Macon, Georgia
Date: 1887
Title: Macon, Ga. County Seat of Bibb County 1887.
Size: 23 × 34½ in. (58.6 × 87.8 cm.)
Artist: H. Wellge
Lithographer:
Printer: Beck & Pauli Lith. Co., Milwaukee, Wis.
Publisher: Henry Wellge & Co., Milwaukee, Wis.
Key/Vignettes/Misc: Refs. A–Z, I–X, 1–55; 12 vignettes
Locations: LC–M; WML–M
Catalogs/Checklists: LC–M, 127

738
Place: Macon, Georgia
Date: 1912
Title: Birdseye View of Macon Ga.
Size: 15¼ × 24 in. (38.8 × 61.1 cm.)
Artist:
Lithographer:
Printer: Barnes Crosby Company, St. Louis, Missouri
Publisher: J. W. Burke Co. Macon, Georgia
Key/Vignettes/Misc:
Locations: WML–M; LC–M
Catalogs/Checklists: LC–M, 128

739
Place: Ocilla, Georgia
Date: 1908
Title: Birds Eye View of Ocilla, Georgia 1908
Size: 19 × 23 in. (48.4 × 58.6 cm.)
Artist: T. M. Fowler
Lithographer:
Printer:
Publisher: T. M. Fowler, Morrisville, Pa.
Key/Vignettes/Misc: 10 vignettes
Locations: LC–M
Catalogs/Checklists: LC–M, 129

740
Place: Pelham, Georgia
Date: Ca. 1885
Title:
Size:
Artist:
Lithographer:
Printer:
Publisher:
Key/Vignettes/Misc:
Locations: Unknown
Catalogs/Checklists:

741
Place: Quitman, Georgia
Date: 1885
Title: Panoramic View of Quitman, Ga. County–Seat of Brooks–County 1885.
Size: 12 × 16½ in. (30.6 × 42 cm.)
Artist:
Lithographer:
Printer: Beck & Pauli, Lith., Milwaukee, Wis.
Publisher: Norris, Wellge & Co., Milwaukee, Wis.

Key/Vignettes/Misc: Refs. 2–33
Locations: LC–M
Catalogs/Checklists: LC–M, 130

742
Place: Savannah, Georgia
Date: 1855
Title: Savannah, Ga. 1855
Size: 24¼ × 37 in. (61.8 × 94.1 cm.)
Artist: J. W. Hill
Lithographer: Chas Parsons
Printer: Endicott & Co., New York
Publisher:
Key/Vignettes/Misc:
Locations: NYP–S; GHS–S; UG–A; MM–NN; NYH–NY
Catalogs/Checklists: Stokes Addenda 1855–Views 9; MM–NN, LP 1000

743
Place: Savannah, Georgia
Date: 1871
Title: Birds Eye View of the City of Savannah Georgia 1871.
Size: 21¼ × 28⅜ in. (54.1 × 72.3 cm.)
Artist: [Albert Ruger]
Lithographer:
Printer:
Publisher: A. Ruger, St. Louis
Key/Vignettes/Misc: Refs. 1–40, A–Y; 2 vignettes
Locations: GHS–S
Catalogs/Checklists:

744
Place: Savannah, Georgia
Date: 1876
Title: City of Savannah, 1776–1876
Size: 10 × 8⅛ in. (25.5 × 20.7 cm.)
Artist: William Brotherhead
Lithographer:
Printer: H. J. Toudy & Co., Philadelphia
Publisher:
Key/Vignettes/Misc:
Locations: UG–A
Catalogs/Checklists:

745
Place: Savannah, Georgia
Date: 1891
Title: Bird's Eye View of Savannah, Ga.
Size: 31 × 39⅛ in. (78.9 × 99.5 cm.)
Artist: Augustus Koch
Lithographer:
Printer: Morning News Lith. Savannah, Ga.
Publisher: Augustus Koch
Key/Vignettes/Misc: Refs. 1–102; 5 vignettes
Locations: GHS–S
Catalogs/Checklists:

746
Place: Tallapoosa, Georgia
Date: 1892
Title: 1892 Tallapoosa, Ga. Haralson Co.
Size: 25 × 31½ in. (63.6 × 80.1 cm.)
Artist: Geo. E. Norris
Lithographer:
Printer: Burleigh Litho. Co., Troy, New York
Publisher: Geo. E. Norris, Brockton, Mass.

Key/Vignettes/Misc: Refs. 1–46; Refs. A–I; 15 vignettes; unnumbered business directory
Locations: LC–M
Catalogs/Checklists: LC–M, 131

747
Place: Thomasville, Georgia
Date: 1885
Title: Thomasville, Ga. County–Seat of Thomas–County 1885. Famous Winter Resort for Northern Invalids and Pleasure Seekers.
Size: 18 × 25½ in. (45.8 × 64.9 cm.)
Artist: H. Wellge
Lithographer:
Printer: Beck & Pauli, Lith., Milwaukee, Wis.
Publisher: Norris, Wellge, & Co., Milwaukee, Wis.
Key/Vignettes/Misc: Refs. 1–30, A–H; 1 vignette; unnumbered business directory
Locations: LC–M
Catalogs/Checklists: LC–M, 132

748
Place: Thomasville, Georgia
Date: 1896
Title: Thomasville, Ga.
Size: 5½ × 9 in. (14 × 22.9 cm.) (photo)
Artist: Henry Moller
Lithographer:
Printer:
Publisher:
Key/Vignettes/Misc: Refs. A–I, K, M–P; R, 1–60; unnumbered business directory
Locations: LC–M (photo)
Catalogs/Checklists: LC–M, 133

749
Place: Valdosta, Georgia
Date: 1885
Title: Panoramic View of Valdosta, Ga. County–Seat of Lowndes–County. 1885.
Size: 10¼ × 17¼ in. (26.1 × 43.9 cm.)
Artist: H. Wellge
Lithographer:
Printer: Beck & Pauli, Milwaukee
Publisher: Norris, Wellge & Co., Milwaukee, Wis.
Key/Vignettes/Misc: Refs. 2–33
Locations: LC–M
Catalogs/Checklists: LC–M, 133.1

750
Place: Honolulu, Hawaii
Date: 1854
Title: No. 1. View of Honolulu. From the Harbor.
Size: 20¼ × 27¼ in. (51.6 × 69.4 cm.)
Artist: Paul Emmert
Lithographer: G. H. Burgess
Printer: Britton & Rey [San Francisco]
Publisher: Paul Emmert
Key/Vignettes/Misc: 14 vignettes
Locations: HHS–H; BML–H; LC–P
Catalogs/Checklists:

751
Place: Honolulu, Hawaii
Date: 1854
Title: No. 2. View of Honolulu. From the

Catholic Church.
Size: 20¾ × 27¼ in. (52.8 × 69.4 cm.)
Artist: Paul Emmert
Lithographer:
Printer: Britton & Rey, San Francisco.
Publisher: Paul Emmert (copyright)
Key/Vignettes/Misc: 16 vignettes
Locations: ACMW–FW; HHS–H; LC–M
(facsimile); BML–H; LC–P
Catalogs/Checklists: ACMW–FW 1074

752
Place: Honolulu, Hawaii
Date: 1854
Title: No. 3. View of Honolulu. From the
Catholic Church.
Size: 20⅜ × 27¼ in. (51.9 × 69.4 cm.)
Artist: Paul Emmert
Lithographer:
Printer: Britton & Rey, Montgomery St.
cor of Commercial [San Francisco]
Publisher: Paul Emmert (copyright)
Key/Vignettes/Misc: 16 vignettes
Locations: HHS–H; ACMW–FW; LC–M
(photo); BML–H; LC–P
Catalogs/Checklists: ACMW–FW 1075

753
Place: Honolulu, Hawaii
Date: 1854
Title: No. 4. View of Honolulu. From the
Catholic Church.
Size: 20¾ × 27¼ in. (52.8 × 69.4 cm.)
Artist: Paul Emmert
Lithographer:
Printer: Britton & Rey, San Francisco
Publisher: Paul Emmert (copyright)
Key/Vignettes/Misc: 16 vignettes
Locations: HHS–H; ACMW–FW; LC–M
(photo); BML–H; LC–P
Catalogs/Checklists: ACMW–FW 1077

754
Place: Honolulu, Hawaii
Date: 1854
Title: No. 5. View of Honolulu. From the
Catholic Church.
Size: 20¾ × 27¼ in. (52.8 × 69.4 cm.)
Artist: P. Emmert
Lithographer: P. Emmert
Printer: Britton & Rey, San Francisco
Publisher: P. Emmert (copyright)
Key/Vignettes/Misc: 16 vignettes
Locations: ACMW–FW; HHS–H; LC–M
(photo); BML–H; LC–P
Catalogs/Checklists: ACMW–FW 1077

755
Place: Honolulu, Hawaii
Date: 1854
Title: No. 6. View of Honolulu. From the
Catholic Church.
Size: 20¾ × 27⅜ in. (52.8 × 69.7 cm.)
Artist: P. Emmert
Lithographer: P. Emmert
Printer: Britton & Rey, San Francisco.
Publisher: P. Emmert (copyright)
Key/Vignettes/Misc: 16 vignettes
Locations: ACMW–FW; HHS–H; LC–M
(photo); BML–H; LC–P
Catalogs/Checklists: ACMW–FW 1078

756
Place: Honolulu, Hawaii
Date: 1857
Title: Diamond Head. from Look–out
Size: 7¾ × 12½ in. (19.7 × 31.8 cm.)
Artist: G. H. Burgess
Lithographer: G. H. Burgess
Printer: Britton & Rey [San Francisco]
Publisher: G. H. Burgess (copyright)
Key/Vignettes/Misc:
Locations: HSL–H; BML–H
Catalogs/Checklists:

757
Place: Honolulu, Hawaii
Date: 1857
Title: Diamond–Head from Honlu Beach
Size: 7¾ × 12½ in. (19.7 × 31.8 cm.)
Artist: G. H. Burgess
Lithographer: G. H. Burgess
Printer: Britton & Rey [San Francisco]
Publisher: G. H. Burgess (copyright)
Key/Vignettes/Misc:
Locations: HSL–H; BML–H
Catalogs/Checklists: Rose, Hawai'i, no. 11

758
Place: Honolulu, Hawaii
Date: 1857
Title: Nuanu Valley. From the New
Church Beritania St.
Size: 7¾ × 12½ in. (19.7 × 31.8 cm.)
Artist: G. H. Burgess
Lithographer: G. H. Burgess
Printer: Britton & Rey [San Francisco]
Publisher: G. H. Burgess (copyright)
Key/Vignettes/Misc:
Locations: HSL–H; BML–H
Catalogs/Checklists:

759
Place: Honolulu, Hawaii
Date: 1857
Title: Port of Honolulu
Size: 7⅝ × 12½ in. (19.4 × 31.8 cm.)
Artist: G. H. Burgess
Lithographer: G. H. Burgess
Printer: Britton & Rey [San Francisco]
Publisher: G. H. Burgess (copyright)
Key/Vignettes/Misc:
Locations: UCBL–B; HSL–H; BML–H
Catalogs/Checklists: Peters, COS, pp. 86,
92; Rose, Hawai'i, no. 10

760
Place: Honolulu, Hawaii
Date: [1857?]
Title: Ewa. From Honolulu
Size: 8 × 12⅜ in. (20.4 × 31.5 cm.)
Artist: G. H. Burgess
Lithographer: G. H. Burgess
Printer: Britton & Rey [San Francisco]
Publisher: G. H. Burgess (copyright)
Key/Vignettes/Misc:
Locations: HSL–H; BML–H
Catalogs/Checklists: Rose, Hawai'i, no. 12

761
Place: Atlanta, Idaho
Date: Ca. 1880
Title: Atlanta. Alturas County—Idaho.

Size: 15⁷⁄₁₆ × 20½ in. (39.2 × 52 cm.)
Artist: E. Green
Lithographer:
Printer: Britton & Rey. S. F. Cal.
Publisher:
Key/Vignettes/Misc:
Locations: ACMW–FW
Catalogs/Checklists: ACMW–FW 1134

762
Place: Boise, Idaho
Date: [1879]
Title: Boise City. Principle Business Houses
and Private Residences
Size: 20 × 26 in. (50.9 × 66.2 cm.)
Artist: Charles Leopold Ostner
Lithographer:
Printer: Britton & Rey, San Francisco
Publisher:
Key/Vignettes/Misc:
Locations: ISHS–B; Boise, Idaho, Public
Library
Catalogs/Checklists:

763
Place: Boise, Idaho
Date: [1890]
Title: Bird's Eye View of Boise City, Ada
County, the Capital of Idaho.
Size: 24½ × 32 in. (62.4 × 81.4 cm.)
Artist: [Augustus Koch]
Lithographer:
Printer:
Publisher:
Key/Vignettes/Misc: Refs. 1–20; 4
vignettes
Locations: Boise, Idaho, Public Library
Catalogs/Checklists:

764
Place: Boise, Idaho
Date: N.D.
Title: View of Boise City, Idaho From the
Court House.
Size: 10¼ × 36½ in. (26 × 92.6 cm.)
Artist: E. Green
Lithographer:
Printer: Britton & Rey, San Francisco
Publisher:
Key/Vignettes/Misc:
Locations: ACMW–FW
Catalogs/Checklists: ACMW–FW 1137;
Reps, Cities on Stone, p. 91

765
Place: Custer, Idaho
Date: 1880
Title: Custer, Idaho—1880.
Size: 15³⁄₁₆ × 22½ in. (38.5 × 57.1 cm.)
Artist: G. W. Hall
Lithographer:
Printer: Omaha Lithographing Co.
Omaha, Neb.
Publisher:
Key/Vignettes/Misc:
Locations: ACMW–FW; ISHS–B
Catalogs/Checklists:

766
Place: Hailey, Idaho
Date: 1884

Title: Wood River Valley with Hailey in the Foreground, 1884
Size: 14½ × 22⅛ in. (36.8 × 56.3 cm.)
Artist:
Lithographer:
Printer: The Collier & Cleaveland Lith. Co., Denver, Col.
Publisher: A. E. Browning, Salt Lake City, Utah (copyright)
Key/Vignettes/Misc: Refs. 1–25, A–Z; description
Locations: Blaine County Historical Museum, Hailey, Idaho; LC–M
Catalogs/Checklists: LC–M, 134

767
Place: Moscow, Idaho
Date: 1897
Title: Bird's Eye View of the City of Moscow, Latah County, Idaho. 1887
Size: 24 × 32 in. (61.1 × 81.4 cm.)
Artist: Augustus Koch
Lithographer:
Printer:
Publisher:
Key/Vignettes/Misc: Refs. 1–32; 1 vignette
Locations: Library, University of Idaho, Moscow, Idaho
Catalogs/Checklists:

768
Place: Quartzburg, Idaho
Date: Ca. 1880
Title: Quartzburgh. Boise Co., Idaho Ty
Size: 9½ × 15 in. (24.2 × 38.2 cm.)
Artist: H. Steinegger
Lithographer:
Printer: Britton & Rey, San Francisco
Publisher:
Key/Vignettes/Misc:
Locations: ISHS–B
Catalogs/Checklists:

769
Place: Rocky Bar, Idaho
Date: Ca. 1880
Title: Rocky Bar. Alturas Co., Idaho
Size: 14 × 23¾ in. (35.6 × 60.5 cm.)
Artist: H. Steinegger, E. Green
Lithographer:
Printer: Britton & Rey, San Francisco
Publisher:
Key/Vignettes/Misc:
Locations: ISHS–B
Catalogs/Checklists:

770
Place: Silver City, Idaho
Date: Ca. 1866
Title: Silver City, Owyhee, I. T.
Size: 23 × 28¼ in (58.6 × 71.9 cm.)
Artist: From photographs by P. F. Castleman
Lithographer:
Printer: Grafton T. Brown & Co. Lith. 543 Clay St., San Francisco
Publisher: P. F. Castleman
Key/Vignettes/Misc: 28 vignettes
Locations: ISHS–B
Catalogs/Checklists:

771
Place: Alton, Illinois
Date: 1841
Title: View of Alton, Illinois.
Size: 5⅝ × 7¹³⁄₁₆ in. (14.3 × 19.8 cm.)
Artist: J. C. Wild
Lithographer: J. C. Wild
Printer: Chambers and Knapp, St. Louis
Publisher: J. C. Wild, St. Louis
Key/Vignettes/Misc:
Locations: SHSM–C; CHS–C
Catalogs/Checklists:

772
Place: Alton, Illinois
Date: [before 1857]
Title: View of Alton, Illinois Taken from the River
Size: 7 × 12 in. (17.8 × 30.6 cm.)
Artist: A. Colon
Lithographer:
Printer:
Publisher: N. Currier
Key/Vignettes/Misc: 12 refs. in two columns
Locations: Unknown
Catalogs/Checklists: Schurre, Currier & Ives Prints, 201

773
Place: Alton, Illinois
Date: [1854–57]
Title: Alton, Jllinois
Size: 5⅞ × 7⅝ in. (15 × 19.4 cm.)
Artist: H. Lewis
Lithographer:
Printer: [C. H. Muller, Aachen]
Publisher: Arnz & Co., Dusseldorf
Key/Vignettes/Misc:
Locations: MHS–SP; SAM–SL; NYH–NY; HEHL; LC–R; NL–C; HNOC–NO
Catalogs/Checklists:

774
Place: Alton, Illinois
Date: 1860
Title: Alton, Ills. 1860
Size: 15½ × 35⅛ in. (39.5 × 89.4 cm.)
Artist: Con Roeder
Lithographer: A. Bottger
Printer: Juls. Hutawa, No. 65 Chestnut St. betw. 3rd & 4th Sts. St. Louis, Mo.
Publisher: Con. Roeder, Alton, Ills.
Key/Vignettes/Misc:
Locations: MHS–SL
Catalogs/Checklists:

775
Place: Alton, Illinois
Date: 1867
Title: Alton. Madison Co. Illinois 1867
Size: 20⅛ × 28½ in. (51.2 × 72.5 cm.)
Artist: A. Ruger
Lithographer:
Printer: Chicago Lithographing Co. [Chicago]
Publisher:
Key/Vignettes/Misc: Refs. 1–17; unnumbered church directory
Locations: LC–M
Catalogs/Checklists: LC–M, 135

776
Place: Aurora, Illinois
Date: 1867
Title: Aurora 1867
Size: 20½ × 27¾ in. (52.1 × 70.5 cm.)
Artist: A. Ruger
Lithographer:
Printer: Chicago Lithographing Co., 154 Clark St., Chicago
Publisher:
Key/Vignettes/Misc:
Locations: LC–M; AHM–A
Catalogs/Checklists: LC–M, 136

777
Place: Aurora, Illinois
Date: 1869
Title: City of Aurora. 1869.
Size: 16¼ × 26¼ in. (41 × 66.5 cm.)
Artist: T. J. Olsaver
Lithographer:
Printer: Chicago Lith. Co. S. Clark St. Chicago
Publisher:
Key/Vignettes/Misc:
Locations: CHS–C; AHM–A; LC–P
Catalogs/Checklists:

778
Place: Aurora, Illinois
Date: 1875
Title: Aurora, Ill. 1875. From Jennings Seminary. Population 16,000
Size: 14½ × 30 in. (36.9 × 76.4 cm.)
Artist: Geo L. Richards
Lithographer:
Printer: National Lith. Institute, Chicago
Publisher: Mason & Richards
Key/Vignettes/Misc: 21 unnumbered refs. below places identified
Locations: AHM–A
Catalogs/Checklists:

779
Place: Aurora, Illinois
Date: 1882
Title: Aurora, Illinois 1882
Size: 18¹⁄₁₆ × 31⁷⁄₁₆ in. (46 × 80 cm.)
Artist: H. Brosius
Lithographer:
Printer: Beck & Pauli, Lith, Milwaukee, Wis.
Publisher: J. J. Stoner, Madison, Wis.
Key/Vignettes/Misc: Refs. 1–66
Locations: LC–M; LC–P
Catalogs/Checklists: LC–M, 137

780
Place: Batavia, Illinois
Date: 1869
Title: Bird's Eye View of Batavia Kane County Illinois Looking South West.
Size: 17¾ × 22 in. (45.1 × 55.9 cm.)
Artist: A. Ruger
Lithographer:
Printer: Merchants Lithographing Co., Chicago
Publisher:
Key/Vignettes/Misc: Refs. 1–11; 3 vignettes
Locations: LC–M
Catalogs/Checklists: LC–M, 138

781
Place: Belleville, Illinois
Date: 1859
Title: Belleville, Ills. Taken from Eimersberg
Size: 21 × 26½ in. (53.5 × 67.4 cm.)
Artist: N. Roesler
Lithographer: N. Roesler
Printer: A. McLean, 15 Chestnut Str, St. Louis
Publisher:
Key/Vignettes/Misc: 10 vignettes
Locations: SCHS–B
Catalogs/Checklists:

782
Place: Belleville, Illinois
Date: Ca. 1860
Title: Belleville, Ill.
Size: 20½ × 30 in. (52.2 × 76.3 cm.)
Artist:
Lithographer:
Printer: Th. Schrader
Publisher: Th. Schrader, St. Louis, Mo.
Key/Vignettes/Misc: 15 vignettes
Locations: SCHS–B
Catalogs/Checklists:

783
Place: Belleville, Illinois
Date: 1867
Title: Bellville St. Clair Co. Illinois 1867.
Size: 19¾ × 27½ in. (50.2 × 69.9 cm.)
Artist: A. Ruger
Lithographer:
Printer: Chicago Lithographing Co., Chicago
Publisher:
Key/Vignettes/Misc:
Locations: LC–M; SCHS–B
Catalogs/Checklists: LC–M, 139

Place: Berlin, Illinois
Date: [1854–57]
See Port Byron, Iowa, [1854–57].

784
Place: Bloomington, Illinois
Date: 1867
Title: Bloomington, Illinois 1867
Size: 19¾ × 28 in. (50.2 × 71.2 cm.)
Artist: A. Ruger
Lithographer:
Printer: Chicago Lithographing Co., Chicago
Publisher:
Key/Vignettes/Misc: Refs. 1–19
Locations: LC–M
Catalogs/Checklists: LC–M, 140

785
Place: Cahokia, Illinois
Date: 1841
Title: Cahokia, Illinois.
Size: 6⅛ × 8⅞ in. (16.0 × 22.6 cm.)
Artist: J. C. Wild
Lithographer: J. C. Wild
Printer: Chambers and Knapp, St. Louis
Publisher: J. C. Wild, St. Louis
Key/Vignettes/Misc:
Locations: SHSM–C; CHS–C
Catalogs/Checklists:

786
Place: Cairo, Illinois
Date: 1838
Title: Prospective View of the City of Cairo, at the Junction of the Ohio with the Mississippi River, Illinois.
Size: 10⁹⁄₁₆ × 19⁷⁄₁₆ in. (25.8 × 49.3 cm.)
Artist: Wm. Strickland
Lithographer: A. Hoffy
Printer: P. S. Duval, Lithogr. Phila.
Publisher:
Key/Vignettes/Misc:
Locations: ACMW–FW; KC–G; ISHL–S; CHS–C; LC–M (facsimile)
Catalogs/Checklists: ACMW–FW 1680; LC–M, 140.1

787
Place: Cairo, Illinois
Date: 1841
Title: Cairo. Illinois.
Size: 5¾ × 9⅛ in. (14.6 × 23.2 cm.)
Artist: J. C. Wild
Lithographer: J. C. Wild
Printer: Chambers and Knapp, St. Louis
Publisher: J. C. Wild, St. Louis
Key/Vignettes/Misc:
Locations: SHSM–C; CHS–C
Catalogs/Checklists:

788
Place: Cairo, Illinois
Date: [1854–57]
Title: Cairo, Illinois, and the Mouth of the Ohio River
Size: 5⅞ × 7¾ in. (14.6 × 19.3 cm.)
Artist: Henry Lewis
Lithographer:
Printer: C. H. Muller, Aachen
Publisher: Arnz & Co., Dusseldorf
Key/Vignettes/Misc:
Locations: MHS–SP; NYH–NY; HEHL; LC–R; NL–C; CHS–C; HNOC–NO
Catalogs/Checklists:

789
Place: Cairo, Illinois
Date: 1867
Title: Cairo. Illinois 1867
Size: 19¾ × 28¼ in. (50.2 × 71.8 cm.)
Artist: A. Ruger
Lithographer:
Printer: Chicago Lithographing Co., Chicago
Publisher:
Key/Vignettes/Misc: Refs. 1–13
Locations: LC–M
Catalogs/Checklists: LC–M, 141

790
Place: Cairo, Illinois
Date: 1888
Title: Perspective Map of the City of Cairo, Ill. 1888.
Size: 18⅞ × 33⅜ in. (48 × 85 cm.)
Artist: H. Wellge
Lithographer:
Printer: Beck & Pauli, lith., Milwaukee
Publisher: Henry Wellge & Co., Milwaukee
Key/Vignettes/Misc: Refs. 1–90; 2 vignettes

Locations: LC–M
Catalogs/Checklists: LC–M, 142

791
Place: Carlinville, Illinois
Date: 1873
Title: Bird's Eye View of Carlinville, Macoupin County, Ill.
Size: 18⅝ × 26 in. (47.4 × 66.2 cm.)
Artist:
Lithographer:
Printer:
Publisher: J. J. Stoner, Madison, Wis.
Key/Vignettes/Misc:
Locations: BPL–R
Catalogs/Checklists:

792
Place: Centralia, Illinois
Date: 1867
Title: Centralia. Mario Co. Illinois 1867
Size: 19½ × 28 in. (49.6 × 71.2 cm.)
Artist: A. Ruger
Lithographer:
Printer: Chicago Lithographing Co. [Chicago]
Publisher:
Key/Vignettes/Misc: Refs. 1–17
Locations: LC–M
Catalogs/Checklists: LC–M, 143

793
Place: Champaign, Illinois
Date: 1869
Title: Bird's Eye View of the City of Champaign Looking from the South East Champaign County Illinois 1869
Size: 20¼ × 26½ in. (51.5 × 67.4 cm.)
Artist: A. Ruger
Lithographer:
Printer: Chicago Lithographing Co., Chicago
Publisher:
Key/Vignettes/Misc: Refs. 1–12, A–B; 2 vignettes
Locations: LC–M
Catalogs/Checklists: LC–M, 144

794
Place: Chenoa, Illinois
Date: 1869
Title: Bird's Eye View of Chenoa McLean County Illinois Looking from the South West
Size: 8¾ × 14¼ in. (22.3 × 36.3 cm.)
Artist: [Albert Ruger]
Lithographer:
Printer:
Publisher:
Key/Vignettes/Misc: Refs. 1–6
Locations: LC–M
Catalogs/Checklists: LC–M, 145

795
Place: Chicago, Illinois
Date: Ca. 1849
Title: View of Chicago as Seen from the Top of St. Mary's College
Size: 6¼ × 9⁵⁄₁₆ in. (15.9 × 23.7 cm.)
Artist: H. Bosse
Lithographer: A. Kollner
Printer: H. Camp, Phila.

Publisher:
Key/Vignettes/Misc:
Locations: NYP–S
Catalogs/Checklists: Stokes C. 1849—
D–9

796

Place: Chicago, Illinois
Date: 1853
Title: Chicago in 1853
Size: 10⅛ × 15⅝ in. (25.7 × 39.8 cm.)
Artist: Geo. J. Robertson
Lithographer: D. W. Moody
Printer: Endicott & Co., New York
Publisher: Smith Bros. & Co., New York
Key/Vignettes/Misc:
Locations: CHS–C
Catalogs/Checklists:

797

Place: Chicago, Illinois
Date: 1853
Title: Chicago, Ill.
Size: 23¹³⁄₁₆ × 37⅞ in. (60.6 × 96.4 cm.)
Artist: Geo. J. Robertson
Lithographer: D. W. Moody
Printer: Endicott & Co., New York
Publisher: Smith Brothers &Co.
Key/Vignettes/Misc:
Locations: CHS–C
Catalogs/Checklists:

798

Place: Chicago, Illinois
Date: 1856
Title: Chicago.
Size: 8½ × 10¾ in. (21.6 × 27.3 cm.)
Artist:
Lithographer:
Printer: Charles Magnus
Publisher: Charles Magnus & Co., New
York
Key/Vignettes/Misc:
Locations: CHS–C
Catalogs/Checklists:

799

Place: Chicago, Illinois
Date: 1856
Title: Chicago.
Size: 4⅜ × 7½ in. (11.1 × 19.1 cm.)
Artist:
Lithographer:
Printer:
Publisher: Charles Magnus & Co., New
York
Key/Vignettes/Misc:
Locations: CHS–C
Catalogs/Checklists:

800

Place: Chicago, Illinois
Date: 1857
Title: Chicago.
Size: 45 × 81⅝ in. (114.3 × 207.3 cm.)
Artist: I. [J.] T. Palmatary
Lithographer: Chr.[istian] Inger
Printer: Herline & Hensel Lith. . .Phila.
Publisher: Braunhold & Sonne, 51–53 La
Salle St. Chicago, Ill.
Key/Vignettes/Misc: Refs. 1–28 & 1–29

Locations: CHS–C; LC–M
Catalogs/Checklists: LC–M, 146

801

Place: Chicago, Illinois
Date: Ca. 1857
Title: Chicago in 1820 Premium to
Palmatary's View of Chicago in 1857
Size: 13¾ × 21½ in. (34.8 × 54.6 cm.)
Artist:
Lithographer: D. Fabronius
Printer: J. Gemmell Lith. 132 Lake St.
[Chicago]
Publisher: Chas. Sonne
Key/Vignettes/Misc:
Locations: CHS–C; NYP–S
Catalogs/Checklists: Stokes P. 1816–20—
F–20

802

Place: Chicago, Illinois
Date: 1860
Title: View of Illinois and Michigan
Central Depot &c. Whitefield's Views of
Chicago. From the Corner of Madison St.
and Michigan Avenue.
Size: 10¾ × 18⅛ in. (27.4 × 46.1 cm.)
Artist: E. Whitefield
Lithographer: Chas. Shober
Printer: Chas. Shober 109 Lake St.
Chicago.
Publisher: E. Whitefield at D. B. Cooke &
Cos. Lake St. Chicago
Key/Vignettes/Misc:
Locations: CHS–C; EI–S; NYH–NY
Catalogs/Checklists: Norton, Whitefield,
no. 75

803

Place: Chicago, Illinois
Date: [1860?]
Title: [Untitled]
Size: 4¾ × 11⅜ in. (12 × 19 cm.)
Artist:
Lithographer:
Printer:
Publisher:
Key/Vignettes/Misc:
Locations: LC–M
Catalogs/Checklists: LC–M, 147

804

Place: Chicago, Illinois
Date: [1860?]
Title: Chicago, Illinois
Size: 9⅝ × 18¾ in. (24.5 × 47.7 cm.)
Artist:
Lithographer:
Printer: Ed. Mendel cor. Lake & La Salle
Strs. Chicago.
Publisher: Rufus Blanchard 52 La Salle St.
Chicago
Key/Vignettes/Misc:
Locations: CHS–C; NYH–NY
Catalogs/Checklists:

805

Place: Chicago, Illinois
Date: 1861
Title: View of the Tremont House nc.
(Corner of Deaborn & Lake Sts.)
Whitefield's Views of Chicago Looking

Down Lake Street.
Size: 10¾ × 18¼ in. (27.4 × 46.4 cm.)
Artist: E. Whitefield
Lithographer: Chas. Shober
Printer: Chas. Shober 109 Lake St.
Chicago
Publisher: E. Whitefield at Rufus
Blanchard 52 La Salle St. Chicago.
Key/Vignettes/Misc:
Locations: CHS–C; EI–S
Catalogs/Checklists: Norton, Whitefield,
no. 88

806

Place: Chicago, Illinois
Date: 1861
Title: View of Clark & Wells St. Bridges E.
Whitefields Views of Chicago From the
Foot of River St.
Size: 10⅝ × 18³⁄₁₆ in. (27 × 46.3 cm.)
Artist: E. Whitefield
Lithographer: Chas. Shober
Printer: Chas. Shober 109 Lake St.
Chicago.
Publisher: E. Whitefield at D. B. Cooke &
Cos. Lake St. Chicago.
Key/Vignettes/Misc:
Locations: CHS–C; EI–S; NYH–NY
Catalogs/Checklists: Norton, Whitefield,
no. 84

807

Place: Chicago, Illinois
Date: 1861
Title: View of Michigan Ave. &c. From
Sturges & Buckingham's Elevator E.
Whitefields Views of Chicago.
Size: 10⁹⁄₁₆ × 18½ in. (26.9 × 47.1 cm.)
Artist: E. Whitefield
Lithographer: Chas. Shober
Printer: Chas. Shober 109 Lake St.
Chicago.
Publisher: E. Whitefield at Rufus
Blanchard, 52 La Salle St. Chicago.
Key/Vignettes/Misc:
Locations: CHS–C; EI–S; MM–NN
Catalogs/Checklists: Norton, Whitefield,
no. 85; MM–NN, LP 2846

808

Place: Chicago, Illinois
Date: 1861
Title: View of Rush St. Bridge &c. E.
Whitefields Views of Chicago From
Nortons Block River St.
Size: 10½ × 18 in. (26.7 × 45.8 cm.)
Artist: E. Whitefield
Lithographer: Chas. Shober
Printer: Chas Shober 109 Lake St.
Chicago.
Publisher: E. Whitefield at Rufus
Blanchard's 52 La Salle St. Chicago
Key/Vignettes/Misc:
Locations: CHS–C; EI–S; MM–NN;
NYH–NY
Catalogs/Checklists: Norton, Whitefield,
no. 87; MM–NN, LP 2845

809

Place: Chicago, Illinois
Date: 1861
Title: View of Sherman House Court

House &c. Looking up Randolph St. Whitefields Views of Chicago.
Size: 10¾ × 18⅜ in. (27.4 × 46.8 cm.)
Artist: E. Whitefield
Lithographer: Chas. Shober
Printer: Chas. Shober 109 Lake St. Chicago.
Publisher: E. Whitefield at Rufus Blanchard 52 La Salle St. Chicago.
Key/Vignettes/Misc:
Locations: CHS−C; EI−S
Catalogs/Checklists: Norton, Whitefield, no. 86

810

Place: Chicago, Illinois
Date: 1863
Title: Michigan Terrace, Michigan Avenue. Looking Towards the Central Depot. Whitefields Views of Chicago.
Size: 10½ × 17⅞ in. (26.7 × 45.5 cm.)
Artist: E. Whitefield
Lithographer: Chas. Shober
Printer: Chas. Shober Chicago
Publisher: E. Whitefield 52 LaSalle St. Chicago.
Key/Vignettes/Misc: Names of occupants
Locations: BPL; CHS−C; EI−S
Catalogs/Checklists: Norton, Whitefield, no. 89

811

Place: Chicago, Illinois
Date: 1864
Title: Chicago, the Metropolis of the Northwest.
Size: 23⅜ × 29 in. (59.5 × 73.8 cm.)
Artist: Louis Kurz
Lithographer: Louis Kurz
Printer:
Publisher:
Key/Vignettes/Misc: 13 (?) vignettes
Locations: CHS−C
Catalogs/Checklists:

812

Place: Chicago, Illinois
Date: [1862−64]
Title: Chicago Ill.
Size: 10 × 19 in. (25.4 × 48.3 cm.)
Artist:
Lithographer:
Printer: Edward Mendel, Cor. Lake & LaSalle Strs., Chicago
Publisher: Rufus Blanchard, 52 LaSalle St. Chicago
Key/Vignettes/Misc: Advertisement
Locations: CHS−C
Catalogs/Checklists:

813

Place: Chicago, Illinois
Date: [1866]
Title: Briggs House
Size: 8¹⁵⁄₁₆ × 11¹³⁄₁₆ in. (22.7 × 29.8 cm.)
Artist:
Lithographer:
Printer: Chicago Lithographing Co. 152 & 154 Clark St. [Chicago]
Publisher: Jevne & Almini [Chicago]
Key/Vignettes/Misc:

Locations: CHS−C; CPL−C; NYH−NY
Catalogs/Checklists:

814

Place: Chicago, Illinois
Date: [1866]
Title: Chamber of Commerce
Size: 8¾ × 12 in. (22.3 × 30.6 cm.)
Artist:
Lithographer:
Printer: Chicago Lith Co. 152 & 154 Clark St. [Chicago]
Publisher: Jevne & Almini [Chicago]
Key/Vignettes/Misc:
Locations: CHS−C; CPL−C; NYH−NY
Catalogs/Checklists:

815

Place: Chicago, Illinois
Date: [1866]
Title: Cor Clark & S. Water Sts
Size: 9¹⁄₁₆ × 12¹⁄₁₆ in. (23.1 × 30.7 cm.)
Artist:
Lithographer:
Printer: Chicago Lithographing Co. 152 & 154 Clark St. [Chicago]
Publisher: Jevne & Almini [Chicago]
Key/Vignettes/Misc:
Locations: CHS−C; CPL−C; NYH−NY
Catalogs/Checklists:

816

Place: Chicago, Illinois
Date: [1866]
Title: Cor Lake & State Sts.
Size: 9 × 11⅞ in. (22.9 × 30.2 cm.)
Artist:
Lithographer:
Printer: Chicago Lithographing Co. 152 & 154 Clark St. [Chicago]
Publisher: Jevne & Almini [Chicago]
Key/Vignettes/Misc:
Locations: CHS−C; CPL−C; NYH−NY
Catalogs/Checklists:

817

Place: Chicago, Illinois
Date: [1866]
Title: Cor Lake St. & Wabash Av.
Size: 9⅝ × 11¾ in. (24.5 × 29.9 cm.)
Artist:
Lithographer:
Printer: Chicago Lithographing Co. 152 & 154 Clark St. [Chicago]
Publisher: Jevne & Almini [Chicago]
Key/Vignettes/Misc:
Locations: CHS−C; CPL−C; NYH−NY
Catalogs/Checklists:

818

Place: Chicago, Illinois
Date: [1866]
Title: Cor. Lake & Wells St
Size: 9⁵⁄₁₆ × 12 in. (23.7 × 30.5 cm.)
Artist:
Lithographer:
Printer: Chicago Lithographing Co. 152 & 154 Clark St. [Chicago]
Publisher: Jevne & Almini [Chicago]
Key/Vignettes/Misc:
Locations: CHS−C; CPL−C; NYH−NY
Catalogs/Checklists:

819

Place: Chicago, Illinois
Date: [1866]
Title: Cor. State & Washington St.
Size: 9¹⁄₁₆ × 12 in. (23 × 30.6 cm.)
Artist:
Lithographer:
Printer: Chicago Lithographing Co. 152 & 154 Clark St. [Chicago]
Publisher: Jevne & Almini [Chicago]
Key/Vignettes/Misc:
Locations: CHS−C; CPL−C; NYH−NY
Catalogs/Checklists:

820

Place: Chicago, Illinois
Date: [1866]
Title: Court House Square
Size: 9³⁄₁₆ × 11¹⁵⁄₁₆ in. (23.4 × 30.4 cm.)
Artist:
Lithographer:
Printer: Chicago Lithographing Co. 152 & 154 Clark St. [Chicago]
Publisher: Jevne & Almini [Chicago]
Key/Vignettes/Misc:
Locations: CHS−C; CPL−C; NYH−NY
Catalogs/Checklists:

821

Place: Chicago, Illinois
Date: [1866]
Title: Crosby's Opera House
Size: 9⅛ × 12¹⁄₁₆ in. (23.2 × 30.7 cm.)
Artist:
Lithographer:
Printer: Chicago Lithographing Co. 152 & 154 Clark St. [Chicago]
Publisher: Jevne & Almini [Chicago]
Key/Vignettes/Misc:
Locations: CHS−C; CPL−C; NYH−NY
Catalogs/Checklists:

822

Place: Chicago, Illinois
Date: [1866]
Title: Custom House
Size: 8¾ × 12 in. (22.3 × 30.6 cm.)
Artist:
Lithographer:
Printer: Chicago Lithographing Co. 152 & 154 Clark St. [Chicago]
Publisher: Jevne & Almini [Chicago]
Key/Vignettes/Misc:
Locations: CHS−C; CPL−C; NYH−NY
Catalogs/Checklists: LC−M, 97.2

823

Place: Chicago, Illinois
Date: [1866]
Title: Great Central Depot Grounds. With Entrance to Harbor
Size: 8¼ × 11¾ in. (21 × 29.9 cm.)
Artist:
Lithographer:
Printer: Chig. Lith. Co. 152 & 154 Clark St. [Chicago]
Publisher: Jevne & Almini [Chicago]
Key/Vignettes/Misc:
Locations: MM−NN; CPL−C; CHS−C; NYH−NY
Catalogs/Checklists: MM−NN, LP 1914

824
Place: Chicago, Illinois
Date: [1866]
Title: Illinois Central Round House
Size: 8⅞ × 11¹⁵⁄₁₆ in. (22.6 × 30.4 cm.)
Artist:
Lithographer:
Printer: Chicago Lithographing Co. 152 & 154 Clark St. [Chicago]
Publisher: Jevne & Almini [Chicago]
Key/Vignettes/Misc:
Locations: CHS–C; CPL–C; NYH–NY
Catalogs/Checklists:

825
Place: Chicago, Illinois
Date: [1866]
Title: Junction of the Chicago River
Size: 8¼ × 11⅝ in. (21 × 29.6 cm.)
Artist:
Lithographer:
Printer: Chicago Lithographing Co. 152 & 154 Clark St. [Chicago]
Publisher: Jevne & Almini [Chicago]
Key/Vignettes/Misc:
Locations: MM–NN; CPL–C; CHS–C; NYH–NY
Catalogs/Checklists: MM–NN, LP 1913

826
Place: Chicago, Illinois
Date: [1866]
Title: La Salle Street From Court House Square
Size: 9 × 11¾ in. (22.9 × 29.9 cm.)
Artist:
Lithographer:
Printer: Chicago Lithographing Co. 152 & 154 Clark St. [Chicago]
Publisher: Jevne & Almini [Chicago]
Key/Vignettes/Misc:
Locations: CHS–C; CPL–C; NYH–NY
Catalogs/Checklists:

827
Place: Chicago, Illinois
Date: [1866]
Title: Lake Street Bridge
Size: 8¼ × 11¾ in. (21 × 29.9 cm.)
Artist:
Lithographer:
Printer: Chicago Lithographing Co. 152 & 154 Clark St. [Chicago]
Publisher: Jevne & Almini [Chicago]
Key/Vignettes/Misc:
Locations: MM–NN; CPL–C; CHS–C; NYH–NY
Catalogs/Checklists: MM–NN, LP 1912

828
Place: Chicago, Illinois
Date: [1866]
Title: Michigan Avenue From the Lake
Size: 8½ × 11⅞ in. (21.6 × 29.9 cm.)
Artist:
Lithographer:
Printer: Chicago Lithographing Co. 152 & 154 Clark St. [Chicago]
Publisher: Jevne & Almini [Chicago]
Key/Vignettes/Misc:
Locations: CHS–C; CPL–C; NYH–NY
Catalogs/Checklists:

829
Place: Chicago, Illinois
Date: [1866]
Title: Michigan Avenue From Park Row
Size: 9¹⁄₁₆ × 12 in. (23 × 30.5 cm.)
Artist:
Lithographer:
Printer: Chicago Lithographing Co. 152 & 154 Clark St. [Chicago]
Publisher: Jevne & Almini [Chicago]
Key/Vignettes/Misc:
Locations: CHS–C; CPL–C; NYH–NY
Catalogs/Checklists:

830
Place: Chicago, Illinois
Date: [1866]
Title: Park Row
Size: 9⁵⁄₁₆ × 11¹⁵⁄₁₆ in. (23.7 × 30.4 cm.)
Artist:
Lithographer:
Printer: Chicago Lithographing Co. 152 & 154 Clark St. [Chicago]
Publisher: Jevne & Almini [Chicago]
Key/Vignettes/Misc:
Locations: CHS–C; CPL–C; NYH–NY
Catalogs/Checklists:

831
Place: Chicago, Illinois
Date: [1866]
Title: Rush Street Bridge From State St.
Size: 8¼ × 11⅞ in. (21 × 30.2 cm.)
Artist:
Lithographer:
Printer: Chicago Litho. Co. 152 & 154 Clark St. [Chicago]
Publisher: Jevne & Almini [Chicago]
Key/Vignettes/Misc:
Locations: MM–NN; CPL–C; CHS–C; NYH–NY
Catalogs/Checklists: MM–NN, LP1911

832
Place: Chicago, Illinois
Date: [1866]
Title: Sherman House
Size: 8¹³⁄₁₆ × 11⅞ in. (22.4 × 30.2 cm.)
Artist:
Lithographer:
Printer: Chicago Lithographing Co. 152 & 154 Clark St. [Chicago]
Publisher: Jevne & Almini [Chicago]
Key/Vignettes/Misc:
Locations: CHS–C; CPL–C; NYH–NY
Catalogs/Checklists:

833
Place: Chicago, Illinois
Date: [1866]
Title: The Chicago Harbor From Rush St Bridge
Size: 8⅛ × 11⅞ in. (20.7 × 30.2 cm.)
Artist:
Lithographer:
Printer: Chicago Lithographing Co. 152 & 154 Clark St. [Chicago]
Publisher: Jevne & Almini [Chicago]
Key/Vignettes/Misc:
Locations: MM–NN; CPL–C; CHS–C; NYH–NY
Catalogs/Checklists: MM–NN, LP 1909

834
Place: Chicago, Illinois
Date: [1866]
Title: Tremont House
Size: 8¾ × 12 in. (22.3 × 30.6 cm.)
Artist:
Lithographer:
Printer: Chicago Lith Co. 152 & 154 Clark St. [Chicago]
Publisher: Jevne & Almini [Chicago]
Key/Vignettes/Misc:
Locations: CHS–C; CPL–C; NYH–NY
Catalogs/Checklists:

835
Place: Chicago, Illinois
Date: [1866]
Title: Union Stock Yards
Size: 8¹⁵⁄₁₆ × 11⅞ in. (22.8 × 30.3 cm.)
Artist:
Lithographer:
Printer: Chicago Lithographing Co. 152 & 154 Clark St. [Chicago]
Publisher: Jevne & Almini [Chicago]
Key/Vignettes/Misc:
Locations: CHS–C; CPL–C; NYH–NY
Catalogs/Checklists:

836
Place: Chicago, Illinois
Date: [1866]
Title: View from 12th Street Bridge
Size: 8¼ × 11⅞ in. (21 × 30.2 cm.)
Artist:
Lithographer:
Printer: Chicago Lithographing Co. 152 & 154 Clark St. [Chicago]
Publisher: Jevne & Almini [Chicago]
Key/Vignettes/Misc:
Locations: MM–NN; CPL–C; CHS–C; NYH–NY
Catalogs/Checklists: MM–NN, LP 1915

837
Place: Chicago, Illinois
Date: [1866]
Title: View From Lake View House
Size: 8¾ × 12⅛ in. (22.3 × 30.8 cm.)
Artist:
Lithographer:
Printer: Chicago Lithographing Co. 152 & 154 Clark St. [Chicago]
Publisher: Jevne & Almini [Chicago]
Key/Vignettes/Misc:
Locations: CHS–C; CPL–C; NYH–NY
Catalogs/Checklists:

838
Place: Chicago, Illinois
Date: 1867
Title: Chicago in 1820.
Size: 14⁹⁄₁₆ × 20¹¹⁄₁₆ in. (37.6 × 52.5 cm.)
Artist:
Lithographer:
Printer: Chicago Lithographing Co. [Chicago]
Publisher: H. Henke (copyright)
Key/Vignettes/Misc:
Locations: CHS–C; LC–P
Catalogs/Checklists:

839
Place: Chicago, Illinois
Date: 1867
Title: Wolf's Point in 1833
Size: 15½ × 19 in. (39.5 × 48.4 cm.)
Artist:
Lithographer:
Printer: Chas Shober & Co., Chicago
Publisher: Rufus Blanchard, Chicago
Key/Vignettes/Misc: 2 vignettes, one with refs. A–H
Locations: CHS–C
Catalogs/Checklists:

840
Place: Chicago, Illinois
Date: [1867]
Title: Chicago Water Works
Size: 9⅛ × 11⅞ in. (23.2 × 30.3 cm.)
Artist:
Lithographer:
Printer: Chicago Lithographing Co. 152 & 154 Clark St. [Chicago]
Publisher: Jevne & Almini [Chicago]
Key/Vignettes/Misc:
Locations: CHS–C; CPL–C; NYH–NY
Catalogs/Checklists:

841
Place: Chicago, Illinois
Date: [1867]
Title: Marine Bank Building
Size: 9⁷⁄₁₆ × 11¾ in. (24 × 29.9 cm.)
Artist:
Lithographer:
Printer: Chicago Lithographing Co. 152 & 154 Clark St. [Chicago]
Publisher: Jevni & Almini [Chicago]
Key/Vignettes/Misc:
Locations: CHS–C; CPL–C; NYH–NY
Catalogs/Checklists:

842
Place: Chicago, Illinois
Date: [1867]
Title: View from Van Buren Street Bridge
Size: 8⅛ × 11⅞ in. (20.7 × 30.2 cm.)
Artist:
Lithographer:
Printer: Chicago Lithographing Co. 152 & 154 Clark St. [Chicago]
Publisher: Jevne & Almini [Chicago]
Key/Vignettes/Misc:
Locations: MM–NN; CPL–C; CHS–C; NYH–NY
Catalogs/Checklists: MM–NN, LP 1910

843
Place: Chicago, Illinois
Date: 1868
Title: Chicago in 1868. From Schiller Street North Side to 12th Street South Side.
Size: 19¼ × 35¼ in. (48.9 × 89.5 cm.)
Artist: A. Ruger
Lithographer:
Printer: Chicago Lithographing Co. 152 & 154 Clark [Chicago]
Publisher:
Key/Vignettes/Misc: 1 vignette
Locations: CHS–C; LC–M
Catalogs/Checklists: LC–M, 148

844
Place: Chicago, Illinois
Date: 1871
Title: The Burning of Chicago. . . .
Size: 11 × 15 in. (28 × 38.2 cm.)
Artist:
Lithographer:
Printer:
Publisher: Currier & Ives, 125 Nassau Street, N. Y.
Key/Vignettes/Misc: Description
Locations: ISHL–S; WRHS–C
Catalogs/Checklists:

845
Place: Chicago, Illinois
Date: 1871
Title: The Great Fire at Chicago Oct. 9th. 1871. View from the West Side
Size: 11⁹⁄₁₆ × 15⅝ in. (29.4 × 39.8 cm.)
Artist:
Lithographer:
Printer: Gibson & Co.s Steam Press. 167 Elm St., Cin. O.
Publisher:
Key/Vignettes/Misc:
Locations: NYP–S; CHS–C
Catalogs/Checklists: Stokes 1871—G–90

846
Place: Chicago, Illinois
Date: 1871
Title: The Great Fire at Chicago, Oct. 8th 1871. (View from the West Side)
Size: 18⁹⁄₁₆ × 24½ in. (47.3 × 62.3 cm.)
Artist:
Lithographer:
Printer: Gibson & Co.'s Steam Press, 167 Elm St., Cin., Ohio
Publisher: Currier & Ives [New York]
Key/Vignettes/Misc:
Locations: LC–P
Catalogs/Checklists:

847
Place: Chicago, Illinois
Date: 1871
Title: The Great Fire at Chicago, Octr. 8th, 1871.
Size: 17¼ × 24⅜ in. (44 × 62 cm.)
Artist:
Lithographer:
Printer:
Publisher: Currier & Ives, New York
Key/Vignettes/Misc:
Locations: CHS–C
Catalogs/Checklists: Conningham 2615

848
Place: Chicago, Illinois
Date: Ca. 1871
Title: Chicago, As it Was.
Size: 9⁷⁄₁₆ × 12⅞ in. (24 × 32.7 cm.)
Artist:
Lithographer:
Printer:
Publisher: Currier & Ives, 125 Nassau St [New York]
Key/Vignettes/Misc: 6 unnumbered refs. below places identified
Locations: MCNY; YUAG–NH
Catalogs/Checklists: Peters, C & I, 3916

849
Place: Chicago, Illinois
Date: 1872
Title: The City of Chicago as it was before the Great Conflagration of October 8th, 9th & 10th, 1871.
Size: 14⅜ × 19⅞ in. (36.6 × 50.5 cm.)
Artist:
Lithographer:
Printer:
Publisher: Wm. Flint (copyright)
Key/Vignettes/Misc:
Locations: MM–NN; CHS–C; YUAG–NH
Catalogs/Checklists: MM–NN, LP 47

850
Place: Chicago, Illinois
Date: 1873
Title: Chicago 1873.
Size: 16¼ × 22⅛ in. (41.3 × 56.2 cm.)
Artist:
Lithographer:
Printer: G. A. Lott & Co., Lith
Publisher: [K.] E. Minger & Fischer, 1281 S. State St.
Key/Vignettes/Misc: 8 vignettes
Locations: CHS–C
Catalogs/Checklists:

851
Place: Chicago, Illinois
Date: 1873
Title: The Illustrated and Historical Map of Chicago.
Size: 16⅛ × 5½ in. (41 × 14 cm.)
Artist:
Lithographer:
Printer:
Publisher: Great Inter–State [Industrial] Exhibition
Key/Vignettes/Misc: 3 vignettes
Locations: CHS–C
Catalogs/Checklists:

852
Place: Chicago, Illinois
Date: 1874
Title: The City of Chicago
Size: 22⅝ × 32½ in. (57.6 × 82.8 cm.)
Artist: Parsons & Atwater
Lithographer: Parsons & Atwater
Printer:
Publisher: Currier & Ives, 125 Nassau St. New York
Key/Vignettes/Misc: Unnumbered refs. below places identified
Locations: CHS–C; LC–P; WIUL–M
Catalogs/Checklists: Peters, C & I, 3914; Conningham 1095; LC–M, 149.2

853
Place: Chicago, Illinois
Date: 1876
Title: Chicago, Ills. 1876
Size: 22¼ × 35¹¹⁄₁₆ in. (56.7 × 90.8 cm.)
Artist:
Lithographer:
Printer:
Publisher:
Key/Vignettes/Misc: 10 vignettes

Locations: CHS—C
Catalogs/Checklists:

854
Place: Chicago, Illinois
Date: 1879
Title: Birds—Eye—View of Chicago 1879 Taken 2,000 Ft. Above the Crib.
Size: 22 × 36¼ in. (56 × 92.2 cm.)
Artist: Louis Klinckerfues & Jacob Richter
Lithographer:
Printer: Shober & Carqueville Lith Co, Chicago
Publisher: Klinckerfues & Richter (copyright)
Key/Vignettes/Misc:
Locations: CHS—C
Catalogs/Checklists:

855
Place: Chicago, Illinois
Date: 1883
Title: Chicago in 1833 Chicago in 1883
Size: 27¹⁵⁄₁₆ × 21¾ in. (71.1 × 55.3 cm.)
Artist:
Lithographer:
Printer:
Publisher: Chicago Varnish Co. [Chicago]
Key/Vignettes/Misc:
Locations: CHS—C; LC—P
Catalogs/Checklists:

856
Place: Chicago, Illinois
Date: 1883
Title: Chicago in 1833.
Size: 19 × 21¹⁄₁₆ in. (48.3 × 53.6 cm.)
Artist:
Lithographer:
Printer:
Publisher: Chicago Varnish Company [Chicago]
Key/Vignettes/Misc:
Locations: CHS—C
Catalogs/Checklists:

857
Place: Chicago, Illinois
Date: 1883
Title: Chicago In 1883
Size: 10½ × 21¹⁵⁄₁₆ in. (26.7 × 55.9 cm.)
Artist:
Lithographer:
Printer: S. D. Childs & Co., Lithog.
Publisher: Chicago Varnish Co. [Chicago]
Key/Vignettes/Misc:
Locations: CHS—C
Catalogs/Checklists:

858
Place: Chicago, Illinois
Date: 1885
Title: Chicago, Ills.
Size: 21⅝ × 35¾ in. (54.9 × 90.8 cm.)
Artist: Jos. Heger
Lithographer:
Printer: Chicago Lithographing Co. [Chicago]
Publisher:
Key/Vignettes/Misc: 11 vignettes
Locations: CHS—C
Catalogs/Checklists:

859
Place: Chicago, Illinois
Date: 1892
Title: Bird's Eye View of Chicago, 1892.
Size: 16⅞ × 32¼ in. (43 × 82 cm.)
Artist:
Lithographer:
Printer:
Publisher: Peter Roy, Chicago
Key/Vignettes/Misc: Refs. 1–23; 1 vignette
Locations: LC—M
Catalogs/Checklists: LC—M, 151

860
Place: Chicago, Illinois
Date: 1892
Title: The City of Chicago.
Size: 22⅜ × 32⅜ in. (56.9 × 82.3 cm.)
Artist: [Parsons & Atwater]
Lithographer:
Printer:
Publisher: Currier & Ives, 115 Nassau St., N. Y.
Key/Vignettes/Misc: 70 unnumbered refs. below places identified
Locations: CHS—C; LC—M; ACMW—FW; YUAG—NH; LC—P; NL—C; NYH—NY
Catalogs/Checklists: LC—M, 150

861
Place: Chicago, Illinois
Date: 1893
Title: Bird's Eye View of Chicago, 1893.
Size: 14⁹⁄₁₆ × 29⅞ in. (37 × 76 cm.)
Artist:
Lithographer:
Printer:
Publisher: Peter Roy, Chicago
Key/Vignettes/Misc: Refs. 2–9, 11–23; 1 vignette
Locations: CHS—C
Catalogs/Checklists:

862
Place: Chicago, Illinois
Date: 1893
Title: 1893 Grand View of Chicago
Size: 27⅞ × 45³⁄₁₆ in. (71 × 115 cm.)
Artist: Th. Treutlein
Lithographer:
Printer: Eagle Lithographing Co., Chicago
Publisher: Reynertson & Beckerman, Chicago
Key/Vignettes/Misc:
Locations: LC—M
Catalogs/Checklists: LC—M, 152

863
Place: Chicago, Illinois
Date: [1893]
Title: Chicago In Early Days. 1779–1857.
Size: 19 × 23¼ in. (47.6 × 59.1 cm.)
Artist: [Louis Kurz ?]
Lithographer:
Printer:
Publisher: Kurz & Allison, 76 & 78 Wabash Ave., Chicago (copyright)
Key/Vignettes/Misc: Refs. 1–15
Locations: CHS—C; MM—NN;

ACMW—FW; ISHL—S; CPL—C; WRHS—C; LC—P; LC—M (facsimile)
Catalogs/Checklists: MM—NN, LP 787; LC—M, 145.1

864
Place: Chicago, Illinois
Date: Ca. 1893
Title: Chicago in 1832. Wolfes Point.
Size: 15½ × 17⅞ in. (39.4 × 45.5 cm.)
Artist: George Davis
Lithographer:
Printer:
Publisher: Rufus Blanchard, 171 Randolph Street, Chicago
Key/Vignettes/Misc: 1 vignette; population 1837–1891; description
Locations: CHS—C; NL—C
Catalogs/Checklists:

865
Place: Chicago, Illinois
Date: 1896
Title: Panorama of Chicago
Size: 14¼ × 48¾ in. (36.3 × 124 cm.)
Artist: Geo W. Melville
Lithographer:
Printer:
Publisher: Geo W. Melville Pontiac Building, Chicago (copyright)
Key/Vignettes/Misc: Unnumbered refs.; 1 vignette; population and area data
Locations: CHS—C
Catalogs/Checklists:

866
Place: Chicago, Illinois
Date: 1897
Title: Panorama of Chicago
Size: 7½ × 26⅝ in. (19.1 × 67.8 cm.)
Artist: George W. Melville
Lithographer: George W. Melville
Printer:
Publisher: George W. Melville
Key/Vignettes/Misc: Refs. 1–105; 1 vignette
Locations: HEHL
Catalogs/Checklists:

867
Place: Chicago, Illinois
Date: [1897]
Title: All Elevated Trains in Chicago Stop at the Chicago Rock Island and Pacific Railway Station Only One on the Loop
Size: 27½ × 30¼ in. (70 × 77 cm.)
Artist:
Lithographer:
Printer:
Publisher: [Chicago, Rock Island & Pacific Railroad]
Key/Vignettes/Misc: Refs. in table keyed to border numbers and letters; 1 vignette
Locations: CHS—C
Catalogs/Checklists:

868
Place: Chicago, Illinois
Date: Ca. 1898
Title: Bird's—Eye—View of the Business District of Chicago.
Size: 36¹⁵⁄₁₆ × 56¹⁵⁄₁₆ in. (94 × 145 cm.)

Artist:
Lithographer:
Printer:
Publisher: Poole Brothers, Inc., Chicago
Key/Vignettes/Misc: Unnumbered business directory and list of elevated railway stations
Locations: LC–M
Catalogs/Checklists: LC–M, 153

869
Place: Chicago, Illinois
Date: Ca. 1900
Title: Chicago 1833
Size: 24 × 39 in. (61 × 99.3 cm.)
Artist:
Lithographer:
Printer:
Publisher: Lanward Specialty Publishing Company
Key/Vignettes/Misc: 7 vignettes
Locations: CHS–C
Catalogs/Checklists:

870
Place: Chicago, Illinois
Date: 1915
Title: Chicago, Central Business Section.
Size: 10⅝ × 16⅞ in. (27 × 43 cm.) (photo)
Artist:
Lithographer:
Printer:
Publisher: Arno B. Reinchke, [Chicago]
Key/Vignettes/Misc:
Locations: LC–M (photo)
Catalogs/Checklists: LC–M, 154

871
Place: Chicago, Illinois
Date: 1916
Title: Chicago, Central Business Section
Size: 17¹¹⁄₁₆ × 29½ in. (45 × 75 cm.)
Artist:
Lithographer:
Printer:
Publisher: Arno B. Reincke, Chicago
Key/Vignettes/Misc:
Locations: LC–M
Catalogs/Checklists: LC–M, 155

872
Place: Chicago, Illinois
Date: N.D.
Title: Chicago in 1820
Size: 5 × 9 in. (12.2 × 22.8 cm.)
Artist:
Lithographer:
Printer:
Publisher:
Key/Vignettes/Misc:
Locations: CHS–C
Catalogs/Checklists:

873
Place: Chicago, Illinois
Date: N.D.
Title: Chicago in 1820.
Size: 11½ × 22⅜ in. (29.2 × 56.9 cm.)
Artist: C. Inger
Lithographer:
Printer: Chas. Shober & Co.

Publisher: Inger & Botker & Co.
Key/Vignettes/Misc: 1 portrait
Locations: CHS–C
Catalogs/Checklists:

874
Place: Chicago, Illinois
Date: N.D.
Title: Chicago in 1833
Size: 23⅞ × 29¾ in. (60.7 × 75.6 cm.)
Artist: J. B. Thomas
Lithographer:
Printer:
Publisher:
Key/Vignettes/Misc:
Locations: WRHS–C
Catalogs/Checklists:

875
Place: Chicago, Illinois
Date: N.D.
Title: Chicago 1833
Size: 26¼ × 39 in. (66.8 × 99.2 cm.)
Artist:
Lithographer:
Printer:
Publisher: Chicago, St. Paul, Minneapolis and Kansas City Line
Key/Vignettes/Misc: 8 vignettes; advertisements
Locations: CHS–C
Catalogs/Checklists:

876
Place: Clinton, Illinois
Date: 1869
Title: Bird's Eye View of the City of Clinton. DeWitt County, Illinois 1869
Size: 17 × 22½ in. (43.2 × 57.3 cm.)
Artist: A. Ruger
Lithographer:
Printer: Merchants Lithographing Co., Chicago
Publisher:
Key/Vignettes/Misc: Refs. 1–9; 2 vignettes
Locations: LC–M
Catalogs/Checklists: LC–M, 156

877
Place: Danville, Illinois
Date: 1869
Title: Bird's Eye View of the City of Danville, Looking Northwest Vermillion County, Illinois
Size: 18¼ × 26 in. (46.4 × 66.1 cm.)
Artist: [Albert Ruger]
Lithographer:
Printer: Chicago Lithographing Co., Chicago
Publisher:
Key/Vignettes/Misc: Refs. 1–14
Locations: LC–M
Catalogs/Checklists: LC–M, 157

878
Place: Decatur, Illinois
Date: 1869
Title: Bird's Eye View of the City of Decatur Macon County, Illinois 1869
Size: 20 × 25½ in. (50.8 × 64.8 cm.)
Artist: A. Ruger

Lithographer:
Printer: Chicago Lithographing Co., Chicago
Publisher:
Key/Vignettes/Misc: Refs. 1–24; 2 vignettes
Locations: LC–M
Catalogs/Checklists: LC–M, 158

879
Place: Decatur, Illinois
Date: 1878
Title: Decatur, Ill.
Size: 18 × 25 in. (45.8 × 63.6 cm.)
Artist:
Lithographer:
Printer:
Publisher: Beck & Pauli, Milwaukee
Key/Vignettes/Misc:
Locations: BPL–R
Catalogs/Checklists:

880
Place: East Joliet, Illinois
Date: ?
Title: East Joliet from West Joliet School
Size:
Artist: P. M. Radfore
Lithographer:
Printer:
Publisher: Edward Mendel, Chicago
Key/Vignettes/Misc:
Locations: ISHL–S
Catalogs/Checklists:

881
Place: East Saint Louis, Illinois
Date: 1841
Title: View at, Illinois Town.
Size: 5¹⁵⁄₁₆ × 8 in. (15.1 × 20.3 cm.)
Artist: J. C. Wild
Lithographer: J. C. Wild
Printer: Chambers and Knapp, St. Louis
Publisher: J. C. Wild, St. Louis
Key/Vignettes/Misc:
Locations: SHSM–C; CHS–C
Catalogs/Checklists:

882
Place: El Paso, Illinois
Date: 1869
Title: Bird's Eye View of the City of El Paso, Woodford County, Illinois 1869.
Size: 14 × 21 in. (35.6 × 53.4 cm.)
Artist: A. Ruger
Lithographer:
Printer: Chicago Lithographing Co., Chicago
Publisher:
Key/Vignettes/Misc: Refs. 1–11
Locations: LC–M
Catalogs/Checklists: LC–M, 160

883
Place: Elgin, Illinois
Date: 1880
Title: Elgin, Kane Co., Illinois. 1880.
Size: 19½ × 24½ in. (49.6 × 62.3 cm.)
Artist: A. B. Upham
Lithographer:
Printer: Shober & Carqueville Lith. Co., Chicago

Publisher: A. B. Upham
Key/Vignettes/Misc: 2 vignettes
Locations: LC–M; CHS–C
Catalogs/Checklists: LC–M, 159

884
Place: Fort Armstrong, Illinois
Date: [1854–57]
Title: Fort Armstrong
Size: 6⅜ × 8⁵⁄₁₆ in. (16.2 × 21.9 cm.)
Artist: Henry Lewis
Lithographer:
Printer: C. H. Muller, Aachen
Publisher: Arnz & Co., Dusseldorf
Key/Vignettes/Misc:
Locations: MHS–SP; NYH–NY; HEHL;
LC–R; NL–C; HNOC–NO
Catalogs/Checklists:

885
Place: Fort Chartres, Illinois
Date: 1841
Title: Ruins of Fort Chartres
Size: 5¾ × 8⅛ in. (14.7 × 20.7 cm.)
Artist: J. C. Wild
Lithographer: J. C. Wild
Printer: Chambers and Knapp, St. Louis
Publisher: J. C. Wild, St. Louis
Key/Vignettes/Misc:
Locations: CHS–C; SHSM–C
Catalogs/Checklists:

886
Place: Galena, Illinois
Date: Ca. 1844
Title: Galena, Illinois
Size: 20⅝ × 30 in. (52.5 × 76.3 cm.)
Artist: J. C. Wild
Lithographer: J. C. Wild
Printer:
Publisher:
Key/Vignettes/Misc:
Locations: PM–D; Galena Historical
Society Museum, Galena, Illinois
Catalogs/Checklists: Stokes C. 1840(?)—
F–62

887
Place: Galena, Illinois
Date: [1851]
Title: Galena, Ill.
Size: 5¹³⁄₁₆ × 7⅞ in. (14.8 × 20)
Artist:
Lithographer: A. Forbriger
Printer: Onken's Lith. Cin. O.
Publisher: [Otto Onken, Cincinnati, Ohio]
Key/Vignettes/Misc:
Locations: CPL–R
Catalogs/Checklists:

888
Place: Galena, Illinois
Date: 1856
Title: View of Galena, Ill.
Size: 19½ × 36 in. (49.5 × 91.5 cm.)
Artist: E. Whitefield
Lithographer:
Printer: Endicott & Co., New York
Publisher: E. Whitefield, Galena
Key/Vignettes/Misc: Refs. 1–10
Locations: NYP–S; CHS–C; MHS–SL;
Galena Historical Society Museum,

Galena, Illinois
Catalogs/Checklists: Stokes P. 1855—
G–44; Norton, Whitefield, no. 68

889
Place: Galena, Illinois
Date: [1854–57]
Title: Galena, Illinois
Size: 5⅞ × 7¾ in. (14.7 × 19.6 cm.)
Artist: Henry Lewis
Lithographer:
Printer: C. H. Muller, Aachen
Publisher: Arnz & Co., Dusseldorf
Key/Vignettes/Misc:
Locations: MHS–SP; NYH–NY; HEHL;
LC–R; NL–C; CHS–C; HNOC–NO
Catalogs/Checklists:

890
Place: Geneva, Illinois
Date: 1869
Title: Bird's Eye View of Geneva Kane
County Illinois 1869
Size: 18¾ × 22½ in. (47.7 × 57.2 cm.)
Artist: A. Ruger
Lithographer:
Printer: Merchants Lithographing Co.,
Chicago
Publisher:
Key/Vignettes/Misc: Refs. 1–14 & 6–10;
4 vignettes
Locations: LC–M
Catalogs/Checklists: LC–M, 161

891
Place: Grafton, Illinois
Date: [1854–57]
Title: Grafton, Illinois
Size: 6⅜ × 8⁵⁄₁₆ in. (16.2 × 21.9 cm.)
Artist: Henry Lewis
Lithographer:
Printer: C. H. Muller, Aachen
Publisher: Arnz & Co., Dusseldorf
Key/Vignettes/Misc:
Locations: MHS–SP; NYH–NY; HEHL;
LC–R; NL–C; HNOC–NO
Catalogs/Checklists:

892
Place: Henry, Illinois
Date: 1873
Title: Bird's Eye View Henry Marshall
County Illinois 1873
Size: 18 × 24 in. (45.8 × 61.1 cm.)
Artist: H. Brosius
Lithographer:
Printer:
Publisher:
Key/Vignettes/Misc: 18 refs.
Locations: Henry, Illinois, Public Library
(facsimile)
Catalogs/Checklists:

893
Place: Highland, Illinois
Date: 1894
Title: Highland, Ill.
Size: 17 × 30½ in. (43.3 × 77.6 cm.)
Artist:
Lithographer:
Printer: Heinicke–Fiegel Lith. Co., St.
Louis

Publisher: J.S. Hoerner, Highland, Illinois
Key/Vignettes/Misc:
Locations: LC–M; Madison County
Historical Museum, Edwardsville, Illinois
Catalogs/Checklists: LC–M, 162

894
Place: Highland, Illinois
Date: N.D.
Title: Highland, Illinois
Size: 18¼ × 22½ in. (46.4 × 57.3 cm.)
Artist:
Lithographer:
Printer: Th. Schrader, 7 Chestnut St. St.
Louis
Publisher: Th. Schrader, 7 Chestnut St. St.
Louis
Key/Vignettes/Misc: 9 vignettes
Locations: Madison County Historical
Museum, Edwardsville, Illinois
Catalogs/Checklists:

895
Place: Homer, Illinois
Date: 1869
Title: Bird's Eye View of the City of
Homer. Champaign County, Illinois.
1869.—Looking North West
Size: 9½ × 12½ in. (24.1 × 31.8 cm.)
Artist: A. Ruger
Lithographer:
Printer: Merchants Lithographing Co.,
Chicago
Publisher:
Key/Vignettes/Misc: Refs. 1–5
Locations: LC–M
Catalogs/Checklists: LC–M, 163

896
Place: Jacksonville, Illinois
Date: Ca. 1861
Title:
Size:
Artist:
Lithographer:
Printer:
Publisher:
Key/Vignettes/Misc:
Locations: ISHL–S (photo)
Catalogs/Checklists:

897
Place: Kankakee, Illinois
Date: 1869
Title: Bird's Eye View of the City of
Kankakee Looking North East Kankakee
County Illinois 1869
Size: 21 × 26 in. (53.4 × 66.1 cm.)
Artist: A. Ruger
Lithographer:
Printer: Chicago Lithog. Co., Chicago
Publisher: Ruger & Stoner, Madison,
Wisconsin
Key/Vignettes/Misc: Refs. 1–17, A; 2
vignettes
Locations: LC–M
Catalogs/Checklists: LC–M, 164

898
Place: Kaskaskia, Illinois
Date: 1841
Title: View of Kaskaskia, Ills.

Size: 5⅜ × 8 in. (13.7 × 20.3 cm.)
Artist: J. C. Wild
Lithographer: J. C. Wild
Printer: Chambers and Knapp, St. Louis
Publisher: J. C. Wild, St. Louis
Key/Vignettes/Misc:
Locations: SHSM–C; CHS–C
Catalogs/Checklists:

899
Place: Lincoln, Illinois
Date: 1869
Title: Bird's Eye View of the City of
Lincoln Logan County, Illinois 1869
Size: 20 × 26 in. (50.8 × 66.1 cm.)
Artist: [Albert Ruger]
Lithographer:
Printer: Merchant's Lithographing Co.,
Chicago, Ills.
Publisher: Ruger & Stoner
Key/Vignettes/Misc: Refs. 1–17; 2
vignettes
Locations: LC–M
Catalogs/Checklists: LC–M, 165

900
Place: Loda, Illinois
Date: 1869
Title: Loda. Iroquois Co. Illinois 1869
Size: 13 × 19¾ in. (33.1 × 50.3 cm.)
Artist: A. Ruger
Lithographer:
Printer: Chicago Lithographing Co.
[Chicago]
Publisher:
Key/Vignettes/Misc: Refs. 1–6
Locations: LC–M
Catalogs/Checklists: LC–M, 166

901
Place: Manteno, Illinois
Date: 1869
Title: Bird's Eye View of the City of
Manteno. Kankakee County Illinois 1869
Size: 9½ × 12½ in. (24.1 × 31.8 cm.)
Artist: A. Ruger
Lithographer:
Printer: Merchants Lithographing Co.,
Chicago
Publisher:
Key/Vignettes/Misc: Refs. 1–5
Locations: LC–M
Catalogs/Checklists: LC–M, 167

902
Place: Marshall, Illinois
Date: 1880
Title: Bird's Eye View of Marshall, C. S. of
Clark Co. Ill. 1880.
Size: 13 × 23 in. (33.1 × 58.6 cm.)
Artist:
Lithographer:
Printer:
Publisher:
Key/Vignettes/Misc: Refs. 1–10, 13,
13–20
Locations: ISHL–S; FSU–T
Catalogs/Checklists:

903
Place: Mattoon, Illinois
Date: 1884

Title: Birds Eye View of Mattoon, Illinois,
1884
Size: 19½ × 29¼ in. (49.6 × 74.4 cm.)
Artist: J. W. Smith
Lithographer:
Printer: Shober & Carqueville
Lithographing Co., Chicago
Publisher:
Key/Vignettes/Misc: Refs. 1–51; 5
vignettes
Locations: LC–M
Catalogs/Checklists: LC–M, 167.1

904
Place: Maywood, Illinois
Date: 1873
Title: Birds Eye View of Maywood 1873.
Size: 12⅛ × 25½ in. (30.5 × 64.5 cm.)
Artist: Augustus Koch
Lithographer:
Printer: Chas. Shober & Co., Prop.
Chicago Lith. Co.
Publisher:
Key/Vignettes/Misc: Refs. 1–6
Locations: CHS–C
Catalogs/Checklists:

905
Place: Moline, Illinois
Date: Ca. 1840
Title: View of Moline, Ill.
Size: 12¾ × 19¾ in. (32.5 × 50.3 cm.)
Artist: After J. C. Wild
Lithographer:
Printer:
Publisher:
Key/Vignettes/Misc:
Locations: Unknown. See Old Print Shop,
Portfolio, XXXII, No. 1, item 34
Catalogs/Checklists:

Place: Moline, Illinois
Date: 1844
See Fort Armstrong, Iowa, 1844.

906
Place: Moline, Illinois
Date: 1854
Title: South View of Moline Ills 1854
Size: 20¼ × 30¼ (51.6 × 76.9 cm.)
Artist: H. C. Ford
Lithographer:
Printer: Schaerff & Bro. St. Louis
Publisher:
Key/Vignettes/Misc:
Locations: CHS–C
Catalogs/Checklists:

907
Place: Moline, Illinois
Date: 1869
Title: Bird's Eye View of the City of
Moline Rock Island County Illinois 1869
Size: 17 × 21¾ in. (43.3 × 55.3 cm.)
Artist: [Albert Ruger]
Lithographer:
Printer: Chicago Lithogr. Co. [Chicago]
Publisher: Ruger & Stoner, Madison,
Wisconsin
Key/Vignettes/Misc: Refs. 1–26; 1
vignette

Locations: LC–M; CHS–C
Catalogs/Checklists: LC–M, 168

908
Place: Moline, Illinois
Date: 1873
Title: Panorama of Moline, Ill. as Seen
from the Island of Rock Island, Ill.
Size: 6⁷⁄₁₆ × 24¾ in. (17 × 63 cm.)
Artist: A. Hageboeck
Lithographer:
Printer: A. Hageboeck, Davenport, Iowa
Publisher: A. Hageboeck, Davenport, Iowa
Key/Vignettes/Misc: Refs. 1–34
Locations: LC–M; WIUL–M
Catalogs/Checklists: LC–M, 169

909
Place: Moline, Illinois
Date: 1889
Title: Moline, Ill. 1889
Size: 15¾ × 26¹¹⁄₁₆ in. (40 × 68 cm.)
Artist: H. Wellge
Lithographer:
Printer:
Publisher: American Publishing Co.,
Milwaukee
Key/Vignettes/Misc: 3 vignettes
Locations: LC–M
Catalogs/Checklists: LC–M, 170

910
Place: Monmouth, Illinois
Date: 1869
Title: Bird's Eye View of the City of
Monmouth. Warren County Illinois 1869.
Size: 20 × 26 in. (50.8 × 66.1 cm.)
Artist: A. Ruger
Lithographer:
Printer: Merchants Lithographing Co.,
Chicago
Publisher:
Key/Vignettes/Misc: Refs. 1–19; 2
vignettes
Locations: LC–M
Catalogs/Checklists: LC–M, 171

911
Place: Mount Sterling, Illinois
Date: 1869
Title: Bird's Eye View of Mount Sterling
Brown County Illinois 1869
Size: 15½ × 22 in. (39.4 × 55.9 cm.)
Artist: A. Ruger
Lithographer:
Printer: Chicago Lithographing Co.
[Chicago]
Publisher:
Key/Vignettes/Misc: Refs. 1–14; 2
vignettes
Locations: LC–M
Catalogs/Checklists: LC–M, 172

912
Place: Mount Vernon, Illinois
Date: 1881
Title: Mount Vernon, Jefferson County,
Illinois 1881.
Size: 12⅝ × 24¼ in. (32.2 × 61.7 cm.)
Artist: H. Brosius
Lithographer:

Printer: Beck & Pauli, Lith., Milwaukee,
Wisconsin
Publisher: J. J. Stoner, Madison, Wisconsin
Key/Vignettes/Misc: Refs. 1–32
Locations: LC–M
Catalogs/Checklists: LC–M, 173

913

Place: Naperville, Illinois
Date: 1869
Title: Bird's Eye View of Naperville,
Dupage County, Illinois
Size: 18¼ × 23¼ in. (46.4 × 59.1 cm.)
Artist: [Albert Ruger]
Lithographer:
Printer: Merchants Lithographing Co.,
Chicago
Publisher: Ruger & Stoner, Madison, Wis.
Key/Vignettes/Misc: Refs. 1–12; 1
vignette
Locations: LC–M
Catalogs/Checklists: LC–M, 174

914

Place: Nauvoo, Illinois
Date: [1854–57]
Title: Nauvoe, Illinois
Size: 5⅞ × 7¾ in. (14.7 × 19.3 cm.)
Artist: Henry Lewis
Lithographer:
Printer: C. H. Muller, Aachen
Publisher: Arnz & Co., Dusseldorf
Key/Vignettes/Misc:
Locations: MHS–SP; NYH–NY; HEHL;
LC–R; NL–C; CHS–C
Catalogs/Checklists:

915

Place: New Salem, Illinois
Date: 1909
Title: [New Salem in 1831–1837]
Size: 19 × 32 in. (48.3 × 81.3 cm.)
Artist: Arthur L. Brown
Lithographer:
Printer: J. W. Franks & Sons, Peoria, Ill.
Publisher: R. J. Onstott, Mason City, Ill.
Key/Vignettes/Misc:
Locations: LC–M
Catalogs/Checklists: LC–M, 176

916

Place: Ottawa, Illinois
Date: 1875
Title: Ottawa, Ills. 1875 Population
10,000
Size: 17¼ × 27⅞ in. (43.5 × 70.5 cm.)
Artist:
Lithographer:
Printer: American Oleographic Co.
Milwaukee
Publisher: Mason & Richards
Key/Vignettes/Misc: 25 unnumbered refs.
in 6 lines
Locations: CHS–C; LC–P
Catalogs/Checklists:

917

Place: Ottawa, Illinois
Date: 1895
Title: Ottawa, Ill., 1895.
Size: 8⅝ × 13⅜ in. (22 × 34 cm.) (photo)

Artist: C. J. Pauli
Lithographer:
Printer:
Publisher: C. J. Pauli, Milwaukee, Wis.
Key/Vignettes/Misc: Refs. 1–32
Locations: LC–M (photo)
Catalogs/Checklists: LC–M, 176.1

918

Place: Pana, Illinois
Date: 1869
Title: Birds Eye View of the City of Pana
Christian County Illinois 1869
Size: 19½ × 25½ in. (49.6 × 64.9 cm.)
Artist: A. Ruger
Lithographer:
Printer: Merchants Lithographing Co.,
Chicago
Publisher:
Key/Vignettes/Misc: Refs. 1–10; 2
vignettes
Locations: Pana, Illinois, Public Library
Catalogs/Checklists:

919

Place: Paxton, Illinois
Date: 1869
Title: Bird's Eye View of the City of
Paxton Ford County Illinois 1869
Size: 15 × 20 in. (38.2 × 50.8 cm.)
Artist: A. Ruger
Lithographer:
Printer: Merchants Lithographing Co.,
Chicago, Ill.
Publisher:
Key/Vignettes/Misc: Refs. 1–8
Locations: LC–M
Catalogs/Checklists: LC–M, 177

920

Place: Pekin, Illinois
Date: 1877
Title: View of Pekin, Ill. 1877. Tazewell
Co.
Size:
Artist:
Lithographer:
Printer: Beck & Pauli, Milwaukee
Publisher:
Key/Vignettes/Misc:
Locations: ISHL–S (photo)
Catalogs/Checklists:

921

Place: Peoria, Illinois
Date: 1858
Title: Peoria. Ill.
Size: 22⅞ × 38 in. (58.0 × 96.5 cm.)
Artist: Charles Peck
Lithographer:
Printer:
Publisher: Reen & Shober, Lithographers
Chicago
Key/Vignettes/Misc:
Locations: CHS–C
Catalogs/Checklists:

922

Place: Peoria, Illinois
Date: 1867
Title: Peoria. Illinois 1867

Size: 20 × 34 in. (50.8 × 86.4 cm.)
Artist: A. Ruger
Lithographer:
Printer: Chicago Lithographing Co.
[Chicago]
Publisher:
Key/Vignettes/Misc: Refs. 1–28
Locations: LC–M; CHS–C; PHS–P
Catalogs/Checklists: LC–M, 178

923

Place: Peoria, Illinois
Date: 1872
Title: Bird's Eye View of the City of
Peoria, Ill. 1872
Size: 25½ × 36 in. (64.9 × 91.6 cm.)
Artist: H. Brosius
Lithographer:
Printer: Chas Shober & Company Props.
Chicago Litho. Co.
Publisher: J. J. Stoner (copyright)
Key/Vignettes/Misc:
Locations: PHS–P
Catalogs/Checklists:

924

Place: Peoria, Illinois
Date: 1877
Title: Peoria, Ill. 1877 Seen from South
West
Size: 16 × 21 in. (40.7 × 53.5 cm.)
Artist:
Lithographer:
Printer:
Publisher: Sicca Soya Paint Company,
3400 South Washington at Krause, Peoria,
Illinois
Key/Vignettes/Misc:
Locations: PHS–P
Catalogs/Checklists:

925

Place: Peoria, Illinois
Date: 1888
Title: Peoria, Ill. 1888
Size: 23½ × 40½ in. (59.8 × 103 cm.)
Artist:
Lithographer:
Printer:
Publisher: [C. J. Pauli & Co.?]
Key/Vignettes/Misc: 16 vignettes
Locations: PHS–P
Catalogs/Checklists:

926

Place: Pontiac, Illinois
Date: 1869
Title: Bird's Eye View of the City of
Pontiac Livingston County Illinois Looking
North West 1869
Size: 17 × 22 in. (43.3 × 55.9 cm.)
Artist: A. Ruger
Lithographer:
Printer: Merchant's Lithographing Co.,
Chicago
Publisher:
Key/Vignettes/Misc: Refs. 1–13; 2
vignettes
Locations: LC–M
Catalogs/Checklists: LC–M, 179

927
Place: Princeton, Illinois
Date: 1870
Title: Bird's Eye View of the City of Princeton Bureau County Illinois 1870 Looking Northeast.
Size: 20 × 26 in. (50.8 × 66.1 cm.)
Artist: Ruger & Stoner
Lithographer:
Printer: Chicago Lithographing Co., Chicago
Publisher:
Key/Vignettes/Misc: Refs. 1–17; 4 vignettes
Locations: LC–M
Catalogs/Checklists: LC–M, 180

928
Place: Quincy, Illinois
Date: 1857
Title: City of Quincy Illinois
Size: 32 × 43 in. (81.4 × 109.3 cm.)
Artist: Edward Everett
Lithographer:
Printer: Sarony, Major & Knapp, 449 Broadway N. Y.
Publisher:
Key/Vignettes/Misc: 2 vignettes
Locations: HSQA–Q
Catalogs/Checklists:

929
Place: Quincy, Illinois
Date: [1854–57]
Title: Quincy, Illinois
Size: ca. 6 × 7½ in. (15.3 × 19.1 cm.)
Artist: H. Lewis
Lithographer:
Printer: [C. H. Muller, Aachen]
Publisher: Arnz & Co., Dusseldorf
Key/Vignettes/Misc:
Locations: MHS–SP; NYH–NY; HEHL; LC–R; NL–C; HNOC–NO; SAM–SL
Catalogs/Checklists:

930
Place: Quincy, Illinois
Date: 1861
Title: Quincy, Illinois, 1861
Size:
Artist:
Lithographer:
Printer:
Publisher:
Key/Vignettes/Misc:
Locations: ISHL–S (photo)
Catalogs/Checklists:

931
Place: Quincy, Illinois
Date: [1860–65]
Title: Quincy, Ills.
Size: 33½ × 48½ in. (85.2 × 123.4 cm.)
Artist:
Lithographer:
Printer: P. S. Duval & Son, Philad.
Publisher:
Key/Vignettes/Misc:
Locations: HSQA–Q
Catalogs/Checklists:

932
Place: Quincy, Illinois
Date: 1870
Title: View of the City of Quincy, Ill.
Size: 23½ × 29½ in. (59.9 × 75 cm.)
Artist: H. L. Haerting
Lithographer:
Printer: L. Gast Bro. & Co., St. Louis, Mo.
Publisher: Haerting and Ortloff
Key/Vignettes/Misc:
Locations: ISHL–S (photo); HSQA–Q
Catalogs/Checklists:

933
Place: Quincy, Illinois
Date: 1878
Title: Quincy, Ill. 1878
Size:
Artist:
Lithographer:
Printer: Beck & Pauli, Milwaukee, Wis.
Publisher:
Key/Vignettes/Misc:
Locations: ISHL–S (photo)
Catalogs/Checklists:

Place: Rock Island, Illinois
Date: 1844
See Fort Armstrong, Iowa, 1844.

934
Place: Rock Island, Illinois
Date: 1869
Title: Bird's Eye View of the City of Rock Island Rock Island County Illinois 1869
Size: 19¾ × 25¾ in. (50.2 × 65.5 cm.)
Artist: [Albert Ruger]
Lithographer:
Printer: Chicago Lithographing Co., Chicago
Publisher: Ruger & Stoner, Madison, Wis.
Key/Vignettes/Misc: Refs. 1–16; 2 vignettes
Locations: LC–M
Catalogs/Checklists: LC–M, 183

935
Place: Rock Island, Illinois
Date: Ca. 1874
Title: Panorama of Rock Island, Ill. as Seen from Davenport, Iowa.
Size: 6¹¹⁄₁₆ × 24⅜ in. (17 × 62 cm.)
Artist: A. Hageboeck
Lithographer:
Printer: A. Hageboeck, Davenport, Iowa
Publisher: A. Hageboeck, Davenport, Iowa
Key/Vignettes/Misc:
Locations: LC–M; WIUL–M
Catalogs/Checklists: LC–M, 184

936
Place: Rock Island, Illinois
Date: 1889
Title: Rock Island, Ill.
Size: 19 × 28 in. (48.4 × 71.2 cm.)
Artist: H. Wellge
Lithographer:
Printer:
Publisher: American Publishing Co., Milwaukee

Key/Vignettes/Misc: Ca. 144 numbered and lettered refs.; 7 vignettes
Locations: LC–M
Catalogs/Checklists: LC–M, 185

937
Place: Rockford, Illinois
Date: [1868–70]
Title: View of Rockford, Ills. From the Seminary.
Size: 16⅛ × 28⅞ in. (41 × 73.4 cm.)
Artist:
Lithographer:
Printer: Western B.[ank] N.[ote] & Engraving Co., Chicago
Publisher: J. H. Wakeman, Rockford, Ills.
Key/Vignettes/Misc:
Locations: CHS–C
Catalogs/Checklists:

938
Place: Rockford, Illinois
Date: 1880
Title: Bird's Eye View of the City of Rockford, Ill. 1880.
Size: 17⅝ × 26¾ in. (44.9 × 68.1 cm.)
Artist:
Lithographer:
Printer: Beck & Pauli, Lith. Milwaukee, Wisconsin
Publisher: J. J. Stoner, Madison, Wisconsin
Key/Vignettes/Misc: Refs. 1–69
Locations: LC–M
Catalogs/Checklists: LC–M, 181

939
Place: Rockford, Illinois
Date: 1891
Title: Perspective Map of the City of Rockford, Ill. 1891.
Size: 20¹⁄₁₆ × 39⁷⁄₁₆ in. (51 × 103 cm.)
Artist:
Lithographer:
Printer:
Publisher:
Key/Vignettes/Misc: 10 vignettes; unnumbered business directory
Locations: LC–M
Catalogs/Checklists: LC–M, 182

940
Place: Sandwich, Illinois
Date: 1869
Title: Bird's Eye View of the City of Sandwich Looking Southwest Dekalb County Illinois 1869
Size: 17½ × 22 in. (44.5 × 55.9 cm.)
Artist: A. Ruger
Lithographer:
Printer: Chicago Lithographing Co., Chicago
Publisher:
Key/Vignettes/Misc: Refs. 1–11; 2 vignettes
Locations: LC–M
Catalogs/Checklists: LC–M, 186

941
Place: Savanna, Illinois
Date: [1854–57]
Title: Savanna, Illinois Savanna in Illinois

Size: 7⅛ × 9¾ in. (18.1 × 24.8 cm.)
Artist: Henry Lewis
Lithographer:
Printer: [C. H. Muller, Aachen]
Publisher: Jnst. Arnz & Co., Dusseldorf
Key/Vignettes/Misc:
Locations: MHS–SP; NYH–NY; HEHL;
NL–C; HNOC–NO; LC–R
Catalogs/Checklists:

942
Place: Shelbyville, Illinois
Date: 1869
Title: Bird's Eye View of the City of
Shelbyville. Shelby County, Illinois 1869
Size: 19¾ × 25¾ in. (50.2 × 65.5 cm.)
Artist: A. Ruger
Lithographer:
Printer: Merchants Lithographing Co.,
Chicago, Ill.
Publisher:
Key/Vignettes/Misc: Refs. 1–7; 3
vignettes
Locations: LC–M
Catalogs/Checklists: LC–M, 187

943
Place: Springfield, Illinois
Date: 1860
Title: Springfield Illinois 1860
Size: 17 × 27 in. (43.3 × 68.7 cm.)
Artist: H. G. Haerting
Lithographer:
Printer: L. Gast, Bro. & Co. St. Louis, Mo.
Publisher:
Key/Vignettes/Misc: 18 vignettes
Locations: CHS–C
Catalogs/Checklists:

944
Place: Springfield, Illinois
Date: 1867
Title: Springfield Illinois 1867.
Size: 20 × 33¾ in. (50.8 × 85.8 cm.)
Artist: A. Ruger
Lithographer:
Printer: Chicago Lithographing Co.
[Chicago]
Publisher:
Key/Vignettes/Misc: Refs. A, 1–34
Locations: LC–M
Catalogs/Checklists: LC–M, 188

945
Place: Springfield, Illinois
Date: Ca. 1870
Title: Springfield, Ill.
Size: 19 × 25⁷⁄₁₆ in. (48.4 × 64.8 cm.)
Artist:
Lithographer:
Printer: Beck & Pauli, Milwaukee, Wis.
Publisher: A. C. Gieseler & Co.
Key/Vignettes/Misc: 40 refs.
Locations: ISHL–S; Sangamon Valley
Collection, Lincoln Library, Springfield,
Illinois
Catalogs/Checklists:

946
Place: Springfield, Illinois
Date: Ca. 1872
Title: Bird's Eye View of Springfield, Ill.

Size: 26¼ × 33½ in. (66.8 × 85.3 cm.)
Artist: Augustus Koch
Lithographer:
Printer:
Publisher:
Key/Vignettes/Misc: 57 refs.
Locations: ISHL–S; Sangamon Valley
Collection, Lincoln Library, Springfield,
Illinois
Catalogs/Checklists:

947
Place: Urbana, Illinois
Date: 1869
Title: Bird's Eye View of the City of
Urbana Champaign County Illinois 1869
Size: 17½ × 22 in. (44.5 × 55.9 cm.)
Artist: A. Ruger
Lithographer:
Printer: Chicago Lithographing Co.,
Chicago
Publisher:
Key/Vignettes/Misc: Refs. 1–10; 2
vignettes
Locations: LC–M
Catalogs/Checklists: LC–M, 189

948
Place: Warsaw, Illinois
Date: [1854–57]
Title: Warsaw, Iowa
Size: 6⅜ × 8⁵⁄₁₆ in. (16.2 × 21.9 cm.)
Artist: Henry Lewis
Lithographer:
Printer: C. H. Muller, Aachen
Publisher: Arnz & Co., Dusseldorf
Key/Vignettes/Misc:
Locations: MHS–SP; NYH–NY; HEHL;
LC–R; NL–C; HNOC–NO
Catalogs/Checklists:

949
Place: Young America, Illinois
Date: 1869
Title: Bird's Eye View of Young America
Warren County Illinois Looking North
West 1869
Size: 14 × 20 in. (35.6 × 50.8 cm.)
Artist: A. Ruger
Lithographer:
Printer: Chicago Lithographing Co.,
Chicago
Publisher: Ruger & Stoner, Madison,
Wisconsin
Key/Vignettes/Misc: Refs. 1–10
Locations: LC–M
Catalogs/Checklists: LC–M, 190

950
Place: Anderson, Indiana
Date: 1871
Title: Bird's Eye View of Anderson,
Indiana 1871.
Size: 19⁹⁄₁₆ × 25³⁄₁₆ in. (49.8 × 64.1 cm.)
Artist: T. M. Fowler and H. H. Bailey
Lithographer: C. H. Vogt
Printer: Milwaukee Lith. and Eng. Co.
[Milwaukee]
Publisher:
Key/Vignettes/Misc: Refs. 1–17; 105
vignettes

Locations: Anderson, Indiana, Public
Library
Catalogs/Checklists:

951
Place: Attica, Indiana
Date: 1869
Title: Bird's Eye View of the City of Attica,
Fountain County, Indiana, Looking
Southeast
Size: 15½ × 21¾ in. (40 × 56 cm.)
Artist: A. Ruger
Lithographer:
Printer: Chicago Lithogr. Co., Chicago
Publisher:
Key/Vignettes/Misc: Refs. 1–11
Locations: LC–M; IHS–I
Catalogs/Checklists: LC–M, 191

952
Place: Auburn, Indiana
Date: ?
Title:
Size:
Artist:
Lithographer:
Printer:
Publisher:
Key/Vignettes/Misc:
Locations:
Catalogs/Checklists:

953
Place: Cambridge City, Indiana
Date: 1871
Title: Cambridge City, Ind. 1871.
Size: 18¾ × 23⅛ in. (47.7 × 58.9 cm.)
Artist: T. M. Fowler & H. H. Bailey
Lithographer: C. H. Vogt
Printer: Milwaukee Lith & Eng. Co.
[Milwaukee]
Publisher: T. M. Fowler & H. H. Bailey
Key/Vignettes/Misc: Refs. 1–13, A–F
Locations: BPL–R; LC–M (photo)
Catalogs/Checklists: LC–M, 191.1

954
Place: Columbus, Indiana
Date: 1871
Title: Columbus, Ind. 1871
Size: 18 × 23 in. (45.8 × 58.6 cm.)
Artist:
Lithographer:
Printer:
Publisher: T. M. Fowler & H. H. Bailey
Key/Vignettes/Misc: Refs. 1–14, A–G
Locations: Bartholomew County
Historical Society, Columbus, Indiana
Catalogs/Checklists:

955
Place: Columbus, Indiana
Date: 1886
Title: Birds Eye View of Columbus, Ind.
1886
Size: 23 × 28¼ in. (58.5 × 71.9 cm.)
Artist: J. Wallis Smith
Lithographer:
Printer: Shober & Carqueville Litho. Co.
Chicago
Publisher:
Key/Vignettes/Misc: 103 refs.; 6 vignettes

Locations: Bartholomew County Historical Society, Columbus, Indiana
Catalogs/Checklists:

956
Place: Crawfordsville, Indiana
Date: 1871
Title: Crawfordsville, Ind.
Size: 16½ × 24½ in. (42 × 62.3 cm.)
Artist: H. H. Bailey
Lithographer:
Printer:
Publisher:
Key/Vignettes/Misc:
Locations: BPL–R
Catalogs/Checklists:

957
Place: Delphi, Indiana
Date: 1868
Title: Birds eye view of the City of Delphi, Carroll Co., Indiana.
Size: 18½ × 24¾ in. (47 × 36 cm.)
Artist: A. Ruger
Lithographer:
Printer: Merchants Lithographing Co., Chicago
Publisher:
Key/Vignettes/Misc: Refs. 1–12; 2 vignettes
Locations: LC–M; IHS–I
Catalogs/Checklists: LC–M, 192

958
Place: Elkhart, Indiana
Date: 1871
Title: Birds Eye View of Elkhart. Ind. 1871 Looking North East.
Size: 15¼ × 18¼ in. (38.8 × 46.4 cm.)
Artist: E. S. Glover
Lithographer:
Printer: The Calvert Lith. Co. Detroit
Publisher:
Key/Vignettes/Misc: Refs. 1–17
Locations: Elkhart, Indiana, Public Library
Catalogs/Checklists:

959
Place: Evansville, Indiana
Date: Ca. 1860
Title: Vue de Evansville
Size: 15 × 21½ in. (38.2 × 54.8 cm.)
Artist: J. Glanz
Lithographer:
Printer: C. Schacher
Publisher:
Key/Vignettes/Misc: 11 vignettes
Locations: CHS–C
Catalogs/Checklists:

960
Place: Evansville, Indiana
Date: 1888
Title: Perspective Map of the City of Evansville, Ind. 1888.
Size: 19¼ × 39¾ in. (49 × 102 cm.)
Artist: H. Wellge
Lithographer:
Printer:
Publisher: American Publishing Co., Milwaukee

Key/Vignettes/Misc: 63 refs.; 14 vignettes
Locations: LC–M; IHS–I
Catalogs/Checklists: LC–M, 193

961
Place: Fort Wayne, Indiana
Date: 1868
Title: Bird's Eye View of the City of Ft. Wayne, Indiana
Size: 19⅝ × 28⅜ in. (50 × 72 cm.)
Artist: A. Ruger
Lithographer:
Printer: Chicago Lithogr. Co. [Chicago]
Publisher:
Key/Vignettes/Misc: Refs. 1–30; 5 vignettes
Locations: LC–M; IHS–I
Catalogs/Checklists: LC–M, 194

962
Place: Fort Wayne, Indiana
Date: 1880
Title: Panoramic View of the City of Fort Wayne Allen County Indiana Looking South East 1880
Size: 21 × 33 in. (53.4 × 84 cm.) (facsimile)
Artist:
Lithographer:
Printer: Beck & Pauli, Milwaukee, Wis.
Publisher: J. J. Stoner, Madison, Wis.
Key/Vignettes/Misc: Refs. 1–190
Locations: City Plan Commission, Ft. Wayne, Indiana; ISL–I (facsimile)
Catalogs/Checklists:

963
Place: Fort Wayne, Indiana
Date: 1907
Title: Griswold's Birdseye View of the City of Fort Wayne, Indiana Indexed for Ready Reference
Size: 30¼ × 41⅝ in. (77 × 106cm.)
Artist: B. J. Griswold
Lithographer:
Printer:
Publisher: W. W. Hixon, Rockford, Ill.
Key/Vignettes/Misc: unnumbered directory of churches, railroads andstreets description;
Locations: LC–M
Catalogs/Checklists: LC–M, 195

964
Place: Frankfort, Indiana
Date: 1885
Title: Birds Eye View of Frankfort, Ind. 1885
Size: 24 × 30 in. (61.1 × 76.3 cm.)
Artist: J. W. Smith
Lithographer:
Printer: Shober & Carqueville Litho Co., Chicago
Publisher: W. S. Van Sickle. . .Frankfort,Indiana (copyright)
Key/Vignettes/Misc: Unnumbered refs.; 6 vignettes
Locations: Frankfort, Indiana, Public Library; ISL–I (photo)
Catalogs/Checklists:

965
Place: Greencastle, Indiana
Date: 1886
Title: Bird's Eye View of Greencastle, Indiana. 1886
Size: 24¼ × 28 in. (61.7 × 71.3 cm.)
Artist: J. Wallis Smith
Lithographer:
Printer: Shober & Carqueville Co., Chicago, Ill.
Publisher:
Key/Vignettes/Misc: 9 vignettes; unnumbered business directory
Locations: DePauw University, Greencastle, Indiana
Catalogs/Checklists:

966
Place: Greensburg, Indiana
Date: 1886
Title: Birds–Eye View of Greensburg, Indiana, 1886
Size: 20⅛ × 27¾ in. (51.2 × 70.6 cm.)
Artist:
Lithographer:
Printer: The Krebs Lithographing Co., Cincinnati, O.
Publisher:
Key/Vignettes/Misc: Unnumbered refs.; 5 vignettes
Locations: ISL–I; IHS–I
Catalogs/Checklists:

967
Place: Indianapolis, Indiana
Date: [1854]
Title: View of Indianapolis
Size: 20⅞ × 33 in. (53.1 × 84 cm.)
Artist: E. Sachse [James T. Palmatary]
Lithographer:
Printer: E. Sachse & Co., Baltimore
Publisher: J. T. Palmatary
Key/Vignettes/Misc: 28 vignettes
Locations: ISL–I; YUAG–NH
Catalogs/Checklists: Stokes C. 1854

968
Place: Indianapolis, Indiana
Date: 1871
Title: Bird's Eye View of Indianapolis, Ind. 1871
Size: 25⅞ × 33⅛ in. (65.9 × 84.3 cm.)
Artist: T. M. Fowler and H. H. Bailey
Lithographer: C. H. Vogt
Printer: Milwaukee Lith. & Eng. Co. [Milwaukee]
Publisher: T. M. Fowler and H. H. Bailey
Key/Vignettes/Misc: Refs. 1–45
Locations: ISL–I
Catalogs/Checklists:

969
Place: Kokomo, Indiana
Date: 1868
Title: Birds Eye View of the City of Kokomo Howard Co. Indiana 1868
Size: 20 × 25½ in. (50.8 × 64.8 cm.)
Artist: A. Ruger
Lithographer:
Printer: Merchants Lithographing Co., Chicago

Publisher:
Key/Vignettes/Misc: Refs. 1–10; 2
vignettes
Locations: LC–M; ISL–I; IHS–I
Catalogs/Checklists: LC–M, 196

970
Place: La Porte, Indiana
Date: 1866
Title: Birds Eye View of La Porte Indiana 1866
Size: 23½ × 34¾ in. (59.8 × 88.5 cm.)
Artist: A. Ruger
Lithographer:
Printer: Chicago Lithographing Co. 152 & 154 Clark St. Chicago
Publisher: A. Ruger, Battle Creek, Mich.
Key/Vignettes/Misc: Refs. 1–26
Locations: LCHM–L
Catalogs/Checklists:

971
Place: La Porte, Indiana
Date: Ca. 1875
Title: La Porte, Indiana
Size: 11 × 20 in. (28 × 50.9 cm.)
Artist:
Lithographer:
Printer: Chas. Shober & Co. Prop's Chicago Lith. Co. [Chicago]
Publisher:
Key/Vignettes/Misc:
Locations: LCHM–L
Catalogs/Checklists:

972
Place: La Porte, Indiana
Date: 1889
Title: La Porte, Ind. 1889 Looking North
Size: 22½ × 30 in. (57.4 × 76.4 cm.)
Artist: C. J. Pauli & Co.
Lithographer:
Printer:
Publisher: C. J. Pauli & Co., Milwaukee, Wis.
Key/Vignettes/Misc: Refs. 1–23; 3 vignettes
Locations: LCHM–L
Catalogs/Checklists:

973
Place: Lafayette, Indiana
Date: 1868
Title: Bird's Eye View of the City of Lafayette, Tippecanoe Co., Indiana
Size: 22 × 27½ in. (55.9 × 69.9 cm.)
Artist: A. Ruger
Lithographer:
Printer: Chicago Lith. Co. [Chicago]
Publisher:
Key/Vignettes/Misc: Refs. 1–35; 2 vignettes
Locations: LC–M; IHS–I
Catalogs/Checklists: LC–M, 197

974
Place: Logansport, Indiana
Date: N.D.
Title: View of Logansport. Indiana.
Size: 18⅞ × 30¼ in. (48.1 × 77 cm.)
Artist: Middleton, Strobridge & Co.

Lithographer:
Printer: Middleton, Strobridge & Co., Cin. O.
Publisher:
Key/Vignettes/Misc:
Locations: ISL–I
Catalogs/Checklists:

975
Place: Madison, Indiana
Date: Ca. 1854
Title: View of Madison, Id.
Size: 17½ × 32 in. (44.5 × 81.4 cm.)
Artist: E. Sachse & Co.
Lithographer:
Printer: E. Sachse & Co.
Publisher: J. T. Palmatary
Key/Vignettes/Misc: Refs. 1–15
Locations: ISL–I; YUAG–NH
Catalogs/Checklists:

976
Place: Madison, Indiana
Date: 1887
Title: Bird's–Eye View of Madison, Indiana, 1887
Size: 23⅝ × 35⅜ in. (60.1 × 90 cm.)
Artist: J. Wallis Smith & Co.
Lithographer:
Printer:
Publisher:
Key/Vignettes/Misc: Unnumbered refs.; 11 vignettes
Locations: IHS–I
Catalogs/Checklists:

977
Place: Michigan City, Indiana
Date: 1869 State I
Title: Bird's Eye View of Michigan City, La Porte County, Indiana.
Size: 20⁷⁄₁₆ × 28⁵⁄₁₆ in. (52 × 72 cm.)
Artist: A. Ruger
Lithographer:
Printer: Merchant's Lithographing Co., Chicago
Publisher:
Key/Vignettes/Misc: Refs. 1–15
Locations: LC–M; IHS–I
Catalogs/Checklists: LC–M, 198

978
Place: Michigan City, Indiana
Date: 1869 State II
Title: Bird's Eye View of Michigan City, Laporte County, Indiana
Size: 19⅝ × 27½ in. (50 × 70 cm.)
Artist: [Albert Ruger]
Lithographer:
Printer: Merchants Lithographing Co., Chicago
Publisher:
Key/Vignettes/Misc: Refs. 1–13; 4 vignettes
Locations: LC–M; IHS–I
Catalogs/Checklists: LC–M, 199

979
Place: Mishawaka, Indiana
Date: 1868
Title: Mishawaka 1868

Size:
Artist:
Lithographer:
Printer:
Publisher:
Key/Vignettes/Misc: Refs. 1–30
Locations: Mishawaka, Indiana, Public Library
Catalogs/Checklists:

980
Place: Mishawaka, Indiana
Date: 1871
Title: Mishawaka 1871 Looking South
Size: 15½ × 19 in. (39.4 × 48.4 cm.)
Artist: [D. D. Morse?]
Lithographer:
Printer: Merchants Lith. Co. Chicago, Ill.
Publisher: D. D. Morse
Key/Vignettes/Misc: Refs. 1–28
Locations: Mishawaka, Indiana, Public Library
Catalogs/Checklists:

981
Place: Muncie, Indiana
Date: 1872
Title: Birds Eye View of Muncie, Ind., 1872
Size: 13 × 19¼ in. (33 × 49 cm.) (photo)
Artist: O. H. Bailey
Lithographer:
Printer: Strobridge & Co. Lith., Cin
Publisher:
Key/Vignettes/Misc: Refs. 1–14
Locations: LC–M (photo)
Catalogs/Checklists: LC–M, 199.2

982
Place: Muncie, Indiana
Date: 1884
Title: Muncie. Indiana. 1884.
Size: 19¾ × 26⅝ in. (50.3 × 67.8 cm.)
Artist:
Lithographer: O. H. Bailey & Co.
Printer: O. H. Bailey & Co., Boston
Publisher: O. H. Bailey & Co., Boston
Key/Vignettes/Misc: Refs. 1–74; 7 vignettes
Locations: BPL–R
Catalogs/Checklists:

983
Place: New Albany, Indiana
Date: Ca. 1848
Title: New Albany, Ind. As seen from the Hills Below the City
Size: 7¾ × 11¹⁄₁₆ in. (19.7 × 28.1 cm.)
Artist: Geo. W. Morrison
Lithographer:
Printer: T. Sinclairs Lith, Philadelphia
Publisher: Jno. R. Nunemacher at the City Bookstore
Key/Vignettes/Misc:
Locations: ISL–I
Catalogs/Checklists:

984
Place: New Albany, Indiana
Date: N.D.
Title: New–Albany, Indiana.

Size: 5½ × 16¼ in. (14 × 41.3 cm.)
Artist:
Lithographer:
Printer: C. Bruder's Lithogr. New Alban. Ind.
Publisher:
Key/Vignettes/Misc:
Locations: ACMW–FW; MM–NN
Catalogs/Checklists: ACMW–FW 1814; MM–NN, LE 559

985
Place: New Castle, Indiana
Date: 1884
Title: New Castle. Indiana. 1884
Size: 20¼ × 24⅜ in. (51.6 × 62 cm.)
Artist:
Lithographer: O. H. Bailey & Co.
Printer: O. H. Bailey & Co., Boston
Publisher: O. H. Bailey & Co., Boston
Key/Vignettes/Misc: Refs. 1–29; 5 vignettes
Locations: BPL–R
Catalogs/Checklists:

986
Place: New Harmony, Indiana
Date: Ca. 1825
Title: A Bird's Eye View of one of the New Communities at Harmony in the State of Indiana North America
Size: 15⅞ × 23⅝ in. (40.4 × 60.0 cm.)
Artist: Stedman Whitwell
Lithographer:
Printer: Ingrey & Madelly, London
Publisher:
Key/Vignettes/Misc: Description
Locations: NYH–NY; LC–P; LC–M (facsimile)
Catalogs/Checklists: LC–M, 199.3

987
Place: Peru, Indiana
Date: 1868
Title: Bird's Eye View of the City of Peru, Miami Co., Indiana.
Size: 20 × 25½ in. (50.8 × 64.8 cm.)
Artist: [Albert Ruger]
Lithographer:
Printer:
Publisher:
Key/Vignettes/Misc: Refs. 1–13; 2 vignettes
Locations: LC–M; IHS–I
Catalogs/Checklists: LC–M, 200

988
Place: Richmond, Indiana
Date: 1859
Title: Richmond, Ind. 1859
Size: 21⅞ × 39³⁄₁₆ in. (55.7 × 99.7 cm.)
Artist: D. E. Jerrold
Lithographer:
Printer: Ehrgott & Forbriger, Cincinnati, O.
Publisher: S. W. Chapman
Key/Vignettes/Misc:
Locations: MRL–R
Catalogs/Checklists:

989
Place: Richmond, Indiana
Date: 1870
Title: View of Richmond, Ind. Looking

South East, 1870
Size: 21⅞ × 28⁵⁄₁₆ in. (55.7 × 72.1 cm.)
Artist: Nordyke & Personett
Lithographer:
Printer: Merchants Lithographing Co., Chicago
Publisher:
Key/Vignettes/Misc: 6 vignettes
Locations: IHS–I; MRL–R
Catalogs/Checklists:

990
Place: Richmond, Indiana
Date: 1884
Title: The City of Richmond, Indiana
Size: 26½ × 38¼ in. (67.4 × 97.3 cm.)
Artist: Albert Downs
Lithographer:
Printer: J. W. C. Gilman & Co.
Publisher: O.H. Bailey & Co., Boston
Key/Vignettes/Misc: Refs. 1–125; 28 vignettes
Locations: LC–M; IHS–I; BPL–R; MRL–R
Catalogs/Checklists: LC–M, 201

991
Place: Seymour, Indiana
Date: 1886
Title: Birds Eye View of Seymour Indiana 1886
Size: 25⅛ × 31¼ in. (63.9 × 79.5 cm.)
Artist: J. Wallis Smith & Co.
Lithographer:
Printer: Shober & Carqueville Litho. Co., Chicago
Publisher:
Key/Vignettes/Misc: 8 vignettes; unnumbered business directory
Locations: Seymour, Indiana, Public Library
Catalogs/Checklists:

992
Place: Shelbyville, Indiana
Date: 1887
Title: Shelbyville, Indiana, 1887
Size: 20⅝ × 32¼ in. (52.5 × 82.1 cm.)
Artist: J. Wallis Smith
Lithographer:
Printer: The Krebs Lithographing Co., Cin. O.
Publisher: Stewart & Blakely. . .Lumber Merchants
Key/Vignettes/Misc: Unnumbered refs.
Locations: ISL–I
Catalogs/Checklists:

993
Place: South Bend, Indiana
Date: 1866
Title: South Bend, Indiana 1866.
Size: 21 × 28½ in. (53.4 × 72.5 cm.)
Artist: A. Ruger
Lithographer:
Printer: Chicago Lithographing Co., Chicago
Publisher: A. Ruger, Battle Creek, Michigan
Key/Vignettes/Misc: Refs. 1–29; 6 vignettes
Locations: LC–M
Catalogs/Checklists: LC–M, 202

994
Place: South Bend, Indiana
Date: 1874
Title: South Bend, Indiana
Size: 19½ × 26 in. (49.6 × 66.1 cm.)
Artist: [Albert Ruger]
Lithographer:
Printer: Chas. Shober & Co., proprietors of Chicago Lith. Co. [Chicago]
Publisher: J. J. Stoner, Madison, Wis., 1874
Key/Vignettes/Misc: Refs. 1–59
Locations: LC–M; IHS–I
Catalogs/Checklists: LC–M, 203

995
Place: South Bend, Indiana
Date: 1890
Title: South Bend, Ind. 1890. Looking West.
Size: 23⅛ × 40 in. (59 × 101 cm.)
Artist: C. J. Pauli
Lithographer:
Printer:
Publisher: C. J. Pauli, 726 Central Avenue, Milwaukee
Key/Vignettes/Misc: Refs. 1–98, A; 2 vignettes
Locations: LC–M; Northern Indiana Historical Museum, South Bend, Indiana
Catalogs/Checklists: LC–M, 204

996
Place: Terre Haute, Indiana
Date: [1856]
Title: View of the City of Terre Haute, Inda.
Size: 28 × 44½ in. (71.3 × 113.2 cm.)
Artist:
Lithographer:
Printer: Middleton, Wallace & Co. Lithos. 115 Walnut St. Cincinnati, O.
Publisher: J. T. Palmatary
Key/Vignettes/Misc:
Locations: NYH–NY
Catalogs/Checklists:

997
Place: Terre Haute, Indiana
Date: 1880
Title: Panoramic View of Terre Haute, Ind. 1880.
Size: 20 × 39⁵⁄₁₆ in. (51 × 100 cm.)
Artist:
Lithographer:
Printer: Beck & Pauli, Milwaukee, Wis.
Publisher:
Key/Vignettes/Misc: Refs. 1–51
Locations: LC–M
Catalogs/Checklists: LC–M, 205

998
Place: Bellevue, Iowa
Date: [1854–57]
Title: Bellevue, Iowa
Size: 7⅛ × 9¾ in. (18.1 × 24.8 cm.)
Artist: Henry Lewis
Lithographer:
Printer: [C. H. Muller, Aachen]
Publisher: Jnst. Arnz & Co., Dusseldorf
Key/Vignettes/Misc:
Locations: MHS–SP; NYH–NY; HEHL;

LC–R; NL–C; HNOC–NO
Catalogs/Checklists:

999
Place: Blairstown, Iowa
Date: 1868
Title: Bird's Eye View of Blairstown, Benton Co., Iowa.
Size: 9¹³⁄₁₆ × 12⁹⁄₁₆ in. (25 × 32 cm.)
Artist: A. Ruger
Lithographer:
Printer: Merchants Lithographing Co. [Chicago]
Publisher:
Key/Vignettes/Misc: Refs. 1–7
Locations: LC–M
Catalogs/Checklists: LC–M, 206

1000
Place: Bloomfield, Iowa
Date: 1869
Title: Bloomfield, Davis County, Iowa.
Size: 15¾ × 23³⁄₁₆ in. (40 × 59 cm.)
Artist: A. Koch
Lithographer:
Printer: Chicago Lith. Co., Chicago
Publisher:
Key/Vignettes/Misc:
Locations: Exchange Bank, Bloomfield, Iowa
Catalogs/Checklists:

Place: Bloomington, Iowa
Date: Ca. 1844
See Muscatine, Iowa, ca. 1844

1001
Place: Boone, Iowa
Date: 1868
Title: Bird's Eye View of the City of Montana, Boone Co., Iowa.
Size: 19⅝ × 26 in. (50 × 66 cm.)
Artist: A. Ruger
Lithographer:
Printer: Chicago Lithographing Co., Chicago
Publisher:
Key/Vignettes/Misc: 2 vignettes
Locations: LC–M
Catalogs/Checklists: LC–M, 223

1002
Place: Burlington, Iowa
Date: 1850
Title: Burlington, Iowa.
Size: 11⅜ × 22¾ in. (29 × 58 cm.)
Artist: Fr. Berchem Lucrode
Lithographer:
Printer: Juls Hutawa & L. Gast, Lith., St. Louis
Publisher:
Key/Vignettes/Misc:
Locations: ISHS–I
Catalogs/Checklists:

1003
Place: Burlington, Iowa
Date: [1851]
Title: Burlington, Iowa.
Size: 5¹³⁄₁₆ × 7⅞ in. (14.8 × 20 cm.)
Artist:
Lithographer: A. Forbriger
Printer: Onken's Lith. Cin. O.

Publisher: [Otto Onken, Cincinnati, Ohio]
Key/Vignettes/Misc:
Locations: CPL–R
Catalogs/Checklists:

1004
Place: Burlington, Iowa
Date: [1854–57]
Title: Burlington, Iowa
Size: 6⅜ × 8⁵⁄₁₆ in. (16.2 × 21.9 cm.)
Artist: Henry Lewis
Lithographer:
Printer: C. H. Muller, Aachen
Publisher: Arnz & Co., Dusseldorf
Key/Vignettes/Misc:
Locations: MHS–SP; NYH–NY; HEHL; LC–R; NL–C; HNOC–NO
Catalogs/Checklists:

1005
Place: Burlington, Iowa
Date: 1858
Title: City of Burlington, Iowa.
Size: 18½ × 26½ in. (47.1 × 67.5 cm.)
Artist: William Bourne
Lithographer:
Printer:
Publisher:
Key/Vignettes/Misc:
Locations:
Catalogs/Checklists: Rathbone, Westward the Way, no. 198

1006
Place: Burlington, Iowa
Date: 1889
Title: 1889 Perspective Map of the City of Burlington, Ia.
Size: 17¼ × 32¼ in. (44 × 82 cm.)
Artist: H. Wellge
Lithographer:
Printer:
Publisher: American Publishing Co., Milwaukee
Key/Vignettes/Misc: Refs. 1–94, A–Q; 7 vignettes
Locations: LC–M
Catalogs/Checklists: LC–M, 207

1007
Place: Cedar Falls, Iowa
Date: 1868
Title: Birdseye View of Cedar Falls, Blackhawk Co., Iowa. 1868.
Size: ca. 18½ × 27 in. (ca. 47.1 × 68.7 cm.)
Artist: A. Koch
Lithographer:
Printer: Merchants Lithographing Co., Chicago
Publisher:
Key/Vignettes/Misc: Refs. 1–24; 1 vignette
Locations: Cedar Falls Historical Society, Cedar Falls, Iowa
Catalogs/Checklists:

1008
Place: Cedar Falls, Iowa
Date: 1880
Title: Directory to the Leading Business Houses of Cedar Falls, Iowa. Birds–Eye

View of Cedar Falls, Blackhawk Co., Iowa, 1880.
Size: 13 × 17½ in. (33.1 × 44.6 cm.) (photo)
Artist: A. Hageboeck
Lithographer:
Printer: A.Hageboeck, Davenport, Iowa
Publisher:
Key/Vignettes/Misc: Advertisements
Locations: Cedar Falls Historical Society, Cedar Falls, Iowa (photo)
Catalogs/Checklists:

1009
Place: Cedar Falls, Iowa
Date: 1881
Title: Bird's–Eye View of Cedar Falls, Black Hawk County, Iowa.
Size:
Artist: W. V. Herancourt
Lithographer:
Printer:
Publisher: [W. V. Herancourt, Dubuque, Iowa?]
Key/Vignettes/Misc: 2 vignettes
Locations: Unknown. see newspaper illustration in files of Cedar Falls Historical Society, Cedar Falls, Iowa
Catalogs/Checklists:

1010
Place: Cedar Rapids, Iowa
Date: 1868
Title: Bird's Eye View of the City of Cedar Rapids, Kingston, Linn Co. Iowa.
Size: 21¼ × 26 in. (54 × 66 cm.)
Artist: A. Ruger
Lithographer:
Printer: Chicago Lith. Co., Chicago
Publisher:
Key/Vignettes/Misc: Refs. 1–16; 2 vignettes
Locations: LC–M
Catalogs/Checklists: LC–M, 208

1011
Place: Cedar Rapids, Iowa
Date: 1889
Title: Cedar Rapids, Iowa
Size: 27¼ × 35 in. (69 × 89 cm.)
Artist: C. J. Pauli
Lithographer:
Printer:
Publisher: C. J. Pauli & Co.
Key/Vignettes/Misc:
Locations: Cedar Rapids, Iowa, Public Library; LC–M (photo)
Catalogs/Checklists: LC–M, 208.1

1012
Place: Clinton, Iowa
Date: 1868
Title: Bird's Eye View of the City of Clinton Clinton Co. Iowa 1868
Size: 18¾ × 25⅞ in. (47.7 × 65.8 cm.)
Artist: A. Ruger
Lithographer:
Printer: Merchants Lithographing Co., Chicago
Publisher:
Key/Vignettes/Misc: Refs. 1–16; 2 vignettes

Locations: MM−NN; LC−M; CHS−C
Catalogs/Checklists: MM−NN, LP 3187

1013
Place: Council Bluffs, Iowa
Date: 1868
Title: Bird's Eye View of the City of
Council Bluffs, Pottawattamie Co., Iowa.
Size: 22⅜ × 27½ in. (57 × 70 cm.)
Artist: A. Ruger
Lithographer:
Printer: Merchants Lithographing Co.,
Chicago
Publisher:
Key/Vignettes/Misc: Refs. 1−11; 2
vignettes
Locations: LC−M
Catalogs/Checklists: LC−M, 209

Place: Davenport, Iowa
Date: 1844
See Fort Armstrong, Iowa, 1844.

1014
Place: Davenport, Iowa
Date: Ca. 1855
Title: Davenport, Iowa
Size: 16¹⁵⁄₁₆ × 25⁵⁄₁₆ in. (43.1 × 64.4 cm.)
Artist: E. P. Gillett
Lithographer:
Printer: J. H. Buffords, 260 Washington
St., Boston
Publisher:
Key/Vignettes/Misc:
Locations: PM−D
Catalogs/Checklists:

1015
Place: Davenport, Iowa
Date: 1856
Title: City of Davenport
Size: 18⅝ × 27¾ in. (47.4 × 70.6 cm.)
Artist: Rufus Wright
Lithographer:
Printer: Sarony, Major & Knapp, N. Y.
Publisher:
Key/Vignettes/Misc: Population for years
1836−1856
Locations: PM−D
Catalogs/Checklists: Rathbone, Westward
the Way, no. 199

1016
Place: Davenport, Iowa
Date: 1857
Title: View of the City of Davenport,
Iowa, 1857
Size: 19¼ × 27 in. (49 × 68.7 cm.)
Artist: J. C. Wolfe
Lithographer: M. Rosenthal
Printer: L. N. Rosenthal
Publisher:
Key/Vignettes/Misc:
Locations: PM−D
Catalogs/Checklists:

1017
Place: Davenport, Iowa
Date: [1854−57]
Title: Fort Armstrong
Size: 7⅛ × 9¾ in. (18.1 × 24.8 cm.)
Artist: Henry Lewis

Lithographer:
Printer:
Publisher: Jnst. Arnz & Co., Dusseldorf
Key/Vignettes/Misc:
Locations: MHS−SP; NYH−NY; HEHL;
NL−C; CHS−C; LC−R
Catalogs/Checklists:

1018
Place: Davenport, Iowa
Date: [1855−57]
Title: [Untitled, possibly proof before
letters]
Size: 17¹⁄₁₆ × 25½ in. (43.4 × 64.8 cm.)
Artist:
Lithographer:
Printer:
Publisher:
Key/Vignettes/Misc:
Locations: NYP−S
Catalogs/Checklists: Stokes C.
1855−57—G−42

1019
Place: Davenport, Iowa
Date: 1858
Title: City of Davenport, Iowa. From the
Original Picture in the Possession of Geo.
L. Davenport
Size: 18⅝ × 27¾ in. (47.4 × 70.6 cm.)
Artist: Rufus Wright
Lithographer:
Printer: Sarony, Major & Knapp, 449
Broadway, N. Y.
Publisher:
Key/Vignettes/Misc: Population for years
1836−1858
Locations: PM−D; CHS−C
Catalogs/Checklists: Rathbone, Westward
the Way, no. 199

1020
Place: Davenport, Iowa
Date: 1865
Title: City of Davenport, Iowa.
Size: 21⅝ × 28⅝ in. (55 × 72.9 cm.)
Artist:
Lithographer: Chas. Vogt & Co.
Printer: J. McKittrick & Co., St. Louis
Publisher: Chas. Vogt & Co., Davenport,
Iowa
Key/Vignettes/Misc: 16 vignettes
Locations: PM−D
Catalogs/Checklists:

1021
Place: Davenport, Iowa
Date: 1866
Title: Davenport, Iowa
Size: 18½ × 29¼ in. (47 × 74.4 cm.)
Artist: [A. Hageboeck]
Lithographer: A. Hageboeck
Printer:
Publisher: A. Hageboeck
Key/Vignettes/Misc: 49 vignettes
Locations: PM−D
Catalogs/Checklists:

1022
Place: Davenport, Iowa
Date: 1872
Title: Panorama of Davenport, Iowa.

Size: 12⅜ × 30¼ in. (31.4 × 76.9 cm.)
Artist: A. Hageboeck
Lithographer: A. Hageboeck
Printer: A. Hageboeck
Publisher:
Key/Vignettes/Misc:
Locations: PM−D
Catalogs/Checklists:

1023
Place: Davenport, Iowa
Date: 1872
Title: Panorama of Davenport, Iowa. As
Seen from the Harper−House, Rock
Island, Ill.
Size: 7⅜ × 24¹⁵⁄₁₆ in. (18.7 × 63.5 cm.)
Artist:
Lithographer: A. Hageboeck
Printer: A. Hageboeck, Davenport, Iowa
Publisher: A. Hageboeck, Davenport, Iowa
Key/Vignettes/Misc:
Locations: LC−P
Catalogs/Checklists:

1024
Place: Davenport, Iowa
Date: 1876
Title: Davenport, Iowa in 1876, From the
East
Size: 17¹³⁄₁₆ × 24 in. (45.3 × 61 cm.)
Artist: C. J. Pauli
Lithographer:
Printer: American Oleograph Co.,
Milwaukee
Publisher:
Key/Vignettes/Misc:
Locations: PM−D
Catalogs/Checklists:

1025
Place: Davenport, Iowa
Date: 1881
Title: View of Davenport, Iowa, 1881
Size: 22⅞ × 28¹⁄₁₆ in. (58.2 × 71.4 cm.)
Artist: A. Hageboeck
Lithographer: A. Hageboeck
Printer: [A. Hageboeck]
Publisher:
Key/Vignettes/Misc:
Locations: PM−D
Catalogs/Checklists:

1026
Place: Davenport, Iowa
Date: 1888
Title: Davenport, Iowa 1888
Size: 20½ × 39¾ in. (52.2 × 101.1 cm.)
Artist: H. Wellge
Lithographer:
Printer:
Publisher: American Publishing Co.,
Milwaukee
Key/Vignettes/Misc: Refs. 1−73; 43
lettered refs.; 5 vignettes
Locations: PM−D; LC−M
Catalogs/Checklists: LC−M, 210

1027
Place: Decorah, Iowa
Date: 1870
Title: Decorah, Winneshiek County, Iowa,

Looking North West.
Size: 18½ × 22 in. (47 × 56 cm.)
Artist: [Albert Ruger]
Lithographer:
Printer: Merchants Lithographing Co., Chicago
Publisher: Ruger & Stoner, Madison, Wisconsin
Key/Vignettes/Misc: Refs. 1–8; 5 vignettes
Locations: LC–M
Catalogs/Checklists: LC–M, 211

1028
Place: Des Moines, Iowa
Date: 1856
Title: View of Des Moines, the Capital of Iowa in 1856.
Size: 19 × 29½ in. (48.3 × 75.1 cm.)
Artist: W. R. Wheeler
Lithographer:
Printer: Hoffman Knickerbocker & Co., Albany, N. Y.
Publisher:
Key/Vignettes/Misc:
Locations: Unknown. See Old Print Shop Portfolio, XXIV, p. 65, No. 28
Catalogs/Checklists:

1029
Place: Des Moines, Iowa
Date: 1858
Title: Des Moines, Iowa, From the Capitol
Size: 23 × 38½ in. (58.6 × 98 cm.)
Artist: G. L. Reynolds
Lithographer:
Printer:
Publisher:
Key/Vignettes/Misc:
Locations:
Catalogs/Checklists: Rathbone, Westward the Way, no. 200

1030
Place: Des Moines, Iowa
Date: 1868
Title: Bird's Eye View of the City of Des Moines the Capital of Iowa.
Size: 22 × 28¾ in. (56 × 73 cm.)
Artist: A. Ruger
Lithographer:
Printer: Merchants Lithographing Co., Chicago
Publisher:
Key/Vignettes/Misc: Refs. 1–8, A–B; 4 vignettes; unnumbered public building directory
Locations: LC–M
Catalogs/Checklists: LC–M, 212

1031
Place: Des Moines, Iowa
Date: 1876
Title: View of Des Moines, Iowa
Size: 19⅜ × 35½ in. (49.3 × 90.3 cm.)
Artist: Senftle
Lithographer:
Printer:
Publisher: Mills & Co.
Key/Vignettes/Misc:
Locations: Des Moines Art Center, Des

Moines, Iowa (on loan from West Des Moines, Iowa, Historical Society)
Catalogs/Checklists:

1032
Place: Dewitt, Iowa
Date: 1868
Title: Bird's Eye View of the City of DeWitt, Clinton Co., Iowa 1868.
Size: 19⅝ × 26 in. (50 × 66 cm.)
Artist: [Albert Ruger]
Lithographer:
Printer:
Publisher:
Key/Vignettes/Misc: Refs. 1–16; 2 vignettes
Locations: LC–M
Catalogs/Checklists: LC–M, 213

1033
Place: Dubuque, Iowa
Date: Ca. 1844
Title: Dubuque, Iowa
Size: 21⅝ × 30¹¹⁄₁₆ in. (55 × 78 cm.)
Artist: J. C. Wild
Lithographer:
Printer:
Publisher:
Key/Vignettes/Misc:
Locations: CHS–C; PM–D
Catalogs/Checklists:

1034
Place: Dubuque, Iowa
Date: Ca. 1856
Title: View of Dubuque, Iowa
Size: 21⅝ × 29⅞ in. (55 × 76 cm.)
Artist: Miss Lucinda Farnham
Lithographer:
Printer: J. Cameron, New York
Publisher:
Key/Vignettes/Misc:
Locations: ISHS–I; CHS–C
Catalogs/Checklists:

1035
Place: Dubuque, Iowa
Date: [1854–57]
Title: Dubuque in Iowa
Size: 7⅛ × 9¾ in. (18.1 × 24.8 cm.)
Artist: Henry Lewis
Lithographer:
Printer: [C. H. Muller, Aachen]
Publisher: Jnst. Arnz & Co., Dusseldorf
Key/Vignettes/Misc:
Locations: MHS–SP; NYH–NY; HEHL; NL–C; CHS–C; LC–R
Catalogs/Checklists:

1036
Place: Dubuque, Iowa
Date: Ca. 1860 State I
Title: Dubuque
Size: 16⅛ × 26⅜ in. (41 × 67.1 cm.)
Artist:
Lithographer:
Printer:
Publisher: W. J. Gilbert, 100 Main St., Dubuque, Iowa
Key/Vignettes/Misc: 16 vignettes; seal of city
Locations: NYP–S

Catalogs/Checklists: Stokes 1859–60—G–58

1037
Place: Dubuque, Iowa
Date: Ca. 1860 State II
Title: Dubuque
Size: 16¼ × 26½ in. (41.4 × 67.4 cm.)
Artist: H. W. Pettit
Lithographer:
Printer: Endicott & Co., 59 Beekman St., NY
Publisher: W. J. Gilbert, 100 Main St. Dubuque, Iowa
Key/Vignettes/Misc: 16 vignettes; seal of city
Locations: MM–NN
Catalogs/Checklists: MM–NN, LP 49

1038
Place: Dubuque, Iowa
Date: 1870
Title: Dubuque, Iowa 1870
Size: 12¼ × 21¾ in. (31.1 × 55.3 cm.)
Artist: Alex. Simplot
Lithographer:
Printer: Chicago Lithographing Co. [Chicago]
Publisher: Alex Simplot, Chicago
Key/Vignettes/Misc:
Locations: MM–NN; ACMW–FW; EI–S
Catalogs/Checklists: MM–NN, LP 4200; ACMW–FW 1654

1039
Place: Dubuque, Iowa
Date: Ca. 1887
Title: Dubuque, Ia.
Size: 13⅜ × 22 in. (34 × 56 cm.)
Artist: Alex Simplot
Lithographer:
Printer:
Publisher: Alex Simplot
Key/Vignettes/Misc:
Locations: ISHS–I
Catalogs/Checklists:

1040
Place: Dubuque, Iowa
Date: 1889
Title: Perspective Map of the City of Dubuque, Ia. 1889.
Size: 21¼ × 39½ in. (54 × 102 cm.)
Artist: H. Wellge
Lithographer:
Printer:
Publisher: American Publishing Co., Milwaukee
Key/Vignettes/Misc: Refs. 1–61, lettered refs.; 8 vignettes
Locations: LC–M
Catalogs/Checklists: LC–M, 214

1041
Place: Elkader, Iowa
Date: 1871
Title: Map of Elkader
Size: 11 × 16⅛ in. (28 × 41 cm.)
Artist: H. H. Bailey
Lithographer:
Printer: Doniat & Zastrow, Milwaukee
Publisher:

Key/Vignettes/Misc:
Locations: Elkader, Iowa, Public Library
Catalogs/Checklists:

1042
Place: Fort Armstrong, Iowa
Date: 1844
Title: Fort Armstrong on Rock–Island, Ill.
East View of Davenport, Iowa T. Town of
Rock–Island, Ill. Moline
Size: 22⅛ × 30¾ in. (56.3 × 78.3 cm.)
Artist: J. C. Wild
Lithographer:
Printer: J. C. Wild, Davenport
Publisher:
Key/Vignettes/Misc:
Locations: NYP–S; PM–D
Catalogs/Checklists:

1043
Place: Fort Dodge, Iowa
Date: 1869
Title: Bird's Eye View of Fort Dodge
Webster County Iowa 1869
Size: 17 × 19⁵⁄₁₆ in. (43.3 × 49.2 cm.)
Artist: A. Koch
Lithographer:
Printer: Merchants Lithographing Co.
Chicago
Publisher:
Key/Vignettes/Misc: Refs. 1–13, A; 1
vignette
Locations: Fort Dodge Historical
Foundation & Fort Museum, Fort Dodge,
Iowa
Catalogs/Checklists:

1044
Place: Fort Dodge, Iowa
Date: 1872
Title: Fort Dodge, Iowa. Taken from the
Bluff Across the Desmoin River.
Size: 17½ × 25⅝ in. (44.5 × 65.1 cm.)
Artist: Bill D. T. Travis
Lithographer:
Printer: Chicago Lith. Co. No. 150, 152 &
154 S. Clark St. [Chicago]
Publisher:
Key/Vignettes/Misc:
Locations: EI–S; Fort Dodge Historical
Foundation & Fort Museum, Fort Dodge,
Iowa
Catalogs/Checklists:

1045
Place: Fort Madison, Iowa
Date: [1854–57]
Title: Fort Madison, Iowa
Size: 6⅜ × 8⁵⁄₁₆ in. (16.2 × 21.9 cm.)
Artist: Henry Lewis
Lithographer:
Printer: C. H. Muller, Aachen
Publisher: Arnz & Co., Dusseldorf
Key/Vignettes/Misc:
Locations: MHS–SP; NYH–NY; HEHL;
LC–R; NL–C; HNOC–NO
Catalogs/Checklists:

1046
Place: Fort Madison, Iowa
Date: 1889
Title: Perspective Map of Fort Madison,
Ia. 1889.
Size: 13⅜ × 37 in. (38 × 96 cm.)

Artist: H. Wellge
Lithographer:
Printer:
Publisher: American Publishing Co.,
Milwaukee
Key/Vignettes/Misc: Refs. 1–44, lettered
refs.; 11 vignettes
Locations: LC–M
Catalogs/Checklists: LC–M, 215

1047
Place: Guttenberg, Iowa
Date: 1869
Title: Bird's Eye View of Guttenberg
Size: 16⅛ × 21⅜ in. (40.9 × 54.3 cm.)
Artist: [Albert Ruger]
Lithographer:
Printer: Merchants Lithographing Co.,
Chicago
Publisher: Ruger & Stoner, Madison Wis.
Key/Vignettes/Misc: Refs. 1–6; 3
vignettes
Locations: ACMW–FW; LC–M
Catalogs/Checklists: ACMW–FW 1727;
LC–M, 216

1048
Place: Indianola, Iowa
Date: 1869
Title: Bird's Eye View of the City of
Indianola, Iowa Warren County 1869
Size: 15¾ × 22¼ in. (40.1 × 56.7 cm.)
Artist:
Lithographer:
Printer: Chicago Lithographing Co.
[Chicago]
Publisher:
Key/Vignettes/Misc:
Locations: Indianola, Iowa, Public Library
Catalogs/Checklists:

1049
Place: Iowa City, Iowa
Date: 1868
Title: Bird's Eye View of Iowa City,
Johnson Co., Iowa.
Size: 20½ × 26 in. (52 × 66 cm.)
Artist: A. Ruger
Lithographer:
Printer: Chicago Lith. Co., Chicago
Publisher:
Key/Vignettes/Misc: Refs.; vignettes
Locations: ISHS–I; LC–M
Catalogs/Checklists: LC–M, 217

1050
Place: Keokuk, Iowa
Date: [1854–57]
Title: Keokuk, Iowa
Size: 6⅜ × 8⁵⁄₁₆ in. (16.2 × 21.9 cm.)
Artist: Henry Lewis
Lithographer:
Printer: C. H. Muller, Aachen
Publisher: Arnz & Co., Dusseldorf
Key/Vignettes/Misc:
Locations: MHS–SP; NYH–NY; HEHL;
LC–R; NL–C; HNOC–NO
Catalogs/Checklists:

1051
Place: Keokuk, Iowa
Date: 1878
Title: View of Keokuk, Iowa, 1878.
Size: 29⅞ × 46⅞ in. (76 × 119 cm.)

Artist:
Lithographer:
Printer:
Publisher:
Key/Vignettes/Misc:
Locations: Lee County Historical Society,
Keokuk, Iowa
Catalogs/Checklists:

1052
Place: Lyons, Iowa
Date: 1868
Title: Bird's Eye View of the City of Lyons,
Clinton Co., Iowa 1868.
Size: 20¹³⁄₁₆ × 28⁵⁄₁₆ in. (53 × 72 cm.)
Artist: A. Ruger
Lithographer:
Printer: Merchants Lithographing Co.,
Chicago
Publisher:
Key/Vignettes/Misc: Refs. 1–12; 2
vignettes
Locations: LC–M
Catalogs/Checklists: LC–M, 218

1053
Place: Maquoketa, Iowa
Date: 1872
Title: Maquoketa, Jackson County Iowa.
1872
Size: 18 × 24 in. (45.8 × 61.1 cm.)
Artist:
Lithographer: C. H. Vogt
Printer: American Oleograph Co.
Publisher: J. J. Stoner [Madison, Wis.]
Key/Vignettes/Misc: Refs. 1–12
Locations: Jackson County Historical
Society Museum, Maquoketa, Iowa
Catalogs/Checklists:

1054
Place: Marengo, Iowa
Date: 1868
Title: Bird's Eye View of the City of
Marengo, Iowa Co., Iowa.
Size: 20⅞ × 25¹⁵⁄₁₆ in. (53 × 66 cm.)
Artist: A. Ruger
Lithographer:
Printer: Merchants Lithographing Co.,
Chicago
Publisher:
Key/Vignettes/Misc: Refs. 1–9; 2
vignettes
Locations: LC–M
Catalogs/Checklists: LC–M, 220

1055
Place: Marion, Iowa
Date: 1868
Title: Bird's Eye View of the City of
Marion, Linn Co., Iowa.
Size: 20½ × 26⅜ in. (52 × 67 cm.)
Artist: A. Ruger
Lithographer:
Printer: Merchants Lithographing Co.
Publisher:
Key/Vignettes/Misc: Refs. 1–17; 2
vignettes
Locations: LC–M
Catalogs/Checklists: LC–M, 221

1056
Place: Marshalltown, Iowa
Date: 1868

Title: Bird's Eye View of the City of
Marshalltown, Marshall Co., Iowa.
Size: 20¹/₁₆ × 26 in. (51 × 66 cm.)
Artist: [Albert Ruger]
Lithographer:
Printer:
Publisher:
Key/Vignettes/Misc: Refs. 1–11; 2
vignettes
Locations: LC–M
Catalogs/Checklists: LC–M, 222

1057
Place: McGregor, Iowa
Date: 1869
Title: Bird's Eye View of the City of
McGregor and North McGregor Clayton
County, Iowa, 1869
Size: 18¹/₁₆ × 22 in. (45.8 × 55.8 cm.)
Artist: [Albert Ruger]
Lithographer:
Printer: Chicago Lithog. Co. Chicago, Ill.
Publisher: Ruger & Stoner, Madison,
Wisconsin
Key/Vignettes/Misc: Refs. 1–11
Locations: ACMW–FW; LC–M; ISHS–I
Catalogs/Checklists: ACMW–FW 1731;
LC–M, 219; Reps, Cities on Stone, p. 94

Place: Montana, Iowa
Date: 1868
See Boone, Iowa, 1868.

1058
Place: Muscatine, Iowa
Date: Ca. 1844
Title: Bloomington, Iowa
Size: 18³/₈ × 24 in. (46.7 × 61 cm.)
Artist: J. C. Wild
Lithographer: J. C. Wild
Printer:
Publisher:
Key/Vignettes/Misc:
Locations: YUAG–NH
Catalogs/Checklists:

1059
Place: Muscatine, Iowa
Date: [1854–57]
Title: Muscadine, Iowa Muscadine in Iowa
Size: 7¹/₈ × 9³/₄ in. (18.1 × 24.8 cm.)
Artist: Henry Lewis
Lithographer:
Printer: [C. H. Muller, Aachen]
Publisher: Jnst. Arnz & Co., Dusseldorf
Key/Vignettes/Misc:
Locations: MHS–SP; NYH–NY; HEHL;
NL–C; HNOC–NO; LC–R
Catalogs/Checklists:

1060
Place: Muscatine, Iowa
Date: 1874
Title: Bird's Eye View of the City of
Muscatine, Muscatine Co., Iowa, 1874.
Size: 15³/₄ × 25³/₄ in. (40.1 × 65.5 cm.)
Artist: Augustus Koch
Lithographer:
Printer:
Publisher:
Key/Vignettes/Misc: Refs. 1–29
Locations: ISHS–I
Catalogs/Checklists:

1061
Place: Newton, Iowa
Date: 1868
Title: Bird's Eye View of Newton, Jasper
Co., Iowa.
Size: 20¹³/₁₆ × 26³/₁₆ in. (53 × 67 cm.)
Artist: A. Ruger
Lithographer:
Printer: Merchants Lithographing Co.,
Chicago
Publisher:
Key/Vignettes/Misc: Refs. 1–10; 2
vignettes
Locations: LC–M
Catalogs/Checklists: LC–M, 224

Place: North McGregor, Iowa
Date: 1869
See McGregor, Iowa, 1869.

1062
Place: Ottumwa, Iowa
Date: 1890
Title: Ottumwa, Iowa.
Size: 16½ × 20⁷/₁₆ in. (42 × 52 cm.)
Artist: J. H. Richmond
Lithographer:
Printer: Courier Printing Co., Ottumwa,
Iowa
Publisher:
Key/Vignettes/Misc:
Locations: Ottumwa, Iowa, Public Library
Catalogs/Checklists:

1063
Place: Port Byron, Iowa
Date: [1854–57]
Title: Port Byron, Iowa and Berlin Illinois
Size: 7¹/₈ × 9³/₄ in. (18.1 × 24.8 cm.)
Artist: Henry Lewis
Lithographer:
Printer: [C. H. Muller, Aachen]
Publisher: Jnst. Arnz & Co., Dusseldorf
Key/Vignettes/Misc:
Locations: MHS–SP; NYH–NY; HEHL;
NL–C; CHS–C; HNOC–NO; LC–R
Catalogs/Checklists:

1064
Place: Sioux City, Iowa
Date: 1888
Title: Perspective Map of Sioux City, Iowa.
1888.
Size: 23⁹/₁₆ × 37³/₄ in. (60 × 96 cm.)
Artist: Henry Wellge
Lithographer:
Printer: The Beck & Pauli Lith Co.,
Milwaukee
Publisher: H. Wellge & Co., Milwaukee
Key/Vignettes/Misc: Refs. 1–15, 17–80,
A–T, I–XVI; 5 vignettes
Locations: LC–M
Catalogs/Checklists: LC–M, 225

1065
Place: Vinton, Iowa
Date: [1868?]
Title: Birds Eye View of Vinton Benton
County Iowa
Size: 21 × 29 in. (53.4 × 73.8 cm.)
Artist: Augustus Koch
Lithographer:

Printer: Chicago Lithographing Co.
[Chicago]
Publisher:
Key/Vignettes/Misc: Refs. 1–17; 30
vignettes; description
Locations: Vinton, Iowa, Public Library
Catalogs/Checklists:

1066
Place: Waterloo, Iowa
Date: 1868
Title: Waterloo Black Hawk County, Iowa
1868
Size: 22¹³/₁₆ × 28⁵/₁₆ in. (58 × 72 cm.)
Artist: A. Koch
Lithographer:
Printer: Merchants Lithographing Co.,
Chicago
Publisher:
Key/Vignettes/Misc: 2 vignettes
Locations: Grout Museum of History &
Science, Waterloo, Iowa
Catalogs/Checklists:

1067
Place: Waterloo, Iowa
Date: 1899
Title: Panoramic Birdseye View of
Waterloo, Iowa.
Size: 19⁵/₈ × 33⁷/₁₆ in. (50 × 85 cm.)
Artist: Bert. J. Griswold
Lithographer:
Printer:
Publisher: Waterloo Daily Courier
(copyright)
Key/Vignettes/Misc: Description
Locations: Grout Museum of History &
Science, Waterloo, Iowa; Cedar Falls,
Iowa, Historical Society
Catalogs/Checklists:

1068
Place: Webster City, Iowa
Date: 1869
Title: Bird's Eye View of Webster City
Hamilton County, Iowa 1869
Size: 16³/₈ × 22⁷/₈ in. (41.7 × 58.3 cm.)
Artist: A. Koch
Lithographer:
Printer: Merchant's Lithographing Co.,
Chicago
Publisher:
Key/Vignettes/Misc: Refs. 1–8
Locations: Kendall Young Library, Webster
City, Iowa
Catalogs/Checklists:

1069
Place: Winterset, Iowa
Date: 1869
Title: Bird's Eye View of the City of
Winterset
Size: 16¹/₈ × 20¹/₁₆ in. (41 × 51 cm.)
Artist: Augustus Koch
Lithographer:
Printer: Chicago Lithographing Co.,
Chicago
Publisher:
Key/Vignettes/Misc:
Locations: Iowa State University Library,
Ames, Iowa
Catalogs/Checklists:

1070
Place: Arkansas City, Kansas
Date: 1870
Title: Arkansas City. Kansas
Size: 14 × 20 in. (35.6 × 50.9 cm.)
Artist: Esther A. Bridge
Lithographer:
Printer:
Publisher:
Key/Vignettes/Misc: 2 vignettes
Locations: KSHS−T
Catalogs/Checklists:

1071
Place: Arkansas City, Kansas
Date: 1890
Title: Bird's Eye View of Arkansas City, Cowley County, Kansas
Size: 11¾ × 16⅛ in. (30 × 41 cm.)
Artist: Augustus Koch
Lithographer:
Printer: Hudson−Kimberly Publishing Co. [Kansas City, Missouri]
Publisher:
Key/Vignettes/Misc:
Locations: Cherokee Strip Museum, Arkansas City, Kansas
Catalogs/Checklists:

1072
Place: Atchison, Kansas
Date: 1869
Title: Bird's Eye View of the City of Atchison Atchison Co. Kansas. 1869.
Size: 20½ × 25½ in. (52.1 × 64.8 cm.)
Artist: A. Ruger
Lithographer:
Printer: Merchants Lithographing Co., Chicago
Publisher:
Key/Vignettes/Misc: Refs. 1−15; 2 vignettes
Locations: LC−M; KSHS−T
Catalogs/Checklists: LC−M, 226

1073
Place: Atchison, Kansas
Date: 1880
Title: Birds Eye View of Atchison Kansas 1880
Size: 21⁵⁄₁₆ × 33¹⁵⁄₁₆ in. (54.1 × 86.1 cm.)
Artist: Augustus Koch
Lithographer:
Printer: Ramsey, Millet & Hudson, Lith, Kansas City, Mo.
Publisher:
Key/Vignettes/Misc: Refs. 1−48
Locations: KSHS−T; LC−M (photo)
Catalogs/Checklists: Reps, Cities on Stone, p. 91; LC−M, 226.1

1074
Place: Cawker City, Kansas
Date: 1879
Title: Birds Eye View of Cawker City, Mitchell County, Kansas. 1879.
Size: 10¼ × 14½ in. (26 × 37 cm.)
Artist:
Lithographer:
Printer:
Publisher: J. J. Stoner, Madison, Wis.

Key/Vignettes/Misc:
Locations: KUL−L
Catalogs/Checklists:

1075
Place: Chetopa, Kansas
Date: 1871
Title: Birds Eye View of the City of Chetopa Kansas.
Size: 15⅛ × 20¹³⁄₁₆ in. (38.5 × 53 cm.)
Artist: E. S. Glover
Lithographer:
Printer: Union Lith. Co. Chicago Ill.
Publisher:
Key/Vignettes/Misc: Refs. 1−12
Locations: ACMW−FW
Catalogs/Checklists:

1076
Place: Clay Center, Kansas
Date: 1880
Title: Clay Center, 1880.
Size: 6¼ × 19¾ in. (15.9 × 50.3 cm.)
Artist: White
Lithographer:
Printer: Moss Co., New York
Publisher:
Key/Vignettes/Misc: 1 vignette
Locations: KSHS−T
Catalogs/Checklists:

1077
Place: Clay Center, Kansas
Date: 1887
Title: Views of Clay Center, Kansas, Summer of 1887
Size: 24 × 37½ in. (61.1 × 95.4 cm.)
Artist: Hough & Ricker
Lithographer:
Printer:
Publisher:
Key/Vignettes/Misc: 53 vignettes
Locations: KSHS−T
Catalogs/Checklists:

1078
Place: Concordia, Kansas
Date: 1879
Title: Concordia Kansas, Cloud Co. 1879.
Size: 10 × 16 in. (25.4 × 40.7 cm.)
Artist:
Lithographer:
Printer:
Publisher: J. J. Stoner, Madison, Wis.
Key/Vignettes/Misc: Refs. 1−20
Locations: KSHS−T
Catalogs/Checklists:

1079
Place: Cottonwood Falls, Kansas
Date: 1878
Title: Cottonwood Falls County Seat of Chase Co. One Mile from the A. T. & S. F. R. R.
Size: 10⅝ × 13⁵⁄₁₆ in. (27 × 34 cm.)
Artist: D. D. Morse
Lithographer:
Printer: Lott & Zeuch, Lith, Chicago
Publisher:
Key/Vignettes/Misc:
Locations: KSHS−T
Catalogs/Checklists:

1080
Place: Council Grove, Kansas
Date: 1873
Title: Bird's Eye View of Council Grove, Kansas From the North West Looking South East 1873
Size: 15⅛ × 22⅛ in. (38.5 × 56.3 cm.)
Artist: E. S. Glover
Lithographer:
Printer: Strobridge & Co., Lith. Cin.
Publisher:
Key/Vignettes/Misc: Refs. 1−10; 6 vignettes
Locations: City Hall, Council Grove, Kansas
Catalogs/Checklists:

1081
Place: Dodge City, Kansas
Date: 1882
Title: Bird's Eye View of Dodge City, Kans. County Seat of Ford County 1882.
Size: 8¼ × 12½ in. (20.9 × 31.7 cm.)
Artist:
Lithographer:
Printer: Beck & Pauli, Lithographers, Milwaukee, Wis.
Publisher: J. J. Stoner, Madison, Wis.
Key/Vignettes/Misc: Refs. 1−7, A−K, X
Locations: KSHS−T; LC−M (photo)
Catalogs/Checklists: Reps, Cities on Stone, p. 92; LC−M, 226.2

1082
Place: El Dorado, Kansas
Date: 1878
Title: Eldorado County seat, Butler Co., Kas.
Size: 12⁹⁄₁₆ × 16½ in. (32 × 42 cm.)
Artist: D. D. Morse
Lithographer:
Printer: Lott & Zeuch, Lith, Chicago
Publisher:
Key/Vignettes/Misc:
Locations: KSHS−T
Catalogs/Checklists:

1083
Place: Great Bend, Kansas
Date: [1878?]
Title: Great Bend. Kansas. County Seat Barton Co. on the A. T. & S. F. R. R. and Arkansas River.
Size: 11 × 14⅞ in. (28 × 37.8 cm.)
Artist: D. D. Morse
Lithographer:
Printer: Lott & Zeuch, Lith. Chicago.
Publisher:
Key/Vignettes/Misc:
Locations: KSHS−T
Catalogs/Checklists:

1084
Place: Halstead, Kansas
Date: 1878
Title: Halstead Harvey Co. 1878. Kansas.
Size: 10¼ × 12½ in. (26.1 × 31.8 cm.)
Artist: D. D. Morse
Lithographer:
Printer: Lott & Zeuch, Lith. Chicago
Publisher:

Key/Vignettes/Misc: Refs. 1−8
Locations: KSHS−T
Catalogs/Checklists:

1085
Place: Hiawatha, Kansas
Date: 1879
Title: Hiawatha, Kansas 1879
Size: 8 × 13¾ in. (20 × 35 cm.)
Artist: T. M. Fowler
Lithographer:
Printer:
Publisher:
Key/Vignettes/Misc: Refs. 1−18
Locations: KUL−L; LC−M (photo)
Catalogs/Checklists: LC−M, 228.1

1086
Place: Hutchinson, Kansas
Date: 1878
Title: Hutchinson, Kansas 1878 County Seat, Reno Co.
Size: 13¾ × 17 in. (35.2 × 43.3 cm.)
Artist: D. D. Morse
Lithographer:
Printer: Lott & Zeuch, Lith. Chicago
Publisher:
Key/Vignettes/Misc: Refs. 1−12, A−B
Locations: KSHS−T
Catalogs/Checklists:

1087
Place: Iola, Kansas
Date: 1872
Title: View of Iola. Kansas, 1872
Size: 17¼ × 21¾ in. (43.9 × 55.3 cm.)
Artist: E. S. Glover
Lithographer:
Printer: Strobridge & Co. Lith. Cin. O.
Publisher:
Key/Vignettes/Misc: Refs. 1−12
Locations: Allen County Historical Society, Iola, Kansas
Catalogs/Checklists:

1088
Place: Iola, Kansas
Date: N.D.
Title: Where the "Sunflower" Brand of Portland Cement is Made, Iola, Kansas
Size: 13¾ × 28¼ in. (35 × 71.9 cm.)
Artist:
Lithographer:
Printer: Hurd Wheeler Co., Detroit
Publisher:
Key/Vignettes/Misc:
Locations: KSHS−T
Catalogs/Checklists:

1089
Place: Junction City, Kansas
Date: 1873
Title: Bird's Eye View of Junction City, Kansas 1873 From the South−East. Looking North−West.
Size: 20¼ × 25⅞ in. (51.5 × 65.8 cm.)
Artist: E. S. Glover
Lithographer:
Printer: Strobridge & Co., Lith. Cin. O.
Publisher:
Key/Vignettes/Misc: Refs., Junction City, 1−18, Fort Riley, 1−16; 4 vignettes

Locations: KSHS−T
Catalogs/Checklists:

1090
Place: Kansas City, Kansas
Date: 1869
Title:
Size: 8 × 13¼ in. (20.4 × 33.8 cm.) (photo)
Artist: G. L. Chadborn (?)
Lithographer:
Printer:
Publisher:
Key/Vignettes/Misc:
Locations: KSHS−T (photo)
Catalogs/Checklists:

1091
Place: Kansas City, Kansas
Date: 1869
Title: Bird's Eye View of Wyandotte Wyandotte Co. Kansas 1869
Size: 11½ × 18 in. (29.2 × 45.8 cm.)
Artist: A. Ruger
Lithographer:
Printer: Merchants Lith. Co., Chicago
Publisher:
Key/Vignettes/Misc: Refs. 1−12; 1 vignette
Locations: LC−M; Wyandotte County Museum, Bonner Springs, Kansas
Catalogs/Checklists: LC−M, 232

1092
Place: Kansas City, Kansas
Date: 1887
Title: Kansas City in 1855 to 1887.
Size: 24 1/16 × 39⅛ in. (61.2 × 99.5 cm.)
Artist:
Lithographer:
Printer:
Publisher: Lanward Specialty Publishing Co., Chicago
Key/Vignettes/Misc: 7 vignettes
Locations: LC−P
Catalogs/Checklists:

1093
Place: Kingman, Kansas
Date: 1883
Title: Birds Eye View of Kingman, Kingman Co. Kan 1883
Size: 12 9/16 × 19⅝ in. (32 × 50 cm.)
Artist: A. Koch
Lithographer:
Printer:
Publisher:
Key/Vignettes/Misc:
Locations: KSHS−T
Catalogs/Checklists:

1094
Place: Kingman, Kansas
Date: 1886
Title: Bird's Eye View of Kingman Kingman County Kansas 1886
Size: 20 13/16 × 26¾ in. (53 × 68 cm.)
Artist: Augustus Koch
Lithographer:
Printer:
Publisher:
Key/Vignettes/Misc:

Locations: KSHS−T
Catalogs/Checklists:

1095
Place: Kinsley, Kansas
Date: 1878
Title: Kinsley, Kas. 1878. County Seat, Edwards Co. on the A. T. & S. F. R. R.
Size: 10½ × 12¾ in. (26.7 × 32.5 cm.)
Artist: D. D. Morse
Lithographer:
Printer: Lott & Zeuch Lith. Chicago.
Publisher:
Key/Vignettes/Misc:
Locations: KSHS−T
Catalogs/Checklists:

1096
Place: Larned, Kansas
Date: 1878
Title: Bird's Eye View of Larned, Kas 1878 County Seat of Pawnee Co.
Size: 11 × 14⅛ in. (28 × 36 cm.)
Artist: D. D. Morse
Lithographer:
Printer: Lott & Zeuch, Lith, Chicago
Publisher:
Key/Vignettes/Misc:
Locations: KSHS−T
Catalogs/Checklists:

1097
Place: Lawrence, Kansas
Date: 1858
Title: View of Lawrence Kansas. Looking South West May 1858
Size: 15 × 23⅛ in. (38 × 58.6 cm.)
Artist:
Lithographer:
Printer: Middleton, Strobridge & Co., Cincinnati
Publisher: Middleton, Strobridge & Co., Cincinnati
Key/Vignettes/Misc: Refs. 1−20; 2 vignettes
Locations: KSHS−T
Catalogs/Checklists: Reps, Cities on Stone, p. 94

1098
Place: Lawrence, Kansas
Date: 1858
Title: View of Lawrence Kansas. Looking South West May 1858.
Size: 11½ × 22¾ in. (29.3 × 57.9 cm.)
Artist:
Lithographer:
Printer:
Publisher:
Key/Vignettes/Misc: 2 vignettes; map of route to gold mines; advertisements
Locations: KSHS−T
Catalogs/Checklists:

1099
Place: Lawrence, Kansas
Date: 1858
Title: View of Lawrence, Kansas. Looking N. E. from the Grounds of the Lawrence University, on Mt. Oread.
Size: 14 × 18 13/16 in. (35.6 × 47.8 cm.)
Artist:

Lithographer:
Printer:
Publisher:
Key/Vignettes/Misc: 7 unnumbered refs. below places identified
Locations: NYP–S
Catalogs/Checklists: Stokes C. 1860—G–60A

1100
Place: Lawrence, Kansas
Date: 1869
Title: Bird's Eye View of the City of Lawrence Kansas 1869
Size: 20¾ × 26½ in. (52.8 × 67.3 cm.)
Artist: [Albert Ruger]
Lithographer:
Printer:
Publisher:
Key/Vignettes/Misc: Refs. 1–16; 2 vignettes
Locations: LC–M; CHS–C; KUL–L
Catalogs/Checklists: LC–M, 229

1101
Place: Lawrence, Kansas
Date: 1880
Title: Bird's Eye View of Lawrence. Kansas, 1880.
Size: 22¼ × 30⅜ in. (56.6 × 77.3 cm.)
Artist: [D. D. Morse?]
Lithographer:
Printer: Wm. Zeuch & Co., Chicago
Publisher: D. D. Morse (copyright)
Key/Vignettes/Misc: Refs. 1–33; 2 vignettes
Locations: KSHS–T; KUL–L
Catalogs/Checklists:

1102
Place: Lawrence, Kansas
Date: Ca. 1882
Title: Lawrence, Kansas
Size: 22½ × 34¾ in. (57.3 × 88.4 cm.)
Artist:
Lithographer:
Printer: Ramsey, Millett & Hudson Lith. Kansas City, Mo.
Publisher:
Key/Vignettes/Misc: 3 views on sectioned sheet
Locations: KSHS–T
Catalogs/Checklists:

1103
Place: Lawrence, Kansas
Date: N.D.
Title: [Bismarck Grove]
Size: 23½ × 34¾ in. (59.8 × 88.4 cm.)
Artist:
Lithographer:
Printer: Ramsey, Millett & Hudson, Kansas City, Mo.
Publisher:
Key/Vignettes/Misc: 4 views on sectioned sheet
Locations: KSHS–T
Catalogs/Checklists:

1104
Place: Leavenworth, Kansas
Date: 1857

Title: Leavenworth City, Kansas Tery. Settled Fall of 1854. 3000 Pop. 1856
Size: 14⁹/₁₆ × 22⅞ in. (37 × 58 cm.)
Artist: R. Ormsby Sweeny
Lithographer: Bachmann
Printer: P. S. Duval & Son's Lith press Phil.
Publisher: R. Ormsby Sweeny (copyright)
Key/Vignettes/Misc:
Locations: LC–P
Catalogs/Checklists:

1105
Place: Leavenworth, Kansas
Date: 1858
Title: View of Leavenworth, K. T. March 1858. Looking West
Size: 31 × 42½ in. (78.8 × 108 cm.)
Artist:
Lithographer:
Printer: Middleton [Strobridge & Co., Cincinnati]
Publisher: Middleton [Strobridge & Co., Cincinnati]
Key/Vignettes/Misc: Refs. 1–12; description
Locations: Leavenworth County Historical Museum, Leavenworth, Kansas
Catalogs/Checklists:

1106
Place: Leavenworth, Kansas
Date: 1869
Title: Bird's Eye View of the City of Leavenworth Kansas 1869
Size: 21¾ × 27¾ in. (55.2 × 70.5 cm.)
Artist: A. Ruger
Lithographer:
Printer: Chicago Lithographing Co. [Chicago]
Publisher:
Key/Vignettes/Misc: Refs. 1–19; 4 vignettes
Locations: LC–M; CHS–C
Catalogs/Checklists: LC–M, 230; Reps, Cities on Stone, p. 94

1107
Place: Neosho Falls, Kansas
Date: 1871
Title: Birds Eye View of Neosho Falls, Woodson Co. Kan 1871
Size: 14⅛ × 18⁷/₁₆ in. (36 × 47 cm.)
Artist: E. S. Glover
Lithographer:
Printer: Merchants Lith Co.
Publisher:
Key/Vignettes/Misc:
Locations: KSHS–T
Catalogs/Checklists:

1108
Place: Newton, Kansas
Date: 1879
Title: Newton, Kas on the Atchison Topeka & Santafe R. R. 1879
Size: 13 × 16⅞ in. (33 × 43 cm.)
Artist: D. D. Morse
Lithographer:
Printer: Lott & Zeuch, Lith, Chicago
Publisher:

Key/Vignettes/Misc: 4 vignettes
Locations: KSHS–T
Catalogs/Checklists:

Place: Oak Dale Park, Kansas
Date: 1879
See Salina, Kansas, 1879.

1109
Place: Oswego, Kansas
Date: 1877
Title: Bird's Eye View of the City of Oswego, Labette County, Kansas 1877
Size: 12⅛ × 19⅝ in. (31 × 50 cm.)
Artist: Augustus Koch
Lithographer:
Printer: Shober & Carqueville, Chicago
Publisher:
Key/Vignettes/Misc:
Locations: KSHS–T
Catalogs/Checklists:

1110
Place: Ottawa, Kansas
Date: 1872
Title: Bird's–Eye View of Ottawa the Largest City of its Age in Kansas 1872
Size: 22 × 31 in. (56 × 79 cm.)
Artist: E. [S.] Glover
Lithographer:
Printer: Strobridge & Co., Cin
Publisher:
Key/Vignettes/Misc: 4 vignettes
Locations: KSHS–T
Catalogs/Checklists:

1111
Place: Paola, Kansas
Date: 1873
Title: Bird's Eye View of Paola, Miami Co., Kan. 1873.
Size: 15 × 22 in. (38.1 × 55.9 cm.)
Artist: E. S. Glover
Lithographer:
Printer: Strobridge & Co., Lith, Cin.
Publisher:
Key/Vignettes/Misc: Refs. 1–10
Locations: KSHS–T
Catalogs/Checklists:

1112
Place: Peabody, Kansas
Date: 1878
Title: Peabody, Kansas Marion County
Size: 11 × 13⁵/₁₆ in. (28 × 34 cm.)
Artist: D. D. Morse
Lithographer:
Printer: Lott & Zeuch, Lith. Chicago
Publisher:
Key/Vignettes/Misc: 1 vignette
Locations: KSHS–T
Catalogs/Checklists:

1113
Place: Salina, Kansas
Date: 1879
Title: Birds Eye View of the Oak Dale Park: Property of W. R. Geis: Adjoining the City of Salina, Kans.
Size: 10¼ × 15¼ in. (26.1 × 38.8 cm.)
Artist: Augustus Koch
Lithographer:

Printer: Ramsey, Millett & Hudson Lith., Kansas City, Mo.
Publisher:
Key/Vignettes/Misc:
Locations: KSHS−T
Catalogs/Checklists:

1114
Place: Sterling, Kansas
Date: 1878
Title: City of Sterling, Kansas 1878
Size: 10⅝ × 13⁵⁄₁₆ in. (27 × 34 cm.)
Artist: D. D. Morse
Lithographer:
Printer: Lott & Zeuch, Lith., Chicago
Publisher:
Key/Vignettes/Misc:
Locations: KSHS−T
Catalogs/Checklists:

1115
Place: Sumner, Kansas
Date: Ca. 1857
Title: View of Sumner Kansas Terry.
Size: 17¹³⁄₁₆ × 28 in. (45.2 × 71.0 cm.)
Artist:
Lithographer:
Printer: Middleton, Strobridge & Co., Cin. O.
Publisher: Middleton, Strobridge & Co., Cin. O.
Key/Vignettes/Misc: 1 vignette
Locations: KSHS−T
Catalogs/Checklists: Reps, Cities on Stone, p. 98

1116
Place: Tecumseh, Kansas
Date: Ca.1859
Title: View of Tecumseh Kansas
Size: 20¼ × 28⅜ in. (51.5 × 72.1 cm.)
Artist:
Lithographer:
Printer: Middleton−Strobridge & Co. Cin. O.
Publisher: Middleton−Strobridge & Co. Cin. O.
Key/Vignettes/Misc: Description
Locations: KSHS−T; LC−M (photo)
Catalogs/Checklists: LC−M, 230.1

1117
Place: Topeka, Kansas
Date: Ca. 1866
Title: Bird's Eye View of the City of Topeka, Shawnee Co. Kansas
Size: 11¾ × 23⁹⁄₁₆ in. (30 × 60 cm.)
Artist: H. Worrall
Lithographer:
Printer: Strickler, Daniels & Pounds, Topeka
Publisher: Investment Banking Company, Topeka
Key/Vignettes/Misc:
Locations: KSHS−T
Catalogs/Checklists:

1118
Place: Topeka, Kansas
Date: 1869
Title: Bird's Eye View of the City of Topeka The Capital of Kansas 1869.

Size: 20 × 26 in. (50.8 × 66 cm.)
Artist: A. Ruger
Lithographer:
Printer: Chicago Lithographing Co., [Chicago]
Publisher:
Key/Vignettes/Misc: Refs. 1−13; 2 vignettes
Locations: LC−M
Catalogs/Checklists: LC−M, 231; Reps, Cities on Stone, p. 98

1119
Place: Topeka, Kansas
Date: 1880
Title: Birds Eye View of Topeka Kansas.
Size: 21⅜ × 33¹⁵⁄₁₆ in. (54.3 × 86.2 cm.)
Artist: Aügustus Koch
Lithographer:
Printer: Ramsey, Millet & Hudson, Lith, Kansas Cy., Mo.
Publisher:
Key/Vignettes/Misc: Refs. 1−48
Locations: KSHS−T; LC−M (photo)
Catalogs/Checklists: Reps, Cities on Stone, p. 98; LC−M, 231.1

1120
Place: Topeka, Kansas
Date: Ca. 1887
Title: Birds Eye View of the City of Topeka Kansas
Size: 11⅞ × 27³⁄₁₆ in. (30.1 × 69.1 cm.)
Artist: H. Worrall
Lithographer:
Printer: Topeka Lithographing and Bank Note Co.
Publisher:
Key/Vignettes/Misc:
Locations: ACMW−FW
Catalogs/Checklists:

1121
Place: Topeka, Kansas
Date: Ca. 1887
Title: Birds Eye View of the City of Topeka, Shawnee Co. Kansas.
Size: 11¾ × 23⁷⁄₁₆ in. (29.7 × 59.5 cm.)
Artist: H. Worrall
Lithographer:
Printer:
Publisher:
Key/Vignettes/Misc: Refs. 1−8
Locations: ACMW−FW
Catalogs/Checklists:

1122
Place: Wichita, Kansas
Date: 1873
Title: Birds Eye View of Wichita, Kansas 1873.
Size: 18¾ × 22½ in. (47.7 × 57.3 cm.)
Artist: E. S. Glover
Lithographer:
Printer: Strobridge & Co. Cin. O.
Publisher:
Key/Vignettes/Misc:
Locations: Private collection; Wichita−Sedgwick Historical Society, Wichita, Kansas (photo)
Catalogs/Checklists:

1123
Place: Wichita, Kansas
Date: 1878
Title: Wichita, Kansas, Sedgwick County, 1878.
Size: 19 × 25½ in. (48.4 × 64.9 cm.)
Artist: D. D. Morse
Lithographer:
Printer: Lott & Zeuch, Chicago
Publisher:
Key/Vignettes/Misc: Refs. 1−16; 1 vignette
Locations: Historic Wichita−Cowtown, Wichita, Kansas; Wichita−Sedgwick County Historical Museum, Wichita, Kansas
Catalogs/Checklists:

Place: Wyandotte, Kansas
Date: 1869
See Kansas City, Kansas, 1869.

1124
Place: Ashland, Kentucky
Date: ?
Title: Ashland, Ky.
Size: 21 × 26 in. (53.4 × 66.2 cm.)
Artist: Riley & Ricker
Lithographer:
Printer: Shober & Carqueville Lith Co. Chicago
Publisher:
Key/Vignettes/Misc: 30 vignettes
Locations: Boyd County Historical Society, Ashland, Kentucky
Catalogs/Checklists:

1125
Place: Bowling Green, Kentucky
Date: 1871
Title: Bird's Eye View of the City of Bowling Green. Warren County Kentucky 1871.
Size: 23 × 26 in. (58.5 × 66.1 cm.)
Artist: A. Ruger
Lithographer:
Printer: Chicago Litho. Co. [Chicago]
Publisher:
Key/Vignettes/Misc: Refs. 1−16; 1 vignette
Locations: LC−M
Catalogs/Checklists: LC−M, 233

Place: Covington, Kentucky
Date: [1851]
See Newport, Kentucky, [1851].

Place: Covington, Kentucky
Date: N.D.
See Cincinnati, Ohio, N. D.

1126
Place: Frankfort, Kentucky
Date: 1854
Title: The City of Frankfort Franklin Co. Ky.
Size: 33 × 38 in. (83.9 × 96.6 cm.)
Artist: Hart & Mapother
Lithographer:
Printer: Robyn & Co., Louisville
Publisher: Hart & Mapother, Civil Engineers, Louisville & New York

Key/Vignettes/Misc:
Locations: Kentucky Historical Society, Frankfort, Kentucky
Catalogs/Checklists:

1127
Place: Frankfort, Kentucky
Date: 1871
Title: Bird's Eye View of the City of Frankfort the Capital of Kentucky 1871. Looking Southeast.
Size: 23 × 24 in. (58.5 × 61 cm.)
Artist: [Albert Ruger]
Lithographer:
Printer: Ehrgott & Krebs, Lith., Cincinnati, Ohio
Publisher:
Key/Vignettes/Misc: Refs. 1–9, A–C; 2 vignettes
Locations: LC–M
Catalogs/Checklists: LC–M, 234

1128
Place: Franklin, Kentucky
Date: 1871
Title: Birds Eye View of the City of Franklin Simpson County 1871.
Size: 17⅞ × 23⁹⁄₁₆ in. (45.1 × 59.9 cm.)
Artist: E. L. Crall
Lithographer:
Printer:
Publisher: E. L. Crall
Key/Vignettes/Misc: Refs. 1–9
Locations: ACMW–FW
Catalogs/Checklists:

1129
Place: Lexington, Kentucky
Date: [1851]
Title: Lexington, Ky. Taken from the Transylvania University.
Size: 5¹⁵⁄₁₆ × 7¹⁵⁄₁₆ in. (13.5 × 18.9 cm.)
Artist: F. v. Laer
Lithographer:
Printer: Onken's Lithography, Cin. O.
Publisher: [Otto Onken, Cincinnati, Ohio]
Key/Vignettes/Misc:
Locations: CPL–R
Catalogs/Checklists:

1130
Place: Lexington, Kentucky
Date: [1856?]
Title: View of the City of Lexington, Ky.
Size: 37 × 46 in. (94.2 × 117 cm.)
Artist:
Lithographer: Middleton, Wallace & Co.
Printer: Middleton, Wallace & Co. Lithos., 115 Walnut St., Cincinnati O.
Publisher: J. T. Palmatary
Key/Vignettes/Misc:
Locations: Kentucky Historical Society, Frankfort, Kentucky (photo)
Catalogs/Checklists:

1131
Place: Lexington, Kentucky
Date: 1871
Title: Bird's Eye View of the City of Lexington Fayette County, Kentucky. 1871. Looking South West.
Size: 23 × 28 in. (58.5 × 71.2 cm.)

Artist: [Albert Ruger]
Lithographer:
Printer: Ehrgott & Krebs, Lith., Cincinnati, Ohio
Publisher:
Key/Vignettes/Misc: Refs. 1–24; 3 vignettes
Locations: LC–M
Catalogs/Checklists: LC–M, 235

1132
Place: Louisville, Kentucky
Date: 1850
Title: Louisville, Ky. From Jeffersonville, Ia.—1850
Size: 23 × 37¼ in. (58.5 × 94.7 cm.)
Artist:
Lithographer: B. F. Smith, Jr.
Printer: P. S. Duval, Philadelphia
Publisher:
Key/Vignettes/Misc:
Locations: Library Company of Philadelphia, Philadelphia, Pennsylvania; FC–L
Catalogs/Checklists: Pyne, no. 441

1133
Place: Louisville, Kentucky
Date: [1851]
Title: Louisville, Ky. Taken from the Public Landing.
Size: 5¾ × 7¾ in. (14.7 × 19.7 cm.)
Artist:
Lithographer: F. v. Laer
Printer: Onken's Lithography, Cincinnati, O.
Publisher: [Otto Onken, Cincinnati, Ohio]
Key/Vignettes/Misc:
Locations: CPL–R
Catalogs/Checklists:

1134
Place: Louisville, Kentucky
Date: 1855
Title: View of the City of Louisville, Ky.
Size: 33½ × 52 in. (85.3 × 132.3 cm.)
Artist:
Lithographer: Middleton, Wallace & Co.
Printer: Middleton, Wallace & Co. 115 Walnut St., Cincinnati, O.
Publisher: J. T. Palmatary
Key/Vignettes/Misc:
Locations: Liberty National Bank & Trust Co., Louisville, Kentucky
Catalogs/Checklists:

1135
Place: Louisville, Kentucky
Date: 1876
Title: Bird's Eye View of Louisville, Kentucky 1876.
Size: 16⅛ × 26 in. (41 × 66 cm.)
Artist: A. Ruger
Lithographer:
Printer: Chas. Shober & Co., props. Chicago Lith. Co. [Chicago]
Publisher:
Key/Vignettes/Misc: Refs. 1–54
Locations: LC–M; FC–L; CHS–C; ACMW–FW
Catalogs/Checklists: LC–M, 236

1136
Place: Louisville, Kentucky
Date: 1883
Title: Birds–Eye View of Louisville from the River Front and Southern Exposition, 1883.
Size: 23⅛ × 36⅛ in. (59 × 92 cm.)
Artist: W. F. Clarke
Lithographer:
Printer:
Publisher: M. P. Levyeau & Co., Cincinnati
Key/Vignettes/Misc: 27 vignettes
Locations: LC–M
Catalogs/Checklists: LC–M, 237

1137
Place: Maysville, Kentucky
Date: [1851]
Title: Maysville, Ky.
Size: 5¾ × 7⅞ in. (14.7 × 20 cm.)
Artist:
Lithographer: E. Bott
Printer: Onken's Lith, Cin. O.
Publisher: [Otto Onken, Cincinnati, Ohio]
Key/Vignettes/Misc:
Locations: CPL–R
Catalogs/Checklists:

1138
Place: Newport, Kentucky
Date: [1851]
Title: View of Newport, Covington and Cincinnati Landing. . . .
Size: 18 (matted) × 28⅝ in. (45.9 × 72.9 cm.)
Artist:
Lithographer:
Printer: Middleton, Wallace & Co. Cincinnati, Ohio
Publisher: Middleton, Wallace & co., Cincinnati, Ohio
Key/Vignettes/Misc:
Locations: COHS
Catalogs/Checklists:

Place: Newport, Kentucky
Date: N.D.
See Cincinnati, Ohio, N. D.

1139
Place: Paducah, Kentucky
Date: 1873
Title: Bird's Eye View of the City of Paducah, Kentucky 1873
Size: 22 × 34½ in. (56 × 87.8 cm.)
Artist: H. Brosius
Lithographer:
Printer: Ehrgott & Krebs Steam Lith. Printers, Cinn.
Publisher:
Key/Vignettes/Misc: 31 refs.
Locations: William Clark Market House Museum, Paducah, Kentucky
Catalogs/Checklists:

1140
Place: Paducah, Kentucky
Date: 1889
Title: Bird's Eye View of Paducah, Kentucky 1889.
Size: 27 × 39⅞ in. (68.7 × 101.4 cm.)

Artist: J. Blanton Postlethwaite
Lithographer:
Printer: The Krebs Lith. Co., Cincinnati, Ohio
Publisher:
Key/Vignettes/Misc: Refs. 1–46; 8 vignettes; unnumbered directory of schools and churches
Locations: LC–M; William Clark Market House Museum, Paducah, Kentucky; Paducah, Kentucky, Public Library
Catalogs/Checklists: LC–M, 238

1141
Place: Paris, Kentucky
Date: 1870
Title: Bird's Eye View of the City of Paris Bourbon County Kentucky 1870 Looking South East
Size: 22 × 25 in. (56 × 63.5 cm.)
Artist: [Albert Ruger]
Lithographer:
Printer:
Publisher:
Key/Vignettes/Misc: Refs. 1–18, A–C
Locations: LC–M
Catalogs/Checklists: LC–M, 239

1142
Place: Baton Rouge, Louisiana
Date: Ca. 1853
Title: View of Baton Rouge Capital of Louisiana
Size: 14¾ × 25⅞ in. (37.7 × 65.9 cm.)
Artist: J. A. Maurel
Lithographer: J. A. Maurel
Printer: X. Magny, Lithor. Exchange Alley N. Or.
Publisher:
Key/Vignettes/Misc:
Locations: TUL–NO
Catalogs/Checklists:

1143
Place: Baton Rouge, Louisiana
Date: Ca. 1857
Title: Baton Rouge (Capital of Louisiana)
Size: 14⅞ × 20⁵⁄₁₆ in. (37.9 × 51.8 cm.)
Artist: A. Persac [Marie Adrien Persac]
Lithographer: A. Persac
Printer: Pessou & Simon, 161 Chartres St. N. Orls
Publisher:
Key/Vignettes/Misc:
Locations: MM–NN; Anglo–American Art Museum, Louisiana State University, Baton Rouge, Louisiana
Catalogs/Checklists: MM–NN, LP 1829

1144
Place: Baton Rouge, Louisiana
Date: [1854–57]
Title: Baton Rouge, Louisiana
Size: 6⅜ × 8⁵⁄₁₆ in. (16.2 × 21.9 cm.)
Artist: Henry Lewis
Lithographer:
Printer: C. H. Muller, Aachen
Publisher: Arnz & Co., Dusseldorf
Key/Vignettes/Misc:
Locations: MHS–SP; NYH–NY; HEHL; LC–R; NL–C; HNOC–NO
Catalogs/Checklists:

1145
Place: Bayou Sara, Louisiana
Date: [1854–57]
Title: Bayon Sacra (Luisiana).
Size: 5⅞ × 7¹¹⁄₁₆ in. (15 × 19.6 cm.)
Artist: H. Lewis
Lithographer:
Printer: [C. H. Muller, Aachen]
Publisher: Arnz & Co. Dusseldorf
Key/Vignettes/Misc:
Locations: MHS–SP; NYH–NY; HEHL; LC–R; NL–C; HNOC–NO; SAM–SL
Catalogs/Checklists:

1146
Place: New Orleans, Louisiana
Date: 1842
Title: Vue de la Nouvelle Orleans Premiere MunicipaliteView of New Orleans First Municipality
Size: 14³⁄₁₆ × 18¹¹⁄₁₆ in. (36.1 × 47.6 cm.)
Artist: P. Cavallier
Lithographer: P. Cavallier
Printer: J. Manouvrier & Chav[in]
Publisher:
Key/Vignettes/Misc:
Locations: MM–NN; TUL–NO
Catalogs/Checklists: MM–NN, LP 1990

1147
Place: New Orleans, Louisiana
Date: 1842
Title: Vue de la Nouvelle Orleans Troisieme Municipalite View of New Orleans Third Municipality
Size: 14⅛ × 18⁹⁄₁₆ in. (36 × 47.3 cm.)
Artist: P. Cavallier
Lithographer: P. Cavallier
Printer: F. Chav[in]
Publisher:
Key/Vignettes/Misc:
Locations: TUL–NO
Catalogs/Checklists:

1148
Place: New Orleans, Louisiana
Date: [1842]
Title: Vue de la Nouvelle Orleans Deuxieme Municipality View of New Orleans Second Municipality
Size: 14³⁄₁₆ × 18⅝ in. (36.1 × 47.4 cm.)
Artist: P. Cavailler
Lithographer: P. Cavailler
Printer: J. Manouvrier & Chav[in]
Publisher:
Key/Vignettes/Misc:
Locations: MM–NN; TUL–NO
Catalogs/Checklists: MM–NN, LP 1989

1149
Place: New Orleans, Louisiana
Date: [1840–49]
Title: Nouvelle–Orleans. Nueva–Orleans
Size: 8³⁄₁₆ × 12⅜ in. (20.7 × 31.4 cm.)
Artist: L. Lebreton
Lithographer: L. Lebreton
Printer: Cosselin, r. St. Jacques 71, Paris
Publisher: Cosselin, Paris and Gadola, Lyon
Key/Vignettes/Misc:
Locations: HNOC–NO; YUAG–NH
Catalogs/Checklists:

1150
Place: New Orleans, Louisiana
Date: 1851
Title: Birds' Eye View of New–Orleans
Size: 24¼ × 31½ in. (61.7 × 80.1 cm.)
Artist: J. Bachman
Lithographer: J. Bachman
Printer: J. Bachman
Publisher: The Agents A. Guerber & Co. 160 Pearl St., New York
Key/Vignettes/Misc:
Locations: NYP–S; YUAG–NH; LC–P; NYH–NY
Catalogs/Checklists: Stokes 1851—G–13; LC–M, 240.1

1151
Place: New Orleans, Louisiana
Date: 1851
Title: Birds' Eye View of New–Orleans
Size: 23¾ × 31⅞ in. (60.3 × 80.9 cm.)
Artist: J Bachman
Lithographer: J Bachman
Printer: J Bachman
Publisher: J Bachman (copyright)
Key/Vignettes/Misc:
Locations: HNOC–NO
Catalogs/Checklists:

1152
Place: New Orleans, Louisiana
Date: [1851]
Title: New Orleans.
Size: 5¾ × 7⅞ in. (14.7 × 20 cm.)
Artist:
Lithographer: F. v. Laer
Printer: Onken's Lithography, Cin. O.
Publisher: [Otto Onken, Cincinnati]
Key/Vignettes/Misc:
Locations: HNOC–NO; CPL–R
Catalogs/Checklists:

1153
Place: New Orleans, Louisiana
Date: Ca. 1851
Title: Vue Generale de la Nouvelle–Orleans Prise d'Algiers
Size: 17⅜ × 25 in. (44.2 × 63.6 cm.)
Artist: Th. Muller
Lithographer: Th. Muller
Printer:
Publisher:
Key/Vignettes/Misc:
Locations: CHS–C
Catalogs/Checklists:

1154
Place: New Orleans, Louisiana
Date: 1852
Title: City of New Orleans
Size: 3¾ (matted) × 7¼ in. (9.6 matted × 8.5 cm.)
Artist:
Lithographer:
Printer: Hammond, Lith. N[ew] O[rleans]
Publisher:
Key/Vignettes/Misc:
Locations: LSM–NO
Catalogs/Checklists:

1155
Place: New Orleans, Louisiana
Date: 1852
Title: New Orleans from the Lower
Cotton Press 1852.
Size: 25¹¹⁄₁₆ × 41⁷⁄₁₆ in. (65.2 × 105.3
cm.)
Artist: J. W. Hill & Smith
Lithographer: D. W. Moody
Printer: Sarony & Major, N[ew] Y[ork]
Publisher: Smith Brothers & Co., 225
Fulton St., New York
Key/Vignettes/Misc:
Locations: MM–NN; HNOC–NO;
LSM–NO; LC–P; NYH–NY
Catalogs/Checklists: MM–NN, LP 953

1156
Place: New Orleans, Louisiana
Date: 1852 State I
Title: View of New Orleans from St.
Patrick's Church 1852.
Size: 25¹¹⁄₁₆ × 40⁵⁄₁₆ in. (65.2 × 102.4
cm.)
Artist: J. W. Hill & Smith
Lithographer: B. F. Smith, Jr.
Printer: [no imprint]
Publisher: Smith Brothers & Co., 225
Fulton St., New York
Key/Vignettes/Misc:
Locations: HNOC–NO; TUL–NO
Catalogs/Checklists:

1157
Place: New Orleans, Louisiana
Date: 1852 State II
Title: New Orleans from St. Patricks
Church 1852.
Size: 23⁷⁄₁₆ × 40⁵⁄₈ in. (59.6 × 103.3 cm.)
Artist: J. W. Hill & Smith
Lithographer: B. F. Smith Jr.
Printer: F. Michelin & Geo. E. Leefe, 225
Fulton St., N. Y.
Publisher: Smith Brothers & Co. 225
Fulton St. New York
Key/Vignettes/Misc:
Locations: NYP–S; CHS–C; LSM–NO;
LC–P
Catalogs/Checklists: Stokes 1852–G–17;
Rathbone, Westward the Way, no. 197

1158
Place: New Orleans, Louisiana
Date: [1854–57]
Title: New–Orleans (Louisiana).
Size: 6³⁄₈ × 18¹⁄₈ in. (16.5 × 46.3 cm.)
Artist: H. Lewis
Lithographer:
Printer: [C. H. Muller, Aachen]
Publisher: Jnst. Arnz & Co., Dusseldorf
Key/Vignettes/Misc:
Locations: MHS–SP; NYH–NY; HEHL;
NL–C; TUL–NO; HNOC–NO;
LSM–NO; LC–R
Catalogs/Checklists:

1159
Place: New Orleans, Louisiana
Date: [1850–59?]
Title: Bird's Eye View of New–Orleans.
Size: 23½ × 31⁷⁄₈ in. (59.6 × 80.9 cm.)

Artist:
Lithographer: C. Matter
Printer: R. Furrer
Publisher: J. U. Locher, St. Gall,
Switzerland, and J. H. Locher, 117 Fulton
St., New York
Key/Vignettes/Misc:
Locations: HNOC–NO; ROM;
LSM–NO
Catalogs/Checklists: Samuel, no. 466

1160
Place: New Orleans, Louisiana
Date: [1850–59?]
Title: Nouvelle–Orleans Vue Prise
d'Algiers Nueva Orleans Vista tomada
desde Algiers
Size: 18¹⁄₁₆ × 24³⁄₄ in. (46 × 63 cm.)
Artist: Th. Muller
Lithographer: Th. Muller
Printer:
Publisher:
Key/Vignettes/Misc:
Locations: CHS–C; HNOC–NO;
MM–NN; TUL–NO; LSM–NO; LC–M
(facsimile)
Catalogs/Checklists: MM–NN, LP 51;
LC–M, 240

1161
Place: New Orleans, Louisiana
Date: [1850–59?] State I
Title: View of the New–Orleans
Size: 17⁷⁄₈ × 24½ in. (45.3 × 62.2 cm.)
Artist: Bachmann
Lithographer: Asselineau
Printer: Auguste Bry, 114 r. du Bac, Paris
Publisher: Wild, Editeur, 15 rue de la
Banque, Place de la Bourse, Paris, and
Alex. Caleppi, 162 Chartres Street corner
of Toulouse [New Orleans]
Key/Vignettes/Misc:
Locations: HNOC–NO
Catalogs/Checklists:

1162
Place: New Orleans, Louisiana
Date: [1850–59?] State II
Title: Vue de la Nouvelle Orleans a Vol
d'Oiseau. [No. 49 at upper right]
Size: 16¹¹⁄₁₆ × 24¼ in. (42.5 × 61.7 cm.)
Artist: Bachmann
Lithographer: Asselineau
Printer: Auguste Bry, 114 r. du Bac, Paris
Publisher:
Key/Vignettes/Misc:
Locations: CHS–C; TUL–NO
Catalogs/Checklists:

1163
Place: New Orleans, Louisiana
Date: [1850–59?] State III
Title: View of the New–Orleans [No. 82
at upper right]
Size: 16¹⁄₁₆ × 24⁷⁄₁₆ in. (40.7 × 62.1 cm.)
Artist: Bachmann
Lithographer: Asselineau
Printer:
Publisher:
Key/Vignettes/Misc:
Locations: HNOC–NO
Catalogs/Checklists:

1164
Place: New Orleans, Louisiana
Date: Ca. 1873
Title: City of New Orleans.
Size: 8¹³⁄₁₆ × 12⁵⁄₈ in. (22.4 × 32.1 cm.)
Artist:
Lithographer:
Printer:
Publisher: Currier & Ives 125 Nassau St.
New York
Key/Vignettes/Misc: 8 unnumbered refs.
below places identified
Locations: CHS–C; MCNY; MM–NN;
HNOC–NO; YUAG–NH
Catalogs/Checklists: MM–NN, LP 48;
Peters, C & I, 3921a; Conningham 1100

1165
Place: New Orleans, Louisiana
Date: 1883
Title: Birds Eye View of the City of New
Orleans. And Suburbs.
Size: 24⁷⁄₈ × 40¼ in. (63.3 × 102.4 cm.)
Artist:
Lithographer:
Printer:
Publisher: Gustave Koeckert
Key/Vignettes/Misc: Refs. 1–30
Locations: NYH–NY; CHS–C;
TUL–NO
Catalogs/Checklists:

1166
Place: New Orleans, Louisiana
Date: 1885
Title: The City of New Orleans, and the
Mississippi River. Lake Ponchartrain in
Distance.
Size: 23⁷⁄₈ × 35 in. (60.8 × 89 cm.)
Artist:
Lithographer:
Printer:
Publisher: Currier & Ives, New York
Key/Vignettes/Misc: 42 unnumbered refs.
in 3 lines
Locations: LC–P; FC–L; CHS–C;
KC–G; TUL–NO; HNOC–NO;
LSM–NO; NYH–NY
Catalogs/Checklists: Conningham 1100;
LC–M, 241.1

1167
Place: New Orleans, Louisiana
Date: N.D.
Title: [untitled]
Size: 8¹⁄₈ × 12³⁄₈ in. (20.5 × 31.3 cm.)
Artist:
Lithographer: C. A. Vanderkamp [spelling
uncertain]
Printer:
Publisher:
Key/Vignettes/Misc:
Locations: New Orleans, Louisiana, Public
Library, Louisiana Division
Catalogs/Checklists:

1168
Place: New Orleans, Louisiana
Date: N.D.
Title: [Untitled]
Size: 21 × 31 in. (53.5 × 78.9 cm.)
Artist:

Lithographer:
Printer:
Publisher:
Key/Vignettes/Misc:
Locations: KC–G
Catalogs/Checklists:

1169
Place: New Orleans, Louisiana
Date: N.D.
Title: View of the News–Orleans
Size: 14½ × 23¼ in. (36.9 × 59.1 cm.)
Artist: Bachmann
Lithographer: Asselineau
Printer: Auguste Bry
Publisher: Wild
Key/Vignettes/Misc:
Locations: MM–NN; CHS–C
Catalogs/Checklists: MM–NN, LP 55

1170
Place: New Orleans, Louisiana
Date: N.D.
Title: Vue General de la Nouvelle Orleans
Size: 18½ × 25¹/₁₆ in. (47.1 × 63.8 cm.)
Artist: Th. Muller
Lithographer: Th. Muller
Printer: Lemercier, Paris
Publisher: Lemiere, Edit. Galerie d'Orleans
19 (Palais Royal) et 14 rue Castiglione
Key/Vignettes/Misc:
Locations: YUAG–NH
Catalogs/Checklists:

1171
Place: Shreveport, Louisiana
Date: 1872
Title: 1872 Bird's Eye View of Shreveport,
Louisiana
Size: 21⅜ × 28¼ in. (54.4 × 71.9 cm.)
(photo)
Artist: H. Brosius, according to the map of
O. L. Van Greelen
Lithographer:
Printer:
Publisher:
Key/Vignettes/Misc: Refs. 1–10, A–M;
population and cotton shipments data
Locations: LC–M (photo)
Catalogs/Checklists: LC–M, 242

1172
Place: The Balize, Louisiana
Date: Ca. 1822
Title: Die Balize an der Mundung des
Mississippi
Size: 11¾ × 16⅝ in. (29.9 × 42.3 cm.)
Artist: Herzog Paul von Wurttemberg
Lithographer:
Printer: der Konig. Lithograph. Anstalt.
Publisher:
Key/Vignettes/Misc:
Locations: NYP–S; MM–NN; TUL–NO
Catalogs/Checklists: Stokes P. 1822–
F–34; MM–NN, LP 4477

1173
Place: Anson, Maine
Date: 1895
Ttle: Anson, and Madison, Me. Somerset
Co. 1895
Size: 14½ × 22⅞ in. (36.9 × 58.3 cm.)

Artist: Geo. E. Norris
Lithographer:
Printer:
Publisher:
Key/Vignettes/Misc: Refs. A–Z; 1 vignette
Locations: MHS–P
Catalogs/Checklists: Farnsworth, p. 34

Place: Auburn, Maine
Date: 1875
See Lewiston, Maine, 1875.

1174
Place: Augusta, Maine
Date: [1854]
Title: Augusta, Me.
Size: 16¹³/₁₆ × 27¹³/₁₆ in. (42.8 × 70.7 cm.)
Artist: F. B. Ladd
Lithographer:
Printer: F. Heppenheimer, 22 North
William Str. N. Y.
Publisher:
Key/Vignettes/Misc:
Locations: NYP–S; MM–NN; MSM–A
Catalogs/Checklists: Stokes C. 1853–
G–26; MM–NN, LP 2946; Farnsworth,
p. 34

1175
Place: Augusta, Maine
Date: 1878
Title: Augusta, 1878
Size: 15 × 25½ in. (38.1 × 64.9 cm.)
Artist: A. Ruger
Lithographer:
Printer: Beck & Pauli, Lith., Milwaukee,
Wis.
Publisher: J. J. Stoner, Madison, Wis.
Key/Vignettes/Misc:
Locations: MSM–A
Catalogs/Checklists: Farnsworth, p. 34

1176
Place: Bangor, Maine
Date: 1835
Title: View of the City of Bangor, Me.
Size: 17¼ × 26¾ in. (43.9 × 68 cm.)
Artist: A. H. Wallace
Lithographer:
Printer: Pendleton's Lithogy, Boston
Publisher: Wm. A. Gilman & Alexr. H.
Wallace (copyright)
Key/Vignettes/Misc:
Locations: LC–P; MHS–P; BA;
YUAG–NH; BAPL–B; NYH–NY
Catalogs/Checklists: Farnsworth, p. 34

1177
Place: Bangor, Maine
Date: 1854
Title: Bangor, Me.
Size: 22⅞ × 39¼ in. (58.2 × 99.9 cm.)
Artist: J. W. Hill
Lithographer: Charles Parsons
Printer: Endicott & Co., N. Y.
Publisher: Smith, Brothers & Co, 59
Beekman St., New York
Key/Vignettes/Misc:
Locations: NYP–S; CHS–C; MHS–P;
BAPL–B; MSM–A
Catalogs/Checklists: Stokes P. 1853–
G–31; Farnsworth, p. 34

1178
Place: Bangor, Maine
Date: 1875
Title: Bird's Eye View of the City of
Bangor Penobscot County, Maine. 1875
Size: 24⅞ × 30¼ in. (63.4 × 77 cm.)
Artist: Augustus Koch
Lithographer:
Printer: Chas Shober & Co., Prop's
Chicago Lith. Co., [Chicago]
Publisher:
Key/Vignettes/Misc: Refs. 1–57
Locations: MHS–P; BAPL–B; MSM–A
Catalogs/Checklists: Farnsworth, p. 34

1179
Place: Bar Harbor, Maine
Date: 1880
Title: Bird's Eye View of Bar Harbor
Hancock Co. Mount Desert Island, Maine.
1880
Size: 15¼ × 23¾ in. (38.8 × 60.5 cm.)
Artist: A. F. Poole
Lithographer:
Printer: Beck & Pauli, Milwaukee
Publisher: J. J. Stoner, Madison, Wis.
Key/Vignettes/Misc: Refs. 1–27, A–C; 6
vignettes
Locations: Bar Harbor Historical Society
Museum, Bar Harbor, Maine
Catalogs/Checklists: Farnsworth, p. 35

1180
Place: Bar Harbor, Maine
Date: 1886
Title: Bar Harbor Mt. Desert Island Maine
Size: 19¼ × 24¾ in. (49 × 63 cm.)
Artist:
Lithographer:
Printer: Geo. H. Walker & Co., Lith.
Boston
Publisher: G. W. Morris, 11 Myrtle St.,
Portland, Me.
Key/Vignettes/Misc: 1 vignette
Locations: LC–M; Bar Harbor Historical
Society Museum, Bar Harbor, Maine; BA;
MSM–A
Catalogs/Checklists: LC–M, 243;
Farnsworth, p. 35

1181
Place: Bar Harbor, Maine
Date: 1886
Title: Bird's Eye View of Bar Harbor.
Mount Desert Island. Hancock Co. Maine.
1886
Size: 15⅛ × 25¼ in. (38.5 × 64.3 cm.)
Artist: A. F. Poole
Lithographer:
Printer: Beck & Pauli Lith. Milwaukee
Publisher: J. J. Stoner, Madison, Wis.
Key/Vignettes/Misc: Refs. 1–27; 6
vignettes
Locations: BPL–R
Catalogs/Checklists:

1182
Place: Bath, Maine
Date: 1877
Title: South End of the City of Bath, Me.
and Winnegance 1877
Size: 7¹/₁₆ × 16³/₁₆ in. (18 × 41.2 cm.)

Artist: A. Ruger
Lithographer:
Printer: Shober & Carqueville Litho. Co.
Chicago
Publisher:
Key/Vignettes/Misc: Refs. 1–14
Locations: MMM–B
Catalogs/Checklists: Farnsworth, p. 35

1183
Place: Bath, Maine
Date: 1878
Title: Bird's eye view of the City of Bath,
Sagadahoc Co., Maine, 1878, looking
North West.
Size: 17 × 34 in. (43.3 × 86.4 cm.)
Artist: A. Ruger
Lithographer:
Printer: Shober & Carqueville Lith. Co.,
Chicago
Publisher: J. J. Stoner, Madison, Wis.
Key/Vignettes/Misc: Refs. 1–42, A–L;
Refs. 1–4 for Woolwich;
Locations: MM–NN; MMM–B;
MSM–A
Catalogs/Checklists: MM–NN, LP 408;
Farnsworth, p. 35

1184
Place: Bath, Maine
Date: N.D.
Title: View of the Town of Bath, Me.
From Opposite the Ferry Landing
Size: 17⅞ × 26 in. (45.5 × 66.2 cm.)
Artist: Cyrus Wm. King
Lithographer:
Printer: Thayer & Co's Lithography,
Boston
Publisher:
Key/Vignettes/Misc:
Locations: MMM–B
Catalogs/Checklists: Farnsworth, p. 35

1185
Place: Belfast, Maine
Date: 1853
Title: View of Belfast, Me. from Roger's
Hill, 1853
Size: 14⅝ × 29¼ in. (37.2 × 74.4 cm.)
Artist: G. H. Swift
Lithographer:
Printer: Tappan & Bradford's Lith., Boston
Publisher:
Key/Vignettes/Misc:
Locations: MM–NN; NHS–R; WM–C;
Belfast Historical Society, Belfast, Maine
Catalogs/Checklists: MM–NN, LP 2947;
Farnsworth, p. 35

1186
Place: Belfast, Maine
Date: Ca. 1860
Title: Belfast
Size: 7 × 20¼ in. (17.8 × 51.6 cm.)
Artist:
Lithographer:
Printer: J. H. Bufford's Sons Lith. Boston
Publisher:
Key/Vignettes/Misc:
Locations: Mystic Seaport Museum,
Mystic, Connecticut
Catalogs/Checklists:

Place: Berwick, Maine
Date: 1877
See Great Falls, New Hampshire, 1877.

1187
Place: Bethel, Maine
Date: 1878
Title: Bethel, Maine. Looking from
Paradise Hill, 1878
Size: 9⅞ × 17¼ in. (25.1 × 43.9 cm.)
Artist: T. M. Fowler
Lithographer:
Printer: Beck & Pauli, Lith. Milwaukee,
Wis.
Publisher: J. J. Stoner, Madison, Wis.
Key/Vignettes/Misc:
Locations: Bethel Historical Society,
Bethel, Maine
Catalogs/Checklists: Farnsworth, p. 35

Place: Biddeford, Maine
Date: Ca. 1855
See Saco, Maine, ca. 1855.

1188
Place: Biddeford, Maine
Date: 1875
Title: Birds–Eye View of the Cities of
Biddeford & Saco, York County, Maine.
As Seen From the North East.
Size: 22⅞ × 30½ in. (58.3 × 77.6 cm.)
Artist:
Lithographer:
Printer: Krebs Lithographing Co.,
Cincinnati
Publisher: J. J. Stoner, Madison, Wis.
Key/Vignettes/Misc: Refs. 1–32, a–i, k–p
R–t, w, z;
Locations: MHS–P; McArthur Library,
Biddeford, Maine
Catalogs/Checklists: Farnsworth, p. 35

1189
Place: Blue Hill, Maine
Date: 1896
Title: Blue Hill, Maine, 1896
Size: 13⁹⁄₁₆ × 22³⁄₁₆ in. (34.5 × 56.5 cm.)
Artist:
Lithographer:
Printer:
Publisher:
Key/Vignettes/Misc: Refs. 1–44; 2
vignettes
Locations: WM–C; Blue Hill Historical
Society, Blue Hill, Maine
Catalogs/Checklists: Farnsworth, p. 35

1190
Place: Boothbay Harbor, Maine
Date: 1885
Title: Boothbay Harbor, Lincoln County,
Maine 1885
Size: 18⅝ × 19¾ in. (47.4 × 50.3 cm.)
Artist:
Lithographer:
Printer: Geo. E. Walker & Co., Boston
Publisher: A. F. Poole and Company,
Brockton, Mass.
Key/Vignettes/Misc: Refs. 1–34; 5
vignettes
Locations: BPL–R
Catalogs/Checklists: Farnsworth, p. 35

1191
Place: Bridgton, Maine
Date: 1888
Title: Bridgton, Maine. U. S. A.
Size: 16⅝ × 23¾ in. (42.3 × 60.4 cm.)
Artist:
Lithographer:
Printer: The Burleigh Lith. Est. Troy, N. Y.
Publisher: Fred C. Gibbs, Bridgton, Maine
Key/Vignettes/Misc: Refs. 1–24; 2
vignettes
Locations: BPL–R; Bridgton Historical
Museum, Bridgton, Maine
Catalogs/Checklists: Farnsworth, p. 37

1192
Place: Brunswick, Maine
Date: 1877
Title: Brunswick and Topsham
Cumberland County Sagadahoc County
Maine 1877
Size: 15⅜ × 21 in. (39.1 × 53.5 cm.)
Artist:
Lithographer:
Printer:
Publisher: [J. J. Stoner, Madison, Wis?]
Key/Vignettes/Misc: Refs. 1–22, A–H,
J–N
Locations: Penobscot Historical Museum,
Brunswick, Maine
Catalogs/Checklists: Farnsworth, p. 37

1193
Place: Bucksport, Maine
Date: 1859
Title: View of Bucksport, Me. 1859. From
Fort Knox. On the Penobscot River.
Size: 15¾ × 29½ in. (40.1 × 75 cm.)
Artist: James Emery
Lithographer:
Printer: Meisel Brothers, Lith., Boston
Publisher: T. B. Emery
Key/Vignettes/Misc:
Locations: YUAG–NH; MM–NN;
Penobscot Heritage Museum of Living
History, Bangor, Maine; CHS–C;
Bucksport Historical Society, Bucksport,
Maine; MSM–A; PM–S
Catalogs/Checklists: MM–NN, LP 12;
Farnsworth, p. 37

1194
Place: Calais, Maine
Date: 1879
Title: Panoramic View of the City of
Calais, Washington Co. Maine St. Stephen
and Milltown Charlotte Co. New
Brunswick 1879.
Size: 19¾ × 25⅞ in. (50.2 × 65.9 cm.)
Artist: AR [Albert Ruger?]
Lithographer:
Printer:
Publisher: J. J. Stoner, Madison, Wis.
Key/Vignettes/Misc: Refs., Calais, 1–20,
St. Stephen & Milltown, 1–19, General,
A–Z; 1 vignette
Locations: BPL–R; Grand Manan
Historical Society, Castalia, New
Brunswick; PANB–F
Catalogs/Checklists: PAC (1976);
Farnsworth, p. 37

Place: Calais, Maine
Date: 1889
See Saint Stephen, New Brunswick, 1889.

1195
Place: Caribou, Maine
Date: 1893
Title: Caribou, Aroostook Co. Maine. 1893
Size: 14¼ × 20¾ in. (36.4 × 52.8 cm.)
Artist: Geo. E. Norris
Lithographer:
Printer:
Publisher:
Key/Vignettes/Misc: Refs. 1–57, A–H; 1 vignette
Locations: BPL–R; Caribou, Maine, Public Library; Nylander Museum, Caribou, Maine
Catalogs/Checklists: Farnsworth, p. 37

1196
Place: Castine, Maine
Date: [1843–44]
Title: View of Castine, Maine. From Hospital Island.
Size: 10⅝ × 15 in. (27 × 38.1 cm.)
Artist: S. V. Homan
Lithographer: W. Sharp
Printer: Bouveau & Sharp, Lithrs. 221 Washington St. Boston
Publisher:
Key/Vignettes/Misc:
Locations: WM–C; NYH–NY
Catalogs/Checklists: Farnsworth, p. 37

1197
Place: Castine, Maine
Date: 1855
Title: Castine from Hospital Island 1855
Size: 24⅜ × 33⁹⁄₁₆ in. (62 × 85.4 cm.)
Artist: F. H. Lane
Lithographer:
Printer: L. H. Bradford & Co. Lith. [Boston]
Publisher: Joseph L. Stevens, Jr.
Key/Vignettes/Misc:
Locations: MM–NN; BMFA; FAM–R; MMM–B; MHS–P; WM–C; BA
Catalogs/Checklists: MM–NN, LP 1101; Wilmerding, no. 176; Farnsworth, p. 37

1198
Place: Castine, Maine
Date: 1889
Title: Castine Maine 1889
Size: 18¼ × 28⅜ in. (46.5 × 72.2 cm.)
Artist:
Lithographer:
Printer:
Publisher:
Key/Vignettes/Misc: 1 vignette
Locations: WM–C
Catalogs/Checklists: Farnsworth, p. 37

1199
Place: Cherryfield, Maine
Date: 1896
Title: Cherryfield, Maine, Washington Co., 1896
Size: 12½ × 22½ in. (31.8 × 57.3 cm.)
Artist:

Lithographer:
Printer:
Publisher: Geo. E. Norris, Brockton, Mass.
Key/Vignettes/Misc: Refs. 1–50
Locations: Union Trust Company, Cherryfield, Maine
Catalogs/Checklists: Farnsworth, p. 37

Place: Cumberland Mills, Maine
Date: 1879
See Saccarappa, Maine, 1879.

Place: Damariscotta, Maine
Date: 1878
See Newcastle, Maine, 1878.

1200
Place: Deering, Maine
Date: 1886
Title: Deering, Cumberland County: Maine. 1886
Size: 21 × 23¾ in. (53.4 × 60.5 cm.)
Artist:
Lithographer:
Printer: Heliotype Printing Co. Boston
Publisher: A. F. Poole & Co., Brockton, Mass.
Key/Vignettes/Misc: Refs. 1–17, A–B; 1 vignette
Locations: BPL–R; MHS–P
Catalogs/Checklists: Farnsworth, p. 37

1201
Place: Dexter, Maine
Date: 1878
Title: Bird's Eye View of Dexter, Maine, 1878
Size: 14 × 23½ in. (35.6 × 59.9 cm.)
Artist:
Lithographer:
Printer:
Publisher: J. J. Stoner, Madison, Wis.
Key/Vignettes/Misc: 39 refs.
Locations: Private collection
Catalogs/Checklists:

1202
Place: Dixfield, Maine
Date: 1896
Title: Dixfield, Maine 1896
Size:
Artist:
Lithographer:
Printer:
Publisher:
Key/Vignettes/Misc: Refs. 1–34
Locations: Unknown. See Early History of Dixfield, Maine, Dixfield, 1976, pp. 46–47
Catalogs/Checklists: Farnsworth, p. 37

1203
Place: Dover–Foxcroft, Maine
Date: 1878
Title: Dover & Foxcroft. Piscataquis Co. Maine 1878.
Size: 14⅝ × 25⅞ in. (37.2 × 65.8 cm.)
Artist: A. Ruger
Lithographer:
Printer: Beck & Pauli, Milwaukee, Wis.
Publisher: J. J. Stoner, Madison, Wis.
Key/Vignettes/Misc: Refs. 1–18, A–H, J–P, R–T

Locations: BPL–R
Catalogs/Checklists: Farnsworth, p. 37

1204
Place: Eastport, Maine
Date: 1879
Title: Bird's Eye View of Eastport Washington Co. Maine, 1879.
Size: 14⅝ × 22¾ in. (37.2 × 53 cm.)
Artist:
Lithographer:
Printer:
Publisher: J. J. Stoner, Madison, Wis.
Key/Vignettes/Misc: Refs. 1–36, A–H
Locations: BPL–R; LC–M
Catalogs/Checklists: LC–M, 244; Farnsworth, p. 38

1205
Place: Ellsworth, Maine
Date: 1879
Title: Bird's Eye View of the City of Ellsworth, 1879, Hancock Co. Maine
Size: 15¾ × 19¾ in. (40.1 × 50.3 cm.)
Artist: A. Ruger
Lithographer:
Printer:
Publisher: J. J. Stoner, Madison, Wis.
Key/Vignettes/Misc:
Locations: MSM–A
Catalogs/Checklists: Farnsworth, p. 38

1206
Place: Fairfield, Maine
Date: 1878
Title: Fairfield, Somerset Co., Maine 1878
Size: 14⅛ × 18⅛ in. (36 × 46.1 cm.)
Artist: Albert Ruger
Lithographer:
Printer: D. Bremner & Co. Lith. Milwaukee, Wis.
Publisher:
Key/Vignettes/Misc:
Locations: Town Office, Fairfield, Maine
Catalogs/Checklists: Farnsworth, p. 38

1207
Place: Fairfield, Maine
Date: 1895
Title: Fairfield, Me. Somerset Co. 1895
Size: 14⅞ × 22⅛ in. (37.6 × 56.4 cm.)
Artist: Geo. E. Norris
Lithographer:
Printer:
Publisher:
Key/Vignettes/Misc: Refs. 1–32
Locations: Lawrence Library, Fairfield, Maine
Catalogs/Checklists: Farnsworth, p. 38

1208
Place: Farmington, Maine
Date: 1878
Title: Farmington and West Farmington, 1878
Size: 12½ × 17⅜ in. (31.8 × 44.2 cm.)
Artist: T. M. Fowler
Lithographer:
Printer:
Publisher: J. J. Stoner, Madison, Wis.
Key/Vignettes/Misc: Refs. 1–21; 1 vignette

Locations: Farmington, Maine, Public Library
Catalogs/Checklists: Farnsworth, p. 38

1209
Place: Fort Fairfield, Maine
Date: 1893
Title: Fort Fairfield, Maine. 1893.
Size: 13⅜ × 20⅝ in. (34 × 52.5 cm.)
Artist: Geo. E. Norris
Lithographer:
Printer:
Publisher:
Key/Vignettes/Misc: Refs. 1–56; 2 vignettes
Locations: BPL–R
Catalogs/Checklists: Farnsworth, p. 38

Place: Foxcroft, Maine
Date: 1878
See Dover–Foxcroft, Maine, 1878.

1210
Place: Gardiner, Maine
Date: 1878
Title: Bird's Eye View of Gardiner and Pittston. Kennebec Co. Maine. 1878
Size: 18¹/₁₆ × 26 in. (46 × 66.2 cm.)
Artist:
Lithographer:
Printer: D. Bremner & Co., Milwaukee
Publisher: J. J. Stoner, Madison, Wis.
Key/Vignettes/Misc: Refs. 1–12, A–L
Locations: MHS–P; LC–M (photo)
Catalogs/Checklists: Farnsworth, p. 38; LC–M, 244.1

Place: Greens Landing, Maine
Date: 1893
See Stonington, Maine, 1893.

1211
Place: Hallowell, Maine
Date: 1878
Title: Bird's Eye View of the City of Hallowell Kennebec Co. Maine 1878
Size: 13⅜ × 26 in. (34 × 66 cm.)
Artist: A. Ruger
Lithographer:
Printer:
Publisher: J. J. Stoner, Madison, Wis.
Key/Vignettes/Misc: Refs. 1–26, A–F; 1 vignette
Locations: LC–M; Hubbard Free Library, Hollowell, Maine
Catalogs/Checklists: Farnsworth, p. 38; LC–M, 244.2

1212
Place: Hartland, Maine
Date: N.D.
Title: Hartland, Maine
Size: 12¾ × 22¼ in. (32.5 × 56.7 cm.)
Artist: Geo. E. Norris
Lithographer:
Printer:
Publisher:
Key/Vignettes/Misc:
Locations: Private collection
Catalogs/Checklists: Farnsworth, p.38

1213
Place: Houlton, Maine
Date: 1887

Title: Houlton, Maine, 1887
Size: 20½ × 27½ in. (52.2 × 69.9 cm.)
Artist: Joseph L. Jones
Lithographer:
Printer: Smith Lithographing Company, Bangor
Publisher: Skillings and Howard
Key/Vignettes/Misc:
Locations: Private collection
Catalogs/Checklists: Farnsworth, p. 38

1214
Place: Houlton, Maine
Date: Ca. 1894
Title: Houlton, Me. Aroostook County Seat.
Size: 15 × 25⅛ in. (38 × 64 cm.)
Artist: Geo. E. Norris
Lithographer:
Printer:
Publisher: Geo. E. Norris, Brockton, Mass.
Key/Vignettes/Misc:
Locations: LC–M; Aroostook Historical and Art Museum, Houlton, Maine
Catalogs/Checklists: LC–M, 245; Farnsworth, p. 38

1215
Place: Islesboro, Maine
Date: Ca.1885
Title: Islesboro, Penobscot Bay, Maine
Size: 16¹³/₁₆ × 21⁹/₁₆ in. (42.8 × 54.9 cm.)
Artist:
Lithographer:
Printer:
Publisher: Mount Desert and Penobscot Real Estate Company
Key/Vignettes/Misc:
Locations: Penobscot Marine Musem, Searsport, Maine
Catalogs/Checklists: Farnsworth, p. 38

1216
Place: Kennebunk, Maine
Date: 1877
Title: Kennebunk, York County, Maine, 1877
Size: 14 × 19 in. (35.5 × 48.2 cm.) (photo)
Artist:
Lithographer:
Printer:
Publisher:
Key/Vignettes/Misc: Refs. A–G
Locations: The Brick Store Museum, Kennebunk, Maine (photo)
Catalogs/Checklists: Farnsworth, p. 40

1217
Place: Kennebunk, Maine
Date: 1895
Title: Kennebunk, Me. 1895
Size: 16½ × 23½ in. (41.8 × 59.6 cm.)
Artist: G. E. Norris
Lithographer:
Printer:
Publisher:
Key/Vignettes/Misc:
Locations: The Brick Store Museum, Kennebunk, Maine
Catalogs/Checklists: Farnsworth, p. 40

1218
Place: Kingfield, Maine
Date: 1895
Title: Kingfield, Maine
Size: 12½ × 19½ in. (31.8 × 49.6 cm.)
Artist: Geo. E. Norris
Lithographer:
Printer:
Publisher:
Key/Vignettes/Misc: 43 refs.
Locations: Kingfield Historical Society, Kingfield, Maine
Catalogs/Checklists: Farnsworth, p. 40

1219
Place: Lewiston, Maine
Date: 1856
Title: Lewiston, Maine, From the Residence of Isaac Haskell (Prospect Hill)
Size: 12½ × 15¾ in. (31.8 × 40.1 cm.)
Artist: J. B. Bachelder
Lithographer:
Printer: Endicott & Co., N. Y.
Publisher: Jno. B. Bachelder, 59 Beekman St. New York
Key/Vignettes/Misc: Refs. 1–10, 1 unnumbered ref.
Locations: BPL–P; MAHS–B; YUAG–NH; BA; MVTM–NA; AHS–A
Catalogs/Checklists: Farnsworth, p. 40

1220
Place: Lewiston, Maine
Date: 1875
Title: Lewiston and Auburn, Maine
Size: 25½ × 31½ in. (64.9 × 80.1 cm.)
Artist:
Lithographer:
Printer: Charles Shober & Co. Prop's Chicago Lith Co. [Chicago]
Publisher: J. J. Stoner, Madison, Wis.
Key/Vignettes/Misc:
Locations: AHS–A
Catalogs/Checklists: Farnsworth, p. 40

1221
Place: Lisbon Falls, Maine
Date: 1896
Title: Lisbon Falls, Me. 1896.
Size: 13 × 21¹⁵/₁₆ in. (33.1 × 55.9 cm.)
Artist:
Lithographer:
Printer:
Publisher:
Key/Vignettes/Misc: Refs. 1–24, A–H
Locations: Private collection
Catalogs/Checklists: Farnsworth, p. 40

1222
Place: Livermore, Maine
Date: 1889
Title: Livermore Falls, Maine.
Size: 10½ × 20¾ in. (26.5 × 52.7 cm.)
Artist: Geo. E. Norris
Lithographer:
Printer: Burleigh Lith. Est., Troy, N. Y.
Publisher: Geo. E. Norris, Brockton, Mass.
Key/Vignettes/Misc: Refs. 1–30
Locations: BPL–R; LC–M; LC–P
Catalogs/Checklists: LC–M, 246; Farnsworth, p. 40

1223
Place: Lubec, Maine
Date: 1896
Title: Lubec, Me
Size: 15½ × 22¾ in. (39.4 × 57.9 cm.)
Artist: Geo. E. Norris
Lithographer:
Printer:
Publisher:
Key/Vignettes/Misc: Refs. 1–62
Locations: Lubec Historical Society, Lubec, Maine
Catalogs/Checklists: Farnsworth, p. 40

1224
Place: Machias, Maine
Date: 1896
Title: Machias 1896
Size: 11½ × 23 in. (29.3 × 58.6 cm.)
Artist: Geo. E. Norris
Lithographer:
Printer:
Publisher: Geo. E. Norris, Brockton, Mass.
Key/Vignettes/Misc:
Locations: Private collection
Catalogs/Checklists:

Place: Madison, Maine
Date: 1895
See Anson, Maine, 1895.

1225
Place: Mechanic Falls, Maine
Date: 1878
Title: Birds Eye View of Mechanic Falls Maine Looking East 1878.
Size: 9½ × 16½ in. (24.2 × 42 cm.)
Artist:
Lithographer:
Printer: D. Bremner & Co. Milw., Wis.
Publisher: J. J. Stoner, Madison, Wis.
Key/Vignettes/Misc: Refs. 1–8, A–K
Locations: AHS–A
Catalogs/Checklists: Farnsworth, p. 40

1226
Place: Monhegan, Maine
Date: 1896
Title: Monhegan, Me.
Size: 17½ × 21¾ in. (44.6 × 55.3 cm.)
Artist: Bert Poole [Albert F. Poole]
Lithographer:
Printer:
Publisher: Bert Poole (copyright)
Key/Vignettes/Misc:
Locations: LC–M; MSL–B; MSM–A
Catalogs/Checklists: Farnsworth, p. 40; LC–M, 246.1

1227
Place: Monson, Maine
Date: 1889
Title: Monson, Maine.
Size: 13½ × 23¾ in. (34.4 × 62 cm.)
Artist: Geo. E. Norris
Lithographer:
Printer: The Burleigh Lith. Est., Troy, N. Y.
Publisher: Geo. E. Norris, Brockton, Mass.
Key/Vignettes/Misc: Refs. 1–32, A–K; 1 vignette
Locations: BPL–R; LC–M; EI–S

Catalogs/Checklists: Farnsworth, p. 40; LC–M, 246.2

1228
Place: Newcastle, Maine
Date: 1878
Title: Birds Eye View of the Villages of Newcastle & Damariscotta Lincoln Co. Maine 1878
Size: 10⅞ × 19⅞ in. (27.7 × 50.6 cm.)
Artist: A. Ruger
Lithographer:
Printer:
Publisher: J. J. Stoner, Madison, Wis.
Key/Vignettes/Misc: Refs., Newcastle, 1–7, Damariscotta, A–I
Locations: Private collection
Catalogs/Checklists: Farnsworth, p. 40; LC–M, 246.3

1229
Place: North Berwick, Maine
Date: 1877
Title: North Berwick York Co. Maine 1877.
Size: 13 × 16⅛ in. (33 × 41 cm.)
Artist: [Albert Ruger]
Lithographer:
Printer:
Publisher: Ruger & Stoner, Madison, Wis.
Key/Vignettes/Misc: Refs. 1–13; 1 vignette
Locations: LC–M
Catalogs/Checklists: Farnsworth, p. 40; LC–M, 246.4

1230
Place: Peak's Island, Maine
Date: [1886]
Title: Peak's Island, Portland Harbor, Maine.
Size: 19½ × 32 in. (41 × 82 cm.)
Artist: JC
Lithographer:
Printer: Geo. H. Walker & Co.
Publisher: G. W. Morris 19 Smith St., Portland, Me.
Key/Vignettes/Misc: Refs. 1–18
Locations: LC–M
Catalogs/Checklists: LC–M, 247; Farnsworth, p. 41

1231
Place: Pittsfield, Maine
Date: 1889
Title: Pittsfield, Maine. Looking Northwest
Size: 12½ × 20¾ in. (32 × 53 cm.)
Artist: Geo. E. Norris
Lithographer:
Printer: Burleigh Lith. Est., Troy, New York
Publisher: Geo. E. Norris, Brockton, Mass.
Key/Vignettes/Misc: Refs. 1–23; 1 vignette
Locations: BPL–R; LC–M
Catalogs/Checklists: LC–M, 248; Farnsworth, p. 41

Place: Pittston, Maine
Date: 1878
See Gardiner, Maine, 1878.

1232
Place: Portland, Maine
Date: Ca. 1849
Title: View of Portland, Me. From the Cape Elizabeth Side.
Size: 16½ × 36 in. (42 × 91.5 cm.)
Artist: E. Whitefield
Lithographer: E. Whitefield
Printer: Jones & Newman, 128 Fulton St., N. Y.
Publisher: Whitefield & Smith, 128 Fulton St., N. Y.
Key/Vignettes/Misc:
Locations: MHS–P; Portland, Maine, Public Library
Catalogs/Checklists: Norton, Whitefield, no. 42; Farnsworth, p. 41

1233
Place: Portland, Maine
Date: 1855
Title: Portland, Me. Portland in 1855, Population 27,000
Size: 25¾ × 39⁷⁄₁₆ in. (65.5 × 100.3 cm.)
Artist: J. W. Hill
Lithographer: Chas. Parsons
Printer: Endicott & Co., New York
Publisher: Smith Brothers & Co., New York
Key/Vignettes/Misc: Dedication; 1 seal
Locations: NYP–S; MM–NN; FAM–R; MMM–B; SSBT–B; BA; LC–P
Catalogs/Checklists: Stokes 1855—G–15; MM–NN, LP 493; Farnsworth, p. 41

1234
Place: Portland, Maine
Date: 1865
Title: View of Portland 1865
Size: 7½ × 16 in. (19 × 40.7 cm.)
Artist: Bailey & Noyes
Lithographer:
Printer:
Publisher: Bailey & Noyes, Portland, Me.
Key/Vignettes/Misc:
Locations: FAM–R
Catalogs/Checklists: Farnsworth, p. 41

1235
Place: Portland, Maine
Date: 1866
Title: Bird's Eye View of Portland, Me. Taken Two Days After the Great Fire of July 4th 1866.
Size: 13⅜ × 18 in. (34 × 45.8 cm.)
Artist: G. Bowker from a photo by Black & Case
Lithographer:
Printer: J. Mayer & Co., Lith. 4 State St. Boston.
Publisher: B. B. Russell & Co., Boston and John Hankerson, Portland
Key/Vignettes/Misc:
Locations: MM–NN; NYH–NY
Catalogs/Checklists: MM–NN, LP 3804

1236
Place: Portland, Maine
Date: 1866
Title: Ruins of the Great Fire at Portland, Me. July 4th and 5th, 1866. View from Corner of Middle and Free Sts.

Size: 22½ × 29¾ in. (57.3 × 75.7 cm.)
Artist: J. E. Baker
Lithographer:
Printer: J. H. Bufford
Publisher: Bufford Brothers, Boston &
New York and S. B. Beckett, Portland
Key/Vignettes/Misc:
Locations: MHS–P
Catalogs/Checklists:

1237
Place: Portland, Maine
Date: Ca. 1866
Title: View of Portland, Me. Taken From
Port Elizabeth Before The Great
Conflagration of July 4th. 1866.
Size: 11 × 18 in. (28 × 45.8 cm.)
Artist: Photo by Edw. F. Smith
Lithographer:
Printer: J. Mayer & Co., Lith, 4 State St.
Boston
Publisher: B. B. Russell & Co., Boston &
John Hankerson, Portland
Key/Vignettes/Misc:
Locations: CHS–C; PAC–P
Catalogs/Checklists: Pyne, no. 480

1238
Place: Portland, Maine
Date: 1876
Title: Bird's Eye View of the City of
Portland Maine, 1876.
Size: 24⅛ × 34³⁄₁₆ in. (61.4 × 86.7 cm.)
Artist: Jos. Warner
Lithographer:
Printer: Chas Shober & Co. Prop's
Chicago Litho'g Co. [Chicago]
Publisher: J. J. Stoner, Madison, Wis.
Key/Vignettes/Misc: Refs.1–91, A–Z
Locations: ACMW–FW; BPL–R; LC–M;
MHS–P; NYH–NY
Catalogs/Checklists: ACMW–FW 1903;
LC–M, 249; Farnsworth, p. 41

1239
Place: Portland, Maine
Date: 1905
Title: Portland, 1905
Size: 18¹⁄₁₆ × 27¹¹⁄₁₆ in. (46 × 70.5 cm.)
Artist:
Lithographer:
Printer: Geo. H. Walker & Co., Boston
Publisher: Maine Central Railroad
Key/Vignettes/Misc:
Locations: EI–S
Catalogs/Checklists: Farnsworth, p. 41

1240
Place: Presque Isle, Maine
Date: Ca. 1894
Title: Presque Isle, Aroostook County,
Maine.
Size: 16 × 23½ in. (41 × 58 cm.)
Artist:
Lithographer:
Printer:
Publisher: Geo. E. Norris, Brockton, Mass.
Key/Vignettes/Misc: 1 vignette
Locations: LC–M
Catalogs/Checklists: LC–M, 250;
Farnsworth, p. 41

1241
Place: Richmond, Maine
Date: 1878
Title: Richmond, Sagadahoc Co., Maine
1878.
Size: 14 × 20⅛ in. (35.6 × 51.2 cm.)
Artist: A. Ruger
Lithographer:
Printer: D. Bremner & Co., Lith,
Milwaukee
Publisher:
Key/Vignettes/Misc: Refs. 1–19
Locations: LC–M; MM–NN; MMM–B
Catalogs/Checklists: Farnsworth, p. 41;
LC–M, 250.1

1242
Place: Rockland, Maine
Date: [1854]
Title: View of Rockland, Me.
Size: 18½ × 36 in. (47.1 × 91.6 cm.)
Artist: G. H. Swift
Lithographer:
Printer: J. H. Bufford's Lith., 260
Washington St., Boston
Publisher:
Key/Vignettes/Misc:
Locations: FAM–R
Catalogs/Checklists: Farnsworth, pp.
41–43

1243
Place: Saccarappa, Maine
Date: 1879
Title: Panorama of Saccarappa and
Cumberland Mills Cumberland Co Maine,
1879. Looking North
Size: 11¼ × 26⅛ in. (28.7 × 66.5 cm.)
Artist:
Lithographer:
Printer: Beck & Pauli, Lith. Milwaukee,
Wis.
Publisher: J. J. Stoner, Madison, Wis.
Key/Vignettes/Misc: Refs. 1–9, A–F
Locations: MHS–P
Catalogs/Checklists: Farnsworth, p. 43

1244
Place: Saco, Maine
Date: Ca. 1855
Title: Sacco and Biddeford, Me.
Size: 21¹⁄₁₆ × 31¹³⁄₁₆ in. (53.6 × 80.9 cm.)
Artist: J. B. Bachelder
Lithographer:
Printer: J. H. Bufford lith. 260 Washington
St. Boston
Publisher:
Key/Vignettes/Misc:
Locations: MM–NN; CHS–C; BA;
LC–P; MHS–P; NYH–NY
Catalogs/Checklists: MM–NN, LP 7;
Farnsworth (ca. 1865), p. 43

Place: Saco, Maine
Date: 1875
See Biddeford, Maine, 1875.

1245
Place: Sanford, Maine
Date: 1889
Title: Sanford, Maine. Looking East.

Size: 13⅝ × 25¼ in. (34.7 × 66 cm.)
Artist: Geo. E. Norris
Lithographer:
Printer: Burleigh Lith. Est., Troy, New
York
Publisher: Geo. E. Norris, Brockton, Mass.
Key/Vignettes/Misc: Refs. 1–27, A–N
Locations: LC–M; BPL–R; NHHS–C
Catalogs/Checklists: LC–M, 251;
Farnsworth, p. 43

1246
Place: Skowhegan, Maine
Date: 1892
Title: Skowhegan, Me., Somerset Co.
Size: 17⅝ × 29¾ in. (44.9 × 75.6 cm.)
Artist: Geo. E. Norris
Lithographer:
Printer: Burleigh Litho Co., Troy, N.Y.
Publisher: Geo. E. Norris, Brockton, Mass.
Key/Vignettes/Misc: Refs. 1–49, A–T; 2
vignettes
Locations: BPL–R; MHS–P
Catalogs/Checklists: Farnsworth, p. 43

1247
Place: South Berwick, Maine
Date: 1877
Title: South Berwick York Co. Maine
1877.
Size: 13⅛ × 15⅞ in. (33.4 × 40.4 cm.)
Artist:
Lithographer:
Printer: Jos. B. Richards Co., Boston,
Mass.
Publisher: Ruger & Stoner, Madison, Wis.
Key/Vignettes/Misc: Refs. 1–12
Locations: Jewett Memorial, South
Berwick, Maine; Old Berwick Historical
Society, South Berwick, Maine
Catalogs/Checklists: Farnsworth, p. 43

1248
Place: Springvale, Maine
Date: 1888
Title: Springvale, Maine. Looking West.
Size: 12⅞ × 22 in. (32.7 × 56 cm.)
Artist: Geo. E. Norris
Lithographer:
Printer: The Burleigh Lith. Est., Troy, N. Y.
Publisher: Geo. E. Norris, Brockton,
Mass.
Key/Vignettes/Misc: Refs. 1–28; 3
vignettes
Locations: BPL–R
Catalogs/Checklists: Farnsworth, p. 43

1249
Place: Stonington, Maine
Date: 1893
Title: Greens Landing, Me.
Size: 15⅞ × 20 in. (40.4 × 50.8 cm.)
Artist: Geo. E. Norris
Lithographer:
Printer:
Publisher:
Key/Vignettes/Misc: Refs. 1–35; 1
vignette
Locations: BPL–R; WM–C
Catalogs/Checklists: Farnsworth, p. 43

1250
Place: Thomaston, Maine
Date: 1878
Title: Thomaston, 1878
Size: 12⅛ × 20⅞ in. (30.8 × 53.2 cm.)
Artist: A. Ruger
Lithographer:
Printer: Beck & Pauli, Lith. Milwaukee, Wis.
Publisher: J. J. Stoner, Madison, Wis.
Key/Vignettes/Misc: 1 vignette
Locations: Private collection
Catalogs/Checklists: Farnsworth, p. 43

1251
Place: Togus, Maine
Date: 1878
Title: National Soldiers Home, Togus, near Augusta. Bird's Eye View Looking North
Size: 11 × 21 in. (28 × 53.4 cm.)
Artist: A. Ruger
Lithographer:
Printer: Beck & Pauli, Lith. Milwaukee, Wis.
Publisher: J. J. Stoner, Madison, Wis.
Key/Vignettes/Misc:
Locations: MHS−P
Catalogs/Checklists: Farnsworth, p. 43

1252
Place: Togus, Maine
Date: 1885
Title: Togus, 1885
Size: 15⁵⁄₁₆ × 23¼ in. (38.9 × 59.2 cm.)
Artist: A. F. Poole
Lithographer:
Printer: Heliotype Printing Co., Boston
Publisher: A. F. Poole & Co., Brockton, Mass.
Key/Vignettes/Misc:
Locations: Private collection
Catalogs/Checklists: Farnsworth, p. 43

Place: Topsham, Maine
Date: 1877
See Brunswick, Maine, 1877.

1253
Place: Vinalhaven, Maine
Date: 1893
Title: Vinalhaven, Me. 1893.
Size: 15½ × 21 in. (39.4 × 54 cm.)
Artist: Geo. E. Norris
Lithographer:
Printer:
Publisher:
Key/Vignettes/Misc: Refs. 1−34
Locations: BPL−R
Catalogs/Checklists: Farnsworth, p. 44

1254
Place: Waldoboro, Maine
Date: 1896
Title:
Size:
Artist:
Lithographer:
Printer:
Publisher:
Key/Vignettes/Misc:
Locations: Unknown. Reproduced in 200 Anniversary: A Pictorial History,

Waldboro: 1873, p. 97
Catalogs/Checklists: Farnsworth, p. 44

1255
Place: Warren, Maine
Date: 1893
Title: Warren, Me.
Size: 10⁹⁄₁₆ × 19 in. (26.9 × 48.3 cm.)
Artist: Geo. E. Norris
Lithographer:
Printer:
Publisher: Geo. E. Norris, Brockton, Mass.
Key/Vignettes/Misc: Refs. A−S
Locations: Private collection
Catalogs/Checklists: Farnsworth, p. 44

1256
Place: Waterville, Maine
Date: 1878
Title: Bird's Eye View of Waterville, Kennebec Co., Maine. Looking North West. 1878
Size: 16⅝ × 25¾ in. (42.3 × 67 cm.)
Artist:
Lithographer:
Printer: Beck & Pauli, Lith., Milwaukee, Wis.
Publisher: J. J. Stoner, Madison, Wis.
Key/Vignettes/Misc: Refs. 1−9, A−F; 1 vignette
Locations: BPL−R; MHS−P; Waterville Historical Society, Waterville, Maine
Catalogs/Checklists: Farnsworth, p. 44

1257
Place: Waterville, Maine
Date: 1895
Title: Central and Northern Part of Waterville, Maine
Size: 18¼ × 26¾ in. (46.5 × 68 cm.)
Artist: Geo. E. Norris
Lithographer:
Printer:
Publisher:
Key/Vignettes/Misc: Refs. 1−27; 1 vignette
Locations: Waterville Historical Society, Waterville, Maine
Catalogs/Checklists: Farnsworth, p. 44

Place: West Farmington, Maine
Date: 1878
See Farmington, Maine, 1878.

1258
Place: West Waterville, Maine
Date: 1878
Title: West Waterville, Kennebec County Maine
Size: 10 × 18⅝ in. (25.5 × 47.4 cm.)
Artist: A. Ruger
Lithographer:
Printer: Beck & Pauli, Lith. Milwaukee, Wis.
Publisher: J. J. Stoner, Madison, Wis.
Key/Vignettes/Misc: 2 vignettes
Locations: MHS−P
Catalogs/Checklists: Farnsworth, p. 44

1259
Place: Wilton, Maine
Date: 1895
Title: Wilton, Me. 1895

Size: 13¼ × 19⅞ in. (33.8 × 50.6 cm.)
Artist: A. D.
Lithographer:
Printer:
Publisher:
Key/Vignettes/Misc: Refs. 1−43; 1 vignette
Locations: Town Office, Wilton, Maine
Catalogs/Checklists: Farnsworth, p. 44

1260
Place: Wiscasset, Maine
Date: 1878
Title: Birds Eye View of the Village of Wiscasset, Lincoln Co., Maine 1878
Size: 10¾ × 16¾ in. (27.4 × 42.6 cm.)
Artist: A. Ruger
Lithographer:
Printer:
Publisher: J. J. Stoner, Madison, Wis.
Key/Vignettes/Misc: Refs. 1−23
Locations: Lincoln County Cultural and Historical Association, Wiscasset, Maine
Catalogs/Checklists: Farnsworth, p. 44

1261
Place: York Beach, Maine
Date: 1888
Title: York Beach, Maine
Size: 24¼ × 16½ in. (61.7 × 41.9 cm.)
Artist: A. Poole
Lithographer:
Printer:
Publisher: Geo. H. Walker & Co., Boston, Mass.
Key/Vignettes/Misc:
Locations: Private collection
Catalogs/Checklists: Farnsworth, p. 44

1262
Place: Emerson, Manitoba
Date: 1880
Title: Bird's Eye View of the City of Emerson, Manitoba. 1880
Size: 7⁷⁄₁₆ × 18⁷⁄₁₆ in. (18 × 47 cm.) (photo)
Artist:
Lithographer:
Printer: Beck & Pauli. Lith., Milwaukee
Publisher: J. J. Stoner, Madison, Wis.
Key/Vignettes/Misc: Refs. 1−22; 3 vignettes
Locations: PAC (photo)
Catalogs/Checklists:

1263
Place: Emerson, Manitoba
Date: [1880−81?]
Title: Emerson, The Gateway City on the Red River
Size: 11¹³⁄₁₆ × 21½ in. (29.8 × 54.7 cm.)
Artist: T. M. Fowler
Lithographer:
Printer: Beck & Pauli Lith. Milwaukee, Wis.
Publisher: Fowler & Rhines
Key/Vignettes/Misc: Refs. 1−32; 2 vignettes
Locations: Provincial Archives of Manitoba, Winnipeg, Manitoba (photo); PAC
Catalogs/Checklists: PAC (1976)

1264
Place: Morris, Manitoba
Date: 1880
Title: Bird's Eye View of Morris, Manitoba, 1880.
Size: 11¾ × 21⅝ in. (30 × 55 cm.)
Artist: T. M. Fowler
Lithographer:
Printer: Beck & Pauli Lith., Milwaukee, Wis.
Publisher: Fowler & Rhines
Key/Vignettes/Misc: 32 refs.; 2 vignettes
Locations: PAC
Catalogs/Checklists: PAC (1976)

1265
Place: Saint Boniface, Manitoba
Date: 1880
Title: Bird's Eye View of Saint Boniface, Manitoba. 1880.
Size:
Artist:
Lithographer:
Printer: Beck & Pauli Lith., Milwaukee, Wis.
Publisher: J. J. Stoner, Madison, Wis.
Key/Vignettes/Misc: Refs. 1–21
Locations: St. Boniface Museum, Saint Boniface, Manitoba; PAC (photo)
Catalogs/Checklists: PAC (1976)

1266
Place: Winnipeg, Manitoba
Date: 1880
Title: Winnipeg. Manitoba. Incorporated in 1873. 1880. Population 10,000
Size: 20⅝ × 31⁹⁄₁₆ in. (52.4 × 80.1 cm.)
Artist: T. M. Fowler
Lithographer:
Printer: Beck & Pauli, Milwaukee, Wis.
Publisher: J. J. Stoner, Madison, Wis.
Key/Vignettes/Misc: Refs. 1–55; 4 vignettes
Locations: PAC; ROM; PAC–P; MCM–M; LC–M (photo)
Catalogs/Checklists: PAC (1976); LC–M, 1078; PAC H²/₅₄₀–Winnipeg–1880

1267
Place: Winnipeg, Manitoba
Date: 1881
Title: Winnipeg, Incorporated in 1873 Manitoba. 1881.
Size: 22½ × 33¼ in. (57.3 × 84.5 cm.)
Artist: [T. M. Fowler]
Lithographer:
Printer: A. Mortimer. Lith. Ottowa.
Publisher: W. G. Fonseca (copyright)
Key/Vignettes/Misc: Refs. 1–67; 4 vignettes
Locations: PAC; LC–M (photo)
Catalogs/Checklists: LC–M, 1079; PAC H2/540–Winnipeg–1881

1268
Place: Winnipeg, Manitoba
Date: 1881
Title: Winnipeg, Incorporated in 1873 Manitoba. 1881.
Size: 22½ × 33³⁄₁₆ in. (57.3 × 84.5 cm.)
Artist: [T. M Fowler]
Lithographer:

Printer: A. Mortimer, Lith. Ottowa
Publisher:
Key/Vignettes/Misc: Refs. 1–76; 4 vignettes
Locations: PAC; LC–M (photo)
Catalogs/Checklists: PAC H2/540–Winnipeg–1881

1269
Place: Winnipeg, Manitoba
Date: 1884
Title: Winnipeg. 1884.
Size: 31¹¹⁄₁₆ × 40½ in. (80.6 × 103 cm.)
Artist:
Lithographer:
Printer: Mortimer & Co. Lith., Ottawa
Publisher: W. G. Fonseca (copyright)
Key/Vignettes/Misc: 22 vignettes; table of population and assessed valuation
Locations: PAC
Catalogs/Checklists: PAC (1976); PAC H1/540–Winnipeg–1884

1270
Place: Winnipeg, Manitoba
Date: 1894
Title: Birds Eye View of the Central Business Portion of Winnipeg, Manitoba.
Size: 27³⁄₁₆ × 41⅛ in. (69.2 × 103.5 cm.)
Artist:
Lithographer:
Printer:
Publisher: Clarence E. Steele, Winnipeg. (copyright)
Key/Vignettes/Misc: 16 vignettes; classified business directory
Locations: PAC
Catalogs/Checklists: PAC V1/540–Winnipeg–1894

1271
Place: Winnipeg, Manitoba
Date: 1900
Title: Bird's Eye View City of Winnipeg.
Size: 24⁷⁄₁₆ × 36⅜ in. (62.2 × 92.5 cm.)
Artist:
Lithographer:
Printer:
Publisher: W. J. Bulman (copyright)
Key/Vignettes/Misc:
Locations: PAC
Catalogs/Checklists: PAC (1976); PAC V1/540–Winnipeg–1900

1272
Place: Winnipeg, Manitoba
Date: 1911
Title: Hathaway's Guide and Birds–eye Maps of Winnipeg.
Size: 21⅞ × 21¹³⁄₁₆ in. (55.7 × 55.6 cm.)
Artist:
Lithographer:
Printer:
Publisher: R. W. Hathaway & J. K. Wright
Key/Vignettes/Misc: 2 vignettes
Locations: PAC
Catalogs/Checklists: PAC H2/540–Winnipeg–1911

1273
Place: Annapolis, Maryland
Date: [1850–58]
Title: View of Annapolis Naval School

Size: 14⅝ × 19¼ in. (37.3 × 49 cm.)
Artist:
Lithographer:
Printer: Sachse Baltimore
Publisher: Sachse Baltimore
Key/Vignettes/Misc: 13 vignettes
Locations: MHS–B
Catalogs/Checklists: McCauley, V 53

1274
Place: Annapolis, Maryland
Date: Ca. 1860
Title: Bird's Eye View of the City of Annapolis, Capital of the State of Maryland.
Size: 19⅜ × 33¼ in. (49.3 × 84.5 cm.)
Artist:
Lithographer:
Printer: E. Sachse & Co.
Publisher: E. Sachse & Co., Baltimore, Md.
Key/Vignettes/Misc: 1 vignette
Locations: PM–B; EPL–B; MHS–B
Catalogs/Checklists: McCauley, V 40

1275
Place: Annapolis, Maryland
Date: 1864
Title: Bird's Eye View of the City of Annapolis, Md.
Size: 10¹³⁄₁₆ × 16¾ in. (27.5 × 42.6 cm.)
Artist:
Lithographer:
Printer:
Publisher: Chas. Magnus 12 Frankfort St. N. Y.
Key/Vignettes/Misc: Refs. 1–3; 1 portrait
Locations: PM–B; NYP–S; LC–M (facsimile); NYH–NY
Catalogs/Checklists: Stokes P. 1863—G–63; LC–M, 252

1276
Place: Annapolis, Maryland
Date: 1871
Title: View of Annapolis in 1797
Size: 3¹⁵⁄₁₆ × 5⅝ in. (10 × 14.4 cm.)
Artist:
Lithographer:
Printer:
Publisher: Chase & Town (copyright)
Key/Vignettes/Misc:
Locations: HEHL
Catalogs/Checklists:

1277
Place: Baltimore, Maryland
Date: 1837
Title: Baltimore
Size: 13¾ × 21½ in. (34.9 × 54.7 cm.)
Artist: P. Haas [and Moses Swett]
Lithographer:
Printer:
Publisher: N. Hickman (copyright)
Key/Vignettes/Misc:
Locations: EPL–B; PM–B
Catalogs/Checklists: McCauley, V 12

1278
Place: Baltimore, Maryland
Date: Ca. 1840
Title: Baltimore
Size: 9¹³⁄₁₆ × 13⅝ in. (25 × 34.7 cm.)

Artist:
Lithographer:
Printer: F. Silber, Berlin
Publisher: F. Silber, Berlin
Key/Vignettes/Misc:
Locations: MHS–B
Catalogs/Checklists: McCauley, V 21

1279
Place: Baltimore, Maryland
Date: Ca. 1840
Title: Baltimore. No. 2
Size: 12½ × 19³⁄₁₆ in. (31.8 × 48.9 cm.)
Artist: Louis Le Breton
Lithographer: Louis Le Breton
Printer: Auguste Bry, 114, Rue du Bac
Publisher: Chez Wild, Passage du Saumon, 38
Key/Vignettes/Misc:
Locations: EPL–B; PM–B; YUAG–NH
Catalogs/Checklists: McCauley, V 22

1280
Place: Baltimore, Maryland
Date: [1842–45]
Title: Baltimore
Size: 12³⁄₁₆ × 17¼ in. (31 × 43.9 cm.)
Artist:
Lithographer:
Printer: Edward Weber & Co. Baltimore
Publisher: Edward Weber & Co. Baltimore
Key/Vignettes/Misc:
Locations: MHS–B; YUAG–NH; LC–P
Catalogs/Checklists: McCauley, V 28

1281
Place: Baltimore, Maryland
Date: 1847
Title: View of Baltimore, Md. From Federal Hill.
Size: 21⁵⁄₁₆ × 39½ in. (54.4 × 103.3 cm.)
Artist: E. Whitefield
Lithographer: E. Whitefield
Printer: F. Michelin, 111 Nassau St., New York
Publisher: E. Whitefield, 32 Ann St., New York
Key/Vignettes/Misc:
Locations: MHS–B; PM–B; EPL–B; LC–P
Catalogs/Checklists: Norton, Whitefield, no. 35; McCauley, V 9

1282
Place: Baltimore, Maryland
Date: 1848
Title: Baltimore 1 N. West View
Size: 7½ × 11 in. (19 × 28 cm.)
Artist: Aug. Kollner
Lithographer: Deroy
Printer: Cattier
Publisher: Goupil, Vibert & Co., New York & Paris
Key/Vignettes/Misc:
Locations: PM–B; MHS–B; EPL–B; JWGL–B; YUAG–NH; LC–P
Catalogs/Checklists: McCauley, V 10

1283
Place: Baltimore, Maryland
Date: 1848
Title: View of Baltimore. Vue de Baltimore. Ansicht von Baltimore.

Size: 8½ × 12⁵⁄₈ in. (21.7 × 32.2 cm.)
Artist:
Lithographer: N. Currier
Printer:
Publisher: N. Currier. 152 Nassau St. Cor. of Spruce N. Y.
Key/Vignettes/Misc:
Locations: EPL–B; PM–B; MCNY; YUAG–NH
Catalogs/Checklists: Peters, C & I, 3925; McCauley, V 23

1284
Place: Baltimore, Maryland
Date: Ca. 1848
Title: View of Baltimore
Size: 16¼ × 25⁵⁄₁₆ in. (41.4 × 64.5 cm.)
Artist:
Lithographer:
Printer: E. Weber & Co. [Baltimore]
Publisher: E. Weber & Co. [Baltimore]
Key/Vignettes/Misc: 18 vignettes
Locations: PM–B; MHS–B
Catalogs/Checklists: McCauley, V 31

1285
Place: Baltimore, Maryland
Date: 1850
Title: View of Baltimore, from Federal Hill
Size: 18 × 27½ in. (45.8 × 69.9 cm.)
Artist: F. H. Lane
Lithographer:
Printer: Sarony and Major, New York
Publisher: A. Conant
Key/Vignettes/Misc:
Locations: PM–B; BMFA; EPL–B
Catalogs/Checklists: Wilmerding, no. 174; McCauley, V 30

1286
Place: Baltimore, Maryland
Date: 1850 State I
Title: View of Baltimore City
Size: 18⅛ × 27½ in. (46.2 × 70 cm.)
Artist:
Lithographer:
Printer: E. Sachse & Co. N. 3 N. Liberty Str. Baltimore Md.
Publisher: Casimir Bohn (copyright)
Key/Vignettes/Misc:
Locations: PM–B; MHS–B; LC–M (facsimile)
Catalogs/Checklists: McCauley, V 13; LC–M, 253

1287
Place: Baltimore, Maryland
Date: 1850 State II
Title: View of Baltimore City
Size: 18⅛ × 27½ in. (46.2 × 70 cm.)
Artist: E. Sachse
Lithographer: E. Sachse & Comp.
Printer: E. Sachse & Comp.
Publisher: E. Sachse & Co., Baltimore M. No. 3 North Liberty Street
Key/Vignettes/Misc:
Locations: Private collection
Catalogs/Checklists: McCauley, V 13

1288
Place: Baltimore, Maryland
Date: 1850 State III
Title: View of Baltimore City

Size: 18⅛ × 27½ in. (46.2 × 70 cm.)
Artist:
Lithographer: E. Sachse & Co.
Printer: E. Sachse & Co. 3 N. Liberty St. Bltm.
Publisher:
Key/Vignettes/Misc:
Locations: EPL–B
Catalogs/Checklists: McCauley, V 13

1289
Place: Baltimore, Maryland
Date: Ca. 1852
Title: View of Baltimore
Size: 10¼ × 15¹⁄₁₆ in. (26.1 × 38.3 cm.)
Artist:
Lithographer:
Printer: E. Sachse & Co. No. 3 N Liberty St. Baltimore
Publisher: E. Sachse & Co. No. 3 N Liberty St. Baltimore
Key/Vignettes/Misc: 13 vignettes
Locations: EPL–B
Catalogs/Checklists: McCauley, note to V 31

1290
Place: Baltimore, Maryland
Date: [1853]
Title: View of Baltimore City. From Fairmount.
Size: 20¾ × 39½ in. (52.9 × 100.4 cm.)
Artist: E. Sachse & Co. [James T. Palmatary]
Lithographer: E. Sachse & Co.
Printer: E. Sachse & Co.
Publisher: E. Sachse & Co. 3 N. Liberty Str. Balto.
Key/Vignettes/Misc: Refs. 1–12
Locations: EPL–B; PM–B; MHS–B
Catalogs/Checklists: McCauley, V 18

1291
Place: Baltimore, Maryland
Date: 1856
Title: Baltimore in 1752
Size: 19⁷⁄₁₆ × 28⁷⁄₁₆ in. (49.5 × 72.4 cm.)
Artist: J. Backman [John Bachmann]
Lithographer:
Printer: P. S. Duval & Co., Lith., Philadelphia
Publisher: John Medary (copyright)
Key/Vignettes/Misc: Refs. 1–22
Locations: MHS–B; PM–B; EPL–B
Catalogs/Checklists: McCauley, V 7

1292
Place: Baltimore, Maryland
Date: 1858
Title: Bird's Eye View of Baltimore City
Size: 23⅛ × 39⁵⁄₁₆ in. (58.9 × 100 cm.)
Artist: E. Sachse & Co.
Lithographer:
Printer: E. Sachse & Co.
Publisher: E. Sachse & Co Sun Iron Building Baltimore Md.
Key/Vignettes/Misc:
Locations: EPL–B; PM–B
Catalogs/Checklists: McCauley, V 33

1293
Place: Baltimore, Maryland
Date: 1858

Title: View of Baltimore
Size: 6¹⁵⁄₁₆ × 23¾ in. (17.7 × 60.5 cm.)
Artist:
Lithographer:
Printer: A. Hoen & Co., Balto.
Publisher: Board of Trade
Key/Vignettes/Misc:
Locations: EPL−B; PM−B; MHS−B; NYH−NY; MM−NN
Catalogs/Checklists: McCauley, V 37; MM−NN, LP 2203

1294
Place: Baltimore, Maryland
Date: 1859
Title: View of Baltimore City From Federal Hill.
Size: 17¹¹⁄₁₆ × 27⅞ in. (45.1 × 71 cm.)
Artist:
Lithographer: T. Sachse
Printer: E. Sachse & Co. Baltimore
Publisher: E. Sachse & Co. Baltimore
Key/Vignettes/Misc:
Locations: EPL−B; PM−B
Catalogs/Checklists: McCauley, V 35

1295
Place: Baltimore, Maryland
Date: 1861
Title: Baltimore
Size: 32¹³⁄₁₆ × 23¹⁵⁄₁₆ in. (83.5 × 61 cm.)
Artist: A. Weidenbach
Lithographer:
Printer: Hunckel & Son, Baltimore
Publisher: Hunckel & Son Baltimore
Key/Vignettes/Misc: 19 vignettes
Locations: PM−B
Catalogs/Checklists: McCauley, V 34

1296
Place: Baltimore, Maryland
Date: 1861
Title: Camp of the Duryea's Zouaves Federal Hill Baltimore Md. Looking North.
Size: 14 × 20¼ in. (35.7 × 51.6 cm.)
Artist:
Lithographer: E. Sachse & Co.
Printer: E. Sachse & Co., 104 S. Charles St. Balto. Md.
Publisher: E. Sachse & Co. (copyright)
Key/Vignettes/Misc:
Locations: Unknown. See Old Print Shop Portfolio, XXVIII, p. 134, No. 24
Catalogs/Checklists:

1297
Place: Baltimore, Maryland
Date: 1861 State I
Title: Camp of the Duryea's Zuaves Federal Hill Baltimore.
Size: 8⅝ × 14½ in. (22 × 36.8 cm.)
Artist:
Lithographer: E. Sachse & Co.
Printer: E. Sachse & Co. 104 S. Charles St. Balto., Md.
Publisher: E. Sachse & Co. . .Maryland (copyright)
Key/Vignettes/Misc:
Locations: PM−B
Catalogs/Checklists: McCauley, E 97

1298
Place: Baltimore, Maryland
Date: 1861 State II
Title: Camp of the Duryea's Zouaves Federal Hill Baltimore Md. Looking North
Size: 8⅝ × 14½ in. (22 × 36.8 cm.)
Artist:
Lithographer: E. Sachse & Co.
Printer: E. Sachse & Co. 104 S. Charles St. Balto., Md.
Publisher: E. Sachse & Co. . .Maryland (copyright)
Key/Vignettes/Misc:
Locations: PM−B; MHS−B
Catalogs/Checklists: McCauley, E 97

1299
Place: Baltimore, Maryland
Date: 1862
Title: Fort Federal Hill, Baltimore, Md.
Size: 13¹⁵⁄₁₆ × 20¹⁄₁₆ in. (35.4 × 51 cm.)
Artist:
Lithographer: E. Sachse & Co.
Printer: E. Sachse & Co. 104 S. Charles St. Balto.
Publisher: E. Sachse & Co. 104 S. Charles St. Balto. (copyright)
Key/Vignettes/Misc:
Locations: PM−B; MM−NN; NYH−NY
Catalogs/Checklists: McCauley, E 99; MM−NN, LP 118

1300
Place: Baltimore, Maryland
Date: 1862
Title: View of Baltimore City, Md. From the North
Size: 18¾ × 27 in. (47.8 × 68.8 cm.)
Artist:
Lithographer: E. Sachse & Co.
Printer: E. Sachse & Co., 104 S. Charles St., Baltimore
Publisher: E. Sachse & Co., 104 S. Charles St., Baltimore
Key/Vignettes/Misc:
Locations: MHS−B; LC−P
Catalogs/Checklists: McCauley, V 14; LC−M, 253.2

1301
Place: Baltimore, Maryland
Date: 1862
Title: View of Baltimore City, Md. From the North.
Size: 9⁵⁄₁₆ × 16³⁄₁₆ in. 23.2 × 41.6 cm.)
Artist:
Lithographer: E. Sachse & Co.
Printer: E. Sachse & Co. 104 S. Charles St. Baltimore
Publisher: E. Sachse & Co. 104 S. Charles St. Baltimore
Key/Vignettes/Misc:
Locations: EPL−B; LC−P
Catalogs/Checklists: McCauley, V 14

1302
Place: Baltimore, Maryland
Date: 1863
Title: Illustrated Album of Baltimore City
Size: 10¾ × 15⁹⁄₁₆ in. (27.3 × 39.6 cm.)
Artist:

Lithographer:
Printer: E. Sachse & Co. 104 S. Charles St.
Publisher: E. Sachse & Co. (copyright)
Key/Vignettes/Misc: 17 vignettes compose entire view
Locations: Private collection
Catalogs/Checklists: McCauley, V 42

1303
Place: Baltimore, Maryland
Date: 1869
Title: E. Sachse & Co.'s Bird's Eye View of the City of Baltimore 1869
Size: 47¾ × 124¾ in. (121.5 × 317.6 cm.)
Artist:
Lithographer:
Printer: E. Sachse & Co., Baltimore
Publisher: E. Sachse & Co. 104 S. Charles St., Baltimore
Key/Vignettes/Misc: 135 vignettes
Locations: PM−B; MHS−B; LC−M; EPL−B
Catalogs/Checklists: LC−M, 254; McCauley, V32

1304
Place: Baltimore, Maryland
Date: 1870
Title: Illustrated Album of Baltimore City and Vicinity.
Size: 11⅝ × 20⅜ in. (29.3 × 51.3 cm.)
Artist:
Lithographer:
Printer: E. Sachse & Co. 5 N. Liberty St. Balto.
Publisher: E. Sachse & Co. Balto (copyright)
Key/Vignettes/Misc: 25 vignettes
Locations: LC−P
Catalogs/Checklists:

1305
Place: Baltimore, Maryland
Date: 1872
Title: Illustrated Album of Baltimore City and Vicinity.
Size: 14¾ × 21 in. (37.5 × 53.3 cm.)
Artist:
Lithographer: E. Sachse & Co.
Printer: E. Sachse & Co. 5 N. Liberty Str. [Baltimore]
Publisher: E. Sachse & Co. [Baltimore]
Key/Vignettes/Misc: 33 vignettes
Locations: LC−P
Catalogs/Checklists:

1306
Place: Baltimore, Maryland
Date: 1872
Title: View of Baltimore City, Md. Looking South.
Size: 9⅜ × 16⁵⁄₁₆ in. (23.2 × 42.1 cm.)
Artist:
Lithographer: E. Sachse & Co.
Printer: E. Sachse & Co. 5 N. Liberty St. Balto.
Publisher: E. Sachse & Co. Balto.
Key/Vignettes/Misc:
Locations: LC−P
Catalogs/Checklists:

1307
Place: Baltimore, Maryland
Date: 1874
Title: View of Baltimore City, Md.
Looking South.
Size: 9⅛ × 16½ in. (23.2 × 42.1 cm.)
Artist:
Lithographer: E. Sachse & Co.
Printer: E. Sachse & Co. 5 N. Liberty St. Balto.
Publisher: E. Sachse & Co., Balto.
Key/Vignettes/Misc:
Locations: MHS–B
Catalogs/Checklists: McCauley, V 15

1308
Place: Baltimore, Maryland
Date: 1880
Title: Baltimore in 1752.
Size: 9⅞ × 13⅛ in. (25.1 × 33.4 cm.)
Artist:
Lithographer:
Printer: R. H. Eichner & Co. Lith & Pub. Balto.
Publisher: R. H. Eichner & Co. Lith & Pub. Balto.
Key/Vignettes/Misc: Refs. 1–31; 5 vignettes; unnumbered list of Baltimore residents in 1752
Locations: PM–B; MHS–B
Catalogs/Checklists:

1309
Place: Baltimore, Maryland
Date: 1880
Title: The City of Baltimore
Size: 22⁹⁄₁₆ × 33⁵⁄₁₆ in. (57.5 × 84.8 cm.)
Artist: C. R. Parsons
Lithographer:
Printer:
Publisher: Currier & Ives, New York
Key/Vignettes/Misc: 40 unnumbered refs. below places identified
Locations: PM–B; LC–P
Catalogs/Checklists: McCauley, V 36

1310
Place: Baltimore, Maryland
Date: 1880
Title: The City of Baltimore, Md. in 1880. View from Washington Monument Looking South. Supplement to the Baltimore American. Population about 400,000.
Size: 17½ × 23½ in. (44.5 × 59.8 cm.)
Artist:
Lithographer: Th. Sachse
Printer: A. Sachse & Co., Baltimore & Eutaw Sts. Balto
Publisher: A. Sachse & Co., Baltimore, Md. (copyright)
Key/Vignettes/Misc: 1 vignette
Locations: PM–B; MHS–B; NYH–NY
Catalogs/Checklists: McCauley, V 16; LC–M, 254.1

1311
Place: Baltimore, Maryland
Date: 1880
Title: View of Baltimore, Md. 1752 (Population about 300.)

Size: 16⅞ × 23⅛ in. (43 × 58.9 cm.)
Artist:
Lithographer: Th[eodore] Sachse
Printer: A. Sachse & Co., Lithographers & Printers Baltimore & Eutaw Sts. Balto.
Publisher: The Baltimore American
Key/Vignettes/Misc: Refs. 1–22; 1 vignette
Locations: NYH–NY; MHS–B
Catalogs/Checklists:

1312
Place: Baltimore, Maryland
Date: 1889
Title: Baltimore in 1889
Size: 17 × 26⅛ in. (43.2 × 65.6 cm.)
Artist: H. P.[helps] Arms
Lithographer:
Printer: Isaac Friedenwald
Publisher: Isaac Friedenwald, 32 S. Paca Street, Baltimore
Key/Vignettes/Misc: Unnumbered refs. keyed to border numbers; 1 vignette
Locations: EPL–B; PM–B; MHS–B
Catalogs/Checklists: McCauley, V 39

1313
Place: Baltimore, Maryland
Date: Ca. 1912
Title: A Birds–Eye View of the Heart of Baltimore
Size: 16⅞ × 30¼ in. (43 × 77 cm.)
Artist: Edward W. Spofford
Lithographer:
Printer: Norman T. A. Munder & Co., Baltimore, Maryland
Publisher: Norman T. A. Munder & Co., Baltimore, Maryland
Key/Vignettes/Misc:
Locations: LC–M; PM–B
Catalogs/Checklists: LC–M, 255

1314
Place: Baltimore, Maryland
Date: N.D.
Title: Baltimore
Size: 10⅞ × 13⁹⁄₁₆ in. (27.6 × 34.5 cm.)
Artist:
Lithographer:
Printer:
Publisher: Louis Rochefort 15 Crown Street Finsbury, London
Key/Vignettes/Misc:
Locations: YUAG–NH
Catalogs/Checklists:

1315
Place: Chestertown, Maryland
Date: 1907
Title: Birds Eye View of Chestertown, Kent Co., Maryland 1907.
Size: 18¹⁄₁₆ × 25⅛ in. (46 × 64 cm.)
Artist: T. M. Fowler
Lithographer:
Printer:
Publisher: Fowler & Kelley, Morrisville, Pennsylvania
Key/Vignettes/Misc: 21 vignettes
Locations: LC–M
Catalogs/Checklists: LC–M, 256

1316
Place: Cumberland, Maryland
Date: 1881
Title: Cumberland, Md. 1881. Viewed from Hill, Back of Rolling Mill.
Size: 13¾ × 26⅛ in. (35.1 × 66.5 cm.)
Artist: C.[harles] L. Fussel
Lithographer:
Printer:
Publisher:
Key/Vignettes/Misc: 7 vignettes
Locations: MHS–B
Catalogs/Checklists: McCauley, V 59

1317
Place: Cumberland, Maryland
Date: Ca. 1906
Title: Bird's Eye View of Cumberland, Maryland 1906.
Size: 12³⁄₁₆ × 20¹⁄₁₆ in. (31 × 51 cm.)
Artist: Thaddeus M. Fowler
Lithographer:
Printer:
Publisher: Fowler & Kelly, Morrisville, Pennsylvania
Key/Vignettes/Misc:
Locations: LC–M
Catalogs/Checklists: LC–M, 257

1318
Place: Elkton, Maryland
Date: 1907
Title: View of Elkton, Maryland
Size: 16⅛ × 22 in. (41 × 56 cm.)
Artist: [T. M. Fowler]
Lithographer:
Printer:
Publisher: Fowler & Kelly, Morrisville, Pennsylvania
Key/Vignettes/Misc: 9 vignettes
Locations: LC–M
Catalogs/Checklists: LC–M, 258

1319
Place: Ellicott's Mills, Maryland
Date: 1854
Title: View of Ellicotts Mills, Md.
Size: 18⅛ × 28 in. (46.1 × 71.2 cm.)
Artist:
Lithographer: E. Sachse & Co.
Printer: E. Sachse & Co., Baltimore
Publisher: John Schofield, Gazette Office, Ellicotts Mills
Key/Vignettes/Misc: 21 vignettes
Locations: PM–B; MHS–B; LC–P
Catalogs/Checklists: McCauley, V 49; LC–M, 258.1

1320
Place: Ellicott's Mills, Maryland
Date: [1859]
Title: Panoramic View of the Scenery on the Patapsco River for 7 Miles Above and Below Ellicott's Mills, Md.
Size: 23⅝ × 32³⁄₁₆ in. (60.1 × 81.9 cm.)
Artist: E. Sachse
Lithographer:
Printer: E. Sachse & Co. Baltimore Md.
Publisher: John Schofield Ellicotts Mills. . ., Md.

Key/Vignettes/Misc: Refs. 1–22; 1
vignette
Locations: PM–B; MHS–B
Catalogs/Checklists: McCauley, V 50

1321
Place: Frederick, Maryland
Date: 1854
Title: View of Frederick, Maryland.
Size: 19⁹⁄₁₆ × 31¼ in. (49.8 × 79.5 cm.)
Artist: E. Sachse & Co.
Lithographer:
Printer: E. Sachse & Co., Baltimore, Md.
Publisher: John Schofield
Key/Vignettes/Misc: 24 vignettes
Locations: MHS–B
Catalogs/Checklists: McCauley, V 46

1322
Place: Frederick, Maryland
Date: 1878
Title: Frederick, Md. 1878. Viewed from
the Top of the Deaf & Dumb Institute.
Size: 12 × 26¾ in. (30.6 × 68.1 cm.)
Artist: W. W. Denslow
Lithographer: [Morris] Traubel
Printer: Thos. Hunter, Lith, Phila.
Publisher: C. J. Corbin
Key/Vignettes/Misc: 18 vignettes
Locations: Commercial Credit Company,
Baltimore, Maryland
Catalogs/Checklists: McCauley, V 48

1323
Place: Frostburg, Maryland
Date: 1905
Title: View of Frostburg, Maryland 1905.
Size: 24⅜ × 28⅝ in. (62 × 73 cm.)
Artist: T. M. Fowler
Lithographer:
Printer:
Publisher: T. M. Fowler, Morrisville, Pa.
Key/Vignettes/Misc: 17 vignettes
Locations: LC–M
Catalogs/Checklists: LC–M, 259

1324
Place: Hagerstown, Maryland
Date: [1856–59]
Title: View of Hagerstown, Md.
Size: 19¹⁄₁₆ × 32⅛ in. (48.5 × 81.8 cm.)
Artist: E. Sachse & Co.
Lithographer: E. Sachse & Co.
Printer: E. Sachse & Co., Sun Iron
Building, Baltimore
Publisher: John Schofield
Key/Vignettes/Misc: 21 vignettes
Locations: PM–B; MHS–B; CHS–C
Catalogs/Checklists: McCauley, V 45

1325
Place: Havre De Grace, Maryland
Date: 1907
Title: Bird's Eye View of Havre de Grace,
Maryland 1907.
Size: 13⅜ × 21⁹⁄₁₆ in. (34 × 55 cm.)
Artist: T. M. Fowler
Lithographer:
Printer:
Publisher: Fowler & Kelly, Morrisville, Pa.
Key/Vignettes/Misc: 15 vignettes

Locations: LC–M
Catalogs/Checklists: LC–M, 260

1326
Place: Lonaconing, Maryland
Date: 1905
Title: Lonaconing, Md. 1905
Size: 14¾ × 21¾ in. (37.6 × 55.3 cm.)
Artist: T. M. Fowler
Lithographer:
Printer:
Publisher: Fowler and Kelly, Morrisville,
Pa.
Key/Vignettes/Misc: 7 vignettes
Locations: NYH–NY
Catalogs/Checklists:

1327
Place: Midland, Maryland
Date: 1905
Title: Midland, Maryland. 1905.
Size: 15⅜ × 19¼ in. (39.1 × 49 cm.)
Artist: T. M. Fowler
Lithographer:
Printer:
Publisher: T. M. Fowler, Morrisville, Pa.
Key/Vignettes/Misc: 8 vignettes
Locations: NYH–NY
Catalogs/Checklists:

1328
Place: Mountain Lake Park, Maryland
Date: 1906
Title: Birds Eye View of Mountain Lake
Park, Garrett Co., Maryland 1906.
Size: 13¾ × 22¾ in. (35 × 58 cm.)
Artist: [T. M. Fowler?]
Lithographer:
Printer:
Publisher: Fowler & Kelly, Morrisville,
Pennsylvania
Key/Vignettes/Misc: 34 vignettes
Locations: LC–M
Catalogs/Checklists: LC–M, 261

1329
Place: Oakland, Maryland
Date: 1906
Title: Bird's Eye View of Oakland,
Maryland 1906.
Size: 13 × 20 in. (33 × 51 cm.)
Artist: Fowler & Kelly
Lithographer:
Printer:
Publisher: Fowler & Kelly, Morrisville, Pa.
Key/Vignettes/Misc:
Locations: LC–M
Catalogs/Checklists: LC–M, 262

1330
Place: Rising Sun, Maryland
Date: 1907
Title: Birds Eye View of Rising Sun, Cecil
County, Maryland 1907.
Size: 10¼ × 20 in. (26 × 51 cm.)
Artist: T. M. Fowler
Lithographer:
Printer:
Publisher: Fowler & Kelly, Morrisville, Pa.
Key/Vignettes/Misc: 12 vignettes
Locations: LC–M
Catalogs/Checklists: LC–M, 263

1331
Place: Allston, Massachusetts
Date: 1899
Title: Allston, Massachusetts. Ward 24
City of Boston. 1899.
Size: 19³⁄₁₆ × 25⅜ in. (48.8 × 64.6 cm.)
Artist:
Lithographer:
Printer: O. H. Bailey & Co. Boston
Publisher: O. H. Bailey & Co. Boston
Key/Vignettes/Misc: Refs. A, 2–40; 17
vignettes
Locations: MSL–B
Catalogs/Checklists:

1332
Place: Amesbury, Massachusetts
Date: 1880
Title: Amesbury and Salisbury Mills,
Mass.
Size: 26¾ × 31⅝ in. (68.1 × 80.5 cm.)
Artist:
Lithographer:
Printer: Beck & Pauli, Milwaukee, Wis.
Publisher: E. H. Bigelow, Framingham,
Mass.
Key/Vignettes/Misc: Refs. 1–75; 34
vignettes
Locations: BPL–R; AAS–W; LC–M
(photo)
Catalogs/Checklists: LC–M, 263.3

1333
Place: Amesbury, Massachusetts
Date: 1890
Title: Amesbury, Mass.
Size: 20 × 33½ in. (50.8 × 85.2 cm.)
Artist: Geo. E. Norris
Lithographer:
Printer: The Burleigh Lith. Est., Troy, N. Y.
Publisher: Geo. E. Norris Brockton, Mass.
Key/Vignettes/Misc: Refs. 1–92
Locations: LC–M; HEHL
Catalogs/Checklists: LC–M, 264

1334
Place: Amesbury, Massachusetts
Date: 1914
Title: Aero View of Amesbury
Massachusetts 1914
Size: 21 × 29½ in. (53.4 × 75 cm.)
Artist: T. M. Fowler
Lithographer:
Printer: Meriden Gravure Co., [Meriden
Conn.]
Publisher: Hughes & Bailey, New York
Key/Vignettes/Misc: Unnumbered business
directory
Locations: LC–M
Catalogs/Checklists: LC–M, 265

1335
Place: Amherst, Massachusetts
Date: Ca. 1855
Title: View of Amherst, Mass.
Size: 16⅞ × 26⅛ in. (43 × 66.5 cm.)
Artist: Ambrotype by E. W. Cowles
Lithographer:
Printer: Endicott & Co., N. Y.
Publisher: John Bachelder
Key/Vignettes/Misc: 6 vignettes

Locations: Amherst Historical Society, Amherst, Massachusetts
Catalogs/Checklists:

1336
Place: Amherst, Massachusetts
Date: 1886
Title: Amherst, Mass. 1886
Size: 15¾ × 29¼ in. (40.1 × 74.4 cm.)
Artist:
Lithographer:
Printer: Burleigh Lith. Est., Troy, N. Y.
Publisher: L. R. Burleigh, Troy, New York
Key/Vignettes/Misc: Refs. 1–43
Locations: LC–M; BPL–R; LC–P
Catalogs/Checklists: LC–M, 266

1337
Place: Andover, Massachusetts
Date: Ca. 1860
Title: Andover, Mass. from the North–West
Size: 16 × 24 in. (40.8 × 61.1 cm.)
Artist: J. P. Newell
Lithographer:
Printer: J. H. Bufford
Publisher: W. F. Draper
Key/Vignettes/Misc: 5 vignettes
Locations: Andover Historical Society, Andover, Massachusetts
Catalogs/Checklists:

1338
Place: Andover, Massachusetts
Date: 1882
Title: View of Andover, Massachusetts. 1882.
Size: 19½ × 25³⁄₁₆ in. (49.6 × 64.2 cm.)
Artist:
Lithographer:
Printer:
Publisher: O. H. Bailey & Co., Boston
Key/Vignettes/Misc: Refs. 1–34
Locations: BPL–R
Catalogs/Checklists:

1339
Place: Arlington, Massachusetts
Date: 1884
Title: Arlington, Massachusetts. 1884.
Size: 19½ × 28¼ in. (49.6 × 71.9 cm.)
Artist:
Lithographer:
Printer:
Publisher: O. H. Bailey & Co., Boston
Key/Vignettes/Misc: Refs. 1–27
Locations: BPL–R
Catalogs/Checklists:

1340
Place: Ashburnham, Massachusetts
Date: 1886
Title: Ashburnham, Mass.
Size: 10½ × 19¾ in. (26.7 × 50.3 cm.)
Artist: L. R. Burleigh
Lithographer:
Printer: C. H. Vogt & Son, Lith. Cleveland
Publisher: L. R. Burleigh, Troy, N. Y.
Key/Vignettes/Misc: Refs. 1–15
Locations: LC–M; BPL–R
Catalogs/Checklists: LC–M, 267

1341
Place: Ashland, Massachusetts
Date: 1878
Title: View of Ashland, Mass. 1878.
Size: 19 × 24½ in. (48.3 × 62 cm.)
Artist: O. H. Bailey & J. C. Hazen
Lithographer:
Printer:
Publisher: O. H. Bailey & J. C. Hazen, Boston
Key/Vignettes/Misc: Refs. A–H, J; 1 vignette
Locations: BPL–R; AAS–W; LC–M
Catalogs/Checklists: LC–M, 268

1342
Place: Athol, Massachusetts
Date: 1878
Title: View of Athol, Mass.
Size: 19⅛ × 26⅞ in. (48.7 × 68.5 cm.)
Artist:
Lithographer:
Printer:
Publisher: O. H. Bailey and Company, Boston
Key/Vignettes/Misc: Refs. 1–30
Locations: BPL–R
Catalogs/Checklists:

1343
Place: Athol, Massachusetts
Date: 1887
Title: Athol, Mass. 1887.
Size: 16¼ × 23¾ in. (41.4 × 60.5 cm.)
Artist: L. R. Burleigh
Lithographer:
Printer:
Publisher: L. R. Burleigh, Troy, N. Y.
Key/Vignettes/Misc: Refs. 1–12
Locations: LC–M; BPL–R
Catalogs/Checklists: LC–M, 269

1344
Place: Attleboro, Massachusetts
Date: 1878
Title: View of Attleborough, Mass. East Village. 1878.
Size: 19 × 25 in. (48.4 × 63.6 cm.)
Artist: O. H. Bailey & J. C.Hazen
Lithographer:
Printer: Beck & Pauli Lith [Milwaukee]
Publisher: O. H. Bailey & J. C. Hazen, Boston
Key/Vignettes/Misc: Refs. 1–32
Locations: BPL–R
Catalogs/Checklists:

1345
Place: Attleboro, Massachusetts
Date: 1891
Title: Attleborough, Mass, 1891.
Size: 22¾ × 29½ in. (57.9 × 75.1 cm.)
Artist:
Lithographer:
Printer: O. H. Bailey & Co. Boston
Publisher: O. H. Bailey & Co. Boston
Key/Vignettes/Misc: Refs. A–B, 2–10, 12–23, 25–33; 45 vignettes
Locations: BA
Catalogs/Checklists:

1346
Place: Avon, Massachusetts
Date: 1899
Title: Avon, Massachusetts. 1899.
Size: 15¹⁄₁₆ × 22¹⁵⁄₁₆ in. (38.3 × 58.4 cm.)
Artist:
Lithographer:
Printer: O. H. Bailey & Co. Boston
Publisher: O. H. Bailey & Co. Boston
Key/Vignettes/Misc: Refs. A, 2–33; 12 vignettes
Locations: MSL–B
Catalogs/Checklists:

1347
Place: Ayer, Massachusetts
Date: 1886
Title: Ayer, Mass.
Size: 11⅞ × 23³⁄₁₆ in. (30.3 × 59.1 cm.)
Artist:
Lithographer:
Printer:
Publisher: L. R. Burleigh, Troy, N. Y. (copyright)
Key/Vignettes/Misc: Refs. 1–19
Locations: LC–M; AAS–W; BPL–R
Catalogs/Checklists: LC–M, 270

Place: Babbatassett Village, Massachusetts
Date: 1851
See Pepperell, Massachusetts, 1851.

1348
Place: Baldwinsville, Massachusetts
Date: 1886
Title: Baldwinville, Mass.
Size: 11½ × 24½ in. (29.3 × 62 cm.)
Artist:
Lithographer:
Printer: Beck & Pauli, Milwaukee
Publisher: L. R. Burleigh, Troy, N. Y. (copyright)
Key/Vignettes/Misc: Refs. 1–12
Locations: BPL–R; LC–M
Catalogs/Checklists: LC–M, 271

1349
Place: Ballardvale, Massachusetts
Date: 1885
Title: Ballardvale, Mass.
Size: 11¾ × 16¾ in. (29.9 × 42.7 cm.)
Artist:
Lithographer:
Printer:
Publisher: A. F. Poole & Co., Brockton, Mass.
Key/Vignettes/Misc: Refs. A–H, J
Locations: BPL–R
Catalogs/Checklists:

1350
Place: Barnstable, Massachusetts
Date: 1884
Title: Village of Barnstable, Seat of Barnstable County Mass. 1884
Size: 12⅝ × 31¾ in. (32.2 × 80.8 cm.)
Artist: A. F. Poole
Lithographer:
Printer: Geo. H. Walker & Co., Lith, Boston
Publisher: A. F. Poole, Brockton, Mass.

Key/Vignettes/Misc: Refs. A–H, J–S; 1
vignette
Locations: BPL–R; LC–M (facsimile)
Catalogs/Checklists: LC–M, 271.1

1351

Place: Barre, Massachusetts
Date: [187–?]
Title: Bird's–Eye View of Village of Barre,
Mass.
Size: 10½ × 24½ in. (26.7 × 62.3 cm.)
Artist:
Lithographer:
Printer:
Publisher: W. R. Spooner
Key/Vignettes/Misc:
Locations: LC–M
Catalogs/Checklists: LC–M, 271.2

1352

Place: Barre, Massachusetts
Date: 1891
Title: Barre, Massachusetts. 1891
Size: 21⁵/₁₆ × 25³/₁₆ in. (54.3 × 64.1 cm.)
Artist:
Lithographer:
Printer: O. H. Bailey & Co. Boston
Publisher: O. H. Bailey & Co. Boston
Key/Vignettes/Misc: Refs. A, 2–31; 35
vignettes
Locations: MSL–B; LC–M
Catalogs/Checklists: LC–M, 271.3

Place: Beverly, Massachusetts
Date: [1843–44]
See Salem, Massachusetts, [1843–44].

Place: Beverly, Massachusetts
Date: 1850
See Salem, Massachusetts, 1850.

1353

Place: Beverly, Massachusetts
Date: 1856
Title: Beverly, Mass. From Fort Lee
(Salem).
Size: 12⁵/₈ × 15⁵/₈ in. (32.1 × 39.7 cm.)
Artist: J. B. Bachelder
Lithographer:
Printer: Endicott & Co., New York
Publisher: Jno. B. Bachelder, 59 Beekman
St. New York
Key/Vignettes/Misc:
Locations: MM–NN; EI–S; AAS–W;
BPL–P; MAHS–B; BA
Catalogs/Checklists: MM–NN, LP 2

1354

Place: Beverly, Massachusetts
Date: 1879
Title: View of Beverly, Mass. 1879.
Size: 18¾ × 24½ in. (47.7 × 62.3 cm.)
Artist:
Lithographer:
Printer:
Publisher: O. H. Bailey & Co., Boston
Key/Vignettes/Misc: Refs. 1–15
Locations: BPL–R; EI–S
Catalogs/Checklists:

1355

Place: Beverly, Massachusetts
Date: 1886
Title: View of Beverly, Massachusetts 1886

Size: 17 × 25 in. (43.3 × 63.6 cm.)
Artist:
Lithographer:
Printer:
Publisher: W. A. Greenough & Co.,
Boston
Key/Vignettes/Misc:
Locations: LC–M
Catalogs/Checklists: LC–M, 271.4

1356

Place: Beverly Farms, Massachusetts
Date: 1886
Title: The Farms. 1886.
Size: 16½ × 30½ in. (41.9 × 77.6 cm.)
Artist:
Lithographer:
Printer:
Publisher: O. W. Walker, Boston
Key/Vignettes/Misc:
Locations: LC–M
Catalogs/Checklists: LC–M, 272

1357

Place: Blackinton, Massachusetts
Date: 1889
Title: Blackington, Mass.
Size: 15¾ × 22⁵/₈ in. (40.1 × 57.6 cm.)
Artist:
Lithographer:
Printer: The Burleigh Lith. Est., Troy, N. Y.
Publisher: L. R. Burleigh, Troy, N. Y.
Key/Vignettes/Misc: Refs. 1–6
Locations: BPL–R
Catalogs/Checklists:

1358

Place: Blackstone, Massachusetts
Date: 1879
Title: Bird's Eye View of Blackstone, Mass.
1879
Size: 16¾ × 22⁷/₈ in. (42.6 × 58.3 cm.)
Artist: O. H. Bailey & J. C. Hazen
Lithographer:
Printer:
Publisher: O. H. Bailey & J. C. Hazen,
Boston
Key/Vignettes/Misc: Refs. A–H, J–K
Locations: BPL–R
Catalogs/Checklists:

1359

Place: Boston, Massachusetts
Date: [1828–29]
Title: View of Boston and the South
Boston Bridge Vue de Boston Prise du Pont
du Sud
Size: 9½ × 11⁷/₁₆ in. (24.2 × 29.1 cm.)
Artist: J. Milbert
Lithographer: Deroy
Printer: Henry Gaugain
Publisher:
Key/Vignettes/Misc:
Locations: CHS–C; BPL–P; BS–B;
MM–NN; YUAG–NH; NYH–NY
Catalogs/Checklists: MM–NN, LP 3699

1360

Place: Boston, Massachusetts
Date: [1825–30?]
Title: Vue de Boston
Size: 9½ × 16 in. (24.2 × 40.7 cm.)
Artist:

Lithographer:
Printer: Englemann pere et fils [Paris]
Publisher:
Key/Vignettes/Misc:
Locations: NYP–S
Catalogs/Checklists: Stokes, C.
1825–30—E26

1361

Place: Boston, Massachusetts
Date: [1835–40]
Title: View in Boston Harbor
Size:
Artist:
Lithographer:
Printer: T. Moore's Lithography, Boston
Publisher:
Key/Vignettes/Misc:
Locations: Unknown. see Goodspeed's
Catalogue, no. 245
Catalogs/Checklists:

1362

Place: Boston, Massachusetts
Date: [1836–40]
Title: Boston, From the S. East.
Size: 15³/₈ × 20¹³/₁₆ in. (39.1 × 53 cm.)
Artist:
Lithographer:
Printer: Jenkins & Colburn's Lith.
[Boston]
Publisher:
Key/Vignettes/Misc:
Locations: BA; YUAG–NH
Catalogs/Checklists:

1363

Place: Boston, Massachusetts
Date: 1848
Title: View of Boston in 1848. From East
Boston.
Size: 22 × 44⅛ in. (56 × 112.2 cm.)
Artist: E. Whitefield
Lithographer: C. Burton
Printer:
Publisher: Whitefield & Smith [Boston]
Key/Vignettes/Misc: Refs. 1–19
Locations: MM–NN; BA; CHS–C; EI–S;
NYH–NY; MAHS–B; BS–B; ROM;
BPL–P; SSBT–B; PAC–P
Catalogs/Checklists: MM–NN, LP 2168;
Norton, Whitefield, no. 37

1364

Place: Boston, Massachusetts
Date: 1848
Title: View of Boston. Vue de Boston
Ansicht von Boston
Size: 8⁵/₈ × 12½ in. (22 × 31.8 cm.)
Artist:
Lithographer: N. Currier
Printer:
Publisher: N. Currier 152 Nassau St. Cor
of Spruce N. Y.
Key/Vignettes/Misc:
Locations: MCNY; YUAG–NH
Catalogs/Checklists: Peters, C & I, 3930

1365

Place: Boston, Massachusetts
Date: Ca. 1848
Title: A South East View of Ye Great Town
of Boston in New England in America.

Exact Copy of an Original Engraving (executed in 1743) in the Possession of Hon. Josiah Quincy Jr.
Size: 23¼ × 40⁹/₁₆ in. (59.2 × 103.1 cm.)
Artist: Wm. Price [William Burgis]
Lithographer:
Printer:
Publisher: A. Tompkins for E. Whitefield, 38 Cornhill, Boston
Key/Vignettes/Misc: Refs. 1–60; description
Locations: BA; BS–B; SSBT–B
Catalogs/Checklists:

1366
Place: Boston, Massachusetts
Date: 1850
Title: Bird's eye view of Boston
Size: 20½ × 27⅝ in. (52 × 70.1 cm.)
Artist: J. Bachmann
Lithographer: J. Bachmann
Printer: Sarony & Major, New York
Publisher: John Bachmann 116 Greenwich St. N. York
Key/Vignettes/Misc:
Locations: MM–NN; CHS–C; BPL–P; BS–B; MAHS–B; YUAG–NH; LC–M (facsimile); LC–P; NYH–NY
Catalogs/Checklists: MM–NN, LP 10; LC–M, 272.3

1367
Place: Boston, Massachusetts
Date: 1854
Title: Boston Harbor, 1854. View taken from Fort Hill.
Size: 25⅝ × 35¾ in. (65.2 × 90.8 cm.)
Artist: J. W. A. Scott
Lithographer:
Printer: J. H. Bufford's Lith., 313 Washington St. Boston
Publisher: Henry A. Page, Boston (copyright)
Key/Vignettes/Misc:
Locations: MM–NN; SSBT–B
Catalogs/Checklists: MM–NN, LP 410

1368
Place: Boston, Massachusetts
Date: [1854]
Title: Environs of Boston, From Corey's Hill, Brookline, Mass.
Size: 18¾ × 38⁵/₁₆ in. (47.8 × 97.5 cm.)
Artist: Freeman Richardson
Lithographer:
Printer: J. H. Bufford's Lith, 313 Washington St. Boston
Publisher: Freeman Richardson, 125 Washington St. Boston
Key/Vignettes/Misc:
Locations: EI–S; SSBT–B; BS–B; MAHS–B
Catalogs/Checklists:

1369
Place: Boston, Massachusetts
Date: [1854]
Title: View of Boston. From Telegraph Hill, S. Boston.
Size: 15 × 22⁵/₁₆ in. (38 × 56.6 cm.)
Artist: B. Spindler
Lithographer:

Printer: Tappan & Bradford's Lith [Boston]
Publisher: Tappan & Bradford's Lith [Boston]
Key/Vignettes/Misc:
Locations: AAS–W; BPL–P; BS–B; MAHS–B; BA; YUAG–NH
Catalogs/Checklists:

1370
Place: Boston, Massachusetts
Date: Ca. 1857
Title: Bird's Eye View of Boston.
Size: 19⅞ × 28³/₁₆ in. (50.6 × 71.7 cm.)
Artist:
Lithographer: C. Matter
Printer: R. Furrer
Publisher: J. H. Locher, 117 Fulton St. New York
Key/Vignettes/Misc:
Locations: BA; CHS–C
Catalogs/Checklists:

1371
Place: Boston, Massachusetts
Date: 1859
Title: South Boston, 1859.
Size: 21½ × 29⅜ in. (54.8 × 74.7 cm.)
Artist: J. F. A. Cole
Lithographer: J. Cole
Printer:
Publisher:
Key/Vignettes/Misc: 5 vignettes; dedication
Locations: BPL–P; BA; YUAG–NH; NYH–NY
Catalogs/Checklists:

1372
Place: Boston, Massachusetts
Date: [1850–59?]
Title: Boston
Size: 14¼ × 19¼ in. (36.3 × 49 cm.)
Artist: Louis Le Breton
Lithographer: Louis Le Breton
Printer: Auguste Bry, 114 rue du bac [Paris]
Publisher:
Key/Vignettes/Misc:
Locations: BPL–P
Catalogs/Checklists:

1373
Place: Boston, Massachusetts
Date: 1866
Title: Bird's Eye View of Boston
Size: 25½ × 34 in. (64.9 × 86.5 cm.)
Artist: B.[enjamin] F. Nutting
Lithographer:
Printer: J. Mayer & Co., Lith. 4 State St. Boston
Publisher: B. B. Russell & Co., 55 Cornhill, Boston
Key/Vignettes/Misc:
Locations: BPL–R; BS–B; MAHS–B; BA
Catalogs/Checklists:

1374
Place: Boston, Massachusetts
Date: 1866
Title: View of the Public Garden & Boston Common From Arlington St.

Size: 17⁹/₁₆ × 29 in. (44.8 × 73.8 cm.)
Artist: E. Whitefield
Lithographer:
Printer: J. H. Bufford's Lith. [Boston]
Publisher: P. R. Stewart & Co. [Boston?]
Key/Vignettes/Misc:
Locations: BA; CHS–C; LC–P; BPL–P; YUAG–NH
Catalogs/Checklists: Norton, Whitefield, no. 90

1375
Place: Boston, Massachusetts
Date: [1870?]
Title: [Bird's eye view of Boston from the west.]
Size: 18¼ × 24¾ in. (46.4 × 63 cm.)
Artist: [F. Fuchs]
Lithographer:
Printer:
Publisher:
Key/Vignettes/Misc:
Locations: BPL–R
Catalogs/Checklists:

1376
Place: Boston, Massachusetts
Date: 1871
Title: View of Boston, July 4th, 1870.
Size: 27¾ × 36 in. (70.6 × 91.6 cm.)
Artist: F. Fuchs
Lithographer: F. Fuchs
Printer: New England Lith. Co., Boston
Publisher: John Weik, 605 Sansom St. Philadelphia
Key/Vignettes/Misc:
Locations: LC–M; BPL–R; BS–B
Catalogs/Checklists: LC–M, 273

1377
Place: Boston, Massachusetts
Date: 1873
Title: The City of Boston.
Size: 22⅜ × 32¾ in. (57.1 × 83.3 cm.)
Artist: Parsons & Atwater
Lithographer:
Printer:
Publisher: Currier & Ives, 125 Nassau St., New York
Key/Vignettes/Misc: 75 unnumbered refs. in 8 lines below places identified
Locations: LC–M; CHS–C; SSBT–B; BPL–P; BS–B; BA; YUAG–NH; LC–P
Catalogs/Checklists: LC–M, 275

1378
Place: Boston, Massachusetts
Date: 1877
Title: Boston Bird's Eye View from the North.
Size: 19¾ × 25 in. (50.3 × 63.6 cm.)
Artist: John Bachmann
Lithographer: John Bachmann
Printer:
Publisher: L. Prang & Co. [Boston] (copyright)
Key/Vignettes/Misc:
Locations: LC–M; BPL–R; BPL–P (cropped); BS–B; BA; LC–P
Catalogs/Checklists: LC–M, 276

1379
Place: Boston, Massachusetts
Date: 1879
Title: Balloon View–Boston Harbor.
Size: 11 × 17⅝ in. (28 × 44.8 cm.)
Artist: F. K. Rogers
Lithographer:
Printer: J.[ohn] H. Daniels
Publisher: J. H. Daniels, Boston.
(copyright)
Key/Vignettes/Misc: 5 vignettes
Locations: BPL–R
Catalogs/Checklists:

1380
Place: Boston, Massachusetts
Date: 1879
Title: The City of Boston 1879.
Size: 28⅝ × 44⅛ in. (72.9 × 112.3 cm.)
Artist:
Lithographer:
Printer: Armstrong & Co., Riverside Press, Cambridge
Publisher: O. H. Bailey & J. C. Hazen, cor. Milk & Congress Sts, Boston, Mass. New England Mutual Life Building
Key/Vignettes/Misc: Refs. A, 2–59
Locations: BPL–R; LC–M; SSBT–B; NYH–NY
Catalogs/Checklists: LC–M, 277

1381
Place: Boston, Massachusetts
Date: 1879
Title: View of East Boston, Mass. 1879.
Size: 19¼ × 23¾ in. (49 × 60.5 cm.)
Artist: O. H. Bailey & Co.
Lithographer:
Printer:
Publisher: O. H. Bailey & Co., Boston
Key/Vignettes/Misc: Refs. 1–36; 2 vignettes
Locations: BPL–R; AAS–W; LC–M
Catalogs/Checklists: LC–M, 285

1382
Place: Boston, Massachusetts
Date: [187–?]
Title: Bird's–Eye View of Boston, United States
Size: 12⁹⁄₁₆ × 19¼ in. (32 × 49 cm.)
Artist: T. Sulman
Lithographer:
Printer:
Publisher:
Key/Vignettes/Misc:
Locations: LC–M
Catalogs/Checklists: LC–M, 274

1383
Place: Boston, Massachusetts
Date: 1880
Title: View of Boston Massachusetts 1880
Size: 32¹¹⁄₁₆ × 54¹⁄₁₆ in. (83 × 137.3 cm.)
Artist: H. H. Rowley & Co.
Lithographer:
Printer: Beck & Pauli, Milwaukee Wis.
Publisher: H. H. Rowley & Co., Hartford, Conn.
Key/Vignettes/Misc: Refs. 1–27
Locations: LC–M; ACMW–FW; BA;

BS–B; MAHS–B
Catalogs/Checklists: LC–M, 278

1384
Place: Boston, Massachusetts
Date: 1883
Title: The Hub, Compliments of A. Shuman & Company
Size: 17 × 23⅛ in. (43.3 × 58.9 cm.)
Artist: T. O. Langerfeldt
Lithographer: T. O. Langerfeldt
Printer: E.[mil] F. Ackermann, Boston, Mass.
Publisher: E. F. Ackermann, Boston, Mass.
Key/Vignettes/Misc: 12 vignettes
Locations: BA
Catalogs/Checklists:

1385
Place: Boston, Massachusetts
Date: 1884
Title: Boston—1884. The Hub.
Size: 16⅜ × 22¼ in. (41.7 × 56.6 cm.)
Artist: T. O. Langerfeldt
Lithographer:
Printer: E.[mil] F. Ackermann, Boston
Publisher: E. F. Ackermann, Boston
Key/Vignettes/Misc: 8 vignettes; 2 portraits; 4 seals
Locations: BPL–P; BS–B
Catalogs/Checklists:

1386
Place: Boston, Massachusetts
Date: 1888
Title: Boston Highlands, Massachusetts. Wards 19, 20, 21 & 22 of Boston.
Size: 31 × 41 in. (78.9 × 104.3 cm.)
Artist: Favour
Lithographer:
Printer:
Publisher: O. H. Bailey & Co. [Boston]
Key/Vignettes/Misc: Refs. A–H, J–M, 2–109; 42 vignettes
Locations: BPL–R; LC–M
Catalogs/Checklists: LC–M, 281

1387
Place: Boston, Massachusetts
Date: 1889
Title: Boston in 1849.
Size: 9⅞ × 16½ in. (25.1 × 42 cm.)
Artist: E. Whitefield
Lithographer:
Printer:
Publisher: E. Whitefield, 211 Tremont St., Boston
Key/Vignettes/Misc:
Locations: BS–B
Catalogs/Checklists:

1388
Place: Boston, Massachusetts
Date: 1897
Title: Boston Harbor
Size: 12 × 21¼ in. (30.6 × 54.1 cm.)
Artist:
Lithographer:
Printer: Geo. H. Walker & Co., Boston
Publisher: Geo. H. Walker & Co., Boston
Key/Vignettes/Misc:
Locations: WHS–M
Catalogs/Checklists:

1389
Place: Boston, Massachusetts
Date: 1899
Title: Boston 1899
Size: 24 × 37⅝ in. (61.1 × 90.8 cm.)
Artist: [A. E. Downs]
Lithographer:
Printer: Geo. H. Walker & Co. Lith Boston
Publisher: E. A. Downs [A. E. Downs] (copyright)
Key/Vignettes/Misc: Refs. 1–16
Locations: LC–M; BPL–R; BPL–P; SSBT–B
Catalogs/Checklists: LC–M, 279

1390
Place: Boston, Massachusetts
Date: Ca. 1902
Title: Bird's Eye View of Boston.
Size: 16½ × 24¾ in. (42 × 63 cm.)
Artist: George Walker & Co.
Lithographer:
Printer: Beach & Clarridge Co., Boston
Publisher: Geo. H. Walker & Co., Boston
Key/Vignettes/Misc: Refs. A–Z, AB, 1–88, 1–14
Locations: LC–M
Catalogs/Checklists: LC–M, 297.1

1391
Place: Boston, Massachusetts
Date: Ca. 1905
Title: Boston and Environs
Size: 19¾ × 27¾ in. (50.2 × 70.6 cm.)
Artist:
Lithographer:
Printer:
Publisher: Geo. H. Walker & Co., Boston (copyright)
Key/Vignettes/Misc:
Locations: LC–M; BPL–R
Catalogs/Checklists: LC–M, 280.1

1392
Place: Boston, Massachusetts
Date: Ca. 1905
Title: Twentieth Century Boston.
Size: 21¼ × 29 in. (54.1 × 73.8 cm.)
Artist: Bert Poole
Lithographer: A. W. Elson & Co.
Printer:
Publisher: F. D. Nichols Company, Boston (copyright)
Key/Vignettes/Misc:
Locations: LC–M; BPL–R; BS–B
Catalogs/Checklists: LC–M, 280

1393
Place: Boston, Massachusetts
Date: [1910?]
Title: The Model of the Metropolitan District of Boston: Bird's Eye View from the East.
Size: 9½ × 24 in. (24.2 × 61.1 cm.)
Artist:
Lithographer:
Printer:
Publisher: George Carroll Curtis, Boston
Key/Vignettes/Misc:
Locations: BPL–R
Catalogs/Checklists:

1394
Place: Boston, Massachusetts
Date: N.D.
Title: Bird's Eye View of Boston Harbor and South Shore to Provincetown Showing Steamboat Routes.
Size: 16 × 20 in. (40.8 × 50.9 cm.)
Artist:
Lithographer:
Printer:
Publisher: John F. Murphy, South Station, Boston, Mass.
Key/Vignettes/Misc:
Locations: Private collection
Catalogs/Checklists:

1395
Place: Boston, Massachusetts
Date: N.D.
Title: Boston.
Size: 11 × 13¾ in. (28 × 35 cm.)
Artist:
Lithographer:
Printer: F. Silber, Post–Str 9 Berlin
Publisher: F. Silber and Max Jacoby & Zeller, 70 John St., New York
Key/Vignettes/Misc:
Locations: BS–B; MM–NN
Catalogs/Checklists: MM–NN, LP 1079

1396
Place: Bradford, Massachusetts
Date: 1857
Title: Bradford and Haverhill, Mass. From the Residence of Hon. E. J. M. Hale
Size: 12½ × 15¾ in. (31.8 × 40.1 cm.)
Artist: J. B. Bachelder
Lithographer:
Printer: Endicott & Co., New York
Publisher: Jno. B. Bachelder, 59 Beekman St. New York
Key/Vignettes/Misc: Refs. 1–6
Locations: EI–S; AAS–W; BPL–P; SSBT–B; MAHS–B; PAC–P; BA; NYH–NY
Catalogs/Checklists:

1397
Place: Bridgewater, Massachusetts
Date: 1887
Title: Bridgewater, Massachusetts. 1887.
Size: 19½ × 30¾ in. (49.7 × 78.3 cm.)
Artist:
Lithographer:
Printer: O. H. Bailey & Co., Boston
Publisher: O. H. Bailey & Co., Boston
Key/Vignettes/Misc: Refs. 1–46; 13 vignettes
Locations: BPL–R
Catalogs/Checklists:

1398
Place: Brockton, Massachusetts
Date: 1878
Title: Brockton, Mass. 1878.
Size: 21¾ × 27⅞ in. (55.4 × 70.9 cm.)
Artist:
Lithographer:
Printer: Beck & Pauli Lith. [Milwaukee]
Publisher:
Key/Vignettes/Misc: Refs. 1–40, 43–44; 6 vignettes

Locations: AAS–W; BPL–R
Catalogs/Checklists:

1399
Place: Brockton, Massachusetts
Date: 1882
Title: Bird's Eye View of the City of Brockton, Plymouth County, Mass. Looking Southwest. 1882.
Size: 26 × 39 in. (66.2 × 99.3 cm.)
Artist: A. F. Poole
Lithographer:
Printer: Beck & Pauli, Milwaukee
Publisher: J. J. Stoner, Madison, Wis.
Key/Vignettes/Misc: Refs. 1–88, A–Z; 24 vignettes
Locations: LC–M
Catalogs/Checklists: LC–M, 282

1400
Place: Brookline, Massachusetts
Date: 1864
Title: Environs of Boston, From Corey's Hill, Brookline, Mass.
Size: 20¹⁵⁄₁₆ × 28⅛ in. (53.3 × 71.6 cm.)
Artist: Freeman Richardson
Lithographer:
Printer: J. H. Bufford's Lith. 313 Washington St. Boston
Publisher: Freeman Richardson, 125 Washington St. Boston
Key/Vignettes/Misc:
Locations: BA
Catalogs/Checklists:

1401
Place: Cambridge, Massachusetts
Date: Ca. 1858
Title: Bird's Eye View of Harvard College, and Old Cambridge.
Size: 20⅛ × 25⅝ in. (51.2 × 65.2 cm.)
Artist: Julius Kummer
Lithographer: Julius Kummer
Printer:
Publisher: Prang & Mayer, Lithographers, 34 Merchants Row, Boston.
Key/Vignettes/Misc: 5 vignettes
Locations: BA; BPL–P; EI–S; NYP–S; SSBT–B
Catalogs/Checklists: Stokes P. 1858–60—G–54

1402
Place: Cambridge, Massachusetts
Date: 1877
Title: City of Cambridge, Mass. 1877
Size: 23 × 34 in. (58.5 × 86.5 cm.)
Artist:
Lithographer:
Printer:
Publisher: Franklin View Company, Boston.
Key/Vignettes/Misc: Refs. 1–32; unnumbered business directory
Locations: BPL–R
Catalogs/Checklists:

1403
Place: Campello, Massachusetts
Date: 1880
Title: Bird's Eye View of the Village of Campello in the Town of Brockton,

Plymouth County, Mass. 1880
Size: 11¾ × 24½ in. (29.9 × 62.3 cm.)
Artist:
Lithographer:
Printer: Beck & Pauli, Milwaukee, Wis.
Publisher: J. J. Stoner, Madison, Wis.
Key/Vignettes/Misc: Refs. 1–17, A–E; 4 vignettes
Locations: BPL–R
Catalogs/Checklists:

1404
Place: Canton, Massachusetts
Date: 1878
Title: View of Canton, Mass.
Size: 19 × 25¾ in. (48.4 × 65.6 cm.)
Artist: O. H. Bailey & J. C. Hazen
Lithographer:
Printer:
Publisher: O. H. Bailey & J. C. Hazen, Boston
Key/Vignettes/Misc: Refs. A–H, J–P R;
Locations: BPL–R; AAS–W
Catalogs/Checklists:

1405
Place: Canton, Massachusetts
Date: 1918
Title: View of Canton, Mass. 1918.
Size: 26 × 36 in. (66.2 × 91.6 cm.)
Artist:
Lithographer:
Printer: [Meriden Gravure Co., Meriden, Conn.]
Publisher: Hughes & Bailey, Boston
Key/Vignettes/Misc: 29 vignettes; unnumbered business directory
Locations: LC–M
Catalogs/Checklists: LC–M, 283

1406
Place: Cape Ann, Massachusetts
Date: 1879
Title: Balloon View–Cape Ann to Boston.
Size: 11¼ × 17⅞ in. (28.6 × 45.5 cm.)
Artist: F. K. Rogers
Lithographer:
Printer: J. H. Daniels
Publisher: J. H. Daniels, Boston (copyright)
Key/Vignettes/Misc: 6 vignettes
Locations:
Catalogs/Checklists:

1407
Place: Chapinville, Massachusetts
Date: 1887
Title: Chapinville, Mass.
Size: 11¼ × 15⅞ in. (28.6 × 40.4 cm.)
Artist: Geo. E. Norris
Lithographer:
Printer: The Burleigh Litho Establishment, Troy, N. Y.
Publisher: Geo. E. Norris, Brockton, Mass.
Key/Vignettes/Misc: Refs. A–K
Locations: BPL–R
Catalogs/Checklists:

1408
Place: Charlton, Massachusetts
Date: 1887
Title: Charlton City & Charlton Depot, Mass.

Size: 12¼ × 20 in. (31.1 × 50.9 cm.)
Artist: Geo. E. Norris
Lithographer:
Printer: The Burleigh Litho Establishment, Troy, N. Y.
Publisher: Geo. E. Norris, Brockton, Mass.
Key/Vignettes/Misc: Refs. 1–24, A–G; 2 vignettes
Locations: BPL–R
Catalogs/Checklists:

Place: Charlton Depot, Massachusetts
Date: 1887
See Charlton, Massachusetts, 1887.

1409
Place: Chelsea, Massachusetts
Date: 1848
Title: View of Chelsea Mass. From Eagle Hill East Boston.
Size: 14⅜ × 20⅛ in. (36.6 × 51.2 cm.)
Artist: S. E. Brown
Lithographer:
Printer: Sharp & Pierce, 251 Washington St. Boston
Publisher: Benjn. Rivers, Winnisimmet Street near the Ferry, Chelsea
Key/Vignettes/Misc:
Locations: MM–NN; AAS–W; BA
Catalogs/Checklists: MM–NN, LP 2810

1410
Place: Chester, Massachusetts
Date: 1885
Title: Chester, Mass. 1885.
Size: 14¼ × 23 in. (36.3 × 58.6 cm.)
Artist: L. R. Burleigh
Lithographer:
Printer: Beck & Pauli, Milwaukee, Wis.
Publisher: L. R. Burleigh, Troy, N. Y.
Key/Vignettes/Misc: Refs. 1–18; 1 vignette
Locations: BPL–R
Catalogs/Checklists:

1411
Place: Chicopee, Massachusetts
Date: 1856
Title: Chicopee, Mass. 1856.
Size: 18¾ × 29⅝ in. (47.8 × 75.3 cm.)
Artist: [D. J. Glasgow]
Lithographer:
Printer: [Endicott]
Publisher:
Key/Vignettes/Misc:
Locations: LC–P
Catalogs/Checklists:

1412
Place: Chicopee, Massachusetts
Date: 1878
Title: Chicopee, Mass. 1878.
Size: 18½ × 25¹⁵⁄₁₆ in. (47 × 66 cm.)
Artist:
Lithographer:
Printer: D. Bremmer & Co. Lith. Milwaukee
Publisher: Galt & Hoy, New York
Key/Vignettes/Misc: Refs. 1–18
Locations: LC–M
Catalogs/Checklists: LC–M, 283.1

1413
Place: Chicopee Falls, Massachusetts
Date: 1857
Title: Chicopee Falls Mass. 1857.
Size: 16½ × 25½ in. (41.8 × 64.6 cm.)
Artist: From an ambrotype by A. F. Daniels
Lithographer:
Printer: Endicott & Co., N. Y.
Publisher: John Bachelder
Key/Vignettes/Misc: Refs. 1–6
Locations: AAS–W
Catalogs/Checklists:

1414
Place: Cliftondale, Massachusetts
Date: 1896
Title: Cliftondale, Saugus, East Saugus, Massachusetts. 1896
Size: 22⅜ × 26¼ in. (57 × 66.8 cm.)
Artist:
Lithographer:
Printer: O. H. Bailey & Co., Boston
Publisher: O. H. Bailey & Co., Boston
Key/Vignettes/Misc: Refs., Cliftondale, 1–35, Saugus, A–H, J–M, 38–64, East Saugus, 1–19; 4 vignettes
Locations: BPL–R
Catalogs/Checklists:

1415
Place: Clinton, Massachusetts
Date: 1876
Title: Bird's Eye View of Clinton, Mass. 1876.
Size: 19½ × 26⅞ in. (49.6 × 68.4 cm.)
Artist: O. H. Bailey & Co.
Lithographer: C. H. Vogt
Printer: J. Knauber & Co.
Publisher: O. H. Bailey & Co.
Key/Vignettes/Misc: 20 refs.
Locations: BPL–R; LC–M (photo)
Catalogs/Checklists: LC–M, 283.2

1416
Place: Cochituate, Massachusetts
Date: 1887
Title: Cochituate, Mass., and North Natick 1887.
Size: 15 × 22 in. (38.2 × 56 cm.)
Artist: Geo. E. Norris
Lithographer:
Printer:
Publisher: George E. Norris, Brockton, Mass.
Key/Vignettes/Misc: Refs. A–Q; 2 vignettes
Locations: BPL–R
Catalogs/Checklists:

1417
Place: Concord Junction, Massachusetts
Date: 1893
Title: Concord Junction, Mass. 1893.
Size: 12¼ × 19½ in. (31.2 × 49.6 cm.)
Artist: Geo. E. Norris
Lithographer:
Printer:
Publisher: Geo. E. Norris, Brockton
Key/Vignettes/Misc:
Locations: BPL–R
Catalogs/Checklists:

Place: Coroaville, Massachusetts
Date: 1887
See Southborough, Massachusetts, 1887.

1418
Place: Cottage City, Massachusetts
Date: 1887
Title: Cottage City Martha's Vineyard Mass 1887.
Size: 19¼ × 24½ in. (49 × 62.3 cm.)
Artist: A. F. Poole
Lithographer:
Printer: Geo. H. Walker & Co. Lith. Boston
Publisher:
Key/Vignettes/Misc: Refs. 1–48
Locations: MSL–B; BPL–R
Catalogs/Checklists:

1419
Place: Cottage City, Massachusetts
Date: [188–?]
Title: Plat & Environs of Lagoon Heights, Cottage City, Mass., Showing Property Owned by Lagoon Heights Land Co.
Size: 19¼ × 26 in. (49 × 66.2 cm.)
Artist: O. H. Bailey & Co.
Lithographer:
Printer:
Publisher: O. H. Bailey & Co., Boston
Key/Vignettes/Misc: 16 vignettes; advertisements
Locations: BPL–R
Catalogs/Checklists:

1420
Place: Cottage City, Massachusetts
Date: 1890
Title: Cottage City, Martha's Vineyard, Mass. 1890.
Size: 16½ × 24⅜ n. (42 × 62 cm.)
Artist:
Lithographer:
Printer:
Publisher: Robert A. Welcke, Lith. 178 Williams St. N. Y.
Key/Vignettes/Misc: Refs.
Locations: LC–M; NYH–NY
Catalogs/Checklists:

1421
Place: Dalton, Massachusetts
Date: 1884
Title: Dalton, Mass.
Size: 14½ × 30 in. (36.9 × 76.4 cm.)
Artist: L. R. Burleigh
Lithographer:
Printer: Beck & Pauli Lith., Milwaukee
Publisher: L. R. Burleigh, Troy, N. Y.
Key/Vignettes/Misc: Refs. 1–17; 1 vignette
Locations: LC–M; BPL–R
Catalogs/Checklists: LC–M, 284

Place: Danvers, Massachusetts
Date: 1850
See Salem, Massachusetts, 1850.

1422
Place: Dedham, Massachusetts
Date: 1876
Title: View of Dedham, Mass. in 1876.
Size: 19⅞ × 31¾ in. (50.5 × 80.7 cm.)

Artist: E. Whitefield
Lithographer:
Printer:
Publisher:
Key/Vignettes/Misc:
Locations: AAS–W; BPL; Dedham
Historical Society, Dedham, Massachusetts
Catalogs/Checklists: Norton, Whitefield,
no. 99

1423
Place: Dedham, Massachusetts
Date: [189–?]
Title: Proposed Development of Fairbanks
Park, Dedham, Mass.
Size: 20¾ × 25⅞ in. (52.8 × 65.9 cm.)
Artist:
Lithographer:
Printer:
Publisher: Fairbanks Park Land Co.,
Boston
Key/Vignettes/Misc: 25 vignettes;
advertisements
Locations: BPL–R
Catalogs/Checklists:

1424
Place: Dodgeville, Massachusetts
Date: 1891
Title: Dodgeville, Massachusetts. 1891
Size: 17½ × 24¹³⁄₁₆ in. (44.6 × 63.2 cm.)
Artist:
Lithographer:
Printer: O. H. Bailey & Co. Boston
Publisher: O. H. Bailey & Co. Boston
Key/Vignettes/Misc: Refs. A–H, J; 5
vignettes
Locations: MSL–B
Catalogs/Checklists:

Place: East Boston, Massachusetts
Date: 1879
See Boston, Massachusetts, 1879.

1425
Place: East Bridgewater, Massachusetts
Date: 1887
Title: East Bridgewater, Massachusetts.
1887
Size: 22½ × 25 in. (57.3 × 63.6 cm.)
Artist:
Lithographer:
Printer: O. H. Bailey & Co. Boston
Publisher: O. H. Bailey & Company,
Boston.
Key/Vignettes/Misc: Refs. A, 2–35; 12
vignettes
Locations: BPL–R
Catalogs/Checklists:

1426
Place: East Cambridge, Massachusetts
Date: 1879
Title: View of East Cambridge, Mass.
1879
Size: 19½ × 24¼ in. (49.7 × 61.7 cm.)
Artist: O. H. Bailey & J. C. Hazen
Lithographer:
Printer:
Publisher: O. H. Bailey & J. C. Hazen,
Boston
Key/Vignettes/Misc:

Locations: BPL–R
Catalogs/Checklists:

1427
Place: East Douglas, Massachusetts
Date: 1886
Title: East Douglas, Mass. 1886.
Size: 12¼ × 23½ in. (31.2 × 59.8 cm.)
Artist: L. R. Burleigh
Lithographer: C. H. Vogt
Printer: The Burleigh Lith. Est., Troy, N. Y.
Publisher:
Key/Vignettes/Misc: Refs. 1–16
Locations: BPL–R; LC–M
Catalogs/Checklists: LC–M, 286

1428
Place: East Pepperell, Massachusetts
Date: 1886
Title: East Pepperell, Mass. 1886.
Size: 12¾ × 20½ in. (32.5 × 52.2 cm.)
Artist: L. R. Burleigh
Lithographer:
Printer: C. H. Vogt & Son, Cleveland
Publisher:
Key/Vignettes/Misc: Refs. 1–17
Locations: BPL–R; LC–M
Catalogs/Checklists: LC–M, 287

Place: East Saugus, Massachusetts
Date: 1896
See Cliftondale, Massachusetts, 1896.

1429
Place: East Stoughton, Massachusetts
Date: 1885
Title: East Stoughton, Norfolk County,
Mass. Looking Northwest. 1885
Size: 13⅜ × 18½ in. (34.1 × 47.1 cm.)
Artist: A. F. Poole
Lithographer:
Printer:
Publisher: A. F. Poole, Brockton, Mass.
Key/Vignettes/Misc: Refs. A–H, J–K
Locations: BPL–R
Catalogs/Checklists:

1430
Place: East Walpole, Massachusetts
Date: 1898
Title: East Walpole, Norfolk County,
Mass. 1898.
Size: 15 × 22½ in. (38.2 × 57.3 cm.)
Artist: The Bert Poole Co.
Lithographer:
Printer:
Publisher: The Bert Poole Co., Boston
Key/Vignettes/Misc: Refs. A–K
Locations: LC–M
Catalogs/Checklists: LC–M, 288

1431
Place: East Weymouth, Massachusetts
Date: 1901
Title: East Weymouth, Massachusetts.
1901.
Size: 14⅞ × 20 in. (37.9 × 50.9 cm.)
Artist:
Lithographer:
Printer:
Publisher: O. H. Bailey & Co. Boston
Key/Vignettes/Misc: Refs. A, 2–59; 12
vignettes

Locations: MSL–B
Catalogs/Checklists:

1432
Place: Easthampton, Massachusetts
Date: 1878
Title: Easthampton, Mass. 1878
Size: 21½ × 25⁷⁄₁₆ in. (54.8 × 64.8 cm.)
Artist:
Lithographer:
Printer:
Publisher: Galt & Hoy, 111 Liberty St., N.
Y.
Key/Vignettes/Misc: Refs. 1–21; 9
vignettes
Locations: BPL–R
Catalogs/Checklists:

1433
Place: Edgartown, Massachusetts
Date: 1886
Title: Edgartown Duke's County Martha's
Vineyard Id. Mass.
Size: 13 × 19 in. (33.1 × 48.3 cm.)
Artist:
Lithographer:
Printer: Geo. H. Walker & Co., Boston
Publisher:
Key/Vignettes/Misc: Refs. A–K, M–Z; 1
vignette
Locations: LC–M; BPL–R; Dukes
County Historical Society, Edgartown,
Massachusetts
Catalogs/Checklists: LC–M, 289

1434
Place: Fall River, Massachusetts
Date: 1852
Title: Fall River, Mass., 1852
Size: 27 × 37½ in. (68.7 × 95.4 cm.)
Artist: B. F. Smith, Jr.
Lithographer:
Printer: Sarony & Major, New York
Publisher: Smith & Jenkins, New York
Key/Vignettes/Misc:
Locations: MM–NN; AAS–W; BA;
NYH–NY
Catalogs/Checklists: MM–NN, LP 192

1435
Place: Fall River, Massachusetts
Date: 1870
Title: Fall–River, Mass.
Size: 19¹¹⁄₁₆ × 33¹⁵⁄₁₆ in. (50.1 × 86.4 cm.)
Artist: J. P. Newell
Lithographer: J. P. Newell
Printer: New England Lith. Co., 109
Summer St., Boston
Publisher: J. P. Newell (copyright)
Key/Vignettes/Misc:
Locations: MM–NN; LC–P
Catalogs/Checklists: MM–NN, LP 2578

1436
Place: Fall River, Massachusetts
Date: 1877
Title: City of Fall River, Mass. 1877.
Size: 25½ × 41 in. (64.9 × 104.2 cm.)
Artist: O. H. Bailey & J. C. Hazen
Lithographer: C. H. Vogt
Printer: J. Knauber & Co.
Publisher: O. H. Bailey & J. C. Hazen,
Boston

Key/Vignettes/Misc: Refs. A, 2–61
Locations: AAS–W; BPL–R; LC–M
Catalogs/Checklists: LC–M, 290

1437
Place: Falmouth, Massachusetts
Date: 1887
Title: Wood's Hole, Falmouth, Mass. 1887
Size: 16½ × 24 in. (41.9 × 61.1 cm.)
Artist:
Lithographer:
Printer:
Publisher: Geo. H. Walker & Co. Lith.
Boston
Key/Vignettes/Misc: Refs. A–R
Locations: BPL–R
Catalogs/Checklists:

Place: Fiskdale, Massachusetts
Date: 1892
See Sturbridge, Massachusetts, 1892.

1438
Place: Fitchburg, Massachusetts
Date: 1856
Title: Fitchburg, Mass. 1856. From
Samuel Hale's Residence.
Size: 19¾ × 30⅛ in. (50.3 × 76.7 cm.)
Artist:
Lithographer:
Printer: J. H. Bufford's Lith. 313
Washington St. Boston
Publisher: John Bachelder
Key/Vignettes/Misc: 16 unnumbered refs.
in 2 lines below places identified
Locations: BA; Fitchburg Historical
Society, Fitchburg, Massachusetts
Catalogs/Checklists:

1439
Place: Fitchburg, Massachusetts
Date: Ca. 1871
Title: [Untitled Proof]
Size: 19⅞ × 35½ in. (50.5 × 90.3 cm.)
Artist: E. Whitefield
Lithographer:
Printer:
Publisher:
Key/Vignettes/Misc:
Locations: Private collection
Catalogs/Checklists: Norton, Whitefield,
no. 91

1440
Place: Fitchburg, Massachusetts
Date: 1875
Title: Bird's Eye View of Fitchburg, Mass.
1875.
Size: 20 × 28⅝ in. (50.8 × 72.9 cm.)
Artist: H. H. Bailey & Co.
Lithographer: C. H. Vogt
Printer: J. Knauber & Co.
Publisher: H. H. Bailey and Company,
New York
Key/Vignettes/Misc: Refs. A–H, J–P R;
Locations: BPL–R
Catalogs/Checklists:

1441
Place: Fitchburg, Massachusetts
Date: 1882
Title: Fitchburg, Mass. 1882.
Size: 20³⁄₁₆ × 30⅞ in. (51.4 × 78.6 cm.)
Artist: L. R. Burleigh

Lithographer:
Printer: C. H. Vogt & Son, Cleveland
Publisher: L. R. Burleigh, Troy, N. Y.
Key/Vignettes/Misc: Refs. 1–53
Locations: BPL–R; LC–M
Catalogs/Checklists: LC–M, 291

1442
Place: Fitchburg, Massachusetts
Date: 1915
Title: Aero View of Fitchburg,
Massachusetts 1915
Size: 24 × 35 in. (61.1 × 89 cm.)
Artist: T. M. Fowler
Lithographer:
Printer: [Meriden Gravure Co., Meriden,
Conn.]
Publisher: Hughes & Bailey, 39 Gold St
New York
Key/Vignettes/Misc: 30 vignettes
Locations: LC–M; Fitchburg Historical
Society, Fitchburg, Massachusetts
Catalogs/Checklists: LC–M, 292

1443
Place: Foxboro, Massachusetts
Date: 1879
Title: Foxborough, Mass. 1879
Size: 20 × 25½ in. (50.8 × 64.9 cm.)
Artist: O. H. Bailey & J. C. Hazen
Lithographer:
Printer:
Publisher: O. H. Bailey & J. C. Hazen,
Boston
Key/Vignettes/Misc: 5 vignettes
Locations: AAS–W; BPL–R; LC–M
Catalogs/Checklists: LC–M, 292.1

1444
Place: Foxboro, Massachusetts
Date: 1888
Title: Foxborough, Massachusetts. 1888.
Size: 21½ × 26 in. (54.8 × 66.1 cm.)
Artist:
Lithographer:
Printer:
Publisher: O. H. Bailey & Co. Boston
Key/Vignettes/Misc: Refs. A, 3–46; 16
vignettes
Locations: BPL–R
Catalogs/Checklists:

1445
Place: Framingham, Massachusetts
Date: 1872
Title: View of Framingham Common in
1808.
Size: 15¹¹⁄₁₆ × 22½ in. (39.9 × 57.3 cm.)
Artist: D. Bell
Lithographer:
Printer: New England Lithographic Co.
109 Summer St., Boston
Publisher:
Key/Vignettes/Misc:
Locations: BA
Catalogs/Checklists:

1446
Place: Franklin, Massachusetts
Date: 1879
Title: View of Franklin, Mass. 1879
Size: 20⅜ × 24¼ in. (51.8 × 61.7 cm.)
Artist: O. H. Bailey & J. C. Hazen

Lithographer:
Printer:
Publisher: O.H. Bailey & J. C. Hazen,
Boston
Key/Vignettes/Misc: Refs. A–H, J–P
R–X;
Locations: BPL–R
Catalogs/Checklists:

1447
Place: Franklin, Massachusetts
Date: 1888
Title: Franklin, Massachusetts. 1888
Size: 22⅞ × 32⅝ in. (58.2 × 83 cm.)
Artist:
Lithographer:
Printer:
Publisher: O. H. Bailey & Co. Boston
Key/Vignettes/Misc: Refs. 2, 4, 6–64; 24
vignettes
Locations: BPL–R
Catalogs/Checklists:

1448
Place: Gardner, Massachusetts
Date: 1880
Title: Gardner,Mass. 1880.
Size: 26¾ × 22³⁄₁₆ in. (68.1 × 56.4 cm.)
Artist:
Lithographer:
Printer: Beck & Pauli, Milwaukee, Wis.
Publisher: E. H. Bigelow, Framingham,
Mass.
Key/Vignettes/Misc: Refs. 1–54, A–O
Locations: AAS–W; BPL–R
Catalogs/Checklists:

1449
Place: Gloucester, Massachusetts
Date: Ca. 1835
Title: View of the Town of Gloucester,
Mass.
Size: 14 × 19¹³⁄₁₆ in. (35.7 × 50.4 cm.)
Artist: F. H. Lane
Lithographer: F. H. Lane
Printer: Pendleton's Lithography, Boston
Publisher:
Key/Vignettes/Misc:
Locations: NYP–S; MM–NN; BA;
YUAG–NH
Catalogs/Checklists: Stokes C. 1835—
F–47; MM–NN, LP 3729; Pyne, no.
432; Wilmerding, no. 143

1450
Place: Gloucester, Massachusetts
Date: Ca. 1837
Title: View of Gloucester, Mass.
Size: 21¾ × 35⅝ in. (55.3 × 90.6 cm.)
Artist: F. H. Lane
Lithographer:
Printer: L. A. Bradford & Co.
Publisher:
Key/Vignettes/Misc:
Locations: MM–NN; SSBT–B
Catalogs/Checklists: MM–NN, LP 18;
Wilmerding, No. 147

1451
Place: Gloucester, Massachusetts
Date: Ca. 1845
Title: View of Gloucester, from Rocky
Neck
Size: 18³⁄₁₆ × 24⁵⁄₁₆ in. (46.3 × 61.9 cm.)

Artist: Fitz H. Lane
Lithographer:
Printer: Lane & Scott's Lithography
Publisher: Fitz H. Lane, Tremont Temple, Boston
Key/Vignettes/Misc:
Locations: BA; MM−NN
Catalogs/Checklists: Wilmerding, no. 167

1452
Place: Gloucester, Massachusetts
Date: Ca. 1853
Title: View of Gloucester, Mass. From Ten Pound Island.
Size:
Artist: [Fitz Hugh Lane?]
Lithographer:
Printer: M. M. Tidd, Boston
Publisher:
Key/Vignettes/Misc:
Locations: BA
Catalogs/Checklists: Wilmerding, no. 175

1453
Place: Gloucester, Massachusetts
Date: Ca. 1855
Title: View of Gloucester, Mass.
Size: 23⁵/₁₆ × 35¹³/₁₆ in. (59.4 × 91.1 cm.)
Artist: F. H. Lane
Lithographer:
Printer: L. H. Bradford & Co's Lith. [Boston]
Publisher: Procter Brothers, 123 Front St. [Gloucester]
Key/Vignettes/Misc:
Locations: BA; MM−NN; SSBT−B
Catalogs/Checklists: Wilmerding, no. 178; MM−NN, LP 18

1454
Place: Gloucester, Massachusetts
Date: [1873?]
Title: City of Gloucester, Mass.
Size: 23¼ × 29⅝ in. (59.2 × 75.4 cm.)
Artist:
Lithographer:
Printer: Franklin Lith. 25 Congress St. Boston
Publisher:
Key/Vignettes/Misc: Unnumbered business directory
Locations: BPL−R
Catalogs/Checklists:

1455
Place: Gloucester, Massachusetts
Date: 1876
Title: View of Gloucester. From Rocky Neck. 1876.
Size: 22¹¹/₁₆ × 34⅞ in. (57.7 × 88.8 cm.)
Artist: F. R. Rogers
Lithographer:
Printer:
Publisher: Geo. Douglas
Key/Vignettes/Misc: 9 unnumbered refs. in 2 lines; 1 vignette; description
Locations: BA; MM−NN; YUAG−NH
Catalogs/Checklists: MM−NN, LP 4268

1456
Place: Gloucester, Massachusetts
Date: 1887
Title: Magnolia, Gloucester, Mass. 1887

Size: 12¼ × 19 in. (31.2 × 48.4 cm.)
Artist:
Lithographer:
Printer: Geo. H. Walker & Co., Boston
Publisher: Geo. H. Walker & Co., Boston
Key/Vignettes/Misc:
Locations: BPL−R
Catalogs/Checklists:

1457
Place: Grafton, Massachusetts
Date: 1887
Title: View of Grafton, Massachusetts.
Size: 23⅜ × 32½ in. (59.5 × 82.7 cm.)
Artist:
Lithographer:
Printer: O. H. Bailey & Co., Boston
Publisher: O. H. Bailey & Co., Boston
Key/Vignettes/Misc: Refs. A−M, O−Y; 17 vignettes
Locations: BPL−R
Catalogs/Checklists:

1458
Place: Graniteville, Massachusetts
Date: 1886
Title: Graniteville, Mass. 1886.
Size: 12⅛ × 21¾ in. (30.8 × 55.3 cm.)
Artist: [Christian] Fausel
Lithographer:
Printer: The Burleigh Lith. Est. Troy, N. Y.
Publisher: L. R. Burleigh, Troy, N. Y.
Key/Vignettes/Misc: Refs. 1−6
Locations: BPL−R; LC−M
Catalogs/Checklists: LC−M, 293

1459
Place: Great Barrington, Massachusetts
Date: 1884
Title: Great Barrington, Mass.
Size: 16½ × 30 in. (41.9 × 76.3 cm.)
Artist: L. R. Burleigh
Lithographer:
Printer: Beck & Pauli, Milwaukee
Publisher: L. R. Burleigh, Troy, N. Y.
Key/Vignettes/Misc: Refs. 1−23; 1 vignette
Locations: BPL−R; LC−M
Catalogs/Checklists: LC−M, 294

1460
Place: Greenfield, Massachusetts
Date: 1877
Title: View of Greenfield, Mass. 1877.
Size: 19⅞ × 24¼ in. (50.6 × 61.7 cm.)
Artist: O. H. Bailey & Co.
Lithographer:
Printer:
Publisher: O. H. Bailey & Co., Boston
Key/Vignettes/Misc: Refs. 1−24; 3 vignettes
Locations: BPL−R; LC−M
Catalogs/Checklists: LC−M, 294.1

Place: Greenville, Massachusetts
Date: 1887
See Rochdale, Massachusetts, 1887.

1461
Place: Groton, Massachusetts
Date: 1886
Title: Groton, Mass. 1886.
Size: 14 × 23⅞ in. (35.6 × 60.8 cm.)
Artist:

Lithographer:
Printer: The Burleigh Lith. Est. Troy, N. Y.
Publisher: L. R. Burleigh, Troy, N. Y.
Key/Vignettes/Misc: Refs. 1−8
Locations: AAS−W; LC−M
Catalogs/Checklists: LC−M, 295

1462
Place: Haverhill, Massachusetts
Date: 1850
Title: View of Haverhill, Mass. From Silver Hill, Nov. 1850
Size: 17⁹/₁₆ × 25⅝ in. (44.8 × 65.2 cm.)
Artist: Gustavus Pfau
Lithographer:
Printer: Tappan & Bradford's Lith., [Boston]
Publisher:
Key/Vignettes/Misc:
Locations: NYP−S; EI−S; BA
Catalogs/Checklists: Stokes 1850—G−4

Place: Haverhill, Massachusetts
Date: 1857
See Bradford, Massachusetts, 1857.

1463
Place: Haverhill, Massachusetts
Date: 1857
Title: Haverhill, Mass. From Bradford.
Size: 12½ × 15¾ in. (31.8 × 40.1 cm.)
Artist: J. B. Bachelder
Lithographer:
Printer: Endicott & Co., N. Y.
Publisher: Jno. B. Bachelder 59 Beekman St New York
Key/Vignettes/Misc: Refs. 1−5
Locations: AAS−W; BPL−P; EI−S; MAHS−B; PAC−P; YUAG−NH; BA
Catalogs/Checklists:

1464
Place: Haverhill, Massachusetts
Date: 1876
Title: Haverhill, Mass. 1876.
Size: 22 × 31¾ in. (55.9 × 80.8 cm.)
Artist: H. H. Bailey & J. C. Hazen
Lithographer: C. H. Vogt
Printer: J. Knauber & Co.
Publisher: H. H. Bailey & J. C. Hazen
Key/Vignettes/Misc: Refs. A−P, R−X
Locations: BPL−R
Catalogs/Checklists:

1465
Place: Haverhill, Massachusetts
Date: 1893
Title: Haverhill, Massachusetts. 1893
Size: 24⅜ × 34¾ in. (62.1 × 88.4 cm.)
Artist:
Lithographer:
Printer: O. H. Bailey & Co. Boston
Publisher: O. H. Bailey & Co. Boston
Key/Vignettes/Misc: Refs. A−B, 2−26; 67 vignettes
Locations: MSL−B; EI−S; LC−M; NYH−NY
Catalogs/Checklists: LC−M, 296

1466
Place: Haverhill, Massachusetts
Date: 1914
Title: Aero View of Haverhill, Massachusetts 1914.

Size: 28 × 31 in. (71.2 × 78.9 cm.)
Artist: Fowler & Downs
Lithographer:
Printer: [Franklin Engraving Co. & Federal Eng. Co. Boston]
Publisher: Hughes & Bailey
Key/Vignettes/Misc: 32 vignettes; unnumbered business directory
Locations: LC–M
Catalogs/Checklists: LC–M, 297

1467
Place: Haydenville, Massachusetts
Date: 1886
Title: Haydenville, Mass. 1886.
Size: 12 × 20⅛ in. (30.5 × 51.2 cm.)
Artist:
Lithographer:
Printer: Northern Lith. Co., Troy, N. Y.
Publisher: L. R. Burleigh
Key/Vignettes/Misc: Refs. 1–10
Locations: BPL–R; LC–M
Catalogs/Checklists: LC–M, 298

1468
Place: Hebronville, Massachusetts
Date: 1891
Title: Hebronville, Massachusetts. 1891
Size: 17¹³⁄₁₆ × 23⅞ in. (45.4 × 60.8 cm.)
Artist:
Lithographer:
Printer: O. H. Bailey & Co. Boston
Publisher: O. H. Bailey & Co. Boston
Key/Vignettes/Misc: Refs. A–F; 6 vignettes
Locations: MSL–B
Catalogs/Checklists:

1469
Place: Highlandville, Massachusetts
Date: 1887
Title: Highlandville, Massachusetts. 1887.
Size: 20¾ × 25 in. (52.8 × 63.6 cm.)
Artist:
Lithographer:
Printer: O. H. Bailey & Co., Boston
Publisher: O. H. Bailey & Co., Boston
Key/Vignettes/Misc: Refs. A–H, J–K, M–O; 12 vignettes
Locations: BPL–R; LC–M
Catalogs/Checklists: LC–M, 298.1

1470
Place: Hingham, Massachusetts
Date: 1885
Title: Town of Hingham, Plymouth County, Mass. 1885.
Size: 24½ × 32⅛ in. (62.4 × 81.7 cm.)
Artist: A. F. Poole
Lithographer: C. E. Jorgenson
Printer: Geo. H. Walker & Co. Lith. Boston
Publisher: A. F. Poole, Brockton, Mass.
Key/Vignettes/Misc: Refs. A–I, K–Z, 1–26, 28, 30–67; 1 vignette
Locations: BPL–R; LC–M; BA
Catalogs/Checklists: LC–M, 299

1471
Place: Hinsdale, Massachusetts
Date: [1887?]
Title: Hinsdale, Mass.
Size: 11⅝ × 21¼ in. (29.6 × 54.1 cm.)

Artist: L. R. Burleigh
Lithographer: C. H. Vogt
Printer: Burleigh Lith. Est. Troy, N. Y.
Publisher: L. R. Burleigh, Troy, N. Y.
Key/Vignettes/Misc: Refs. 1–8
Locations: LC–M; BPL–R
Catalogs/Checklists: LC–M, 300

1472
Place: Holbrook, Massachusetts
Date: 1882
Title: Bird's Eye View of the Town of Holbrook. Norfolk County, Mass. Looking East. 1882.
Size: 12 × 24¾ in. (30.5 × 63 cm.)
Artist:
Lithographer:
Printer: Beck & Pauli, Milwaukee, Wis.
Publisher: J. J. Stoner, Madison, Wis.
Key/Vignettes/Misc: Refs. 1–24; 2 vignettes
Locations: BPL–R
Catalogs/Checklists:

1473
Place: Holden, Massachusetts
Date: 1892
Title: Holden, Massachusetts. 1892.
Size: 20⅜ × 26⅛ in. (51.9 × 66.5 cm.)
Artist:
Lithographer:
Printer: O. H. Bailey & Co. Boston
Publisher: O. H. Bailey & Co. Boston
Key/Vignettes/Misc: Refs. 1–26; 26 vignettes
Locations: MSL–B; AAS–W
Catalogs/Checklists:

1474
Place: Holliston, Massachusetts
Date: 1878
Title: View of Holliston, Mass. 1878
Size: 21¼ × 27 in. (54.1 × 68.7 cm.)
Artist: I. J.
Lithographer:
Printer:
Publisher: D. Bremner Co. Milwaukee, Wis.
Key/Vignettes/Misc: Refs. 1–29
Locations: AAS–W; BPL–R
Catalogs/Checklists:

1475
Place: Holliston, Massachusetts
Date: 1898
Title: Holliston, Massachusetts. 1898
Size: 17⅝ × 26½ in. (44.9 × 67.4 cm.)
Artist:
Lithographer:
Printer: O. H. Bailey & Co. Boston
Publisher: O. H. Bailey & Co. Boston
Key/Vignettes/Misc: 26 vignettes
Locations: MSL–B
Catalogs/Checklists:

Place: Holmes' Hole, Massachusetts
Date: 1856
See Tisbury, Massachusetts, 1856.

1476
Place: Holyoke, Massachusetts
Date: 1856
Title: Holyoke and South Hadley Falls, Mass., Southeast View.

Size: 12½ × 15⅝ in. (31.8 × 39.8 cm.)
Artist: J. B. Bachelder
Lithographer:
Printer: Endicott & Co., New York
Publisher: Jno. B. Bachelder, 59 Beekman St. New York
Key/Vignettes/Misc: Refs. 1–14; 1 vignette
Locations: AAS–W; BPL–P; MAHS–B; PAC–P; BA; NYH–NY
Catalogs/Checklists:

1477
Place: Holyoke, Massachusetts
Date: 1877
Title: Bird's Eye View of Holyoke, Mass. 1877.
Size: 26½ × 34½ in. (67.4 × 87.8 cm.)
Artist: H. H. Bailey & J. C. Hazen
Lithographer: C. H. Vogt
Printer: J. Knauber & Co.
Publisher: H. H. Bailey & J. C. Hazen, N. Y.
Key/Vignettes/Misc: Refs. 1–46
Locations: AAS–W; BPL–R
Catalogs/Checklists:

1478
Place: Holyoke, Massachusetts
Date: 1881
Title: Bird's Eye View of the City of Holyoke, and Village of South Hadley Falls Mass. Looking North. 1881
Size: 25⁹⁄₁₆ × 37⅛ in. (65.1 × 94.5 cm.)
Artist: A. F. Poole
Lithographer:
Printer: Beck & Pauli, Lith., Milwaukee, Wis.
Publisher: J. J. Stoner, Madison, Wis.
Key/Vignettes/Misc: Refs. 1–61, A–Z, A–J; 29 vignettes
Locations: LC–M; CHS–C; BA
Catalogs/Checklists: LC–M, 301

1479
Place: Hopedale, Massachusetts
Date: 1888
Title: View of Hopedale, Massachusetts. 1888.
Size: 20 × 25¹⁄₁₆ in. (50.8 × 63.8 cm.)
Artist:
Lithographer:
Printer: O. H. Bailey & Co., Boston
Publisher: O. H. Bailey & Co., Boston
Key/Vignettes/Misc: Refs. 1–17; 8 vignettes
Locations: BPL–R
Catalogs/Checklists:

1480
Place: Hopedale, Massachusetts
Date: 1899
Title: Hopedale, Mass. 1899 Works of the Draper Company
Size: 16 × 22½ in. (40.7 × 57.3 cm.)
Artist: The Bert Poole Co.
Lithographer:
Printer:
Publisher: The Bert Poole Co., Boston
Key/Vignettes/Misc:
Locations: LC–M
Catalogs/Checklists: LC–M, 302

1481
Place: Hopkinton, Massachusetts
Date: 1880
Title: Hopkinton, Mass. 1880.
Size: 19⅜ × 25½ in. (49.3 × 64.9 cm.)
Artist:
Lithographer:
Printer:
Publisher: O. H. Bailey & J. C. Hazen, Boston
Key/Vignettes/Misc: Refs. A–H, J–K; 5 vignettes
Locations: AAS–W; BPL–R
Catalogs/Checklists:

1482
Place: Housatonic, Massachusetts
Date: 1890
Title: Housatonic, Mass.
Size: 17 × 23 in. (43.2 × 58.5 cm.)
Artist: L. R. Burleigh
Lithographer:
Printer:
Publisher: L. R. Burleigh, Troy, N. Y.
Key/Vignettes/Misc: Refs. 1–19; 1 vignette
Locations: LC–M
Catalogs/Checklists: LC–M, 303

1483
Place: Hudson, Massachusetts
Date: 1878
Title: Bird's Eye View of Hudson, Mass. 1878.
Size: 18¾ × 24¼ in. (47.8 × 61.7 cm.)
Artist: O. H. Bailey & J. C. Hazen
Lithographer:
Printer:
Publisher: O. H. Bailey and J. C. Hazen, Boston
Key/Vignettes/Misc: Refs. A–P R;
Locations: BPL–R; NYH–NY
Catalogs/Checklists:

1484
Place: Huntington, Massachusetts
Date: 1886
Title: Huntington, Mass. 1886.
Size: 13 × 21 in. (33.1 × 53.4 cm.)
Artist: L. R. Burleigh
Lithographer:
Printer: The Burleigh Lith. Establishment, Troy, N. Y.
Publisher:
Key/Vignettes/Misc: Refs. 1–7
Locations: BPL–R; LC–M
Catalogs/Checklists: LC–M, 304

1485
Place: Hyannis, Massachusetts
Date: 1884
Title: Bird's Eye View of the Village of Hyannis, Barnstable County, Mass. 1884.
Size: 12¼ × 20¼ in. (31.2 × 51.6 cm.)
Artist: A. F. Poole
Lithographer:
Printer: Geo. H. Walker & Co. Lith, Boston
Publisher: A. F. Poole, Brockton, Mass.
Key/Vignettes/Misc: Refs. A–X
Locations: BPL–R
Catalogs/Checklists:

1486
Place: Hyde Park, Massachusetts
Date: 1879
Title: View of Hyde Park, Mass. 1879.
Size: 18⅜ × 25⅝ in. (46.8 × 65.2 cm.)
Artist: O. H. Bailey & J. C. Hazen
Lithographer:
Printer:
Publisher: O. H. Bailey & J. C. Hazen, Boston
Key/Vignettes/Misc: Refs. A–H, J–P, R–T
Locations: AAS–W; BPL–R
Catalogs/Checklists:

1487
Place: Hyde Park, Massachusetts
Date: 1890
Title: Hyde Park, Massachusetts. 1890
Size: 20⅝ × 27 in. (52.5 × 68.7 cm.)
Artist:
Lithographer:
Printer: O. H. Bailey & Co., Boston
Publisher: O. H. Bailey & Co., Boston
Key/Vignettes/Misc: Refs. 1–53; 18 vignettes
Locations: BPL–R
Catalogs/Checklists:

1488
Place: Ipswich, Massachusetts
Date: 1893
Title: Ipswich, Mass. Incorporated 1634
Size: 15¼ × 23⅝ in. (38.8 × 60.2 cm.)
Artist: Geo. E. Norris
Lithographer:
Printer:
Publisher:
Key/Vignettes/Misc: Refs. 1–37
Locations: BPL–R
Catalogs/Checklists:

1489
Place: Jamaica Plain, Massachusetts
Date: [1891?] State I
Title: Jamaica Plain, Massachusetts. Ward 23 City of Boston
Size: 21¹⁵⁄₁₆ × 28⅛ in. (55.8 × 71.6 cm.)
Artist:
Lithographer:
Printer:
Publisher: [O. H. Bailey & Co. Boston]
Key/Vignettes/Misc: Refs. A, 2–31; 33 vignettes
Locations: MSL–B
Catalogs/Checklists:

1490
Place: Jamaica Plain, Massachusetts
Date: 1891 State II
Title: Jamaica Plain, Massachusetts. Ward 23, City of Boston. 1891.
Size: 21⅞ × 28⅛ in. (55.7 × 71.6 cm.)
Artist:
Lithographer:
Printer: O. H. Bailey & Co., Boston
Publisher: O. H. Bailey & Co., Boston
Key/Vignettes/Misc: Refs. A, 2–31; 33 vignettes
Locations: BPL–R
Catalogs/Checklists:

1491
Place: Kingston, Massachusetts
Date: 1885
Title: Village of Kingston Plymouth County Mass. 1885.
Size: 12 × 17⅝ in. (30.5 × 44.8 cm.)
Artist:
Lithographer:
Printer:
Publisher: A. F. Poole & Co., Brockton, Mass.
Key/Vignettes/Misc: Refs. A–Y; 1 vignette
Locations: BPL–R
Catalogs/Checklists:

1492
Place: Kingston, Massachusetts
Date: 1896
Title: Kingston. Massachusetts. 1896
Size: 16¾ × 26⅝ in. (42.7 × 67.8 cm.)
Artist:
Lithographer:
Printer:
Publisher:
Key/Vignettes/Misc: Refs. A, 1–47; 15 vignettes
Locations: MSL–B
Catalogs/Checklists:

1493
Place: Lawrence, Massachusetts
Date: 1848
Title: View of the Town of Lawrence (From the East) April, 1848
Size: 11 × 16¼ in. (28 × 41.5 cm.)
Artist: A. Conant
Lithographer:
Printer: J. W. A. Scott 16 Tremont Temple [Boston]
Publisher:
Key/Vignettes/Misc:
Locations: EI–S; NYH–NY
Catalogs/Checklists:

1494
Place: Lawrence, Massachusetts
Date: [1854?]
Title: View of the City of Lawrence, Mass. Dedicated to Samuel Lawrence Esquire.
Size: 24¼ × 34¹⁵⁄₁₆ in. (61.7 × 88.9 cm.)
Artist: Ed. Hoffman
Lithographer:
Printer: S. W. Chandler & Bro. Lith. Boston
Publisher: A. J. Wondra
Key/Vignettes/Misc: 14 unnumbered refs. of industries; 14 unnumbered refs. to churches; description
Locations: BA; SSBT–B
Catalogs/Checklists: MVTM, Lawrence, 11

1495
Place: Lawrence, Massachusetts
Date: 1856
Title: Lawrence, Mass. From the residence of Wm. C. Chapin, Esq.
Size: 12½ × 15¹⁵⁄₁₆ in. (31.8 × 40.5 cm.)
Artist: J. B. Bachelder
Lithographer:
Printer: Endicott & Co., New York, 1856

Publisher: Jno. B. Bachelder 59 Beekman St. New York
Key/Vignettes/Misc: Refs. 1–12
Locations: MVTM–NA; EI–S; AAS–W; CHS–C; BPL–P; MAHS–B; YUAG–NH; BA; NYH–NY
Catalogs/Checklists: MVTM, Lawrence, 14

1496
Place: Lawrence, Massachusetts
Date: 1876
Title: Lawrence, Mass. 1876.
Size: 22¼ × 30¹¹⁄₁₆ in. (56.7 × 78 cm.)
Artist: H. H. Bailey & J. C. Hazen
Lithographer: C. H. Vogt
Printer: J. Knauber & Co., Milwaukee
Publisher: H. H. Bailey & J. C. Hazen
Key/Vignettes/Misc: Refs. 1–39
Locations: MVTM–NA; BPL–R; LC–M (facsimile)
Catalogs/Checklists: MVTM, Lawrence, 26; LC–M, 304.1

1497
Place: Lee, Massachusetts
Date: 1878
Title: Lee Mass. 1878.
Size: 22¼ × 25¹⁵⁄₁₆ in. (56.7 × 66 cm.)
Artist: H. H. Rowley & Co.
Lithographer:
Printer: Beck & Pauli Lith. Milwaukee, Wis.
Publisher: H. H. Rowley & Co. Hartford, Conn.
Key/Vignettes/Misc: Refs. 1–36; 6 vignettes
Locations: MSL–B
Catalogs/Checklists:

1498
Place: Leicester, Massachusetts
Date: 1891
Title: Leicester, Massachusetts. 1891
Size: 21 × 25⅞ in. (53.4 × 65.9 cm.)
Artist:
Lithographer:
Printer: O. H. Bailey & Co. Boston
Publisher: O. H. Bailey & Co. Boston
Key/Vignettes/Misc: Refs. A, 2–24; refs. for Cherry Valley, A, 2–13; 25 vignettes
Locations: MSL–B
Catalogs/Checklists:

1499
Place: Leominster, Massachusetts
Date: 1876
Title: View of Leominster, Mass. 1876
Size: 20³⁄₁₆ × 25¹⁄₁₆ in. (51.4 × 66.3 cm.)
Artist: O. H. Bailey & Co.
Lithographer: C. H. Vogt
Printer: J. Knauber & Co.
Publisher: O. H. Bailey & Co. [Boston]
Key/Vignettes/Misc: Refs. 1–28
Locations: MSL–B; AAS–W; BA
Catalogs/Checklists:

1500
Place: Leominster, Massachusetts
Date: 1886
Title: Leominster, Mass. 1886.
Size: 15¾ × 29⅛ in. (40.1 × 74.1 cm.)

Artist: L. R. Burleigh
Lithographer:
Printer: Burleigh Lith. Est. Troy, N. Y.
Publisher: L. R. Burleigh, Troy, N. Y.
Key/Vignettes/Misc: Refs. 1–53; 2 vignettes
Locations: BPL–R; LC–M
Catalogs/Checklists: LC–M, 305

Place: Linden, Massachusetts
Date: 1897
See Maplewood, Massachusetts, 1897.

1501
Place: Lowell, Massachusetts
Date: 1830
Title: View of the Town of Lowell, Mass. Taken from Mr. Z. Rogers House, near Fort Hill, Tewksbury.
Size: 13 × 21½ in. (33.1 × 54.7 cm.)
Artist: James Kidder
Lithographer:
Printer: Senefelder Lithographic Co., Boston, 1830
Publisher:
Key/Vignettes/Misc:
Locations: LHS–L
Catalogs/Checklists: LHS–L, Views of Lowell

1502
Place: Lowell, Massachusetts
Date: 1834
Title: View of Lowell, Mass. Taken from the House of Elisha Fuller Esq: in Dracutt, by E. A. Farrar.
Size: 15¹¹⁄₁₆ × 23⅞ in. (39.9 × 60.8 cm.)
Artist: E. A. Farrar
Lithographer:
Printer: Pendleton's Lithography, Boston
Publisher: Jacob Farrar (copyright)
Key/Vignettes/Misc:
Locations: NYP–S; Lowell, Massachusetts, Public Library; BA
Catalogs/Checklists: Stokes P. 1833—F–21; LHS–L, Views of Lowell; Pyne, no. 442

1503
Place: Lowell, Massachusetts
Date: 1834
Title: View of Lowell, Mass., 1834
Size: 16 × 24 in. (40.7 × 61 cm.)
Artist:
Lithographer:
Printer:
Publisher:
Key/Vignettes/Misc:
Locations: Worcester Art Museum, Worcester, Massachusetts
Catalogs/Checklists:

1504
Place: Lowell, Massachusetts
Date: Ca. 1840
Title: View of Lowell, Mass.
Size: 9 × 15¾ in. (22.9 × 40.1 cm.)
Artist: F. H. Lane
Lithographer:
Printer: T. Moore, [Boston]
Publisher: E. A. Rice & Co., Lowell
Key/Vignettes/Misc:

Locations: LHS–L; AAS–W
Catalogs/Checklists: LHS–L, Views of Lowell

1505
Place: Lowell, Massachusetts
Date: 1856
Title: Lowell, Mass. Sketched from the Residence of Thomas L. Tuxbury Esq. (Dracut Heights).
Size: 23⅜ × 36⁵⁄₁₆ in. (59.5 × 92.4 cm.)
Artist: J. B. Bachelder
Lithographer:
Printer: Endicott & Co., N. Y.
Publisher: J. B. Bachelder, 59 Beekman St. N. Y.
Key/Vignettes/Misc: 1 vignette; dedication
Locations: LSH–L; BA; NYH–NY
Catalogs/Checklists: LHS–L, Views of Lowell

1506
Place: Lowell, Massachusetts
Date: 1876
Title: Bird's Eye View of Lowell Mass.
Size: 25 × 34½ in. (66.2 × 87.7 cm.)
Artist: H. H. Bailey & J. C. Hazen
Lithographer: C. H. Vogt
Printer: J. Knauber & Co.
Publisher: H. H. Bailey & J. C. Hazen
Key/Vignettes/Misc: Refs. 1–60
Locations: MVTM–NA; BPL–R; LC–M (photo)
Catalogs/Checklists: LC–M, 305.1

Place: Lynn, Massachusetts
Date: 1850
See Salem, Massachusetts, 1850.

1507
Place: Lynn, Massachusetts
Date: 1856
Title: East View from near High Rock. Lynn, Mass.
Size: 12¾ × 15¹⁵⁄₁₆ in. (32.5 × 40.5 cm.)
Artist: J. B. Bachelder from daguerreotype by C. Hill
Lithographer:
Printer: Endicott & Co.
Publisher: J. B. Bachelder, 59 Beekman St., N. Y.
Key/Vignettes/Misc: Refs. 1–8; 1 vignette
Locations: AAS–W; BPL–P; MAHS–B; BA; NYH–NY
Catalogs/Checklists:

1508
Place: Lynn, Massachusetts
Date: 1856
Title: Lynn Mass. West View from Near High Rock
Size: 12⅝ × 15⅝ in. (32.1 × 39.8 cm.)
Artist: J. B. Bachelder, from daguerreotype by C. G. Hill
Lithographer:
Printer: Endicott & Co., New York
Publisher: Jno. B. Bachelder, 59 Beekman St., New York
Key/Vignettes/Misc: Refs. 1–8; 1 vignette
Locations: EI–S; AAS–W; BPL–P; MAHS–B; PAC–P; BA; NYH–NY
Catalogs/Checklists:

1509
Place: Lynn, Massachusetts
Date: Ca. 1871
Title: View of Lynn, Mass. in 1849. From High Rock
Size: 9¹³⁄₁₆ × 28⁹⁄₁₆ in. (25 × 72.7 cm.)
Artist: John L. Robinson
Lithographer:
Printer: J. H. Bufford's Lith, 490 Washington St. Boston
Publisher:
Key/Vignettes/Misc: Refs. 1–33, A–K; 5 cols. of data
Locations: EI–S; LYHS–L
Catalogs/Checklists:

1510
Place: Lynn, Massachusetts
Date: 1874
Title: Market Street, Lynn Mass. As it Appeared in 1820
Size: 6 × 16 in. (15.3 × 40.7 cm.)
Artist: Wm. T. Oliver
Lithographer:
Printer:
Publisher: Wm. T. Oliver
Key/Vignettes/Misc:
Locations: LC–M
Catalogs/Checklists: LC–M, 306

1511
Place: Lynn, Massachusetts
Date: 1879
Title: Manufacturing Center of Lynn, Mass. 1879
Size: 20½ × 25¾ in. (52.1 × 65.5 cm.)
Artist: O. H. Bailey & J. C. Hazen
Lithographer:
Printer:
Publisher: O. H. Bailey & J. C. Hazen, Boston
Key/Vignettes/Misc: Refs. A, 2–31, 35–48; 4 vignettes
Locations: EI–S; AAS–W; BA; LYHS–L (no vignettes); BPL–R (no vignettes)
Catalogs/Checklists:

1512
Place: Lynn, Massachusetts
Date: 1881
Title: Home of the Hutchinson Family, High Rock, Lynn, Mass. U. S. A.
Size: 27 × 39 in. (68.7 × 99.3 cm.)
Artist:
Lithographer:
Printer: Armstrong & Co., Lith. Boston
Publisher: C. A. Shaw & H. J. Hutchinson
Key/Vignettes/Misc: 2 vignettes
Locations: LC–M
Catalogs/Checklists: LC–M, 307

1513
Place: Lynn, Massachusetts
Date: 1904
Title: Lynn Woods, Lynn, Massachusetts
Size: 18⅛ × 25⅝ in. (46.1 × 65.2 cm.)
Artist: O. H. Bailey & J. C. Hazen
Lithographer:
Printer:
Publisher: Geo. H.Walker & Co., Boston (copyright)
Key/Vignettes/Misc: Description

Locations: BPL–R
Catalogs/Checklists:

1514
Place: Lynn, Massachusetts
Date: 1916
Title: Aero View of Lynn, Mass. 1916 Looking North
Size: 22⅜ × 34¾ in. (57 × 88.4 cm.)
Artist: Fowler and Downs
Lithographer:
Printer:
Publisher: Hughes and Bailey, Boston
Key/Vignettes/Misc: 46 vignettes; alphabetical business directory
Locations: LYHS–L
Catalogs/Checklists:

1515
Place: Malden, Massachusetts
Date: 1881
Title: City of Malden. 1881
Size: 20½ × 25¾ in. (52.2 × 65.6 cm.)
Artist: A. E. D.
Lithographer:
Printer:
Publisher: O. H. Bailey & Co., Boston
Key/Vignettes/Misc: Refs. 1–28
Locations: BPL–R
Catalogs/Checklists:

1516
Place: Manchaug, Massachusetts
Date: 1891
Title: Manchaug, Massachusetts. 1891.
Size: 18 × 25⅛ in. (45.8 × 63.9 cm.)
Artist:
Lithographer:
Printer: O. H. Bailey & Co. Boston
Publisher: O. H. Bailey & Co. Boston
Key/Vignettes/Misc: Refs. A–H, K–P; 13 vignettes
Locations: MSL–B; LC–M (photo)
Catalogs/Checklists: LC–M, 307.1

1517
Place: Mansfield, Massachusetts
Date: 1879
Title: View of Mansfield, Mass. 1879
Size: 18⅝ × 23¾ in. (47.5 × 60.4 cm.)
Artist: O. H. Bailey & J. C. Hazen
Lithographer:
Printer:
Publisher: O. H. Bailey & J. C. Hazen, Boston
Key/Vignettes/Misc: Refs. A–H, J–P
Locations: BPL–R
Catalogs/Checklists:

1518
Place: Mansfield, Massachusetts
Date: 1888
Title: Mansfield, Massachusetts. 1888
Size: 22⅜ × 31¼ in. (56.9 × 79.5 cm.)
Artist:
Lithographer:
Printer:
Publisher: O. H. Bailey & Co., Boston
Key/Vignettes/Misc: Refs. A, 2–53; 18 vignettes
Locations: BPL–R
Catalogs/Checklists:

1519
Place: Maplewood, Massachusetts
Date: 1897
Title: Maplewood and Linden, Massachusetts. 1897.
Size: 19 × 26½ in. (48.3 × 67.5 cm.)
Artist:
Lithographer:
Printer: O. H. Bailey & Co., Boston
Publisher: O. H. Bailey & Co., Boston
Key/Vignettes/Misc: 26 vignettes
Locations: BPL–R
Catalogs/Checklists:

Place: Marblehead, Massachusetts
Date: [1843–44]
See Salem, Massachusetts, [1843–44].

1520
Place: Marblehead, Massachusetts
Date: 1856
Title: Marblehead, Mass.
Size: 12¾ × 15⅝ in. (32.5 × 39.8 cm.)
Artist: J. B. Bachelder
Lithographer:
Printer: Endicott & Co., N. Y.
Publisher: Jno. B. Bachelder, 59 Beekman St. New York
Key/Vignettes/Misc:
Locations: MM–NN; EI–S; AAS–W; BPL–P; MAHS–B; BA; NYH–NY
Catalogs/Checklists: MM–NN, LP 991

1521
Place: Marblehead, Massachusetts
Date: 1882
Title: Marblehead, Massachusetts. 1882.
Size: 16¼ × 25¼ in. (41.4 × 64.3 cm.)
Artist: O. H. Bailey & Co.
Lithographer:
Printer: O. H. Bailey & Co., Boston
Publisher: M. H. Graves
Key/Vignettes/Misc: Refs. 1–48; 4 vignettes
Locations: BPL–R
Catalogs/Checklists:

1522
Place: Marblehead, Massachusetts
Date: 1886
Title: The Farms 1886
Size: 16⅛ × 30⁵⁄₁₆ in. (41 × 77.2 cm.)
Artist:
Lithographer:
Printer:
Publisher: O. W. Walker, Boston
Key/Vignettes/Misc:
Locations: MSL–B; LC–M
Catalogs/Checklists:

1523
Place: Marblehead, Massachusetts
Date: 1909
Title: Marblehead
Size: ["folio"]
Artist: A. E. Downs
Lithographer:
Printer:
Publisher: Merrill H. Graves, Marblehead
Key/Vignettes/Misc:
Locations: Unknown. see Goodspeed's Catalogue No. 224, item 535
Catalogs/Checklists:

1524
Place: Marblehead Shore, Massachusetts
Date: 1886
Title:
Size: 17½ × 30 in. (44.5 × 76.3 cm.)
Artist:
Lithographer:
Printer:
Publisher: O. W. Walker, Boston
Key/Vignettes/Misc:
Locations: LC−M
Catalogs/Checklists: LC−M, 308

1525
Place: Marlborough, Massachusetts
Date: 1878
Title: View of Marlborough, Mass. 1878
Size: 20½ × 26⅝ in. (52.2 × 67.8 cm.)
Artist: O. H. Bailey & J. C. Hazen
Lithographer: J. Knauber & Co.
Printer: J. Knauber & Co., Milwaukee, Wis.
Publisher: O. H. Bailey & J. C. Hazen, Boston
Key/Vignettes/Misc: Refs. A−P, R−X, Z, 1−8
Locations: AAS−W; BPL−R
Catalogs/Checklists:

1526
Place: Mattapan, Massachusetts
Date: 1890
Title: Mattapan, Massachusetts. 1890.
Size: 20⅜ × 25⅝ in. (51.9 × 65.2 cm.)
Artist:
Lithographer:
Printer: O. H. Bailey & Co., Boston
Publisher: O. H. Bailey & Co., Boston
Key/Vignettes/Misc: Refs. A, 2−30; 13 vignettes
Locations: BPL−R
Catalogs/Checklists:

1527
Place: Maynard, Massachusetts
Date: 1879
Title: Maynard, Mass. 1879.
Size: 21½ × 24⅞ in. (54.7 × 63.3 cm.)
Artist: O. H. Bailey & J. C. Hazen
Lithographer:
Printer:
Publisher: O. H. Bailey & J. C. Hazen, Boston
Key/Vignettes/Misc: Refs. C−H; 1 vignette
Locations: AAS−W; BPL−R; LC−M
Catalogs/Checklists: LC−M, 309

1528
Place: Medford, Massachusetts
Date: 1880
Title: Medford Massachusetts 1880.
Size: 19 × 25⅜ in. (48.4 × 64.6 cm.)
Artist:
Lithographer:
Printer:
Publisher: O. H. Bailey & Co., Boston
Key/Vignettes/Misc: Refs. A−H, J−V
Locations: AAS−W; BPL−R; EI−S; BA
Catalogs/Checklists:

1529
Place: Medway, Massachusetts
Date: 1887
Title: View of Medway, Massachusetts. 1887
Size: 21¼ × 26 in. (54.1 × 66.2 cm.)
Artist:
Lithographer:
Printer: O. H. Bailey & Co., Boston
Publisher: O. H. Bailey & Co., Boston
Key/Vignettes/Misc: Refs. A−H, J−P, R−W, Y−Z; 13 vignettes
Locations: BPL−R
Catalogs/Checklists:

1530
Place: Merrimac, Massachusetts
Date: 1889
Title: Merrimac, Mass.
Size: 14½ × 26¾ in. (36.9 × 68.1 cm.)
Artist: Geo. E. Norris
Lithographer:
Printer:
Publisher: Geo. E. Norris, Brockton, Mass.
Key/Vignettes/Misc: Refs. 1−46; 2 vignettes
Locations: BPL−R; LC−M
Catalogs/Checklists: LC−M, 310

1531
Place: Methuen, Massachusetts
Date: 1882
Title: View of Methuen, Massachusetts. 1882.
Size: 19⅛ × 23¾ in. (48.7 × 60.4 cm.)
Artist:
Lithographer:
Printer:
Publisher: O. H. Bailey & Co., Boston
Key/Vignettes/Misc: Refs. 1−16; unnumbered business directory
Locations: BPL−R
Catalogs/Checklists:

1532
Place: Middleborough, Massachusetts
Date: 1881
Title: Middleboro, Mass. 1881
Size: 20½ × 22 in. (52.1 × 56 cm.)
Artist:
Lithographer:
Printer: Beck & Pauli, Milwaukee, Wis.
Publisher:
Key/Vignettes/Misc: Refs. 1−12; 8 vignettes
Locations: BPL−R
Catalogs/Checklists:

1533
Place: Middleborough, Massachusetts
Date: 1889
Title: Middleborough, Massachusetts. 1889.
Size: 20¼ × 30 in. (51.5 × 76.3 cm.)
Artist:
Lithographer:
Printer:
Publisher: O. H. Bailey & Co., Boston
Key/Vignettes/Misc: Refs. A, 2−57
Locations: BPL−R
Catalogs/Checklists:

1534
Place: Middleborough, Massachusetts
Date: N.D.
Title: An Eastern View of the Village at Middleborough. At the Four Corners
Size: 8 × 11¼ in. (20.3 × 28.7 cm.)
Artist: A. Conant
Lithographer:
Printer: Bufford [Boston]
Publisher:
Key/Vignettes/Misc:
Locations: Unknown. see Goodspeed's Catalogue No. 127 (Oct.−Nov., 1918), item 800
Catalogs/Checklists:

1535
Place: Milford, Massachusetts
Date: 1857
Title: Milford, Mass.
Size: 12¾ × 15⁷⁄₁₆ in. (32.4 × 39.3 cm.)
Artist: J. B. Bachelder
Lithographer:
Printer: Endicott & Co., New York
Publisher: Jno. B. Bachelder, 59 Beekman St., New York
Key/Vignettes/Misc:
Locations: AAS−W; BPL−P; SSBT−B; MAHS−B; PAC−P; BA; NYH−NY
Catalogs/Checklists:

1536
Place: Milford, Massachusetts
Date: 1876
Title: View of Milford, Mass. 1876
Size: 20 × 24¼ in. (50.9 × 61.7 cm.)
Artist:
Lithographer:
Printer: The Forbes Lith M'f'g. Co., Boston
Publisher:
Key/Vignettes/Misc: Refs. 1−32
Locations: AAS−W; BPL−R
Catalogs/Checklists:

1537
Place: Milford, Massachusetts
Date: 1888
Title: Milford, Massachusetts.
Size: 24¾ × 33 in. (63 × 84 cm.)
Artist:
Lithographer:
Printer: O. H. Bailey & Co., Boston
Publisher: O. H. Bailey & Co., Boston
Key/Vignettes/Misc: Refs. 1−60; 30 vignettes
Locations: BPL−R
Catalogs/Checklists:

1538
Place: Millbury, Massachusetts
Date: [1836−40?]
Title: Millbury Village.
Size: 11⁷⁄₁₆ × 16⅞ in. (29.1 × 43 cm.)
Artist: F. H. Lane
Lithographer:
Printer: Moore's Lithography Boston, successor to Pendleton
Publisher:
Key/Vignettes/Misc:
Locations: BA
Catalogs/Checklists:

1539
Place: Millbury, Massachusetts
Date: 1880
Title: Millbury, Mass. 1880.
Size: 21¾ × 27¼ in. (55.1 × 69.4 cm.)
Artist:
Lithographer:
Printer: Beck & Pauli, Milwaukee, Wis.
Publisher:
Key/Vignettes/Misc: Refs. 1–62; 13
vignettes
Locations: BPL–R
Catalogs/Checklists:

1540
Place: Millbury, Massachusetts
Date: 1891
Title: Millbury. Massachusetts. 1891
Size: 21³⁄₁₆ × 26¹⁵⁄₁₆ in. (53.9 × 68.6 cm.)
Artist:
Lithographer:
Printer: O. H. Bailey & Co. Boston
Publisher: O. H. Bailey & Co. Boston
Key/Vignettes/Misc: Refs. A, 2–32; 38
vignettes
Locations: MSL–B
Catalogs/Checklists:

1541
Place: Millers Falls, Massachusetts
Date: 1889
Title: Millers Falls, Mass.
Size: 15⅞ × 21 in. (40.4 × 53.4 cm.)
Artist:
Lithographer:
Printer:
Publisher: L. R. Burleigh, Troy, N. Y.
Key/Vignettes/Misc:
Locations: BPL–R
Catalogs/Checklists:

1542
Place: Millis, Massachusetts
Date: 1890
Title: Millis, Massachusetts. 1890.
Size: 17¾ × 26 in. (45.2 × 66.2 cm.)
Artist:
Lithographer:
Printer: O. H. Bailey & Co., Boston
Publisher: O. H. Bailey & Co., Boston
Key/Vignettes/Misc: Refs. A–H, K–L; 15
vignettes
Locations: BPL–R
Catalogs/Checklists:

1543
Place: Millville, Massachusetts
Date: 1887
Title: Millville, Massachusetts. 1887
Size: 17¼ × 24⅞ in. (43.9 × 63.3 cm.)
Artist:
Lithographer:
Printer: O. H. Bailey & Co., Boston,
Mass.
Publisher: O. H. Bailey & Co., Boston,
Mass.
Key/Vignettes/Misc: Refs. A–H, J–S; 1
vignette
Locations: BPL–R
Catalogs/Checklists:

1544
Place: Milton, Massachusetts
Date: 1890
Title: Milton Lower Mills, Massachusetts.
1890
Size: 20½ × 30¾ in. (52.2 × 78.3 cm.)
Artist:
Lithographer:
Printer: O. H. Bailey & Co., Boston
Publisher: O. H. Bailey & Co., Boston
Key/Vignettes/Misc: Refs. A, 2–49; 33
vignettes
Locations: BPL–R; BA
Catalogs/Checklists:

1545
Place: Mittineague, Massachusetts
Date: 1889
Title: Mittineague, Mass.
Size: 15⁵⁄₁₆ × 26⅜ in. (39 × 67.2 cm.)
Artist: L. R. Burleigh
Lithographer:
Printer: The Burleigh Lith. Est., Troy, N. Y.
Publisher: L. R. Burleigh, Troy, N. Y.
Key/Vignettes/Misc: Refs. 1–22
Locations: BPL–R
Catalogs/Checklists:

1546
Place: Monson, Massachusetts
Date: 1879
Title: Monson, Mass. 1879.
Size: 18⅝ × 25⁵⁄₁₆ in. (47.4 × 64.4 cm.)
Artist:
Lithographer:
Printer:
Publisher: O. H. Bailey & Co., Boston
Key/Vignettes/Misc: Refs. 1–33; 4
vignettes
Locations: LC–M; BPL–R; NYH–NY
Catalogs/Checklists: LC–M, 301.1

1547
Place: Nantasket Beach, Massachusetts
Date: 1879
Title: View of Nantasket Beach, Landing
Place of the Boats of the Boston &
Hingham Steam Boat Co.
Size: 16½ × 25½ in. (42 × 64.9 cm.)
Artist: R. P. Mallory
Lithographer:
Printer: [George H. Walker & Co. Boston]
Publisher: George H. Walker & Co.
[Boston] (copyright)
Key/Vignettes/Misc: 5 unnumbered refs.
Locations: AAS–W; BA; LC–M;
MM–NN
Catalogs/Checklists: LC–M, 311;
MM–NN, LP 3598

1548
Place: Nantasket Beach, Massachusetts
Date: [1879?]
Title: View of Nantasket Beach, Looking
s. e. from Sagmore Hill.
Size: 14¹⁵⁄₁₆ × 24¾ in. (38 × 63 cm.)
Artist: R. P. Mallory
Lithographer:
Printer:
Publisher: Geo. H. Walker & Co. [Boston]

Key/Vignettes/Misc:
Locations: LC–M
Catalogs/Checklists: LC–M, 311.1

1549
Place: Nantucket, Massachusetts
Date: 1881
Title: Bird's Eye View of the Town of
Nantucket State of Massachusetts.
Looking Southwest 1881.
Size: 20 × 28½ in. (51.1 × 72.5 cm.)
Artist:
Lithographer:
Printer: Beck & Pauli, Milwaukee
Publisher: J. J. Stoner, Madison, Wis.
Key/Vignettes/Misc: Refs. 1–36, A–E; 5
vignettes
Locations: LC–M; CHS–C; MM–NN
Catalogs/Checklists: LC–M, 312;
MM–NN, LP 13

1550
Place: Natick, Massachusetts
Date: 1877
Title: View of Natick, Mass. 1877
Population about 8,000
Size: 18¾ × 26⅜ in. (47.7 × 67.2 cm.)
Artist:
Lithographer:
Printer: D. Bremner & Co., Milwaukee,
Wis.
Publisher: O. H. Bailey & Co., Boston
Key/Vignettes/Misc: Refs. 1–21, A–H
Locations: AAS–W; BPL–R
Catalogs/Checklists:

1551
Place: Needham, Massachusetts
Date: 1887
Title: Needham, Massachusetts. 1887.
Size: 19 × 24½ in. (48.4 × 62.4 cm.)
Artist:
Lithographer:
Printer:
Publisher: O. H. Bailey & Co., Boston
Key/Vignettes/Misc: Refs. A–H, J–P; 8
vignettes
Locations: BPL–R
Catalogs/Checklists:

1552
Place: New Bedford, Massachusetts
Date: 1845
Title: View of New Bedford. From the Fort
Near Fairhaven.
Size: 18 × 25⁵⁄₁₆ in. (45.8 × 64.4 cm.)
Artist: A. Conant
Lithographer: F. H. Lane
Printer: Lane & Scott's Lith. Tremont
Temple, Boston
Publisher: A. Conant [Boston]
Key/Vignettes/Misc:
Locations: BA; MM–NN; ODHS–NB;
YUAG–NH
Catalogs/Checklists: MM–NN, LP 17;
Wilmerding, no. 172; Pyne, no. 448

1553
Place: New Bedford, Massachusetts
Date: 1858
Title: New Bedford Fifty Years Ago.

Size: 15¹⁵⁄₁₆ × 23¹¹⁄₁₆ in. (40.5 × 60.2 cm.)
Artist: William A. Wall
Lithographer:
Printer: Endicott & Co., New York
Publisher:
Key/Vignettes/Misc:
Locations: NYP–S; CHS–C; YUAG–NH
Catalogs/Checklists: Stokes C. 1807–F–3

1554
Place: New Bedford, Massachusetts
Date: [1858–60]
Title: New Bedford, Mass.
Size: 17⅝ × 32⁵⁄₁₆ in. (44.9 × 82.2 cm.)
Artist: J. F. A. Cole
Lithographer:
Printer: J. F. A. Cole, 265 Washington St. Boston
Publisher: Prang & Mayer, 34 Merchants Row, Boston
Key/Vignettes/Misc:
Locations: MM–NN; SSBT–B; BA; YUAG–NH
Catalogs/Checklists: MM–NN, LP 28

1555
Place: New Bedford, Massachusetts
Date: 1876
Title: View of the City of New Bedford, Mass. 1876
Size: 25¹⁄₁₆ × 33⅜ in. (63.8 × 84.9 cm.)
Artist: O. H. Bailey & Co.
Lithographer: C. H. Vogt
Printer: J. Knauber Co.
Publisher: O. H. Bailey & Co. [Boston]
Key/Vignettes/Misc: Refs. 1–76; 6 vignettes
Locations: MSL–B; ODHS–NB; BPL–R; AAS–W; MM–NN; NYH–NY
Catalogs/Checklists: New Bedford & Old Dartmouth, no. 172

1556
Place: New Bedford, Massachusetts
Date: 1907
Title: Buzzards Bay
Size: 20 × 27 in. (50.9 × 68.7 cm.)
Artist:
Lithographer:
Printer: Geo. H. Walker & Co. Lith. Boston
Publisher: Geo. H. Walker & Co. Boston (copyright)
Key/Vignettes/Misc:
Locations: MSL–B
Catalogs/Checklists:

1557
Place: Newburyport, Massachusetts
Date: Ca. 1845
Title: View of Newburyport (from Salisbury).
Size: 15½ × 24⅞ in. (39.4 × 63.2 cm.)
Artist: F. H. Lane after A. Conant
Lithographer:
Printer: Lane & Scott's Lith., Boston
Publisher: A. Conant
Key/Vignettes/Misc:
Locations: MM–NN; EI–S; CHS–C; SSBT–B; YUAG–NH
Catalogs/Checklists: MM–NN, LP 11

1558
Place: Newburyport, Massachusetts
Date: 1880
Title: Newburyport, Mass. 1880.
Size: 17⁵⁄₁₆ × 22¾ in. (44.1 × 57.9 cm.)
Artist:
Lithographer:
Printer:
Publisher: Bigelow and Hazen, [Boston]
Key/Vignettes/Misc: Refs. A–H, J–P, R–T
Locations: BPL–R
Catalogs/Checklists:

1559
Place: Newton, Massachusetts
Date: 1878
Title: View of Newton, Mass., Comprising Wards 1 & 7 & Environs of the City of Newton.
Size: 20⅜ × 25 in. (51.9 × 63.6 cm.)
Artist:
Lithographer:
Printer:
Publisher: O. H. Bailey & Co., Boston
Key/Vignettes/Misc: Refs. 1–16
Locations: BPL–R; MAHS–B; LC–M
Catalogs/Checklists: LC–M, 312.2

1560
Place: Newton, Massachusetts
Date: 1897
Title: Wards 1 and 7, Newton, Massachusetts 1897.
Size: 14⅛ × 24¾ in. (36 × 63 cm.)
Artist:
Lithographer:
Printer:
Publisher: O. H. Bailey & Co., Boston
Key/Vignettes/Misc:
Locations: LC–M
Catalogs/Checklists: LC–M, 312.3

1561
Place: Newton Center, Massachusetts
Date: Ca. 1845
Title: A View of Newton Center, as seen from Fiske Hill.
Size: 9 × 14½ in. (22.8 × 36.9 cm.)
Artist: A. Conant
Lithographer:
Printer: Lane & Scotts Lith. 16 Tremont Temple, Boston
Publisher:
Key/Vignettes/Misc:
Locations: AAS–W; BA
Catalogs/Checklists: Wilmerding, no. 170

1562
Place: Newton Center, Massachusetts
Date: 1897
Title: Newton Centre, Massachusetts 1897.
Size: 19¹³⁄₁₆ × 27 in. (50.4 × 68.7 cm.)
Artist:
Lithographer:
Printer: O. H. Bailey & Co. Boston
Publisher: O. H. Bailey & Co. Boston
Key/Vignettes/Misc: 29 vignettes
Locations: MSL–B; LC–M
Catalogs/Checklists: LC–M, 312.4

1563
Place: Newton Lower Falls, Massachusetts
Date: 1880
Title: Newton Lower Falls. Massachusetts. 1880.
Size: 20 × 22½ in. (50.9 × 57.3 cm.)
Artist:
Lithographer:
Printer:
Publisher: O. H. Bailey & Co., Boston
Key/Vignettes/Misc: Refs. A–Z
Locations: BPL–R
Catalogs/Checklists:

1564
Place: Newton Upper Falls, Massachusetts
Date: 1888
Title: Newton Upper Falls, Massachusetts. 1888.
Size: 21 × 24½ in. (53.5 × 62.4 cm.)
Artist:
Lithographer:
Printer:
Publisher: O. H. Bailey & Co., Boston
Key/Vignettes/Misc: Refs. A, 2–27; 13 vignettes
Locations: BPL–R
Catalogs/Checklists:

1565
Place: Newton Upper Falls, Massachusetts
Date: [189–?]
Title: Map of River Park, Newton Upper Falls.
Size: 15¾ × 20¾ in. (40.1 × 52.8 cm.)
Artist:
Lithographer:
Printer:
Publisher:
Key/Vignettes/Misc: 14 vignettes; advertisements
Locations: BPL–R
Catalogs/Checklists:

1566
Place: North Abington, Massachusetts
Date: 1885
Title: North Abington, Plymouth County, Mass., Looking West. 1885
Size: 13¾ × 21¾ in. (35 × 55.4 cm.)
Artist:
Lithographer:
Printer:
Publisher: A. F. Poole and Company, Brockton, Mass.
Key/Vignettes/Misc: Refs. A–U
Locations: BPL–R
Catalogs/Checklists:

1567
Place: North Abington, Massachusetts
Date: 1899
Title: North Abington, Massachusetts. 1899.
Size: 16¹⁄₁₆ × 22⅞ in. (40.9 × 58.3 cm.)
Artist:
Lithographer:
Printer: O. H. Bailey & Co. Boston
Publisher: O. H. Bailey & Co. Boston
Key/Vignettes/Misc: Refs. A, 2–28; 6 vignettes

Locations: MSL–B
Catalogs/Checklists:

1568
Place: North Adams, Massachusetts
Date: 1841
Title: North Adams 1841.
Size: 8½ × 11 in. (21.6 × 28 cm.)
Artist: Jas. C. Clapp
Lithographer:
Printer:
Publisher: E. B. and E. C. Kellogg
Key/Vignettes/Misc:
Locations: YUAG–NH
Catalogs/Checklists:

1569
Place: North Adams, Massachusetts
Date: 1881
Title: North Adams, Mass. 1881
Size: 19 × 26¾ in. (48.4 × 68.1 cm.)
Artist: H. H. Rowley & Co.
Lithographer:
Printer:
Publisher: H. H. Rowley & Co., Hartford, Conn.
Key/Vignettes/Misc: 55 refs.; 6 vignettes
Locations: Unknown. See Old Print Shop Portfolio, XXXIII, p. 61, No. 18
Catalogs/Checklists:

1570
Place: North Attleboro, Massachusetts
Date: 1878
Title: North Attleborough, Mass. 1878.
Size: 22 × 27 in. (56 × 68.7 cm.)
Artist: O. H. Bailey & J. C. Hazen
Lithographer: C. H. Vogt
Printer:
Publisher: O. H. Bailey & J. C. Hazen, Boston
Key/Vignettes/Misc: Refs. 1–29, A–H, J–L; 4 vignettes
Locations: AAS–W; BPL–R; LC–M
Catalogs/Checklists: LC–M, 313

1571
Place: North Attleboro, Massachusetts
Date: 1891
Title: North Attleborough, Masachusetts
Size: 24 × 31¼ in. (61.1 × 79.5 cm.)
Artist:
Lithographer:
Printer:
Publisher: O. H. Bailey & Co., Boston
Key/Vignettes/Misc:
Locations: BPL–R
Catalogs/Checklists:

1572
Place: North Billerica, Massachusetts
Date: 1887
Title: North Billerica, Mass. 1887.
Size: 12¾ × 23⅞ in. (32.5 × 60.8 cm.)
Artist: L. R. Burleigh
Lithographer:
Printer: Burleigh Litho. Est. Troy, N. Y.
Publisher: Burleigh Litho. Est., Troy, N. Y.
Key/Vignettes/Misc: Refs. 1–17
Locations: BPL–R; LC–M
Catalogs/Checklists: LC–M, 314

1573
Place: North Bridgewater, Massachusetts
Date: [1844]
Title: East View of the Village of North Bridgewater, Ma.
Size: 13¹⁄₁₆ × 20⁵⁄₁₆ in. (33.1 × 51.5 cm.)
Artist: A. Conant
Lithographer:
Printer: E. W. Bouve
Publisher:
Key/Vignettes/Misc:
Locations: AAS–W
Catalogs/Checklists:

1574
Place: North Bridgewater, Massachusetts
Date: 1882
Title: East View of the Village of North Bridgewater, Mass., 1844. From a Lithograph in Possession of Mr. R. C. Kimball
Size: 11 × 16¼ in. (28 × 41.4 cm.)
Artist: A. F. Poole
Lithographer:
Printer: Beck & Pauli, Lith., Milwaukee, Wis.
Publisher: J. J. Stoner, Madison, Wis.
Key/Vignettes/Misc: Refs. 1–5
Locations: LC–M; AAS–W; BA
Catalogs/Checklists: LC–M, 315

1575
Place: North Brookfield, Massachusetts
Date: 1878
Title: North Brookfield, Mass. 1878
Size: 17½ × 25½ in. (44.5 × 64.9 cm.)
Artist: O. H. Bailey & J. C. Hazen
Lithographer: C. H. Vogt
Printer:
Publisher: O. H. Bailey and J. C. Hazen, Boston
Key/Vignettes/Misc: Refs. A–G; 1 vignette
Locations: AAS–W; BPL–R
Catalogs/Checklists:

1576
Place: North Chelmsford, Massachusetts
Date: 1893
Title: No. Chelmsford, Mass. (On the Merrimac River) 1893.
Size: 12⅜ × 17¾ in. (31.5 × 45.2 cm.)
Artist:
Lithographer:
Printer:
Publisher: George E. Norris, Brockton, Mass.
Key/Vignettes/Misc: Refs. A–Q; 1 vignette
Locations: BPL–R
Catalogs/Checklists:

1577
Place: North Dighton, Massachusetts
Date: 1881
Title: View of North Dighton, Massachusetts
Size: 18⁷⁄₁₆ × 22¹⁵⁄₁₆ in. (46.8 × 58.2 cm.)
Artist:
Lithographer:
Printer:

Publisher: O. H. Bailey & Co., Boston
Key/Vignettes/Misc: Refs. A–Q; 2 vignettes
Locations: AAS–W
Catalogs/Checklists:

1578
Place: North Easton, Massachusetts
Date: 1881
Title: View of North Easton, Massachusetts. 1881
Size: 19⅝ × 23¼ in. (50 × 59.2 cm.)
Artist:
Lithographer:
Printer:
Publisher: O. H. Bailey & Co., Boston
Key/Vignettes/Misc: Refs. 1–35
Locations: BPL–R
Catalogs/Checklists:

1579
Place: North Easton, Massachusetts
Date: 1891
Title: North Easton, Massachusetts. 1891.
Size: 19⅞ × 26 in. (50.6 × 66.2 cm.)
Artist:
Lithographer:
Printer: O. H. Bailey & Co., Boston
Publisher: O. H. Bailey & Co., Boston
Key/Vignettes/Misc: Refs. A–H, J–Y; 31 vignettes
Locations: BPL–R; BA
Catalogs/Checklists:

1580
Place: North Leominster, Massachusetts
Date: 1887
Title: North Leominster, Mass.
Size: 11 × 19⅞ in. (28 × 50.6 cm.)
Artist: L. R. Burleigh
Lithographer:
Printer: Burleigh Lith. Est., Troy, N. Y.
Publisher: L. R. Burleigh, Troy, N. Y.
Key/Vignettes/Misc: Refs. 1–11
Locations: BPL–R; LC–M
Catalogs/Checklists: LC–M, 316

Place: North Natick, Massachusetts
Date: 1887
See Cochituate, Massachusetts, 1887.

1581
Place: Northampton, Massachusetts
Date: 1875
Title: Northampton, Mass. 1875
Size: 20⅜ × 24⅝ in. (51.8 × 62.7 cm.)
Artist: H. H. Bailey & Co.
Lithographer: C. H. Vogt
Printer: J. Knauber & Co.
Publisher: H. H. Bailey & Co., Milwaukee
Key/Vignettes/Misc: Refs. A–I, K–P
Locations: BPL–R
Catalogs/Checklists:

1582
Place: Northborough, Massachusetts
Date: 1887
Title: Northboro, Mass. 1887.
Size: 14¼ × 26⅛ in. (36.3 × 66.5 cm.)
Artist: Geo. E. Norris
Lithographer:
Printer: Burleigh Litho., Troy, N. Y.

Publisher: Geo. E. Norris
Key/Vignettes/Misc: Refs. 1–15, A–Z; 1 vignette
Locations: LC–M (photo); Northborough Historical Society, Inc., Northborough, Massachusetts
Catalogs/Checklists: LC–M, 314.1

1583
Place: Northborough, Massachusetts
Date: 1887
Title: View of Northborough, Massachusetts, 1887.
Size: 18¼ × 26⅛ in. (46.5 × 66.5 cm.)
Artist:
Lithographer:
Printer:
Publisher:
Key/Vignettes/Misc: Refs. A–H, J–K; 2 vignettes
Locations: BPL–R; LC–M
Catalogs/Checklists: LC–M, 314.2

1584
Place: Norton, Massachusetts
Date: 1891
Title: Norton, Massachusetts. 1891
Size: 17½ × 24¼ in. (44.6 × 61.7 cm.)
Artist:
Lithographer:
Printer: O. H. Bailey & Co., Boston
Publisher: O. H. Bailey & Co., Boston
Key/Vignettes/Misc: Refs. A, 2–25; 19 vignettes
Locations: LC–M; BPL–R
Catalogs/Checklists: LC–M, 316.1

1585
Place: Norwood, Massachusetts
Date: 1882
Title: Norwood, Massachusetts. 1882
Size: 19 × 25½ in. (48.4 × 64.9 cm.)
Artist:
Lithographer: O. H. Bailey & Co.
Printer: O. H. Bailey & Co., Boston
Publisher: O. H. Bailey & Co., Boston
Key/Vignettes/Misc: Refs. 1–39; 4 vignettes
Locations: BPL–R
Catalogs/Checklists:

1586
Place: Norwood, Massachusetts
Date: 1898
Title: Norwood, Massachusetts. 1898.
Size: 18⅜ × 25¾ in. (46.8 × 65.5 cm.)
Artist:
Lithographer:
Printer: O. H. Bailey & Co. Boston
Publisher: O. H. Bailey & Co. Boston
Key/Vignettes/Misc: 28 vignettes
Locations: MSL–B
Catalogs/Checklists:

1587
Place: Oakdale, Massachusetts
Date: 1891
Title: Oakdale, Massachusetts. 1891.
Size: 19⅛ × 22¹¹⁄₁₆ in. (48.7 × 57.7 cm.)
Artist:
Lithographer:
Printer: O. H. Bailey & Co. Boston
Publisher: O. H. Bailey & Co. Boston

Key/Vignettes/Misc: Refs. A, 2–10, 12–14; 13 vignettes
Locations: MSL–B
Catalogs/Checklists:

1588
Place: Orange, Massachusetts
Date: 1878
Title: Bird's Eye View of Orange, Massachusetts. 1878.
Size: 18½ × 24⅞ in. (47.1 × 63.3 cm.)
Artist: O. H. Bailey & Co.
Lithographer:
Printer:
Publisher: O. H. Bailey & Co., Boston
Key/Vignettes/Misc: Refs. 1–22
Locations: BPL–R
Catalogs/Checklists:

1589
Place: Orange, Massachusetts
Date: 1883
Title: Orange, Mass.
Size: 16³⁄₁₆ × 23⅞ in. (41.2 × 60.8 cm.)
Artist: L. R. Burleigh
Lithographer:
Printer: Beck & Pauli, Milwaukee, Wis.
Publisher: L. R. Burleigh, Troy, N. Y.
Key/Vignettes/Misc: Refs. 1–24
Locations: AAS–W; BPL–R
Catalogs/Checklists:

1590
Place: Oxford, Massachusetts
Date: Ca. 1850
Title: Oxford, Ms
Size: 8 × 13 in. (20.3 × 33.1 cm.)
Artist: G. F. Daniels
Lithographer:
Printer: Thayer & Co.
Publisher:
Key/Vignettes/Misc:
Locations: Unknown. see Goodspeed's Catalogue No. 449, p. 14, item 214
Catalogs/Checklists:

1591
Place: Oxford, Massachusetts
Date: Ca. 1850
Title: View of Oxford from Fort Hill.
Size: 13 × 21 in. (33.1 × 53.4 cm.)
Artist: G. F. Daniels
Lithographer:
Printer: Thayer & Co.
Publisher:
Key/Vignettes/Misc:
Locations: Unknown. see Goodspeed's Catalogue, No. 449, p. 14, item 213
Catalogs/Checklists:

1592
Place: Oxford, Massachusetts
Date: 1891
Title: Oxford, Massachusetts. 1891
Size: 20⅞ × 24⅞ in. (53.2 × 63.3 cm.)
Artist:
Lithographer:
Printer: O. H. Bailey & Co., Boston
Publisher: O. H. Bailey & Co., Boston
Key/Vignettes/Misc: Refs. A, 2–32
Locations: BPL–R
Catalogs/Checklists:

1593
Place: Palmer, Massachusetts
Date: 1879
Title: View of Palmer, Mass. 1879
Size: 19 × 23⅜ in. (48.4 × 59.5 cm.)
Artist:
Lithographer:
Printer:
Publisher: O. H. Bailey & Company, Boston
Key/Vignettes/Misc: Refs. 1–52; 2 vignettes
Locations: BPL–R; NYH–NY
Catalogs/Checklists:

1594
Place: Peabody, Massachusetts
Date: 1856
Title: South Danvers, Mass. From Buxton's Hill.
Size: 12⅜ × 15¾ in. (31.3 × 40.1 cm.)
Artist: J. B. Bachelder
Lithographer:
Printer: Endicott & Co., New York
Publisher: Jno. B. Bachelder, 59 Beekman St. N. Y.
Key/Vignettes/Misc:
Locations: AAS–W; BPL–P; EI–S; MAHS–B; PAC–P; BA
Catalogs/Checklists:

1595
Place: Peabody, Massachusetts
Date: 1877
Title: View of Peabody, Mass. 1877
Size: 19¾ × 25½ in. (50.3 × 64.9 cm.)
Artist: O. H. Bailey & J. C. Hazen
Lithographer: J. Knauber & Co.
Printer: J. Knauber & Co., Milwaukee
Publisher: O. H. Bailey and J. C. Hazen, Boston
Key/Vignettes/Misc: Refs. A–I, K–N
Locations: AAS–W; BPL–R; LC–M
Catalogs/Checklists: LC–M, 318

1596
Place: Pepperell, Massachusetts
Date: 1851
Title: View of Babbatassett Village, Pepperell Mass. 1851
Size: 13⅜ × 20⅞ in. (34 × 53.1 cm.)
Artist: Uriah Smith
Lithographer:
Printer: Tappan & Bradford's Lith. [Boston]
Publisher:
Key/Vignettes/Misc:
Locations: BA
Catalogs/Checklists:

1597
Place: Pittsfield, Massachusetts
Date: [1854–60]
Title: Pittsfield (Massachusetts)
Size: 13¹⁄₁₆ × 20¹³⁄₁₆ in. (33.2 × 52.9 cm.)
Artist: James C. Clapp
Lithographer: J. Jacottet & Aubrun
Printer: Lemercier, Paris
Publisher: Goupil & Co. 366 Broadway, New York
Key/Vignettes/Misc:
Locations: NYP–S; YUAG–NH

Catalogs/Checklists: Stokes P. 1854–60—
G–33

1598
Place: Pittsfield, Massachusetts
Date: 1876
Title: Bird's Eye View of Pittsfield, Mass.
1876
Size: 20¾ × 27⅝ in. (52.9 × 70.3 cm.)
Artist: H. H. Bailey & J. C. Hazen
Lithographer: C. H. Vogt
Printer: J. Knauber & Co.
Publisher: H. H. Bailey & J. C. Hazen
Key/Vignettes/Misc: Refs. A–T
Locations: BPL–R; Berkshire Athenaeum,
Pittsfield, Massachusetts
Catalogs/Checklists:

1599
Place: Pittsfield, Massachusetts
Date: 1899
Title: Pittsfield, Massachusetts
Size: 22 × 33⅜ in. (55.9 × 84.9 cm.)
Artist: A. E. Rapp
Lithographer: C. Fausel
Printer: Weed–Parsons Printing Company,
Albany, New York
Publisher: A. M. Van Decarr, South
Schodack, New York
Key/Vignettes/Misc: Refs. 1–33
Locations: Berkshire Athenaeum,
Pittsfield, Massachusetts
Catalogs/Checklists:

1600
Place: Plainville, Massachusetts
Date: 1887
Title: Plainville, Mass. 1887.
Size: 14½ × 22¼ in. (36.9 × 56.7 cm.)
Artist: Geo. E. Norris
Lithographer:
Printer: L. R. Burleigh Lith. Troy, N. Y.
Publisher: Geo. E. Norris, Brockton, Mass.
Key/Vignettes/Misc: Refs. 1–22; 1
vignette
Locations: BPL–R
Catalogs/Checklists:

1601
Place: Plymouth, Massachusetts
Date: [1851–55]
Title: A View of Plymouth, From the
Beach East of the Harbor—the Oldest
Town in New England and Landing Place
of the Pilgrim Fathers, Dec. 22d. 1620.
Size: 14³⁄₁₆ × 19⅝ in. (36.1 × 50 cm.)
Artist: Timothy Barry
Lithographer:
Printer: J. H. Bufford's Lith. 160
Washington St. Boston
Publisher: Timothy Barry
Key/Vignettes/Misc:
Locations: MM–NN; NYP–S; BA
Catalogs/Checklists: Stokes P. 1845—
G–9; MM–NN, LP 22

1602
Place: Plymouth, Massachusetts
Date: 1882
Title: Plymouth, Mass. 1882
Size: 20⁹⁄₁₆ × 26¹⁄₁₆ in. (52.3 × 66.3 cm.)
Artist:

Lithographer:
Printer:
Publisher: O. H. Bailey & Company,
Boston
Key/Vignettes/Misc: Refs. 1–35; 6
vignettes
Locations: BPL–R; LC–M (photo)
Catalogs/Checklists: LC–M, 318.1

1603
Place: Plymouth, Massachusetts
Date: 1897
Title: Plymouth, Massachusetts. 1897
Size: 20¾ × 31⅞ in. (52.8 × 81.1 cm.)
Artist:
Lithographer:
Printer: O. H. Bailey & Co. Boston
Publisher: O. H. Bailey & Co. Boston
Key/Vignettes/Misc: Refs. 1–60; 45
vignettes
Locations: MSL–B
Catalogs/Checklists:

1604
Place: Plymouth, Massachusetts
Date: 1910
Title: Plymouth, Mass.
Size: 19⅞ × 39 in. (50.6 × 99.2 cm.)
Artist:
Lithographer:
Printer:
Publisher: Walker Lith. & Pub. Co.,
Boston
Key/Vignettes/Misc:
Locations: BPL–R
Catalogs/Checklists:

1605
Place: Provincetown, Massachusetts
Date: 1877
Title: Provincetown, from Long Point.
Size: 16½ × 25⅜ in. (42.1 × 64.5 cm.)
Artist:
Lithographer:
Printer:
Publisher: F. K. Rogers, Boston
Key/Vignettes/Misc: Unnumbered
directory of churches and public buildings
Locations: MM–NN; LC–M; LC–P
Catalogs/Checklists: MM–NN, LP 14;
LC–M, 319

1606
Place: Provincetown, Massachusetts
Date: 1879
Title: Balloon View–Provincetown to
Boston. Massachusetts Bay.
Size: 11 × 18¼ in. (28 × 46.4 cm.)
Artist:
Lithographer:
Printer: J. H. Daniels
Publisher: John H. Daniels, Boston
(copyright)
Key/Vignettes/Misc:
Locations: BPL–R
Catalogs/Checklists:

1607
Place: Provincetown, Massachusetts
Date: 1882
Title: Bird's Eye View of the Town of
Provincetown, Barnstable County, Mass.

Size: 16⅞ × 38¼ in. (42.9 × 97.3 cm.)
Artist: A. F. Poole
Lithographer:
Printer: Beck & Pauli Lith. Milwaukee,
Wis.
Publisher: J. J. Stoner, Madison, Wis.
Key/Vignettes/Misc: Refs. 1–40, B; 6
vignettes
Locations: BPL–R; SSBT–B
Catalogs/Checklists:

1608
Place: Provincetown, Massachusetts
Date: 1910
Title: Provincetown, Mass.
Size: 10⁹⁄₁₆ × 17 in. (26.8 × 43.1 cm.)
Artist:
Lithographer:
Printer: Walker Lith & Pub Co., Boston
Publisher: Walker Lith & Pub Co. Boston
(copyright)
Key/Vignettes/Misc:
Locations: BA; LC–M
Catalogs/Checklists:

1609
Place: Provincetown, Massachusetts
Date: Ca. 1910
Title: Provincetown, Mass. Barnstable Co.
Size: 17⅜ × 27 in. (44.2 × 68.7 cm.)
Artist:
Lithographer:
Printer:
Publisher: Walker Lith. & Pub. Co.,
Boston (copyright)
Key/Vignettes/Misc: Refs. 1–24
Locations: BPL–R; BA (proof); LC–M
(photo)
Catalogs/Checklists: LC–M, 320

1610
Place: Quincy, Massachusetts
Date: 1877
Title: Quincy, Mass.
Size: 20 × 33 in. (50.8 × 83.9 cm.)
Artist: E. Whitefield
Lithographer:
Printer:
Publisher: E. Whitefield
Key/Vignettes/Misc:
Locations: LC–M; ACMW–FW; BPL–R;
MAHS–B
Catalogs/Checklists: LC–M, 321; Norton,
Whitefield, no. 100

1611
Place: Randolph, Massachusetts
Date: 1882
Title: View of Randolph Mass. 1882
Size: 20¼ × 24 in. (51.6 × 61.1 cm.)
Artist: J. C. Hazen & E. H. Bigelow
Lithographer:
Printer: Beck & Pauli, Milwaukee, Wis.
Publisher: J. C. Hazen & E. H. Bigelow,
Boston
Key/Vignettes/Misc: 6 vignettes
Locations: BPL–R
Catalogs/Checklists:

1612
Place: Rochdale, Massachusetts
Date: 1887

Title: Rochdale and Greenville, Mass. 1887.
Size: 14¼ × 21⅜ in. (36.3 × 54.4 cm.)
Artist: Geo. E. Norris
Lithographer:
Printer: The Burleigh Litho Establishment, Troy, N. Y.
Publisher: Geo. E. Norris, Brockton, Mass.
Key/Vignettes/Misc: Refs. 1–20, A–T; 2 vignettes
Locations: BPL–R
Catalogs/Checklists:

1613
Place: Rockland, Massachusetts
Date: 1881
Title: Bird's Eye View of the Town of Rockland, Plymouth County Mass. 1881 Looking Northeast.
Size: 16³⁄₁₆ × 20¾ in. (41.2 × 52.9 cm.)
Artist: A. F. Poole
Lithographer:
Printer: Beck & Pauli, Milwaukee, Wis.
Publisher: J. J. Stoner, Madison, Wis.
Key/Vignettes/Misc: Refs. 1–14, A–H, J–R, T–U; 5 vignettes
Locations: MSL–B; Rockland Savings Bank, Rockland, Massachusetts
Catalogs/Checklists:

1614
Place: Rockland, Massachusetts
Date: 1901
Title: Rockland, Massachusetts. 1901
Size: 18⅝ × 24¹⁄₁₆ in. (47.4 × 61.3 cm.)
Artist:
Lithographer:
Printer:
Publisher: O. H. Bailey, Boston
Key/Vignettes/Misc: Refs. A, 2–67; 27 vignettes
Locations: MSL–B
Catalogs/Checklists:

1615
Place: Rockport, Massachusetts
Date: 1886
Title: Pigeon Cove. Rockport: Essex County, Mass. 1886.
Size: 13¾ × 24 in. (35 × 61.1 cm.)
Artist: JC
Lithographer:
Printer:
Publisher: Geo. H. Walker & Co.
Key/Vignettes/Misc: 1 vignette
Locations: BPL–R; EI–S; BA
Catalogs/Checklists:

1616
Place: Rockport, Massachusetts
Date: [188–?]
Title: Land's End, Rockport, Mass.
Size: 20⅛ × 26¼ in. (51.2 × 66.8 cm.)
Artist:
Lithographer:
Printer:
Publisher:
Key/Vignettes/Misc: 5 vignettes
Locations: BPL–R
Catalogs/Checklists:

1617
Place: Salem, Massachusetts
Date: [1843–44]
Title: Salem, Beverly & Marblehead as Seen from Browne's Hill, Beverly. Southern View.
Size: 20¼ × 29⁹⁄₁₆ in. (51.6 × 75.3 cm.)
Artist: J. Sheldon Jr.
Lithographer:
Printer: Bouve & Sharp, 221 Washington St., Boston
Publisher:
Key/Vignettes/Misc: Refs. 1–32
Locations: EI–S; BA
Catalogs/Checklists:

1618
Place: Salem, Massachusetts
Date: 1849
Title: View of Salem, Mass.
Size: 14¹⁵⁄₁₆ × 38½ in. (38 × 97.9 cm.)
Artist: E. Whitefield
Lithographer: E. Whitefield
Printer: F. Mich[e]lin 111 Nassau St., N. Y.
Publisher: E. Whitefield, New York
Key/Vignettes/Misc:
Locations: EI–S
Catalogs/Checklists: Norton, Whitefield, no. 45

1619
Place: Salem, Massachusetts
Date: 1850
Title: View of Salem, Mass. View of Lynn, Mass. View of Beverly, Mass. View of Danvers, Mass.
Size: 22 × 33⅛ in. (56 × 84.3 cm.)
Artist: E. Whitefield
Lithographer:
Printer: Wm. Endicott & Co., New York
Publisher:
Key/Vignettes/Misc: 4 views on a single sheet
Locations: EI–S; NYP–S
Catalogs/Checklists: Stokes C. 1850—G–7; Norton, Whitefield, no. 49

1620
Place: Salem, Massachusetts
Date: 1854
Title: Salem, Mass.
Size: 24³⁄₁₆ × 38 in. (61.6 × 96.6 cm.)
Artist: J. W. Hill
Lithographer: J. H. Colen
Printer: Endicott & Co., N. Y.
Publisher: Smith Brothers & Co., 59 Beekman St. New York
Key/Vignettes/Misc:
Locations: MM–NN; CHS–C; EI–S; SSBT–B; BA; LC–P
Catalogs/Checklists: MM–NN, LP 1832; Stokes P. 1853—G–18

1621
Place: Salem, Massachusetts
Date: 1856
Title: Salem Mass. West View.
Size: 9⅞ × 15⅜ in. (25.2 × 39.2 cm.)
Artist: J. B. Bachelder
Lithographer:

Printer: Endicott & Co., New York
Publisher: Jno. B. Bachelder, 59 Beekman St. New York
Key/Vignettes/Misc:
Locations: EI–S; AAS–W; BPL–P; PAC–P; BA
Catalogs/Checklists:

1622
Place: Salem, Massachusetts
Date: 1856
Title: South View—Salem, Mass.
Size: 12⅝ × 15⅝ in. (32.1 × 39.8 cm.)
Artist: J. B. Bachelder
Lithographer:
Printer: Endicott & Co., N. Y.
Publisher: J. B. Bachelder, 59 Beekman St. New York
Key/Vignettes/Misc:
Locations: MM–NN; AAS–W; BPL–P; MAHS–B; PAC–P; BA
Catalogs/Checklists: MM–NN, LP 4

1623
Place: Salem, Massachusetts
Date: Ca. 1856
Title: East View, Salem, Mass.
Size: 12½ × 15⅝ in. (31.8 × 39.8 cm.)
Artist: J. B. Bachelder
Lithographer:
Printer: Endicott & Co., New York
Publisher: Jno. B. Bachelder, New York
Key/Vignettes/Misc:
Locations: MM–NN; MAHS–B
Catalogs/Checklists: MM–NN, LP 3

1624
Place: Salem, Massachusetts
Date: 1883
Title: Salem, Mass. 1883
Size: 23¹⁵⁄₁₆ × 39¹⁵⁄₁₆ in. (61 × 101.6 cm.)
Artist: L. R. Burleigh
Lithographer: J. Lyth
Printer:
Publisher: D. Mason & Co., Syracuse, N. Y.
Key/Vignettes/Misc: Refs. 1–56; 1 vignette
Locations: EI–S; LC–M (facsimile)
Catalogs/Checklists: LC–M, 321.1

Place: Salisbury, Massachusetts
Date: 1880
See Amesbury, Massachusetts, 1880.

1625
Place: Sandwich, Massachusetts
Date: 1884
Title: Sandwich Village, Barnstable County Mass., Looking West. 1884
Size: 12½ × 18¾ in. (31.8 × 47.7 cm.)
Artist: A. F. Poole
Lithographer:
Printer: George H. Walker & Co., Lith. Boston
Publisher: A. F. Poole, Brockton, Mass.
Key/Vignettes/Misc: 36 refs.
Locations: BPL–R
Catalogs/Checklists:

Place: Saugus, Massachusetts
Date: 1896
See Cliftondale, Massachusetts, 1896.

1626
Place: Saxonville, Massachusetts
Date: 1882
Title: View of Saxonville, Mass. 1882.
Size: 18⅝ × 23¾ in. (47.4 × 60.4 cm.)
Artist:
Lithographer:
Printer:
Publisher: O. H. Bailey & Co., Boston
Key/Vignettes/Misc: Refs. 1–35
Locations: BPL–R
Catalogs/Checklists:

1627
Place: Sharon, Massachusetts
Date: 1890
Title: Sharon, Massachusetts. 1890.
Size: 21 × 26 in. (53.5 × 66.1 cm.)
Artist:
Lithographer:
Printer: O. H. Bailey & Co. Boston
Publisher: O. H. Bailey & Co. Boston
Key/Vignettes/Misc: Refs. A, 2–23; 23 vignettes
Locations: MSL–B
Catalogs/Checklists:

1628
Place: Shirley, Massachusetts
Date: 1892
Title: Shirley, Massachusetts. 1892
Size: 18 × 23 in. (45.8 × 58.6 cm.)
Artist:
Lithographer:
Printer: O. H. Bailey & Co. Boston
Publisher: O. H. Bailey & Co. Boston
Key/Vignettes/Misc: Refs. A, 2–13; 16 vignettes
Locations: MSL–B
Catalogs/Checklists:

1629
Place: South Abington, Massachusetts
Date: 1882
Title: Bird's Eye View of the Town of South Abington, Plymouth Co. Mass. 1882. Looking Southeast.
Size: 15⅝ × 20⅞ in. (39.8 × 53.2 cm.)
Artist: [A. F. Poole?]
Lithographer:
Printer: Beck & Pauli, Milwaukee, Wis.
Publisher: J. J. Stoner, Madison, Wis.
Key/Vignettes/Misc: Refs. 1–22; 5 vignettes
Locations: MSL–B; BPL–R
Catalogs/Checklists:

1630
Place: South Acton, Massachusetts
Date: 1886
Title: South Acton, Mass., 1886.
Size: 10⅝ × 21⅝ in. (27 × 55.1 cm.)
Artist:
Lithographer:
Printer: The Burleigh Lith. Est., Troy, N. Y.
Publisher: L. R. Burleigh, Troy, N. Y.
Key/Vignettes/Misc: Refs. 1–6
Locations: BPL–R; LC–M
Catalogs/Checklists: LC–M, 322

Place: South Boston, Massachusetts
Date: 1859
See Boston, Massachusetts, 1859.

1631
Place: South Braintree, Massachusetts
Date: 1882
Title: View of South Braintree, Massachusetts. 1892
Size: 19¼ × 23⁷⁄₁₆ in. (49 × 59.7 cm.)
Artist:
Lithographer:
Printer:
Publisher: O. H. Bailey & Co., Boston
Key/Vignettes/Misc: Refs. 1–22; 4 vignettes
Locations: BPL–R
Catalogs/Checklists:

Place: South Danvers, Massachusetts
Date: 1856
See Peabody, Massachusetts, 1856.

1632
Place: South Easton, Massachusetts
Date: 1888
Title: South Easton, Massachusetts. 1888
Size: 20¼ × 21⅜ in. (51.6 × 54.4 cm.)
Artist:
Lithographer:
Printer:
Publisher: O. H. Bailey and Co., Boston
Key/Vignettes/Misc: Refs. 1–18; 9 vignettes
Locations: BPL–R
Catalogs/Checklists:

1633
Place: South Framingham, Massachusetts
Date: 1882
Title: South Framingham, Massachusetts. 1882
Size: 19⅝ × 25¼ in. (49.9 × 64.3 cm.)
Artist:
Lithographer:
Printer:
Publisher: O. H. Bailey & Co., Boston
Key/Vignettes/Misc: Refs. 1–47; 4 vignettes
Locations: BPL–R
Catalogs/Checklists:

1634
Place: South Framingham, Massachusetts
Date: 1898
Title: South Framingham, Massachusetts. 1898
Size: 22⅜ × 31⅛ in. (57 × 79.2 cm.)
Artist:
Lithographer:
Printer: O. H. Bailey & Co. Boston
Publisher: O. H. Bailey & Co. Boston
Key/Vignettes/Misc: Refs. A, 2–45; 34 vignettes
Locations: MSL–B
Catalogs/Checklists:

Place: South Hadley Falls, Massachusetts
Date: 1856
See Holyoke, Massachusetts, 1856.

Place: South Hadley Falls, Massachusetts
Date: 1881
See Holyoke, Massachusetts, 1881.

1635
Place: South Weymouth, Massachusetts
Date: 1885

Title: South Weymouth, Norfolk County, Mass. 1885 From the Fair Grounds.
Size: 19¼ × 23¾ in. (49 × 63 cm.)
Artist: C. E. Jorgensen
Lithographer:
Printer: Geo. H. Walker & Co., Boston
Publisher: A. F. Poole & Co., Brockton, Mass.
Key/Vignettes/Misc: Refs. A–Z, 1–23
Locations: BPL–R; LC–M
Catalogs/Checklists: LC–M, 323

1636
Place: Southboro, Massachusetts
Date: 1887
Title: Southville and Coroaville, Massachusetts.1887
Size: 19¼ × 25¾ in. (49 × 65.5 cm.)
Artist:
Lithographer:
Printer: O. H. Bailey & Co. Boston
Publisher: O. H. Bailey & Co. Boston
Key/Vignettes/Misc: Refs. 1–4, A–E
Locations: MSL–B; BPL–R
Catalogs/Checklists:

1637
Place: Southbridge, Massachusetts
Date: 1878
Title: View of Southbridge, Mass., Center & Globe Village, 1878
Size: 22³⁄₁₆ × 26⅝ in. (56.5 × 67.8 cm.)
Artist:
Lithographer:
Printer: Beck and Pauli, Lith., Mil.[waukee]
Publisher: J. L. Galt and Co., 111 Liberty St., New York
Key/Vignettes/Misc: Refs. 1–40; 5 vignettes
Locations: BPL–R
Catalogs/Checklists:

Place: Southville, Massachusetts
Date: 1887
See Southboro, Massachusetts, 1887.

1638
Place: Spencer, Massachusetts
Date: 1877
Title: Spencer, Mass. 1877.
Size: 20 × 24½ in. (50.9 × 62.4 cm.)
Artist: O. H. Bailey & J. C. Hazen
Lithographer:
Printer:
Publisher: O. H. Bailey & J. C. Hazen, Boston
Key/Vignettes/Misc: Refs. A–H, J–N, P, R–T, V–Z; 2 vignettes
Locations: AAS–W; BPL–R; LC–M
Catalogs/Checklists: LC–M, 324

1639
Place: Spencer, Massachusetts
Date: 1892
Title: Spencer, Massachusetts. 1892
Size: 19¹³⁄₁₆ × 24¾ in. (50.4 × 63 cm.)
Artist:
Lithographer:
Printer: O. H. Bailey & Co. Boston
Publisher: O. H. Bailey & Co. Boston
Key/Vignettes/Misc: Refs. A, 2–29; 24 vignettes

Locations: MSL–B
Catalogs/Checklists:

1640
Place: Springfield, Massachusetts
Date: [1847–49]
Title: View of Springfield from Long Hill.
Size: 9½ × 13¹¹⁄₁₆ in. (24.1 × 34.4 cm.)
Artist: C. W. King
Lithographer:
Printer: Sharp, Peirce & Co. Boston
Publisher:
Key/Vignettes/Misc:
Locations: BA
Catalogs/Checklists:

1641
Place: Springfield, Massachusetts
Date: 1850
Title: Springfield. 1850
Size: 20⁵⁄₁₆ × 35⅞ in. (51.7 × 91.3 cm.)
Artist:
Lithographer: D. W. Moody
Printer: Sarony & Major, New York
Publisher: Smith Brothers & Co. New
York
Key/Vignettes/Misc:
Locations: NYP–S; LC–P
Catalogs/Checklists: Stokes 1850—G–8

1642
Place: Springfield, Massachusetts
Date: [185–?]
Title: Springfield, Mass.
Size: 12⅜ × 18⅝ in. (31.5 × 47.4 cm.)
Artist:
Lithographer:
Printer:
Publisher:
Key/Vignettes/Misc: 3 vignettes
Locations: BA
Catalogs/Checklists:

1643
Place: Springfield, Massachusetts
Date: 1875
Title: View of Springfield, Mass. 1875
Size: 26⅞ × 35 in. (68.4 × 89.1 cm.)
Artist: O. H. Bailey & Co.
Lithographer:
Printer:
Publisher: O. H. Bailey & Co.
Key/Vignettes/Misc: Refs. 1–67; 4
vignettes
Locations: BPL–R; LC–M
Catalogs/Checklists: LC–M, 325

1644
Place: Springfield, Massachusetts
Date: 1875
Title: View of Springfield, Mass. 1875
Size: 21⅞ × 35³⁄₁₆ in. (55.7 × 89.5 cm.)
Artist:
Lithographer:
Printer:
Publisher: Whitney & Adams
Key/Vignettes/Misc: Refs. 1–67; 4
vignettes
Locations: CHS–C; NYH–NY
Catalogs/Checklists:

1645
Place: Stoneham, Massachusetts
Date: 1878

Title: View of Stoneham, Mass.
Size: 19 × 25¼ in. (48.4 × 64.3 cm.)
Artist: O. H. Bailey & J. C. Hazen
Lithographer: J. Knauber & Co.
Printer: J. Knauber & Co., Milwaukee,
Wis.
Publisher: O. H. Bailey & J. C. Hazen,
Boston
Key/Vignettes/Misc: Refs. A–H, J–M
Locations: BPL–R
Catalogs/Checklists:

1646
Place: Stoughton, Massachusetts
Date: 1879
Title: Stoughton, Mass. 1879.
Size: 19⅞ × 25⅜ in. (50.6 × 64.6 cm.)
Artist: O. H. Bailey & J. C. Hazen
Lithographer:
Printer:
Publisher: O. H. Bailey and J. C. Hazen,
Boston
Key/Vignettes/Misc: Refs. A–H, J–P, S; 1
vignette
Locations: AAS–W; BPL–R; BA
Catalogs/Checklists:

1647
Place: Stoughton, Massachusetts
Date: 1890
Title: Stoughton, Massachusetts. 1890.
Size: 21 × 26¾ in. (53.5 × 68.1 cm.)
Artist:
Lithographer:
Printer: O. H. Bailey & Co., Boston
Publisher: O. H. Bailey & Co., Boston
Key/Vignettes/Misc: Refs. A, 2–32; 22
vignettes; unnumbered business directory
Locations: BPL–R
Catalogs/Checklists:

1648
Place: Sturbridge, Massachusetts
Date: 1892
Title: Sturbridge and Fiskdale,
Massachusetts. 1892
Size: 16 × 30¾ in. (40.8 × 78.2 cm.)
Artist:
Lithographer:
Printer:
Publisher: [O. H. Bailey & Co. Boston?]
Key/Vignettes/Misc: Refs. A, 2–20; 30
vignettes
Locations: MSL–B
Catalogs/Checklists:

1649
Place: Swampscott, Massachusetts
Date: 1856
Title: Swampscott Mass.
Size: 12⅝ × 15½ in. (32.2 × 39.4 cm.)
Artist: J. B. Bachelder
Lithographer:
Printer: Endicott & Co., New York
Publisher: Jno. B. Bachelder 59 Beekman
St. New York
Key/Vignettes/Misc: Refs. 1–6
Locations: EI–S; AAS–W; BPL–P;
MAHS–B; BA
Catalogs/Checklists:

1650
Place: Swampscott, Massachusetts
Date: 1871

Title: Swampscott. Essex County, Mass.
View from Inner Edge of Phillips Point.
View from Lincoln House towards Lynn.
View from the Heights. . . .
Size: 16¹¹⁄₁₆ × 18⁷⁄₁₆ in. (42.5 × 46.9 cm.)
Artist: E. Burrill Jr., from photo by F. M.
Smith
Lithographer:
Printer: J. H. Bufford's Premium Lith,
Boston, Mass.
Publisher: J. L. Robinson (copyright)
Key/Vignettes/Misc: 4 views on a single
sheet
Locations: EI–S; BA; LC–P
Catalogs/Checklists:

1651
Place: Swampscott, Massachusetts
Date: 1871
Title: Swampscott, Essex County, Mass.
11 Miles from Boston, View from Red
Rock, Lynn.
Size: 14⅝ × 18 in. (37.2 × 45.8 cm.)
Artist: From a photograph by F. M. Smith
Lithographer:
Printer: J. H. Bufford's Premium Lith.
Publisher: J. L. Robinson
Key/Vignettes/Misc:
Locations: Unknown. See Old Print Shop
Portfolio, XXXVII, p. 63, No. 29
Catalogs/Checklists:

1652
Place: Taunton, Massachusetts
Date: 1875
Title: City of Taunton, Mass. 1875.
Size: 22 × 30¾ in. (56 × 78.2 cm.)
Artist: O. H. Bailey & Co.
Lithographer:
Printer: American Oleograph Co.,
Milwaukee
Publisher: O. H. Bailey & Co.
Key/Vignettes/Misc: Refs. 1–36; 5
vignettes
Locations: LC–M; BPL–R
Catalogs/Checklists: LC–M, 325.1

Place: The Farms, Massachusetts
Date: 1886
See Marblehead, Massachusetts, 1886.

1653
Place: Tisbury, Massachusetts
Date: 1853
Title: Vineyard Haven 1853—Front View
of the Village of Holmes' Hole, Martha's
Vineyard, Mass., 1853.
Size: 15½ × 27½ in. (38.5 × 70 cm.)
Artist: G. F. Danforth
Lithographer:
Printer: Moore & Crosby
Publisher:
Key/Vignettes/Misc:
Locations: Town Hall, Tisbury,
Massachusetts
Catalogs/Checklists:

1654
Place: Tisbury, Massachusetts
Date: 1856
Title: View of the Village of Holmes' Hole,
Martha's Vineyard, Mass. 1856
Size: 18³⁄₁₆ × 27¹⁵⁄₁₆ in. (46.3 × 71.1 cm.)
Artist: Wm. H. Sturtevant

Lithographer:
Printer: J. H. Bufford's Lith. 313
Washington St. Boston.
Publisher:
Key/Vignettes/Misc:
Locations: BA; Dukes County Historical
Society, Edgartown, Massachusetts;
NYH–NY
Catalogs/Checklists:

1655
Place: Tisbury, Massachusetts
Date: [189–?]
Title: Vineyard Haven, Duke's County.
Martha's Vineyard, Massachusetts. The
Popular Seaside Summer Resort.
Size: 15½ × 18 in. (39.4 × 45.8 cm.)
Artist:
Lithographer:
Printer:
Publisher: Geo. H. Walker & Co. Lith,
Boston
Key/Vignettes/Misc: Refs. A–J, L–V
Locations: AAS–W; BPL–R
Catalogs/Checklists:

1656
Place: Townsend, Massachusetts
Date: 1889
Title: Townsend Center, Mass.
Size: 13⅞ × 24⅜ in. (35.4 × 62.1 cm.)
Artist: Geo. E. Norris
Lithographer:
Printer: The Burleigh Lith. Est., Troy, N. Y.
Publisher: Geo. E. Norris, Brockton, Mass.
Key/Vignettes/Misc: Refs. A–V
Locations: BPL–R
Catalogs/Checklists:

1657
Place: Turners Falls, Massachusetts
Date: 1877
Title: Turners Falls, Mass. 1877
Size: 19¾ × 27¼ in. (50.3 × 69.4 cm.)
Artist:
Lithographer: C. H. Vogt & Co.
Printer:
Publisher: O. H. Bailey & Co., Boston
Key/Vignettes/Misc: Refs. 1–15; 3
vignettes
Locations: AAS–W; BPL–R; LC–M
Catalogs/Checklists: LC–M, 325.2

1658
Place: Upton, Massachusetts
Date: 1888
Title: Upton, Massachusetts. 1888
Size: 23¼ × 30¼ in. (59.2 × 77 cm.)
Artist:
Lithographer:
Printer:
Publisher: O. H. Bailey & Co., Boston
Key/Vignettes/Misc: Refs. A, 2–39; 18
vignettes
Locations: BPL–R
Catalogs/Checklists:

1659
Place: Uxbridge, Massachusetts
Date: 1880
Title: Uxbridge, Mass. 1880.
Size: 23½ × 24½ in. (59.9 × 62.3 cm.)
Artist:

Lithographer:
Printer: Beck & Pauli, Milwaukee, Wis.
Publisher: E. H. Bigelow, Framingham,
Mass.
Key/Vignettes/Misc: Refs. 1–39; 13
vignettes
Locations: AAS–W; LC–M
Catalogs/Checklists: LC–M, 326

Place: Vineyard Haven, Massachusetts
Date: 1853
See Tisbury, Massachusetts, 1853.

1660
Place: Wakefield, Massachusetts
Date: 1882
Title: View of Wakefield, Mass. 1882
Size: 19⅞ × 22¼ in. (50.6 × 56.6 cm.)
Artist: J. C. Hazen & E. H. Bigelow
Lithographer:
Printer: Beck & Pauli. Lith, Milwaukee,
Wis.
Publisher: J. C. Hazen & E. H. Bigelow,
Boston
Key/Vignettes/Misc: 2 vignettes
Locations: BPL–R
Catalogs/Checklists:

1661
Place: Walpole, Massachusetts
Date: 1882
Title: Walpole, Massachusetts. 1882.
Size: 20½ × 24⅜ in. (52.2 × 62 cm.)
Artist: J. M.
Lithographer:
Printer:
Publisher: O. H. Bailey & Co., Boston
Key/Vignettes/Misc: Refs. A–H, J–X; 5
vignettes
Locations: BPL–R
Catalogs/Checklists:

1662
Place: Waltham, Massachusetts
Date: 1877
Title: View of Waltham, Mass.
Size: 19⅞ × 25⅞ in. (50.6 × 65.9 cm.)
Artist: O. H. Bailey & Co.
Lithographer: C. H. Vogt
Printer: J. Knauber & Co.
Publisher: O. H. Bailey and Co., [Boston]
Key/Vignettes/Misc: Refs. 1–26
Locations: AAS–W; BPL–R
Catalogs/Checklists:

1663
Place: Waltham, Massachusetts
Date: 1898
Title: Waltham Massachusetts. 1898
Size: 23¹¹⁄₁₆ × 33⁷⁄₁₆ in. (60.3 × 85.1 cm.)
Artist:
Lithographer:
Printer: O. H. Bailey & Co. Boston
Publisher: O. H. Bailey & Co. Boston
Key/Vignettes/Misc: Refs. A, 2–58; 77
vignettes
Locations: MSL–B
Catalogs/Checklists:

1664
Place: Ware, Massachusetts
Date: 1837
Title: View of Ware Village, Mass. Taken

From Prospect Hill Near the Northampton
Road.
Size: 16¾ × 25⁵⁄₁₆ in. (42.6 × 67 cm.)
Artist: P. Anderson
Lithographer: R. Cooke
Printer: Moore's Lith. Boston
Publisher: Peter Anderson (copyright)
Key/Vignettes/Misc:
Locations: BA
Catalogs/Checklists:

1665
Place: Ware, Massachusetts
Date: 1878
Title: View of Ware, Mass. 1878
Size: 18⅛ × 25⅜ in. (46.1 × 64.6 cm.)
Artist:
Lithographer:
Printer: Beck & Pauli, Milwaukee, Wis.
Publisher: J. L. Galt & Co.
Key/Vignettes/Misc:
Locations: LC–M (photo)
Catalogs/Checklists: LC–M, 326.1

1666
Place: Wareham, Massachusetts
Date: 1885
Title: Onset Bay Grove, Wareham, Mass.
1885.
Size: 16⅞ × 23⅞ in. (42.9 × 60.8 cm.)
Artist:
Lithographer:
Printer: Geo. H. Walker & Co., Boston
Publisher: O. W. Walker, [Boston]
Key/Vignettes/Misc: Refs. A–Z; 1 vignette
Locations: BPL–R; LC–M
Catalogs/Checklists: LC–M, 327

1667
Place: Warren, Massachusetts
Date: 1879
Title: View of Warren, Mass. 1879.
Size: 19½ × 25³⁄₁₆ in. (49.7 × 64.1 cm.)
Artist: O. H. Bailey & Co.
Lithographer:
Printer:
Publisher: O. H. Bailey & Co., Boston
Key/Vignettes/Misc: Refs. 1–48
Locations: AAS–W; BPL–R; BA;
NYH–NY
Catalogs/Checklists:

1668
Place: Watertown, Massachusetts
Date: 1879
Title: View of Watertown, Mass. 1879
Size: 20 × 25⅝ in. (50.8 × 65.2 cm.)
Artist:
Lithographer:
Printer:
Publisher: O. H. Bailey & Co., Boston
Key/Vignettes/Misc: Refs. A–R; 2
vignettes
Locations: BPL–R
Catalogs/Checklists:

1669
Place: Watertown, Massachusetts
Date: 1898
Title: Watertown, Massachusetts. 1898.
Size: 17⅞ × 29⁹⁄₁₆ in. (45.5 × 75.3 cm.)
Artist:
Lithographer:

Printer: O. H. Bailey & Co. Boston
Publisher: O. H. Bailey & Co. Boston
Key/Vignettes/Misc: 28 vignettes
Locations: MSL−B
Catalogs/Checklists:

1670
Place: Webster, Massachusetts
Date: 1878
Title: View of Webster, Mass. 1878
Size: 22⅞ × 30⅞ in. (58.1 × 78.4 cm.)
Artist: I. J.
Lithographer:
Printer: Beck & Pauli
Publisher: J. L. Galt & Co. 111 Liberty
St., N. Y.
Key/Vignettes/Misc: Refs. 1−40; 5
vignettes
Locations: AAS−W; BPL−R
Catalogs/Checklists:

1671
Place: Webster, Massachusetts
Date: 1892
Title: Webster, Massachusetts 1892.
Size: 20¹³⁄₁₆ × 27⅛ in. (53 × 69 cm.)
Artist:
Lithographer:
Printer:
Publisher: O. H. Bailey & Co., Boston
Key/Vignettes/Misc: Refs. A, 2, 4−6, 10,
13−16, 18−35; 1 vignette
Locations: LC−M
Catalogs/Checklists: LC−M, 327.1

1672
Place: West Boylston, Massachusetts
Date: 1891
Title: West Boylston, Massachusetts. 1891.
Size: 17¼ × 26¾ in. (43.9 × 68.1 cm.)
Artist:
Lithographer:
Printer: O. H. Bailey & Co., Boston
Publisher: O. H. Bailey & Co., Boston
Key/Vignettes/Misc: Refs. A−H, J−R; 11
vignettes
Locations: AAS−W; BPL−R
Catalogs/Checklists:

1673
Place: West Medford, Massachusetts
Date: 1897
Title: West Medford, Massachusetts. 1897
Size: 16¼ × 25⅛ in. (41.4 × 64 cm.)
Artist:
Lithographer:
Printer: O. H. Bailey & Co., Boston
Publisher: O. H. Bailey & Co., Boston
Key/Vignettes/Misc: Refs. A, 2−21; 21
vignettes
Locations: BPL−R
Catalogs/Checklists:

1674
Place: West Medway, Massachusetts
Date: 1887
Title: West Medway, Massachusetts. 1887
Size: 19 × 25 in. (48.3 × 63.6 cm.)
Artist:
Lithographer:
Printer: O. H. Bailey & Co., Boston
Publisher: O. H. Bailey & Co., Boston

Key/Vignettes/Misc: Refs. A−H, J−Z,
2−4; 4 vignettes
Locations: BPL−R; LC−P; LC−M
Catalogs/Checklists: LC−M, 328.1

1675
Place: West Newbury, Massachusetts
Date: 1847
Title: [untitled fragment of lithograph laid
down on sheet with sky added in pencil]
Size:
Artist: John Appleton
Lithographer:
Printer:
Publisher:
Key/Vignettes/Misc:
Locations: EI−S
Catalogs/Checklists:

1676
Place: West Newton, Massachusetts
Date: 1890
Title: West Newton, Massachusetts.
Size: 19¾ × 25½ in. (50.3 × 64.9 cm.)
Artist:
Lithographer:
Printer: O. H. Bailey & Co., Boston
Publisher: O. H. Bailey & Co., Boston
Key/Vignettes/Misc: Refs. A, 2−31
Locations: BPL−R
Catalogs/Checklists:

1677
Place: Westborough, Massachusetts
Date: 1880
Title: Westboro, Mass. 1880
Size: 21⅝ × 23⅞ in. (57.6 × 60.8 cm.)
Artist:
Lithographer:
Printer: Beck & Pauli, Lith. Milwaukee,
Wis.
Publisher: E. H. Bigelow, Framingham,
Mass.
Key/Vignettes/Misc: Refs. 1−45; 8
vignettes
Locations: BPL−R
Catalogs/Checklists:

1678
Place: Westborough, Massachusetts
Date: 1888
Title: Westborough, Massachusetts. 1888.
Size: 23⅞ × 31⅞ in. (60.8 × 81.1 cm.)
Artist:
Lithographer:
Printer: O. H. Bailey & Co. Boston
Publisher: O. H. Bailey & Co. Boston
Key/Vignettes/Misc: Refs. A, 2−51; 22
vignettes
Locations: MSL−B; AAS−W; BPL−R
Catalogs/Checklists:

1679
Place: Westfield, Massachusetts
Date: 1875
Title: Westfield, Mass. 1875.
Size: 20¾ × 27⅞ in. (52.9 × 70.9 cm.)
Artist: O. H. Bailey & Co.
Lithographer: C. H. Vogt
Printer: J. Knauber & Co.
Publisher: O. H. Bailey & Co., Boston
Key/Vignettes/Misc: Refs. 1−21

Locations: BPL−R; LC−M
Catalogs/Checklists: LC−M, 327.2

1680
Place: Westford, Massachusetts
Date: 1886
Title: Westford, Mass. 1886.
Size: 11 × 19¹¹⁄₁₆ in. (28 × 50.1 cm.)
Artist:
Lithographer:
Printer: The Burleigh Lith. Est., Troy, N. Y.
Publisher: L. R. Burleigh, Troy, N. Y.
Key/Vignettes/Misc: Refs. 1−5
Locations: BPL−R; LC−M
Catalogs/Checklists: LC−M, 328

1681
Place: Westwood, Massachusetts
Date: 1898
Title: Westwood, Norfolk County, Mass.
1898.
Size: 14⁵⁄₁₆ × 20¾ in. (36.4 × 52.9 cm.)
Artist: Bert Poole
Lithographer:
Printer:
Publisher: The Bert Poole Co., Boston
Key/Vignettes/Misc: Refs. A−I, K−P, R
Locations: MSL−B
Catalogs/Checklists:

1682
Place: Weymouth, Massachusetts
Date: 1880
Title: Weymouth, Mass. 1880
Size: 20⁷⁄₁₆ × 23¾ in. (52 × 60.4 cm.)
Artist: F. F.
Lithographer:
Printer: Beck & Pauli Lith, Milwaukee,
Wis.
Publisher: E. H. Bigelow, Framingham,
Mass.
Key/Vignettes/Misc: Ref. Q; 1 vignette
Locations: AAS−W; BPL−R
Catalogs/Checklists:

1683
Place: Whitinsville, Massachusetts
Date: 1891
Title: Whitinsville, Massachusetts. 1891
Size: 22¼ × 26⅞ in. (56.6 × 68.4 cm.)
Artist:
Lithographer:
Printer: O. H. Bailey & Co., Boston
Publisher: O. H. Bailey & Co., Boston
Key/Vignettes/Misc: Refs. A, 2−19
Locations: AAS−W; BPL−R
Catalogs/Checklists:

1684
Place: Whitman, Massachusetts
Date: 1889
Title: Whitman, Massachusetts. 1889
Size: 20⅝ × 30⅞ in. (52.5 × 78.6 cm.)
Artist:
Lithographer:
Printer: O. H. Bailey & Co., Boston
Publisher: O. H. Bailey & Co., Boston
Key/Vignettes/Misc: Refs. A, 2−47; 24
vignettes
Locations: BPL−R
Catalogs/Checklists:

1685
Place: Williamstown, Massachusetts
Date: Ca. 1846
Title: View of Williamstown Mass.
Size: 13⅞ × 16⅜ in. (35.3 × 41.7 cm.)
Artist: E. Valois
Lithographer: E. Valois
Printer: E. Valois 89 7th Ave. New York
Publisher:
Key/Vignettes/Misc: 8 vignettes
Locations: BA
Catalogs/Checklists:

1686
Place: Williamstown, Massachusetts
Date: [1855–56]
Title: Williamstown, Mass. As seen from Stone Hill
Size: 15¾ × 26⅜ in. (40.1 × 67.1 cm.)
Artist: George Yeomans
Lithographer:
Printer: P. S. Duval & Co., Philadelphia
Publisher:
Key/Vignettes/Misc:
Locations: NYP–S
Catalogs/Checklists: Stokes C. 1855–56—G–47

1687
Place: Williamstown, Massachusetts
Date: 1889
Title: Williamstown, Mass.
Size: 17⅝ × 28 9/16 in. (44.8 × 72.7 cm.)
Artist: L. R. Burleigh
Lithographer:
Printer: Burleigh Lith. Est., Troy, N. Y.
Publisher: L. R. Burleigh, Troy,N.Y.
Key/Vignettes/Misc: Refs. 1–35 & 1–4
Locations: BPL–R; LC–M
Catalogs/Checklists: LC–M, 329

1688
Place: Winchendon, Massachusetts
Date: 1860
Title: Winchendon, Mass, 1860, From Residence of Henry Wyman
Size: 17⅞ × 29⅛ in. (45.5 × 74.1 cm.)
Artist: R. M. Shurtleff
Lithographer:
Printer: J. H. Bufford's Lith. 383 Washington St. Boston
Publisher:
Key/Vignettes/Misc:
Locations: BA; Winchendon Historical Society, Winchendon, Massachusetts
Catalogs/Checklists:

1689
Place: Winchendon, Massachusetts
Date: 1878
Title: View of Winchendon, Mass. 1878
Size: 18¾ × 23⅛ in. (47.8 × 58.9 cm.)
Artist: O. H. Bailey & J. C. Hazen
Lithographer:
Printer:
Publisher: O. H. Bailey & J. C. Hazen, Boston
Key/Vignettes/Misc: Refs. A–H, J–P, R–T
Locations: BPL–R; Winchendon Historical Society, Winchendon,

Massachusetts
Catalogs/Checklists:

1690
Place: Winchester, Massachusetts
Date: 1886
Title: Winchester, Middlesex County, Mass. 1886.
Size: 19¼ × 26⅛ in. (49 × 66.5 cm.)
Artist: A. F. P. [Albert F. Poole?]
Lithographer:
Printer: Geo. H. Walker & Co.
Publisher: A. F. Poole and Co., Brockton, Mass.
Key/Vignettes/Misc: Refs. 1–34
Locations: BPL–R
Catalogs/Checklists:

1691
Place: Winchester, Massachusetts
Date: 1898
Title: Winchester, Massachusetts 1898.
Size: 16⅞ × 25 15/16 in. (43 × 66 cm.)
Artist: Robbins
Lithographer:
Printer: Heliotype Co., Boston
Publisher: Robbins & Enrich
Key/Vignettes/Misc: Refs. 1–11; 9 vignettes
Locations: LC–M
Catalogs/Checklists: LC–M, 330

1692
Place: Winthrop, Massachusetts
Date: Ca. 1894
Title: Winthrop, Mass.
Size: 15 × 24½ in. (37 × 61 cm.)
Artist:
Lithographer:
Printer:
Publisher: Bert [Albert F.] Poole
Key/Vignettes/Misc:
Locations: LC–M
Catalogs/Checklists: LC–M, 331

1693
Place: Woburn, Massachusetts
Date: Ca. 1860
Title: View of Woburn, Mass. From Academy Hill. In 1820
Size: 16 × 22 in. (40.7 × 56 cm.)
Artist: Bowen Buckman
Lithographer: M. M. Tidd
Printer:
Publisher: Hastings & Parker
Key/Vignettes/Misc: Refs. 1–33 on separately printed key with outline drawing of view
Locations: NYP–S; SSBT–B; BA; YUAG–NH; LC–P; NYH–NY
Catalogs/Checklists:

1694
Place: Woburn, Massachusetts
Date: 1863
Title: Horn Pond and Environs of Boston, Taken From Rag Rock in Woburn, Embracing Scenes and Objects in Twenty Different Towns.
Size: 18½ × 24 13/16 in. (47.1 × 63.2 cm.)
Artist: F. Richardson

Lithographer: J. F. Cole
Printer: J. Mayer & Co. 97 State St. Boston
Publisher: F. Richardson, 19 Tremont Row, Boston
Key/Vignettes/Misc: Refs. 1–54 on separately printed key with outline drawing of view
Locations: BA
Catalogs/Checklists:

1695
Place: Woburn, Massachusetts
Date: 1883
Title: Woburn, Mass., 1883
Size: 18 1/16 × 31 13/16 in. (46 × 81 cm.)
Artist: L. R. Burleigh
Lithographer: J. Lyth
Printer:
Publisher: D. Mason & Co., Syracuse, N. Y.
Key/Vignettes/Misc:
Locations: LC–M
Catalogs/Checklists: LC–M, 331.1

1696
Place: Wollaston, Massachusetts
Date: 1890
Title: Wollaston, Massachusetts. 1890
Size: 19¾ × 26⅜ in. (50.3 × 67.2 cm.)
Artist:
Lithographer:
Printer: O. H. Bailey & Co. Boston
Publisher: O. H. Bailey & Co. Boston
Key/Vignettes/Misc: Refs. A–D, 2–34; 20 vignettes
Locations: MSL–B; BPL–R; LC–M (facsimile)
Catalogs/Checklists: LC–M, 331.2

1697
Place: Worcester, Massachusetts
Date: [1837?]
Title: View of Worcester, Mass. Taken from Union Hill
Size: 19¾ × 27 11/16 in. (50.3 × 70.5 cm.)
Artist: P.[eter] Anderson
Lithographer: R. Cooke
Printer: T. Moore's Lithography, Boston
Publisher:
Key/Vignettes/Misc:
Locations: NYP–S; EI–S; AAS–W; BA; LC–P
Catalogs/Checklists: Stokes P. 1837–38—F–51

1698
Place: Worcester, Massachusetts
Date: 1849
Title: View of Worcester, Mass. From the Insane Hospital
Size: 19 7/16 × 37 9/16 in. (49.5 × 95.6 cm.)
Artist: E. Whitefield
Lithographer: E. Whitefield
Printer: Buchanan & Co., 128 Fulton St., New York
Publisher: E. Whitefield, N. Y.
Key/Vignettes/Misc: 4 vignettes
Locations: AAS–W; BA
Catalogs/Checklists: Norton, Whitefield, No. 44

1699
Place: Worcester, Massachusetts
Date: 1858
Title: Worcester Mass.
Size: 12⅝ × 15⅞ in. (32 × 40.2 cm.)
Artist: J. B. Bachelder
Lithographer:
Printer: Endicott & Co.
Publisher: J.B. Bachelder, 59 Beekman St., N. Y.
Key/Vignettes/Misc: Refs. 1–4; 1 vignette
Locations: AAS–W; MAHS–B; BA
Catalogs/Checklists:

1700
Place: Worcester, Massachusetts
Date: 1864
Title: City of Worcester Mass.
Size: 18⅛ × 31⅝ in. (46 × 80.4 cm.)
Artist: Photgr. by Black & Batchelder
Lithographer:
Printer: J. H. Bufford's Lith
Publisher: D. B. Tarr, Boston
Key/Vignettes/Misc:
Locations: AAS–W; CHS–C
Catalogs/Checklists:

1701
Place: Worcester, Massachusetts
Date: 1878
Title: The City of Worcester, Mass. 1878
Size: 25¾ × 33¾ in. (65.6 × 85.9 cm.)
Artist: O. H. Bailey & J. C. Hazen
Lithographer:
Printer: Beck & Pauli [Milwaukee]
Publisher: O. H. Bailey & J. C. Hazen, Boston
Key/Vignettes/Misc: Refs. A–B, 2–51
Locations: AAS–W; BPL–R
Catalogs/Checklists:

1702
Place: Wrentham, Massachusetts
Date: 1888
Title: Wrentham, Massachusetts. 1888
Size: 18 × 25¼ in. (45.8 × 64.3 cm.)
Artist:
Lithographer:
Printer: O. H. Bailey & Co., Boston
Publisher: O. H. Bailey & Co., Boston
Key/Vignettes/Misc: Refs. 1–19; 9 vignettes
Locations: BPL–R
Catalogs/Checklists:

1703
Place: Adrian, Michigan
Date: 1866
Title: Adrian, Michigan. 1866.
Size: 22 × 34 in. (56 × 86.4 cm.)
Artist: A. Ruger
Lithographer:
Printer: Chicago Lithographing Company [Chicago]
Publisher: A. Ruger, Battle Creek, Mich.
Key/Vignettes/Misc: Refs. 1–15; 11 vignettes
Locations: LC–M; MHSA–L
Catalogs/Checklists: Cumming; LC–M, 332

1704
Place: Adrian, Michigan
Date: 1889
Title: Adrian, Michigan. 1889.
Size: 18⅜ × 36 in. (46.7 × 91.5 cm.)
Artist: C. J. Pauli
Lithographer:
Printer:
Publisher: C. J. Pauli, Milwaukee
Key/Vignettes/Misc: Refs. 1–81; 2 vignettes
Locations: CMU–MP
Catalogs/Checklists: Cumming

1705
Place: Albion, Michigan
Date: [1866]
Title: Birds Eye View of the City of Albion, Calhoun County, Michigan.
Size: 19¼ × 28 in. (48.3 × 71.2 cm.)
Artist: A. Ruger
Lithographer:
Printer:
Publisher: A. Ruger, Battle Creek, Michigan
Key/Vignettes/Misc: Refs. 1–12
Locations: CMU–MP; Albion Historical Society, Albion, Michigan; MHC; LC–M
Catalogs/Checklists: Cumming; LC–M, 333

1706
Place: Allegan, Michigan
Date: N.D.
Title: Allegann in 1840; After a Sketch from Nature by O. O. Goodrich.
Size: 6 × 12 in. (15.2 × 30.4 cm.)
Artist: O. O. Goodrich
Lithographer:
Printer: O. H. Krumbism
Publisher:
Key/Vignettes/Misc:
Locations: Allegan, Michigan, Public Library
Catalogs/Checklists: Cumming

1707
Place: Alma, Michigan
Date: 1885
Title: Alma, Michigan, 1885.
Size: 12 × 22 in. (30.4 × 55.9 cm.)
Artist:
Lithographer:
Printer:
Publisher: O. H. Bailey & Co., Boston
Key/Vignettes/Misc: Refs. 1–24; 3 vignettes
Locations: CMU–MP; Alma, Michigan, Public Library
Catalogs/Checklists: Cumming

1708
Place: Alpena, Michigan
Date: 1880
Title: Alpena, Michigan, 1880.
Size: 20 × 33 in. (50.8 × 84 cm.)
Artist:
Lithographer:
Printer:
Publisher:
Key/Vignettes/Misc: Refs. 1–36
Locations: CMU–MP
Catalogs/Checklists: Cumming

1709
Place: Ann Arbor, Michigan
Date: 1853
Title: Ann Arbor
Size: 7¾ × 13 in. (19.7 × 33.1 cm.)
Artist: R. Burger
Lithographer: R. Burger
Printer: R. Burger, Detroit
Publisher: R. Burger, Detroit
Key/Vignettes/Misc:
Locations: MHC–AA
Catalogs/Checklists:

1710
Place: Ann Arbor, Michigan
Date: 1866
Title: Ann Arbor, Michigan, 1866.
Size: 20¾ × 20⅛ in. (52.7 × 51.1 cm.)
Artist: A. Ruger
Lithographer:
Printer: Chicago Lithographing Company [Chicago]
Publisher: A. Ruger
Key/Vignettes/Misc: Refs. 1–18; 10 vignettes
Locations: MHC–AA; CHS–C
Catalogs/Checklists: Cumming

1711
Place: Ann Arbor, Michigan
Date: 1874
Title: University of Michigan.
Size: 17 × 23⅞ in. (43.2 × 60.7 cm.)
Artist: Clarence L. Smith
Lithographer:
Printer: Duval & Hunter, Philadelphia
Publisher: Everts & Stewart (copyright)
Key/Vignettes/Misc:
Locations: MHC; LC–P
Catalogs/Checklists: Cumming

1712
Place: Ann Arbor, Michigan
Date: 1880
Title: Panoramic View of the City of Ann Arbor, Washtenaw Co., Michigan. 1880.
Size: 14¾ × 27 in. (37.5 × 68.6 cm.)
Artist: [Albert Ruger]
Lithographer:
Printer: Beck and Pauli, Milwaukee, Wis.
Publisher: J. J. Stoner, Madison, Wis.
Key/Vignettes/Misc: Refs. 1–52, X
Locations: CMU–MP; LC–M; MCH–AA
Catalogs/Checklists: Cumming; LC–M, 334

1713
Place: Ann Arbor, Michigan
Date: 1881
Title: University of Michigan, Ann Arbor. 1881.
Size: 15¾ × 23 in. (40 × 58.4 cm.)
Artist: A. Ruger
Lithographer:
Printer: Beck and Pauli, Milwakee, Wis.
Publisher: J. J. Stoner, Madison, Wis.
Key/Vignettes/Misc: 9 vignettes

Locations: CMU–MP; MHC; LC–P
Catalogs/Checklists: Cumming

1714
Place: Ann Arbor, Michigan
Date: 1890
Title: Ann Arbor, Michigan, 1890.
Size: 12⁹⁄₁₆ × 21⁵⁄₁₆ in. (32 × 54.3 cm.)
Artist: C. J. Pauli
Lithographer:
Printer:
Publisher: C. J. Pauli
Key/Vignettes/Misc: Refs. 1–76; 9
vignettes
Locations: MCH–AA
Catalogs/Checklists: Cumming

1715
Place: Au Sable, Michigan
Date: 1880
Title: Au Sable and Oscoda, Michigan,
1880.
Size: 17 × 28 in. (43.2 × 71.1 cm.)
Artist: H. Brosius
Lithographer:
Printer: Beck & Pauli, Milwaukee, Wis.
Publisher: J. J. Stoner, Madison, Wis.
Key/Vignettes/Misc: Refs. 1–23
Locations: CMU–MP
Catalogs/Checklists: Cumming

1716
Place: Bangor, Michigan
Date: 1880
Title: Bangor, Van Buren County,
Michigan, 1880.
Size: 9⅞ × 21¹⁵⁄₁₆ in. (25.1 × 55.8 cm.)
Artist:
Lithographer:
Printer: Beck & Pauli Lith. Milwaukee,
Wis.
Publisher: J. J. Stoner, Madison, Wis.
Key/Vignettes/Misc: Refs. 1–21
Locations: CMU–MP; UML–AA
Catalogs/Checklists: Cumming

1717
Place: Battle Creek, Michigan
Date: [1866]
Title: Birds Eye View of the City, Battle
Creek, Calhoun, Co., Mich.
Size: 13 × 18 in. (33 × 45.8 cm.)
Artist: A. Ruger
Lithographer: A. Ruger
Printer:
Publisher: A. Ruger
Key/Vignettes/Misc:
Locations: Willard Library, Battle Creek,
Michigan; LC–M
Catalogs/Checklists: Cumming; LC–M,
335

1718
Place: Battle Creek, Michigan
Date: [1870?]
Title: Mill & Manufacturing
Establishments of the City of Battle Creek,
Calhoun County, Michigan.
Size: 12¾ × 20⅛ in. (32.4 × 51.1 cm.)
Artist: A. Ruger
Lithographer:

Printer:
Publisher: A. Ruger
Key/Vignettes/Misc: 3 vignettes;
advertisements
Locations: CHS–C; LC–M
Catalogs/Checklists: Cumming;
LC–M, 336

1719
Place: Battle Creek, Michigan
Date: [188–?]
Title: [Battle Creek.]
Size: 26 × 41 in. (66 × 101.2 cm.)
Artist:
Lithographer:
Printer:
Publisher:
Key/Vignettes/Misc: Bottom of sheet
cropped eliminating title and other
information
Locations: LC–M
Catalogs/Checklists: Cumming; LC–M,
337

1720
Place: Bay City, Michigan
Date: 1867
Title: Bird's Eye View of Bay City,
Portsmouth, Wenona & Salzburg. Bay Co.
Michigan 1867.
Size: 19¾ × 28 in. (50.3 × 71.2 cm.)
Artist: A. Ruger
Lithographer:
Printer: Chicago Lithographing Co.
[Chicago]
Publisher:
Key/Vignettes/Misc: Refs. 1–12
Locations: LC–M; MM–NN; Bay City,
Michigan, Public Library
Catalogs/Checklists: LC–M, 338;
Cumming

1721
Place: Bay City, Michigan
Date: 1879
Title: Panoramic View of the City of Bay
City Bay County, Michigan 1879.
Size: 17⅝ × 32¼ in. (45 × 82 cm.)
Artist: A. Ruger
Lithographer:
Printer: Beck & Pauli, Lith. Milwaukee,
Wis.
Publisher: J. J. Stoner, Madison, Wis.
Key/Vignettes/Misc: Refs. 1–71, A–T; 4
vignettes
Locations: CMU–MP; Bay County
Museum, Bay City, Michigan; Museum of
the Great Lakes, Bay City, Michigan
Catalogs/Checklists: Cumming

1722
Place: Bay City, Michigan
Date: 1890
Title: Bay City, Mich., 1890 Looking East
Size: 24⅜ × 39⁵⁄₁₆ in. (62 × 100 cm.)
Artist: Clemens J. Pauli
Lithographer:
Printer:
Publisher: Clemens J. Pauli
Key/Vignettes/Misc: Refs. 1–64; 1
vignette

Locations: Museum of the Great Lakes,
Bay City, Michigan
Catalogs/Checklists:

1723
Place: Belding, Michigan
Date: 1880
Title: Bird's Eye View of Belding, Ionia
Co., Michigan. 1880.
Size: 8¼ × 20½ in. (20.9 × 52.1 cm.)
Artist: H. Brosius
Lithographer:
Printer: Beck & Pauli, Milwaukee, Wis.
Publisher: J. J. Stoner, Madison, Wis.
Key/Vignettes/Misc: Refs. 1–28
Locations: CMU–MP; Alvah N. Belding
Library, Belding, Michigan; UML–AA
Catalogs/Checklists: Cumming

1724
Place: Benton Harbor, Michigan
Date: 1870
Title: Birds Eye View of Benton Harbor,
Michigan, The Great Peach Region, 1870.
Size: 17¹¹⁄₁₆ × 15⁵⁄₁₆ in. (45 × 39 cm.)
Artist:
Lithographer:
Printer: Merchants Lithographing Co.,
Chicago
Publisher: D. D. Morse
Key/Vignettes/Misc: Refs. 1–12; 1
vignette
Locations: Benton Harbor, Michigan,
Public Library
Catalogs/Checklists:

1725
Place: Benton Harbor, Michigan
Date: 1889
Title: Benton Harbor, Mich. 1889.
Looking North West.
Size: 23 × 29 in. (58.4 × 73.7 cm.)
Artist: C. J. Pauli & Co.
Lithographer:
Printer:
Publisher: C. J. Pauli & Co., Milwaukee,
Wis.
Key/Vignettes/Misc: Refs. 1–37; 3
vignettes
Locations: LC–M
Catalogs/Checklists: LC–M, 339

1726
Place: Berrien Springs, Michigan
Date: [1870–75?]
Title: Berrien Springs, County Seat of
Berrien Co. Mich.
Size: 11 × 14⅜ in. (28 × 36.6 cm.)
Artist: D. D. Morse
Lithographer:
Printer: Lott & Zeuch, Lith. Chicago
Publisher: Berrien Springs Era
Key/Vignettes/Misc: Refs. A–C; 2
vignettes
Locations: Berrien County Historical
Association, Berrien Springs, Michigan
Catalogs/Checklists:

1727
Place: Bessemer, Michigan
Date: 1886
Title: Bird's Eye View of Bessemer, Mich.

Ontonagon County 1886.
Size: 10 × 16¾ in. (25.4 × 42.6 cm.)
Artist:
Lithographer:
Printer: Beck & Pauli, Litho. Milwaukee, Wis.
Publisher: Norris, Wellge & Co. Milwaukee
Key/Vignettes/Misc: Refs. 1–12, A–D, H, M–N, P; 4 vignettes
Locations: LC–M
Catalogs/Checklists: Cumming; LC–M, 340

1728
Place: Big Rapids, Michigan
Date: 1870
Title: Bird's Eye View of Big Rapids, Michigan 1870.
Size: 13 × 17½ in. (33 × 44.5 cm.)
Artist: E. S. Glover
Lithographer:
Printer: Merchants Lithographing Company, Chicago
Publisher:
Key/Vignettes/Misc: Refs.
Locations: Mecosta County Historical Society, Big Rapids, Michigan
Catalogs/Checklists: Cumming

1729
Place: Big Rapids, Michigan
Date: 1880
Title: Bird's Eye View of the City of Big Rapids, Mich. 1880.
Size: 9¼ × 19¾ in. (23.5 × 50.2 cm.)
Artist:
Lithographer:
Printer: Beck & Pauli, Milwaukee, Wis.
Publisher: J. J. Stoner, Madison, Wis.
Key/Vignettes/Misc: Refs.
Locations: MHC; Mecosta County Historical Society, Big Rapids, Michigan; UML–AA
Catalogs/Checklists: Cumming

1730
Place: Birmingham, Michigan
Date: 1881
Title: Panoramic View of Birmingham, Oakland Co., Michigan. 1881. Looking Southwest.
Size: 8 × 12 in. (20.3 × 30.5 cm.)
Artist:
Lithographer:
Printer: Beck & Pauli, Milwaukee, Wis.
Publisher: J. J. Stoner, Madison, Wis.
Key/Vignettes/Misc: Refs. 1–23
Locations: CMU–MP
Catalogs/Checklists: Cumming

1731
Place: Buchanan, Michigan
Date: 1873
Title: View of Buchanan, Michigan, 1873.
Size:
Artist: D. D. Morse
Lithographer:
Printer: Strobridge & Co.
Publisher:
Key/Vignettes/Misc:
Locations: Lemke Photographic Studio,

Buchanan, Michigan (photo)
Catalogs/Checklists:

1732
Place: Cadillac, Michigan
Date: 1882
Title: Cadillac, Mich.
Size: 14 × 18¾ in. (35.6 × 47.7 cm.)
Artist: Riley and Ricker
Lithographer:
Printer: Shober & Carqueville
Publisher:
Key/Vignettes/Misc: 12 vignettes
Locations: CMU–MP (photo); private collection
Catalogs/Checklists:

1733
Place: Calumet, Michigan
Date: 1881
Title: Calumet Hecla & Red Jacket Mich. 1881.
Size: 12½ × 24½ in. (31.8 × 62.4 cm.)
Artist: H. Wellge
Lithographer:
Printer: Beck & Pauli, Milwaukee, Wis.
Publisher: J. J. Stoner, Madison, Wis.
Key/Vignettes/Misc: Refs. 1–22, A–H, K–P, R–S, X
Locations: LC–M
Catalogs/Checklists: LC–M, 340.1

1734
Place: Caro, Michigan
Date: ?
Title:
Size:
Artist:
Lithographer:
Printer:
Publisher:
Key/Vignettes/Misc:
Locations: Indian Fields Township Library, Caro, Michigan
Catalogs/Checklists:

1735
Place: Charlevoix, Michigan
Date: 1889
Title: Charlevoix, Michigan, 1889.
Size: 15 × 21 in. (38.1 × 53.4 cm.)
Artist: Fred Lubow
Lithographer:
Printer: Hughes Lithographing Company
Publisher:
Key/Vignettes/Misc: Refs. 1–18
Locations: CMU–MP
Catalogs/Checklists: Cumming

1736
Place: Charlotte, Michigan
Date: 1870
Title: Birds Eye View of Charlotte Eaton Co. Mich. 1870.
Size: 16 × 20 in. (40.7 × 50.8 cm.)
Artist: Eli S. Glover
Lithographer:
Printer: Merchants Lithographing Co., Chicago
Publisher:
Key/Vignettes/Misc: Refs. 1–11
Locations: Private collection
Catalogs/Checklists: Cumming

1737
Place: Cheboygan, Michigan
Date: N.D.
Title: Cheboygan, Mich.
Size: 19 × 25 in. (48.3 × 63.5 cm.)
Artist:
Lithographer:
Printer: Shober and Carqueville
Publisher: Riley & Ricker
Key/Vignettes/Misc: Vignettes
Locations: Private collection
Catalogs/Checklists: Cumming

1738
Place: Chelsea, Michigan
Date: 1881
Title: Panoramic View of Chelsea, Washtenaw Co., Michigan. 1881. Looking South West.
Size: 9½ × 15½ in. (24.1 × 39.4 cm.)
Artist:
Lithographer:
Printer: Beck & Pauli, Milwaukee, Wis.
Publisher: J. J. Stoner, Madison, Wis.
Key/Vignettes/Misc: Refs. 1–34, A–F
Locations: UML–AA
Catalogs/Checklists: Cumming

1739
Place: Clare, Michigan
Date: 1884
Title: Clare, Mich. 1884.
Size: 16 × 22⅛ in. (40.7 × 56.4 cm.)
Artist: O. H. Bailey
Lithographer:
Printer:
Publisher: O. H. Bailey & Co., Boston
Key/Vignettes/Misc: Refs. 1–16; 2 vignettes
Locations: CMU–MP
Catalogs/Checklists:

1740
Place: Coldwater, Michigan
Date: Ca. 1868
Title: Birds Eye View of the City of Coldwater Branch Co. Michigan.
Size: 19 × 28½ in. (48.3 × 72.5 cm.)
Artist: A. Ruger
Lithographer:
Printer: Chicago Lithographing Co., 152–154 Clark, Chicago
Publisher: A. Ruger, Battle Creek, Michigan
Key/Vignettes/Misc: Refs. 1–14
Locations: CMU–MP; LC–M
Catalogs/Checklists: LC–M, 341; Cumming

1741
Place: Coldwater, Michigan
Date: 1883
Title: Panoramic View of the City of Coldwater Branch County, Michigan 1883.
Size: 27 × 29 in. (68.6 × 73.7 cm.)
Artist:
Lithographer:
Printer: Beck & Pauli, Lithographers, Milwaukee, Wis.
Publisher: J. J. Stoner, Madison, Wis.
Key/Vignettes/Misc: Refs. 1–36, A–F, H; 2 vignettes

Locations: LC–M (facsimile); private collection
Catalogs/Checklists: Cumming; LC–M, 341.2

1742
Place: Coleman, Michigan
Date: 1884
Title: Coleman, Michigan. 1884.
Size: 11 × 22 in. (28 × 56 cm.)
Artist:
Lithographer:
Printer:
Publisher: O. H. Bailey & Co., Boston
Key/Vignettes/Misc: Refs. 1–21; 2 vignettes
Locations: Midland County Historical Museum, Midland, Michigan; CMU–MP
Catalogs/Checklists: Cumming

1743
Place: Constantine, Michigan
Date: 1874
Title: View of Constantine, St. Joseph Co., Mich. 1874. The Most Extensive Water Power on the St. Joseph River.
Size: 13⅛ × 18⅜ in. (33.4 × 46.8 cm.)
Artist: D. D. Morse
Lithographer:
Printer:
Publisher: Strobridge & Company [Cincinnati]
Key/Vignettes/Misc: Refs. 1–11
Locations: CMU–MP
Catalogs/Checklists: Cumming

1744
Place: Corunna, Michigan
Date: 1881
Title: Panoramic View of Corunna County Seat of Shiawasse County, Michigan, 1881
Size: 9 × 18 in. (22.8 × 45.8 cm.)
Artist:
Lithographer:
Printer: Beck & Pauli, Lith., Milwaukee, Wis.
Publisher: J. J. Stoner, Madison, Wis.
Key/Vignettes/Misc: Refs.
Locations: Private collection
Catalogs/Checklists:

1745
Place: Decatur, Michigan
Date: 1875
Title: Birds Eye View of Decatur, Michigan, 1875. On the Michigan Central R. R., 116 Miles from Chicago.
Size: 13¼ × 18 in. (33.7 × 45.7 cm.)
Artist: D. D. Morse
Lithographer:
Printer: Strobridge & Company, Cincinnati
Publisher:
Key/Vignettes/Misc: Refs. 1–16
Locations: CMU–MP; Webster Memorial Library, Decatur, Michigan
Catalogs/Checklists: Cumming

1746
Place: Delhi Mills, Michigan
Date: N.D.
Title: Bird's Eye View of Delhi Mills, Scio Tp. (Washtenaw Co.)

Size: 10 × 15⅛ in. (25.5 × 38.5 cm.)
Artist:
Lithographer:
Printer:
Publisher:
Key/Vignettes/Misc: Refs. 1–44
Locations: MHC–AA
Catalogs/Checklists: Cumming

1747
Place: Detroit, Michigan
Date: [1834–38]
Title: View of the City of Detroit, M. T.
Size: 12¹¹⁄₁₆ × 19 in. (32.3 × 48.4 cm.)
Artist: C. F. Davis
Lithographer: A. Fleetwood
Printer: M. Bancroft, 389 Broadway, N. Y.
Publisher:
Key/Vignettes/Misc:
Locations: NYP–S; NYH–NY
Catalogs/Checklists: Stokes P. 1834—F–13; Cumming

1748
Place: Detroit, Michigan
Date: 1852
Title: Detroit in 1852
Size: 16¾ × 22³⁄₁₆ in. (42.6 × 56.5 cm.)
Artist: R. Burger
Lithographer: R. Burger
Printer:
Publisher: R. Burger & C. Dix, Detroit
Key/Vignettes/Misc: 20 vignettes
Locations: LC–P
Catalogs/Checklists: Cumming

1749
Place: Detroit, Michigan
Date: [1854–55]
Title: Detroit, Michigan
Size: 22½ × 39 in. (57.2 × 99.2 cm.)
Artist: George J. Robertson
Lithographer: Charles Parsons
Printer: Endicott & Co., N. Y.
Publisher: Smith Brothers & Company, 59 Beekman St. New York
Key/Vignettes/Misc:
Locations: MHC; Detroit Institute of Arts, Detroit, Michigan; CHS–C
Catalogs/Checklists: Cumming

1750
Place: Detroit, Michigan
Date: 1871
Title: Detroit in 1820, From an Original Sketch Made in 1820 by George W. Whistler, C. E., With View of "Walk–in–the–Water."
Size: 16¾ × 23¼ in. (42.6 × 59.1 cm.)
Artist: George W. Whistler
Lithographer:
Printer:
Publisher: Calvert Lithographing Company, Detr.
Key/Vignettes/Misc: 10 unnumbered refs.
Locations: CMU–MP; BDPL–D; CHS–C
Catalogs/Checklists: Cumming

1751
Place: Detroit, Michigan
Date: [1872?]
Title: Detroit in 1820, with View of "Walk–in–the–Water".

Size: 15⅝ × 22⅞ in. (39.7 × 55.8 cm.)
Artist:
Lithographer:
Printer: Corrie's Detroit Lithographic Office
Publisher:
Key/Vignettes/Misc:
Locations: CMU–MP; MTLB–T; YUAG–NH
Catalogs/Checklists: Stokes 1820—F–14; Cumming; Robertson, no. 144

1752
Place: Detroit, Michigan
Date: 1889
Title: All Roads Will Lead to Detroit in September. Why?
Size: 5¾ × 12¾ in. (13.9 × 32.4 cm.)
Artist:
Lithographer:
Printer: Calvert Lithographing Company, Detroit
Publisher:
Key/Vignettes/Misc:
Locations: CMU–MP; LC–M
Catalogs/Checklists: Cumming;

1753
Place: Detroit, Michigan
Date: [1889?]
Title: Bird's Eye View—Showing About Three Miles Square—of the Central Portion of the City of Detroit, Michigan.
Size: 11½ × 19½ in. (29.2 × 49.6 cm.)
Artist:
Lithographer:
Printer: Calvert Lith Co. Detroit
Publisher:
Key/Vignettes/Misc:
Locations: LC–M; LC–P
Catalogs/Checklists: Cumming; LC–M, 342

1754
Place: Detroit, Michigan
Date: 1891
Title: Bird's Eye View of Detroit, "The City of the Straits."
Size: 12¼ × 20¼ in. (31.1 × 51.5 cm.)
Artist:
Lithographer:
Printer: Poole Bros., Chicago
Publisher: Knight, Leonard & Company, Chicago, 1891
Key/Vignettes/Misc: Refs. 1–33
Locations: Lansing, Michigan, Public Library
Catalogs/Checklists: Cumming

1755
Place: Detroit, Michigan
Date: 1906
Title: [Principal Business Section of Detroit . . . .]
Size:
Artist:
Lithographer:
Printer:
Publisher: Hurd–Wheeler Co., Detroit (copyright)
Key/Vignettes/Misc:
Locations: LC–M (photo)
Catalogs/Checklists: LC–M, 342.1

1756
Place: Detroit, Michigan
Date: 1906
Title: Detroit 1818 & 1906
Size: 5½ × 9½ in. (8.5 × 24.1 cm.)
Artist:
Lithographer:
Printer:
Publisher: Hurd Wheeler & co., Detroit
Key/Vignettes/Misc:
Locations: LC–M (photo)
Catalogs/Checklists: LC–M, 343

1757
Place: Detroit, Michigan
Date: Ca. 1906
Title: [Business Section of Detroit]
Size:
Artist:
Lithographer:
Printer:
Publisher: Hurd–Wheeler Co., Detroit
(copyright)
Key/Vignettes/Misc:
Locations: LC–M (photo)
Catalogs/Checklists: LC–M, 343.1

1758
Place: Detroit, Michigan
Date: N.D.
Title: A View of Detroit, July 25th. 1794.
Size: 11¼ × 18 in. (28.7 × 45.8 cm.)
(photo)
Artist:
Lithographer:
Printer:
Publisher:
Key/Vignettes/Misc:
Locations: NYP–S (photo)
Catalogs/Checklists: Stokes 1794—
B–119; Cumming

1759
Place: Detroit, Michigan
Date: N.D.
Title: Detroit
Size: 4⅝ × 7⅝ in. (11.8 × 19.4 cm.)
Artist:
Lithographer:
Printer: Charles Magnus, New York
Publisher:
Key/Vignettes/Misc:
Locations: CMU–MP
Catalogs/Checklists: Cumming

1760
Place: Dowagiac, Michigan
Date: 1890
Title: Dowagiac, Cass Co., 1890.
Size: 18 × 30 in. (45.8 × 76.3 cm.)
Artist:
Lithographer:
Printer: C. J. Pauli
Publisher: C. J. Pauli
Key/Vignettes/Misc: Refs.
Locations: Private collection
Catalogs/Checklists: Cumming

1761
Place: Dowagiac, Michigan
Date: ?

Title: Birds Eye View of Dowagiac
Size:
Artist:
Lithographer:
Printer:
Publisher:
Key/Vignettes/Misc:
Locations: Unknown. Reproduced in W.
A. Norton's Directory of Dowagiac,
Cassapolis, and Lagrage,
Pokagon. . .Townships. A. B. Morse
Printers, St. Joseph, Michigan, 1899
Catalogs/Checklists:

1762
Place: East Saginaw, Michigan
Date: 1867
Title: East Saginaw. Michigan. 1867.
Size: 21⅝ × 28½ in. (55.1 × 72.5 cm.)
Artist: A. Ruger
Lithographer:
Printer: Chicago Lithographing Co. 152 &
154 Clark St. Chicago
Publisher: A. Ruger, Chicago
Key/Vignettes/Misc: Refs. 1–8
Locations: SCHS–S; CMU–MP
Catalogs/Checklists: Cumming

1763
Place: East Saginaw, Michigan
Date: [1866–71]
Title: East Saginaw, 1849.
Size: 9⅜ × 12 in. (23.8 × 30.6 cm.)
Artist:
Lithographer:
Printer: Chicago Lithographing Co.
[Chicago]
Publisher:
Key/Vignettes/Misc:
Locations: CHS–C
Catalogs/Checklists: Cumming

1764
Place: East Saginaw, Michigan
Date: 1885
Title: Cities of East Saginaw and Saginaw.
Michigan 1885
Size: 26⁹⁄₁₆ × 36⁵⁄₁₆ in. (75.3 × 92.4 cm.)
Artist:
Lithographer:
Printer: O. H. Bailey & Co. Boston
Publisher: O. H. Bailey & Co. Boston
Key/Vignettes/Misc: Refs., Saginaw, 1–13,
East Saginaw, 1–88, A–X; 34 vignettes
Locations: SCHS–S; CMU–MP; Hoyt
Public Library, Saginaw, Michigan; LC–M
(photo)
Catalogs/Checklists: Cumming; LC–M,
374

1765
Place: Escanaba, Michigan
Date: 1871
Title: Escanaba, Mich. 1871.
Size:
Artist:
Lithographer:
Printer:
Publisher:
Key/Vignettes/Misc:

Locations: MHC (photo)
Catalogs/Checklists: Cumming

1766
Place: Escanaba, Michigan
Date: 1881
Title: Escanaba, Mich. 1881
Size: 12 × 22¼ in. (30.6 × 56.6 cm.)
Artist:
Lithographer:
Printer: Beck & Pauli, Milwaukee, Wis.
Publisher: J. J. Stoner, Madison, Wis.
Key/Vignettes/Misc: 22 refs.; 1 vignette
Locations: LC–M (photo); BDPL–D
Catalogs/Checklists: Cumming; LC–M,
343.2

1767
Place: Fenton, Michigan
Date: 1880
Title: Bird's Eye View of Fenton, Genesee
County, Michigan. 1880.
Size: 16½ × 22 in. (42 × 55.9 cm.)
Artist: Joseph Warner
Lithographer:
Printer:
Publisher: J. J. Stoner, Madison, Wis.
Key/Vignettes/Misc: Refs. 1–28
Locations: CMU–MP; LC–M (photo)
Catalogs/Checklists: Cumming; LC–M,
344

Place: Ferrysburg, Michigan
Date: 1894
See Grand Haven, Michigan, 1894.

1768
Place: Flint, Michigan
Date: 1867
Title: Flint, Genessee Co., Michigan. 1867.
Size: 21⅜ × 28¼ in. (54.3 × 71.9 cm.)
Artist: A. Ruger
Lithographer:
Printer: Chicago Lithographing Company
[Chicago]
Publisher: A. Ruger
Key/Vignettes/Misc: Refs. 1–12; 4
vignettes
Locations: CMU–MP; A. P. Sloan
Panorama of Transportation,
Flint, Michigan; LC–M (photo)
Catalogs/Checklists: Cumming; LC–M,
345

1769
Place: Flint, Michigan
Date: 1880
Title: Panoramic View of the City of Flint,
Genessee County, Michigan, 1880.
Size: 15¼ × 26¾ in. (38.8 × 68 cm.)
Artist:
Lithographer:
Printer:
Publisher:
Key/Vignettes/Misc: Refs. 1–43, A–H, K
Locations: Sloan Panorama of
Transportation, Flint, Michigan; LC–M
(photo)
Catalogs/Checklists: LC–M, 346;
Cumming

1770

Place: Flint, Michigan
Date: 1890
Title: Flint Michigan 1890. Population 10,000. Looking East.
Size: 19 × 35 in. (48.3 × 89 cm.)
Artist: C. J. Pauli
Lithographer:
Printer:
Publisher: C. J. Pauli, Milwaukee
Key/Vignettes/Misc: Refs. 1–65; 4 vignettes
Locations: Flint, Michigan, Public Library; LC–M (photo)
Catalogs/Checklists: LC–M, 347; Cumming

Place: Franklin, Michigan
Date: 1873
See Ripley, Michigan, 1873.

1771

Place: Grand Haven, Michigan
Date: 1868
Title: Birds Eye View of the City of Grand Haven, Ottowa Co., Michigan, 1868
Size: 16¾ × 23⅞ in. (42.6 × 60.7 cm.)
Artist: A. Ruger
Lithographer:
Printer: Merchants Lithographing Company, Chicago
Publisher: E. S. Glover
Key/Vignettes/Misc: Refs. 1–10
Locations: Loutit Library, Grand Haven, Michigan; LC–M (photo)
Catalogs/Checklists: LC–M, 348; Cumming

1772

Place: Grand Haven, Michigan
Date: 1874
Title: Grand Haven, Ottawa County Michigan, 1874.
Size: 18¹/₁₆ × 23⅞ in. (45.8 × 60.6 cm.)
Artist:
Lithographer:
Printer: Chas. Shober & Co. Props. Chicago Lithographing Co. [Chicago]
Publisher: J. J. Stoner, Madison, Wis.
Key/Vignettes/Misc: Refs. 1–33; 1 vignette
Locations: LC–M; ACMW–FW; Loutit Library, Grand Haven, Michigan; CHS–C
Catalogs/Checklists: Cumming; LC–M, 349

1773

Place: Grand Haven, Michigan
Date: 1894
Title: Grand Haven, Mich., Spring Lake and Ferrysburg, 1894
Size: 20¹³/₁₆ × 34¹⁵/₁₆ in. (53 × 89 cm.)
Artist: Clemens J. Pauli
Lithographer: Clemens J. Pauli
Printer:
Publisher: Clemens J. Pauli
Key/Vignettes/Misc: Refs., Grand Haven, 1–48, Ferrysburg and Spring Lake, A–L; vignettes
Locations: Grand Haven, Michigan, Public Library
Catalogs/Checklists:

1774

Place: Grand Ledge, Michigan
Date: 1880
Title: Panoramic View of the Village of Grand Ledge, 1880.
Size:
Artist:
Lithographer:
Printer: Beck & Pauli, Milwaukee, Wis.
Publisher: J. J. Stoner, Madison, Wis.
Key/Vignettes/Misc:
Locations: MHC
Catalogs/Checklists:

1775

Place: Grand Ledge, Michigan
Date: 1881
Title: Panoramic View of the Village of Grand Ledge, Eaton Co., Michigan 1881.
Size: 11 × 19½ in. (27.9 × 49.6 cm.)
Artist:
Lithographer:
Printer: Beck & Pauli, Milwaukee, Wis.
Publisher: J. J. Stoner, Madison, Wis.
Key/Vignettes/Misc: Refs. 2–44, A–E
Locations: MHSA–L; LC–M (facsimile)
Catalogs/Checklists: LC–M, 349.1

1776

Place: Grand Rapids, Michigan
Date: 1860
Title: View of the City of Grand Rapids. Mich. in 1860. From the West
Size: 7⅞ × 32 in. (20 × 81.4 cm.)
Artist: From photographs by E. S. Wykes
Lithographer:
Printer: E. Mendel, Chicago
Publisher: C. F. Dietrich
Key/Vignettes/Misc:
Locations: GRPM–GR
Catalogs/Checklists: Cumming

1777

Place: Grand Rapids, Michigan
Date: 1868
Title: Grand Rapids Michigan 1868.
Size: 22 × 33⅞ in. (56 × 86.2 cm.)
Artist: A. Ruger
Lithographer:
Printer: Chicago Lithographing Co. 152 and 154 Clark St., Chicago
Publisher:
Key/Vignettes/Misc: Refs. 1–32
Locations: GRPM–GR; LC–M
Catalogs/Checklists: Cumming; LC–M, 350

1778

Place: Grand Rapids, Michigan
Date: 1874
Title: Grand Rapids Michigan. 1874
Size: 14½ × 27¹⁵/₁₆ in. (36.9 × 71.1 cm.)
Artist: [Herman Brosius?]
Lithographer:
Printer: Chas. Shober and Co. Props.
Chicago Lith. Co. [Chicago]
Publisher:
Key/Vignettes/Misc: Refs. a–u, 1–60
Locations: CMU–MP; GRPM–GR; MHC; LC–M
Catalogs/Checklists: Cumming

1779

Place: Grand Rapids, Michigan
Date: 1886
Title: Grand Rapids, Michigan. 1886.
Size: 28⅜ × 43¼ in. (72.2 × 110.1 cm.)
Artist:
Lithographer:
Printer: Cole and Demar, Grand Rapids
Publisher: Cole and Demar, Grand Rapids
Key/Vignettes/Misc: Refs. 1–32; 33 vignettes
Locations: GRPM–GR
Catalogs/Checklists: Cumming

Place: Gratiot, Michigan
Date: 1867
See Port Huron, Michigan, 1867.

1780

Place: Greenville, Michigan
Date: 1880
Title: Greenville, Moncalm Co. Michigan. 1880.
Size: 13 × 27½ in. (33 × 69.9 cm.)
Artist:
Lithographer:
Printer: Beck & Pauli Lith., Milwaukee, Wis.
Publisher: J. J. Stoner, Madison, Wis.
Key/Vignettes/Misc: Refs. A–H, 1–30
Locations: Flat River Historical Museum, Greenville, Michigan
Catalogs/Checklists: Cumming

1781

Place: Hancock, Michigan
Date: 1873
Title: Bird's Eye View of Hancock, L. S. Mich. 1873. Looking North West.
Size: 15⅝ × 22 in. (39.8 × 55.9 cm.)
Artist: A. J. Cleveland
Lithographer: C. H. Vogt
Printer: American Oleograph Co.
Publisher: A. J. Clevelwand, Milaukee
Key/Vignettes/Misc: Refs. 1–13, A–D
Locations: ACMW–FW; CMU–MP; HCHS–LL; Detroit Institute of Arts, Detroit, Michigan
Catalogs/Checklists: ACMW–FW 1028; Cumming

1782

Place: Hancock, Michigan
Date: 1881
Title: Hancock, Mich 1881 Population 3200
Size: 12⅜ × 24⅜ in. (31.5 × 62.1 cm.)
Artist: H. Wellge
Lithographer:
Printer: Beck & Pauli Lith., Milwaukee, Wis.
Publisher: J. J. Stoner, Madison, Wis.
Key/Vignettes/Misc: Refs.

Locations: HCHS—LL
Catalogs/Checklists:

1783
Place: Hancock, Michigan
Date: 1890
Title: Hancock, Mich Population 6000 1890
Size: 17 × 29¼ in. (43.3 × 74.4 cm.)
Artist: Edward Demar
Lithographer: Edward Demar
Printer:
Publisher: B. H. Pierce & Co., Hancock, Mich.
Key/Vignettes/Misc: Refs.; vignettes
Locations: HCHS—LL
Catalogs/Checklists:

1784
Place: Hart, Michigan
Date: 1880
Title: Birds Eye View of Hart, Mich., C. S., of Oceana County, 1880.
Size: 7⅜ × 18¼ in. (18.7 × 46.4 cm.)
Artist:
Lithographer:
Printer:
Publisher: J. J. Stoner, Madison, Wis.
Key/Vignettes/Misc: Refs.
Locations: Private collection
Catalogs/Checklists: Cumming

1785
Place: Hartford, Michigan
Date: 1880
Title: Hartford, Van Buren County, Michigan. 1880.
Size: 8 × 20 in. (20.3 × 50.8 cm.)
Artist:
Lithographer:
Printer: Beck and Pauli, Milwaukee, Wis.
Publisher: J. J. Stoner, Madison, Wis.
Key/Vignettes/Misc: Refs. 1–19
Locations: CMU—MP
Catalogs/Checklists: Cumming

1786
Place: Hastings, Michigan
Date: 1870
Title: Birds Eye View of Hastings, Barry Co., Mich. 1870.
Size: 13½ × 17⅛ in. (34.3 × 43.6 cm.)
Artist: E. S. Glover
Lithographer:
Printer: Merchants Lithographing Company [Chicago]
Publisher:
Key/Vignettes/Misc: Refs. 1–11
Locations: Hastings Press, Inc., Hastings, Michigan
Catalogs/Checklists: Cumming

Place: Hecla, Michigan
Date: 1881
See Calumet, Michigan, 1881.

1787
Place: Hillsdale, Michigan
Date: 1866
Title: Birds Eye View of the City of Hillsdale. Hillsdale Co. Mich. 1866
Size: 21 × 28¼ in. (53.5 × 71.9 cm.)

Artist: A. Ruger
Lithographer:
Printer: Chicago Lithographic Co. 152 & 154 Clark St., Chicago
Publisher: A. Ruger, Battle Creek, Mich.
Key/Vignettes/Misc: Refs. 1–12
Locations: LC—M; Mitchell Public Library, Hillsdale, Michigan
Catalogs/Checklists: LC—M, 351; Cumming

1788
Place: Holland, Michigan
Date: 1875
Title: Bird's Eye View of Holland, Michigan, 1875
Size: 17 × 21¼ in. (43.2 × 55.3 cm.)
Artist: D. D. Morse
Lithographer:
Printer: Chicago Lithographing Company [Chicago]
Publisher: Charles Shober & Company
Key/Vignettes/Misc: Refs. 1–24
Locations: Netherlands Museum, Holland, Michigan
Catalogs/Checklists: Cumming

1789
Place: Holly, Michigan
Date: 1873
Title: Bird's Eye View of Holly, Oakland Co., Michigan. 1873. Looking Southwest.
Size: 13 × 20 in. (33 × 50.8 cm.)
Artist: E. S. Glover
Lithographer:
Printer: Strobridge & Company, Cincinnati
Publisher:
Key/Vignettes/Misc: Refs. 1–10
Locations: CMU—MP
Catalogs/Checklists: Cumming

1790
Place: Houghton, Michigan
Date: 1872
Title: Birds Eye View of Houghton, L. S. Michigan. 1872 Looking South East
Size: 15 × 22⅜ in. (38.2 × 57 cm.)
Artist: Cleveland
Lithographer: C. H. Vogt
Printer: American Oleograph Co.
Publisher: Cleveland & Porter
Key/Vignettes/Misc: Refs.
Locations: Michigan Technological University Library, Houghton, Michigan; HCHS—LL
Catalogs/Checklists:

1791
Place: Houghton, Michigan
Date: 1881
Title: Houghton, Mich 1881 Population 2500
Size: 12⅜ × 23½ in. (31.5 × 59.8 cm.)
Artist: H. Wellge
Lithographer:
Printer: Beck & Pauli, Lith. Milwaukee, Wis.
Publisher: J. J. Stoner, Madison, Wis.
Key/Vignettes/Misc:
Locations: HCHS—LL
Catalogs/Checklists:

1792
Place: Howell, Michigan
Date: 1877
Title: Howell, County Seat of Livingston Co., Michigan. 1877. Looking Southwest.
Size: 16 × 20½ in. (40.7 × 52.1 cm.)
Artist: D. D. Morse
Lithographer:
Printer: Lott & Zeuch, Chicago
Publisher:
Key/Vignettes/Misc: Refs. 1–12
Locations: CMU—MP
Catalogs/Checklists: Cumming

1793
Place: Hudson, Michigan
Date: 1868
Title: Hudson, Lenawee Co., Michigan, 1868.
Size: 17½ × 23½ in. (44.5 × 59.7 cm.)
Artist: A. Ruger
Lithographer:
Printer: Chicago Lithographing Company [Chicago]
Publisher: E. S. Glover
Key/Vignettes/Misc: Refs. 1–16; 1 vignette
Locations: LC—M
Catalogs/Checklists: Cumming; LC—M, 352

1794
Place: Ionia, Michigan
Date: 1868
Title: Ionia, Ionia Co., Michigan. 1868.
Size: 24 × 30 in. (61 × 76.3 cm.)
Artist: A. Ruger
Lithographer:
Printer: Chicago Lithographing Company [Chicago]
Publisher:
Key/Vignettes/Misc:
Locations: CMU—MP; LC—M
Catalogs/Checklists: Cumming; LC—M, 353

1795
Place: Ionia, Michigan
Date: 1879
Title: Panoramic View of Ionia, Ionia County, Michigan. 1879.
Size: 11½ × 24½ in. (29.2 × 62.3 cm.)
Artist:
Lithographer:
Printer: Beck and Pauli, Milwaukee, Wis.
Publisher: J. J. Stoner, Madison, Wis.
Key/Vignettes/Misc: Refs. 1–25, A–K; 1 vignette
Locations: CMU—MP
Catalogs/Checklists: Cumming

1796
Place: Iron Mountain, Michigan
Date: 1886
Title: Iron Mountain. Menominee County, Michigan.
Size: 12⅞ × 21⅛ in. (32.7 × 53.8 cm.)
Artist:
Lithographer:
Printer: Beck & Pauli, Lith., Milwaukee, Wis.

Publisher: Norris Wellge & Co., Milwaukee
Key/Vignettes/Misc: Refs. 1–52, I–V
Locations: Menominee Range Historical Foundation Museum, Iron Mountain, Michigan
Catalogs/Checklists:

1797
Place: Ironwood, Michigan
Date: 1886
Title: Ironwood, Mich., Ontonagon County, 1886.
Size: 9½ × 18 in. (24.1 × 45.8 cm.)
Artist: H. Wellge
Lithographer:
Printer: Beck & Pauli, Litho. Milwaukee, Wis.
Publisher: Norris Wellge, & Co. Milwaukee, Wis.
Key/Vignettes/Misc: Refs. 1–28, A–C, P; vignettes
Locations: LC–M
Catalogs/Checklists: Cumming; LC–M, 354

1798
Place: Ishpeming, Michigan
Date: 1871
Title: Bird's Eye View of Ishpeming, L. S., Michigan. 1871.
Size: 14½ × 19½ in. (36.5 × 49.6 cm.) (photo)
Artist: H. H. Bailey
Lithographer: C. H. Vogt
Printer: Milwaukee Lithographing and Engraving Co., [Milwaukee]
Publisher:
Key/Vignettes/Misc: Refs. 1–14
Locations: Marquette County Historical Society, Marquette, Michigan (photo); LC–M (photo)
Catalogs/Checklists: Cumming; LC–M, 354.1

1799
Place: Ishpeming, Michigan
Date: 1881
Title: Ishpeming, Michigan. 1881
Size: 14 × 17 in. (35.7 × 43.3 cm.)
Artist:
Lithographer:
Printer: Beck & Pauli, Milwaukee, Wis.
Publisher: J. J. Stoner, Madison, Wis.
Key/Vignettes/Misc: Refs. 1–27, A–I
Locations: Marquette County Historical Society, Marquette, Michigan
Catalogs/Checklists: Cumming

1800
Place: Jackson, Michigan
Date: [1868]
Title: Birds Eye View of the City of Jackson, Michigan.
Size: 20½ × 33¾ in. (52.1 × 85.8 cm.)
Artist: A. Ruger
Lithographer:
Printer: Chicago Lithographing Company, Chicago
Publisher: A. Ruger
Key/Vignettes/Misc: Refs. 1–16
Locations: LC–M

Catalogs/Checklists: Cumming; LC–M, 355

1801
Place: Jackson, Michigan
Date: 1881
Title: Panoramic View of the City of Jackson, Michigan 1881. Looking North East.
Size: 15¼ × 30½ in. (38.8 × 77.5 cm.)
Artist: A. Ruger
Lithographer:
Printer: Beck & Pauli, Milwaukee, Wis.
Publisher: J. J. Stoner, Madison, Wis.
Key/Vignettes/Misc: Refs. 1–36, A–H, K–R; unnumbered directory of newspapers and printers
Locations: LC–M
Catalogs/Checklists: Cumming; LC–M, 356

1802
Place: Jonesville, Michigan
Date: 1872
Title: Birdseye View of Jonesville, Hillsdale Co., Mich. 1872. Looking North–West
Size: 17¼ × 25¹⁵⁄₁₆ in. (44 × 66 cm.)
Artist: E. S. Glover
Lithographer:
Printer: Strobridge & Co. [Cincinnati]
Publisher:
Key/Vignettes/Misc: Refs. 1–12; 2 vignettes
Locations: MHSA–L
Catalogs/Checklists:

1803
Place: Kalamazoo, Michigan
Date: 1874
Title: Kalamazoo, Michigan. 1874.
Size: 20½ × 28¼ in. (52.1 × 71.8 cm.)
Artist: [Herman Brosius]
Lithographer:
Printer: Chas. Shober & Co. props. Chicago Litho. Co. [Chicago]
Publisher: J. J. Stoner, Madison, Wis.
Key/Vignettes/Misc: Refs. 1–45
Locations: CHS–C; LC–M
Catalogs/Checklists: Cumming; LC–M, 357

1804
Place: Kalamazoo, Michigan
Date: 1883
Title: Birdseye View of Kalamazoo, Mich. 1883.
Size: 16¾ × 28¼ in. (42.6 × 71.8 cm.)
Artist: H. Wellge and A. F. Poole
Lithographer:
Printer: Beck & Pauli, Lithographers, Milwaukee, Wis.
Publisher: J. J. Stoner, Madison, Wis.
Key/Vignettes/Misc: Refs. 1–41, A–V; 9 vignettes
Locations: Kalamazoo Public Museum, Kalamazoo, Michigan; Kalamazoo, Michigan, Public Library; LC–M
Catalogs/Checklists: Cumming; LC–M, 358

1805
Place: Kalamazoo, Michigan
Date: N.D.

Title: Kalamazoo, Michigan.
Size: 24 × 35¾ in. (61 × 90.9 cm.)
Artist:
Lithographer:
Printer: Charles Shober
Publisher: J. C. S. Fitzpatrick, Gazette Office, Kalamazoo.
Key/Vignettes/Misc:
Locations: Kalamazoo Public Museum, Kalamazoo, Michigan
Catalogs/Checklists: Cumming

1806
Place: L'Anse, Michigan
Date: 1881
Title: L'Anse, L. S. Mich. C. S. of Baraga Co. 1881
Size: 17¾ × 23⅝ in. (45.2 × 60.2 cm.)
Artist:
Lithographer:
Printer:
Publisher: J. J. Stoner
Key/Vignettes/Misc: Refs.
Locations: Private collection
Catalogs/Checklists:

1807
Place: Lake Linden, Michigan
Date: 1873
Title: Bird's Eye View of Torch Lake, Houghton Co Mich 1873
Size: 19 × 23½ in. (48.4 × 59.8 cm.)
Artist: A. J. Cleveland
Lithographer:
Printer: Am Oleograph Co.
Publisher: A. J. Cleveland
Key/Vignettes/Misc: Refs.
Locations: HCHS–LL; Marquette County Historical Society, Marquette, Michigan
Catalogs/Checklists:

1808
Place: Lake Linden, Michigan
Date: 1881
Title: Lake Linden, Torch Lake Lake Superior, Michigan 1881 Population 2500
Size: 13¾ × 21½ in. (35 × 54.7 cm.)
Artist:
Lithographer:
Printer: Beck & Pauli, Lith, Milwaukee, Wis.
Publisher: J. J. Stoner, Madison, Wis
Key/Vignettes/Misc: Refs.
Locations: HCHS–LL
Catalogs/Checklists:

1809
Place: Lansing, Michigan
Date: 1866
Title: Birds Eye View of the City of Lansing, Michigan, 1866.
Size: 23¼ × 30 in. (59.2 × 76.3 cm.)
Artist: A. Ruger
Lithographer:
Printer: Chicago Lithographing Company [Chicago]
Publisher: A. Ruger
Key/Vignettes/Misc: Refs. 1–18; 3 vignettes
Locations: LC–M; MHS; MHC; Lansing, Michigan, Public Library; MHSA–L
Catalogs/Checklists: Cumming; LC–M, 359

1810
Place: Lansing, Michigan
Date: 1880
Title: New State Capitol, Lansing, Michigan.
Size: 16⅞ × 22¾ in. (43 × 57.9 cm.)
Artist:
Lithographer:
Printer: Shober & Carqueville Lithographing Company, Chicago
Publisher:
Key/Vignettes/Misc:
Locations: LC–P
Catalogs/Checklists: Cumming

1811
Place: Lansing, Michigan
Date: N.D.
Title: New State Capitol, Lansing, Michigan.
Size: 17 × 23 in. (43.3 × 58.5 cm.)
Artist:
Lithographer:
Printer:
Publisher: Kalamazoo Publishing Company, Kalamazoo, Michigan
Key/Vignettes/Misc:
Locations: CMU–MP
Catalogs/Checklists: Cumming

1812
Place: Lapeer, Michigan
Date: 1880
Title: Bird's Eye View of the City of Lapeer, Lapeer Co., Michigan. 1880.
Size: 13 × 22½ in. (33 × 57.3 cm.)
Artist:
Lithographer:
Printer:
Publisher:
Key/Vignettes/Misc:
Locations: Lapeer, Michigan, Public Library
Catalogs/Checklists: Cumming

1813
Place: Lapeer, Michigan
Date: N.D.
Title: Henry Stephens' White Pine Lumber Mills and Yard, Stephens, Lapeer Co., Michigan.
Size: 19¾ × 25½ in. (50.2 × 64.9 cm.)
Artist:
Lithographer:
Printer: Calvert Lithographing Company, Detroit
Publisher:
Key/Vignettes/Misc: 8 vignettes
Locations: CMU–MP
Catalogs/Checklists: Cumming

1814
Place: Leslie, Michigan
Date: 1883
Title: Panoramic View of Leslie, Ingham Co., Michigan, 1883. From Position N. E. of Town Looking South West
Size: 12½ × 16 in. (31.8 × 40.7 cm.)
Artist:
Lithographer:
Printer:
Publisher:

Key/Vignettes/Misc: Refs. 1–44
Locations: Private collection
Catalogs/Checklists:

1815
Place: Lowell, Michigan
Date: 1870
Title: Bird's Eye View of Lowell, Kent Co., Michigan, 1870. Looking South–west.
Size: 13½ × 18½ in. (34.4 × 47.1 cm.)
Artist: Eli S. Glover
Lithographer:
Printer: Merchants Lithographing Company, Chicago
Publisher:
Key/Vignettes/Misc: Refs. 1–14
Locations: CMU–MP
Catalogs/Checklists: Cumming

1816
Place: Ludington, Michigan
Date: 1880
Title: Bird's Eye View of Ludington, C. S. of Mason Co., Mich., 1880.
Size: 10½ × 18 in. (26.7 × 45.9 cm.)
Artist:
Lithographer:
Printer: Beck and Pauli, Milwaukee, Wis.
Publisher: J. J. Stoner, Madison, Wis.
Key/Vignettes/Misc: Refs. 1–25, A–I; 1 vignette
Locations: CMU–MP; MHC; MM–NN; Rose Hawley Museum, Ludington, Michigan; LC–M (photo)
Catalogs/Checklists: Cumming; MM–NN, LP 1876; LC–M, 359.1

1817
Place: Ludington, Michigan
Date: 1892
Title: Ludington, Michigan, 1892.
Size: 20 × 36 in. (50.8 × 91.5 cm.)
Artist: C. J. Pauli
Lithographer:
Printer:
Publisher: C. J. Pauli
Key/Vignettes/Misc: Refs. 1–74
Locations: Rose Hawley Museum, Ludington, Michigan; LC–M (photo)
Catalogs/Checklists: Cumming; LC–M, 359.2

1818
Place: Mackinac Island, Michigan
Date: N.D.
Title: The Island of Mackinac.
Size: 14 × 18⅚ in. (35.7 × 48.2 cm.)
Artist:
Lithographer:
Printer: Shober & Carqueville
Publisher: Shober & Carqueville
Key/Vignettes/Misc:
Locations: CHS–C
Catalogs/Checklists: Cumming

1819
Place: Manchester, Michigan
Date: 1872
Title: Birds–Eye View of Manchester, Washtenaw County, Michigan, 1872.
Size:
Artist:

Lithographer:
Printer:
Publisher:
Key/Vignettes/Misc: Refs.; vignettes
Locations: Manchester Township Library, Manchester, Michigan
Catalogs/Checklists: Cumming

1820
Place: Manistee, Michigan
Date: 1880
Title: Bird's Eye View of Manistee, C. S. of Manistee Co., Mich. 1880.
Size: 11 × 22½ in. (28 × 57.9 cm.)
Artist:
Lithographer:
Printer: Beck & Pauli, Milwaukee, Wis.
Publisher: J. J. Stoner, Madison, Wis.
Key/Vignettes/Misc: Refs. 1–54
Locations: Manistee County Historical Society Museum, Manistee, Michigan; LC–M (photo)
Catalogs/Checklists: Cumming; LC–M, 359.3

1821
Place: Manistee, Michigan
Date: 1891
Title: Manistee, Mich. 1891. Looking East.
Size: 19⅞ × 34⅝ in. (50.6 × 88.1 cm.)
Artist: C. J. Pauli
Lithographer:
Printer:
Publisher: C. J. Pauli 729 Central Ave. Milwaukee, Wis.
Key/Vignettes/Misc: Numbered and lettered refs.
Locations: Manistee County Historical Society, Manistee, Michigan; LC–M (photo)
Catalogs/Checklists: Cumming; LC–M, 359.4

1822
Place: Marquette, Michigan
Date: 1871
Title: Birds Eye View of Marquette, 1871.
Size: 20 × 31 in. (50.9 × 78.9 cm.)
Artist: H. H. Bailey
Lithographer:
Printer: Chicago Lithographing Company [Chicago]
Publisher: T. M. Fowler and H. H. Bailey, Chicago
Key/Vignettes/Misc: Refs. 1–22
Locations: CMU–MP; MM–NN; MARH–M
Catalogs/Checklists: Cumming; MM–NN, LP 4047

1823
Place: Marquette, Michigan
Date: 1881
Title: Marquette, L. S. Mich., 1881.
Size: 13½ × 27 in. (34.4 × 68.6 cm.)
Artist:
Lithographer:
Printer: Beck & Pauli, Milwaukee, Wis.
Publisher: J. J. Stoner, Madison, Wis.
Key/Vignettes/Misc: Refs. 1–36

Locations: CMU–MP; MARH–M
Catalogs/Checklists: Cumming

1824
Place: Marquette, Michigan
Date: 1886
Title: Marquette, L. S. Mich. 1886.
Size: 22 × 30½ in. (56 × 77.6 cm.)
Artist: E. Demar
Lithographer:
Printer: Beck & Pauli, Milwaukee, Wis.
Publisher:
Key/Vignettes/Misc: Refs. 1–72; 26
vignettes
Locations: CMU–MP; MHSA–L;
MARH–M
Catalogs/Checklists: Cumming

1825
Place: Marquette, Michigan
Date: 1897
Title: Lake Superior's Queen City
(Marquette, Mich.) 1897.
Size: 23 × 41 in. (58.5 × 104.3 cm.)
Artist:
Lithographer:
Printer:
Publisher:
Key/Vignettes/Misc: Refs. 1–57; 2
vignettes
Locations: LC–M; MARH–M
Catalogs/Checklists: Cumming; LC–M,
360

1826
Place: Marshall, Michigan
Date: [1866]
Title: Bird's Eye View of the City of
Marshall, Calhoun Co., Michigan.
Size: 19 × 28 in. (48.4 × 71.2 cm.)
Artist: A. Ruger
Lithographer:
Printer: Chicago Lithographing Company
[Chicago]
Publisher: A. Ruger, Battle Creek,
Michigan
Key/Vignettes/Misc: Refs. 1–16
Locations: LC–M
Catalogs/Checklists: Cumming; LC–M,
361

1827
Place: Mason, Michigan
Date: 1883
Title: Panoramic View of Mason, County
Seat of Ingham County, Michigan, 1883.
Looking South West
Size: 13 × 19½ in. (33.1 × 49.6 cm.)
Artist:
Lithographer:
Printer:
Publisher:
Key/Vignettes/Misc: Refs. 1–28, A–E
Locations: Private collection
Catalogs/Checklists:

1828
Place: Mendon, Michigan
Date: 1880
Title: Bird's Eye View of the Village of
Mendon, St. Joseph Co., Michigan, 1880.
Size: 8 × 16½ in. (20.3 × 42 cm.)

Artist:
Lithographer:
Printer: Beck & Pauli, Milwaukee, Wis.
Publisher: J. J. Stoner, Madison, Wis.
Key/Vignettes/Misc: Refs. 1–32
Locations: UML–AA
Catalogs/Checklists: Cumming

Place: Menominee, Michigan
Date: [1871]
See Marinette, Wisconsin, [1871].

1829
Place: Menominee, Michigan
Date: 1886
Title: Menominee, County Seat of
Menominee County, Michigan. 1886.
Size: 18½ × 25 in. (47.1 × 63.6 cm.)
Artist:
Lithographer:
Printer:
Publisher: Norris, Wellge & Co.,
Milwaukee
Key/Vignettes/Misc: Refs. 1–70; 1
vignette
Locations: MM–NN
Catalogs/Checklists: Cumming;
MM–NN, LP 1248

1830
Place: Menominee, Michigan
Date: [1886]
Title: Menominee, County Seat of
Menominee County, Michigan. 1860.
Size: 18½ × 25 in. (47.1 × 63.6 cm.)
Artist:
Lithographer:
Printer:
Publisher: Norris, Wellge & Co.,
Milwaukee
Key/Vignettes/Misc: Refs. 1–70; 1
vignette
Locations: CMU–MP
Catalogs/Checklists: Cumming

1831
Place: Midland, Michigan
Date: 1884
Title: Midland City, Michigan. 1884.
Size: 19½ × 23½ in. (49.6 × 59.8 cm.)
Artist:
Lithographer:
Printer:
Publisher: O. H. Bailey and Co., Boston
Key/Vignettes/Misc: Refs. 1–40; 11
vignettes
Locations: Midland County Historical
Museum, Midland City, Michigan; LC–M
(photo)
Catalogs/Checklists: Cumming; LC–M,
361.1

1832
Place: Monroe, Michigan
Date: 1866
Title: Monroe. Monroe Co. Michigan
1866
Size: 19 × 27½ in. (48.4 × 70 cm.)
Artist: A. Ruger
Lithographer:
Printer: Chicago Lithographing Co. 152 &
154 Clark St. Chicago

Publisher: A. Ruger, Battle Creek, Mich.
Key/Vignettes/Misc: Refs. 1–13
Locations: LC–M; Monroe County
Historical Commission, Monroe,
Michigan
Catalogs/Checklists: LC–M, 362;
Cumming

1833
Place: Monroe, Michigan
Date: 1894
Title: Monroe, Mich., 1894
Size: 20¼ × 35 in. (54.1 × 89 cm.)
Artist: C. J. Pauli
Lithographer: C. J. Pauli
Printer:
Publisher: C. J. Pauli, 726 Central Avenue,
Milwaukee, Wis.
Key/Vignettes/Misc: Refs. 1–60; 1
vignette
Locations: Monroe County Historical
Commission, Monroe, Michigan
Catalogs/Checklists:

1834
Place: Montague, Michigan
Date: ?
Title:
Size:
Artist:
Lithographer:
Printer:
Publisher:
Key/Vignettes/Misc:
Locations: Montague Museum, Montague,
Michigan
Catalogs/Checklists:

1835
Place: Mount Clemens, Michigan
Date: 1881
Title: Panoramic View of Mt. Clemens,
Macomb Co. Michigan. Looking North
West. 1881
Size: 12¹³⁄₁₆ × 22⅜ in. (32.6 × 57 cm.)
Artist:
Lithographer:
Printer: Beck & Pauli, Milwaukee, Wis.
Publisher: J. J. Stoner, Madison, Wis.
Key/Vignettes/Misc: Refs. A–F, 1–27; 4
vignettes; unnumbered business directory;
description
Locations: UML–AA; Mt. Clemens,
Michigan, Public Library; LC–M
Catalogs/Checklists: Cumming; LC–M,
363

1836
Place: Mount Pleasant, Michigan
Date: 1884
Title: Mt. Pleasant, Michigan. 1884.
Size: 16 × 22½ in. (40.7 × 57.3 cm.)
Artist: O. H. Bailey
Lithographer:
Printer: O. H. Bailey & Company, Boston
Publisher:
Key/Vignettes/Misc: Refs. 1–26; 7
vignettes
Locations: CMU–MP
Catalogs/Checklists: Cumming

1837

Place: Muir, Michigan
Date: 1881
Title: Panoramic View of Muir, Ionia County, Michigan. 1881.
Size:
Artist:
Lithographer:
Printer:
Publisher:
Key/Vignettes/Misc: Refs.
Locations: CMU–MP (photo)
Catalogs/Checklists: Cumming

1838

Place: Mullet Lake, Michigan
Date: 1884
Title: Mullet Lake House, Head of Mullet Lake, Cheboygan County, Michigan. 1884.
Size: 14 × 19⅛ in. (35.7 × 48.7 cm.)
Artist: Riley
Lithographer:
Printer: Shober & Carqueville
Publisher:
Key/Vignettes/Misc:
Locations: CHS–C
Catalogs/Checklists: Cumming

1839

Place: Muskegon, Michigan
Date: 1868
Title: Bird's Eye View of the City of Muskegon, Muskegon Co., Michigan, 1868.
Size: 19¼ × 27¾ in. (49 × 70.5 cm.)
Artist: A. Ruger
Lithographer:
Printer: Chicago Lithographing Company [Chicago]
Publisher: A. Ruger
Key/Vignettes/Misc: Refs. 1–34
Locations: LC–M
Catalogs/Checklists: Cumming; LC–M, 364

1840

Place: Muskegon, Michigan
Date: 1874
Title: Muskegon, Michigan. 1874.
Size: 18 × 26 in. (45.8 × 66.1 cm.)
Artist: [Herman Brosius]
Lithographer:
Printer: Chas. Shober & Co. props. Chicago Lithographing Co. [Chicago]
Publisher:
Key/Vignettes/Misc: Refs. 1–39
Locations: LC–M
Catalogs/Checklists: Cumming; LC–M, 365

1841

Place: Muskegon, Michigan
Date: 1889
Title: Bird's Eye View of Muskegon, Michigan, From Muskegon Lake Looking East. 1889.
Size: 21 × 37¼ in. (53.4 × 94.7 cm.)
Artist: E. S. Glover
Lithographer:
Printer: Shober & Carqueville Lithographing Co. [Chicago]

Publisher: A. J. Little
Key/Vignettes/Misc: Refs. 1–9; 7 vignettes
Locations: LC–M
Catalogs/Checklists: LC–M, 366; Cumming

1842

Place: Negaunee, Michigan
Date: 1871
Title: Negaunee, Mich. 1871.
Size: 16½ × 24 in. (42 × 61 cm.)
Artist: H. H. Bailey
Lithographer: C. H. Vogt
Printer: Milwaukee Lithographing and Engraving Company [Milwaukee]
Publisher:
Key/Vignettes/Misc: Refs. 1–14
Locations: LC–M
Catalogs/Checklists: LC–M, 367; Cumming

1843

Place: Negaunee, Michigan
Date: 1881
Title: Negaunee, Mich. 1881
Size: 12 × 23½ in. (30.5 × 59.8 cm.)
Artist:
Lithographer:
Printer: Beck & Pauli, Lith. Milwaukee, Wis.
Publisher: J. J. Stoner, Madison, Wis.
Key/Vignettes/Misc: Refs. 1–24
Locations: Negaunee, Michigan, Public Library
Catalogs/Checklists: Cumming

1844

Place: Niles, Michigan
Date: [1868?]
Title: Niles Berrien County, Michigan
Size: 21 × 28 in. (53.4 × 71.2 cm.)
Artist: A. Ruger
Lithographer:
Printer: Chicago Lithographing Co. 152 & 154 Clark St. Chicago
Publisher: A. Ruger, Battle Creek, Mich.
Key/Vignettes/Misc: Refs. 1–17
Locations: LC–M; Fort St. Joseph Museum, Niles, Michigan
Catalogs/Checklists: LC–M, 368; Cumming

1845

Place: Niles, Michigan
Date: 1889
Title: Niles Michigan 1889
Size: 22 × 30 in. (56 × 76.4 cm.)
Artist: C. J. Pauli & Co.
Lithographer:
Printer:
Publisher: C. J. Pauli & Co. 726 Central Ave. Milwaukee, Wis.
Key/Vignettes/Misc: Refs. 1–41; 1 vignette
Locations: LC–M; Fort St. Joseph Museum, Niles, Michigan
Catalogs/Checklists: Cumming

1846

Place: Ontonagon, Michigan
Date: 1855

Title: Southview of Town of Ontonagon Lake Superior, Mich.
Size: 13 × 28 in. (33 × 71.2 cm.)
Artist: G. L. Brunschweiler
Lithographer:
Printer: F. Mayer & Company, 96 Fulton St. N. Y.
Publisher:
Key/Vignettes/Misc:
Locations: BDPL–D; CMU–MP; MM–NN
Catalogs/Checklists: Cumming; MM–NN, LP 1055

1847

Place: Ontonagon, Michigan
Date: 1858
Title: View of Minesota Mine County of Ontonagon State of Michigan Taken from the South September 1858
Size:
Artist: G. L. Brunschweiler, T. E.
Lithographer:
Printer: J. Bien, 60 Fulton St., N. Y.
Publisher:
Key/Vignettes/Misc:
Locations: HCHS–LL
Catalogs/Checklists:

1848

Place: Ontonagon, Michigan
Date: 1859
Title: View of Minesota Mine. Sept. 1859.
Size: 26½ × 40 in. (67.4 × 101.6 cm.)
Artist: G. L. Brunschweiler
Lithographer:
Printer: J. Bien
Publisher:
Key/Vignettes/Misc:
Locations: Ontonagon Museum, Ontonagon, Michigan
Catalogs/Checklists: Cumming

1849

Place: Orchard Lake, Michigan
Date: N.D.
Title: Michigan Military Academy, Orchard Lake, Oakland County, Michigan.
Size: 12⅜ × 20⅜ in. (31.5 × 51.8 cm.)
Artist:
Lithographer:
Printer:
Publisher: L. H. Everts
Key/Vignettes/Misc:
Locations: CHS–C
Catalogs/Checklists: Cumming

Place: Oscoda, Michigan
Date: 1880
See Au Sable, Michigan, 1880.

1850

Place: Otsego, Michigan
Date: 1880
Title: Otsego, Allegan County, Michigan. 1880.
Size: 9¹⁵⁄₁₆ × 20½ in. (25.3 × 52.2 cm.)
Artist:
Lithographer:
Printer: Beck & Pauli Lith. Milwaukee, Wis.

Publisher: J. J. Stoner, Madison, Wis.
Key/Vignettes/Misc: Refs. 1–34
Locations: UML–AA; CHS–C
Catalogs/Checklists: Cumming

1851

Place: Ovid, Michigan
Date: 1881
Title: Panoramic View of Ovid, Clinton Co., Michigan, 1881. Looking North West.
Size: 8½ × 15½ in. (21.7 × 39.5 cm.)
Artist:
Lithographer:
Printer: Beck & Pauli, Milwaukee, Wis.
Publisher: J. J. Stoner, Madison, Wis.
Key/Vignettes/Misc: Refs. 1–41
Locations: CMU–MP; UML–AA; Ovid, Michigan, Public Library
Catalogs/Checklists: Cumming

1852

Place: Owosso, Michigan
Date: 1873
Title: Bird's–Eye View of Owosso, Shiawassee County, Mich. 1873.
Size: 15½ × 22 in. (39.5 × 56 cm.)
Artist:
Lithographer:
Printer: Strobridge & Co. Lith, Cin.
Publisher:
Key/Vignettes/Misc: Refs. 1–17; 2 vignettes
Locations: CMU–MP
Catalogs/Checklists: Cumming

1853

Place: Owosso, Michigan
Date: 1894
Title: Birds Eye View of Owosso, Michigan. 1894. Looking North–west.
Size: 26 × 38 in. (66.2 × 96.6 cm.)
Artist: C. J. Pauli
Lithographer:
Printer:
Publisher: C. J. Pauli, Milwaukee
Key/Vignettes/Misc: Refs. 1–74
Locations: MHC; MHSA–L
Catalogs/Checklists: Cumming

1854

Place: Paw Paw, Michigan
Date: 1875
Title: Paw Paw, Michigan, 1875. From Prospect Hill.
Size: 14 × 18¾ in. (35.6 × 47.7 cm.)
Artist: D. D. Morse
Lithographer:
Printer: Strobridge & Company, Cincinnati
Publisher:
Key/Vignettes/Misc: Refs. 1–15
Locations: CMU–MP
Catalogs/Checklists: Cumming

1855

Place: Pentwater, Michigan
Date: 1880
Title: Bird's Eye View of Pentwater, Oceana Co., Michigan. 1880.
Size: 10⅞ × 16½ in. (27.7 × 42 cm.)
Artist:

Lithographer:
Printer: Beck & Pauli, Milwaukee, Wis.
Publisher: J. J. Stoner, Madison, Wis.
Key/Vignettes/Misc: 15 refs.
Locations: CHS–C
Catalogs/Checklists: Cumming

1856

Place: Petoskey, Michigan
Date: 1880
Title: Birds Eye View of Petoskey, Michigan 1880
Size: 15¾ × 25 in. (40.1 × 63.6 cm.)
Artist:
Lithographer:
Printer: Beck & Pauli Lith., Milwaukee, Wis.
Publisher: J. J. Stoner, Madison, Wis.
Key/Vignettes/Misc:
Locations: Little Traverse Regional Historical Society, Petoskey, Michigan
Catalogs/Checklists:

1857

Place: Petoskey, Michigan
Date: 1880
Title: Petoskey and Surroundings.
Size: 14 × 19 in. (35.6 × 48.3 cm.)
Artist:
Lithographer:
Printer: Shober & Carqueville
Publisher: Shober & Carqueville
Key/Vignettes/Misc: Refs. 1–12
Locations: CMU–MP
Catalogs/Checklists: Cumming

Place: Pewabic, Michigan
Date: 1873
See Ripley, Michigan, 1873.

1858

Place: Pontiac, Michigan
Date: 1867
Title: Pontiac, Oakland Co., Michigan. 1867.
Size: 18¼ × 28½ in. (46.5 × 72.5 cm.)
Artist: A. Ruger
Lithographer:
Printer: Chicago Lithographing Company [Chicago]
Publisher: A. Ruger
Key/Vignettes/Misc: Refs. 1–14; 9 vignettes
Locations: LC–M
Catalogs/Checklists: Cumming; LC–M, 369

1859

Place: Port Huron, Michigan
Date: 1867
Title: Birds Eye View of the City of Port Huron, Sarnia and Gratiot, St. Clair Co., Michigan, 1867, and Point Edwards, Lambton Co., Canada West.
Size: 19½ × 28½ in. (49.6 × 72.5 cm.)
Artist: A. Ruger
Lithographer:
Printer: Chicago Lithograhing Company [Chicago]
Publisher: A. Ruger
Key/Vignettes/Misc: Refs. 1–19
Locations: CMU–MP; LC–M

Catalogs/Checklists: Cumming; LC–M, 370; PAC (1976); PAC H¾₄₄₀–Sarnia–1867

1860

Place: Port Huron, Michigan
Date: 1894
Title: Port Huron, Mich. 1894.
Size: 20½ × 39 in. (52.2 × 99.1 cm.)
Artist: C. J. Pauli
Lithographer: C. J. Pauli
Printer:
Publisher: C. J. Pauli
Key/Vignettes/Misc: Refs. 1–67, A–Z, XX
Locations: LC–M
Catalogs/Checklists: Cumming; LC–M, 371

1861

Place: Portland, Michigan
Date: 1881
Title: Portland, Ionia Co., Michigan, 1881.
Size: 10 × 20 in. (25.4 × 50.8 cm.)
Artist:
Lithographer:
Printer: Beck & Pauli Lith. Milwaukee, Wis.
Publisher: J. J. Stoner, Madison, Wis.
Key/Vignettes/Misc: Refs. 1–46
Locations: CMU–MP; LC–M (facsimile)
Catalogs/Checklists: Cumming; LC–M, 371.1

Place: Portsmouth, Michigan
Date: 1867
See Bay City, Michigan, 1867.

Place: Quincy, Michigan
Date: 1873
See Ripley, Michigan, 1873.

1862

Place: Quincy, Michigan
Date: 1883
Title: Panoramic View of Quincy, Branch Co. Michigan, 1883. Looking South–West.
Size: 11¹⁵⁄₁₆ × 18⁵⁄₁₆ in. (30.4 × 46.6 cm.) (facsimile)
Artist: [Albert Ruger?]
Lithographer:
Printer:
Publisher:
Key/Vignettes/Misc: Refs. 1–25
Locations: CMU–MP (facsimile); Branch County Historical Society, Coldwater, Michigan (facsimile); LC–M (facsimile)
Catalogs/Checklists: LC–M, 371.2

1863

Place: Quinnesec, Michigan
Date: 1881
Title: Bird's Eye View of Quinnesec, Mich., 1881
Size: 6⅞ × 12 in. (17.5 × 30.6 cm.)
Artist:
Lithographer:
Printer:
Publisher: J. J. Stoner, Madison, Wis.
Key/Vignettes/Misc: Refs. 1–13

Locations: ACMW–FW
Catalogs/Checklists:

Place: Red Jacket, Michigan
Date: 1881
See Calumet, Michigan, 1881.

1864
Place: Reed City, Michigan
Date: 1880
Title: Bird's Eye View of Reed City, Michigan 1880
Size:
Artist:
Lithographer:
Printer: Beck & Pauli Lith., Milwaukee, Wis.
Publisher: J. J. Stoner, Madison, Wis.
Key/Vignettes/Misc:
Locations: Unknown. See White, Marjorie Brown, One Hundred Going on Two Hundred Reed City Centennial. Reed City, Michigan: Reed City Chamber of Commerce, [1975?]
Catalogs/Checklists:

1865
Place: Ripley, Michigan
Date: 1873
Title: Birds Eye View of Ripley, Quincy, Pewabic & Franklin, L. S. Mich 1873
Size: 19½ × 26½ in. (49.6 × 67.4 cm.)
Artist: A. J. Cleveland
Lithographer: C. H. Vogt
Printer: American Oleograph Co.
Publisher: A. J. Cleveland
Key/Vignettes/Misc:
Locations: HCHS–LL
Catalogs/Checklists:

1866
Place: Rockford, Michigan
Date: 1880
Title: Bird's Eye View of Rockford, Michigan, 1880.
Size: 9 × 10¼ in. (23 × 27.4 cm.)
Artist:
Lithographer:
Printer:
Publisher: J. J. Stoner, Madison, Wis.
Key/Vignettes/Misc: Refs. 1–10
Locations: CMU–MP
Catalogs/Checklists: Cumming

1867
Place: Romeo, Michigan
Date: 1868
Title: Birds Eye View of Romeo.
Size: 17 × 27 in. (43.3 × 68.6 cm.)
Artist: A. Ruger
Lithographer:
Printer: Chicago Lithogr. Co. [Chicago]
Publisher: E. S. Glover
Key/Vignettes/Misc: Refs. 1–8
Locations: Romeo, Michigan, Public Library; LC–M
Catalogs/Checklists: Cumming; LC–M, 372

1868
Place: Saginaw, Michigan
Date: Ca. 1855
Title: View of Saginaw City. Michigan

Size: 16½ × 26½ in. (42 × 67.5 cm.)
Artist: Chas H. Brower
Lithographer: L. Brown, Jr.
Printer: A. Robertson, 121 Fulton St. N. Y.
Publisher:
Key/Vignettes/Misc:
Locations: SCHS–S
Catalogs/Checklists:

1869
Place: Saginaw, Michigan
Date: 1867
Title: Saginaw City. Michigan 1867
Size: 23¼ × 28½ in. (59.2 × 72.5 cm.)
Artist: A. Ruger
Lithographer:
Printer: Chicago Lithographing Co. 152 & 154 Clark St. Chicago
Publisher:
Key/Vignettes/Misc: Refs. 1–10; 9 vignettes
Locations: SCHS–S; CMU–MP; CHS–C; LC–M
Catalogs/Checklists: Cumming; LC–M, 373

Place: Saginaw, Michigan
Date: 1885
See East Saginaw, Michigan, 1885.

1870
Place: Saint Clair, Michigan
Date: 1868
Title: Bird's Eye View of Saint Clair, St. Clair Co., Michigan, 1868.
Size: 16¾ × 23½ in. (42.7 × 59.8 cm.)
Artist: A. Ruger
Lithographer:
Printer: Chicago Lithographing Company [Chicago]
Publisher: E. S. Glover
Key/Vignettes/Misc:
Locations: CMU–MP; LC–M
Catalogs/Checklists: Cumming; LC–M, 375

1871
Place: Saint Clair, Michigan
Date: N.D.
Title: St. Clair Mineral Spring and Oakland Hotel, St. Clair, Michigan. The Great Health Resort of Michigan. Open Winter and Summer
Size: 18¹⁄₁₆ × 29⅜ in. (46 × 74.7 cm.)
Artist:
Lithographer:
Printer: Calvert Lithographing Company, Detroit
Publisher:
Key/Vignettes/Misc:
Locations: CHS–C
Catalogs/Checklists: Cumming

1872
Place: Saint Johns, Michigan
Date: 1868
Title: Saint Johns, Clinton Co., Michigan. 1868.
Size: 16 × 25½ in. (40.8 × 64.9 cm.)
Artist: A. Ruger
Lithographer:
Printer: Chicago Lithographing Company [Chicago]

Publisher:
Key/Vignettes/Misc: Refs. 1–12
Locations: Bement Public Library, St. Johns, Michigan; LC–M
Catalogs/Checklists: Cumming; LC–M, 376

1873
Place: Saint Johns, Michigan
Date: 1881
Title: Panoramic View of St. Johns, Clinton Co., Michigan, 1881.
Size: 12 × 18½ in. (30.6 × 47.1 cm.)
Artist:
Lithographer:
Printer: Beck & Pauli, Milwaukee, Wis.
Publisher: J. J. Stoner, Madison, Wis.
Key/Vignettes/Misc: Refs. 1–55, A–G
Locations: UML–AA
Catalogs/Checklists: Cumming

1874
Place: Saint Joseph, Michigan
Date: 1870
Title: Birds Eye View of Saint Joseph, Michigan, 1870.
Size: 12¾ × 19 in. (32.5 × 48.4 cm.)
Artist:
Lithographer:
Printer: Merchants Lithographing Company, Chicago
Publisher: D. D. Morse
Key/Vignettes/Misc: Refs. 1–11
Locations: Fort Miama Heritage Society, Benton Harbor, Michigan; Benton Harbor, Michigan, Public Library
Catalogs/Checklists: Cumming

1875
Place: Saint Joseph, Michigan
Date: 1883
Title: St. Joseph, Michigan 60 Feet Above Level of Lake 1883
Size: 14¼ × 28⅛ in. (36.3 × 71.6 cm.)
Artist:
Lithographer:
Printer: Rand McNally & Co. Chicago
Publisher: St. Joseph Mich, Traveler–Herald
Key/Vignettes/Misc: Refs. 1–36
Locations: Fort St. Joseph Museum, Niles, Michigan
Catalogs/Checklists:

1876
Place: Saint Joseph, Michigan
Date: 1895
Title: St. Joseph, Mich. County Seat of Berrien County. 1895.
Size: 12¾ × 21¼ in. (32.4 × 54.1 cm.)
Artist: C. J. Pauli
Lithographer:
Printer:
Publisher: C. J. Pauli
Key/Vignettes/Misc:
Locations: City Hall, St. Joseph, Michigan
Catalogs/Checklists: Cumming

1877
Place: Saint Louis, Michigan
Date: 1880
Title: Saint Louis, Gratiot Co., Michigan, 1880.

Size: 11¼ × 21 in. (28.7 × 53.4 cm.)
Artist:
Lithographer:
Printer: Beck & Pauli, Milwaukee, Wis.
Publisher: J. J. Stoner, Madison, Wis.
Key/Vignettes/Misc: Refs. 1–22
Locations: CMU–MP
Catalogs/Checklists: Cumming

1878

Place: Saline, Michigan
Date: 1872
Title: Birds Eye View of Saline, Washtenaw Co., Mich., 1872. Looking Southeast.
Size: 12¾ × 18¼ in. (32.5 × 46.5 cm.)
Artist: E. S. Glover
Lithographer:
Printer: Strobridge & Company [Cincinnati]
Publisher:
Key/Vignettes/Misc: Refs. 1–12
Locations: Saline, Michigan, Public Library; MHSA–L
Catalogs/Checklists: Cumming

Place: Salzburg, Michigan
Date: 1867
See Bay City, Michigan, 1867.

1879

Place: Sand Beach, Michigan
Date: N.D.
Title: Bird's Eye View of Sand Beach Harbor of Refuge.
Size: 10 × 17⅜ in. (25.5 × 44.3 cm.)
Artist:
Lithographer:
Printer: Van Leyden Co., So. Detroit.
Publisher:
Key/Vignettes/Misc:
Locations: MHC
Catalogs/Checklists: Cumming

1880

Place: Saranac, Michigan
Date: 1910
Title: The Village of Saranac Mich 1910
Size: ca. 10 × 16 in. (25.4 × 40.7 cm.)
Artist:
Lithographer:
Printer:
Publisher: H. Peake (copyright)
Key/Vignettes/Misc:
Locations: LC–M (photo); Saranac, Michigan, Public Library
Catalogs/Checklists: LC–M, 377

Place: Sarnia, Michigan
Date: 1867
See Port Huron, Michigan, 1867.

1881

Place: South Haven, Michigan
Date: 1880
Title: South Haven, Van Buren County, Michigan 1880
Size: 10¾ × 21¼ in. (27.4 × 52.9 cm.)
Artist: H. Brosius
Lithographer: Swift
Printer: Beck & Pauli, Milwaukee, Wis.
Publisher: J. J. Stoner, Madison, Wis.
Key/Vignettes/Misc:

Locations: South Haven, Michigan, Memorial Library; Liberty Hyde Bailey Museum, South Haven, Michigan
Catalogs/Checklists: Cumming

Place: Spring Lake, Michigan
Date: 1894
See Grand Haven, Michigan, 1894.

1883

Place: Stanton, Michigan
Date: 1880
Title: Stanton. Montcalm County, Michigan. 1880.
Size: 9½ × 24 in. (24.2 × 61 cm.)
Artist:
Lithographer:
Printer: Beck & Pauli, Milwaukee, Wis.
Publisher: J. J. Stoner, Madison, Wis.
Key/Vignettes/Misc: Refs. 1–40; 1 vignette
Locations: UML–AA
Catalogs/Checklists: Cumming

1884

Place: Sturgis, Michigan
Date: 1881
Title: Bird's Eye View of Sturgis. St. Joseph Co., Michigan, 1881.
Size: 9⅝ × 17½ in. (24.5 × 44.5 cm.)
Artist:
Lithographer:
Printer: Beck & Pauli, Milwaukee, Wis.
Publisher: J. J. Stoner, Madison, Wis.
Key/Vignettes/Misc: Refs. 1–24
Locations: UML–AA
Catalogs/Checklists: Cumming

1885

Place: Tecumseh, Michigan
Date: 1868
Title: Tecumseh, Lenawee Co., Michigan, 1868.
Size: 17¼ × 23¼ in. (43.9 × 59.1 cm.)
Artist: A. Ruger
Lithographer:
Printer: Chicago Lithogr. Co. [Chicago]
Publisher: E. S. Glover
Key/Vignettes/Misc: Refs. 1–11; 1 vignette
Locations: CMU–MP; LC–M; MHSA–L
Catalogs/Checklists: Cumming; LC–M, 378

1886

Place: Three Rivers, Michigan
Date: 1871
Title: Three Rivers, Michigan, 1871. Looking North East.
Size: 15⅞ × 26 in. (40.5 × 66.1 cm.)
Artist:
Lithographer:
Printer: Merchant's Lithographing Company, Chicago
Publisher:
Key/Vignettes/Misc:
Locations: CHS–C
Catalogs/Checklists: Cumming

Place: Torch Lake, Michigan
Date: 1873
See Lake Linden, Michigan, 1873.

Place: Torch Lake, Michigan
Date: 1881
See Lake Linden, Michigan, 1881.

1887

Place: Traverse City, Michigan
Date: 1879
Title: Bird's Eye View of Traverse City, Michigan.
Size: 17 × 28 in. (43.3 × 71.2 cm.)
Artist: H. Brosius
Lithographer:
Printer: Beck & Pauli, Milwaukee, Wis.
Publisher: J. J. Stoner, Madison, Wis.
Key/Vignettes/Misc: Refs. 1–16; 1 vignette
Locations: Con Foster Museum, Traverse City, Michigan
Catalogs/Checklists: Cumming

1888

Place: Traverse City, Michigan
Date: N.D.
Title: Traverse City and Its Pioneers.
Size: 16 × 13 in. (40.8 × 33.1 cm.)
Artist: Willie S. Holdsworth
Lithographer:
Printer: Willie S. Holdsworth
Publisher:
Key/Vignettes/Misc: 6 vignettes
Locations: CMU–MP
Catalogs/Checklists: Cumming

1889

Place: Union City, Michigan
Date: 1880
Title: Panoramic View of Union City Branch County Michigan 1880
Size: 10 × 18 in. (25.5 × 45.8 cm.)
Artist:
Lithographer:
Printer: Beck & Pauli, Lith., Milwaukee, Wis.
Publisher: J. J. Stoner, Madison, Wis.
Key/Vignettes/Misc: Refs. 1–38, A–D
Locations: UML–AA; LC–M (facsimile)
Catalogs/Checklists: Cumming; LC–M, 378.1

1890

Place: Vassar, Michigan
Date: ?
Title:
Size:
Artist:
Lithographer:
Printer:
Publisher:
Key/Vignettes/Misc:
Locations: Unknown
Catalogs/Checklists:

1891

Place: Vicksburg, Michigan
Date: 1880
Title: Bird's Eye View of Vicksburg, Kalamazoo Co., Michigan, 1880.
Size: 7 × 14 in. (17.8 × 35.6 cm.)
Artist:
Lithographer:
Printer: Beck & Pauli, Milwaukee, Wis.
Publisher: J. J. Stoner, Madison, Wis.

Key/Vignettes/Misc: Refs. 1–26
Locations: CMU–MP; UML–AA
Catalogs/Checklists: Cumming

Place: Wenona, Michigan
Date: 1867
See Bay City, Michigan, 1867.

1892
Place: Whitehall, Michigan
Date: 1880
Title: Bird's Eye View of Whitehall, 1880
Size: 14 × 30 in. (35.7 × 76.3 cm.)
Artist:
Lithographer:
Printer:
Publisher:
Key/Vignettes/Misc:
Locations: City Hall, Whitehall, Michigan
Catalogs/Checklists:

1893
Place: Wyandotte, Michigan
Date: 1896
Title: Wyandotte, MIchigan, 1896.
Size: 22⁵⁄₁₆ × 32⁵⁄₁₆ in. (56.7 × 82 cm.)
Artist: T. M. Fowler
Lithographer:
Printer:
Publisher: T. M. Fowler & James B. Moyer
Key/Vignettes/Misc: Refs. 1–38; 2
vignettes
Locations: ACMW–FW; LC–M
Catalogs/Checklists: Cumming; LC–M,
379

1894
Place: Ypsilanti, Michigan
Date: 1865
Title: Ypsilanti Washtenaw Co. Michigan
1865
Size: 22 × 27¾ in. (56 × 70.6 cm.)
Artist:
Lithographer:
Printer:
Publisher:
Key/Vignettes/Misc: Refs. 1–11
Locations: Ypsilanti, Michigan, Historical
Museum
Catalogs/Checklists:

1895
Place: Ypsilanti, Michigan
Date: [1867]
Title: Ypsilanti, Washtenaw Co.,
Michigan.
Size: 20½ × 28 in. (52.2 × 71.2 cm.)
Artist: A. Ruger
Lithographer:
Printer: Chicago Lithographing Company
Chicago
Publisher: A. Ruger, Battle Creek, Mich.
Key/Vignettes/Misc: Refs. 1–11
Locations: LC–M
Catalogs/Checklists: Cumming; LC–M,
380

1896
Place: Ypsilanti, Michigan
Date: 1879
Title: Michigan State Normal School,
Ypsilanti.
Size: 13⅜ × 17⁷⁄₁₆ in. (35.3 × 44.4 cm.)

Artist:
Lithographer: James McCoy
Printer:
Publisher: James McCoy (copyright)
Key/Vignettes/Misc:
Locations: LC–P
Catalogs/Checklists: Cumming

1897
Place: Ypsilanti, Michigan
Date: 1890
Title: Ypsilanti, Mich. 1890
Size: 20 × 36 in. (50.9 × 91.4 cm.)
Artist: C. J. Pauli
Lithographer:
Printer: C. J. Pauli
Publisher: C. J. Pauli
Key/Vignettes/Misc: Refs. 1–45; 2
vignettes
Locations: Ypsilanti, Michigan, Historical
Museum
Catalogs/Checklists: Cumming

1898
Place: Zeeland, Michigan
Date: 1907
Title: Bird's Eye View of Zeeland, 1907
Size: 12 × 17 in. (30.5 × 43.3 cm.)
Artist: Jos. Warner
Lithographer:
Printer:
Publisher:
Key/Vignettes/Misc: Refs.; 2 vignettes
Locations: Netherlands Museum, Holland,
Michigan
Catalogs/Checklists:

1899
Place: Albert Lea, Minnesota
Date: 1879
Title: Bird's Eye View of the City of Albert
Lea, Freeborn Co., Minnesota, 1879.
Looking South West.
Size: 10½ × 16¾ in. (26.7 × 42.6 cm.)
Artist:
Lithographer:
Printer: Beck & Pauli Lith. Milwaukee,
Wis.
Publisher: J. J. Stoner, Madison, Wis.
Key/Vignettes/Misc: Refs. 1–14, A–H
Locations: LC–M (facsimile); Albert Lea,
Minnesota, Public Libary
Catalogs/Checklists: LC–M, 380.1

1900
Place: Anoka, Minnesota
Date: 1869
Title: Bird's Eye View of noka, Anoka
County, Minnesota, 1869.
Size: 17½ × 20 in. (44.5 × 50.8 cm.)
Artist: A. Ruger
Lithographer:
Printer: Merchant's Lith. Co. [Chicago]
Publisher:
Key/Vignettes/Misc: Refs. 1–9; 1 vignette
Locations: LC–M; MHS–SP
Catalogs/Checklists: LC–M, 381

1901
Place: Austin, Minnesota
Date: 1870
Title: Bird's Eye View of Austin, Mower
County Minnesota, 1879.

Size: 17 × 20 in. (43.2 × 50.8 cm.)
Artist: [Albert Ruger]
Lithographer:
Printer: Chicago Lith. Co., Chicago
Publisher: Ruger & Stoner, Madison,
Wisconsin
Key/Vignettes/Misc: Refs. 1–11; 1
vignette
Locations: LC–M
Catalogs/Checklists: LC–M, 383

1902
Place: Brainerd, Minnesota
Date: Ca. 1914
Title: Brainerd, "City of Mines."
Size: 20 × 26½ in. (50.8 × 67.4 cm.)
Artist: McCoy
Lithographer:
Printer: Duluth Photo–Engraving Co.,
Duluth, Minnesota
Publisher: Brainerd Townsite Company
Key/Vignettes/Misc:
Locations: LC–M
Catalogs/Checklists: LC–M, 384

1903
Place: Duluth, Minnesota
Date: 1883
Title: View of Duluth, Minn. 1883.
Size: 16 × 40 in. (40.7 × 101.7 cm.)
Artist: H. Wellge
Lithographer:
Printer: Beck & Pauli, Lith. Milwaukee
Publisher: J. J. Stoner, Madison
Key/Vignettes/Misc: Refs. 1–84; 2
vignettes
Locations: LC–M
Catalogs/Checklists: LC–M, 385

1904
Place: Duluth, Minnesota
Date: 1887
Title: Perspective Map of Duluth, Minn.
1887.
Size: 22 × 41 in. (55.9 × 104.2 cm.)
Artist: H. Wellge
Lithographer:
Printer: The Beck & Pauli, Lith. Co.,
Milwaukee
Publisher: Duluth News Co., Duluth
Key/Vignettes/Misc: Refs. 1–61
Locations: LC–M
Catalogs/Checklists: LC–M, 386

1905
Place: Duluth, Minnesota
Date: [1893?]
Title: Perspective Map of the City of
Duluth, Minn.
Size: 27⅞ × 47½ in. (71 × 124.7 cm.)
Artist:
Lithographer:
Printer:
Publisher: American Publishing Co.,
Milwaukee
Key/Vignettes/Misc: Refs. 1–49; 6
vignettes
Locations: MHS–SP
Catalogs/Checklists:

Place: Duluth, Minnesota
Date: 1910
See Superior, Wisconsin, 1910.

Place: Duluth, Minnesota
Date: 1915
See Superior, Wisconsin, 1915.

1906
Place: Elk River, Minnesota
Date: Ca. 1870
Title: View of Elk River, Sherburne
Size: 11¾ × 13¾ in. (30 × 35 cm.)
Artist:
Lithographer:
Printer: Beck & Pauli, Lith. Milwaukee
Publisher: J. J. Stoner, Madison
Key/Vignettes/Misc: Refs. 1–31; 1
vignette
Locations: MHS–SP
Catalogs/Checklists:

1907
Place: Fairmont, Minnesota
Date: 1879
Title: Fairmont Martin Co. Minnesota,
1879. From Position North East of Town
Size: 7¾ × 12⁵⁄₁₆ in. (19.7 × 31.3 cm.)
Artist:
Lithographer:
Printer: Beck & Pauli, Lith. Milwaukee,
Wis.
Publisher: J. J. Stoner, Madison, Wis.
Key/Vignettes/Misc: Refs. 1–10, 12–17
Locations: ACMW–FW
Catalogs/Checklists: ACMW–FW 1773

1908
Place: Faribault, Minnesota
Date: 1869
Title: Bird's Eye View of the City of
Faribault, Rice County, Minnesota, 1869:
Looking North West
Size: 21 × 22½ in. (53.4 × 57.2 cm.)
Artist: Prof. A. Ruger
Lithographer:
Printer: Merchant's Lithogr. Co., Chicago
Publisher:
Key/Vignettes/Misc: Refs. 1–13; 3
vignettes
Locations: LC–M; MHS–SP
Catalogs/Checklists: LC–M, 387

1909
Place: Faribault, Minnesota
Date: 1874
Title: Faribault, Minn.
Size: 22⅜ × 32¼ in. (57 × 82 cm.)
Artist: Geo. L. Richards
Lithographer:
Printer: Milwaukee Lith. & Eng. Co.
Publisher: Joseph M. Wolfe
Key/Vignettes/Misc: Refs. 1–29; 4
vignettes
Locations: MHS–SP
Catalogs/Checklists:

1910
Place: Faribault, Minnesota
Date: 1888
Title: Faribault, Rice Co., Minn.
Size: 24⅜ × 33¾ in. (62 × 86 cm.)
Artist: C. J. Pauli & Co.
Lithographer:
Printer:
Publisher: C. J. Pauli & Co.

Key/Vignettes/Misc: Refs. 1–59; 1
vignette
Locations: MHS–SP
Catalogs/Checklists:

1911
Place: Fergus Falls, Minnesota
Date: 1880
Title: Fergus Falls, Minn., 1880.
Size: 13¼ × 22½ in. (33.8 × 57.3 cm.)
Artist: T. M. Fowler
Lithographer:
Printer: Beck & Pauli, Milwaukee
Publisher: Fowler & Rhines [Asbury Park,
N. J.]
Key/Vignettes/Misc: Refs. 1–21; 3
vignettes
Locations: MHS–SP; CHS–C
Catalogs/Checklists:

1912
Place: Hastings, Minnesota
Date: 1867
Title: Bird's Eye View of the City of
Hastings, Dakota Co., Minnesota, 1867.
Size: 20 × 24 in. (50.8 × 61 cm.)
Artist: A. Ruger
Lithographer:
Printer: Chicago Lith. Co., Chicago
Publisher:
Key/Vignettes/Misc: Refs. 1–14, A–C
Locations: LC–M; MHS–SP
Catalogs/Checklists: LC–M, 389

1913
Place: Kandotta, Minnesota
Date: [1858]
Title: Kandotta, M. T. Fairy Lake in the
Distance
Size: 10¼ × 14¾ in. (26.1 × 37.6 cm.)
Artist: E. Whitefield
Lithographer:
Printer: J. Gemmell 132 Lake St. Chicago
Publisher:
Key/Vignettes/Misc:
Locations: MHS–P
Catalogs/Checklists: Norton, Whitefield,
no. 72

1914
Place: Lake Benton, Minnesota
Date: 1883
Title: Lake Benton, Minn. County Seat of
Lincoln Co., 1883.
Size: 11⅜ × 14¹⁵⁄₁₆ in. (29 × 38 cm.)
Artist: H. Wellge
Lithographer:
Printer: Beck & Pauli, Lith, Milwaukee,
Wis.
Publisher: J. J. Stoner, Madison, Wis.
Key/Vignettes/Misc: Refs. 2–21, A–F; 1
vignette
Locations: MHS–SP
Catalogs/Checklists:

1915
Place: Lake City, Minnesota
Date: 1867
Title: Lake City, Wabasha Co., Minnesota,
1867
Size: 19 × 24 in. (48.3 × 61.0 cm.)
Artist: A. Ruger

Lithographer:
Printer: Chicago Lith. Co., Chicago
Publisher:
Key/Vignettes/Misc: Refs. 1–10
Locations: LC–M
Catalogs/Checklists: LC–M, 390

1916
Place: Lanesboro, Minnesota
Date: 1879
Title: Lanesboro, Fillmore Co., Minnesota,
1879.
Size: 7½ × 13¾ in. (19 × 35 cm.)
Artist:
Lithographer:
Printer: Beck & Pauli, Lith, Milwaukee
Publisher: J. J. Stoner, Madison
Key/Vignettes/Misc: Refs. 1–13
Locations: MHS–SP
Catalogs/Checklists:

1917
Place: Little Crow's Village, Minnesota
Date: [1854–57]
Title: Little Crow's Village
Size: 6⅜ × 8⁵⁄₁₆ in. (16.2 × 21.9 cm.)
Artist: Henry Lewis
Lithographer:
Printer: C. H. Muller, Aachen
Publisher: Arnz & Co., Dusseldorf
Key/Vignettes/Misc:
Locations: MHS–SP; NYH–NY; HEHL;
LC–R; NL–C; HNOC–NO
Catalogs/Checklists:

1918
Place: Luverne, Minnesota
Date: 1883
Title: 1883 Bird's Eye View of Luverne.
County Seat of Rock County, Minnesota.
Size: 14 × 21½ in. (35.6 × 54.7 cm.)
Artist: H. Brosius
Lithographer:
Printer: Beck & Pauli, Lith. Milwaukee,
Wis.
Publisher: J. J. Stoner, Madison, Wis
Key/Vignettes/Misc: Refs. 1–16
Locations: LC–M; MHS–SP
Catalogs/Checklists: LC–M, 391

1919
Place: Mankato, Minnesota
Date: 1870
Title: Bird's Eye View of the City of
Mankato Blue Earth County Minnesota
1870
Size: 20⅞ × 25⅞ in. (53 × 65.6 cm.)
Artist: [Albert Ruger]
Lithographer:
Printer: Merchants Lithographing Co.,
Chicago
Publisher: Ruger & Stoner, Madison, Wis.
Key/Vignettes/Misc: Refs. 1–12; 2
vignettes
Locations: ACMW–FW; LC–M
Catalogs/Checklists: ACMW–FW 1732;
LC–M, 392

1920
Place: Medicine Bottle's Village,
Minnesota
Date: [1854–57]

Title: Medicine Bottle's Village
Size: 6⅜ × 8⁵⁄₁₆ in. (16.2 × 21.9 cm.)
Artist: Henry Lewis
Lithographer:
Printer: C. H. Muller, Aachen
Publisher: Arnz & Co., Dusseldorf
Key/Vignettes/Misc:
Locations: MHS–SP; NYH–NY; HEHL;
LC–R; NL–C; HNOC–NO
Catalogs/Checklists:

Place: Minneapolis, Minnesota
Date: 1857
See Saint Anthony, Minnesota, 1857.

1921

Place: Minneapolis, Minnesota
Date: 1867
Title: Minneapolis and Saint Anthony
Minnesota 1867
Size: 22 × 27¾ in. (55.9 × 70.5 cm.)
Artist: A. Ruger
Lithographer:
Printer: Chicago Lithographing Company
[Chicago]
Publisher:
Key/Vignettes/Misc: Refs. 1–24
Locations: LC–M
Catalogs/Checklists: LC–M, 393

1922

Place: Minneapolis, Minnesota
Date: 1873
Title: Panorama of Minneapolis, Minn.
Size: 7¼ × 24¼ in. (18.4 × 61.6 cm.)
Artist: A. Hageboeck
Lithographer:
Printer: A. Hageboeck, Davenport, Iowa
Publisher: A. Hageboeck, Davenport, Iowa
Key/Vignettes/Misc:
Locations: LC–M
Catalogs/Checklists: LC–M, 394

1923

Place: Minneapolis, Minnesota
Date: 1874
Title: Minneapolis, Minn.
Size: 16⅝ × 29⅜ in. (42.3 × 74.8 cm.)
Artist:
Lithographer: Hoffman
Printer: Chas. Shober & Co. Prop's.
Chicago Litho Co.
Publisher: Geo. H. Ellsbury & V. Green
(copyright)
Key/Vignettes/Misc: 85 unnumbered refs.
in 12 lines below places identified
Locations: ACMW–FW; LC–P
Catalogs/Checklists: LC–M, 394.1

1924

Place: Minneapolis, Minnesota
Date: 1879
Title: Panoramic View of the City of
Minneapolis, Minnesota, 1879 Looking
North West.
Size: 20½ × 32½ in. (52.1 × 82.6 cm.)
Artist: A. Ruger
Lithographer:
Printer: Beck & Pauli, Lith., Milwaukee
Publisher: J. J. Stoner, Madison, Wisconsin
Key/Vignettes/Misc: Refs. 1–124; 1
vignette
Locations: LC–M; CHS–C

Catalogs/Checklists: LC–M, 395;
Rathbone, Westward the Way, no. 208

1925

Place: Minneapolis, Minnesota
Date: 1879
Title: View of South Minneapolis, 1879.
Size: 9¹⁄₁₆ × 12⁹⁄₁₆ in. (23 × 32 cm.)
Artist:
Lithographer:
Printer: Beck & Pauli, Lith. Milwaukee
Publisher: J. J. Stoner, Madison, Wis.
Key/Vignettes/Misc:
Locations: MHS–SP
Catalogs/Checklists:

1926

Place: Minneapolis, Minnesota
Date: 1885
Title: Minneapolis, Minnesota.
Size: 27½ × 40½ in. (69.9 × 103 cm.)
Artist: W. V. Herancourt
Lithographer:
Printer:
Publisher: I.[sador] Monasch, Minneapolis
Key/Vignettes/Misc:
Locations: LC–M
Catalogs/Checklists: LC–M, 396

1927

Place: Minneapolis, Minnesota
Date: 1891
Title: Bird's Eye View of the City of
Minneapolis, Minn.
Size: 15½ × 21½ in. (39.4 × 54.7 cm.)
Artist: Frank Pezolt
Lithographer:
Printer:
Publisher: A. M. Smith [Minneapolis]
Key/Vignettes/Misc: 1 vignette
Locations: LC–M (photo); MHS–SP
Catalogs/Checklists: LC–M, 398

1928

Place: Minneapolis, Minnesota
Date: 1891
Title: Bird's Eye View of Minneapolis,
Minn.
Size: 29 × 41 in. (73.7 × 104.2 cm.)
Artist: F. Pezolt
Lithographer:
Printer: F. G. Christoph Lith. Co, Chicago
Publisher: A. M. Smith Co. [Minneapolis]
Key/Vignettes/Misc: Refs. 1–49, A–B
Locations: Minneapolis, Minnesota, Public
Library; LC–M; MHS–SP
Catalogs/Checklists: LC–M, 397

1929

Place: Minnehaha, Minnesota
Date: 1858
Title: Minnehaha Whitefield's Series of
Minnesota Scenery, No. 3
Size: 14¼ × 10⅛ in. (36.3 × 25.8 cm.)
Artist: E. Whitefield
Lithographer:
Printer: Gemmell Lith. 132 Lake St.
Chicago.
Publisher: E. Whitefield & Rufus
Blanchard (copyright)
Key/Vignettes/Misc:
Locations: MHS–SP; BPL–P
Catalogs/Checklists: Norton, Whitefield,
no. 73

1930

Place: Minnehaha, Minnesota
Date: 1858
Title: Minnehaha Whitefield's Series of
Minnesota Scenery, No. 4
Size: 14½ × 10¼ in. (36.9 × 26.1 cm.)
Artist: E. Whitefield
Lithographer:
Printer: J. Gemmell Lith. 132 Lake St.
Chicago.
Publisher: Rufus Blanchard Chicago Ill.
Key/Vignettes/Misc:
Locations: BPL–P
Catalogs/Checklists: Norton, Whitefield,
no. 74

1931

Place: Moorhead, Minnesota
Date: 1882
Title: Moorhead, Clay Co., Minnesota,
1882.
Size: 17¼ × 24⅜ in. (44 × 62 cm.)
Artist:
Lithographer:
Printer:
Publisher:
Key/Vignettes/Misc: Refs. 1–28
Locations: MHS–SP
Catalogs/Checklists:

1932

Place: New Ulm, Minnesota
Date: 1860
Title: Ansicht von New Ulm, Minnesota.
1860
Size: 13⅝ × 18⁷⁄₁₆ in. (34.5 × 46.7 cm.)
Artist: J. Berndt
Lithographer:
Printer: Ehrgott, Forbriger & Co.,
Cincinnati, O
Publisher: Nagele, Gerstenhauer & Co.,
New Ulm
Key/Vignettes/Misc: 8 vignettes
Locations: ACMW–FW; MHS–SP;
CPL–AM
Catalogs/Checklists:

1933

Place: New Ulm, Minnesota
Date: 1870
Title: Bird's Eye View of New Ulm Brown
County Minnesota 1870.
Size: 15½ × 20½ in. (39.4 × 52.1 cm.)
Artist: A. Ruger
Lithographer:
Printer: Chicago Lithog. Co., Chicago
Publisher: A. Ruger & Stoner, Madison,
Wisconsin
Key/Vignettes/Misc: Refs. 1–13; 3
vignettes
Locations: LC–M
Catalogs/Checklists: LC–M, 400

1934

Place: Northfield, Minnesota
Date: 1869
Title: Bird's Eye View of Northfield, Rice
County, Minnesota, 1869. Looking South
East.
Size: 17 × 20 in. (43.2 × 50.8 cm.)
Artist: [Albert Ruger]
Lithographer:
Printer: Chicago Lith. Co., Chicago

Publisher: Ruger & Stoner, Madison, Wisconsin
Key/Vignettes/Misc: Refs. 1–10
Locations: MHS–SP; LC–M
Catalogs/Checklists: LC–M, 401

1935
Place: Owatonna, Minnesota
Date: 1870
Title: Bird's Eye View of Owatonna, Steele County, Minnesota, 1879, Looking North East
Size: 18 × 20½ in. (45.8 × 52.1 cm.)
Artist: [Albert Ruger]
Lithographer:
Printer: Merchant's Lith. Co., Chicago
Publisher: Ruger & Stoner, Madison, Wisconsin
Key/Vignettes/Misc: Refs. 1–10; 2 vignettes
Locations: LC–M
Catalogs/Checklists: LC–M, 402

1936
Place: Red Wing, Minnesota
Date: [1854–57]
Title: Red Wing's Village
Size: 6⅜ × 8⁵⁄₁₆ in. (16.2 × 21.9 cm.)
Artist: Henry Lewis
Lithographer:
Printer: C. H. Muller, Aachen
Publisher: Arnz & Co., Dusseldorf
Key/Vignettes/Misc:
Locations: MHS–SP; NYH–NY; HEHL; LC–R; NL–C; HNOC–NO
Catalogs/Checklists:

1937
Place: Red Wing, Minnesota
Date: 1868
Title: Bird's Eye View of the City of Red Wing, Goodhue Co., Minnesota, 1868
Size: 18½ × 24½ in. (47.1 × 62.3 cm.)
Artist: A. Ruger
Lithographer:
Printer: Robert Teufel & Co., Chicago
Publisher:
Key/Vignettes/Misc: Refs. 1–11; 3 vignettes
Locations: LC–M; MHS–SP
Catalogs/Checklists: LC–M, 404

1938
Place: Red Wing, Minnesota
Date: 1874
Title: Red Wing, Minn.
Size: 16⅝ × 27⅞ in. (42.3 × 70.9 cm.)
Artist: Geo. L. Richards
Lithographer:
Printer: Milwaukee Lith & Eng. Co. [Milwaukee]
Publisher: Joseph M. Wolfe
Key/Vignettes/Misc: Refs. 1–30
Locations: MHS–SP; CHS–C
Catalogs/Checklists: Rathbone, Westward the Way, no. 210

1939
Place: Rochester, Minnesota
Date: 1868
Title: Rochester, Minn. 1868.
Size: 9¼ × 18 in. (23.6 × 45.9 cm.)

Artist: Geo. H. Ellsbury
Lithographer:
Printer: Chas. Shober & Co., Chicago
Publisher:
Key/Vignettes/Misc:
Locations: OCHS–R
Catalogs/Checklists:

1940
Place: Rochester, Minnesota
Date: 1869
Title: Bird's Eye View of the City of Rochester, Olmsted County, Minnesota, 1869. Looking North West.
Size: 20½ × 22 in. (52.1 × 55.9 cm.)
Artist: [Albert Ruger]
Lithographer:
Printer: Merchant's Lith. Co., Chicago
Publisher: Ruger & Stoner, Madison, Wisconsin
Key/Vignettes/Misc: Refs. 1–11; 2 vignettes
Locations: LC–M; OCHS–R
Catalogs/Checklists: LC–M, 405

1941
Place: Rochester, Minnesota
Date: 1874
Title: Rochester, Minn. 1874 Population About 5000
Size: 14½ × 27 in. (36.9 × 68.7 cm.)
Artist: Geo. L. Richards
Lithographer:
Printer: Milwaukee Lith & Eng. Co. [Milwaukee]
Publisher: J. Curle & A. Baer
Key/Vignettes/Misc: Refs. 1–27; 2 vignettes
Locations: OCHS–R
Catalogs/Checklists:

1942
Place: Saint Anthony, Minnesota
Date: 1857
Title: View of St. Anthony, Minneapolis, and St. Anthony's Falls. From Cheever's Tower. 1857.
Size: 24 × 36 in. (61 × 91.5 cm.)
Artist: E. Whitefield
Lithographer:
Printer: Endicott & Co., New York
Publisher: E. Whitefield
Key/Vignettes/Misc: 9 refs.
Locations: MHS–SP; NYP–S
Catalogs/Checklists: Norton, Whitefield, no. 70

Place: Saint Anthony, Minnesota
Date: 1867
See Minneapolis, Minnesota, 1867.

1943
Place: Saint Charles, Minnesota
Date: N.D.
Title: St. Charles, Minn.
Size: 8⁹⁄₁₆ × 10⅛ in. (21.8 × 25.7 cm.)
Artist:
Lithographer:
Printer:
Publisher:
Key/Vignettes/Misc:
Locations: ACMW–FW
Catalogs/Checklists:

1944
Place: Saint Cloud, Minnesota
Date: 1869
Title: Bird's Eye View of the City of Saint Cloud, Stearns County, Minnesota 1869.
Size: 21 × 24 in. (53.4 × 61 cm.)
Artist: A. Ruger
Lithographer:
Printer: Merchant's Lith. Co., Chicago
Publisher:
Key/Vignettes/Misc: Refs. 1–12; 2 vignettes
Locations: LC–M; MHS–SP
Catalogs/Checklists: LC–M, 406

1945
Place: Saint Paul, Minnesota
Date: 1853
Title: City of St. Paul, Capital of Minnesota.
Size: 13⅛ × 19¾ in. (33.4 × 50.3 cm.)
Artist: Strobel
Lithographer: J. Queen
Printer: P. S. Duval & Co. steam lith press, Phila.
Publisher: Thompson Ritchie
Key/Vignettes/Misc:
Locations: MHS–SP; NYP–S; CHS–C; LC–M; NYH–NY
Catalogs/Checklists: Stokes P. 1852—E–36; LC–M, 406.1

1946
Place: Saint Paul, Minnesota
Date: 1853
Title: Saint Paul, Capital of Minnesota August 1853. From "Daytons Bluff."
Size: 15½ × 20⅝ in. (39.5 × 52.5 cm.)
Artist: From daguerreotype by J. E. Whitney
Lithographer:
Printer: Endicott & Co., New York
Publisher: Whitney & LeDuc [St. Paul, Minn.]
Key/Vignettes/Misc: 5 vignettes; description
Locations: HEHL; MHS–SP; NYP–S; CHS–C; NYH–NY
Catalogs/Checklists: Stokes 1853—G–24

1947
Place: Saint Paul, Minnesota
Date: 1856
Title: Saint Paul. Capitol of Minnesota, May, 1856
Size: 14⅝ × 22¾ in. (37.2 × 57.9 cm.)
Artist: S. H.[olmes] Andrews
Lithographer:
Printer: Endicott & Co. N. Y.
Publisher: C. Hamilton & Co.
Key/Vignettes/Misc:
Locations: MHS–SP; CHS–C
Catalogs/Checklists:

1948
Place: Saint Paul, Minnesota
Date: [1854–57]
Title: St. Paul, Minnesota
Size: 6⅜ × 8⁵⁄₁₆ in. (16.2 × 21.9 cm.)
Artist: Henry Lewis
Lithographer:
Printer: C. H. Muller, Aachen
Publisher: Arnz & Co., Dusseldorf

Key/Vignettes/Misc:
Locations: MHS−SP; NYH−NY; HEHL;
LC−R; NL−C; HNOC−NO
Catalogs/Checklists:

1949

Place: Saint Paul, Minnesota
Date: 1867
Title: Saint Paul, Minnesota, 1867
Size: 22½ × 28 in. (57.2 × 71.1 cm.)
Artist: A. Ruger
Lithographer:
Printer: Chicago Lithographing Co.,
Chicago
Publisher:
Key/Vignettes/Misc: Refs. 1−28
Locations: LC−M; MHS−SP
Catalogs/Checklists: LC−M, 407

1950

Place: Saint Paul, Minnesota
Date: 1873
Title: Panorama of St. Paul, Minn.
Size: 7½ × 24½ in. (19 × 62.3 cm.)
Artist: A. Hageboeck
Lithographer: A. Hageboeck
Printer: A. Hageboeck, Davenport, Iowa
Publisher: A. Hageboeck, Davenport, Iowa
Key/Vignettes/Misc:
Locations: LC−M
Catalogs/Checklists: LC−M, 408

1951

Place: Saint Paul, Minnesota
Date: 1874
Title: St. Paul, Minn.
Size: 16½ × 29⁷⁄₁₆ in. (42 × 74.9 cm.)
Artist: Geo. H. Ellsbury
Lithographer: Hoffman
Printer: Chas. Shober & Co. proprietors of
Chicago Lith. Co. [Chicago]
Publisher:
Key/Vignettes/Misc: 62 unnumbered refs.
in 7 lines below places identified
Locations: ACMW−FW; LC−M;
CHS−C; LC−P
Catalogs/Checklists: ACMW−FW 1072;
Rathbone, Westward the Way, no. 207;
LC−M, 409

1952

Place: Saint Paul, Minnesota
Date: 1883
Title: St. Paul State Capital, County Seat
of Ramsey Co., Minnesota
Size: 29¹⁄₁₆ × 51¹³⁄₁₆ in. (74 × 112 cm.)
Artist: H. Wellge
Lithographer:
Printer: Beck & Pauli, Lithographers,
Milwaukee, Wis.
Publisher: J. J. Stoner, Madison, Wis.
Key/Vignettes/Misc: Refs. 1−102, A−F;
18 vignettes
Locations: MHS−SP; LC−P (19 vignettes,
publisher imprint only)
Catalogs/Checklists:

1953

Place: Saint Paul, Minnesota
Date: 1883
Title: St. Paul, Minnesota, 1883 State
Capital and County Seat of Ramsey Co.
Size: 25½ × 40¹⁄₁₆ in. (65 × 102 cm.)

Artist: H. Wellge. Vignettes by H. Brosius
Lithographer:
Printer: Beck & Pauli, Lithographers,
Milwaukee, Wis.
Publisher: J. J. Stoner, Madison, Wis.
Key/Vignettes/Misc: Refs. 1−115; 18
vignettes
Locations: MHS−SP; LC−M
Catalogs/Checklists: LC−M, 409.1

1954

Place: Saint Paul, Minnesota
Date: Ca. 1884
Title: View of the City of St. Paul in 1853
Size: 12³⁄₁₆ × 19⁵⁄₈ in. (31 × 50 cm.)
Artist: Max Strobel
Lithographer:
Printer: St. Paul Lith. Co. St. Paul
Publisher: L. P. C. Godfrey
Key/Vignettes/Misc: List of territorial
officers & election results in 1853
Locations: MHS−SP
Catalogs/Checklists:

1955

Place: Saint Paul, Minnesota
Date: 1887
Title: St. Paul, Minn., 1887. Ice Palace and
Winter Carnival Souvenir
Size: 13⅜ × 27½ in. (34 × 70 cm.)
Artist:
Lithographer:
Printer: Marr−Richards Engravers,
Milwaukee
Publisher: Baker, Collins & Co., St. Paul
Key/Vignettes/Misc:
Locations: MHS−SP
Catalogs/Checklists:

1956

Place: Saint Paul, Minnesota
Date: 1888
Title: St. Paul, Minn., 1888. Ice Palace and
Winter Carnival Souvenir.
Size: 13⅜ × 27½ in. (34 × 70 cm.)
Artist:
Lithographer:
Printer: Marr−Richards, Engravers,
Milwaukee
Publisher: Baker, Collins & Co., St. Paul
Key/Vignettes/Misc:
Locations: LC−M
Catalogs/Checklists: LC−M, 409.2

1957

Place: Saint Paul, Minnesota
Date: 1888
Title: St. Paul, Minn, January, 1888
Size: 20¹³⁄₁₆ × 39¹¹⁄₁₆ in. (53 × 101 cm.)
Artist:
Lithographer:
Printer: Orcutt Litho. Co., Chicago
Publisher: J. H. Mahler Co., St. Paul
Key/Vignettes/Misc: Refs. 0−344;
advertisement
Locations: MHS−SP
Catalogs/Checklists:

1958

Place: Saint Paul, Minnesota
Date: 1893
Title: Bird's−Eye View of St. Paul Looking
West from Dayton's Bluff

Size: 8 × 10½ in. (20.3 × 26.7 cm.)
Artist:
Lithographer:
Printer:
Publisher: Brown, Tracy & Co. [St. Paul]
Key/Vignettes/Misc:
Locations: LC−M
Catalogs/Checklists: LC−M, 410

1959

Place: Saint Paul, Minnesota
Date: 1906
Title: St. Paul, Minn.
Size: 16½ × 30½ in. (42 × 77.5 cm.)
Artist:
Lithographer:
Printer:
Publisher: Robert M. Saint, St. Paul
Key/Vignettes/Misc:
Locations: LC−M
Catalogs/Checklists: LC−M, 411

1960

Place: Saint Peter, Minnesota
Date: 1870
Title: Bird's Eye View of the City of Saint
Peter, Nicollet County, Minnesota, 1870.
Size: 17½ × 20½ in. (44.5 × 52.1 cm.)
Artist: [Albert Ruger]
Lithographer:
Printer: Merchant's Lith. Co., Chicago
Publisher: Ruger & Stoner, Madison,
Wisconsin
Key/Vignettes/Misc: Refs. 1−14; 1
vignette
Locations: LC−M; MHS−SP
Catalogs/Checklists: LC−M, 412

1961

Place: Sauk Center, Minnesota
Date: [1868]
Title: View of Sauk Centre, Minnesota.
Size: 11¾ × 19⁵⁄₈ in. (30 × 50 cm.)
Artist: W.[ilford] J. Whitefield
Lithographer:
Printer: Endicott & Co., New York
Publisher:
Key/Vignettes/Misc:
Locations: NYH−NY; MHS−SP
Catalogs/Checklists:

1962

Place: Shakopee, Minnesota
Date: 1869
Title: Bird's Eye View of Shakopee, Scott
County, Minnesota, 1869
Size: 16 × 20½ in. (40.7 × 52.1 cm.)
Artist: A. Ruger & Stoner
Lithographer:
Printer: Chicago Lith. Co., Chicago
Publisher:
Key/Vignettes/Misc: Refs. 1−10
Locations: LC−M
Catalogs/Checklists: LC−M, 413

Place: South Minneapolis, Minnesota
Date: 1879
See Minneapolis, Minnesota, 1879.

1963

Place: Stillwater, Minnesota
Date: 1870
Title: Bird's Eye View of the City of

Stillwater, Washington County, Minnesota, 1879.
Size: 20½ × 22½ in. (52.1 × 57.2 cm.)
Artist: A. Ruger
Lithographer:
Printer: Merchant's Lith. Co., Chicago
Publisher:
Key/Vignettes/Misc: Refs. 1–10; 3 vignettes
Locations: LC–M; MHS–SP
Catalogs/Checklists: LC–M, 414

1964

Place: Stockton, Minnesota
Date: 1866
Title: Stockton, Minn. 1866.
Size: 4⅞ × 9 in. (12.4 × 22.8 cm.)
Artist:
Lithographer:
Printer:
Publisher:
Key/Vignettes/Misc:
Locations: ACMW–FW
Catalogs/Checklists: ACMW–FW 1844

1965

Place: Waconia, Minnesota
Date: Ca. 1870
Title: Coney Island of the West in Clear Water Lake, Waconia, Minnesota.
Size: 17¹¹⁄₁₆ × 23¹⁵⁄₁₆ in. (45 × 61 cm.)
Artist:
Lithographer:
Printer: I.[sador] Monasch
Publisher:
Key/Vignettes/Misc: 1 vignette
Locations: MHS–SP
Catalogs/Checklists:

1966

Place: Winona, Minnesota
Date: 1866
Title: Winona, Minn. 1866
Size: 5⅞ × 20⁹⁄₁₆ in. (15 × 52.3 cm.)
Artist: Geo H. Ellsbury
Lithographer:
Printer: Chas Shober, Chicago.
Publisher:
Key/Vignettes/Misc:
Locations: ACMW–FW
Catalogs/Checklists: ACMW–FW 1073

1967

Place: Winona, Minnesota
Date: 1867
Title: Birds Eye View of the City of Winona, Minnesota, 1867
Size: 22½ × 28½ in. (57.2 × 72.4 cm.)
Artist: A. Ruger
Lithographer:
Printer: Chicago Lithographing Co., Chicago
Publisher:
Key/Vignettes/Misc: Refs. 1–16; 2 vignettes
Locations: LC–M
Catalogs/Checklists: LC–M, 415

1968

Place: Winona, Minnesota
Date: 1874
Title: Winona, Minn.

Size: 17⅛ × 28¼ in. (43.5 × 72 cm.)
Artist:
Lithographer:
Printer: Chas. Shober & Co. props. Chicago Lith. Co. [Chicago]
Publisher: Geo. H. Ellsbury & Vernon Green (copyright)
Key/Vignettes/Misc: 58 unnumbered refs. in 6 lines below places identified
Locations: MM–NN; LC–M; ACMW–FW; MHS–SP; CHS–C; YUAG–NH; LC–P
Catalogs/Checklists: MM–NN, LP 2702; ACMW–FW 1877; Rathbone, Westward the Way, no. 209; LC–M, 416

1969

Place: Winona, Minnesota
Date: 1889
Title: Winona, Minn. 1889.
Size: 18 × 40 in. (45.8 × 101.7 cm.)
Artist: C. J. Pauli
Lithographer:
Printer:
Publisher: C. J. Pauli & Co.
Key/Vignettes/Misc:
Locations: LC–M
Catalogs/Checklists: LC–M, 417

1970

Place: Columbus, Mississippi
Date: [1871?]
Title: Bird's Eye View of Columbus Mississippi
Size: 18½ × 26⅛ in. (47.1 × 66.5 cm.) (cropped)
Artist: C. Drie
Lithographer:
Printer: A. McLean
Publisher: Braughtsman
Key/Vignettes/Misc:
Locations: Private collection
Catalogs/Checklists:

1971

Place: Farmington, Mississippi
Date: 1862
Title: Farmington, Miss.
Size: 10¾ × 15⅛ in. (27.3 × 38.5 cm.)
Artist: A. E. Mathews
Lithographer:
Printer: Middleton Strobridge & Co. Lith., Cin., O.
Publisher:
Key/Vignettes/Misc:
Locations: WHPL–D
Catalogs/Checklists:

1972

Place: Grand Gulf City, Mississippi
Date: 1862
Title: Grand Gulf City. Return of the 4th Wis,. and 6th Mich. Volunteers on the Evening of the 26th of May 1862, in Pursuit of a Rebel Battery
Size: 8½ × 16 in. (21.6 × 40.7 cm.)
Artist: Baldwin
Lithographer:
Printer:
Publisher:
Key/Vignettes/Misc:
Locations: Unknown. See Old Print Shop

Portfolio, XV, p. 105, No. 10
Catalogs/Checklists:

1973

Place: Natchez, Mississippi
Date: [1816–19]
Title: Vue d'un Village a un Mille des Natchez
Size: 4⅜ × 6³⁄₁₆ in. (11.2 × 15.8 cm.)
Artist: Ed[ouard] de Montule
Lithographer: Ed de Montule
Printer:
Publisher:
Key/Vignettes/Misc:
Locations: Natchez Historical Society, Natchez, Mississippi
Catalogs/Checklists:

1974

Place: Natchez, Mississippi
Date: [1833–36]
Title: Natchez. On the Hill, from the Old Fort
Size: 14⅝ × 21³⁄₁₆ in. (37.2 × 53.9 cm.)
Artist: James Tooley
Lithographer:
Printer: Risso & Browne. N. Y.
Publisher:
Key/Vignettes/Misc:
Locations: NYP–S; Natchez Historical Society, Natchez, Mississippi
Catalogs/Checklists: Stokes C. 1835—F–49; Pyne, no. 447

1975

Place: Natchez, Mississippi
Date: [1854–57]
Title: Natchez, Mississippi
Size: 6⅜ × 8⁵⁄₁₆ in. (16.2 × 21.9 cm.)
Artist: Henry Lewis
Lithographer:
Printer: C. H. Muller, Aachen
Publisher: Arnz & Co., Dusseldorf
Key/Vignettes/Misc:
Locations: MHS–SP; NYH–NY; HEHL; LC–R; NL–C; HNOC–NO
Catalogs/Checklists: Stokes 1846–47—F–77

1976

Place: Vicksburg, Mississippi
Date: [1851]
Title: Vicksburgh, Miss.
Size: 5¾ × 7¹⁵⁄₁₆ in. (14.7 × 20.2 cm.)
Artist:
Lithographer: A. Forbriger
Printer: Onken's Lith. Cin. O.
Publisher: [Otto Onken, Cincinnati, Ohio]
Key/Vignettes/Misc:
Locations: CPL–R
Catalogs/Checklists:

1977

Place: Vicksburg, Mississippi
Date: [1854–57]
Title: Vicksburg, Mississippi
Size: 6⅜ × 8⁵⁄₁₆ in. (16.2 × 21.9 cm.)
Artist: Henry Lewis
Lithographer:
Printer: C. H. Muller, Aachen
Publisher: Arnz & Co., Dusseldorf
Key/Vignettes/Misc:

Locations: MHS–SP; NYH–NY; HEHL;
LC–R; NL–C; HNOC–NO
Catalogs/Checklists: Stokes 1846–47—
F–77

1978
Place: Vicksburg, Mississippi
Date: 1871
Title: Bird's Eye View of the City of
Vicksburg Mississippi, 1871
Size: 23⅞ × 29 in. (60.8 × 73.8 cm.)
Artist: [C. Drie?]
Lithographer:
Printer: Chicago Lithography Co., 150,
152 & 154 S. Clark St., Chicago
Publisher: C. Drie, New Orleans
Key/Vignettes/Misc:
Locations: Old Court House
Museum–Eva W. Davis Memorial,
Vicksburg, Mississippi
Catalogs/Checklists:

1979
Place: Vicksburg, Mississippi
Date: 1891
Title: Vicksburg, Miss. 1891
Size: 21⅛ × 33 1/16 in. (53.8 × 84.2 cm.)
Artist: C. J. Pauli
Lithographer:
Printer:
Publisher: C. J. Pauli, 726 Central Avenue,
Milwaukee
Key/Vignettes/Misc: Refs. 1–55
Locations: Old Court House Museum,
Vicksburg, Mississippi
Catalogs/Checklists:

1980
Place: Alexandria, Missouri
Date: N.D.
Title: City of Alexandria, Mo.
Size: 14⅜ × 25 3/16 in. (36.5 × 64 cm.)
Artist: J. B. Miller
Lithographer:
Printer: Wm. Schuchman, Pittsburgh
Publisher:
Key/Vignettes/Misc:
Locations: ACMW–FW
Catalogs/Checklists: ACMW–FW 1431

1981
Place: Aurora, Missouri
Date: 1891
Title: Aurora, Missouri 1891.
Size: 14 9/16 × 26 in. (37 × 66 cm.)
Artist: T. M. Fowler
Lithographer:
Printer:
Publisher: T. M. Fowler & James B.
Moyer, Morrisville, Pa.
Key/Vignettes/Misc: Refs. 1–14
Locations: LC–M
Catalogs/Checklists: LC–M, 417.1

1982
Place: Brookfield, Missouri
Date: 1869
Title: Bird's–Eye–View of Brookfield,
Linn Co., Missouri, 1869
Size: 17 × 20½ in. (43.2 × 52.1 cm.)
Artist: A. Ruger
Lithographer:
Printer:

Publisher:
Key/Vignettes/Misc:
Locations: LC–M
Catalogs/Checklists: LC–M, 418

1983
Place: California, Missouri
Date: 1869
Title: Bird's Eye View of California,
Moniteau Co., Missouri, 1869
Size: 17 × 18 in. (43.2 × 45.8 cm.)
Artist: A. Ruger
Lithographer:
Printer:
Publisher:
Key/Vignettes/Misc:
Locations: LC–M
Catalogs/Checklists: LC–M, 419

1984
Place: Cape Girardeau, Missouri
Date: 1858 State I
Title: Capital View of Cape Girardeau
Size: 20 5/16 × 27⅛ in. (51.8 × 69.1 cm.)
Artist:
Lithographer:
Printer: Chas. Robyn & Co. Lith. 51
Chestnut St. cor. of 3d. St. Louis, Mo.
Publisher:
Key/Vignettes/Misc: 28 vignettes
Locations: MHS–SL
Catalogs/Checklists:

1985
Place: Cape Girardeau, Missouri
Date: 1858 State II
Title: Capital View of Cape Girardeau
Size: 20 5/16 × 27⅛ in. (51.8 × 69.1 cm.)
Artist: A. Bottger
Lithographer: A. Bottger
Printer: Chas. Robyn & Co. Lith. 51
Chestnut St. cor. of 3d. St. Louis, Mo.
Publisher:
Key/Vignettes/Misc: 28 vignettes
Locations: MHS–SL
Catalogs/Checklists:

1986
Place: Carondelet, Missouri
Date: 1841
Title: View of Carandolet. (Vuide Poche.)
Size: 6½ × 8½ in. (16.5 × 21.6 cm.)
Artist: J. C. Wild
Lithographer: J. C. Wild
Printer: Chambers and Knapp, St. Louis
Publisher: J. C. Wild, St. Louis
Key/Vignettes/Misc:
Locations: SHSM–C; CHS–C
Catalogs/Checklists:

1987
Place: Carondelet, Missouri
Date: [1854–57]
Title: Carondelet or Vide–Poche,
Missouri. Carondelet oder Vide–Poche.
(Die leere Tasche) Missouri.
Size: 6⅛ × 7 11/16 in. (15.6 × 19.6 cm.)
Artist: H. Lewis
Lithographer:
Printer: [C. H. Muller, Aachen]
Publisher: Arnz & Co., Dusseldorf
Key/Vignettes/Misc:
Locations: MHS–SP; SAM–SL;

NYH–NY; HEHL; LC–R; NL–C;
HNOC–NO
Catalogs/Checklists:

1988
Place: Carondelet, Missouri
Date: Ca. 1859
Title: Carondelet, Mo.
Size: 21½ × 26⅝ in. (54.8 × 67.8 cm.)
Artist:
Lithographer:
Printer:
Publisher: Th. Schrader, Lithr. No. 42
North 2nd Street St. Louis.
Key/Vignettes/Misc: 12 vignettes
Locations: MHS–SL
Catalogs/Checklists:

1989
Place: Carondelet, Missouri
Date: Ca. 1860
Title:
Size:
Artist: E. Robyn
Lithographer:
Printer:
Publisher:
Key/Vignettes/Misc:
Locations: Unknown. See Charles van
Ravenswaay, Arts & Architecture in
Missouri, p. 491
Catalogs/Checklists:

1990
Place: Carthage, Missouri
Date: 1891
Title: Carthage, Missouri 1891.
Size: 16¼ × 32 in. (41.3 × 81.4 cm.)
Artist: T. M. Fowler
Lithographer:
Printer:
Publisher: T. M. Fowler & James B. Moyer
Key/Vignettes/Misc: Refs. 1–31
Locations: LC–M
Catalogs/Checklists: LC–M, 420

1991
Place: Chillicothe, Missouri
Date: 1869
Title: Bird's Eye View of the City of
Chillicothe, Livingston Co., Missouri,
1869.
Size: 21 × 26 in. (53.4 × 66.1 cm.)
Artist: A. Ruger
Lithographer:
Printer:
Publisher:
Key/Vignettes/Misc: Refs. 1–15; 2
vignettes
Locations: LC–M
Catalogs/Checklists: LC–M, 421

1992
Place: Columbia, Missouri
Date: 1869
Title: Bird's Eye View of the City of
Columbia, Boone Co., Missouri 1869
Size: 17½ × 22 in. (44.5 × 55.9 cm.)
Artist: A. Ruger
Lithographer:
Printer:
Publisher:

Key/Vignettes/Misc: Refs. 1–13; 2 vignettes
Locations: LC–M
Catalogs/Checklists: LC–M, 422

1993
Place: Hannibal, Missouri
Date: [1854–57]
Title: Hanibal, Missouri. Hannibal in Missouri.
Size: 5⅞ × 7⅝ in. (15 × 19.4 cm.)
Artist: H. Lewis
Lithographer:
Printer: [C. H. Muller, Aachen]
Publisher: Arnz & Co., Dusseldorf
Key/Vignettes/Misc:
Locations: MHS–SP; SAM–SL; NYH–NY; HEHL; LC–R; NL–C; HNOC–NO
Catalogs/Checklists:

1994
Place: Hannibal, Missouri
Date: 1869
Title: Bird's Eye View of the City of Hannibal, Marion Co. Missouri. 1869.
Size: 20⅛ × 25¾ in. (51.1 × 65.4 cm.)
Artist: A. Ruger
Lithographer:
Printer:
Publisher:
Key/Vignettes/Misc: Refs. 1–31
Locations: ACMW–FW; LC–M
Catalogs/Checklists: LC–M, 423; ACMW–FW 1638; Reps, Cities on Stone, p. 93

1995
Place: Herculaneum, Missouri
Date: [1854–57]
Title: Herculaneum, Missouri
Size: ca. 6 × 7½ in. (15.3 × 19.1 cm.)
Artist: H. Lewis
Lithographer:
Printer: [C. H. Muller, Aachen]
Publisher: Arnz & Co., Dusseldorf
Key/Vignettes/Misc:
Locations: MHS–SP; SAM–SL; NYH–NY; HEHL; LC–R; NL–C; HNOC–NO
Catalogs/Checklists:

1996
Place: Hermann, Missouri
Date: Ca. 1860
Title: Hermann Missouri
Size: 20⅝ × 25⅞ in. (52.5 × 65.9 cm.)
Artist: E. Robyn [Eduard Robyn]
Lithographer: E. Robyn
Printer: Th. Schrader, 7 Chestnut St., St. Louis
Publisher: Th. Schrader, 7 Chestnut St., St. Louis
Key/Vignettes/Misc: 20 vignettes
Locations: MHS–SL; ACMW–FW
Catalogs/Checklists: Rathbone, Westward the Way, no. 196

1997
Place: Hermann, Missouri
Date: 1869
Title: Bird's Eye View of the City of

Hermann, Gasconade Co., Missouri 1869.
Size: 14 × 16½ in. (35.6 × 42 cm.)
Artist: A. Ruger
Lithographer:
Printer:
Publisher:
Key/Vignettes/Misc: Refs. 1–13; 2 vignettes
Locations: LC–M
Catalogs/Checklists: LC–M, 424

1998
Place: Holden, Missouri
Date: 1869
Title: Bird's Eye View of the City of Holden, Johnson Co., Missouri 1869.
Size: 11 × 12 in. (27.9 × 30.5 cm.)
Artist: A. Ruger
Lithographer:
Printer:
Publisher:
Key/Vignettes/Misc:
Locations: LC–M; LC–P
Catalogs/Checklists: LC–M, 425

1999
Place: Independence, Missouri
Date: 1868
Title: Bird's Eye View of the City of Independence, Jackson Co., Missouri 1868.
Size: 21½ × 26½ in. (54.7 × 67.4 cm.)
Artist: A. Ruger
Lithographer:
Printer:
Publisher:
Key/Vignettes/Misc: Refs. 1–18; 2 vignettes
Locations: LC–M
Catalogs/Checklists: LC–M, 426

2000
Place: Jefferson City, Missouri
Date: [1859?]
Title: Jefferson City, Capital of Missouri
Size: 21¾ (cropped) × 25¹³⁄₁₆ in. (55.3 × 65.7 cm.)
Artist: [E. Robyn?]
Lithographer: [E. Robyn?]
Printer: [Th. Schrader, Lithr. 7 Chestnut Str. St. Louis?]
Publisher: Th. Schrader Lithr. 7 Chestnut Str. St.Louis
Key/Vignettes/Misc: 20 vignettes
Locations: Missouri State Museum, Jefferson City, Missouri
Catalogs/Checklists:

2001
Place: Jefferson City, Missouri
Date: 1869
Title: Bird's Eye View of Jefferson City, the Capitol of Missouri 1869.
Size: 20 × 26 in. (50.8 × 66.1 cm.)
Artist: A. Ruger
Lithographer:
Printer:
Publisher:
Key/Vignettes/Misc: Refs. 1–20; 2 vignettes
Locations: LC–M
Catalogs/Checklists: LC–M, 427

2002
Place: Joplin, Missouri
Date: 1877
Title: Birds Eye View of the City of Joplin Jasper County, Mo. 1877.
Size: 22 × 32½ in. (56 × 82.7 cm.)
Artist: Augustus Koch
Lithographer:
Printer: Shober & Carqueville Lith. Chicago
Publisher:
Key/Vignettes/Misc: Refs. 1–33
Locations: MHS–SL
Catalogs/Checklists:

2003
Place: Kansas City, Missouri
Date: 1855
Title: Kansas City 1855
Size: 7⅜ × 33¼ in. (18.8 x84.6 cm.)
Artist: F. Buckridge
Lithographer:
Printer: John H. Bufford, 313 Washington St. Boston
Publisher:
Key/Vignettes/Misc:
Locations: MHS–SL
Catalogs/Checklists:

2004
Place: Kansas City, Missouri
Date: 1869
Title: Bird's Eye View of Kansas City, Missouri. Jan'y. 1869.
Size: 22 × 28 in. (55.8 × 71.1 cm.)
Artist: A. Ruger
Lithographer:
Printer: Merchants Lith. Co., Chicago
Publisher: Ruger & Stoner, Madison, Wisconsin
Key/Vignettes/Misc: Refs. 1–25; 2 vignettes
Locations: LC–M; KCPL–KC
Catalogs/Checklists: Reps, Cities on Stone, p. 94; LC–M, 428

2005
Place: Kansas City, Missouri
Date: Ca. 1878
Title: Birds Eye View of Kansas City, Missouri
Size: 26¼ × 37¾ in. (66.8 × 96.1 cm.)
Artist:
Lithographer:
Printer:
Publisher:
Key/Vignettes/Misc: 80 refs.
Locations: KCPL–KC
Catalogs/Checklists:

2006
Place: Kansas City, Missouri
Date: [1884?]
Title: Kansas City
Size:
Artist:
Lithographer:
Printer:
Publisher:
Key/Vignettes/Misc: Refs.
Locations: KCPL–KC (photo)
Catalogs/Checklists:

2007
Place: Kansas City, Missouri
Date: 1887
Title: Case & Norman's Stranger's Guide
to Kansas City Missouri, Showing
Principal Points of Interest Correctly
Drawn and Located. . . .
Size: 22 × 39⁵⁄₁₆ in. (56 × 100 cm.)
Artist: W. L. Bloomer
Lithographer:
Printer: A. Zeese Co. Photo Zinc Eng.
Chicago
Publisher: Theo. S. Case [Kansas City,
Missouri]
Key/Vignettes/Misc: 13 vignettes
Locations: KCPL–KC (photo); University
of Missouri, Kansas City, Missouri
Catalogs/Checklists:

2008
Place: Kansas City, Missouri
Date: 1887
Title: Kansas City in 1855 to 1887.
Size: 24¹⁄₁₆ × 39⅛ in. (61.2 × 99.5 cm.)
Artist:
Lithographer:
Printer:
Publisher: Lanward Specialty Publishing
Co., Chicago
Key/Vignettes/Misc: 7 vignettes
Locations: LC–P
Catalogs/Checklists:

2009
Place: Kansas City, Missouri
Date: 1895
Title: Panoramic View of the West
Bottoms, Kansas City, Missouri & Kansas
Showing Stock Yards, Packing &
Wholesale Houses.
Size: 32½ × 49½ in. (82.6 × 125.9 cm.)
Artist: Augustus Koch
Lithographer:
Printer:
Publisher:
Key/Vignettes/Misc: Refs. 1–35; 1
vignette
Locations: LC–M
Catalogs/Checklists: LC–M, 429

2010
Place: Lexington, Missouri
Date: 1869
Title: Bird's Eye View of the City of
Lexington, Lafayette Co., Missouri 1869.
Size: 20½ × 25⅞ in. (52.2 × 65.9 cm.)
Artist: A. Ruger
Lithographer:
Printer:
Publisher:
Key/Vignettes/Misc: Refs. 1–18; 2
vignettes
Locations: LC–M; MHS–SL
Catalogs/Checklists: LC–M, 430

2011
Place: Louisiana, Missouri
Date: [1854–57]
Title: The Town of Louisiana, Missouri
Louisiana, in Missouri
Size: ca. 6 × 7½ in. (15.3 × 19.1 cm.)
Artist: H. Lewis
Lithographer:

Printer: [C. H. Muller, Aachen]
Publisher: Arnz & Co., Dusseldorf
Key/Vignettes/Misc:
Locations: MHS–SP; SAM–SL;
NYH–NY; HEHL; LC–R; NL–C;
HNOC–NO
Catalogs/Checklists:

2012
Place: Louisiana, Missouri
Date: 1876
Title: Birds Eye View of the City of
Louisiana. Pike County Mo. 1876
Size: 16¾ × 20¹¹⁄₁₆ in. (42.6 × 52.7 cm.)
Artist: Augustus Koch
Lithographer:
Printer: Charles Shober & Co., Props,
Chicago Lith Co. [Chicago]
Publisher:
Key/Vignettes/Misc:
Locations: Louisiana, Missouri, Public
Library (photo)
Catalogs/Checklists:

2013
Place: Macon, Missouri
Date: 1869
Title: Bird's Eye View of Macon City,
Macon County, Missouri 1869.
Size: 20½ × 26 in. (52.1 × 66.1 cm.)
Artist: A. Ruger
Lithographer:
Printer:
Publisher:
Key/Vignettes/Misc: Refs. 1–14; 2
vignettes
Locations: LC–M
Catalogs/Checklists: LC–M, 431

2014
Place: Mexico, Missouri
Date: 1869
Title: Bird's Eye View of the City of
Mexico, Audrian Co., Missouri 1869.
Size: 20 × 26 in. (50.8 × 66.1 cm.)
Artist: A. Ruger
Lithographer:
Printer:
Publisher:
Key/Vignettes/Misc: Refs. 1–13; 2
vignettes
Locations: LC–M
Catalogs/Checklists: LC–M, 432

2015
Place: New Madrid, Missouri
Date: [1854–57]
Title: New Madrid, Missouri.
Size: ca. 6 × 7½ in. (ca. 15.3 × 19.1 cm.)
Artist: H. Lewis
Lithographer:
Printer: [C. H. Muller, Aachen]
Publisher: Arnz & Co., Dusseldorf
Key/Vignettes/Misc:
Locations: MHS–SP; SAM–SL;
NYH–NY; HEHL; LC–R; NL–C;
HNOC–NO
Catalogs/Checklists:

2016
Place: Pacific, Missouri
Date: 1869
Title: Pacific, Formerly Franklin, Franklin
Co., Missouri 1869.

Size: 10 × 12 in. (25.4 × 30.5 cm.)
Artist: A. Ruger
Lithographer:
Printer:
Publisher:
Key/Vignettes/Misc:
Locations: LC–M
Catalogs/Checklists: LC–M, 433

2017
Place: Palmyra, Missouri
Date: 1869
Title: Bird's Eye View of the City of
Palmyra, Marion Co., Missouri, A. D.
1869.
Size: 20 × 26 in. (50.8 × 66.1 cm.)
Artist: A. Ruger
Lithographer:
Printer:
Publisher:
Key/Vignettes/Misc: Refs. 1–19; 4
vignettes
Locations: LC–M
Catalogs/Checklists: LC–M, 434

2018
Place: Pleasant Hill, Missouri
Date: 1869
Title: Bird's Eye View of the City of
Pleasant Hill, Case Co., Missouri 1869.
Size: 14 × 18 in. (35.6 × 45.8 cm.)
Artist: A. Ruger
Lithographer:
Printer:
Publisher:
Key/Vignettes/Misc: Refs. 1–10
Locations: LC–M
Catalogs/Checklists: LC–M, 435

2019
Place: Saint Charles, Missouri
Date: 1841
Title: View of St. Charles. Missouri.
Size: 6⅛ × 8⅜ in. (15.6 × 21.3 cm.)
Artist: J. C. Wild
Lithographer: J. C. Wild
Printer: Chambers and Knapp, St. Louis
Publisher: J. C. Wild, St. Louis
Key/Vignettes/Misc:
Locations: SHSM–C; CHS–C
Catalogs/Checklists:

2020
Place: Saint Charles, Missouri
Date: 1850
Title: View of the City of St. Charles, Mo.
Size: 14⅛ × 24½ in. (36 × 62.4 cm.)
Artist:
Lithographer: H. G. Haerting
Printer: A. Janicke & Co. Lith. 41
Chestnut St. [St. Louis]
Publisher: Ortloff
Key/Vignettes/Misc:
Locations: MHS–SL
Catalogs/Checklists: Rathbone, Westward
the Way, no. 190

2021
Place: Saint Charles, Missouri
Date: 1869
Title: Bird's Eye View of the City of Saint
Charles, St. Charles Co., Missouri 1869.
Size: 20½ × 26 in. (52.1 × 66.1 cm.)

Artist: A. Ruger
Lithographer:
Printer:
Publisher:
Key/Vignettes/Misc: Refs. 1–14; 2
vignettes
Locations: LC–M
Catalogs/Checklists: LC–M, 436

2022
Place: Saint Joseph, Missouri
Date: 1868
Title: Bird's Eye View of the City of Saint
Joseph, Missouri 1868.
Size: 22½ × 28 in. (57.2 × 71.2 cm.)
Artist: A. Ruger
Lithographer:
Printer: Merchants Lithographing Co.,
Chicago
Publisher:
Key/Vignettes/Misc: Refs. 1–25; 4
vignettes
Locations: LC–M; St. Joseph, Missouri,
Public Library
Catalogs/Checklists: LC–M, 437

2023
Place: Saint Joseph, Missouri
Date: 1874
Title: Saint Joseph, Mo.
Size: 21½ × 32½ in. (54.8 × 82.7 cm.)
Artist:
Lithographer: Wm. T. Keller
Printer: St. Joseph Steam Printing Co. [St.
Joseph]
Publisher: St. Joseph Steam Printing Co.
[St. Joseph]
Key/Vignettes/Misc: 10 vignettes
Locations: MHS–SL
Catalogs/Checklists:

2024
Place: Saint Joseph, Missouri
Date: N.D.
Title: View of St. Joseph, Mo. From the
Kansas Shore
Size: 7 × 15⅜ in. (17.8 × 39.2 cm.)
Artist:
Lithographer:
Printer:
Publisher:
Key/Vignettes/Misc: 3 views on 1 sheet
Locations: NYH–NY
Catalogs/Checklists:

2025
Place: Saint Louis, Missouri
Date: [1839]
Title: View of St. Louis Taken from
Illinois
Size: 20½ × 27⅝ in. (52.2 × 70.3 cm.)
Artist: J. C. Wild
Lithographer: J. C. Wild
Printer: Lithographic Establishment of E
Dupre St. Louis Mo.
Publisher:
Key/Vignettes/Misc:
Locations: CHS–C; NYP–S; NYH–NY
Catalogs/Checklists: Stokes C. 1840—
E–37; Rathbone, Westward the Way, no.
188

2026
Place: Saint Louis, Missouri
Date: 1840
Title: View of Front St. Looking North
from Walnut
Size: 9¾ × 15 in. (24.8 × 38.1 cm.)
Artist:
Lithographer:
Printer: J. C. Wild
Publisher: J. C. Wild, Mo. Republican
Office
Key/Vignettes/Misc:
Locations: MHS–SL; NYH–NY
Catalogs/Checklists:

2027
Place: Saint Louis, Missouri
Date: 1840
Title: View of St. Louis from South of
Chouteaus Lake
Size: 10⅞ × 15³⁄₁₆ in. (27.7 × 38.7 cm.)
Artist: [J. C. Wild]
Lithographer:
Printer: J. C. Wild, Missouri Republican
Office [St. Louis]
Publisher: J. C. Wild, Missouri Republican
Office [St. Louis]
Key/Vignettes/Misc:
Locations: MHS–SL; KC–G; NYH–NY
Catalogs/Checklists: Pyne, no. 494

2028
Place: Saint Louis, Missouri
Date: [1840]
Title: North East View of St. Louis. From
the Illinois Shore
Size: 11¹⁄₁₆ × 15⁵⁄₁₆ in. (28.1 × 39 cm.)
Artist: J. C. Wild
Lithographer: J. C. Wild
Printer:
Publisher: Republican Office, [St. Louis]
Key/Vignettes/Misc:
Locations: MHS–SL; NYH–NY
Catalogs/Checklists:

2029
Place: Saint Louis, Missouri
Date: [1840?]
Title: South East View of St. Louis From
the Illinois Shore
Size: 11¹⁵⁄₁₆ × 15³⁄₁₆ in. (30.4 × 38.7 cm.)
Artist: J. C. Wild
Lithographer:
Printer:
Publisher:
Key/Vignettes/Misc:
Locations: NYH–NY; MHS–SL
Catalogs/Checklists:

2030
Place: Saint Louis, Missouri
Date: 1841
Title: View of St. Louis. From the Illinois
Shore.
Size: 6¼ × 8¼ in. (15.9 × 21 cm.)
Artist: J. C. Wild
Lithographer: J. C. Wild
Printer: Chambers and Knapp, St. Louis
Publisher: J. C. Wild, St. Louis
Key/Vignettes/Misc:
Locations: SHSM–C; CHS–C
Catalogs/Checklists:

2031
Place: Saint Louis, Missouri
Date: [1841]
Title: Panorama of St. Louis and Vicinity.
Size: 10¾ × 70½ in. (27.3 × 179.3 cm.)
[4 sheets]
Artist: J. C. Wild
Lithographer: J. C. Wild
Printer:
Publisher: J. C. Wild, St. Louis, Mo.
Key/Vignettes/Misc: Refs. 1–4 & 1–10 &
1–5 & 1–8
Locations: SHSM–C; CHS–C; MHS–SL;
NYH–NY
Catalogs/Checklists:

2032
Place: Saint Louis, Missouri
Date: [1839–41?]
Title: A View of St. Louis
Size: 10 × 15 in. (25.4 × 38.2 cm.)
Artist: J. C. Wild
Lithographer: J. C. Wild
Printer: Missouri Republican Office [St.
Louis]
Publisher:
Key/Vignettes/Misc:
Locations: KC–G
Catalogs/Checklists:

2033
Place: Saint Louis, Missouri
Date: [1839–41?]
Title: South View of S. Louis. From the
Mouth of the Cahokia, Illinois
Size:
Artist: J. C. Wild
Lithographer:
Printer:
Publisher: J. C. Wild, St. Louis
Key/Vignettes/Misc:
Locations: Unknown. See Old Print Shop
Negative File
Catalogs/Checklists:

2034
Place: Saint Louis, Missouri
Date: [1846?]
Title: Northeast View of St. Louis from
the Illinois Shore
Size: 11½ × 15⅝ in. (29.2 × 39.7 cm.)
Artist: [J. C. Wild?]
Lithographer:
Printer:
Publisher: George Wooll, No 71, Market,
St. Louis, Mo.
Key/Vignettes/Misc:
Locations: KC–G
Catalogs/Checklists:

2035
Place: Saint Louis, Missouri
Date: [1846?]
Title: South East View of St. Louis. From
the Illinois Shore.
Size: 11¹⁵⁄₁₆ × 15⁵⁄₁₆ in. (30.4 × 38.7 cm.)
Artist: [J. C. Wild]
Lithographer:
Printer: George Wooll, No 71 Market
Street [St. Louis]
Publisher:
Key/Vignettes/Misc:

Locations: MHS–SL
Catalogs/Checklists: Pyne, no. 493

2036
Place: Saint Louis, Missouri
Date: [1846–47]
Title: View of St. Louis
Size: 17¼ × 20¼ in. (43.9 × 51.6 cm.)
Artist:
Lithographer:
Printer: Julius Hutawa
Publisher:
Key/Vignettes/Misc:
Locations: CHS–C
Catalogs/Checklists:

2037
Place: Saint Louis, Missouri
Date: [1848]
Title: Map and View of St. Louis, Mo.
Size: 8½ × 10½ in. (21.6 × 26.7 cm.)
Artist: J. M. Kershaw
Lithographer:
Printer: J. M. Kershaw, St. Louis
Publisher: J. M. Kershaw, St. Louis
Key/Vignettes/Misc: 22 vignettes
Locations: LC–M
Catalogs/Checklists: LC–M, 438

2038
Place: Saint Louis, Missouri
Date: [1848?]
Title: St. Louis & New Orleans Packet
Steamer Grand Turk, N. Robirds,
Master. . . .
Size: 18 × 26½ in. (45.8 × 67.5 cm.)
Artist: H. S. Blood
Lithographer:
Printer: Fishbourne, Lithog. 46 Canal
Street, New Orleans
Publisher:
Key/Vignettes/Misc: Description
Locations: MHS–SL
Catalogs/Checklists:

2039
Place: Saint Louis, Missouri
Date: 1849
Title: Great Fire at St. Louis, Mo.
Thursday Night May 17 1849.
Size: 8¹³⁄₁₆ × 12¾ in. (22.4 × 32.5 cm.)
Artist:
Lithographer:
Printer: N. Currier
Publisher: N. Currier 252 Nassau St. cor
of Spruce N. Y.
Key/Vignettes/Misc:
Locations: NYH–NY
Catalogs/Checklists:

2040
Place: Saint Louis, Missouri
Date: [1840–50]
Title: View of St Louis, Mo.
Size: 13 × 19¼ in. (33.1 × 49 cm.)
Artist: E. W. Playter
Lithographer:
Printer: T. Moore, lith., Boston
Publisher:
Key/Vignettes/Misc:
Locations: MHS–SL; LC–P
Catalogs/Checklists:

2041
Place: Saint Louis, Missouri
Date: 1852
Title: St. Louis, 1852.
Size: 26 × 41⅞ in. (66.2 × 106.5 cm.)
Artist: J. W. Hill and Smith
Lithographer:
Printer: F. Michelin 225 Fulton St., N. Y.
Publisher: Smith Brothers & Co., New
York
Key/Vignettes/Misc:
Locations: MM–NN; MHS–SL
Catalogs/Checklists: MM–NN, LP 1864

2042
Place: Saint Louis, Missouri
Date: 1853
Title: St. Louis Mo. 1853.
Size: 13⅞ × 26 in. (35.2 × 65.8 cm.)
Artist: E. Robyn
Lithographer: E. Robyn
Printer: E. & C. Robyn Lithogrs. No. 44
n. 2nd St. [St. Louis]
Publisher: E. & C. Robyn [St. Louis]
Key/Vignettes/Misc:
Locations: ACMW–FW; MHS–SL
Catalogs/Checklists:

2043
Place: Saint Louis, Missouri
Date: 1854
Title: View of St. Louis, Mo.
Size: 22⅝ × 34¹⁄₁₆ in. (57.6 × 86.7 cm.)
Artist:
Lithographer:
Printer: Juls. Hutawa, Lithr. Second St.
No. 45, St. Louis, Mo.
Publisher:
Key/Vignettes/Misc:
Locations: MHS–SL
Catalogs/Checklists:

2044
Place: Saint Louis, Missouri
Date: 1855
Title: Saint Louis, Mo. in 1855
Size: 7¾ × 51⅜ in. (19.7 × 130.5 cm.)
Artist:
Lithographer: Leopold Gast & Brother
Printer:
Publisher: Leopold Gast & Bros.
Key/Vignettes/Misc:
Locations: LC–P
Catalogs/Checklists:

2045
Place: Saint Louis, Missouri
Date: 1855
Title: Saint Louis, Mo. in 1855.
Size: 12¾ × 84¼ in. (32.4 × 214.3 cm.)
Artist:
Lithographer: Leopold Gast & Brother
Printer:
Publisher: Leopold Gast & Brother [St.
Louis] (copyright)
Key/Vignettes/Misc:
Locations: St. Louis, Missouri, Public
Library
Catalogs/Checklists:

2046
Place: Saint Louis, Missouri
Date: [1854–57]

Title: St. Louis.
Size: 5⅞ × 7¹³⁄₁₆ in. (15 × 19.9 cm.)
Artist: [Henry Lewis]
Lithographer:
Printer: [C. H. Muller, Aachen]
Publisher: Arnz & Co., Dusseldorf
Key/Vignettes/Misc:
Locations: MHS–SP; SAM–SL;
NYH–NY; HEHL; LC–R; NL–C;
HNOC–NO
Catalogs/Checklists:

2047
Place: Saint Louis, Missouri
Date: [1854–57]
Title: The Great Fire in St. Louis May
17th 1849. Der Grosse Brand in St. Louis
am 17, Mei 1849.
Size: ca. 6 × 7½ in. (ca. 15.3 × 19.1 cm.)
Artist: H. Lewis
Lithographer:
Printer: [C. H. Muller, Aachen]
Publisher: Arnz & Co., Dusseldorf
Key/Vignettes/Misc:
Locations: MHS–SP; NYH–NY; HEHL;
SAM–SL; LC–R; HNOC–NO;
MHS–SL
Catalogs/Checklists:

2048
Place: Saint Louis, Missouri
Date: 1858
Title: Bird's Eye View of St. Louis Mo.
Size: 54 × 93 in. (137.5 × 236.7 cm.)
Artist: J. T. Palmatary
Lithographer:
Printer: Middleton Strobridge & Co., Cin.
O.
Publisher:
Key/Vignettes/Misc:
Locations: MHS–SL
Catalogs/Checklists:

2049
Place: Saint Louis, Missouri
Date: 1859
Title: Our City (St. Louis, Mo.)
Size: 17 × 22 in. (43.2 × 55.8 cm.)
Artist:
Lithographer:
Printer: A. Janicke & Co. 3rd St. opp the
Post Office [St. Louis]
Publisher: Hagen & Pfau
Key/Vignettes/Misc:
Locations: LC–P
Catalogs/Checklists: LC–M, 438.1

2050
Place: Saint Louis, Missouri
Date: [1865]
Title: View of St. Louis from Lucas
Place
Size: 18½x 30⅞ in. (47.1 × 78.5 cm.)
Artist:
Lithographer:
Printer: E. Sachse & Co., Baltimore
Publisher: Edw. Buehler, 15 S. 4th. Str. St.
Louis
Key/Vignettes/Misc:
Locations: MM–NN; CHS–C; MHS–SL
Catalogs/Checklists: MM–NN, LP 490;
Rathbone, Westward the Way, no. 194

2051
Place: Saint Louis, Missouri
Date: Ca. 1871
Title: St. Louis, Mo.
Size: 7¹/₁₆ × 9¹/₁₆ in. (18 × 23 cm.) (photo)
Artist:
Lithographer:
Printer:
Publisher: G. Hofmann (copyright)
Key/Vignettes/Misc:
Locations: MHS–SL (photo)
Catalogs/Checklists:

2052
Place: Saint Louis, Missouri
Date: 1873
Title: St. Louis
Size: 15¹/₁₆ × 22¹³/₁₆ in. (38.3 × 58.2 cm.)
Artist:
Lithographer:
Printer:
Publisher: Geo. Degan, New York (copyright)
Key/Vignettes/Misc:
Locations: LC–P
Catalogs/Checklists: LC–M, 438.2

2053
Place: Saint Louis, Missouri
Date: [1873?]
Title: St. Louis
Size: 14 × 22⁵/₁₆ in. (35.6 × 56.8 cm.)
Artist:
Lithographer:
Printer:
Publisher: [Illegible]
Key/Vignettes/Misc:
Locations: KC–G
Catalogs/Checklists:

2054
Place: Saint Louis, Missouri
Date: 1874
Title: Saint Louis, Mo.
Size: 9⁵/₁₆ × 24⁷/₈ in. (23.7 × 63.4 cm.)
Artist:
Lithographer: A. Hageboek
Printer:
Publisher: A. Hageboek
Key/Vignettes/Misc:
Locations: LC–P
Catalogs/Checklists:

2055
Place: Saint Louis, Missouri
Date: 1874
Title: The Bridge at St. Louis
Size: 27¾ × 38½ in. (70.6 × 98 cm.)
Artist:
Lithographer:
Printer:
Publisher:
Key/Vignettes/Misc: 8 vignettes; 1 portrait
Locations: LC–P; The Old Cathedral, St. Louis, Missouri
Catalogs/Checklists: Rathbone, Westward the Way, no. 206

2056
Place: Saint Louis, Missouri
Date: 1874
Title: The City of St. Louis
Size: 21¾ × 32⁵/₈ in. (55.3 × 83 cm.)

Artist: Parsons & Atwater
Lithographer: Parsons & Atwater
Printer:
Publisher: Currier & Ives, New York
Key/Vignettes/Misc: 32 unnumbered refs. below places identified
Locations: ACMW–FW; MM–NN; FC–L; KC–G; SHSM–C; CHS–C; SAM–SL; MHS–SL; Mercantile Library, St. Louis, Missouri; LC–P; NYH–NY
Catalogs/Checklists: ACMW–FW 1578; MM–NN, LP 45; Reps, Cities on Stone, p. 96; LC–M, 438.3

2057
Place: Saint Louis, Missouri
Date: 1875
Title: Pictorial Saint Louis
Size: 110 sheets, each 13 × 18½ in. (33 × 47 cm.)
Artist: Camille N. Dry
Lithographer:
Printer: St. Louis Globe–Democrat Job Printing Co.
Publisher: Compton & Co. [St. Louis]
Key/Vignettes/Misc:
Locations: LC–M; ACMW–FW; Washington University Library, St. Louis, Missouri
Catalogs/Checklists: LC–M, 439

2058
Place: Saint Louis, Missouri
Date: 1876
Title: Saint Louis, 1832
Size: 11¾ × 18⁷/₈ in. (29.9 × 48 cm.)
Artist: L. D. Pomarede, 1832
Lithographer: C. Becker, 1875
Printer:
Publisher: Compton & Co. [St. Louis] (copyright)
Key/Vignettes/Misc:
Locations: MM–NN
Catalogs/Checklists: MM–NN, LP 1166

2059
Place: Saint Louis, Missouri
Date: Ca. 1876
Title: Birds Eye View of St. Louis Showing the New Line of the St. Louis, Kansas City & Northern Ry.
Size: 12 × 23¾ in. (30.5 × 60.5 cm.)
Artist: C. K. Lord
Lithographer:
Printer:
Publisher:
Key/Vignettes/Misc: 15 refs.; 2 vignettes
Locations: MHS–SL; LC–M
Catalogs/Checklists: LC–M, 439.1

2060
Place: Saint Louis, Missouri
Date: 1884
Title: A Pen Picture of the Progress of the City of Saint Louis, Mo
Size: 18½ × 26 in. (47 × 66.1 cm.)
Artist: Henry M. Vogel
Lithographer:
Printer: J. E. Lawton Printing Co.
Publisher: Henry M. Vogel
Key/Vignettes/Misc: 37 vignettes
Locations: LC–M; CHS–C
Catalogs/Checklists: LC–M, 440

2061
Place: Saint Louis, Missouri
Date: 1893
Title: St. Louis in '93
Size: 25½ × 39¼ in. (64.8 × 99.8 cm.)
Artist: Fred Graf
Lithographer:
Printer: Fred Graf, St. Louis
Publisher: Fred Graf, St. Louis
Key/Vignettes/Misc: Refs. 1–74
Locations: LC–M; LC–P
Catalogs/Checklists: LC–M, 441

2062
Place: Saint Louis, Missouri
Date: 1894
Title: The Panorama of St. Louis
Size: 18 × 24 in. (45.8 × 61 cm.)
Artist: Chas. Juehne
Lithographer:
Printer:
Publisher: Chas. Juehne
Key/Vignettes/Misc: Refs. 1–40
Locations: LC–M
Catalogs/Checklists: LC–M, 442

2063
Place: Saint Louis, Missouri
Date: 1895
Title: St. Louis in 1895
Size: 23 × 40 in. (58.5 × 101.7 cm.)
Artist:
Lithographer:
Printer: Chas. Juehne
Publisher: Chas. Juehne
Key/Vignettes/Misc: Refs. 1–48
Locations: LC–M
Catalogs/Checklists: LC–M, 443

2064
Place: Saint Louis, Missouri
Date: 1896
Title: Saint Louis in 1896
Size: 26 × 40½ in. (66.1 × 103 cm.)
Artist: Fred Graf
Lithographer:
Printer:
Publisher: Graf Eng. Co., St. Louis
Key/Vignettes/Misc: 20 vignettes
Locations: LC–M
Catalogs/Checklists: LC–M, 444

2065
Place: Saint Louis, Missouri
Date: 1896
Title: St. Louis in 1896
Size: 23½ × 40 in. (59.8 × 101.7 cm.)
Artist: Chas. Juehne
Lithographer:
Printer: Chas. Juehne
Publisher: Chas. Juehne
Key/Vignettes/Misc: Refs. 1–50
Locations: LC–M
Catalogs/Checklists: LC–M, 445

2066
Place: Saint Louis, Missouri
Date: [1897?]
Title: [St. Louis]
Size: 8½ × 9½ in. (21.6 × 24.1 cm.) (photo)
Artist:
Lithographer:

Printer:
Publisher:
Key/Vignettes/Misc:
Locations: LC–M (photo)
Catalogs/Checklists: LC–M, 446

2067
Place: Saint Louis, Missouri
Date: Ca. 1904
Title: Panoramic View of the Wholesale
and Office District of St. Louis.
Size: 5 × 10½ in. (12.7 × 26.7 cm.)
Artist: Charles Juehne
Lithographer:
Printer:
Publisher: Charles Juehne
Key/Vignettes/Misc:
Locations: LC–M
Catalogs/Checklists: LC–M, 447

2068
Place: Saint Louis, Missouri
Date: Ca. 1907
Title: The Heart of St. Louis
Size: 19½ × 24½ in. (49.6 × 62.3 cm.)
Artist: Fred Graf
Lithographer:
Printer:
Publisher: Fred Graf Engraving Co., St.
Louis
Key/Vignettes/Misc: Refs. 1–72; 4 seals
Locations: LC–M
Catalogs/Checklists: LC–M, 448

2069
Place: Saint Louis, Missouri
Date: N.D.
Title: [Untitled. View of St. Louis
Waterfront. Steamboat St. Louis in
foreground]
Size: 20⅞ × 35¾ in. (53.1 × 90.9 cm.)
Artist:
Lithographer:
Printer:
Publisher:
Key/Vignettes/Misc:
Locations: KC–G
Catalogs/Checklists:

2070
Place: Saint Louis, Missouri
Date: N.D.
Title: St. Louis in 1832. From an original
Painting by Geo. Catlin in Possession of
the Mercantile Library Association.
Size: 12½ × 19¼ in. (31.8 × 48.9 cm.)
Artist: Geo. Catlin
Lithographer:
Printer:
Publisher:
Key/Vignettes/Misc:
Locations: MM–NN; CHS–C
Catalogs/Checklists: MM–NN, LP 2809

2071
Place: Saint Louis, Missouri
Date: N.D.
Title: St. Louis [title in ms.]
Size: 15½ × 25⅛ in. (39.4 × 64 cm.)
Artist:
Lithographer:
Printer:
Publisher:

Key/Vignettes/Misc:
Locations: Unknown
Catalogs/Checklists: Pyne, no. 495

2072
Place: Sedalia, Missouri
Date: 1869
Title: Bird's Eye View of the City of
Sedalia, Pettis Co., Missouri 1869.
Size: 21 × 26½ in. (53.4 × 67.3 cm.)
Artist: A. Ruger
Lithographer:
Printer:
Publisher:
Key/Vignettes/Misc: Refs. 1–14; 4
vignettes
Locations: LC–M
Catalogs/Checklists: LC–M, 449

2073
Place: Selma, Missouri
Date: 1841
Title: View of Selma. Missouri.
Size: 6⅜ × 8½ in. (16.2 × 21.6 cm.)
Artist: J. C. Wild
Lithographer: J. C. Wild
Printer: Chambers and Knapp, St. Louis
Publisher: J. C. Wild, St. Louis
Key/Vignettes/Misc:
Locations: SHSM–C
Catalogs/Checklists:

2074
Place: Tipton, Missouri
Date: 1869
Title: Bird's Eye View of Tipton, Missouri,
Moniteau Co., 1869.
Size: 9¹/₁₆ × 11¹³/₁₆ in. (23 × 30 cm.)
Artist:
Lithographer:
Printer:
Publisher:
Key/Vignettes/Misc:
Locations: LC–M
Catalogs/Checklists:

2075
Place: Warrensburg, Missouri
Date: 1869
Title: Bird's Eye View of the City of
Warrensburg, Johnson Co., Missouri
1869.
Size: 16 × 20 in. (40.7 × 50.8 cm.)
Artist: A. Ruger
Lithographer:
Printer:
Publisher:
Key/Vignettes/Misc: Refs. 1–13
Locations: LC–M
Catalogs/Checklists: LC–M, 450

2076
Place: Washington, Missouri
Date: [1857–59]
Title: Washington, Mo.
Size: 20 × 26 in. (50.9 × 66.2 cm.)
Artist: E.[duard] Robyn
Lithographer: E. Robyn
Printer: Th. Schrader Lith, No. 7. Chestnut
Street [St. Louis]
Publisher: Th. Schrader, Lith. No. 7.
Chestnut Street [St. Louis]
Key/Vignettes/Misc: 20 vignettes

Locations: MHS–SL
Catalogs/Checklists: Rathbone, Westward
the Way, no. 195

2077
Place: Washington, Missouri
Date: 1869
Title: Bird's Eye View of the City of
Washington, Franklin County, Missouri,
1869.
Size: 21 × 26 in. (53.4 × 66.1 cm.)
Artist: A. Ruger
Lithographer:
Printer:
Publisher:
Key/Vignettes/Misc: Refs. 1–11; 2
vignettes
Locations: LC–M
Catalogs/Checklists: LC–M, 451

2078
Place: Billings, Montana
Date: 1904
Title: Birds Eye View Looking South from
"Country Club." Billings, Montana.
County–Seat of Yellowstone County.
1904.
Size: 16⅛ × 28⁵/₁₆ in. (41 × 72 cm.)
Artist: H. Wellge
Lithographer:
Printer:
Publisher: H. Wellge, Milwaukee, Wis.
Key/Vignettes/Misc: Bank advertisement
Locations: LC–M; ACMW–FW
Catalogs/Checklists: LC–M, 452;
ACMW–FW 1296; Reps, Cities on
Stone, p. 91

2079
Place: Bozeman, Montana
Date: 1884
Title: Bird's Eye View of Bozeman, Mon.
1884 County Seat of Gallatin County
Size: 20 × 23 in. (50.9 × 58.5 cm.)
Artist: H. Wellge
Lithographer:
Printer: Beck & Pauli, Litho. Milwaukee,
Wis.
Publisher: J. J. Stoner, Madison, Wis.
Key/Vignettes/Misc: Refs. A–C, 1–6; 4
vignettes; unnumbered business directory
Locations: Bozeman, Montana, Public
Library; RU–NB
Catalogs/Checklists:

2080
Place: Bozeman, Montana
Date: 1898
Title: Bird's Eye View of the City of
Bozeman Gallatin County, Mont. 1898.
Size: 24¾ × 29¾ in. (63 × 75.7 cm.)
Artist: Augustus Koch
Lithographer:
Printer:
Publisher:
Key/Vignettes/Misc: Refs. 1–21
Locations: Chamber of Commerce,
Bozeman, Montana; Montana State
University Library, Bozeman, Montana;
Museum of the Rockies, Bozeman,
Montana
Catalogs/Checklists:

2081
Place: Butte, Montana
Date: 1884
Title: Bird's Eye View of Butte-City
Montana County Seat of Silver Bow Co.
1884
Size: 20 × 29 in. (50.8 × 73.7 cm.)
Artist: H. Wellge
Lithographer:
Printer: Beck & Pauli, Litho. Milwaukee,
Wis.
Publisher: J. J. Stoner, Madison, Wisconsin
Key/Vignettes/Misc: Refs. 1–95; 8
vignettes
Locations: LC–M; MHS–H;
ACMW–FW
Catalogs/Checklists: LC–M, 453; Reps,
Cities on Stone, p. 91

2082
Place: Butte, Montana
Date: ?
Title: Bird's Eye View of Butte City,
Montana
Size: 9 (cropped) × 17⅞ in. (22.6 × 45.5
cm.)
Artist:
Lithographer:
Printer:
Publisher:
Key/Vignettes/Misc:
Locations: UML–M
Catalogs/Checklists:

2083
Place: Deer Lodge, Montana
Date: [1883–84]
Title: Bird's Eye View of Deer Lodge City.
County Seat of Deer Lodge Co. Montana
1883–4
Size: 18 × 23½ in. (45.8 × 59.8 cm.)
Artist:
Lithographer:
Printer: Beck & Pauli, Litho., Milwaukee
Publisher: J. J. Stoner, Madison, Wis.
Key/Vignettes/Misc: Refs. 1–32; 1
vignette
Locations: MHS–H
Catalogs/Checklists:

2084
Place: Glendale, Montana
Date: 1883
Title: Bird's Eye View of Glendale, Mon.
Beaver Head Co. 1883.
Size: 11½ × 23½ in. (29.3 × 59.8 cm.)
Artist:
Lithographer:
Printer: Beck & Pauli, Litho. Milwaukee,
Wis.
Publisher: J. J. Stoner, Madison, Wis.
Key/Vignettes/Misc: Refs. 1–27; 2
vignettes
Locations: Beaverhead County Museum,
Dillon, Montana
Catalogs/Checklists:

2085
Place: Great Falls, Montana
Date: 1891
Title: Perspective Map of Great Falls,
Mont. 1891

Size: 18¹¹⁄₁₆ × 32¾ in. (47.4 × 83.1 cm.)
Artist:
Lithographer:
Printer:
Publisher: American Publishing Co.,
Milwaukee, Wis.
Key/Vignettes/Misc: Description;
advertisement
Locations: ACMW–FW; LC–M
Catalogs/Checklists: ACMW–FW 1821;
LC–M, 454; Reps, Cities on Stone, p. 93

2086
Place: Helena, Montana
Date: 1865
Title: Helena. (in 1865) (Montana
Territory.)
Size: 12¾ × 22⅞ in. (32.5 × 58 cm.)
Artist: G.[ustave] R. Bechler
Lithographer:
Printer: Herline & Hensel, Lith. 632
Chestnut St. Philada.
Publisher: G. R. Bechler (copyright)
Key/Vignettes/Misc:
Locations: ACMW–FW; NYH–NY
Catalogs/Checklists: ACMW–FW 828;
Reps, Cities on Stone, p. 93

2087
Place: Helena, Montana
Date: 1868
Title: Helena.
Size: 9¾ × 20 in. (24.8 × 50.8 cm.)
Artist: [A. E. Mathews]
Lithographer: A. E. Mathews
Printer:
Publisher:
Key/Vignettes/Misc:
Locations: ACMW–FW; NL–C
Catalogs/Checklists: ACMW–FW 1402

2088
Place: Helena, Montana
Date: 1875
Title: Birds–Eye View of Helena,
Montana From the North East Looking
South West.
Size: 20½ × 27 in. (52.1 × 68.6 cm.)
Artist: E. S. Glover
Lithographer:
Printer: A. L. Bancroft & Co.,
Lithographers, San Francisco, California
Publisher: C. K. Wells, Helena
Key/Vignettes/Misc: Refs. 1–14;
description
Locations: LC–M; ACMW–FW;
MHS–H
Catalogs/Checklists: LC–M, 455

2089
Place: Helena, Montana
Date: 1883
Title: 1883 Bird's Eye View of Helena,
Montana. The Capitol of Montana
and County Seat of Lewis and Clark Co.
Size: 12⁹⁄₁₆ × 25¹⁵⁄₁₆ in. (32 × 66 cm.)
Artist:
Lithographer:
Printer: Beck & Pauli, Milwaukee
Publisher: J. J. Stoner, Madison, Wisconsin
Key/Vignettes/Misc: Refs. 1–20, A–J; 5
vignettes

Locations: LC–M; HEHL
Catalogs/Checklists: LC–M, 456

2090
Place: Helena, Montana
Date: 1890
Title: Perspective Map of the City of
Helena, Mont. Capital of State, County
Seat of Lewis & Clarke Co. 1890.
Size: 26¼ × 39⅜ in. (66.7 × 100 cm.)
Artist:
Lithographer:
Printer:
Publisher: American Publishing Co.,
Milwaukee
Key/Vignettes/Misc: Refs. 1–36, A–P; 17
vignettes; description; advertisement
Locations: ACMW–FW; WHPL–D;
LC–M; MHS–H; HEHL
Catalogs/Checklists: ACMW–FW 1822;
LC–M, 457; Reps, Cities on Stone, p. 93

2091
Place: Kalispell, Montana
Date: 1897
Title: Bird's Eye View of the City of
Kalispell, Flathead County, Montana.
1897 Looking Southwest
Size: 21¾ × 27¼ in. (55.3 × 69.3 cm.)
Artist: Augustus Koch
Lithographer:
Printer:
Publisher:
Key/Vignettes/Misc: Refs. 1–32
Locations: UML–M
Catalogs/Checklists:

2092
Place: Livingston, Montana
Date: 1883
Title: Bird's Eye View of Livingston, Mon.
Gallatin County 1883.
Size: 10⅝ × 22⅜ in. (27 × 57 cm.)
Artist:
Lithographer:
Printer: Beck & Pauli, Milwaukee
Publisher: J. J. Stoner, Madison, Wisconsin
Key/Vignettes/Misc:
Locations: LC–M
Catalogs/Checklists: LC–M, 458

2093
Place: Miles City, Montana
Date: 1883
Title: Bird's Eye View of Miles City, c. s. of
Custer County, Montana 1883.
Size: 10¼ × 21⅝ in. (26 × 55 cm.)
Artist:
Lithographer:
Printer: Beck & Pauli, Milwaukee
Publisher: J. J. Stoner, Madison, Wisconsin
Key/Vignettes/Misc:
Locations: LC–M
Catalogs/Checklists: LC–M, 459

2094
Place: Missoula, Montana
Date: 1884
Title: Bird's Eye View of Missoula, Mon.
County Seat of Missoula County 1884.
Size: 13¹⁄₁₆ × 24¹⁄₁₆ in. (33.5 × 61.3 cm.)
Artist: H. Wellge

Lithographer:
Printer: Beck & Pauli, Litho. Milwaukee, Wis.
Publisher: J. J. Stoner, Madison, Wisconsin
Key/Vignettes/Misc: Refs. 1–18; 3 vignettes; unnumbered business directory
Locations: ACMW–FW; LC–M; UML–M
Catalogs/Checklists: LC–M, 460; Reps, Cities on Stone, p. 94

2095
Place: Missoula, Montana
Date: 1891
Title: Perspective Map of Missoula, Mont. County Seat of Missoula County.
Size: 18½ × 33 in. (47 × 84 cm.)
Artist:
Lithographer:
Printer:
Publisher: American Publishing Co., Milwaukee
Key/Vignettes/Misc: 3 vignettes
Locations: LC–M; ACMW–FW; UML–M
Catalogs/Checklists: LC–M, 461

2096
Place: Union City, Montana
Date: 1868
Title: Union City.
Size: 5⅜ × 9 in. (13.6 × 22.8 cm.)
Artist: A. E. Mathews
Lithographer: A. E. Mathews
Printer:
Publisher:
Key/Vignettes/Misc:
Locations: ACMW–FW
Catalogs/Checklists: ACMW–FW 1412

2097
Place: Unionville, Montana
Date: 1868
Title: Unionville.
Size: 7⅞ × 5⅜ in. (20 × 13.6 cm.)
Artist: A. E. Mathews
Lithographer: A. E. Mathews
Printer:
Publisher:
Key/Vignettes/Misc:
Locations: ACMW–FW; WHPL–D
Catalogs/Checklists: ACMW–FW 1413

2098
Place: Virginia City, Montana
Date: 1868
Title: Virginia City.
Size: 9 × 17¼ in. (22.8 × 43.5 cm.)
Artist: A. E. Mathews
Lithographer: A. E. Mathews
Printer:
Publisher: A. E. Mathews (copyright)
Key/Vignettes/Misc:
Locations: ACMW–FW; NL–C
Catalogs/Checklists: ACMW–FW 1414; Reps, Cities on Stone, p. 98; LC–M, 461.1

2099
Place: Virginia City, Montana
Date: 1875
Title: View of Virginia City, Montana Ty,

1875. From Alder Gulch, Looking East.
Size: 14¾ × 20½ in. (37.1 × 52 cm.)
Artist: E. S. Glover
Lithographer:
Printer: Chas. Shober & Co. Prop's Chicago Lith Co. [Chicago]
Publisher:
Key/Vignettes/Misc: Refs. 1–11; description
Locations: MHS–H; ACMW–FW; UML–M; LC–M (photo)
Catalogs/Checklists: LC–M, 461.2

2100
Place: Alma, Nebraska
Date: 1884
Title: Birds Eye View of Alma, Harlan County, Neb. 1884
Size:
Artist: Aug. Koch
Lithographer:
Printer: Ramsey, Millett & Hudson Lith. [Kansas City, Mo.]
Publisher:
Key/Vignettes/Misc: Refs. 1–3
Locations: NSHS–L (photo)
Catalogs/Checklists:

2101
Place: Aurora, Nebraska
Date: 1880
Title: Bird's Eye View of Aurora, Hamilton County Neb. 1880
Size: 12¾ × 17¼ in. (32.4 × 43.9 cm.)
Artist: Augustus Koch
Lithographer:
Printer: Ramsey Millet & Hudson, Lith. Kan. Cy., Mo.
Publisher:
Key/Vignettes/Misc: Refs. 1–8
Locations: Plainsman Museum, Aurora, Nebraska
Catalogs/Checklists:

2102
Place: Beatrice, Nebraska
Date: 1874
Title: Bird's eye View of Beatrice Gage County, Neb, 1874
Size: 16⅞ × 22⅜ in. (43 × 57 cm.)
Artist: Augustus Koch
Lithographer:
Printer: Chas. Shober & Co. Prop. Chicago Lith. Co. [Chicago]
Publisher:
Key/Vignettes/Misc: Refs. 1–16
Locations: HNM–B
Catalogs/Checklists:

2103
Place: Beatrice, Nebraska
Date: 1881
Title: Birds Eye View of the City of Beatrice Gage County, Neb. Looking North East
Size: 21⅝ × 27¹⁵⁄₁₆ in. (55 × 71 cm.)
Artist: Augustus Koch
Lithographer:
Printer:
Publisher:
Key/Vignettes/Misc: Refs. 1–16
Locations: HNM–B
Catalogs/Checklists:

2104
Place: Blair, Nebraska
Date: 1876
Title: Birds Eye View of Blair Washington County Neb. 1876 Looking Towards the South West
Size: 12⁷⁄₁₆ × 16⅛ in. (32 × 41 cm.)
Artist: Augustus Koch
Lithographer:
Printer:
Publisher:
Key/Vignettes/Misc: Refs. 1–13
Locations: Washington County Historical Society, Ft. Calhoun, Nebraska
Catalogs/Checklists:

2105
Place: Blue Springs, Nebraska
Date: 1881
Title: Birds Eye View of Blue Springs Gage County, Neb. 1881
Size: 12³⁄₁₆ × 20¹³⁄₁₆ in. (31 × 53 cm.)
Artist: Augustus Koch
Lithographer:
Printer:
Publisher:
Key/Vignettes/Misc: Refs. 1–4
Locations: HNM–B
Catalogs/Checklists:

2106
Place: Cedar Rapids, Nebraska
Date: 1884
Title: Bird's Eye View of Cedar Rapids, Boone Co. Neb. 1884
Size: 10¾ × 15¼ in. (27.4 × 38.8 cm.) (facsimile)
Artist: Aug. Koch
Lithographer:
Printer: Ramsay, Millett & Hudson, lith. Kan. Cy. Mo.
Publisher:
Key/Vignettes/Misc:
Locations: Cedar Rapids, Nebraska, Public Library (facsimile)
Catalogs/Checklists:

2107
Place: Columbus, Nebraska
Date: 1874
Title: Bird's Eye View of Columbus Platte County Neb. 1874
Size: 11¹¹⁄₁₆ × 17⅞ in. (29.7 × 45.4 cm.)
Artist: Augustus Koch
Lithographer:
Printer:
Publisher:
Key/Vignettes/Misc: Refs. 1–12
Locations: NSHS–L
Catalogs/Checklists: Reps, Cities on Stone, p. 92

2108
Place: Columbus, Nebraska
Date: 1880
Title: Birds Eye View of Columbus, Platt County Neb. 1880. Looking South West
Size:
Artist: August Koch
Lithographer:
Printer: Ramsey, Millett & Hudson Lith. [Kansas City, Mo.]
Publisher:

Key/Vignettes/Misc: Refs. 1–20
Locations: NSHS–L (photo)
Catalogs/Checklists:

2109
Place: Edgar, Nebraska
Date: 1881
Title:
Size:
Artist:
Lithographer:
Printer:
Publisher:
Key/Vignettes/Misc: Refs. 1–5
Locations: NSHS–L (photo of Edgar centennial postcard)
Catalogs/Checklists:

2110
Place: Fairbury, Nebraska
Date: 1881
Title:
Size: 13½ × 18⅞ in. (34.4 × 48.1 cm.)
Artist: Augustus Koch
Lithographer:
Printer:
Publisher:
Key/Vignettes/Misc: Refs. 1–12
Locations: Fairbury City Museum, Fairbury, Nebraska
Catalogs/Checklists:

2111
Place: Fairmont, Nebraska
Date: 1879
Title: Fairmont, Nebraska 1879
Size:
Artist: T. M. Fowler
Lithographer:
Printer:
Publisher: J. J. Stoner, Madison, Wis.
Key/Vignettes/Misc:
Locations: Unknown. Photo in Wilbur Gaffney (ed.), The Fillmore County Story, Geneva, Neb.: Geneva Community Grange No. 403, 1968, p. 134
Catalogs/Checklists:

2112
Place: Falls City, Nebraska
Date: 1876
Title: Birds Eye View of Falls City Richardson County Neb. 1876
Size: 15⁵⁄₁₆ × 20¹⁄₁₆ in. (39 × 51 cm.) (facsimile)
Artist: Augustus Koch
Lithographer:
Printer:
Publisher:
Key/Vignettes/Misc: Refs. 1–12
Locations: NSHS–L (facsimile)
Catalogs/Checklists:

2113
Place: Fremont, Nebraska
Date: 1874
Title: Bird's Eye View of Fremont Dodge County, Neb. 1874
Size: 19⅝ × 24 in. (50 × 61 cm.)
Artist: Aug. Koch
Lithographer:
Printer:
Publisher:

Key/Vignettes/Misc: Refs. 1–20
Locations: Dodge County Historical Society, Fremont, Nebraska
Catalogs/Checklists:

2114
Place: Fremont, Nebraska
Date: 1884
Title: Bird's Eye View of Fremont Dodge Co. Neb. 1884
Size: 21⅝ × 27½ in. (55 × 70 cm.)
Artist: Aug. Koch
Lithographer:
Printer: Ramsay, Millett & Hudson, K[ansas] C[ity], Mo.
Publisher:
Key/Vignettes/Misc: Refs. 1–35
Locations: Dodge County Historical Society, Fremont, Nebraska
Catalogs/Checklists:

2115
Place: Fremont, Nebraska
Date: 1889
Title: Perspective Map of Fremont, Neb. 1889.
Size: 19 × 25½ in. (48.3 × 64.8 cm.)
Artist: H.[enry] W.[ellge?]
Lithographer:
Printer:
Publisher: American Publishing Co., Milwaukee
Key/Vignettes/Misc: Refs. 1–37, A–Y; 3 vignettes
Locations: NSHS–L
Catalogs/Checklists:

2116
Place: Friend, Nebraska
Date: 1879
Title: Birds Eye View of Friend, Nebraska 1879
Size: 12 × 16 in. (30.6 × 40.7 cm.)
Artist: T. M. Fowler
Lithographer:
Printer:
Publisher: J. J. Stoner, Madison, Wis.
Key/Vignettes/Misc:
Locations: Gilbert Public Library, Friend, Nebraska
Catalogs/Checklists:

2117
Place: Grand Island, Nebraska
Date: 1880
Title: Birds Eye View of Grand Island, Hall County Neb. 1880
Size: 19⅝ × 23⁹⁄₁₆ in. (50 × 60 cm.)
Artist: Augustus Koch
Lithographer:
Printer: Ramsey Millett & Hudson, Kan[sas] C[it]y, Mo.
Publisher:
Key/Vignettes/Misc: Refs. 1–14
Locations: Stuhr Museum of the Prairie Pioneer, Grand Island, Nebraska
Catalogs/Checklists:

2118
Place: Harvard, Nebraska
Date: 1879
Title: Harvard, Nebraska. 1879.

Size: 9½ × 12⅞ in. (24.1 × 32.7 cm.)
Artist: T. M. Fowler
Lithographer:
Printer:
Publisher: J. J. Stoner, Madison, Wis.
Key/Vignettes/Misc: Refs. 1–12
Locations: NSHS–L
Catalogs/Checklists:

2119
Place: Hastings, Nebraska
Date: 1879
Title: Hastings, Nebraska. 1879.
Size: 14¹⁵⁄₁₆ × 21¼ in. (38 × 54 cm.)
Artist: T. M. Fowler
Lithographer:
Printer:
Publisher: J. J. Stoner, Madison, Wisconsin
Key/Vignettes/Misc: Refs. 1–21; 1 vignette
Locations: Hastings Museum, Hastings, Nebraska
Catalogs/Checklists:

2120
Place: Hebron, Nebraska
Date: 1883
Title: Bird's Eye View of Hebron Thayer Co., Neb. 1883
Size: 12 × 22½ in. (30.6 × 57.3 cm.)
Artist: Aug. Koch
Lithographer:
Printer: Ramsey, Millett, & Hudson, lith. Kan. Cy. Mo.
Publisher:
Key/Vignettes/Misc: Refs. 1–9
Locations: Thayer County Museum, Belvidere, Nebraska
Catalogs/Checklists:

2121
Place: Holdrege, Nebraska
Date: 1884
Title: Birds Eye View of Holdrege Phelps County, Neb. 1884
Size: 12¼ × 18⅞ in. (31 × 48 cm.)
Artist: Aug. Koch
Lithographer:
Printer:
Publisher:
Key/Vignettes/Misc: Refs. 1–4
Locations: Holdrege Public Library, Holdrege, Nebraska
Catalogs/Checklists:

2122
Place: Humboldt, Nebraska
Date: 1879
Title:
Size:
Artist:
Lithographer:
Printer:
Publisher:
Key/Vignettes/Misc:
Locations: Unknown. Illus. in Lewis Edwards, History of Richardson County. Indianapolis: B. F. Bower & Co., 1917, p. 704
Catalogs/Checklists:

2123
Place: Kearney, Nebraska
Date: 1889
Title: Perspective Map of the City of Kearney, Neb. County Seat of Buffalo Co. 1889.
Size: 24 × 36½ in. (61 × 92.8 cm.)
Artist: H. Wellge
Lithographer:
Printer:
Publisher: American Publishing Co., Milwaukee
Key/Vignettes/Misc: Refs. 1–33, A–Z, AA–AC; 8 vignettes
Locations: LC–M; NSHS–L
Catalogs/Checklists: LC–M, 462

2124
Place: Lincoln, Nebraska
Date: 1874
Title: Birds Eye View of the City of Lincoln. The Capital of Nebraska. 1874.
Size: 21 × 28 in. (53.4 × 71.2 cm.)
Artist: Augustus Koch
Lithographer:
Printer: Chas Shober & Co. Prop. Chicago Lith Co. [Chicago]
Publisher:
Key/Vignettes/Misc: Refs. 1–41; 3 vignettes
Locations: LPL–L
Catalogs/Checklists:

2125
Place: Lincoln, Nebraska
Date: 1880
Title: Birds Eye View of Lincoln, Nebraska
Size: 20½ × 25¾ in. (52.1 × 65.9 cm.)
Artist: Augustus Koch
Lithographer:
Printer: Ramsey, Millett & Hudson, Kansas City, Missouri
Publisher:
Key/Vignettes/Misc: Refs. 1–29; 3 vignettes
Locations: LPL–L; LC–M (facsimile)
Catalogs/Checklists: Reps, Cities on Stone, p. 94; LC–M, 463

2126
Place: Lincoln, Nebraska
Date: 1885
Title: Bird's Eye View of Lincoln Nebraska 1885.
Size: 26½ × 39¼ in. (67.4 × 99.7 cm.)
Artist: Augustus Koch
Lithographer:
Printer: Ramsey, Millett & Hudson, Litho., K. C., Mo.
Publisher:
Key/Vignettes/Misc: Refs. 1–42; 3 vignettes
Locations: LPL–L; NSHS–L
Catalogs/Checklists: Reps, Cities on Stone, p. 94

2127
Place: Lincoln, Nebraska
Date: 1889
Title: Lincoln, Neb. State Capitol of

Nebraska, County Seat of Lancaster Co. 1889.
Size: 22¼ × 31⅞ in. (56.6 × 81 cm.)
Artist: H. Wellge
Lithographer:
Printer:
Publisher: American Publishing Co., Milwaukee
Key/Vignettes/Misc: Refs. A–Z, AA–CD, 1–35, 42–44; 4 vignettes
Locations: LC–M
Catalogs/Checklists: LC–M, 464

2128
Place: Long Pine, Nebraska
Date: 1884
Title: Bird's Eye View of Long Pine, Brown Co., Neb. 1884
Size: 4⅜ × 5½ in. (11 × 14 cm.)
Artist: Aug. Koch
Lithographer:
Printer: Ramsay, Millett & Hudson, Kan. Cy. Mo.
Publisher:
Key/Vignettes/Misc: Refs. 1–5
Locations: Brown County Historical Society, Ainsworth, Nebraska
Catalogs/Checklists:

2129
Place: Madison, Nebraska
Date: 1881
Title: Birds Eye View of Madison, Madison County, Neb. 1881
Size:
Artist: Augustus Koch
Lithographer:
Printer:
Publisher:
Key/Vignettes/Misc:
Locations: NSHS–L (photo)
Catalogs/Checklists:

2130
Place: Nebraska City, Nebraska
Date: 1865
Title: Nebraska City. As Seen From Kearney Heights in 1865.
Size: 11¾ × 16¾ in. (29.9 × 42.6 cm.)
Artist: A. E. Mathews
Lithographer:
Printer: Donaldson & Elmes, 22 Court St, Cincinnati, O.
Publisher:
Key/Vignettes/Misc:
Locations: NSHS–L
Catalogs/Checklists: Taft, p. 76 No. 4

2131
Place: Nebraska City, Nebraska
Date: 1865
Title: Nebraska City. The Landing and City as Seen from the Iowa Side of the Missouri River in 1865.
Size: 12⅛ × 17⅝ in. (30.8 × 44.8 cm.)
Artist: A. E. Matthews
Lithographer:
Printer:
Publisher:
Key/Vignettes/Misc:

Locations: NSHS–L
Catalogs/Checklists: Taft, p. 75 No. 1

2132
Place: Nebraska City, Nebraska
Date: 1865
Title: Nebraska City. View of Main Street—North Side.
Size: ca. 12 × 16 in. (30.6 × 40.7 cm.)
Artist: A. E. Matthews
Lithographer:
Printer: Donaldson & Elmes, 22 Court St., Cincinnati, O.
Publisher:
Key/Vignettes/Misc:
Locations: NSHS–L
Catalogs/Checklists: Taft, p. 75 No. 3

2133
Place: Nebraska City, Nebraska
Date: 1865
Title: Nebraska City. View on Main Street—Looking West.
Size: ca. 12 × 16 in. (30.6 × 40.7 cm.)
Artist: A. E. Matthews
Lithographer:
Printer: Donaldson & Elmes, 22 Court St., Cincinnati, O.
Publisher:
Key/Vignettes/Misc:
Locations: NSHS–L
Catalogs/Checklists: Taft, p. 75 No. 2

2134
Place: Nebraska City, Nebraska
Date: 1868
Title: Bird's Eye View of the City of Nebraska City, Otoe County Nebraska 1868
Size: 21 × 26 in. (53.3 × 66 cm.)
Artist: A. Ruger
Lithographer:
Printer: Merchant's Lithogr. Co. Chicago.
Publisher:
Key/Vignettes/Misc: Refs. 1–16; 2 vignettes
Locations: LC–M
Catalogs/Checklists: Reps, Cities on Stone, p. 94; LC–M, 465

2135
Place: Nebraska City, Nebraska
Date: 1880
Title: Bird's Eye View of Nebraska City Otoe County Nebraska 1880.
Size: 24 × 36⅛ in. (61 × 92 cm.) (sheet)
Artist: Aug. Koch
Lithographer:
Printer:
Publisher:
Key/Vignettes/Misc: Refs. 1–20
Locations: NSHS–L
Catalogs/Checklists:

2136
Place: Neligh, Nebraska
Date: 1881
Title: Birds Eye View of Neligh Antelope County, Neb.
Size: 12½ × 18 in. (31.8 × 45.8 cm.)
Artist: Augustus Koch

Lithographer:
Printer:
Publisher:
Key/Vignettes/Misc:
Locations: Antelope County Museum, Neligh, Nebraska
Catalogs/Checklists:

Place: New York, Nebraska
Date: 1879
See York, Nebraska, 1879.

2137
Place: Norfolk, Nebraska
Date: 1881
Title: Bird's—EyeView of Norfolk Madison County, Neb. 1881
Size: 14½ × 21⅝ in. (36.8 × 54.7 cm.)
Artist: Augustus Koch
Lithographer:
Printer:
Publisher:
Key/Vignettes/Misc: Refs. 1–7
Locations: Norfolk, Nebraska, Public Library NYH–NY
Catalogs/Checklists:

2138
Place: Norfolk, Nebraska
Date: 1889
Title: 1889 Perspective Map of Norfolk, Neb.
Size: 14⅛ × 24⅜ in. (36 × 62 cm.)
Artist: H. Wellge
Lithographer:
Printer:
Publisher: American Publishing Co., Milwaukee
Key/Vignettes/Misc:
Locations: LC–M
Catalogs/Checklists: LC–M, 466

2139
Place: North Platte, Nebraska
Date: 1888
Title: North Platte, Lincoln County, Neb., Fall of 1888.
Size: 14⁹⁄₁₆ × 23⅝ in. (37 × 60 cm.)
Artist: J. A. Ricker
Lithographer:
Printer:
Publisher: North Platte Telegraph
Key/Vignettes/Misc: 30 vignettes
Locations: WHPL–D
Catalogs/Checklists: Reps, Cities on Stone, p. 95

2140
Place: Omaha, Nebraska
Date: 1867
Title: Omaha Nebraska 1867 Looking North From Forest Hill.
Size: 12¹³⁄₁₆ × 26⅞ in. (32.5 × 68.2 cm.)
Artist: H. Lambach
Lithographer:
Printer: Gast, Moeller & Co. Lith., St. Louis.
Publisher:
Key/Vignettes/Misc:
Locations: ACMW–FW; NYP–S
Catalogs/Checklists: ACMW–FW 1285;

Reps, Cities on Stone, p. 95; Stokes 1867—G–79

2141
Place: Omaha, Nebraska
Date: 1868
Title: Bird's Eye View of the City of Omaha Nebraska 1868.
Size: 22¹⁄₁₆ × 28 in. (55.9 × 71 cm.)
Artist: A. Ruger
Lithographer:
Printer: Chicago Lithographing Co., Chicago
Publisher:
Key/Vignettes/Misc: Refs. 1–19; 4 vignettes
Locations: ACMW–FW; LC–M; CHS–C; Omaha, Nebraska, Public Library
Catalogs/Checklists: LC–M, 467; Reps, Cities on Stone, p. 95

2142
Place: Omaha, Nebraska
Date: 1876
Title: Birds Eye View of the City of Omaha Douglas County Neb. 1876.
Size: 23⁹⁄₁₆ × 39⁵⁄₁₆ in. (69 × 100 cm.)
Artist: Augustus Koch
Lithographer:
Printer: Charles Shober & Co., Chicago
Publisher:
Key/Vignettes/Misc: Refs. 1–50
Locations: LC–M (photo); Omaha, Nebraska, Public Library
Catalogs/Checklists: LC–M, 467.2

2143
Place: Omaha, Nebraska
Date: 1906
Title: Panoramic View of Omaha
Size: 21½ × 42⁵⁄₁₆ in. (54.5 × 107.4 cm.)
Artist: Edw. J. Austen
Lithographer:
Printer: Manz Engraving Co., Chicago and New York
Publisher: Omaha Daily Bee
Key/Vignettes/Misc:
Locations: Joslyn Art Musem, Omaha, Nebraska; NSHS–L; LC–M
Catalogs/Checklists: Reps, Cities on Stone, p. 95; LC–M, 468

2144
Place: Osceola, Nebraska
Date: Ca. 1882
Title: [Osceola, Nebraska]
Size: 12 × 18 in. (30.6 × 45.8 cm.)
Artist: Augustus Koch
Lithographer:
Printer: Ramsey, Millet & Hudson Lith Kansas City Mo.
Publisher:
Key/Vignettes/Misc:
Locations: Polk County Museum, Osceola, Nebraska
Catalogs/Checklists:

2145
Place: Pawnee City, Nebraska
Date: 1879

Title: Birds Eye View of Pawnee City Neb. 1879
Size:
Artist:
Lithographer:
Printer:
Publisher: J. J. Stoner, Madison, Wisconsin
Key/Vignettes/Misc: Refs. 1–17
Locations: NSHS–L (photo); Pawnee City, Nebraska, Republican
Catalogs/Checklists:

2146
Place: Pierce, Nebraska
Date: 1884
Title: Birds Eye View of Pierce Co., Neb. 1884
Size: 10¼ × 17½ in. (26.1 × 44.6 cm.)
Artist: Aug. Koch
Lithographer:
Printer: Ramsay, Millett & Hudson, lith. K. Cy. Mo.
Publisher:
Key/Vignettes/Misc: 24 vignettes
Locations: Pierce Museum, Pierce, Nebraska
Catalogs/Checklists:

2147
Place: Plattsmouth, Nebraska
Date: 1880
Title: Birds Eye View of Plattsmouth, Cass County, Neb. 1880
Size: 19⅝ × 23³⁄₁₆ in. (50 × 59 cm.)
Artist: Augustus Koch
Lithographer:
Printer: Ramsey Millett & Hudson, Lith., Kan Cy, Mo.
Publisher:
Key/Vignettes/Misc: Refs. 1–15
Locations: NSHS–L
Catalogs/Checklists:

2148
Place: Red Cloud, Nebraska
Date: 1881
Title: Birds Eye View of Red Cloud Webster County, Neb. 1881
Size: 21⅝ × 27½ in. (55 × 70 cm.)
Artist: Augustus Koch
Lithographer:
Printer:
Publisher:
Key/Vignettes/Misc: Refs. 1–3
Locations: Willa Cather Pioneer Memorial, Red Cloud, Nebraska
Catalogs/Checklists:

2149
Place: Schuyler, Nebraska
Date: 1884
Title: Bird's Eye View of Schuyler Colfax County, Neb. 1884
Size: 16¹³⁄₁₆ × 22⅝ in. (42.8 × 57.6 cm.) (facsimile)
Artist: Aug. Koch
Lithographer:
Printer: Ramsay, Millett & Hudson lith. Kan. Cy. Mo.
Publisher:
Key/Vignettes/Misc:

Locations: Schuyler, Nebraska, Public Library (facsimile)
Catalogs/Checklists:

2150
Place: Seward, Nebraska
Date: [1874–76?]
Title: Bird's Eye View of Seward. Seward County, Neb.
Size: 11¹¹⁄₁₆ × 16⅛ in. (29.7 × 40.8 cm.)
Artist: Augustus Koch
Lithographer:
Printer: Chas. Shober & Co. Prop. Chicago Lith. Co. [Chicago]
Publisher:
Key/Vignettes/Misc: Refs. 1–12
Locations: ACMW–FW; NSHS–L
Catalogs/Checklists:

2151
Place: Sutton, Nebraska
Date: 1879
Title: Sutton, Nebraska 1879
Size:
Artist: T. M. Fowler
Lithographer:
Printer:
Publisher: J. J. Stoner, Madison, Wis.
Key/Vignettes/Misc: Refs. 1–18
Locations: T. C. Wenzlaff, Sutton, Nebraska (photo)
Catalogs/Checklists:

2152
Place: York, Nebraska
Date: 1879
Title: Birds Eye View of York & New York Nebraska 1879
Size: 17¹¹⁄₁₆ × 21⅝ in. (45 × 55 cm.)
Artist: T. M. Fowler
Lithographer:
Printer: Beck & Pauli lith., Milwaukee
Publisher: J. J. Stoner, Madison, Wis.
Key/Vignettes/Misc: Refs. 1–13
Locations: Anna Palmer Museum, York, Nebraska
Catalogs/Checklists:

2153
Place: Carson City, Nevada
Date: 1875
Title: Birds Eye View of Carson City Ormsby County Nevada 1875 Looking Southwest.
Size: 15⅝ × 24⅛ in. (39.8 × 61.4 cm.)
Artist: Augustus Koch
Lithographer:
Printer: Britton, Rey & Co., Lith. S. F.
Publisher:
Key/Vignettes/Misc: Refs. 1–27
Locations: UCBL–B; NHS–R; Nevada State Museum, Carson City, Nevada; LC–M (photo)
Catalogs/Checklists: Reps, Cities on Stone, p. 91; LC–M, 468.1

2154
Place: Ely, Nevada
Date: ?
Title: Ely District, Nev.
Size:
Artist: F. E. Durand

Lithographer:
Printer: Britton & Rey, S. F.
Publisher:
Key/Vignettes/Misc: Refs. 0–26; map of mining region
Locations: Unknown. See Stanley Poher, Nevada Ghost Towns and Mining Camps. Berkeley: Howell–North Books, 1970
Catalogs/Checklists:

2155
Place: Eureka, Nevada
Date: 1879
Title: Eureka, Eureka County, Nevada.
Size: ["folio"]
Artist:
Lithographer:
Printer: Shober & Carqueville, Chicago
Publisher:
Key/Vignettes/Misc:
Locations: Unknown. American Art Association, Anderson Galleries, Pioneer & Mining Days of California, Sales Catalog No. 3834, March 31 and April 1, 1930, no. 47
Catalogs/Checklists:

2156
Place: Reno, Nevada
Date: [1890]
Title: Birds Eye View of Reno Nevada
Size: 20⅞ × 34½ in. (53 × 87.6 cm.)
Artist:
Lithographer:
Printer: H. S. Crocker & Co.
Publisher: C. C. Powning
Key/Vignettes/Misc: Refs. 1–58; 24 vignettes
Locations: NHS–R; Washoe County School District, Reno, Nevada; LC–M (facsimile)
Catalogs/Checklists: Reps, Cities on Stone, p. 96; LC–M, 468.2

2157
Place: Reno, Nevada
Date: N.D.
Title: A Bird's–Eye View of Reno The Commercial Center of Nevada
Size: 14¹⁵⁄₁₆ × 29⅞ in. (38 × 76 cm.)
Artist: G. T. Brown
Lithographer:
Printer: Journal Print, Reno, Nevada
Publisher: B. M. Barndollar
Key/Vignettes/Misc: 30 vignettes
Locations: NHS–R
Catalogs/Checklists:

2158
Place: Treasure Hill, Nevada
Date: 1869
Title: View of the West Side of Treasure Hill.
Size: 23 × 30½ in. (58.6 × 77.6 cm.)
Artist: Samuel C. Lewis
Lithographer:
Printer: Britton & Rey, San Francisco
Publisher: Samuel C. Lewis (copyright)
Key/Vignettes/Misc: Refs. 1–190
Locations: UN–R
Catalogs/Checklists:

2159
Place: Treasure Hill, Nevada
Date: 1869
Title: View of Treasure Hill White Pine, Nev.
Size: 9⅝ × 16½ in. (24.5 × 42 cm.)
Artist: E. W. Peet
Lithographer:
Printer: Britton & Rey, San Francisco
Publisher: H. H. Bancroft & Co., San Francisco
Key/Vignettes/Misc:
Locations: UCBL–B
Catalogs/Checklists:

2160
Place: Treasure Hill, Nevada
Date: N.D.
Title: View of Eastern Slope of Treasure Hill Showing the Works of the Hamilton Hydraulic & Tunnel Co.
Size: 11¹⁵⁄₁₆ × 19⁹⁄₁₆ in. (30.4 × 49.8 cm.)
Artist: R. M. Wilson
Lithographer:
Printer: Britton & Rey, San Francisco
Publisher:
Key/Vignettes/Misc: Refs. 1–20
Locations: UCBL–B
Catalogs/Checklists:

2161
Place: Virginia City, Nevada
Date: 1861
Title: Virginia City, Nevada Territory. 1861.
Size: 7¼ × 10¹¹⁄₁₆ in. (18.4 × 27.2 cm.)
Artist: Grafton T. Brown
Lithographer: C. C.Kuchel
Printer: Britton & Co. [San Francisco]
Publisher: Grafton T. Brown [San Francisco]
Key/Vignettes/Misc: 30 vignettes
Locations: UCBL–B; LC–P; NYP–S
Catalogs/Checklists: Stokes 1861—G–59; Peters, COS, pp. 88, 90, 147; LC–M, 468.2

2162
Place: Virginia City, Nevada
Date: 1864
Title: Virginia City, N. T. 1864.
Size: 26½ × 39½ in. (67.5 × 100.5 cm.)
Artist: Grafton T. Brown
Lithographer: C. C. Kuchel
Printer: Britton & Co. [San Francisco]
Publisher:
Key/Vignettes/Misc: 9 vignettes
Locations: UCBL–B; UN–R
Catalogs/Checklists: Peters, COS, p. 90

2163
Place: Virginia City, Nevada
Date: 1875
Title: Birds Eye View of Virginia City Storey County, Nevada. 1875
Size: 22 × 28⁵⁄₁₆ in. (56 × 72 cm.)
Artist: Augustus Koch
Lithographer:
Printer: Britton, Rey & Co., S. F.
Publisher:
Key/Vignettes/Misc: Refs. 1–46

Locations: LC–M; Nevada State Musem, Carson City, Nevada; UN–R
Catalogs/Checklists: LC–M, 469; Reps, Cities on Stone, p. 98

2164
Place: Virginia City, Nevada
Date: 1875
Title: Treadwell's Birds Eye View of the Comstock Mines and Vicinity. Storey & Lyon Counties. State of Nevada
Size: 24⅞ × 33³⁄₁₆ in. (63.3 × 84.5 cm.)
Artist: H. Stggr [Steinegger]
Lithographer:
Printer: Britton Rey & Co., San Francisco
Publisher: J. B. Treadwell, Washington
Key/Vignettes/Misc:
Locations: UCBL–B; UN–R; HEHL; LC–M
Catalogs/Checklists: Peters, COS, p. 85

2165
Place: Virginia City, Nevada
Date: 1877
Title: Virginia City Storey County, Nevada 1877
Size: 22¼ × 34½ in. (56.6 × 87.8 cm.)
Artist:
Lithographer:
Printer: Britton, Rey & Co., San Francisco
Publisher:
Key/Vignettes/Misc:
Locations: UCBL–B
Catalogs/Checklists:

2166
Place: Winnemucca, Nevada
Date: 1881
Title: Bird's–Eye View of Winnemucca County Seat of Humboldt County, Nevada. 1881.
Size: 20¹⁄₁₆ × 27¹⁵⁄₁₆ in. (51 × 71 cm.)
Artist: G. T. Brown
Lithographer:
Printer: W. T. Galloway, San Francisco
Publisher:
Key/Vignettes/Misc: 13 vignettes
Locations: NHS–R
Catalogs/Checklists:

2167
Place: Bathurst, New Brunswick
Date: 1860
Title: The Town of Bathurst
Size: 7½ × 11¾ in. (19.1 × 29.8 cm.)
Artist: W. Hickman
Lithographer: F. Jones
Printer: Day & Sons Lithrs to the Queen, [London]
Publisher:
Key/Vignettes/Misc:
Locations: PAC–P; MTLB–T
Catalogs/Checklists: Robertson, no. 2214

2168
Place: Bathurst, New Brunswick
Date: Ca. 1866
Title: Bathurst, N. B.
Size: ca. 8 × 11⅛ in. (20.4 × 28.4 cm.)
Artist: Thomas Pye
Lithographer:

Printer:
Publisher: Roberts and Reinhold, Place d'Armes, Mtl.
Key/Vignettes/Misc:
Locations: PAC–P; MTLB–T
Catalogs/Checklists: Robertson, no. 1581; Spendlove, Face of Early Canada, p. 35 and Plate 52

2169
Place:(ppp Buctouche, New Brunswick
Date: 1888
Title: Buctouche, New Brunswick. 1888.
Size: 19⅜ × 25¼ in. (49.3 × 64.2 cm.)
Artist:
Lithographer:
Printer:
Publisher: D.[uncan] D.[unbar] Currie, Moncton, N. B.
Key/Vignettes/Misc: Refs. A–H, J–P; 16 vignettes
Locations: BPL–R; Archives Acadiennes, Universite de Moncton, Moncton, New Brunswick
Catalogs/Checklists: PAC (1976)

2170
Place: Chatham, New Brunswick
Date: 1881
Title: View of Chatham. New Brunswick. 1881.
Size: 20⅜ × 24¼ in. (51.8 × 61.7 cm.)
Artist:
Lithographer:
Printer:
Publisher: O. H. Bailey & Co., [Boston]
Key/Vignettes/Misc: Refs. 1–28, A–E; 8 vignettes
Locations: BPL–R; New Brunswick Museum, St. John, New Brunswick
Catalogs/Checklists: PAC (1976)

2171
Place: Dalhousie, New Brunswick
Date: Ca. 1866
Title: Dalhousie, N. B.
Size: 8 × 11¼ in. (20.4 × 28.3 cm.)
Artist: Thomas Pye
Lithographer:
Printer:
Publisher: Roberts and Reinhold, Place d'Armes, Mtl.
Key/Vignettes/Misc:
Locations: PAC–P; MTLB–T
Catalogs/Checklists: Robertson, no. 1580; Spendlove, Face of Early Canada, p. 35

2172
Place: Dorchester, New Brunswick
Date: 1888
Title: Dorchester, New Brunswick 1888.
Size: 21 × 26½ in. (53.4 × 67.5 cm.)
Artist:
Lithographer:
Printer:
Publisher: D. D. Currie, Moncton, N. B.
Key/Vignettes/Misc: 25 vignettes
Locations: Keillor House Musum, Dorchester, New Brunswick
Catalogs/Checklists: PAC (1976)

2173
Place: Fredericton, New Brunswick
Date: Ca. 1837
Title: Fredericton, N. B. From the Oromocto Road
Size: 7 × 10 in. (17.8 × 25.4 cm.)
Artist: R. Petley
Lithographer: R. Petley
Printer: C. Hullmandel Lith., London
Publisher: J. Dickinson, NewBond Street
Key/Vignettes/Misc:
Locations: MCM–M; ROM; MTLB–T
Catalogs/Checklists: Samuel, no. 736; Robertson, no. 2266; Spendlove, Face of Early Canada, p. 34

2174
Place: Fredericton, New Brunswick
Date: 1882
Title: City of Fredericton, N. B. 1882.
Size: 21¼ × 26½ in. (54.1 × 67.4 cm.)
Artist: Alexander M. Hubly
Lithographer:
Printer: O. H. Bailey & Co., Boston
Publisher: A. M. Hubly
Key/Vignettes/Misc: Refs. 1–79; 10 vignettes
Locations: BPL–R; PANB–F; PAC (photo)
Catalogs/Checklists: PAC (1976)

2175
Place: Marysville, New Brunswick
Date: Ca. 1885
Title: Marysville, N. B.
Size:
Artist:
Lithographer:
Printer:
Publisher: E. Russell [pub., printer, or artist]
Key/Vignettes/Misc: 1 vignette
Locations: PANB–F (photo)
Catalogs/Checklists:

Place: Milltown, New Brunswick
Date: 1879
See Calais, Maine, 1879.

2176
Place: Moncton, New Brunswick
Date: 1881
Title: Moncton, New Brunswick. 1881.
Size: 24½ × 32¼ in. (62.3 × 82 cm.)
Artist:
Lithographer:
Printer:
Publisher: O. H. Bailey & Co., [Boston]
Key/Vignettes/Misc: Refs. 1–88; 26 vignettes
Locations: BPL–R
Catalogs/Checklists:

2177
Place: Moncton, New Brunswick
Date: 1888
Title: Moncton, New Brunswick, 1888.
Size: 25½ × 34¼ in. (64.9 × 87.1 cm.)
Artist:
Lithographer:
Printer:

Publisher: D. D. Currie
Key/Vignettes/Misc: Refs. 1–191; 49 vignettes
Locations: PANB–F; BPL–R
Catalogs/Checklists: PAC (1976)

2178
Place: Newcastle, New Brunswick
Date: 1881
Title: Newcastle, New Brunswick. 1881.
Size: 17⅛ × 20¼ in. (43.5 × 51.6 cm.)
Artist:
Lithographer:
Printer:
Publisher:
Key/Vignettes/Misc: Refs. 1–49; 5 vignettes
Locations: BPL–R; Miramichi Historical Society, Newcastle, New Brunswick
Catalogs/Checklists: PAC (1976)

2179
Place: Saint Andrews, New Brunswick
Date: [1840]
Title: View of the Town of St. Andrew's, New Brunswick, With its Manificent Harbour and Bay.
Size: 15¹⁄₁₆ × 19 in. (38.3 × 48.2 cm.)
Artist: Frederick Wells
Lithographer:
Printer: Day & Son [London]
Publisher:
Key/Vignettes/Misc: Description
Locations: PAC–P
Catalogs/Checklists:

2180
Place: Saint Andrews, New Brunswick
Date: [187–?]
Title: View of the Town and Harbour of St. Andrew's, N, B, America Taken from Navy Island.
Size: 11¹³⁄₁₆ × 28½ in. (30 × 72.4 cm.)
Artist: W. M. Buck
Lithographer: I. Tashenhurst
Printer: John Kelly, 45 Upr. Gloucester St. Dublin.
Publisher:
Key/Vignettes/Misc:
Locations: MTLB–T; PAC–P; MCM–M
Catalogs/Checklists: Robertson, no. 2220

2181
Place: Saint John, New Brunswick
Date: [1827]
Title: City of St. John, Province of New Brunswick
Size: 13⅛ × 32 in. (33.4 × 81.4 cm.)
Artist: [L.] W.[illiam] Hunt
Lithographer: A. Robinson
Printer:
Publisher:
Key/Vignettes/Misc:
Locations: PAC–P; MTLB–T (cropped and lacking title)
Catalogs/Checklists:

2182
Place: Saint John, New Brunswick
Date: [1835]
Title: The City of St. John–New Brunswick

Size: 6⅛ × 9 in. (15.6 × 22.9 cm.)
Artist: M. G. Hall
Lithographer:
Printer: Pendleton's Lithography, Boston
Publisher: [M. G. Hall, St. John, New Brunswick]
Key/Vignettes/Misc:
Locations: PAC–P; MTLB–T
Catalogs/Checklists: Robertson, no. 2268

2183
Place: Saint John, New Brunswick
Date: Ca. 1835
Title: The Northern and Eastern Panoramic View of St. John, N. B.
Size: 14⅛ × 22¹⁄₁₆ in. (35.9 × 56 cm.)
Artist:
Lithographer:
Printer: Pendleton's Lithography, Boston
Publisher:
Key/Vignettes/Misc:
Locations: PAC–P
Catalogs/Checklists:

2184
Place: Saint John, New Brunswick
Date: 1838
Title: View of the Great Conflagration.
Size: 18¹³⁄₁₆ × 26³⁄₁₆ in. (47.9 × 66.7 cm.)
Artist: Thos. W. Wentworth and Wm. H. Wentworth
Lithographer: F. H. Lane
Printer: Thos Moore's establishment, Boston
Publisher: Thos. Moore (copyright)
Key/Vignettes/Misc: Description
Locations: BA
Catalogs/Checklists:

2185
Place: Saint John, New Brunswick
Date: [1848]
Title: View of the City of St. John, New Brunswick. From the Rock in Rear of Sandpoint, Carleton.
Size: 17³⁄₁₆ × 24⁵⁄₁₆ in. (43.7 × 61.8 cm.)
Artist: Geo. N. Smith
Lithographer:
Printer: J. H. Bufford's Lithography, Boston
Publisher:
Key/Vignettes/Misc:
Locations: PAC–P
Catalogs/Checklists:

2186
Place: Saint John, New Brunswick
Date: 1851
Title: View of Saint John, N. B. 1851. This Picture is Most Respectfully Dedicated to the Liberal and Enterprising Citizens of St. John and Vicinity. . . .
Size: 28⁹⁄₁₆ × 38¹¹⁄₁₆ in. (72.5 × 98.3 cm.)
Artist: J. W. Hill
Lithographer: N. Sarony
Printer: Sarony & Major, 117 Fulton St. N. York
Publisher: Francis Smith & Co., New York
Key/Vignettes/Misc: 4 vignettes; description
Locations: NYP–S; PAC–P; NYH–NY
Catalogs/Checklists: Stokes 1851—H–7

2187
Place: Saint John, New Brunswick
Date: [1860–69]
Title: City of St. John New Brunswick
Size: 14¾ × 46³⁄₁₆ in. (37.5 × 117.3 cm.)
Artist: From a photograph by Bowron & Cox
Lithographer:
Printer: Day & Son Limited. . .London, W. C.
Publisher: Bowron & Cox, Photographers, 16 King Street, St. John's, New Brunswick
Key/Vignettes/Misc:
Locations: PAC–P; MCM–M
Catalogs/Checklists:

2188
Place: Saint John, New Brunswick
Date: 1877
Title: The Great Fire at St. John, N. B. June 20th 1877
Size: 7⅞ × 12¾ in. (20.2 × 32.3 cm.)
Artist:
Lithographer:
Printer:
Publisher: Currier & Ives, 115 Nassau St. New York
Key/Vignettes/Misc: Description
Locations: PAC–P; MCM–M; MTLB–T; ROM
Catalogs/Checklists: Robertson, no. 44; Samuel, no. 613

2189
Place: Saint John, New Brunswick
Date: 1882
Title: The City of St. John. New Brunswick. 1882.
Size: 24⅞ × 31¼ in. (63.3 × 79.5 cm.)
Artist: [illegible initials in lower right of principal view]
Lithographer:
Printer:
Publisher: O. H. Bailey & Co., [Boston]
Key/Vignettes/Misc: Refs. 1–132; 18 vignettes
Locations: BPL–R; PANB–F; PAC–P (cropped)
Catalogs/Checklists:

Place: Saint Stephen, New Brunswick
Date: 1879
See Calais, Maine, 1879.

2190
Place: Saint Stephen, New Brunswick
Date: 1889
Title: St. Stephen, New Brunswick, and Calais, Maine. 1889.
Size: 23 × 29¼ in. (58.5 × 74.4 cm.)
Artist:
Lithographer:
Printer:
Publisher: L. W. McAnn, Moncton, N. B.
Key/Vignettes/Misc: 41 vignettes; unnumbered business directory
Locations: BPL–R
Catalogs/Checklists: Farnsworth, p. 37

2191
Place: Stanley, New Brunswick
Date: 1836
Title: General View of Stanley

Size: ca. $7\frac{1}{4} \times 11$ in. (18.5×28 cm.)
Artist: P. Harry
Lithographer:
Printer: Day & Haghe, Lithrs. to the King. [London]
Publisher: Ackermann & Co, Strand [London]
Key/Vignettes/Misc:
Locations: MTLB–T
Catalogs/Checklists: Robertson, no. 2232; Spendlove, Face of Early Canada, p. 35

2192
Place: Stanley, New Brunswick
Date: 1836
Title: Process of Clearing the Town Plot at Stanley. Octr., 1834
Size: 8×15 in. (20.3×38.1 cm.)
Artist: W. P. Kay
Lithographer: S. Russell
Printer: Day and Haghe, Lithrs. to the King [London]
Publisher: Ackermann and Co. Strand, [London]
Key/Vignettes/Misc:
Locations: MTLB–T
Catalogs/Checklists: Robertson, no. 2237

2193
Place: Woodstock, New Brunswick
Date: 1889
Title: Woodstock, New Brunswick. 1889.
Size: $22\frac{1}{4} \times 29\frac{1}{4}$ in. (56.6×74.4 cm.)
Artist:
Lithographer:
Printer: O. H. Bailey & Co. [Boston]
Publisher: L. W. McAnn & Co., Moncton, N. B.
Key/Vignettes/Misc: Refs., Upper Woodstock, A, 2–5, Victoria Corner, A, 2–8; 42 vignettes; unnumbered business directory
Locations: BPL–R; L. P. Fisher Library, Woodstock, New Brunswick
Catalogs/Checklists: PAC (1976)

2194
Place: Alton, New Hampshire
Date: 1888
Title: Alton and Alton Bay, N. H. 1888.
Size: $14\frac{1}{8} \times 22\frac{3}{8}$ in. (35.9×57 cm.)
Artist: Geo. E. Norris
Lithographer:
Printer: The Burleigh Lith. Est.
Publisher: Geo. E. Norris, Brockton, Mass.
Key/Vignettes/Misc: Refs. 1–16; 2 vignettes
Locations: LC–M; BPL–R
Catalogs/Checklists: LC–M, 469.2

2195
Place: Antrim, New Hampshire
Date: 1887
Title: Antrim, N. H., and Clinton Village. 1887
Size: $16\frac{1}{8} \times 26$ in. (41×66.1 cm.)
Artist: Geo. E. Norris
Lithographer:
Printer: The Burleigh Litho Establishment, Troy, N. Y.
Publisher: Geo. E. Norris, Brockton, Mass.
Key/Vignettes/Misc: Refs. A–H, J–V, 1–11; 1 vignette
Locations: BPL–R; LC–M; NHHS–C
Catalogs/Checklists: LC–M, 469.3

2196
Place: Ashland, New Hampshire
Date: 1883
Title: Ashland, Grafton Co., N. H. 1883.
Size: $14\frac{1}{8} \times 13\frac{5}{8}$ in. (35.9×34.7 cm.)
Artist:
Lithographer:
Printer: Beck & Pauli, Milwaukee, Wis.
Publisher: Poole & Norris, Brockton, Mass.
Key/Vignettes/Misc: Refs. 1–24
Locations: LC–M; BPL–R; NHHS–C (facsimile); LC–P
Catalogs/Checklists: LC–M, 470

2197
Place: Ashuelot, New Hampshire
Date: 1887
Title: Ashuelot, N. H. 1887
Size: ca. 10×15 in. (25.4×38.1 cm.)
Artist:
Lithographer:
Printer:
Publisher: Geo. H. Walker & Co., Boston
Key/Vignettes/Misc:
Locations: Thayer Public Library, Ashuelot, New Hampshire
Catalogs/Checklists:

2198
Place: Bartlett, New Hampshire
Date: 1896
Title: Bartlett, N. H. 1896
Size: $14\frac{1}{16} \times 21\frac{1}{4}$ in. (35.8×54.1 cm.)
Artist:
Lithographer:
Printer:
Publisher:
Key/Vignettes/Misc: Refs. 1–39; 1 vignette
Locations: NHHS–C
Catalogs/Checklists:

2199
Place: Bennington, New Hampshire
Date: 1887
Title: Bennington, N. H.
Size: $10\frac{1}{4} \times 19$ in. (26.1×48.3 cm.)
Artist: Geo. E. Norris
Lithographer:
Printer: The Burleigh Litho. Establishment, Troy, N. Y.
Publisher: Geo. E. Norris, Brockton, Mass.
Key/Vignettes/Misc: Refs. A–M
Locations: BPL–R
Catalogs/Checklists:

2200
Place: Berlin Falls, New Hampshire
Date: 1888
Title: Berlin Falls, N. H. and Berlin Mills. 1888
Size: $17\frac{1}{8} \times 30\frac{5}{16}$ in. (43.4×77 cm.)
Artist: Geo. E. Norris
Lithographer:
Printer: Burleigh Lith. Est., Troy, N. Y.
Publisher: Geo. E. Norris, Brockton, Mass.
Key/Vignettes/Misc: Refs. 1–31, A–P; 12 vignettes
Locations: BPL–R; NHHS–C
Catalogs/Checklists:

2201
Place: Bethlehem, New Hampshire
Date: 1883
Title: Bird's Eye View of Bethlehem, Grafton County, N. H. 1883.
Size: 16×20 in. (40.7×50.8 cm.)
Artist: A. F. Poole
Lithographer:
Printer: Beck & Pauli, Milwaukee
Publisher: Poole & Norris, Brockton, Mass.
Key/Vignettes/Misc: Refs. 1–53
Locations: LC–M
Catalogs/Checklists: LC–M, 471; Cobb, New Hampshire Maps, no. 382

2202
Place: Bristol, New Hampshire
Date: 1884
Title: Bristol, Grafton County, N. H. 1884
Size: $15\frac{3}{4} \times 22\frac{13}{16}$ in. (40×58 cm.)
Artist: Geo. E. Norris
Lithographer:
Printer: Beck & Pauli, Milwaukee
Publisher: Geo. E. Norris, Brockton, Mass.
Key/Vignettes/Misc: Refs. 1–60; 1 vignette
Locations: LC–M; WHS–M
Catalogs/Checklists: LC–M, 471.1

2203
Place: Claremont, New Hampshire
Date: 1857
Title: Claremont, N. H. 1857
Size: $17\frac{3}{16} \times 27\frac{1}{2}$ in. (43.8×70 cm.)
Artist: From ambrotype by Charles Allen
Lithographer:
Printer: Endicott & Co. N. Y.
Publisher: John Bachelder
Key/Vignettes/Misc: 4 unnumbered refs. below places identified
Locations: BA; NHHS–C; NYH–NY
Catalogs/Checklists:

2204
Place: Claremont, New Hampshire
Date: 1877
Title: Birds Eye View of Claremont, Sullivan County, N. H. 1877
Size: $20 \times 24\frac{1}{2}$ in. (50.8×62.3 cm.)
Artist: A. Ruger
Lithographer:
Printer: Shober & Carqueville Litho. Co., Chicago
Publisher: [J. J. Stoner, Madison, Wis.]
Key/Vignettes/Misc: Refs. 1–22; 1 vignette
Locations: LC–M
Catalogs/Checklists: LC–M, 472

2205
Place: Colebrook, New Hampshire
Date: 1887
Title: Colebrook, N. H., Coos Co.
Size: $14\frac{1}{4} \times 20\frac{1}{4}$ in. (36.2×51.5 cm.)
Artist: Geo. E. Norris
Lithographer:

Printer:
Publisher: Geo. E. Norris, Brockton, Mass.
Key/Vignettes/Misc: Refs. 1–25, A–T; 1 vignette
Locations: BPL–R; NHHS–C
Catalogs/Checklists:

2206
Place: Concord, New Hampshire
Date: 1853
Title: Concord, New Hampshire. From an Original Painting by G. Harvey, A. N. A.
Size: 16⅞ × 26¾ in. (43 × 67.7 cm.)
Artist: G. Harvey
Lithographer:
Printer: M. & H. Hanhart, London
Publisher: V. Bartholomew, 23, Charlotte St. Portland Place, London
Key/Vignettes/Misc:
Locations: BA; NYP–S; YUAG–NH; ROM; NHHS–C; NYH–NY
Catalogs/Checklists: Samuel, no. 432; Stokes P. 1852—G–23

2207
Place: Concord, New Hampshire
Date: 1855
Title: City of Concord, N. H. From the High Bluff about 80 Rods North East of the Free Bridge.
Size: 18⅞ × 25⅝ in. (48 × 65.2 cm.)
Artist: Henry P. Moore
Lithographer:
Printer: J. H. Bufford's Lith, 260 Washington St., Boston
Publisher:
Key/Vignettes/Misc:
Locations: EI–S; BA; YUAG–NH; NHHS–C; NYH–NY
Catalogs/Checklists:

2208
Place: Concord, New Hampshire
Date: 1860
Title: South West View Concord, N. H. 1860
Size: 14⁹⁄₁₆ × 18¾ in. (36.8 × 47.7 cm.)
Artist: H. P. Moore
Lithographer:
Printer: Endicott & Co. New York
Publisher: H. P. Moore, Concord, N.H. 1860
Key/Vignettes/Misc:
Locations: MM–NN; NHHS–C
Catalogs/Checklists: MM–NN, LP 2699

2209
Place: Concord, New Hampshire
Date: 1875
Title: Bird's Eye View of Concord, N. H. 1875
Size: 21⅛ × 29½ in. (53.8 × 75.1 cm.)
Artist: H. H. Bailey & Co.
Lithographer: C. H. Vogt
Printer: J. Knauber & Co.
Publisher: H. H. Bailey & Co.
Key/Vignettes/Misc: Refs. 1–17
Locations: BPL–R; NHHS–C
Catalogs/Checklists:

2210
Place: Concord, New Hampshire
Date: 1899 State I
Title: Concord, N. H. 1899

Size: 22½ × 28 in. (57.2 × 71.2 cm.)
Artist: [Bert Poole]
Lithographer:
Printer:
Publisher: G. M. Clough, Boston
Key/Vignettes/Misc: 3 vignettes
Locations: LC–M
Catalogs/Checklists: LC–M, 474; Cobb, New Hampshire Maps, no. 510

2211
Place: Concord, New Hampshire
Date: 1899 State II
Title: Concord, N. H. 1899.
Size: 22½ × 28 in. (57.2 × 71.2 cm.)
Artist: [Bert Poole]
Lithographer:
Printer:
Publisher: Bert Poole
Key/Vignettes/Misc:
Locations: LC–M
Catalogs/Checklists: LC–M, 473

2212
Place: Conway, New Hampshire
Date: 1896
Title: Conway, N. H. 1896.
Size: 14⁹⁄₁₆ × 23⅛ in. (37 × 56 cm.)
Artist: Geo. E. Norris
Lithographer:
Printer:
Publisher:
Key/Vignettes/Misc: Refs. 1–54
Locations: NHHS–C
Catalogs/Checklists:

2213
Place: Derry, New Hampshire
Date: 1898
Title: Derry, N. H. 1898
Size: 18¾ × 26⅝ in. (47.7 × 67.7 cm.)
Artist: [O. H. Bailey]
Lithographer:
Printer:
Publisher: Charles Bartlett, Derry, N. H.
Key/Vignettes/Misc: 29 vignettes
Locations: NHHS–C; Derry, New Hampshire, Public Library
Catalogs/Checklists:

2214
Place: Derry Depot, New Hampshire
Date: 1887
Title: Derry Depot, N. H., Rockingham County. 1887.
Size: 13⁵⁄₁₆ × 20½ in. (33.7 × 52.2 cm.)
Artist: Geo. E. Norris
Lithographer:
Printer: The Burleigh Litho. Establishment, Troy, N. Y.
Publisher: Geo. E. Norris, Brockton, Mass.
Key/Vignettes/Misc: Refs. 1–24; 1 vignette
Locations: BPL–R; NHHS–C
Catalogs/Checklists:

2215
Place: Dover, New Hampshire
Date: 1855
Title: View of Dover, N. H. Taken from Garrison Hill.
Size: 22⅜ × 30¼ in. (56.7 × 77.8 cm.)
Artist: J. B. Bachelder
Lithographer:

Printer: J. H. Bufford's Lith. 260 Washington St., Boston
Publisher: J. B. Bachelder (copyright)
Key/Vignettes/Misc:
Locations: BPL–P; BA; NHHS–C; NYH–NY
Catalogs/Checklists:

2216
Place: Dover, New Hampshire
Date: 1877
Title: Bird's Eye View of Dover Stafford Co. New Hampshire. Looking Southwest 1877
Size: 23½ × 24¼ in. (59.8 × 61.7 cm.)
Artist: A. Ruger
Lithographer:
Printer: D. Bremner & Co., Lith., Milwaukee
Publisher:
Key/Vignettes/Misc: Refs. 1–46, A–H, J–K
Locations: BPL–R; LC–M
Catalogs/Checklists: LC–M, 475

2217
Place: Dover, New Hampshire
Date: 1888
Title: Dover, Stafford County, New Hampshire 1888.
Size: 20¹⁄₁₆ × 27⅞ in. (51 × 71 cm.)
Artist: Bert Poole
Lithographer:
Printer:
Publisher: Interstate Art Publishing Co., Boston
Key/Vignettes/Misc: Refs. A–H, J–Z, 1–87
Locations: LC–M; Dover, New Hampshire, Public Library
Catalogs/Checklists: LC–M, 475.1

Place: East Rochester, New Hampshire
Date: 1884
See Rochester, New Hampshire, 1884.

2218
Place: Exeter, New Hampshire
Date: 1884
Title: Exeter, N. H. County Seat of Rockingham County. 1884.
Size: 15⅞ × 21½ in. (40.4 × 54.7 cm.)
Artist: H. Wellge
Lithographer:
Printer:
Publisher: Norris & Wellge, Brockton, Mass,.
Key/Vignettes/Misc: Refs. 1–43
Locations: BPL–R; LC–M; NHHS–C
Catalogs/Checklists: LC–M, 476; Cobb, New Hampshire Maps, no. 394

2219
Place: Exeter, New Hampshire
Date: 1896
Title: Exeter New Hampshire. 1896
Size: 27½ × 32 in. (69.9 × 81.3 cm.)
Artist:
Lithographer:
Printer:
Publisher: A. W. Moore Co., lith Boston
Key/Vignettes/Misc: Refs. 1–32; 35 vignettes
Locations: LC–M

Catalogs/Checklists: LC−M, 477; Cobb,
New Hampshire Maps, no. 502

2220
Place: Farmington, New Hampshire
Date: 1877
Title: Bird's Eye View of the Village of
Farmington, Stafford County, New
Hampshire 1877.
Size: 14⅛ × 17¼ in. (36 × 44 cm.)
Artist: [Albert Ruger]
Lithographer:
Printer:
Publisher: [J. J. Stoner, Madison, Wis.]
Key/Vignettes/Misc: Refs. 1−25; 1
vignette
Locations: LC−M
Catalogs/Checklists: LC−M, 477.1

2221
Place: Franklin, New Hampshire
Date: 1856
Title: Franklin, N. H. 1856 from Cemetery
Hill Paper Mill Village Franklin Mill
Village
Size: 29½ × 23½ in. (75.1 × 59.8 cm.)
Artist: H. P. Moore
Lithographer:
Printer:
Publisher:
Key/Vignettes/Misc: 3 views in vertical
format on a single sheet
Locations: Unknown. See Old Print Shop
Portfolio, XXXVIII, p. 38, No. 25
Catalogs/Checklists:

2222
Place: Franklin, New Hampshire
Date: 1884
Title: Franklin and Franklin Falls, N. H.,
Merrimack County. 1884.
Size: 16 × 19¾ in. (40.7 × 50.2 cm.)
Artist: H. Wellge
Lithographer:
Printer:
Publisher: Norris & Wellge, Brockton,
Mass.
Key/Vignettes/Misc: Refs. 1−53; 1
vignette
Locations: LC−M; BPL−R; NHHS−C
Catalogs/Checklists: LC−M, 478; Cobb,
New Hampshire Maps, no. 395

2223
Place: Goffstown, New Hampshire
Date: 1887
Title: Goffstown, N. H. 1887.
Size: 15¼ × 19⅝ in. (38.8 × 50 cm.)
Artist: Geo. E. Norris
Lithographer:
Printer: The Burleigh Litho. Establishment
Publisher: Geo. E. Norris, Brockton, Mass.
Key/Vignettes/Misc: Refs. 1−26, A−L
Locations: LC−M; BPL−R; NHHS−C
Catalogs/Checklists: LC−M, 478.1

Place: Gonic, New Hampshire
Date: 1884
See Rochester, New Hampshire, 1884.

2224
Place: Gorham, New Hampshire
Date: 1888
Title: Gorham, N. H. 1888.

Size: 19⅞ × 24¾ in. (50.6 × 63 cm.)
Artist: Geo. E. Norris
Lithographer:
Printer: The Burleigh Lith. Est.
Publisher: Geo. E. Norris, Brockton, Mass.
Key/Vignettes/Misc: Refs. 1−42, A−K; 8
vignettes
Locations: LC−M; BPL−R
Catalogs/Checklists: LC−M, 478.2

2225
Place: Great Falls, New Hampshire
Date: 1877
Title: Bird's Eye View of Great Falls,
Strafford Co., New Hampshire & Berwick,
York Co., Maine 1877.
Size: 22¼ × 24 in. (56.6 × 61 cm.)
Artist: A. Ruger
Lithographer:
Printer: C. H. Vogt & Co., Lith
[Milwaukee]
Publisher: J. J. Stoner, Madison, Wisconsin
Key/Vignettes/Misc: Refs. 1−36
Locations: LC−M; BPL−R
Catalogs/Checklists: LC−M, 479;
Farnsworth, p. 38

2226
Place: Greenville, New Hampshire
Date: 1886
Title: Greenville, N. H. 1886.
Size: 14 × 20 in. (35.6 × 50.8 cm.)
Artist:
Lithographer:
Printer: The Burleigh Lith. Establishment,
Troy, N. Y.
Publisher: L. R. Burleigh, Troy, N. Y.
Key/Vignettes/Misc: Refs. 1−9; 1 vignette
Locations: LC−M; BPL−R
Catalogs/Checklists: LC−M, 480; Cobb,
New Hampshire Maps, no. 410

2227
Place: Groton, New Hampshire
Date: 1897
Title: Groveton, N. H. Coos Co. 1897
Size: 15¼ × 22½ in. (38.9 × 57.3 cm.)
Artist: [George E. Norris]
Lithographer:
Printer:
Publisher: [George E. Norris, Brockton,
Mass.]
Key/Vignettes/Misc: Refs. 1−36
Locations: Town Office, Groveton, New
Hampshire
Catalogs/Checklists:

2228
Place: Henniker, New Hampshire
Date: 1889
Title: Henniker, N. H.
Size: 14¹⁄₁₆ × 20½ in. (35.7 × 52 cm.)
Artist: Geo. E. Norris
Lithographer:
Printer: The Burleigh Lith. Est., Troy, N. Y.
Publisher: Geo. E. Norris, Brockton, Mass.
Key/Vignettes/Misc: Refs. 1−30; 3
vignettes
Locations: LC−M; BPL−R; NHHS−C
Catalogs/Checklists: LC−M, 480.1

2229
Place: Hillsborough Bridge, New
Hampshire

Date: 1884
Title: Hillsborough−Bridge, Hillsborough
County, N. H. 1884.
Size: 13⅜ × 18 in. (34 × 45.8 cm.)
Artist: H.[enry?] W.[ellge?]
Lithographer:
Printer:
Publisher: Norris & Wellge, Brockton,
Mass.
Key/Vignettes/Misc: Refs. 1−28
Locations: LC−M; BPL−R
Catalogs/Checklists: Cobb, New
Hampshire Maps, no. 396; LC−M, 481

2230
Place: Hinsdale, New Hampshire
Date: 1886
Title: Hinsdale, N. H.
Size: 13½ × 24½ in. (34.3 × 62.3 cm.)
Artist: L. R. Burleigh
Lithographer:
Printer: C. H. Vogt & Son, Cleveland
Publisher: L. R. Burleigh, Troy, New York
Key/Vignettes/Misc: Refs. 1−30
Locations: LC−M; BPL−R; NHHS−C
Catalogs/Checklists: LC−M, 482; Cobb,
New Hampshire Maps, no. 411

2231
Place: Jefferson, New Hampshire
Date: 1883
Title: Jefferson, Coos County N. H. 1883
Size: 11¾ × 20 in. (30.7 × 50.8 cm.)
Artist: A. F. Poole
Lithographer:
Printer: Geo. H. Walker & Co., Boston
Publisher: Poole & Norris, Brockton,
Mass.
Key/Vignettes/Misc: Refs. A−O; 3
vignettes
Locations: NHHS−C
Catalogs/Checklists:

2232
Place: Keene, New Hampshire
Date: 1877
Title: From Position West of the City
Bird's Eye View of Keene, Cheshire Co.
New Hampshire 1877
Size: 23⅞ × 28⁵⁄₁₆ in. (60.7 × 72 cm.)
Artist: A. Ruger
Lithographer:
Printer: D. Bremner and Co., Milwaukee
Publisher:
Key/Vignettes/Misc: Refs. 1−32, A−H; 1
vignette
Locations: NHHS−C
Catalogs/Checklists:

2233
Place: Keene, New Hampshire
Date: N.D.
Title: View of Keene, N. H. and Valley of
the Ashvelot Taken from Beach Hill.
Size: 15³⁄₁₆ × 20³⁄₁₆ in. (38.6 × 51.4 cm.)
Artist: B. Champney
Lithographer:
Printer: J. H. Bufford & Cos. Lith.
Boston
Publisher:
Key/Vignettes/Misc:
Locations: YUAG−NH; NHHS−C
Catalogs/Checklists:

2234
Place: Laconia, New Hampshire
Date: 1883
Title: Bird's Eye View of Laconia, Belknap County, N. H. 1883.
Size: 16 × 21 in. (40.7 × 53.4 cm.)
Artist:
Lithographer:
Printer: Beck & Pauli, Milwaukee
Publisher: Poole & Norris, Brockton, Mass.
Key/Vignettes/Misc: Refs. 2–21, A–Y
Locations: LC–M; BPL–R; NHHS–C
Catalogs/Checklists: LC–M, 483; Cobb, New Hampshire Maps, no. 383

2235
Place: Lake Village, New Hampshire
Date: 1883
Title: Bird's Eye View of Lake Village, Belknap County N H 1883
Size: 12½ × 17⅞ in. (31.8 × 45.5 cm.)
Artist:
Lithographer:
Printer: Beck & Pauli, Milwaukee
Publisher: Poole & Norris, Brockton, Mass.
Key/Vignettes/Misc: Refs. 1–20, A–R
Locations: LC–M; BPL–R; Thompson Ames Historical Society, Gilford, New Hampshire
Catalogs/Checklists: LC–M, 484; Cobb, New Hampshire Maps, no. 384

2236
Place: Lancaster, New Hampshire
Date: 1883
Title: Bird's Eye View of the Village of Lancaster, Coos County, N. H. 1883.
Size: 16 × 19½ in. (40.3 × 49.6 cm.)
Artist: A. F. Poole
Lithographer:
Printer: Beck & Pauli, Milwaukee
Publisher: Poole & Norris, Brockton, Mass.
Key/Vignettes/Misc: Refs. 1–30, A; 2 vignettes
Locations: LC–M
Catalogs/Checklists: LC–M, 485; Cobb, New Hampshire Maps, no. 386

2237
Place: Lebanon, New Hampshire
Date: 1884
Title: Lebanon Grafton County. 1884 N. H. 1884
Size: 19 × 20⅛ in. (48.3 × 51 cm.)
Artist: [George E. Norris]
Lithographer:
Printer: Beck & Pauli, Milwaukee
Publisher: Geo. E. Norris, Brockton, Mass.
Key/Vignettes/Misc: Refs. 1–41; 3 vignettes
Locations: ACMW–FW; BPL–R; DCL–H
Catalogs/Checklists: ACMW–FW 1801

2238
Place: Lisbon, New Hampshire
Date: 1883 State I
Title: Lisbon Grafton County N. H. 1883
Size: 13 × 17⅛ in. (33.1 × 43.5 cm.)
Artist:

Lithographer:
Printer: Beck & Pauli, Milwaukee, Wis.
Publisher: Poole & Norris, Brockton, Mass.
Key/Vignettes/Misc: Refs. 1–30; [no vignettes]
Locations: BPL–R; New Hampshire State Library, Concord, New Hampshire
Catalogs/Checklists:

2239
Place: Lisbon, New Hampshire
Date: 1883 State II
Title: Lisbon Grafton County N. H. 1883
Size: 15⁵⁄₁₆ × 17¼ in. (38.9 × 43.8 cm.)
Artist:
Lithographer:
Printer: Beck & Pauli, Milwaukee, Wis.
Publisher: Geo. E. Norris, Brockton, Mass.
Key/Vignettes/Misc: Refs. 1–30; 1 vignette
Locations: NHHS–C
Catalogs/Checklists:

2240
Place: Littleton, New Hampshire
Date: 1883
Title: Bird's Eye View of Littleton, Grafton County, N. H. Looking East, 1883
Size: 18¼ × 21½ in. (46.4 × 54.7 cm.)
Artist: A. Poole
Lithographer:
Printer: Beck & Pauli, Milwaukee
Publisher: Poole & Norris, Brockton, Mass.
Key/Vignettes/Misc: Refs. A–Z, a–b, 1–15; 3 vignettes
Locations: LC–M; NHHS–C
Catalogs/Checklists: LC–M, 486; Cobb, New Hampshire Maps, no. 385

2241
Place: Manchester, New Hampshire
Date: 1847
Title: View of Manchester City N. H. from Rock Raymond, 1847.
Size: 11¼ × 17⁷⁄₁₆ in. (28.5 × 44.3 cm.)
Artist: Uriah Smith
Lithographer:
Printer: Sharp, Pierce & Co., Boston
Publisher:
Key/Vignettes/Misc:
Locations: BA; Manchester Historic Association, Manchester, New Hampshire
Catalogs/Checklists:

2242
Place: Manchester, New Hampshire
Date: 1855
Title: A View of Manchester N. H.
Size: 9⅞ × 16 in. (25.1 × 40.7 cm.)
Artist: J. B. Bachelder
Lithographer:
Printer: Endicott & Co., New York
Publisher: J. B. Bachelder. . .New Hampshire (copyright)
Key/Vignettes/Misc: 16 refs.
Locations: BPL–P; YUAG–NH
Catalogs/Checklists:

2243
Place: Manchester, New Hampshire
Date: 1855
Title: A View of Manchester N. H.

Composed from Sketches Taken near Rock Raymond. . .
Size: 25¹⁵⁄₁₆ × 33¹³⁄₁₆ in. (65.9 × 85.8 cm.)
Artist: J. B. Bachelder
Lithographer:
Printer: Endicott & Co., New York
Publisher: J. B. Bachelder [copyright]
Key/Vignettes/Misc: 27 unnumbered refs.
Locations: NHHS–C; Manchester, New Hampshire, City Library; LC–P; EI–S
Catalogs/Checklists:

2244
Place: Manchester, New Hampshire
Date: 1855
Title: Manchester, N. H.
Size: 12⅝ × 15⅞ in. (32.1 × 40.4 cm.)
Artist: J. B. Bachelder
Lithographer:
Printer: Endicott & Co., N. Y.
Publisher: Jno. B. Bachelder 59 Beekman St. New York
Key/Vignettes/Misc: Refs. 1–16
Locations: CHS–C; MAHS–B; PAC–P; BA; NHHS–C
Catalogs/Checklists:

2245
Place: Manchester, New Hampshire
Date: 1856
Title: From the Amoskeag Bridge Downward View. Amoskeag Falls. Manchester, N. H.
Size: 12¼ × 15⅝ in. (31.2 × 39.8 cm.)
Artist: J. B. Bachelder
Lithographer:
Printer: Endicott and Co., N. Y.
Publisher: Jno. B. Bachelder, 59 Beekman St., New York
Key/Vignettes/Misc:
Locations: MAHS–B; PAC–P; BA; NHHS–C
Catalogs/Checklists:

2246
Place: Manchester, New Hampshire
Date: 1876
Title: Manchester, N. H. 1876.
Size: 22⅝ × 34⅛ in. (57.6 × 86.8 cm.)
Artist: H. H. Bailey & J. C. Hazen
Lithographer: C. H. Vogt
Printer: J. Knauber Co.
Publisher: H. H. Bailey & J. C. Hazen
Key/Vignettes/Misc: Refs. 1–32
Locations: NHHS–C; BPL–R; DCL–H
Catalogs/Checklists:

2247
Place: Mason, New Hampshire
Date: 1847
Title: View of Mason Vill. N. H., 1847. From the North.
Size: 11¾ × 20¹¹⁄₁₆ in. (30 × 52.7 cm.)
Artist: Uriah Smith
Lithographer:
Printer: Sharp Pierce & Co. Boston
Publisher:
Key/Vignettes/Misc:
Locations: NHHS–C
Catalogs/Checklists:

2248
Place: Meredith, New Hampshire
Date: 1889

Title: Meredith Village, N. H.
Size: 13⅝ × 24¼ in. (34.7 × 62.3 cm.)
Artist: Geo. E. Norris
Lithographer:
Printer: The Burleigh Lith. Est., Troy, N. Y.
Publisher: Geo E. Norris, Brockton, Mass.
Key/Vignettes/Misc: 1–26, A–J
Locations: LC–M; BPL–R
Catalogs/Checklists: LC–M, 487; Cobb, New Hampshire Maps, no. 434

2249

Place: Milford, New Hampshire
Date: 1886
Title: Milford, N. H.
Size: 12⅜ × 23¾ in. (31.5 × 60.4 cm.)
Artist: L. R. Burleigh
Lithographer:
Printer: C. H. Vogt & Son, Cleveland
Publisher: L. R. Burleigh, Troy, N. Y.
Key/Vignettes/Misc: Refs. 1–28
Locations: BPL–R; LC–M; NHHS–C
Catalogs/Checklists: LC–M, 488; Cobb, New Hampshire Maps, no. 412

2250

Place: Milton, New Hampshire
Date: 1888
Title: Milton, N. H. 1888
Size: 13⁹⁄₁₆ × 22¹³⁄₁₆ in. (34.4 × 57.9 cm.)
Artist: George Norris
Lithographer:
Printer: The Burleigh Lith. Est., Troy, N. Y.
Publisher: Geo. E. Norris, Brockton, Mass.
Key/Vignettes/Misc: Refs. 1–17; 1 vignette
Locations: BPL–R; LC–M; NHHS–C
Catalogs/Checklists: LC–M, 488.1

2251

Place: Nashua, New Hampshire
Date: [1851–]
Title: Nashua Village, N. H. From the South.
Size: 18½ × 30 in. (47.1 × 76.4 cm.)
Artist: J. D.[enison] Crocker
Lithographer:
Printer: J. H. Bufford, 260 Washington St. Boston.
Publisher:
Key/Vignettes/Misc: Description
Locations: BA; YUAG–NH; NYH–NY
Catalogs/Checklists:

2252

Place: Nashua, New Hampshire
Date: 1875
Title: Nashua, N. H. 1875
Size: 21¾ × 32¾ in. (55.4 × 83.3 cm.)
Artist: H. H. Bailey & Co.
Lithographer: C. H. Vogt
Printer: J. Knauber & Co.
Publisher: H. H. Bailey & Co., Boston
Key/Vignettes/Misc: Refs. A–P, R–X, Z
Locations: NHHS–C; BPL–R
Catalogs/Checklists:

2253

Place: Nashua, New Hampshire
Date: 1883
Title: Nashua, New Hampshire
Size: 22 × 32⅞ in. (56 × 83.5 cm.)
Artist:

Lithographer:
Printer: O. H. Bailey & Co., Boston
Publisher: O. H. Bailey & Co., Boston
Key/Vignettes/Misc: Refs. A–Z, 2–5; 16 vignettes
Locations: BPL–R; NHHS–C; LC–M
Catalogs/Checklists: LC–M, 488.2

2254

Place: Newport, New Hampshire
Date: 1857
Title: Newport, N. H. 1857. From Hill Back of South Congregational Church.
Size: 14 × 18⁹⁄₁₆ in. (35.7 × 47.3 cm.)
Artist: Henry P. Moore
Lithographer:
Printer: L. H. Bradford and Co., Boston
Publisher:
Key/Vignettes/Misc: 1 seal
Locations: BA; NHHS–C
Catalogs/Checklists: LC–M, 504.1

2255

Place: Newport, New Hampshire
Date: 1877
Title: Bird's Eye View Newport, New Hampshire 1877
Size: 15 × 22¼ in. (38.2 × 56.7 cm.)
Artist: [T. M. Fowler]
Lithographer:
Printer: Shober & Carqueville, Chicago
Publisher: Ruger & Stoner, Madison, Wis.
Key/Vignettes/Misc: Refs. 1–26
Locations: Newport Historical Society, Newport, New Hampshire
Catalogs/Checklists:

2256

Place: Newport, New Hampshire
Date: 1895
Title: Newport, N. H. 1895.
Size: 12¼ × 21¹¹⁄₁₆ in. (31 × 55.1 cm.)
Artist: [George E. Norris]
Lithographer:
Printer:
Publisher: [George E. Norris, Brockton, Mass.]
Key/Vignettes/Misc:
Locations: NHHS–C
Catalogs/Checklists:

2257

Place: Penacook, New Hampshire
Date: [1886]
Title: Penacook, N. H.
Size: 14⅛ × 24⅜ in. (36 × 61.9 cm.)
Artist: L. R. Burleigh
Lithographer:
Printer:
Publisher: L. R. Burleigh, Troy, N. Y.
Key/Vignettes/Misc: Refs. 1–22
Locations: LC–M; NHHS–C; BPL–R
Catalogs/Checklists: LC–M, 489; Cobb, New Hampshire Maps, no. 420

2258

Place: Peterborough, New Hampshire
Date: 1841
Title: View of Peterboro', N. H. 1841
Size: 8 × 12¼ in. (20.4 × 31.2 cm.)
Artist: C. Hill
Lithographer:
Printer: B. W. Thayer & Co's Lithography, Boston

Publisher:
Key/Vignettes/Misc:
Locations: Peterborough Historical Society, Peterborough, New Hampshire
Catalogs/Checklists:

2259

Place: Peterborough, New Hampshire
Date: 1886
Title: Peterborough, N. H. 1886.
Size: 14⅝ × 24 in. (37.2 × 61 cm.)
Artist: L. R. Burleigh
Lithographer:
Printer: Burleigh Lith. Establishment, Troy, N. Y.
Publisher: L. R. Burleigh, Troy, N. Y.
Key/Vignettes/Misc: Refs. 1–31; 4 vignettes
Locations: LC–M; BPL–R; Peterborough Historical Society, Peterborough, New Hampshire; NHHS–C
Catalogs/Checklists: LC–M, 490; Cobb, New Hampshire Maps, no. 413

2260

Place: Pittsfield, New Hampshire
Date: 1856
Title: South View Pittsfield N. H.
Size: 12⅝ × 15⅝ in. (32.1 × 39.8 cm.)
Artist: J. B. Bachelder
Lithographer:
Printer: Endicott & Co., N. Y.
Publisher: Jno. B. Bachelder, 59 Beekman St., New York
Key/Vignettes/Misc:
Locations: BPL–P; MAHS–B; PAC–P; YUAG–NH; BA; NHHS–C; LC–P; NYH–NY
Catalogs/Checklists:

2261

Place: Pittsfield, New Hampshire
Date: 1884
Title: Pittsfield, Merrimack County N. H. 1884
Size: 16½ × 23⅝ in. (42 × 60.1 cm.)
Artist: [George E. Norris]
Lithographer:
Printer: Beck & Pauli, Milwaukee, Wis.
Publisher: Geo. E. Norris, Brockton, Mass.
Key/Vignettes/Misc: Refs. 1–54
Locations: LC–M; BPL–R; NHHS–C
Catalogs/Checklists: LC–M, 491; Cobb, New Hampshire Maps, no. 397

2262

Place: Plymouth, New Hampshire
Date: 1883
Title: Plymouth Grafton County, N. H.
Size: 13¾ × 16¼ in. (35 × 41.3 cm.)
Artist: A. F. Poole
Lithographer: J. (?) Jones
Printer: Geo. H. Walker & Co. Lith. Boston
Publisher: Poole & Norris, Brockton, Mass.
Key/Vignettes/Misc: Refs. A–Z; 1 vignette
Locations: BPL–R; New Hampshire State Library, Concord, New Hampshire
Catalogs/Checklists:

2263

Place: Portsmouth, New Hampshire
Date: 1854

Title: Portsmouth, N. H. From the Navy Yard, Kittery Me. 1854
Size: 23¾ × 37⁷⁄₁₆ in. (60.5 × 95.3 cm.)
Artist: C. Parsons
Lithographer: C. Parsons
Printer: Endicott & Co. N. Y.
Publisher: Smith Brothers & Co., 59 Beekman St., New York
Key/Vignettes/Misc:
Locations: NYP–S; MM–NN; CHS–C; BA; NHHS–C; LC–P; NYH–NY
Catalogs/Checklists: Stokes 1854—G–19; MM–NN, LP 24

2264
Place: Portsmouth, New Hampshire
Date: 1876
Title: City of Portsmouth New Hampshire 1776 1876
Size: 9¾ × 7¹⁵⁄₁₆ in. (24.8 × 20.2 cm.) (photo)
Artist: W. Brotherhead
Lithographer:
Printer: H. J. Toudy & Co Steam Lith
Publisher:
Key/Vignettes/Misc: 1 vignette
Locations: NHHS–C
Catalogs/Checklists:

2265
Place: Portsmouth, New Hampshire
Date: 1877
Title: Bird's Eye View of Portsmouth, Rockingham Co., New Hampshire 1877.
Size: 21¼ × 26⅜ in. (54 × 67 cm.)
Artist: A. Ruger
Lithographer:
Printer: D. Bremner & Co., Lith., Milwaukee, Wis.
Publisher: J. J. Stoner, Madison, Wis.
Key/Vignettes/Misc: Refs. 1–10, 12–24, A–H, J–N
Locations: LC–M; NHHS–C
Catalogs/Checklists: LC–M, 492; Cobb, New Hampshire Maps, no. 340

2266
Place: Raymond, New Hampshire
Date: 1887
Title: Raymond, N. H. 1887
Size: 12³⁄₁₆ × 18 in. (31 × 45.7 cm.)
Artist: Geo. E. Norris
Lithographer:
Printer: Burleigh Litho. Establishment, Troy, N. Y.
Publisher: Geo. E. Norris, Brockton, Mass.
Key/Vignettes/Misc: Refs. 1–18, A–I
Locations: NHHS–C
Catalogs/Checklists:

2267
Place: Rochester, New Hampshire
Date: 1877
Title: Bird's Eye View of Rochester Strafford County, New Hampshire, 1877, From a Position East of Town.
Size: 18¼ × 22 in. (46.5 × 55.9 cm.)
Artist: [Albert Ruger]
Lithographer:
Printer: C. H. Vogt & Co., Lith., Milwaukee
Publisher: J. J. Stoner, Madison, Wisconsin
Key/Vignettes/Misc: Refs. 1–24

Locations: BPL–R; NHHS–C; LC–M
Catalogs/Checklists: LC–M, 492.2

2268
Place: Rochester, New Hampshire
Date: 1884
Title: Rochester, N. H. Gonic and East–Rochester, 1884.
Size: 15¾ × 19⅞ in. (40.1 × 50.5 cm.)
Artist: H. Wellge
Lithographer:
Printer:
Publisher: Norris & Wellge, Brockton, Mass.
Key/Vignettes/Misc: Refs. Rochester, 1–29, Gonic, 1–9, East Rochester, 1–9; 2 vignettes
Locations: LC–M; BPL–R
Catalogs/Checklists: LC–M, 493; Cobb, New Hampshire Maps, no. 400

2269
Place: Salem Depot, New Hampshire
Date: 1887
Title: Salem Depot, N. H.
Size: 10⅞ × 19¹⁄₁₆ in. (27.5 × 48.5 cm.)
Artist: Geo. E. Norris
Lithographer:
Printer: Burleigh Litho. Est. Troy, N. Y.
Publisher: Geo. E. Norris, Brockton, Mass.
Key/Vignettes/Misc: Refs. 1–18
Locations: BPL–R; NHHS–C
Catalogs/Checklists:

2270
Place: Salmon Falls, New Hampshire
Date: 1877
Title: Salmon Falls, Strafford Co., New Hampshire 1877.
Size: 10 × 12³⁄₁₆ in. (25.3 × 31 cm.)
Artist: [Albert Ruger]
Lithographer:
Printer: Jos. B. Richards & Co., Lith, 424 Washn. St. Boston
Publisher:
Key/Vignettes/Misc: Refs. 1–8
Locations: LC–M; NHHS–C
Catalogs/Checklists: LC–M, 494

2271
Place: Somersworth, New Hampshire
Date: 1856
Title: Great Falls, Somersworth, N. H.
Size: 12½ × 15⅞ in. (31.8 × 40.4 cm.)
Artist: J. B. Bachelder
Lithographer:
Printer: Endicott & Co., N. Y.
Publisher: Jno. B. Bachelder, 59 Beekman St, New York
Key/Vignettes/Misc: 1 vignette
Locations: MAHS–B; PAC–P; YUAG–NH; BA; NHHS–C
Catalogs/Checklists:

2272
Place: South New Market, New Hampshire
Date: 1884
Title: South–New–Market, Rockingham County, N. H. 1884.
Size: 13½ × 17⅞ in. (34.4 × 45.5 cm.)
Artist:
Lithographer:

Printer:
Publisher: Norris & Wellge, Brockton, Mass.
Key/Vignettes/Misc: Refs. 1–24
Locations: LC–M; BPL–R
Catalogs/Checklists: LC–M, 495; Cobb, New Hampshire Maps, no. 398

2273
Place: Temple, New Hampshire
Date: 1847
Title: View of Temple, N. H. 1847.
Size: 10½ × 15½ in. (26.7 × 39.6 cm.)
Artist: Uriah Smith
Lithographer:
Printer: Sharp, Pierce & Co., Boston
Publisher:
Key/Vignettes/Misc:
Locations: NHHS–C; Historical Society of Temple, Temple, New Hampshire
Catalogs/Checklists:

2274
Place: Tilton, New Hampshire
Date: 1884
Title: Tilton, N. H., Belknap County, 1884.
Size: 15½ × 19⅞ in. (39.4 × 55 cm.)
Artist: H. Wellge
Lithographer:
Printer:
Publisher: Norris & Wellge, Brockton, Mass.
Key/Vignettes/Misc: Refs. 1–29
Locations: LC–M; BPL–R
Catalogs/Checklists: LC–M, 496; Cobb, New Hampshire Maps, no. 399

2275
Place: Warner, New Hampshire
Date: 1887
Title: Warner, N. H. 1887.
Size: 14¼ × 23⅞ in. (36.3 × 60.7 cm.)
Artist: Geo. E. Norris
Lithographer:
Printer: The Burleigh Litho. Establishment, Troy, N. Y.
Publisher: Geo. E. Norris, Brockton, Mass.
Key/Vignettes/Misc: Refs. 1–16, A–L
Locations: BPL–R; NHHS–C
Catalogs/Checklists:

2276
Place: West Lebanon, New Hampshire
Date: 1889
Title: West Lebanon, N. H. and White River Juncton, Vermont.
Size: 16 × 25½ in. (40.5 × 65.2 cm.)
Artist: Geo. E. Norris
Lithographer:
Printer: Burleigh Lith. Est., Troy, N. Y.
Publisher: Geo. E. Norris, Brockton, Mass.
Key/Vignettes/Misc: Refs. 1–17, A–F
Locations: LC–M; BPL–R; VHS–M; NHHS–C
Catalogs/Checklists: LC–M, 497; Cobb, New Hampshire Maps, no. 435

2277
Place: Whitefield, New Hampshire
Date: 1883
Title: Bird's Eye View of Whitefield Coos County N. H. 1883

Size: 13¹⁵⁄₁₆ × 17⅝ in. (35.6 × 44.9 cm.)
Artist: A. F. Poole
Lithographer:
Printer: Beck & Pauli, Milwaukee
Publisher: Poole & Norris, Brockton, Mass.
Key/Vignettes/Misc: Refs. 1–39
Locations: LC–M; NHHS–C
Catalogs/Checklists: LC–M, 498; Cobb, New Hampshire Maps, no. 387

2278
Place: Wilton, New Hampshire
Date: 1847
Title: View of Wilton, West Village, 1847.
Size:
Artist: Uriah Smith
Lithographer:
Printer:
Publisher: Sharp, Pierce & Co. Boston
Key/Vignettes/Misc:
Locations: Wilton Historical Society, Wilton, New Hampshire
Catalogs/Checklists:

2279
Place: Wilton, New Hampshire
Date: [1886]
Title: Wilton, N. H.
Size: 11⅛ × 19¾ in. (28.4 × 50.2 cm.)
Artist: L. R. Burleigh
Lithographer:
Printer:
Publisher: L. R. Burleigh, Troy, N. Y.
Key/Vignettes/Misc: Refs. 1–10
Locations: BPL–R; NHHS–C
Catalogs/Checklists:

2280
Place: Winchester, New Hampshire
Date: 1887
Title: Winchester, N. H., Cheshire County.
Size: 13⁹⁄₁₆ × 20¹⁵⁄₁₆ in. (34.4 × 53.2 cm.)
Artist: Geo. E. Norris
Lithographer:
Printer: The Burleigh Litho. Establishment, Troy, N. Y.
Publisher: Geo. E. Norris, Brockton, Mass.
Key/Vignettes/Misc: Refs. 1–32
Locations: BPL–R; NHHS–C; LC–M
Catalogs/Checklists: LC–M, 498.1

2281
Place: Wolfeboro, New Hampshire
Date: 1889
Title: Wolfeborough, N. H., Lake Winnipesaukee.
Size: 13¾ × 25⁵⁄₁₆ in. (35 × 65 cm.)
Artist: Geo. E. Norris
Lithographer:
Printer: Burleigh Lith. Est., Troy, N. Y.
Publisher: Geo. E. Norris, Brockton, Mass
Key/Vignettes/Misc: Refs. 1–49; 1 vignette
Locations: LC–M
Catalogs/Checklists: LC–M, 499; Cobb, New Hampshire Maps, no. 436

2282
Place: Absecon, New Jersey
Date: 1924
Title: Aero–View of Absecon New Jersey 1924

Size: 25 × 35 in. (63.5 × 89 cm.)
Artist: Rene Cinquin
Lithographer:
Printer: [Meriden Gravure Co., Meriden, Conn.]
Publisher: Hughes & Cinquin, New York
Key/Vignettes/Misc: 7 vignettes; unnumbered business directory; 1 map
Locations: LC–M
Catalogs/Checklists: LC–M, 500

2283
Place: Annandale, New Jersey
Date: 1886
Title: Annandale, New Jersey
Size: 14 × 19½ in. (35.6 × 49.6 cm.)
Artist: T. M. Fowler
Lithographer:
Printer: A. E. Downs
Publisher: T. M. Fowler
Key/Vignettes/Misc: Refs. 1–22; 3 vignettes
Locations: Grandin Library, Clinton, New Jersey
Catalogs/Checklists:

2284
Place: Arlington, New Jersey
Date: 1907
Title: [Untitled]
Size: 14½ × 26 in. (36.9 × 66.1 cm.)
Artist:
Lithographer:
Printer:
Publisher:
Key/Vignettes/Misc:
Locations: LC–M
Catalogs/Checklists: LC–M, 501

Place: Asbury Park, New Jersey
Date: 1877
See Ocean Grove, New Jersey, 1877.

Place: Asbury Park, New Jersey
Date: 1881
See Ocean Grove, New Jersey, 1881.

2285
Place: Asbury Park, New Jersey
Date: 1881
Title: Bird's Eye View of Asbury Park, New Jersey. 1881.
Size: 16½ × 24½ in. (42.5 × 62.4 cm.)
Artist:
Lithographer:
Printer: Beck & Pauli, Lith. Milwaukee, Wis.
Publisher: T. M. Fowler, Asbury Park, N. J.
Key/Vignettes/Misc: Refs. 1–7; 1 vignette; description
Locations: NJHS–N (photo); LC–P; LC–M; BPL–R
Catalogs/Checklists: LC–M, 501.1

2286
Place: Asbury Park, New Jersey
Date: 1897
Title: Asbury Park, Ocean Grove and Vicinity, New Jersey 1897
Size: 33 × 40½ in. (83.9 × 103 cm.)
Artist:
Lithographer:

Printer:
Publisher: Landis & Hughes, New York
Key/Vignettes/Misc: 65 vignettes; unnumbered business directory
Locations: LC–M
Catalogs/Checklists: LC–M, 503

2287
Place: Asbury Park, New Jersey
Date: Ca. 1910
Title: Aeroplane View of Asbury Park, N. J. Showing Location of 'Asbury Park Estates' Among the Hills on Asbury Ave.
Size: 7½ × 9½ in. (19.1 × 24.1 cm.)
Artist:
Lithographer:
Printer:
Publisher: Barton & Spooner Co., New York
Key/Vignettes/Misc:
Locations: LC–M
Catalogs/Checklists: LC–M, 504

2288
Place: Atlantic City, New Jersey
Date: 1875?
Title:
Size:
Artist: H. H. Bailey
Lithographer:
Printer:
Publisher:
Key/Vignettes/Misc:
Locations:
Catalogs/Checklists: Warren & Wise

2289
Place: Atlantic City, New Jersey
Date: 1880
Title: Atlantic City, N. J. 1880
Size: 20⁷⁄₁₆ × 31⁷⁄₁₆ in. (52 × 80 cm.)
Artist:
Lithographer:
Printer:
Publisher: T. J. Shepherd Landis, Philadelphia
Key/Vignettes/Misc: 23 vignettes
Locations: LC–M
Catalogs/Checklists: LC–M, 504.1

2290
Place: Atlantic City, New Jersey
Date: 1900
Title: Atlantic City, New Jersey
Size: 38 × 55½ in. (96.7 × 141.2 cm.)
Artist:
Lithographer:
Printer:
Publisher: Landis & Alsop, Newark, N. J.
Key/Vignettes/Misc: Refs. 1–71; 32 vignettes
Locations: LC–M
Catalogs/Checklists: LC–M, 505

2291
Place: Atlantic City, New Jersey
Date: 1904
Title: Atlantic City's New Suburbs Bird's–Eye View of Atlantic City. . . .
Size: 17³⁄₁₆ × 21⅝ in. (43.8 × 55.1 cm.)
Artist:
Lithographer:

Printer:
Publisher: Victor J. Humbrecht (copyright)
Key/Vignettes/Misc:
Locations: NJHS–N
Catalogs/Checklists:

2292
Place: Atlantic City, New Jersey
Date: 1905
Title: Atlantic City, N. J.
Size: 10 × 24 in. (25.4 × 61.1 cm.)
Artist:
Lithographer:
Printer:
Publisher: National Publishing Co., New York
Key/Vignettes/Misc:
Locations: LC–M
Catalogs/Checklists: LC–M, 506

2293
Place: Atlantic City, New Jersey
Date: 1908
Title: Atlantic City, New Jersey, U. S. A.
Size: 4 × 7 in. (10.1 × 17.8 cm.) (photo)
Artist:
Lithographer:
Printer:
Publisher: W. Adickes
Key/Vignettes/Misc:
Locations: LC–M (photo)
Catalogs/Checklists: LC–M, 507

2294
Place: Atlantic City, New Jersey
Date: 1909
Title: Aero View of Atlantic City, New Jersey 1909
Size: 20 × 38 in. (50.9 × 96.7 cm.)
Artist:
Lithographer:
Printer:
Publisher: Hughes & Bailey, New York
Key/Vignettes/Misc: Refs. 1–9; 1 vignette
Locations: LC–M
Catalogs/Checklists: LC–M, 508

2295
Place: Atlantic City, New Jersey
Date: 1910
Title: Aero View of Atlantic City, New Jersey 1910.
Size: 20 × 42 in. (50.8 × 106.8 cm.)
Artist: T. M. Fowler
Lithographer:
Printer:
Publisher: Hughes & Bailey, New York
Key/Vignettes/Misc:
Locations: LC–M
Catalogs/Checklists: LC–M, 509

2296
Place: Atlantic Highlands, New Jersey
Date: 1894
Title: Atlantic Highlands, New Jersey 1894
Size: 13⅜ × 26⅜ in. (34 × 67 cm.)
Artist:
Lithographer:
Printer:
Publisher: O. H. Bailey & Co., Boston
Key/Vignettes/Misc: 30 vignettes

Locations: LC–M; MCHA–F
Catalogs/Checklists: LC–M, 510

2297
Place: Belvidere, New Jersey
Date: Ca. 1860
Title: Belvidere.
Size: 16½ × 21½ in. (42 × 54.7 cm.)
Artist:
Lithographer:
Printer: P. S. Duval & Co's Steam Lith Press, Phila.
Publisher:
Key/Vignettes/Misc: Description
Locations: NJHS–N
Catalogs/Checklists:

2298
Place: Belvidere, New Jersey
Date: 1883
Title: Belvidere, New Jersey. 1883
Size: 18⅝ × 24¼ in. (47.4 × 61.7 cm.)
Artist:
Lithographer:
Printer: O. H. Bailey & Co., Boston
Publisher: O. H. Bailey & Co., Boston
Key/Vignettes/Misc: Refs. 1–38
Locations: BPL–R
Catalogs/Checklists:

2299
Place: Blairstown, New Jersey
Date: [1883]
Title: Blairstown, New Jersey
Size: 15⅞ × 20¾ in. (40.4 × 52.7 cm.)
Artist:
Lithographer:
Printer: O. H. Bailey & Co., Boston
Publisher: O. H. Bailey & Co., Boston
Key/Vignettes/Misc: Refs. 1–13; 1 vignette
Locations: BPL–R; NJHS–N
Catalogs/Checklists:

Place: Bloomington, New Jersey
Date: 1887
See Bound Brook, New Jersey, 1887.

2300
Place: Bound Brook, New Jersey
Date: 1887
Title: Bound Brook, and Bloomington, New Jersey, 1887
Size: 17 × 22 in. (43.3 × 56 cm.)
Artist: T. M. Fowler
Lithographer:
Printer:
Publisher:
Key/Vignettes/Misc: Refs. 1–23; 4 vignettes
Locations: RU–NB
Catalogs/Checklists:

2301
Place: Burlington, New Jersey
Date: [1847]
Title: Burlington College
Size: 5⅝ × 7¾ in. (14.3 × 19.7 cm.)
Artist:
Lithographer: John Collins
Printer: T. Sinclair, Phila.
Publisher:
Key/Vignettes/Misc:

Locations: YUAG–NH
Catalogs/Checklists:

2302
Place: Burlington, New Jersey
Date: [1847]
Title: Burlington Steam Mills and Water Works
Size: 5⅝ × 8⅛ in. (14.3 × 20.6 cm.)
Artist:
Lithographer: John Collins
Printer: T. Sinclair, Phila.
Publisher:
Key/Vignettes/Misc:
Locations: YUAG–NH
Catalogs/Checklists:

2303
Place: Burlington, New Jersey
Date: [1847]
Title: City Hall. Built 1797
Size: 5⅞ × 7¹⁵⁄₁₆ in. (14.9 × 20.2 cm.)
Artist:
Lithographer: John French
Printer: T. Sinclair Phila
Publisher:
Key/Vignettes/Misc:
Locations: YUAG–NH
Catalogs/Checklists:

2304
Place: Burlington, New Jersey
Date: [1847]
Title: Friends' meeting House
Size: 5⅝ × 7¾ in. (14.3 × 19.7 cm.)
Artist:
Lithographer: John Collins
Printer: T. Sinclair. Phila
Publisher:
Key/Vignettes/Misc:
Locations: YUAG–NH
Catalogs/Checklists:

2305
Place: Burlington, New Jersey
Date: [1847]
Title: Green Bank
Size: 5⅝ × 8⁵⁄₁₆ in. (14.3 × 21.1 cm.)
Artist:
Lithographer:
Printer: T. Sinclair, Phila.
Publisher:
Key/Vignettes/Misc:
Locations: YUAG–NH
Catalogs/Checklists:

2306
Place: Burlington, New Jersey
Date: [1847]
Title: Presbyterian Church
Size: 5⅝ × 7¹³⁄₁₆ in. (14.3 × 19.8 cm.)
Artist:
Lithographer: John Collins
Printer: T. Sinclair, Phila.
Publisher:
Key/Vignettes/Misc:
Locations: YUAG–NH
Catalogs/Checklists:

2307
Place: Burlington, New Jersey
Date: [1847]
Title: Residence of the Late Joseph

Bloomfield Governor of New Jersey
Size: 5¹⁵⁄₁₆ × 7¾ in. (15.1 × 19.7 cm.)
Artist:
Lithographer: John Collins
Printer: T. Sinclair, Phila
Publisher:
Key/Vignettes/Misc:
Locations: YUAG–NH
Catalogs/Checklists:

2308
Place: Burlington, New Jersey
Date: [1847]
Title: Residence of Susan V. Bradford
Size: 5½ × 7¾ in. (14 × 19.6 cm.)
Artist:
Lithographer:
Printer: T. Sinclair, Phila.
Publisher:
Key/Vignettes/Misc:
Locations: YUAG–NH
Catalogs/Checklists:

2309
Place: Burlington, New Jersey
Date: [1847]
Title: Riverside
Size: 5⅝ × 7¹¹⁄₁₆ in. (14.3 × 19.5 cm.)
Artist:
Lithographer: John Collins
Printer: T. Sinclair, Phila
Publisher:
Key/Vignettes/Misc:
Locations: YUAG–NH
Catalogs/Checklists:

2310
Place: Burlington, New Jersey
Date: [1847]
Title: St. Mary's Church. Founded 1703
Enlarged 1834.
Size: 5¹³⁄₁₆ × 7¾ in. (14.8 × 19.7 cm.)
Artist:
Lithographer: John Collins
Printer: T. Sinclair, Phila.
Publisher:
Key/Vignettes/Misc:
Locations: YUAG–NH
Catalogs/Checklists:

2311
Place: Burlington, New Jersey
Date: 1874
Title: Burlington, N. J. 1874
Size: 21 × 21 in. (53.4 × 53.4 cm.)
Artist: H. H. Bailey
Lithographer: H. J. Toudy & Co.
Printer: H. J. Toudy & Co. Steam Lith
Phila.
Publisher: Fowler & Bailey
Key/Vignettes/Misc: Refs. 1–29
Locations: Library Company of
Burlington, Burlington, New Jersey
Catalogs/Checklists:

Place: Camden, New Jersey
Date: 1856
See Philadelphia, Pennsylvania, 1856.

2312
Place: Camden, New Jersey
Date: 1873
Title:

Size:
Artist: H. H. Bailey
Lithographer:
Printer:
Publisher:
Key/Vignettes/Misc:
Locations:
Catalogs/Checklists: Warren & Wise

2313
Place: Camden, New Jersey
Date: 1876
Title: Bird's Eye View of Camden, N. J. in
the Centennial Year 1876
Size: 19¾ × 31⅞ in. (50.3 × 81.1 cm.)
Artist: C. G.
Lithographer: Traubel
Printer:
Publisher:
Key/Vignettes/Misc: Refs. 1–49, A–M; 6
vignettes
Locations: CCHS–C
Catalogs/Checklists:

2314
Place: Cape May, New Jersey
Date: Ca. 1883
Title: Cape May, N. J.
Size: ca. 24 × 32 in. (61.1 × 81.4 cm.)
Artist: S. Landis
Lithographer:
Printer: Weise Lith Phila., Pa.
Publisher: T. J. Shepherd Landis, Phila., Pa
Key/Vignettes/Misc:
Locations: Private collection
Catalogs/Checklists:

2315
Place: Clinton, New Jersey
Date: [1886]
Title: Clinton
Size: 20¼ × 24½ in. (51.5 × 62.3 cm.)
Artist: T. M. Fowler
Lithographer:
Printer: A. E. Downs
Publisher: T. M. Fowler
Key/Vignettes/Misc: Refs. 1–16; 8
vignettes
Locations: Grandin Library, Clinton, New
Jersey; LC–M (photo)
Catalogs/Checklists: LC–M, 510.1

Place: Columbia, New Jersey
Date: 1885
See Portland, Pennsylvania, 1885.

2316
Place: Darlington, Deal Beach, New
Jersey
Date: N.D.
Title: Darlington. Conceded to be the
Most Beautiful Location on the Jersey
Coast. . . .
Size: 28 × 36½ in. (71 × 92 cm.)
Artist:
Lithographer:
Printer:
Publisher: National View Company,
Boston
Key/Vignettes/Misc: 7 vignettes
Locations: RU–NB
Catalogs/Checklists:

2317
Place: Dover, New Jersey
Date: Ca. 1860
Title: Dover, N. J.
Size: 15⅜ × 24 in. (39.1 × 61.1 cm.)
Artist:
Lithographer:
Printer:
Publisher:
Key/Vignettes/Misc:
Locations: YUAG–NH; NJHS–N (photo)
Catalogs/Checklists:

2318
Place: Dover, New Jersey
Date: 1903
Title: Dover, New Jersey 1903.
Size: 17½ × 20 in. (44.5 × 50.8 cm.)
Artist: [T. M. Fowler]
Lithographer:
Printer:
Publisher: Fowler & Bailey, Boston
Key/Vignettes/Misc: Refs. A, 2–30; 15
vignettes
Locations: LC–M
Catalogs/Checklists: LC–M, 511

2319
Place: Egg Harbor City, New Jersey
Date: 1858
Title: Gedenkblatt der Grundung Von Egg
Harbor City.
Size: 4⅞ × 9¹⁄₁₆ in. (12.4 × 23.1 cm.)
Artist: From ambrotype by A. Morhart
Lithographer:
Printer: F. Wogram, 54 Chatham St. N. Y.
Publisher:
Key/Vignettes/Misc:
Locations: RU–NB
Catalogs/Checklists:

2320
Place: Egg Harbor City, New Jersey
Date: 1865
Title: Birds Eye View of Egg Harbor City,
N. J.
Size: 21⅜ × 26⅞ in. (54.4 × 68.4 cm.)
Artist:
Lithographer:
Printer: Herline & Hensel, 632 Chestnut
St. Philadelphia
Publisher: F. Scheu, Egg Harbor City, N. J.
Key/Vignettes/Misc:
Locations: LC–M; NJHS–N
Catalogs/Checklists: LC–M, 512

2321
Place: Egg Harbor City, New Jersey
Date: 1866
Title: Birds Eye View of Egg Harbor, N. J.
Size: 8½ × 10½ in. (21.6 × 26.7 cm.)
Artist:
Lithographer:
Printer:
Publisher: Charles Magnus, New York
Key/Vignettes/Misc:
Locations: RU–NB
Catalogs/Checklists:

2322
Place: Egg Harbor City, New Jersey
Date: 1924

Title: Aero View of Egg Harbor City. New Jersey
Size: 20 × 34½ in. (50.8 × 87.7 cm.)
Artist: Rene Cinquin
Lithographer:
Printer: [Meriden Gravure Co., Meriden, Conn.]
Publisher: Hughes & Cinquin, Brooklyn, N. Y.
Key/Vignettes/Misc: Refs. 1–10; 8 vignettes; 1 map
Locations: LC–M
Catalogs/Checklists: LC–M, 513

2323
Place: Elizabeth, New Jersey
Date: 1892
Title: Map of 400 Buildings Lots Owned by William H. Moffitt, in the City of Elizabeth, N. J.
Size: 22 × 29 in. (56 × 73.5 cm.)
Artist:
Lithographer:
Printer: O. H. Bailey & Co., Boston
Publisher: William H. Moffitt
Key/Vignettes/Misc: 10 vignettes; description
Locations: RU–NB
Catalogs/Checklists:

2324
Place: Elizabeth, New Jersey
Date: 1898
Title: Elizabeth, N. J. 1898
Size: 32 × 44 in. (81.4 × 111.9 cm.)
Artist:
Lithographer:
Printer:
Publisher: Landis & Hughes, New York
Key/Vignettes/Misc: 52 vignettes; unnumbered business directory; description
Locations: LC–M
Catalogs/Checklists: LC–M, 514

2325
Place: Flemington, New Jersey
Date: 1883
Title: Flemington, New Jersey. 1883.
Size: 19⅝ × 25 in. (49.9 × 63.6 cm.)
Artist:
Lithographer:
Printer: O. H. Bailey & Co., Boston
Publisher: O. H. Bailey & Co., Boston
Key/Vignettes/Misc: Refs. 1–17; 7 vignettes
Locations: BPL–R
Catalogs/Checklists:

2326
Place: Flemington, New Jersey
Date: 1903
Title: Flemington, N. J., 1903
Size: 22 × 28 in. (56.5 × 71 cm.)
Artist: T. M. Fowler
Lithographer:
Printer:
Publisher: T. M. Fowler, Morrisville, Pa.
Key/Vignettes/Misc: Refs. 1–98; 27 vignettes
Locations: RU–NB
Catalogs/Checklists:

2327
Place: Florence, New Jersey
Date: N.D.
Title: Florence, N. J.
Size: 8 × 12 in. (20.4 × 30.5 cm.)
Artist:
Lithographer:
Printer: T. Sinclair's Lith Phil
Publisher:
Key/Vignettes/Misc:
Locations: RU–NB; NJHS–N
Catalogs/Checklists:

2328
Place: Freehold, New Jersey
Date: 1895
Title: Freehold, New Jersey 1895
Size: 29 × 32 in. (73.8 × 81.4 cm.)
Artist:
Lithographer:
Printer:
Publisher: National View Co., 36 Columbus Ave., Boston
Key/Vignettes/Misc: Refs. A–L, 2–35; 34 vignettes
Locations: MCHA–F
Catalogs/Checklists:

2329
Place: Freehold, New Jersey
Date: 1928
Title: Aero–View of Freehold, Monmouth County, New Jersey
Size: 27 × 29 in. (68.7 × 73.8 cm.)
Artist:
Lithographer:
Printer:
Publisher: Hughes and Cinquin, 23 Duane Street, New York
Key/Vignettes/Misc: 37 vignettes; unnumbered business directory
Locations: MCHA–F
Catalogs/Checklists:

2330
Place: Freehold, New Jersey
Date: N.D.
Title: [View of Freehold, New Jersey]
Size: 9 × 14 in. (22.9 × 35.6 cm.)
Artist: T. M. Fowler
Lithographer:
Printer: Edward Bierstadt, N. Y. Artotype
Publisher: Fowler & Evans, Box 208, Asbury Park, N. J.
Key/Vignettes/Misc:
Locations: MCHA–F
Catalogs/Checklists:

2331
Place: Frenchtown, New Jersey
Date: 1883
Title: Frenchtown, New Jersey
Size: 18⅝ × 21¾ in. (47.4 × 55.3 cm.)
Artist:
Lithographer:
Printer:
Publisher: O. H. Bailey & Co., Boston
Key/Vignettes/Misc: Refs. 1–14 & 1–12 (vignette view of Uhlertown); 7 vignettes
Locations:
Catalogs/Checklists:

2332
Place: Garfield, New Jersey
Date: 1909
Title: Birds Eye View of Garfield, New Jersey 1909.
Size: 20 × 28 in. (50.8 × 71.1 cm.)
Artist: T. M. Fowler
Lithographer:
Printer:
Publisher: T. M. Fowler, Morrisville, Pa.
Key/Vignettes/Misc: 10 vignettes
Locations: LC–M
Catalogs/Checklists: LC–M, 515

2333
Place: Garwood, New Jersey
Date: 1903
Title: Garwood, New Jersey, 1903
Size: 18 × 25 in. (45.8 × 63.6 cm.)
Artist:
Lithographer:
Printer:
Publisher: Fowler & Bailey, New York
Key/Vignettes/Misc: 19 refs.; 5 vignettes
Locations: RU–NB
Catalogs/Checklists:

Place: Greenville, New Jersey
Date: 1876
See Jersey City, New Jersey, 1876.

2334
Place: Hackensack, New Jersey
Date: 1875
Title: Bird's Eye View of Hackensack 1875
Size: 20½ × 31½ in. (52.2 × 80.2 cm.)
Artist:
Lithographer:
Printer:
Publisher:
Key/Vignettes/Misc: Refs. 1–28, A–L
Locations: Johnson Public Library, Hackensack, New Jersey; NJHS–N (photo)
Catalogs/Checklists:

2335
Place: Hackensack, New Jersey
Date: 1896
Title: Hackensack, New Jersey, 1896
Size: 25¼ × 33½ in. (64.3 × 85.3 cm.)
Artist:
Lithographer:
Printer: O. H. Bailey & Co., Boston
Publisher: O. H. Bailey & Co., Boston
Key/Vignettes/Misc: Refs. A, 2–13, B–G, 14–54; 35 vignettes
Locations: RU–NB; LC–M
Catalogs/Checklists: LC–M, 515.1

2336
Place: Hackettstown, New Jersey
Date: 1845
Title: Hackett's Town
Size:
Artist: J. W. Hill
Lithographer:
Printer: G. & W. Endicott
Publisher:
Key/Vignettes/Misc:
Locations: Unknown
Catalogs/Checklists: Peters, America on Stone, p. 173

2337
Place: Hackettstown, New Jersey
Date: 1883
Title: Hackettstown. New Jersey. 1883
Size: 20¾ × 24 in. (52.8 × 61.1 cm.)
Artist: O. H. Bailey & Co.
Lithographer:
Printer: O. H. Bailey & Co.
Publisher: Bailey & Fowler, Boston
Key/Vignettes/Misc: Refs. 1–21; 8
vignettes
Locations: BPL–R
Catalogs/Checklists:

2338
Place: Haddonfield, New Jersey
Date: 1899
Title: Haddonfield, N. J.
Size: 22 × 28 in. (56 × 71.2 cm.)
Artist:
Lithographer:
Printer: O. H. Bailey & Co., Boston
Publisher: O. H. Bailey & Co., Boston
Key/Vignettes/Misc: 13 vignettes
Locations: Historical Society of
Haddonfield, Haddonfield, New Jersey
Catalogs/Checklists:

2339
Place: Hammonton, New Jersey
Date: 1926
Title: Aero View of Hammonton, New
Jersey 1926
Size: 26 × 31 in. (66.2 × 78.9 cm.)
Artist:
Lithographer:
Printer: [Stankovits & Co., Brooklyn, N.
Y.]
Publisher: Hughes & Bailey, Brooklyn, N.
Y.
Key/Vignettes/Misc: 21 vignettes;
unnumbered business directory
Locations: LC–M
Catalogs/Checklists: LC–M, 516

Place: Harrison, New Jersey
Date: 1895
See Newark, New Jersey, 1895.

2340
Place: Highland Park, New Jersey
Date: N.D.
Title: Livingston Manor Comprising 1090
Building Lots. Property of Livingston
Manor Corp.
Size: 24½ × 28 in. (62.3 × 71.2 cm.)
Artist:
Lithographer:
Printer: O. H. Bailey & Co., Boston
Publisher: Livingston Manor Corp.
Key/Vignettes/Misc: 3 vignettes;
description
Locations: RU–NB
Catalogs/Checklists:

2341
Place: Hightstown, New Jersey
Date: 1895
Title: Hightstown, N. J., 1895
Size: 24 × 30 in. (61 × 76.3 cm.)
Artist:
Lithographer:
Printer:

Publisher: [National View Company, New
York]
Key/Vignettes/Misc: Refs. A–D, 2–5, E,
6–32; 30 vignettes
Locations: RU–NB
Catalogs/Checklists:

2342
Place: Hightstown, New Jersey
Date: Ca. 1895
Title: Peddie Institute: A School of High
Rank for Both Sexes
Size: 24 × 32 in. (61.1 × 81.4 cm.)
Artist:
Lithographer:
Printer:
Publisher: National View Co., New York
Key/Vignettes/Misc: 16 vignettes;
description
Locations: RU–NB
Catalogs/Checklists:

Place: Hoboken, New Jersey
Date: 1856
See New York, New York, 1856.

Place: Hoboken, New Jersey
Date: 1858
See New York, New York, 1858.

2343
Place: Hoboken, New Jersey
Date: 1860
Title: Birds Eye View of Hoboken.
Size: 13½ × 20¹³⁄₁₆ in. (34.3 × 52.9 cm.)
Artist: J. Bachmann
Lithographer: J. Bachmann
Printer:
Publisher: J. Bachmann, 9 Irving Place,
Hoboken
Key/Vignettes/Misc:
Locations: NYP–S
Catalogs/Checklists: Stokes P. 1859—
G–57

Place: Hoboken, New Jersey
Date: Ca. 1868
See New York, New York, ca. 1868.

2344
Place: Hoboken, New Jersey
Date: 1874
Title: Hoboken.
Size: 16¼ × 20¼ in. (41.4 × 51.5 cm.)
Artist: J. Bachmann
Lithographer:
Printer:
Publisher: F. Luthin, 197 Washington St
Hoboken, N. J.
Key/Vignettes/Misc:
Locations: MM–NN; CHS–C; NJHS–N;
YUAG–NH; NYH–NY
Catalogs/Checklists: MM–NN, LP 326

Place: Hoboken, New Jersey
Date: 1877
See New York, New York, 1877.

2345
Place: Hoboken, New Jersey
Date: 1881
Title: The City of Hoboken. New Jersey.
1881.
Size: 22⅛ × 25⅜ in. (56.3 × 64.6 cm.)

Artist: O. H. Bailey & A. Ward
Lithographer:
Printer:
Publisher: O. H. Bailey & Co., Boston
Key/Vignettes/Misc: Refs. 1–87; 6
vignettes
Locations: BPL–R; LC–M
Catalogs/Checklists: LC–M, 517

2346
Place: Hoboken, New Jersey
Date: [1881–85]
Title: [Hoboken]
Size:
Artist:
Lithographer:
Printer:
Publisher:
Key/Vignettes/Misc: Litho view with
penciled title: Bird's–eye looking south
from vicinity of Stevens Institute
Locations: NYP–P
Catalogs/Checklists: Eno 426

Place: Hoboken, New Jersey
Date: 1892
See New York, New York, 1892.

2347
Place: Hoboken, New Jersey
Date: 1904
Title: City of Hoboken, New Jersey 1904
Size: 26½ × 32 in. (67.4 × 81.4 cm.)
Artist:
Lithographer:
Printer:
Publisher: Hughes & Bailey, N. Y.
Key/Vignettes/Misc: Refs. 1–123, A–H,
J–T; 27 vignettes
Locations: LC–M
Catalogs/Checklists: LC–M, 518

2348
Place: Hopewell, New Jersey
Date: 1887
Title: Hopewell, New Jersey, 1887
Size: 21½ × 27 in. (54.7 × 68.7 cm.)
Artist: T. M. Fowler
Lithographer:
Printer:
Publisher: T. M. Fowler, Morrisville, Pa.
Key/Vignettes/Misc: 29 refs.
Locations: RU–NB
Catalogs/Checklists:

Place: Jersey City, New Jersey
Date: 1849
See New York, New York, 1849.

2349
Place: Jersey City, New Jersey
Date: Ca. 1851
Title: View of Jersey City, N. J., Taken
from a Ship's Mast lying Directly Opposite
Montgomery St.
Size: 19⅝ × 33⅛ in. (49.9 × 84.3 cm.)
Artist:
Lithographer:
Printer: Endicott & Co. New York
Publisher: J. Parsons & Co., New Jersey
Key/Vignettes/Misc: Refs. 1–15
Locations: NYP–S (ca. 1866); MM–NN;
NJHS–N; NYH–NY

Catalogs/Checklists: MM–NN, LP 2189;
Stokes C. 1866—E–139

Place: Jersey City, New Jersey
Date: 1856
See New York, New York, 1856.

Place: Jersey City, New Jersey
Date: 1858
See New York, New York, 1858.

Place: Jersey City, New Jersey
Date: Ca. 1868
See New York, New York, ca. 1868.

2350
Place: Jersey City, New Jersey
Date: 1876
Title: Greenville J. C., New Jersey, 1876
Size: 17 × 24 in. (43.3 × 61.1 cm.)
Artist: T. M. Fowler
Lithographer: D. Bremner & Co.
Printer: D. Bremner & Co., Milwaukee,
Wisc.
Publisher: Fowler & Bulger
Key/Vignettes/Misc: Refs. 1–12
Locations: RU–NB
Catalogs/Checklists:

Place: Jersey City, New Jersey
Date: 1877
See New York, New York, 1877.

2351
Place: Jersey City, New Jersey
Date: 1883
Title: Jersey City, N. J. 1883.
Size: 28 × 39 in. (71.2 × 99.2 cm.)
Artist:
Lithographer:
Printer:
Publisher: O. H. Bailey & Co., Boston
Key/Vignettes/Misc: Refs. 1–99, A–I; 33
vignettes
Locations: BPL–R; Jersey City, New
Jersey, Public Library
Catalogs/Checklists:

Place: Jersey City, New Jersey
Date: 1892
See New York, New York, 1892.

2352
Place: Jersey City, New Jersey
Date: N.D.
Title: Panorama of the Harbor of New
York, Staten Island and the Narrows.
Size: ca. 14 × 20 in. (ca. 35.7 × 50.9 cm.)
Artist: John Bornet
Lithographer: John Bornet
Printer: Nagel & Weingartner, N. Y.
Publisher: Goupil & Co. 366 Broadway,
New York
Key/Vignettes/Misc: 12 unnumbered refs.
below places identified
Locations: NYP–P; NJHS–N (photo)
Catalogs/Checklists: Eno 469

2353
Place: Jersey City, New Jersey
Date: ?
Title: Jersey City—New York New York
from Staten Island, Brooklyn City
Size: 35 × 45 in. (89.1 × 114.5 cm.)

Artist:
Lithographer:
Printer: Horron, Sarony, and Major
Publisher: Horron, Sarony and Major
Key/Vignettes/Misc:
Locations: SIHS–R
Catalogs/Checklists:

Place: Kearney, New Jersey
Date: 1895
See Newark, New Jersey, 1895.

2354
Place: Keyport, New Jersey
Date: 1894
Title: Keyport, New Jersey, 1894
Size: 25 × 30 in. (63.6 × 76.4 cm.)
Artist:
Lithographer:
Printer:
Publisher: National View Co., Boston
Key/Vignettes/Misc: Refs. A, 2–29; 13
vignettes
Locations: RU–NB
Catalogs/Checklists:

2355
Place: Lambertville, New Jersey
Date: 1883
Title: View of Lambertville, New Jersey.
1883.
Size: 20⅜ × 26¾ in. (51.9 × 68.1 cm.)
Artist:
Lithographer:
Printer:
Publisher: O. H. Bailey & Co., Boston
Key/Vignettes/Misc: Refs. A, 2–25; 11
vignettes
Locations: BPL–R
Catalogs/Checklists:

2356
Place: Long Branch, New Jersey
Date: 1882
Title: Off Long Branch
Size: 20⅛ × 27 in. (51.1 × 68.6 cm.)
Artist:
Lithographer:
Printer: Cadwell Lith. Co., New York
Publisher: E. G. Rideout & Co., 10
Barclay St. New York
Key/Vignettes/Misc:
Locations: MM–NN
Catalogs/Checklists: MM–NN, LP 3924

2357
Place: Maplewood, New Jersey
Date: 1910
Title: Bird's–Eye–View of Maplewood,
N. J. Looking West
Size: 10⅞ × 14⁵⁄₁₆ in. (27.7 × 36.5 cm.)
Artist: H[enry] S[haw] Wyllie
Lithographer:
Printer:
Publisher: H. S. Wyllie, Newark, N. J.
Key/Vignettes/Misc:
Locations: LC–M
Catalogs/Checklists: LC–M, 519

2358
Place: Margate City, New Jersey
Date: 1925
Title: Aero View of Margate City New
Jersey 1925

Size: 21 × 34½ in. (53.4 × 87.7 cm.)
Artist: Rene Cinquin
Lithographer:
Printer:
Publisher: Hughes & Cinquin, Brooklyn,
N. Y.
Key/Vignettes/Misc: 2 vignettes; 1 map
Locations: LC–M
Catalogs/Checklists: LC–M, 520

2359
Place: Morristown, New Jersey
Date: 1876
Title: Bird's Eye View of Morristown,
Morris Co. New Jersey. 1876.
Size: 19½ × 28¼ in. (49.6 × 71.9 cm.)
Artist: T. M. Fowler
Lithographer: C. H. Vogt
Printer: Fowler & Bulger
Publisher:
Key/Vignettes/Misc: Refs. 1–13, A–M
Locations: BPL–R
Catalogs/Checklists:

2360
Place: Morristown, New Jersey
Date: 1899
Title: Morristown, N. J. 1899
Size: 33 × 46 in. (83.9 × 117 cm.)
Artist:
Lithographer:
Printer:
Publisher: Landis & Alsop, Newark, N. J.
Key/Vignettes/Misc: 41 vignettes;
unnumbered business directory
Locations: LC–M
Catalogs/Checklists: LC–M, 521

2361
Place: Mountain Lakes, New Jersey
Date: N.D.
Title: Bird's–Eye View of Mountain
Lakes, Boonton, New Jersey
Size: 12½ × 19 in. (31.8 × 48.3 cm.)
Artist: A. T. Holton
Lithographer:
Printer:
Publisher: Mountain Lakes, Incorporated,
New York
Key/Vignettes/Misc:
Locations: RU–NB
Catalogs/Checklists:

2362
Place: New Brunswick, New Jersey
Date: Ca. 1870
Title: New Brunswick, N. J.
Size: 6 × 8½ in. (15.2 × 21.6 cm.)
Artist:
Lithographer:
Printer:
Publisher: Charles Magnus
Key/Vignettes/Misc:
Locations: RU–NB
Catalogs/Checklists:

2363
Place: New Brunswick, New Jersey
Date: 1874
Title: Bird's Eye View of New Brunswick,
N. J. 1874.
Size: 23½ × 27½ in. (59.8 × 70 cm.)
Artist: O. H. Bailey

Lithographer:
Printer: Breuker & Kessler Lith, Phila.
Publisher: Fowler & Bailey
Key/Vignettes/Misc: Refs. 1–29, A–H
Locations: RU–NB
Catalogs/Checklists:

2364
Place: New Brunswick, New Jersey
Date: 1880
Title: City of New Brunswick, New Jersey, 1880
Size: 19⅝ × 30⁹⁄₁₆ in. (50 × 77.8 cm.)
Artist:
Lithographer:
Printer: Packer & Butler, Lith, Philadelphia
Publisher:
Key/Vignettes/Misc: 7 vignettes
Locations: RU–NB; NJHS–N; LC–P
Catalogs/Checklists: LC–M, 523.1

2365
Place: New Brunswick, New Jersey
Date: 1892
Title: Livingston Terrace, Comprising 352 Building Lots Owned by Wm. H. Moffitt. . . .
Size: 22 × 28 in. (55.9 × 71.2 cm.)
Artist:
Lithographer:
Printer: [O. H. Bailey & Co., Boston]
Publisher: Wm. H. Moffitt
Key/Vignettes/Misc: 8 vignettes
Locations: RU–NB
Catalogs/Checklists:

2366
Place: New Brunswick, New Jersey
Date: 1910
Title: Aero View of New–Brunswick, New Jersey 1910
Size: 35 × 44 in. (89.1 × 111.9 cm.)
Artist:
Lithographer:
Printer:
Publisher: Hughes & Bailey, New York
Key/Vignettes/Misc: 130 unnumbered refs.; 64 vignettes
Locations: LC–M; RU–NB
Catalogs/Checklists: LC–M, 524

2367
Place: New Brunswick, New Jersey
Date: N.D.
Title: View of the City of New Brunswick, N. J. Taken from the Rail Road Hotel at East Brunswick.
Size: 13½ × 20½ in. (34.4 × 52.2 cm.)
Artist: J. H. Bufford
Lithographer: J. H. Bufford
Printer: Bufford's Lith, 126 Nassau St, New York
Publisher:
Key/Vignettes/Misc: 8 unnumbered refs. below places identified
Locations: RU–NB
Catalogs/Checklists:

2368
Place: Newark, New Jersey
Date: 1847
Title: View of Newark, N. J. from the North.

Size: 17¾ × 35¾ in. (45.2 × 90.9 cm.)
Artist: E. Whitefield
Lithographer: E. Whitefield
Printer: F. Michelin, New York
Publisher: E. Whitefield, 32 Ann St. N. Y.
Key/Vignettes/Misc: 4 vignettes
Locations: MM–NN; NJHS–N; NM–N
Catalogs/Checklists: MM–NN, LP 516; Norton, Whitefield, no. 34

2369
Place: Newark, New Jersey
Date: [1852]
Title: Newark, N. J. From the Residence of T. V. Johnson, Esqr.
Size: 18½ × 37⁷⁄₁₆ in. (47 × 95.2 cm.)
Artist: B. F. Smith, Jr.
Lithographer: B. F. Smith, Jr.
Printer: Geo E. Leffe, 225 Fulton St., New York
Publisher: Smith, Fern & Co. 218 Fulton St., New York
Key/Vignettes/Misc:
Locations: NYP–S
Catalogs/Checklists: Stokes C. 1853—G–22

2370
Place: Newark, New Jersey
Date: [1854–]
Title: Newark, (East of Mulberry St. 1820–5)
Size: 25⅝ × 20³⁄₁₆ in. (65.2 × 51.4 cm.)
Artist:
Lithographer:
Printer: Ferd Mayer, Gen'l Lith'r, 96 & 98 Fulton St., N. Y.
Publisher:
Key/Vignettes/Misc: Refs. 1–38
Locations: NYP–S; MM–N; NJHS–N; YUAG–NH
Catalogs/Checklists: Stokes 1820–25—F–22

2371
Place: Newark, New Jersey
Date: [1874]
Title: City of Newark, N. J.
Size: 22¼ × 28⅞ in. (56.6 x 73.4 cm.)
Artist: Parsons & Atwater
Lithographer:
Printer:
Publisher: Parsons & Atwater, 57 Beekman St., New York
Key/Vignettes/Misc: 39 unnumbered refs. below places identified
Locations: LC–P; NJHS–N
Catalogs/Checklists: LC–M, 521.1

2372
Place: Newark, New Jersey
Date: 1895
Title: Newark, N. J., Harrison–Kearney 1895
Size: 30 × 43½ in. (76.3 × 110.6 cm.)
Artist:
Lithographer:
Printer:
Publisher: T. J. S. Landis, 294 Roseville Ave. Newark
Key/Vignettes/Misc: 96 unnumbered refs.
Locations: LC–M; NJHS–N
Catalogs/Checklists: LC–M, 522

2373
Place: Newark, New Jersey
Date: 1916
Title: Newark–New Jersey and Suburbs
Size: 22 × 30¾ in. (56 × 78.2 cm.)
Artist:
Lithographer:
Printer:
Publisher: T. J. S. Landis, Newark, N. J.
Key/Vignettes/Misc:
Locations: LC–M
Catalogs/Checklists: LC–M, 523

2374
Place: Newark, New Jersey
Date: N.D.
Title: City of Newark, N. J.
Size: 14⅛ × 35⅝ in. (35.9 × 90.5 cm.)
Artist: Otto Gsantntner from ambrotype by Hopper & Freeman
Lithographer:
Printer: A. Weingartner's Lithography, N. Y.
Publisher: F. Keer, 350 Broad St., Newark, N. J.
Key/Vignettes/Misc:
Locations: MM–N; NJHS–N
Catalogs/Checklists:

2375
Place: Newark, New Jersey
Date: N.D.
Title: Newark, N. J. Part I.
Size: 5⅛ × 7⅞ in. (13 × 20 cm.)
Artist:
Lithographer:
Printer:
Publisher: Charles Magnus, New York
Key/Vignettes/Misc:
Locations: MM–NN
Catalogs/Checklists: MM–NN, LP 3611

2376
Place: Newark, New Jersey
Date: N.D.
Title: Newark, N. J. Part II.
Size: 5⅛ × 7⅞ (13 × 20 cm.)
Artist:
Lithographer:
Printer:
Publisher: Charles Magnus, New York
Key/Vignettes/Misc:
Locations: MM–NN
Catalogs/Checklists: MM–NN, LP 3612

2377
Place: Newton, New Jersey
Date: 1883
Title: Newton, New Jersey. 1883
Size: 20⅝ × 24¼ in. (52.5 × 61.7 cm.)
Artist:
Lithographer:
Printer:
Publisher: O. H. Bailey & Co., Boston
Key/Vignettes/Misc: Refs. 1–51, A–E; 8 vignettes
Locations: BPL–R
Catalogs/Checklists:

2378
Place: Newton, New Jersey
Date: 1927
Title: Aero–View of Newton–1927–Sussex County, New Jersey

Size: 11 × 17 in. (28 × 43.3 cm.)
Artist: Rene Cinquin
Lithographer:
Printer:
Publisher: Standard Aero–View Co., New York
Key/Vignettes/Misc: 1 vignette; description
Locations: RU–NB
Catalogs/Checklists:

Place: North Plainfield, New Jersey
Date: 1899
See Plainfield, New Jersey, 1899.

2379
Place: Ocean Grove, New Jersey
Date: 1877
Title: Ocean Grove & Asbury Park, New Jersey, 1877
Size: 20 × 27½ in. (50.8 × 70 cm.)
Artist: T. M. Fowler
Lithographer:
Printer: D. Bremner & Co., Milwaukee, Wis.
Publisher: Fowler & Crosbie
Key/Vignettes/Misc: 5 vignettes; description
Locations: RU–NB; MCHA–F
Catalogs/Checklists:

2380
Place: Ocean Grove, New Jersey
Date: 1881
Title: Bird's Eye View of Ocean Grove
Size: 15⅞ × 20⅜ in. (40.5 × 51.9 cm.)
Artist:
Lithographer:
Printer: Beck & Pauli, Lith., Milwaukee, Wis.
Publisher: T. M. Fowler, Asbury Park, N. J. (copyright)
Key/Vignettes/Misc: Refs. 1–5; 1 vignette
Locations: LC–P
Catalogs/Checklists:

2381
Place: Ocean Grove, New Jersey
Date: 1881
Title: Bird's Eye View of Ocean Grove and Asbury Park, New Jersey 1881
Size: 18¾ × 34⅞ in. (47.8 × 88.7 cm.)
Artist: T. M. Fowler
Lithographer:
Printer: Beck & Pauli, Lith., Milwaukee, Wis.
Publisher: T. M. Fowler, Asbury Park, N. J.
Key/Vignettes/Misc: Ocean Grove refs., 1–5, Asbury Park refs., 1–7; 7 vignettes
Locations: NJHS–N (photo); LC–M
Catalogs/Checklists: LC–M, 502

Place: Ocean Grove, New Jersey
Date: 1897
See Asbury Park, New Jersey, 1897.

2382
Place: Orange, New Jersey
Date: 1877
Title: City of Orange, N. J. 1877
Size: 20¾ (cropped) × 27⅛ in. (52.9 × 69 cm.)
Artist: T. M. Fowler
Lithographer:

Printer: D. Bremner & Co. Lith., Milwaukee, Wis.
Publisher: Jos. B. Bray, Orange
Key/Vignettes/Misc: Refs. 1–30 (cropped), A–P
Locations: NJHS–N
Catalogs/Checklists:

2383
Place: Paterson, New Jersey
Date: 1834
Title: Paterson, N. J.
Size: 9⁹⁄₁₆ × 13¾ in. (24.3 × 35 cm.)
Artist: J. W. Hill
Lithographer:
Printer: Endicott, 359 Broadway, New York
Publisher:
Key/Vignettes/Misc:
Locations: NYP–S; FL–P
Catalogs/Checklists: Stokes P. 1833—F–32; Pyne, no. 458

2384
Place: Paterson, New Jersey
Date: 1853
Title: View of Paterson, N. J. from the Manchester side (Totowa) side
Size: 24 × 33 in. (framed) (61.1 × 84 cm.)
Artist: E. Whitefield
Lithographer: E. Whitefield
Printer: Nagel and Weingartner
Publisher: I.[saac] Prindle (copyright)
Key/Vignettes/Misc: 9 refs.
Locations: Paterson, New Jersey, Free Public Library; YUAG–NH
Catalogs/Checklists: Norton, Whitefield, no. 52

2385
Place: Paterson, New Jersey
Date: 1875
Title: Birds Eye View of Paterson, N. J. 1875
Size: 22³⁄₁₆ × 31⅞ in. (56.5 × 81.1 cm.)
Artist: H. H. Bailey
Lithographer:
Printer: Breuker & Kessler, Lithograph, Phila. Pa.
Publisher:
Key/Vignettes/Misc: 66 refs.; 4 vignettes
Locations: Paterson, New Jersey, Free Public Library; Passaic County Historical Society, Paterson, New Jersey
Catalogs/Checklists:

2386
Place: Paterson, New Jersey
Date: 1880
Title: Paterson, N. J. 1880 17 Miles from New York on the N. Y. L. E. & W. Ry.
Size: 19¾ × 33⅞ in. (50.3 × 86.2 cm.)
Artist:
Lithographer:
Printer: Packard & Butler, Lith, Phila.
Publisher:
Key/Vignettes/Misc: 16 vignettes
Locations: YUAG–NH; LC–P
Catalogs/Checklists: LC–M, 524.1

2387
Place: Paulsboro, New Jersey
Date: 1898
Title: Paulsboro, New Jersey

Size: 22 × 27¹⁵⁄₁₆ in. (56 × 71.1 cm.)
Artist:
Lithographer:
Printer: O. H. Bailey & Co., Boston
Publisher: O. H. Bailey & Co., Boston
Key/Vignettes/Misc: Refs. A, 2–46; 18 vignettes
Locations: GCHS–W (facsimile)
Catalogs/Checklists:

2388
Place: Perth Amboy, New Jersey
Date: Ca. 1860
Title: Perth Amboy, New–Jersey.
Size: 10½ × 16½ in. (26.7 × 42 cm.)
Artist: H. Knecht
Lithographer:
Printer:
Publisher: W. Faust, 59 Fulton St. New York
Key/Vignettes/Misc:
Locations: MM–NN
Catalogs/Checklists: MM–NN, LP 4606

Place: Phillipsburg, New Jersey
Date: 1900
See Easton, Pennsylvania, 1900.

Place: Phillipsburg, New Jersey
Date: N.D.
See Easton, Pennsylvania, n.d.

2389
Place: Plainfield, New Jersey
Date: 1899
Title: Plainfield and North Plainfield, N. J. 1899
Size: 31 × 47½ in. (78.9 × 120.9 cm.)
Artist:
Lithographer:
Printer:
Publisher: Landis & Hughes, N. Y.
Key/Vignettes/Misc: 40 vignettes; unnumbered business directory
Locations: LC–M
Catalogs/Checklists: LC–M, 525

2390
Place: Pleasantville, New Jersey
Date: 1924
Title: Aero–View of Pleasantville, Atlantic County N. J.—The City of Homes and Industry
Size: 7¹⁵⁄₁₆ × 10¼ in. (20.2 × 26.1 cm.) (facsimile)
Artist:
Lithographer:
Printer:
Publisher: Hughes & Cinquin, 557–4th St., Brooklyn, N. Y.
Key/Vignettes/Misc: 1 vignette; description
Locations: Atlantic County Historical Society, Somers Point, New Jersey (facsimile)
Catalogs/Checklists:

2391
Place: Port Au Peck, New Jersey
Date: N.D.
Title: Port Au Peck, Near Long Branch
Size: 21 × 26 in. (53.4 × 66.2 cm.)
Artist:

Lithographer:
Printer:
Publisher: National View Co., 36
Columbus Ave., Boston
Key/Vignettes/Misc: 8 vignettes;
description
Locations: MCHA−F
Catalogs/Checklists:

Place: Progress, New Jersey
Date: Ca. 1855
See Riverside, New Jersey, ca. 1855.

2392
Place: Rahway, New Jersey
Date: 1874
Title: Rahway, N. J. 1874.
Size: 17¾ × 22⅜ in. (45.2 × 57 cm.)
Artist:
Lithographer:
Printer: G. W. Lewis, 452 Broadway,
Albany, N. Y.
Publisher: H. H. Bailey & J. C. Hazen
[Hazen's name in ms]
Key/Vignettes/Misc: Refs. 1−22
Locations: BPL−R
Catalogs/Checklists:

2393
Place: Red Bank, New Jersey
Date: 1881
Title: Red Bank, New Jersey, 1881
Size: 15 × 24 in. (38.2 × 61.1 cm.)
Artist: T. M. Fowler
Lithographer:
Printer:
Publisher: Fowler & Rhines
Key/Vignettes/Misc: Refs. 1−32
Locations: MCHA−F
Catalogs/Checklists:

2394
Place: Red Bank, New Jersey
Date: 1894
Title: Red Bank, New Jersey, 1894
Size: 26¼ × 32½ in. (66.9 × 82.7 cm.)
Artist:
Lithographer:
Printer:
Publisher: National View Company, 36
Columbus Ave., Boston, Mass.
Key/Vignettes/Misc: Refs. A−C, 2−42; 44
vignettes
Locations: MCHA−F
Catalogs/Checklists:

2395
Place: Riverside, New Jersey
Date: Ca. 1855
Title: [View of the Town of Progress, N.
J.]
Size: 12⁹⁄₁₆ × 20⅛ in. (32 × 51.2 cm.)
Artist:
Lithographer:
Printer: P. S. Duval & Co., Steam Lith.
Press, Phila.
Publisher:
Key/Vignettes/Misc:
Locations: National Maritime Museum,
Greenwich, England; NJHS−N (photo)
Catalogs/Checklists:

2396
Place: Rutherford, New Jersey
Date: 1904
Title: Rutherford, New Jersey 1904
Size: 22 × 27 in. (55.9 × 68.6 cm.)
Artist:
Lithographer:
Printer:
Publisher: T. J. Hughes, New York
Key/Vignettes/Misc:
Locations: LC−M; NJHS−N
Catalogs/Checklists: LC−M, 526

2397
Place: Sea Isle City, New Jersey
Date: 1885
Title: View of Sea Isle City. New Jersey.
1885.
Size: 15⅝ × 24½ in. (39.8 × 62.3 cm.)
Artist:
Lithographer:
Printer:
Publisher: O. H. Bailey & Co., Boston
Key/Vignettes/Misc: Refs. 1−30; 6
vignettes
Locations: BPL−R
Catalogs/Checklists:

2398
Place: Seabright, New Jersey
Date: N.D.
Title: Seabright, N. J.
Size: 24 × 30 in. (61.1 × 76.4 cm.)
Artist:
Lithographer:
Printer:
Publisher:
Key/Vignettes/Misc: Refs. A, 2−15; 13
vignettes
Locations: MCHA−F
Catalogs/Checklists:

Place: Shreveville, New Jersey
Date: [1830?]
See Smithville, New Jersey, [1830?].

2399
Place: Smithville, New Jersey
Date: [1830?]
Title: View of Shreveville, N. J.
Size: 12 × 19 in. (30.5 × 48.3 cm.)
Artist:
Lithographer:
Printer:
Publisher:
Key/Vignettes/Misc:
Locations: RU−NB
Catalogs/Checklists:

2400
Place: Somers Point, New Jersey
Date: 1925
Title: Aero−View of Somers Point New
Jersey 1925
Size: 25 × 34 in. (63.5 × 86.4 cm.)
Artist: R. Cinquin
Lithographer:
Printer: [Meriden Gravure Co., Meriden,
Conn.]
Publisher: Hughes & Cinquin, 557 Fourth
Street, Brooklyn, N. Y.

Key/Vignettes/Misc: 3 vignettes
Locations: LC−M
Catalogs/Checklists: LC−M, 527

2401
Place: Somerville, New Jersey
Date: 1882
Title: Somerville, New Jersey, 1882
Size: 15 × 25 in. (38.1 × 63.5 cm.)
Artist: T. M. Fowler
Lithographer:
Printer: Beck & Pauli, Lithographers,
Milwaukee
Publisher: Fowler & Evans, Asbury Park,
N. J.
Key/Vignettes/Misc: Refs. 1−32
Locations: LC−M; RU−NB
Catalogs/Checklists: LC−M, 527.1

2402
Place: South Orange, New Jersey
Date: 1877
Title: Bird's Eye View of South Orange, N.
J. 1877
Size: 18 × 23 in. (45.8 × 58.6 cm.)
Artist: T. M. Fowler
Lithographer:
Printer: D. Bremner & Co. Lith,
Milwaukee, Wis.
Publisher: T. M. Fowler
Key/Vignettes/Misc: Refs. 1−17
Locations: NJHS−N; LC−M (facsimile)
Catalogs/Checklists: LC−M, 527.2

2403
Place: Swedesboro, New Jersey
Date: 1886
Title: View of Swedesboro New Jersey
Size: 20⅞ × 26¾ in. (53.2 × 68.1 cm.)
Artist:
Lithographer:
Printer: O. H. Bailey & Co., Boston
Publisher: T. M. Fowler
Key/Vignettes/Misc: Refs. 1−38; 13
vignettes
Locations: GCHS−W
Catalogs/Checklists:

2404
Place: Trenton, New Jersey
Date: 1851
Title: View of Trenton, N. J. from
Morrisville, Pa.
Size: 21⅞ × 34¼ in. (55.7 × 87.1 cm.)
Artist: E. Whitefield
Lithographer: E. Whitefield
Printer:
Publisher: Wm. Endicott & Co., New
York
Key/Vignettes/Misc: 27 unnumbered refs.
below places identified; 6 vignettes
Locations: MM−NN; NJHS−N; NYP−S;
Trenton, New Jersey, Free Public Library
Catalogs/Checklists: MM−NN, LP 4335;
Norton, Whitefield, no. 51

2405
Place: Trenton, New Jersey
Date: 1872
Title:
Size:

Artist:
Lithographer:
Printer:
Publisher: Fowler & Bailey
Key/Vignettes/Misc:
Locations:
Catalogs/Checklists: Warren & Wise

2406

Place: Trenton, New Jersey
Date: 1874
Title: Trenton, N. J. 1874
Size: 23 × 32 in. (58.5 × 81.4 cm.)
Artist: T. M. Fowler
Lithographer: H. J. Toudy & Co.
Printer: H. J. Toudy & Co. Steam Lith.,
Philadelphia, Pa.
Publisher: Fowler & Bailey
Key/Vignettes/Misc: Refs. 1–44, A–V; 1
vignette
Locations: LC–M(photo); Trenton, New
Jersey, Free Public Library
Catalogs/Checklists: LC–M, 527.3

2407

Place: Trenton, New Jersey
Date: Ca. 1876
Title: New Jersey 1776–1876 City of
Trenton
Size: 10 × 8⅛ in. (25.4 × 20.6 cm.)
Artist: W. Brotherhead
Lithographer:
Printer: H. J. Toudy & Co., Philadelphia
Publisher:
Key/Vignettes/Misc:
Locations: MM–NN
Catalogs/Checklists: MM–NN, LP 879

2408

Place: Vineland, New Jersey
Date: 1870
Title: Vineland, N. J. 1870. View from the
Seminary
Size: 19½ × 33¼ in. (49.6 × 84.6 cm.)
Artist: J. H. Sawyer
Lithographer:
Printer: Duval & Hunter, Lith. Phila.
Publisher:
Key/Vignettes/Misc:
Locations: HEHL; RU–NB
Catalogs/Checklists:

2409

Place: Vineland, New Jersey
Date: 1885
Title: The City of Vineland, New Jersey.
1885
Size: 23½ × 32½ in. (59.8 × 82.6 cm.)
Artist:
Lithographer:
Printer: O. H. Bailey & Co., Boston
Publisher: O. H. Bailey & Co., Boston
Key/Vignettes/Misc: Refs. 1–87; 21
vignettes
Locations: BPL–R; LC–M
Catalogs/Checklists: LC–M, 528

2410

Place: Wenonah, New Jersey
Date: 1886
Title: Wenonah, New Jersey, 1886
Size: 20⅞ × 24³⁄₁₆ in. (53.1 × 61.6 cm.)

Artist:
Lithographer:
Printer: O. H. Bailey & Co., Boston
Publisher: O. H. Bailey & Co., Boston
Key/Vignettes/Misc: Refs. 1–6; 10
vignettes
Locations: GCHS–W
Catalogs/Checklists:

2411

Place: Westfield, New Jersey
Date: 1878
Title: Westfield, New Jersey, 1878
Size: 13 × 17½ in. (33 × 44.5 cm.)
Artist: T. M. Fowler
Lithographer:
Printer:
Publisher: Fowler & Evans, Box 208
Asbury Park, N. J.
Key/Vignettes/Misc: Refs. 1–10, 12–45,
A–T; 16 vignettes
Locations: RU–NB (facsimile); NJHS–N
(photo)
Catalogs/Checklists:

2412

Place: Westfield, New Jersey
Date: 1903
Title: Westfield, New Jersey, 1903
Size: 22 × 28 in. (56 × 71.2 cm.)
Artist:
Lithographer:
Printer:
Publisher: T. J. Hughes, 359 52nd St.
Brooklyn, N. Y.
Key/Vignettes/Misc: Refs. 1–45, A–T; 16
vignettes
Locations: RU–NB
Catalogs/Checklists:

2413

Place: Westfield, New Jersey
Date: 1929
Title: Aero–View of Westfield, N. J. 1929
Size: 27 × 31 in. (68.6 × 78.8 cm.)
Artist: Rene Cinquin
Lithographer:
Printer: [Meriden Gravure Co., Meriden,
Conn.]
Publisher: Hughes & Cinquin, 106 Park
Row, New York, N. Y.
Key/Vignettes/Misc: Refs. 1–26; 45
vignettes; unnumbered business directory;
1 map
Locations: LC–M
Catalogs/Checklists: LC–M, 529

2414

Place: Westwood, New Jersey
Date: 1924
Title: Aeroview of Westwood, New Jersey
1924
Size: 22½ × 34 in. (57.3 × 86.5 cm.)
Artist: Rene Cinquin
Lithographer:
Printer: [Meriden Gravure Co., Meriden,
Conn.]
Publisher: Hughes & Cinquin
Key/Vignettes/Misc: Refs.; 5 vignettes;
unnumbered business directory; 1 map
Locations: LC–M
Catalogs/Checklists: LC–M, 530

2415

Place: Woodbury, New Jersey
Date: 1886
Title: The City of Woodbury, New Jersey
1886
Size: 23⅜ × 30⅜ in. (59.5 × 77.3 cm.)
Artist:
Lithographer:
Printer: O. H. Bailey & Co., Boston
Publisher: O. H. Bailey & Co., Boston
Key/Vignettes/Misc: Refs. 1–64, A–D; 27
vignettes
Locations: LC–M; GCHS–W
Catalogs/Checklists: LC–M, 531

2416

Place: Albuquerque, New Mexico
Date: 1886
Title: Bird's Eye View of Albuquerque
Bernalillo Co. New Mex. 1886
Size: 22⁷⁄₁₆ × 29 in. (58.3 × 73.8 cm.)
Artist: Augustus Koch
Lithographer:
Printer:
Publisher:
Key/Vignettes/Misc: Refs. 1–30;
advertisement
Locations: UCBL–B; LC–M (photo)
Catalogs/Checklists: LC–M, 531.1

2417

Place: Las Vegas, New Mexico
Date: 1882
Title: Bird's Eye View of Las Vegas, N. M.
C. S. San Miguel County 1882.
Size: 13⅜ × 21⅝ in. (34 × 55 cm.)
Artist:
Lithographer:
Printer: Beck & Pauli, Lithographers,
Milwaukee, Wis.
Publisher: J. J. Stoner, Madison, Wis.
Key/Vignettes/Misc: Refs. 1–31; 1
vignette
Locations: LC–M; ACMW–FW
Catalogs/Checklists: LC–M, 532

2418

Place: Santa Fe, New Mexico
Date: 1882
Title: Bird's Eye View of the City of Santa
Fe, N. M. 1882.
Size: 9⁹⁄₁₆ × 19¹⁄₁₆ in. (24.2 × 48.3 cm.)
Artist: H. Wellge
Lithographer:
Printer: Beck & Pauli, Lithographers,
Milwaukee, Wis.
Publisher: J. J. Stoner, Madison, Wis.
Key/Vignettes/Misc: Refs. 1–30
Locations: ACMW–FW; LC–M; Museum
of New Mexico, Santa Fe, New Mexico
Catalogs/Checklists: LC–M, 533; Reps,
Cities on Stone, p. 97

2419

Place: Socorro, New Mexico
Date: Ca. 1877
Title: Bird's Eye View of the City of
Socorro, N. M. Socorro County
Size:
Artist:
Lithographer:
Printer:

Publisher: J. J. Stoner, Madison (?)
Key/Vignettes/Misc:
Locations: Private collection
Catalogs/Checklists:

2420
Place: Addison, New York
Date: Ca. 1850
Title: View of Addison, Steuben Co., N. Y.
Size: 13½ × 19 in. (34.4 × 48.4 cm.)
Artist: H. Walton
Lithographer: H. Walton
Printer:
Publisher:
Key/Vignettes/Misc:
Locations: NYH−NY
Catalogs/Checklists: Rehner, Walton, no. 63

2421
Place: Albania, New York
Date: [1918]
Title: Albania.
Size: 20 × 30 in. (50.9 × 76.4 cm.)
Artist:
Lithographer:
Printer:
Publisher: American Geographical Society, New York City
Key/Vignettes/Misc:
Locations: BPL−R
Catalogs/Checklists:

2422
Place: Albany, New York
Date: [1828−29]
Title: Albany—Capital of the State of New York
Size: 7½ × 11¼ in. (19.1 × 28.6 cm.)
Artist: [Jacques] Milbert
Lithographer: Deroy
Printer:
Publisher:
Key/Vignettes/Misc:
Locations: YUAG−NH; AIHA−A
Catalogs/Checklists:

2423
Place: Albany, New York
Date: 1844
Title: View of the City of Albany, N. Y. From the N. East
Size: 12¼ × 17¼ in. (31.2 × 43.9 cm.)
Artist: S. Palmer, Jr.
Lithographer: S. Palmer, Jr.
Printer:
Publisher: Wm Green, Exchange, Albany
Key/Vignettes/Misc:
Locations: AIHA−A
Catalogs/Checklists:

2424
Place: Albany, New York
Date: Ca. 1845
Title: View of Albany, N. Y. from the East.
Size: 15³⁄₁₆ × 24 in. (38.6 × 61 cm.)
Artist: E. Whitefield
Lithographer:
Printer: Lewis & Brown, Lith. New York
Publisher: Lewis & Brown, 272 Pearl St. New York
Key/Vignettes/Misc: Refs. 1−34

Locations: MM−NN; YUAG−NH; NYSH−C; AIHA−A
Catalogs/Checklists: MM−NN, LP 27; Hemenway; Norton, Whitefield, no. 29

2425
Place: Albany, New York
Date: 1850
Title: Albany General View
Size: 9⁹⁄₁₆ × 11¾ in. (24.3 × 29.9 cm.)
Artist: August Kollner
Lithographer: Deroy
Printer: Cattier
Publisher: Goupil, Vibert & Co., New York & Paris
Key/Vignettes/Misc:
Locations: NYP−S; PAC−P; YUAG−NH; ROM; AIHA−A
Catalogs/Checklists: Samuel, no. 423; Stokes P. 1849—G−2

2426
Place: Albany, New York
Date: 1852
Title: View of Albany, Capital of the Empire State. From the Hills East Side the Hudson.
Size: 22 × 32¾ in. (56 × 83.3 cm.)
Artist: From daguerreotypes
Lithographer: E. Brown Jr.
Printer: A. Robertson 121 Fulton St. N. Y.
Publisher: C. C. Schoonmaker, Exchange Building, Albany, New York
Key/Vignettes/Misc: 20 unnumbered refs. below places identified
Locations: AIHA−A
Catalogs/Checklists:

2427
Place: Albany, New York
Date: Ca.1853
Title: Albany, N. Y.
Size: 26⁹⁄₁₆ × 38 in. (67.6 × 96.7 cm.)
Artist: J. W. Hill
Lithographer: Hatch & Severyn
Printer: Michelin 225 Fulton St., N. Y.
Publisher: Smith Bros. & Co., New York
Key/Vignettes/Misc:
Locations: MM−NN; CHS−C; LC−M (facsimile); AIHA−A; NYSL−A; CSNY−S; LC−P; NYH−NY
Catalogs/Checklists: MM−NN, LP 494; LC−M, 533.2

2428
Place: Albany, New York
Date: Ca. 1855
Title: View of Albany, N. Y.
Size: 25⅞ × 38¹⁄₁₆ in. (65.9 × 96.8 cm.)
Artist:
Lithographer: C. Masson
Printer:
Publisher:
Key/Vignettes/Misc:
Locations: AIHA−A
Catalogs/Checklists:

2429
Place: Albany, New York
Date: 1879
Title: Albany, New York. 1879
Size: 28¾ × 44⅛ in. (73.2 × 112.3 cm.)
Artist: H. H. Rowley

Lithographer:
Printer: Beck & Pauli, Milwaukee, Wis.
Publisher: H. H. Rowley & Co., Hartford, Conn.
Key/Vignettes/Misc: Refs. 1−88; 1 vignette
Locations: BPL−R; LC−M; NYSL−A
Catalogs/Checklists: LC−M, 534

2430
Place: Altamont, New York
Date: 1889 State I
Title: Altamont, N. Y.
Size: 15⅝ × 24¹⁵⁄₁₆ in. (39.8 × 63.5 cm.)
Artist: L. R. Burleigh
Lithographer:
Printer:
Publisher: L. R. Burleigh, Troy, N.Y.
Key/Vignettes/Misc: Refs. 1−16; [no vignettes]
Locations: NYH−NY; LAHS−L
Catalogs/Checklists:

2431
Place: Altamont, New York
Date: 1890 State II
Title: Altamont, N. Y.
Size: 15⅝ × 24¹⁵⁄₁₆ in. (39.8 × 63.5 cm.)
Artist: L. R. Burleigh
Lithographer:
Printer:
Publisher: L. R. Burleigh, Troy, N. Y.
Key/Vignettes/Misc: Refs. 1−19; 1 vignette; description
Locations: NYSL−A; NYSM−A
Catalogs/Checklists:

2432
Place: Altamont, New York
Date: 1890 State III
Title: Altamont, N. Y.
Size: 11½ × 23¹³⁄₁₆ in. (29.3 × 60.6 cm.)
Artist: L. R. Burleigh
Lithographer:
Printer:
Publisher: L. R. Burleigh, Troy, N. Y.
Key/Vignettes/Misc: Refs. 1−19; 1 vignette; description
Locations: NYH−NY
Catalogs/Checklists:

2433
Place: Amityville, New York
Date: 1925
Title: Aero−View of Amityville, Suffolk County, Long Island, N. Y. 1925.
Size: 16½ × 31¹⁄₁₆ in. (42 × 79 cm.)
Artist: Rene Cinquin
Lithographer:
Printer:
Publisher: Metropolitan Aero−View Co., N. Y.
Key/Vignettes/Misc: 46 vignettes; unnumbered business directory; 1 map; description
Locations: LC−M
Catalogs/Checklists: LC−M, 535

2434
Place: Amsterdam, New York
Date: 1875
Title: Amsterdam, N. Y. 1875.
Size: 17½ × 24⅝ in. (44.5 × 62.7 cm.)

Artist: H. H. Bailey [& J. C. Hazen]
Lithographer:
Printer: G. W. Lewis 452 Bdwy. Albany, N. Y.
Publisher:
Key/Vignettes/Misc: Refs. A–F, 1–5
Locations: BPL–R; MCDH–F; NYH–NY
Catalogs/Checklists:

2435
Place: Amsterdam, New York
Date: 1881
Title: Amsterdam & Port Jackson, N. Y. 1881
Size: 18⅝ × 26⅝ in. (47.4 × 67.8 cm.)
Artist: H. H. Rowley & Co.
Lithographer:
Printer: C. H. Vogt, Lith, Cleveland, O.
Publisher: H. H. Rowley & Co., Hartford, Conn.
Key/Vignettes/Misc: Refs. 1–39
Locations: NYSH–C; NYSM–A; NYH–NY
Catalogs/Checklists:

2436
Place: Antwerp, New York
Date: 1888
Title: Bird's–Eye View of Antwerp, N. Y.
Size: 15¼ × 23½ in. (38.8 × 59.8 cm.)
Artist: C.[hristian] F.[ausel]
Lithographer:
Printer: The Burleigh Lith. Est., Troy, N. Y.
Publisher:
Key/Vignettes/Misc: Refs. 1–16; 1 vignette
Locations: LC–M; NYH–NY
Catalogs/Checklists: LC–M, 536

2437
Place: Astoria, New York
Date: 1862
Title: View of Astoria, L. I. From the New York Side.
Size: 12 × 15⅝ in. (30.5 × 39.8 cm.)
Artist: F. F. Palmer
Lithographer:
Printer:
Publisher: Currier & Ives, New York
Key/Vignettes/Misc:
Locations: MCNY; YUAG–NH
Catalogs/Checklists:

2438
Place: Babylon, New York
Date: 1901 State I
Title: Babylon, Long Island, N. Y. 1901
Size: 12⁹⁄₁₆ × 21¾ in. (32 × 55.3 cm.)
Artist: O. H. Bailey & Co.
Lithographer:
Printer:
Publisher: O. H. Bailey & Co. Boston
Key/Vignettes/Misc: 1 vignette
Locations: NYH–NY
Catalogs/Checklists:

2439
Place: Babylon, New York
Date: 1901 State II
Title: Babylon, Long Island, N. Y. 1901
Size: 12⁹⁄₁₆ × 21¾ in. (32 × 55.3 cm.)

Artist: O. H. Bailey & Co.
Lithographer:
Printer:
Publisher: O. H. Bailey & Co. Boston
Key/Vignettes/Misc: Refs. A, 2–60; 22 vignettes
Locations: NYH–NY
Catalogs/Checklists:

2440
Place: Bainbridge, New York
Date: 1889
Title: Bainbridge, N. Y.
Size: 11 × 21⅝ in. (27.9 × 55 cm.)
Artist: L. R. Burleigh
Lithographer:
Printer: The Burleigh Lith. Est., Troy, N. Y.
Publisher: L. R. Burleigh, Troy, N. Y.
Key/Vignettes/Misc: Refs. 1–28
Locations: LC–M; LC–P
Catalogs/Checklists: LC–M, 537

2441
Place: Ballston Spa, New York
Date: [1899?]
Title: Ballston Spa, N. Y.
Size: 17⅞ × 28⅛ in. (45.5 × 71.6 cm.)
Artist: C.[hristian] Fausel
Lithographer:
Printer: [Weed–Parsons Printing Company, Albany, New York?]
Publisher: A. M. Vandecarr, South Shodack, Rens. Co., N. Y.
Key/Vignettes/Misc: Refs. 1–38
Locations: NYSL–A; NYH–NY; LC–M; LAHS–L
Catalogs/Checklists: LC–M, 536

2442
Place: Batavia, New York
Date: 1873
Title: Bird's Eye View of Batavia, Genesee County, N. Y. 1873
Size: 20 × 25⅞ in. (50.8 × 65.9 cm.)
Artist: Augustus Koch
Lithographer:
Printer: National Lithographic Institute, N. E. Cor. 5th Ave. & Washington St. Chicago
Publisher:
Key/Vignettes/Misc: Refs. 1–25
Locations: Holland Land Office Museum, Batavia, New York
Catalogs/Checklists:

2443
Place: Batavia, New York
Date: 1882
Title: Batavia, N. Y. 1882
Size: 19 × 30⅛ in. (48.4 × 76.7 cm.)
Artist: L. R. Burleigh
Lithographer: Lyth
Printer:
Publisher:
Key/Vignettes/Misc:
Locations: Holland Land Office Museum, Batavia, New York
Catalogs/Checklists:

2444
Place: Bath, New York
Date: 1878
Title: Bath, N. Y. 1878. From Mossy Bank

Size: 16 × 24¾ in. (40.7 × 63.1 cm.)
Artist: W. W. Denslow
Lithographer:
Printer: Thos Hunter, Lith, Phila.
Publisher: C. J. Corbin
Key/Vignettes/Misc: 10 vignettes
Locations: Bath Village Museum, Bath, New York; RMSC–R
Catalogs/Checklists:

2445
Place: Binghamton, New York
Date: 1873
Title: Birds Eye View of Binghamton. Broome County New York. 1873.
Size: 23½ × 31 in. (59.8 × 78.9 cm.)
Artist: H. Brosius
Lithographer:
Printer:
Publisher: J. J. Stoner, Madison, Wis.
Key/Vignettes/Misc: Refs. 1–36, A; 2 vignettes
Locations: BCHS–B; CSNY–S
Catalogs/Checklists:

2446
Place: Binghamton, New York
Date: 1882
Title: Binghamton, N. Y. 1882
Size: 23⅝ × 34 in. (60.1 × 86.5 cm.)
Artist: Burleigh
Lithographer: J. Lyth
Printer:
Publisher:
Key/Vignettes/Misc:
Locations: BCHS–B
Catalogs/Checklists:

2447
Place: Binghamton, New York
Date: 1901
Title: Binghamton, N. Y. 1901
Size: 39⅞ × 56⅜ in. (101.3 × 145.7 cm.)
Artist:
Lithographer:
Printer:
Publisher: Landis & Alsop, Newark, New Jersey
Key/Vignettes/Misc: 61 vignettes; unnumbered business directory
Locations: LC–M
Catalogs/Checklists: LC–M, 538

2448
Place: Binghamton, New York
Date: N.D.
Title: View of Binghamton. From the Inebriate Asylum.
Size: 17 × 25 in. (43.3 × 63.6 cm.)
Artist: H.[enry] W.[alcott] Boss
Lithographer:
Printer: Ferd. Mayer & Co. Lithographers, 96 Fulton St., N. Y.
Publisher:
Key/Vignettes/Misc:
Locations: BCHS–B
Catalogs/Checklists:

2449
Place: Brewster, New York
Date: 1887
Title: Brewster, N. Y. 1887

Size: 13 × 21 in. (33 × 53.5 cm.)
Artist:
Lithographer:
Printer:
Publisher: The Burleigh Litho. Est., Troy, N. Y.
Key/Vignettes/Misc: Refs. 1–12
Locations: LC–M; LC–P
Catalogs/Checklists: LC–M, 539

2450
Place: Brockport, New York
Date: [1879–81?]
Title: View Showing the Works of D. S. Morgan & Co. Brockport, N. Y.
Size: 21 × 24¹/₁₆ in. (53.4 × 61.3 cm.)
Artist: H. H. Rowley & Co.
Lithographer:
Printer:
Publisher: H. H. Rowley and Co.
Key/Vignettes/Misc: 4 vignettes
Locations: BPL–R
Catalogs/Checklists:

2451
Place: Brooklyn, New York
Date: 1846
Title: View of Brooklyn, L. I. from U. S. Hotel, New York.
Size: 17¼ × 36⅝ in. (43.8 × 93.3 cm.)
Artist: E. W. Whitefield
Lithographer: E. W. Whitefield
Printer: F. Michelin 111 Nassau St. [New York]
Publisher: E. W. Whitefield
Key/Vignettes/Misc:
Locations: MM–NN; NYH–NY; NYP–S; CHS–C; NYP–P; LC–P
Catalogs/Checklists: Eno 454; MM–NN, LP 3581; Norton, Whitefield, no. 33; Pyne, no. 180

Place: Brooklyn, New York
Date: 1849
See New York, New York, 1849.

2452
Place: Brooklyn, New York
Date: 1853
Title: (The Wall Street Ferry and South St.). Brooklyn, L. I. 1853.
Size: 23½ × 39 in. (59.8 × 99.2 cm.)
Artist: J. W. Hill
Lithographer:
Printer: Endicott & Co., New York
Publisher: Smith Brothers & Co. 225 Fulton St. N. Y.
Key/Vignettes/Misc:
Locations: Unknown. See Old Print Shop Portfolio, XIV, p. 54, No. 6
Catalogs/Checklists: Pyne, no. 181

2453
Place: Brooklyn, New York
Date: 1853
Title: Brooklyn, L. I., as seen from Trinity Church, New York
Size: 23¾ × 38⅞ in. (60.4 × 98.8 cm.)
Artist: J. W. Hill
Lithographer: Smith
Printer: Endicott & Co.
Publisher: Smith Brothers & Co., 225 Fulton St. N. Y.

Key/Vignettes/Misc:
Locations: NYP–P; LIHS–B; MM–NN
Catalogs/Checklists: Eno 457; MM–NN, LP 495

2454
Place: Brooklyn, New York
Date: 1855
Title: City of Brooklyn, L. I. Taken from Rush Street.
Size: 17⅝ × 23 in. (44.8 × 58.5 cm.)
Artist: John Bornet
Lithographer: John Bornet
Printer: A. Weingartner
Publisher: John Bornet (copyright)
Key/Vignettes/Misc:
Locations: NYP–P; LIHS–B; YUAG–NH; NYH–NY
Catalogs/Checklists: Eno 460

Place: Brooklyn, New York
Date: 1856
See New York, New York, 1856.

Place: Brooklyn, New York
Date: 1858
See New York, New York, 1858.

Place: Brooklyn, New York
Date: 1859
See New York, New York, 1859.

Place: Brooklyn, New York
Date: 1868
See New York, New York, 1868.

Place: Brooklyn, New York
Date: Ca. 1868
See New York, New York, ca. 1868.

Place: Brooklyn, New York
Date: 1877
See New York, New York, 1877.

2455
Place: Brooklyn, New York
Date: 1879
Title: The City of Brooklyn
Size: 20⅞ × 33⅞ in. (53 × 86 cm.)
Artist: C. R. Parsons
Lithographer: C. R. Parsons
Printer:
Publisher: Currier & Ives, New York
Key/Vignettes/Misc: Unnumbered refs. below places identified
Locations: LC–M; LC–P
Catalogs/Checklists: LC–M, 541; Peters, C & I, 4094; Conningham 1092

2456
Place: Brooklyn, New York
Date: 1897
Title: Bird's–Eye–View of the Borough of Brooklyn Showing Parks, Cemeteries, Principal Buildings, Suburbs.
Size: 20⁷/₁₆ × 34⁹/₁₆ in. (52 × 88 cm.)
Artist: Geo. Welch
Lithographer:
Printer:
Publisher:
Key/Vignettes/Misc:
Locations: LC–M
Catalogs/Checklists: LC–M, 541.1

2457
Place: Brooklyn, New York
Date: Ca. 1908
Title: [Bird's–Eye–View of Brooklyn] Compliments of Woldmere Realty Co.
Size: 20¹/₁₆ × 19¼ in. (51 × 49 cm.)
Artist:
Lithographer:
Printer:
Publisher: August R. Ohman & Co., New York
Key/Vignettes/Misc:
Locations: LC–M
Catalogs/Checklists: LC–M, 541.2

2458
Place: Buffalo, New York
Date: [1847]
Title: View of Buffalo, N. Y., from the old Lighthouse.
Size: 14¼ × 37 in. (36.3 × 94.1 cm.)
Artist: E. Whitefield
Lithographer: E. Whitefield
Printer: F. Michelin, New York
Publisher: E. Whitefield
Key/Vignettes/Misc: Refs. 1–15
Locations: MM–NN; NYH–NY; ROM; BECH–B
Catalogs/Checklists: MM–NN, LP 1001; Norton, Whitefield, no. 38

2459
Place: Buffalo, New York
Date: 1853
Title: Buffalo.
Size: 25⁵/₁₆ × 39¹/₁₆ in. (64.3 × 99.3 cm.)
Artist: J. W. Hill
Lithographer: J. H. Colen
Printer: E. Michelin & Shattuck, New York
Publisher: Smith Bros. & Co. 225 Fulton St., New York
Key/Vignettes/Misc:
Locations: NYP–S; MM–NN; CHS–C; PAC–P; NYH–NY; BECH–B
Catalogs/Checklists: Stokes Addenda P. 1852—Views–16; MM–NN, LP 1227

2460
Place: Buffalo, New York
Date: 1863
Title: Bird's Eye View of the City of Buffalo, N. Y.
Size: 40⅜ × 81½ in. (102.8 × 207.3 cm.)
Artist:
Lithographer:
Printer:
Publisher: Charles Magnus, 12 Frankfort St. New York
Key/Vignettes/Misc:
Locations: BECH–B; NYH–NY
Catalogs/Checklists:

2461
Place: Buffalo, New York
Date: 1872
Title: View of Buffalo, N. Y. Ansicht von Buffalo, N. Y.
Size: 18 × 23⅛ in. (45.7 × 58.9 cm.)
Artist: R. Buerger
Lithographer: R. Buerger
Printer:

Publisher: Ernst Besser & Brother, Buffalo, N. Y.
Key/Vignettes/Misc: 6 vignettes
Locations: LC–P; NYH–NY
Catalogs/Checklists:

2462
Place: Buffalo, New York
Date: 1880
Title: The City of Buffalo, N. Y. 1880.
Size: 24⅞ × 37¹¹⁄₁₆ in. (63.4 × 95.9 cm.)
Artist:
Lithographer:
Printer: Maerz Lithographing Co., Buffalo
Publisher: E. H. Hutchinson, Buffalo
Key/Vignettes/Misc: Refs. 1–60
Locations: LC–M; BECH–B; LC–P
Catalogs/Checklists: LC–M, 542

2463
Place: Buffalo, New York
Date: 1880
Title: Views of Buffalo, 1880
Size: 13 × 16½ in. (32.8 × 41.8 cm.)
Artist: R. Buerger and W. J. Baker
Lithographer:
Printer: Gies & Co., Lithographers, Buffalo, N. Y.
Publisher:
Key/Vignettes/Misc:
Locations: BECH–B
Catalogs/Checklists:

2464
Place: Buffalo, New York
Date: 1895
Title: Buffalo and Its Waterfront, The Illustrated Buffalo Express
Size: 5½ × 44 in. (13.9 × 111.2 cm.)
Artist: Chapin
Lithographer:
Printer: Matthews, Northrup Co., Buffalo, N. Y.
Publisher:
Key/Vignettes/Misc:
Locations: BECH–B
Catalogs/Checklists:

2465
Place: Buffalo, New York
Date: 1902
Title: Buffalo, Erie Co., N. Y.
Size: 41 × 58½ in. (104.3 × 148.5 cm.)
Artist:
Lithographer:
Printer:
Publisher: Landis & Alsop, 294 Roseville Ave, Newark, New Jersey
Key/Vignettes/Misc: 60 vignettes; business directory keyed to border numbers and letters
Locations: LC–M
Catalogs/Checklists: LC–M, 543

2466
Place: Caldwell, New York
Date: [1828–29]
Title: Lake George and the Village of Caldwell
Size: 10 × 12¾ in. (25.4 × 32.5 cm.)
Artist: [Jacques] Milbert

Lithographer:
Printer: L. Sabatier
Publisher:
Key/Vignettes/Misc:
Locations: CHS–C; YUAG–NH
Catalogs/Checklists:

2467
Place: Caledonia, New York
Date: 1892
Title: Caledonia, N. Y.
Size: 15⅛ × 24⅞ in. (38.5 × 63.3 cm.)
Artist:
Lithographer:
Printer:
Publisher: Burleigh Litho. Co., Troy, N. Y.
Key/Vignettes/Misc: Refs. 1–48
Locations: LC–M; NYH–NY; NYSM–A
Catalogs/Checklists: LC–M, 544

2468
Place: Cambridge, New York
Date: 1886
Title: Cambridge, N. Y. 1886
Size: 17 × 27½ in. (43.3 × 70 cm.)
Artist:
Lithographer:
Printer: Burleigh Lith. Est., Troy, N. Y.
Publisher: L. R. Burleigh, Troy, N. Y.
Key/Vignettes/Misc: Refs. 1–15; 1 vignette
Locations: LC–M; LAHS–L
Catalogs/Checklists: LC–M, 545

2469
Place: Camden, New York
Date: 1885
Title: Camden, N. Y.
Size: 12¼ × 24¾ in. (31 × 63 cm.)
Artist: L.R. Burleigh
Lithographer: L. R. Burleigh
Printer: Beck & Pauli, Litho, Milwaukee, Wis.
Publisher: L. R. Burleigh, Troy, N. Y.
Key/Vignettes/Misc: Refs. 1–36
Locations: LC–M
Catalogs/Checklists: LC–M, 545.1

2470
Place: Canajoharie, New York
Date: 1881
Title: Canajoharie & Palatine Bridge, N. Y. 1881.
Size: 18¾ × 24⅜ in. (47.7 × 62.1 cm.)
Artist: [L. R. Burleigh]
Lithographer:
Printer: C. H. Vogt, Cleveland
Publisher:
Key/Vignettes/Misc:
Locations: CSNY–S
Catalogs/Checklists:

2471
Place: Canandaigua, New York
Date: 1873
Title: Bird's Eye View of Canandaigua. Ontario County, N. Y. 1873.
Size: 17¾ × 20½ in. (45.2 × 52.2 cm.)
Artist: Aug. Koch.
Lithographer:
Printer:

Publisher: J. J. Stoner
Key/Vignettes/Misc: Refs. 1–26; 1 vignette
Locations: Ontario County Historical Society, Canandaigua, New York (photo)
Catalogs/Checklists:

2472
Place: Canastota, New York
Date: 1885
Title: Canastota, N. Y. 1885.
Size: 14½ × 24 in. (36.9 × 61 cm.)
Artist: L. R. Burleigh
Lithographer:
Printer: C. H. Vogt & Son, Lith. [Cleveland]
Publisher: L. R. Burleigh, Troy, N. Y.
Key/Vignettes/Misc: Refs. 1–20
Locations: LC–M
Catalogs/Checklists: LC–M, 546

2473
Place: Canton, New York
Date: 1885
Title: Canton, N. Y.
Size: 15 × 24½ in. (38.2 × 62.4 cm.)
Artist: L. R. Burleigh
Lithographer:
Printer: C. H. Vogt & Son [Cleveland]
Publisher: L. R. Burleigh, Troy, N. Y.
Key/Vignettes/Misc: Refs. 1–19
Locations: LC–M; Archives of St. Lawrence County, New York Historian, Canton, New York
Catalogs/Checklists: LC–M, 547

2474
Place: Carthage, New York
Date: 1888
Title: Carthage, N. Y. 1888
Size: 18 × 28 in. (45.8 × 71.3 cm.)
Artist: L. R. Burleigh
Lithographer:
Printer: Burleigh Lith. Est., Troy, N. Y.
Publisher: L. R. Burleigh, Troy, N. Y.
Key/Vignettes/Misc: Refs. 1–40
Locations: LC–M; NYH–NY LAHS–L
Catalogs/Checklists: LC–M, 548

2475
Place: Catskill, New York
Date: 1854
Title: Catskill, Green Co. N. Y. South west view,—1854.
Size: 18⅝ × 32⅛ in. (47.4 × 81.7 cm.)
Artist: C. Kelsey
Lithographer: C. Kelsey
Printer: R. H. Pease, Albany, N. Y.
Publisher:
Key/Vignettes/Misc:
Locations: MM–NN; AIHA–A
Catalogs/Checklists: MM–NN, LP 2186

2476
Place: Catskill, New York
Date: 1882
Title: Catskill on the Hudson and Its Magnificent Mountains
Size:
Artist: W. Van Loan
Lithographer:

Printer: Charles Hart
Publisher:
Key/Vignettes/Misc:
Locations: NYSH–C
Catalogs/Checklists: Hemenway

2477
Place: Catskill, New York
Date: 1889
Title: Catskill, N. Y.
Size: 18¼ × 27⅞ in. (46.4 × 73.5 cm.)
Artist: L. R. Burleigh
Lithographer:
Printer: The Burleigh Lith. Est., Troy, N. Y.
Publisher: L. R. Burleigh, Troy, New York
Key/Vignettes/Misc: Refs. 1–44
Locations: NYSL–A; MM–NN; LC–M; LC–P
Catalogs/Checklists: MM–NN, LP 2204; LC–M, 549

2478
Place: Cazenovia, New York
Date: 1890
Title: Cazenovia, N. Y.
Size: 16½ × 30 in. (41.9 × 76.3 cm.)
Artist:
Lithographer:
Printer: Burleigh Lithographing Establishment, Troy, N. Y.
Publisher: L. R. Burleigh, Troy, N. Y.
Key/Vignettes/Misc: 28 refs.
Locations: LAHS–L
Catalogs/Checklists:

2479
Place: Cazenovia, New York
Date: 1890
Title: Cazenovia, N. Y.
Size: 14½ × 31 in. (37 × 79 cm.)
Artist:
Lithographer:
Printer: Burleigh Lithographing Establishment, Troy, N. Y.
Publisher: L. R. Burleigh, Troy, N. Y.
Key/Vignettes/Misc:
Locations: LC–M
Catalogs/Checklists: LC–M, 550

2480
Place: Chatham, New York
Date: 1886
Title: Chatham, N. Y. 1886
Size: 14 × 29½ in. (35.7 × 75.1 cm.)
Artist:
Lithographer:
Printer: The Burleigh Lith. Est. Troy, N. Y.
Publisher: L. R. Burleigh, Troy, N. Y.
Key/Vignettes/Misc: Refs. 1–17
Locations: LC–M; NYSM–A
Catalogs/Checklists: LC–M, 551

2481
Place: Chautauqua, New York
Date: 1885
Title: Lake Chautauqua Chautauqua, Jamestown, Dewittville, and Mayville
Size: 20 × 37¹/₁₆ in. (50.9 × 94.3 cm.)
Artist:
Lithographer:
Printer:

Publisher: Matthews, Northrop & Co. Buffalo, N. Y. (copyright)
Key/Vignettes/Misc:
Locations: LC–P
Catalogs/Checklists:

2482
Place: Cleveland, New York
Date: 1890
Title: Cleveland, N. Y.
Size: 15¼ × 24¾ in. (38.8 × 63 cm.)
Artist:
Lithographer:
Printer: Burleigh Lithographing Establishment, Troy, N. Y.
Publisher: L. R. Burleigh, Troy, N. Y.
Key/Vignettes/Misc: Refs. 1–27
Locations: NYSL–A
Catalogs/Checklists:

2483
Place: Clifton Springs, New York
Date: 1892
Title: Clifton Springs, N. Y.
Size: 14½ × 27⅞ in. (37 × 71 cm.)
Artist:
Lithographer:
Printer: Burleigh Litho. Co., Troy, N. Y.
Publisher: Burleigh Litho. Co., Troy, N. Y.
Key/Vignettes/Misc: Refs. 1–35
Locations: LC–M
Catalogs/Checklists: LC–M, 551.1

2484
Place: Clinton, New York
Date: 1885
Title: Clinton, N. Y.
Size: 15 × 26 in. (38.2 × 66.2 cm.)
Artist: L. R. Burleigh
Lithographer:
Printer: Beck & Pauli, Lith., Milwaukee
Publisher: L. R. Burleigh
Key/Vignettes/Misc: Refs. 1–28; 1 vignette
Locations: LC–M; LC–P
Catalogs/Checklists: LC–M, 552

2485
Place: Clyde, New York
Date: 1892
Title: Clyde, N. Y.
Size: 17 × 26½ in. (43.3 × 67.5 cm.)
Artist:
Lithographer:
Printer: Burleigh Litho. Co., Troy, N. Y.
Publisher:
Key/Vignettes/Misc: Refs. 1–56; 1 vignette
Locations: NYSL–A
Catalogs/Checklists:

2486
Place: Cobleskill, New York
Date: 1883
Title: Cobleskill, N. Y. 1883
Size: 18⅞ × 25⅜ in. (47.8 × 64.5 cm.)
Artist: J. McGregor & Co. and J. J. Dunphy
Lithographer:
Printer: J. McGregor & Co, 481 B,way, Albany, N. Y. J. J. Dunphy, Litho. Printer
Publisher: J. McGregor & Co., 481 B,way,

Albany, N. Y. J. J. Dunphy, Litho. Printer
Key/Vignettes/Misc:
Locations: NYSM–A
Catalogs/Checklists:

2487
Place: Cohoes, New York
Date: [1860–67]
Title: View of Cohoes, N. Y. from Prospect Hill. Waterford, Lansingburgh, Mt. Rafenesque and Troy, in the Distance
Size: 19⅜ × 35⅜ in. (49.3 × 90 cm.)
Artist:
Lithographer:
Printer: Lewis 452 Broadway Albany, N. Y.
Publisher: Lewis 452 Broadway Albany, N. Y.
Key/Vignettes/Misc: 22 unnumbered refs. below places identified
Locations: MM–NN; NYSH–C
Catalogs/Checklists: MM–NN, LP 999; Hemenway

2488
Place: Cohoes, New York
Date: 1879
Title: Cohoes, N. Y. 1879
Size: 25⁹/₁₆ × 34½ in. (65.1 × 87.8 cm.)
Artist: Galt & Hoy
Lithographer:
Printer:
Publisher: Galt and Hoy, 111 Liberty St. N. Y.
Key/Vignettes/Misc: Refs. 1–48; 6 vignettes
Locations: BPL–R
Catalogs/Checklists:

2489
Place: College Point, New York
Date: 1876
Title: View of College Point, L. I. 1876.
Size: 18⅛ × 25⅛ in. (46.1 × 64 cm.)
Artist: T. M. Fowler
Lithographer: C. H. Vogt
Printer:
Publisher: Fowler & Bulger
Key/Vignettes/Misc: Refs. 1–17
Locations: BPL–R
Catalogs/Checklists:

2490
Place: Cooperstown, New York
Date: 1862
Title: Cooperstown, N. Y.
Size: 19⅛ × 27¹/₁₆ in. (48.7 × 68.8 cm.)
Artist: M. DeV. Martin
Lithographer: M. DeV. Martin
Printer: Lewis and Goodwin, Albany, N. Y.
Publisher: M. DeV. Martin (copyright)
Key/Vignettes/Misc: 17 unnumbered refs. below places identified
Locations: NYSH–C; NYH–NY
Catalogs/Checklists: Hemenway

2491
Place: Cooperstown, New York
Date: 1890
Title: Cooperstown, N. Y.
Size: 17 × 28½ in. (43.3 × 72.5 cm.)

Artist:
Lithographer:
Printer: Burleigh Lith. Est., Troy, N. Y.
Publisher: L. R. Burleigh, Troy, N. Y.
Key/Vignettes/Misc: Refs. 1–40
Locations: LC–M; NYSH–C; NYH–NY
Catalogs/Checklists: LC–M, 553;
Hemenway

2492
Place: Corinth, New York
Date: 1888
Title: Corinth, N. Y. 1888 and Palmer
Falls
Size: 17 × 27 in. (43.3 × 68.7 cm.)
Artist: L. R. Burleigh
Lithographer:
Printer: The Burleigh Lith. Est., Troy, N. Y.
Publisher: L. R. Burleigh, Troy, N. Y.
Key/Vignettes/Misc: Refs. 1–13
Locations: LC–M; NYH–NY; LAHS–L
Catalogs/Checklists: LC–M, 554

2493
Place: Cortland, New York
Date: 1873
Title: Cortland, N. Y.
Size: 16¾ × 20¾ in. (42.6 × 52.8 cm.)
Artist: Fowler & Bailey
Lithographer:
Printer: Am. Oleograph Co. [Milwaukee]
Publisher: Fowler & Bailey
Key/Vignettes/Misc: Refs. 1–14
Locations: BPL–R; CCHS–CO
Catalogs/Checklists:

2494
Place: Cortland, New York
Date: 1882
Title: Cortland, N. Y. 1882 Looking South
From Benham's Hill
Size: 19¼ × 28 in. (49 × 71.2 cm.)
Artist:
Lithographer:
Printer:
Publisher: Philadelphia Publishing House,
925 Chestnut St., Philadelphia
Key/Vignettes/Misc: 14 vignettes
Locations: CCHS–CO
Catalogs/Checklists:

2495
Place: Cortland, New York
Date: 1892
Title: Cortland, N. Y. 1892
Size: 20¾ × 33⅝ in. (52.8 × 85.5 cm.)
Artist: Geo. E. Norris
Lithographer:
Printer:
Publisher: Burleigh Litho. Co., Troy, N. Y.
Key/Vignettes/Misc: Refs. 1–60, A–R
Locations: CCHS–CO; DWHS–I
Catalogs/Checklists:

2496
Place: Croton–On–Hudson, New York
Date: [1846]
Title: View Near Croton, N. Y., Hudson
River
Size: 6½ × 9½ in. (16.5 × 24.1 cm.)
Artist: E. Whitefield
Lithographer: E. Whitefield

Printer:
Publisher:
Key/Vignettes/Misc:
Locations: NYH–NY
Catalogs/Checklists: Hufeland, Checklist,
272; Norton, Whitefield, no. 18

2497
Place: Cuba, New York
Date: 1882
Title: Bird's Eye View of the Village of
Cuba, Alegany County, N. Y. 1882.
Size: 13 × 24⅜ in. (33 × 62 cm.)
Artist: H. Brosius
Lithographer:
Printer: Beck & Pauli, Milwaukee, Wis.
Publisher: J. J. Stoner, Madison, Wis.
Key/Vignettes/Misc: Refs. A–H, J–X
Locations: LC–M (facsimile); Cuba
Historical Society, Cuba, New York
Catalogs/Checklists: LC–M, 554.1

2498
Place: Delhi, New York
Date: 1887
Title: Delhi, N. Y. 1887
Size: 13 × 20¹⁄₁₆ in. (33 × 51 cm.)
Artist: L. R. Burleigh
Lithographer:
Printer: The Burleigh Litho. Establishment,
Troy, N. Y.
Publisher: L. R. Burleigh, Troy, N. Y.
Key/Vignettes/Misc: Refs. 1–29
Locations: LC–M; NYH–NY; Delaware
County Historical Society, Delhi, New
York; LC–P
Catalogs/Checklists: LC–M, 555

2499
Place: Depew, New York
Date: 1898
Title: Depew, N. Y.
Size: 31 × 46 in. (78.2 × 116.3 cm.)
Artist:
Lithographer:
Printer:
Publisher: Matthews, Northrup Co.,
Buffalo
Key/Vignettes/Misc:
Locations: BECH–B; LC–M
Catalogs/Checklists: LC–M, 555.1

2500
Place: Deposit, New York
Date: 1887
Title: Deposit, N. Y. 1887
Size: 15 × 24½ in. (38.2 × 62.4 cm.)
Artist: L. R. Burleigh
Lithographer:
Printer: The Burleigh Lith. Est., Troy, N. Y.
Publisher: L. R. Burleigh, Troy, N. Y.
Key/Vignettes/Misc: Refs. 1–34
Locations: LC–M; LC–P
Catalogs/Checklists: LC–M, 556

Place: Despatch, New York
Date: N.D.
See East Rochester, New York, n. d.

Place: Dewittville, New York
Date: 1885
See Chautauqua, New York, 1885.

2501
Place: Dolgeville, New York
Date: 1890
Title: Dolgeville, N. Y.
Size: 14⅜ × 25⅜ in. (36.6 × 64.6 cm.)
Artist:
Lithographer:
Printer: Burleigh Litho. Est., Troy, N. Y.
Publisher: Alfred Dolge, Dolgeville
Key/Vignettes/Misc: Refs. 1–2; 1 vignette
Locations: LC–M; NYH–NY; LAHS–L
Catalogs/Checklists: LC–M, 556.1

2502
Place: Earlville, New York
Date: 1892
Title: Earlville, N. Y.
Size: 15 × 26 in. (38.2x 66.2 cm.)
Artist:
Lithographer:
Printer: Burleigh Litho. Co., Troy, N. Y.
Publisher:
Key/Vignettes/Misc: 30 refs.
Locations: LAHS–L NYSL–A
Catalogs/Checklists:

2503
Place: East New York, New York
Date: 1859
Title: View of Brooklyn City Water Works
and Cypress Hills from Ridgewood
Reservoir. 1859
Size: 14⁹⁄₁₆ × 22¾ in. (37 × 58 cm.)
Artist:
Lithographer: F. Blummer
Printer:
Publisher: G. Kraetzer, Sheffield Ave. East
New York
Key/Vignettes/Misc:
Locations: LIHS–B
Catalogs/Checklists:

2504
Place: East New York, New York
Date: 1867
Title: East New York. 1867
Size: 16¹⁄₁₆ × 24⁵⁄₁₆ in. (40.8 × 61.8 cm.)
Artist:
Lithographer:
Printer:
Publisher: G. Kraetzer, Sheffield Av. [East
New York]
Key/Vignettes/Misc:
Locations: NYP–S; MCNY; NYSM–A;
LISH–B; NYH–NY
Catalogs/Checklists: Stokes 1867—G–73

2505
Place: East New York, New York
Date: Ca. 1867
Title: East New York
Size: 16½ × 24¼ in. (42 × 61.7 cm.)
Artist:
Lithographer: Kraetzer & Flumner
Printer: J. Rau 333 Broadway
Publisher: G. Kraetzer
Key/Vignettes/Misc:
Locations: BM–NY; YUAG–NH
Catalogs/Checklists: Eno 461 [Dates ca.
1860]

2506

Place: East New York, New York
Date: 1873
Title: East New York, N. Y. Eastern Section. East New York Western Section.
Size: 18¼ × 22¾ in. (46.4 × 57.9 cm.)
Artist:
Lithographer:
Printer: Chas. Hart Lith. 36 Vesey St. N. Y.
Publisher: W. Shapter (copyright)
Key/Vignettes/Misc:
Locations: MCNY; NYH−NY
Catalogs/Checklists:

2507

Place: East Rochester, New York
Date: N.D.
Title: Despatch, N. . Y. Rochester's Great Industrial Suburb
Size: 20 × 27 in. (50.9 × 68.7 cm.)
Artist:
Lithographer:
Printer: O. H. Bailey & Co., Lith. Boston
Publisher:
Key/Vignettes/Misc: 9 vignettes
Locations: RMSC−R
Catalogs/Checklists:

2508

Place: East Syracuse, New York
Date: 1885
Title: East Syracuse N. Y.
Size: 12½ × 25 in. (31.9 × 63.6 cm.)
Artist: L. R. Burleigh
Lithographer:
Printer: C. H. Vogt & Son, Cleveland, Ohio
Publisher: L. R. Burleigh, Troy, N. Y.
Key/Vignettes/Misc: Refs. 1−17
Locations: LC−M; CSNY−S
Catalogs/Checklists: LC−M, 557

2509

Place: Ellenville, New York
Date: 1887
Title: Ellenville, N. Y. 1887
Size: 15⅛ × 25¼ in. (38.5 × 64.3 cm.)
Artist: L. R. Burleigh
Lithographer:
Printer: The Burleigh Lith. Est., Troy, N. Y.
Publisher: L. R. Burleigh, Troy, N. Y.
Key/Vignettes/Misc: Refs. 1−21
Locations: LC−M; NYH−NY; CSNY−S
Catalogs/Checklists: LC−M, 558

2510

Place: Elmira, New York
Date: Ca. 1840
Title: View of Elmira Ch. Co., N. Y., Looking West.
Size: 17⅞ × 24½ in. (45.5 × 62.3 cm.)
Artist: H. Walton
Lithographer: H. Walton
Printer:
Publisher:
Key/Vignettes/Misc:
Locations: NYSM−A; Arnot Art Gallery, Elmira, New York
Catalogs/Checklists: Rehner, Walton, no. 59

2511

Place: Elmira, New York
Date: 1862
Title: Elmira, N. Y. 1862. From the East Hill
Size: 17½ × 26 in. (44.5 × 66.2 cm.)
Artist:
Lithographer: B. F. Smith, Jr. & Co.
Printer: Lewis & Goodwin
Publisher: B. F. Smith, Jr. & Co. Albany, N. Y.
Key/Vignettes/Misc:
Locations: NYSL−A
Catalogs/Checklists:

2512

Place: Elmira, New York
Date: 1873
Title: Elmira N. Y. 1873
Size: 19⅞ × 28¾ in. (50.6 × 73.2 cm.)
Artist: H. H. Bailey
Lithographer:
Printer: Strobridge & Co Lith. Cin. O.
Publisher:
Key/Vignettes/Misc:
Locations: CCHS−E
Catalogs/Checklists:

2513

Place: Elmira, New York
Date: 1882
Title: Elmira N Y 1882
Size: 16¾ × 27⅝ in. (42.6 × 70.3 cm.)
Artist: Burleigh
Lithographer: J. H. Kirby
Printer:
Publisher:
Key/Vignettes/Misc:
Locations: CCHS−E
Catalogs/Checklists:

2514

Place: Elmira, New York
Date: 1884
Title: City of Elmira 1884.
Size: 16³⁄₁₆ × 23³⁄₁₆ in. (41.2 × 59 cm.)
Artist: John Moray
Lithographer:
Printer: Mensing & Stechep, Roch. N. Y.
Publisher:
Key/Vignettes/Misc:
Locations: NYH−NY
Catalogs/Checklists:

2515

Place: Elmira, New York
Date: 1901
Title: Elmira, N. Y. 1901
Size: 4 sheets, each 18 × 26 in. (45.9 × 66.2 cm.)
Artist:
Lithographer:
Printer:
Publisher: Landis & Alsop, Newark, New Jersey
Key/Vignettes/Misc: 51 vignettes; unnumbered business directory
Locations: LC−M
Catalogs/Checklists: LC−M, 559

2516

Place: Essex, New York
Date: [1846]

Title: Village of Essex N. Y.
Size: 6½ × 9¼ in. (16.5 × 23.6 cm.)
Artist: E. Whitefield
Lithographer:
Printer:
Publisher:
Key/Vignettes/Misc:
Locations: NYSM−A; NYH−NY
Catalogs/Checklists: Norton, Whitefield, no. 19

2517

Place: Fairport, New York
Date: 1884 State I
Title: Fairport, N. Y.
Size: 15 × 24 in. (38.2 × 61.1 cm.)
Artist: L. R. Burleigh
Lithographer:
Printer: Beck & Pauli, Milwaukee
Publisher: L. R. Burleigh, Troy, N. Y.
Key/Vignettes/Misc: Refs. 1−21
Locations: LC−M
Catalogs/Checklists: LC−M, 560

2518

Place: Fairport, New York
Date: 1885 State II
Title: Fairport, N. Y.
Size: 15½ × 24 in. (39.4 × 61.1 cm.)
Artist: L. R. Burleigh
Lithographer:
Printer: Beck & Pauli, Litho., Milwaukee, Wis.
Publisher: L. R. Burleigh, Troy, N. Y.
Key/Vignettes/Misc: Refs. 1−21
Locations: LC−M
Catalogs/Checklists: LC−M, 560.1

2519

Place: Far Rockaway, New York
Date: 1902
Title: Far Rockaway, Long Island, N. Y. 1902
Size: 20 × 29½ in. (50.8 × 75 cm.)
Artist:
Lithographer:
Printer:
Publisher: O. H. Bailey & Co. Boston
Key/Vignettes/Misc: Refs. A−B, 2−60; 42 vignettes
Locations: NYH−NY
Catalogs/Checklists:

2520

Place: Farmingdale, New York
Date: 1925
Title: Aero−View of Farmingdale, Nassau County, Long Island, N. Y. 1925.
Size: 22 × 34 in. (55.9 × 86.5 cm.)
Artist: Rene Cinquin
Lithographer:
Printer:
Publisher: Metropolitan Aero−View Co., N. Y.
Key/Vignettes/Misc: Refs. A−M, 1−32
Locations: LC−M
Catalogs/Checklists: LC−M, 561

2521

Place: Fishkill, New York
Date: 1886
Title: Fishkill−on−the−Hudson, U. S. A. 1886

Size: 15½ × 24 in. (39.5 × 61.1 cm.)
Artist: L. R. Burleigh
Lithographer:
Printer: Burleigh Lithographic Establishment, Troy, N. Y.
Publisher: L. R. Burleigh, Troy, N. Y.
Key/Vignettes/Misc: Refs. 1–12
Locations: LC–M; NYH–NY
Catalogs/Checklists: LC–M, 562

2522
Place: Fonda, New York
Date: 1889
Title: Fonda, N. Y.
Size: 13½ × 24 in. (34.3 × 61.1 cm.)
Artist: L. R. Burleigh
Lithographer:
Printer: The Burleigh Lith. Est. Troy, N. Y.
Publisher: L. R. Burleigh, Troy, N. Y.
Key/Vignettes/Misc: Refs. 1–27
Locations: NYH–NY; NYSM–A; MCDH–F
Catalogs/Checklists:

2523
Place: Fort Edward, New York
Date: 1875
Title: Bird's Eye View of Fort Edward, New York. 1875
Size: 19¾ × 25⁹⁄₁₆ in. (50.3 × 65.1 cm.)
Artist: H. H. Bailey & Co.
Lithographer: C. H. Vogt
Printer: J. Knauber & Co.
Publisher: H. H. Bailey & Co.
Key/Vignettes/Misc: Refs. 1–6
Locations: BPL–R; NYH–NY
Catalogs/Checklists:

2524
Place: Fort Edward, New York
Date: 1892
Title: Fort Edward, N. Y.
Size: 16½ × 30¾ in. (42 × 78.2 cm.)
Artist:
Lithographer:
Printer: Burleigh Litho. Co. Troy, N. Y.
Publisher:
Key/Vignettes/Misc: Refs. 1–34
Locations: NYSL–A; RCHS–T
Catalogs/Checklists:

2525
Place: Fort Plain, New York
Date: 1879
Title: Fort Plain, N. Y.
Size: 21⅞ × 23 in. (55.7 × 58.6 cm.)
Artist: H. H. Rowley & Co.
Lithographer:
Printer: Beck & Pauli, Lith. Milwaukee, Wis.
Publisher: H. H. Rowley & Co. Hartford, Conn.
Key/Vignettes/Misc: Refs. 1–24; 2 vignettes
Locations: AIHA–A
Catalogs/Checklists:

2526
Place: Fort Plain, New York
Date: 1879
Title: Fort Plain, N. Y. 1879 From Prospect Hill

Size: 18⅛ × 34 in. (46.1 × 86.5 cm.)
Artist: W. B. Lindsay
Lithographer:
Printer:
Publisher: Clay and Richmond, Buffalo, N. Y.
Key/Vignettes/Misc: 2 vignettes
Locations: NYSH–C; AIHA–A; NYH–NY
Catalogs/Checklists: Hemenway

2527
Place: Fort Plain, New York
Date: 1891
Title: Fort Plain, N. Y. and Nelliston
Size: 20 × 27 in. (50.9 × 68.7 cm.)
Artist:
Lithographer:
Printer: Burleigh Lithographing Est., Troy, N. Y.
Publisher: L. R. Burleigh, Troy, N. Y.
Key/Vignettes/Misc: Refs. 1–77
Locations: LC–M; AIHA–A; CSNY–S; Fort Plain Museum, Fort Plain, New York; LC–P NYH–NY
Catalogs/Checklists: LC–M, 563

2528
Place: Fort Plain, New York
Date: N.D.
Title: [Title possibly obscured by mat]
Size: 17¹⁄₁₆ × 32⅜ in. (43.4 × 82.4 cm.) (matted)
Artist: Stanley Fox
Lithographer:
Printer: Harry E. Pease, Albany, N. Y.
Publisher:
Key/Vignettes/Misc:
Locations: AIHA–A
Catalogs/Checklists:

2529
Place: Frankfort, New York
Date: 1887
Title: Frankfort, N. Y. 1887
Size: 17 × 24 in. (43.3 × 61.1 cm.)
Artist: L. R. Burleigh
Lithographer:
Printer: Burleigh Lith. Est., Troy, N. Y.
Publisher: L. R. Burleigh, Troy, N. Y.
Key/Vignettes/Misc: Refs. 1–9
Locations: LC–M; NYH–NY
Catalogs/Checklists: LC–M, 564

2530
Place: Freeport, New York
Date: 1909
Title: Aero View of Freeport, Long Island, N. Y. 1909
Size: 21 × 34½ in. (53.5 × 87.8 cm.)
Artist:
Lithographer:
Printer:
Publisher: Hughes & Bailey, New York
Key/Vignettes/Misc: 21 vignettes; unnumbered business directory
Locations: LC–M
Catalogs/Checklists: LC–M, 565

2531
Place: Freeport, New York
Date: 1925
Title: Freeport L. I. 1925 N. Y.

Size: 23½ × 34 in. (28.8 × 56 cm.)
Artist: R. Cinquin
Lithographer:
Printer:
Publisher: Metropolitan Aero–View Co., N. Y.
Key/Vignettes/Misc: 33 vignettes; unnumbered business directory; list of public officials; description
Locations: LC–M
Catalogs/Checklists: LC–M, 566

2532
Place: Fulton, New York
Date: Ca. 1860
Title: View of Fulton, N. Y.
Size: 18½ × 24¾ in. (47.1 × 63 cm.)
Artist:
Lithographer:
Printer: M. de V. Martin
Publisher: M. de V. Martin
Key/Vignettes/Misc:
Locations: Fulton, New York, Public Library; CSNY–S; NYH–NY
Catalogs/Checklists:

2533
Place: Fulton, New York
Date: 1880
Title: Birds Eye View of Fulton, N. Y. 1880
Size: 24 × 30 in. (61.1 × 76.4 cm.)
Artist: H. H. Rowley & Co.
Lithographer:
Printer: C. H. Vogt
Publisher: H. H. Rowley & Company, Hartford, Connecticut
Key/Vignettes/Misc: Refs. 1–16; 3 vignettes
Locations: OCHS–O; CSNY–S; NYH–NY
Catalogs/Checklists:

2534
Place: Geneva, New York
Date: 1836
Title: View of Geneva, Ontario County, N. Y. Taken From the Foot of Seneca Lake in July, 1836.
Size: 9¾ × 16½ in. (24.8 × 41.9 cm.)
Artist: H. Walton
Lithographer: E. Brown, Jr.
Printer: Bufford's Press
Publisher: Bogerts & Wynkoop, Geneva, N. Y.
Key/Vignettes/Misc:
Locations: CHS–C; MM–NN; Geneva Historical Society, Geneva, New York; YUAG–NH
Catalogs/Checklists: MM–NN, LP 4108; Rehner, Walton, no. 58

2535
Place: Geneva, New York
Date: 1873
Title: Bird's Eye View of Geneva Ontario County N. Y. 1873
Size: 17¾ × 24¾ in. (45.2 × 63 cm.)
Artist: Augustus Koch
Lithographer:
Printer:
Publisher:

Key/Vignettes/Misc: Refs. 1–39; 2 vignettes
Locations: NYSL–A
Catalogs/Checklists:

2536
Place: Geneva, New York
Date: 1893
Title: Geneva, N. Y. 1893
Size: 18 × 30 in. (45.8 × 76.3 cm.)
Artist:
Lithographer:
Printer: Burleigh Litho. Co., Troy, N. Y.
Publisher:
Key/Vignettes/Misc: 99 refs. 1 vignette
Locations: Private collection
Catalogs/Checklists:

2537
Place: Glen Island, New York
Date: Ca. 1885
Title: Glen Island, Long Island Sound, N. Y. The World Famous Day Summer Resort
Size: 21³⁄₁₆ × 34¼ in. (53.8 × 87.1 cm.)
Artist:
Lithographer:
Printer: Metropolitan Print, New York
Publisher:
Key/Vignettes/Misc:
Locations: MM–NN
Catalogs/Checklists: MM–NN, LP 205

2538
Place: Glens Falls, New York
Date: 1834
Title: Glennville, on the Hudson.
Size: 9½ × 13¾ in. (24.1 × 35 cm.)
Artist: J. W. Hill
Lithographer:
Printer: [Endicott] 359 Broadway [New York]
Publisher: George Endicott (copyright)
Key/Vignettes/Misc:
Locations: NYP–S; NYH–NY
Catalogs/Checklists: Stokes P. 1833—F–33

2539
Place: Glens Falls, New York
Date: 1875
Title: Glens Falls, N. Y. 1875
Size: 19¾ × 26¼ in. (50.3 × 66.8 cm.)
Artist: H. H. Bailey [& J. C. Hazen]
Lithographer:
Printer: G. W. Lewis, Albany, N. Y.
Publisher: H. H. Bailey [& J. C. Hazen]
Key/Vignettes/Misc: Refs. 1–13
Locations: NYSL–A; BPL–R
Catalogs/Checklists:

2540
Place: Glens Falls, New York
Date: 1884
Title: Glens Falls, N. Y.
Size: 18½ × 30 in. (47.1 × 76.3 cm.)
Artist: L. R. Burleigh
Lithographer:
Printer: Beck & Pauli, Lith., Milwaukee, Wis.
Publisher: L. R. Burleigh, Troy, N. Y.
Key/Vignettes/Misc: Refs. 1–39

Locations: LC–M; NYH–NY
Catalogs/Checklists: LC–M, 567

2541
Place: Gloversville, New York
Date: 1875
Title: Gloversville, N. Y. 1875
Size: 17¹⁵⁄₁₆ × 23¾ in. (45.6 × 60.5 cm)
Artist:
Lithographer:
Printer: G. W. Lewis, 452 Broadway, Albany, N. Y.
Publisher: H. H. Bailey [& J. C. Hazen]
Key/Vignettes/Misc: Refs. 1–20
Locations: BPL–R; LC–M; NYSL–A
Catalogs/Checklists: LC–M, 568

2542
Place: Gloversville, New York
Date: 1881
Title: Gloversville, N. Y. 1881.
Size: 20½ × 26¾ in. (25.2 × 68.1 cm.)
Artist:
Lithographer:
Printer:
Publisher:
Key/Vignettes/Misc: Refs. 1–21; 9 vignettes
Locations: NYSM–A
Catalogs/Checklists:

2543
Place: Goshen, New York
Date: 1874
Title: Goshen, N. Y. 1874
Size: 16½ × 22⁵⁄₁₆ in. (42 × 56.8 cm.)
Artist: O. H. Bailey
Lithographer:
Printer: J. Knauber & Co. Print, Milwaukee
Publisher: O. H. Bailey
Key/Vignettes/Misc: Refs. 1–9; list of municipal officials
Locations: BPL–R; NYH–NY
Catalogs/Checklists:

2544
Place: Goshen, New York
Date: 1922
Title: Aero View of Goshen New York 1922
Size:
Artist:
Lithographer:
Printer:
Publisher: Hughes & Fowler, 357 4th St Brooklyn, N. Y.
Key/Vignettes/Misc: Vignettes; unnumbered business directory
Locations:
Catalogs/Checklists: Warren & Wise

2545
Place: Gouverneur, New York
Date: 1885
Title: Gouverneur, N. Y.
Size: 13⅝ × 29⅞ in. (35.2 × 75.7 cm.)
Artist: L. R. Burleigh
Lithographer:
Printer: Beck & Pauli, Litho., Milwaukee, Wis.
Publisher: L. R. Burleigh, Troy, N. Y.

Key/Vignettes/Misc: Refs. 1–18; 1 vignette
Locations: LC–M; LC–P
Catalogs/Checklists: LC–M, 569

2546
Place: Gouverneur, New York
Date: ?
Title: Gouverneur as it was in 1888
Size: 8¼ × 15¾ in. (21 × 40.1 cm.)
Artist:
Lithographer:
Printer:
Publisher:
Key/Vignettes/Misc:
Locations: Edward Case, 107 E. Main St., Gouverneur, New York
Catalogs/Checklists:

2547
Place: Granville, New York
Date: 1873
Title: The Mettowee Valley From Salte Hill Granville, N. Y.
Size: 23⅞ × 37¼ in. (60.8 × 94.8 cm.)
Artist: Prof. F. Childs
Lithographer:
Printer: J. H. Bufford's Lith. 490 Washn St. Boston
Publisher: Prof. F. Childs
Key/Vignettes/Misc:
Locations: NYSM–A
Catalogs/Checklists:

2548
Place: Granville, New York
Date: 1886
Title: Granville, N. Y.
Size: 12½ × 23⅞ in. (31.8 × 60.5 cm.)
Artist:
Lithographer:
Printer: Beck & Pauli, Litho., Milwaukee, Wis.
Publisher: L. R. Burleigh, Troy, N. Y.
Key/Vignettes/Misc: Refs. 1–16; 1 vignette
Locations: LC–M; NYH–NY; LC–P; LAHS–L
Catalogs/Checklists: LC–M, 570

2549
Place: Greene, New York
Date: 1890
Title: Greene, N. Y.
Size: 14⅛ × 25⅛ in. (36 × 64 cm.)
Artist:
Lithographer:
Printer: Burleigh Lithographing Establishment, Troy, N. Y.
Publisher: L. R. Burleigh, Troy, N. Y.
Key/Vignettes/Misc: Refs. 1–39
Locations: LC–M; RCHS–T
Catalogs/Checklists: LC–M, 570.1

2550
Place: Greenwich, New York
Date: 1868
Title: Greenwich, Washington Co., N. Y.
Size: 14 × 19 in. (35.5 × 48.2 cm.)
Artist: B. W. Jennens
Lithographer:
Printer: J & R McClellan, N. Y.

Publisher: B. W. Jennens, Greenwich, Washington Co. N. Y.
Key/Vignettes/Misc:
Locations: NYH–NY
Catalogs/Checklists:

2551
Place: Groton, New York
Date: [1885]
Title: Groton. N. Y.
Size: ca. 14 × 25 in. (ca. 35.6 × 63.6 cm.)
Artist: L. R. Burleigh
Lithographer:
Printer: Beck & Pauli, Milwaukee, Wis.
Publisher: L. R. Burleigh, Troy, N. Y.
Key/Vignettes/Misc: Refs. 1–21; 1 vignette
Locations: Groton, New York, Public Library
Catalogs/Checklists:

Place: Hadley, New York
Date: 1888
See Luzerne, New York, 1888.

2552
Place: Hagamans Mills, New York
Date: 1890
Title: Hagamans Mills, N. Y.
Size: 12⅞ × 25³⁄₁₆ in. (32.8 × 64.1 cm.)
Artist: L. R. Burleigh
Lithographer:
Printer:
Publisher: L. R. Burleigh, Troy, N. Y.
Key/Vignettes/Misc: Refs. 1–11
Locations: NYH–NY; NYSM–A; LAHS–L
Catalogs/Checklists:

2553
Place: Hamilton, New York
Date: 1885
Title: Hamilton, N. Y.
Size: 13¾ × 24½ in. (35 × 62.4 cm.)
Artist: L. R. Burleigh
Lithographer:
Printer: C. H. Vogt & Son, Lith. Cleve'd. O.
Publisher: L. R. Burleigh, Troy, N. Y.
Key/Vignettes/Misc: Refs. 1–29; 1 vignette
Locations: CSNY–S
Catalogs/Checklists:

2554
Place: Hempstead, New York
Date: 1876
Title: Hempstead, N. Y. Long Island. 1876
Size: 14⁵⁄₁₆ × 22⅛ in. (36.4 × 56.3 cm.)
Artist: Fowler & Bulger
Lithographer: C. H. Vogt
Printer: J. Knauber & Co.
Publisher: Fowler & Bulger
Key/Vignettes/Misc: Refs. 1–8
Locations: NYP–S; NCM–EM; BPL–R; LC–M (photo)
Catalogs/Checklists: Stokes 1876—G–96; LC–M, 570.2

2555
Place: Herkimer, New York
Date: 1884
Title: Herkimer, N. Y.

Size: 16 × 24 in. (40.7 × 61.1 cm.)
Artist: L. R. Burleigh
Lithographer:
Printer: Beck & Pauli, Litho. Milwaukee, Wisc.
Publisher: L. R. Burleigh, Troy, N. Y.
Key/Vignettes/Misc: 33 refs.
Locations: HCHS–H
Catalogs/Checklists:

2556
Place: Hicksville, New York
Date: 1925
Title: 1925 Aero View of Hicksville, Long Island, Nassau County, New York
Size: 25 × 36½ in. (63.6 × 92.9 cm.)
Artist: Rene Cinquin
Lithographer:
Printer:
Publisher: Metropolitan Aero–View Co., 505 Fifth Ave., New York, N. Y.
Key/Vignettes/Misc: 59 vignettes
Locations: NCM–EM; LC–M
Catalogs/Checklists: LC–M, 571

2557
Place: Holley, New York
Date: 1890
Title: Holley, N. Y.
Size: 15⅞ × 24⁵⁄₁₆ in. (40.5 × 61.9 cm.)
Artist:
Lithographer:
Printer: Burleigh Lithographing Establishment, Troy, N. Y.
Publisher: L. R. Burleigh, Troy, N. Y.
Key/Vignettes/Misc: Refs. 1–22
Locations: NYSM–A
Catalogs/Checklists:

2558
Place: Homer, New York
Date: 1851
Title: View of Homer, Cortland Co., N. Y. Looking West.
Size: 14¼ × 17¾ in. (36.3 × 45.2 cm.)
Artist: F. N. Otis
Lithographer: C. Parsons
Printer: Endicott & Co., N. Y.
Publisher: F. N. Otis (copyright)
Key/Vignettes/Misc: 1 portrait
Locations: CCHS–CO; NYH–NY
Catalogs/Checklists:

2559
Place: Honeoye Falls, New York
Date: 1892
Title: Honeoye Falls, N. Y.
Size: 15⅜ × 27⅛ in. (39.1 × 69 cm.)
Artist: The Burleigh Lith. Co.
Lithographer:
Printer:
Publisher: The Burleigh Lith Co., Troy, N. Y.
Key/Vignettes/Misc: Refs. 1–55; 1 vignette
Locations: NYSM–A
Catalogs/Checklists:

2560
Place: Hoosick Falls, New York
Date: 1889
Title: Hoosick Falls, N. Y.

Size: 19 × 31½ in. (48.3 × 80.1 cm.)
Artist: L. R. Burleigh
Lithographer:
Printer: The Burleigh Lith. Est., Troy, N. Y.
Publisher: L. R. Burleigh, Troy, N. Y.
Key/Vignettes/Misc: Refs. 1–40
Locations: LC–M; LC–P; LAHS–L
Catalogs/Checklists: LC–M,572

2561
Place: Hornell, New York
Date: 1878
Title: Hornellsville, N. Y. 1878. Viewed from Hartshorns Hill
Size: 15 × 29 in. (38.2 × 73.8 cm.)
Artist: W. W. Denslow
Lithographer:
Printer: Krebs Lithographing Co., Cincinnati, O.
Publisher: C. J. Corbin
Key/Vignettes/Misc: 14 vignettes
Locations: NYH–NY
Catalogs/Checklists:

2562
Place: Hudson, New York
Date: [1828–29]
Title: Town of Hudson
Size: 9¾ × 12¾ in. (24.8 × 32.5 cm.)
Artist: [Jacques] Milbert
Lithographer:
Printer: L. Sabatier
Publisher:
Key/Vignettes/Misc:
Locations: CHS–C
Catalogs/Checklists:

2563
Place: Hudson Falls, New York
Date: 1884
Title: Sandy Hill, N. Y.
Size: 16³⁄₁₆ × 30¼ in. (41.2 × 76.8 cm.)
Artist: L. R. Burleigh
Lithographer:
Printer: Beck & Pauli, Litho., Milwaukee
Publisher: L. R. Burleigh, Troy, N. Y.
Key/Vignettes/Misc: Refs. 1–33
Locations: LC–M; LC–P
Catalogs/Checklists: LC–M, 629

2564
Place: Hunter, New York
Date: 1890
Title: Hunter, N. Y.
Size: 17½ × 26½ in. (44.5 × 67.5 cm.)
Artist:
Lithographer:
Printer: Burleigh Lith. Est., Troy, N. Y.
Publisher: L. R. Burleigh, Troy, N. Y.
Key/Vignettes/Misc: Refs. 1–35
Locations: LC–M; NYH–NY
Catalogs/Checklists: LC–M, 573

2565
Place: Ilion, New York
Date: 1881
Title: Bird's Eye View of Illion, N. Y. Population 4500 1881
Size: 20 × 24 in. (50.9 × 61.1 cm.)
Artist: H. H. Rowley & Co.
Lithographer:
Printer: C. H. Vogt & Son, Cleveland

Publisher: H. H. Rowley & Co., Hartford, Conn.
Key/Vignettes/Misc: 12 refs. (6ppLocations: HCHS−H
Catalogs/Checklists:

2566
Place: Ithaca, New York
Date: 1836
Title: East View of Ithaca, Tompkins County, N. Y. Taken in Septr 1836
Size: 11 × 17½ in. (27.9 × 34.5 cm.)
Artist: H. Walton
Lithographer: H. Walton
Printer: Bufford's Lithography 114 Nassau St. N. Y.
Publisher:
Key/Vignettes/Misc:
Locations: LC−M (facsimile); NYP−S; DWHS−I; YUAG−NH; NYH−NY; LC−P
Catalogs/Checklists: LC−M, 574; Rehner, Walton, no. 55

2567
Place: Ithaca, New York
Date: 1838
Title: View of Ithaca. Tompkins County, N. Y. Taken From The South Hill, in November. 1838.
Size: 14 × 16 in. (35.6 × 40.7 cm.)
Artist: Henry Walton
Lithographer: Henry Walton
Printer: J. H. Bufford, 114 Nassau St., N. Y.
Publisher:
Key/Vignettes/Misc: description
Locations: DWHS−I; NYH−NY
Catalogs/Checklists: Rehner, Walton, no. 56A

2568
Place: Ithaca, New York
Date: 1839
Title: View of Ithaca, Tompkins County N. Y. Taken From The West Hill 1839.
Size: 16 × 27 in. (40.7 × 68.6 cm.)
Artist: Henry Walton
Lithographer: Henry Walton
Printer: Daniel S. Jenkins 136 Nassau St. Cor. Beekman. N. York
Publisher:
Key/Vignettes/Misc:
Locations: DWHS−I
Catalogs/Checklists: Rehner, Walton, no. 57

2569
Place: Ithaca, New York
Date: 1873
Title: Bird's Eye View of Ithaca, N. Y. 1873
Size: 19³⁄₁₆ × 25⁵⁄₁₆ in. (48.8 × 64.4 cm.)
Artist: [O. H. Bailey]
Lithographer:
Printer:
Publisher:
Key/Vignettes/Misc: Refs. 1−24, A−G, O−P, R−U
Locations: DWHS−I; LC−M (facsimile)
Catalogs/Checklists: LC−M, 574.2

2570
Place: Ithaca, New York
Date: 1882 State I
Title: Ithaca, N. Y. 1882
Size: 20 × 29 in. (55.9 × 71.1 cm.)
Artist: L. R. Burleigh
Lithographer: J. Lyth
Printer:
Publisher: [D. H. Mason & Co., Syracuse, N. Y.]
Key/Vignettes/Misc: [no refs]
Locations: DWHS−I; CSNY−S; NYH−NY
Catalogs/Checklists: LC−M, 574.3

2571
Place: Ithaca, New York
Date: 1882 State II
Title: Ithaca, N. Y. 1882
Size: 20 × 29 in. (55.9 × 71.1 cm.)
Artist: L. R. Burleigh
Lithographer: J. Lyth
Printer:
Publisher: [D. H. Mason & Co., Syracuse, N. Y.]
Key/Vignettes/Misc: Refs. 1−56
Locations: Tompkins County Trust Co., Ithaca, New York; LC−M (facsimile)
Catalogs/Checklists: LC−M, 574.3

2572
Place: Jamestown, New York
Date: Ca. 1882
Title: Bird's Eye View of the Village of Jamestown, Chautauqua County, New York. Looking North East
Size: 26³⁄₈ × 41³⁄₁₆ in. (67.2 × 104.9 cm.)
Artist: H. Brosius & A. F. Poole
Lithographer:
Printer: Beck & Pauli, Litho., Milwaukee
Publisher: J. J. Stoner, Madison, Wisconsin
Key/Vignettes/Misc: Refs. A−X, 1−36; 18 vignettes
Locations: LC−M; NYH−NY
Catalogs/Checklists: LC−M, 575

Place: Jamestown, New York
Date: 1885
See Chautauqua, New York, 1885.

Place: Jefferson, New York
Date: 1847
See Watkins Glen, New York, 1847.

2573
Place: Johnsonville, New York
Date: 1887
Title: Johnsonville, N. Y. 1887
Size: 11³⁄₁₆ × 21⅛ in. (28.5 × 53.8 cm.)
Artist: L. R. Burleigh
Lithographer:
Printer: Burleigh Lith. Est., Troy, N. Y.
Publisher: L. R. Burleigh, Troy, N. Y.
Key/Vignettes/Misc: Refs. 1−9
Locations: LC−M; NYH−NY; NYSM−A
Catalogs/Checklists: LC−M, 576

2574
Place: Johnstown, New York
Date: 1874
Title: Johnstown, N. Y. 1874

Size: 18⅞ × 23⅛ in. (48.1 × 58.9 cm.)
Artist: H. H. Bailey [& J. C. Hazen]
Lithographer:
Printer: G. W. Lewis, 452 Broadway, Albany, N. Y.
Publisher:
Key/Vignettes/Misc: Refs. 1−13
Locations: BPL−R; NYSL−A; NYH−NY
Catalogs/Checklists:

2575
Place: Johnstown, New York
Date: 1888
Title: Johnstown, N. Y. 1888
Size: 16⅝ × 28⅞ in. (42.3 × 73.5 cm.)
Artist: L. R. Burleigh
Lithographer:
Printer: Burleigh Lith., Troy, N. Y.
Publisher: L. R. Burleigh, Troy, N. Y.
Key/Vignettes/Misc: Refs. 1−33; 1 vignette
Locations: LC−M; NYSL−A; NYH−NY; MCDH−F; LAHS−L
Catalogs/Checklists: LC−M, 577

2576
Place: Keeseville, New York
Date: 1887
Title: Keeseville, N. Y. 1887
Size: 15 × 24 in. (38.2 × 61.1 cm.)
Artist: L. R. Burleigh
Lithographer:
Printer: Burleigh Lith. Est., Troy, N. Y.
Publisher: L. R. Burleigh, Troy, N. Y.
Key/Vignettes/Misc: Refs. 1−13
Locations: LC−M; NYH−NY
Catalogs/Checklists: LC−M, 578

2577
Place: Kingston, New York
Date: Ca. 1888
Title: City of Kingston, N. Y.
Size: 21 × 30 in. (53.4 × 76.3 cm.)
Artist:
Lithographer:
Printer: Thos. Hunter, Lith. 716, Filbert St. Phila.
Publisher: [L. R.] Burleigh [Troy, N. Y.]
Key/Vignettes/Misc:
Locations: MM−NN; NYH−NY
Catalogs/Checklists: MM−NN, LP 2603

2578
Place: Kingston, New York
Date: 1894
Title: The Wellesley Parker View of Kingston.
Size: 28³⁄₈ × 38⅛ in. (72.2 × 97 cm.)
Artist:
Lithographer:
Printer: Kingston Lithographic Print
Publisher: Kingston Freeman
Key/Vignettes/Misc: 50 vignettes; advertisements
Locations: NYH−NY
Catalogs/Checklists:

2579
Place: Lake George, New York
Date: 1827
Title: Road to Lake George

Size: 9½ × 14½ in. (24.1 × 36.8 cm.)
Artist: [Jacques] Milbert
Lithographer:
Printer:
Publisher:
Key/Vignettes/Misc:
Locations: Unknown. See American Art Association, Auction Catalog no. 411
Catalogs/Checklists:

2580
Place: Lancaster, New York
Date: 1892
Title: Lancaster, N. Y.
Size: 18½ × 28¹¹⁄₁₆ in. (47.1 × 73 cm.)
Artist:
Lithographer:
Printer: Burleigh Litho. Co., Troy, N. Y.
Publisher: Burleigh Litho. Co., Troy, N. Y.
Key/Vignettes/Misc: Refs. 1–72, 4 unnumbered refs.
Locations: LC–M; NYH–NY
Catalogs/Checklists: LC–M, 578.1

Place: Lansingburgh, New York
Date: [1860–67]
See Cohoes, New York, [1860–67]

2582
Place: Lansingburgh, New York
Date: 1879
Title: Lansingburgh, N. Y. 1879
Size: 18½ × 27 in. (47.1 × 68.7 cm.)
Artist: Galt & Hoy
Lithographer:
Printer:
Publisher: Galt & Hoy, 111 Liberty Street, New York
Key/Vignettes/Misc: 24 refs. 3 vignettes
Locations: LAHS–L
Catalogs/Checklists:

2583
Place: Lansingburgh, New York
Date: 1891
Title: Lansingburgh, N. Y. First Ward 9th to 15th Sts. Second Ward, 15th to 18th Sts.
Size: 17¾ × 25⅛ in. (45.2 × 63.9 cm.)
Artist:
Lithographer:
Printer: Burleigh Litho Est. Troy, N. Y.
Publisher: L. R. Burleigh, Troy, N. Y.
Key/Vignettes/Misc: Refs. 1–60
Locations: RCHS–T; NYSM–A; NYH–NY; LAHS–L
Catalogs/Checklists:

2584
Place: Lansingburgh, New York
Date: 1891
Title: Lansingburgh, N. Y. Third Ward, 18th Street North
Size: 16⅞ × 25 in. (42.9 × 63.6 cm.)
Artist:
Lithographer:
Printer: Burleigh Litho. Est. Troy, N. Y.
Publisher: L. R. Burleigh, Troy, N. Y.
Key/Vignettes/Misc: Refs. 1–16
Locations: RCHS–T; NYSM–A; NYH–NY; LAHS–L
Catalogs/Checklists:

2585
Place: Lansingburgh, New York
Date: 1891
Title: Lansingburgh, N. Y., Fourth Ward 1st Street to 9th Street
Size: 17½ × 26 in. (44.5 × 66.2 cm.)
Artist:
Lithographer:
Printer: Burleigh Litho. Est. Troy, N. Y.
Publisher: L. R. Burleigh, Troy, N. Y.
Key/Vignettes/Misc: Refs. 1–22
Locations: RCHS–T; NYSM–A; LAHS–L
Catalogs/Checklists:

2586
Place: Larchmont, New York
Date: 1904
Title: View of the Borough of Larchmont, New York
Size: 21 × 25 in. (53.5 × 63.6 cm.)
Artist:
Lithographer:
Printer:
Publisher: Hughes & Bailey, New York
Key/Vignettes/Misc: Refs. 1–31; 10 vignettes
Locations: LC–M
Catalogs/Checklists: LC–M, 579

2587
Place: Le Roy, New York
Date: 1892
Title: Le Roy, N. Y.
Size: 18¾ × 30¼ in. (47.8 × 77 cm.)
Artist:
Lithographer:
Printer:
Publisher: Burleigh Litho. Co., Troy, N. Y.
Key/Vignettes/Misc: Refs. 1–71
Locations: LC–M; NYSL–A; Le Roy Historical Society, Le Roy, New York
Catalogs/Checklists: LC–M, 580

2588
Place: Lima, New York
Date: [1895?]
Title: Lima, N. Y.
Size: 14¼ × 26 in. (36.3 × 66.2 cm.)
Artist:
Lithographer:
Printer: The Burleigh Lith. Co. Troy, N. Y.
Publisher:
Key/Vignettes/Misc: Refs. 1–36
Locations: LC–M (facsimile); NYSM–A
Catalogs/Checklists: LC–M, 580.1

2589
Place: Lindenhurst, New York
Date: 1900
Title: Lindenhurst, Long Island, N. Y. 1900
Size: 15⅝ × 19⅞ in. (39.8 × 50.6 cm.)
Artist:
Lithographer:
Printer:
Publisher: O. H. Bailey, Boston, Mass.
Key/Vignettes/Misc: Refs. A, 2–35; 18 vignettes
Locations: NYH–NY
Catalogs/Checklists:

2590
Place: Lindenhurst, New York
Date: 1926
Title: Aero–View of Lindenhurst Long Island 1926
Size: 27 × 32 in. (68.6 × 81.3 cm.)
Artist: R. Cinquin
Lithographer:
Printer:
Publisher: Metropolitan Aero–View Co., N. Y.
Key/Vignettes/Misc: 21 vignettes; unnumbered business directory; description
Locations: LC–M
Catalogs/Checklists: LC–M, 581

2591
Place: Little Falls, New York
Date: 1862
Title: Little Falls Herkimer Co. N. Y. 1862. From the South Side of the River
Size: 22⅞ × 33⅞ in. (58.3 × 86.3 cm.)
Artist: Stanley Fox
Lithographer: Stanley Fox
Printer:
Publisher:
Key/Vignettes/Misc:
Locations: CSNY–S
Catalogs/Checklists:

2592
Place: Little Falls, New York
Date: 1881
Title: Little Falls, N. Y. 1881
Size: 19⅞ × 28⁵⁄₁₆ in. (50.6 × 72.1 cm.)
Artist: H. H. Rowley & Co.
Lithographer:
Printer: C. H. Vogt & Son, Cleveland
Publisher: H. H. Rowley & Co. Hartford, Conn.
Key/Vignettes/Misc: Refs. 1–42; 10 vignettes; names and addresses of 2 dentists
Locations: BPL–R; CSNY–S
Catalogs/Checklists:

2593
Place: Little Falls, New York
Date: N.D.
Title: View of Little–Falls.
Size: 20¾ × 30⅜ in. (52.8 × 77.3 cm.)
Artist: N. J. Barber
Lithographer: D. W. Moody
Printer: F. Michelin, 111 Nassau St. N. Y.
Publisher:
Key/Vignettes/Misc:
Locations: CSNY–S
Catalogs/Checklists:

2594
Place: Lockport, New York
Date: 1836
Title: View of the Upper Village of Lockport, Niagara Co. N.Y. From Above the Race, Showing the Ten Combined Locks on the Erie Canal 1836.
Size: 15⅛ × 20 in. (38.5 × 50.9 cm.)
Artist: W. Wilson
Lithographer:
Printer: Bufford's Lith, 144 Nassau St. N. Y.

Publisher: W. Wilson (copyright)
Key/Vignettes/Misc:
Locations: CHS−C; CSNY−S; LC−P; NYH−NY
Catalogs/Checklists:

2595
Place: Lockport, New York
Date: N.D.
Title: Birds Eye View of the City of Lockport Niagara County N. Y.
Size: 21¼ × 28½ in. (54.1 × 72.6 cm.)
Artist:
Lithographer:
Printer: M. C. Richardson & Co., Lockport, N. Y. Lith
Publisher:
Key/Vignettes/Misc: Refs. 1−51
Locations: CSNY−S; Niagara County Historical Society, Lockport, New York
Catalogs/Checklists:

2596
Place: Loudonville, New York
Date: 1883
Title: Loudonville 1883
Size: 18 × 25½ in. (45.8 × 64.9 cm.)
Artist: James MacGregor
Lithographer: James MacGregor
Printer: John J. Dunphy, Litho−Printer
Publisher: James MacGregor, 481 Broadway, Albany, N. Y.
Key/Vignettes/Misc: 36 refs.
Locations: Office of Town Historian, Colonie, New York
Catalogs/Checklists:

2597
Place: Lowville, New York
Date: Ca. 1885
Title: Lowville, N. Y.
Size: 17 × 24 in. (43.3 × 61.1 cm.)
Artist: L. R. Burleigh
Lithographer:
Printer: Beck & Pauli, Litho., Milwaukee, Wis.
Publisher: L. R. Burleigh, Troy, N. Y.
Key/Vignettes/Misc: Refs. 1−4
Locations: LC−M
Catalogs/Checklists: LC−M, 582

2598
Place: Luzerne, New York
Date: 1888
Title: Luzerne, N. Y. and Hadley
Size: 18 × 24½ in. (45.8 × 62.3 cm.)
Artist: L. R. Burleigh
Lithographer:
Printer:
Publisher: L. R. Burleigh, Troy, N. Y.
Key/Vignettes/Misc: Refs. 1−37
Locations: LC−M
Catalogs/Checklists: LC−M, 583

2599
Place: Lyons, New York
Date: 1880
Title: View of Lyons, N. Y. 1880.
Size: 18¼ × 24¾ in. (46.4 × 63 cm.)
Artist: H. H. Rowley & Co.
Lithographer:
Printer:

Publisher: H. H. Rowley & Co., Hartford, Conn.
Key/Vignettes/Misc: Refs. 1−18
Locations: Wayne County Historical Society, Lyons, New York
Catalogs/Checklists:

2600
Place: Malone, New York
Date: 1886
Title: Malone, N. Y.
Size: 17³⁄₁₆ × 33¹⁵⁄₁₆ in. (43.7 × 86.4 cm.)
Artist: L. R. Burleigh
Lithographer:
Printer: C. H. Vogt & Son, Cleveland, Ohio
Publisher: L. R. Burleigh
Key/Vignettes/Misc: Refs. 1−14
Locations: LC−M; Franklin County Historical Society and Museum, Malone, New York
Catalogs/Checklists: LC−M, 584

Place: Manhattanville, New York
Date: 1834
See New York, New York, 1834.

2601
Place: Matteawan, New York
Date: 1886
Title: Matteawan, N. Y. 1886.
Size: 15 × 21½ in. (38.2 × 54.8 cm.)
Artist: L. R. Burleigh
Lithographer:
Printer: Burleigh Lithograph Establishment, Troy, N. Y.
Publisher: L. R. Burleigh, Troy, N. Y.
Key/Vignettes/Misc: Refs. 1−12
Locations: LC−M; NYH−NY
Catalogs/Checklists: LC−M, 585

Place: Mayville, New York
Date: 1885
See Chautauqua, New York, 1885.

2602
Place: Mechanicville, New York
Date: [1885?]
Title: Mechanicville, N. Y.
Size: 14½ × 25⅛ in. (36.9 × 64 cm.)
Artist: L. R. Burleigh
Lithographer: L. R. Burleigh
Printer: Beck & Pauli, Litho, Milwaukee
Publisher: L. R. Burleigh, Troy, N.Y.
Key/Vignettes/Misc: Refs. 1−29
Locations: MM−NN; LC−M; NYSL−A; NYH−NY; CSNY−S; LAHS−L
Catalogs/Checklists: MM−NN, LP 1925; LC−M, 586

2603
Place: Melrose, New York
Date: 1868
Title: View of Melrose And Surroundings. Taken From the Ursuline Convent, Westchester Co N. Y. 1868.
Size: 17 × 25⅛ in. (43.3 × 63.9 cm.)
Artist: Valois
Lithographer: Valois
Printer: G. Schlegel 97 William St N. Y.
Publisher:
Key/Vignettes/Misc: Refs.

Locations:
Catalogs/Checklists: Goldsmith, no. 390

2604
Place: Middleburg, New York
Date: 1890
Title: Middleburgh, N. Y.
Size: 14¾ × 28⅛ in. (37.6 × 71.6 cm.)
Artist:
Lithographer:
Printer: Burleigh Lithographing Establishment, Troy, N. Y.
Publisher: L. R. Burleigh, Troy, N. Y.
Key/Vignettes/Misc: Refs. 1−28
Locations: NYSM−A
Catalogs/Checklists:

2605
Place: Middletown, New York
Date: 1874
Title: View of Middletown, N. Y. 1874
Size: 20½ × 26¾ in. (52.2 × 68.1 cm.)
Artist:
Lithographer:
Printer:
Publisher: American Oleograph Co. Milwaukee
Key/Vignettes/Misc: Refs. 1−21; 4 vignettes
Locations: BPL−R; HSMW−M; NYH−NY
Catalogs/Checklists:

2606
Place: Middletown, New York
Date: 1887
Title: Middletown, N. Y. 1887.
Size: 18 × 30½ in. (45.8 × 77.6 cm.)
Artist: L. R. Burleigh
Lithographer:
Printer:
Publisher: L. R. Burleigh, Troy, N. Y.
Key/Vignettes/Misc: Refs. 1−53
Locations: LC−M; HSMW−M; NYH−NY
Catalogs/Checklists: LC−M, 587

2607
Place: Middletown, New York
Date: 1921
Title: Middletown, N. Y.
Size: 23 × 35 in. (58.6 × 89.1 cm.)
Artist: T. M. Fowler
Lithographer:
Printer:
Publisher: Hughes & Fowler
Key/Vignettes/Misc: 26 vignettes; 1 map
Locations: LC−M
Catalogs/Checklists: LC−M, 588

2608
Place: Middletown, New York
Date: 1922
Title: Middletown, N. Y. 1922
Size: 26½ × 36½ in. (67.5 × 92.9 cm.)
Artist: [T. M. Fowler]
Lithographer:
Printer:
Publisher: Hughes & Fowler, 30−32 Bridge St., Brooklyn, N. Y.
Key/Vignettes/Misc: Refs. 1−21; 32 vignettes; unnumbered business directory; description

Locations: LC–M; HSMW–M
Catalogs/Checklists: LC–M, 589

2609
Place: Middleville, New York
Date: [1890?]
Title: Middleville, N. Y.
Size: 17 × 23 in. (43.3 × 58.5 cm.)
Artist:
Lithographer:
Printer: Burleigh Lith. Est., Troy, N. Y.
Publisher: L. R. Burleigh, Troy, N. Y.
Key/Vignettes/Misc: Refs. 1–15
Locations: LC–M; LAHS–L
Catalogs/Checklists: LC–M, 590

2610
Place: Millerton, New York
Date: 1887
Title: Millerton, N. Y. 1887
Size: 13¼ × 18 in. (33.7 × 45.8 cm.)
Artist: L. R. Burleigh
Lithographer:
Printer: The Burleigh Lith. Est., Troy, N.Y.
Publisher: L. R. Burleigh, Troy, N. Y.
Key/Vignettes/Misc: Refs. 1–12; 1
vignette
Locations: LC–M; NYH–NY
Catalogs/Checklists: LC–M, 591

2611
Place: Mohawk, New York
Date: 1893
Title: Mohawk, New York
Size: 17 × 22½ in. (43.2 × 57.3 cm.)
Artist:
Lithographer:
Printer: Burleigh Litho Co., Troy, N. Y.
Publisher:
Key/Vignettes/Misc: 30 refs.
Locations: HCHS–H; LAHS–L
Catalogs/Checklists:

2612
Place: Monroe, New York
Date: 1923
Title: Aero–View of Monroe, New York
1923
Size: 16 × 31⅞ in. (40.7 × 81.1 cm.)
Artist:
Lithographer:
Printer: [Meriden Gravure Co., Meriden,
Connecticut]
Publisher: Hughes & Bailey (copyright)
Key/Vignettes/Misc: 1 vignette;
unnumbered business directory;
description
Locations: LC–M; NYH–NY
Catalogs/Checklists: LC–M, 592

2613
Place: Moravia, New York
Date: 1885
Title: Moravia, N. Y.—1885
Size: 13½ × 22¼ in. (34.4 × 56.6 cm.)
Artist: L. R. Burleigh
Lithographer:
Printer:
Publisher: L. R. Burleigh, Troy, N. Y.
Key/Vignettes/Misc:
Locations: NYSM–A
Catalogs/Checklists:

2614
Place: Morris, New York
Date: Ca. 1855
Title: Morris, N. Y.
Size: 16 × 22⅛ in. (40.7 × 56.3 cm.)
Artist: A. S. Avery
Lithographer:
Printer: J. Bien
Publisher:
Key/Vignettes/Misc:
Locations: NYSH–C; NYH–NY
Catalogs/Checklists: Hemenway

2615
Place: Morrisania, New York
Date: [1861] State I
Title: Historical Morrisania (Village.)
Size: 12¾ × 20¹/₁₆ in. (32.5 × 51 cm.)
Artist:
Lithographer:
Printer:
Publisher:
Key/Vignettes/Misc:
Locations: NYH–NY
Catalogs/Checklists:

2616
Place: Morrisania, New York
Date: [1861] State II
Title: Historical Morrisania (Village.)
Size: 12⅞ × 19¹³/₁₆ in. (32.8 × 50.4 cm.)
Artist:
Lithographer:
Printer:
Publisher:
Key/Vignettes/Misc: Refs. 1–32
Locations: NYH–NY
Catalogs/Checklists:

2617
Place: Morrisania, New York
Date: 1861 State III
Title: Historical Morrisania (Village.)
1861.
Size: 13⅞ × 19¹³/₁₆ in. (35.3 × 50.4 cm.)
Artist:
Lithographer:
Printer:
Publisher:
Key/Vignettes/Misc: Refs. 1–32
Locations: NYH–NY
Catalogs/Checklists:

2618
Place: Morrisania, New York
Date: N.D.
Title: Morrisania (Village.)
Size: 14 × 16 in. (35.6 × 40.6 cm.)
Artist:
Lithographer:
Printer:
Publisher:
Key/Vignettes/Misc:
Locations: NYH–NY
Catalogs/Checklists: Hufeland, Checklist,
1035

2619
Place: Mount Morris, New York
Date: 1893
Title: Mount Morris, N. Y.
Size: 16⅝ × 30¹/₁₆ in. (42.3 × 76.5 cm.)

Artist:
Lithographer:
Printer: Burleigh Litho. Co., Troy, N. Y.
Publisher:
Key/Vignettes/Misc: Refs. 1–60
Locations: NYH–NY; NYSM–A;
NYSL–A
Catalogs/Checklists:

2620
Place: Mount Vernon, New York
Date: 1883
Title: Mt. Vernon. New York. 1883
Size: 18⅞ × 25½ in. (48 × 64.9 cm.)
Artist:
Lithographer:
Printer: O. H. Bailey & Co., Boston
Publisher: O. H. Bailey & Co., Boston
Key/Vignettes/Misc: Refs. 1–41; 5
vignettes
Locations: BPL–R
Catalogs/Checklists:

2621
Place: Mount Vernon, New York
Date: 1898
Title: Mt. Vernon, N. Y. 1898
Size: 26½ × 39¾ in. (67.5 × 101.2 cm.)
Artist:
Lithographer:
Printer: E. B. Barguet, 54 S. 4th Ave. Mt.
Vernon, N. Y.
Publisher: Landis and Hughes, 134
Mulberry St. N. Y.
Key/Vignettes/Misc: Refs.; 39 vignettes
Locations: Mt. Vernon, New York, Public
Library
Catalogs/Checklists: Hufeland, Checklist,
1302

Place: Nelliston, New York
Date: 1891
See Fort Plain, New York, 1891.

2622
Place: New Brighton, New York
Date: ?
Title: New Brighton, Staten Island
Size: 14 × 24½ in. (35.7 × 62.4 cm.)
Artist:
Lithographer:
Printer: P. A. Mesier Litho Co., 28 Wall
St., New York, N. Y.
Publisher: P. A. Mesier Litho Co., 28 Wall
St., New York, N. Y.
Key/Vignettes/Misc:
Locations: SIHS–R
Catalogs/Checklists:

2623
Place: New Rochelle, New York
Date: 1911
Title: Bird's–Eye View of New Rochelle
Size:
Artist:
Lithographer:
Printer:
Publisher:
Key/Vignettes/Misc:
Locations:
Catalogs/Checklists: Hufeland, Checklist,
1490

2624
Place: New York, New York
Date: [1821]
Title: New–York vue de l'Ouest.
Size: 6⁵⁄₁₆ × 9⁷⁄₁₆ in. (16.1 × 24 cm.)
Artist: Ed. de Montulé
Lithographer:
Printer: Ed. de Montulé
Publisher:
Key/Vignettes/Misc:
Locations:
Catalogs/Checklists: Eno 79; Pyne, no. 49

2625
Place: New York, New York
Date: [1825]
Title: View of the City of New–York
taken from Brooklyn Hills.
Size: 7³⁄₈ × 11³⁄₄ in. (18.8 × 29.9 cm.)
Artist: J. Milbert
Lithographer:
Printer: C. Motte
Publisher:
Key/Vignettes/Misc:
Locations: NYSH–C; YUAG–NH
Catalogs/Checklists: Goldsmith, no. 35;
Hemenway; Pyne, no. 53; Stokes, Icon.,
III, Supp. List, no. 24

2626
Place: New York, New York
Date: [1828]
Title: New–York From Weehawk.
Size: 9⁹⁄₁₆ × 14³⁄₄ in. (24.3 × 37.6 cm.)
Artist: Alex. J. Davis.
Lithographer:
Printer: M. Williams No. 49 Sulivan Street
New York
Publisher:
Key/Vignettes/Misc:
Locations: NYH–NY; MCNY
Catalogs/Checklists: Eno 113; Goldsmith,
no. 36; Pyne, no. 56; Stokes, Icon., III,
Supp. List, no. 27

2627
Place: New York, New York
Date: [1828]
Title: Vue de New–York prise de
Weahawk.—No. 1—View of New–York
Taken from Weahawk. [Title repeated in
Latin and German]
Size: 7⁹⁄₁₆ × 11¹⁄₈ in. (19.2 × 28.3 cm.)
Artist: I Milbert.
Lithographer: Deroy
Printer: Lith deBove dirigee par Noel aine
& Ce.
Publisher:
Key/Vignettes/Misc:
Locations: NYH–NY
Catalogs/Checklists: Eno 80 (dates c.
1819); Pyne, no. 54; Stokes, Icon., III,
Supp. List, no. 26

2628
Place: New York, New York
Date: [1825–28]
Title: Vue de New York Prise de Weekawk
(N. J.)
Size: 11¹⁄₈ × 15³⁄₈ in. (28.3 × 39.1 cm.)

Artist: J. Milbert
Lithographer:
Printer:
Publisher:
Key/Vignettes/Misc:
Locations: SIHS–R
Catalogs/Checklists:

2629
Place: New York, New York
Date: [1825–30?]
Title: Vue de New York
Size: 9¹⁄₂ × 16 in. (24.2 × 40.7 cm.)
Artist:
Lithographer:
Printer: Engelmann pere et fils [Paris]
Publisher:
Key/Vignettes/Misc:
Locations: NYP–S
Catalogs/Checklists: Stokes, C.
1825–30—E26

2630
Place: New York, New York
Date: 1834
Title: Manhattanville, New York
Size: 10¹⁄₈ × 13⁵⁄₈ in. (25.7 × 34.6 cm.)
Artist: J. W. Hill
Lithographer:
Printer: Endicott, 359, Broadway
Publisher: George Endicott, New York
(copyright)
Key/Vignettes/Misc:
Locations: FL–P; YUAG–NH
Catalogs/Checklists: Goldsmith, no. 383;
Stokes, Icon., III, Pl. 112; Pyne, no. 322

2631
Place: New York, New York
Date: 1835
Title: New York From Weehawken
Size:
Artist:
Lithographer:
Printer:
Publisher: C. Currier, New York
Key/Vignettes/Misc:
Locations:
Catalogs/Checklists: Peters, C & I, 3976

2632
Place: New York, New York
Date: Ca. 1840
Title: New York.
Size: 9¹¹⁄₁₆ × 14 in. (24.6 × 35.6 cm.)
Artist:
Lithographer:
Printer:
Publisher: E. L. Kling, Tuttlingen
Key/Vignettes/Misc:
Locations: MCNY
Catalogs/Checklists:

2633
Place: New York, New York
Date: Ca. 1840
Title: New–York
Size: 10¹⁄₈ × 12⁷⁄₈ in. (25.8 × 32.7 cm.)
Artist:
Lithographer:
Printer: Thierry Fs. Cite Ergeret, Paris

Publisher: Victor Co, Paris et St.
Petersbourg; C. Luckhardt Cassel
Key/Vignettes/Misc:
Locations: MCNY
Catalogs/Checklists:

2634
Place: New York, New York
Date: 1844
Title: City of New York
Size:
Artist:
Lithographer:
Printer:
Publisher: N. Currier, New York
Key/Vignettes/Misc:
Locations:
Catalogs/Checklists: Peters, C & I, 3977

2635
Place: New York, New York
Date: 1846
Title: New–York. Taken from the North
West Angle of Fort Columbus. Governors
Island
Size:
Artist:
Lithographer:
Printer:
Publisher:
Key/Vignettes/Misc:
Locations: MCNY
Catalogs/Checklists:

2636
Place: New York, New York
Date: 1848
Title: New York, in 1849.
Size: 15³⁄₄ × 39⁵⁄₈ in. (40 × 100.6 cm.)
Artist: E. Purcell
Lithographer: S. Weekes
Printer:
Publisher: Robert Sears, 128 Nassau St.,
N. Y.
Key/Vignettes/Misc:
Locations: LC–P
Catalogs/Checklists:

2637
Place: New York, New York
Date: 1848
Title: New–York and Environs. From
Williamsburg
Size: 22¹⁄₈ × 32¹³⁄₁₆ in. (56.3 × 83.5 cm.)
Artist: E. W. Foreman and E. Brown Jr.
Lithographer: E. W. Foreman and E.
Brown Jr.
Printer: Sarony & Major, 117 Fulton St.,
New York
Publisher: Williams & Stevens, 353
Broadway, New York and Ackermann &
Co., 96 Strand, London.
Key/Vignettes/Misc: 14 unnumbered refs.
below places identified; 2 vignettes
Locations: NYP–E; MM–NN; CHS–C;
MCNY; YUAG–NH; ROM; NYH–NY
Catalogs/Checklists: Goldsmith, no. 47;
Eno 221; Stokes P. 1847—E–130;
MM–NN, LP 2105; Pyne, no. 74; Stokes,
Icon., III, Supp. List, no. 42; Samuel, no.
710

2638
Place: New York, New York
Date: 1848
Title: View of New York, From
Weehawken. Vue De New York, de
Weehawken Ansicht Von New York, von
Weehawken
Size: 8⅞ × 12½ in. (22.6 × 31.8 cm.)
Artist:
Lithographer:
Printer:
Publisher: N. Currier (copyright)
Key/Vignettes/Misc:
Locations: MCNY; YUAG–NH
Catalogs/Checklists: Peters, C & I, 3978;
Pyne, no. 75

2639
Place: New York, New York
Date: 1849
Title: City of New York, From Jersey City
Size: 8⁹⁄₁₆ × 12¹³⁄₁₆ in. (21.8 × 32.6 cm.)
Artist:
Lithographer:
Printer:
Publisher: N. Currier, 152 Nassau St. Cor
of Spruce N. Y.
Key/Vignettes/Misc: 9 unnumbered refs. in
2 lines below places identified
Locations: NYH–NY; MCNY;
YUAG–NH; LC–P
Catalogs/Checklists: Stokes, Icon., III,
Supp. List, no. 44; Eno 235; Peters, C & I,
3981; Pyne, no. 80

2640
Place: New York, New York
Date: 1849
Title: Jersey City[,] New York From Staten
Island [and] Brooklyn City
Size: 26¼ × 37½ in. (66.7 × 95:3 cm.)
Artist: C. W. Burton
Lithographer: C. W. Burton
Printer: Sarony & Major, New York
Publisher: C. W. Burton and Sarony &
Major, New York
Key/Vignettes/Misc: 26 unnumbered refs.
in 2 lines
Locations: MM–NN; NYP–P; MCNY;
LC–P; NYH–NY
Catalogs/Checklists: MM–NN, LP 1993;
Pyne, no. 83; Eno 232–233; Stokes, Icon.,
III, Pl. 134

2641
Place: New York, New York
Date: 1849
Title: New York from Heights above St.
George's, Staten Island.
Size: 20 × 45 in. (50.9 × 114.4 cm.)
(framed)
Artist: C. W. Burton
Lithographer: C. W. Burton
Printer:
Publisher:
Key/Vignettes/Misc:
Locations: MCNY
Catalogs/Checklists:

2642
Place: New York, New York
Date: 1849

Title: View of New York from Brooklyn
Heights.
Size: 12⅝ × 17 in. (32.2 × 43.3 cm.)
Artist: Palmer
Lithographer:
Printer: N. Currier, New York
Publisher: N. Currier, New York
Key/Vignettes/Misc: 16 unnumbered refs.
in 2 lines below places identified
Locations: MM–NN; NYH–NY;
CHS–C; MCNY
Catalogs/Checklists: MM–NN, LP 1036;
Eno 236; Peters, C& I, 3980; Pyne, no.
78; Stokes, Icon., III, Supp. List, no. 4

2643
Place: New York, New York
Date: 1849
Title: View of New York from
Weehawken–North River
Size: 14¹⁄₁₆ × 21⅝ in. (35.8 × 55.1 cm.)
Artist: Palmer
Lithographer:
Printer:
Publisher: N. Currier, 152 Nassau St.,
New York
Key/Vignettes/Misc: 25 unnumbered refs.
in 3 lines below places identified
Locations: NYP–P; MCNY; YUAG–NH;
NYH–NY
Catalogs/Checklists: Peters, C & I, 3979;
Pyne, no. 77; Eno 234

2644
Place: New York, New York
Date: 1849
Title: View of Union Park, New York from
the head of Broadway. . . .
Size: 11⅞ × 16⁵⁄₁₆ in. (30.2 × 41.5 cm.)
Artist: James Smillie
Lithographer:
Printer: Sarony & Major, New York
Publisher: Williams & Stevens, 353
Broadway, New York
Key/Vignettes/Misc:
Locations: NYP–S
Catalogs/Checklists: Stokes P. 1848—
E–135

2645
Place: New York, New York
Date: 1849 State I
Title: New–York
Size: 19¼ × 28½ in. (49 × 72.4 cm.)
Artist: C. Bachman
Lithographer: C. Bachman
Printer: Sarony & Major 117 Fulton St.
Publisher: John Bachman, 5 Rector St. N.
York
Key/Vignettes/Misc:
Locations: LC–P; MCNY
Catalogs/Checklists: Eno 237; Stokes P.
1848—E–134; Pyne, no. 82

2646
Place: New York, New York
Date: 1849 State II
Title: New–York
Size: 19¼ × 28½ in. (49 × 72.4 cm.)
Artist: C. Bachman
Lithographer: C. Bachman
Printer: Sarony & Major 117 Fulton St.,
New York

Publisher: Williams & Stevens, 353
Broadway, New York
Key/Vignettes/Misc:
Locations: NYP–S; CHS–C; YUAG–NH
Catalogs/Checklists: Stokes P. 1848—
E–134; Stokes, Icon., III, Pl. 135

2647
Place: New York, New York
Date: 1850
Title: Birds Eye View of New–York &
Brooklyn
Size: 24⅜ × 32⁷⁄₁₆ in. (62 × 82.5 cm.)
Artist: J. Bachman
Lithographer: J. Bachman
Printer: J. Bachman 218 William Street
New York
Publisher: John Bachman 218 William St.
N. York
Key/Vignettes/Misc:
Locations: NYH–NY; MCNY
Catalogs/Checklists: Pyne, no. 86; Stokes,
Icon., III, Supp. List, no. 49

2648
Place: New York, New York
Date: 1850
Title: New York General View (From
Governor's Island.)
Size: 7⅜ × 11¹⁄₁₆ in. (18.8 × 28.2 cm.)
Artist: Aug. Kollner
Lithographer: Deroy
Printer: Cattier
Publisher: Goupil & Co., New–York &
Paris
Key/Vignettes/Misc:
Locations: NYP–P; MCNY; YUAG–NH;
ROM
Catalogs/Checklists: Eno 247; Samuel, no.
424; Stokes, Icon., III, Supp. List, no. 47

2649
Place: New York, New York
Date: 1850
Title: New–York Bay and the Narrows.
Size: 7⁷⁄₁₆ × 11⅛ in. (18.9 × 28.3 cm.)
Artist: Aug. Kollner
Lithographer: Deroy
Printer: Cattier
Publisher: Goupil, Vibert & Co., New
York & Paris
Key/Vignettes/Misc:
Locations: NYP–P; MCNY; ROM
Catalogs/Checklists: Samuel, no. 421; Eno
245

2650
Place: New York, New York
Date: 1850
Title: New–York General View (from
Brooklyn)
Size: 8¹¹⁄₁₆ × 11¹¹⁄₁₆ in. (22.1 × 29.7 cm.)
Artist: Aug. Kollner
Lithographer: Deroy
Printer: Cattier
Publisher: Goupil & Co., New York &
Paris
Key/Vignettes/Misc:
Locations: NYP–P; MCNY; ROM
Catalogs/Checklists: Samuel, no. 426;
Pyne, no. 85; Stokes, Icon., III, Supp. List,
no. 48; Eno 250; Goldsmith, no. 50

2651
Place: New York, New York
Date: 1850 State III
Title: New York
Size: 19¼ × 28⅜ in. (49 × 72.2 cm.)
Artist: C. Bachman
Lithographer: C. Bachman
Printer: Sarony & Major
Publisher: Williams & Stevens
Key/Vignettes/Misc:
Locations: CHS–C
Catalogs/Checklists: Stokes P. 1848—
E–134; Goldsmith, no. 49

2652
Place: New York, New York
Date: Ca. 1850
Title: New York von der Seeseite aus
gesehen Des Auswanderers Sehnsucht
Size: 11³⁄₁₆ × 15¾ in. (28.5 × 40.1 cm.)
Artist:
Lithographer:
Printer: A. Felgner, Berlin
Publisher: A. Felgner, Berlin
Key/Vignettes/Misc:
Locations: NYH–NY
Catalogs/Checklists: Pyne, no. 92

2653
Place: New York, New York
Date: Ca. 1850
Title: New–York
Size: 8⅞ × 11⁵⁄₁₆ in. (22.6 × 28.8 cm.)
Artist:
Lithographer:
Printer:
Publisher: G. N. Renner & Co., Nurnberg
Key/Vignettes/Misc:
Locations: NYH–NY
Catalogs/Checklists: Pyne, no. 88

2654
Place: New York, New York
Date: Ca. 1850
Title: New–York. Arrivee du Paquebot
Transatlantique
Size: 12¹⁵⁄₁₆ × 19⁷⁄₁₆ in. (32.9 × 49.5 cm.)
Artist: Louis Le Breton
Lithographer: Louis Le Breton
Printer: Auguste Bry, 134, rue du Bac.
Publisher: E. Savary, Paris & Gambart,
London
Key/Vignettes/Misc:
Locations: MCNY; ROM
Catalogs/Checklists: Pyne, no. 90; Samuel,
no. 462

2655
Place: New York, New York
Date: Ca. 1850
Title: Vue Generale de New York, Prise a
Vol d'Oiseau.
Size: 16 × 22¾ in. (40.7 × 57.9 cm.)
Artist: J. Bachmann
Lithographer: Asselineau
Printer: Lemercier, rue de Seine 5, Paris
Publisher: Wild, Editeur, 36 Passage du
Saumon
Key/Vignettes/Misc:
Locations: Unknown. See Old Print Shop
Portfolio, I, p. 20, No. 14
Catalogs/Checklists:

2656
Place: New York, New York
Date: 1851
Title: Birds' Eye View of New York &
Brooklyn
Size: 22¼ × 32¾ in. (56.6 × 83.3 cm.)
Artist: J. Bachman
Lithographer: J. Bachman
Printer: Schedler & Liebler
Publisher:
Key/Vignettes/Misc: Refs. 1–12
Locations: CHS–C
Catalogs/Checklists:

2657
Place: New York, New York
Date: 1851
Title: Birds' Eye View of New–York &
Brooklyn
Size: 21⁷⁄₁₆ × 31⁵⁄₁₆ in. (54.6 × 79.7 cm.)
Artist: J. Bachman
Lithographer:
Printer: J. Bachman
Publisher: A. Guerber & Co. 160 Pearl Stt.
N. York (copyright)
Key/Vignettes/Misc: Refs. 1–12
Locations: EI–S; LC–P
Catalogs/Checklists: LC–M, 594.3

2658
Place: New York, New York
Date: 1851
Title: Birds' Eye View of New–York &
Brooklyn.
Size: 22⅛ × 32⁷⁄₁₆ in. (56.3 × 82.6 cm.)
Artist: J. Bachman
Lithographer: J. Bachman
Printer: J. Bachman
Publisher: John Bachman, 72 Beekman St.
New York
Key/Vignettes/Misc: 12 refs. in 2 cols. at
sides of title
Locations: Unknown
Catalogs/Checklists: Pyne, no. 87 (dates
1850)

2659
Place: New York, New York
Date: 1851
Title: New York
Size: 24¾ × 37⁵⁄₁₆ in. (62.8 × 94.7 cm.)
Artist: Heine, J. Kummer & Dopler
Lithographer: Himley
Printer: Goupil & Co., Paris
Publisher: W. Schaus
Key/Vignettes/Misc:
Locations: LC–P
Catalogs/Checklists: LC–M, 594.2

2660
Place: New York, New York
Date: 1851
Title: Souvenir of New York
Size: 17¼ × 21½ in. (43.9 × 54.8 cm.)
Artist: J. Bornet
Lithographer: C. Gildemeister
Printer: Nagel & Weingartner
Publisher: J. Haasis 26 Spruce St. New
York.
Key/Vignettes/Misc: 18 vignettes
Locations: NYH–NY
Catalogs/Checklists:

2661
Place: New York, New York
Date: 1851
Title: Souvenir of New York
Size: 16¹⁄₁₆ × 21⁷⁄₁₆ in. (40.8 × 54.5 cm.)
Artist: J. Bornet
Lithographer: J. Bornet
Printer: D. McLellan, 26 Spruce St., New
York
Publisher: Powell & Haasis, 115 Nassau
St., New York
Key/Vignettes/Misc:
Locations: NYP–S; CHS–C
Catalogs/Checklists: Stokes P. 1850—
G–30

2662
Place: New York, New York
Date: 1851
Title: Souvenir Of New York.
Size: 16 × 21¼ in. (40.7 × 54.1 cm.)
Artist: J. Bornet
Lithographer: J. Bornet
Printer: Nagel & Weingartner
Publisher: Frash & Haasis, 90 Fulton St.,
New York
Key/Vignettes/Misc: 18 vignettes
Locations: NYH–NY (publisher's imprint
cropped)
Catalogs/Checklists: Goldsmith, no. 52

2663
Place: New York, New York
Date: 1851
Title: View of New York From Governor's
Island
Size: 16 × 21¼ in. (40.7 × 54.1 cm.)
Artist: J. Bornet
Lithographer: C. Gildemeister
Printer: Nagel & Weingartner
Publisher: J. Haasis [copyright]
Key/Vignettes/Misc: 18 vignettes
Locations:
Catalogs/Checklists: Pyne, no. 94

2664
Place: New York, New York
Date: 1851
Title: View of New York From West
Hoboken
Size: 16 × 21¼ in. (40.7 × 54.1 cm.)
Artist: J. Bornet
Lithographer: C. Gildemeister
Printer: Nagel & Weingartner
Publisher: J. Haasis 26 Spruce St. N. Y.
Key/Vignettes/Misc:
Locations: LC–P
Catalogs/Checklists: Pyne, no. 94

2665
Place: New York, New York
Date: 1852
Title: View of Williamsburgh, L. I. from
Grand St. N. Y.
Size: 16 × 33¾ in. (40.8 × 85.8 cm.)
Artist: E. Whitefield
Lithographer:
Printer: Endicott & Co., New York
Publisher: I. Prindle, New York (copyright)
Key/Vignettes/Misc: Refs. 1–24, A–B
Locations: MM–NN; CHS–C;
NYH–NY; LIHS–B

Catalogs/Checklists: MM–NN, LP 3183; Norton, Whitefield, no.55

2666
Place: New York, New York
Date: Ca. 1852
Title: Bird's Eye View of New–York & Brooklyn.
Size: 22⅞ × 28½ in. (58.3 × 72.5 cm.)
Artist:
Lithographer: C. Matter
Printer: I. Schaerer
Publisher: J. U. Locher St Gall Switzerland [and] J. H. Locher 117 Fulton Street New–York
Key/Vignettes/Misc:
Locations: MCNY; MM–NN; NYH–NY
Catalogs/Checklists: MM–NN, LP 36

2667
Place: New York, New York
Date: Ca. 1852
Title: New–York
Size: 11⅝ × 15⁹⁄₁₆ in. (29.6 × 39.6 cm.)
Artist:
Lithographer:
Printer: A. Gocht, Neu–Gersdorf
Publisher: H. Trommer, Neu–Gersdorf
Key/Vignettes/Misc:
Locations: MCNY; NYH–NY
Catalogs/Checklists: Pyne, no. 95

2668
Place: New York, New York
Date: 1853
Title: The City of New York from Union Hill, New Jersey
Size: 20⅞ × 27⅞ in. (53.1 × 69.7 cm.)
Artist: J. Bornet
Lithographer: J. Bornet
Printer: David McLellan, 26 Spruce Street, New York
Publisher: David McLellan, 26 Spruce Street, New York
Key/Vignettes/Misc: 3 unnumbered refs. below places identified
Locations: NYH–NY
Catalogs/Checklists: Pyne, no. 96

2669
Place: New York, New York
Date: 1854
Title: Bird's–Eye View of New York City
Size: 24¼ × 35⅜ in. (61.7 × 90 cm.)
Artist: Charles Parsons
Lithographer:
Printer:
Publisher:
Key/Vignettes/Misc: [3 views on a single sheet]
Locations: BPL–R
Catalogs/Checklists:

2670
Place: New York, New York
Date: 1854
Title: Panorama of the Harbor of New York, Staten Island and the Narrows.
Size: 27⁹⁄₁₆ × 38³⁄₁₆ in. (70 × 97 cm.)
Artist: John Bornet
Lithographer: John Bornet
Printer: Nagel & Weingartner, N. Y.

Publisher: Goupil & Co. 366 Broadway, N. Y.
Key/Vignettes/Misc: Unnumbered refs.
Locations: MM–NN; MCNY; LC–P; NYH–NY
Catalogs/Checklists: MM–NN, LP 4270

2671
Place: New York, New York
Date: 1854
Title: Panorama of Manhattan Island, City of New York and Environs 1854.
Size: 24 × 36½ in. (61.1 × 92.9 cm.)
Artist: John Bornet
Lithographer: John Bornet
Printer: Nagel & Weingartner (copyright)
Publisher: Goupil & Co., 366 Broadway, New York
Key/Vignettes/Misc: 48 unnumbered refs. below and 24 refs. above places identified
Locations: NYP–P; MCNY
Catalogs/Checklists: Eno 334; Stokes, Icon., III, Supp. List, no. 56

2672
Place: New York, New York
Date: 1854 State IV
Title: New–York
Size: 18½ × 27½ in. (47.1 × 70 cm.)
Artist: C. Bachman
Lithographer: C. Bachman
Printer: Sarony and Major
Publisher: Williams & Stevens
Key/Vignettes/Misc:
Locations: Unknown. See Old Print Shop Portfolio, XVIII, p. 83, No. 13
Catalogs/Checklists:

2673
Place: New York, New York
Date: 1855
Title: City of New York
Size: 20⅞ × 29 in. (53.1 × 73.8 cm.)
Artist: C. Parsons
Lithographer: C. Parsons
Printer:
Publisher: N. Currier, New York
Key/Vignettes/Misc: 33 unnumbered refs. in 5 lines
Locations:
Catalogs/Checklists: Peters, C & I, 3982; Conningham 1102

2674
Place: New York, New York
Date: 1855
Title: New York
Size: 23¼ × 33⅞ in. (59.2 × 86.2 cm.)
Artist: J. Bachmann
Lithographer: J. Bachmann
Printer: A. Weingartner's Lithy., N. Y.
Publisher: L. W. Schmidt, 191 William St. New–York
Key/Vignettes/Misc: 9 unnumbered refs. below places identified
Locations: NYP–P
Catalogs/Checklists: Eno 335; Pyne, no. 99

2675
Place: New York, New York
Date: 1855
Title: The Empire City, Birdseye View of

New–York and Environs.
Size: 23¼ × 33⅝ in. (59.2 × 85.6 cm.)
Artist: J. Bachman
Lithographer: J. Bachman
Printer: A. Weingartner's Lithy, N. Y.
Publisher: J. Bachman, 134 Spring St & 134 Fulton St., N. Y.
Key/Vignettes/Misc:
Locations: Unknown. See Old Print Shop Portfolio, VII, pp. 156–57, No. 7
Catalogs/Checklists:

2676
Place: New York, New York
Date: Ca. 1855
Title: New–York et Brooklyn Vue Prise au Dessus de la Batterie. Nueva York y Brooklyn Vista Tomada en Cima de la Bateria
Size: 17⅞ × 24½ in. (45.6 × 62.4 cm.)
Artist: Simpson
Lithographer: Th. Muller
Printer:
Publisher:
Key/Vignettes/Misc:
Locations: MM–NN; LC–P; MCNY; CHS–C; YUAG–NH; LC–M (facsimile); NYH–NY
Catalogs/Checklists: Goldsmith, no. 51; LC–M, 594.1

2677
Place: New York, New York
Date: 1856
Title: City of New York
Size: 22¾ × 29¼ in. (57.8 × 74.3 cm.)
Artist: C. Parsons
Lithographer: C. Parsons
Printer: N. Currier, 152 Nassau Street, New York
Publisher: N. Currier, 152 Nassau Street, New York
Key/Vignettes/Misc: 33 unnumbered refs. in 5 lines
Locations: YUAG–NH; NYH–NY; LC–P; LC–M (facsimile)
Catalogs/Checklists: Peters, C & I, 3983; Conningham 1103; Pyne, no. 100; LC–M, 594.4

2678
Place: New York, New York
Date: 1856
Title: View of New York, Jersey City, Hoboken & Brooklyn—1856.
Size: 19½ × 33 in. (49.6 × 84 cm.)
Artist:
Lithographer:
Printer:
Publisher: Currier & Ives, New York
Key/Vignettes/Misc:
Locations: Unknown. See Old Print Shop Portfolio, XVIII, p. 40, No. 18
Catalogs/Checklists:

2679
Place: New York, New York
Date: 1858
Title: View of New York. Jersey City, Hoboken and Brooklyn
Size: 19¹¹⁄₁₆ × 33¼ in. (50.1 × 84.6 cm.)
Artist: C. Parsons

Lithographer: C. Parsons
Printer:
Publisher: Currier & Ives, New York
Key/Vignettes/Misc:
Locations: CHS–C (lacks title); LC–P
Catalogs/Checklists: Peters, C & I, 3984;
Conningham 6406; Pyne, no. 101;
LC–M, 594.5

2680
Place: New York, New York
Date: 1859
Title: Bird's Eye View of the City of New
York
Size: 23⅜ × 35⁹⁄₁₆ in. (59.4 × 90.4 cm.)
Artist: J. Bachmann
Lithographer: J. Bachmann
Printer:
Publisher: C. Magnus & Co. 12 Frankfort
St., New York
Key/Vignettes/Misc:
Locations: NYP–S; CSNY–S; NYH–NY
Catalogs/Checklists: Stokes P. 1858–
G–81

2681
Place: New York, New York
Date: 1859
Title: Brooklyn. Bird's Eye View of the
City of New York. Williamsburg
Size: 23½ × 35⁹⁄₁₆ in. (59.8 × 90 cm.)
Artist: J. Bachmann
Lithographer: J. Bachmann
Printer:
Publisher: C. Magnus & Co., 12 Frankfort
St., N York.
Key/Vignettes/Misc:
Locations: NYP–P; MCNY (stamped:
printed by C. Fatzer)
Catalogs/Checklists: Eno 354

2682
Place: New York, New York
Date: 1859
Title: New York City, From Weehawken.
Size: 18⅝ × 12¹⁄₁₆ in. (47.4 × 30.7 cm.)
Artist:
Lithographer:
Printer: W. Gauci, Lith—London
Publisher: E. Gembart & Co. 25, Berners
St. Oxford St. & 8, Rue De Bruxelles,
Paris.—M & N Hanhart, Impt.
Key/Vignettes/Misc:
Locations:
Catalogs/Checklists: Pyne, no. 103

2683
Place: New York, New York
Date: 1859
Title: New–York and Environs
Size: 22 in. in diameter (56 cm. in
diameter)
Artist: Bachman
Lithographer: Bachman
Printer: C. Fatzer 216 William St. N. Y.
Publisher: Bachman No. 73 Nassau St N.
Y.
Key/Vignettes/Misc: 22 refs. around print
Locations: NYP–P; MCNY
Catalogs/Checklists: Eno 352

2684
Place: New York, New York
Date: 1859
Title: View of New York
Size: 8½ × 13 in. (21.6 × 33.1 cm.)
Artist:
Lithographer:
Printer:
Publisher: Currier & Ives, 152 Nassau St.
New York
Key/Vignettes/Misc:
Locations: YUAG–NH
Catalogs/Checklists: Peters, C & I, 3985

2685
Place: New York, New York
Date: [185–?]
Title: A View of New–York And Its
Environs Taken from the Heights of West
Hoboken.
Size: 16¼ × 22½ in. (41.4 × 57.3 cm.)
Artist: Charmaille
Lithographer: Jacottet, figures by Bayot
Printer: Auguste Bry
Publisher:
Key/Vignettes/Misc:
Locations: NYP–P; NYH–NY
Catalogs/Checklists: Stokes, Icon., III,
Supp. List 40; Eno 273; Pyne, no. 71

2686
Place: New York, New York
Date: [185–?]
Title: New–York Vue Generale.
Size:
Artist: Louis le Breton
Lithographer: L. Le Breton
Printer: Aug. Bry, 142, rue du Bac
Publisher: [obliterated], et Cie. 10, Place
du Louvre, London, Gambart et Co. 25
Berners St. Oxford St.
Key/Vignettes/Misc:
Locations: NYP–P
Catalogs/Checklists: Eno 275

2687
Place: New York, New York
Date: [185–?]
Title: Vue Generale de New–York et
Brooklyn. Prise au Dessus de la Batterie.
Size:
Artist: Simpson
Lithographer: T. Muller
Printer: Lemercier, Paris
Publisher: Lemercier (Palais Royal) Galerie
d'Orleans, 19, et rue Castiglione, 14
Key/Vignettes/Misc:
Locations: NYP–P
Catalogs/Checklists: Eno 274

2688
Place: New York, New York
Date: [185–?]
Title: Vue Generale de New–York Prise a
Vol d'Oiseau
Size: 17½ × 23⅝ in. (44.5 × 60.1 cm.)
Artist: Bachmann
Lithographer: Asselineau
Printer: Lemercier, r. de Seine [Paris]
Publisher: Wild, r. de la Banque 15 Pl de la
Bourse, Paris

Key/Vignettes/Misc:
Locations: YUAG–NH
Catalogs/Checklists: Pyne, no. 93

2689
Place: New York, New York
Date: 1860
Title: Bird's Eye View of the City of New
York.
Size: 18 × 30¹¹⁄₁₆ in. (45.9 × 78.1 cm.)
Artist:
Lithographer:
Printer:
Publisher: Chas. Magnus, 12 Frankfort St.,
N. York
Key/Vignettes/Misc:
Locations: MCNY
Catalogs/Checklists:

2690
Place: New York, New York
Date: Ca. 1860
Title: New–York
Size: 9¾ × 14½ in. (24.8 × 36.9 cm.)
Artist:
Lithographer:
Printer:
Publisher: Fr. Wentzel, Wissembourg &
Paris
Key/Vignettes/Misc:
Locations: MM–NN
Catalogs/Checklists: MM–NN, LP 116

2691
Place: New York, New York
Date: 1861
Title: New–York & Environs
Size: 20¼ in. in diameter (51.6 cm. in
diameter)
Artist:
Lithographer:
Printer:
Publisher: Bachman No. 115 Nassau St.
New–York
Key/Vignettes/Misc:
Locations: NYH–NY
Catalogs/Checklists:

2692
Place: New York, New York
Date: 1865
Title: Bird's Eye View of New York and
Environs.
Size: 11½ × 15⅜ (oval) 29.3 × 39.1 cm.)
Artist: J. Bachmann
Lithographer:
Printer:
Publisher: Kummel & Forster, N Y
Key/Vignettes/Misc:
Locations: LC–M; MCNY
Catalogs/Checklists: LC–M, 594.6

2693
Place: New York, New York
Date: 1865
Title: Birds Eye View of New York and
Environs
Size: 12⅝ × 18 in. (32.1 × 45.8 cm.)
Artist: John Bachmann
Lithographer:
Printer:

Publisher: John Bachmann, 76 Nassau Street New York
Key/Vignettes/Misc:
Locations: NYH–NY
Catalogs/Checklists:

2694
Place: New York, New York
Date: 1865
Title: Birds Eye View of New–York & Environs
Size: 21¾ (cropped) × 32¼ in. (55.4 × 82.1 cm.)
Artist:
Lithographer:
Printer:
Publisher: Charles Magnus 12 Frankfort Street N. Y.
Key/Vignettes/Misc:
Locations: NYH–NY
Catalogs/Checklists:

2695
Place: New York, New York
Date: 1865
Title: Central Park.
Size: 13¾ × 19½ in. (35 × 49.6 cm.)
Artist: John Bachmann
Lithographer:
Printer: J. Bien, Lith [New York]
Publisher: John Bachmann (copyright)
Key/Vignettes/Misc:
Locations: NYH–NY
Catalogs/Checklists:

2696
Place: New York, New York
Date: 1866 State I
Title: Panorama of New York and Vicinity
Size: 22¼ × 35¹³⁄₁₆ in. (56.6 × 91 cm.)
Artist: John Bachmann
Lithographer:
Printer: J. Bien
Publisher: John Bachmann, 76 Nassau St. N. Y.
Key/Vignettes/Misc:
Locations: NYP–P; CHS–C
Catalogs/Checklists: Eno 382

2697
Place: New York, New York
Date: 1866 State II
Title: Panorama of New York and Vicinity
Size: 22¼ × 35¹³⁄₁₆ in. (56.6 × 91 cm.)
Artist: John Bachmann
Lithographer:
Printer: J. Bien
Publisher: John Bachmann, Nassau St., N. Y.
Key/Vignettes/Misc:
Locations: NYP–S
Catalogs/Checklists: Stokes P. 1865—G–83

2698
Place: New York, New York
Date: 1868
Title: New York and Environs, und Umebung
Size: 16⅞ × 22 in. (42.9 × 56 cm.)
Artist:
Lithographer:

Printer: Deutz Bros. 197 William St. N. Y.
Publisher: George Degen, 51 Chatam St., New York
Key/Vignettes/Misc: Refs. 1–14
Locations: CHS–C; MCNY; NYH–NY
Catalogs/Checklists:

2699
Place: New York, New York
Date: 1868
Title: Panorama of New York and Vicinity
Size: 24¾ × 36 in. (63 × 91.6 cm.)
Artist: J. Bachman
Lithographer: J. Bachman
Printer: P. S. Duval Son & Co. Philada.
Publisher: John Weik 607 Sansom Str. Phila
Key/Vignettes/Misc: Advertisements
Locations: NYH–NY (untitled); CHS–C
Catalogs/Checklists:

2700
Place: New York, New York
Date: Ca. 1868
Title: New York and Environs. New York und Umgegend.
Size: 9¹³⁄₁₆ × 14¹⁵⁄₁₆ in. (25 × 38 cm.)
Artist: Harnisch
Lithographer:
Printer:
Publisher:
Key/Vignettes/Misc:
Locations: MCNY
Catalogs/Checklists:

2701
Place: New York, New York
Date: Ca. 1868
Title: View of New York, Jersey City, Hoboken & Brooklyn
Size: 22⅛ × 33¹⁄₁₆ in. (56.3 × 84.2 cm.)
Artist: C. Parsons
Lithographer: C. Parsons
Printer:
Publisher: Currier and Ives, New York
Key/Vignettes/Misc:
Locations: LC–P
Catalogs/Checklists:

2702
Place: New York, New York
Date: 1869
Title: View of New York
Size: 9 × 12⅞ in. (22.9 × 32.8 cm.)
Artist:
Lithographer:
Printer:
Publisher: Currier & Ives, New York
Key/Vignettes/Misc:
Locations: MCNY
Catalogs/Checklists: Peters, C & I, 3986

2703
Place: New York, New York
Date: [186–?]
Title: New York
Size:
Artist:
Lithographer:
Printer: J. H. Bufford & Sons Lith. Boston, Mass.
Publisher:

Key/Vignettes/Misc:
Locations: NYP–P
Catalogs/Checklists: Eno 361

2704
Place: New York, New York
Date: 1870
Title: The City of New York
Size:
Artist:
Lithographer:
Printer:
Publisher: Currier & Ives, 125 Nassau St.
Key/Vignettes/Misc: Refs. in 5 lines
Locations: NYP–P
Catalogs/Checklists: Eno 398

2705
Place: New York, New York
Date: 1870
Title: The City of New York
Size: 20³⁄₁₆ × 32¹³⁄₁₆ in. (51.4 × 83.4 cm.)
Artist:
Lithographer:
Printer:
Publisher: Currier & Ives, New York
Key/Vignettes/Misc: 46 refs. in 6 lines
Locations: LC–M
Catalogs/Checklists: LC–M, 595; Peters, C & I, 3988; Conningham 1104 [48 refs.]

2706
Place: New York, New York
Date: 1870
Title: The City of New York
Size: 20⁵⁄₁₆ × 32¹³⁄₁₆ in. (51.7 × 83.4 cm.)
Artist:
Lithographer:
Printer:
Publisher: Currier & Ives, New York
Key/Vignettes/Misc: 40 unnumbered refs. in 6 lines below places identified
Locations:
Catalogs/Checklists: Conningham 1105; Peters, C & I, 3989

2707
Place: New York, New York
Date: 1870
Title: View of New York and Environs
Size: 13 × 26 in. (33.1 × 66.2 cm.)
Artist: [J. Bachmann?]
Lithographer:
Printer:
Publisher: L. W. Schmidt
Key/Vignettes/Misc:
Locations: MCNY
Catalogs/Checklists:

2708
Place: New York, New York
Date: Ca. 1870
Title: City of New York
Size: 20¼ × 28½ in. (51.6 × 72.5 cm.)
Artist: C. Parsons
Lithographer:
Printer:
Publisher:
Key/Vignettes/Misc:
Locations: Unknown. See Old Print Shop Portfolio, XXVI, p. 51, No. 5
Catalogs/Checklists:

2709

Place: New York, New York
Date: Ca. 1870
Title: Vue Generale de New—York Vista General de New—York
Size: 14⅝ × 19⅜ in. (37.2 × 49.3 cm.)
Artist:
Lithographer:
Printer: L. Turgis Jne. r. des Ecoles 60 [Paris]
Publisher: L. Turgis Jne. r. des Ecoles 60 [Paris] and Park Place, 46, New York
Key/Vignettes/Misc:
Locations: YUAG—NH
Catalogs/Checklists: Goldsmith, no. 57; Pyne, no. 107

2710

Place: New York, New York
Date: 1872
Title: The Great East River Bridge. To Connect the Cities of New York & Brooklyn
Size: 8½ × 12⅜ in. (21.7 × 31.5 cm.)
Artist:
Lithographer:
Printer:
Publisher: Currier & Ives, 125 Nassau St. New York
Key/Vignettes/Misc: 6 lines of description on each side of title
Locations: NYP—P; MCNY; YUAG—NH
Catalogs/Checklists: Eno 408

2711

Place: New York, New York
Date: 1872
Title: The Port of New York, Bird's—Eye View from the Battery, Looking South.
Size: 20⅜ × 32¹⁵⁄₁₆ in. (51.8 × 83.8 cm.)
Artist: Parsons & Atwater
Lithographer:
Printer:
Publisher: Currier & Ives, 125 Nassau St. New York
Key/Vignettes/Misc: 52 unnumbered refs. in 6 lines below places identified
Locations: NYP—P
Catalogs/Checklists: Peters, C & I, 4010; Conningham 4847; Emo, 49 (48 refs.)

2712

Place: New York, New York
Date: 1873
Title: New York
Size: 17 × 24 in. (43.2 × 61.1 cm.)
Artist:
Lithographer:
Printer: G. Schlegel, N. Y.
Publisher: Geo. Degen, N. Y.
Key/Vignettes/Misc:
Locations: LC—P
Catalogs/Checklists: LC—M, 595.2

2713

Place: New York, New York
Date: 1873
Title: New York
Size: 16¾ × 23¾ in. (42.6 × 60.4 cm.)
Artist:
Lithographer:

Printer: G. Schlegel, 97 William St., N. Y.
Publisher: Geo. Degen, 22 Beckman St., N. Y.
Key/Vignettes/Misc:
Locations: LC—P
Catalogs/Checklists: LC—M, 595.2

2714

Place: New York, New York
Date: 1874
Title: New York
Size: 21¹³⁄₁₆ × 31¹¹⁄₁₆ in. (55.4 × 80.5 cm.)
Artist: J. Bachmann
Lithographer:
Printer: G. Schlegel, 97 William St., N. Y.
Publisher:
Key/Vignettes/Misc:
Locations: LC—P
Catalogs/Checklists: LC—M, 595.3

2715

Place: New York, New York
Date: 1874
Title: New York
Size: 21¹³⁄₁₆ × 31¾ in. (55.5 × 80.7 cm.)
Artist:
Lithographer:
Printer: G. Schlegel, 97 William St., N. Y.
Publisher: Tamsen, No. 52 Ave. A, N. Y.
Key/Vignettes/Misc:
Locations: LC—P
Catalogs/Checklists: LC—M, 595.4

2716

Place: New York, New York
Date: 1874
Title: New York Taken from Central Park
Size: 17 (matted) × 23½ in. (43.3 × 59.8 cm.)
Artist:
Lithographer:
Printer: G. Schlegel, 97 William St. N. Y.
Publisher: Geo. Degen, 22 Beekman St. N. Y.
Key/Vignettes/Misc:
Locations: NYH—NY
Catalogs/Checklists:

2717

Place: New York, New York
Date: 1874
Title: New York, Taken From Battery Place.
Size: 15⅛ × 23¾ in. (38.5 × 60.4 cm.)
Artist:
Lithographer:
Printer: G. Schlegel, 97 William St., N. Y.
Publisher: Geo. Degen, 22 Beekman St. N. Y.
Key/Vignettes/Misc:
Locations: Unknown. See Old Print Shop Portfolio, XXXV, p. 54, No. 9
Catalogs/Checklists: Pyne 108

2718

Place: New York, New York
Date: 1874
Title: The Great East River Suspension Bridge Connecting the Cities of New York and Brooklyn.
Size: 20⁷⁄₁₆ × 32¹³⁄₁₆ in. (52 × 83.4 cm.)
Artist: Parsons & Atwater

Lithographer:
Printer:
Publisher: Currier & Ives, New York
Key/Vignettes/Misc:
Locations:
Catalogs/Checklists: Peters, C & I, 4020; Conningham 2592

2719

Place: New York, New York
Date: 1875
Title: City of New York and Environs
Size: 9½ × 13⅛ in. (24.2 × 33.4 cm.)
Artist:
Lithographer:
Printer:
Publisher: Currier & Ives, 115 Nassau, New York
Key/Vignettes/Misc: 10 unnumbered refs. in 2 lines below places identified
Locations: CHS—C; MM—NN; MCNY; YUAG—NH; NYH—NY
Catalogs/Checklists: MM—NN, LP 29; Peters, C & I, 3990

2720

Place: New York, New York
Date: 1875
Title: New York and Brooklyn.
Size: 22¹⁵⁄₁₆ × 32¹³⁄₁₆ in. (58.3 × 83.3 cm.)
Artist: Parsons & Atwater
Lithographer: Parsons & Atwater
Printer:
Publisher: Currier & Ives 125 Nassau St. New York
Key/Vignettes/Misc: 103 refs. in 7 lines below places identified
Locations: LC—M; LC—P
Catalogs/Checklists: LC—M, 596; Conningham, 4433; Peters, C & I, 3991

2721

Place: New York, New York
Date: 1876
Title: The City of New York
Size: 23⁵⁄₁₆ × 33½ in. (59.2 × 85.2 cm.)
Artist: Parsons & Atwater
Lithographer: Parsons & Atwater
Printer:
Publisher: Currier & Ives, New York
Key/Vignettes/Misc: 76 unnumbered refs. below places identified
Locations: NYH—NY; CHS—C; LC—M (facsimile); LC—P
Catalogs/Checklists: LC—M, 597; Conningham 1107

2722

Place: New York, New York
Date: 1876
Title: The City of New York Showing the Building of Equitable Life Assurance Society of the United States. No. 120 Broadway.
Size: 21½ × 33¾ in. (54.7 × 85.8 cm.)
Artist:
Lithographer:
Printer:
Publisher: Currier & Ives, New York
Key/Vignettes/Misc:
Locations: MCNY; YUAG—NH

Catalogs/Checklists: Peters, C & I, 3992; Conningham 1113

2723
Place: New York, New York
Date: 1876
Title: The City of New York, Showing the Building of the Equitable Life Assurance Society of the United States, No. 120 Broadway
Size: 22¼ × 35¹⁄₁₆ in. (56.6 × 89.3 cm.)
Artist:
Lithographer:
Printer:
Publisher: Currier & Ives, New York
Key/Vignettes/Misc:
Locations: Unknown
Catalogs/Checklists: Conningham 1114

2724
Place: New York, New York
Date: 1876
Title: Vista de la Ciudad de New York Mostrando el Edificiode la Equitiva. . .Broadway 120.
Size: 21 × 33½ in. (53.4 × 85.2 cm.)
Artist:
Lithographer:
Printer:
Publisher: Currier & Ives, New York
Key/Vignettes/Misc:
Locations: Unknown. See Old Print Shop Portfolio, XXIII, p. 40, No. 21
Catalogs/Checklists: variation of Conningham, 1113

2725
Place: New York, New York
Date: Ca. 1876
Title: 1776–1876. New York, City of New York
Size: 7¹⁵⁄₁₆ × 10 in. (20.2 × 25.5 cm.)
Artist: W. Brotherhead
Lithographer:
Printer: H. J. Toudy & Co. Steam Lith. Philadelphia
Publisher:
Key/Vignettes/Misc:
Locations: MM–NN; MCNY; LC–P
Catalogs/Checklists: MM–NN, LP 874

2726
Place: New York, New York
Date: 1877
Title: New York and Brooklyn, with Jersey City and Hoboken Water Front.
Size: 23⁵⁄₁₆ × 32¾ in. (59.4 × 83.4 cm.)
Artist: Parsons & Atwater
Lithographer: Parsons & Atwater
Printer:
Publisher: Currier & Ives 125 Nassau New York
Key/Vignettes/Misc: 100 unnumbered refs. in 7 lines below places identified
Locations: LC–M; LC–P
Catalogs/Checklists: LC–M, 598; Peters, C & I, 3993; Conningham 4434

2727
Place: New York, New York
Date: 1877
Title: The City of New–York. View from Fort Green, Brooklyn.
Size: 17 × 25 in. (43.3 × 63.6 cm.)
Artist:
Lithographer:
Printer: Charles Magnus, 550 Pearl Street, N. Y.
Publisher: Charles Magnus, 550 Pearl Street, N. Y.
Key/Vignettes/Misc: 11 refs. in 3 lines
Locations: MCNY; NYH–NY
Catalogs/Checklists:

2728
Place: New York, New York
Date: 1877
Title: The Great East River Suspension Bridge Connecting the Cities of New York and Brooklyn—From New York, Looking South–East
Size: 20⁵⁄₈ × 33¹⁄₁₆ in. (52.5 × 84.1 cm.)
Artist: Parsons & Atwater
Lithographer:
Printer:
Publisher: Currier & Ives, New York
Key/Vignettes/Misc:
Locations:
Catalogs/Checklists: Peters, C & I, 4021; Conningham 2593

2729
Place: New York, New York
Date: 1877
Title: View of New–York
Size: 20 × 29½ in. (50.8 × 75 cm.)
Artist: John Bachmann
Lithographer:
Printer: H. Bencke Lith., 207 Fulton St, N. Y.
Publisher: John Bachmann (copyright)
Key/Vignettes/Misc:
Locations: NYH–NY
Catalogs/Checklists:

2730
Place: New York, New York
Date: 1878
Title: The Port of New York Bird's–Eye View from the Battery, Looking South
Size: 20⁵⁄₈ × 33¼ in. (52.5 × 84.6 cm.)
Artist: Parsons and Atwater
Lithographer:
Printer:
Publisher: Currier & Ives, New York
Key/Vignettes/Misc: 55 unnumbered refs. in 6 lines below places identified
Locations: CHS–C; MCNY
Catalogs/Checklists: Peters, C & I, 4011; Conningham 4848

2731
Place: New York, New York
Date: 1878
Title: View of New York and Vicinity 1878.
Size: 22¼ × 30½ in. (56.7 × 77.6 cm.)
Artist: John Bachmann
Lithographer:
Printer:
Publisher: H. Bencke
Key/Vignettes/Misc:
Locations: MCNY
Catalogs/Checklists:

2732
Place: New York, New York
Date: 1879
Title: New York
Size: 24 × 17⅛ in. (61.1 × 43.5 cm.)
Artist: J. W. Williams
Lithographer:
Printer:
Publisher: Rogers, Peet & Co., . . .New York
Key/Vignettes/Misc: 25 refs. keyed to marginal numbers
Locations: NYH–NY
Catalogs/Checklists:

2733
Place: New York, New York
Date: 1879
Title: New York
Size: 24 × 17⅛ in. (61.1 × 43.5 cm.)
Artist: J. W. Williams
Lithographer:
Printer:
Publisher: Root & Tinker, New York
Key/Vignettes/Misc: 25 refs. keyed to marginal numbers and letters
Locations: LC–M
Catalogs/Checklists: LC–M, 600

2734
Place: New York, New York
Date: 1879
Title: New York A Birdseye View Showing Manhattan and the Rogers Peet & Co.'s Building, the Exact Center of the Clothing Trade in New York City
Size: 16 × 23¼ in. (40.7 × 59.2 cm.)
Artist:
Lithographer:
Printer:
Publisher: Currier & Ives
Key/Vignettes/Misc: 18 refs.
Locations: Unknown
Catalogs/Checklists: Schurre, Currier & Ives Prints, no. 143

2735
Place: New York, New York
Date: 1879
Title: New York, New York
Size: 13³⁄₁₆ × 26⅛ in. (33.5 × 66.4 cm.)
Artist: J. Bachmann
Lithographer: J. Bachmann
Printer:
Publisher: J. Bachmann
Key/Vignettes/Misc:
Locations: LC–P
Catalogs/Checklists:

2736
Place: New York, New York
Date: 1879
Title: The City of New York
Size: 73⅞ × 39⅝ in. (188 × 100.7 cm.)
Artist: Will L. Taylor
Lithographer:
Printer:
Publisher: Galt & Hoy111 Liberty St. New York
Key/Vignettes/Misc: 19 vignettes; numbered and unnumbered business

directory; 1 map; 7 advertisements
Locations: LC–M
Catalogs/Checklists: LC–M, 599

2737

Place: New York, New York
Date: 1879
Title: View of New–York. and Vicinity.
Size: 17⅜ × 26³⁄₁₆ in. (44.2 × 66.7 cm.)
Artist: John Bachmann
Lithographer:
Printer:
Publisher: J. Bachmann (copyright) H.
Bencke, 207 Fulton St. (copyright)
Key/Vignettes/Misc:
Locations: MCNY
Catalogs/Checklists:

2738

Place: New York, New York
Date: Ca. 1879
Title: The City of New York
Size: 9⅞ × 7½ in. (25.1 × 19.1 cm.)
Artist: J. W. Williams
Lithographer:
Printer:
Publisher: The Cottager Editors,
Baldwinville, Mass.
Key/Vignettes/Misc: 24 refs. identified by
marginal letters and numbers
Locations: LC–M
Catalogs/Checklists: LC–M, 601

2739

Place: New York, New York
Date: 1880
Title: New York (A Birds Eye View from
the Harbor)
Size: 18⅞ × 23⅜ in. (48 × 59.5 cm.)
Artist:
Lithographer:
Printer:
Publisher: Rogers, Peet & Co., Broadway,
Broome & Meree Stss., N. Y.
Key/Vignettes/Misc:
Locations: LC–P
Catalogs/Checklists:

2740

Place: New York, New York
Date: 1880
Title: New York.
Size: 20⁵⁄₁₆ × 31⅞ in. (51.7 × 81.1 cm.)
Artist:
Lithographer:
Printer: G. Schlegel, & Son, 75 & 77
Duane St. N. Y.
Publisher: J. H. Tamsen, No. 52 Ave A, N.
Y.
Key/Vignettes/Misc:
Locations: MCNY
Catalogs/Checklists:

2741

Place: New York, New York
Date: 1880
Title: New York. A Birdseye View from
the Harbor.
Size: 18⅞ × 23⅜ in. (48 × 59.5 cm.)
Artist:
Lithographer:
Printer:

Publisher: Rogers, Peet & Co., Broadway,
Broome & Mereer Streets N.Y.
Key/Vignettes/Misc: Refs. A–P
Locations: LC–P
Catalogs/Checklists:

2742

Place: New York, New York
Date: 1881
Title: The Great East River Suspension
Bridge. Connecting the Cities of New York
and Brooklyn.
Size: 10½ × 12⅞ in. (26.7 × 32.8 cm.)
Artist:
Lithographer:
Printer:
Publisher: Currier & Ives 115 Nassau St.
New York
Key/Vignettes/Misc: Description
Locations: MCNY
Catalogs/Checklists: Peters, C & I, 4023

2743

Place: New York, New York
Date: 1881
Title: The Great East River Suspension
Bridge. Connecting the Cities of New York
and Brooklyn. View from Brooklyn
Looking West
Size:
Artist:
Lithographer:
Printer:
Publisher: Currier & Ives, New York
Key/Vignettes/Misc:
Locations: MCNY
Catalogs/Checklists: Peters, C & I, 4025a

2744

Place: New York, New York
Date: 1883
Title: Bird's–Eye View of the Great
Suspension Bridge, Connecting the
Cities—of New York and Brooklyn—from
New York Looking South–East.
Size: 18 × 36½ in. (45.8 × 92.8 cm.)
Artist:
Lithographer:
Printer: The Franklin Square Lithographic
Co., New York
Publisher: A. Major, New York, 1883
Key/Vignettes/Misc:
Locations: MM–NN; CHS–C; SAM–M
Catalogs/Checklists: MM–NN, LP 3586

2745

Place: New York, New York
Date: 1883
Title: Bird's–Eye View of the Great
Suspension Bridge, Connecting the Cities
of New York and Booklyn, from New
York Looking South–East
Size: 18 × 36 in. (45.8 × 91.6 cm.)
Artist:
Lithographer:
Printer:
Publisher: Currier & Ives, New York
Key/Vignettes/Misc:
Locations: Unknown. See Old Print Shop
Portfolio, XXV, p. 41, No. 30
Catalogs/Checklists:

2746

Place: New York, New York
Date: 1883
Title: Bird's–Eye View of the Great
Suspension Bridge, Connecting the Cities
of New York and Brooklyn.
Size: 20 × 26¾ in. (50.9 × 68.1 cm.)
Artist:
Lithographer:
Printer:
Publisher: Currier & Ives, New York
Key/Vignettes/Misc:
Locations:
Catalogs/Checklists: Conningham 2596

2747

Place: New York, New York
Date: 1883
Title: Birds–Eye View of the Great
Suspension Bridge Connecting the Cities of
New York and Brooklyn From New York
Looking South East
Size: 20⅝ × 36 in. (52.5 × 91.6 cm.)
Artist:
Lithographer:
Printer:
Publisher: The Judge Publishing Co of N.
Y. 324–28 Pearl Street
Key/Vignettes/Misc: Description
Locations: BM–NY
Catalogs/Checklists:

2748

Place: New York, New York
Date: 1883
Title: The City of New York—Showing
the Building of the Equitable Life
Assurance Society of the U. S.
Size: 23½ × 33⅝ in. (59.7 × 85.6 cm.)
Artist:
Lithographer:
Printer:
Publisher: Currier & Ives [New York]
Key/Vignettes/Misc:
Locations: LC–P
Catalogs/Checklists:

2749

Place: New York, New York
Date: 1883
Title: The Great East River Suspension
Bridge Connecting the Cities of New York
and Brooklyn. View From Brooklyn,
Looking West.
Size: 18⁵⁄₁₆ × 32¹⁵⁄₁₆ in. (46.6 × 83.8 cm.)
Artist:
Lithographer:
Printer:
Publisher: Currier & Ives, New York
Key/Vignettes/Misc:
Locations: MCNY
Catalogs/Checklists: Peters, C & I, 4025;
Conningham 2597

2750

Place: New York, New York
Date: Ca. 1883
Title: Bird's–eye view of the great New
York and Brooklyn Bridge.
Size: 15¼ × 24³⁄₁₆ in. (38.8 × 61.5 cm.)
Artist:

Lithographer:
Printer:
Publisher: Major, New York
Key/Vignettes/Misc:
Locations: MM–NN
Catalogs/Checklists: MM–NN, LP 700

2751
Place: New York, New York
Date: Ca. 1883
Title: The Great East River Bridge with entrance from the New York side.
Size: 18⁹⁄₁₆ × 23⁹⁄₁₆ in. . (47.2 × 59.9 cm.)
Artist: R. Schwarz
Lithographer: Shugg Bros.
Printer: Burrow–Giles Litho. Co., New York
Publisher: Shugg Bros., New York
Key/Vignettes/Misc:
Locations: MM–NN
Catalogs/Checklists: MM–NN, LE 244

2752
Place: New York, New York
Date: 1884
Title: The City of New York
Size: 24½ × 35⅛ in. (62.4 × 89.3 cm.)
Artist:
Lithographer:
Printer:
Publisher: Currier & Ives, New York
Key/Vignettes/Misc: 58 unnumbered refs. in 6 lines below places identified
Locations: LC–M; CHS–C; LC–P
Catalogs/Checklists: LC–M, 602; Peters, C & I, 3994; Conningham 1106

2753
Place: New York, New York
Date: 1885
Title: Grand Birds Eye View of the Great East River Suspension Bridge. Connecting the Cities of New York & Brooklyn. . . .
Size: 21³⁄₁₆ × 34³⁄₁₆ in. (54 × 87 cm.)
Artist:
Lithographer:
Printer:
Publisher: Currier & Ives, New York
Key/Vignettes/Misc: 12 unnumbered refs. below places identified
Locations: LC–M; NYH–NY
Catalogs/Checklists: Conningham 2599

2754
Place: New York, New York
Date: 1885
Title: New York
Size: 12⅞ × 18¹⁵⁄₁₆ in. (32.8 × 48.2 cm.)
Artist:
Lithographer:
Printer:
Publisher: Charles Magnus (copyright)
Key/Vignettes/Misc:
Locations: LC–P
Catalogs/Checklists:

2755
Place: New York, New York
Date: 1885
Title: View of New York
Size: 18½ × 32 in. (47.1 × 81.4 cm.)
Artist: J. Bachmann

Lithographer:
Printer:
Publisher: J. Bachmann
Key/Vignettes/Misc:
Locations: Unknown. See Old Print Shop Portfolio, I, No. 10, p. 23, unnumbered
Catalogs/Checklists:

2756
Place: New York, New York
Date: Ca. 1885
Title: View of New York and Vicinity
Size: 17⅜ × 26½ in. (44.2 × 66.5 cm.)
Artist: John Bachmann
Lithographer:
Printer:
Publisher: H. Bencke, 207 Fulton St. N. Y.
Key/Vignettes/Misc:
Locations: MCNY; NYH–NY
Catalogs/Checklists:

2757
Place: New York, New York
Date: 1886
Title: The City of New York
Size: 21³⁄₁₆ × 33¾ in. (54 × 86 cm.)
Artist: Parsons & Atwater
Lithographer:
Printer:
Publisher: Currier & Ives, New York
Key/Vignettes/Misc:
Locations: LC–M
Catalogs/Checklists: LC–M, 603; Conningham 1108

2758
Place: New York, New York
Date: 1886
Title: The Great East River Suspension Bridge Connecting the Cities of New York and Brooklyn. View from Brooklyn, looking west.
Size: 18⅞ × 33 in. (48 × 83.9 cm.)
Artist:
Lithographer:
Printer:
Publisher: Currier & Ives, New York, 1886
Key/Vignettes/Misc: Description
Locations: MM–NN; NYH–NY
Catalogs/Checklists: MM–NN, LP 2619; Peters, C & I, 4028; Conningham 2500

2759
Place: New York, New York
Date: 1889
Title: The City of New York
Size: 21³⁄₁₆ × 33¾ in. (54 × 86 cm.)
Artist: Parsons & Atwater
Lithographer:
Printer:
Publisher: Currier & Ives, New York
Key/Vignettes/Misc: 75 unnumbered refs. below places identified
Locations: LC–M; NYSM–A
Catalogs/Checklists: LC–M, 604; Conningham 1109

2760
Place: New York, New York
Date: 1890
Title: The Great East River Suspension

Bridge Connecting the Cities of New York and Brooklyn, From New York Looking South Bird's Eye View. . . .
Size: 18³⁄₁₆ × 25¼ in. (46.3 × 64.3 cm.)
Artist:
Lithographer:
Printer:
Publisher: Currier & Ives, New York
Key/Vignettes/Misc:
Locations: Unknown. See Old Print Shop Portfolio, XXV, p. 41, No. 29
Catalogs/Checklists: Conningham 2601

2761
Place: New York, New York
Date: Ca. 1891
Title: Gracie Emmett in her Great Play the Pulse of New York
Size: 40⅛ × 23⅛ in. (102 × 59 cm.)
Artist: Howard P. Taylor
Lithographer:
Printer: Courier Lith. Co., Buffalo, N. Y.
Publisher:
Key/Vignettes/Misc:
Locations: LC–M
Catalogs/Checklists: LC–M, 605

2762
Place: New York, New York
Date: 1892
Title: New York and Brooklyn, with Jersey City and Hoboken Water Front.
Size: 20¹³⁄₁₆ × 33 in. (53 × 84 cm.)
Artist: Parsons & Atwater
Lithographer:
Printer:
Publisher: Currier and Ives, New York
Key/Vignettes/Misc:
Locations: LC–M
Catalogs/Checklists: LC–M, 607

2763
Place: New York, New York
Date: 1892
Title: The City of New York
Size: 22⅜ × 34¹⁵⁄₁₆ in. (57 × 89 cm.)
Artist:
Lithographer:
Printer:
Publisher: Currier & Ives, New York
Key/Vignettes/Misc:
Locations: LC–M
Catalogs/Checklists: LC–M, 606; Conningham 1110

2764
Place: New York, New York
Date: 1892
Title: The Great East River Bridge. To Connect the Cities of New York & Brooklyn
Size: 8½ × 12⅜ in. (21.7 × 31.5 cm.)
Artist:
Lithographer:
Printer:
Publisher: Currier & Ives, 125 Nassau St. New York
Key/Vignettes/Misc: 6 lines of description on each side of title
Locations: NYP–P; MCNY; YUAG–NH
Catalogs/Checklists: Eno 408

2765

Place: New York, New York
Date: 1892
Title: The Great East River Suspension Bridge. Connecting the Cities of New York & Brooklyn—From New York Looking South—East.
Size: 23⁵/₁₆ × 32¹³/₁₆ in. (59.3 × 83.5 cm.)
Artist:
Lithographer:
Printer:
Publisher: Currier & Ives, 115 Nassau St. New York
Key/Vignettes/Misc: 2 refs. below places identified; description; list of bridge officials & engineers
Locations: MM–NN; NJHS–N
Catalogs/Checklists: Conningham 2602; MM–NN, LP 2378

2766

Place: New York, New York
Date: 1892
Title: The Port of New York Bird's–Eye View From The Battery, Looking South
Size: 20⁵/₈ × 33¼ in. (52.5 × 84.6 cm.)
Artist:
Lithographer:
Printer:
Publisher: Currier & Ives, New York
Key/Vignettes/Misc: 57 unnumbered refs. in 6 lines below places identified
Locations: MM–NN; NYSM–A
Catalogs/Checklists: MM–NN, LP 31; Peters, C & I, 4013; Conningham 4849

2767

Place: New York, New York
Date: 1892
Title: The Port of New York, Bird's Eye View From the Battery, Looking South.
Size:
Artist: Parsons & Atwater
Lithographer:
Printer:
Publisher: Currier & Ives, 125 Nassau St. [New York]
Key/Vignettes/Misc: 48 unnumbered refs. below places identified
Locations: NYP–P
Catalogs/Checklists: Eno 409

2768

Place: New York, New York
Date: 1896
Title: The Sky Line of New York
Size:
Artist: Chas. Graham
Lithographer:
Printer: G. H. Buek & Co. N. Y. Lith
Publisher: New York Journal
Key/Vignettes/Misc:
Locations: NYP–P
Catalogs/Checklists: Eno 442

2769

Place: New York, New York
Date: 1897
Title: Birds Eye View of that Portion of the 23rd and 24th Wards of the City of New York, Lying Westerly of the New York and Harlem Railroad, and of the Grand Boulevard. . . .

Size: 16⁷/₈ × 70¾ in. (43 × 180 cm.)
Artist: Wm. W. Klein
Lithographer:
Printer: Robert A. Welcke, photo–lith
Publisher: Dept. of Street Improvements, New York
Key/Vignettes/Misc:
Locations: LC–M
Catalogs/Checklists:

2770

Place: New York, New York
Date: 1897
Title: Greater New York
Size: 24½ × 37⁵/₁₆ in. (62.3 × 94.9 cm.)
Artist:
Lithographer:
Printer: Charles Hart Lith., 36 Vesey St. N. Y.
Publisher: E. M. Parsons, 36 Vesey St. N. Y.
Key/Vignettes/Misc: 41 refs. on 5 lines below places identified
Locations: NYH–NY
Catalogs/Checklists:

2771

Place: New York, New York
Date: [1899–1900?]
Title: [Manhattan]
Size: 87 × 42 in. (221.3 × 106.8 cm.)
Artist:
Lithographer:
Printer:
Publisher:
Key/Vignettes/Misc:
Locations: LC–M
Catalogs/Checklists: LC–M, 584.1

2772

Place: New York, New York
Date: 1903
Title: New York and Brooklyn Bridge
Size: 21½ × 37 in. (54.6 × 94.1 cm.)
Artist:
Lithographer:
Printer:
Publisher: Joseph Koehler, New York
Key/Vignettes/Misc:
Locations: MM–NN
Catalogs/Checklists: MM–NN, LP 3559

2773

Place: New York, New York
Date: 1905
Title: The City of Greater New York
Size: 25⁷/₁₆ × 37⁵/₁₆ in. (64.8 × 94.9 cm.)
Artist:
Lithographer:
Printer: Charles Hart, 36 Vesey St., N. Y.
Publisher: Joseph Koehler, 150 Park Row, N. Y.
Key/Vignettes/Misc: Unnumbered refs.
Locations: NYSM–A; LC–P; MM–NN
Catalogs/Checklists: MM–NN, LP 4171; LC–M, 584.2

2774

Place: New York, New York
Date: 1907
Title: View of the City of New York and Vicinity
Size: 26⁷/₁₆ × 38¹⁵/₁₆ in. (67.3 × 99 cm.)

Artist:
Lithographer:
Printer:
Publisher: August R. Ohman & Co. 97–101 Warren Street, N. Y.
Key/Vignettes/Misc:
Locations: MCNY; LC–M
Catalogs/Checklists: LC–M, 607.1

2775

Place: New York, New York
Date: 1911
Title: View of New York
Size: 20 × 31 in. (50.9 × 78.8 cm.)
Artist: Richard Rummell
Lithographer:
Printer:
Publisher: Detroit Publishing Co. (copyright)
Key/Vignettes/Misc:
Locations: MCNY
Catalogs/Checklists:

2776

Place: New York, New York
Date: 1912
Title:
Size: 16¹⁵/₁₆ × 27½ in. (43 × 70 cm.)
Artist: Jacob Ruppert
Lithographer:
Printer: U. S. Printing & Lithographing Co., New York
Publisher:
Key/Vignettes/Misc:
Locations: WHS–M
Catalogs/Checklists:

2777

Place: New York, New York
Date: 1916
Title: New York and Brooklyn Bridge.
Size: 15½ × 23 in. (39.5 × 58.6 cm.)
Artist:
Lithographer:
Printer: Chas. Hart, N. Y.
Publisher: Joseph Koehler, Inc., N. Y.
Key/Vignettes/Misc:
Locations: Unknown. See Old Print Gallery, Showcase, IV, No. 3 (May–June, 1977) p. 71
Catalogs/Checklists:

2778

Place: New York, New York
Date: N.D.
Title:
Size: 12⁵/₁₆ × 19 in. (31.3 × 48.3 cm.)
Artist:
Lithographer:
Printer:
Publisher: L. Turgis, New York & Paris
Key/Vignettes/Misc:
Locations: MM–NN
Catalogs/Checklists: MM–NN, LP 3913

2779

Place: New York, New York
Date: N.D.
Title: Ansicht von New–York. View of New–York.
Size: 11³/₈ × 14⁵/₈ in. (28.9 × 37.2 cm.)
Artist:
Lithographer:

Printer:
Publisher: F. Lenz, Berlin
Key/Vignettes/Misc:
Locations: Unknown
Catalogs/Checklists:

2780
Place: New York, New York
Date: N.D.
Title: New York
Size: 11⅞ × 16¾ in. (30.3 × 42.6 cm.)
Artist:
Lithographer:
Printer: Wentzel & Wissembourg
Publisher:
Key/Vignettes/Misc:
Locations: CHS–C
Catalogs/Checklists:

2781
Place: New York, New York
Date: N.D.
Title: New York Bay, from Bay Ridge
Size: 9⅜ × 12½ in. (23.8 × 31.8 cm.)
Artist:
Lithographer:
Printer:
Publisher: Currier & Ives 125 Nassau St.
New York
Key/Vignettes/Misc: 5 unnumbered refs.
below places identified
Locations: MCNY
Catalogs/Checklists: Peters, C & I, 4006

2782
Place: New York, New York
Date: N.D.
Title: New York Harbour from Staten
Island. [Title also in French]
Size: 12⅝ × 19⅝ in. (32.2 × 50 cm.)
Artist: J. W. C. Williams
Lithographer:
Printer:
Publisher: L. Turgis, Paris
Key/Vignettes/Misc:
Locations:
Catalogs/Checklists: Stokes, Icon., III,
Supp. List, no. 55

2783
Place: New York, New York
Date: N.D.
Title: New York 1643. Conquered and
Named New Orange
Size: 11¼ × 16½ in. (28.6 × 42 cm.)
Artist: Jos. W. Moulton
Lithographer: Rob't M. Gaw
Printer:
Publisher:
Key/Vignettes/Misc: Refs. 1–11, A–I,
K–T
Locations: NCM–EM
Catalogs/Checklists:

2784
Place: New York, New York
Date: N.D.
Title: New–York
Size: 7¹¹⁄₁₆ × 11⅜ in. (19.6 × 29 cm.)
Artist:
Lithographer:
Printer:

Publisher:
Key/Vignettes/Misc:
Locations:
Catalogs/Checklists: Pyne, no. 55

2785
Place: New York, New York
Date: N.D.
Title: New–York Et Brooklyn——New
York And Brooklyn Vue Prise de
Williamsburg——From Williamsburg
Size: 12⅝ × 19⅝ in. (32.2 × 49.9 cm.)
Artist: J. W. C. Williams
Lithographer:
Printer: Turgis, Paris
Publisher: L. Turgis, rue Serpente 10, Paris
& 300 Broadway, N. Y.
Key/Vignettes/Misc:
Locations: LIHS–B
Catalogs/Checklists: Stokes, Icon., III,
Supp. List, no. 54

2786
Place: New York, New York
Date: N.D.
Title: New–York Vue Pris du Fort de
William–Castle. New–York Tomado
desde el castille de William–Castle.
Size: 16 × 24¼ in. (40.7 × 61.8 cm.)
Artist: Lebreton
Lithographer: L. Lebreton
Printer: Becquet a Paris
Publisher: Bulla Freres, 16, rue
Tiquetonne, Paris
Key/Vignettes/Misc:
Locations: NYH–NY; CHS–C
Catalogs/Checklists: Pyne, no. 89; Stokes,
Icon., III, Supp. List, no. 50

2787
Place: New York, New York
Date: N.D.
Title: New–York——New–York Vue
Prise des Hauteurs de Brooklyn.——from
Brooklyn Heights
Size: 12⁹⁄₁₆ × 19⁵⁄₁₆ in. (32 × 49.2 cm.)
Artist: J. W. C. Williams
Lithographer:
Printer: Turgis, Paris
Publisher: L. Turgis, rue Serpente, 10 Paris
& 300 Broadway, N. Y.
Key/Vignettes/Misc:
Locations:
Catalogs/Checklists: Stokes, Icon., III,
Supp. List, no. 53

2788
Place: New York, New York
Date: N.D.
Title: The Harbor of New York. From the
Brooklyn Bridge Tower—Looking
South–West.
Size: 10 × 12⅞ in. (25.4 × 32.8 cm.)
Artist:
Lithographer:
Printer:
Publisher: Currier & Ives. 115 Nassau St.
New York
Key/Vignettes/Misc: 9 unnumbered refs.
below places identified
Locations: MCNY; MM–NN

Catalogs/Checklists: Peters, C & I, 4012;
MM–NN, LP 3353

2789
Place: New York, New York
Date: N.D.
Title: View of New York
Size: 8⁵⁄₁₆ × 12¹³⁄₁₆ in. (21.2 × 32.6 cm.)
Artist:
Lithographer:
Printer:
Publisher: George Stinson & Co.,
Portland, Maine
Key/Vignettes/Misc:
Locations:
Catalogs/Checklists: Goldsmith, no. 58

2790
Place: New York, New York
Date: N.D.
Title: View of New York
Size: 9 × 12⅞ in. (22.9 × 32.8 cm.)
Artist:
Lithographer:
Printer:
Publisher: Currier & Ives, New York
Key/Vignettes/Misc:
Locations: MCNY
Catalogs/Checklists: Peters, C & I, 3987

2791
Place: New York, New York
Date: N.D.
Title: View of New York
Size: 18½ × 32 in. (47.1 × 81.4 cm.)
Artist: J. Bachman
Lithographer:
Printer: Snyder & Black
Publisher: J. Bachman, 80 Bower St.,
Jersey City Heights.
Key/Vignettes/Misc: 26 refs. in 4 lines.
Locations:
Catalogs/Checklists: Pyne, no. 109

2792
Place: New York, New York
Date: N.D.
Title: View of The City of New York From
Governors Island
Size: 10³⁄₁₆ × 18⁵⁄₁₆ in. (25.9 × 46.6 cm.)
Artist:
Lithographer:
Printer:
Publisher:
Key/Vignettes/Misc:
Locations:
Catalogs/Checklists: Pyne, no. 102

2793
Place: New York, New York
Date: N.D.
Title: Views of New–York New–York
From Governor's Island.
Size: 6¹⁄₁₆ × 8¹³⁄₁₆ in. (15.4 × 22.4 cm.)
Artist:
Lithographer:
Printer:
Publisher: Henry Hoff No. 180 William St.
N. Y.
Key/Vignettes/Misc:
Locations:

Catalogs/Checklists: Stokes, Icon., III, Supp. List, no. 46

2794
Place: New York, New York
Date: N.D.
Title: Vue de New–York et de l'Entree de la Riviere de l'Est Prise de l'Ile Ellis Vista de New–York y de la Entrada del Ryo de l'Est Tomada de la Ysla Ellis
Size: 13½ × 18¼ in. (34.4 × 46.4 cm.)
Artist:
Lithographer:
Printer: Chez Gosselin. . .Paris
Publisher: Gosselin, Paris and Chez Gadola, Cours de Brosse 1, Lyon
Key/Vignettes/Misc:
Locations: YUAG–NH
Catalogs/Checklists:

2795
Place: New York, New York
Date: N.D.
Title: Vue Generale de New–York
Size: 17⁷⁄₁₆ × 23⅝ in. (44.4 × 60.1 cm.)
Artist:
Lithographer: Walter
Printer: Lemercier, Paris
Publisher: Wild, Passage du Saumon, 38 [Paris]
Key/Vignettes/Misc:
Locations: YUAG–NH
Catalogs/Checklists:

2796
Place: New York, New York
Date: N.D.
Title: Vue Generale de New–York Pris de l'Union Square
Size: 14¹¹⁄₁₆ × 23 in. (37.3 × 58.5 cm.)
Artist:
Lithographer: Walter
Printer:
Publisher: Lemercier
Key/Vignettes/Misc:
Locations: MM–NN
Catalogs/Checklists: MM–NN, LP 1185

Place: New York, New York
Date: ?
See Jersey City, New Jersey, ?

2797
Place: Newburgh, New York
Date: 1846
Title: View of Newburgh, N. Y.
Size: 14 × 25⅝ in. (40.7 × 65.2 cm.)
Artist: E. Whitefield
Lithographer: E. Whitefield
Printer:
Publisher: E. Whitefield, New York, 1846 (copyright)
Key/Vignettes/Misc: Refs. 1–6
Locations: MM–NN; NYH–NY; NYP–S
Catalogs/Checklists: MM–NN, LP 2187; Norton, Whitefield, no. 32

2798
Place: Newburgh, New York
Date: 1852
Title: View of Newburgh, N. Y.
Size: 10¹⁵⁄₁₆ × 15¹⁄₁₆ in. (26.2 × 38.2 cm.)

Artist: B. Hess
Lithographer:
Printer: Wiltsie & Hess, Newburgh, N. Y.
Publisher: Wiltsie & Hess, Newburgh,N. Y.
Key/Vignettes/Misc: 2 vignettes
Locations: NYSM–A; NYSH–C; LC–P; NYH–NY
Catalogs/Checklists: Hemenway

2799
Place: Newburgh, New York
Date: 1875 State I
Title: Newburgh, N. Y. 1875.
Size: 21¹³⁄₁₆ × 31¹¹⁄₁₆ in. (55.5 × 80.6 cm.)
Artist: H. H. Bailey [& J. C. Hazen]
Lithographer:
Printer: G. W. Lewis, 452 Broadway, Albany, N. Y.
Publisher: H. H. Bailey [& J. C. Hazen]
Key/Vignettes/Misc: Refs. 1–38
Locations: BPL–R; NYH–NY
Catalogs/Checklists:

2800
Place: Newburgh, New York
Date: 1875 State II
Title: Newburgh, N. Y. 1875.
Size: 21¹³⁄₁₆ × 31¹¹⁄₁₆ in. (55.5 × 80.6 cm.)
Artist: H. H. Bailey [& J. C. Hazen]
Lithographer:
Printer: G. W. Lewis, 452 Broadway, Albany, N. Y.
Publisher: H. H. Bailey [& J. C. Hazen]
Key/Vignettes/Misc: Refs. 1–38; 1 vignette
Locations: NYH–NY
Catalogs/Checklists:

2801
Place: Newburgh, New York
Date: 1899
Title: Newburgh, N. Y.
Size: 17³⁄₁₆ × 32½ in. (43.7 × 82.7 cm.)
Artist:
Lithographer:
Printer:
Publisher: T. J. Hughes, New York
Key/Vignettes/Misc:
Locations: MM–NN; LC–M (cropped); NYH–NY
Catalogs/Checklists: MM–NN, LP 2055; LC–M, 593

2802
Place: Newburgh, New York
Date: N.D.
Title: City of Newburgh, N. Y.
Size: 21⅜ × 31⅞ in. (54.3 × 81 cm.)
Artist: Ray
Lithographer:
Printer: Traubel, Camden, New Jersey
Publisher: Amweg & Ray, Philadelphia
Key/Vignettes/Misc: 10 vignettes
Locations: MM–NN; NYH–NY
Catalogs/Checklists: MM–NN, LP 1201

2803
Place: Newport, New York
Date: 1890
Title: Newport, N. Y.
Size: 16 × 25 in. (40.7 × 63.6 cm.)
Artist:

Lithographer:
Printer: Burleigh Lith. Est. Troy, N. Y.
Publisher: L. R. Burleigh, Troy, N. Y.
Key/Vignettes/Misc: Refs.
Locations: LC–M; LAHS–L
Catalogs/Checklists: LC–M, 594

2804
Place: Niagara Falls, New York
Date: 1882
Title: Niagara–Falls, N. Y. 1882
Size: 19½ × 28¹³⁄₁₆ in. (49.6 × 73.3 cm.)
Artist: H. Wellge
Lithographer:
Printer: Beck & Pauli, Milwaukee, Wis.
Publisher: J. J. Stoner, Madison, Wisc.
Key/Vignettes/Misc: Refs. 1–48
Locations: LC–M; Niagara County Historical Society, Niagara Falls, New York; NYH–NY
Catalogs/Checklists: LC–M, 608

2805
Place: Niagara Falls, New York
Date: N.D.
Title: Niagara Falls, N. Y.
Size: 20¼ × 24⅞ in. (51.6 × 63.3 cm.)
Artist: T. M. Fowler
Lithographer:
Printer: Charles Hart, N. Y.
Publisher: Simmons–Baker Company, Niagara Falls, N.Y.
Key/Vignettes/Misc: 17 vignettes
Locations: NYH–NY
Catalogs/Checklists:

2806
Place: Norwich, New York
Date: 1879
Title: Norwich, New York, 1879, Junction of N. Y. & O. M. and D. L. & W. Rail Roads Viewed from West Hill.
Size: 16 × 26 in. (40.7 × 66.2 cm.)
Artist: W. W. Denslow
Lithographer: Traubel
Printer: [Thomas Hunter Lith. Phila.?]
Publisher: [C. J. Corbin?]
Key/Vignettes/Misc: 18 vignettes
Locations: Chenango County Museum, Norwich, New York; NYH–NY
Catalogs/Checklists:

2807
Place: Ogdensburg, New York
Date: 1857
Title: Ogdensburg, N. Y., 1857 From the St. Lawrence River
Size: 16¹³⁄₁₆ × 23⅞ in. (41.2 × 60.8 cm.)
Artist: Henry P. Moore
Lithographer:
Printer: L. H. Bradford & Co. Lith, Boston
Publisher:
Key/Vignettes/Misc: 1 seal
Locations: Ogdensburg, New York, Public Library; NYH–NY
Catalogs/Checklists:

2808
Place: Olean, New York
Date: 1882
Title: Bird's Eye View of Olean Cattaraugus County New York Looking

North West 1882.
Size: 26 × 40 in. (66.2 × 101.7 cm.)
Artist: H. Brosius
Lithographer:
Printer: Beck & Pauli, Milwaukee, Wis.
Publisher: J. J. Stoner, Madison, Wis.
Key/Vignettes/Misc: Refs. 1–23, A–Q; 15 vignettes; 4 newspaper titles
Locations: LC–M; NYH–NY
Catalogs/Checklists: LC–M, 609

2809
Place: Oneida, New York
Date: 1874
Title: View of Oneida, N. Y. 1874.
Size: 19¹¹⁄₁₆ × 24⅜ in. (50.1 × 62.1 cm.)
Artist: O. H. Bailey
Lithographer: C. H. Vogt
Printer: J. Knauber & Co.
Publisher: O. H. Bailey
Key/Vignettes/Misc: Refs. 1–13; 4 vignettes
Locations: BPL–R
Catalogs/Checklists:

2810
Place: Oneida, New York
Date: 1885
Title: Oneida, N. Y. 1885
Size: ca. 16½ × 30½ in. (ca. 42 × 77.6 cm.)
Artist: L. R. Burleigh
Lithographer:
Printer: Beck & Pauli, Lith. Milwaukee, Wis.
Publisher: L. R. Burleigh, Troy, N. Y.
Key/Vignettes/Misc: Refs. 1–22; 1 vignette
Locations: Madison County Historical Society, Oneida, New York
Catalogs/Checklists:

2811
Place: Oneonta, New York
Date: 1884
Title: Oneonta, N. Y.
Size: 16⁵⁄₁₆ × 33 in. (41.5 × 83.9 cm.)
Artist: L. R. Burleigh
Lithographer: L. R. Burleigh
Printer: Beck & Pauli, Lith. Milwaukee, Wis.
Publisher: L. R. Burleigh, Troy, N. Y.
Key/Vignettes/Misc: Refs. 1–36
Locations: NYSH–C; NYH–NY
Catalogs/Checklists: Hemenway

2812
Place: Oriskany Falls, New York
Date: 1891
Title: Oriskany Falls, N. Y.
Size: 14 × 25½ in. (35.7 × 64.9 cm.)
Artist:
Lithographer:
Printer: Burleigh Lithographing Establishment, Troy, N. Y.
Publisher: L. R. Burleigh, Troy, N. Y.
Key/Vignettes/Misc: 28 refs.
Locations: Private collection
Catalogs/Checklists:

2813
Place: Ossining, New York
Date: 1884
Title: Sing Sing, N. Y.

Size: 17 × 26¾ in. (43.3 × 68.1 cm.)
Artist: L. R. Burleigh
Lithographer:
Printer: Beck & Pauli, Litho. Milwaukee, Wis.
Publisher: L. R. Burleigh, Troy, N. Y.
Key/Vignettes/Misc: Refs. 1–42
Locations: MM–NN
Catalogs/Checklists:

2814
Place: Oswego, New York
Date: [1855]
Title: Oswego, N. Y.
Size: 23¾ × 35¼ in. (60.3 × 89.6 cm.)
Artist: Lewis Bradley
Lithographer: D. W. Moody
Printer:
Publisher: Smith Brothers & Company, 225 Fulton Street, New York, New York
Key/Vignettes/Misc:
Locations: MM–NN; CHS–C; OCHS–O; PAC–P; NYSH–C; CSNY–S; LC–P; NYH–NY
Catalogs/Checklists: MM–NN, LP 15; Hemenway; LC–M, 609.1

2815
Place: Oswego, New York
Date: 1873
Title: Bird's Eye View of Oswego, N. Y. 1873
Size: 20⅝ × 25⅛ in. (52.5 × 63.9 cm.)
Artist:
Lithographer:
Printer:
Publisher:
Key/Vignettes/Misc: Refs. 1–33, A–H
Locations: CSNY–S
Catalogs/Checklists:

2816
Place: Oswego, New York
Date: N.D.
Title: Oswego, New York.
Size: 16⅜ × 26⅝ in. (41.7 × 67.8 cm.)
Artist: John F. Forman
Lithographer:
Printer: G. Endicott Litho. New York
Publisher:
Key/Vignettes/Misc:
Locations: NYH–NY
Catalogs/Checklists:

2817
Place: Owego, New York
Date: 1869
Title: Owego The County Seat of Tioga Co. N. Y. From Cemetery Hill 1869
Size: 18½ × 23⅞ in. (47.1 × 60.8 cm.)
Artist: John Moray
Lithographer:
Printer: Chas. Hart, 99 Fulton St., N. Y.
Publisher: John Moray (copyright)
Key/Vignettes/Misc:
Locations: YUAG–NH; Tioga County Historical Society Museum, Owego, New York
Catalogs/Checklists:

2818
Place: Oxford, New York
Date: 1888
Title: Oxford, N. Y.

Size: 13⅜ × 24¾ in. (34 × 63 cm.)
Artist: L.R. Burleigh
Lithographer:
Printer: Burleigh Litho. Establishment, Troy, N. Y.
Publisher: L. R. Burleigh
Key/Vignettes/Misc: Refs. 1–29
Locations: LC–M NYSL–A
Catalogs/Checklists: LC–M, 610

2819
Place: Oyster Bay, New York
Date: 1900
Title: Oyster Bay, Long Island, N. Y. 1900
Size: 20½ × 25½ in. (52.2 × 64.8 cm.)
Artist:
Lithographer:
Printer:
Publisher: O. M. Bailey Map Co, Boston, Mass.
Key/Vignettes/Misc: Refs.; 22 vignettes
Locations: Oyster Bay Historical Society, Oyster Bay, New York
Catalogs/Checklists:

2820
Place: Painted Post, New York
Date: [1850]
Title: View of Painted Post, Steuben Co. N. Y. From the North Side.
Size: 16½ × 22¼ in. (41.9 × 56.6 cm.)
Artist: H. Walton
Lithographer: H. Walton
Printer: Sarony, N. Y.
Publisher:
Key/Vignettes/Misc:
Locations: YUAG–NH; NYH–NY
Catalogs/Checklists: Rehner, Walton, no. 64

Place: Palatine Bridge, New York
Date: 1881
See Canajoharie, New York, 1881.

Place: Palmer Falls, New York
Date: 1888
See Corinth, New York, 1888.

2821
Place: Palmyra, New York
Date: [1880]
Title: View of Palmyra, N. Y. From Walkers Hill.
Size: 16⅛ × 25⅞ in. (41 × 65.9 cm.) (matted)
Artist: H. H. Rowley & Co.
Lithographer:
Printer:
Publisher: H. H. Rowley & Co. Hartford, Conn.
Key/Vignettes/Misc: Refs. 1–6, 8–13
Locations: CSNY–S
Catalogs/Checklists:

2822
Place: Parishville, New York
Date: [1838?]
Title: Parishville
Size: 12 × 14¾ in. (30.6 × 37.6 cm.)
Artist: S.[alathiel] Ellis
Lithographer:
Printer: Speckter & Co. Lith.
Publisher:
Key/Vignettes/Misc:

Locations: NYH–NY
Catalogs/Checklists:

2823

Place: Patchogue, New York
Date: Ca. 1905
Title: Bird's Eye View of Patchogue, Long Island, N. Y.
Size: 28 × 33 in. (71.2 × 84 cm.)
Artist:
Lithographer:
Printer:
Publisher: Hughes & Bailey, New York
Key/Vignettes/Misc: Refs. 1–71, A, C, E, G, I, K–V, VA, W–Z, AA; 29 vignettes
Locations: LC–M
Catalogs/Checklists: LC–M, 611

2824

Place: Patchogue, New York
Date: 1911
Title:
Size: 14½ × 30 in. (36.8 × 76.2 cm.)
Artist:
Lithographer:
Printer: Moessner–Blanchard Art Service, N. Y.
Publisher: Great South Bay Development Co.
Key/Vignettes/Misc:
Locations: LC–M
Catalogs/Checklists: LC–M, 612

2825

Place: Pawling, New York
Date: 1909
Title: Pawling, N. Y. 1909
Size: 19 × 25 in. (48.4 × 63.6 cm.)
Artist: P. H. Smith
Lithographer:
Printer: Knickerbocker Litho. Co., New York
Publisher: W. G. Tice
Key/Vignettes/Misc: Refs. 1–4, 7, 11–14, 17–18
Locations: LC–M
Catalogs/Checklists: LC–M, 613

2826

Place: Pearl River, New York
Date: 1924
Title: Aero–View of Pearl River New York 1924
Size: 19 × 32 in. (48.4 × 81.4 cm.)
Artist: Rene Cinquin
Lithographer:
Printer: Stankovits & Co., N. Y.
Publisher: Hughes & Bailey, Brooklyn, N. Y.
Key/Vignettes/Misc: Refs. A–L; 9 vignettes; unnumbered business directory
Locations: LC–M
Catalogs/Checklists: LC–M, 614

2827

Place: Peekskill, New York
Date: [1846]
Title: View from Peekskill, N. Y. (Regatta).
Size: 6 × 9 in. (15.2 × 22.8 cm.)
Artist: E. Whitefield
Lithographer:
Printer: F. Michelin, N. Y.
Publisher:

Key/Vignettes/Misc:
Locations: NYH–NY
Catalogs/Checklists: Hufeland, Checklist, 217; Norton, Whitefield, no. 7

2828

Place: Peekskill, New York
Date: 1851
Title: View of Peekskill 1851.
Size: 19¼ × 25¹⁵⁄₁₆ in. (49 × 66 cm.)
Artist: from daguerreotype by S. L. Walker
Lithographer: Gildemeister
Printer: Endicott & Co, New York
Publisher:
Key/Vignettes/Misc:
Locations: NYP–S; NYH–NY
Catalogs/Checklists:

2829

Place: Peekskill, New York
Date: 1883
Title: Peekskill, N. Y., Bird's Eye View
Size: 18 × 26 in. (45.8 × 66.2 cm.)
Artist: L. R. Burleigh
Lithographer:
Printer: Beck & Pauli, Lith. Milwaukee, Wis.
Publisher: L. R. Burleigh, Troy, N. Y.
Key/Vignettes/Misc:
Locations: Unknown
Catalogs/Checklists: Hufeland, Checklist, 279

2830

Place: Peekskill, New York
Date: 1911
Title: Aero View of Peekskill, New York 1911
Size: 25 × 33 in. (63.6 × 84 cm.)
Artist: Fowler and Hughes
Lithographer:
Printer: [Consolidated Engraving Co., N. Y.]
Publisher: Hughes & Bailey, New York
Key/Vignettes/Misc: 8 vignettes; description
Locations: LC–M
Catalogs/Checklists: LC–M, 615

2831

Place: Penn Yan, New York
Date: 1874
Title: Bird's Eye View of Penn Yan, N. Y. 1874
Size: 19¾ × 25 in. (50.3 × 63.6 cm.)
Artist: O. H. Bailey
Lithographer: H. J. Toudy & Co.
Printer: H. J. Toudy & Co., Philadelphia
Publisher: T. M. Fowler & Co.
Key/Vignettes/Misc:
Locations: Yates County Genealogical & Historical Society, Penn Yan, New York; CSNY–S
Catalogs/Checklists:

2832

Place: Perry, New York
Date: 1892
Title: Perry, N. Y., Wyoming Co. 1892
Size: 17 × 25 in. (43.3 × 63.6 cm.)
Artist:
Lithographer:
Printer: Burleigh Litho Co., Troy, N. Y.

Publisher: Geo. E. Norris, Brockton, Mass.
Key/Vignettes/Misc: Refs. 1–20, A–O
Locations: LC–M (photo); Perry, New York, Public Library
Catalogs/Checklists: LC–M, 615.1

2833

Place: Phelps, New York
Date: 1892
Title: Phelps, N. Y.
Size: 15⅛ × 28⅝ in. (38.5 × 72.9 cm.)
Artist: C.[hristian] Fausel
Lithographer:
Printer: Burleigh Litho. Co. Troy N. Y.
Publisher:
Key/Vignettes/Misc: Refs. 1–37
Locations: NYSL–A
Catalogs/Checklists:

2834

Place: Phoenix, New York
Date: 1887
Title: Phoenix, N. Y.
Size: 13½ × 24⅛ in. (34.3 × 61.4 cm.)
Artist: L. R. Burleigh
Lithographer:
Printer: Burleigh Litho. Troy, N. Y.
Publisher: L. R. Burleigh, Troy, N. Y.
Key/Vignettes/Misc: Refs. 1–27
Locations: CSNY–S
Catalog/Checklists:

2835

Place: Plattsburgh, New York
Date: 1877
Title: Bird's Eye View of Plattsburgh Clinton Co. New York 1877.
Size: 22¼ × 24³⁄₁₆ in. (56.6 × 61.6 cm.)
Artist: A. Ruger
Lithographer: C. H. Vogt & Co.
Printer:
Publisher: J. J. Stoner, Madison, Wis.
Key/Vignettes/Misc: Refs. 1–25, A–H, L
Locations: BPL–R; CCHM–P; LC–M
Catalogs/Checklists: LC–M, 616

2836

Place: Plattsburgh, New York
Date: 1899
Title: 1899 Plattsburgh, N. Y.
Size: 20¼ × 32¼ in. (51.6 × 82 cm.)
Artist: C[hristian] Fausel
Lithographer:
Printer: L. R. Burleigh, Lith, Troy, N. Y.
Publisher:
Key/Vignettes/Misc: Refs. 1–52
Locations: LC–M; NYSL–A; CCHM–P; NYH–NY
Catalogs/Checklists: LC–M, 617

2837

Place: Pleasantville, New York
Date: 1927
Title: Aero–View of Pleasantville, N. Y.
Size: 23½ × 33½ in. (59.8 × 85.2 cm.)
Artist:
Lithographer:
Printer:
Publisher:
Key/Vignettes/Misc:
Locations:
Catalogs/Checklists: Hufeland, Checklist, 1109

2838
Place: Poestenkill, New York
Date: Ca. 1865
Title: Poestenkill, Rens. Co. N. Y.
Size: 12⅝ × 18⅞ in. (32.1 × 48 cm.)
Artist: J.[oseph] H. Hidley
Lithographer:
Printer: G. W. Lewis, Albany
Publisher:
Key/Vignettes/Misc:
Locations: NYP–S; YUAG–NH;
NYSH–C; AIHA–A; NYH–NY
Catalogs/Checklists: Stokes Addenda C.
1860–70—Views–15; Hemenway

2839
Place: Poland, New York
Date: 1890
Title: Poland, N. Y.
Size: 16 × 23 in. (40.7 × 58.6 cm.)
Artist:
Lithographer:
Printer: Burleigh Lith. Est., Troy, N. Y.
Publisher: L. R. Burleigh, Troy, N. Y.
Key/Vignettes/Misc: 15 refs.
Locations: LC–M; HCHS–H
Catalogs/Checklists: LC–M, 618

2840
Place: Port Chester, New York
Date: 1882
Title: Port Chester. New York 1882
Size: 20⅜ × 25½ in. (51.9 × 64.9 cm.)
Artist:
Lithographer: O. H. Bailey & Co.
Printer: O. H. Bailey & Co.
Publisher: O. H. Bailey & Co. [Boston]
Key/Vignettes/Misc: Refs. 1–23; 3
vignettes
Locations: BPL–R
Catalogs/Checklists:

2841
Place: Port Henry, New York
Date: 1889
Title: Port Henry, N. Y.
Size: 17 × 28¾ in. (43.3 × 73.2 cm.)
Artist: L. R. Burleigh
Lithographer:
Printer:
Publisher: L. R. Burleigh, Troy, N. Y.
Key/Vignettes/Misc: Refs. 1–42
Locations: LC–M; NYSL–A; RCHS–T;
LAHS–L
Catalogs/Checklists: LC–M, 619

Place: Port Jackson, New York
Date: 1881
See Amsterdam, New York, 1881.

2842
Place: Port Jervis, New York
Date: Ca. 1854
Title: Port Jervis N. Y.
Size: 14½ × 24½ in. (36.9 × 62.4 cm.)
Artist: S. W. Corwin
Lithographer:
Printer: Endicott & Co. N. Y.
Publisher:
Key/Vignettes/Misc:
Locations: CSNY–S; Minisink Valley

Historical Society, Port Jervis, New York;
NYH–NY
Catalogs/Checklists:

2843
Place: Port Jervis, New York
Date: 1874
Title: Port Jervis, N. Y.
Size: 17¾ × 25½ in. (45.2 × 64.9 cm.)
Artist: O. H. Bailey & Co.
Lithographer: C. H. Vogt
Printer: J. Knauber & Co. Print,
Milwaukee
Publisher: O. H. Bailey & Co., Boston
Key/Vignettes/Misc:
Locations: Minisink Valley Historical
Society, Port Jervis, New York
Catalogs/Checklists:

2844
Place: Port Jervis, New York
Date: 1920
Title: Aero View of Port Jervis, New York
1920
Size: 24 × 32 in. (61.1 × 81.4 cm.)
Artist: T. M. Fowler
Lithographer:
Printer:
Publisher: Hughes & Fowler, Brooklyn, N.
Y.
Key/Vignettes/Misc:
Locations: LC–M
Catalogs/Checklists: LC–M, 620

2845
Place: Potsdam, New York
Date: 1885
Title: Potsdam, N. Y. 1885
Size: 16 × 26½ in. (40.7 × 67.4 cm.)
Artist: L. R. Burleigh
Lithographer:
Printer: Beck & Pauli, Litho., Milwaukee,
Wis.
Publisher: L. R. Burleigh, Troy, N. Y.
Key/Vignettes/Misc: Public building
directory
Locations: LC–M; Postdam, New York,
Public Library
Catalogs/Checklists: LC–M, 621

2846
Place: Poughkeepsie, New York
Date: 1852
Title: View of Poughkeepsie, N. Y.
Size: 7¼ × 14¹⁵⁄₁₆ in. (18.4 × 38 cm.)
Artist: B. Hess
Lithographer:
Printer: Wiltsie & Hess, Newburg.
Publisher: Wiltsie & Hess, Newburg.
Key/Vignettes/Misc:
Locations: YUAG–NH; LC–P;
NYH–NY
Catalogs/Checklists:

2847
Place: Poughkeepsie, New York
Date: Ca. 1852
Title: Poughkeepsie. From the Opposite
Side of the Hudson River.
Size: 16⅜ × 34¼ in. (41.6 × 87 cm.)
Artist: E. Whitefield
Lithographer: E. Whitefield

Printer: Endicott & Co., New York
Publisher: E. Whitefield, New York, 1852.
Key/Vignettes/Misc: 4 unnumbered refs.
below places identified
Locations: MM–NN; NYH–NY; NYP–S
Catalogs/Checklists: MM–NN, LP 480;
Norton, Whitefield, no. 57; Pyne, no. 482

2848
Place: Poughkeepsie, New York
Date: 1874
Title: Poughkeepsie, N. Y. 1874
Size: 23½ × 31 in. (59.8 × 78.9 cm.)
Artist: H. H. Bailey [& J. C. Hazen]
Lithographer:
Printer: G. W. Lewis, 452 Broadway,
Albany, N. Y.
Publisher: H. H. Bailey & J. C. Hazen
Key/Vignettes/Misc: Refs. A–R, 1–52; 1
vignette
Locations: BPL–R; Dutchess County
Historical Society, Poughkeepsie, New
York
Catalogs/Checklists:

2849
Place: Prattsville, New York
Date: 1850
Title: Prattsville, Greene County, N. Y.
Size: 16¼ × 25½ in. (41.3 × 64.8 cm.)
Artist:
Lithographer:
Printer: Wm. Endicott & Co. N. York
Publisher:
Key/Vignettes/Misc: Description
Locations: NYH–NY
Catalogs/Checklists:

2850
Place: Prattsville, New York
Date: [1849–52]
Title: View of Prattsville, Green Co. N. Y.
1844.
Size: 19⅝ × 26⅜ in. (49.9 × 67.2 cm.)
Artist:
Lithographer: C. Parsons
Printer: Wm. Endicott & Co. 59 Beekman
St. N. Y.
Publisher:
Key/Vignettes/Misc:
Locations: NYSH–C; LC–P
Catalogs/Checklists: Hemenway

2851
Place: Pulaski, New York
Date: 1885
Title: Pulaski, N. Y. 1885
Size: 17 × 24½ in. (43.3 × 62.4 cm.)
Artist: L. R. Burleigh
Lithographer:
Printer: C. H. Vogt & Son, Lith, Cleveland
Publisher: L. R. Burleigh, Troy, N. Y.
Key/Vignettes/Misc: Refs. 1–26; 3
vignettes
Locations: LC–M; OCHS–O (facsimile)
Catalogs/Checklists: LC–M, 622

2852
Place: Rensselaerville, New York
Date: N.D.
Title: Rensselaerville, N. Y.
Size: 8½ × 15½ in. (21.7 × 39.4 cm.)

Artist: [Joseph H. Hidley?]
Lithographer:
Printer:
Publisher: Ferd. Mayer & Sons, Lithographers, 96 & 98 Fulton St. N. Y.
Key/Vignettes/Misc:
Locations: Unknown. See Old Print Shop Portfolio, XV, p. 86, No. 17
Catalogs/Checklists:

2853
Place: Rhinebeck, New York
Date: 1890
Title: Rhinebeck, N. Y.
Size: 14¼ × 24¾ in. (36.3 × 63 cm.)
Artist: L. R. Burleigh
Lithographer:
Printer:
Publisher: L. R. Burleigh, Troy, N. Y.
Key/Vignettes/Misc: Refs. 1–26
Locations: LC–M; NYH–NY
Catalogs/Checklists: LC–M, 623

2854
Place: Richfield Springs, New York
Date: 1865
Title: Richfield Springs (Taken from North Hill), Otsego County, N. Y.
Size: 18⅝ × 25⅝ in. (47.4 × 65.2 cm.)
Artist:
Lithographer:
Printer:
Publisher: M. DeV. Martin (copyright)
Key/Vignettes/Misc: 17 unnumbered refs. below places identified
Locations: YUAG–NH; NYSH–C; NYH–NY
Catalogs/Checklists: Hemenway

2855
Place: Richfield Springs, New York
Date: 1885
Title: Richfield Springs, N. Y.
Size: 16 × 26½ in. (40.7 × 67.5 cm.)
Artist: L. R. Burleigh
Lithographer:
Printer: C. H. Vogt & Son, Cleveland
Publisher: L. R. Burleigh, Troy, N. Y.
Key/Vignettes/Misc: Refs. 1–30
Locations: LC–M; NYH–NY
Catalogs/Checklists: LC–M, 624

Place: Riverhead, New York
Date: Ca. 1890
See Southampton, New York, ca. 1890.

2856
Place: Rochester, New York
Date: [1836]
Title: The Upper Falls of the Genesee at Rochester N. Y. From the East
Size: 16⁵⁄₁₆ × 19⅜ in. (41.5 × 49.3 cm.)
Artist: J. Young
Lithographer: J. H. Bufford
Printer: Bufford's Lithography, 114 Nassau St., N. Y.
Publisher: C. & M. Morse, Rochester
Key/Vignettes/Misc:
Locations: NYP–S; CHS–C; YUAG–NH; RMSC–R; NYH–NY
Catalogs/Checklists: Stokes P. 1835–F–48; Genesee Country, no. 58

2857
Place: Rochester, New York
Date: [1836]
Title: The Upper Falls of the Genesee at Rochester N. Y. From the East Bank Looking N. W.
Size: 16¾ × 20³⁄₁₆ in. (42.6 × 51.3 cm.)
Artist: J. Young
Lithographer: J. H. Bufford
Printer: Bufford's Lithography, 114 Nassau St. N. Y.
Publisher: C. & M. Morse, Rochester
Key/Vignettes/Misc:
Locations: YUAG–NH; RMSC–R; NYH–NY
Catalogs/Checklists: Genesee Country, no. 57

2858
Place: Rochester, New York
Date: Ca. 1836
Title: The Lower Falls of the Genesee at Rochester, N. Y. From the West Bank Looking S E.
Size: 14⅝ × 19½ in. (37.2 × 49.7 cm.)
Artist: J. Young
Lithographer: Bufford
Printer: Bufford's Lithog 114 Nassau St. N. Y.
Publisher: C & M. Morse, 17 Exchange St., Rochester, N. Y.
Key/Vignettes/Misc:
Locations: NYH–NY
Catalogs/Checklists: Genesee Country, no. 56

2859
Place: Rochester, New York
Date: Ca. 1838
Title: View of Rochester, N. Y. From the Residence of George A. Tiffany, Esq., Near Mt. Hope Cemetery
Size: 14½ × 20 in. (36.9 × 50.8 cm.)
Artist: F. Sowerby
Lithographer:
Printer: Steele's Lithographic Press [Buffalo]
Publisher:
Key/Vignettes/Misc:
Locations: Rochester Historical Society, Rochester, New York
Catalogs/Checklists: Genesee Country, no. 59

2860
Place: Rochester, New York
Date: Ca. 1847
Title: View of Rochester, N. Y., Taken from the Neighborhood of Mt. Hope.
Size: 14⅝ × 38½ in. (37.2 × 98 cm.)
Artist: E. Whitefield
Lithographer: E. Whitefield
Printer: F. Michelin, 111, Nassau St., New York
Publisher:
Key/Vignettes/Misc: 14 refs.
Locations: Rochester Historical Society, Rochester, New York; University of Rochester Library, Rochester, New York;

Rochester, New York, Public Library; RMSC–R
Catalogs/Checklists: Norton, Whitefield, no. 36; Genesee Country, no. 69

2861
Place: Rochester, New York
Date: [1845–47]
Title: The Upper Falls of the Genesee at Rochester
Size: 8¼ × 12⅞ in. (21 × 32.8 cm.)
Artist:
Lithographer:
Printer: J. Baillie, 81st St. near 3d. Avenue, N. Y.
Publisher: J. Baillie, 81st St. near 3d. Avenue, N. Y.
Key/Vignettes/Misc:
Locations: CHS–C; NYH–NY
Catalogs/Checklists:

2862
Place: Rochester, New York
Date: 1853
Title: Rochester. From the West. 1853
Size: 23¹³⁄₁₆ × 39¹¹⁄₁₆ in. (60.6 × 100.9 cm.)
Artist: J. W. Hill
Lithographer: D. W. Moody
Printer:
Publisher: Smith Bros. & Co. 225 Fulton St., New York
Key/Vignettes/Misc:
Locations: NYP–S; CHS–C; Rush Rhees Library, University of Rochester, Rochester, New York; NYSH–C; LC–M (facsimile); CSNY–S; NYH–NY; RMSC–R
Catalogs/Checklists: Stokes 1853—G–14; Hemenway; LC–M, 624.1

2863
Place: Rochester, New York
Date: [1867–68]
Title: [Untitled proof of view of Rochester, New York]
Size:
Artist: William Henry Robinson
Lithographer:
Printer:
Publisher:
Key/Vignettes/Misc:
Locations: Private collection
Catalogs/Checklists: Memorial Art Gallery of the University of Rochester, Made in Rochester, pp. 20–21

2864
Place: Rochester, New York
Date: 1880
Title: View of Rochester, New York 1880
Size: 36 × 44½ in. (91.6 × 113.1 cm.)
Artist: H. H. Rowley & Co.
Lithographer:
Printer: Beck & Pauli, Milwaukee, Wis.
Publisher: H. H. Rowley & Co., Hartford, Conn.
Key/Vignettes/Misc:
Locations: LC–M; OHA–S; RMSC–R
Catalogs/Checklists: LC–M, 625

2865
Place: Rochester, New York
Date: 1884
Title: 1834 Semi−Centennial Memorial 1884
Size: 26 × 20 in. (66.1 × 50.8 cm.)
Artist:
Lithographer:
Printer: Meising & Stecher, Rochester, N. Y.
Publisher:
Key/Vignettes/Misc:
Locations: RMSC−R
Catalogs/Checklists: Genesee Country, no. 77

2866
Place: Rockaway Beach, New York
Date: ?
Title: [Rockaway Beach, Long Island, New York]
Size: 17¹¹⁄₁₆ × 24¹¹⁄₁₆ in. (cropped) (45.1 × 62.9 cm.)
Artist:
Lithographer:
Printer: O. H. Bailey Co. Lith. Boston
Publisher:
Key/Vignettes/Misc:
Locations: NYH−NY
Catalogs/Checklists:

2867
Place: Rockland Lake, New York
Date: [1845−49]
Title: Rockland Lake
Size: 11¾ × 17⅝ in. (29.7 × 44.7 cm.)
Artist: John W. Hill
Lithographer:
Printer: G. & W. Endicott
Publisher:
Key/Vignettes/Misc:
Locations: YUAG−NH
Catalogs/Checklists:

2868
Place: Rockton, New York
Date: 1890
Title: Rockton, N. Y.
Size: 13¾ × 23¹⁄₁₆ in. (35 × 58.7 cm.)
Artist:
Lithographer:
Printer: Burleigh Lithographing Establishment
Publisher: L. R. Burleigh, Troy, N. Y.
Key/Vignettes/Misc: Refs. 1−12
Locations: NYSL−A
Catalogs/Checklists:

2869
Place: Rockville Centre, New York
Date: 1895
Title: Rockville Centre, Long Island, N. Y. 1895
Size: 17 × 22 in. (43.2 × 56 cm.)
Artist: O. H. Bailey & Co.
Lithographer:
Printer: O. H. Bailey & Co., Boston
Publisher: O. H. Bailey & Co., Boston
Key/Vignettes/Misc: Refs. 1−44; 37 vignettes
Locations: NCM−EM
Catalogs/Checklists:

2870
Place: Rome, New York
Date: 1886
Title: Rome, N. Y.
Size: 15½ × 33⅝ in. (39.4 × 85.6 cm.)
Artist: L. R. Burleigh
Lithographer:
Printer: Beck & Pauli, Litho., Milwaukee, Wis.
Publisher: L. R. Burleigh, Troy, N. Y.
Key/Vignettes/Misc: Refs. 1−45; 1 vignette
Locations: LC−M; NYSL−A
Catalogs/Checklists: LC−M, 626

2871
Place: Rondout, New York
Date: Ca. 1852
Title: Rondout, N. Y.
Size: 10¼ × 15¹⁄₁₆ in. (26.1 × 38.3 cm.)
Artist: B. Hess
Lithographer:
Printer: J. R. Wiltsie & B. Hess, Newburgh, N. Y.
Publisher: J. R. Wiltsie & B. Hess, Newburgh, N. Y.
Key/Vignettes/Misc: 2 vignettes
Locations: NYH−NY
Catalogs/Checklists:

2872
Place: Rondout, New York
Date: N.D.
Title: Rondout, New York
Size: 10¼ × 17³⁄₁₆ in. (26.1 × 43.8 cm.)
Artist: S. Quilliard
Lithographer:
Printer: Endicott [New York]
Publisher:
Key/Vignettes/Misc:
Locations: NYH−NY
Catalogs/Checklists:

2873
Place: Rossie, New York
Date: [1838?]
Title: Rossie
Size: 11 × 14¼ in. (28 × 36.3 cm.)
Artist: Salathiel Ellis
Lithographer:
Printer: Sprecht & Co.
Publisher:
Key/Vignettes/Misc:
Locations: YUAG−NH; NYH−NY
Catalogs/Checklists:

2874
Place: Round Lake, New York
Date: [1877?]
Title: Round Lake Grounds, Saratoga Co., N. Y.
Size: 10¼ × 15 in. (26.1 × 38.2 cm.)
Artist:
Lithographer:
Printer:
Publisher:
Key/Vignettes/Misc:
Locations: NYSM−A
Catalogs/Checklists:

2875
Place: Sacketts Harbor, New York

Date: ?
Title: South−East View of Sackett's Harbour
Size:
Artist:
Lithographer:
Printer:
Publisher:
Key/Vignettes/Misc:
Locations: NYSH−C
Catalogs/Checklists: Hemenway

2876
Place: Sag Harbor, New York
Date: N.D.
Title: Sag Harbor, (L. I.) N. Y. View from the North.
Size: 16 × 24¾ in. (40.7 × 63 cm.)
Artist: O. H. Beers
Lithographer:
Printer: D. W. Kellogg & Co., Hartford, Ct.
Publisher:
Key/Vignettes/Misc:
Locations: CHS−H
Catalogs/Checklists: CHS−H, 41

2877
Place: Saint Johnsville, New York
Date: 1890
Title: St. Johnsville, N. Y.
Size: 15⅝ × 22¾ in. (39.8 × 57.9 cm.)
Artist:
Lithographer:
Printer: Burleigh Lithographing Establishment, Troy, N. Y.
Publisher: L. R. Burleigh, Troy, N. Y.
Key/Vignettes/Misc: Refs. 1−33; 1 vignette
Locations: LC−M; NYH−NY; LAHS−L
Catalogs/Checklists: LC−M, 627

2878
Place: Salem, New York
Date: 1889
Title: Salem, N. Y.
Size: 19 × 29½ in. (48.4 × 75.1 cm.)
Artist: L. R.Burleigh
Lithographer:
Printer: The Burleigh Lith. Est., Troy, N. Y.
Publisher: L. R. Burleigh, Troy, N. Y.
Key/Vignettes/Misc: Refs. 1−29, A−G; 1 vignette
Locations: LC−M NYSL−A
Catalogs/Checklists: LC−M, 628

Place: Sandy Hill, New York
Date: 1884
See Hudson Falls, New York, 1884.

2879
Place: Saratoga Springs, New York
Date: 1848
Title: Saratoga
Size: 8⅛ × 11¹¹⁄₁₆ in. (20.7 × 29.8 cm.)
Artist: Augustus Kollner
Lithographer:
Printer: Deroy
Publisher: Goupil, Vibert & Co.
Key/Vignettes/Misc:
Locations: CHS−C
Catalogs/Checklists: Stokes P. 1847−G−1 (note)

2880
Place: Saratoga Springs, New York
Date: Ca. 1865
Title: Saratoga Springs, N. Y.
Size: 8⅛ × 12⅝ in. (20.6 × 32.1 cm.)
Artist:
Lithographer:
Printer:
Publisher: Currier & Ives, New York
Key/Vignettes/Misc:
Locations: NYP−S; YUAG−NH
Catalogs/Checklists: Stokes C. 1865—
F−100; Peters, C & I, 4179

2881
Place: Saratoga Springs, New York
Date: 1888
Title: Saratoga Springs, N. Y. 1888
Size: 20¼ × 33¾ in. (51.6 × 85.9 cm.)
Artist: L. R. Burleigh
Lithographer:
Printer: The Burleigh Lith. Est., Troy, N. Y.
Publisher: L. R. Burleigh, Troy, N. Y.
Key/Vignettes/Misc: Refs. 1−75; 1
vignette
Locations: LC−M; NYSL−A; RCHS−T;
NYH−NY; LAHS−L
Catalogs/Checklists: LC−M, 630

2882
Place: Sayville, New York
Date: 1901
Title: Sayville, Long Island, N. Y. 1901
Size: 16⅜ × 19⅞ in. (41.7 × 50.6 cm.)
Artist:
Lithographer:
Printer:
Publisher: O. H. Bailey & Co. Boston
Key/Vignettes/Misc: Refs. A, 2−56; West
Sayville refs. A−H, J; 25 vignettes
Locations: NYH−NY
Catalogs/Checklists:

2883
Place: Schaghticoke, New York
Date: 1889 State I
Title: Schaghticoke, N. Y.
Size: 12¾ × 20½ in. (32.5 × 52 cm.)
Artist:
Lithographer:
Printer:
Publisher:
Key/Vignettes/Misc: Refs. 1−14
Locations: LC−M; LC−P
Catalogs/Checklists: LC−M, 631

2884
Place: Schaghticoke, New York
Date: 1889 State II
Title: Schaghticoke, N. Y.
Size: 15⅛ × 21⁷⁄₁₆ in. (38.5 × 54.6 cm.)
Artist:
Lithographer:
Printer:
Publisher: L. R. Burleigh, Troy, N. Y.
Key/Vignettes/Misc: Refs. 1−14
Locations: NYH−NY; LAHS−L
Catalogs/Checklists:

2885
Place: Schenectady, New York
Date: 1875

Title: Schenectady, N. Y. 1875
Size: 19¾ × 24¾ in. (50.3 × 63 cm.)
Artist: H. H. Bailey [& J. C. Hazen]
Lithographer:
Printer: G. W. Lewis 452 Broadway
Albany, N. Y.
Publisher:
Key/Vignettes/Misc: Refs. 1−22
Locations: BPL−R; CHS−C; NYSM−A;
NYH−NY
Catalogs/Checklists:

2886
Place: Schenectady, New York
Date: [1882]
Title: Schenectady, N. Y.
Size: 18⅞ × 31⅞ in. (48.1 × 81.1 cm.)
Artist: Burleigh
Lithographer: Lyth
Printer:
Publisher:
Key/Vignettes/Misc:
Locations: NYSL−A; NYH−NY
Catalogs/Checklists:

2887
Place: Schuylerville, New York
Date: 1834
Title: Schuylersville.
Size: 10¹⁄₁₆ × 13¾ in. (25.6 × 35 cm.)
Artist: J. W. Hill
Lithographer:
Printer: Endicott, 359, Broadway, N. Y.
Publisher: G. Endicott
Key/Vignettes/Misc:
Locations: NYH−NY
Catalogs/Checklists: Van Zandt,
Chronicles of the Hudson, no. 9

2888
Place: Schuylerville, New York
Date: 1835
Title: Schuylerville, Saratoga Co. N. Y.
Size: 8¼ x 12¼ in. (20.9 × 31.1 cm.)
Artist:
Lithographer:
Printer: J. N. Graham Lith. Johns St. N.
Y., N. Y.
Publisher:
Key/Vignettes/Misc:
Locations: Private collection
Catalogs/Checklists:

2889
Place: Schuylerville, New York
Date: 1889
Title: Schuylerville, N. Y.
Size: 11½ × 24¼ in. (29.3 × 61.8 cm.)
Artist: L. R. Burleigh
Lithographer:
Printer: The Burleigh Lith. Est., Troy, N. Y.
Publisher: L. R. Burleigh, Troy, N. Y.
Key/Vignettes/Misc: Refs. 1−22, A−I;
description
Locations: LC−M; CSNY−S; LAHS−L
Catalogs/Checklists: LC−M, 632

2890
Place: Sea Cliff, New York
Date: 1899
Title: Sea Cliff, Long Island, N. Y. 1899
Size: 22 × 29 in. (56 × 73.8 cm.)
Artist: O. H. Bailey & Co.

Lithographer:
Printer: O. H. Bailey & Co., Boston
Publisher: O. H. Bailey & Co., Boston
Key/Vignettes/Misc: Refs. 1−71; 34
vignettes
Locations: NCM−EM
Catalogs/Checklists:

2891
Place: Seneca Falls, New York
Date: 1873
Title: Bird's Eye View of Seneca Falls, N.
Y. 1873.
Size: 20¼ × 26¼ in. (51.5 × 66.8 cm.)
Artist: O. H. Bailey
Lithographer: Parsons & Atwater
Printer: Endicott & Co., New York
Publisher:
Key/Vignettes/Misc: Refs. 1−18, A−P; R;
1 vignette
Locations: Seneca Falls Historical Society,
Seneca Falls, New York; CSNY−S
Catalogs/Checklists:

2892
Place: Sherburne, New York
Date: 1887
Title: Sherburne, N. Y. 1887
Size: 15 × 24½ in. (38.2 × 62.4 cm.)
Artist: L. R. Burleigh
Lithographer:
Printer: The Burleigh Lith. Est., Troy, N.Y.
Publisher: L. R. Burleigh, Troy, N. Y.
Key/Vignettes/Misc: Refs. 1−15
Locations: LC−M; NYH−NY
Catalogs/Checklists: LC−M, 633

2893
Place: Shortsville, New York
Date: 1892
Title: Shortsville, N. Y.
Size: 16¾ × 27¾ in. (42.6 × 70.6 cm.)
Artist:
Lithographer:
Printer: Burleigh Litho. Co., Troy, N. Y.
Publisher:
Key/Vignettes/Misc: Refs. 1−31
Locations: NYSL−A
Catalogs/Checklists:

2894
Place: Shushan, New York
Date: 1890
Title: Shushan, N. Y.
Size: 10 × 16 in. (25.4 × 40.8 cm.)
(facsimile)
Artist:
Lithographer:
Printer: Burleigh Lithographing Est., Troy,
N. Y.
Publisher: L. R. Burleigh, Troy, N. Y.
Key/Vignettes/Misc: Refs. 1−12
Locations: LC−M (facsimile)
Catalogs/Checklists: LC−M, 633.1

2895
Place: Sidney, New York
Date: 1887
Title: Sidney, N. Y. 1887
Size: 14³⁄₁₆ × 22¹⁵⁄₁₆ in. (36.1 × 58.4 cm.)
Artist: L. R. Burleigh
Lithographer:

Printer: The Burleigh Lith. Est., Troy, N. Y.
Publisher: L. R. Burleigh, Troy, N. Y.
Key/Vignettes/Misc: Refs. 1–14
Locations: LC–M; NYH–NY
Catalogs/Checklists: LC–M, 634

2896
Place: Silver Creek, New York
Date: 1892
Title: Silver Creek, N. Y.
Size: 16¼ × 27½ in. (41.4 × 70 cm.)
Artist:
Lithographer:
Printer: Burleigh Litho. Co., Troy, N. Y.
Publisher:
Key/Vignettes/Misc: Refs. 1–54
Locations: NYH–NY; NYSL–A; LC–M
Catalogs/Checklists:

Place: Sing Sing, New York
Date: 1884
See Ossining, New York, 1884.

2897
Place: Skaneateles, New York
Date: [1855]
Title: View of Skaneateles Village, from the South
Size: 11 × 14¹⁵⁄₁₆ in. (28 × 38.1 cm.)
Artist: W. M. Beauchamp
Lithographer: W. M. Beauchamp
Printer:
Publisher:
Key/Vignettes/Misc:
Locations: Unknown. See Old Print Shop Portfolio, XXXII, p. 79, No. 10
Catalogs/Checklists:

2898
Place: Skaneateles, New York
Date: 1884
Title: Skaneateles, N. Y.
Size: 12¼ × 29⅛ in. (31.1 × 74.1 cm.)
Artist: L. R. Burleigh
Lithographer:
Printer: Beck & Pauli, Litho., Milwaukee, Wis.
Publisher: L. R. Burleigh, Troy, N.Y.
Key/Vignettes/Misc: Refs. 1–16; 1 vignette
Locations: LC–M; NYSH–C; NYH–NY; CSNY–S
Catalogs/Checklists: Hemenway; LC–M, 635

2899
Place: Sleepy Hollow, New York
Date: [1828–29]
Title:
Size: 9½ × 13 in. (24.2 × 33 cm.)
Artist: [Jacques] Milbert
Lithographer:
Printer:
Publisher:
Key/Vignettes/Misc: 3 other views on same sheet: Road to Kingbridge, Falls of Owasco, Croton River
Locations: Unknown
Catalogs/Checklists: American Art Association Auction, 410

2900
Place: Southampton, New York

Date: Ca. 1890
Title: Riverhead, The Home Resort of Long Island, Property of the Riverhead Investement Co. 30 Ann Street, New York City, N. Y.
Size: 22¾ × 33⅜ in. (57.9 × 84.9 cm.)
Artist:
Lithographer:
Printer:
Publisher:
Key/Vignettes/Misc: 16 vignettes
Locations: Suffolk County Historical Society, Riverhead, New York
Catalogs/Checklists:

2901
Place: Springville, New York
Date: 1892
Title: Springville, N. Y.
Size: 16½ × 29⅝ in. (42 × 75.4 cm.)
Artist:
Lithographer:
Printer: Burleigh Lithographic Co., Troy, N. Y.
Publisher:
Key/Vignettes/Misc: Refs. 1–54
Locations: BECH–B; NYSL–A
Catalogs/Checklists:

2902
Place: Stamford, New York
Date: 1890
Title: Stamford, N. Y.
Size: 12⅝ × 24¼ in. (32.2 × 61.7 cm.)
Artist:
Lithographer:
Printer: Burleigh Lithographing Establishment, Troy, N. Y.
Publisher: L. R. Burleigh, Troy, N. Y.
Key/Vignettes/Misc: Refs. 1–27
Locations: LC–M; NYH–NY; LAHS–L
Catalogs/Checklists: LC–M, 636

2903
Place: Stapleton, New York
Date: 1905
Title: Bird's Eye View of Stapleton, Staten Island, N. Y., 1905
Size: 31 × 32½ in. (78.9 × 82.7 cm.)
Artist: T. J. Hughes
Lithographer:
Printer: T. J. Hughes, 43 Gold St., New York, N. Y.
Publisher: T. J. Hughes, 43 Gold St., New York, N. Y.
Key/Vignettes/Misc: 56 vignettes
Locations: SIHS–R
Catalogs/Checklists:

2904
Place: Staten Island, New York
Date: [1864–67]
Title: Staten Island, N. Y.
Size: 13⅛ × 18½ in. (33.4 × 47.1 cm.)
Artist: H. Knecht
Lithographer:
Printer:
Publisher:
Key/Vignettes/Misc: Sectioned print consisting of 7 views of locations on Staten Island
Locations: NYP–S; SIHS–R

Catalogs/Checklists: Stokes C. 1864–67—E–133

2905
Place: Stillwater, New York
Date: 1889
Title: Stillwater, N. Y.
Size: 12 × 25¹¹⁄₁₆ in. (30.5 × 65.3 cm.)
Artist: L. R. Burleigh
Lithographer:
Printer: Burleigh Lith. Est., Troy, N. Y.
Publisher: L. R. Burleigh, Troy, N. Y., 1889
Key/Vignettes/Misc:
Locations: MM–NN; LC–M
Catalogs/Checklists: MM–NN, LP 1926; LC–M, 637

2906
Place: Stottville, New York
Date: 1889
Title: Stottville, N. Y.
Size: 14⅝ x 23½ in. (37.3 × 59.8 cm.)
Artist: L. R. Burleigh
Lithographer:
Printer: The Burleigh Lith. Est. Troy, N. Y.
Publisher: L. R. Burleigh, N. Y.
Key/Vignettes/Misc: Refs. 1–12
Locations: NYH–NY; NYSM–A; LAHS–L
Catalogs/Checklists:

2907
Place: Stuyvesant Falls, New York
Date: N.D.
Title: Stuyvesant Falls, N. Y.
Size: 14⅛ × 24 in. (36 × 61.1 cm.)
Artist: F. [Christian Fausel?]
Lithographer:
Printer: [Burleigh Lithographing Establishment, Troy, N. Y.?]
Publisher:
Key/Vignettes/Misc: Refs. 1–11
Locations: NYSM–A
Catalogs/Checklists:

2908
Place: Syracuse, New York
Date: [1852]
Title: Syracuse, N. Y.
Size: 21½ × 35⅝ in. (54.7 × 90.6 cm.)
Artist: Lewis Bradley
Lithographer: D. W. Moody
Printer: F. Michelin
Publisher: Smith Bros & Co. 225 Fulton St., New York
Key/Vignettes/Misc:
Locations: NYP–S; NYSH–C; CHS–C; OHA–S; CM–S; NYH–NY
Catalogs/Checklists: Stokes C. 1850–53—G–35; Hemenway

2909
Place: Syracuse, New York
Date: [1859]
Title: Syracuse, N. Y.
Size: 22¾ × 33 in. (57.8 × 84 cm.)
Artist: M.[elville] DeV. Martin
Lithographer:
Printer: M. De V. Martin, Syracuse, N. Y.
Publisher: M. De V. Martin, Syracuse, N. Y.
Key/Vignettes/Misc:

Locations: OHA–S
Catalogs/Checklists:

2910
Place: Syracuse, New York
Date: 1868
Title: Bird's Eye View of Syracuse, N. Y.
Size: 51½ × 78¼ in. (131 × 199 cm.) (4 sheets)
Artist: J.[ulius] C.[aesar] Lass and L.[eopold] Laass
Lithographer: E. Sachse & Co.
Printer: E. Sachse & Co., Baltimore, Md.
Publisher: J. C. Laass and L. Laass (copyright)
Key/Vignettes/Misc: 12 vignettes
Locations: LC–M; OHA–S (upper 2 sheets); Syracuse, New York, Savings Bank (lower 2 sheets)
Catalogs/Checklists: LC–M, 638

2911
Place: Syracuse, New York
Date: 1874
Title: Birds Eye View of Syracuse, New York. 1874
Size: 25 × 35½ in. (63.6 × 90.4 cm.)
Artist: H. H. Bailey
Lithographer:
Printer: American Oleograph Co., Milwaukee Wis.
Publisher:
Key/Vignettes/Misc: Refs. 1–81; 2 vignettes; 1 seal
Locations: BPL–R; OHA–S; CM–S
Catalogs/Checklists:

2912
Place: Tarrytown, New York
Date: [1828–29]
Title: Where Major Andre Was Captured
Size: 9½ × 12 in. (24.1 × 30.5 cm.)
Artist: [Jacques] Milbert
Lithographer:
Printer:
Publisher:
Key/Vignettes/Misc:
Locations: Unknown
Catalogs/Checklists: Hufeland, Checklist, 768

2913
Place: Ticonderoga, New York
Date: 1884
Title: Ticonderoga, N. Y.
Size: 18 × 24½ in. (45.8 × 62.4 cm.)
Artist: L. R. Burleigh
Lithographer:
Printer: Beck & Pauli, Litho., Milwaukee
Publisher: L. R. Burleigh, Troy, N. Y.
Key/Vignettes/Misc: 34 refs.; 1 vignette
Locations: LC–M; NYH–NY; LAHS–L
Catalogs/Checklists: LC–M, 639

2914
Place: Ticonderoga, New York
Date: 1891
Title: Ticonderoga, N. Y.
Size: 18½ × 25 in. (47.1 × 63.6 cm.)
Artist:
Lithographer:

Printer: Burleigh Lithographing Establishment, Troy, N. Y.
Publisher: R. M. Adkins, Ticonderoga, New York
Key/Vignettes/Misc: Refs. 1–34; 1 vignette
Locations: LC–M; LAHS–L
Catalogs/Checklists: LC–M, 640

2915
Place: Tivoli, New York
Date: [1846]
Title: Tivoli, or Upper Red Hook, Hudson River, N. Y.
Size: 6¹¹⁄₁₆ × 9 in. (17 × 22.8 cm.)
Artist: E. Whitefield
Lithographer:
Printer: E. Jones & G. W. Newman, N. York
Publisher:
Key/Vignettes/Misc:
Locations: NYSH–C; NYH–NY
Catalogs/Checklists: Hemenway; Norton, Whitefield, no. 14

2916
Place: Tottenville, New York
Date: Ca. 1880
Title: Tottenville. Staten Island
Size: 19 × 22⅞ in. (48.4 × 58.3 cm.)
Artist:
Lithographer:
Printer: Beck & Pauli, Lith., Milwaukee, Wis.
Publisher: Fowler & Evans, Asbury Park, N. J.
Key/Vignettes/Misc: Refs. 1–26
Locations: SIHS–R
Catalogs/Checklists:

2917
Place: Tottenville, New York
Date: 1902
Title: Tottenville, Borough of Richmond, New York. 1902
Size: 17¼ × 19¾ in. (43.9 × 50.3 cm.)
Artist: O. H. Bailey & Co.
Lithographer:
Printer:
Publisher: O. H. Bailey & Co.
Key/Vignettes/Misc: Refs. 1–57; 24 vignettes
Locations: NYH–NY
Catalogs/Checklists:

2918
Place: Troy, New York
Date: 1845
Title: View of Troy, N. Y. From the West.
Size: 16³⁄₁₆ × 26¼ in. (41.2 × 66.7 cm.)
Artist: E. Whitefield
Lithographer:
Printer: Lewis & Brown, 272 Pearl St. New–York
Publisher: Lewis & Brown, 272 Pearl St. New–York
Key/Vignettes/Misc: Refs. 1–4
Locations: MM–NN; RCHS–T; Troy, New York, Public Library
Catalogs/Checklists: MM–NN, LP 865; Norton, Whitefield, no. 30

2919
Place: Troy, New York
Date: 1850
Title: Troy General View
Size: 9⁹⁄₁₆ × 11¾ in. (24.3 × 29.9 cm.)
Artist: Aug. Kollner
Lithographer: Deroy
Printer: Cattier
Publisher: Goupil, Vibert & Co., New–York & Paris
Key/Vignettes/Misc:
Locations: PAC–P; YUAG–NH; RCHS–T
Catalogs/Checklists:

2920
Place: Troy, New York
Date: 1850
Title: View of Troy, N. Y. 1848. From Mount Ida.
Size: 23¾ × 39⅛ in. (60.5 × 99.5 cm.)
Artist: H. & D. P. Barringer
Lithographer:
Printer: Sarony & Major, New York
Publisher: H. & D. P. Barringer, Troy, N. Y. (copyright)
Key/Vignettes/Misc:
Locations: MM–NN; CHS–C; RCHS–T
Catalogs/Checklists: MM–NN, LP 1078

2921
Place: Troy, New York
Date: Ca. 1850
Title: View of Troy, N. Y. in 1848 From Mount Ida.
Size: 22½ × 39½ in. (57.3 × 100.5 cm.)
Artist: Edwin Whitefield
Lithographer:
Printer: Sarony & Major, New York
Publisher:
Key/Vignettes/Misc:
Locations: Unknown. Publication assumed on basis of tracing in private collection
Catalogs/Checklists: Norton, Whitefield, no. 46

Place: Troy, New York
Date: [1860–67]
See Cohoes, New York, [1860–67].

2922
Place: Troy, New York
Date: 1877
Title: Troy, N. Y. 1877
Size: 25⅝ × 43⁹⁄₁₆ in. (65.2 × 110.6 cm.)
Artist: H. H. Bailey & J. C. Hazen
Lithographer: C. H. Vogt
Printer: J. Knauber & Co.
Publisher: H. H. Bailey & J. C. Hazen, New York
Key/Vignettes/Misc: Refs. A–H, J–P, R–V
Locations: BPL–R; NYSL–A; RCHS–T; NYH–NY
Catalogs/Checklists:

2923
Place: Troy, New York
Date: 1881
Title: Troy, N. Y. 1881
Size: 28⅜ × 36⅛ in. (72.2 × 91.9 cm.)

Artist:
Lithographer:
Printer: Beck & Pauli, Milwaukee, Wis.
Publisher: Beck & Pauli [Milwaukee]
(copyright)
Key/Vignettes/Misc:
Locations: LC–M; NYH–NY
Catalogs/Checklists: LC–M, 641

2924
Place: Tuckahoe, New York
Date: 1902
Title: Tuckahoe, New York. 1902
Size: 17⅜ × 24⅛ in. (44.2 × 61.4 cm.)
Artist:
Lithographer:
Printer:
Publisher: O. H. Bailey & Co. Boston
Key/Vignettes/Misc: Refs. A, 2–32; 16
vignettes
Locations: NYH–NY
Catalogs/Checklists:

2925
Place: Unadilla, New York
Date: 1887
Title: Unadilla, N. Y. 1887
Size: 13½ × 22¼ in. (34.4 × 56.7 cm.)
Artist: L. R. Burleigh
Lithographer:
Printer: The Burleigh Lith. Est., Troy, N. Y.
Publisher: L. R. Burleigh, Troy, N. Y.
Key/Vignettes/Misc: Refs. 1–12
Locations: LC–M; NYH–NY
Catalogs/Checklists: LC–M, 642

2926
Place: Utica, New York
Date: Ca. 1850
Title: Utica, N. Y.
Size: 22⅝ × 36³⁄₁₆ in. (57.5 × 92 cm.)
Artist: Lewis Bradley
Lithographer: D. W. Moody
Printer: F. Michelin, New York
Publisher: Smith, Brothers & Co., New
York
Key/Vignettes/Misc:
Locations: NYP–S; NYSH–C; CHS–C;
OHS–U; CSNY–S; NYSL–A; NYH–NY
Catalogs/Checklists: Stokes C. 1850—
G–25; Hemenway

2927
Place: Utica, New York
Date: 1873
Title: Bird's Eye View of the City of Utica,
Oneida County, New York. 1873.
Size: 26½ × 36½ in. (67.5 × 92.9 cm.)
Artist: H. Brosius
Lithographer:
Printer:
Publisher:
Key/Vignettes/Misc: Refs. 1–63, A–B; 1
vignette
Locations: OHS–U; LC–M
Catalogs/Checklists: LC–M, 643

2928
Place: Utica, New York
Date: 1894
Title: Birdseye View of the City of Utica,
Oneida County, N. Y. 1894. Compliments
of the Utica Deutsche Zeitung Company.
Size: 28 × 44 in. (71.2 × 112 cm.)

Artist: C.[harles] F. Graneis
Lithographer: Minor
Printer: Utica Deutsche Zeitung Co.
[Utica, New York]
Publisher: Utica Deutsche Zeitung
Company [Utica, New York]
Key/Vignettes/Misc: Refs. 1–195; 21
vignettes
Locations: OHS–U
Catalogs/Checklists:

2929
Place: Valatie, New York
Date: 1881
Title: Valatie, N. Y. 1881
Size: 15 × 20½ in. (38.2 × 52.2 cm.)
Artist: H. H. Rowley & Co.
Lithographer:
Printer: C. H. Vogt & Son, Cleveland
Publisher: H. H. Rowley & Co., Hartford,
Conn.
Key/Vignettes/Misc: Refs. 1–19; 6
vignettes
Locations: BPL–R; Columbia County
Historical Society, Kinderhook, New York
Catalogs/Checklists:

2930
Place: Valley Falls, New York
Date: 1887
Title: Valley Falls, N. Y. 1887
Size: 11 × 19¾ in. (28 × 50.3 cm.)
Artist: L. R. Burleigh
Lithographer:
Printer: Burleigh Lith. Est., Troy, N. Y.
Publisher: L. R. Burleigh, Troy, N. Y.
Key/Vignettes/Misc: Refs. 1–11
Locations: LC–M; NYH–NY
Catalogs/Checklists: LC–M, 644

2931
Place: Valley Stream, New York
Date: 1924
Title: Aero–View of Valley Stream Long
Island 1924
Size: 22 × 34½ in. (55.9 × 57.1 cm.)
Artist: Rene Cinquin
Lithographer: Meriden Gravure Co.
Printer:
Publisher: Hughes & Cinquin, Brooklyn,
N. Y.
Key/Vignettes/Misc: Refs. A–G, H, K–M,
U; 2 vignettes; unnumbered business
directory
Locations: LC–M
Catalogs/Checklists: LC–M, 645

2932
Place: Verplanck, New York
Date: 1836
Title: Verplanck (from the Hudson)
Size: 21½ × 14½ in. (54.6 × 36.8 cm.)
Artist:
Lithographer:
Printer: Bakers Lith, 8 Wall St., N. Y.
Publisher:
Key/Vignettes/Misc:
Locations:
Catalogs/Checklists: Hufeland, Checklist,
305

2933
Place: Walden, New York
Date: 1887

Title: Walden, Orange County, N. Y. 1887
Size: 15 × 24½ in. (38.2 × 62.4 cm.)
Artist: L. R. Burleigh
Lithographer:
Printer: The Burleigh Lith. Est., Troy, N. Y.
Publisher: L. R. Burleigh, Troy, N. Y.
Key/Vignettes/Misc: Refs. 1–22
Locations: LC–M
Catalogs/Checklists: LC–M, 646

2934
Place: Walton, New York
Date: 1887
Title: Walton, N. Y. 1887
Size: 14 × 24 in. (35.7 × 61.1 cm.)
Artist: L. R. Burleigh
Lithographer:
Printer: The Burleigh Litho. Establishment,
Troy, N. Y.
Publisher: L. R. Burleigh, Troy, N. Y.
Key/Vignettes/Misc: Refs. 1–33
Locations: LC–M; NYH–NY; NYSL–A;
LAHS–L
Catalogs/Checklists: LC–M, 647

2935
Place: Wappingers Falls, New York
Date: 1889
Title: Wappingers Falls, N. Y.
Size: 16³⁄₁₆ × 27¹³⁄₁₆ in. (41.2 × 70.8 cm.)
Artist: L. R. Burleigh
Lithographer:
Printer: The Burleigh Lith. Est., Troy, N. Y.
Publisher: L. R. Burleigh, Troy, N.Y.
Key/Vignettes/Misc: Refs. 1–45
Locations: LC–M; NYH–NY; NYSM–A
Catalogs/Checklists: LC–M, 648

2936
Place: Warrensburg, New York
Date: 1891
Title: Warrensburgh, N. Y.
Size: 13 × 29⁷⁄₁₆ in. (33.1 × 74.9 cm.)
Artist:
Lithographer:
Printer: Burleigh Lith. Est., Troy, N. Y.
Publisher: L. R. Burleigh, Troy, N. Y.
Key/Vignettes/Misc: Refs. 1–45
Locations: LC–M; Adirondack Museum,
Blue Mountain Lake, New York;
RCHS–T; NYH–NY
Catalogs/Checklists: LC–M, 649

2937
Place: Warsaw, New York
Date: 1885
Title: Warsaw, N. Y.
Size: 15 × 28 in. (38.2 × 71.2 cm.)
Artist: L. R. Burleigh
Lithographer:
Printer: Beck & Pauli, Litho., Milwaukee
Publisher: L. R. Burleigh, Troy, N. Y.
Key/Vignettes/Misc: Refs. 1–38; 1
vignette
Locations: LC–M
Catalogs/Checklists: LC–M, 650

2938
Place: Warwick, New York
Date: 1887
Title: Warwick, N. Y. 1887
Size: 14 × 20½ in. (35.6 × 52.2 cm.)
Artist: L. R. Burleigh
Lithographer:

Printer: The Burleigh Lith. Est., Troy, N. Y.
Publisher: L. R. Burleigh, Troy, N. Y.
Key/Vignettes/Misc: Refs. 1–33
Locations: LC–M; NYH–NY
Catalogs/Checklists: LC–M, 651

Place: Waterford, New York
Date: [1860–67]
See Cohoes, New York, [1860–67].

2939
Place: Waterloo, New York
Date: 1873
Title: Bird's Eye View of Waterloo. Seneca County N. Y. 1873
Size: 17½ × 21⅝ in. (44.5 × 55.1 cm.)
Artist: Aug. Koch
Lithographer:
Printer:
Publisher: J. J. Stoner
Key/Vignettes/Misc: Refs. 1–30; 2 vignettes
Locations: BPL–R; CHS–C
Catalogs/Checklists:

2940
Place: Watertown, New York
Date: 1891
Title: Watertown, N. Y. Looking Northeast
Size: 20 × 35½ in. (55.9 × 90.3 cm.)
Artist:
Lithographer:
Printer: Burleigh Litho. Co., Troy, N. Y.
Publisher: J. C. Kimball, Watertown, N. Y.
Key/Vignettes/Misc: Refs. 1–92
Locations: LC–M
Catalogs/Checklists: LC–M, 652

2941
Place: Waterville, New York
Date: 1885
Title: Waterville, N. Y. 1885
Size: 14½ × 24⅛ in. (36.9 × 61.4 cm.)
Artist: L. R. Burleigh
Lithographer:
Printer: C. H. Vogt & Son, Lith., Cleveland
Publisher: L. R. Burleigh, Troy, N. Y.
Key/Vignettes/Misc: Refs. 1–19; 1 vignette
Locations: LC–M; NYH–NY
Catalogs/Checklists: LC–M, 652.1

2942
Place: Watkins Glen, New York
Date: 1847
Title: View of Jefferson, Chemung Co., N. Y. Looking North.
Size: 15 × 21½ in. (38.1 × 54.6 cm.)
Artist: H. Walton
Lithographer: H. Walton
Printer: G. & W. Endicott N. York
Publisher:
Key/Vignettes/Misc:
Locations: Unknown
Catalogs/Checklists: Rehner, Walton, no. 60

2943
Place: Watkins Glen, New York
Date: N.D.
Title: Bird's Eye View of Watkins, N. Y.

Size: 21½ × 26¼ in. (54.8 × 66.8 cm.)
Artist: S. F. Bailey
Lithographer:
Printer: Jones & Potsdamer, Lith, 321 Chestnut St. Phila.
Publisher: Fowler & Bailey
Key/Vignettes/Misc: Refs. 1, 2, 7–8, a–e; 1 vignette; description
Locations: CSNY–S
Catalogs/Checklists:

2944
Place: Waverly, New York
Date: 1874
Title: Bird's Eye View of Waverly, N. Y.
Size: ca. 22 × 24 in. (ca. 56 × 61.1 cm.)
Artist: O. H. Bailey
Lithographer: J. H. Toudy & Co.
Printer: J. H. Toudy & Co., Philadelphia
Publisher: T. M. Fowler & Co.
Key/Vignettes/Misc:
Locations: Private collection
Catalogs/Checklists:

2945
Place: Waverly, New York
Date: 1881
Title: Waverly, N. Y. 1881
Size: 17¹⁄₁₆ × 23 in. (43.4 × 58.6 cm.)
Artist: John Moray
Lithographer:
Printer: Thomas Hunter Lith. Phila. Pa.
Publisher: John Moray
Key/Vignettes/Misc: 6 vignettes
Locations: LC–M; Tioga County Historical Society Museum, Owego, New York; NYH–NY
Catalogs/Checklists: LC–M, 653

2946
Place: Weedsport, New York
Date: 1885
Title: Weedsport, N. Y. 1885
Size: 13 × 26½ in. (33.1 × 67.4 cm.)
Artist: L. R. Burleigh
Lithographer:
Printer: C. H. Vogt & Son, Cleveland
Publisher: L. R. Burleigh, Troy, N. Y.
Key/Vignettes/Misc: Refs. 1–33
Locations: LC–M; NYSL–A
Catalogs/Checklists: LC–M, 654

2947
Place: West Chazy, New York
Date: 1899
Title: West Chazy, N. Y.
Size: 15⅛ × 24⅜ in. (38.5 × 62.1 cm.)
Artist: C.[hristian] Fausel
Lithographer:
Printer: L. R. Burleigh Lith, Troy, N. Y.
Publisher: C. Fausel
Key/Vignettes/Misc: Refs. 1–17
Locations: NYSL–A; LC–M; CCHM–P; NYH–NY
Catalogs/Checklists: LC–M, 654.1

2948
Place: White Plains, New York
Date: 1887
Title: White Plains, N. Y. 1887
Size: 14½ × 27¹¹⁄₁₆ in. (36.9 × 70.4 cm.)
Artist: L. R. Burleigh
Lithographer:

Printer: The Burleigh Lith. Est., Troy, N. Y.
Publisher: L. R. Burleigh, Troy, N. Y.
Key/Vignettes/Misc: Refs. 1–10
Locations: LC–M; NYH–NY
Catalogs/Checklists: LC–M, 655

2949
Place: White Plains, New York
Date: 1901
Title: Bird's–Eye View of White Plains
Size: 28 × 40 in. (71.2 × 100.7 cm.)
Artist:
Lithographer:
Printer: T. J. Hughes, N. Y.
Publisher:
Key/Vignettes/Misc:
Locations: Unknown
Catalogs/Checklists: Hufeland, Checklist, 2210

2950
Place: Whitehall, New York
Date: [1828–29]
Title: White–Hall, Lake Champlain
Size: 7½ × 11¼ in. (19.1 × 28.7 cm.)
Artist: [Jacques] Milbert
Lithographer: Bichebois
Printer:
Publisher:
Key/Vignettes/Misc:
Locations: Unknown. See Old Print Shop Portfolio, XXVIII, p. 56, No. 9
Catalogs/Checklists:

2951
Place: Whitehall, New York
Date: 1875
Title: Bird's Eye View of Whitehall, N. Y. 1875.
Size: 20 × 28 in. (50.9 × 71.3 cm.)
Artist: H. H. Bailey & Co.
Lithographer: C. H. Vogt
Printer: J. Knauber & Co.
Publisher: H. H. Bailey & Co.
Key/Vignettes/Misc: Refs. 1–6, A–D
Locations: Skenesborough Museum, Whitehall(?), New York
Catalogs/Checklists:

2952
Place: Whitesboro, New York
Date: 1891
Title: Whitesboro, N. Y.
Size: 16³⁄₁₆ × 28⅝ in. (41.2 × 72.9 cm.)
Artist:
Lithographer:
Printer: Burleigh Lithographing Establishment, Troy, N. Y.
Publisher: L. R. Burleigh, Troy, N. Y.
Key/Vignettes/Misc:
Locations: NYSL–A
Catalogs/Checklists:

Place: Williamsburg, New York
Date: 1852
See New York, New York, 1852.

Place: Williamsburg, New York
Date: 1859
See New York, New York, 1859.

2953
Place: Windsor, New York

Date: 1887
Title: Windsor, N. Y. 1887
Size: 15 × 20⅝ in. (38.2 × 52.5 cm.)
Artist: L. R. Burleigh
Lithographer:
Printer: The Burleigh Lith. Est., Troy, N. Y.
Publisher: L. R. Burleigh, Troy, N. Y.
Key/Vignettes/Misc: Refs. 1–35
Locations: LC–M; BCHS–B; NYH–NY
Catalogs/Checklists: LC–M, 656

2954
Place: Worcester, New York
Date: 1890
Title: Worcester, N. Y.
Size: 14½ × 24⅜ in. (36.9 × 62 cm.)
Artist: L. R. Burleigh
Lithographer:
Printer: Burleigh Lithographing
Establishment, Troy, N. Y.
Publisher: L. R. Burleigh, Troy, N. Y.
Key/Vignettes/Misc: Refs. 1–24
Locations: NYSH–C
Catalogs/Checklists: Hemenway

2955
Place: Yonkers, New York
Date: [1853–55]
Title: View of Yonkers, New York
Size: 16¼ × 24¾ in. (41.3 × 63 cm.)
Artist:
Lithographer:
Printer: Sarony & Co., N. Y.
Publisher:
Key/Vignettes/Misc: Description
Locations: NJHS–N; NYP–P;
YUAG–NH; Hudson River Museum,
Yonkers, New York
Catalogs/Checklists: Eno 493; Hufeland,
Checklist 2436

2956
Place: Yonkers, New York
Date: 1899
Title: Yonkers, N. Y. 1899
Size: 43⅝ × 59 in. (111 × 150 cm.)
Artist:
Lithographer:
Printer:
Publisher: Landis & Hughes, New York
Key/Vignettes/Misc: 24 vignettes;
unnumbered business directory
Locations: LC–M
Catalogs/Checklists: LC–M, 657

2957
Place: Greenspond, Newfoundland
Date: 1846
Title: Greenspond Newfoundland. 1846.
Size: 8 × 14¹⁵⁄₁₆ in. (20.3 × 38 cm.)
Artist: B. Smith
Lithographer:
Printer: T. Whitaker
Publisher:
Key/Vignettes/Misc:
Locations: MTLB–T
Catalogs/Checklists: Robertson, no. 2259

2958
Place: Harbour Grace, Newfoundland
Date: 1879
Title: Panoramic View of Harbour Grace,
Newfoundland, 1879

Size: 8 × 18⁷⁄₁₆ in. (20 × 47 cm.) (photo)
Artist:
Lithographer:
Printer:
Publisher:
Key/Vignettes/Misc: Refs.
Locations: PAC (photo)
Catalogs/Checklists: PAC (1976); deVolpi,
Newfoundland, Plate 154

2959
Place: Saint John's, Newfoundland
Date: [1841–42]
Title: Harbour, Town and Narrows of St.
John's, Newfoundland
Size: 15¹⁄₁₆ × 20 in. (38.3 × 50.9 cm.)
Artist: Wm. P.[ado] Clarke
Lithographer: T. Picken
Printer: Day & Haghe Lithrs. to the
Queen [London]
Publisher:
Key/Vignettes/Misc:
Locations: PAC–P; MTLB–T
Catalogs/Checklists: Robertson, no. 2300

2960
Place: Saint John's, Newfoundland
Date: 1857
Title: South Side of West End of St. John's,
Newfoundland, 1857. Looking
North–East
Size: 8 × 13 in. (20.3 × 33 cm.)
Artist: Rev. William Grey
Lithographer:
Printer: S. D. Cowell, Anastatic Press,
Ipswich
Publisher: S. D. Cowell, Anastatic Press,
Ipswich
Key/Vignettes/Misc:
Locations: MTLB–T
Catalogs/Checklists: Robertson, no. 2276

2961
Place: Saint John's, Newfoundland
Date: 1857
Title: St. John's, Newfoundland, 1857.
Looking to the Sea from the
West–north–west
Size: 9 × 10 in. (22.8 × 25.4 cm.)
Artist: Rev. William Grey
Lithographer:
Printer: S. D. Cowell, Anastatic Press,
Ipswich
Publisher: S. D. Cowell, Anastatic Press,
Ipswich
Key/Vignettes/Misc:
Locations: MTLB–T
Catalogs/Checklists: Robertson, no. 2277

2962
Place: Saint John's, Newfoundland
Date: [1859]
Title: Free St. Andrew's Church, Bank, B.
N. A. &c. &c. Duckworth Street, St.
John's Newfoundland
Size: 11⅛ × 14⁷⁄₁₆ in. (28.3 × 36.8 cm.)
Artist: W. R. Best
Lithographer: W. Spreat
Printer: W. Spreat's Litho. Establishment.
High St. Exeter
Publisher:
Key/Vignettes/Misc:

Locations: PAC–P; MTLB–T
Catalogs/Checklists: Robertson, no. 2260

2963
Place: Saint John's, Newfoundland
Date: [1859]
Title: St. John's, Newfoundland. From the
Freshwater Road, Looking East
Size: 8 × 13 in. (20.3 × 33 cm.)
Artist: W. R. Best
Lithographer: W. Spreat
Printer: W. Spreat's litho. establishment,
High Street, Exeter
Publisher:
Key/Vignettes/Misc:
Locations: MTLB–T
Catalogs/Checklists: Robertson, no. 2261

2964
Place: Saint John's, Newfoundland
Date: [1859]
Title: St. Johns Newfoundland From the
Domain of Government House, Looking
West.
Size: 10¹⁄₁₆ × 13½ in. (25.6 × 34.4 cm.)
Artist: W. R. Best
Lithographer: W. Spreat
Printer: W. Spreat's Litho. Establishment
High St. Exeter
Publisher:
Key/Vignettes/Misc:
Locations: PAC–P
Catalogs/Checklists:

2965
Place: Saint John's, Newfoundland
Date: [1859]
Title: St. Thomas's Church, The Narrows,
&c. From Government House, St. John's
Newfoundland.
Size: 10⅜ × 13⅞ (cropped) in. (26.4 ×
35.3 cm.)
Artist: W. R. Best
Lithographer: W. Spreat
Printer: W. Spreat's Litho. Establishment.
High St. Exeter.
Publisher:
Key/Vignettes/Misc:
Locations: PAC–P; MTLB–T
Catalogs/Checklists: Robertson, no. 2257

2966
Place: Saint John's, Newfoundland
Date: 1865
Title: A View of the Town and Harbour of
St. John's, Newfoundland. . . .
Size: 19½ × 28¾ in. (49.6 × 73.2 cm.)
Artist: From photographs
Lithographer: W. Spreat
Printer: W. Spreat, Exeter
Publisher: F. R. Page
Key/Vignettes/Misc: Refs. A–C
Locations: PAC–P; MCM–M ([1860])
Catalogs/Checklists: deVolpi,
Newfoundland, Plate 79

2967
Place: Saint John's, Newfoundland
Date: 1879
Title: Panoramic View of St. John's,
Newfoundland. 1879
Size: 19⁹⁄₁₆ × 30½ in. (49.7 × 77.4 cm.)

Artist: A. Ruger
Lithographer:
Printer:
Publisher:
Key/Vignettes/Misc: Refs. 1–21, A–P; 1 vignette
Locations: PAC–P; LC–M (photo)
Catalogs/Checklists: PAC (1976); PAC H3/140–St. John's–1879; LC–M, 1073.5

2968
Place: Asheville, North Carolina
Date: 1891
Title: 1891 Bird's–Eye View of the City of Asheville, North Carolina.
Size: 26 × 31 in. (66.2 × 78.9 cm.)
Artist:
Lithographer:
Printer: Burleigh Lith. Est., Troy, New York
Publisher: Ruger & Stoner, Madison, Wis.
Key/Vignettes/Misc: 4 vignettes
Locations: LC–M; NYH–NY
Catalogs/Checklists: LC–M, 658

2969
Place: Asheville, North Carolina
Date: 1912
Title: Asheville, Buncombe Co. N. C. 1912
Size: 24 × 4 in. (61.1 × 86.5 cm.)
Artist: T. M. Fowler
Lithographer:
Printer: Charles Hart, Photo., New York
Publisher: T. M. Fowler, Passaic, N. J.
Key/Vignettes/Misc: 5 vignettes; description
Locations: LC–M
Catalogs/Checklists: LC–M, 659

2970
Place: Black Mountain, North Carolina
Date: 1912
Title: Black Mountain, N. C. 1912
Size: 24 × 32 in. (61.1 × 81.4 cm.)
Artist: [T. M. Fowler]
Lithographer:
Printer: Manhattan Photo Engraving Co., New York
Publisher: Fowler & Browning, Asheville, N. C.
Key/Vignettes/Misc: 6 vignettes; unnumbered business directory; list of Board of Trade Officers; description
Locations: LC–M
Catalogs/Checklists: LC–M, 660

2971
Place: Durham, North Carolina
Date: 1891
Title: Bird's–Eye View of the City of Durham, North Carolina. 1891.
Size: 18 × 29½ in. (45.9 × 75.1 cm.)
Artist:
Lithographer:
Printer: Burleigh Lith. Est., Troy, New York
Publisher: Ruger & Stoner, Madison, Wis.
Key/Vignettes/Misc: Refs. 1–51; 3 vignettes; unnumbered business directory
Locations: LC–M; Duke University Library, Durham, North Carolina
Catalogs/Checklists: LC–M, 661

2972
Place: Greensboro, North Carolina
Date: 1891
Title: Bird's Eye View of the City of Greensboro, North Carolina. 1891. Looking North East Population 8000
Size: 17½ × 29 in. (44.5 × 73.8 cm.)
Artist:
Lithographer:
Printer: Burleigh Lith. Est., Troy, New York
Publisher: Ruger & Stoner, Madison, Wis.
Key/Vignettes/Misc: Refs. A–Z, 1–24, 26; 2 vignettes; unnumbered business directory
Locations: LC–M
Catalogs/Checklists: LC–M, 662

2973
Place: Hendersonville, North Carolina
Date: 1913
Title: Hendersonville, N. C. 1913.
Size: 21½ × 31½ in. (54.8 × 80.1 cm.)
Artist: [T. M. Fowler]
Lithographer:
Printer: [Manhattan Photo Engraving Co., New York]
Publisher: Fowler & Browning, Asheville, N. C.
Key/Vignettes/Misc: 9 vignettes; unnumbered business directory; description
Locations: LC–M
Catalogs/Checklists: LC–M, 663

2974
Place: High Point, North Carolina
Date: 1913
Title: Aero View of High Point, North Carolina
Size: 15⁵⁄₁₆ × 27¹⁵⁄₁₆ in. (39 × 71 cm.)
Artist: T. M. Fowler
Lithographer:
Printer: Charles Hart Lith. N. Y.
Publisher: J. J. Farris, High Point, N. C.
Key/Vignettes/Misc: Refs. 1–59, A–H, J–M
Locations: LC–M
Catalogs/Checklists: LC–M, 665

2975
Place: Marion, North Carolina
Date: 1912
Title:
Size:
Artist: T. M. Fowler
Lithographer:
Printer:
Publisher:
Key/Vignettes/Misc:
Locations:
Catalogs/Checklists: Warren

2976
Place: New Bern, North Carolina
Date: 1864
Title: New Berne, N. C.
Size: 20½ × 30⁵⁄₁₆ in. (52.1 × 77.2 cm.)
Artist: [Voltaire] Combe
Lithographer:
Printer: Major & Knapp 499 Broadway New York

Publisher: V. Combe (copyright)
Key/Vignettes/Misc: 23 refs. in 5 lines
Locations: MM–NN; NYP–S; CHS–C; Tryon Palace Restoration Complex, New Bern, North Carolina; LC–M (facsimile); LC–P; CSNY–S; NYH–NY
Catalogs/Checklists: MM–NN, LP 50; Stokes P. 1863–G–75; LC–M, 665.1

2977
Place: Raleigh, North Carolina
Date: 1872
Title: Bird's Eye View of the City of Raleigh, North Carolina 1872.
Size: 20⁷⁄₁₆ × 28⁵⁄₁₆ in. (52 × 72 cm.)
Artist: C. Drie
Lithographer:
Printer:
Publisher: C. Drie
Key/Vignettes/Misc: Refs. 1–47; 2 vignettes
Locations: LC–M
Catalogs/Checklists: LC–M, 666

2978
Place: Rocky Mount, North Carolina
Date: 1907
Title: Bird's Eye View of Rocky Mount, North Carolina 1907.
Size: 20⁷⁄₁₆ × 27⁵⁄₈ in. (52 × 70.4 cm.)
Artist: T. M. Fowler
Lithographer:
Printer: Charles Hart Photo–Litho. 36 Vessey St., N. Y.
Publisher: T. M. Fowler, Morrisville, Pa.
Key/Vignettes/Misc: 18 vignettes
Locations: LC–M; North Carolina Division of Archives & History, Raleigh, North Carolina; LC–P
Catalogs/Checklists: LC–M, 667

2979
Place: South Rocky Mount, North Carolina
Date: 1907
Title: Property of the South Rocky Mount Land Co. at South Rocky Mount, N. C.
Size: 13½ × 18 in. (34.3 × 45.8 cm.)
Artist: T. M. Fowler
Lithographer:
Printer:
Publisher:
Key/Vignettes/Misc:
Locations: LC–M
Catalogs/Checklists: LC–M, 666

2980
Place: Weaverville, North Carolina
Date: 1908
Title:
Size:
Artist: T. M. Fowler
Lithographer:
Printer:
Publisher:
Key/Vignettes/Misc:
Locations:
Catalogs/Checklists: Warren

2981
Place: Wilson, North Carolina
Date: 1908

Title: Birds Eye View of Wilson, North Carolina 1908.
Size: 19¹¹⁄₁₆ × 30¼ in. (50 × 77 cm.)
Artist: T. M. Fowler
Lithographer:
Printer:
Publisher: T. M. Fowler, Morrisville, Pa.
Key/Vignettes/Misc: 29 vignettes
Locations: LC–M
Catalogs/Checklists: LC–M, 670

2982
Place: Winston–Salem, North Carolina
Date: 1891
Title: Bird's Eye View of the Twin Cities, Winston–Salem, North Carolina 1891.
Size: 16½ × 34⅝ in. (42 × 88.1 cm.)
Artist:
Lithographer:
Printer:
Publisher: Ruger & Stoner, Madison
Key/Vignettes/Misc: Refs. A–N, 1–62; unnumbered business directory
Locations: LC–M; North Carolina Division of Archives and History, Raleigh, North Carolina; University of North Carolina Library, Chapel Hill, North Carolina
Catalogs/Checklists: LC–M, 671

2983
Place: Bismarck, North Dakota
Date: 1883
Title: View of the City of Bismarck, Dak. Capital of Dakota and County–Seat of Burleigh–County. 1883.
Size: 14⅛ × 25½ in. (35.9 × 64.9 cm.)
Artist:
Lithographer:
Printer: Beck & Pauli, Lithographers, Milwaukee, Wis.
Publisher: J. J. Stoner, Madison, Wis.
Key/Vignettes/Misc: Refs. 1–25, A–E; 4 vignettes
Locations: LC–M; SDHS–P (photo); LC–P
Catalogs/Checklists: LC–M, 672; Reps, Cities on Stone, p. 91; SDH VIII–3, p. 228

2984
Place: Fargo, North Dakota
Date: 1880
Title: Bird's Eye View of Fargo Dakota 1880.
Size: 12¼ × 22½ in. (31.2 × 57.3 cm.)
Artist: T. M. Fowler
Lithographer:
Printer: Beck & Pauli, Milwaukee, Wis.
Publisher: J. J. Stoner, Madison, Wis.
Key/Vignettes/Misc: Refs. 1–28; 1 vignette
Locations: NYP–P; LC–M (photo)
Catalogs/Checklists: LC–M, 672.2

2985
Place: Grand Forks, North Dakota
Date: 1880
Title: Birds' Eye View of Grand Forks, Dakota, 1880
Size: 9¹³⁄₁₆ × 23³⁄₁₆ in. (25 × 59 cm.)
Artist: T. M. Fowler
Lithographer:

Printer: D. Bremner & Co. Lith. [Chicago]
Publisher:
Key/Vignettes/Misc: 21 refs.
Locations: North Dakota Historical Society, Bismarck, North Dakota
Catalogs/Checklists:

2986
Place: Jamestown, North Dakota
Date: 1883
Title: Bird's Eye View of Jamestown, Dak., C. S. of Stutsman County 1883.
Size: 13⅜ × 25½ in. (34 × 65 cm.)
Artist:
Lithographer:
Printer: Beck & Pauli, Lithographers, Milwaukee, Wis.
Publisher: J. J. Stoner, Madison, Wis.
Key/Vignettes/Misc: Refs. 1–24; 1 vignette; unnumbered business directory
Locations: LC–M; ACMW–FW
Catalogs/Checklists: LC–M, 673

2987
Place: Mandan, North Dakota
Date: 1883
Title: Bird's Eye View of Mandan, Dak. County Seat of Morton Co. 1883.
Size: 12⅞ × 21¾ in. (32.8 × 55.4 cm.)
Artist:
Lithographer:
Printer: Beck & Pauli, Milwaukee, Wis.
Publisher: J. J. Stoner, Madison, Wis.
Key/Vignettes/Misc: Refs. 1–10, A–F; 2 vignettes
Locations: LC–M; ACMW–FW
Catalogs/Checklists: LC–M, 674

2988
Place: Annapolis, Royal, Nova Scotia
Date: 1878
Title: Bird's Eye View of Annapolis Royal & Granville, Nova Scotia, 1878.
Size: 14¼ × 18³⁄₁₆ in. (36.4 × 46.3 cm.)
Artist: T. M. Fowler
Lithographer:
Printer:
Publisher:
Key/Vignettes/Misc: Refs. 1–16, A–F
Locations: NSM–H; PANS–H (facsimile)
Catalogs/Checklists: PAC (1976)

2989
Place: Digby, Nova Scotia
Date: 1835
Title: View of Digby,—Nova Scotia
Size: 6⅛ × 9 in. (15.6 × 22.9 cm.)
Artist: M.[ary] G. Hall
Lithographer: Mrs. Hall
Printer: Pendleton's Lithography, Boston
Publisher: [M. G. Hall, St. John, New Brunswick]
Key/Vignettes/Misc:
Locations: PAC–P; MTLB–T
Catalogs/Checklists: deVolpi, Nova Scotia, Plate 60; Robertson, no. 2143

2990
Place: Digby, Nova Scotia
Date: 1878
Title: Bird's Eye View of Digby, Nova Scotia. 1878
Size:

Artist: T. M. Fowler
Lithographer:
Printer:
Publisher:
Key/Vignettes/Misc: Refs. 1–14
Locations: NSM–H (photo)
Catalogs/Checklists:

2991
Place: Grand Pré, Nova Scotia
Date: [1840]
Title: View from the Horton Mountains, Looking Over Grand Pre.
Size: 6½ × 9½ in. (16.5 × 24.2 cm.)
Artist: Wm Eagar
Lithographer: Wm Eagar
Printer: T. Moore's Lithography, Boston
Publisher: [C. H. Belcher, Hollis St., Halifax]
Key/Vignettes/Misc:
Locations: PAC–P
Catalogs/Checklists: deVolpi, Nova Scotia, Plate 87

Place: Granville, Nova Scotia
Date: 1878
See Annapolis, Royal, Nova Scotia, 1878.

2992
Place: Halifax, Nova Scotia
Date: 1831
Title: View of Halifax from Dartmouth Cove
Size: 6⅛ × 8⅛ in. (15.5 × 20.8 cm.)
Artist:
Lithographer: L. Haghe
Printer: Day & Haghe, Lithrs. to the King. 17 Gate St. Linc. Inn Fds. [London]
Publisher:
Key/Vignettes/Misc:
Locations: PAC–P; MCM–M; NSM–H; MTLB–T
Catalogs/Checklists: deVolpi, Nova Scotia, Plate 59; Robertson, no. 2195

2993
Place: Halifax, Nova Scotia
Date: Ca. 1837
Title: Halifax from Point Pleasant.
Size: ca. 7 × 10 in. (17.8 × 25.4 cm.)
Artist: R.[obert] Petley
Lithographer: R.[obert] Petley
Printer: Day & Haghe Lithrs. to the King. [London]
Publisher:
Key/Vignettes/Misc:
Locations: PAC–P; ROM
Catalogs/Checklists: Samuel, no. 738; deVolpi, Nova Scotia, Plate 72; Spendlove, Face of Early Canada, p. 34, Plate 50

2994
Place: Halifax, Nova Scotia
Date: Ca. 1837
Title: View of Halifax. From the Indian Encampment at Dartmouth.
Size: ca. 7 × 10 in. (17.8 × 25.4 cm.)
Artist: R.[obert] Petley
Lithographer: R.[obert] Petley
Printer: Day & Haghe Lithrs to the King [London]
Publisher:

Key/Vignettes/Misc:
Locations: PAC–P; ROM; MTLB–T
Catalogs/Checklists: deVolpi, Nova Scotia, Plate 63; Spendlove, Face of Early Canada, p. 34; Samuel, no. 730 Robertson, no. 2208

2995
Place: Halifax, Nova Scotia
Date: [1839]
Title: Entrance to Halifax Harbour From Reeve's Hill, Dartmouth.
Size: 8$\frac{1}{16}$ × 10$\frac{13}{16}$ in. (20.5 × 27.6 cm.)
Artist: Wm Eagar
Lithographer: Wm Eagar
Printer: Thos. Moore's Lithography, Boston
Publisher: [C. H. Belcher, Hollis St., Halifax]
Key/Vignettes/Misc:
Locations: PAC–P; NSM–H; MTLB–T; PANS–H; ROM; DHM–D
Catalogs/Checklists: deVolpi, Nova Scotia, Plate 80

2996
Place: Halifax, Nova Scotia
Date: [1839]
Title: Halifax, From the Red Mill, Dartmouth.
Size: 8$\frac{3}{8}$ × 10$\frac{7}{8}$ in. (21.3 × 27.7 cm.)
Artist: Wm. Eagar
Lithographer: Wm. Eagar
Printer: T. Moore's Lithogy. Boston
Publisher: [C. H. Belcher, Hollis St., Halifax]
Key/Vignettes/Misc:
Locations: PAC–P; MCM–M; MTLB–T; NSM–H; DU–H
Catalogs/Checklists: Robertson, no. 2174; deVolpi, Nova Scotia, Plate 79

2997
Place: Halifax, Nova Scotia
Date: [1839]
Title: View of Halifax, N. S. From McNab's Island.
Size: 10 × 13 in. (25.4 × 33 cm.)
Artist: Wm. Eagar
Lithographer: Wm. Eagar
Printer: T. Moore's Lithography, Boston
Publisher: [C. H. Belcher, Halifax]
Key/Vignettes/Misc:
Locations: PAC–P; NSM–H; MTLB–T; PANS–H; DU–H
Catalogs/Checklists: Robertson, no. 2171; deVolpi, Nova Scotia, Plate 83

2998
Place: Halifax, Nova Scotia
Date: Ca. 1854 State I
Title: Halifax, From McNab's Island.
Size: 14 × 18$\frac{3}{4}$ in. (35.7 × 47.7 cm.)
Artist: W.[estcote Whitechurch Lewis] Lyttleton
Lithographer: Hullmandel & Walton
Printer:
Publisher:
Key/Vignettes/Misc:
Locations: PANS–H; DU–H
Catalogs/Checklists:

2999
Place: Halifax, Nova Scotia
Date: Ca. 1855
Title: Halifax, N. S. Dedicated by Permission to His Excellency Sir Gaspard Le Marchant, Lt. Governor of Nova Scotia. . . .
Size: 26$\frac{11}{16}$ × 42 in. (68 × 106.6 cm.)
Artist: J. W. Hill
Lithographer: C. Parsons
Printer: Endicott & Co., N. Y.
Publisher: Smith Bros. & Co. 59 Beekman Street, N. Y.
Key/Vignettes/Misc:
Locations: NYP–S; PAC–P; PANS–H; DHM–D; NSM–H; DU–H
Catalogs/Checklists: Stokes C. 1854—H–8; deVolpi, Nova Scotia, Plate 108

3000
Place: Halifax, Nova Scotia
Date: Ca. 1855 State II
Title: Halifax, From McNab's Island.
Size: 14$\frac{11}{16}$ × 18$\frac{3}{4}$ in. (37.4 × 47.8 cm.)
Artist: W.[estcote Whitechurch Lewis] Lyttleton
Lithographer:
Printer: S. W. Chandler & Bro. Lith. Boston
Publisher: E. G. Fuller, Halifax, N. W.
Key/Vignettes/Misc:
Locations: PAC–P; DU–H; PANS–H; MTLB–T
Catalogs/Checklists: Robertson, no. 57; deVolpi, Nova Scotia, Plate 118 (ca. 1862 and R. R. Wetmore, publisher)

3001
Place: Halifax, Nova Scotia
Date: Ca. 1860
Title: Halifax, Nova Scotia.
Size: 14$\frac{1}{8}$ × 23$\frac{13}{16}$ in. (35.9 × 60.6 cm.)
Artist: William Hickman
Lithographer:
Printer: Day & Son, Chromolithographers to the Queen
Publisher: John B. Strong, Bookseller Librarian, Halifax
Key/Vignettes/Misc:
Locations: MTLB–T; PAC–P; NSM–H; DU–H
Catalogs/Checklists: deVolpi, Nova Scotia, Plate 113; Spendlove, Face of Early Canada, p. 72; Robertson, no. 2163

3002
Place: Halifax, Nova Scotia
Date: 1865
Title: City of Halifax—Nova Scotia as Seen From the Cupola of the Mount Hope Asylum.
Size: 28$\frac{1}{8}$ × 49$\frac{9}{16}$ in. (71.2 × 125.9 cm.)
Artist: F. Day & Photo by J. R. Woodburn
Lithographer: A. Arnst
Printer: W. H. McFarland, Edinburgh
Publisher: R. T. Muir. . ., 125 Granville Street, Halifax, N. S.
Key/Vignettes/Misc:
Locations: PAC–P; PANS–H; DHM–D
Catalogs/Checklists: deVolpi, Nova Scotia, Plate 121; Samuel, no. 757

3003
Place: Halifax, Nova Scotia
Date: 1879
Title: Panoramic View of the City of Halifax, Nova Scotia 1879
Size: 18$\frac{15}{16}$ × 35$\frac{3}{8}$ in. (48.3 × 90.1 cm.)
Artist: A. Ruger
Lithographer:
Printer:
Publisher:
Key/Vignettes/Misc: Refs. 1–114
Locations: LC–M; PANS–H; MCM–M; NSM–H; PAC
Catalogs/Checklists: LC–M, 1071; PAC H3/240–Halifax–1879

3004
Place: Halifax, Nova Scotia
Date: 1890
Title: The City of Halifax, Nova Scotia. 1890.
Size: 22$\frac{3}{4}$ × 35$\frac{3}{4}$ in. (58 × 91 cm.)
Artist:
Lithographer:
Printer:
Publisher: D.[uncan] D. Currie, Moncton, N. B.
Key/Vignettes/Misc: Refs. A, 2–102; 57 vignettes; directory of public officials and important citizens
Locations: NSM–H; PANS–H; PAC (facsimile); MCM–M; LC–M (facsimile)
Catalogs/Checklists: PAC (1976); PAC V1/240–Halifax–1890; LC–M, 1071.1

3005
Place: Halifax, Nova Scotia
Date: 1933
Title: Illustrated Plan of the City of Halifax, Nova Scotia. . . .
Size: 13$\frac{1}{16}$ × 17$\frac{1}{8}$ in. (33.2 × 43.6 cm.)
Artist:
Lithographer:
Printer:
Publisher: Arthur W. Wallace
Key/Vignettes/Misc:
Locations: PAC
Catalogs/Checklists:

3006
Place: Halifax, Nova Scotia
Date: 1935
Title: Halifax/Nova Scotia
Size: 19$\frac{3}{4}$ × 27$\frac{3}{4}$ in. (50.3 x 70.7 cm.)
Artist: Arthur W. Wallace
Lithographer:
Printer:
Publisher: The Canadian Civic Map Service
Key/Vignettes/Misc: Street index for Halifax and Dartmouth; directory; tram routes for Halifax; bus routes for Dartmouth
Locations: NSM–H
Catalogs/Checklists:

3007
Place: Kentville, Nova Scotia
Date: 1879
Title: Bird's Eye View of Kentville Nova Scotia. 1879.

Size: 12½ × 17³⁄₁₆ in. (31.7 × 43.8 cm.)
(facsimile)
Artist: T. M. Fowler
Lithographer:
Printer:
Publisher:
Key/Vignettes/Misc: Refs. 1–20
Locations: PAC (facsimile); NSM–H
(facsimile); LC–M (facsimile)
Catalogs/Checklists: LC–M, 1071.3

3008

Place: Londonderry, Nova Scotia
Date: 1889
Title: Acadia Iron Mines Nova Scotia.
1889
Size: 14¹¹⁄₁₆ × 21⅜ in. (37.4 × 54.5 cm.)
Artist:
Lithographer:
Printer:
Publisher: D. D. Currie, Moncton, N. B.
Key/Vignettes/Misc: 9 vignettes
Locations: PANS–H; NSM–H
Catalogs/Checklists: PAC (1976)

3009

Place: Lunenburg, Nova Scotia
Date: 1879
Title: Bird's Eye View of Lunenburg
Lunenburg Co. Nova Scotia 1879
Size: 12⁹⁄₁₆ × 16⅞ in. (32 × 43 cm.)
Artist: A. Ruger
Lithographer:
Printer:
Publisher:
Key/Vignettes/Misc: Refs. 1–22, A–E
Locations: PAC (newspaper reproduction);
NSM–H
Catalogs/Checklists: PAC
H3/240–Lunenburg–1879

3010

Place: Lunenburg, Nova Scotia
Date: 1890
Title: Lunenburg, Nova Scotia. 1890
Size: 22¾ × 31½ in. (57.9 × 80.1 cm.)
Artist:
Lithographer: O. H. Bailey & Co.
Printer: O. H. Bailey & Co. Lith. & Print.
Boston.
Publisher: D. D. Currie, Moncton, N. B.
Key/Vignettes/Misc: Refs. 1–34; 61
vignettes; unnumbered list of public
officials and important citizens
Locations: BPL–R; NSM–H; PANS–H
Catalogs/Checklists: PAC (1976)

3011

Place: New Glasgow, Nova Scotia
Date: 1878
Title: Panoramic View of New Glasgow
Pictou County Nova Scotia, 1878.
Size: 13 × 18⅛ in. (33 × 46.1 cm.)
Artist:
Lithographer:
Printer:
Publisher:
Key/Vignettes/Misc: Refs. 1–22
Locations: NSM–H
Catalogs/Checklists: PAC (1976)

3012

Place: New Glasgow, Nova Scotia
Date: 1889
Title: New Glasgow Nova Scotia, 1889.
Size: 22¼ × 30⅛ in. (56.7 × 76.8 cm.)
Artist:
Lithographer:
Printer: [O. H. Bailey & Co., Boston?]
Publisher: D. D. Currie, Moncton, N.B.
Key/Vignettes/Misc: Refs. 1–28; 44
vignettes
Locations: BPL–R; NSM–H
Catalogs/Checklists:

3013

Place: Pictou, Nova Scotia
Date: [1840]
Title: Pictou from Fort Hill
Size: 8½ × 10¾ in. (21.6 × 27.4 cm.)
Artist: Wm. Eagar
Lithographer: B. Champney
Printer: Thayer, successor to Moore,
Boston
Publisher: [C. H. Belcher, Hollis St.
Halifax]
Key/Vignettes/Misc:
Locations: PAC–P; NSM–H; PANS–H;
ROM; DU–H; MTLB–T
Catalogs/Checklists: Robertson, no. 2170;
deVolpi, Nova Scotia, Plate 90

3014

Place: Pictou, Nova Scotia
Date: [1840]
Title: Pictou, From the Road to Halifax.
Size: 8½ × 10¾ in. (21.6 × 27.3 cm.)
Artist: Wm. Eagar
Lithographer: B. Champney
Printer: Thayer, Successor to Moore,
Boston
Publisher: [C. H. Belcher, Hollis St.,
Halifax]
Key/Vignettes/Misc:
Locations: PAC–P; NSM–H; MTLB–T;
DU–H; PANS–H; ROM
Catalogs/Checklists: Robertson, no. 2177;
deVolpi, Nova Scotia, Plate 89

3015

Place: Pictou, Nova Scotia
Date: [1840]
Title: Pictou, From Mortimer's Point.
Size: 5¼ × 10¹³⁄₁₆ in. (21 × 27.5 cm.)
Artist: Wm. Eagar
Lithographer: B. Champney
Printer: Thayer, successor to Moore,
Boston
Publisher: [C. H. Belcher, Hollis St.,
Halifax]
Key/Vignettes/Misc:
Locations: PAC–P; NSM–H; MTLB–T;
ROM; DU–H; DHM–D
Catalogs/Checklists: Robertson, no. 2181;
deVolpi, Nova Scotia, Plate 88

3016

Place: Pictou, Nova Scotia
Date: 1878
Title: Panoramic View of Pictou Pictou
County Nova Scotia 1878
Size: 15⅛ × 24¹¹⁄₁₆ in. (38.6 × 62.9 cm.)

Artist: A. Ruger
Lithographer:
Printer:
Publisher: [J. J. Stoner, Madison, Wis.]
Key/Vignettes/Misc: Refs. 1–34; 1
vignette drawn by T. M. Fowler
Locations: PAC (facsimile); NSM–H
Catalogs/Checklists: PAC (1976)

3017

Place: Truro, Nova Scotia
Date: 1878
Title: Panoramic View of Truro Colchester
County Nova Scotia Looking from
Foundry Hill
Size: 20¾ × 30⅝ in. (52.8 × 77.9 cm.)
Artist:
Lithographer:
Printer:
Publisher:
Key/Vignettes/Misc: Refs. 1–24, A–H; 1
vignette
Locations: PANB–F; PANS–H (facsimile)
Catalogs/Checklists:

3018

Place: Truro, Nova Scotia
Date: 1889
Title: Truro, Nova Scotia. 1889.
Size: 22⅞ × 30⅜ in. (58.2 × 77.3 cm.)
Artist:
Lithographer:
Printer:
Publisher: D. D. Currie, Moncton, N. B.
Key/Vignettes/Misc: Refs. A, 2–55; 60
vignettes
Locations: BPL–R; Colchester Historical
Museum, Truro, Nova Scotia; PANS–H
(facsimile); NSM–H (facsimile)
Catalogs/Checklists: PAC (1976)

3019

Place: Windsor, Nova Scotia
Date: 1837
Title: Windsor N. S. From the Barracks
Size: 7 × 10 in. (17.8 × 25.4 cm.)
Artist: R.[obert] Petley
Lithographer: R.[obert] Petley
Printer: C. Hullmandel [London]
Publisher: J. Dickinson, London. . .
Key/Vignettes/Misc:
Locations: PAC–P; MTLB–T
Catalogs/Checklists: Robertson, no. 2198;
deVolpi, Nova Scotia, Plate 68

3020

Place: Windsor, Nova Scotia
Date: [1840]
Title: Windsor, N. S. From Fort Hill
Size: 8⅛ × 10¹³⁄₁₆ in. (20.8 × 27.6 cm.)
Artist: W. Eagar
Lithographer: W. Eagar
Printer: Thayer, successor to Moore,
Boston
Publisher: [C. H. Belcher, Hollis St.,
Halifax]
Key/Vignettes/Misc:
Locations: PAC–P; NSM–H; PANS–H;
ROM; MTLB–T; DHM–D; DU–H
Catalogs/Checklists: Robertson, no. 2178;
deVolpi, Nova Scotia, Plate 85

3021
Place: Windsor, Nova Scotia
Date: 1868
Title: Nova Scotia Scenery
Size: 9¾ × 16¹⁵⁄₁₆ in. (24.7 × 43.1 cm.)
Artist:
Lithographer:
Printer:
Publisher: Currier & Ives, 152 Nassau St. New York
Key/Vignettes/Misc:
Locations: PAC–P; NSM–H
Catalogs/Checklists: deVolpi, Nova Scotia, Plate 122

3022
Place: Windsor, Nova Scotia
Date: 1868
Title: Windsor, N. S. Looking West from Ferry Hill, 1868
Size: 10 × 17 in. (25.4 × 43.3 cm.)
Artist:
Lithographer:
Printer:
Publisher:
Key/Vignettes/Misc:
Locations: MTLB–T
Catalogs/Checklists: Robertson, no. 2239

3023
Place: Windsor, Nova Scotia
Date: 1878
Title: Bird's Eye View of Windsor, Nova Scotia.
Size: 16¼ × 22³⁄₁₆ in. (41.4 × 56.5 cm.)
Artist: T. M. Fowler
Lithographer:
Printer:
Publisher:
Key/Vignettes/Misc: Refs. 1–27
Locations: PANS–H; LC–M (photo)
Catalogs/Checklists: PAC (1976); LC–M, 1077.1

3024
Place: Yarmouth, Nova Scotia
Date: 1878
Title: Panoramic View of Yarmouth, Yarmouth County, Nova Scotia, 1878
Size: 16½ × 29½ in. (41.9 × 75.1 cm.)
Artist: Ruger
Lithographer:
Printer:
Publisher:
Key/Vignettes/Misc: Refs. 1–51, A–L
Locations: Yarmouth County Museum, Yarmouth, Nova Scotia
Catalogs/Checklists:

3025
Place: Yarmouth, Nova Scotia
Date: 1889
Title: Yarmouth, Nova Scotia. 1889.
Size: 23 × 32¼ in. (58.5 × 82 cm.)
Artist:
Lithographer:
Printer:
Publisher: Duncan D. Currie, Moncton, New Brunswick
Key/Vignettes/Misc: Refs. A, 2–40; 64 vignettes
Locations: BPL–R; Yarmouth County

Museum, Yarmouth, Nova Scotia; NSM–H (facsimile)
Catalogs/Checklists: PAC (1976)

3026
Place: Akron, Ohio
Date: 1870
Title: Bird's eye view of the city of Akron. Summit County Ohio 1870.
Size: 22 × 28¼ in. (56 × 72 cm.)
Artist: A. Ruger
Lithographer:
Printer: Chicago Lithographing Co. [Chicago]
Publisher: Ruger & Stoner, Madison, Wis.
Key/Vignettes/Misc: Refs. 1–20; 5 vignettes
Locations: LC–M
Catalogs/Checklists: LC–M, 675

3027
Place: Akron, Ohio
Date: 1882
Title: Panoramic view of the city of Akron, Summit County, Ohio, 1882.
Size: 19¼ × 28¹¹⁄₁₆ in. (49 × 73 cm.)
Artist: [Albert Ruger]
Lithographer:
Printer: Beck & Pauli, Milwaukee, Wis.
Publisher: Ruger & Stoner, Madison, Wis.
Key/Vignettes/Misc: Refs. 1–55, A–H, K–U, W, X
Locations: LC–M
Catalogs/Checklists: LC–M, 677

3028
Place: Akron, Ohio
Date: 1882
Title: Sixth ward of Akron, formerly Middlebury, Summit Co., Ohio 1882.
Size: 9⁷⁄₁₆ × 16⁷⁄₈ in. (24 × 43 cm.)
Artist: [Albert Ruger]
Lithographer:
Printer: Beck & Pauli, Milwaukee, Wis.
Publisher: Ruger & Stoner, Madison, Wis.
Key/Vignettes/Misc: Refs. 1–6, A–G
Locations: LC–M
Catalogs/Checklists: LC–M, 676

3029
Place: Ashland, Ohio
Date: N.D.
Title: Bird's–Eye View of Ashland, Ohio
Size: 17⁵⁄₈ × 25¹⁵⁄₁₆ in. (44.9 × 66 cm.)
Artist:
Lithographer:
Printer: Thos. Hunter, Lith. 716 Filbert St. Phila.
Publisher: Howland & Germann
Key/Vignettes/Misc: 13 vignettes
Locations: OHS–C; WRHS–C
Catalogs/Checklists:

3030
Place: Ashtabula, Ohio
Date: 1896
Title: Ashtabula Harbor, Ohio 1896.
Size: 16⁷⁄₈ × 26⁵⁄₁₆ in. (43 × 67 cm.)
Artist: T. M. Fowler
Lithographer:
Printer:
Publisher: T. M. Fowler & James B. Moyer, Morrisville, Pa.

Key/Vignettes/Misc: Refs. 1–10, A–I
Locations: LC–M; CHS–C
Catalogs/Checklists: LC–M, 678

3031
Place: Barnesville, Ohio
Date: 1899
Title: Barnesville, Ohio 1899.
Size: 12³⁄₁₆ × 25⅛ in. (31 × 64 cm.)
Artist: T. M. Fowler
Lithographer:
Printer:
Publisher: T. M. Fowler & James B. Moyer, Morrisville, Pa.
Key/Vignettes/Misc: Refs. A–D, 1–13
Locations: LC–M; OHS–C
Catalogs/Checklists: LC–M, 679

3032
Place: Bedford, Ohio
Date: 1885
Title: Birdseye View of Bedford 1885
Size: 15 × 20 in. (38.2 × 50.8 cm.)
Artist:
Lithographer:
Printer:
Publisher:
Key/Vignettes/Misc:
Locations: Bedford Historical Society, Bedford, Ohio; OHS–C
Catalogs/Checklists:

3033
Place: Bellaire, Ohio
Date: 1882
Title: Bird's eye view of Bellaire, Ohio, 1882.
Size: 9⁷⁄₁₆ × 24⅜ in. (24 × 62 cm.)
Artist: H. Wellge
Lithographer:
Printer: Beck & Pauli, Milwaukee, Wis.
Publisher: J. J. Stoner, Madison, Wis.
Key/Vignettes/Misc: Refs. 1–34, A–X; 1 vignette; unnumbered business directory
Locations: LC–M
Catalogs/Checklists: LC–M, 680

3034
Place: Bellevue, Ohio
Date: 1888
Title: Bellevue, Ohio, Sandusky & Huron counties 1888.
Size: 14½ × 28¼ in. (37 × 72 cm.)
Artist:
Lithographer:
Printer: Burleigh Lith. Est, Troy, N. Y.
Publisher: Burleigh & Norris, Troy, N. Y.
Key/Vignettes/Misc: Refs. 1–52; 3 vignettes
Locations: LC–M
Catalogs/Checklists: LC–M, 681

3035
Place: Bowling Green, Ohio
Date: 1888
Title: Bowling Green, Ohio 1888.
Size: 14½ × 25⅛ in. (37 × 64 cm.)
Artist:
Lithographer:
Printer: Burleigh Lith. Est., Troy, N. Y.
Publisher: Burleigh & Norris, Troy, N. Y.
Key/Vignettes/Misc: Refs. 1–60, A–H; 1 vignette

Locations: LC–M
Catalogs/Checklists: LC–M, 682

3036
Place: Burlington, Ohio
Date: N.D.
Title: Burlington. Formerly the County Seat of Lawrence Co., Ohio
Size: 15½ × 19⅛ in. (39.5 × 48.7 cm.)
Artist: Theo. Strong
Lithographer:
Printer: Strobridge & Co. Lith. Cinci. Ohio
Publisher:
Key/Vignettes/Misc: 4 vignettes
Locations: Unknown. Old Print Shop, 9/21/79
Catalogs/Checklists:

3037
Place: Cambridge, Ohio
Date: 1899
Title: Cambridge, Ohio 1899.
Size: 18¹⁄₁₆ × 31¹³⁄₁₆ in. (46 × 81 cm.)
Artist: T. M. Fowler
Lithographer:
Printer:
Publisher: Fowler & Jas. B. Moyer, Morrisville, Pa.
Key/Vignettes/Misc: Refs. 1–20, A–L; 2 vignettes
Locations: LC–M
Catalogs/Checklists: LC–M, 683

3038
Place: Canal Dover, Ohio
Date: 1899
Title: Canal Dover, Tuscarawas County, Ohio 1899.
Size: 20¹⁄₁₆ × 28⁵⁄₁₆ in. (51 × 72 cm.)
Artist: A. E. Downs
Lithographer:
Printer:
Publisher: T. M. Fowler & A. E. Downs, Boston
Key/Vignettes/Misc:
Locations: LC–M; OHS–C
Catalogs/Checklists: LC–M, 684

3039
Place: Canton, Ohio
Date: N.D.
Title: View of Canton, State of Ohio, North America
Size: 14⅜ × 19¾ in. (36.6 × 50.3 cm.)
Artist: Adolphus Wever
Lithographer:
Printer: Klauprech & Menzel, Cincinnati, O.
Publisher:
Key/Vignettes/Misc:
Locations: Unknown
Catalogs/Checklists: Pyne, no. 409

3040
Place: Chillicothe, Ohio
Date: 1854
Title: View of Chillicothe, O.
Size: 21½ × 35 in. (54.7 × 89.1 cm.)
Artist: E. Sachse Co. [James T. Palmatary]
Lithographer:
Printer: E. Sachse Co., Baltimore, Md.

Publisher: J. T. Palmatary
Key/Vignettes/Misc: Refs. 1–28
Locations: Ross County Historical Society, Chillicothe, Ohio
Catalogs/Checklists:

3041
Place: Chillicothe, Ohio
Date: 1889
Title: Chillicothe, O, 1889.
Size: 28½ × 35¹⁄₁₆ in. (72.5 × 89.2 cm.)
Artist: Smith & Buckingham
Lithographer:
Printer: The Krebs Litho. Co. Cincinnati, O.
Publisher:
Key/Vignettes/Misc: Unnumbered business and public building directory
Locations: Ross County Historical Society, Chillicothe, Ohio
Catalogs/Checklists:

3042
Place: Cincinnati, Ohio
Date: Ca. 1841
Title: Cincinnati in 1841, For the Family Magazine.
Size: 6 × 9⅜ in. (15.3 × 23.8 cm.)
Artist:
Lithographer:
Printer: Klauprech & Menzel's Lithy., Cincinnati
Publisher:
Key/Vignettes/Misc:
Locations: NYP–S; CHS–C; CAM–C; CPL–AM
Catalogs/Checklists: Stokes 1841—F–37

3043
Place: Cincinnati, Ohio
Date: [1847?]
Title: Flood of 1847. A View of the City of Cincinnati and the Ohio River, taken from Mrs. W. W. Southgate's, in Covington. . . .
Size: 15⅛ × 24¼ in. (38.5 × 61.7 cm.)
Artist:
Lithographer: J. B. Rowse
Printer: Onken Print. [Cincinnati]
Publisher: Sherer & Rowse, Lith. College Hall, Walnut Street, Cincinnati, Ohio
Key/Vignettes/Misc:
Locations: COHS; CPL–R
Catalogs/Checklists:

3044
Place: Cincinnati, Ohio
Date: 1848
Title: View of Cincinnati, Ohio. From Covington, Ky.
Size: 20⅜ × 38 in. (51.8 × 96.8 cm.)
Artist: E. Whitefield
Lithographer: E. Whitefield
Printer: Jones & Newman, 128 Fulton St., New York
Publisher: E. Whitefield, 32 Ann St., New York
Key/Vignettes/Misc:
Locations: MM–NN; LC–P
Catalogs/Checklists: MM–NN, LP 2940; Norton, Whitefield, no. 39

3045
Place: Cincinnati, Ohio
Date: Ca. 1850
Title: Burnet House
Size: ca. 8⅞ × 11¼ in. (22.6 × 28.6 cm.)
Artist:
Lithographer:
Printer: Onkens Lith Cincinnati O.
Publisher:
Key/Vignettes/Misc:
Locations: NYH–NY
Catalogs/Checklists:

3046
Place: Cincinnati, Ohio
Date: Ca. 1850
Title: Cincinnati Broadway
Size: 8¼ × 11 in. (21 × 28 cm.)
Artist:
Lithographer: Engels
Printer: Onkens Lith. Cincinnati O.
Publisher:
Key/Vignettes/Misc:
Locations: COHS; YUAG–NH
Catalogs/Checklists:

3047
Place: Cincinnati, Ohio
Date: Ca. 1850
Title: Cincinnati Fifth Street Market
Size: 9 × 11½ in. (22.9 × 29.3 cm.)
Artist:
Lithographer: Schnicke
Printer: Onkens Lith. Cincinnati. O.
Publisher:
Key/Vignettes/Misc:
Locations: CAM–C; YUAG–NH
Catalogs/Checklists:

3048
Place: Cincinnati, Ohio
Date: Ca. 1850
Title: Cincinnati Main Street Betw. Second & Fifth
Size: 9 × 11½ in. (22.9 × 29.3 cm.)
Artist:
Lithographer: Schnicke
Printer: Onkens Lith. Cincinnati. O.
Publisher:
Key/Vignettes/Misc:
Locations: CAM–C
Catalogs/Checklists:

3049
Place: Cincinnati, Ohio
Date: Ca. 1850
Title: Cincinnati Main Street. Betw. Fourth & Fifth
Size: 9 × 11½ in. (22.9 × 29.3 cm.)
Artist:
Lithographer: Schnicke
Printer: Onkens Lith Cincinnati
Publisher:
Key/Vignettes/Misc:
Locations: CAM–C; COHS
Catalogs/Checklists:

3050
Place: Cincinnati, Ohio
Date: Ca. 1850
Title: Cincinnati Public Landing
Size: 8⅞ × 11¼ in. (22.6 × 28.6 cm.)

Artist:
Lithographer: Schnicke
Printer: Onkens Lith Cincinnati O.
Publisher:
Key/Vignettes/Misc:
Locations: COHS; YUAG–NH
Catalogs/Checklists:

3051
Place: Cincinnati, Ohio
Date: Ca. 1850
Title: Cincinnati Third Street, Betw. Main & Vine
Size: 8⅞ × 11¼ in. (22.6 × 28.6 cm.)
Artist:
Lithographer: Schnicke
Printer: Onkens Lith. Cincinnati O.
Publisher:
Key/Vignettes/Misc:
Locations: CAM–C; COHS; YUAG–NH
Catalogs/Checklists:

3052
Place: Cincinnati, Ohio
Date: Ca. 1850
Title: View of Cincinnati, Ohio. From Covington, Ky.
Size: 8⅜ × 11⅜ in. (21.3 × 29 cm.)
Artist:
Lithographer: [En]gels
Printer: Onkens Lith Cincinnati
Publisher:
Key/Vignettes/Misc:
Locations: CAM–C; NYH–NY
Catalogs/Checklists:

Place: Cincinnati, Ohio
Date: [1851]
See Newport, Kentucky, [1851].

3053
Place: Cincinnati, Ohio
Date: [1851]
Title: Cincinnati. Taken from Covington, Ky.
Size: 4⅝ × 7¼ in. (11.8 × 18.9 cm.)
Artist: F. von Laer
Lithographer:
Printer: Onken's Lithography, Cincinnati
Publisher: [Otto Onken, Cincinnati,Ohio?]
Key/Vignettes/Misc:
Locations: Unknown. See Old Print Shop Portfolio, X, p. 201, No. 11
Catalogs/Checklists:

3054
Place: Cincinnati, Ohio
Date: [1851]
Title: Cincinnati, Taken from Belle Vue on Sycamore Hill
Size: 5⅞ × 7⅞ in. (15 × 20.1 cm.)
Artist: A Forbriger
Lithographer:
Printer: Onken's Lithography, Cincinnati
Publisher: [Otto Onken, Cincinnati, Ohio]
Key/Vignettes/Misc:
Locations: COHS; CPL–R
Catalogs/Checklists:

3055
Place: Cincinnati, Ohio
Date: 1852
Title: Cincinnati. Covington & Newport. From M't. Adam—1852.

Size: 25⅜ × 40³⁄₁₆ in. (64.5 × 102 cm.)
Artist: J. W. Hill
Lithographer:
Printer: F. Michelin & Geo E. Leefe, 180 Fulton St., N. Y.
Publisher: Smith Brothers & Co.
Key/Vignettes/Misc:
Locations: NYP–S; MM–NN; CHS–C; CPL–R; NYH–NY
Catalogs/Checklists: MM–NN, LP 1830; Stokes 1852—G–36

3056
Place: Cincinnati, Ohio
Date: 1853
Title: Cincinnati, Covington & Newport. 1853.
Size: 27⁹⁄₁₆ × 39¾ in. (70.2 × 101.1 cm.)
Artist: J. W. Hill
Lithographer: D. W. Moody
Printer: Michelin & Shattuck
Publisher: Smith Brothers & Co. 225 Fulton St. New York
Key/Vignettes/Misc:
Locations: COHS
Catalogs/Checklists:

3057
Place: Cincinnati, Ohio
Date: [1855?]
Title: Cincinnati, Covington & Newport.
Size: 11⅝ × 15½ in. (29.6 × 39.4 cm.)
Artist:
Lithographer:
Printer:
Publisher:
Key/Vignettes/Misc:
Locations: COHS; CAM–C; CPL–AM
Catalogs/Checklists:

3058
Place: Cincinnati, Ohio
Date: [1855?]
Title: View of Cincinnati, Ohio
Size: 9 × 23¾ in. (22.9 × 60.5 cm.)
Artist: E. Sachse
Lithographer: A. Krebs
Printer: Onken's Lithography, Cincinnati
Publisher: Otto Onken, north side of Fifth street, betw. Vine and Race, Cincinnati, O.
Key/Vignettes/Misc:
Locations: COHS
Catalogs/Checklists:

3059
Place: Cincinnati, Ohio
Date: Ca. 1855
Title: Cincinnati, Covington & Newport
Size: 11¹⁄₁₆ × 15⁹⁄₁₆ in. (28.1 × 39.6 cm.)
Artist:
Lithographer:
Printer:
Publisher:
Key/Vignettes/Misc:
Locations: NYP–S; CHS–C; COHS; CPL–AM; NYH–NY
Catalogs/Checklists: Stokes C. 1855—G–32

3060
Place: Cincinnati, Ohio
Date: [1856]
Title: Cincinnati, From a Point West of Covington Ky.

Size: 18¼ × 27¼ in. (46.5 × 69.4 cm.)
Artist:
Lithographer:
Printer: Middleton, Wallace & Co., 115 Walnut St. . . .Cin.
Publisher: Middleton, Wallace & Co., 115 Walnut St. . . .Cin.
Key/Vignettes/Misc:
Locations: LC–P; COHS; YUAG–NH; LC–M (facsimile)
Catalogs/Checklists: LC–M, 684.1

3061
Place: Cincinnati, Ohio
Date: Ca. 1857
Title: Cincinnati.
Size: 11 × 15⁷⁄₁₆ in. (28 × 39.3 cm.)
Artist:
Lithographer:
Printer: Fr. Wentzel a Wissembourg
Publisher: Chez Humbert rue St. Jacques 65, Paris
Key/Vignettes/Misc:
Locations: COHS; NYH–NY
Catalogs/Checklists:

3062
Place: Cincinnati, Ohio
Date: [1840–59]
Title: Cincinnati in 1840
Size: 6¾ × 13⅜ in. (17.2 × 34 cm.)
Artist:
Lithographer:
Printer: Klauprech & Menzel
Publisher:
Key/Vignettes/Misc:
Locations: CHS–C
Catalogs/Checklists:

3063
Place: Cincinnati, Ohio
Date: [1867–]
Title: Cincinnati
Size: 14⅛ × 20⅜ in. (35.9 × 51.9 cm.)
Artist:
Lithographer:
Printer: Fr. Wentzel, Wissembourg and Paris
Publisher: Fr. Wentzel, Wissembourg and Paris
Key/Vignettes/Misc:
Locations: MM–NN; CHS–C
Catalogs/Checklists: MM–NN, LP 56

3064
Place: Cincinnati, Ohio
Date: 1868
Title: Cincinnati, Ohio.
Size: 13 × 18 in. (33.1 × 45.8 cm.)
Artist:
Lithographer:
Printer: Ehrgott, Forbriger & Co., Cincinnati
Publisher: Ehrgott, Forbriger & Co., Cincinnati
Key/Vignettes/Misc:
Locations: COHS; CPL–R; LC–P
Catalogs/Checklists:

3065
Place: Cincinnati, Ohio
Date: 1869
Title: Cincinnati
Size: 16⁵⁄₁₆ × 21¹¹⁄₁₆ in. (41.6 × 55.3 cm.)

Artist:
Lithographer:
Printer: Deutz Brothers, 197 William St. N. Y.
Publisher: George Degen, 51 Chatham St. N. Y.
Key/Vignettes/Misc:
Locations: CHS–C; COHS; CAM–C; YUAG–NH; NYH–NY
Catalogs/Checklists: Pyne, no. 419

3066
Place: Cincinnati, Ohio
Date: [1878]
Title: Cincinnati.
Size: 11¹¹⁄₁₆ × 23¹¹⁄₁₆ in. (29.7 × 60.2 cm.)
Artist:
Lithographer: F. Achert
Printer:
Publisher: F. Achert 119 W. 5th St. Cincinnati O. (copyright)
Key/Vignettes/Misc:
Locations: LC–P
Catalogs/Checklists:

3067
Place: Cincinnati, Ohio
Date: 1880
Title: Cincinnati—1800.
Size: 19³⁄₁₆ × 34½ in. (framed) (48.9 × 87.8 cm.)
Artist: A. J. Swing
Lithographer:
Printer: The Strobridge Lith. Co. Cin.
Publisher:
Key/Vignettes/Misc: Refs. 1–15
Locations: COHS; CPL–R; NYH–NY
Catalogs/Checklists:

3068
Place: Cincinnati, Ohio
Date: 1900
Title: Panoramic View, City of Cincinnati, U. S. A. 1900
Size: 26¾ × 45⅛ in. (68 × 115 cm.)
Artist: J. L. Trout
Lithographer:
Printer:
Publisher: Henderson Lithographing Co., Cincinnati
Key/Vignettes/Misc:
Locations: LC–M
Catalogs/Checklists: LC–M, 685

3069
Place: Cincinnati, Ohio
Date: 1909
Title: Cincinnati—1800.
Size: 11⅛ × 19¹⁵⁄₁₆ in. (28.3 × 50.8 cm.)
Artist: A. J. Swing
Lithographer:
Printer: The Strobridge Lith. Co. [Cincinnati]
Publisher:
Key/Vignettes/Misc: Refs. 1–15
Locations: CPL–AM
Catalogs/Checklists:

3070
Place: Cincinnati, Ohio
Date: 1909
Title: Cincinnati, U. S. A.
Size: 8¹⁄₁₆ × 37⅛ in. (20.5 × 94.4 cm.)

Artist:
Lithographer:
Printer: Chas. F. Ulrich
Publisher: A. O. Kraemer, Cin. O.
Key/Vignettes/Misc:
Locations: LC–P
Catalogs/Checklists:

3071
Place: Cincinnati, Ohio
Date: N.D.
Title: Cincinnati & Covington Suspension Bridge
Size: 16 × 22¼ in. (40.7 × 56.7 cm.)
Artist:
Lithographer:
Printer: Strobridge & Co. Lith. Cin. O.
Publisher:
Key/Vignettes/Misc: Description
Locations: COHS
Catalogs/Checklists:

3072
Place: Cincinnati, Ohio
Date: N.D.
Title: Cincinnati. From Forest Hill. Ky
Size: 10⅞ × 16¹⁵⁄₁₆ in. (27.6 × 43.1 cm.)
Artist:
Lithographer:
Printer: Ehrgott & Forbriger S. W. Cor. of 4th & Main Sts. Cincinnati, O.
Publisher: Ehrgott & Forbriger S. W. Cor. of 4th & Main Sts. Cincinnati, O.
Key/Vignettes/Misc:
Locations: YUAG–NH
Catalogs/Checklists:

3073
Place: Cincinnati, Ohio
Date: N.D.
Title: Cincinnati, Covington & Newport in Kentucky
Size: 15¾ (cropped) × 23¾ in. (40.1 × 60.5 cm.)
Artist:
Lithographer:
Printer:
Publisher:
Key/Vignettes/Misc:
Locations: CPL–AM
Catalogs/Checklists:

3074
Place: Cincinnati, Ohio
Date: N.D.
Title: Cincinnati, Queen of the West.
Size: 14½ × 20⅛ in. (36.9 × 51.2 cm.)
Artist: J. Jollasse
Lithographer: J. Jollasse
Printer: Klauprech & Menzel's Lith, Johnston's Row, Cincinnati
Publisher:
Key/Vignettes/Misc:
Locations: NYH–NY
Catalogs/Checklists:

3075
Place: Cincinnati, Ohio
Date: N.D.
Title: View of Cincinnati. Taken From the Residence Of. Wm. Southgate, Esq, Covington, Ky.
Size: 17 × 22 in. (43.2 × 56 cm.)

Artist:
Lithographer:
Printer:
Publisher:
Key/Vignettes/Misc:
Locations: Unknown
Catalogs/Checklists: Pyne, no. 417

3076
Place: Cincinnati, Ohio
Date: N.D.
Title: Vue Generale de Cincinnati (Ohio) Prise Derriere Newport, (Ky).
Size: 17¹¹⁄₁₆ × 24 in. (45 × 61 cm.)
Artist: Forbriger
Lithographer: Asselineau
Printer: Lemercier, Paris
Publisher: Wild 15 rue de la Banque [Paris]
Key/Vignettes/Misc:
Locations: CHS–C; YUAG–NH
Catalogs/Checklists:

3077
Place: Circleville, Ohio
Date: 1876
Title: Birds eye view of the city of Circleville, Pickaway County, Ohio 1876.
Size: 18¹⁄₁₆ × 24⅜ in. (46 × 62 cm.)
Artist:
Lithographer:
Printer: Krebs Lithographing Company
Publisher: J. J. Stoner, Madison, Wis.
Key/Vignettes/Misc: Refs. 1–35, G, O
Locations: LC–M
Catalogs/Checklists: LC–M, 686

3078
Place: Circleville, Ohio
Date: 1889
Title: Circleville, Ohio 1889
Size: 27 × 34½ in. (68.7 × 87.9 cm.).
Artist: Smith & Buckingham
Lithographer:
Printer: Smith & Buckingham
Publisher: The Krebs Lith. Company
Key/Vignettes/Misc:
Locations: OHS–C
Catalogs/Checklists:

3079
Place: Cleveland, Ohio
Date: Ca. 1834
Title: Panorama of Cleveland and Ohio city. Taken from Scrantons Height.
Size: 14⁹⁄₁₆ × 18⅛ in. (37 × 46.1 cm.)
Artist: J.[acob] Mueller
Lithographer:
Printer: Onken's Lithography, Cincinnati
Publisher: J. Mueller [Cleveland, Ohio]
Key/Vignettes/Misc:
Locations: WRHS–C
Catalogs/Checklists:

3080
Place: Cleveland, Ohio
Date: 1851
Title: Cleveland
Size: 12⁹⁄₁₆ × 17½ in. (31.9 × 44.5 cm.)
Artist:
Lithographer:
Printer:
Publisher:
Key/Vignettes/Misc:

Locations: NYP–S
Catalogs/Checklists: Stokes P. 1850—
G–21

3081
Place: Cleveland, Ohio
Date: 1853
Title: Cleveland 1853
Size: 25½ × 37 in. (64.9 × 94.2 cm.)
Artist: J. W. Hill
Lithographer: B. F. Smith, Jr.
Printer: Michelin & Shattuck 225 Fulton
[New York]
Publisher: Smith Bros. & Co. 225 Fulton
St, N. Y.
Key/Vignettes/Misc:
Locations: MM–NN; WRHS–C;
CHS–C; NYH–NY
Catalogs/Checklists: MM–NN, LP 2775

3082
Place: Cleveland, Ohio
Date: 1868
Title: Cleveland, Ohio. From the Buffalo
Road, East of the Court House. [in 1833.]
Size: 10⁹⁄₁₆ × 14¹¹⁄₁₆ in. (26.9 × 37.4 cm.)
Artist: Thos. Whelpley
Lithographer: Sanford & Hayward
Printer: Sanford & Hayward, Cleveland,
Ohio
Publisher: Thomas Whelpley
Key/Vignettes/Misc: 2 vignettes
Locations: WRHS–C
Catalogs/Checklists:

3083
Place: Cleveland, Ohio
Date: 1868
Title: Cleveland, Ohio. From the Corner
of Bank and St. Clair Str Looking East [in
1833]
Size: 10¹³⁄₁₆ × 14¹¹⁄₁₆ in. (27.5 × 37.4 cm.)
Artist: Thos. Whelpley
Lithographer: Sanford & Hayward
Printer: Sanford & Hayward, Cleveland,
Ohio
Publisher: Thomas Whelpley
Key/Vignettes/Misc: 2 vignettes
Locations: WRHS–C
Catalogs/Checklists:

3084
Place: Cleveland, Ohio
Date: 1868
Title: Cleveland, Ohio. From the Court
House Looking West [in 1833]
Size: 10¾ × 14⁹⁄₁₆ in. (27.4 × 37 cm.)
Artist: Thos Whelpley
Lithographer: Sanford & Hayward
Printer: Sanford & Hayward, Cleveland,
Ohio
Publisher: Thomas Whelpley
Key/Vignettes/Misc: 2 vignettes
Locations: WRHS–C
Catalogs/Checklists:

3085
Place: Cleveland, Ohio
Date: 1868
Title: Cleveland, Ohio. From Brooklyn
Hill Looking East. [in 1833.]
Size: 10⅝ × 14¹¹⁄₁₆ in. (27.1 × 37.4 cm.)
Artist: Thos Whelpley

Lithographer: Sanford & Hayward
Printer: Sanford & Hayward, Cleveland,
Ohio
Publisher: Thomas Whelpley
Key/Vignettes/Misc: 2 vignettes
Locations: WRHS–C
Catalogs/Checklists:

3086
Place: Cleveland, Ohio
Date: 1874
Title: Cleveland Ohio.
Size: 18⅜ × 25⅛ in. (46.7 × 63.9 cm.)
Artist: Orlando Schubert
Lithographer: Orlando Schubert
Printer:
Publisher: C. Schubert (copyright)
Key/Vignettes/Misc: 8 vignettes
Locations: LC–P; WRHS–C
Catalogs/Checklists:

3087
Place: Cleveland, Ohio
Date: 1877
Title: Birds Eye View of Cleveland, Ohio
1877.
Size: 18¹⁄₁₆ × 33¾ in. (46 × 86 cm.)
Artist: A. Ruger
Lithographer:
Printer: Shober & Carqueville [Chicago]
Publisher: J. J. Stoner, Madison, Wis.
Key/Vignettes/Misc: Refs. 1–108
Locations: LC–M; WRHS–C; OHS–C
Catalogs/Checklists: LC–M, 687

3088
Place: Cleveland, Ohio
Date: 1883
Title: The City of Cleveland, Ohio.
Population 1883, 200,000
Size: 29 × 39½ in. (73.8 × 100.3 cm.)
Artist: C. H. Vogt and Son
Lithographer:
Printer: W. J. Morgan and Company,
Cleveland
Publisher: C. H. Vogt and Son, Cleveland,
Ohio
Key/Vignettes/Misc: Refs. 1–149, A–F
Locations: LC–M (photo); WRHS–C
Catalogs/Checklists: LC–M, 688

3089
Place: Cleveland, Ohio
Date: [1881–85?]
Title: Cleveland, O.
Size: 15⅞ × 25 in. (39.8 × 63.6 cm.)
Artist:
Lithographer: M. M. Tidd
Printer: Beck & Pauli, Milwaukee, Wis.
Publisher:
Key/Vignettes/Misc: 10 vignettes
Locations: NYP–S
Catalogs/Checklists:

3090
Place: Cleveland, Ohio
Date: 1887
Title: Cleveland, Ohio.
Size: 11⅜ × 19¼ in. (29 × 49 cm.)
Artist:
Lithographer:
Printer:
Publisher: C. H. Vogt & Son, Cleveland

Key/Vignettes/Misc:
Locations: LC–M; WRHS–C
Catalogs/Checklists: LC–M, 689

3091
Place: Cleveland, Ohio
Date: [1881–91]
Title: Cleveland, O.
Size: 16½ × 25⅞ in. (42 × 65.8 cm.)
Artist:
Lithographer:
Printer: Beck & Pauli, Milwaukee
Publisher: Die Clevelander Anzeiger
Key/Vignettes/Misc: 10 vignettes
Locations: WRHS–C
Catalogs/Checklists:

3092
Place: Columbus, Ohio
Date: [1854]
Title: View of Columbus O. From Capitol
University
Size: 22½ × 39⅝ in. (57.3 × 100.7 cm.)
Artist: E. Sachse [James T. Palmatary?]
Lithographer:
Printer: E. Sachse & Co., Baltimore
Publisher: J. T. Palmatary
Key/Vignettes/Misc: 31 refs.
Locations: NYP–S; OHS–C
Catalogs/Checklists: Stokes C. 1865—
G–77

3093
Place: Columbus, Ohio
Date: 1872
Title: Bird's Eye View of Columbus, Ohio.
Size: 23¼ × 36 in. (59.2 × 91.6 cm.)
Artist: H. H. & O. H. Bailey
Lithographer:
Printer: Strobridge & Co., Cincinnati
Publisher: Fowler & Bailey
Key/Vignettes/Misc:
Locations: OHS–C
Catalogs/Checklists:

3094
Place: Conneaut, Ohio
Date: 1896
Title: Conneaut, Ohio 1896.
Size: 17⁵⁄₁₆ × 28¾ in. (44 × 73 cm.)
Artist: T. M. Fowler
Lithographer:
Printer:
Publisher: T. M. Fowler & James B.
Moyer, Morrisville, Pa.
Key/Vignettes/Misc:
Locations: LC–M; OHS–C
Catalogs/Checklists: LC–M, 690

3095
Place: Cuyahoga Falls, Ohio
Date: 1882
Title: Panoramic View of Cuyahoga Falls,
Summit Co. Ohio 1882 Population 2500
Size: 15½ × 22½ in. (39.4 × 57.3 cm.)
Artist:
Lithographer:
Printer: Beck & Pauli, Milwaukee, Wis.
Publisher: Ruger & Stoner, Madison, Wis.
Key/Vignettes/Misc: Refs. 1–30, A–F; 1
vignette; advertisement
Locations: Taylor Memorial Public
Library, Cuyahoga Falls, Ohio (facsimile);

Summit County Historical Society, Akron, Ohio
Catalogs/Checklists:

3096
Place: Dayton, Ohio
Date: [1854]
Title: View of Dayton, O.
Size: 20½ × 33¼ in. (52.2 × 84.6 cm.)
Artist: E. Sachse [James T. Palmatary?]
Lithographer: E. Sachse & Co.
Printer:
Publisher: J. T. Palmatary
Key/Vignettes/Misc: Description
Locations: OHS−C
Catalogs/Checklists:

3097
Place: Dayton, Ohio
Date: 1870
Title: Dayton, Ohio 1870.
Size: 20¹³/₁₆ × 30⅝ in. (53 × 78 cm.)
Artist: [Albert Ruger]
Lithographer:
Printer: Merchant's Lith. Co., Chicago
Publisher:
Key/Vignettes/Misc: 9 vignettes
Locations: LC−M
Catalogs/Checklists: LC−M, 691

3098
Place: East Liverpool, Ohio
Date: 1886
Title: Panoramic View of the City of East Liverpool Columbiana Co. Ohio. Population: 8000. 1886
Size: 17¾ × 21½ in. (45.2 × 54.7 cm.)
Artist:
Lithographer:
Printer: Beck & Pauli Litho. Milwaukee, Wis.
Publisher: Ruger & Stoner, Madison, Wis.
Key/Vignettes/Misc: Refs. 2−66, A−H; 1 vignette
Locations: OHS−C
Catalogs/Checklists:

3099
Place: Edgerton, Ohio
Date: 1881
Title: Looking North West Bird's Eye View of Edgerton Williams Co. Ohio 1881.
Size: 9 × 14½ in. (22.9 × 36.9 cm.) (photo)
Artist:
Lithographer:
Printer: Beck & Pauli, Lith. Milwaukee, Wis
Publisher: J. J. Stoner, Madison, Wis.
Key/Vignettes/Misc: Refs. A, 1−41
Locations: LC−M (photo); Edgerton Historical Society, Edgerton, Ohio
Catalogs/Checklists: LC−M, 691.2

3100
Place: Elyria, Ohio
Date: 1868
Title: Bird's Eye View of the Town of Elyria, Lorain Co., Ohio 1868
Size: 22 × 28¼ in. (56 × 72 cm.)
Artist: A. Ruger
Lithographer:

Printer: Chicago Lithographing Co. [Chicago]
Publisher:
Key/Vignettes/Misc: Refs. 1−12; 3 vignettes
Locations: LC−M
Catalogs/Checklists: LC−M, 692

3101
Place: Findlay, Ohio
Date: 1889
Title: Findlay, Ohio. The Gas City
Size: 21 × 33½ in. (53.4 × 85.2 cm.)
Artist:
Lithographer:
Printer: The Burleigh Lith. Est., Troy, N. Y.
Publisher: Burleigh & Norris, Troy, N. Y.
Key/Vignettes/Misc: Refs. 1−95; 3 vignettes
Locations: LC−M; WRHS−C
Catalogs/Checklists: LC−M, 693

3102
Place: Fostoria, Ohio
Date: 1872
Title: Fostoria, Seneca County, O.
Size: 13½ × 18⁹/₁₆ in. (34.3 × 47.3 cm.)
Artist: T. M. Fowler & H. H. Bailey
Lithographer: C. H. Vogt
Printer: American Oleograph Co.
Publisher: T. M. Fowler & H. H. Bailey
Key/Vignettes/Misc: Refs. 1−4, A−E
Locations: BPL−R
Catalogs/Checklists:

3103
Place: Garrettsville, Ohio
Date: 1883
Title: Bird's Eye View of Garrettesville, Portage Co. Ohio. 1883.
Size: 11 × 17½ in. (28 × 44.5 cm.)
Artist:
Lithographer:
Printer: Beck & Pauli, Milwaukee, Wis.
Publisher: Ruger & Stoner, Madison, Wis.
Key/Vignettes/Misc: Refs. 1−19, A−H
Locations: PCHS−R
Catalogs/Checklists:

3104
Place: Glendale, Ohio
Date: [1858−65]
Title: View of Glendale, Near Cincinnati
Size: 18¾ × 29 in. [matted] (47.4 × 73.8 cm.)
Artist: Middleton, Strobridge & Co.
Lithographer:
Printer: Middleton, Strobridge & Co. Cincinnati, O.
Publisher:
Key/Vignettes/Misc:
Locations: COHS
Catalogs/Checklists:

3105
Place: Greenville, Ohio
Date: 1886
Title: Greenville, Ohio 1886
Size: 20 × 28 in. (50.9 × 71.3 cm.)
Artist:
Lithographer:
Printer: O. H. Bailey & Co. Boston
Publisher: O. H. Bailey & Co., Boston

Key/Vignettes/Misc: Refs. 1−37; 12 vignettes
Locations: Darke County Historical Society, Greenville, Ohio
Catalogs/Checklists:

3106
Place: Hamilton, Ohio
Date: [1856]
Title: View of Hamilton, Ohio.
Size: 24½ × 37½ in. (62.3 × 95.4 cm.)
Artist:
Lithographer: Middleton, Wallace & Co.
Printer: Middleton, Wallace & Co. Lithos. 115 Walnut St. Cincinnati, O.
Publisher: Middleton, Wallace & Co. Lithos. 115 Walnut St. Cincinnati, O.
Key/Vignettes/Misc:
Locations: NYH−NY
Catalogs/Checklists:

3107
Place: Hamilton, Ohio
Date: 1870
Title: Birds−Eye View of Hamilton, Ohio, 1870. Looking East from the West.
Size: 24¼ × 40¼ in. (61.7 × 102.4 cm.)
Artist: P. A. Gross
Lithographer:
Printer: Ehrgott & Krebs, Lith. Cincinnati
Publisher:
Key/Vignettes/Misc: Refs. A−Z, A1−A11; 30 vignettes
Locations: Private collection
Catalogs/Checklists:

3108
Place: Jefferson, Ohio
Date: 1883
Title: Panoramic View of Jefferson, County Seat of Ashtabula County, Ohio
Size: 8⅝ × 17¹¹/₁₆ in. (22 × 45 cm.)
Artist:
Lithographer:
Printer:
Publisher:
Key/Vignettes/Misc:
Locations: OHS−C
Catalogs/Checklists:

3109
Place: Kent, Ohio
Date: 1882
Title: Panoramic View of the City of Kent, Portage County, Ohio 1882. Looking North East.
Size: 13 × 25½ in. (33 × 65 cm.)
Artist: [Albert Ruger]
Lithographer:
Printer: Beck & Pauli, Milwaukee, Wis.
Publisher: Ruger & Stoner, Madison, Wis.
Key/Vignettes/Misc: Refs. 1−27, A−H, J−K, X, XX
Locations: LC−M; PCHS−R; OHS−C
Catalogs/Checklists: LC−M, 695

3110
Place: Lakeside, Ohio
Date: [1884]
Title: Lakeside. Summer Resort and Campground
Size: 19¼ × 24 in. (49 × 61.1 cm.)
Artist:

Lithographer:
Printer: Sinz & Fausel Lith. Cleveland, O.
Publisher: A. J. Hare, Sandusky, O.
Key/Vignettes/Misc:
Locations: LC–M
Catalogs/Checklists: LC–M, 696

3111
Place: Lancaster, Ohio
Date: 1885
Title: Lancaster. Ohio. 1885
Size: 20 1/16 × 25 11/16 in. (51.1 × 65.4 cm.)
Artist:
Lithographer:
Printer: O. H. Bailey & Co. Boston
Publisher: O. H. Bailey & Co. Boston
Key/Vignettes/Misc: Refs. 1–32; 8
vignettes
Locations: BPL–R
Catalogs/Checklists:

3112
Place: Lima, Ohio
Date: 1881
Title: Birds Eye View of Lima, O.
Size: 24 1/16 × 36 in. (61.2 × 91.6 cm.)
Artist:
Lithographer:
Printer: Thos. Hunter, Lith. 716 Filbert St.
Phila.
Publisher: Howland & Germann
Key/Vignettes/Misc: 16 vignettes
Locations: Allen County Museum, Lima,
Ohio
Catalogs/Checklists:

3113
Place: Lima, Ohio
Date: 1892
Title: City of Lima, O. 1892.
Size: 25 1/8 × 38 15/16 in. (64 × 99 cm.)
Artist:
Lithographer:
Printer: Geo. S. Harris & Sons
Publisher: Smith & Buckingham [Mt.
Vernon, Ohio]
Key/Vignettes/Misc: 6 vignettes;
unnumbered business directory
Locations: LC–M; Allen County
Museum, Lima, Ohio
Catalogs/Checklists: LC–M, 697

3114
Place: Madison, Ohio
Date: 1883
Title: Panoramic View of Madison Lake
County Ohio 1883
Size:
Artist:
Lithographer:
Printer:
Publisher: Ruger & Stoner, Madison,
Wisconsin
Key/Vignettes/Misc: Refs. 1–10, A–H
Locations: Lake County Historical Society,
Mentor, Ohio (photo)
Catalogs/Checklists:

3115
Place: Mansfield, Ohio
Date: Ca. 1865
Title:
Size:

Artist:
Lithographer:
Printer:
Publisher:
Key/Vignettes/Misc:
Locations: [Existence assumed from small
illustration in Mansfield Sesqu–Centennial
Souvenir Book, 1958]
Catalogs/Checklists:

3116
Place: Mansfield, Ohio
Date: 1884
Title: Panoramic View of the City of
Mansfield Richland County, Ohio.
Size:
Artist:
Lithographer:
Printer:
Publisher:
Key/Vignettes/Misc: Refs. 1–47, A–H, K,
M–P, R–S
Locations: Richland County Auditor,
Mansfield, Ohio
Catalogs/Checklists:

3117
Place: Marietta, Ohio
Date: Ca. 1836
Title: Marietta, Ohio
Size: 9 11/16 × 12 in. (24.7 × 30.6 cm.)
Artist:
Lithographer:
Printer:
Publisher:
Key/Vignettes/Misc:
Locations: OHS–C
Catalogs/Checklists:

3118
Place: Marietta, Ohio
Date: Ca. 1840
Title: Marietta
Size: 19 1/8 × 22 1/4 in. (48.7 × 56.7 cm.)
Artist:
Lithographer: C. Sullivan
Printer:
Publisher: P. S. Duval Lith.
Key/Vignettes/Misc:
Locations: OHS–C
Catalogs/Checklists:

3119
Place: Martins Ferry, Ohio
Date: 1899
Title: Martin's Ferry, Ohio 1899.
Size: 17 1/4 × 24 3/8 in. (44 × 62 cm.)
Artist: T. M. Fowler
Lithographer:
Printer:
Publisher: Fowler & Jas. B. Moyer,
Morrisville, Pa.
Key/Vignettes/Misc: Refs. 1–16, A–H; 7
vignettes
Locations: LC–M
Catalogs/Checklists: LC–M, 698

3120
Place: Massillon, Ohio
Date: 1870
Title: Bird's eye view of Massillon, Stark
County, Ohio 1870

Size: 20 × 23 15/16 in. (51 × 61 cm.)
Artist: [Albert Ruger]
Lithographer:
Printer: Merchants Lith. Co.
Publisher: Ruger & Stoner, Madison, Wis.
Key/Vignettes/Misc: Refs. 1–33; 2
vignettes
Locations: LC–M
Catalogs/Checklists: LC–M, 699

Place: Middlebury, Ohio
Date: 1882
See Akron, Ohio, 1882.

3121
Place: Middleport, Ohio
Date: 1884
Title: Panoramic View of Middleport
Meigs Co. Ohio 1884 Looking North
West
Size: 14 1/4 × 21 9/16 in. (36.3 × 54.9 cm.)
Artist:
Lithographer:
Printer: Beck & Pauli, Litho, Milwaukee,
Wis.
Publisher: Ruger & Stoner, Madison, Wis.
Key/Vignettes/Misc: Refs. 1–45, A–L; 3
vignettes
Locations: Meigs County Musem,
Pomeroy, Ohio
Catalogs/Checklists:

3122
Place: Mingo Junction, Ohio
Date: 1899
Title: Mingo Junction, Ohio 1899.
Size: 15 5/16 × 22 3/4 in. (39 × 58 cm.)
Artist: T. M. Fowler
Lithographer:
Printer:
Publisher: Fowler & Jas. B. Moyer,
Morrisville, Pa.
Key/Vignettes/Misc: Refs. 1–12
Locations: LC–M
Catalogs/Checklists: LC–M, 700

3123
Place: Mount Vernon, Ohio
Date: 1870
Title: Bird's eye view of the city of Mount
Vernon, Knox County, Ohio 1870.
Size: 20 7/16 × 23 15/16 in. (52 × 61 cm.)
Artist: [Albert Ruger]
Lithographer:
Printer: Merchants Lith. Co. [Chicago]
Publisher: Ruger & Stoner, Madison, Wis.
Key/Vignettes/Misc: Refs. 1–18; 2
vignettes
Locations: LC–M
Catalogs/Checklists: LC–M, 701

3124
Place: Niles, Ohio
Date: 1882
Title: Panoramic view of the city of Niles,
Trumbull Co., Ohio 1882.
Size: 12 9/16 × 22 in. (32 × 56 cm.)
Artist: [Albert Ruger]
Lithographer:
Printer: Beck & Pauli Lith. Milwaukee,
Wis.
Publisher: Ruger & Stoner, Madison, Wis.

Key/Vignettes/Misc: Refs. 1–25, A–H, X
Locations: LC–M
Catalogs/Checklists: LC–M, 702

3125
Place: Norwalk, Ohio
Date: 1870
Title: Bird's eye view of Norwalk, Huron County, Ohio 1870.
Size: 18⅞ × 23¹⁵⁄₁₆ in. (48 × 61 cm.)
Artist: [Albert Ruger]
Lithographer:
Printer: Merchants Lithographing Co. [Chicago]
Publisher: Ruger & Stoner, Madison, Wis.
Key/Vignettes/Misc: Refs. 1–16; 2 vignettes
Locations: LC–M
Catalogs/Checklists: LC–M, 703

3126
Place: Oberlin, Ohio
Date: 1868
Title: Bird's Eye View of the Town of Oberlin Lorain County, 1866.
Size: 21 × 27 in. (53.5 × 68.7 cm.)
Artist: A. Ruger
Lithographer:
Printer: Chicago Lith. Co. [Chicago]
Publisher: A. Ruger
Key/Vignettes/Misc:
Locations: OHS–C
Catalogs/Checklists:

3127
Place: Ohio White Sulphur Springs, Ohio
Date: Ca. 1859
Title: Ohio White Sulphur Springs. With Improvements of 1858–59
Size:
Artist:
Lithographer: Ehrgott & Forbriger
Printer: Ehrgott & Forbriger, Carlisles Building S. W. Cor of 4th & Walnut Sts. Cincinnati, O.
Publisher:
Key/Vignettes/Misc: 4 vignettes; description
Locations: Unknown. Old Print Shop, Negative File
Catalogs/Checklists:

3128
Place: Painesville, Ohio
Date: 1871
Title: Bird's Eye View of Painesville Lake County Ohio 1871
Size: 21¾ × 25¾ in. (55.4 × 65.6 cm.)
Artist: [Albert Ruger?]
Lithographer:
Printer: Chicago Lith. Co. 152 & 154 Clark St. [Chicago]
Publisher: Ruger & Stoner, St. Louis
Key/Vignettes/Misc: Refs. 1–14; 2 vignettes
Locations: Private collection; Lake County Historical Society, Mentor, Ohio (cropped)
Catalogs/Checklists:

3129
Place: Piqua, Ohio
Date: 1872
Title: Birds Eye View of Piqua, Ohio, 1872

Size: 19½ × 24⅞ in. (49.6 x 63.4 cm.)
Artist: H. H. Bailey
Lithographer:
Printer: Strobridge & Co Lith, Cincinnati, Ohio
Publisher:
Key/Vignettes/Misc: Refs. 1–31, A–L
Locations: Old Canal Book Shop, Piqua, Ohio
Catalogs/Checklists:

3130
Place: Piqua, Ohio
Date: 1888
Title: Piqua, Ohio 1888
Size: 23¼ × 29⅝ in. (59.2 × 75.4 cm.) (facsimile)
Artist:
Lithographer:
Printer:
Publisher:
Key/Vignettes/Misc: Refs.
Locations: Old Canal Book Shop, Piqua, Ohio (facsimile)
Catalogs/Checklists:

3131
Place: Portsmouth, Ohio
Date: [1854–55]
Title: View of Portsmouth, O. From the Kentucky Hills
Size: 18 × 32½ in. (45.8 × 82.7 cm.)
Artist: J. T. Palmatary
Lithographer: Klauprech & Menzel
Printer: Klauprech & Menzel, Cincinnati
Publisher: J. T. Palmatary
Key/Vignettes/Misc:
Locations: WRHS–C
Catalogs/Checklists:

3132
Place: Portsmouth, Ohio
Date: Ca. 1870
Title: Portsmouth, Ohio
Size: 26¼ × 32 in. (66.8 × 81.4 cm.)
Artist: Riley and Ricker
Lithographer:
Printer: Riley & Ricker
Publisher: Shober & Carqueville Lith.
Key/Vignettes/Misc:
Locations: OHS–C
Catalogs/Checklists:

Place: Putnam, Ohio
Date: [1854–55?] 18554
See Zanesville, Ohio, [1854–55?].

3133
Place: Ravenna, Ohio
Date: 1882
Title: Panoramic View of the City of Ravenna, County Seat of Portage Co., Ohio 1882. Looking South East.
Size: 14⁹⁄₁₆ × 20¹⁄₁₆ in. (37 × 51 cm.)
Artist: [A. Ruger]
Lithographer:
Printer:
Publisher:
Key/Vignettes/Misc:
Locations: LC–M; OHS–C
Catalogs/Checklists: LC–M, 704

3134
Place: Sandusky, Ohio
Date: [1855]
Title: View of the City of Sandusky, O
Size: 21 × 44 in. (53 × 112 cm.)
Artist: [James T. Palmatary]
Lithographer: Middleton, Wallace & Co.
Printer: Middleton, Wallace & Co. Lithos. 115 Walnut St. Cincinnati, O.
Publisher: J. T. Palmatary
Key/Vignettes/Misc:
Locations: WHS–M; NYH–NY
Catalogs/Checklists:

3135
Place: Sandusky, Ohio
Date: [1856?]
Title: View of the City of Sandusky, O
Size: 20¼ × 33⅜ in. (51.6 × 84.9 cm.)
Artist: E. Sachse & Co.
Lithographer:
Printer: E. Sachse & Co. Sun Iron Building, Balto. Md.
Publisher: J. T. Palmatary
Key/Vignettes/Misc:
Locations: Follett House Museum, Sandusky, Ohio
Catalogs/Checklists:

3136
Place: Sandusky, Ohio
Date: 1864
Title: Panoramic View of Sandusky City and Bay and Depot for Prisoners of War on Johnson's Island
Size: 22 × 29 in. (56 × 73.8 cm.)
Artist: Philip Nunan
Lithographer:
Printer: Sage & Sons & Co., Buffalo, N. Y.
Publisher: Philip Nunan
Key/Vignettes/Misc: Refs. 1–16; 4 vignettes
Locations: Follett House Museum, Sandusky, Ohio
Catalogs/Checklists:

3137
Place: Sandusky, Ohio
Date: 1870
Title: Bird's–eye–view of the City of Sandusky, Erie County, Ohio 1870
Size: 20¹³⁄₁₆ × 25¹⁵⁄₁₆ in. (53 × 66 cm.)
Artist: A. Ruger
Lithographer:
Printer: Chicago Lithographing Co. [Chicago]
Publisher: Ruger & Stoner, Madison, Wis.
Key/Vignettes/Misc: Refs. 1–16, A–I, K–P; 2 vignettes
Locations: LC–M
Catalogs/Checklists: LC–M, 705

3138
Place: Sandusky, Ohio
Date: 1883
Title: City of Sandusky, O.
Size: 26½ × 39½ in. (67.5 × 100.5 cm.)
Artist:
Lithographer:
Printer: W. J. Morgan & Co., Cleveland, Ohio
Publisher: A. J. Hare, Sandusky, Ohio

Key/Vignettes/Misc: Refs. 1–65
Locations: LC–M
Catalogs/Checklists: LC–M, 706

3139
Place: Sandusky, Ohio
Date: [1898?]
Title: Sandusky, Ohio
Size: 14¹⁵⁄₁₆ × 35¾ in. (38 × 91 cm.)
Artist:
Lithographer:
Printer: Gugler Litho. Co. [Milwaukee]
Publisher: Alvord–Peters Co., Sandusky
Key/Vignettes/Misc:
Locations: LC–M
Catalogs/Checklists: LC–M, 707

3140
Place: Scio, Ohio
Date: 1899 State I
Title: Scio, Harrison Conty, Ohio 1899.
Size: 13⅜ × 24⅜ in. (34 × 62 cm.)
Artist: T. M. Fowler
Lithographer:
Printer: Wheeling News Publishing Co.
Publisher: T. M. Fowler, Morrisville, Pa.
Key/Vignettes/Misc: Refs. 1–52, A–K
Locations: LC–M
Catalogs/Checklists: LC–M, 708

3141
Place: Scio, Ohio
Date: 1899 State II
Title: Scio, Harrison County, Ohio.
Size: 13⅜ × 24⅜ in. (34 × 62 cm.)
Artist: T. M. Fowler
Lithographer:
Printer:
Publisher: Fowler & Jas. B. Moyer,
Morrisville, Pa.
Key/Vignettes/Misc: Refs. 1–59, A–O
Locations: LC–M
Catalogs/Checklists: LC–M, 709

3142
Place: Sherrodsville, Ohio
Date: 1904
Title: Sherrodsville, Ohio. 1904.
Size: 11¾ × 17 in. (29.9 × 43.3 cm.)
Artist:
Lithographer:
Printer:
Publisher:
Key/Vignettes/Misc: Refs. 1–7; 4
vignettes
Locations: Unknown. Old Print Shop,
9/21/79
Catalogs/Checklists:

3143
Place: Sidney, Ohio
Date: 1884
Title: Sidney, Ohio. 1884
Size: 22 × 30½ in. (56 × 77.6 cm.)
Artist:
Lithographer: C. H. Vogt
Printer: W. J. Morgan & Co. Cleveland,
O.
Publisher: Howland & Zuver
Key/Vignettes/Misc: Refs. 1–41
Locations: Amos Memorial Public Library,
Sidney, Ohio
Catalogs/Checklists:

3144
Place: Springfield, Ohio
Date: [1855–56]
Title: View of Springfield, O.
Size: 23¾ × 35 in. (60.5 × 89.1 cm.)
Artist: J. T. Palmatery
Lithographer: Middleton, Wallace & Co.
Printer: Middleton, Wallace & Co., 115
Walnut St., Odd Fellows Hall, Cinc., Ohio
Publisher: Middleton, Wallace & Co.
Key/Vignettes/Misc: 20 vignettes
Locations: CCHS–S
Catalogs/Checklists:

3145
Place: Springfield, Ohio
Date: 1870
Title: View of Springfield, Ohio, Looking
South West. 1870
Size: 22 × 32½ in. (56 × 82.7 cm.)
Artist:
Lithographer:
Printer: Chicago Litho. Co. 150, 152 &
154 S. Clark St., Chicago
Publisher:
Key/Vignettes/Misc: Refs. 1–20, A–M;
14 vignettes
Locations: CCHS–S
Catalogs/Checklists:

3146
Place: Springfield, Ohio
Date: Ca. 1875
Title: Springfield, the Champion City,
Ohio, U. S. A.
Size: 21¼ × 34 in. (54.1 × 86.5 cm.)
Artist:
Lithographer:
Printer:
Publisher:
Key/Vignettes/Misc:
Locations: OHS–C
Catalogs/Checklists:

3147
Place: Springfield, Ohio
Date: 1884
Title: Springfield. Ohio 1884
Size: 29½ × 33 in. (75.1 × 84 cm.)
Artist:
Lithographer:
Printer:
Publisher: O. H. Bailey & Co., Boston
Key/Vignettes/Misc: Refs., 1–160; 17
vignettes
Locations: CCHS–S; BPL–R
Catalogs/Checklists:

3148
Place: Steubenville, Ohio
Date: [1846]
Title: Part of Steubenville, Ohio
Size: 9½ × 11¾ in. (23.5 × 29.8 cm.)
Artist: E. Whitefield
Lithographer:
Printer:
Publisher:
Key/Vignettes/Misc:
Locations: BECH–B; NYH–NY
Catalogs/Checklists: Norton, Whitefield,
no. 10

3149
Place: Steubenville, Ohio
Date: 1883
Title: Bird's Eye View of Steubenville, O.
1883
Size: 12¼ × 21¾ in. (31.2 × 55.3 cm.)
Artist:
Lithographer:
Printer: Beck & Pauli Lithographers,
Milwaukee, Wis.
Publisher: J. J. Stoner, Madison, Wis.
Key/Vignettes/Misc:
Locations: Public Library of Steubenville
and Jefferson County, Steubenville, Ohio
Catalogs/Checklists:

3150
Place: Toledo, Ohio
Date: [1856]
Title: View of the City of Toledo. O.
Size: 29½ × 46¼ in. (75 × 117.7 cm.)
Artist:
Lithographer: Middleton, Wallace & Co.
Printer: Middleton, Wallace & Co. Lithos.
115 Walnut St. Cincinnati, O.
Publisher: J. T. Palmatary
Key/Vignettes/Misc:
Locations: NYH–NY
Catalogs/Checklists:

3151
Place: Toledo, Ohio
Date: 1870
Title: Bird's Eye View of the City of
Toledo, Ohio 1870
Size: ca. 24 × 36 in. (61.1 × 91.6 cm.)
Artist: Albert Ruger
Lithographer:
Printer: Chicago Lithograph Company,
150–54 So. Clark St., Chicago
Publisher: Ruger & Stoner, Madison,
Wisconsin
Key/Vignettes/Misc:
Locations: Toledo–Lucas County Public
Library, Toledo, Ohio
Catalogs/Checklists:

3152
Place: Toledo, Ohio
Date: 1876
Title: Toledo, Ohio, 1876
Size: 12 × 25⅞ in. (30.5 × 65.8 cm.)
Artist: A. Ruger
Lithographer:
Printer: Chas. Shober & Co. props
Chicago Lith. Co. [Chicago]
Publisher: J. J. Stoner, Madison, Wis.
Key/Vignettes/Misc:
Locations: MM–NN; LC–M; CHS–C;
Toledo–Lucas County Public Library,
Toledo, Ohio
Catalogs/Checklists: MM–NN, LP 1219;
LC–M, 710

3153
Place: Toronto, Ohio
Date: 1899
Title: Toronto, Ohio 1899.
Size: 18½ × 33¾ in. (47 × 86 cm.)
Artist: A. E. Downs
Lithographer:
Printer:

Publisher: A. E. Downs & Jas. B. Moyer, Boston
Key/Vignettes/Misc: Refs. 1–13, A–G; 18 vignettes
Locations: LC–M
Catalogs/Checklists: LC–M, 711

3154
Place: Van Wert, Ohio
Date: 1881
Title: Birdseye View of Van Wert, O
Size: 15½ × 30⅜ in. (39.4 × 77.3 cm.)
Artist: FGT
Lithographer:
Printer: Thos. Hunter, Lith. 716 Filbert St. Phila.
Publisher: Howland & Germann
Key/Vignettes/Misc: 12 vignettes
Locations: Van Wert County Historical Society, Van Wert, Ohio; Brumback Library, Van Wert, Ohio
Catalogs/Checklists:

3155
Place: Wapakoneta, Ohio
Date: Ca. 1870
Title: Bird's eye view of Wapakoneta, Auglaize County Ohio
Size: 16½ × 25⅜ in. (42 × 64.6 cm.)
Artist:
Lithographer:
Printer:
Publisher:
Key/Vignettes/Misc:
Locations: OHS–C
Catalogs/Checklists:

3156
Place: Warren, Ohio
Date: 1870
Title: Bird's eye view of Warren, Trumbull County, Ohio 1870.
Size: 20⁷⁄₁₆ × 25¹⁵⁄₁₆ in. (52 × 66 cm.)
Artist: [Albert Ruger]
Lithographer:
Printer: Merchants Lithographing Co. [Chicago]
Publisher: Ruger & Stoner, Madison, Wis.
Key/Vignettes/Misc: Refs. 1–16; 2 vignettes
Locations: LC–M
Catalogs/Checklists: LC–M, 712

3157
Place: Washington Court House, Ohio
Date: N.D.
Title: Bird's–Eye View of the City of Washington C. H. Fayette Co., Ohio, Looking to the East
Size: 22⅜ × 27¾ in. (57 × 70.6 cm.)
Artist: E. L. Crall
Lithographer:
Printer:
Publisher: Crall & Nemme
Key/Vignettes/Misc:
Locations: OHS–C
Catalogs/Checklists:

3158
Place: Wauseon, Ohio
Date: 1881
Title: Bird's Eye View of Wauseon, County Seat of Fulton Co. Ohio 1881

Size: 12½ × 18½ in. (31.8 × 47.1 cm.)
Artist:
Lithographer:
Printer: Beck & Pauli, Milwaukee, Wisc.
Publisher: J. J. Stoner, Madison, Wisc.
Key/Vignettes/Misc: Refs. 1–42, A–G
Locations: Wauseon, Ohio, Public Library
Catalogs/Checklists:

3159
Place: Willoughby, Ohio
Date: 1883
Title: Panoramic View of Willoughby, Lake County, Ohio, 1883
Size:
Artist:
Lithographer:
Printer:
Publisher: J. J. Stoner, Madison, Wis.
Key/Vignettes/Misc: Refs. 1–13, A–G
Locations: Lake County Historical Society, Mentor, Ohio (photo)
Catalogs/Checklists:

3160
Place: Youngstown, Ohio
Date: 1870
Title: Bird's Eye View of the City of Youngstown Looking West Mahoning County Ohio 1870 Population 8,100
Size: 21⅝ × 26 in. (55.1 × 66.2 cm.)
Artist: [Albert Ruger]
Lithographer:
Printer: Merchants Lith. Co., Chicago
Publisher: Ruger & Stoner, Madison, Wisconsin
Key/Vignettes/Misc: Refs. 1–24, A–T; 2 vignettes
Locations: Mahoning Valley Historical Society, Youngstown, Ohio
Catalogs/Checklists:

3161
Place: Youngstown, Ohio
Date: 1882
Title: Panoramic View of the City of Youngstown County Seat of Mahoning Co. Ohio Looking South West 1882
Size: 16½ × 28 in. (42 × 71 cm.)
Artist: A. Ruger
Lithographer:
Printer: Beck & Pauli Lithographers, Milwaukee, Wis.
Publisher: Ruger & Stoner, Madison, Wis.
Key/Vignettes/Misc: Refs. 1–64, X, XX, OO, O, A–H, K–P, R–W
Locations: LC–M; Mahoning Valley Historical Society, Youngstown, Ohio
Catalogs/Checklists: LC–M, 713

3162
Place: Zanesville, Ohio
Date: [1854–55?]
Title: View of Zanesville & Putnam O.
Size: 17⅛ × 29⅜ in. (43.5 × 74.7 cm.)
Artist: E. Sachse [James T. Palmatary?]
Lithographer:
Printer: E. Sachse & Co., Baltimore
Publisher: J. T. Palmatary
Key/Vignettes/Misc:
Locations: ACMW–FW
Catalogs/Checklists: ACMW–FW 1641

3163
Place: Zanesville, Ohio
Date: 1885
Title: Panoramic View of the City of Zanesville, Muskingum County, Ohio 1885.
Size: 18⅛ × 29⅞ in. (46 × 76 cm.) (facsimile)
Artist:
Lithographer:
Printer: Beck & Pauli, Litho. Madison, Wis.
Publisher: Ruger & Stoner, Madison, Wis.
Key/Vignettes/Misc: Refs.
Locations: LC–M (facsimile); OHS–C; PAC; Zane Grey Museum, Norwich, Ohio
Catalogs/Checklists: LC–M, 713.1

3164
Place: Ardmore, Oklahoma
Date: 1891
Title: Ardmore, Indian Territory. 1891
Size: 11½ × 23½ in. (29.5 × 59.7 cm.)
Artist: T. M. Fowler
Lithographer:
Printer:
Publisher: T. M. Fowler & James B. Moyer
Key/Vignettes/Misc: Refs. 1–9, A–C
Locations: ACMW–FW; LC–M
Catalogs/Checklists: ACMW–FW 1096; LC–M, 713.2

3165
Place: Bartlesville, Oklahoma
Date: 1917
Title: Bartlesville Oklahoma 1917
Size: 11¹³⁄₁₆ × 29¹⁄₁₆ in. (29.9 × 73.8 cm.)
Artist: T. M. Fowler
Lithographer:
Printer:
Publisher: Fowler & Kelley, Passaic, N. J.
Key/Vignettes/Misc: Unnumbered business directory
Locations: ACMW–FW; LC–M
Catalogs/Checklists: ACMW–FW 1097; LC–M, 714

3166
Place: Edmond, Oklahoma
Date: 1891
Title: Edmond, Oklahoma Territory 1891.
Size: 9¹⁄₁₆ × 19⅛ in. (22.9 × 48.5 cm.)
Artist: T. M. Fowler
Lithographer:
Printer:
Publisher: T. M. Fowler & James B. Moyer
Key/Vignettes/Misc: Refs. 1–7
Locations: ACMW–FW; LC–M
Catalogs/Checklists: ACMW–FW 1100; LC–M, 714.1

3167
Place: El Reno, Oklahoma
Date: 1891
Title: Fort Reno, Oklahoma Territory. 1891
Size: 9⁹⁄₁₆ × 23¹⁄₁₆ in. (24.2 × 58.6 cm.)
Artist: T. M. Fowler
Lithographer:
Printer: A. E. Downs Lith. Boston
Publisher: T. M. Fowler & James B. Moyer
Key/Vignettes/Misc: Refs. 1–29

Locations: ACMW−FW
Catalogs/Checklists: ACMW−FW 1101

3168
Place: Guthrie, Oklahoma
Date: [1891]
Title: Guthrie Oklahoma's Capital and Largest City. Age 2 ½ Years Population 10,350.
Size: 23 × 23⅛ in. (58.6 × 58.9 cm.)
Artist:
Lithographer:
Printer:
Publisher: Robbins & Thomas
Key/Vignettes/Misc: 32 vignettes; description
Locations: Oklahoma Historical Society, Oklahoma City, Oklahoma
Catalogs/Checklists:

3169
Place: Lawton, Oklahoma
Date: 1910
Title: Birds Eye View of Lawton, Okla. Showing Chamber of Commerce Industrial Addition.
Size: 6¼ × 13⅜ in. (16 × 34 cm.)
Artist: J. P. Hathaway
Lithographer:
Printer: Joslyn Engraving, Okla City
Publisher:
Key/Vignettes/Misc:
Locations: LC−M
Catalogs/Checklists: LC−M, 715

3170
Place: Oklahoma City, Oklahoma
Date: 1890
Title: Oklahoma City, Indian Territory, 1890
Size: 15¹³⁄₁₆ × 29⅜ in. (40.1 × 74.6 cm.)
Artist: T. M. Fowler
Lithographer:
Printer: A. E. Downs Lith Boston
Publisher:
Key/Vignettes/Misc: Refs. 1−8, A−K; description
Locations: NYP−S; Oklahoma City University, Oklahoma City, Oklahoma; LC−M (facsimile)
Catalogs/Checklists: LC−M, 715.2; Stokes 1890—G−93; Reps, Cities on Stone, p. 95

3171
Place: Sand Springs, Oklahoma
Date: 1917
Title:
Size:
Artist: T. M. Fowler
Lithographer:
Printer:
Publisher:
Key/Vignettes/Misc:
Locations: Unknown
Catalogs/Checklists: Warren

3172
Place: Tulsa, Oklahoma
Date: 1918
Title: Aero View of Tulsa Oklahoma, 1918.

Size: 13³⁄₁₆ × 35 in. (33.4 × 88.8 cm.)
Artist: T. M. Fowler
Lithographer:
Printer: [Meriden Gravure Co., Meriden, Conn.]
Publisher: Fowler & Kelly
Key/Vignettes/Misc: Refs. A−F; 2 vignettes
Locations: LC−M; ACMW−FW
Catalogs/Checklists: LC−M, 716; ACMW−FW 1095; Reps, Cities on Stone, p. 98

3173
Place: Barrie, Ontario
Date: 1853
Title: Barrie, on Lake Simcoe Canada West.
Size: 8⅞ × 24 in. (22.5 × 61.1 cm.)
Artist: Capt. W. H. Grubbe
Lithographer:
Printer: H. Scobie, Toronto
Publisher:
Key/Vignettes/Misc:
Locations: MTLB−T; ROM
Catalogs/Checklists: Spendlove, Face of Early Canada, p. 72; Samuel, no. 612

3174
Place: Barrie, Ontario
Date: 1857
Title: Barrie. County of Simcoe. 1857.
Size: 8¹⁄₁₆ × 15⅝ in. (20.4 × 39.8 cm.)
Artist:
Lithographer:
Printer: J[ohn] Ellis [8 King St. W.] Toronto
Publisher:
Key/Vignettes/Misc:
Locations: UTR−T
Catalogs/Checklists:

3175
Place: Barrie, Ontario
Date: 1875
Title: Barrie, Ont., 1875
Size: 18⁹⁄₁₆ × 39¾ in. (47.2 × 101 cm.)
Artist: Edgar A. Dickinson
Lithographer: J. Wilson
Printer: The Burland−Desbarats Litho. Comp. Montreal
Publisher: Edgar A. Dickinson (copyright)
Key/Vignettes/Misc:
Locations: PAC−P
Catalogs/Checklists:

3176
Place: Belleville, Ontario
Date: 1874
Title: Bird's Eye View of Belleville, Ontario, Canada. 1874
Size: 14⁹⁄₁₆ × 22 in. (37 × 56 cm.) (facsimile)
Artist:
Lithographer:
Printer:
Publisher:
Key/Vignettes/Misc: Refs.; vignettes
Locations: PAC (facsimile)
Catalogs/Checklists: PAC (1976)

Place: Berlin, Ontario
Date: 1875
See Kitchener, Ontario, 1875.

3177
Place: Brantford, Ontario
Date: 1875
Title: Bird's Eye View of Brantford, Province Ontario. Canada. 1875.
Size: 20¹³⁄₁₆ × 24⅜ in. (53 × 62 cm.)
Artist: H. Brosius
Lithographer:
Printer: Chas. Shober & Co. prop's Chicago Lith Co. [Chicago]
Publisher:
Key/Vignettes/Misc: Refs. 1−61, A; 1 vignette
Locations: LC−M; Brant County Musem, Brantford, Ontario; PAC (photo)
Catalogs/Checklists: LC−M, 1069; PAC H3/440−Brantford−1875

3178
Place: Brantford, Ontario
Date: 1893
Title: City of Brantford, Can.
Size: 23⁹⁄₁₆ × 35⅛ in. (60 × 89.5 cm.)
Artist:
Lithographer:
Printer: Toronto Lithographing Co.
Publisher: Toronto Lithographing Co., Toronto (copyright)
Key/Vignettes/Misc:
Locations: PAC
Catalogs/Checklists: PAC (1976); PAC H2/440−Brantford−1893

3179
Place: Brantford, Ontario
Date: [1893−]
Title: City of Brantford, Canada.
Size: 23 × 34¾ in. (58.5 × 88.5 cm.)
Artist:
Lithographer:
Printer: Toronto Lithographing Co.
Publisher:
Key/Vignettes/Misc:
Locations: PAC
Catalogs/Checklists: PAC H2/440−Brantford−[post 1893]

3180
Place: Brantford, Ontario
Date: ?
Title:
Size:
Artist: [Edwin Whitefield]
Lithographer:
Printer:
Publisher:
Key/Vignettes/Misc:
Locations: Unknown. Not located by Norton
Catalogs/Checklists: Norton, Whitefield, no. 63

3181
Place: Brockville, Ontario
Date: 1874
Title: Bird's Eye View of Brockville Province, Ontario, Canada.
Size: 22¾ × 31 in. (58 × 79 cm.)

Artist: H. Brosius
Lithographer:
Printer: Chas. Shober & Co. Props, Chicago Lith Co. [Chicago]
Publisher:
Key/Vignettes/Misc: Refs. 1–42; 1 vignette
Locations: PAC; AO–T; Brockville and District Historical Society, Brockville, Ontario; LC–M (photo)
Catalogs/Checklists: PAC (1976); PAC H2/440–Brockville–1874; LC–M, 1069.1

3182
Place: Cambridge, Ontario
Date: 1875
Title: Bird's Eye View of Galt, Province Ontario. Canada, 1875.
Size: 21¹¹⁄₁₆ × 28⅛ in. (55.2 × 71.6 cm.)
Artist:
Lithographer:
Printer: Chicago Lith Co., Chas. Shober & Co. [Chicago]
Publisher:
Key/Vignettes/Misc: Refs. 1–32, A–H, K–M; 1 vignette
Locations: ROM; Cambridge, Ontario, Public Library
Catalogs/Checklists: PAC (1976)

3183
Place: Chatham, Ontario
Date: 1875
Title: Chatham. Province Ontario Canada, 1875
Size: 25¹⁵⁄₁₆ × 34⅜ in. (66 × 87.5 cm.)
Artist:
Lithographer:
Printer:
Publisher: L. J. Stones
Key/Vignettes/Misc:
Locations: PAC (photo); Archives of Ontario, Toronto, Ontario
Catalogs/Checklists:

3184
Place: Chatham, Ontario
Date: [1895]
Title: [Title trimmmed] [Birdseye View of Chatham, Ontario]
Size: 29¹⁄₁₆ × 39⅜ in. (74 × 99 cm.)
Artist:
Lithographer:
Printer:
Publisher:
Key/Vignettes/Misc: 29 vignettes
Locations: LC–M [dates 1870–1880]
Catalogs/Checklists: LC–M, 1070; PAC (1976); PAC H3/440–Chatham–[1895]

3185
Place: Cobourg, Ontario
Date: 1874
Title: Bird's Eye View of Cobourg, Ontario, Canada. 1874
Size: 19¾ × 25¾ in. (50.2 × 65.5 cm.)
Artist:
Lithographer:
Printer:
Publisher:
Key/Vignettes/Misc: Refs. 1–32; 2 vignettes

Locations: AO–T
Catalogs/Checklists: PAC (1976)

3186
Place: Collingwood, Ontario
Date: 1875
Title: Bird's Eye View of Collingwood, Ontario, Canada
Size: 16⅞ × 24 in. (42.9 × 61.1 cm.)
Artist:
Lithographer:
Printer:
Publisher: J. J. Stoner, Madison, Wis.
Key/Vignettes/Misc: 2 vignettes
Locations: BPL–R
Catalogs/Checklists:

3187
Place: Dundas, Ontario
Date: 1848
Title: Dundas, Canada West
Size: 10½ × 16½ in. (26.7 × 42 cm.)
Artist: J. Gillespie
Lithographer: J. Gillespie
Printer: Scobie & Balfour Lith. Toronto
Publisher: Scobie & Balfour, Toronto
Key/Vignettes/Misc:
Locations: PAC–P
Catalogs/Checklists: Allodi, Printmaking in Canada, no. 97

3188
Place: Fergus, Ontario
Date: 1835
Title: Fergus, U. C.
Size: 8 × 13 in. (20.3 × 33 cm.)
Artist: Miss J. D. Fordyce
Lithographer:
Printer: Forrester & Nichol, Edinburgh
Publisher:
Key/Vignettes/Misc:
Locations: MTLB–T
Catalogs/Checklists: Robertson, no. 1051

Place: Galt, Ontario
Date: 1875
See Cambridge, Ontario, 1875.

3189
Place: Guelph, Ontario
Date: 1872
Title: Bird's Eye View of Guelph, Ontario, Canada. 1872.
Size:
Artist: H. Brosius.
Lithographer:
Printer:
Publisher:
Key/Vignettes/Misc: Refs. 1–19; 2 vignettes
Locations: PAC (photo)
Catalogs/Checklists: PAC (1976)

3190
Place: Guelph, Ontario
Date: 1873
Title: Bird's Eye View of Guelph Ontario Canada 1873.
Size: 17¹⁵⁄₁₆ × 23⅜ in. (45.7 × 59.5 cm.) (photo)
Artist: H. Brosius
Lithographer:

Printer:
Publisher:
Key/Vignettes/Misc: 19 refs.; 2 vignettes
Locations: PAC (photo)
Catalogs/Checklists: PAC H3/440–Guelph–1873

3191
Place: Hamilton, Ontario
Date: Ca. 1849
Title: Hamilton. From the Mountain Road.
Size: 5⅝ × 7½ in. (14.4 × 19.1 cm.)
Artist: T.[homas] Young
Lithographer:
Printer: Sarony & Major, N. York
Publisher:
Key/Vignettes/Misc:
Locations: PAC–P
Catalogs/Checklists: deVolpi, Niagara Peninsula, Plate 33

3192
Place: Hamilton, Ontario
Date: 1854
Title: Hamilton, Canada West. From the Mountain
Size: 22⁷⁄₁₆ × 35⅜ in. (57.1 × 89.9 cm.)
Artist: E. Whitefield
Lithographer:
Printer: Endicott & Co., New York
Publisher: E. Whitefield, Hamilton
Key/Vignettes/Misc: Refs. 1–10
Locations: ROM; MTLB–T; PAC–P
Catalogs/Checklists: Robertson, no. 235; Samuel, no. 298; Norton, Whitefield, no. 59; deVolpi, Niagara Peninsula, Plate 40; Spendlove, Face of Early Canada, p. 71

3193
Place: Hamilton, Ontario
Date: Ca. 1857
Title: Hamilton, C. W.
Size:
Artist:
Lithographer:
Printer:
Publisher: Charles Magnus, 12 Frankfort Street N. Y.
Key/Vignettes/Misc:
Locations: Unknown
Catalogs/Checklists: deVolpi, Niagara Peninsula, Plate 46

3194
Place: Hamilton, Ontario
Date: 1859
Title: Hamilton, C. W.
Size: 23¹³⁄₁₆ × 35¹³⁄₁₆ in. (60.6 × 91.1 cm.)
Artist: G. S. Rice
Lithographer:
Printer: Endicott & Co. N. Y.
Publisher:
Key/Vignettes/Misc: Refs. 1–18
Locations: LC–P
Catalogs/Checklists: LC–M, 1071.2

3195
Place: Hamilton, Ontario
Date: Ca. 1861
Title: City of Hamilton, C. W.
Size: 23³⁄₁₆ × 35⅝ in. (58.8 × 89.8 cm.)

Artist: Whale
Lithographer: Fuller & Bencke
Printer: Fuller & Bencke, Victoria Hall, Toronto
Publisher: Geo. E. Pell
Key/Vignettes/Misc:
Locations: PAC–P; MCM–M
Catalogs/Checklists: deVolpi, Niagara Peninsula, Plate 49

3196

Place: Ingersoll, Ontario
Date: [1885?]
Title: Town of Ingersoll
Size:
Artist:
Lithographer:
Printer: W. Wesbroom [Toronto]
Publisher: J. C. Young
Key/Vignettes/Misc: Refs. 1–78; 23 vignettes
Locations: Oxford Museum, Woodstock, Ontario (facsimile); PAC (photo)
Catalogs/Checklists:

3197

Place: Kingston, Ontario
Date: 1851
Title: Canada Kingston on Kingsriver
Size: 9⁹⁄₁₆ × 11¾ in. (24.2 × 29.9 cm.)
Artist: Aug. Kollner
Lithographer: Deroy
Printer: Jacomme & Co.
Publisher: Goupil & Co., New York & Paris
Key/Vignettes/Misc:
Locations: NYP–S; MTLB–T; PAC–P; ROM
Catalogs/Checklists: Samuel, no. 591; Stokes P. 1850—H–11; Robertson, no. 1349

3198

Place: Kingston, Ontario
Date: 1855
Title: Kingston, Canada West. From Fort Henry.
Size: 22¼ × 34½ in. (56.5 × 87.8 cm.)
Artist: E. Whitefield
Lithographer:
Printer:
Publisher: E. Whitefield, Kingston
Key/Vignettes/Misc: Refs. 1–11
Locations: ROM; Musee Chateau de Ramezay, Montreal, Quebec; Douglas Library, Queen's University, Kingston, Ontario; PAC–P; MTLB–T
Catalogs/Checklists: Norton, Whitefield, no. 64; Robertson, no. 50; Spendlove, Face of Early Canada, p. 71

3199

Place: Kingston, Ontario
Date: 1875
Title: Kingston Ontario, Canada. 1875 View Over the Kingston Harbour, From Gunn's Warehouse.
Size: 24⁷⁄₁₆ × 32 in. (62.1 × 81 cm.)
Artist: H. Brosius
Lithographer:
Printer: Chas Shober & Co. prop's Chicago Lith. Co. [Chicago]

Publisher: J. J. Stoner, Madison, Wis.
Key/Vignettes/Misc: Refs. 1–49, A–O
Locations: PAC–P; PAC (photo); LC–M (facsimile)
Catalogs/Checklists: PAC (1976); PAC H3/440–Kingston–1875; LC–M,1071.4

3200

Place: Kitchener, Ontario
Date: 1875
Title: Berlin, Province Ontario Canada 1875
Size: 15 × 20 in. (38.2 × 50.9 cm.)
Artist: H. Brosius
Lithographer:
Printer: C. H. Vogt Lith., Milwaukee
Publisher: J. J. Stoner, Madison, Wis.
Key/Vignettes/Misc: Refs. 1–44; 1 vignette
Locations: Waterloo Historical Society Archives, Kitchener, Ontario; Kitchener, Ontario, Public Library
Catalogs/Checklists: PAC (1976)

3201

Place: Lindsay, Ontario
Date: 1875
Title: Bird's Eye View of Lindsay, Ontario, Canada, 1875
Size: 13¾ × 17⁷⁄₁₆ in. (35 × 44.4 cm.) (photo)
Artist:
Lithographer:
Printer: Chas. Shober & Co. prop's Chicago Lith Co. [Chicago]
Publisher:
Key/Vignettes/Misc: Refs. 1–45, B; 1 vignette
Locations: PAC (photo); Lindsay, Ontario, Public Library
Catalogs/Checklists:

3202

Place: London, Ontario
Date: [1847–50]
Title: London, Canada West.
Size: 10⅜ × 15½ in. (26.4 × 39.5 cm.)
Artist:
Lithographer:
Printer: Lith. Press of Scobie & Balfour
Publisher: Thomas Craig, London, C. W.
Key/Vignettes/Misc:
Locations: PAC–P
Catalogs/Checklists: Allodi, Printmaking in Canada, no. 103

3203

Place: London, Ontario
Date: 1855
Title: London, Canada West
Size: 21¾ × 36¾ in. (55.3 × 93.4 cm.)
Artist: E. Whitefield
Lithographer:
Printer:
Publisher: E. Whitefield, London [Ontario]
Key/Vignettes/Misc: Refs. 1–11
Locations: NYP–S; PAC; ROM; London, Ontario, Public Library and Art Museum; AO–T; MTLB–T; PAC–P
Catalogs/Checklists: Norton, Whitefield, no. 67; Spendlove, Face of Early Canada, p. 71; Robertson, no. 226

3204

Place: London, Ontario
Date: 1872
Title: Bird's Eye View of London, Ontario, Canada, 1872. Looking North–East. Population 20,000.
Size: 14¹⁵⁄₁₆ × 25⁵⁄₁₆ in. (38 × 64.5 cm.) (facsimile)
Artist: E. S. Glover
Lithographer:
Printer:
Publisher:
Key/Vignettes/Misc: Refs. 1–28
Locations: LC–M (facsimile); PAC (facsimile); MTLB–T (facsimile); MGUR–M (facsimile); London, Ontario, Public Library and Art Museum
Catalogs/Checklists: LC–M, 1072; PAC H2/440–London–1872

3205

Place: London, Ontario
Date: 1890
Title: City of London, Ont. Canada.
Size: 22¼ × 35¹⁵⁄₁₆ in. (56.6 × 91.4 cm.)
Artist:
Lithographer:
Printer:
Publisher:
Key/Vignettes/Misc:
Locations: PAC
Catalogs/Checklists: PAC H2/440–London–1890

3206

Place: London, Ontario
Date: 1893
Title: City of London, Canada
Size: 27¹⁄₁₆ × 41⅛ in. (68.9 × 104.5 cm.)
Artist:
Lithographer:
Printer: Toronto Lithographing Co. [Toronto]
Publisher: Toronto Lithographing Co., Toronto [copyright]
Key/Vignettes/Misc:
Locations: PAC
Catalogs/Checklists: PAC (1976); PAC V1/440–London–1893

3207

Place: Napanee, Ontario
Date: 1874
Title: Bird's Eye View of Napanee, Ontario, Canada. 1874.
Size: 16⁵⁄₁₆ × 22¾ in. (41.4 × 57.8 cm.)
Artist: H. Brosius
Lithographer:
Printer: Chas. Shober & Co., Prop's Chicago Lith. Co. [Chicago]
Publisher:
Key/Vignettes/Misc: Refs. 1–30; 1 vignette
Locations: PAC–P; PAC (photo)
Catalogs/Checklists: PAC (1976); PAC H3/440–Napanee–1874

3208

Place: Norwich, Ontario
Date: 1881
Title: Norwich, Ontario. 1881.
Size: 13 × 23¼ in. (33.1 × 59.2 cm.)

Artist: T. M. Fowler
Lithographer:
Printer: Beck & Pauli, Lith, Milwaukee, Wis.
Publisher: Fowler & Tidey
Key/Vignettes/Misc: Refs. 1–25; 9 vignettes
Locations: LC–M (photo); PAC
Catalogs/Checklists: PAC (1976); LC–M, 1072.3

3209
Place: Orillia, Ontario
Date: 1875
Title: Orille, Ontario, Canada.
Size: 13⁵⁄₁₆ × 17⁷⁄₈ in. (34 × 45.5 cm.) (photo)
Artist: H. Brosius
Lithographer:
Printer: Chas. Shober & Co. Prop's Chicago Lith. Co. [Chicago]
Publisher: J. J. Stoner, Madison, Wis.
Key/Vignettes/Misc:
Locations: Archives of Ontario, Toronto, Ontario; PAC (photo)
Catalogs/Checklists: PAC (1976)

3210
Place: Ottawa, Ontario
Date: 1855
Title: Ottawa City, Canada West Lower Town. From Government Hill Looking down the Ottawa River and Showing the Locks of the Rideau Canal.
Size: 22¾ × 36⅛ in. (57.8 × 91.6 cm.)
Artist: E. Whitefield
Lithographer:
Printer: Endicott & Co., N. Y.
Publisher: E. Whitefield, Ottawa
Key/Vignettes/Misc: Refs. 1–9
Locations: ROM; MCM–M; PAC–P; MTLB–T
Catalogs/Checklists: Norton, Whitefield, no. 66; deVolpi, Ottawa, Plate 20; Spendlove, Face of Early Canada, p. 71; Robertson, no. 205

3211
Place: Ottawa, Ontario
Date: 1855
Title: Ottawa City, Canada West. (Late Bytown.) View of the Uppertown, Looking up the Ottawa River from Government Hill.
Size: 22⁹⁄₁₆ × 35¹⁵⁄₁₆ in. (57.4 × 91.2 cm.)
Artist: E. Whitefield
Lithographer:
Printer: Endicott & Co., N. Y.
Publisher: E. Whitefield, Ottawa
Key/Vignettes/Misc: Refs. 1–5
Locations: NYP–S; ROM; MTLB–T; PAC–P
Catalogs/Checklists: deVolpi, Ottawa, Plate 21; Norton, Whitefield, no. 65; Stokes P. 1855—H–32; Spendlove, Face of Early Canada, p. 71; Robertson, no. 194

3212
Place: Ottawa, Ontario
Date: [1858–61] State I
Title: City of Ottawa, Canada West.
Size: 27⁵⁄₁₆ × 37¼ in. (69.4 × 94.5 cm.)

Artist:
Lithographer:
Printer: Sarony, Major & Knapp. Lith. 449 Broadway, N. Y.
Publisher: Stent & Laver, Architects &c., Ottawa, C. W.
Key/Vignettes/Misc:
Locations: PAC–P; ROM; MCM–M
Catalogs/Checklists: deVolpi, Ottawa, Plate 43; Spendlove, Face of Early Canada, p. 72; Samuel, no. 596

3213
Place: Ottawa, Ontario
Date: [1858–61] State II
Title: City of Ottawa, Canada West
Size: 27¼ × 37⅛ in. (69.3 × 94.4 cm.)
Artist:
Lithographer:
Printer: Sarony, Major & Knapp. Lith. 449 Broadway, N. Y.
Publisher: Stent & Laver, Achitects &c., Ottawa, C. W.
Key/Vignettes/Misc:
Locations: PAC–P
Catalogs/Checklists: Spendlove, Face of Early Canada, p. 72

3214
Place: Ottawa, Ontario
Date: 1876
Title: Bird's Eye View of the City of Ottawa Province Ontario. Canada 1876
Size: 26⅛ × 34¹⁄₁₆ in. (66.4 × 86.6 cm.)
Artist: Herm. Brosius
Lithographer:
Printer: Chas. Shober & Co props Chicago Litho. Co. [Chicago]
Publisher:
Key/Vignettes/Misc: Refs. 1–66, A–W; 1 vignette
Locations: LC–M (facsimile); PAC; MTLB–T; Douglas Library, Queen's University, Kingston, Ontario; PAC–P
Catalogs/Checklists: deVolpi, Ottawa, Plate 86; PAC (1976); PAC H2/440–Ottawa–1876; LC–M, 1072.4

3215
Place: Ottawa, Ontario
Date: [1893]
Title: City of Ottawa, Canada. With Views of Principal Business Buildings
Size: 31¼ × 42⅝ in. (79.5 × 108.5 cm.)
Artist: [Walter Raine]
Lithographer:
Printer: Toronto Lithographing Co. [Toronto]
Publisher:
Key/Vignettes/Misc: 28 vignettes
Locations: LC–M; PAC
Catalogs/Checklists: PAC (1976); PAC–H1/440–Ottawa–[1893]

3216
Place: Ottawa, Ontario
Date: 1895
Title: City of Ottawa, Canada with Views of Principal Business Buildings.
Size: 33 × 42 in. (84 × 106.8 cm.)
Artist:
Lithographer:

Printer: Toronto Lithographing Co. [Toronto]
Publisher:
Key/Vignettes/Misc: 28 vignettes
Locations: LC–M
Catalogs/Checklists: LC–M, 1073; PAC H3/440–Ottawa–[1895]

3217
Place: Ottawa, Ontario
Date: [1893–98]
Title: City of Ottawa, Canada, with Views of Principal Business Buildings
Size: 30⁹⁄₁₆ × 41¼ in. (77.7 × 104.7 cm.)
Artist: [Walter Raine]
Lithographer:
Printer: Toronto Lithographing Co. [Toronto]
Publisher:
Key/Vignettes/Misc: 26 vignettes
Locations: PAC (photo); PAC–P
Catalogs/Checklists: PAC H3/440–Ottawa–[1893–98]

3218
Place: Ottawa, Ontario
Date: 1908
Title: Ottawa, 1908.
Size: 19⅝ × 43⅜ in. (50 × 110.4 cm.)
Artist:
Lithographer:
Printer:
Publisher: J. L. Wiseman (copyright)
Key/Vignettes/Misc:
Locations: PAC
Catalogs/Checklists: PAC V1/440–Ottawa–1908

3219
Place: Paris, Ontario
Date: Ca. 1870
Title: Paris, Ont. Lower Town from the Central School
Size: 14½ x 17¼ in. (36.9 × 43.8 cm.)
Artist: M[ichael] A. F[arrar]
Lithographer:
Printer: Brown & Bautz, Hamilton
Publisher:
Key/Vignettes/Misc:
Locations: Private collection
Catalogs/Checklists:

3220
Place: Perth, Ontario
Date: 1874
Title: Bird's Eye View of Perth, Province Ontario, Canada.
Size: 17⅝ × 20⅛ in. (44.9 × 51.2 cm.)
Artist: H. Brosius
Lithographer:
Printer: J. Knauber Co., Milwaukee, Wisconsin
Publisher: J. J. Stoner
Key/Vignettes/Misc: Refs. 1–34; 1 vignette
Locations: Perth Museum, Perth, Ontario
Catalogs/Checklists: PAC (1976)

3221
Place: Peterborough, Ontario
Date: 1875
Title: Bird's Eye View of Peterborough Ontario,—Canada 1875.

Size: 21¼ × 32¼ in. (54.1 × 82.1 cm.)
Artist: H. Brosius
Lithographer:
Printer: Chas. Shober & Co. props.
Chicago Lith Co. [Chicago]
Publisher:
Key/Vignettes/Misc: Refs. 1–35, A, O; 2
vignettes
Locations: PAC (facsimile); Peterborough
Centennial Museum & Archives,
Peterborough, Ontario; LC–M (photo)
Catalogs/Checklists: PAC
V1/440–Peterborough–1875; LC–M,
1073.1

3222
Place: Peterborough, Ontario
Date: [1900]
Title: City of Peterborough Canada. With
Views of Principal Business Buildings
Size: 29 × 39½ in. (73.8 × 100.5 cm.)
Artist:
Lithographer:
Printer: The Howell Lith. Co., Hamilton,
Ont.
Publisher:
Key/Vignettes/Misc: 25 vignettes
Locations: PAC (photo); Peterborough
Centennial Museum & Archives,
Peterborough, Ontario
Catalogs/Checklists: PAC (1976); PAC
V1/440–Peterborough–[1900]

Place: Point Edwards, Ontario
Date: 1867
See Port Huron, Michigan, 1867. Key/
Vignettes/Misc: Refs.

3223
Place: Port Arthur, Ontario
Date: 1885
Title: Port Arthur, Ont., 1885 Population
6000
Size: 29¾ × 39¾ in. (75.7 × 101.1 cm.)
Artist: R. J. Edwards and E. Demar
Lithographer:
Printer: Rolph Smith & Co., Toronto, Ont.
Publisher: J. C. Young, Port Arthur Ont.
Key/Vignettes/Misc: Refs. 1–123; 23
vignettes
Locations: PAC; Thunder Bay Historical
Museum Society, Thunder Bay, Ontario;
LC–M (photo)
Catalogs/Checklists: LC–M, 1073.2

3224
Place: Port Hope, Ontario
Date: 1874
Title: Bird's Eye View of Port Hope,
Ontario, Canada
Size: 17¼ × 23⅛ in. (44 × 59 cm.)
(photo)
Artist: H. Brosius
Lithographer:
Printer:
Publisher:
Key/Vignettes/Misc: Refs. 1–36, A
Locations: PAC (photo)
Catalogs/Checklists: PAC (1976)

3225
Place: Preston, Ontario
Date: [1900]

Title: Town of Preston With Views of
Principal Business Buildings
Size:
Artist:
Lithographer:
Printer: Howell Lith. Co., Hamilton
Publisher:
Key/Vignettes/Misc: 19 vignettes
Locations: PAC (photo); Doon Pioneer
Village, Kitchener, Ontario
Catalogs/Checklists:

3226
Place: Saint Catherines, Ontario
Date: 1875
Title: St. Catherines 1875 Province
Ontario, Canada
Size: 22¾ × 30¼ in. (57.9 × 77 cm.)
Artist: H. Brosius
Lithographer:
Printer: Chas. Shober & Co. Prop's
Chicago Lith. Co. [Chicago]
Publisher:
Key/Vignettes/Misc: Refs. 1–52; 1
vignette
Locations: St. Catharines Historical
Museum, St. Catharines, Ontario
Catalogs/Checklists: PAC (1976)

3227
Place: Saint Thomas, Ontario
Date: 1875
Title: St. Thomas, Province Ontario,
Canada.
Size: 20¼ × 31½ in. (51.6 × 80.1 cm.)
Artist:
Lithographer:
Printer:
Publisher: J. J. Stoner, Madison, Wis.
Key/Vignettes/Misc: 1 vignette
Locations: BPL–R
Catalogs/Checklists:

3228
Place: Saint Thomas, Ontario
Date: [1876?]
Title: St. Thomas.
Size: 22⅛ × 31¹³⁄₁₆ in. (56.3 × 80.9 cm.)
Artist: H. Brosius
Lithographer: C. H. Vogt
Printer: J. Knauber & Co. Milwaukee
Publisher: J. J. Stoner, Madison, Wis.
Key/Vignettes/Misc: Refs. 1–37; 1
vignette
Locations: LC–M
Catalogs/Checklists: LC–M, 1074

3229
Place: Sarnia, Ontario
Date: 1872
Title: Bird's Eye View of Sarnia, Lambton
County Ontario. Dominion of Canada.
1872.
Size: 19¾ × 25⅛ in. (50.3 × 64 cm.)
Artist:
Lithographer: C. H. Vogt
Printer: American Oleograph Co. Print
Publisher: J. J. Stoner
Key/Vignettes/Misc: Refs. A–G, 1–7; 2
vignettes
Locations: PAC (photo); private collection
Catalogs/Checklists:

3230
Place: Simcoe, Ontario
Date: 1881
Title: Simcoe, Ont. 1881.
Size: 11⅜ × 24⅜ in. (29 × 62 cm.)
Artist: T. M. Fowler
Lithographer:
Printer:
Publisher: Fowler & Coombs
Key/Vignettes/Misc: Refs. 1–26; 7
vignettes
Locations: AO–T; PAC (photo); LC–M
(photo)
Catalogs/Checklists: PAC (1976); PAC
H3/440–Simcoe–1881; LC–M, 1074.1

3231
Place: Smiths Falls, Ontario
Date: 1874
Title: Birds Eye View of Smith's Falls,
Province Ontario. Canada. 1874
Size: 14⅜ × 18¼ in. (36.5 × 46.4 cm.)
Artist:
Lithographer:
Printer:
Publisher:
Key/Vignettes/Misc: Refs. 1–30
Locations: Smith's Falls & District
Historical Society, Smith's Falls, Ontario;
PAC (redrawing)
Catalogs/Checklists: PAC(1976)

3232
Place: Stratford, Ontario
Date: 1872
Title: Birds Eye View of Stratford Ontario
1872
Size: 24 × 30 in. (61.1 × 76.3 cm.)
Artist: H. Brosius
Lithographer:
Printer:
Publisher:
Key/Vignettes/Misc:
Locations: Beacon Herald Archives,
Stratford, Ontario
Catalogs/Checklists:

3233
Place: Tillsonburg, Ontario
Date: 1881
Title: Tilsonburg, Ontario. 1881.
Size: ca. 11 × 20 in. (28 × 50.9 cm.)
Artist: T. M. Fowler
Lithographer:
Printer: Beck & Pauli, Lith., Milwaukee,
Wis.
Publisher: Fowler & Rhines
Key/Vignettes/Misc: Refs. 1–29; 3
vignettes
Locations: LC–M (photo); Tillsonburg
and District Historical Museum Society,
Tillsonburg, Ontario; PAC (photo)
Catalogs/Checklists: PAC (1976); LC–M,
1074.2

3234
Place: Toronto, Ontario
Date: [1835]
Title: General View of the City of Toronto,
U. C.
Size: 12¹³⁄₁₆ × 17¹³⁄₁₆ in. (32.6 × 45.3 cm.)
Artist: T.[homas] Young
Lithographer: J. H. Bufford

Printer:
Publisher: N. Currier Lith. No 1 Wall St. N. Y.
Key/Vignettes/Misc:
Locations: MTLB–T; PAC–P; ROM
Catalogs/Checklists: deVolpi, Toronto, Plate 5; Spendlove, Face of Early Canada, pp. 58–9 and Plate 83; Samuel, no. 524

3235
Place: Toronto, Ontario
Date: 1842
Title: City of Toronto
Size: 14½ × 24⅜ in. (36.9 × 62.1 cm.)
Artist: John Gillespie
Lithographer: Dodson
Printer: Day & Haghe Lithrs to the Queen [London]
Publisher:
Key/Vignettes/Misc: Refs. 1–29
Locations: PAC–P
Catalogs/Checklists: deVolpi, Toronto, Plate 12

3236
Place: Toronto, Ontario
Date: 1842
Title: West View of the City of Toronto, in the Province of Canada
Size: 14½ × 24⅜ in. (37 × 62.1 cm.)
Artist: John Gilespie
Lithographer: Dodson
Printer: Day & Haghe [London]
Publisher: F. C. Capreol, London
Key/Vignettes/Misc:
Locations: PAC–P; MTLB–T
Catalogs/Checklists: Robertson, no. 274

3237
Place: Toronto, Ontario
Date: 1851
Title: Canada Toronto
Size: 9½ × 11¾ in. (24.2 × 29.9 cm.)
Artist: Aug. Kollner
Lithographer: Deroy
Printer: Jacomme & Co.
Publisher: Goupil & Co., New–York & Paris
Key/Vignettes/Misc:
Locations: NYP–S; MTLB–T; PAC–P; ROM
Catalogs/Checklists: deVolpi, Toronto, Plate 20; Stokes P. 1850—H–6; Samuel, no. 625; Robertson, no. 889

3238
Place: Toronto, Ontario
Date: 1851
Title: Canada Toronto
Size: 9½ × 11¾ in. (24.2 × 29.9 cm.)
Artist: Aug. Kollner
Lithographer: Deroy
Printer: Cattier
Publisher: Goupil, Vibert & Co., New York & Paris
Key/Vignettes/Misc:
Locations: ROM
Catalogs/Checklists: Samuel, no. 295

3239
Place: Toronto, Ontario
Date: 1854
Title: Toronto, Canada West. From the

Top of the Jail.
Size: 22⅜ × 36¼ in. (56.8 × 92.1 cm.)
Artist: E. Whitefield
Lithographer:
Printer: Endicott & Co. N. Y.
Publisher: E. Whitefield, Toronto
Key/Vignettes/Misc: Refs. 1–16
Locations: MM–NN; ROM; MCM–M; Musee Chateau de Ramezay, Montreal, Quebec; AO–T; MTLB–T; MGUR–M; PAC–P
Catalogs/Checklists: deVolpi, Toronto, Plate 27; Norton, Whitefield, no. 60; Robertson, no. 338; Spendlove, Face of Early Canada, p. 71; Samuel, nos. 534, 626

3240
Place: Toronto, Ontario
Date: [1856]
Title: Toronto Canada West.
Size: 21¾ × 40½ in. (55.4 × 102.9 cm.)
Artist: Wm. Armstrong
Lithographer: C. Parsons
Printer: Endicott & Co. N. Y.
Publisher: Wm. Armstrong, for the City Council
Key/Vignettes/Misc:
Locations: MTLB–T; PAC–P; ROM
Catalogs/Checklists: Volpi, Toronto, Plate 17 (dated 1851); Samuel, no. 296; Spendlove, Face of Early Canada, p. 61 and Plate 88

3241
Place: Toronto, Ontario
Date: 1876
Title: Birds–Eye View of Toronto, 1876.
Size: 35¹⁵⁄₁₆ × 56⅝ in. (91.4 × 144.3 cm.)
Artist: P. A. Gross
Lithographer: P. A. Gross
Printer: [Copp, Clark & Co., Toronto]
Publisher: P. A. Gross, Toronto, Ont.
Key/Vignettes/Misc: 133 refs.; 124 vignettes
Locations: PAC; MTLB–T; Toronto Historical Board, Toronto, Ontario; LC–M (photo)
Catalogs/Checklists: PAC (1976); PAC V3/440–Toronto–1876; LC–M, 1074.3

3242
Place: Toronto, Ontario
Date: [1876]
Title: City of Toronto. (From the Northern Railway Elevator)
Size: 14⅛ × 28½ in. (35.9 × 72.5 cm.)
Artist: G. Gascard
Lithographer:
Printer: Alexr. Craig, Steam Lith, 13 Adelaide St. East
Publisher:
Key/Vignettes/Misc:
Locations: MTLB–T (title cropped); PAC–P; ROM
Catalogs/Checklists: Samuel, no. 585; deVolpi, Toronto, Plate 101; Robertson, no. 745

3243
Place: Toronto, Ontario
Date: 1877
Title: Toronto, in 1877. (Looking West)

Size: 13½ × 21⁷⁄₁₆ in. (34.3 × 54.5 cm.)
Artist:
Lithographer:
Printer: Rolph, Smith & Co. Toronto.
Publisher: Jas. Timperlake, Toronto.
Key/Vignettes/Misc:
Locations: MTLB–T
Catalogs/Checklists:

3244
Place: Toronto, Ontario
Date: 1884
Title: 1884 Toronto 1884.
Size:
Artist:
Lithographer:
Printer:
Publisher:
Key/Vignettes/Misc:
Locations: MTLB–T (photo)
Catalogs/Checklists:

3245
Place: Toronto, Ontario
Date: [1886]
Title: City of Toronto.
Size: 17 × 30⅞ in. (43.2 × 78.5 cm.)
Artist: W. Wesbroom
Lithographer:
Printer:
Publisher: Toronto Lithographing Co. [Toronto]
Key/Vignettes/Misc:
Locations: MTLB–T; UTR–T; City of Toronto Archives, Toronto, Ontario
Catalogs/Checklists:

3246
Place: Toronto, Ontario
Date: [188–?]
Title: 1834 Toronto 1834
Size: 12⅜ × 21⁷⁄₁₆ in. (31.5 × 54.5 cm.)
Artist:
Lithographer:
Printer:
Publisher:
Key/Vignettes/Misc:
Locations: MTLB–T
Catalogs/Checklists:

3247
Place: Toronto, Ontario
Date: [1892?]
Title: Toronto Railway Company's map Showing Street Railway Lines
Size: 18¾ × 57¾ in. (47.7 × 147 cm.)
Artist:
Lithographer:
Printer:
Publisher:
Key/Vignettes/Misc: Description
Locations: MTLB–T; PAC (photo)
Catalogs/Checklists:

3248
Place: Toronto, Ontario
Date: 1893
Title: City of Toronto
Size: 39¾ × 76¾ in. (101 × 195 cm.)
Artist:
Lithographer:
Printer: Barclay, Clark & Co.

Lithographers, Toronto
Publisher: Barclay, Clark & Co. (copyright)
Key/Vignettes/Misc:
Locations: MTLB–T; City of Toronto Archives, Toronto, Ontario (photo)
Catalogs/Checklists:

3249
Place: Windsor, Ontario
Date: 1878
Title: Bird's Eye View of Windsor, Ontario. 1878
Size: 17³/₁₆ × 27¼ in. (43.8 × 69.4 cm.)
Artist: T. M. Fowler
Lithographer:
Printer:
Publisher:
Key/Vignettes/Misc: Refs. 1–35; 1 vignette
Locations: PAC; LC–M (photo)
Catalogs/Checklists: PAC (1976); LC–M, 1077.2

3250
Place: Woodstock, Ontario
Date: Ca. 1890
Title: Woodstock
Size: 25½ × 38 in. (64.9 × 96.7 cm.)
Artist:
Lithographer:
Printer:
Publisher:
Key/Vignettes/Misc: 22 vignettes
Locations: Oxford Museum, Woodstock, Ontario
Catalogs/Checklists: PAC (1976)

3251
Place: Albany, Oregon
Date: 1889
Title: Bird's Eye View of Albany, Linn County, Oregon, 1889.
Size: 18⅞ × 23⅝ in. (48 × 60 cm.)
Artist:
Lithographer:
Printer: Elliott Publ. Co., San Francisco
Publisher: Albany Board of Trade
Key/Vignettes/Misc:
Locations: OUL–E
Catalogs/Checklists:

3252
Place: Ashland, Oregon
Date: 1884
Title: Bird's Eye View of Ashland, Jackson County, Oregon 1884. Looking South East. Population 1500
Size: 14 × 21½ in. (35.5 × 54.5 cm.)
Artist: [Fred A. Walpole]
Lithographer:
Printer: Beck & Pauli, Milwaukee, Wis.
Publisher:
Key/Vignettes/Misc: Refs. 1–12
Locations: SOHS–J
Catalogs/Checklists:

3253
Place: Ashland, Oregon
Date: 1890
Title: Birdseye View of Ashland, Oregon
Size: 19⅛ × 22⅝ in. (48.5 × 57 cm.)

Artist: E. S. Moore
Lithographer:
Printer:
Publisher:
Key/Vignettes/Misc: 5 vignettes
Locations: SOHS–J
Catalogs/Checklists:

3254
Place: Astoria, Oregon
Date: 1846
Title: Fort George Formerly Astoria.
Size: 8 × 12 in. (20.4 × 30.6 cm.)
Artist: [Henry James Warre]
Lithographer:
Printer:
Publisher:
Key/Vignettes/Misc:
Locations: Unknown. See Old Print Shop, Negative File
Catalogs/Checklists: Spendlove, Face of Early Canada, p. 77

3255
Place: Astoria, Oregon
Date: [1870]
Title: Astoria Clatsop Co. Oregon. The Proposed Terminus of the North Pacific R. R.
Size: 14³/₁₆ × 22⁵/₁₆ in. (36.1 × 56.8 cm.)
Artist: Castleman & Talbot
Lithographer:
Printer: G. T. Brown & Co. Lith. 540 Clay St. S. F.
Publisher: Capt. J. G. Hustler
Key/Vignettes/Misc: 2 vignettes
Locations: UCBL–B; OHS–P
Catalogs/Checklists:

3256
Place: Astoria, Oregon
Date: 1887
Title: Oregon.–General View of Astoria, Looking Inland.
Size: 8¼ × 15⅞ in. (21 × 40.4 cm.)
Artist:
Lithographer:
Printer: West Shore Litho. & Eng. Co. Portland, Or.
Publisher: [The West Shore, Portland, Oregon]
Key/Vignettes/Misc:
Locations: PUL–P
Catalogs/Checklists:

3257
Place: Astoria, Oregon
Date: 1887
Title: Oregon–General View of Astoria, Looking Seaward
Size: 8¼ × 15⅞ in. (21 × 40.4 cm.)
Artist:
Lithographer:
Printer: West Shore Litho. & Eng Co. Portland Or.
Publisher: [The West Shore, Portland, Oregon]
Key/Vignettes/Misc:
Locations: OUL–E
Catalogs/Checklists:

3258
Place: Astoria, Oregon
Date: 1890
Title: Stengele's View of Astoria Oregon 1890
Size: 22⅜ × 35⅞ in. (57 × 91.3 cm.)
Artist: [B. W.] Pierce
Lithographer:
Printer:
Publisher: J. W. Stengle (copyright)
Key/Vignettes/Misc: Refs. 1–60; 26 vignettes
Locations: MM–NN; ACMW–FW; OUL–E; SOHS–J; Clatsop County Historical Museum, Astoria, Oregon; OHS–P; UCBL–B; UCBL–B
Catalogs/Checklists: MM–NN, LP 4303; ACMW–FW 1677

3259
Place: Eugene, Oregon
Date: 1859
Title: Eugene City, Lane County, Oregon. 1859
Size: 13¾ × 20⅝ in. (34.9 × 52.3 cm.)
Artist: Kuchel & Dresel
Lithographer: Kuchel & Dresel
Printer: [Britton & Rey, San Francisco?]
Publisher: Danforth & Bro.
Key/Vignettes/Misc: 12 vignettes
Locations: ACMW–FW (proof before tone stone); LCM–E (cropped)
Catalogs/Checklists:

3260
Place: Eugene, Oregon
Date: 1859
Title: Eugene City, Lane County, Oregon. 1859
Size: 7⅞ × 14⅛ in.(20 × 36 cm.)
Artist: Kuchel & Dresel
Lithographer: Kuchel & Dresel
Printer:
Publisher:
Key/Vignettes/Misc: [no vignettes]
Locations: UCBL–B
Catalogs/Checklists:

3261
Place: Eugene, Oregon
Date: [1859?]
Title: Eugene City, Oregon
Size: ["medium"]
Artist: Kuchel & Dresel
Lithographer: Kuchel & Dresel
Printer: Britton & Rey
Publisher:
Key/Vignettes/Misc: [no vignettes]
Locations: Unknown
Catalogs/Checklists: Peters, COS, p. 143

3262
Place: Eugene, Oregon
Date: 1890
Title: Eugene, Oregon, 1890
Size: 24 × 32 in. (61.1 × 81.4 cm.)
Artist:
Lithographer:
Printer: Elliot Pub. Co. 120 Sutter St., S. F.
Publisher: Geo. M. Miller, Eugene, Or.
Key/Vignettes/Misc: Refs. 1–43; 1 vignette; description

3263
Place: Eugene, Oregon
Date: [1890?]
Title: Eugene, Lane County, Oregon.
Size: 21 × 28 in. (53.4 × 71.2 cm.)
Artist:
Lithographer:
Printer: Elliott Pub. Co. S. F.
Publisher: J. A. Straight & Co. . .Eugene, Or.
Key/Vignettes/Misc: Refs. 1–35; 14 vignettes; description
Locations: LCM–E; OHS–P (photo)
Catalogs/Checklists:

3264
Place: Grants Pass, Oregon
Date: [1890]
Title: Birdseye View of Grants Pass, Oregon.
Size: 22⅞ × 31⅞ in. (58 × 81 cm.)
Artist: E. S. Moore
Lithographer:
Printer:
Publisher: Arthur Conklin, Real Estate, Loans and Investment
Key/Vignettes/Misc:
Locations: OUL–E
Catalogs/Checklists:

3265
Place: Jacksonville, Oregon
Date: 1856
Title: Jacksonville, Jackson County, Oregon T. 1856
Size: 15½ × 21½ in. (39.5 × 55 cm.)
Artist: Kuchel & Dresel
Lithographer: Kuchel & Dresel
Printer: Britton & Rey [San Francisco]
Publisher: W. W. Fowler & C. C. Beekman [Jacksonville, Ore.]
Key/Vignettes/Misc: 19 vignettes
Locations: SOHS–J; OHS–P (photo)
Catalogs/Checklists:

3266
Place: Jacksonville, Oregon
Date: Ca. 1856
Title: Jacksonville, O. T.
Size: 9¹⁄₁₆ × 15⅛ in. (23 × 38.3 cm.)
Artist: Kuchel & Dresel
Lithographer: Kuchel & Dresel
Printer: Britton & Rey [San Francisco]
Publisher:
Key/Vignettes/Misc:
Locations: ACMW–FW
Catalogs/Checklists: ACMW–FW 1260

3267
Place: Jacksonville, Oregon
Date: 1883
Title: Bird's Eye View of Jacksonville and the Rogue River Valley, Oregon. Looking North East. Population 1000 1883.
Size: 14 × 21½ in. (35.5 × 54.5 cm.)
Artist: Fred A. Walpole
Lithographer:
Printer: Beck & Pauli, Milwaukee, Wis.
Publisher: Fred A. Walpole (copyright)

Key/Vignettes/Misc: Refs. 1–12; 1 vignette
Locations LC–M; SOHS–J; OHS–P (facsimile); LC–P
Catalogs/Checklists: LC–M, 717

3268
Place: La Grande, Oregon
Date: [1889]
Title: The Grande Ronde Valley as Seen from La Grande Oregon
Size: 13⅞ × 20 in. (35.3 × 50.9 cm.)
Artist:
Lithographer:
Printer:
Publisher: The West Shore Magazine, Portland–Or.
Key/Vignettes/Misc:
Locations: OHS–P
Catalogs/Checklists:

3269
Place: Marshfield, Oregon
Date: 1884
Title: View of Marshfield, Coos County, Oregon
Size: 15¼ × 27½ in. (38.8 × 70 cm.)
Artist: E. F. Cook
Lithographer:
Printer: Britton & Rey, S. F.
Publisher:
Key/Vignettes/Misc:
Locations: Coos–Curry Museum, North Band, Oregon
Catalogs/Checklists:

3270
Place: Oregon City, Oregon
Date: 1846
Title: The American Village
Size: 9¹³⁄₁₆ × 13⅛ in. (24.8x 33.3 cm.)
Artist: H[enry] J.[ames] Warre
Lithographer:
Printer: Dickinson & Co., [London]
Publisher:
Key/Vignettes/Misc:
Locations: ACMW–FW; PAC–P; ROM
Catalogs/Checklists: Samuel, no. 270; ACMW–FW 1904; Reps, Cities on Stone, p. 95; Spendlove, Face of Early Canada, p. 77 MM–NN, LP 592

3271
Place: Oregon City, Oregon
Date: Ca. 1857
Title: Oregon City, Oregon
Size: ["medium"]
Artist: Kuchel & Dresel
Lithographer: Kuchel & Dresel
Printer: Britton & Rey [San Francisco]
Publisher:
Key/Vignettes/Misc: [no vignettes]
Locations: Unknown
Catalogs/Checklists: Peters, COS, p. 144

3272
Place: Oregon City, Oregon
Date: 1858
Title: Oregon City, Clackamas County, Oregon. 1858.
Size: 15¹⁵⁄₁₆ × 25¹⁄₁₆ in. (40.5 × 65.2 cm.)
Artist: Kuchel & Dresel
Lithographer:

Printer: Kuchel & Dresel, Lithographers. 176 Clay St. S. E.
Publisher: Charman & Warner, Oregon City.
Key/Vignettes/Misc: 26 vignettes
Locations: ACMW–FW; UCBL–B; LC–M (facsimile)
Catalogs/Checklists: ACMW–FW 1264; Reps, Cities on Stone, p. 95; LC–M, 719.1

3273
Place: Pendleton, Oregon
Date: 1884
Title: Panoramic View of Pendleton, Or. County Seat of Umatilla County. 1884.
Size: 13 × 21¹⁵⁄₁₆ in. (33.1 × 55.9 cm.)
Artist: H. Wellge
Lithographer:
Printer: Beck & Pauli, Milwaukee, Wis.
Publisher: J. J. Stoner, Madison, Wis.
Key/Vignettes/Misc: Refs. 2–13; 2 vignettes; unnumbered business directory
Locations: ACMW–FW; LC–M; OHS–P; LC–P
Catalogs/Checklists: ACMW–FW 1928; Reps, Cities on Stone, p. 95; LC–M, 720

3274
Place: Pendleton, Oregon
Date: [1888]
Title: Bird's Eye View of Pendleton, Umatilla County, Ore.
Size: 19³⁄₁₆ × 27½ in. (48.8 × 70 cm.)
Artist:
Lithographer:
Printer: Dakin Publishing Co., S. F.
Publisher: East Oregonian Publishing Co., Pendleton Or.
Key/Vignettes/Misc: Refs. 1–33
Locations: LC–M; OHS–P
Catalogs/Checklists: LC–M, 721

3275
Place: Portland, Oregon
Date: 1855
Title: Portland, Multnomah County, Oregon. 1855.
Size: ["large"]
Artist: Kuchel & Dresel
Lithographer: Kuchel & Dresel
Printer: Britton & Rey [San Francisco]
Publisher:
Key/Vignettes/Misc: 40 vignettes
Locations: Unknown
Catalogs/Checklists: Peters, COS, p. 145

3276
Place: Portland, Oregon
Date: 1858
Title: Portland, Multnomah County, Oregon. 1858
Size: 21¼ × 34⅜ in. (54.1 × 87.5 cm.)
Artist: Kuchel & Dresel
Lithographer:
Printer: Kuchel & Dresel, Lithographers, 176 Clay St. San Francisco, Cal.
Publisher: S. J. McCormick, Franklin Book Store
Key/Vignettes/Misc: 40 vignettes
Locations: ACMW–FW; MM–NN; UCBL–B (lacks publisher's imprint);

OHS–P; LC–M (facsimile)
Catalogs/Checklists: ACMW–FW 1266; MM–NN, LP 491; LC–M, 721.1

3277
Place: Portland, Oregon
Date: Ca. 1861
Title: City of Portland, Oregon.
Size: 19¹⁄₁₆ × 29½ in. (48.4 × 74.9 cm.)
Artist: Grafton T. Brown
Lithographer: C. C. Kuchel
Printer: Britton & Co., [San Francisco]
Publisher:
Key/Vignettes/Misc: 22 vignettes
Locations: ACMW–FW
Catalogs/Checklists: Reps, Cities on Stone, p. 96

3278
Place: Portland, Oregon
Date: 1870
Title: Bird's Eye View of the City of Portland, Oregon.
Size: 27¹⁵⁄₁₆ × 37⅝ in. (71.1 × 95.7 cm.)
Artist: C. B. Talbot
Lithographer:
Printer: G. T. Brown & Co. Lith. 540 Clay St. S. F.
Publisher: P. F. Castleman
Key/Vignettes/Misc: Refs. 1–26, A–E
Locations: OHS–P
Catalogs/Checklists: Reps, Cities on Stone, p. 96

3279
Place: Portland, Oregon
Date: 1879 State I
Title: Portland, Oregon. Population 23,000. Looking East to the Cascade Mountains. Price $10.
Size: 24 × 40⅜ in. (61.1 × 102.6 cm.)
Artist: E. S. Glover
Lithographer:
Printer: A. L. Bancroft & Co., Lithographers, San Francisco, Cal.
Publisher: E. S. Glover
Key/Vignettes/Misc: Refs. 1–16, 6 unnumbered refs. below places identified; unnumbered church directory
Locations: UCBL–B; LC–M; OHS–P; LC–P
Catalogs/Checklists:

3280
Place: Portland, Oregon
Date: 1879 State II
Title: Portland, Oregon. Showing Also. East Portland and the Cascade Mountains
Size: 25 × 40½ in. (63.6 × 103 cm.)
Artist: E. S. Glover
Lithographer:
Printer: A. L. Bancroft & Co., San Francisco
Publisher: J. K. Gill & Co., Portland
Key/Vignettes/Misc: Refs. 1–27; unnumbered church directory
Locations: LC–M; UCBL–B; OHS–P
Catalogs/Checklists: LC–M, 722

3281
Place: Portland, Oregon
Date: 1881 State III
Title: Portland, Oregon. Showing Also,

East Portland and the Cascade Mountains. Price $10
Size: 25 × 40⅜ in. (63.7 × 102.6 cm.)
Artist:
Lithographer:
Printer: A. L. Bancroft & Co., San Francisco
Publisher: J. K. Gill & Co., Portland
Key/Vignettes/Misc: Refs. 1–27; unnumbered church directory
Locations: LC–M; CHS–C; OHS–P
Catalogs/Checklists: LC–M,723

3282
Place: Portland, Oregon
Date: 1888
Title: Portland, Oregon, the Metropolis of the Pacific Northwest, as Seen from the Northwestern Residence Portion.
Size: 10 × 30¼ in. (25.4 × 76.9 cm.)
Artist: C. L. Smith
Lithographer:
Printer: West Shore Litho & Eng. Co., Portland
Publisher: The West Shore, Portland, Oregon
Key/Vignettes/Misc:
Locations: OUL–E; HEHL; ACMW–FW; LC–P
Catalogs/Checklists:

3283
Place: Portland, Oregon
Date: 1889
Title: Portland, Oregon, and its Surroundings, 1889.
Size: 12⅝ × 19⅛ in. (32.2 × 48.7 cm.)
Artist:
Lithographer:
Printer: Lewis & Dryden Print Co. Lith. Portland Or.
Publisher: Oregon Immigration Board
Key/Vignettes/Misc:
Locations: OHS–P
Catalogs/Checklists:

3284
Place: Portland, Oregon
Date: 1890
Title: Portland, Oregon 1890.
Size: 30⅛ × 44⁷⁄₁₆ in. (76.7 × 113 cm.)
Artist: B. W. Pierce
Lithographer:
Printer: Elliott Publishing Co., San Francisco
Publisher: Clohessy & Strengele, Portland
Key/Vignettes/Misc: Refs. 1–130; 29 vignettes
Locations: OHS–P; LC–M; UCBL–B; WHPL–D
Catalogs/Checklists: LC–M, 724; Reps, Cities on Stone, p. 96

3285
Place: Portland, Oregon
Date: 1890
Title: Portland, Oregon; and Surroundings. 1890. Looking North
Size: 18¼ × 24⅞ in. (46.4 × 63.4 cm.)
Artist:
Lithographer:
Printer: Elliott Pub. Co. 120 Sutter St. S. F.

Publisher:
Key/Vignettes/Misc:
Locations: OHS–P
Catalogs/Checklists:

3286
Place: Portland, Oregon
Date: Ca. 1890
Title: Portland's Willamette–Columbia Peninsula, Portland, Or.
Size: 22⅛ × 34¾ in. (56.3 × 88.4 cm.)
Artist: Elliott Pub. Co.
Lithographer:
Printer: Elliott Pub Co. 120 Sutter St. S. F. Cal.
Publisher:
Key/Vignettes/Misc: Refs. 1–2; 1 vignette
Locations: OHS–P
Catalogs/Checklists:

3287
Place: Portland, Oregon
Date: 1893
Title: Portland, Or. Population 80,000
Size: 34¾ × 47¾ in. (88.3 × 121.5 cm.)
Artist:
Lithographer:
Printer: The Lewis & Dryden Lithographing Co., Portland, Oregon
Publisher: The Oregon Immigration Board
Key/Vignettes/Misc: 5 unnumbered refs. above places identified; 31 vignettes; description
Locations: OHS–P
Catalogs/Checklists:

3288
Place: Portland, Oregon
Date: 1904
Title: Bird's–Eye View Portland, Oregon, "The Rose City." Looking in North–Easterly Direction, Showing 4 1/2 Miles of Willamette River.
Size: 38¼ × 56½ in. (97.3 × 143.7 cm.)
Artist:
Lithographer:
Printer: Mutual Label & Lith Co., Portland, Or.
Publisher: Lawrence Publishing Co. (copyright)
Key/Vignettes/Misc: 27 vignettes; 2 portraits; description
Locations: OHS–P
Catalogs/Checklists:

3289
Place: Portland, Oregon
Date: 1909
Title: [Untitled View of Portland, Oregon, Vancouver, Washington, and the Willamette Valley]
Size: 17⁷⁄₁₆ × 47¹³⁄₁₆ in. (44.4 × 121.7 cm.)
Artist: Gibson Catlett
Lithographer:
Printer: The James Printing Co.
Publisher: A. E. Chisholm, 212 Henry Building, Portland, Oregon
Key/Vignettes/Misc:
Locations: OHS–P
Catalogs/Checklists:

3290
Place: Roseburg, Oregon
Date: [1888]
Title: Roseburg, Oregon
Size: 13⅞ × 19 in. (35.3 × 48.4 cm.)
Artist:
Lithographer:
Printer:
Publisher: The West Shore [Portland]
Key/Vignettes/Misc:
Locations: OHS–P
Catalogs/Checklists:

3291
Place: Roseburg, Oregon
Date: [1890–91]
Title: Birds Eye View of Roseburg, Douglas County, Oregon—Compliments of the Hendricks Review Real Estate Company, Roseburg, Oregon
Size: 14 × 18 in. (35.6 × 45.9 cm.)
Artist:
Lithographer:
Printer:
Publisher: W. W. Elliott, Pub. Co. 120 Sutter St., S. F.
Key/Vignettes/Misc: 12 vignettes
Locations: Douglas County Museum, Roseburg, Oregon
Catalogs/Checklists:

3292
Place: Salem, Oregon
Date: 1858
Title: Salem, Marion County, Oregon. 1858.
Size: 15¹³⁄₁₆ × 25⅝ in. (40.2 × 65.1 cm.)
Artist: Kuchel & Dresel
Lithographer:
Printer: Kuchel & Dresel, San Francisco
Publisher: W. C. Griswold & Co., Salem
Key/Vignettes/Misc: 26 vignettes
Locations: ACMW–FW; CHS–C; LC–M (facsimile)
Catalogs/Checklists: ACMW–FW 1268; Peters, COS, p. 145; LC–M, 724.1

3293
Place: Salem, Oregon
Date: 1876
Title: Bird's Eye View of Salem, Oregon From the West Looking East. 1876.
Size: 20¾ × 29⁹⁄₁₆ in. (52.8 × 75.2 cm.)
Artist: E. S. Glover, from photograph by F. A. Smith
Lithographer:
Printer: A. L. Bancroft & Co., Lithographers, San Francisco, California
Publisher: F. A. Smith, Salem, Oregon
Key/Vignettes/Misc: Refs. A–C, E, F, H, I; unnumbered directory
Locations: LC–M; UCBL–B
Catalogs/Checklists: LC–M, 725; Reps, Cities on Stone, p. 96

3294
Place: Salem, Oregon
Date: 1890 State I
Title: The City of Salem, Capital of Oregon
Size: 23⅞ × 32¹¹⁄₁₆ in. (60.8 × 83.2 cm.)
Artist: E. S. Moore

Lithographer:
Printer:
Publisher: [n.p.]
Key/Vignettes/Misc: Refs. 1–19; 25 vignettes
Locations: OHS–P
Catalogs/Checklists:

3295
Place: Salem, Oregon
Date: 1890 State II
Title: The City of Salem, Capital of Oregon
Size: 23⅞ × 32¹¹⁄₁₆ in. (60.8 × 83.2 cm.)
Artist: E. S. Moore
Lithographer:
Printer:
Publisher: Salem Board of Trade
Key/Vignettes/Misc: Refs. 1–19; 25 vignettes
Locations: OHS–P
Catalogs/Checklists:

3296
Place: Salem, Oregon
Date: [1905]
Title: Capital City of Oregon, Salem.
Size: 27 × 35 in. (68.6 × 89 cm.)
Artist:
Lithographer:
Printer: Mutual L. & Lith. Co., Portland
Publisher: E. Koppe & Ch. Fromm
Key/Vignettes/Misc: 2 vignettes
Locations: LC–M
Catalogs/Checklists: LC–M, 726

3297
Place: Stanley, Oregon
Date: [1890]
Title: Map and Plainly Stated Facts About Stanley.
Size: 23⅝ × 18⅛ in. (60 × 46 cm.)
Artist:
Lithographer:
Printer: Dickman–Jones, San Francisco
Publisher: Stites, Kerr & Co., Portland
Key/Vignettes/Misc:
Locations: OUL–E
Catalogs/Checklists:

3298
Place: The Dalles, Oregon
Date: 1858
Title: The Dalles, Wasco Couniy, Oricon, 1858.
Size: 13¾ × 20 in. (34.8 × 50.7 cm.)
Artist: Kuchel & Dresel
Lithographer: Kuchel & Dresel
Printer: Kuchel & Dresel, Lithographers, 176 Clay St. S. Francisco
Publisher: W. L. Demoss
Key/Vignettes/Misc: 16 vignettes
Locations: ACMW–FW; UCBL–B; CHS–C; OHS–P (title cropped)
Catalogs/Checklists: ACMW–FW 1256; Reps, Cities on Stone, p. 92

3299
Place: The Dalles, Oregon
Date: 1884
Title: Panoramic View of the City of The Dalles, Or. County Seat of Wasco County 1884.

Size: 13½ × 24⅛ in. (34.4 × 61.4 cm.)
Artist: H. Wellge
Lithographer:
Printer: Beck & Pauli, Litho. Milwaukee, Wis.
Publisher: J. J. Stoner, Madison, Wis.
Key/Vignettes/Misc: Refs. 1–17
Locations: LC–M; OHS–P
Catalogs/Checklists: LC–M, 727

3300
Place: The Dalles, Oregon
Date: N.D.
Title: Panoramic view of the Dalles, Oregon
Size: 10 × 16 in. (25.4 × 40.7 cm.)
Artist:
Lithographer:
Printer: The West Shore, Portland, Oregon
Publisher: The West Shore, Portland, Oregon
Key/Vignettes/Misc:
Locations: MM–NN
Catalogs/Checklists: MM–NN, LP 860

3301
Place: Alburtis, Pennsylvania
Date: 1893
Title: Alburtis and Lockridge, Lehigh County Pennsylvania. 1893.
Size: 9¾ × 17½ in. (24.7 × 44.5 cm.)
Artist: T. M. Fowler
Lithographer:
Printer:
Publisher: T. M. Fowler & James B. Moyer
Key/Vignettes/Misc: Refs. 1–9
Locations: LC–M; PHMC–H; PSU
Catalogs/Checklists: Stout, no. 165; LC–M, 728

Place: Allegheny, Pennsylvania
Date: 1849
See Pittsburgh, Pennsylvania, 1849.

Place: Allegheny, Pennsylvania
Date: [1871]
See Pittsburgh, Pennsylvania, [1871].

Place: Allegheny, Pennsylvania
Date: 1874
See Pittsburgh, Pennsylvania, 1874.

Place: Allegheny, Pennsylvania
Date: 1876
See Pittsburgh, Pennsylvania, 1876.

3302
Place: Allentown, Pennsylvania
Date: Ca. 1830
Title: South View of Allentown
Size: 15¼ × 20¼ in. (38.7 × 51.5 cm.)
Artist:
Lithographer: A. Grunewald
Printer: Childs & Lehman [Philadelphia]
Publisher:
Key/Vignettes/Misc:
Locations: YO
Catalogs/Checklists:

3303
Place: Allentown, Pennsylvania
Date: 1879
Title: Bird's Eye View of the City of Allentown, Pa.

Size: 19¼ × 26⅜ in. (49 × 67 cm.)
Artist: O. H. Bailey
Lithographer:
Printer:
Publisher: Fowler & Bailey, Boston
Key/Vignettes/Misc: Numbered refs.
Locations: LC–M (imperfect impression)
Catalogs/Checklists: Stout, no. 297;
LC–M, 728.1

3304
Place: Allentown, Pennsylvania
Date: 1901
Title: Allentown Penna, 1901.
Size: 49½ × 34½ in. (125.9 × 87.8 cm.)
Artist:
Lithographer:
Printer:
Publisher: Landis & Alsop, Newark, N. J.
Key/Vignettes/Misc: 34 vignettes; list of
84 professional and business people
Locations: LC–M
Catalogs/Checklists: Stout, no. 166;
LC–M, 729

3305
Place: Allentown, Pennsylvania
Date: Ca. 1922
Title: [Bird's–Eye–View of Allentown,
Pennsylvania.]
Size: 13¾ × 35⅜ in. (35 × 90 cm.)
Artist: [T. M. Fowler]
Lithographer:
Printer:
Publisher: Hughes & Fowler [Brooklyn?]
Key/Vignettes/Misc:
Locations: LC–M
Catalogs/Checklists: Stout, no. 167b;
LC–M, 731

3306
Place: Altoona, Pennsylvania
Date: 1872
Title: Bird's Eye View of Altoona, Pa.,
1872
Size: 16½ × 25½ in. (42 × 64.9 cm.)
Artist: Fowler & Bailey
Lithographer:
Printer: American Oleograph Co.
Publisher: Fowler & Bailey
Key/Vignettes/Misc: Refs. 1–6
Locations: YO; LC–M (photo)
Catalogs/Checklists: Stout, no. 48; PP;
LC–M, 731.1

3307
Place: Altoona, Pennsylvania
Date: 1881
Title: Altoona and Tyrone Pa. 1881. On
the Pennsylvania Rail Road.
Size: 19⅞ × 30⅞ in. (50.6 × 78.6 cm.)
Artist: Wils Porter from photos by R. A.
Boning
Lithographer: C. L. Fussell
Printer:
Publisher: Philadelphia Publishing House,
923 Chestnut St. [Philadelphia]
Key/Vignettes/Misc: 17 vignettes
Locations: YO
Catalogs/Checklists: Stout, no. 49; PP, no.
73

3308
Place: Ambler, Pennsylvania
Date: 1894
Title: Ambler, Montgomery County
Pennsylvania. 1894
Size: 13¾ × 24¾ in. (35 × 63 cm.)
Artist: T. M. Fowler
Lithographer:
Printer:
Publisher: T. M. Fowler & James B. Moyer
Key/Vignettes/Misc: Refs. 1–9, A–E
Locations: PHMC–H; PSU; LC–M
(facsimile)
Catalogs/Checklists: Stout, no. 197;
LC–M, 731.3

3309
Place: Annville, Pennsylvania
Date: 1888
Title: View of Annville, Pennsylvania.
1888.
Size: 21 × 24⅛ in. (53.4 × 61.4 cm.)
Artist: [T. M. Fowler]
Lithographer:
Printer:
Publisher: T. M. Fowler & James B. Moyer
Key/Vignettes/Misc: Refs. 1–17; 11
vignettes
Locations: YO
Catalogs/Checklists: Stout, no. 163;
LC–M, 817; PP

3310
Place: Apollo, Pennsylvania
Date: 1896
Title: Apollo, Armstrong County
Pennsylvania 1896
Size: 18⅝ × 23⁵⁄₁₆ in. (47.5 × 59.4 cm.)
Artist: T. M. Fowler
Lithographer:
Printer:
Publisher: T. M. Fowler & James B. Moyer
Key/Vignettes/Misc: Refs. 1–12, A–I
Locations: LC–M; PHMC–H; PSU;
UPDL–P; LC–P
Catalogs/Checklists: Stout, no. 22;
LC–M, 732

3311
Place: Archbald, Pennsylvania
Date: 1892
Title: Archbald, Lackawana County Pa.
1892.
Size: 16⅜ × 25⅝ in. (41.6 × 65.2 cm.)
Artist: T. M. Fowler
Lithographer:
Printer: A. E. Downs, Lith.
Publisher: T. M. Fowler & James B. Moyer
Key/Vignettes/Misc: Refs. 1–5, A–C; 1
vignette
Locations: LC–M; PHMC–H; PSU
Catalogs/Checklists: Stout, no. 144;
LC–M, 733

3312
Place: Athens, Pennsylvania
Date: 1881
Title: Athens, Bradford Co. Pa. 1881.
Size: 18⅝ × 22½ in. (47.5 × 57.4 cm.)
Artist: John Moray

Lithographer: Thos. Hunter Lith.
Printer:
Publisher: John Moray
Key/Vignettes/Misc: 7 vignettes
Locations: YO; LC–P
Catalogs/Checklists: Stout, no. 56; PP

3313
Place: Avoca, Pennsylvania
Date: 1892
Title: Avoca, Luzerne County
Pennsylvania. 1892.
Size: 14⅞ × 26½ in. (37.9 × 67.4 cm.)
Artist: T. M. Fowler
Lithographer:
Printer: A. E. Downs, Lith. Boston
Publisher: T. M. Fowler
Key/Vignettes/Misc: Refs. 1–16
Locations: PHMC–H; LC–M (photo)
Catalogs/Checklists: Stout, no. 173;
LC–M, 733.1

3314
Place: Bangor, Pennsylvania
Date: 1885
Title: Bangor. Pennsylvania. 1885.
Size: 14¼ × 23¼ in. (36.3 × 59.1 cm.)
Artist: [T. M. Fowler?]
Lithographer:
Printer: O. H. Bailey & Co.
Publisher: O. H. Bailey & Co.
Key/Vignettes/Misc: Refs. 1–19; 19
vignettes
Locations: BPL–R
Catalogs/Checklists: Stout, no. 208

3315
Place: Bangor, Pennsylvania
Date: 1918
Title: Aero View of Bangor Pennsylvania
1918
Size: 21 × 32 in. (53.4 × 81.4 cm.)
Artist: T. M. Fowler
Lithographer:
Printer:
Publisher: Hughes & Bailey, Boston & N.
Y.
Key/Vignettes/Misc: 22 vignettes;
unnumbered business directory
Locations: HSP–P; LC–M
Catalogs/Checklists: Stout, no. 209;
LC–M, 734

3316
Place: Bath, Pennsylvania
Date: 1885
Title: Bath, Penn. 1885.
Size: 14¼ × 20⅛ in. (36.3 × 51.2 cm.)
Artist: [T. M. Fowler?]
Lithographer:
Printer:
Publisher: O. H. Bailey & Co., Boston
Key/Vignettes/Misc: Refs. 1–39; 1
vignette
Locations: BPL–R
Catalogs/Checklists: Stout, no. 210

3317
Place: Beaver, Pennsylvania
Date: 1842
Title: Scenery on the Ohio River, viz.

Beaver, Bridgewater, Sharon, Fallston, New
Brighton, Rochester & Phillipsburgh
Size: 16⅜ × 20¾ in. (41.7 × 52.8 cm.)
Artist: [Adolph Wever]
Lithographer:
Printer:
Publisher: Adolph Wever (copyright)
Key/Vignettes/Misc:
Locations: YO
Catalogs/Checklists: PP, no. 24

3318
Place: Beaver, Pennsylvania
Date: 1886
Title: Beaver and Bridgewater, 1886
Size: 15½ × 22¼ in. (39.5 × 56.7 cm.)
(photo)
Artist: A. Ruger
Lithographer:
Printer: Beck & Pauli, Milwaukee, Wis.
Publisher: Ruger & Stoner, Madison, Wis.
Key/Vignettes/Misc: Refs. 1–10, 1–10,
A–E, X
Locations: LC–M (photo)
Catalogs/Checklists: Stout, no. 27;
LC–M, 734.1

3319
Place: Beaver, Pennsylvania
Date: 1900
Title: Beaver, Pennsylvania 1900
Size: 14 × 24 in. (35.6 × 61 cm.)
Artist: T. M. Fowler
Lithographer:
Printer:
Publisher: T. M. Fowler and James B.
Moyer
Key/Vignettes/Misc: Refs. 1–13, A–D
Locations: CLP–P; HSP–P; LC–M;
PHMC–H; PSU; UPDL–P; Beaver Area
Heritage Foundation, Beaver, Pennsylvania
Catalogs/Checklists: Stout, no. 26;
LC–M, 735

3320
Place: Beaver Falls, Pennsylvania
Date: 1882
Title: Beaver Falls, Penna. 1882
Size: 25 × 35 in. (63.6 × 89 cm.)
Artist: [C. L. Fussell]
Lithographer:
Printer: Karle & Reichenbach, Rochester,
N. Y.
Publisher: Philadelphia Publishing House
Key/Vignettes/Misc: 19 vignettes
Locations: LC–M
Catalogs/Checklists: Stout, no. 28;
LC–M, 735.2

3321
Place: Bedford County, Pennsylvania
Date: 1906
Title: Bird's–Eye View of Bedford County,
Pennsylvania 1906
Size: 13⅞ × 22⅜ in. (35.2 × 56.8 cm.)
Artist: T. M. Fowler
Lithographer:
Printer:
Publisher: Fowler & Kelly, Morrisville, Pa.
(copyright)
Key/Vignettes/Misc: 5 vignettes
Locations: YO; LC–M (photo)

Catalogs/Checklists: Stout, no. 33; PP;
LC–M, 735.3

3322
Place: Belle Vernon, Pennsylvania
Date: 1902 State I
Title: Belle Vernon, Pennsylvania. 1902
Size: 10⅝ × 23⅜ in. (27 × 59.5 cm.)
Artist: T. M. Fowler
Lithographer:
Printer:
Publisher: T. M. Fowler & James B. Moyer
Key/Vignettes/Misc: Refs. 1–15, A–E
Locations: PHMC–H
Catalogs/Checklists: Stout, no. 120b

3323
Place: Belle Vernon, Pennsylvania
Date: 1902 State II
Title: Belle Vernon, Pennsylvania. 1902.
Size: 10⅝ × 23⅜ in. (27 × 59.5 cm.)
Artist: T. M. Fowler
Lithographer:
Printer:
Publisher: T. M. Fowler & James B. Moyer
Key/Vignettes/Misc: Refs. 1–15, A–E
Locations: CLP–P; HSP–P; LC–M;
PHMC–H; PSU; UPDL–P
Catalogs/Checklists: Stout, no. 120c;
LC–M, 736

3324
Place: Bellefonte, Pennsylvania
Date: 1878
Title: Bellefonte, Pa., 1878. Viewed From
Half Moon Hill.
Size: 17½ × 21½ in. (44.5 × 54.7 cm.)
Artist: W. W. Denslow
Lithographer: Traubel
Printer: Thos. Hunter, Lith. Phila.
Publisher: C. J. Corbin & Co.
[Philadelphia]
Key/Vignettes/Misc: 9 vignettes
Locations: PSU; YO
Catalogs/Checklists: PP, no. 70; Stout, no.
75

3325
Place: Bellwood, Pennsylvania
Date: 1895
Title: Bird's Eye View of the Borough of
Bellwood, Blair County Pennsylvania
1895.
Size: 14⅝ × 26 in. (37.2 × 66.2 cm.)
Artist: T. M. Fowler
Lithographer:
Printer:
Publisher: T. M. Fowler & James B. Moyer
Key/Vignettes/Misc: Refs. 1–7, A–F; 1
vignette
Locations: PHMC–H; PSU; YO; LC–M
(photo)
Catalogs/Checklists: Stout, no. 50; PP;
LC–M, 736.1

3326
Place: Berlin, Pennsylvania
Date: 1905
Title: Berlin, Somerset County,
Pennsylvania 1905.
Size: 16 × 26 in. (40.8 × 66.1 cm.)
Artist: T. M. Fowler
Lithographer:

Printer:
Publisher: T. M. Fowler, Morrisville, Pa.
Key/Vignettes/Misc: Refs. 1–10; 21
vignettes
Locations: LC–M; PHMC–H; YO;
NYH–NY
Catalogs/Checklists: Stout, no. 250;
LC–M, 737; PP

3327
Place: Bernville, Pennsylvania
Date: 1898
Title: Bernville, Pennsylvania. 1898
Size: 9 × 22⅛ in. (22.9 × 56.3 cm.)
Artist: [T. M. Fowler?]
Lithographer:
Printer:
Publisher: Bailey & Moyer, Boston
Key/Vignettes/Misc:
Locations: LC–M; PHMC–H; PSU; YO
Catalogs/Checklists: Stout, no. 37; PP;
LC–M, 737.1

3328
Place: Berwick, Pennsylvania
Date: 1884
Title: Berwick, Pennsylvania. 1884.
Size: 17⅛ × 23⅞ in. (43.6 × 60.7 cm.)
Artist: [T. M. Fowler?]
Lithographer:
Printer:
Publisher: O. H. Bailey & Co. Pub. Boston
Key/Vignettes/Misc: Refs. 1–16; 5
vignettes
Locations: BPL–R
Catalogs/Checklists: Stout, no. 92

3329
Place: Bethlehem, Pennsylvania
Date: 1830
Title: Bethlehem.
Size: 10³⁄₁₆ × 13⁹⁄₁₆ in. (25.9 × 33.8 cm.)
Artist: Geo Lehman
Lithographer:
Printer: C. G. Childs Lithr.
Publisher: C. G. Childs & R. H. Hobson,
Philadelphia
Key/Vignettes/Misc:
Locations: NYP–S; YO
Catalogs/Checklists: Stokes P. 1829—
F–23; McClintock, no. 75; PP

3330
Place: Bethlehem, Pennsylvania
Date: [1830–33]
Title: South West View of Bethlehem
Penna
Size: 14¼ × 20¼ in. (36.3 × 56.6 cm.)
Artist: Gustavus Grunewald
Lithographer:
Printer: Childs & Inman
Publisher:
Key/Vignettes/Misc:
Locations: CHS–C
Catalogs/Checklists:

3331
Place: Bethlehem, Pennsylvania
Date: [1856?]
Title: Bethlehem, Pa. From the West.
Size: 15⅝ × 18½ in. (39.8 × 47.1 cm.)
Artist: Fr. Kilian
Lithographer: Fr. Kilian

Printer:
Publisher:
Key/Vignettes/Misc: 12 vignettes
Locations: YO; HSP–P; PHMC–H
Catalogs/Checklists: PP, no. 54; Stout, no. 211

3332
Place: Bethlehem, Pennsylvania
Date: 1877
Title: Bethlehem and South Bethlehem, Pa. 1877. Looking North East.
Size: 12¾ × 18¹⁵⁄₁₆ in. (32.4 × 48 cm.)
Artist: G. A. Rudd
Lithographer:
Printer:
Publisher: Schwartz & Weaver (copyright)
Key/Vignettes/Misc:
Locations: YO; LC–P
Catalogs/Checklists: PP; LC–M, 737.3

3333
Place: Bethlehem, Pennsylvania
Date: 1886
Title: The Boroughs of Bethlehem South and West Bethlehem, Pennsylvania, 1886
Size: 18⅜ × 31¾ in. (46.8 × 80.8 cm.)
Artist: O. H. Bailey
Lithographer:
Printer: O. H. Bailey
Publisher:
Key/Vignettes/Misc: 32 refs.
Locations: Unknown. See Old Print Shop Portfolio, XXXVIII, p. 50, No. 2
Catalogs/Checklists:

3334
Place: Birdsboro, Pennsylvania
Date: 1890
Title: Birdsboro, Berks County, Pa. 1890.
Size: 14⅞ × 23⅛ in. (37.9 × 58.8 cm.)
Artist: T. M. Fowler
Lithographer:
Printer: A. E. Downs, Boston
Publisher: T. M. Fowler & James B. Moyer
Key/Vignettes/Misc: Refs. 1–11, A–G
Locations: HSP–P; LC–M; PHMC–H; PSU; YO
Catalogs/Checklists: Stout, no. 38; LC–M, 738; PP

Place: Birmingham, Pennsylvania
Date: [1871]
See Pittsburgh, Pennsylvania, [1871].

3335
Place: Birmingham, Pennsylvania
Date: 1876
Title: Birmingham, 1876.
Size:
Artist: Bailey
Lithographer:
Printer:
Publisher:
Key/Vignettes/Misc:
Locations:
Catalogs/Checklists: Stout, no. 298

3336
Place: Blair, Pennsylvania
Date: 1904
Title: Blair, Allegheny Co. Pennsylvania 1904

Size: 13 × 15¹⁵⁄₁₆ in. (33.1 × 40.6 cm.)
Artist: T. M. Fowler
Lithographer:
Printer:
Publisher: T. M. Fowler, Box 128, Morrisville, Pa.
Key/Vignettes/Misc: 9 vignettes
Locations: NYH–NY
Catalogs/Checklists:

3337
Place: Bloomsburg, Pennsylvania
Date: 1873
Title: Bloomsburg, 1873
Size:
Artist: H. H. Bailey
Lithographer:
Printer:
Publisher:
Key/Vignettes/Misc:
Locations:
Catalogs/Checklists: Stout, no. 299

3338
Place: Boiling Spring, Pennsylvania
Date: 1876
Title: View of Boiling Spring Cumberland Penn 1876
Size: 12 × 19¼ in. (30.6 × 49 cm.)
Artist:
Lithographer:
Printer:
Publisher:
Key/Vignettes/Misc: 6 vignettes
Locations: YO
Catalogs/Checklists: Stout, no. 97; PP

3339
Place: Boswell, Pennsylvania
Date: 1905
Title: Boswell, Somerset County, Pennsylvania. 1905.
Size: 12⅞ × 19⅞ in. (32.7 × 50.6 cm.)
Artist: T. M. Fowler
Lithographer:
Printer:
Publisher: T. M. Fowler, Morrisville, Pa.
Key/Vignettes/Misc: 15 vignettes
Locations: PHMC–H; LC–M (photo); NYH–NY
Catalogs/Checklists: Stout, no. 251b; LC–M, 738.1

3340
Place: Boyertown, Pennsylvania
Date: 1893
Title: Boyertown, Berks County Pennsylvania 1893.
Size: 13⅜ × 19¾ in. (34.1 × 50.2 cm.)
Artist: T. M. Fowler
Lithographer:
Printer:
Publisher: James B. Moyer, Myerstown, Pa.
Key/Vignettes/Misc: Refs. 1–11, A–E
Locations: YO
Catalogs/Checklists: Stout, no. 39; PP

3341
Place: Bradford, Pennsylvania
Date: 1895
Title: Bradford, McKean County Pennsylvania. 1895.

Size: 18⅛ × 32⅞ in. (46.2 × 83.6 cm.)
Artist: T. M. Fowler
Lithographer:
Printer:
Publisher: T. M. Fowler & James B. Moyer
Key/Vignettes/Misc: Refs. 1–23, A–N
Locations: CLP–P; HSP–P; LC–M; PHMC–H; PSU; UPDL–P; FL–P; YO
Catalogs/Checklists: Stout, no. 187; LC–M, 739; PP

3342
Place: Brandonville, Pennsylvania
Date: N.D.
Title: Brandonville East Union Township Penna. Nelson Brandon Proprietor
Size:
Artist: H. S. P.
Lithographer:
Printer: Chas. Hart, N. Y.
Publisher:
Key/Vignettes/Misc: 2 vignettes
Locations: YO
Catalogs/Checklists: Stout, no. 242; PP

Place: Bridgeport, Pennsylvania
Date: 1883
See Brownsville, Pennsylvania, 1883.

Place: Bridgewater, Pennsylvania
Date: 1842
See Beaver, Pennsylvania, 1842.

Place: Bridgewater, Pennsylvania
Date: 1886
See Beaver, Pennsylvania, 1886.

3343
Place: Brookville, Pennsylvania
Date: 1895
Title: Brookville, Jefferson County, Penn. 1895.
Size: 18⅝ × 26⅜ in. (47.4 × 67.1 cm.)
Artist: T. M. Fowler
Lithographer:
Printer:
Publisher: T. M. Fowler & James B. Moyer
Key/Vignettes/Misc: Refs. 1–21, A–H
Locations: LC–M; LC–P
Catalogs/Checklists: Stout, no. 139; LC–M, 740

3344
Place: Brownsville, Pennsylvania
Date: 1883
Title: Birds Eye View of Brownsville, Bridgeport, W. Brownsville, Pa. 1883.
Size: 13½ × 25⅜ in. (34.4 × 64.6 cm.)
Artist: [Henry Wellge?]
Lithographer:
Printer: Beck & Pauli, Lithographers, Milwaukee, Wis.
Publisher: J. J. Stoner, Madison, Wis.
Key/Vignettes/Misc: Refs. 1–32, A–H, J–L; 1 vignette; unnumbered business directory
Locations: LC–M
Catalogs/Checklists: PP, no. 74; Stout, no. 121; LC–M, 740.1

3345
Place: Brownsville, Pennsylvania
Date: 1902
Title: Brownsville, Pennsylvania. 1902.

Size: 11⅞ × 26¾ in. (30.2 × 68 cm.)
Artist: T. M. Fowler
Lithographer:
Printer:
Publisher: T. M. Fowler & James B. Moyer
Key/Vignettes/Misc: Refs. 1–16, A–H
Locations: CLP–P; HSP–P; LC–M;
PHMC–H; PSU; UPDL–P; YO
Catalogs/Checklists: Stout, no. 122;
LC–M, 741; PP

3346
Place: Burnham, Pennsylvania
Date: 1906
Title: Birds Eye View of Burnham and
Yeagertown Mifflin Co., Pa. 1906.
Size: 15 × 20 in. (38.2 × 50.9 cm.)
Artist: T. M. Fowler
Lithographer:
Printer:
Publisher: Fowler & Kelly, Morrisville, Pa.
Key/Vignettes/Misc: 6 vignettes
Locations: LC–M
Catalogs/Checklists: Stout, no. 192;
LC–M, 742

3347
Place: Burnside, Pennsylvania
Date: N.D.
Title: Burnside. Clearfield Co, Pa.
Size: 16 × 10⅝ in. (41.3 × 27.1 cm.)
Artist:
Lithographer:
Printer:
Publisher:
Key/Vignettes/Misc: 3 vignettes
Locations: YO
Catalogs/Checklists: Stout, no. 85; PP

3348
Place: Butler, Pennsylvania
Date: 1896
Title: Butler, Butler County, Penn. 1896.
Size: 19½ × 29½ in. (49.6 × 75.1 cm.)
Artist: T. M. Fowler
Lithographer:
Printer:
Publisher: T. M. Fowler & James B. Moyer
Key/Vignettes/Misc: Refs. 1–30, A–N
Locations: CLP–P; HSP–P; LC–M;
PHMC–H; PSU; UPDL–P; LC–P
Catalogs/Checklists: Stout, no. 65;
LC–M, 743

3349
Place: California, Pennsylvania
Date: 1902
Title: California, Washington County
Pennsylvania 1902
Size: 12⅜ × 19⅛ in. (31.4 × 48.7 cm.)
Artist: T. M. Fowler
Lithographer:
Printer:
Publisher: T. M. Fowler & James B. Moyer
Key/Vignettes/Misc: Refs. 1–10, 12–13,
A–E
Locations: CLP–P; HSP–P; LC–M;
PHMC–H; PSU; UPDL–P; YO
Catalogs/Checklists: PP, no. 79; Stout, no.
269; LC–M, 744

3350
Place: Cambridgeboro, Pennsylvania
Date: 1895
Title: Cambridgeboro, Crawford County
Pennsylvania. 1895.
Size: 15 × 27½ in. (38.2 × 70 cm.)
Artist: T. M. Fowler
Lithographer:
Printer:
Publisher: T. M. Fowler & James B. Moyer
Key/Vignettes/Misc: Refs. 1–24
Locations: LC–M; PHMC–H; PSU; YO
Catalogs/Checklists: Stout, no. 94;
LC–M, 745; PP

3351
Place: Canonsburg, Pennsylvania
Date: 1897
Title: Canonsburg, Washington County
Pennsylvania. 1897.
Size: 15 × 24½ in. (38.1 × 62.3 cm.)
Artist: T. M. Fowler
Lithographer:
Printer:
Publisher: T. M. Fowler & James B. Moyer
Key/Vignettes/Misc: Refs. 1–14, A–F
Locations: LC–M; PHMC–H; PSU; YO
Catalogs/Checklists: Stout, no. 270;
LC–M, 746; PP

3352
Place: Carbondale, Pennsylvania
Date: [187–?]
Title: Bird's Eye View of Carbondale Pa.
Size: 15¼ × 19¾ in. (38.8 × 50.2 cm.)
Artist: Fowler & Bailey
Lithographer: C. H. Vogt
Printer: American Oleograph Co.
Publisher: Fowler & Bailey
Key/Vignettes/Misc: Refs. 1–9, A–H
Locations: BPL–R
Catalogs/Checklists: Stout, no. 145

3353
Place: Carbondale, Pennsylvania
Date: 1890
Title: Carbondale, Pennsylvania, 1890.
Size: 19⅛ × 35¾ in. (48.1 × 90.8 cm.)
Artist: T. M. Fowler
Lithographer:
Printer: A. E. Downs, Lith., Boston
Publisher: T. M. Fowler & James B. Moyer
Key/Vignettes/Misc: Refs. 1–13, A–J
Locations: LC–M; PHMC–H; PSU
Catalogs/Checklists: Stout, no. 146;
LC–M, 747

3354
Place: Carlisle, Pennsylvania
Date: 1877
Title: Carlisle, Pa. 1877
Size: 17¾ × 24 in. (45.2 x 61 cm.)
Artist: W. W. Denslow
Lithographer:
Printer: Thos. Hunter, Lith. Phila.
Publisher: C. J. Corbin & Co.
[Philadelphia]
Key/Vignettes/Misc: 10 vignettes
Locations: YO
Catalogs/Checklists: Stout, no. 98; PP

3355
Place: Carnegie, Pennsylvania
Date: 1897
Title: Carnegie, Allegheny County,
Pennsylvania. 1897.
Size: 16⅞ × 28¾ in. (43 × 73.1 cm.)
Artist: T. M. Fowler
Lithographer:
Printer:
Publisher: T. M. Fowler & James B. Moyer
(copyright)
Key/Vignettes/Misc: Refs. 1–15, A–K
Locations: LC–M; PHMC–H; PSU;
UPDL–P; YO; LC–P
Catalogs/Checklists: Stout, no. 2; LC–M,
748; PP

3356
Place: Catasauqua, Pennsylvania
Date: 1873
Title: Catasauqua, Pa. 1873
Size: 12 × 18⅛ in. (30 × 46.2 cm.)
Artist: Fowler & Bailey
Lithographer: C. H. Vogt
Printer: American Oleograph Co.
Publisher: Fowler & Bailey
Key/Vignettes/Misc: Refs. 1–27
Locations: HSP–P; YO
Catalogs/Checklists: Stout, no. 168; PP

3357
Place: Central Park, Pennsylvania
Date: [1890?]
Title: Central Park, Located 20 Miles from
Pittsburg, Pa. up the Monongahela Vlley
Size: 12⅝ × 18⅞ in. (32 × 48 cm.)
(photo)
Artist: T. M. Fowler
Lithographer:
Printer:
Publisher: T. M. Fowler & J. B. Moyer,
Morrisville, Pa.
Key/Vignettes/Misc:
Locations: LC–M (photo)
Catalogs/Checklists: Stout, no. 300;
LC–M, 748.1

3358
Place: Chambersburg, Pennsylvania
Date: 1877
Title: Chambersburg, Pa.
Size: 16½ × 22¾in. (41.9 × 58 cm.)
Artist: W. W. Denslow
Lithographer:
Printer: Thos. Hunter Lith. Phila.
Publisher: D. F. Pursel, Chambersburg
(copyright)
Key/Vignettes/Misc: 6 vignettes
Locations: PHMC–H; YO; LC–P
Catalogs/Checklists: Stout, no. 131; PP

3359
Place: Chambersburg, Pennsylvania
Date: 1894
Title: Chambersburg, Pennsylvania,
Burned by Rebel Cavalry July 30th 1864.
Size: 17¼ × 29⅛ in. (44 × 74 cm.)
Artist: T. M. Fowler
Lithographer:
Printer:
Publisher: T. M. Fowler & James B. Moyer

Key/Vignettes/Misc: Refs. 1–21, A–R
Locations: CLP–P; PHMC–H; PSU; LC–M
Catalogs/Checklists: Stout, no. 132; LC–M, 749

3360
Place: Chapmans Quarries, Pennsylvania
Date: 1885
Title: Chapmans' Quarries. Pennsylvania. 1885.
Size: 13 × 21⅝ in. (33.1 × 55 cm.)
Artist: [T. M. Fowler?]
Lithographer:
Printer: O. H. Bailey & Co., Boston
Publisher: O. H. Bailey & Co., Boston
Key/Vignettes/Misc: Refs. 1–8; 1 vignette
Locations: BPL–R
Catalogs/Checklists: Stout, no. 212

3361
Place: Charleroi, Pennsylvania
Date: 1897
Title: Charleroi, Washington County Pennsylvania. 1897.
Size: 14⅛ × 23⅝ in. (36 × 60.1 cm.)
Artist: T. M. Fowler
Lithographer:
Printer:
Publisher: T. M. Fowler & James B. Moyer
Key/Vignettes/Misc: Refs. 1–20, A–F
Locations: LC–M; PHMC–H; UPDL–P; LC–P
Catalogs/Checklists: Stout, no. 271; LC–M, 750

3362
Place: Chester, Pennsylvania
Date: 1885
Title: The City of Chester, Pennsylvania, 1885.
Size: 22¾ × 29¾ in. (57.8 × 75.7 cm.)
Artist:
Lithographer:
Printer: O. H. Bailey & Co., Boston
Publisher: O. H. Bailey & Co., Boston
Key/Vignettes/Misc: Refs. 1–36, A–M; 11 vignettes
Locations: LC–M; PHMC–H
Catalogs/Checklists: Stout, no. 108; LC–M, 751

3363
Place: Clairton, Pennsylvania
Date: 1904
Title: Bird's Eye View of Clairton, Pennsylvania. 1904.
Size: 11 × 18¹⁄₁₆ in. (28 × 46 cm.) (photo)
Artist: T. M. Fowler
Lithographer:
Printer:
Publisher: T. M. Fowler, Morrisville, Pa.
Key/Vignettes/Misc: 7 vignettes
Locations: LC–M (photo); NYH–NY
Catalogs/Checklists: LC–M, 751.1

3364
Place: Clarion, Pennsylvania
Date: 1896
Title: Clarion, Clarion County Pennsylvania. 1896.
Size: 13⅞ × 23 in. (35.4 × 58.5 cm.)
Artist: T. M. Fowler

Lithographer:
Printer:
Publisher: T. M. Fowler & James B. Moyer
Key/Vignettes/Misc: Refs. 1–18, A–E
Locations: CLP–P; HSP–P; LC–M; PHMC–H; PSU; UPDL–P; YO
Catalogs/Checklists: Stout, no. 82; LC–M, 752; PP

3365
Place: Clearfield, Pennsylvania
Date: 1895
Title: Clearfield, Clearfield County Penn.
Size: 16¼ × 26½ in. (41.5 × 67.4 cm.)
Artist: T. M. Fowler
Lithographer:
Printer:
Publisher: T. M. Fowler & James B. Moyer
Key/Vignettes/Misc: Refs. 1–17, A–H
Locations: LC–M; PHMC–H; YO; LC–P
Catalogs/Checklists: Stout, no. 86; LC–M, 753; PP

3366
Place: Collegeville, Pennsylvania
Date: 1894
Title: Collegeville, Montgomery County Pennsylvania. 1894.
Size: 16 × 26⅛ in. (40.8 × 66.5 cm.)
Artist: T. M. Fowler
Lithographer:
Printer:
Publisher: T. M. Fowler & James B. Moyer
Key/Vignettes/Misc: Refs. 1–12, A–D; 2 vignettes
Locations: LC–M; PHMC–H; PSU
Catalogs/Checklists: Stout, no. 198; LC–M, 754

3367
Place: Columbia, Pennsylvania
Date: Ca. 1850
Title: Columbia, Lancaster Co. Pa.
Size: 18⅝ × 23½ in. (47.4 × 59.9 cm.)
Artist: W.[illiam] Sanford Mason
Lithographer: Js. Queen
Printer: P. S. Duval & Co. Steam Lith. Press, Phila.
Publisher:
Key/Vignettes/Misc:
Locations: YO; NYH–NY
Catalogs/Checklists: PP, no. 38

3368
Place: Columbia, Pennsylvania
Date: 1894 State I
Title: Columbia, Pennsylvania 1894.
Size: 17⅜ × 25¾ in. (44.3 × 68 cm.)
Artist: T. M. Fowler
Lithographer:
Printer:
Publisher: T. M. Fowler & James B. Moyer
Key/Vignettes/Misc: Refs. 1–18, A–P; 1 vignette
Locations: YO
Catalogs/Checklists: Stout, no. 153a; PP

3369
Place: Columbia, Pennsylvania
Date: 1894 State II
Title: Columbia, Pennsylvania 1894.
Size: 17⅜ × 26¾ in. (44.3 × 68 cm.)

Artist: T. M. Fowler
Lithographer:
Printer:
Publisher: T. M. Fowler & James B. Moyer
Key/Vignettes/Misc: Refs. 1–18, A–P; 1 vignette
Locations: HSP–P; LC–M; PSU
Catalogs/Checklists: Stout, no. 153b; LC–M, 755

3370
Place: Confluence, Pennsylvania
Date: 1905
Title: Confluence, Pennsylvania. 1905.
Size: 11⅜ × 20¹⁄₁₆ in. (39 × 51 cm.)
Artist: T. M. Fowler
Lithographer:
Printer:
Publisher: T. M. Fowler, Morrisville, Pa.
Key/Vignettes/Misc: 10 vignettes
Locations: LC–M; PHMC–H; YO; NYH–NY
Catalogs/Checklists: Stout, no. 252; LC–M, 756; PP

3371
Place: Connellsville, Pennsylvania
Date: 1897
Title: Connellsville, Fayette County Pennsylvania. 1897.
Size: 17⅛ × 30⅜ in. (43.5 × 77.2 cm.)
Artist: T. M. Fowler
Lithographer:
Printer:
Publisher: T. M. Fowler & James B. Moyer
Key/Vignettes/Misc: Refs. 1–23, A–M
Locations: CLP–P; LC–M; PHMC–H; PSU; UPDL–P; YO
Catalogs/Checklists: Stout, no. 123; LC–M, 757; PP

3372
Place: Corry, Pennsylvania
Date: 1870
Title: Bird's Eye View of the City of Corry Erie County Pennsylvania. Looking South West 1870
Size: 22 × 25¾ in. (56 × 65.5 cm.)
Artist: [Albert Ruger]
Lithographer:
Printer: Chicago Lithographing Co. No. 150, 152 & 154. . .Chicago
Publisher: Ruger & Stoner, Madison, Wis.
Key/Vignettes/Misc: Refs. 1–17, A–I, K–N; 4 vignettes
Locations: LC–M; YO
Catalogs/Checklists: LC–M, 758; Stout, no. 112; PP, no. 65

3373
Place: Corry, Pennsylvania
Date: 1895
Title: Corry, Pennsylvania 1895.
Size: 16⅝ × 29⅞ in. (42.3 × 76 cm.)
Artist: T. M. Fowler
Lithographer:
Printer:
Publisher: T. M. Fowler & James B. Moyer
Key/Vignettes/Misc: Refs. 1–27, A–K
Locations: LC–M; PHMC–H; PSU; UPDL–P; YO
Catalogs/Checklists: Stout, no. 113; LC–M, 759; PP

3374
Place: Curwensville, Pennsylvania
Date: 1895
Title: Curwensville, Clearfield County Pennsylvania. 1895.
Size: 13½ × 25½ in. (34.3 × 64.9 cm.)
Artist: T. M. Fowler
Lithographer:
Printer:
Publisher: T. M. Fowler & James B. Moyer
Key/Vignettes/Misc: Refs. 1–18, A–F
Locations: LC–M; PHMC–H; YO
Catalogs/Checklists: Stout, no. 87; LC–M, 760; PP

3375
Place: Danville, Pennsylvania
Date: Ca. 1855
Title: Danville, Pa., as Seen From the Blue Hill.
Size: 19 × 25½ in. (48.3 × 64.8 cm.)
Artist: A. Yeomans
Lithographer:
Printer: P. S. Duval's Steam Lithography Press, Philadelphia
Publisher: E. W. Conklin, Danville
Key/Vignettes/Misc:
Locations: YO
Catalogs/Checklists: PP

3376
Place: Dauphin County, Pennsylvania
Date: 1878
Title: Bird's Eye View of Steel Works and Vicinity Dauphin Co. Pennsylvania. 1878
Size: 13½ × 21⅞ in. (34.4 × 55.6 cm.)
Artist: A. Ruger
Lithographer:
Printer: Beck & Pauli Lith. Milwaukee, Wisc.
Publisher: J. J. Stoner, Madison, Wisc.
Key/Vignettes/Misc:
Locations: PHMC–H
Catalogs/Checklists: Stout, no. 107

3377
Place: Dawson, Pennsylvania
Date: 1902
Title: Dawson, Pennsylvania. 1902.
Size: 15½ × 19¼ in. (39.4 × 49.1 cm.)
Artist: T. M. Fowler
Lithographer:
Printer:
Publisher: T. M. Fowler, Morrisville, Pa.
Key/Vignettes/Misc: Refs. 1–35; 9 vignettes
Locations: LC–M; PHMC–H; NYH–NY
Catalogs/Checklists: Stout, no. 124; LC–M, 761

3378
Place: Derry, Pennsylvania
Date: 1900
Title: Derry Station, Pennsylvania 1900
Size: 12½ × 22½ in. (31.8 × 57.3 cm.)
Artist: T. M. Fowler
Lithographer:
Printer:
Publisher: T. M. Fowler & James B. Moyer
Key/Vignettes/Misc: Refs. 1–7, A–F
Locations: LC–M; PHMC–H; PSU; UPDL–P

3379
Place: Dillsburg, Pennsylvania
Date: 1903
Title: View of Dillsburg, York Co., Pennsylvania. 1903.
Size: 14⅛ × 17³⁄₁₆ in. (35.9 × 43.7 cm.)
Artist: T. M. Fowler
Lithographer:
Printer:
Publisher: T. M. Fowler, Morrisville, Pa.
Key/Vignettes/Misc: Refs. 1–12; 15 vignettes
Locations: YO; NYH–NY
Catalogs/Checklists: PP

3380
Place: Donora, Pennsylvania
Date: 1901 State I
Title: Donora, Washington County Pennsylvania. 1901.
Size: 10¼ × 18⅝ in. (26 × 47.5 cm.)
Artist: T. M. Fowler
Lithographer:
Printer:
Publisher: T. M. Fowler & James B. Moyer
Key/Vignettes/Misc: Refs. 1–10; description
Locations: PHMC–H
Catalogs/Checklists: Stout, no. 272a

3381
Place: Donora, Pennsylvania
Date: 1901 State II
Title: Donora, Washington County Pennsylvania. 1901.
Size: 10¼ × 18⅝ in. (26 × 47.5 cm.)
Artist: T. M. Fowler
Lithographer:
Printer:
Publisher: T. M. Fowler & James B. Moyer
Key/Vignettes/Misc: Refs. 1–10; description
Locations: PHMC–H; UPDL–P; LC–M (photo)
Catalogs/Checklists: Stout, no. 272b; LC–M, 761.2

3382
Place: Downingtown, Pennsylvania
Date: 1893
Title: Downington, Chester County Pennsylvania 1893.
Size: 15⅞ × 26⅛ in. (41 × 71 cm.)
Artist: T. M. Fowler
Lithographer:
Printer:
Publisher: James B. Moyer, Myerstown, Pa.
Key/Vignettes/Misc: Refs. 1–15, A–F
Locations: HSP–P; LC–M; PHMC–H; PSU
Catalogs/Checklists: Stout, no. 78; LC–M, 762

3383
Place: Doylestown, Pennsylvania
Date: 1886
Title: Doylestown, 1886.
Size:
Artist:
Lithographer:
Catalogs/Checklists: Stout, no. 279; LC–M, 761.1

3383 (cont.)
Printer: O. H. Bailey & Co., Boston
Publisher:
Key/Vignettes/Misc:
Locations:
Catalogs/Checklists: Stout, no. 301

3384
Place: Du Bois, Pennsylvania
Date: 1895
Title: Du Bois, Clearfield County Pennsylvania 1895
Size: 17⅞ × 33¾ in. (45.6 × 86 cm.)
Artist: T. M. Fowler
Lithographer:
Printer:
Publisher: T. M. Fowler & James B. Moyer
Key/Vignettes/Misc: Refs. 1–17, A–L
Locations: LC–M; PHMC–H; PSU; UPDL–P; LC–P
Catalogs/Checklists: Stout, no. 88; LC–M, 763

3385
Place: Dunbar, Pennsylvania
Date: 1900
Title: Dunbar, Fayette County Pennsylvania 1900
Size: 11¼ × 22⁷⁄₁₆ in. (28.7 × 57 cm.)
Artist: T. M. Fowler
Lithographer:
Printer:
Publisher: T. M. Fowler & James B. Moyer
Key/Vignettes/Misc: Refs. 1–12, A–E
Locations: CLP–P; HSP–P; LC–M; PHMC–H; PSU; UPDL–P
Catalogs/Checklists: Stout, no. 125; LC–M, 764

3386
Place: Duncannon, Pennsylvania
Date: 1903
Title: View of Duncannon, Pennsylvania. 1903.
Size: 14⅝ × 20 in. (37.2 × 50.9 cm.)
Artist: T. M. Fowler
Lithographer:
Printer:
Publisher: T. M. Fowler, Morrisville, Pa.
Key/Vignettes/Misc: Refs. 1–10; 11 vignettes
Locations: LC–M; YO; NYH–NY
Catalogs/Checklists: Stout, no. 225; LC–M, 765; PP

3387
Place: Duquesne, Pennsylvania
Date: 1897
Title: Duquesne, Allegheny County Pennsylvania 1897.
Size: 18¼ × 26¾ in. (46.6 × 68.1 cm.)
Artist: T. M. Fowler
Lithographer:
Printer:
Publisher: T. M. Fowler & James B. Moyer
Key/Vignettes/Misc: Refs. 1–12, A–I
Locations: CLP–P; HSP–P; LC–M; PHMC–H; PSU; UPDL–P; LC–P
Catalogs/Checklists: Stout, no. 4; LC–M, 766

3388
Place: East Stroudsburg, Pennsylvania
Date: 1885
Title: East Stroudsburg. Pennsylvania. 1885.

Size: 12¼ × 21½ in. (31.2 × 54.7 cm.)
Artist: [T. M. Fowler?]
Lithographer:
Printer:
Publisher: [O. H. Bailey & Co.]
Key/Vignettes/Misc: Refs. 1–11; 5 vignettes
Locations: BPL–R
Catalogs/Checklists: Stout, no. 195

3389

Place: Easton, Pennsylvania
Date: Ca. 1832
Title: Easton
Size: 8½ × 13 in. (21.6 × 33.1 cm.)
Artist: George Lehman
Lithographer: George Lehman
Printer:
Publisher: Childs & Inman, Lithrs. [Philadelphia]
Key/Vignettes/Misc:
Locations: YUAG–NH; OHA–S
Catalogs/Checklists: McClintock, no. 102

3390

Place: Easton, Pennsylvania
Date: [1856?]
Title: View of Easton Pa.
Size: 12⅜ × 17⅜ in. (31.5 × 44.3 cm.)
Artist: Fr. Kilian
Lithographer: Fr. Kilian
Printer: E. Valois, N. Y.
Publisher:
Key/Vignettes/Misc: 10 vignettes
Locations: YO
Catalogs/Checklists: Stout, no. 213; PP

3391

Place: Easton, Pennsylvania
Date: [1861]
Title: Explosion of the Alfred Thomas at Easton Pa. March 6th. 1860.
Size: 14½ × 21¼ in. (36.9 × 54.1 cm.)
Artist: J. Queen
Lithographer:
Printer: P. S. Duval & Son Phila.
Publisher: Bixler & Corwin, Easton, Pa.
Key/Vignettes/Misc:
Locations: YO
Catalogs/Checklists: PP, no. 58; McClintock, no. 104

3392

Place: Easton, Pennsylvania
Date: 1873
Title: Easton, 1873.
Size:
Artist:
Lithographer:
Printer:
Publisher: Fowler & Bailey
Key/Vignettes/Misc:
Locations:
Catalogs/Checklists: Stout, no. 302

3393

Place: Easton, Pennsylvania
Date: 1876
Title: Easton Pa. in 1876. Viewed from Mt. Parnassus. Phillipsburg, N. J.
Size: 12⅜ × 21⅞ in. (31.5 × 55.7 cm.)
Artist: W. W. Denslow
Lithographer:

Printer:
Publisher: Peter Fritts
Key/Vignettes/Misc: 2 vignettes
Locations: YO
Catalogs/Checklists: PP, no. 68

3394

Place: Easton, Pennsylvania
Date: 1900
Title: Easton Pa. and Phillipsurg N. J.
Size: 31¼ × 39½ in. (79.5 × 100.5 cm.)
Artist:
Lithographer:
Printer:
Publisher: Landis & Alsop, Newark, N. J.
Key/Vignettes/Misc: 158 refs. of professionals and business people; 51 vignettes
Locations: LC–M
Catalogs/Checklists: Stout, no. 214; LC–M, 767

3395

Place: Easton, Pennsylvania
Date: N.D.
Title: View of Easton. (From Phillipsburg Rock) Showing Part of Phillipsburg, the Lehigh and the Delaware Rivers, Morris & Delaware Canals. . . .
Size: 10 × 17¾ in. (25.4 × 45.2 cm.)
Artist: Js. Queen, from ambrotype by H. P. Osborn, Bethlehem
Lithographer:
Printer: P. S. Duval & Son's Lith, Phila.
Publisher:
Key/Vignettes/Misc:
Locations: FL–P; YO
Catalogs/Checklists: PP

3396

Place: Easton, Pennsylvania
Date: ?
Title: View on the Delaware Near Easton, Pa.
Size: 8½ × 12⅜ in. (21.6 × 37.4 cm.)
Artist:
Lithographer:
Printer:
Publisher: Currier & Ives, 125 Nassau St., N. Y.
Key/Vignettes/Misc:
Locations: YO
Catalogs/Checklists: McClintock, no. 92; PP

3397

Place: Edinboro, Pennsylvania
Date: 1898
Title: Edinboro, Pa. 1898.
Size: 8⅞ × 21⅝ in. (22.6 × 55 cm.)
Artist:
Lithographer:
Printer: John J. O'Brien, Erie, Pa.
Publisher: H. H. Rowley, Erie, Pa. (copyright)
Key/Vignettes/Misc: Refs. 1–10
Locations: LC–M
Catalogs/Checklists: Stout, no. 114; LC–M, 768

3398

Place: Edwardsville, Pennsylvania
Date: 1892

Title: Edwardsville, Pa. 1892.
Size: 13½ × 24 in. (34.4 × 61 cm.)
Artist: T. M. Fowler
Lithographer:
Printer:
Publisher: T. M. Fowler & James B. Moyer
Key/Vignettes/Misc: Refs. 1–8, A–G; 1 vignette
Locations: LC–M; PHMC–H; PSU
Catalogs/Checklists: Stout, no. 174; LC–M, 769

3399

Place: Elizabeth, Pennsylvania
Date: 1897
Title: Elizabeth and West Elizabeth, Allegheny County Pennsylvania, 1897
Size: 16¼ × 26¼ in. (41.4 × 66.8 cm.)
Artist: T. M. Fowler
Lithographer:
Printer:
Publisher: T. M. Fowler & James B. Moyer
Key/Vignettes/Misc: Refs. 1–14, A–F
Locations: LC–M; PHMC–H; PSU; LC–P
Catalogs/Checklists: Stout, no. 5; LC–M, 770

3400

Place: Elizabethtown, Pennsylvania
Date: 1894
Title: Elizabethtown, Lancaster County Pennsylvania. 1894.
Size: 12¼ × 21⅛ in. (31.2 × 53.2 cm.)
Artist: T. M. Fowler
Lithographer:
Printer:
Publisher: T. M. Fowler & James B. Moyer
Key/Vignettes/Misc: Refs. 1–13, A–G
Locations: PHMC–H; LC–M (facsimile)
Catalogs/Checklists: Stout, no. 154; LC–M, 770.1

3401

Place: Ellwood City, Pennsylvania
Date: 1896
Title: Ellwood City, Lawrence County Pennsylvania. 1896.
Size: 14 × 26⅛ in. (35.6 × 66.4 cm.)
Artist: T. M. Fowler
Lithographer:
Printer:
Publisher: T. M. Fowler & James B. Moyer
Key/Vignettes/Misc: Refs. 1–18, A–F
Locations: PHMC–H; LC–M (photo)
Catalogs/Checklists: Stout, no 161; LC–M, 770.2

3402

Place: Ellwood City, Pennsylvania
Date: 1901
Title:
Size:
Artist: T. M. Fowler
Lithographer:
Printer:
Publisher:
Key/Vignettes/Misc:
Locations:
Catalogs/Checklists: Stout, no. 303

3403
Place: Elmhurst, Pennsylvania
Date: N.D.
Title:
Size:
Artist: T. M. Fowler ?
Lithographer:
Printer:
Publisher:
Key/Vignettes/Misc:
Locations:
Catalogs/Checklists: Stout, no. 304

3404
Place: Emaus, Pennsylvania
Date: 1893
Title: Emaus, Pennsylvania, Lehigh County. 1893.
Size: 14½ × 25⅛ in. (36.9 × 63.9 cm.)
Artist: T. M. Fowler
Lithographer:
Printer:
Publisher: T. M. Fowler & James B. Moyer
Key/Vignettes/Misc: Refs. 1–12, A–E; 2 vignettes
Locations: PHMC–H; HSP–P; LC–M (photo)
Catalogs/Checklists: Stout, no. 169; LC–M, 770.3

3405
Place: Emlenton, Pennsylvania
Date: 1897
Title: Emlenton, Venango County Pennsylvania. 1897.
Size: 14¾ × 19¼ in. (37.7 × 49 cm.)
Artist: T. M. Fowler
Lithographer:
Printer:
Publisher: T. M. Fowler & James B. Moyer
Key/Vignettes/Misc: Refs. 1–11, A–E
Locations: CLP–P; LC–M; PHMC–H; PSU; UPDL–P; LC–P
Catalogs/Checklists: Stout, no. 263; LC–M, 771

3406
Place: Ephrata, Pennsylvania
Date: 1887
Title: View of Ephrata, Pennsylvania
Size: 23½ × 34 in. (59.8 × 86.5 cm.)
Artist: T. M. Fowler
Lithographer:
Printer:
Publisher: T. M. Fowler, Morrisville, Pa.
Key/Vignettes/Misc: Refs. 1–20, A–H, J–O; 22 vignettes
Locations: YO; LC–M
Catalogs/Checklists: PP, no. 78; LC–M, 771.1

3407
Place: Erie, Pennsylvania
Date: 1855
Title: Erie City & Harbour, Penna. 1855
Size: 14¼ × 25⅜ in. (36.3 × 64.6 cm.)
Artist: W. Bourne
Lithographer:
Printer: P. S. Duval & Co's Steam Lith Press, Philada.
Publisher:
Key/Vignettes/Misc:

Locations: Unknown. See Old Print Shop, 9/21/79
Catalogs/Checklists:

3408
Place: Erie, Pennsylvania
Date: [1855]
Title: View of Presque Isle Bay, Erie City & Harbor, Erie City, Penna.
Size: 14⅞ × 25⅜ in. (37.6 × 64.6 cm.)
Artist: P. F. Goist
Lithographer:
Printer:
Publisher: Everts, Ensign & Everts, Philadelphia
Key/Vignettes/Misc:
Locations: MM–NN; YO
Catalogs/Checklists: MM–NN, LP 40; Stout, no. 115; PP

3409
Place: Erie, Pennsylvania
Date: 1870
Title: Bird's Eye View of the City of Erie Erie County, Pennsylvania 1870
Size: 22 × 33¾ in. (56 × 85.8 cm.)
Artist: [Albert Ruger]
Lithographer:
Printer: Chicago Lithographing Co. [Chicago]
Publisher: Ruger & Stoner, Madison, Wis.
Key/Vignettes/Misc: Refs. 1–16, A–K; 2 vignettes
Locations: LC–M
Catalogs/Checklists: Stout, no. 116; LC–M, 772

3410
Place: Erie, Pennsylvania
Date: 1909
Title: Birdseye View of Erie, Penna. 1909
Size: 28 × 40 in. (71.1 × 101.6 cm.)
Artist: Chas. Lederle
Lithographer:
Printer: Erie Litho. Co. Erie, Pa.
Publisher: Chas. Lederle & Co., Erie Pa.
Key/Vignettes/Misc:
Locations: LC–M
Catalogs/Checklists: Stout, no. 117; LC–M, 773

3411
Place: Evans City, Pennsylvania
Date: 1900
Title: Evans City, Pennsylvania 1900.
Size: 11¾ × 21⅞ in. (29.9 × 55.7 cm.)
Artist: T. M. Fowler
Lithographer:
Printer:
Publisher: T. M. Fowler & James B. Moyer
Key/Vignettes/Misc: Refs. 1–10, A–G
Locations: CLP–P; LC–M; PHMC–H; PSU; UPDL–P
Catalogs/Checklists: Stout, no. 66; LC–M, 774

3412
Place: Everett, Pennsylvania
Date: 1905
Title: Bird's–Eye View of Everett, Bedford County, Pa. 1905.
Size: 23 × 24 in. (58.4 × 61 cm.)
Artist: T. M. Fowler

Lithographer:
Printer:
Publisher: T. M. Fowler
Key/Vignettes/Misc: 23 vignettes
Locations: LC–M; YO; NYH–NY
Catalogs/Checklists: Stout, no. 34; LC–M, 775; PP

3413
Place: Everson, Pennsylvania
Date: [1890]
Title: [Everson & Scottdale]
Size: 5⅝ × 8¾ in. (14.3 × 22.2 cm.) (photo)
Artist:
Lithographer:
Printer:
Publisher: [Scottdale & Everson Land Co.]
Key/Vignettes/Misc:
Locations: LC–M (photo)
Catalogs/Checklists: Stout, no. 126; LC–M, 843

3414
Place: Factoryville, Pennsylvania
Date: 1891
Title: Factoryville, Wyoming County Penna. 1891.
Size: 13¾ × 24⅛ in. (35 × 61.4 cm.)
Artist: T. M. Fowler
Lithographer:
Printer:
Publisher: T. M. Fowler & James B. Moyer
Key/Vignettes/Misc: Refs. 1–12
Locations: PHMC–H
Catalogs/Checklists: Stout, no. 292

Place: Fallston, Pennsylvania
Date: 1842
See Beaver, Pennsylvania, 1842.

3415
Place: Fayette City, Pennsylvania
Date: 1904
Title: Fayette City. Pennsylvania. 1904
Size: 15⁷⁄₁₆ × 19⁷⁄₁₆ in. (39.3 × 49.5 cm.)
Artist: T. M. Fowler
Lithographer:
Printer:
Publisher: T. M. Fowler, Morrisville, Pa.
Key/Vignettes/Misc: Refs. 1–28, A–C; 10 vignettes
Locations: NYH–NY
Catalogs/Checklists:

3416
Place: Fleetwood, Pennsylvania
Date: 1893
Title: Fleetwood, Berks County Pennsylvania. 1893.
Size: 10½ × 18¾ in. (26.7 × 47.7 cm.)
Artist: T. M. Fowler
Lithographer:
Printer:
Publisher: T. M. Fowler & James B. Moyer
Key/Vignettes/Misc: Refs. 1–9, A–D
Locations: PHMC–H; YO; LC–M
Catalogs/Checklists: Stout, no. 40; PP; LC–M, 775.1

3417
Place: Ford City, Pennsylvania
Date: 1896

Title: Ford City, Armstrong County
Pennsylvania. 1896.
Size: 14 × 22⅛ in. (35.6 × 56.2 cm.)
Artist: T. M. Fowler
Lithographer:
Printer:
Publisher: T. M. Fowler & James B. Moyer
Key/Vignettes/Misc: Refs. 1–7, A–E;
description
Locations: LC–M; PHMC–H; PSU;
UPDL–P; LC–P
Catalogs/Checklists: Stout, no. 23;
LC–M, 776

3418
Place: Forest City, Pennsylvania
Date: 1889
Title: Forest City, Susquehanna County Pa.
1889.
Size: 14½ × 25⅝ in. (36.9 × 65.6 cm.)
Artist: T. M. Fowler
Lithographer:
Printer: A. E. Downs, Lith. Boston
Publisher: T. M. Fowler & James B. Moyer
Key/Vignettes/Misc: Refs. 1–12
Locations: HSP–P; LC–M; PHMC–H;
PSU; UPDL–P
Catalogs/Checklists: Stout, no. 257;
LC–M, 777

3419
Place: Foxburg, Pennsylvania
Date: 1878
Title: Foxburg, Clarion County, Pa. 1878.
Size: 13¾ × 28⅝ in. (35 × 72.9 cm.)
Artist: E. Bott
Lithographer:
Printer: Armor, Feurhake & Co. Lith. Pbg.
[Pittsburgh]
Publisher:
Key/Vignettes/Misc:
Locations: YO
Catalogs/Checklists: Stout, no. 83; PP

3420
Place: Frackville, Pennsylvania
Date: 1889
Title: Frackville, Pennsylvania 1889.
Size: 16¾ × 23⅞ in. (42.7 × 60.8 cm.)
Artist: T. M. Fowler
Lithographer:
Printer:
Publisher:
Key/Vignettes/Misc: Refs. 1–9; 6
vignettes
Locations: PHMC–H; PSU; LC–M
Catalogs/Checklists: Stout, no. 243;
LC–M, 777.1

3421
Place: Franklin, Pennsylvania
Date: 1901
Title: View of the City of Franklin, Pa.
1901.
Size: 15½ × 30⅞ in. (39.4 × 78.5 cm.)
Artist: T. M. Fowler
Lithographer:
Printer:
Publisher: T. M. Fowler & James B. Moyer
Key/Vignettes/Misc: Refs. 1–30, A–L; 1
vignette
Locations: CLP–P; HSP–P; LC–M;

PHMC–H; PSU; UPDL–P; YO
Catalogs/Checklists: Stout, no. 264;
LC–M, 778; PP

3422
Place: Gallitzin, Pennsylvania
Date: 1901
Title: Gallitzin, Cambria County
Pennsylvania. 1901.
Size: 11 × 24½ in. (28 × 62.3 cm.)
Artist: T. M. Fowler
Lithographer:
Printer:
Publisher: T. M. Fowler & James B. Moyer
Key/Vignettes/Misc: Refs. 1–14, A–C
Locations: CLP–P; HSP–P; LC–M;
PHMC–H; PSU; UPDL–P; YO
Catalogs/Checklists: Stout, no. 71;
LC–M, 779; PP

Place: Gaysport, Pennsylvania
Date: 1878
See Hollidaysburg, Pennsylvania, 1878.

3423
Place: Gettysburg, Pennsylvania
Date: 1863
Title: Gettysburg Battle–Field
Size: 20¹³⁄₁₆ × 35¹³⁄₁₆ in. (53 × 91 cm.)
Artist: Jno. B. Bachelder
Lithographer:
Printer: Endicott & Co., New York
Publisher:
Key/Vignettes/Misc:
Locations: WHS–M
Catalogs/Checklists:

3424
Place: Gettysburg, Pennsylvania
Date: 1888
Title: Gettysburg, Pennsylvania. 1888.
Size: 22½ × 35½ in. (57.2 × 90.2 cm.)
Artist: T. M. Fowler and A. E. Downs
Lithographer:
Printer: A. E. Downs, Lith.
Publisher: T. M. Fowler and A. E. Downs,
Boston
Key/Vignettes/Misc: Refs. 1–9, A–H; 80
vignettes
Locations: LC–M; PSU; YO
Catalogs/Checklists: Stout, no. 1; LC–M,
780; PP

3425
Place: Girardville, Pennsylvania
Date: 1889
Title: Girardville, Pennsylvania 1889.
Size: 20 × 24⅞ in. (50.8 × 63.3 cm.)
Artist: T. M. Fowler
Lithographer:
Printer:
Publisher: T. M. Fowler & James B. Moyer
Key/Vignettes/Misc: Refs. 1–17; 6
vignettes
Locations: PHMC–H; PSU; LC–M
Catalogs/Checklists: Stout, no. 244;
LC–M, 780.1

3426
Place: Glassport, Pennsylvania
Date: 1902
Title: Glassport, Allegheny County,
Pennsylvania. 1902

Size: 10⅜ × 21½ in. (26.4 × 54.6 cm.)
Artist: T. M. Fowler
Lithographer:
Printer:
Publisher: T. M. Fowler & James B. Moyer
Key/Vignettes/Misc: Refs. 1–8, A–D
Locations: CLP–P; HSP–P; LC–M;
PHMC–H; PSU; UPDL–P; YO
Catalogs/Checklists: Stout, no. 6; LC–M,
781; PP

3427
Place: Great Bend, Pennsylvania
Date: 1887
Title: Great Bend, Penn. 1887.
Size: 14½ × 25⅝ in. (36.9 × 65.2 cm.)
Artist: L. R. Burleigh
Lithographer:
Printer: The Burleigh Litho. Establishment,
Troy, N. Y.
Publisher: L. R. Burleigh
Key/Vignettes/Misc: Refs. 1–20
Locations: LC–M; YO
Catalogs/Checklists: Stout, no. 258;
LC–M, 782; PP

3428
Place: Greensburg, Pennsylvania
Date: 1901
Title: Greensburg, Pennsylvania. 1901.
Size: 15½ × 31 in. (39.5 × 78.9 cm.)
Artist: T. M. Fowler
Lithographer:
Printer:
Publisher: T. M. Fowler & James B. Moyer
Key/Vignettes/Misc: Refs. 1–21, A–H
Locations: LC–M; PHMC–H; PSU;
UPDL–P; YO
Catalogs/Checklists: Stout, no. 280;
LC–M, 783; PP

3429
Place: Greenville, Pennsylvania
Date: 1896
Title: Greenville, Mercer County
Pennsylvania.
Size: 15½ × 30⅞ in. (39.5 × 78.5 cm.)
Artist: T. M. Fowler
Lithographer:
Printer:
Publisher: T. M. Fowler & James B. Moyer
Key/Vignettes/Misc: Refs. 1–20, A–H
Locations: PHMC–H; LC–M (photo)
Catalogs/Checklists: Stout, no. 188;
LC–M, 783.1

3430
Place: Grove City, Pennsylvania
Date: 1901
Title: Grove City, Mercer County
Pennsylvania.
Size: 11¾ × 22 in. (39.9 × 56 cm.)
Artist: T. M. Fowler
Lithographer:
Printer:
Publisher: T. M. Fowler & James B. Moyer
Key/Vignettes/Misc: Refs. 1–14, A–D
Locations: CLP–P; HSP–P; LC–M;
PHMC–H; PSU; UPDL–P; LC–P
Catalogs/Checklists: Stout, no. 189;
LC–M, 784

3431
Place: Hallstead, Pennsylvania
Date: 1887
Title: Hallstead, Penn. 1887.
Size: 11¹⁵⁄₁₆ × 17⅞ in. (30.4 × 45.5 cm.)
Artist: L. R. Burleigh
Lithographer:
Printer: The Burleigh Litho. Establishment, Troy, N. Y.
Publisher: L. R. Burleigh
Key/Vignettes/Misc: Refs. 1–14
Locations: LC–M; LC–P
Catalogs/Checklists: Stout, no. 259; LC–M, 785

3432
Place: Hamburg, Pennsylvania
Date: 1889 State I
Title: Hamburg Berks Co., Penn'a. 1889.
Size: 16¾ × 27¼ in. (42.6 × 69.3 cm.)
Artist: T. M. Fowler
Lithographer:
Printer:
Publisher: T. M. Fowler & F. P. Henry
Key/Vignettes/Misc: Refs. 1–22; 4 vignettes
Locations: HSP–P; LC–M; PHMC–H; PSU
Catalogs/Checklists: Stout, no. 41a; LC–M, 786

3433
Place: Hamburg, Pennsylvania
Date: 1889 State II
Title: Hamburg Berks Co. Penna. 1889.
Size: 19¾ × 27¼ in. (42.6 × 69.3 cm.)
Artist: T. M. Fowler
Lithographer:
Printer:
Publisher: T. M. Fowler & F. P. Henry
Key/Vignettes/Misc: Refs. 1–22; 9 vignettes
Locations: YO
Catalogs/Checklists: Stout, no. 41b; PP

3434
Place: Harmony, Pennsylvania
Date: 1901
Title: Harmony, Butler County Pennsylvania. 1901.
Size: 9⅝ × 16¾ in. (24.5 × 42.7 cm.)
Artist: T. M. Fowler
Lithographer:
Printer:
Publisher: T. M. Fowler & James B. Moyer
Key/Vignettes/Misc: Refs. 1–9
Locations: CLP–P; LC–M; PHMC–H; PSU; UPDL–P; HSWP–P; YO; LC–P
Catalogs/Checklists: Stout, no. 67; LC–M, 787; PP

3435
Place: Harrisburg, Pennsylvania
Date: 1846
Title: View of Harrisburg, Pa. From the West.
Size: 16½ × 23 in. (42 × 58.5 cm.)
Artist: E. Whitefield
Lithographer:
Printer: Lewis & Brown, 37 John St., New York
Publisher: Lewis & Brown, New York
Key/Vignettes/Misc:

Locations: YO; Historical Society of Dauphin County, Harrisburg, Pennsylvania
Catalogs/Checklists: Norton, Whitefield, no. 31; Pyne, no. 435; PP, no. 28

3436
Place: Harrisburg, Pennsylvania
Date: [1846]
Title: View of Harrisburg, Pa. From the S. W.
Size: 7½ × 10⅛ in. (19.1 × 25.8 cm.)
Artist: E. Whitefield
Lithographer:
Printer: [E. Jones & G. W. Newman]
Publisher:
Key/Vignettes/Misc:
Locations: YO; NYH–NY
Catalogs/Checklists: PP, no. 33; Norton, Whitefield, no. 24

3437
Place: Harrisburg, Pennsylvania
Date: Ca. 1850
Title: S. W. View of Harrisburg, Pa.
Size: 19⅛ × 26 in. (48.2 × 66.2 cm.)
Artist: J.[ames] A.[rthur] Benade
Lithographer: J. A. Benade
Printer: P. S. Duval, Phila.
Publisher:
Key/Vignettes/Misc:
Locations: NYH–NY
Catalogs/Checklists:

3438
Place: Harrisburg, Pennsylvania
Date: 1855
Title: View of Harrisburg. Penn.
Size: 21 × 31½ in. (53.4 × 80.1 cm.)
Artist: J. T. Williams
Lithographer: J. T. Williams
Printer: E. Sachse & Co. 3 N. Liberty St. Baltimore, Md.
Publisher:
Key/Vignettes/Misc: 21 vignettes
Locations: LC–M; PHMC–H; NYH–NY
Catalogs/Checklists: Stout, no. 102; LC–M, 788

3439
Place: Harrisburg, Pennsylvania
Date: 1865
Title: Harrisburg and the Susquehanna. From Bridgeport Heights.
Size: 16¾ × 21⅛ in. (42.6 × 53.8 cm.)
Artist: F. F. Palmer
Lithographer:
Printer: Currier & Ives, Lith. N. Y.
Publisher: Currier & Ives, 152 Nassau St., New York
Key/Vignettes/Misc:
Locations: CHS–C; YO
Catalogs/Checklists: PP, no. 63; Peters, C & I, 4209; Conningham 2733

3440
Place: Harrisburg, Pennsylvania
Date: 1879
Title: Harrisburg, Pa. 1879. Viewed From Ft. Washington.
Size: 19 × 30 in. (48.3 × 76.3 cm.)
Artist:
Lithographer:
Printer: Thos. Hunter Lith. Phila.

Publisher: C. J. Corbin
Key/Vignettes/Misc: 21 vignettes
Locations: HSP–P
Catalogs/Checklists: Stout, no. 103

3441
Place: Harrisburg, Pennsylvania
Date: 1881
Title: Harrisburgh, Penna. 1881
Size: 23½ × 37¾ in. (59.8 × 95.9 cm.)
Artist:
Lithographer:
Printer: Knauber & Co. Lith. Milwaukee
Publisher: John R. Fender & Co. N. Y.
Key/Vignettes/Misc: Refs. 1–119
Locations: PHMC–H
Catalogs/Checklists: Stout, no. 104

3442
Place: Hazelton, Pennsylvania
Date: 1884
Title: Hazelton. Pennsylvania. 1884.
Size: 13¾ × 25 in. (35 × 63.6 cm.)
Artist: [T. M. Fowler?]
Lithographer:
Printer:
Publisher: O. H. Bailey & Co., Boston
Key/Vignettes/Misc: Refs. 1–33; 12 vignettes
Locations: BPL–R; LC–M (facsimile)
Catalogs/Checklists: Stout, no. 175; LC–M, 788.1

3443
Place: Highspire, Pennsylvania
Date: [186–?]
Title: Mill and residence of J. Buser, Highspire, Dauphin Co., Pa.
Size: 19 × 38 in. (48.3 × 96.7 cm.)
Artist: A. Ruger
Lithographer:
Printer:
Publisher:
Key/Vignettes/Misc:
Locations: LC–M
Catalogs/Checklists:

3444
Place: Highspire, Pennsylvania
Date: 1873
Title: Bird's Eye View of Highspire Duphin Co. Pennsylvania 1873
Size: 16⅝ × 20¹⁄₁₆ in. (41.6 × 51.1 cm.)
Artist: H. Brosius
Lithographer:
Printer:
Publisher: J. J. Stoner, Madison, Wis.
Key/Vignettes/Misc:
Locations: YO
Catalogs/Checklists:

3445
Place: Hollidaysburg, Pennsylvania
Date: [1852]
Title: Hollidaysburg Taken From the Chimney Rocks.
Size: 16¾ × 19¼ in. (42.6 × 49 cm.)
Artist: E. Schellhorn
Lithographer:
Printer: Wegner & Braum lith. 60 Market St. Pittsburgh
Publisher:
Key/Vignettes/Misc:

Locations: YO; PHMC-H; LC-M
(photo)
Catalogs/Checklists: PP, no. 42; LC-M,
788.3

3446
Place: Hollidaysburg, Pennsylvania
Date: 1878
Title: Hollidaysburg and Gaysport, Pa.
1878.
Size: 15⅝ × 22 in. (39.8 × 56 cm.)
Artist: W. W. Denslow
Lithographer: Traubel
Printer: Thos. Hunter Lith. Phila.
Publisher: C. J. Corbin [Philadelphia]
Key/Vignettes/Misc: 5 vignettes
Locations: YO
Catalogs/Checklists: Stout, no. 52; PP

3447
Place: Homestead, Pennsylvania
Date: 1902
Title: Homestead, Pennsylvania. 1902
Size: 16⅛ × 27⅜ in. (41 × 69.5 cm.)
Artist: T. M. Fowler
Lithographer:
Printer:
Publisher: T. M. Fowler & James B. Moyer
Key/Vignettes/Misc: Refs. 1–14, A–T
Locations: CLP-P; HSP-P; LC-M;
PHMC-H; PSU; UPDL-P; YO
Catalogs/Checklists: Stout, no. 8; LC-M,
789; PP

3448
Place: Honesdale, Pennsylvania
Date: 1882
Title: Honesdale, Pa. 1882. Looking West.
Size: 16 × 28 in. (40.8 × 71.2 cm.)
Artist: C. L. Fussell, from photo by R. B.
Whittaker
Lithographer:
Printer:
Publisher: Philadelphia Publishing House
Key/Vignettes/Misc: 13 vignettes
Locations: YO
Catalogs/Checklists: Stout, no. 277;
LC-M, 790; PP

3449
Place: Honesdale, Pennsylvania
Date: 1890 State I
Title: Honesdale, Pennsylvania 1890.
Size: 16½ × 33⅞ in. (42 × 86.1 cm.)
Artist: T. M. Fowler
Lithographer:
Printer:
Publisher: T. M. Fowler & James B. Moyer
Key/Vignettes/Misc: Refs. 1–17, A–H
Locations: LC-M; PHMC-H; PSU
Catalogs/Checklists: Stout, no. 278a;
LC-M, 790

3450
Place: Honesdale, Pennsylvania
Date: 1890 State II
Title: Honesdale, Pennsylvania 1890.
Size: 16½ × 33⅞ in. (42 × 86.1 cm.)
Artist: [T. M. Fowler]
Lithographer:
Printer:
Publisher: T. M. Fowler & James B. Moyer
Key/Vignettes/Misc: Refs. 1–17, A–H; 1

vignette; overprint advertisement in sky
Locations: HSP-P
Catalogs/Checklists: Stout, no. 278b

3451
Place: Hopewell, Pennsylvania
Date: 1906
Title: Birds Eye View of Hopewell,
Bedford Co., Pa. 1906
Size: 15¾ × 17⁵⁄₁₆ in. (40 × 44 cm.)
Artist: T. M. Fowler
Lithographer:
Printer:
Publisher: T. M. Fowler, Morrisville, Pa.
Key/Vignettes/Misc: 11 vignettes
Locations: YO
Catalogs/Checklists: PP

3452
Place: Huntingdon, Pennsylvania
Date: 1878
Title: Huntingdon, Pa. 1878.
Size: 17¾ × 26⅛ in. (45.2 × 66.5 cm.)
Artist: W. W. Denslow
Lithographer: Traubel
Printer: Thos. Hunter, Lith. Phila.
Publisher: C. J. Corbin & Co.
[Philadelphia]
Key/Vignettes/Misc: 22 vignettes
Locations: YO; PSU
Catalogs/Checklists: PP, no. 71; Stout, no.
135

3453
Place: Hyndman, Pennsylvania
Date: 1906
Title: Bird's–Eye View of Hyndman,
Bedford Co., Pa.
Size: 16¼ × 18⅞ in. (41.3 × 47.9 cm.)
Artist: [T. M. Fowler]
Lithographer:
Printer:
Publisher: Fowler & Kelly, Morrisville, Pa.
(copyright)
Key/Vignettes/Misc: 12 vignettes
Locations: LC-M
Catalogs/Checklists: Stout, no. 35;
LC-M, 791

3454
Place: Indiana, Pennsylvania
Date: 1878
Title:
Size:
Artist: W. W. Denslow
Lithographer:
Printer:
Publisher:
Key/Vignettes/Misc:
Locations:
Catalogs/Checklists: Stout, no. 305

3455
Place: Indiana, Pennsylvania
Date: 1900
Title: Indiana, Pennsylvania. 1900.
Size: 14 × 28⅝ in. (35.6 × 72.8 cm.)
Artist: T. M. Fowler
Lithographer:
Printer:
Publisher: T. M. Fowler & James B. Moyer
Key/Vignettes/Misc: Refs. 1–18, A–J; 1
vignette

Locations: CLP-P; LC-P; PHMC-H;
PSU; UPDL-P; LC-M
Catalogs/Checklists: Stout, no. 138;
LC-M, 792

3456
Place: Indiantown Gap, Pennsylvania
Date: N.D.
Title: View of Indiantown Gap
Size: 10¹⁄₁₆ × 16 in. (25.6 × 40.7 cm.)
Artist:
Lithographer: H. von Hodenberg
Printer:
Publisher: H. von Hodenberg, Philadelphia
Key/Vignettes/Misc: 2 vignettes
Locations: LCHS-L
Catalogs/Checklists:

3457
Place: Irvona, Pennsylvania
Date: 1895
Title: Irvona, Clearfield County
Pennsylvania 1895.
Size: 15⁵⁄₁₆ × 22⁵⁄₁₆ in. (39 × 56.8 cm.)
Artist: T. M. Fowler
Lithographer:
Printer:
Publisher: T. M. Fowler & James B. Moyer
Key/Vignettes/Misc: Refs. 1–11
Locations: PHMC-H; YO; LC-M
Catalogs/Checklists: Stout, no. 89; PP;
LC-M, 792.1

3458
Place: Irwin, Pennsylvania
Date: 1897
Title: Irwin, Pennsylvania 1897.
Size: 15 × 23¾ in. (38.2 × 60.4 cm.)
Artist: T. M. Fowler
Lithographer:
Printer:
Publisher: T. M. Fowler & James B. Moyer
Key/Vignettes/Misc: Refs. 1–11, A–I
Locations: LC-M; PHMC-H; PSU;
UPDL-P; YO
Catalogs/Checklists: Stout, no. 281;
LC-M, 793; PP

3459
Place: Jeannette, Pennsylvania
Date: 1897
Title: Jeannette, Westmoreland County
Pennsylvania. 1897.
Size: 18⅜ × 29½ in. (46.9 × 75.1 cm.)
Artist: T. M. Fowler
Lithographer:
Printer:
Publisher: T. M. Fowler & James B. Moyer
Key/Vignettes/Misc: Refs. 1–18, A–J
Locations: CLP-P; HSP-P; LC-M;
PHMC-H; PSU; UPDL-P; YO; LC-P
Catalogs/Checklists: Stout, no. 282;
LC-M, 794; PP

3460
Place: Jermyn, Pennsylvania
Date: 1889
Title: Jermyn, Lackawanna County Pa.
1889.
Size: 16⅜ × 26⅝ in. (41.7 × 67.7 cm.)
Artist: T. M. Fowler
Lithographer:
Printer:

Publisher: T. M. Fowler & James B. Moyer
Key/Vignettes/Misc: Refs. 1–18
Locations: PSU; PHMC–H; LC–M
Catalogs/Checklists: Stout, no. 147;
LC–M, 794.2

3461
Place: Jersey Shore, Pennsylvania
Date: 1854
Title: Jersey Shore Looking South West
LycomingCo. Pa. 1854
Size: 19¾ × 24⅜ in. (50.3 × 62 cm.)
Artist: J. B. Bachelder
Lithographer: W. H. Rease
Printer: Wagner & McGuigan
[Philadelphia]
Publisher:
Key/Vignettes/Misc:
Locations: YO; HSP–P; PHMC–H
Catalogs/Checklists: PP, no. 45; Stout, no.
183

3462
Place: Jim Thorpe, Pennsylvania
Date: 1858
Title: Pass of the Lehigh, at Maugh Chunk
Size: 7⅛ × 9½ in. (18.1 × 24.1 cm.)
Artist: George Lehman
Lithographer: George Lehman
Printer:
Publisher:
Key/Vignettes/Misc:
Locations:
Catalogs/Checklists: McClintock, no. 64

3463
Place: Jim Thorpe, Pennsylvania
Date: N.D.
Title: Bird's Eye View of Mauch Chunk,
From Mount Pisgah, Showing the Lehigh
Gap in the Distance
Size: 5⁵⁄₁₆ × 7¹³⁄₁₆ in. (13.5 × 18.3 cm.)
Artist: James Queen, from ambrotype by
H. P. Osborn
Lithographer:
Printer: P. S. Duval & Son's lith Philad.
Publisher:
Key/Vignettes/Misc:
Locations: FL–P
Catalogs/Checklists:

3464
Place: Johnsonburg, Pennsylvania
Date: 1895
Title: Johnsonburg, Elk County
Pennsylvania. 1895.
Size: 15 × 26¾ in. (38.2 × 68 cm.)
Artist: T. M. Fowler
Lithographer:
Printer:
Publisher: T. M. Fowler & James B. Moyer
Key/Vignettes/Misc: Refs. 1–16, A–G
Locations: PHMC–H; PSU; UPDL–P;
LC–M; YO
Catalogs/Checklists: Stout, no. 109; PP;
LC–M, 794.3

3465
Place: Johnstown, Pennsylvania
Date: 1889
Title: Birds Eye View of the Conemaugh
Valley, from Neneveh to the Lake.
Johnstown, Pa.

Size: 14⅛ × 28 in. (36 × 71.2 cm.)
Artist: Alex. Y. Lee
Lithographer:
Printer:
Publisher: Alex. Y. Lee
Key/Vignettes/Misc: 4 vignettes
Locations: BPL–R
Catalogs/Checklists: Stout, no. 70

3466
Place: Kane, Pennsylvania
Date: 1895
Title: Kane, McKean County,
Pennsylvania, 1895
Size:
Artist: T. M. Fowler
Lithographer:
Printer:
Publisher: T. M. Fowler & James B. Moyer
Key/Vignettes/Misc: Refs.
Locations: McKean County Historical
Society, Smethport, Pennsylvania; LC–M
(photo)
Catalogs/Checklists: Stout, no. 306;
LC–M, 794.4

3467
Place: Kittanning, Pennsylvania
Date: 1878
Title: Kittaning, Pa. 1878.
Size: 14 × 20 in. (35.7 × 50.9 cm.)
Artist: W. W. Denslow
Lithographer: Traubel
Printer: Thos. Hunter, Lith. Phila.
Publisher: C. J. Corbin & Co.
Key/Vignettes/Misc: 7 vignettes
Locations: YO
Catalogs/Checklists: Stout, no. 24; PP

3468
Place: Kittanning, Pennsylvania
Date: 1896
Title: Kittanning, Armstrong County
Pennsylvania. 1896.
Size: 14⅛ × 26⅜ in. (35.9 × 67 cm.)
Artist: T. M. Fowler
Lithographer:
Printer:
Publisher: T. M. Fowler & James B. Moyer
Key/Vignettes/Misc: Refs. 1–19, A–I
Locations: LC–M; PHMC–H; YO
Catalogs/Checklists: Stout, no. 25;
LC–M, 795; PP

3469
Place: Knox, Pennsylvania
Date: 1896
Title: Knox, Clarion County Pa. 1896.
Size: 11 × 18 in. (28 × 45.8 cm.)
Artist: T. M. Fowler
Lithographer:
Printer:
Publisher: T. M. Fowler & James B. Moyer
Key/Vignettes/Misc: Refs. 1–7, A–C
Locations: CLP–P; UPDL–P; PSU;
PHMC–H; LC–M (photo)
Catalogs/Checklists: Stout, no. 84;
LC–M, 795.1

3470
Place: Kutztown, Pennsylvania
Date: 1893
Title: Kutztown, Berks County,
Pennsylvania, 1893

Size: 15⅜ × 25⅛ in. (39.1 × 63.9 cm.)
Artist: T. M. Fowler
Lithographer:
Printer:
Publisher: T. M. Fowler & James B. Moyer
Key/Vignettes/Misc: Refs. 1–18, A–C; 2
vignettes
Locations: PHMC–H; YO; LC–M
(photo)
Catalogs/Checklists: Stout, no. 42; PP;
LC–M, 795.2

3471
Place: Lancaster, Pennsylvania
Date: Ca. 1842
Title: Southwest View of Lancaster, Pa.
Size: 15 × 18⅞ in. (38.2 × 48.1 cm.)
Artist: Jas. Benade
Lithographer: Jas. Benade
Printer: P. S. Duval, Lith. Phila.
Publisher:
Key/Vignettes/Misc:
Locations: NYP–S (ca. 1835); YO
Catalogs/Checklists: Stokes C. 1835—
F–46; PP, no. 22

3472
Place: Lancaster, Pennsylvania
Date: 1853
Title: View of Lancaster, Pa.
Size: 17¾ × 33½ in. (45.1 × 85.3 cm.)
Artist: Chas. Parsons
Lithographer:
Printer: Endicott & Co. Lith. N. Y.
Publisher: Jas. T. Palmatary, N. Y.
Key/Vignettes/Misc: Refs. 1–19
Locations: PHMC–H; YO
Catalogs/Checklists: Stout, no. 155; PP

3473
Place: Lansdale, Pennsylvania
Date: 1885
Title: Lansdale. Pennsylvania. 1885.
Size: 17 × 23 in. (43.3 × 58.5 cm.)
Artist: [T. M. Fowler?]
Lithographer:
Printer: O. H. Bailey & Co., Boston
Publisher: O. H. Bailey & Co., Boston
Key/Vignettes/Misc: Refs. 1–43
Locations: BPL–R; HSP–P; LC–M
(photo)
Catalogs/Checklists: Stout, no. 199;
LC–M, 795.3

3474
Place: Latrobe, Pennsylvania
Date: 1900
Title: Latrobe, Pennsylvania 1900
Size: 16 × 30⅛ in. (40.7 × 76.7 cm.)
Artist: T. M. Fowler
Lithographer:
Printer:
Publisher: T. M. Fowler & James B. Moyer
Key/Vignettes/Misc: Refs. A–G
Locations: CLP–P; LC–M; PHMC–H;
PSU; UPDL–P
Catalogs/Checklists: Stout, no. 283;
LC–M, 796

3475
Place: Lebanon, Pennsylvania
Date: 1840
Title: Lebanon, Pa., in 1840
Size: 8⅛ × 15³⁄₁₆ in. (20.6 × 38.7 cm.)

Artist: B. B. Lehman
Lithographer:
Printer:
Publisher: Ed. M. Miller
Key/Vignettes/Misc:
Locations: LCHS–L
Catalogs/Checklists: LC–M, 1063.1

3476
Place: Lebanon, Pennsylvania
Date: 1873
Title: Lebanon, Pa. 1873
Size: 16⅞ × 23⅜ in. (42.9 × 59.5 cm.)
Artist: Fowler & Bailey
Lithographer: C. H. Vogt
Printer: Am. Oleograph Company
[Milwaukee]
Publisher: Fowler & Bailey
Key/Vignettes/Misc: Refs. 1–22, A–N
Locations: LCHS–L
Catalogs/Checklists:

3477
Place: Lebanon, Pennsylvania
Date: 1888
Title: Lebanon, Pennsylvania—1888
Size: 21¹¹⁄₁₆ × 32¾ in. (55.2 × 83.3 cm.)
Artist: T. M. Fowler
Lithographer:
Printer:
Publisher: Fowler & Moyer, Lebanon,
Pennsylvania
Key/Vignettes/Misc: Refs. 1–25, A–P; 8
vignettes
Locations: LCHS–L
Catalogs/Checklists: Stout, no. 307

3478
Place: Lebanon, Pennsylvania
Date: N.D.
Title: Lebanon, Pa.
Size: 16¼ × 25¹⁄₁₆ in. (41.4 × 63.8 cm.)
Artist:
Lithographer: H. von Hodenberg
Printer:
Publisher: H. von Hodenberg, Philadelphia
Key/Vignettes/Misc: 14 vignettes
Locations: LCHS–L
Catalogs/Checklists:

3479
Place: Lehighton, Pennsylvania
Date: 1883
Title: Lehighton, Pennsylvania. 1883
Size: 14¼ × 21¾ in. (36.3 × 55.4 cm.)
Artist: [T. M. Fowler?]
Lithographer: O. H. Bailey & Co.
Printer: O. H. Bailey & Co.
Publisher: Bailey & Fowler, Publishers,
Boston
Key/Vignettes/Misc: Refs. 1–19
Locations: BPL–R
Catalogs/Checklists: Stout, no. 74

3480
Place: Lewisburg, Pennsylvania
Date: 1884
Title: Lewisburgh. Pennsylvania. 1884
Size: 20 × 24½ in. (50.8 × 62.3 cm.)
Artist: O. H. Bailey & Co.
Lithographer:
Printer: O. H. Bailey & Co., Boston
Publisher: O. H. Bailey & Co. Publishers,
Boston

Key/Vignettes/Misc: Refs. 1–24; 5
vignettes
Locations: BPL–R; PHMC–H; YO;
LC–M (photo)
Catalogs/Checklists: PP, no. 76; Stout, no.
261; LC–M, 796.1

3481
Place: Lewistown, Pennsylvania
Date: 1842
Title: View of Lewistown, Taken from
Ard's Hill. . . .
Size: 15 × 20¼ in. (38.2 × 51.6 cm.)
Artist:
Lithographer: J. Benade
Printer: P. S. Duval, Philada.
Publisher: G. W. Draper
Key/Vignettes/Misc:
Locations: YO
Catalogs/Checklists: PP, no. 23

3482
Place: Lewistown, Pennsylvania
Date: 1879
Title: Lewistown, Pa. 1879 viewed from
the Pennsylvania Rail Road.
Size: 17⅜ × 27¼ in. (45.2 × 69.3 cm.)
Artist: P. R. Robjohns
Lithographer:
Printer: Thos. Hunter Lith. Phila.
Publisher: C. J. Corbin, Phila.
Key/Vignettes/Misc: 17 vignettes
Locations: HSP–P; PHMC–H
Catalogs/Checklists: Stout, no. 193

3483
Place: Lewistown, Pennsylvania
Date: 1895
Title: Lewistown, Mifflin County
Pennsylvania 1895.
Size: 14½ × 25⅛ in. (36.9 × 64 cm.)
Artist: T. M. Fowler
Lithographer:
Printer:
Publisher: T. M. Fowler & James B. Moyer
Key/Vignettes/Misc: Refs. 1–20, A–H
Locations: PHMC–H; YO
Catalogs/Checklists: Stout, no. 194; PP

3484
Place: Ligonier, Pennsylvania
Date: 1900
Title: Ligonier, Pennsylvania. 1900.
Size: 12 × 22 in. (30.5 × 56 cm.)
Artist: T. M. Fowler
Lithographer:
Printer:
Publisher: T. M. Fowler & James B. Moyer
Key/Vignettes/Misc: Refs. 1–10, A–F
Locations: CLP–P; HSP–P; LC–M;
PHMC–H; PSU; UPDL–P; PAC; YO
Catalogs/Checklists: Stout, no. 284;
LC–M, 797; PP

3485
Place: Lincoln, Pennsylvania
Date: 1887
Title: Lincoln, Lancaster Co.,
Pennsylvania, 1887.
Size: 14⅜ × 20³⁄₁₆ in. (36.6 × 48.8 cm.)
(facsimile)
Artist: T. M. Fowler
Lithographer:

Printer:
Publisher:
Key/Vignettes/Misc: Refs. 1–26; 5
vignettes
Locations: LC–M (facsimile)
Catalogs/Checklists: LC–M, 797.2

3486
Place: Lindsey, Pennsylvania
Date: 1895
Title: Lindsey, Jefferson County
Pennsylvania 1895.
Size: 15 × 24¾ in. (38.2 × 62.9 cm.)
Artist: T. M. Fowler
Lithographer:
Printer:
Publisher: T. M. Fowler & James B. Moyer
Key/Vignettes/Misc: Refs. 1–13
Locations: PHMC–H; LC–M
Catalogs/Checklists: Stout, no. 140;
LC–M, 797.3

3487
Place: Lititz, Pennsylvania
Date: Ca. 1855
Title: Litiz, Lancaster Co. Pennsylvania.
Size: 16½ × 21⅞ in. (42 × 55.7 cm.)
Artist: F. Fuchs
Lithographer: F. Fuchs
Printer: L. N. Rosenthal's Lithographic
Establishment. . .Phila.
Publisher: B. de Sweinitz, Litiz. . . .
Key/Vignettes/Misc: 2 vignettes
Locations: YO
Catalogs/Checklists: PP, no. 49

3488
Place: Lititz, Pennsylvania
Date: 1887
Title: View of Lititz, and Warwick.
Lancaster County Pa. 1887
Size: 16 × 19½ in. (40.7 × 49.6 cm.)
(facsimile)
Artist: T. M. Fowler
Lithographer:
Printer:
Publisher:
Key/Vignettes/Misc: Refs. 1–36; 10
vignettes
Locations: LC–M (facsimile)
Catalogs/Checklists: LC–M, 797.4

3489
Place: Lititz, Pennsylvania
Date: 1894
Title:
Size:
Artist: T. M. Fowler ?
Lithographer:
Printer:
Publisher:
Key/Vignettes/Misc:
Locations:
Catalogs/Checklists: Stout, no. 308

3490
Place: Littlestown, Pennsylvania
Date: 1888
Title: Littlestown, Pennsylvania. 1888
Size: 17¾ × 21⅞ in. (45.2 × 55.7 cm.)
Artist: T. M. Fowler
Lithographer:
Printer:

Publisher: T. M. Fowler, Morrisville, Pa.
Key/Vignettes/Misc: Refs. 1–39; 6
vignettes
Locations: Adams County Historical
Society, Gettysburg, Pennsylvania
Catalogs/Checklists: Stout, no. 309

3491
Place: Lock Haven, Pennsylvania
Date: 1854
Title: A View of Lock Haven Clinton Co.
Pa. 1854. Looking East.
Size: 19¼ × 24 in. (49 × 61.1 cm.)
Artist: J. B. Bachelder
Lithographer:
Printer: Endicott & Co. N. Y.
Publisher:
Key/Vignettes/Misc:
Locations: HSP–P; YO; YUAG–NH
Catalogs/Checklists: Stout, no. 90; PP, no.
47

3492
Place: Lock Haven, Pennsylvania
Date: 1872
Title: Lock Haven, Pa. 1872.
Size: 15½ × 24 in. (39.5 × 61 cm.)
Artist: H. H. Bailey
Lithographer:
Printer: Strobridge & Co. Lith. Cincinnati
Ohio.
Publisher:
Key/Vignettes/Misc: Refs. 1–5, A–G
Locations: YO; Heisey Museum, Lock
Haven, Pennsylvania
Catalogs/Checklists: Stout, no. 91; PP

3493
Place: Lock Haven, Pennsylvania
Date: 1880
Title:
Size:
Artist:
Lithographer:
Printer:
Publisher:
Key/Vignettes/Misc:
Locations:
Catalogs/Checklists: Stout, no. 310

3494
Place: Lock Haven, Pennsylvania
Date: 1881
Title: Lock Haven, Pa. Viewed From the
Central State Normal School.
Size: 16½ × 24¾ in. (41.9 × 62.9 cm.)
Artist: C. L. Fussell
Lithographer:
Printer: W. Bracher Lithography,
Philadelphia
Publisher:
Key/Vignettes/Misc: 12 vignettes
Locations: YO
Catalogs/Checklists: PP

Place: Lockridge, Pennsylvania
Date: 1893
See Alburtis, Pennsylvania, 1893.

3495
Place: Macungie, Pennsylvania
Date: 1893
Title: Macungie, Lehigh County
Pennsylvania, 1893.

Size: 11⅜ × 20 in. (29 × 50.8 cm.)
Artist: T. M. Fowler
Lithographer:
Printer:
Publisher: T. M. Fowler & James B. Moyer
Key/Vignettes/Misc: Refs. 1–11, A–F
Locations: HSP–P; LC–M; PHMC–H;
PSU; YO
Catalogs/Checklists: Stout, no. 170;
LC–M, 801; PP

3496
Place: Mahanoy City, Pennsylvania
Date: 1889
Title: Mahanoy City, Pennsylvania. 1889
Size: 19½ × 28 in. (48.4 × 71.2 cm.)
Artist: T. M. Fowler
Lithographer:
Printer:
Publisher: T. M. Fowler & James B. Moyer
Key/Vignettes/Misc: Refs. 1–30; 11
vignettes
Locations: PHMC–H; LC–M
Catalogs/Checklists: Stout, no. 245;
LC–M, 801.1

3497
Place: Manayunk, Pennsylvania
Date: 1840
Title: Manayunk.
Size: 6⅛ × 6¾ in. (15.5 × 17.1 cm.)
Artist:
Lithographer:
Printer: J. T. Bowen
Publisher: J. T. Bowen Lithographic &
Print Coloring Establishment, Philadelphia
Key/Vignettes/Misc:
Locations: YO
Catalogs/Checklists: PP

3498
Place: Manayunk, Pennsylvania
Date: 1907
Title: Birds Eye View of Manayunk
Wissahickon–Roxboro From West Laurel
Cemetery Philadelphia, Pennsylvania 1907.
Size: 14½ × 28⅞ in. (36.9 × 73.4 cm.)
Artist: T. M. Fowler
Lithographer:
Printer:
Publisher: Fowler & Kelly, Morrisville, Pa.
Key/Vignettes/Misc:
Locations: LC–M
Catalogs/Checklists: Stout, no. 277;
LC–M, 802

3499
Place: Marysville, Pennsylvania
Date: 1904
Title: Marysville, Pennsylvania 1904
Size: 14 × 20 in. (35.6 × 50.8 cm.)
Artist: T. M. Fowler
Lithographer:
Printer:
Publisher: T. M. Fowler, Morrisville, Pa.
Key/Vignettes/Misc: Refs. 1–10; 12
vignettes
Locations: PHMC–H; LC–M (photo);
NYH–NY
Catalogs/Checklists: Stout, no. 226;
LC–M, 802.2

Place: Mauch Chunk, Pennsylvania
Date: 1858
See Jim Thorpe, Pennsylvania, 1858.

Place: Mauch Chunk, Pennsylvania
Date: N.D.
See Jim Thorpe, Pennsylvania, n.d.

3500
Place: Mcdonald, Pennsylvania
Date: 1897 State I
Title: McDonald, Washington County
Pennsylvania 1897.
Size: 13 × 22¾ in. (33.1 × 57.8 cm.)
Artist: T. M. Fowler
Lithographer:
Printer:
Publisher: T. M. Fowler & James B. Moyer
Key/Vignettes/Misc: Refs. 1–10, A–D
Locations: PSU
Catalogs/Checklists: Stout, no. 274a

3501
Place: Mcdonald, Pennsylvania
Date: 1897 State II
Title: McDonald, Washington County
Pennsylvania 1897.
Size: 12 × 22¾ in. (33.1 × 57.8 cm.)
Artist: T. M. Fowler
Lithographer:
Printer:
Publisher: T. M. Fowler & James B. Moyer
Key/Vignettes/Misc: Refs. 1–10, A–D
Locations: LC–M; PHMC–H; PSU;
LC–P
Catalogs/Checklists: Stout, no. 274b;
LC–M, 798

3502
Place: Mckees Rocks, Pennsylvania
Date: 1901
Title: McKee's Rocks, Allegheny County
Pennsylvania 1901.
Size: 18 × 25⅞ in. (45.7 × 65.7 cm.)
Artist: T. M. Fowler
Lithographer:
Printer:
Publisher: T. M. Fowler & James B. Moyer
Key/Vignettes/Misc: Refs. 1–19, A–H
Locations: CLP–P; HSP–P; LC–M;
PHMC–H; PSU; UPDL–P; YO; LC–P
Catalogs/Checklists: Stout, no. 9; LC–M,
800; PP

3503
Place: Mckeesport, Pennsylvania
Date: 1883
Title: Bird's Eye View of McKeesport, Pa.
1883.
Size: 15 × 21⅝ in. (38.2 × 55 cm.)
Artist: H. Wellge
Lithographer:
Printer: Beck & Pauli, Lithographers,
Milwaukee
Publisher: J. J. Stoner, Madison, Wis.
Key/Vignettes/Misc: Refs. A–H, J–L,
2–10, 12–21; unnumbered business
directory
Locations: YO
Catalogs/Checklists: PP, no. 75

3504
Place: Mckeesport, Pennsylvania
Date: 1893

Title: City of McKeesport & Vicinity
Size: 14¾ × 30⁹⁄₁₆ in. (37.5 × 77.8 cm.)
Artist: H. Morgenroth
Lithographer:
Printer: Otto Krebs Sons & Co., Pittsburgh, Pa.
Publisher: Otto Krebs Sons & Co., Pittsburgh, Pa.
Key/Vignettes/Misc: 13 unnumbered refs. in lower margin
Locations: LC–M; LC–P
Catalogs/Checklists: Stout, no. 10; LC–M, 799

3505
Place: Meadville, Pennsylvania
Date: 1870
Title:
Size:
Artist:
Lithographer:
Printer:
Publisher:
Key/Vignettes/Misc:
Locations:
Catalogs/Checklists: Stout, no. 311

3506
Place: Mechanicsburg, Pennsylvania
Date: 1903
Title: Mechanicsburg, Pa. 1903
Size: 14¼ × 20 in. (36.3 × 50.9 cm.)
Artist: T. M. Fowler
Lithographer:
Printer:
Publisher: T. M. Fowler
Key/Vignettes/Misc: Refs. 1–24, A–L; 13 vignettes
Locations: PHMC–H; LC–M; YO; NYH–NY
Catalogs/Checklists: Stout, no. 99; PP; LC–M, 802.3

Place: Mendelssohn, Pennsylvania
Date: 1902
See Wilson, Pennsylvania, 1902.

3507
Place: Meyersdale, Pennsylvania
Date: 1900
Title: Meyersdale, Pennsylvania 1900.
Size: 15¾ x 27¼ in. (40.1 × 69.4 cm.)
Artist: T. M. Fowler
Lithographer:
Printer:
Publisher: T. M. Fowler & James B. Moyer
Key/Vignettes/Misc: Refs. 1–14, A–I
Locations: PHMC–H; PSU; LC–M
Catalogs/Checklists: Stout, no. 253; LC–M, 802.5

3508
Place: Middletown, Pennsylvania
Date: 1894
Title: Middletown, Pennsylvania. 1894
Size: 16½ × 25⅝ in. (42 × 65.2 cm.)
Artist: T. M. Fowler
Lithographer:
Printer:
Publisher: T. M. Fowler & James B. Moyer
Key/Vignettes/Misc: Refs. 1–19, A–K
Locations: PHMC–H; LC–M (photo)
Catalogs/Checklists: Stout, no. 105; LC–M, 802.6

3509
Place: Mifflinburg, Pennsylvania
Date: 1884
Title: Mifflinburg, Union County, Pa. 1884.
Size: 15 × 22¼ in. (38.2 × 56.6 cm.)
Artist: [T. M. Fowler?]
Lithographer: O. H. Bailey & Co.
Printer: O. H. Bailey & Co., Boston
Publisher: O. H. Bailey & Co., Boston
Key/Vignettes/Misc: Refs. 1–12; 2 vignettes
Locations: BPL–R
Catalogs/Checklists: Stout, no. 262

3510
Place: Mifflintown, Pennsylvania
Date: 1895
Title: Mifflintown, Juniata County Pennsylvania. 1895.
Size: 8½ × 13¹⁄₁₆ in. (21.6 × 33.2 cm.)
Artist: T. M. Fowler
Lithographer:
Printer:
Publisher: T. M. Fowler & James B. Moyer
Key/Vignettes/Misc: Refs. 1–10, A–C
Locations: PHMC–H; LC–M; YO
Catalogs/Checklists: Stout, no. 142; PP; LC–M, 802.7

Place: Mill Creek, Pennsylvania
Date: 1892
See Miner's Mills, Pennsylvania, 1892.

3511
Place: Millersburg, Pennsylvania
Date: 1894
Title: Millersburg, Dauphin County Pennsylvania 1894.
Size: 12 × 20¾ in. (31 × 52.8 cm.)
Artist: T. M. Fowler
Lithographer:
Printer:
Publisher: T. M. Fowler & James B. Moyer
Key/Vignettes/Misc: Refs. 1–9, A–D
Locations: HSP–P; PHMC–H; PSU; LC–M
Catalogs/Checklists: Stout, no. 106; LC–M, 803

3512
Place: Millersville, Pennsylvania
Date: 1894
Title: Millersville, Lancaster County Pennsylvania. 1894.
Size: 14 × 26⅝ in. (35.6 × 65.2 cm.)
Artist: T. M. Fowler
Lithographer:
Printer:
Publisher: T. M. Fowler & James B. Moyer
Key/Vignettes/Misc: Refs. 1–9, A–E
Locations: LC–M; PHMC–H; PSU
Catalogs/Checklists: Stout, no. 156; LC–M, 803.1

3513
Place: Milton, Pennsylvania
Date: 1883
Title: Milton, Pa. 1883.
Size: 19¼ × 26⅞ in. (49 × 68.4 cm.)
Artist: [T. M. Fowler]
Lithographer: O. H. Bailey & Co.
Printer: O. H. Bailey & Co., Boston

Publisher: O. H. Bailey & Co., Boston
Key/Vignettes/Misc: Refs. 1–37; 12 vignettes
Locations: BPL–R; YO
Catalogs/Checklists: Stout, no. 221; PP

3514
Place: Miner's Mills, Pennsylvania
Date: 1892
Title: Miner's Mills, and Mill Creek
Size: 14 × 21⅝ in. (35.6 × 55 cm.)
Artist: T. M. Fowler
Lithographer:
Printer:
Publisher: T. M. Fowler & James B. Moyer
Key/Vignettes/Misc: Refs. 1–7
Locations: LC–M; PHMC–H; PSU
Catalogs/Checklists: Stout, no. 176; LC–M, 804

3515
Place: Minersville, Pennsylvania
Date: 1889
Title: Minersville, Pennsylvania. 1889.
Size: 17 × 25½ in. (43.3 × 64.9 cm.)
Artist: T. M. Fowler
Lithographer:
Printer:
Publisher:
Key/Vignettes/Misc: Refs. 1–19; 5 vignettes
Locations: LC–M; PHMC–H; PSU; YO
Catalogs/Checklists: Stout, no. 246; LC–M, 805; PP

3516
Place: Mohrsville, Pennsylvania
Date: 1898
Title: Mohnsville, Pennsylvania 1898
Size: 15¾ × 26½ in. (40.1 × 64.8 cm.)
Artist:
Lithographer:
Printer:
Publisher: Bailey & Moyer, Boston, Mass.
Key/Vignettes/Misc: Refs. A, 2–21; 27 vignettes
Locations: LC–M; PHMC–H; PSU; YO
Catalogs/Checklists: Stout, no. 43; PP; LC–M, 805.1

3517
Place: Monaca, Pennsylvania
Date: 1900
Title: Monaca, Pennsylvania. 1900.
Size: 12½ × 20½ in. (31.7 × 52 cm.)
Artist: T. M. Fowler
Lithographer:
Printer:
Publisher: T. M. Fowler & James B. Moyer
Key/Vignettes/Misc: Refs. 1–12, A–E
Locations: CLP–P; HSP–P; LC–M; PHMC–H; PSU; UPDL–P; YO
Catalogs/Checklists: Stout, no. 29; LC–M, 806; PP

3518
Place: Monessen, Pennsylvania
Date: 1900
Title: Monessen, Pennsylvania 1900.
Size: 13 × 24 in. (33 × 61 cm.)
Artist: T. M. Fowler
Lithographer:
Printer:

Publisher: T. M. Fowler & James B. Moyer
Key/Vignettes/Misc: Refs. 1–17
Locations: PSU; UPDL–P
Catalogs/Checklists: Stout, no. 285

3519
Place: Monessen, Pennsylvania
Date: 1904
Title: Monessen, Pennsylvania. 1904.
Size: 16¾ × 26⅛ in. (42.6 × 66.5 cm.)
Artist: T. M. Fowler
Lithographer:
Printer:
Publisher: T. M. Fowler, Morrisville, Pa.
Key/Vignettes/Misc: Refs. 1–27; 5
vignettes
Locations: NYH–NY
Catalogs/Checklists:

3520
Place: Monongahela, Pennsylvania
Date: 1902
Title: Monongahela City, Pennsylvania.
1902.
Size: 12⅝ × 27½ in. (32.1 × 69.9 cm.)
Artist: T. M. Fowler
Lithographer:
Printer:
Publisher: T. M. Fowler & James B. Moyer
Key/Vignettes/Misc: Refs. 1–24, A–H
Locations: CLP–P; HSP–P; LC–M;
PHMC–H; PSU; UPDL–P; YO
Catalogs/Checklists: Stout, no. 275;
LC–M, 807; PP

3521
Place: Montrose, Pennsylvania
Date: 1890
Title: Montrose, Susquehanna County Pa.
1890
Size: 16¼ × 25¾ in. (41.4 × 65.5 cm.)
Artist: T. M. Fowler
Lithographer:
Printer: A. E. Downs, Lith. Boston
Publisher: T. M. Fowler & James B. Moyer
Key/Vignettes/Misc: Refs. 1–10, A–H
Locations: PHMC–H; UPDL–P; LC–M
Catalogs/Checklists: Stout, no. 260;
LC–M, 807.1

3522
Place: Moosic, Pennsylvania
Date: 1892
Title: Moosic, Pennsylvania 1892.
Size: 13⅞ × 22 in. (35.4 × 55.9 cm.)
Artist: T. M. Fowler
Lithographer:
Printer: A. E. Downs Lith. Boston
Publisher: T. M Fowler
Key/Vignettes/Misc: Refs. 1–9
Locations: LC–M
Catalogs/Checklists: Stout, no. 148;
LC–M, 808

3523
Place: Morrisville, Pennsylvania
Date: 1893
Title: Morrisville Bucks County.
Pennsylvania. 1893.
Size: 20 × 31⅛ in. (51.4 × 79.2 cm.)
Artist: T. M. Fowler
Lithographer:
Printer:

Publisher: T. M. Fowler, Morrisville, Pa.
Key/Vignettes/Misc: Refs. 1–17; 13
vignettes
Locations: LC–M
Catalogs/Checklists: Stout, no. 60;
LC–M, 809

3524
Place: Morrisville Island, Pennsylvania
Date: [1900]
Title: Properties of the Delaware River
Improvement Company on Morrisville
Island, Pa. Opposite Trenton, N. J.
Size: 15⁵⁄₁₆ × 22¾ in. (39 × 68 cm.)
Artist: T. M. Fowler
Lithographer:
Printer: O. H. Bailey & Co.
Publisher:
Key/Vignettes/Misc:
Locations: LC–M
Catalogs/Checklists: LC–M, 809.3

3525
Place: Moscow, Pennsylania
Date: 1891
Title: Moscow, Lackawanna County
Penn'a. 1891.
Size: 13⅜ × 20⅜ in. (34 × 51.8 cm.)
Artist: T. M. Fowler
Lithographer:
Printer:
Publisher:
Key/Vignettes/Misc: Refs. 1–14, A–T
Locations: LC–M; PSU; YO
Catalogs/Checklists: Stout, no. 149;
LC–M, 810; PP

3526
Place: Mount Carbon, Pennsylvania
Date: 1833
Title: View of Mount Carbon Taken from
Second Mountain. . . .
Size: 14 × 18½ in. (35.6 × 47 cm.)
Artist: J. R. Smith, Jun. and J. R. Smith,
Sen.
Lithographer:
Printer:
Publisher: J. R. Smith, Phil.
Key/Vignettes/Misc:
Locations: RU–NB
Catalogs/Checklists:

3527
Place: Mount Carmel, Pennsylvania
Date: 1884
Title: Mt. Carmel, Pennsylvania. 1884.
Size: 18½ × 20 in. (47 × 51 cm.)
Artist: [T. M. Fowler?]
Lithographer:
Printer:
Publisher: [O. H. Bailey & Co.]
Key/Vignettes/Misc: Refs. 1–23; 10
vignettes
Locations: BPL–R
Catalogs/Checklists: Stout, no. 93

3528
Place: Mount Holly Springs, Pennsylvania
Date: 1903
Title: View of Mt. Holly Springs,
Pennsylvania. 1903.
Size: 12¹⁵⁄₁₆ × 26⁷⁄₁₆ in. (32.8 × 67.3 cm.)
Artist: T. M. Fowler

Lithographer:
Printer:
Publisher: T. M. Fowler, Morrisville, Pa.
Key/Vignettes/Misc: Refs. 1–14; 17
vignettes
Locations: YO; NYH–NY
Catalogs/Checklists: PP

3529
Place: Mount Joy, Pennsylvania
Date: 1894
Title: Mount Joy, Lancaster County
Pennsylvania. 1894.
Size: 12¾ × 23⅝ in. (32.4 × 60.1 cm.)
Artist: T. M. Fowler
Lithographer:
Printer:
Publisher: T. M. Fowler & James B. Moyer
Key/Vignettes/Misc: Refs. 1–21, A–H
Locations: LC–M; PHMC–H; PSU; YO
Catalogs/Checklists: Stout, no. 157; PP;
LC–M, 810.1

3530
Place: Mount Pleasant, Pennsylvania
Date: 1900
Title: Mount Pleasant, Pennsylvania 1900.
Size: 16 × 31⅝ in. (40.3 × 80.4 cm.)
Artist: T. M. Fowler
Lithographer:
Printer:
Publisher: T. M. Fowler & James B. Moyer
Key/Vignettes/Misc: Refs. 1–18, A–L
Locations: PHMC–H; PSU; UPDL–P;
LC–M
Catalogs/Checklists: Stout, no. 286;
LC–M, 810.2

3531
Place: Mount Union, Pennsylvania
Date: 1906
Title: Mount Union Huntington Co., Pa.
1906
Size: 18 × 23 in. (45.8 × 58.5 cm.)
Artist: T. M. Fowler
Lithographer:
Printer:
Publisher: Fowler & Kelly, Morrisville, Pa.
Key/Vignettes/Misc: 10 vignettes
Locations: LC–M
Catalogs/Checklists: Stout, no. 136;
LC–M, 811

3532
Place: Mountville, Pennsylvania
Date: 1894
Title: Mountville, Lancaster Co.,
Pennsylvania. 1894.
Size: 9 × 14 in. (22.9 × 35.6 cm.)
Artist: T. M. Fowler
Lithographer:
Printer:
Publisher: T. M. Fowler & James B. Moyer
Key/Vignettes/Misc: Refs. 1–15
Locations: LC–M; PHMC–H
Catalogs/Checklists: Stout, no. 158;
LC–M, 812

3533
Place: Muncy, Pennsylvania
Date: 1883
Title: Muncy. Pennsylvania 1883.
Size: 17 × 24 in. (43.3 × 61.1 cm.)

Artist: O. H. Bailey & Co.
Lithographer:
Printer: O. H. Bailey & Co., Boston
Publisher: O. H. Bailey & Co., Boston
Key/Vignettes/Misc: Refs. 1–22; 4
vignettes
Locations: BPL–R; YO
Catalogs/Checklists: Stout, no. 184; PP

3534
Place: Myerstown, Pennsylvania
Date: 1888
Title: Myerstown, Pa. 1888.
Size: 22 × 25¹¹⁄₁₆ in. (56 × 65.4 cm.)
Artist: T. M. Fowler
Lithographer:
Printer:
Publisher: T. M. Fowler, Morrisville, Pa.
Key/Vignettes/Misc: Refs. 1–28; 12
vignettes
Locations: LCHS–L
Catalogs/Checklists:

3535
Place: Nazareth, Pennsylvania
Date: 1885
Title: Nazareth. Pennsylvania. 1885.
Size: 19⅛ × 21⅛ in. (48.2 × 53.8 cm.)
Artist: [T. M. Fowler?]
Lithographer:
Printer: O. H. Bailey & Co., Boston
Publisher: O. H. Bailey & Co., Boston
Key/Vignettes/Misc: Refs. 1–22; 11
vignettes
Locations: BPL–R
Catalogs/Checklists: Stout, no. 216

3536
Place: New Berlin, Pennsylvania
Date: 1847
Title: New Berlin, Union Co.
Size: 4 × 6½ in. (10.2 × 16.5 cm.)
Artist:
Lithographer:
Printer: T. Sinclair
Publisher:
Key/Vignettes/Misc:
Locations: YO
Catalogs/Checklists: PP

3537
Place: New Bloomfield, Pennsylvania
Date: 1903
Title: New Bloomfield, Perry Co. Pa 1903.
Size: 13⁹⁄₁₆ × 17¹⁵⁄₁₆ in. (34.5 × 45.6 cm.)
Artist: T. M. Fowler
Lithographer:
Printer:
Publisher: T. M. Fowler, Morrisville, Pa.
Key/Vignettes/Misc: Refs. 1–13; 12
vignettes
Locations: NYH–NY
Catalogs/Checklists:

Place: New Brighton, Pennsylvania
Date: 1842
See Beaver, Pennsylvania, 1842.

3538
Place: New Brighton, Pennsylvania
Date: Ca. 1850
Title: New Brighton.
Size: 18⅜ × 26 in. (46.8 × 66.2 cm.)

Artist: Rudolph Leonhart
Lithographer:
Printer: Wm. Schuchman lith. Pittsburgh,
Pa.
Publisher:
Key/Vignettes/Misc:
Locations: YO
Catalogs/Checklists: PP, no. 39

3539
Place: New Brighton, Pennsylvania
Date: 1883
Title: New Brighton, Pa. 1883
Size: 18 × 28 in. (45.7 × 71.1 cm.)
Artist: C. L. Fussell
Lithographer:
Printer:
Publisher: Philadelphia Publishing House
Key/Vignettes/Misc: Refs. 1–34; 13
vignettes
Locations: LC–M
Catalogs/Checklists: Stout, no. 30;
LC–M, 812.1

3540
Place: New Brighton, Pennsylvania
Date: 1901
Title: New Brighton, Pennsylvania 1901
Size: 15 × 28⅝ in. (38.1 × 72.7 cm.)
Artist: T. M. Fowler
Lithographer:
Printer:
Publisher: T. M. Fowler & James B. Moyer
Key/Vignettes/Misc: Refs. 1–15, A–M
Locations: LC–M; PHMC–H; PSU; YO
Catalogs/Checklists: Stout, no. 31;
LC–M, 813; PP

3541
Place: New Castle, Pennsylvania
Date: 1896
Title: New Castle, Pennsylvania 1896.
Size: 20⅞ × 37³⁄₁₆ in. (53.2 × 94.6 cm.)
Artist: T. M. Fowler
Lithographer:
Printer:
Publisher: T. M. Fowler & James B. Moyer
Key/Vignettes/Misc: Refs. 1–34, A–R
Locations: CLP–P; LC–M; PHMC–H;
PSU; UPDL–P; YO; LC–P
Catalogs/Checklists: Stout, no. 162;
LC–M, 814; PP

3542
Place: New Kensington, Pennsylvania
Date: 1896
Title: New Kensington, Westmoreland
County, Pennsylvania, 1896.
Size: 19⅛ × 27⅜ in. (48.7 × 69.7 cm.)
Artist: T. M. Fowler
Lithographer:
Printer:
Publisher: T. M. Fowler & James B. Moyer
Key/Vignettes/Misc: Refs. 1–20, A–F
Locations: LC–M; LC–P
Catalogs/Checklists: Stout, no. 287;
LC–M, 815

3543
Place: New Kensington, Pennsylvania
Date: 1902 State I
Title: New Kensington, Pennsylvania,
1902.

Size: 10 × 20 in. (25.4 × 50.8 cm.)
Artist: T. M. Fowler
Lithographer:
Printer:
Publisher: T. M. Fowler & James B. Moyer
Key/Vignettes/Misc: Refs. 1–19, A–N
Locations: CLP–P
Catalogs/Checklists: Stout, no. 288a;
LC–M, 816

3544
Place: New Kensington, Pennsylvania
Date: 1902 State II
Title: New Kensington, Pennsylvania,
1902.
Size: 10 × 20 in. (25.4 × 50.8 cm.)
Artist: T. M. Fowler
Lithographer:
Printer:
Publisher: T. M. Fowler & James B. Moyer
Key/Vignettes/Misc: Refs. 1–19, A–N
Locations: LC–M; PHMC–H; PSU;
UPDL–P
Catalogs/Checklists: Stout, no. 288b;
LC–M, 816

3545
Place: Newmanstown, Pennsylvania
Date: 1898
Title: Newmanstown and Sheridan,
Pennsylvania.
Size: 10 × 19¼ in. (25.4 × 49 cm.)
Artist:
Lithographer:
Printer:
Publisher: Bailey & Moyer Publishers,
Boston
Key/Vignettes/Misc:
Locations: LC–M; PHMC–H; PSU;
UPDL–P; YO
Catalogs/Checklists: Stout, no. 164;
LC–M, 817; PP

3546
Place: Newtown, Pennsylvania
Date: 1893
Title: Newtown, Bucks County,
Pennsylvania.
Size: 21¼ × 32¼ in. (54 × 82 cm.)
Artist: T. M. Fowler
Lithographer:
Printer:
Publisher:
Key/Vignettes/Misc: Refs. 1–28; 10
vignettes
Locations: LC–M
Catalogs/Checklists: Stout, no. 312;
LC–M, 817.2

3547
Place: Newville, Pennsylvania
Date: 1903
Title: View of Newville, Cumberland Co.
Pennsylvania 1903
Size: 15¼ × 20 in. (38.9 × 50.8 cm.)
Artist: T. M. Fowler
Lithographer:
Printer:
Publisher: T. M. Fowler, Morrisville, Pa.
Key/Vignettes/Misc: Refs. 1–12; 9
vignettes
Locations: LC–M; NYH–NY

Catalogs/Checklists: Stout, no. 100; LC–M, 818

3548
Place: Nicholson, Pennsylvania
Date: 1891
Title: Nicholson, Wyoming County Pennsylvania 1891.
Size: 13¼ × 23½ in. (33.7 × 59.8 cm.)
Artist: T. M. Fowler
Lithographer:
Printer:
Publisher: T. M. Fowler & James B. Moyer
Key/Vignettes/Misc: Refs. 1–8, A–D
Locations: PHMC–H; LC–M (photo)
Catalogs/Checklists: Stout, no. 293; LC–M, 818.1

3549
Place: Norristown, Pennsylvania
Date: [1869–74]
Title: Norristown, Pa.
Size: 20½ × 31⅝ in. (52.2 × 80.5 cm.)
Artist:
Lithographer:
Printer: Duval & Hunter, Phila.
Publisher: Richter & Koehler, Phila.
Key/Vignettes/Misc:
Locations: HSP–P
Catalogs/Checklists: Stout, no. 200

3550
Place: Norristown, Pennsylvania
Date: 1881
Title: Norristown, Penna.
Size: 19¼ × 32⅝ in. (49 × 83 cm.)
Artist:
Lithographer:
Printer:
Publisher: Packard & Butler, Phila.
Key/Vignettes/Misc: 15 vignettes
Locations: LC–M; BPL–R
Catalogs/Checklists: Stout, no. 201b; LC–M, 819

3551
Place: North East, Pennsylvania
Date: 1896
Title: North East, Erie County Pennsylvania. 1896.
Size: 16½ × 27¾ in. (42 × 71 cm.)
Artist: T. M. Fowler
Lithographer:
Printer:
Publisher: T. M. Fowler & James B. Moyer
Key/Vignettes/Misc: Refs. 1–18, A–G
Locations: HSP–P; LC–M; PHMC–H; PSU; UPDL–P
Catalogs/Checklists: Stout, no. 188; LC–M, 820

3552
Place: Northumberland, Pennsylvania
Date: [1853]
Title: Northumberland Northumberland County Pa. Shewing the Junctions of the North and West Branches of the Susquehanna.
Size: 15 × 18¾ in. (38.2 × 47.7 cm.)
Artist: R. B. McKay
Lithographer: James I. Glasgow
Printer: Endicott & Co., N. Y.
Publisher: James Taggart & Son, Northumberland, Pa.
Key/Vignettes/Misc:
Locations: YO
Catalogs/Checklists: PP, no. 44; McClintock, no. 50

Place: Oakmont, Pennsylvania
Date: 1896
See Verona, Pennsylvania, 1896.

3553
Place: Oil City, Pennsylvania
Date: 1896
Title: Oil City, Pennsylvania 1896.
Size: 21¹⁄₁₆ × 32¹⁄₁₆ in. (53.6 × 81.6 cm.)
Artist: T. M. Fowler
Lithographer:
Printer:
Publisher: T. M. Fowler & James B. Moyer
Key/Vignettes/Misc: Refs. 1–25, A–L
Locations: CLP–P; LC–M; PHMC–H; PSU; UPDL–P; YO; LC–P
Catalogs/Checklists: Stout, no. 265; LC–M, 821; PP

3554
Place: Orbisonia, Pennsylvania
Date: 1906
Title: Bird's Eye View of Orbisonia and Rock Hill 1906
Size: 13⅜ × 19⅞ in. (34 × 50.5 cm.)
Artist: [T. M. Fowler]
Lithographer:
Printer:
Publisher: Fowler & Kelly, Morrisville, Pa. (copyright)
Key/Vignettes/Misc: 8 vignettes
Locations: LC–M; YO
Catalogs/Checklists: Stout, no. 137; LC–M, 822; PP

3555
Place: Oxford, Pennsylvania
Date: 1907
Title: Bird's Eye View of Oxford Chester Co., Pennsylvania
Size: 18¼ × 22⅞ in. (45 × 58.2 cm.)
Artist: [T. M. Fowler]
Lithographer:
Printer:
Publisher: Fowler & Kelly, Morrisville, Pa.
Key/Vignettes/Misc: 16 vignettes
Locations: LC–M
Catalogs/Checklists: Stout, no. 79; LC–M, 823

3556
Place: Patterson, Pennsylvania
Date: 1895
Title: Patterson, Juniata County Pennsylvania. 1895.
Size: 8½ × 13½ in. (21.6 × 34.3 cm.)
Artist: T. M. Fowler
Lithographer:
Printer:
Publisher: T. M. Fowler & James B. Moyer
Key/Vignettes/Misc: Refs. 1–6, A
Locations: PHMC–H; LC–M; YO
Catalogs/Checklists: Stout, no. 143; PP; LC–M, 823.1

3557
Place: Patton, Pennsylvania
Date: 1900
Title: Patton, Cambria County Pennsylvania. 1900.
Size: 11⅛ × 24¼ in. (28.3 × 61.6 cm.)
Artist: T. M. Fowler
Lithographer:
Printer:
Publisher: T. M. Fowler & James B. Moyer
Key/Vignettes/Misc: Refs. 1–10, A–E
Locations: PHMC–H; PSU; YO; LC–M (photo)
Catalogs/Checklists: Stout, no. 72; PP; LC–M, 823.2

3558
Place: Peckville, Pennsylvania
Date: 1892
Title: Peckville, Lackawanna County Pa. 1892.
Size: 15 × 25 in. (38.1 × 63.5 cm.)
Artist: T. M. Fowler
Lithographer:
Printer: A. E. Downs Lith. Boston.
Publisher: T. M. Fowler & James B. Moyer
Key/Vignettes/Misc: Refs. 1–10
Locations: LC–M; PHMC–H; PSU
Catalogs/Checklists: Stout, no. 150; LC–M, 824

3559
Place: Pen Argyl, Pennsylvania
Date: 1885
Title: Pen Argyl, Pennsylvania. 1885.
Size: 15½ × 24⅞ in. (39.5 × 63.3 cm.)
Artist: [T. M. Fowler?]
Lithographer:
Printer: O. H. Bailey & Co., Boston
Publisher: O. H. Bailey & Co., Boston
Key/Vignettes/Misc: Refs. 1–40, A–O
Locations: BPL–R
Catalogs/Checklists: Stout, no. 217

3560
Place: Pen Argyl, Pennsylvania
Date: 1894
Title: Pen Argyl, Pennsylvania 1894.
Size: 15⅝ × 26⅝ in. (39.8 × 67.7 cm.)
Artist: T. M. Fowler
Lithographer:
Printer:
Publisher: T. M. Fowler & James B. Moyer
Key/Vignettes/Misc: Refs. 1–11, A–E
Locations: LC–M; PHMC–H; PSU; YO
Catalogs/Checklists: Stout, no. 218; LC–M, 825; PP

3561
Place: Pen Argyl, Pennsylvania
Date: 1916
Title: Aero View of Pen Argyl Pennsylvania 1916
Size: 17 × 34 in. (43.3 × 86.6 cm.)
Artist: T. M. Fowler
Lithographer:
Printer: [Meriden Gravure Co., Meriden, Conn. & Tudor Press, Boston]
Publisher: Hughes & Bailey
Key/Vignettes/Misc: 15 vignettes; unnumbered directory
Locations: LC–M; PSU

Catalogs/Checklists: Stout, no. 219;
LC–M, 826

3562
Place: Pennsburg, Pennsylvania
Date: 1894
Title: Pennsburgh, Montgomery County Pennsylvania 1894.
Size: 10½ × 20⅛ in. (26.2 × 51.2 cm.)
Artist: T. M. Fowler
Lithographer:
Printer:
Publisher: T. M. Fowler & James B. Moyer
Key/Vignettes/Misc: Refs. 1–9; 1 vignette
Locations: LC–M; PSU; YO
Catalogs/Checklists: Stout, no. 202; PP; LC–M, 826.1

3563
Place: Perkasie, Pennsylvania
Date: 1894
Title: Perkasie, Pennsylvania Bucks County. 1894.
Size: 15¾ × 22¼ in. (40.1 × 56.6 cm.)
Artist: T. M. Fowler
Lithographer:
Printer:
Publisher: T. M. Fowler & James B. Moyer
Key/Vignettes/Misc: Refs. 1–25, A–J; 1 vignette
Locations: LC–M; PHMC–H; PSU; YO
Catalogs/Checklists: Stout, no. 61; PP; LC–M, 826.2

3564
Place: Perryopolis, Pennsylvania
Date: 1904
Title: View of Perryopolis, Fayette County, Pennsylvania. 1904.
Size: 12¹⁄₁₆ × 17 in. (30.7 × 43.3 cm.)
Artist: T. M. Fowler
Lithographer:
Printer:
Publisher: T. M. Fowler, Morrisville, Pa.
Key/Vignettes/Misc: 9 vignettes
Locations: NYH–NY
Catalogs/Checklists:

3565
Place: Philadelphia, Pennsylvania
Date: 1838 State I
Title: Panorama of Philadelphia from the State House Steeple. East.
Size: 8½ × 12⅝ in. (21.6 × 32.2 cm.)
Artist: J. C. Wild
Lithographer:
Printer: Wild & Chevalier
Publisher: Wild & Chevalier
Key/Vignettes/Misc:
Locations: HSP–P; FL–P; CHS–C
Catalogs/Checklists: Wainwright, no. 264

3566
Place: Philadelphia, Pennsylvania
Date: 1838 State I
Title: Panorama of Philadelphia from the State House Steeple. North.
Size: 8⅜ × 12⅝ in. (21.3 × 32.2 cm.)
Artist: J. C. Wild
Lithographer:
Printer: Wild & Chevalier
Publisher: Wild & Chevalier

Key/Vignettes/Misc:
Locations: HSP–P; FL–P
Catalogs/Checklists: Wainwright, no. 265

3567
Place: Philadelphia, Pennsylvania
Date: 1838 State I
Title: Panorama of Philadelphia from the State House Steeple. South.
Size: 8⅜ × 12⅜ in. (21.3 × 31.5 cm.)
Artist: J. C. Wild
Lithographer:
Printer: Wild & Chevalier
Publisher: Wild & Chevalier
Key/Vignettes/Misc:
Locations: HSP–P; FL–P; CHS–C
Catalogs/Checklists: Wainwright, no. 266

3568
Place: Philadelphia, Pennsylvania
Date: 1838 State I
Title: Panorama of Philadelphia from the State House Steeple. West.
Size: 8⅜ × 12⅜ in. (21.3 × 31.5 cm.)
Artist: J. C. Wild
Lithographer:
Printer: Wild & Chevalier
Publisher: Wild & Chevalier
Key/Vignettes/Misc:
Locations: HSP–P; FL–P
Catalogs/Checklists: Wainwright, no. 267

3569
Place: Philadelphia, Pennsylvania
Date: 1838 State II
Title: Panorama of Philadelphia from the State House Steeple. East.
Size: 8½ × 12⅝ in. (21.6 × 32.2 cm.)
Artist: J. C. Wild
Lithographer:
Printer:
Publisher: J. T. Bowen (copyright)
Key/Vignettes/Misc: Refs. 1–11
Locations: HSP–P; NYH–NY
Catalogs/Checklists: Wainwright, no. 264

3570
Place: Philadelphia, Pennsylvania
Date: 1838 State II
Title: Panorama of Philadelphia from the State House Steeple. North.
Size: 8⅜ × 12⅝ in. (21.3 × 32.2 cm.)
Artist: J. C. Wild
Lithographer:
Printer:
Publisher: J. T. Bowen (copyright)
Key/Vignettes/Misc: Refs. 1–5
Locations: HSP–P; NYH–NY
Catalogs/Checklists: Wainwright, no. 265

3571
Place: Philadelphia, Pennsylvania
Date: 1838 State II
Title: Panorama of Philadelphia from the State House Steeple. South.
Size: 8⅜ × 12⅜ in. (21.3 × 31.5 cm.)
Artist: J. C. Wild
Lithographer:
Printer:
Publisher: J. T. Bowen (copyright)
Key/Vignettes/Misc: Refs. 1–7
Locations: HSP–P; NYH–NY
Catalogs/Checklists: Wainwright, no. 266

3572
Place: Philadelphia, Pennsylvania
Date: 1838 State II
Title: Panorama of Philadelphia from the State House Steeple. West.
Size: 8⅜ × 12⅜ in. (21.3 × 31.5 cm.)
Artist: J. C. Wild
Lithographer:
Printer:
Publisher: J. T. Bowen (copyright)
Key/Vignettes/Misc: Refs. 1–15
Locations: HSP–P; NYH–NY
Catalogs/Checklists: Wainwright, no. 267

3573
Place: Philadelphia, Pennsylvania
Date: 1842
Title: View of the City of Philadelphia, And its Principal Buildings.
Size: 11⅜ × 17 in. (29 × 43.3 cm.)
Artist: A. Koellner
Lithographer:
Printer: F. Kuhl
Publisher: F. Kuhl
Key/Vignettes/Misc: 10 vignettes
Locations: First Pennsylvania Banking & Trust Co., Philadelphia
Catalogs/Checklists: Wainwright, no. 425

3574
Place: Philadelphia, Pennsylvania
Date: 1848
Title: S. E. View of Philadelphia
Size: 7⅜ × 10¹⁵⁄₁₆ in. (18.7 × 27.9 cm.)
Artist: Aug. Kollner
Lithographer: Deroy
Printer: Cattier
Publisher: Goupil, Vibert & Co., New York & Paris
Key/Vignettes/Misc:
Locations: EI–S; YUAG–NH; LC–P
Catalogs/Checklists:

3575
Place: Philadelphia, Pennsylvania
Date: 1849
Title: Philadelphia, From the State House Steeple, North, East and South.
Size: 18 × 35¼ in. (45.8 × 89.7 cm.)
Artist: Joseph Thoma
Lithographer: Leo Elliot
Printer: T. Sinclair's Litho. Establishmt. [Philadelphia]
Publisher: J. C. Sidney, No. 80, Walnut Street, Philada.
Key/Vignettes/Misc:
Locations: Library Company of Philadelphia, Philadelphia, Pennsylvania
Catalogs/Checklists:

3576
Place: Philadelphia, Pennsylvania
Date: 1850
Title: Birds Eye View of Philadelphia
Size: 20½ × 27⅞ in. (52.2 × 70.9 cm.)
Artist: J. Bachman
Lithographer: J. Bachman
Printer: Sarony & Major, 117 Fulton St., New York
Publisher: Williams & Stevens, 353 Broadway, N. Y.
Key/Vignettes/Misc:

Locations: CHS–C; PHMC–H; YO;
NYH–NY
Catalogs/Checklists: Stout, no. 228a; PP

3577

Place: Philadelphia, Pennsylvania
Date: 1850
Title: Birds Eye View of Philadelphia
Size: 20⅞ × 27½ in. (53.1 × 70 cm.)
Artist: J. Bachman
Lithographer: J. Bachman
Printer: Sarony & Major, 117 Fulton St.,
N. Y.
Publisher: John Bachmann, 116 Greenwich
St. New York.
Key/Vignettes/Misc:
Locations: NYH–NY
Catalogs/Checklists:

3578

Place: Philadelphia, Pennsylvania
Date: 1850
Title: Philadelphia. From Camden–1850
Size: 27¼ × 41 in. (69.4 × 104.2 cm.)
Artist: J. W. Hill and Smith
Lithographer: B. F. Smith, Jr.
Printer: Sarony, N. Y.
Publisher: Smith Brothers & Co.
Key/Vignettes/Misc:
Locations: HSP–P; MM–NN; YO;
NYH–NY
Catalogs/Checklists: MM–NN, LP 243;
Stout, no. 229; PP, no. 40

3579

Place: Philadelphia, Pennsylvania
Date: 1850
Title: Philadelphia, From Girard College—
1850
Size: 26¼ × 40¾ in. (66.7 × 103.6 cm.)
Artist: J. W. Hill & Smith
Lithographer: B. F. Smith Jr.
Printer: F. Michelin [New York]
Publisher: Francis Smith (copyright)
Key/Vignettes/Misc:
Locations: Library Company of
Philadelphia, Philadelphia, Pennsylvania;
CHS–C; LC–P
Catalogs/Checklists:

3580

Place: Philadelphia, Pennsylvania
Date: [1850]
Title: Panoramic Views of Philadelphia
From the State House. East View Looking
Down Chestnut St. Across the Delaware—
Camden, N. J. in the Distance.
Size: 10½ × 19 in. (26.7 × 48.3cm.)
Artist: E. Whitefield
Lithographer:
Printer: Wm. Endicott & Co., N. Y.
Publisher:
Key/Vignettes/Misc:
Locations: LC–P; FL–P
Catalogs/Checklists: Norton, Whitefield,
no. 47

3581

Place: Philadelphia, Pennsylvania
Date: [1850]
Title: Panoramic Views of Philadelphia
From the State House. North View
Looking Across Chestnut St. Towards

Spring Garden, Northern Liberties, and
Kensington.
Size: 10½ × 19 in. (26.7 × 48.3 cm.)
Artist: E. Whitefield
Lithographer:
Printer: Wm. Endicott & Co., N. Y.
Publisher:
Key/Vignettes/Misc:
Locations: LC–P; FL–P
Catalogs/Checklists: Norton, Whitefield,
no. 47

3582

Place: Philadelphia, Pennsylvania
Date: [1850]
Title: Panoramic Views of Philadelphia
From the State House. South View
Looking Towards Navy Yard, Southwark
and Moyamensing.
Size: 10½ × 19 in. (26.7 × 48.3 cm.)
Artist: E. Whitefield
Lithographer:
Printer: Wm. Endicott & Co., N. Y.
Publisher:
Key/Vignettes/Misc:
Locations: LC–P; FL–P
Catalogs/Checklists: Norton, Whitefield,
no. 47

3583

Place: Philadelphia, Pennsylvania
Date: [1850]
Title: Panoramic Views of Philadelphia
From the State House. West View Looking
up Chestnut St. Towards West
Philadelphia.
Size: 10½ × 19 in. (26.7 × 48.3 cm.)
Artist: E. Whitefield
Lithographer:
Printer: Wm. Endicott & Co., N. Y.
Publisher:
Key/Vignettes/Misc:
Locations: LC–P; FL–P
Catalogs/Checklists: Norton, Whitefield,
no. 47

3584

Place: Philadelphia, Pennsylvania
Date: Ca. 1850
Title: Bird's Eye View of Philadelphia
Size: 20¹³⁄₁₆ × 27 in. (53 × 68.7 cm.)
Artist:
Lithographer: G. Matter
Printer: R. Furrer
Publisher: J. U. Locher, St. Gall,
Switzerland & J. H. Locher 117 Fulton St.
New York
Key/Vignettes/Misc:
Locations: YUAG–NH
Catalogs/Checklists:

3585

Place: Philadelphia, Pennsylvania
Date: Ca. 1850
Title: Bird's Eye View of Philadelphia.
Size: 18¾ × 27 in. (47.7 × 68.6 cm.)
Artist:
Lithographer: G. Matter
Printer: I Schaerer
Publisher: J. U. Locher, Switzerland & J.
H. Locher, N. Y.
Key/Vignettes/Misc:

Locations: MM–NN; ACMW–FW;
HSP–P
Catalogs/Checklists: Stout, no. 228b;
MM–NN, LP 38; ACMW–FW 1416

3586

Place: Philadelphia, Pennsylvania
Date: Ca. 1855
Title: Philadelphia
Size: 15¼ × 22¾ in. (38.8 × 57.8 cm.)
Artist:
Lithographer: Asselineau
Printer: Lemercier, Paris
Publisher:
Key/Vignettes/Misc:
Locations: MM–NN; YUAG–NH;
LC–M (facsimile); NYH–NY
Catalogs/Checklists: MM–NN, LP 1184;
Stout, no. 231b; LC–M, 826.6

3587

Place: Philadelphia, Pennsylvania
Date: 1856
Title: East View of Philadelphia,
Pennsylva. and Part of Camden New
Jersey.
Size: 17 × 29¾ in. (43.3 × 75.7 cm.)
Artist: A. Kollner
Lithographer:
Printer: A. Kollner, Dock St. Phila.
Publisher: Augs. Kollner (copyright)
Key/Vignettes/Misc:
Locations: HSP–P; NJHS–N (photo);
NYP–S
Catalogs/Checklists: Stout, no. 230;
Stokes P. 1855—G–41

3588

Place: Philadelphia, Pennsylvania
Date: 1857
Title: Bird's Eye View of Philadelphia.
Size: 28 × 35¾ in. (71.2 × 91 cm.)
Artist: J. Bachman
Lithographer: J. Bachman
Printer: P. S. Duval & Sons lith. Philad.
Publisher: John Weik, Phila.
Key/Vignettes/Misc:
Locations: HSP–P; LC–M; BPL–R;
CHS–C; LC–P
Catalogs/Checklists: Stout, no. 213a;
LC–M, 827

3589

Place: Philadelphia, Pennsylvania
Date: 1868
Title: Bird's Eye View of Philadelphia
Size: 24⅞ × 35⅞ in. (63.1 × 91 cm.)
Artist: J. Bachman
Lithographer: J. Bachman
Printer: P. S. Duval Son & Co. Lith.
Philada.
Publisher: John Weik No. 607. Sansom
Street (copyright)
Key/Vignettes/Misc:
Locations: LC–P
Catalogs/Checklists: LC–M, 827.1

3590

Place: Philadelphia, Pennsylvania
Date: [1870?]
Title: Birds Eye View of Philadelphia and
Vicinity

Size: 14½ × 21⁹⁄₁₆ in. (37 × 55 cm.)
Artist:
Lithographer:
Printer:
Publisher:
Key/Vignettes/Misc:
Locations: LC−M
Catalogs/Checklists: LC−M, 827.2

3591
Place: Philadelphia, Pennsylvania
Date: 1875
Title: Birds Eye View of Philadelphia
Size: 9⅜ × 13⅜ in. (23.9 × 34.1 cm.)
Artist:
Lithographer:
Printer:
Publisher: Currier & Ives, N. Y.
Key/Vignettes/Misc: 12 unnumbered refs.
Locations: HSP−P; YUAG−NH
Catalogs/Checklists: Stout, no. 233

3592
Place: Philadelphia, Pennsylvania
Date: 1875
Title: Birds Eye View of Philadelphia and Centennial Grounds
Size: 19⅛ × 28½ in. (48.7 × 72.5 cm.)
Artist: John Bachman
Lithographer: John Bachman
Printer: Pelletreau & Raynor
Publisher: John Bachman (copyright)
Key/Vignettes/Misc:
Locations: CHS−C; LC−P
Catalogs/Checklists:

3593
Place: Philadelphia, Pennsylvania
Date: 1875
Title: Philadelphia in the Olden Time
Size: 18⅜ × 24¹⁄₁₆ in. (46.8 × 61.2 cm.)
Artist: S. S. S. & D. C.
Lithographer:
Printer: F. J. Wade, 230 S. 5th St. Phila.
Publisher: Smith and Cremens, Washington, 1875
Key/Vignettes/Misc: 3 vignettes
Locations: MM−NN; CCHS−C; RMSC−R
Catalogs/Checklists: MM−NN, LP 37

3594
Place: Philadelphia, Pennsylvania
Date: 1875
Title: The City of Philadelphia.
Size: 20⅝ × 32½ in. (52.4 × 82.6 cm.)
Artist: Parsons & Atwater
Lithographer: Parsons & Atwater
Printer:
Publisher: Currier & Ives, N. Y.
Key/Vignettes/Misc: 65 unnumbered refs. in 9 lines below places identified
Locations: HSP−P; LC−P; LC−M (facsimile)
Catalogs/Checklists: Stout, no. 234; Peters, C & I, 4212; LC−M, 828.1

3595
Place: Philadelphia, Pennsylvania
Date: [1875]
Title: Philadelphia in 1702
Size: 20 × 26 in. (50.9 × 66.2 cm.)

Artist:
Lithographer:
Printer: F. J. Wade Lith 230 So. 5th St. Phila. Pa.
Publisher: Smith & Cremens
Key/Vignettes/Misc: 3 vignettes
Locations: CCHS−C; LCO−P; RMSC−R; LC−M (facsimile)
Catalogs/Checklists: LC−M, 826.3

3596
Place: Philadelphia, Pennsylvania
Date: 1876
Title: Bird's Eye view, Philadelphia.
Size: 25⅜ × 36⁵⁄₁₆ in. (64.5 × 92.4 cm.)
Artist:
Lithographer:
Printer: H. J. Toudy & Co. 621 & 623 Commerce St. Phila.
Publisher: John P. Hunt & Co. 29 South 9th St., Philad.
Key/Vignettes/Misc: 9 vignettes
Locations: LC−P
Catalogs/Checklists:

3597
Place: Philadelphia, Pennsylvania
Date: 1876
Title: Panorama of Philadelphia and Centennial Exhibition Grounds.
Size: 6⅞ × 34¹⁵⁄₁₆ in. (17.4 × 88.9 cm.)
Artist: H. Bachmann
Lithographer: H. Bachmann
Printer: A. L. Weise. Phila.
Publisher: H. Bachmann, 401 Ranstead Place, Phila. (copyright)
Key/Vignettes/Misc: 30 unnumbered refs.
Locations: LC−P
Catalogs/Checklists:

3598
Place: Philadelphia, Pennsylvania
Date: 1876
Title: Philadelphia 1876.
Size: 18 × 33¾ in. (45.8 × 85.8 cm.)
Artist:
Lithographer:
Printer: H. J. Toudy
Publisher: John P. Hunt (copyright)
Key/Vignettes/Misc: 9 vignettes
Locations: LC−P
Catalogs/Checklists: Stout, no. 236; LC−M, 828.3

3599
Place: Philadelphia, Pennsylvania
Date: 1876
Title: Philadelphia, 1876
Size: 17¼ × 25⅛ in. (44 × 63.9 cm.)
Artist: C. Inger
Lithographer:
Printer:
Publisher: D. Hensel, Philad[elphi]a
Key/Vignettes/Misc: 24 unnumbered refs.
Locations: HSP−P; LC−M; LC−P
Catalogs/Checklists: Stout, no. 235; LC−M, 829

3600
Place: Philadelphia, Pennsylvania
Date: Ca. 1876
Title: Pennsylvania, City of Philadelphia

Size: 10 × 8 in. (25.4 × 20.3 cm.)
Artist: W. Brotherhead
Lithographer:
Printer: H. J. Toudy & Co., Philadelphia
Publisher:
Key/Vignettes/Misc:
Locations: MM−NN
Catalogs/Checklists: MM−NN, LP 875

3601
Place: Philadelphia, Pennsylvania
Date: 1886 State I
Title: Philadelphia in 1886
Size: 40¾ × 71½ in. (103.6 × 182 cm.)
Artist: H. S. P.[ackard]
Lithographer:
Printer:
Publisher: Burk & McFetridge, Phila. (copyright)
Key/Vignettes/Misc: ca. 290 refs. of textile−related industries keyed to marginal numbers; 28 vignettes
Locations: LC−M
Catalogs/Checklists: Stout, no. 238a; LC−M, 829.1

3602
Place: Philadelphia, Pennsylvania
Date: 1886 State II
Title: Philadelphia in 1886
Size: 40¾ × 71½ in. (103.6 × 182 cm.)
Artist: H. S. P.[ackard]
Lithographer:
Printer:
Publisher: Burk & McFetridge, Phila. (copyright)
Key/Vignettes/Misc: ca. 290 refs. of bank and insurance companies keyed to marginal numbers; 40 vignettes
Locations: LC−M
Catalogs/Checklists: Stout, no. 238b; LC−M, 829.2

3603
Place: Philadelphia, Pennsylvania
Date: 1887
Title: Philadelphia of To−Day.
Size: 18⅛ × 33⅜ in. (46.1 × 84.9 cm.)
Artist: [H. S. Packard?]
Lithographer:
Printer: Burk & McFetridge, Lith., Phila.
Publisher: Burk & McFetridge, Phila. (copyright)
Key/Vignettes/Misc: Refs. 1−52
Locations: LC−M
Catalogs/Checklists: Stout, no. 238c; LC−M, 830

3604
Place: Philadelphia, Pennsylvania
Date: [1888?]
Title: Philadelphia in 1888.
Size: 18⅛ × 33⅜ in. (46.1 × 84.9 cm.)
Artist: [H. S. Packard?]
Lithographer:
Printer: Burk & McFetridge, Lith. Phila.
Publisher: Burk & McFetridge (copyright)
Key/Vignettes/Misc: 134 refs. to railroad terminals
Locations LC−M
Catalogs/Checklists: LC−M, 831

3605
Place: Philadelphia, Pennsylvania
Date: 1908
Title: The Philadelphia of To–Day The World's Greatest Workshop
Size: 23½ × 34½ in. (59.8 × 87.8 cm.)
Artist:
Lithographer:
Printer: W. T. Littig & Co. N. Y.
Publisher: Executive Committee, 225th Anniversary of the City of Philadelphia (copyright)
Key/Vignettes/Misc:
Locations: LC–M
Catalogs/Checklists: LC–M, 831.1

3606
Place: Philadelphia, Pennsylvania
Date: [1926?]
Title: Hammond's Bird's–eye View Map of Philadelphia and Vicinity
Size: 17 × 24½ in. (43.3 × 62.3 cm.)
Artist: [Edward W.] Spofford
Lithographer:
Printer:
Publisher: C. S. Hammond & Co. (copyright)
Key/Vignettes/Misc:
Locations: LC–M
Catalogs/Checklists: LC–M, 831.2

Place: Phillipsburg, Pennsylvania
Date: 1842
See Beaver, Pennsylvania, 1842.

3607
Place: Pitcairn, Pennsylvania
Date: 1901
Title: Pitcairn, Allegheny County, Pa. 1901.
Size: 11¾ × 19⅞ in. (29.8 × 50.5 cm.)
Artist: T. M. Fowler
Lithographer:
Printer:
Publisher: T. M. Fowler & James B. Moyer
Key/Vignettes/Misc: Refs. 1–10
Locations: LC–M; PHMC–H; PSU; UPDL–P; YO
Catalogs/Checklists: Stout, no. 11; LC–M, 832; PP

3608
Place: Pittsburgh, Pennsylvania
Date: 1849
Title: Pittsburgh and Allegheny, From Coal Hill—1849.
Size: 22½ × 41½ in. (57.3 × 105.5 cm.)
Artist: B. F. Smith Jr.
Lithographer:
Printer: Tappan & Bradford's Lith. Boston
Publisher: G. Warren Smith & Co., New York
Key/Vignettes/Misc: 75 refs.
Locations: NYP–S; YO
Catalogs/Checklists: Stokes 1849—F–59; PP, no. 37

3609
Place: Pittsburgh, Pennsylvania
Date: Ca. 1850
Title: View of Pittsburg, Pa.
Size: 17¾ × 37 in. (45.1 × 94.1 cm.)
Artist: E. Whitefield

Lithographer:
Printer:
Publisher: Hudson & Smith, Fulton, St., N. Y.
Key/Vignettes/Misc:
Locations: Raymond C. Wright, Pittsburgh, Pa.
Catalogs/Checklists: Norton, Whitefield, no. 50

3610
Place: Pittsburgh, Pennsylvania
Date: [1851]
Title: Pittsburgh, Pa.
Size: 5¾ × 7⅞ in. (14.7 × 20 cm.)
Artist:
Lithographer: E. Bott
Printer: Onken's Lith. Cin. O.
Publisher: [Otto Onken, Cincinnati, Ohio]
Key/Vignettes/Misc:
Locations: CPL–R
Catalogs/Checklists:

3611
Place: Pittsburgh, Pennsylvania
Date: 1859
Title: View of Pittsburgh, Pa.
Size: 20⅜ × 31⅛ in. (51.9 × 79.2 cm.)
Artist: William Schuchman
Lithographer: William Schuchman
Printer:
Publisher: William Schuchman
Key/Vignettes/Misc: 12 vignettes
Locations: CHS–C
Catalogs/Checklists:

3612
Place: Pittsburgh, Pennsylvania
Date: 1871
Title: Pittsburgh, Allegheny & Birmingham. 1871.
Size: 19⅛ × 42⅞ in. (48.7 × 108.9 cm.)
Artist: Otto Krebs
Lithographer:
Printer: Otto Krebs, Pittsburgh, Pa.
Publisher: Otto Krebs, Pittsburgh, Pa.
Key/Vignettes/Misc:
Locations: ACMW–FW; CHS–C; LC–P
Catalogs/Checklists: Stout, no. 12; LC–M, 832.1

3613
Place: Pittsburgh, Pennsylvania
Date: [1871]
Title: Pittsburgh, Allegheny & Birmingham.
Size: 12½ × 41½ in. (31.8 × 105.7 cm.)
Artist:
Lithographer: [W. G. Armor]
Printer: Otto Krebs
Publisher:
Key/Vignettes/Misc:
Locations: CLP–P
Catalogs/Checklists: Stout, no. 13

3614
Place: Pittsburgh, Pennsylvania
Date: 1874
Title: View of Pittsburgh & Allegheny.
Size: 14 × 26¼ in. (35.7 × 66.8 cm.)
Artist:
Lithographer: J. W.
Printer: Otto Krebs Lith. Pittsbg.

Publisher: Otto Krebs [Pittsburgh] (copyright)
Key/Vignettes/Misc:
Locations: HSWP–P; MM–NN; LC–P
Catalogs/Checklists: Stout, no. 14; MM–NN, LP 2183; LC–M, 832.2

3615
Place: Pittsburgh, Pennsylvania
Date: 1876
Title: Pittsburgh & Allegheny
Size: 20⅜ × 26¾ in. (51.9 × 68.1 cm.)
Artist:
Lithographer: [A. Marcus]
Printer: Otto Krebs, Pittsburgh
Publisher: Otto Krebs [Pittsburgh]
Key/Vignettes/Misc:
Locations: LC–P
Catalogs/Checklists:

3616
Place: Pittsburgh, Pennsylvania
Date: 1877
Title: View of the City of Pittsburgh in 1817 Taken from a Sketch Drawn by Mrs. E. C. Gibson, Wife of Jas. Gibson, Esq. the Philad'a Bar While on her Wedding Tour in 1817
Size: 12⅝ × 18⁵⁄₁₆ in. (32.1 × 46.6 cm.)
Artist: Mrs. E. C. Gibson
Lithographer:
Printer: Pittsburgh Lith. Co.
Publisher: Charles O. Lappe
Key/Vignettes/Misc:
Locations: MM–NN
Catalogs/Checklists: MM–NN, LP 21

3617
Place: Pittsburgh, Pennsylvania
Date: [1890?] State I
Title: Pittsburgh
Size: 12 × 29¼ in. (30.5 × 74.4 cm.)
Artist: [A. Y. Lee?]
Lithographer:
Printer:
Publisher:
Key/Vignettes/Misc: Refs. 1–193
Locations: CLP–P
Catalogs/Checklists: Stout, no. 15a

3618
Place: Pittsburgh, Pennsylvania
Date: [1890?] State II
Title: Birds–Eye View of Pittsburgh & Vicinity
Size: 11¼ × 26 in. (28.6 × 66.1 cm.)
Artist: A. Y. Lee
Lithographer:
Printer:
Publisher: Freight Department, Pennsylvania Railroad
Key/Vignettes/Misc: Refs. 1–143
Locations: YO
Catalogs/Checklists: Stout, no. 15b; PP

3619
Place: Pittsburgh, Pennsylvania
Date: 1902
Title: Pittsburgh, Pennsylvania. 1902.
Size: 15⅛ × 22¾ in. (38.5 × 57.9 cm.)
Artist: T. M. Fowler
Lithographer:
Printer:

Publisher: T. M. Fowler & James B. Moyer
Key/Vignettes/Misc: Refs. 1–10, 12–16
Locations: HSWP–P; YO; LC–M; LC–P
Catalogs/Checklists: PP, no. 80; Stout, no. 16; LC–M, 833

3620
Place: Pittsburgh, Pennsylvania
Date: Ca. 1904
Title: Pittsburgh, Pa., 1904
Size: 6¹⁵⁄₁₆ × 35⁹⁄₁₆ in. (17.7 × 90.5 cm.)
Artist:
Lithographer:
Printer: Colonial Litho., Pittsburgh
Publisher:
Key/Vignettes/Misc:
Locations: LC–P
Catalogs/Checklists:

3621
Place: Pittston, Pennsylvania
Date: 1892
Title: Pittston, and West Pittston Pennsylvania 1892.
Size: 14 × 26¾ in. (35.6 × 68.1 cm.)
Artist: [T. M. Fowler]
Lithographer:
Printer: A. E. Downs. Lith. Boston
Publisher: T. M. Fowler & James B. Moyer
Key/Vignettes/Misc: Refs. 1–17, A–N
Locations: PHMC–H; LC–M
Catalogs/Checklists: Stout, no. 177; LC–M, 833.1

3622
Place: Plains, Pennsylvania
Date: 1892
Title: Plains, Luzerne County Pa. 1892.
Size: 15⅛ × 25⅝ in. (38 × 65.2 cm.)
Artist: T. M. Fowler
Lithographer:
Printer: A. E. Downs, Lith. Boston
Publisher:
Key/Vignettes/Misc: Refs. 1–14
Locations: PHMC–H; LC–M
Catalogs/Checklists: Stout, no. 178; LC–M, 833.2

3623
Place: Plymouth, Pennsylvania
Date: 1884
Title: Plymouth. Pennsylvania. 1884.
Size: 17⅛ × 25¼ in. (43.6 × 61.7 cm.)
Artist: [T. M. Fowler?]
Lithographer:
Printer:
Publisher: O. H. Bailey & Co., Publishers, Boston.
Key/Vignettes/Misc: Refs. 1–28; 3 vignettes
Locations: BPL–R
Catalogs/Checklists: Stout, no. 179

3624
Place: Point Marion, Pennsylvania
Date: 1902
Title: Point Marion, Pennsylvania 1902
Size: 14 × 19¾ in. (35.6 × 50.2 cm.)
Artist: T. M. Fowler
Lithographer:
Printer:
Publisher: T. M. Fowler, Morrisville, Pa.

Key/Vignettes/Misc: Refs. 1–6, A–H; 6 vignettes
Locations: LC–M; LC–P
Catalogs/Checklists: Stout, no. 127; LC–M, 834

3625
Place: Portland, Pennsylvania
Date: 1885
Title: Portland, Penn. 1885 [and Columbia, N. J.]
Size: 15⅜ × 24½ in. (39.2 × 62.3 cm.)
Artist: [T. M. Fowler?]
Lithographer:
Printer:
Publisher: O. H. Bailey & Co., Boston
Key/Vignettes/Misc: Portland Refs., 1–38, Columbia Refs., A–F; 3 vignettes
Locations: BPL–R
Catalogs/Checklists: Stout, no. 220; Warren & Wise

3626
Place: Pottstown, Pennsylvania
Date: 1893
Title: Pottstown, Pennsylvania, 1893.
Size: 18⅛ × 32½ in. (46.2 × 82.2 cm.)
Artist: T. M. Fowler
Lithographer:
Printer:
Publisher: James B. Moyer, Myerstown, Pa.
Key/Vignettes/Misc: Refs. 1–22, A–S
Locations: PHMC–H; PSU; LC–M (photo)
Catalogs/Checklists: Stout, no. 203; LC–M, 834.1

3627
Place: Pottsville, Pennsylvania
Date: Ca. 1831
Title: View of Part of the Borough, & Environs of Pottsville, Schuylkill Coy.
Size: 12 × 19½ in. (30.5 × 49.6 cm.)
Artist: T. P. Ashwin
Lithographer: C. Lehman
Printer: Childs & Inman, Lithographers, Philadelphia
Publisher:
Key/Vignettes/Misc:
Locations: Unknown. See The Month at Goodspeed's, XXXVI, No. 8, May 1965, pp. 253–55
Catalogs/Checklists:

3628
Place: Pottsville, Pennsylvania
Date: Ca. 1855
Title: View of Pottsville, Pa.
Size: 19⅝ × 25¾ in. (49.9 × 65.6 cm.)
Artist: [A. Kollner?]
Lithographer: [A. Kollner?]
Printer: A. Kollner's Lithy, Phila.
Publisher: F. Alstadt, Pottsville, Pa.
Key/Vignettes/Misc:
Locations: YO
Catalogs/Checklists: PP, no. 53

3629
Place: Pottsville, Pennsylvania
Date: [1855–60]
Title: View of Pottsville
Size: 11⅞ × 13⅞ in. (30.2 × 35.3 cm.)

Artist: J. R. Smith Junr.
Lithographer:
Printer:
Publisher:
Key/Vignettes/Misc:
Locations: NYP–S
Catalogs/Checklists: Stokes C. 1855–60—G–101

3630
Place: Pottsville, Pennsylvania
Date: 1889
Title: Pottsville, Pennsylvania 1889.
Size: 17⅛ × 34¼ in. (43.6 × 87.1 cm.)
Artist: T. M. Fowler
Lithographer:
Printer: A. E. Downs Lith. Boston
Publisher: T. M. Fowler & James B. Moyer
Key/Vignettes/Misc: Refs. 1–22, A–O
Locations: HSP–P; LC–M; PHMC–H; PSU; BPL–R; YO
Catalogs/Checklists: Stout, no. 247; LC–M, 835; PP

3631
Place: Providence, Pennsylvania
Date: 1892
Title: Providence, Pennsylvania. 1892.
Size: 19⅝ × 34¾ in. (50 × 88.4 cm.)
Artist: A. E. Downs
Lithographer:
Printer:
Publisher:
Key/Vignettes/Misc: 2 blank vignettes
Locations: BPL–R
Catalogs/Checklists: Stout, no. 151; LC–M, 836

3632
Place: Punxsutawney, Pennsylvania
Date: 1895
Title: Punxsutawney, Jefferson County Pennsylvania 1895.
Size: 13¾ × 26½ in. (35 × 67.4 cm.)
Artist: T. M. Fowler
Lithographer:
Printer:
Publisher: T. M. Fowler & James B. Moyer
Key/Vignettes/Misc: Refs. 1–19, A–H
Locations: PHMC–H; YO
Catalogs/Checklists: Stout, no. 141; PP

3633
Place: Quakertown, Pennsylvania
Date: 1885
Title: Quakertown. Pennsylvania. 1885.
Size: 12½ × 22½ in. (31.8 × 57.3 cm.)
Artist:
Lithographer:
Printer: O. H. Bailey & Co., Boston
Publisher: O. H. Bailey & Co., Boston
Key/Vignettes/Misc: Refs. 1–18; 2 vignettes
Locations: BPL–R
Catalogs/Checklists: Stout, no. 62

3634
Place: Quarryville, Pennsylvania
Date: 1903
Title: Quarryville, Pennsylvania. 1903
Size: 12 × 17¾ in. (30.5 × 45.2 cm.)
Artist: T. M. Fowler
Lithographer:

Printer:
Publisher: T. M. Fowler, Morrisville, Pa.
Key/Vignettes/Misc: Refs. 1–31, A–D; 6 vignettes
Locations: NYH–NY
Catalogs/Checklists:

3635
Place: Reading, Pennsylvania
Date: 1837
Title: A View of Reading Taken from the West Side of Schuylkill.
Size: 15 × 22¹⁵⁄₁₆ in. (38.1 × 58.3 cm.)
Artist: F. A. Holzwart
Lithographer: F. A. Holzwart
Printer: Lehman & Duval Lithrs., Philadelphia
Publisher:
Key/Vignettes/Misc:
Locations: NYP–S
Catalogs/Checklists: Stokes C. 1836—F–63; PP, no. 12

3636
Place: Reading, Pennsylvania
Date: 1838
Title: Reading from the South
Size: 10³⁄₁₆ × 13³⁄₁₆ in. (26 × 33.5 cm.)
Artist: T. K. Wharton
Lithographer: T. K. Wharton
Printer: P. S. Duval, Lith. Philada.
Publisher:
Key/Vignettes/Misc:
Locations: NYP–S
Catalogs/Checklists: Stokes C. 1838—F–42

3637
Place: Reading, Pennsylvania
Date: 1839
Title: View of Reading, Pa. From the Neversink in the Neighborhood of White Cottage.
Size: 17⅝ × 22⅛ in. (44.9 × 56.3 cm.)
Artist: [John Caspar Wild?]
Lithographer:
Printer: J. T. Bowen's Lithographic Establishment Philadelphia
Publisher: J. T. Bowen, No. 94 Walnut St., Philadelphia
Key/Vignettes/Misc:
Locations: YO
Catalogs/Checklists: PP, no. 15

3638
Place: Reading, Pennsylvania
Date: 1879
Title: Reading, Pa. 1879. View from the White Spot.
Size: 18¾ × 31¾ in. (47.6 × 80.7 cm.)
Artist:
Lithographer:
Printer: Thos. Hunter Lith, Phila.
Publisher: C. J. Corbin [Philadelphia]
Key/Vignettes/Misc: 14 vignettes
Locations: LC–M; YO
Catalogs/Checklists: Stout, no. 44; PP

3639
Place: Reading, Pennsylvania
Date: 1881
Title: Topographic View of the City of Reading, Pa. 1881.

Size: 22⅞ × 31¼ in. (58.2 × 79.4 cm.)
Artist: J. Hanold Kendall
Lithographer:
Printer:
Publisher:
Key/Vignettes/Misc: 21 vignettes
Locations: LC–M
Catalogs/Checklists: Stout, no. 45; LC–M, 837

3640
Place: Reading, Pennsylvania
Date: 1898
Title: The City of Reading, Pennsylvania. 1898.
Size: 17 × 30⅜ in. (43.3 × 77.2 cm.)
Artist: O. H. Bailey
Lithographer:
Printer:
Publisher: Bailey & Moyer, Boston
Key/Vignettes/Misc:
Locations: LC–M; BPL–R; YO
Catalogs/Checklists: Stout, no. 46b; PP; LC–M, 837.1

3641
Place: Ridgway, Pennsylvania
Date: 1895
Title: Ridgway, Elk County Pennsylvania. 1895.
Size: 18⁹⁄₁₆ × 29⁵⁄₁₆ in. (47.3 × 74.6 cm.)
Artist: T. M. Fowler
Lithographer:
Printer:
Publisher: T. M. Fowler & James B. Moyer
Key/Vignettes/Misc: Refs. 1–23, A–H
Locations: LC–M; PHMC–H; PSU; LC–P
Catalogs/Checklists: Stout, no. 110; LC–M, 838

Place: Rochester, Pennsylvania
Date: 1842
See Beaver, Pennsylvania, 1842.

3642
Place: Rochester, Pennsylvania
Date: 1886
Title: Panoramic View of Rochester, Beaver County, Pennsylvania
Size: 13 × 20¹³⁄₁₆ in. (33 × 53 cm.) (facsimile)
Artist:
Lithographer:
Printer: Beck & Pauli, Litho. Milwaukee, Wis.
Publisher: Ruger & Stoner, Madison, Wis.
Key/Vignettes/Misc: Refs. A–H, J–K, 0–28; 1 vignette
Locations: LC–M (facsimile); Rochester Historical Society, Rochester, Pennsylvania
Catalogs/Checklists: LC–M, 838.1

3643
Place: Rochester, Pennsylvania
Date: 1900
Title: Rochester, Pennsylvania 1900
Size: 17 × 30 in. (43.2 × 76.2 cm.)
Artist: T. M. Fowler
Lithographer:
Printer:
Publisher: T. M. Fowler & James B. Moyer

Key/Vignettes/Misc: Refs. 1–13, A–N; 3 vignettes
Locations: CLP–P; HSP–P; LC–M; PHMC–H; PSU; UPDL–P
Catalogs/Checklists: Stout, no. 32; LC–M, 839

Place: Rock Hill, Pennsylvania
Date: 1906
See Orbisonia, Pennsylvania, 1906.

3644
Place: Rockwood, Pennsylvania
Date: 1905
Title: View of Rockwood, Pennsylvania. 1905.
Size: 15⅞ × 19½ in. (40.3 × 49.5 cm.)
Artist: T. M. Fowler
Lithographer:
Printer:
Publisher: T. M. Fowler, Morrisville, Pa.
Key/Vignettes/Misc: 16 vignettes
Locations: YO; NYH–NY
Catalogs/Checklists: PP

3645
Place: Roscoe, Pennsylvania
Date: 1902
Title: Roscoe, Washington Co. Pennsylvania 1902
Size: 9⅝ × 18½ in. (24.5 × 47.1 cm.)
Artist: T. M. Fowler
Lithographer:
Printer:
Publisher: T. M. Fowler & James B. Moyer
Key/Vignettes/Misc: Refs. 1–9, A–B
Locations: CLP–P; HSP–P; LC–M; PSU; UPDL–P
Catalogs/Checklists: Stout, no. 273; LC–M, 840

Place: Roxborough, Pennsylvania
Date: 1907
See Manayunk, Pennsylvania, 1907.

3646
Place: Royersford, Pennsylvania
Date: 1893
Title: Royersford, Montgomery County Pennsylvania 1893
Size: 14 × 23 in. (35.7 × 58.5 cm.)
Artist: T. M. Fowler
Lithographer:
Printer:
Publisher: James B. Moyer, Myerstown, Pa.
Key/Vignettes/Misc: Refs. 1–22, A–E
Locations: LC–M; PHMC–H; PSU; YO
Catalogs/Checklists: Stout, no. 204; PP; LC–M, 840.1

3647
Place: Saint Marys, Pennsylvania
Date: 1895
Title: St. Mary's, Elk County Pennsylvania. 1895.
Size: 15¼ × 25 in. (38.8 × 63.6 cm.)
Artist: T. M. Fowler
Lithographer:
Printer:
Publisher: T. M. Fowler & James B. Moyer
Key/Vignettes/Misc: Refs. 1–17

Locations: HSP–P; LC–M; PHMC–H; PSU; UPDL–P; YO
Catalogs/Checklists: Stout, no. 111; LC–M, 841; PP

3648
Place: Salisbury, Pennsylvania
Date: 1905
Title: Salisbury, Post Office Elk Lick: Somerset County: Pennsylvania (2300 Feet Above Mean Tide). 1905
Size: 16¾ × 26¾ in. (42.6 × 68 cm.)
Artist: T. M. Fowler
Lithographer:
Printer:
Publisher: T. M. Fowler, Morrisville, Pa.
Key/Vignettes/Misc: Refs. 1–11; 24 vignettes
Locations: PHMC–H; YO; NYH–NY
Catalogs/Checklists: Stout, no. 254; PP

3649
Place: Saxton, Pennsylvania
Date: 1906
Title: Saxton Bedford Co., Pennsylvania 1906
Size: 13¾ × 21⅛ in. (34.9 × 53.6 cm.)
Artist: [T. M. Fowler?]
Lithographer:
Printer:
Publisher: Fowler & Kelly, Morrisville, Pa.
Key/Vignettes/Misc: 15 vignettes
Locations: LC–M (photo)
Catalogs/Checklists: Stout, no. 36; LC–M, 841.1

3650
Place: Sayre, Pennsylvania
Date: 1881
Title: Sayre, Penna. 1881
Size: 14 × 21⅝ in. (35.6 × 55.1 cm.)
Artist: John Moray
Lithographer:
Printer: Thos. Hunter Lith. Phila.
Publisher: John Moray
Key/Vignettes/Misc:
Locations: YO
Catalogs/Checklists: Stout, no. 57; PP

3651
Place: Schwenksville, Pennsylvania
Date: [1894]
Title: Schwenksville, Montgomery County Pennsylvania. 1894.
Size: 11¾ × 20⅛ in. (29.4 × 51.2 cm.)
Artist: T. M. Fowler
Lithographer:
Printer:
Publisher: T. M. Fowler & James B. Moyer
Key/Vignettes/Misc: Refs. 1–14
Locations: HSP–P; LC–M; PHMC–H; PSU
Catalogs/Checklists: Stout, no. 205; LC–M, 842

Place: Scottdale, Pennsylvania
Date: [1890]
See Everson, Pennsylvania, 1890.

3652
Place: Scottdale, Pennsylvania
Date: 1900
Title: Scottdale, Pennsylvania 1900.

Size: 15½ × 28 in. (39.4 × 71.2 cm.)
Artist: T. M. Fowler
Lithographer:
Printer:
Publisher: T. M. Fowler & James B. Moyer
Key/Vignettes/Misc: Refs. 1–24, A–M
Locations: PHMC–H; UPDL–P; LC–M (photo)
Catalogs/Checklists: Stout, no. 289; LC–M, 843.1

3653
Place: Scranton, Pennsylvania
Date: 1872
Title:
Size:
Artist:
Lithographer:
Printer:
Publisher:
Key/Vignettes/Misc:
Locations:
Catalogs/Checklists: Stout, no. 314; Warren & Wise

3654
Place: Scranton, Pennsylvania
Date: 1882
Title: Scranton, Pa. 1882.Size: 18½ × 32 in. (47.1 × 81.4 cm.)
Artist:
Lithographer:
Printer:
Publisher: C. J. Corbin
Key/Vignettes/Misc: 18 vignettes
Locations: Lackawanna Historical Society, Scranton, Pennsylvania
Catalogs/Checklists: Stout, no. 315

3655
Place: Scranton, Pennsylvania
Date: 1890
Title: Scranton, Penn. 1890.
Size: 20¾ × 40 in. (52.8 × 101.6 cm.)
Artist: T. M. Fowler & A. E. Downs
Lithographer:
Printer: A. E. Downs Lith. Boston
Publisher: T. M. Fowler & James B. Moyer
Key/Vignettes/Misc: Refs. 1–38, A–X
Locations: LC–M; PHMC–H
Catalogs/Checklists: Stout, no. 152; LC–M, 844

3656
Place: Sellersville, Pennsylvania
Date: 1894
Title: Sellersville, Bucks County, Pa. 1894.
Size: 12⅝ × 24⅜ in. (32.8 × 62 cm.)
Artist: T. M. Fowler
Lithographer:
Printer:
Publisher: T. M. Fowler & James B. Moyer
Key/Vignettes/Misc: Refs. 1–28
Locations: HSP–P; LC–M; PHMC–H; PSU; YO
Catalogs/Checklists: Stout, no. 63; LC–M, 845; PP

3657
Place: Shamokin, Pennsylvania
Date: 1884
Title: Shamokin. Pennsylvania. 1884.
Size: 19⅞ × 32 in. (50.1 × 81.4 cm.)

Artist:
Lithographer:
Printer:
Publisher: O. H. Bailey & Co., Boston
Key/Vignettes/Misc: Refs. 1–29; 21 vignettes
Locations: BPL–R
Catalogs/Checklists: Stout, no. 222

Place: Sharon, Pennsylvania
Date: 1842
See Beaver, Pennsylvania, 1842.

3658
Place: Sharon, Pennsylvania
Date: 1901
Title: Sharon, Mercer County Pennsylvania. 1901.
Size: 15⅛ × 30⅜ in. (38.5 × 77.3 cm.)
Artist: T. M. Fowler
Lithographer:
Printer:
Publisher: T. M. Fowler & James B. Moyer
Key/Vignettes/Misc: Refs. 1–22, A–N
Locations: CLP–P; HSP–P; LC–M; PHMC–H; PSU; UPDL–P; YO
Catalogs/Checklists: Stout, no. 190; LC–M, 846; PP

3659
Place: Sharpsville, Pennsylvania
Date: 1901
Title: Sharpsville, Mercer County Pennsylvania 1901.
Size: 12 × 23¾ in. (30.5 × 60.4 cm.)
Artist: T. M. Fowler
Lithographer:
Printer:
Publisher: T. M. Fowler & James B. Moyer
Key/Vignettes/Misc: Refs. 1–18, A–G
Locations: LC–M; PHMC–H; LC–P
Catalogs/Checklists: Stout, no. 191; LC–M, 847

3660
Place: Sheffield, Pennsylvania
Date: 1895
Title: Sheffield, Warren County Pennsylvania 1895.
Size: 14 × 24⅝ in. (35.7 × 62.7 cm.)
Artist: T. M. Fowler
Lithographer:
Printer:
Publisher: T. M. Fowler & James B. Moyer
Key/Vignettes/Misc: Refs. 1–12, A–D
Locations: HSP–P; LC–M; PHMC–H; PSU
Catalogs/Checklists: Stout, no. 266; LC–M, 848

3661
Place: Shenandoah, Pennsylvania
Date: 1889
Title: Shenandoah, Pa. 1889.
Size: 20⅛ × 28¼ in. (51.2 × 71.9 cm.)
Artist: T. M. Fowler
Lithographer:
Printer:
Publisher: T. M. Fowler & James B. Moyer
Key/Vignettes/Misc: Refs. 1–19, A–P; 13 vignettes
Locations: LC–M; PHMC–H; PSU; YO
Catalogs/Checklists: Stout, no. 248; LC–M, 849; PP

Place: Sheridan, Pennsylvania
Date: 1898
See Newsmanstown, Pennsylvania, 1898.

3662
Place: Shippensburg, Pennsylvania
Date: 1894
Title: Shippensburg, Pennsylvania. 1894.
Size: 14 × 25¼ in. (35.6 × 64.2 cm.)
Artist: T. M. Fowler
Lithographer:
Printer:
Publisher: T. M. Fowler & James B. Moyer
Key/Vignettes/Misc: Refs. 1–22, A–I
Locations: PHMC–H; LC–M (photo)
Catalogs/Checklists: Stout, no. 101;
LC–M, 850

3663
Place: Sinking Spring, Pennsylvania
Date: 1898
Title:
Size:
Artist: T. M. Fowler
Lithographer:
Printer:
Publisher:
Key/Vignettes/Misc:
Locations:
Catalogs/Checklists: Warren

3664
Place: Slatington, Pennsylvania
Date: 1883
Title: Slatington, Pennsylvania. 1883.
Size: 15½ × 23½ in. (39.5 × 59.8 cm.)
Artist: O. H. Bailey & Co.
Lithographer:
Printer: O. H. Bailey & Co., Boston
Publisher: Bailey & Fowler
Key/Vignettes/Misc: Refs. 1–32
Locations: BPL–R
Catalogs/Checklists: Stout, no. 171

3665
Place: Somerset, Pennsylvania
Date: 1900
Title: Somerset, Pennsylvania 1900
Size: 16⅜ × 23⅛ in. (41.6 × 58.9 cm.)
Artist: T. M. Fowler
Lithographer:
Printer:
Publisher: T. M. Fowler & James B. Moyer
Key/Vignettes/Misc: Refs. 1–15, A–G; 11
vignettes
Locations: CLP–P; HSP–P; LC–M;
PHMC–H; PSU; UPDL–P
Catalogs/Checklists: Stout, no. 255;
LC–M, 851

3666
Place: Souderton, Pennsylvania
Date: 1894
Title: Souderton, Montgomery County,
Pennsylvania. 1894.
Size: 12⅝ × 19⅝ in. (32.2 × 50 cm.)
Artist: T. M. Fowler
Lithographer:
Printer:
Publisher: T. M. Fowler & James B. Moyer
Key/Vignettes/Misc: Refs. 1–29
Locations: HSP–P; LC–M; PHMC–H;
PSU; YO

Catalogs/Checklists: Stout, no. 206;
LC–M, 852; PP

Place: South Bethlehem, Pennsylvania
Date: 1877
See Bethlehem, Pennsylvania, 1877.

Place: South Bethlehem, Pennsylvania
Date: 1886
See Bethlehem, Pennsylvania, 1886.

3667
Place: South Bethlehem, Pennsylvania
Date: 1894
Title: Lehigh University, South Bethlehem
Pa. 1894.
Size: 10 × 15½ in. (25.5 × 39.5 cm.)
Artist: T. M. Fowler
Lithographer:
Printer:
Publisher: T. M. Fowler & James B. Moyer
Key/Vignettes/Misc: Refs. 1–6
Locations: PHMC–H; PSU
Catalogs/Checklists: Stout, no. 215

3668
Place: South Fork, Pennsylvania
Date: 1900
Title: South Fork, Cambria County
Pennsylvania 1900
Size: 12¾ × 22½ in. (32.5 × 57.3 cm.)
Artist: T. M. Fowler
Lithographer:
Printer:
Publisher: T. M. Fowler & James B. Moyer
Key/Vignettes/Misc: Refs. 1–14, A–C
Locations: CLP–P; HSP–P; LC–M;
PHMC–H; PSU; UPDL–P
Catalogs/Checklists: Stout, no. 73;
LC–M, 853

3669
Place: Spring City, Pennsylvania
Date: 1893
Title: Spring City, Chester County, Pa.
1893.
Size: 15 × 23¾ in. (38.1 × 60.4 cm.)
Artist: T. M. Fowler
Lithographer:
Printer:
Publisher: James B. Moyer, Myerstown,
Pa.
Key/Vignettes/Misc: Refs. 1–17, A–D
Locations: PHMC–H; PSU; LC–M
(photo)
Catalogs/Checklists: Stout, no. 80;
LC–M, 853.1

3670
Place: Star Junction, Pennsylvania
Date: 1904
Title: View of Star Junction. Fayette
County, Pennsylvania. 1904.
Size: 13¾ × 17¹⁵⁄₁₆ in. (35 × 45.7 cm.)
Artist: T. M. Fowler
Lithographer:
Printer:
Publisher: T. M. Fowler, Morrisville, Pa.
Key/Vignettes/Misc: Refs. 1–10; 7
vignettes
Locations: NYH–NY
Catalogs/Checklists:

3671
Place: State College, Pennsylvania
Date: 1910
Title: The Pennsylvania State College.
Size: 13⅛ × 27¼ in. (33.4 × 69.3 cm.)
Artist: [Richard Rummelly]
Lithographer:
Printer:
Publisher: W. T. Littig & Co., N. Y.
(copyright)
Key/Vignettes/Misc:
Locations: PSU
Catalogs/Checklists: Stout, no. 77b

3672
Place: Strasburg, Pennsylvania
Date: 1903
Title: Strasburg, Lancaster Co. Pa. 1903.
Size: 12¾ × 17¾ in. (32.4 × 45.2 cm.)
Artist: T. M. Fowler
Lithographer:
Printer:
Publisher: T. M. Fowler, Morrisville, Pa.
Key/Vignettes/Misc: Refs. 1–31; 9
vignettes
Locations: LC–M; YO; NYH–NY
Catalogs/Checklists: Stout, no. 159;
LC–M, 854; PP

3673
Place: Stroudsburg, Pennsylvania
Date: 1884
Title: Stroudsburg, Pennsylvania. 1884.
Size: 17¼ × 24 in. (43.9 × 61 cm.)
Artist:
Lithographer: O. H. Bailey & Co.
Printer: O. H. Bailey & Co., Boston
Publisher: O. H. Bailey & Co., Boston
Key/Vignettes/Misc: Refs. 1–23; 3
vignettes
Locations: BPL–R; LC–M (photo)
Catalogs/Checklists: Stout, no. 196;
LC–M, 854.1

3674
Place: Sunbury, Pennsylvania
Date: Ca. 1850
Title: Sunbury, Northumberland Co. Penn.
The Point of Junction of the Philadelphia
and Sunbury Rail Road–and the
Susquehanna and Baltimore Rail
Road. . . .
Size: 23⅞ × 31⅝ in. (60.8 × 80.5 cm.)
Artist: Mrs. Donnell
Lithographer:
Printer: P. S. Duval & Co's. Steam Lith
Press Philada.
Publisher:
Key/Vignettes/Misc:
Locations: MM–NN; YO
Catalogs/Checklists: MM–NN, LP 2806;
PP, no. 41

3675
Place: Sunbury, Pennsylvania
Date: 1873
Title: Birds Eye View of Sunbury, Pa.
1873.
Size: 17¼ x 25⅞ in. (43.9 × 65.8 cm.)
Artist: O. H. Bailey
Lithographer:

Printer: J. H. Touvy [H. J. Toudy] & Co.
Phila.
Publisher:
Key/Vignettes/Misc: Refs. 1–19
Locations: HSP–P; LC–M (photo)
Catalogs/Checklists: Stout, no. 223;
LC–M, 854.2

3676
Place: Susquehanna, Pennsylvania
Date: 1882
Title: Susquehanna, Pa. Viewed From
Oakland. 1882.
Size: 16⅛ × 24⅜ in. (41 × 61.9 cm.)
Artist: W. W. Denslow
Lithographer:
Printer:
Publisher: Philadelphia Publishing House
[Philadelphia]
Key/Vignettes/Misc: 13 vignettes
Locations: YO
Catalogs/Checklists: PP

3677
Place: Tacony, Pennsylvania
Date: 1898
Title: Tacony, Pennsylvania. 1898
Size: 16⅜ × 30½ in. (41.7 × 77.6 cm.)
Artist: T. M. Fowler
Lithographer:
Printer:
Publisher: T. M. Fowler, Morrisville, Pa.
Key/Vignettes/Misc: Refs. 1–21; 21
vignettes
Locations: PHMC–H; LC–M (photo)
Catalogs/Checklists: Stout, no. 239;
LC–M, 854.3

3678
Place: Tarentum, Pennsylvania
Date: 1901
Title: Tarentum. Allegheny County
Pennsylvania. 1901.
Size: 14 × 29⅛ in. (35.6 × 74.1 cm.)
Artist: T. M. Fowler
Lithographer:
Printer:
Publisher: T. M. Fowler & James B. Moyer
Key/Vignettes/Misc: Refs. 1–15, A–K
Locations: LC–M; PHMC–H; PSU;
UPDL–P
Catalogs/Checklists: Stout, no. 17;
LC–M, 855

3679
Place: Telford, Pennsylvania
Date: 1894
Title: Telford, Montgomery County
Pennsylvania. 1894.
Size: 10⅛ × 19½ in. (25.8 × 49.7 cm.)
Artist: T. M. Fowler
Lithographer:
Printer:
Publisher: T. M. Fowler & James B.
Moyer
Key/Vignettes/Misc: Refs. 1–19; 1
vignette
Locations: HSP–P; LC–M; PHMC–H;
PSU; YO
Catalogs/Checklists: Stout, no. 207;
LC–M, 856; PP

3680
Place: Terre Hill, Pennsylvania
Date: 1894
Title: Terre Hill, Lancaster County
Pennsylvania. 1894.
Size: 13½ × 21¼ in. (34.3 × 54 cm.)
Artist: T. M. Fowler
Lithographer:
Printer:
Publisher: T. M. Fowler & James B. Moyer
Key/Vignettes/Misc: Refs. 1–17, A–B
Locations: LC–M; PSU; YO
Catalogs/Checklists: Stout, no. 160; PP;
LC–M, 857

3681
Place: Tidioute, Pennsylvania
Date: 1896
Title: Tidioute, Warren County
Pennsylvania. 1896.
Size: 15¾ × 24 in. (40.2 × 61 cm.)
Artist: T. M. Fowler
Lithographer:
Printer:
Publisher: T. M. Fowler & James B. Moyer
Key/Vignettes/Misc: Refs. 1–14, A–H
Locations: LC–M; PHMC–H; PSU; YO;
LC–P
Catalogs/Checklists: Stout, no. 267;
LC–M, 858; PP

3682
Place: Tionesta, Pennsylvania
Date: 1896
Title: Tionesta. Forest County Pa. 1896.
Size: 11 × 17¾ in. (28 × 45.7 cm.)
Artist: T. M. Fowler
Lithographer:
Printer:
Publisher: T. M. Fowler & James B. Moyer
Key/Vignettes/Misc: Refs. 1–11, A–D
Locations: HSP–P; LC–M; PHMC–H;
PSU; UPDL–P; YO
Catalogs/Checklists: Stout, no. 130;
LC–M, 859; PP

3683
Place: Titusville, Pennsylvania
Date: 1871
Title: Birds Eye View of the City of
Titusville Crawford County Pennsylvania
Looking Northeast 1871.
Size: 21 × 25¾ in. (53.4 × 65.5 cm.)
Artist: A. Ruger
Lithographer:
Printer: Chicago Lithographing Co.,
Chicago
Publisher:
Key/Vignettes/Misc: Refs. 1–15, A–D
Locations: LC–M
Catalogs/Checklists: Stout, no. 95;
LC–M, 860

3684
Place: Titusville, Pennsylvania
Date: 1896
Title: Titusville, Pennsylvania 1896
Size: 19¾ × 33⁹⁄₁₆ in. (50.2 × 85.4 cm.)
Artist: T. M. Fowler
Lithographer:
Printer:

Publisher: T. M. Fowler & James B. Moyer
Key/Vignettes/Misc: Refs. 1–32, A–N
Locations: LC–M; PHMC–H; PSU;
UPDL–P; LC–P
Catalogs/Checklists: Stout, no. 96;
LC–M, 861

3685
Place: Topton, Pennsylvania
Date: 1893
Title: Topton, Berks County Pennsylvania.
1893.
Size: 10⅞ × 19⅝ in. (27.7 × 50 cm.)
Artist: T. M. Fowler
Lithographer:
Printer:
Publisher: T. M. Fowler & James B. Moyer
Key/Vignettes/Misc: Refs. 1–12
Locations: LC–M
Catalogs/Checklists: Stout, no. 47;
LC–M, 862

3686
Place: Towanda, Pennsylvania
Date: 1867
Title: Towanda the County Seat of
Bradford Co. Penna. 1867
Size: 16⅝ × 30 in. (43 × 76.3 cm.)
Artist: John Mornay
Lithographer:
Printer: P. S. Duval & Sons Lith. Phila.
Publisher: John Mornay
Key/Vignettes/Misc:
Locations: YO
Catalogs/Checklists: Stout, no. 58; PP

3687
Place: Towanda, Pennsylvania
Date: 1880
Title: Towanda, Pa. 1880.
Size: 14¼ × 27 in. (36.3 × 68.7 cm.)
Artist:
Lithographer:
Printer:
Publisher: Philadelphia Publishing House
[Philadelphia]
Key/Vignettes/Misc: 17 vignettes
Locations: LC–M; YO
Catalogs/Checklists: Stout, no. 59; PP;
LC–M, 862.1

3688
Place: Tower City, Pennsylvania
Date: 1888
Title: Tower City, And Suburbs. 1888.
Size: 19¼ × 22⅞ in. (49 × 58.2 cm.)
Artist: [T. M. Fowler]
Lithographer:
Printer:
Publisher: T. M. Fowler, Morrisville, Pa.
Key/Vignettes/Misc: Refs. 1–29; 12
vignettes
Locations: HSP–P
Catalogs/Checklists: Stout, no. 249

3689
Place: Tullytown, Pennsylvania
Date: 1887
Title: Tullytown. Pennsylvania. 1887.
Size: 10⅜ × 17 in. (26.4 × 43.3 cm.)
Artist: T. M. Fowler
Lithographer:

Printer:
Publisher: [T. M. Fowler, Morrisville, Pa.?]
Key/Vignettes/Misc: Refs. 1–15; 3 vignettes
Locations: LC–M
Catalogs/Checklists: Stout, no. 64; LC–M, 863

3690
Place: Tunkhannock, Pennsylvania
Date: 1890
Title:
Size:
Artist: T. M. Fowler
Lithographer:
Printer:
Publisher:
Key/Vignettes/Misc:
Locations:
Catalogs/Checklists: Stout, no. 316

3691
Place: Turtle Creek, Pennsylvania
Date: 1897
Title: Turtle Creek, Allegheny County Pennsylvania 1897.
Size: 13¼ × 22 in. (33.6 × 55.9 cm.)
Artist: T. M. Fowler
Lithographer:
Printer:
Publisher: T. M. Fowler & James B. Moyer
Key/Vignettes/Misc: Refs. 1–16, A–F
Locations: CLP–P; HSP–P; LC–M; PHMC–H; PSU; UPDL–P; YO; LC–P
Catalogs/Checklists: Stout, no. 18; LC–M, 864; PP

Place: Tyrone, Pennsylvania
Date: 1881
See Altoona, Pennsylvania, 1881.

3692
Place: Tyrone, Pennsylvania
Date: 1895
Title: Tyrone, Blair County Pennsylvania. 1895.
Size: 15¾ × 24¾ in. (40.1 × 63 cm.)
Artist: T. M. Fowler
Lithographer:
Printer:
Publisher: T. M. Fowler & James B. Moyer
Key/Vignettes/Misc: Refs. 1–11, A–K
Locations: LC–M; PHMC–H; PSU
Catalogs/Checklists: Stout, no. 54; LC–M, 864.1

3693
Place: Union City, Pennsylvania
Date: 1895
Title: Union City, Erie County, Pennsylvania. 1895.
Size: 15⅝ × 26⅜ in. (39.8 × 67.1 cm.)
Artist: T. M. Fowler
Lithographer:
Printer:
Publisher: T. M. Fowler & James B. Moyer
Key/Vignettes/Misc: Refs. 1–20, A–E
Locations: HSP–P; LC–M; PHMC–H; PSU; UPDL–P
Catalogs/Checklists: Stout, no. 119; LC–M, 865

3694
Place: Uniontown, Pennsylvania
Date: 1879
Title: Uniontown, Pa. 1879.
Size: 14¼ × 25⅛ in. (36.2 × 63.9 cm.)
Artist: F. Robjohns
Lithographer:
Printer: Thos. Hunter Lith. Phila.
Publisher: C. J. Corbin
Key/Vignettes/Misc: 11 vignettes
Locations: HSP–P; LC–M (photo)
Catalogs/Checklists: Stout, no. 128; LC–M, 865.1

3695
Place: Uniontown, Pennsylvania
Date: 1897
Title: Uniontown, Pennsylvania. 1897.
Size: 19⁷⁄₁₆ × 26⅝ in. (49.5 × 67.7 cm.)
Artist: T. M. Fowler
Lithographer:
Printer:
Publisher: T. M. Fowler & James B. Moyer
Key/Vignettes/Misc: Refs. 1–29, A–N
Locations: LC–M; PHMC–H; PSU; LC–P
Catalogs/Checklists: Stout, no. 129; LC–M, 866

3696
Place: Unlerstown, Pennsylvania
Date: N.D.
Title:
Size:
Artist:
Lithographer:
Printer:
Publisher:
Key/Vignettes/Misc:
Locations:
Catalogs/Checklists: Stout, no. 317

3697
Place: Valley Forge, Pennsylvania
Date: 1890
Title: Valley Forge, Pa. 1890.
Size: 19 × 26¼ in. (48.4 × 66.8 cm.)
Artist: [T. M. Fowler]
Lithographer:
Printer: A. E. Downs Lith. Boston
Publisher: James B. Moyer, Myerstown, Pa.
Key/Vignettes/Misc: Refs. A–F; 5 vignettes
Locations: LC–M; YO; LC–P
Catalogs/Checklists: Stout, no. 81; LC–M, 867; PP

3698
Place: Verona, Pennsylvania
Date: 1896
Title: Verona & Oakmont, Allegheny County Pennsylvania 1896.
Size: 17⅛ × 28⅛ in. (43.6 × 71.5 cm.)
Artist: T. M. Fowler
Lithographer:
Printer:
Publisher: T. M. Fowler & James B. Moyer
Key/Vignettes/Misc: Refs. 1–8, A–H
Locations: LC–M; PHMC–H; PSU; UPDL–P; BPL–R; YO

Catalogs/Checklists: Stout, no. 19; LC–M, 868; PP

3699
Place: Warren, Pennsylvania
Date: 1895
Title: Warren, Pennsylvania 1895.
Size: 20⅝ × 31¾ in. (52.5 × 80.6 cm.)
Artist: T. M. Fowler
Lithographer:
Printer:
Publisher: T. M. Fowler & James B. Moyer
Key/Vignettes/Misc: Refs. 1–31, A–L
Locations: PHMC–H; LC–M (photo)
Catalogs/Checklists: Stout, no. 268; LC–M, 868.1

3700
Place: Washington, Pennsylvania
Date: 1897 State I
Title: Washington, Pennsylvania. 1897
Size: 16⅞ × 37⅜ in. (43 × 95 cm.)
Artist: T. M. Fowler
Lithographer:
Printer:
Publisher: T. M. Fowler & James B. Moyer
Key/Vignettes/Misc: Refs. 1–34, A–U
Locations: PHMC–H
Catalogs/Checklists: Stout, no. 276a

3701
Place: Washington, Pennsylvania
Date: 1897 State II
Title: Washington, Pennsylvania, 1897.
Size: 19⅝ × 38¹⁄₁₆ in. (50 × 96.9 cm.)
Artist: T. M. Fowler
Lithographer:
Printer:
Publisher: T. M. Fowler & James B. Moyer
Key/Vignettes/Misc: Refs. 1–34, A–U
Locations: CLP–P; LC–M; PHMC–H; UPDL–P; BPL–R; YO; LC–P
Catalogs/Checklists: Stout, no. 276b; LC–M, 869; PP

3702
Place: Watertown, Pennsylvania
Date: 1918
Title:
Size:
Artist:
Lithographer:
Printer:
Publisher:
Key/Vignettes/Misc:
Locations:
Catalogs/Checklists: Stout, no. 318

3703
Place: Watsontown, Pennsylvania
Date: N.D.
Title: Watsontown, Pennsylvania.
Size: 19 × 25½ in. (48.4 × 64.9 cm.)
Artist:
Lithographer:
Printer: O. H. Bailey & Co.
Publisher: O. H. Bailey & Co., Boston
Key/Vignettes/Misc: Refs. 1–28; 6 vignettes
Locations: YO; LC–M (photo)
Catalogs/Checklists: Stout, no. 224; PP

3704
Place: Waynesboro, Pennsylvania
Date: 1894
Title: Waynesboro, Franklin County
Pennsylvania 1894.
Size: 15⅝ × 26¼ in. (39.8 × 66.7 cm.)
Artist: T. M. Fowler
Lithographer:
Printer:
Publisher: T. M. Fowler & James B. Moyer
Key/Vignettes/Misc: Refs. 1–14, A–I
Locations: HSP–P; PHMC–H; LC–M
(photo)
Catalogs/Checklists: Stout, no. 133;
LC–M, 869.1

3705
Place: Waynesburg, Pennsylvania
Date: 1875
Title:
Size:
Artist:
Lithographer:
Printer:
Publisher:
Key/Vignettes/Misc:
Locations:
Catalogs/Checklists: Stout, no. 320

3706
Place: Waynesburg, Pennsylvania
Date: 1897
Title: Waynesburg, Green County
Pennsylvania. 1897.
Size: 14 × 22⅝ in. (35.6 × 57.5 cm.)
Artist: T. M. Fowler
Lithographer:
Printer:
Publisher: T. M. Fowler & James B. Moyer
Key/Vignettes/Misc: Refs. 1–24
Locations: LC–M; PHMC–H; LC–P
Catalogs/Checklists: Stout, no. 134;
LC–M, 870

3707
Place: Waynesburg, Pennsylvania
Date: 1906
Title:
Size:
Artist: T. M. Fowler
Lithographer:
Printer:
Publisher:
Key/Vignettes/Misc:
Locations:
Catalogs/Checklists: Stout, no. 321

3708
Place: Webster, Pennsylvania
Date: 1904
Title: Webster, Westmoreland Co.
Pennsylvania. 1904.
Size: 12 × 16¾ in. (30.5 × 42.6 cm.)
Artist: T. M. Fowler
Lithographer:
Printer:
Publisher: T. M. Fowler, Morrisville, Pa.
Key/Vignettes/Misc: Refs. 1–18; 8
vignettes
Locations: BPL–R; LC–M (photo);
NYH–NY

Catalogs/Checklists: Stout, no. 290;
LC–M, 870.1

3709
Place: Wellsville, Pennsylvania
Date: 1903
Title: View of Wellsville, Pennsylvania.
1903
Size: 14⅛ × 17¹⁵⁄₁₆ in. (35.9 × 45.7 cm.)
Artist: T. M. Fowler
Lithographer:
Printer:
Publisher: T. M. Fowler, Morrisville, Pa.
Key/Vignettes/Misc: 13 vignettes
Locations: NYH–NY
Catalogs/Checklists:

Place: West Bethlehem, Pennsylvania
Date: 1886
See Bethlehem, Pennsylvania, 1886.

3710
Place: West Bethlehem, Pennsylvania
Date: 1894
Title: West Bethlehem, Lehigh County
Pennsylvania. 1894.
Size: 13½ × 21¾ in. (34.4 × 55.3 cm.)
Artist: T. M. Fowler
Lithographer:
Printer:
Publisher: T. M. Fowler & James B. Moyer
Key/Vignettes/Misc: Refs. 1–7, A–C
Locations: PHMC–H; BPL–R; LC–M
Catalogs/Checklists: Stout, no. 172;
LC–M, 870.2

Place: West Brownsville, Pennsylvania
Date: 1883
See Brownsville, Pennsylvania, 1883.

Place: West Elizabeth, Pennsylvania
Date: 1897
See Elizabeth, Pennsylvania, 1897.

3711
Place: West Newton, Pennsylvania
Date: 1900
Title: West Newton, Pennsylvania 1900
Size: 13½ × 22¾ in. (34.3 × 57.9 cm.)
Artist: T. M. Fowler
Lithographer:
Printer:
Publisher: T. M. Fowler
Key/Vignettes/Misc: Refs. 1–13, A–H
Locations: CLP–P; HSP–P; LC–M;
PHMC–H; PSU; UPDL–P; BPL–R
Catalogs/Checklists: Stout, no. 291;
LC–M, 871

3712
Place: West Pittston, Pennsylvania
Date: 1885
Title: West Pittston, Pa. Wyoming Valley
Size: 18⅞ × 31 in. (48.1 × 78.8 cm.)
Artist: H. H. Rowley
Lithographer:
Printer: C. H. Vogt & Son Lith. Cleveland
Publisher: H. H. Rowley, Utica
Key/Vignettes/Misc:
Locations: YO
Catalogs/Checklists: PP, no. 77

Place: West Pittston, Pennsylvania
Date: 1892
See Pittston, Pennsylvania, 1892.

3713
Place: West Union, Pennsylvania
Date: 1899
Title:
Size:
Artist: T. M. Fowler
Lithographer:
Printer:
Publisher:
Key/Vignettes/Misc:
Locations:
Catalogs/Checklists: Warren

3714
Place: Wilkes–Barre, Pennsylvania
Date: 1864
Title: Valley of Wyoming. From Prospect
Rock
Size: 11⅛ × 35⅞ in. (28.3 × 91.3 cm.)
Artist: Eugene J. Adams
Lithographer:
Printer: Endicott & Co. Lith. 59 Beekman
St. New York
Publisher: Eugene J. Adams,
Wilkes–Barre, Pa.
Key/Vignettes/Misc: Refs. 1–7; 1 vignette
Locations: YO
Catalogs/Checklists: PP, no. 60

3715
Place: Wilkes–Barre, Pennsylvania
Date: 1872
Title: Bird's Eye View of Wilkes–Barre,
Pa. 1872
Size: 18¼ × 25 in. (46.5 × 63.6 cm.)
Artist: [H. H. Bailey?]
Lithographer: C. H. Vogt
Printer: American Oleograph Co.
Publisher: Fowler & Bailey
Key/Vignettes/Misc: Refs. 1–7, A–M
Locations: BPL–R
Catalogs/Checklists: Stout, no. 180

3716
Place: Wilkes–Barre, Pennsylvania
Date: 1882
Title: Wilkes–Barre, Pa. 1882.
Size: 18 × 32⅛ in. (45.9 × 81.7 cm.)
Artist: C. L. Fussell
Lithographer:
Printer:
Publisher: Philadelphia Publishing House,
Phila.
Key/Vignettes/Misc: 14 vignettes
Locations: PSU
Catalogs/Checklists: Stout, no. 181

3717
Place: Wilkes–Barre, Pennsylvania
Date: 1889
Title: Wilkes–Barre Pennsylvania. 1889
Size: 24⅝ × 42½ in. (62.7 × 108.1 cm.)
Artist: Fowler, Downs and Moyer
Lithographer:
Printer: A. E. Downs Lith. Boston
Publisher: Fowler, Downs, and Moyer
Key/Vignettes/Misc: Refs. 1–31, A–X

Locations: HSP–P; LC–M; PHMC–H
Catalogs/Checklists: Stout, no. 182;
LC–M, 872

3718
Place: Williamsburg, Pennsylvania
Date: 1906
Title: Birds Eye View of Williamsburg
Blair Co., Pa. 1906
Size: 20⅛ × 23¾ in. (51.2 × 60.4 cm.)
Artist: T. M. Fowler
Lithographer:
Printer:
Publisher: Fowler & Kelly, Morrisville, Pa.
Key/Vignettes/Misc: 9 vignettes
Locations: LC–M
Catalogs/Checklists: Stout, no. 55;
LC–M, 873

3719
Place: Williamsport, Pennsylvania
Date: 1854
Title: View of Williamsport, Pa. 1854.
Size: 19½ × 24¾ in. (49.6 × 63 cm.)
Artist: J. B. Bachelder
Lithographer:
Printer: P. S. Duval & Co. Steam Lith
Press Phila.
Publisher:
Key/Vignettes/Misc:
Locations: YO
Catalogs/Checklists: PP, no. 48; Stout, no.
185

3720
Place: Williamsport, Pennsylvania
Date: 1872
Title: Williamsport, Pa. 1872.
Size: 17¾ × 30⅞ in. (45.2 × 78.5 cm.)
Artist: H. H. Bailey
Lithographer:
Printer: Strobridge & Co. Lith.
Cin[cinnati]
Publisher:
Key/Vignettes/Misc: Refs. 1–29, A–Z
Locations: YO; LC–M (facsimile)
Catalogs/Checklists: Stout, no. 186; PP;
LC–M, 873.1

3721
Place: Williamsport, Pennsylvania
Date: 1880
Title:
Size:
Artist: C. L. Fussell
Lithographer:
Printer:
Publisher:
Key/Vignettes/Misc:
Locations:
Catalogs/Checklists: Stout, no. 322

3722
Place: Wilmerding, Pennsylvania
Date: 1897
Title: Wilmerding, Allegheny County
Pennsylvania. 1897
Size: 22⅞ × 14⅝ in. (58.1 × 37.1 cm.)
Artist: T. M. Fowler
Lithographer:
Printer:
Publisher: T. M. Fowler & James B. Moyer

Key/Vignettes/Misc: Refs. 1–8, A–D
Locations: LC–M; PHMC–H; UPDL–P;
LC–P
Catalogs/Checklists: Stout, no. 20;
LC–M, 874

3723
Place: Wilson, Pennsylvania
Date: 1902
Title: Wilson and Mendelssohn,
Pennsylvania 1902.
Size: 8¼ × 13 in. (21 × 33 cm.)
Artist: T. M. Fowler
Lithographer:
Printer:
Publisher: T. M. Fowler & James B. Moyer
Key/Vignettes/Misc: Refs. 1–8
Locations: BPL–R; CLP–P; HSP–P;
LC–M; PHMC–H; PSU; UPDL–P
Catalogs/Checklists: Stout, no. 21;
LC–M, 875

3724
Place: Windber, Pennsylvania
Date: 1900
Title: Bird's Eye View of Windber,
Somerset County Pa. 1900
Size: 15½ × 28⅝ in. (39.5 × 72.8 cm.)
Artist: T. M. Fowler
Lithographer:
Printer:
Publisher: T. M. Fowler & James B. Moyer
Key/Vignettes/Misc: Refs. 1–16, A–H; 2
vignettes
Locations: CLP–P; PHMC–H; PSU;
UPDL–P; YO; LC–M (photo)
Catalogs/Checklists: Stout, no. 256;
LC–M, 875.1

Place: Wissahickon, Pennsylvania
Date: 1907
See Manayunk, Pennsylvania, 1907.

3725
Place: Womelsdorf, Pennsylvania
Date: 1898
Title: Womelsdorf
Size: 11¹⁵⁄₁₆ × 17 in. (30.4 × 43.2 cm.)
Artist:
Lithographer:
Printer:
Publisher: Bailey & Moyer, Boston, Mass.
Key/Vignettes/Misc:
Locations: YO
Catalogs/Checklists:

3726
Place: Wrightsville, Pennsylvania
Date: 1894
Title: Wrightsville, York County
Pennsylvania. 1894.
Size: 13 × 21¼ in. (33.1 × 54 cm.)
Artist: T. M. Fowler
Lithographer:
Printer:
Publisher: T. M. Fowler & James B. Moyer
Key/Vignettes/Misc: Refs. 1–15, A–F
Locations: HSP–P; LC–M; PHMC–H;
PSU; HSYC–Y
Catalogs/Checklists: Stout, no. 294;
LC–M, 876

3727
Place: Wyoming, Pennsylvania
Date: 1885
Title: Village of Wyoming, Wyoming
Valley, Penn'a., 1885, Scene of the
Massacre of July 3rd 1778.
Size: 16¹³⁄₁₆ × 29⅛ in. (42.8 × 74.1 cm.)
Artist: H. H. Rowley
Lithographer:
Printer: C. H. Vogt & Son, Lith
Publisher: H. H. Rowley, Utica, N. Y.
Key/Vignettes/Misc:
Locations: LC–M (facsimile); Wyoming
Historical and Geological Society,
Wilkes–Barre, Pennsylvania
Catalogs/Checklists: LC–M, 876.1

Place: Yeagertown, Pennsylvania
Date: 1906
See Burnham, Pennsylvania, 1906.

3728
Place: York, Pennsylvania
Date: 1852
Title: View of York Pa.
Size: 20 × 27⅜ in. (50.9 × 69.7 cm.)
Artist: From daguerreotype by Williams
Lithographer:
Printer: E. Sachse & Co. . . .Balto.
Publisher: J. Thomas Williams
Key/Vignettes/Misc: 18 vignettes
Locations: HSP–P; LC–M; BPL–R; YO
Catalogs/Checklists: Stout, no. 295;
LC–M, 876.2 PP, No. 43

3729
Place: York, Pennsylvania
Date: 1873
Title: Bird's Eye View of York, Penn. 1873
Size: 20¼ × 26 in. (51.6 × 66.2 cm.)
Artist: H. H. Bailey
Lithographer:
Printer: Strobridge & Co. Lith Cin. O.
Publisher:
Key/Vignettes/Misc: Refs. 1–43, A–T
Locations: HSYC–Y
Catalogs/Checklists: Stout, no. 323

3730
Place: York, Pennsylvania
Date: 1879
Title: York, Pa.
Size: 22¾ × 36¾ in. (57.9 × 93.4 cm.)
Artist: Davoust Kern
Lithographer:
Printer: A. Hoen & Co., Lith., Baltimore,
Md.
Publisher: Davoust Kern
Key/Vignettes/Misc: 25 vignettes;
description
Locations: LC–M; LC–P; BPL–R;
HSYC–Y
Catalogs/Checklists: Stout, no. 296;
LC–M, 877

3731
Place: York, Pennsylvania
Date: 1888
Title:
Size:
Artist: Davoust Kern

Lithographer:
Printer:
Publisher:
Key/Vignettes/Misc:
Locations:
Catalogs/Checklists: Stout, no. 324

3732
Place: York, Pennsylvania
Date: 1888
Title: York. Pennsylvania
Size:
Artist:
Lithographer:
Printer:
Publisher: Fowler & Downs Boston
Key/Vignettes/Misc: Refs. 1–40, A–Y; 14 vignettes
Locations: HSYC–Y (facsimile)
Catalogs/Checklists:

3733
Place: Zelienople, Pennsylvania
Date: 1901
Title: Zelienople. Butler County Pennsylvania, 1901.
Size: 11 × 27⅞ in. (28 × 70.9 cm.)
Artist: T. M. Fowler
Lithographer:
Printer:
Publisher: T. M. Fowler & James B. Moyer
Key/Vignettes/Misc: Refs. 1–9, A–E; 1 vignette
Locations: PHMC–H; CLP–P; LC–M; PSU; UPDL–P
Catalogs/Checklists: Stout, no. 69; LC–M, 878

3734
Place: Charlottetown, Prince Edward Island
Date: 1878
Title: Panoramic View of Charlottetown, Prince Edward Island. 1878
Size: 16½ × 25⁹⁄₁₆ in. (41.8 × 65 cm.)
Artist: A. Ruger
Lithographer:
Printer:
Publisher: [J. J. Stoner, Madison, Wis.]
Key/Vignettes/Misc: Refs. A–H, J–M, 1–49
Locations: PAC–P; Prince Edward Island Public Archives, Charlottetown, Prince Edward Island; LC–M (photo)
Catalogs/Checklists: PAC (1976); LC–M, 1069.2

3735
Place: Summerside, Prince Edward Island
Date: 1878
Title: Panoramic View of Summerside, Prince County, Prince Edward Island.
Size: 16⅛ × 22 in. (41 × 56 cm.)
Artist: A. Ruger
Lithographer:
Printer:
Publisher: [J. J. Stoner, Madison, Wis.]
Key/Vignettes/Misc: Refs. 1–37
Locations: PAC (facsimile); private collection
Catalogs/Checklists: PAC (1976)

3736
Place: San Juan, Puerto Rico
Date: [1842]
Title: Puerto–Rico
Size: 13 × 20½ in. (33.1 × 52.2 cm.)
Artist:
Lithographer: A. de Vaudicourt
Printer: P. S. Duval, Lith. Phila.
Publisher:
Key/Vignettes/Misc:
Locations: NYP–P
Catalogs/Checklists:

3737
Place: San Juan, Puerto Rico
Date: Ca. 1850
Title: Panorama de San Juan de Puerto–Rico. Propriedad de Cl. Marsal
Size: 17⁷⁄₁₆ × 29⅝ in. (44.4 × 75.4 cm.)
Artist:
Lithographer: Deroy
Printer: Lemercier, Paris
Publisher:
Key/Vignettes/Misc:
Locations: NYP–S (imprint lacking)
Catalogs/Checklists: Stokes C. 1860—H–38

3738
Place: San Juan, Puerto Rico
Date: Ca. 1850
Title: Vue Generale de Porto–Rico Vista General de Puerto–Rico
Size: 12 × 19 in. (30.6 × 48.3 cm.)
Artist:
Lithographer:
Printer:
Publisher: L. Turgis, Paris
Key/Vignettes/Misc:
Locations: Unknown. See Old Print Shop Portfolio, XXVI, p. 65, No. 29
Catalogs/Checklists:

3739
Place: San Juan, Puerto Rico
Date: Ca. 1855
Title: San Juan Porto Rico Puerto Rico Pinturesco—Capital, Vista Tomada Desde el Olimpo
Size: 14¾ × 19½ in. (37.6 × 49.6 cm.)
Artist: Jacottet
Lithographer:
Printer: Lemercier, Paris
Publisher:
Key/Vignettes/Misc:
Locations: Unknown. See Old Print Shop Portfolio, XIX, p. 81, No. 10
Catalogs/Checklists:

3740
Place: San Juan, Puerto Rico
Date: Ca. 1860
Title: Vue Generale de Porto–Rico, Grandes Antilles
Size: 12½ × 19 in. (31.8 × 48.4 cm.)
Artist:
Lithographer:
Printer: Deroy
Publisher: Turgis, Paris
Key/Vignettes/Misc:
Locations: Unknown. See Old Print Shop Portfolio, XXX, p. 156, No. 18
Catalogs/Checklists:

3741
Place: Amherst Harbour, Quebec
Date: 1866
Title: Amherst Harbour, Magdalen Islands, C. E.
Size: 8⅛ × 11¼ in. (20.5 × 28.4 cm.)
Artist: Thomas Pye
Lithographer:
Printer: Roberts & Reinhold, Place d'Armes, Mtl.
Publisher:
Key/Vignettes/Misc:
Locations: PAC–P; MTLB–T
Catalogs/Checklists: Robertson, no. 1592

3742
Place: Bedford, Quebec
Date: 1881
Title: Bird's Eye View of Bedford, P. Q. Chef Lieu of Missisquoi County.
Size:
Artist: H. Wellge
Lithographer:
Printer:
Publisher: J. J. Stoner, Madison, Wis.
Key/Vignettes/Misc: Refs. 1–17; 3 vignettes
Locations: PAC (photo)
Catalogs/Checklists: PAC (1976); deVolpi & Scowen, Eastern Townships, Plate 102

3743
Place: Berthierville, Quebec
Date: 1881
Title: Vue a vol d'oiseau de la Ville de Berthier, P. Q. 1881
Size: 6¾ × 15⅞ in. (17.3 × 40.5 cm.)
Artist:
Lithographer:
Printer:
Publisher:
Key/Vignettes/Misc: Refs. 1–20; 1 vignette
Locations: PAC (photo)
Catalogs/Checklists: PAC (1976)

3744
Place: Cape Cove, Quebec
Date: Ca. 1866
Title: Cape Cove, C. E.
Size: 8⅛ × 11⅛ in. (20.6 × 28.3 cm.)
Artist: Thomas Pye
Lithographer:
Printer: Roberts & Reinhold, lith. Place d'Armes, Mtl.
Publisher:
Key/Vignettes/Misc:
Locations: PAC–P; MTLB–T
Catalogs/Checklists: Robertson, no. 1583

3745
Place: Carleton, Quebec
Date: Ca. 1866
Title: Carleton, C. E.
Size: 8 × 11¼ in. (20.4 × 28.4 cm.)
Artist: Thomas Pye
Lithographer:
Printer: Roberts & Reinhold, Lith., Place d'Armes, Mtl.
Publisher:
Key/Vignettes/Misc:
Locations: PAC–P; MTLB–T

Catalogs/Checklists: Robertson, no. 1593; Spendlove, Face of Early Canada, p. 35

3746
Place: Chambly, Quebec
Date: Ca. 1841
Title: View in the Seignory of Chambly, Canada
Size: 9⅜ × 13¹⁵⁄₁₆ in. (23.7 × 35.4 cm.)
Artist:
Lithographer:
Printer:
Publisher: Bourne [Montreal]
Key/Vignettes/Misc:
Locations: PAC–P
Catalogs/Checklists: Allodi, Printmaking in Canada, no. 66

3747
Place: Chambly, Quebec
Date: Ca. 1841
Title: View of the Village of Chambly, Seignory of Chambly.
Size: 10⁵⁄₁₆ × 13⅞ in. (26.2 × 35.2 cm.)
Artist:
Lithographer:
Printer:
Publisher: Bourne
Key/Vignettes/Misc:
Locations: MTLB–T
Catalogs/Checklists: Robertson, no. 1999; Allodi, Printmaking in Canada, no. 67

3748
Place: Coaticook, Quebec
Date: 1881
Title: Bird's Eye View of Coaticook, P. Q. 1881.
Size: 13 × 24⅛ in. (33 × 61.5 cm.)
Artist: H. Wellge
Lithographer:
Printer:
Publisher: J. J. Stoner, Madison, Wis.
Key/Vignettes/Misc: Refs. 1–23, A–E
Locations: ROM
Catalogs/Checklists: PAC (1976); deVolpi & Scowen, Eastern Townships, Plate 103

3749
Place: Farnham, Quebec
Date: 1881
Title: Bird's Eye View of Town of Farnham, P. Q. 1881.
Size: 10⁷⁄₁₆ × 17½ in. (26.5 × 44.5 cm.) (photo)
Artist:
Lithographer:
Printer:
Publisher:
Key/Vignettes/Misc: Refs. 1–17; 2 vignettes
Locations: PAC (photo)
Catalogs/Checklists: PAC (1976)

3750
Place: Fox River, Quebec
Date: Ca. 1866
Title: Fox River, C. E.
Size: 8 × 11⅛ in. (20.5 × 28.3 cm.)
Artist: Thomas Pye
Lithographer:
Printer: Roberts & Reinhold, Place d'Armes, Mtl.

Publisher:
Key/Vignettes/Misc:
Locations: PAC–P; MTLB–T
Catalogs/Checklists: Robertson, no. 1589

3751
Place: Grand Greve, Quebec
Date: Ca. 1866
Title: Grand Greve, C. E.
Size: 8 × 11¼ in. (20.3 × 28.5 cm.)
Artist: Thomas Pye
Lithographer:
Printer: Roberts & Reinhold, Place d'Armes, Mtl.
Publisher:
Key/Vignettes/Misc:
Locations: PAC–P; MTLB–T
Catalogs/Checklists: Robertson, no. 1590

3752
Place: Grand River, Quebec
Date: Ca. 1866
Title: Grand River, C. E.
Size: 8 × 11¼ in. (20.4 × 28.4 cm.)
Artist: Thomas Pye
Lithographer:
Printer: Roberts & Reinhold, Place d'Armes, Mtl.
Publisher:
Key/Vignettes/Misc:
Locations: PAC–P
Catalogs/Checklists:

3753
Place: Joliette, Quebec
Date: 1881
Title: Vue a vol d'oiseau de la Ville de Joliette, P. Q. 1881
Size: 11⅝ (cropped) × 21¾ in. (29.6 × 55.4 cm.)
Artist:
Lithographer:
Printer:
Publisher:
Key/Vignettes/Misc: Refs. 1–30
Locations: PAC (cropped)
Catalogs/Checklists: PAC (1976)

3754
Place: Lennoxville, Quebec
Date: 1832
Title: Lennoxville District of Saint Francis L. C. in 1832.
Size: 11 × 17⅞ in. (28 × 45.5 cm.) (photo)
Artist: C. B. Felton
Lithographer:
Printer:
Publisher:
Key/Vignettes/Misc:
Locations: PAC (photo)
Catalogs/Checklists: deVolpi & Scowen, Eastern Townships, Plate 3

3755
Place: Lennoxville, Quebec
Date: 1881
Title: Bird's Eye View of Lennoxville, P. Q. 1881
Size: 11 × 17⅞ in. (28 × 45.5 cm.) (photo)
Artist: H. Wellge
Lithographer:

Printer:
Publisher: J. J. Stoner, Madison, Wis.
Key/Vignettes/Misc: Refs. 1–25
Locations: PAC (photo)
Catalogs/Checklists: PAC (1976); deVolpi & Scowen, Eastern Townships, Plate 104

3756
Place: Levis, Quebec
Date: 1881
Title: Vue a vol d'oiseau de Bird's Eye View of Levis, P. Q. 1881.
Size: 12⁹⁄₁₆ × 17¹¹⁄₁₆ in. (32 × 45 cm.) (photo)
Artist:
Lithographer:
Printer:
Publisher:
Key/Vignettes/Misc: Refs. 1–25; 2 vignettes
Locations: PAC (photo)
Catalogs/Checklists: PAC (1976)

3757
Place: Montmagny, Quebec
Date: 1881
Title: Vue a vol d'oiseau de Montmagny, P. Q.
Size: 10 × 15⅜ in. (25.4 × 39.2 cm.)
Artist:
Lithographer:
Printer: The Burland Lith. Co., Montreal
Publisher:
Key/Vignettes/Misc:
Locations: Archives Nationales, Quebec, Quebec; PAC (photo)
Catalogs/Checklists: PAC (1976)

3758
Place: Montreal, Quebec
Date: Ca.1830
Title: Montreal. From the Mount, Lower Canada North America.
Size: 9⅜ × 14⅛ in. (23.8 × 35.9 cm.)
Artist: Lt. Hornbrook, R. M.
Lithographer: T. M. Baynes
Printer: C. Hullmandel
Publisher:
Key/Vignettes/Misc:
Locations: MTLB–T; MGUR–M; PAC–P
Catalogs/Checklists: Robertson, no. 1881; deVolpi, Montreal, I, Plate 18; Bellman, Fig. 4

3759
Place: Montreal, Quebec
Date: 1831
Title: View of the City of Montreal, Taken from the Mountain
Size: 7¼ × 15½ in. (18.5 × 39.4 cm.)
Artist: Jos. Bouchette Junr.
Lithographer: L. Haghe
Printer: Day & Haghe, 17 Gate St. [London]
Publisher:
Key/Vignettes/Misc:
Locations: PAC–P; MCM–M
Catalogs/Checklists:

3760
Place: Montreal, Quebec
Date: 1841
Title: Sleighing in Canada, on the River St.

Lawrence Facing Montreal, 1841.
Size: 12¾ × 25¼ in. (32.5 × 64.1 cm.)
(cropped)
Artist: Mrs. Shirley and Mr. Warre, A. D.
C.
Lithographer:
Printer: [C. Warren, London]
Publisher:
Key/Vignettes/Misc: Refs. 1–11
Locations: MGUR–M; MCM–M
Catalogs/Checklists: deVolpi, Montreal, I,
Plate 81

3761
Place: Montreal, Quebec
Date: [1841]
Title: View of the Port of Montreal
Size: 8 × 13⁹⁄₁₆ in. (20.4 × 34.5 cm.)
Artist: Crehen
Lithographer:
Printer: Bourne, Lithogy. [Montreal]
Publisher:
Key/Vignettes/Misc:
Locations: MCM–M
Catalogs/Checklists: deVolpi, Montreal, I,
Plate 83; Allodi, Printmaking in Canada,
no. 62

3762
Place: Montreal, Quebec
Date: [1840–42]
Title: Montreal
Size: ca. 10½ × 15 in. (ca. 26.7 × 38.2
cm.)
Artist: Coke Smyth
Lithographer:
Printer: A. Ducote's Lithographic
Establishment, 70, St. Martins Lane,
London
Publisher: Thos. McLean, 26, Haymarket,
London
Key/Vignettes/Misc:
Locations: MCM–M; ROM; MTLB–T
Catalogs/Checklists: Samuel, no. 243
(XIX); Spendlove, Face of Early Canada,
p. 42 and Plate 66; Robertson, no. 1876

3763
Place: Montreal, Quebec
Date: [1843]
Title: Montreal. (From the Mountain).
Size: 10⅝ × 14⅞ in. (27.1 × 38 cm.)
Artist:
Lithographer: J[ames] Duncan
Printer: Mathews Lithography [Montreal]
Publisher:
Key/Vignettes/Misc:
Locations: MGUR–M; PAC–P (title &
imprint cropped); MCM–M; ROM
Catalogs/Checklists: Allodi, Printmaking
in Canada, no. 75; Spendlove, Face of
Early Canada, p. 66 and Plate 101;
deVolpi, Montreal, I, Plate 90; Samuel, no.
294

3764
Place: Montreal, Quebec
Date: [1843]
Title: Notre–Dame–Street
Size: 9¹⁵⁄₁₆ × 15¼ in. (25.2 × 38.8 cm.)
Artist:
Lithographer: J[ames] Duncan
Printer: Matthews Lith. [Montreal]

Publisher:
Key/Vignettes/Misc:
Locations: MGUR–M; MTLB–T; ROM
Catalogs/Checklists: Allodi, Printmaking
in Canada, no. 74; Spendlove, Face of
Early Canada, p. 66 and Plate 104;
deVolpi, Montreal, I, Plate 91

3765
Place: Montreal, Quebec
Date: [1843]
Title: Steam Boat Wharf.
Size: 10³⁄₁₆ × 15⅛ in. (25.9 × 38.5 cm.)
Artist:
Lithographer: J[ames] Duncan
Printer: Matthews' Lith. Montreal
Publisher:
Key/Vignettes/Misc:
Locations: MGUR–M; MTLB–T
Catalogs/Checklists: Robertson, no. 2851;
Allodi, Printmaking in Canada, no. 76;
Spendlove, Face of Early Canada, p. 66
and Plate 103

3766
Place: Montreal, Quebec
Date: [1844]
Title: Montreal From the Indian
Encamping–Ground
Size: 10⁷⁄₁₆ × 14⁹⁄₁₆ in. (26.5 × 36.8 cm.)
Artist:
Lithographer: J[ames] Duncan
Printer: Matthews Lithy. [Montreal]
Publisher:
Key/Vignettes/Misc:
Locations: MGUR–M; ROM
Catalogs/Checklists: deVolpi, Montreal, I,
Plate 92; Spendlove, Face of Early Canada,
p. 66; Allodi, Printmaking in Canada, no.
79; Samuel, no. 293

3767
Place: Montreal, Quebec
Date: [1844]
Title: Notre Dame Street–West
Size: 10³⁄₁₆ × 14¹³⁄₁₆ in. (25.9 x 37.7 cm.)
Artist:
Lithographer: J[ames] Duncan
Printer: Matthews' Lith. [Montreal]
Publisher:
Key/Vignettes/Misc:
Locations: ROM
Catalogs/Checklists: Spendlove, Face of
Early Canada, p. 66 and Plate 102; Allodi,
Printmaking in Canada, no. 77

3768
Place: Montreal, Quebec
Date: [1844]
Title: Winter Scene on the River St.
Lawrence.
Size: 10⅜ × 13¹⁵⁄₁₆ in. (26.4 × 35.5 cm.)
Artist:
Lithographer: J.[ames] Duncan
Printer: Matthews Lith. [Montreal]
Publisher:
Key/Vignettes/Misc:
Locations: Private collection
Catalogs/Checklists: Allodi, Printmaking
in Canada, no. 78

3769
Place: Montreal, Quebec
Date: [1851]

Title: Montreal
Size: 9½ × 11¹³⁄₁₆ in. (24.1 × 30 cm.)
Artist: Aug. Kollner
Lithographer: Deroy
Printer: Jacomme & Co.
Publisher: Goupil & Co., New York &
Paris
Key/Vignettes/Misc:
Locations: MTLB–T; MGUR–M;
PAC–P; MCM–M
Catalogs/Checklists: Spendlove, Face of
Early Canada, p. 72; Robertson, no. 1874;
deVolpi, Montreal, I, Plate 107

3770
Place: Montreal, Quebec
Date: 1852
Title: Montreal, Canada East. From the
Mountain
Size: 22½ × 35⁷⁄₁₆ in. (47.2 × 90 cm.)
Artist: E. Whitefield
Lithographer:
Printer: Endicott & Co., New York
Publisher: E. Whitefield, Gt. St. James St.,
Montreal
Key/Vignettes/Misc: 20 refs.; description
Locations: PAC–P; MCM–M; ROM;
NYP–S; MTLB–T; MGUR–M
Catalogs/Checklists: Stokes P. 1851—
H–39; Norton, Whitefield, no. 54;
deVolpi, Montreal, I, Plate 108; Samuel,
no. 780

3771
Place: Montreal, Quebec
Date: 1854
Title: City of Montreal From the
Mountain [in 1840]
Size: 20⅜ × 24½ in. (51.9 × 62.4 cm.)
Artist: Jas Duncan
Lithographer: Gauci
Printer: M. & N. Hanhart, [London]
Publisher: John Armour, Montreal and E.
Gambart & Co., London
Key/Vignettes/Misc:
Locations: MGUR–M; MTLB–T;
MCM–M; PAC–P
Catalogs/Checklists: Spendlove, Face of
Early Canada, p. 72; deVolpi, Montreal, I,
Plate 116; Bellman, Fig. 10

3772
Place: Montreal, Quebec
Date: [1854]
Title: Grand Trunk Railway of Canada,
Victoria Bridge, now Constructing Across
the River St. Lawrence at Montreal.
Size: 16¼ × 31¼ in. (41.2 × 79.3 cm.)
Artist: S. Russell
Lithographer:
Printer: Day & Son Lithrs. to the Queen
[London]
Publisher:
Key/Vignettes/Misc:
Locations: MCM–M
Catalogs/Checklists:

3773
Place: Montreal, Quebec
Date: 1855
Title: Montreal, Canada East. From the
Mountain.
Size: 22⅝ × 35¼ in. (57.4 × 89.5 cm.)

Artist: E. Whitefield
Lithographer:
Printer: Endicott & Co., New York
Publisher: E. Whitefield, Gt. St. James St.,
Montreal
Key/Vignettes/Misc: Refs. 1–19, A–B;
description
Locations: MM–NN; NYP–S; ROM;
PAC–P; MCM–M; Musee Chateau de
Ramezay, Montreal, Quebec; MGUR–M;
Musee du Quebec, Quebec, Quebec;
ACMW–FW
Catalogs/Checklists: Samuel, no. 297;
Norton, Whitefield, no. 61; Spendlove,
Face of Early Canada, p. 71, Plate 106

3774
Place: Montreal, Quebec
Date: Ca. 1859
Title: Montreal, C. E.
Size: 5 × 8⅜ in. (12.7 × 21.3 cm.)
Artist:
Lithographer:
Printer:
Publisher: Charles Magnus & Co. 12
Frankfurt St. N. Y.
Key/Vignettes/Misc:
Locations: MCM–M
Catalogs/Checklists:

3775
Place: Montreal, Quebec
Date: 1860
Title: Montreal. From the Lower Slope of
the Mountain
Size: 8⅛ × 19¹¹⁄₁₆ in. (20.7 × 47.6 cm.)
Artist: J. H. Walker
Lithographer: J. H. Walker
Printer:
Publisher: Chas. Magnus & Co., 12
Frankfort St., N. Y.
Key/Vignettes/Misc:
Locations: NYP–S
Catalogs/Checklists: Stokes 1860—H–2

3776
Place: Montreal, Quebec
Date: 1860
Title: Victoria Bridge, Over the River St.
Lawrence at Montreal
Size: 14 × 20¹³⁄₁₆ in. (35.7 × 53 cm.)
Artist: S. Russel
Lithographer:
Printer: Kell Bros. Lithrs. Castle St.
Holborn [London]
Publisher: John Weale
Key/Vignettes/Misc: Description on 10
lines
Locations: MGUR–M; MCM–M
Catalogs/Checklists: Spendlove, Face of
Early Canada, pp. 67–68

3777
Place: Montreal, Quebec
Date: Ca. 1860
Title: Montreal
Size:
Artist:
Lithographer:
Printer: William Collins, Sons & Co.,
London, Glasgow, & Edinburgh
Publisher:
Key/Vignettes/Misc:

Locations: MCM–M
Catalogs/Checklists: Bellman, Fig. 11;
deVolpi, Montreal, I, Plate 116

3778
Place: Montreal, Quebec
Date: Ca.1860
Title: Victoria Brucke uber den St. Lorenz
Strom bei Montreal
Size: 14¼ × 20⅝ in. (36.3 × 52.5 cm.)
Artist:
Lithographer: A. Oesterlein
Printer: J. Veith, Karlsruhe
Publisher: J. Veith, Karlsruhe
Key/Vignettes/Misc: Description
Locations: MGUR–M
Catalogs/Checklists:

3779
Place: Montreal, Quebec
Date: Ca. 1870
Title: City and Harbour of Montreal
Size: 12 × 21½ in. (30.5 × 54.6 cm.)
Artist: Roberts & Reinhold
Lithographer: R&R
Printer: Roberts & Reinhold, Montreal
Publisher: F. E. Grafton, 82 Gt. St. James
Street
Key/Vignettes/Misc:
Locations: PAC–P; MCM–M
Catalogs/Checklists: deVolpi, Montreal, II,
Plate 178

3780
Place: Montreal, Quebec
Date: 1871
Title: Notre Dame Street Montreal [in
1830]
Size: 10⅜ × 13⁵⁄₁₆ in. (26.3 × 33.9 cm.)
(matted)
Artist: R. A. Sproule
Lithographer: [W. L. Leney and A. Bourne]
Printer: [Leggo & Co., Montreal]
Publisher: A. Bourne, Montreal
Key/Vignettes/Misc:
Locations: MGUR–M; MCM–M; ROM
Catalogs/Checklists: Samuel, no. 228;
Spendlove, Face of Early Canada, pp.
62–64

3781
Place: Montreal, Quebec
Date: 1871
Title: Place D'Armes Montreal [in 1830]
Size: 10¹⁄₁₆ × 13³⁄₁₆ in. (25.5 × 33.4 cm.)
(matted)
Artist: R. A. Sproule
Lithographer: [W. L. Leney and A. Bourne]
Printer: [Leggo & Co., Montreal]
Publisher: A. Bourne, Montreal
Key/Vignettes/Misc:
Locations: MGUR–M; MCM–M; ROM
Catalogs/Checklists: Samuel, no. 224;
Spendlove, Face of Early Canada, pp.
62–64

3782
Place: Montreal, Quebec
Date: 1871
Title: St. James Street Montreal [in 1830]
Size: 10¹⁵⁄₁₆ × 13⁷⁄₁₆ in. (26.2 × 34.1 cm.)
(matted)

Artist: R. A. Sproule
Lithographer: [W. L. Leney and A. Bourne]
Printer: [Leggo & Co., Montreal]
Publisher: A. Bourne, Montreal
Key/Vignettes/Misc:
Locations: MGUR–M; MCM–M; ROM
Catalogs/Checklists: Samuel, no. 227;
Spendlove, Face of Early Canada, pp.
62–64

3783
Place: Montreal, Quebec
Date: 1871
Title: View of the Champ de Mars
Montreal [in 1830]
Size: 10¹⁄₁₆ × 13⅛ in. (25.6 × 33.5 cm.)
(matted)
Artist: R. A. Sproule
Lithographer: [W. L. Leney and A. Bourne]
Printer: [Leggo & Co., Montreal]
Publisher: A. Bourne, Montreal
Key/Vignettes/Misc:
Locations: MGUR–M; MCM–M; ROM
Catalogs/Checklists: Samuel, no. 226;
Spendlove, Face of Early Canada, pp.
62–64

3784
Place: Montreal, Quebec
Date: 1871
Title: View of the Harbour of Montreal [in
1830]
Size: 10¹⁄₁₆ × 13⅛ in. (25.6 × 33.5 cm.)
(matted)
Artist: R. A. Sproule
Lithographer: [W. L. Leney and A. Bourne]
Printer: [Leggo & Co., Montreal]
Publisher: A. Bourne, Montreal
Key/Vignettes/Misc:
Locations: MGUR–M; MCM–M; ROM
Catalogs/Checklists: Samuel, no. 225;
Spendlove, Face of Early Canada, pp.
62–64

3785
Place: Montreal, Quebec
Date: 1871
Title: View of Montreal, From Saint
Helens Island.
Size: 10⁵⁄₁₆ × 13³⁄₁₆ in. (26.2 × 33.4 cm.)
(matted)
Artist: R. A. Sproule
Lithographer: W. L. Leney and A. Bourne
Printer: Leggo & Co., Montreal
Publisher: A. Bourne, Montreal
Key/Vignettes/Misc:
Locations: MGUR–M; PAC–P;
MCM–M; ROM
Catalogs/Checklists: Samuel, no. 229;
Spendlove, Face of Early Canada, pp.
62–64

3786
Place: Montreal, Quebec
Date: 1878
Title: View of Montreal from St. Helen's
Island.
Size: 13¹¹⁄₁₆ × 16¾ in. (34.7 × 42.5 cm.)
Artist: James Duncan
Lithographer:
Printer: The Burland–Desbarats Lith. Co.

Publisher: Adolphus Bourne
Key/Vignettes/Misc:
Locations: MCM–M; PAC–P
Catalogs/Checklists: deVolpi, Montreal, II, Plate 279; Bellman, Fig. 13; Spendlove, Face of Early Canada, p. 66

3787
Place: Montreal, Quebec
Date: 1888 State I
Title: City of Montreal.
Size: 23 1/16 × 35 15/16 in. (58.6 × 91.2 cm.)
Artist:
Lithographer:
Printer: Toronto Lithographing Co.
Publisher: A. W. Morris & Bro.
Key/Vignettes/Misc: Description
Locations: MCM–M
Catalogs/Checklists:

3788
Place: Montreal, Quebec
Date: 1889
Title: Bird's Eye View of the City of Montreal. 1889
Size: 28 3/16 × 45 5/16 in. (71.6 × 115.1 cm.)
Artist: George Bishop Eng. & Ptg. Co.
Lithographer:
Printer: George Bishop Eng. & Ptg. Co.
Publisher: George Bishop Eng. & Ptg. Co.
Key/Vignettes/Misc:
Locations: PAC; PAC–P; LC–M (photo)
Catalogs/Checklists: PAC (1976); PAC H3/340–Montreal–1889; LC–M, 1072.2

3789
Place: Montreal, Quebec
Date: 1892 State II
Title: City of Montreal.
Size: 23 1/16 × 35 15/16 in. (58.6 × 91.2 cm.)
Artist:
Lithographer:
Printer: Toronto Lithographing Co.
Publisher: A. W. Morris & Bro.
Key/Vignettes/Misc: Description
Locations: Chateau Dufresne, Montreal, Quebec
Catalogs/Checklists:

3790
Place: Montreal, Quebec
Date: 1904
Title: The Harbour of Montreal
Size: 14 1/16 × 42 1/4 in. (35.8 × 107.5 cm.)
Artist:
Lithographer:
Printer:
Publisher:
Key/Vignettes/Misc:
Locations: PAC
Catalogs/Checklists: PAC V1/340–Montreal–1904

3791
Place: Montreal, Quebec
Date: ?
Title: Place d'Armes, Montreal
Size: 14 × 19 in. (35.6 × 48.3 cm.)
Artist: C. Krieghoff
Lithographer:
Printer: A. Borum [Montreal]
Publisher:

Key/Vignettes/Misc:
Locations: MTLB–T
Catalogs/Checklists: Robertson, no. 1878

3792
Place: New Carlisle, Quebec
Date: Ca. 1866
Title: New Carlisle, C. E.
Size: 8 1/8 × 11 1/8 in. (20.5 × 28.3 cm.)
Artist: Thomas Pye
Lithographer:
Printer: Roberts & Reinhold, lith. Place d'Armes, Mtl.
Publisher:
Key/Vignettes/Misc:
Locations: PAC–P; MTLB–T
Catalogs/Checklists: Robertson, no. 1585; Spendlove, Face of Early Canada, p. 35

3793
Place: Paspebiac, Quebec
Date: Ca. 1866
Title: Paspebiac, C. E., Pl. 1.
Size: 8 × 11 1/4 in. (20.4 × 28.5 cm.)
Artist: Thomas Pye
Lithographer:
Printer: Roberts & Reinhold, Place d'Armes, Mtl.
Publisher:
Key/Vignettes/Misc:
Locations: PAC–P
Catalogs/Checklists:

3794
Place: Perce, Quebec
Date: Ca. 1866
Title: Perce, C. E. Pl. 1
Size: 8 × 11 1/4 in. (20.5 × 28.5 cm.)
Artist: Thomas Pye
Lithographer:
Printer: Roberts & Reinhold, Place d'Armes, Mtl.
Publisher:
Key/Vignettes/Misc:
Locations: PAC–P
Catalogs/Checklists:

3795
Place: Perce, Quebec
Date: Ca. 1866
Title: Perce, C. E., Pl. 2
Size: 8 1/8 × 11 1/4 in. (20.5 × 28.7 cm.)
Artist: Thomas Pye
Lithographer:
Printer: Roberts & Reinhold, Place d'Armes, Mtl.
Publisher:
Key/Vignettes/Misc:
Locations: PAC–P
Catalogs/Checklists:

3796
Place: Point Saint Peter, Quebec
Date: Ca. 1866
Title: Point St. Peter, C. E.
Size: 8 1/8 × 11 1/8 in. (20.6 × 28.4 cm.)
Artist: Thomas Pye
Lithographer:
Printer: Roberts & Reinhold, Place d'Armes, Mtl.
Publisher:
Key/Vignettes/Misc:

Locations: PAC–P; MTLB–T
Catalogs/Checklists: Robertson, no. 1584

3797
Place: Quebec City, Quebec
Date: 1832
Title: Quebec. Lower Canada. View of the Esplanade and Fortifications of Quebec, With Part of the Surrounding Country. [Title also in French]
Size: ca. 10 1/4 × 14 1/2 in. (26.1 × 36.9 cm.)
Artist: R. A. Sproule
Lithographer: W. Walton
Printer: C. Hullmandel
Publisher: A. Bourne, London
Key/Vignettes/Misc:
Locations: PAC–P; ROM
Catalogs/Checklists: deVolpi, Quebec, Plate 76; Spendlove, Face of Early Canada, p. 64; Samuel, no. 514

3798
Place: Quebec City, Quebec
Date: 1832
Title: Quebec. Lower Canada. View of the Market Place and Catholic Church, Taken from the Barracks Fabrique Street. [Title also in French]
Size: ca. 10 1/4 × 14 1/2 in. (ca. 26.1 × 36.9 cm.)
Artist: R. A. Sproule
Lithographer: W. Walton
Printer: C. Hullmandel
Publisher: A. Bourne, London
Key/Vignettes/Misc:
Locations: PAC–P; ROM
Catalogs/Checklists: deVolpi, Quebec, Plate 78; Spendlove, Face of Early Canada, p. 64 and Plate 96; Samuel, no. 517

3799
Place: Quebec City, Quebec
Date: 1832
Title: Quebec. Lower Canada. View of the Place d'Armes & of the Episcopal Church of England, From the Garden of the Governor. [Title also in French]
Size: ca. 10 1/4 × 14 1/2 in. (26.1 × 36.9 cm.)
Artist: R. A. Sproule
Lithographer: W. Walton
Printer: C. Hullmandel
Publisher: A. Bourne, London
Key/Vignettes/Misc:
Locations: ACMW–FW; PAC–P; ROM
Catalogs/Checklists: deVolpi, Quebec, Plate 77; Spendlove, Face of Early Canada, p. 64 and Plate 97; Samuel, no. 516

3800
Place: Quebec City, Quebec
Date: 1832
Title: Quebec. Lower Canada. Vue de Quebec Prise de la Pointe Levi. View of Quebec from Point Levy.
Size: 10 1/2 × 15 in. (26.7 × 38.2 cm.)
Artist: R. A. Sproule
Lithographer: W. Walton
Printer: C. Hullmandel
Publisher: A. Bourne, Montreal
Key/Vignettes/Misc:
Locations: PAC–P; ROM

Catalogs/Checklists: deVolpi, Quebec, Plate 75; Spendlove, Face of Early Canada, p. 64; Samuel, no. 515

3801
Place: Quebec City, Quebec
Date: [1830–37]
Title: City of Quebec Taken from the Harbour.
Size: 5½ × 8⅛ in. (14 × 20.7 cm.)
Artist: R. S. M. Bouchette
Lithographer:
Printer: Day & Haghe Lithos to the King, 17 Gate St. Linc Inn Fds. [London]
Publisher:
Key/Vignettes/Misc:
Locations: PAC–P; MTLB–T
Catalogs/Checklists: Robertson, no. 2041

3802
Place: Quebec City, Quebec
Date: 1838
Title: Quebec With the Arrival of H. M. S. Hastings Conveying the Earl of Durham Governor General of Canada May 1838.
Size: 11½ × 17¼ in. (29.3 × 43.9 cm.)
Artist: Captain Digby Morton
Lithographer:
Printer: [Day and Haghe, London]
Publisher:
Key/Vignettes/Misc:
Locations: MGUR–M
Catalogs/Checklists: deVolpi, Quebec, Plate 94

3803
Place: Quebec City, Quebec
Date: [1840–42]
Title: Quebec
Size: ca. 10½ × 15 in. (26.7 × 38.2 cm.)
Artist: Coke Smyth
Lithographer:
Printer: A. Ducote's Lithographic Establishment, 70, St. Martin's Lane, London
Publisher: Thos. McLean, 26, Haymarket, London
Key/Vignettes/Misc:
Locations: ROM; PAC–P
Catalogs/Checklists: Spendlove, Face of Early Canada, p. 42 and Plate 64; Samuel, no. 243(V)

3804
Place: Quebec City, Quebec
Date: [1840–42]
Title: Quebec from the Chateau
Size: ca. 10½ × 15 in. (26.7 × 38.2 cm.)
Artist: Coke Smyth
Lithographer:
Printer: A. Ducote's Lithographic Establishment, 70, St. Martin's Lane, London
Publisher: Thos. McLean, 26, Haymarket, London
Key/Vignettes/Misc:
Locations: ROM; MTLB–T
Catalogs/Checklists: Samuel, no. 243(VI); Spendlove, Face of Early Canada, p. 42 and Plate 65; Robertson, no. 1973

3805
Place: Quebec City, Quebec
Date: Ca. 1844 State I
Title: View of Quebec
Size: 16 × 20¹¹⁄₁₆ in. (40.6 × 52.5 cm.)
Artist: Captain B. Beaufoy
Lithographer:
Printer:
Publisher:
Key/Vignettes/Misc:
Locations: PAC–P
Catalogs/Checklists:

3806
Place: Quebec City, Quebec
Date: Ca. 1844 State II
Title: View of Quebec
Size: 15¹³⁄₁₆ × 20½ in. (40.3 × 52 cm.)
Artist: Captain B. Beaufoy
Lithographer: T. Picken
Printer: Day & Haghe. Lithrs to the Queen [London]
Publisher:
Key/Vignettes/Misc:
Locations: PAC–P; MCM–M; MTLB–T; ROM
Catalogs/Checklists: deVolpi, Quebec, Plate 95; Spendlove, Face of Early Canada, p. 53; Robertson, no. 2014; Samuel, no. 245

3807
Place: Quebec City, Quebec
Date: 1845 State I
Title: View of Quebec, Canada, from the River St. Charles, Shewing the Conflagration of June 28th 1845, and the Ruins of the Fire of May 28th, 1845.
Size: 15¹⁵⁄₁₆ × 20⁷⁄₁₆ in. (40.5 × 51.9 cm.)
Artist: J. Murray
Lithographer: G.[eorge] T. Sanford
Printer: G. & W. Endicott, New York
Publisher: A. Bourne, Montreal
Key/Vignettes/Misc:
Locations: PAC–P; MCM–M; Art Gallery of Ontario
Catalogs/Checklists: deVolpi, Quebec, Plate 122

3808
Place: Quebec City, Quebec
Date: 1845 State II
Title: View of Quebec, Canada, from the River St. Charles Shewing the Conflagration of June 28th 1845, and the Ruins of the Fire of May 28th, 1845.
Size: 16¼ × 20⅜ in. (41.2 × 51.7 cm.) (cropped)
Artist: J. Murray & C. Cruhen [Crehen?]
Lithographer: G.[eorge] T. Sanford
Printer: G. & W. Endicott, New York
Publisher: A. Bourne, Montreal
Key/Vignettes/Misc:
Locations: MTLB–T; PAC–P; ROM
Catalogs/Checklists: Samuel, no. 461; Robertson, no. 1983

3809
Place: Quebec City, Quebec
Date: Ca. 1850
Title: French Cathedral and Market Square, Quebec

Size: 7 × 9¾ in. (17.8 × 24.9 cm.)
Artist: [James Duncan?]
Lithographer:
Printer: Sarony & Major, N. Y.
Publisher:
Key/Vignettes/Misc:
Locations: PAC–P
Catalogs/Checklists: deVolpi, Quebec, Plate 125

3810
Place: Quebec City, Quebec
Date: Ca. 1850
Title: Monument to Wolfe &, Montcalm, Quebec
Size: 7 × 9¾ in. (17.8 × 24.9 cm.)
Artist: [James Duncan?]
Lithographer:
Printer: Sarony & Major, New York
Publisher:
Key/Vignettes/Misc:
Locations: PAC–P
Catalogs/Checklists: deVolpi, Quebec, Plate 128

3811
Place: Quebec City, Quebec
Date: Ca. 1850
Title: Parliament Buildings, Quebec
Size: 7 × 9¾ in. (17.8 × 24.9 cm.)
Artist: [James Duncan?]
Lithographer:
Printer: Sarony & Major, N. Y.
Publisher:
Key/Vignettes/Misc:
Locations: PAC–P
Catalogs/Checklists: deVolpi, Quebec, Plate 126

3812
Place: Quebec City, Quebec
Date: Ca. 1850
Title: St. Johns Gate, Quebec
Size: 7 × 9¾ in. (17.8 × 24.9 cm.)
Artist:
Lithographer:
Printer: Sarony & Major, New York
Publisher:
Key/Vignettes/Misc:
Locations: PAC–P
Catalogs/Checklists: deVolpi, Quebec, Plate 130

3813
Place: Quebec City, Quebec
Date: Ca. 1850
Title: View from Esplanade, Quebec
Size: 7 × 9¾ in. (17.8 × 24.9 cm.)
Artist:
Lithographer:
Printer: Sarony & Major, N. Y.
Publisher:
Key/Vignettes/Misc:
Locations: PAC–P
Catalogs/Checklists: deVolpi, Quebec, Plate 129

3814
Place: Quebec City, Quebec
Date: Ca. 1850
Title: View of the Parliament Buildings, Quebec.

Size: 7 × 9⅞ in. (17.8 × 25.2 cm.)
Artist: [James Duncan?]
Lithographer:
Printer: Sarony and Major, New York
Publisher:
Key/Vignettes/Misc:
Locations: MGUR–M
Catalogs/Checklists:

3815
Place: Quebec City, Quebec
Date: Ca. 1850
Title: View From Parliament Buildings, Quebec
Size: 7 × 9⅞ in. (17.8 × 25.2 cm.)
Artist: [James Duncan?]
Lithographer:
Printer: Sarony & Major, New York
Publisher:
Key/Vignettes/Misc:
Locations: Unknown
Catalogs/Checklists: deVolpi, Quebec, Plate 127

3816
Place: Quebec City, Quebec
Date: 1851
Title: Canada. Quebec & Fort
Size: 9½ × 11¾ in. (24.2 × 29.9 cm.)
Artist: Aug. Kollner
Lithographer: Deroy
Printer: Jacomme & Co.
Publisher: Goupil & Co. New–York & Paris
Key/Vignettes/Misc:
Locations: PAC–P; ROM
Catalogs/Checklists: Samuel, no. 606

3817
Place: Quebec City, Quebec
Date: 1852 State I
Title: Quebec. From Beauport.
Size: 22¼ × 34⅞ in. (56.6 × 88.6 cm.)
Artist: E. Whitefield
Lithographer:
Printer: Endicott & Co., New York
Publisher: E. Whitefield, Quebec
Key/Vignettes/Misc: Refs. 1–20
Locations: MM–NN; NYP–S; ROM; Musee du Quebec, Quebec, Quebec; PAC–P
Catalogs/Checklists: deVolpi, Quebec, Plate 131; Norton, Whitefield, no. 56; Stokes P. 1851—H–30; Spendlove, Face of Early Canada, p.71; Samuel, no. 429

3818
Place: Quebec City, Quebec
Date: 1854
Title: Quebec, Vue Prise de Beauport.
Size: 19¹³⁄₁₆ × 28⅝ in. (50.4 × 72.9 cm.)
Artist: [P. L. Morin? after Whitefield]
Lithographer: Hub. Clerget
Printer: Villain, r. de Sevres 19, Paris
Publisher: Massard, 53 rue de Seine; J. et O. Cremanzie, rue de la Fabrique, Paris
Key/Vignettes/Misc:
Locations: MTLB–T; PAC–P (title cropped); ROM; NYH–NY
Catalogs/Checklists: Samuel, no. 302 & 430; Spendlove, Face of Early Canada, p. 72; Robertson, no. 2017

3819
Place: Quebec City, Quebec
Date: 1855 State II
Title: Quebec. From Beauport.
Size: 22 × 36¼ in. (55.9 × 92.2 cm.)
Artist: E. Whitefield
Lithographer: E. Whitefield
Printer: Maclear & Co., Toronto, C. W.
Publisher: E. Whitefield, 16 King St., Toronto
Key/Vignettes/Misc: Refs. 1–19
Locations: MM–NN; AO–T; MTLB–T; PAC–P
Catalogs/Checklists: Norton, Whitefield, no. 62; Robertson, no. 103; Spendlove, Face of Early Canada, p. 71

3820
Place: Quebec City, Quebec
Date: 1855 State III
Title: Quebec. From Beauport.
Size: 22 × 36¼ in. (55.9 × 92.2 cm.)
Artist: E. Whitefield
Lithographer: E. Whitefield
Printer: Maclear & Co., Toronto, C. W.
Publisher: E. Whitefield, Quebec
Key/Vignettes/Misc: Refs. 1–19
Locations: PAC–P
Catalogs/Checklists:

3821
Place: Quebec City, Quebec
Date: 1858
Title: Topographical and Pictural Map of the City of Quebec from Actual Survey
Size: 34⁹⁄₁₆ × 45³⁄₁₆ in. (88 × 115 cm.)
Artist: Alfred Hamel
Lithographer:
Printer: Hatch & Co. N. Y.
Publisher:
Key/Vignettes/Misc:
Locations: Archives de la Ville de Quebec
Catalogs/Checklists:

3822
Place: Quebec City, Quebec
Date: 1862
Title: Quebec Augt. 1860.
Size: 7 × 9⅛ in. (17.8 × 23.2 cm.)
Artist: W. L. Walton
Lithographer:
Printer:
Publisher:
Key/Vignettes/Misc:
Locations: PAC–P
Catalogs/Checklists:

3823
Place: Quebec City, Quebec
Date: 1862
Title: View of Quebec, Canada. From the Railway Station Opposite Quebec, the City.
Size: 16³⁄₁₆ × 23¾ in. (41.1 × 66.3 cm.)
Artist: C. Krieghoff
Lithographer:
Printer: M. & H. Hanhart [London]
Publisher: Morre McQueen & Co. 25 Berners St. [London]
Key/Vignettes/Misc:
Locations: MCM–M

Catalogs/Checklists: deVolpi, Quebec, Plate 132 (ca. 1853)

3824
Place: Quebec City, Quebec
Date: 1874
Title: Modern Street View of Point Levi and Quebec in the Distance.
Size: ca. 10¼ × 14½ in. (26.1 × 36.9 cm.)
Artist: James Duncan
Lithographer:
Printer: C. G. Crehan
Publisher: A. Bourne, Montreal
Key/Vignettes/Misc:
Locations: MCM–M; ROM; MTLB–T
Catalogs/Checklists: Robertson, no. 2837; Samuel, no. 230; deVolpi, Quebec, Plate 184; Spendlove, Face of Early Canada, p. 64 and Plate 98

3825
Place: Quebec City, Quebec
Date: 1874
Title: View of the Esplanade and Fortifications of Quebec [in 1832]
Size: ca. 10¼ × 14½ in. (26.1 × 36.9 cm.)
Artist: James Duncan
Lithographer:
Printer: C. G. Crehan
Publisher: A. Bourne, Montreal
Key/Vignettes/Misc:
Locations: MCM–M; ROM; MTLB–T
Catalogs/Checklists: Samuel, no. 231; Spendlove, Face of Early Canada, p. 64; Robertson, no. 2842

3826
Place: Quebec City, Quebec
Date: 1874
Title: View of the Market Place and Catholic Church, Taken from the Barracks, Fabrique Street [in 1832]
Size: ca. 10¼ × 14½ in. (26.1 × 36.9 cm.)
Artist: R. A. Sproule
Lithographer:
Printer: C. G. Crehan
Publisher: A. Bourne, Montreal
Key/Vignettes/Misc:
Locations: MCM–M; ROM
Catalogs/Checklists: Samuel, no. 233; Spendlove, Face of Early Canada, p. 64

3827
Place: Quebec City, Quebec
Date: 1874
Title: View of the Market Place and Catholic Church, Uppertown, Quebec [in 1832]
Size: 10 × 14 in. (25.4 × 35.6 cm.)
Artist: R. A. Sproule
Lithographer:
Printer: C. G. Crehan
Publisher: Adolphus Bourne, Montreal, Canada
Key/Vignettes/Misc:
Locations: ROM; MTLB–T
Catalogs/Checklists: Robertson, no. 2849; Samuel, no. 234

3828
Place: Quebec City, Quebec
Date: 1874
Title: View of the Place d'Armes & of the

Episcopal Church of England, From the Garden of the Governor. [in 1832]
Size: ca. 10¼ × 14½ in. (26.1 × 36.9 cm.)
Artist: R. A. Sproule
Lithographer:
Printer: C. G. Crehan
Publisher: A. Bourne, Montreal
Key/Vignettes/Misc:
Locations: MCM–M; ROM; MTLB–T
Catalogs/Checklists: Samuel, no. 235; Robertson, no. 2850; Spendlove, Face of Early Canada, p. 64

3829
Place: Quebec City, Quebec
Date: 1874
Title: View of Quebec from Point Levy. [in 1832]
Size: ca. 10¼ × 14½ in. (26.1 × 36.9 cm.)
Artist: R. A. Sproule
Lithographer:
Printer: C. G. Crehan
Publisher: A. Bourne, Montreal
Key/Vignettes/Misc:
Locations: MCM–M; ROM; MTLB–T
Catalogs/Checklists: Samuel, no. 232; Spendlove, Face of Early Canada, p. 64; Robertson, no. 2843

3830
Place: Quebec City, Quebec
Date: 1905
Title: Quebec Tercentenary, 1908
Size: 13¹³⁄₁₆ × 27⅞ in. (35.2 × 70.9 cm.)
Artist: J. L. Wiseman
Lithographer:
Printer:
Publisher: J. L. Wiseman [copyright, 1905]
Key/Vignettes/Misc:
Locations: PAC
Catalogs/Checklists: PAC (1976); PAC V1/340–Quebec–1905

3831
Place: Quebec City, Quebec
Date: 1905
Title: Quebec, A. D. MDCCCCV (Bird's Eye View)
Size: 23¹⁵⁄₁₆ × 53⅞ in. (61 × 137 cm.)
Artist: J. L. Wiseman
Lithographer:
Printer:
Publisher:
Key/Vignettes/Misc:
Locations: Archives de la Ville de Quebec
Catalogs/Checklists:

Place: Rock Island, Quebec
Date: 1881
See Derby Line, Vermont, 1881.

3832
Place: Saint Hyacinthe, Quebec
Date: [1830–37]
Title: Village of St. Hyacinthe, Co. of St. Hyacinthe.
Size: 5⅜ × 8⅜ in. (13.7 × 21.3 cm.)
Artist: R. S. M. Bouchette
Lithographer:
Printer: Day & Haghe Lithrs to the King, 17 Gate Street, Linc Inn Fds. [London]
Publisher:
Key/Vignettes/Misc:

Locations: PAC–P; MTLB–T
Catalogs/Checklists: Robertson, no. 2029

3833
Place: Saint Hyacinthe, Quebec
Date: 1881
Title: Vue a vol d'Oiseau de St. Hyacinthe, P. Q.
Size: 13⁵⁄₁₆ × 25½ in. (34.9 × 64.9 cm.)
Artist: H. Wellge
Lithographer:
Printer:
Publisher:
Key/Vignettes/Misc: Refs. 1–16, X
Locations: Seminaire de Saint–Hyacinthe, St. Hyacinthe, Quebec
Catalogs/Checklists: PAC (1976)

3834
Place: Saint–Jean, Quebec
Date: 1881
Title: Bird's Eye View of St. Johns, P. Q. Domin. of Canada. 1881
Size: 16⅞ × 27½ in. (43 × 70 cm.)
Artist: H. Wellge
Lithographer:
Printer:
Publisher:
Key/Vignettes/Misc: Refs. 1–21; 6 vignettes
Locations: PAC
Catalogs/Checklists: PAC (1976); PAC V1/340–Saint Jean–1881

3835
Place: Saint Jérôme, Quebec
Date: 1881
Title: Vue a vol d'Oiseau de St. Jerome, P. Q. 1881
Size: 5⅞ × 15⁵⁄₁₆ in. (12 × 39 cm.) (photo)
Artist:
Lithographer:
Printer:
Publisher:
Key/Vignettes/Misc: Refs. 1–17
Locations: PAC (photo)
Catalogs/Checklists: PAC (1976)

3836
Place: Sainte Anne De Beaupré, Quebec
Date: 1904
Title: Ste. Anne de Beaupre
Size: 13¾ × 21⅝ in. (35 × 55 cm.)
Artist:
Lithographer:
Printer:
Publisher: F. S. McKay, Sherbrooke, Quebec, Canada
Key/Vignettes/Misc: 2 vignettes
Locations: ROM
Catalogs/Checklists:

3837
Place: Sherbrooke, Quebec
Date: 1834
Title: Panoramic View of Sherbrooke, From the East Side of the River St. Francis, in the District of St. Francis, Province of Lower Canada, Canada East,—in 1834.
Size:
Artist: C. B. Felton
Lithographer:

Printer:
Publisher:
Key/Vignettes/Misc: Refs. 1–38, A
Locations:
Catalogs/Checklists: deVolpi & Scowen, Eastern Townships, Plate 3

3838
Place: Sherbrooke, Quebec
Date: 1836
Title: Sherbrooke, Eastern Townships, Lower Canada. Principal Station of the British American Land Company
Size: 8 × 10 in. (20.3 × 25.4 cm.)
Artist:
Lithographer:
Printer: W. Day, 17 Gate St.
Publisher:
Key/Vignettes/Misc:
Locations: MTLB–T
Catalogs/Checklists: Robertson, no. 2245

3839
Place: Sherbrooke, Quebec
Date: 1881
Title: Bird's Eye View of Sherbrooke, P. Q. 1881.
Size: 21 × 28¼ in. (53.5 × 72 cm.)
Artist: H. Wellge
Lithographer:
Printer:
Publisher: J. J. Stoner, Madison, Wis.
Key/Vignettes/Misc: Refs. 1–49; 1 vignette
Locations: PAC
Catalogs/Checklists: deVolpi & Scowen, Eastern Townships, Plate 106; PAC (1976); PAC H2/340–Sherbrooke–1881

3840
Place: Sorel, Quebec
Date: 1881
Title: Vue a vol d'Oiseau de la Ville de Sorel, P. Q. 1881.
Size: 17⅝ × 25¾ in. (45 × 65.5 cm.)
Artist:
Lithographer:
Printer:
Publisher:
Key/Vignettes/Misc: 24 refs.
Locations: PAC
Catalogs/Checklists: PAC (1976); PAC H12/340–Sorel–1881

3841
Place: Trois Rivieres, Quebec
Date: 1881
Title: Vue a Vol d'Oiseau des Trois Rivieres, P. Q. 1881
Size: 15¼ × 24⅞ in. (38.7 × 63.1 cm.)
Artist:
Lithographer:
Printer:
Publisher:
Key/Vignettes/Misc: Refs. 1–24
Locations: PAC–P; PAC (photo)
Catalogs/Checklists: PAC (1976); PAC H3/340–Trois Rivieres–1881

3842
Place: Waterloo, Quebec
Date: 1881
Title: Bird's Eye View of Waterloo, P. Q. 1881.

Size: 12⁹⁄₁₆ × 23¾ in. (32 × 60.5 cm.)
Artist: H. Wellge
Lithographer:
Printer:
Publisher: J. J. Stoner, Madison, Wis.
Key/Vignettes/Misc: Refs. 1–18; 1
vignette
Locations: PAC (photo); private collection
Catalogs/Checklists: PAC (1976); deVolpi
& Scowen, Eastern Townships, Plate 107

Place: Arctic, Rhode Island
Date: 1889
See Clyde, Rhode Island, 1889.

Place: Arctic Centre, Rhode Island
Date: 1889
See Centerville, Rhode Island, 1889.

Place: Arkwright, Rhode Island
Date: 1889
See Hope, Rhode Island, 1889.

3843
Place: Auburn, Rhode Island
Date: 1890
Title: Auburn, Rhode Island. 1890
Size: 20½ × 24 in. (52.1 × 61 cm.)
Artist:
Lithographer:
Printer: O. H. Bailey & Co., Boston
Publisher: O. H. Bailey & Co., Boston
Key/Vignettes/Misc: Refs. A, 2–20; 35
vignettes
Locations: BPL–R
Catalogs/Checklists:

3844
Place: Bristol, Rhode Island
Date: 1877
Title: Bird's Eye View of Bristol, R. I. 1877
Size: 18¾ × 25⅛ in. (47.7 × 63.8 cm.)
Artist: O. H. Bailey and J. C. Hazen
Lithographer: C. H. Vogt
Printer:
Publisher: O. H. Bailey & J. C. Hazen,
Boston
Key/Vignettes/Misc: Refs. A–H, J–W
Locations: BPL–R
Catalogs/Checklists:

3845
Place: Bristol, Rhode Island
Date: 1891
Title: Bristol, Rhode Island. 1891.
Size: 19⅝ × 30⅜ in. (47.4 × 77.3 cm.)
Artist:
Lithographer:
Printer: O. H. Bailey & Co., Boston
Publisher: O. H. Bailey & Co., Boston
Key/Vignettes/Misc: Refs. 1–30; 31
vignettes
Locations: LC–M
Catalogs/Checklists: LC–M, 878.1

3846
Place: Bristol, Rhode Island
Date: N.D.
Title: Bristol, R. I. View from Pappoose
Squaw's Neck.
Size: 13⅜ × 33⅜ in. (34 × 84.8 cm.)
Artist: J. P. Newell
Lithographer: J. P. Newell
Printer: J. H. Bufford's

Publisher:
Key/Vignettes/Misc:
Locations: MM–NN
Catalogs/Checklists: MM–NN, LP 1163

3847
Place: Centerville, Rhode Island
Date: 1889
Title: Centerville, and Arctic Centre,
Rhode Island. 1889.
Size: 21 × 26⅝ in. (53.4 × 67.8 cm.)
Artist:
Lithographer:
Printer:
Publisher: O. H. Bailey & Co. Boston
Key/Vignettes/Misc: Refs. A, 2–46; 20
vignettes
Locations: BPL–R
Catalogs/Checklists:

Place: Central Falls, Rhode Island
Date: 1877
See Pawtucket, Rhode Island, 1877.

3848
Place: Clyde, Rhode Island
Date: 1889
Title: Clyde, River Point and Arctic,
Rhode Island. 1889
Size: 19¾ × 25½ in. (50.2 × 64.9 cm.)
Artist:
Lithographer:
Printer: O. H. Bailey & Co., Boston
Publisher: O. H. Bailey & Co., Boston
Key/Vignettes/Misc: Refs. A, 2–36; 17
vignettes
Locations: BPL–R
Catalogs/Checklists:

3849
Place: Crompton, Rhode Island
Date: 1889
Title: Crompton, Rhode Island. 1889
Size: 10⅞ × 23⅞ in. (27.7 × 60.7 cm.)
Artist:
Lithographer:
Printer: O. H. Bailey & Co., Boston
Publisher: O. H. Bailey & Co., Boston
Key/Vignettes/Misc: Refs. A, 2–21
Locations: BPL–R
Catalogs/Checklists:

3850
Place: East Greenwich, Rhode Island
Date: 1879
Title: View of East Greenwich, R. I.
Size: 19⅜ × 24½ in. (49.3 × 62.3 cm.)
Artist: O. H. Bailey & J. C. Hazen
Lithographer:
Printer:
Publisher: O. H. Bailey & J. C. Hazen,
Boston
Key/Vignettes/Misc: Refs. A–X
Locations: RIHS–P
Catalogs/Checklists:

Place: Fiskeville, Rhode Island
Date: 1889
See Hope, Rhode Island, 1889.

3851
Place: Harrisville, Rhode Island
Date: 1889
Title: Harris, Phenix and Lippitt, Rhode
Island. 1889.

Size: 21 × 26⅛ in. (53.4 × 66.5 cm.)
Artist:
Lithographer:
Printer: O. H. Bailey & Co., Boston
Publisher: O. H. Bailey & Co., Boston
Key/Vignettes/Misc: Refs. A, 2–40; 25
vignettes
Locations: BPL–R; RIHS–P
Catalogs/Checklists:

3852
Place: Hope, Rhode Island
Date: 1889
Title: Hope, Jackson, Fiskville and
Arkwright, Rhode Island. 1889.
Size: 20½ × 25 in. (52.2 × 63.5 cm.)
Artist:
Lithographer:
Printer: O. H. Bailey & Co., Boston
Publisher: O. H. Bailey & Co., Boston
Key/Vignettes/Misc: Refs. A, 2–17; 12
vignettes
Locations: BPL–R
Catalogs/Checklists:

Place: Jackson, Rhode Island
Date: 1889
See Hope, Rhode Island, 1889.

Place: Lippitt, Rhode Island
Date: 1889
See Harris, Rhode Island, 1889.

3853
Place: Lonsdale, Rhode Island
Date: 1888
Title: Lonsdale, Rhode Island. 1888.
Size: 21 × 25⅝ in. (53.4 × 65.2 cm.)
Artist:
Lithographer:
Printer: O. H. Bailey & Co., Boston
Publisher: O. H. Bailey & Co., Boston
Key/Vignettes/Misc: Refs. A, 2–31; 18
vignettes
Locations: BPL–R; RIHS–P (facsimile)
Catalogs/Checklists:

3854
Place: Narragansett, Rhode Island
Date: N.D.
Title: Narragansett Village, South Ferry
South Kingston, R. I.
Size: 11½ × 16½ in. (29.2 × 41.9 cm.)
Artist: J. P. Newell
Lithographer: J. P. Newell
Printer: Robertson, Seibert & Shearman,
New York
Publisher:
Key/Vignettes/Misc:
Locations: RIHS–P
Catalogs/Checklists:

3855
Place: Narragansett Bay, Rhode Island
Date: 1907
Title: Chromatic Balloon View of
Narragansett Bay
Size: 10¾ × 12½ in. (27.3 × 31.8 cm.)
Artist:
Lithographer:
Printer: Providence Lithograph Co.
Publisher: J. C. Thompson, 269
Westminster St. Providence, R. I.
Key/Vignettes/Misc:

Locations: RIHS–P
Catalogs/Checklists:

3856
Place: Narragansett Bay, Rhode Island
Date: 1907
Title: Narragansett Bay
Size: 19½ × 26¾ in. (49.6 × 68.1 cm.)
Artist:
Lithographer:
Printer: George H. Walker Lith. & Pub. Co. . . ., Boston
Publisher: George H. Walker Lith. & Pub. Co. 400 Newbury St. Boston
Key/Vignettes/Misc:
Locations: RIHS–P
Catalogs/Checklists:

3857
Place: Narragansett Pier, Rhode Island
Date: 1888
Title: Narragansett Pier, Rhode Island. 1888
Size: 19½ × 24 in. (49.6 × 61 cm.)
Artist:
Lithographer:
Printer: O. H. Bailey & Co., Boston
Publisher: O. H. Bailey & Co., Boston
Key/Vignettes/Misc: Refs. A, 2–45; 8 vignettes
Locations: BPL–R
Catalogs/Checklists:

3858
Place: Narragansett Pier, Rhode Island
Date: 1890
Title: Narragansett Pier, Rhode Island 1890
Size: 20½ × 25 in. (52.1 × 63.6 cm.)
Artist:
Lithographer:
Printer: O. H. Bailey & Co., Boston, Mass.
Publisher: O. H. Bailey & Co., Boston, Mass
Key/Vignettes/Misc: Refs. 1–25, A–Z; 19 vignettes
Locations: South County Museum, North Kingstown, Rhode Island
Catalogs/Checklists:

3859
Place: Natick, Rhode Island
Date: 1889
Title: Natick, Rhode Island. 1889
Size: 20¼ × 23⅝ in. (51.6 × 60.1 cm.)
Artist:
Lithographer:
Printer: O. H. Bailey & Co., Boston
Publisher: O. H. Bailey & Co., Boston
Key/Vignettes/Misc: Refs. A, 2–21; 16 vignettes
Locations: BPL–R
Catalogs/Checklists:

3860
Place: Newport, Rhode Island
Date: Ca. 1860
Title: Newport, R. I. View from Fort Wolcott GoatIsland
Size: 11 × 33¹³⁄₁₆ in. (27.9 × 85.9 cm.)
Artist: J. P. Newell

Lithographer: J. P. Newell
Printer: J. H. Bufford [Boston]
Publisher:
Key/Vignettes/Misc:
Locations: NYP–S; Library Company of Philadelphia, Philadelphia, Pennsylvania; RIHS–P; BA; YUAG–NH
Catalogs/Checklists: Stokes C. 1860—G–76; Pyne, no. 452

3861
Place: Newport, Rhode Island
Date: 1864
Title: Newport, R. I. in 1730.
Size: 19¼ × 28⅛ in. (49 × 71.6 cm.)
Artist: J. P. Newell
Lithographer: J. P. Newell
Printer: J. H. Bufford's Lith. 313 Washington St. Boston
Publisher: J. P. Newell (copyright)
Key/Vignettes/Misc: 19 unnumbered refs. in 2 lines
Locations: BA; YUAG–NH
Catalogs/Checklists:

3862
Place: Newport, Rhode Island
Date: 1870
Title: Newport, R. I.
Size: 19 × 33⅞ in. (48.4 × 86.2 cm.)
Artist: J. P. Newell
Lithographer: J. P. Newell
Printer: New Eng. Lith. Co., 109 Summer St. Boston
Publisher: J. P. Newell, Newport, R. I. (copyright)
Key/Vignettes/Misc:
Locations: MM–NN; RIHS–P; BA; YUAG–NH; LC–P
Catalogs/Checklists: MM–NN, LP 9

3863
Place: Newport, Rhode Island
Date: 1876
Title: Newport, Rhode Island
Size: 14¹¹⁄₁₆ × 20⁹⁄₁₆ in. (37.4 × 52.3 cm.)
Artist:
Lithographer:
Printer: I. F. W. Gleason
Publisher:
Key/Vignettes/Misc:
Locations: BPL–R
Catalogs/Checklists:

3864
Place: Newport, Rhode Island
Date: Ca. 1876
Title: Rhode Island. City of Newport.
Size: 8 × 10 in. (20.3 × 25.4 cm.)
Artist: W. Brotherhead
Lithographer:
Printer: H. J. Toudy & Co., Philadelphia
Publisher:
Key/Vignettes/Misc:
Locations: MM–NN
Catalogs/Checklists: MM–NN, LP 877

3865
Place: Newport, Rhode Island
Date: 1878
Title: Newport, R. I. 1878.
Size: 25 × 27½ in. (63.6 × 69.9 cm.)

Artist: Galt & Hoy
Lithographer:
Printer:
Publisher: Galt & Hoy, 111 Liberty St. N. Y.
Key/Vignettes/Misc:
Locations: LC–M; LC–P
Catalogs/Checklists: LC–M, 879

3866
Place: Newport, Rhode Island
Date: 1884
Title: Newport, R. I. in 1730
Size: 19⅜ × 28⅛ in. (49.3 × 71.5 cm.)
Artist: J. P. Newell
Lithographer: J. P. Newell
Printer: J. H. Bufford's Lith. 313 Washn. St. Boston
Publisher: J. P. Newell (copyright)
Key/Vignettes/Misc: 20 unnumbered refs. below places identified
Locations: RIHS–P
Catalogs/Checklists:

3867
Place: Pascoag, Rhode Island
Date: 1895
Title: Pascoag and Vicinity, Rhode Island 1895.
Size:
Artist:
Lithographer:
Printer:
Publisher: O. H. Bailey & Co.
Key/Vignettes/Misc:
Locations: LC–M (photo)
Catalogs/Checklists: LC–M, 879.1

3868
Place: Pawtucket, Rhode Island
Date: 1877
Title: Bird's Eye View of Pawtucket & Central Falls, R. I. 1877.
Size: 24¾ × 31¾ in. (63 × 80.8 cm.)
Artist: O. H. Bailey & J. C. Hazen
Lithographer: C. H. Vogt
Printer: J. Knauber & Co.
Publisher: O. H. Bailey & J. C. Hazen, Boston
Key/Vignettes/Misc: Refs. 1–56
Locations: LC–M; BPL–R; RIHS–P; LC–P
Catalogs/Checklists: LC–M, 880

3869
Place: Pawtuxet, Rhode Island
Date: 1890
Title: Pawtuxet, Rhode Island. 1890
Size: 21¼ × 25 in. (54.1 × 63.5 cm.)
Artist:
Lithographer:
Printer: O. H. Bailey & Co., Boston
Publisher: O. H. Bailey & Co., Boston
Key/Vignettes/Misc: Refs. A, 2–27; 26 vignettes
Locations: BPL–R
Catalogs/Checklists:

Place: Peace Dale, Rhode Island
Date: 1888
See Wakefield, Rhode Island, 1888.

Place: Phenix, Rhode Island
Date: 1889
See Harris, Rhode Island, 1889.

3870
Place: Pontiac, Rhode Island
Date: 1889
Title: Pontiac, Rhode Island. 1889
Size: 16 × 24½ in. (40.7 × 62.3 cm.)
Artist:
Lithographer:
Printer: O. H. Bailey & Co., Boston
Publisher: O. H. Bailey & Co., Boston
Key/Vignettes/Misc: Refs. A, 2–11; 6 vignettes
Locations: BPL–R; RIHS–P
Catalogs/Checklists:

3871
Place: Providence, Rhode Island
Date: [1828–29]
Title: Vue du Cote du Nord de la Ville de Providence. . . .
Size: 7½ × 11⁵⁄₁₆ in. (19 × 28.8 cm.)
Artist: J. Milbert
Lithographer: Deroy
Printer:
Publisher:
Key/Vignettes/Misc:
Locations: NYP–S; RIHS–P
Catalogs/Checklists: Stokes C. 1817—F–26

3872
Place: Providence, Rhode Island
Date: 1848
Title: View of Providence, R. I. 1848.
Size: 10⅞ × 15½ in. (27.7 × 39.4 cm.)
Artist: F. H. Lane
Lithographer:
Printer: Scott's Lith. 16 Tremont Temple, Boston
Publisher:
Key/Vignettes/Misc:
Locations: BA
Catalogs/Checklists:

3873
Place: Providence, Rhode Island
Date: 1849
Title: View of Providence, R. I. From the South, 1849.
Size: 16¼ × 37½ in. (41.3 × 95.4 cm.)
Artist: E. Whitefield
Lithographer: C. W. Burton
Printer: F. Michelin, 111 Nassau St., N. Y.
Publisher: Whitefield & Smith, New York
Key/Vignettes/Misc:
Locations: MM–NN; RIHS–P; AAS–W; BA; Providence Athenaeum, Providence, Rhode Island; CHS–C; LC–P; NYH–NY
Catalogs/Checklists: MM–NN, LP 1105; Pyne, no. 483; Norton, Whitefield, no. 40

3874
Place: Providence, Rhode Island
Date: 1849
Title: View of Providence, R. I., from the North. 1849.
Size: 16¼ × 37½ in. (41.3 × 95.4 cm.)
Artist: E. Whitefield
Lithographer: C. W. Burton
Printer: F. Michelin, 111 Nassau St. N. Y.

Publisher: Whitefield & Smith, New York
Key/Vignettes/Misc:
Locations: MM–NN; PAC–P; AAS–W; NYH–NY; Providence Athenaeum, Providence, Rhode Island; BA; RIHS–P; LC–P
Catalogs/Checklists: MM–NN, LP 1104; Norton, Whitefield, no. 41; Pyne, no. 483

3875
Place: Providence, Rhode Island
Date: 1858
Title: Providence, R. I. Harbor View. Taken from the Grounds of Geo. W. Rhodes, Esq.
Size: 12⅝ × 15¾ in. (32.1 × 40.1 cm.)
Artist: J. B. Batchelder
Lithographer:
Printer: Endicott & Co., N. Y.
Publisher: Jno. B. Batchelder, 59 Beekman St., New York
Key/Vignettes/Misc: 1 vignette
Locations: MAHS–B; MM–NN; RIHS–P; BPL–P; PAC–P; BA
Catalogs/Checklists: MM–NN, LP 5

3876
Place: Providence, Rhode Island
Date: [1858–60]
Title: Providence, R. I. View from the West Bank of the River
Size: 16¹¹⁄₁₆ × 33¹¹⁄₁₆ in. (42.4 × 85.6 cm.)
Artist: J. P. Newell
Lithographer: J. P. Newell
Printer: J. H. Bufford's
Publisher:
Key/Vignettes/Misc:
Locations: NYP–S; RIHS–P; NYH–NY
Catalogs/Checklists: Stokes P. 1858–60—G–56

3877
Place: Providence, Rhode Island
Date: 1877
Title: City of Providence, R. I.
Size: 22 × 35½ in. (55.9 × 90.3 cm.)
Artist: J. Schwegler (?)
Lithographer: Louis E. Neuman
Printer:
Publisher: H. W. Burgett & Co., Boston and New York
Key/Vignettes/Misc:
Locations: RIHS–P
Catalogs/Checklists:

3878
Place: Providence, Rhode Island
Date: 1877
Title: Providence. From Prospect Terrace—1877
Size: 10⅜ × 28⅞ in. (26.4 × 73.5 cm.)
Artist:
Lithographer:
Printer: J. H. Bufford's Sons Lith, 141 Franklin St. Boston
Publisher: G. A. Miller (copyright)
Key/Vignettes/Misc:
Locations: ACMW–FW; RIHS–P; BA
Catalogs/Checklists: ACMW–FW 1830

3879
Place: Providence, Rhode Island
Date: 1882

Title: Providence, R. I.
Size: 29 × 40¼ in. (73.8 × 102.4 cm.)
Artist:
Lithographer:
Printer:
Publisher: O. H. Bailey & Co., Boston
Key/Vignettes/Misc: Refs. A–Z, 1–81; 11 vignettes
Locations: BPL–R; RIHS–P
Catalogs/Checklists:

3880
Place: Providence, Rhode Island
Date: 1895
Title: A Bird's Eye View of Providence Showing the New Railroad Station and State House.
Size: 20 × 30 in. (50.8 × 76.3 cm.)
Artist: J. B. Chapin
Lithographer:
Printer: Providence Albertype Co. [Providence]
Publisher: Providence Sunday Journal [Providence]
Key/Vignettes/Misc:
Locations: RIHS–P
Catalogs/Checklists:

3881
Place: Providence, Rhode Island
Date: 1896
Title: View of the City of Providence as Seen from the Dome of the New State House
Size: 13 × 19⅝ in. (33 × 50 cm.)
Artist: M. D. Mason
Lithographer:
Printer:
Publisher: Providence Journal Co., Providence
Key/Vignettes/Misc:
Locations: LC–M
Catalogs/Checklists: LC–M, 881

Place: River Point, Rhode Island
Date: 1889
See Clyde, Rhode Island, 1889.

3882
Place: Rocky Point, Rhode Island
Date: 1878
Title: Birds Eye or Baloon View of Rocky Point, Narragansett Bay, R. I.
Size: 11 × 19 in. (28 × 48.3 cm.)
Artist:
Lithographer:
Printer: L. Sunderland, Providence, R. I.
Publisher: L. Sunderland, Providence, R. I., 1878
Key/Vignettes/Misc:
Locations: MM–NN
Catalogs/Checklists: MM–NN, LP 2620

3883
Place: Slatersville, Rhode Island
Date: 1895
Title: Slatersville, Rhode Island
Size: 16⅝ × 20⅜ in. (42.3 × 51.8 cm.) (facsimile)
Artist:
Lithographer:
Printer: O. H. Bailey & Co., Boston
Publisher: O. H. Bailey & Co., Boston

Key/Vignettes/Misc: Refs. A, 2–18; 8 vignettes
Locations: RIHS–P (facsimile)
Catalogs/Checklists:

3884
Place: Wakefield, Rhode Island
Date: 1888
Title: Wakefield and Peacedale, Rhode Island. 1888.
Size: 20⅞ × 25⅝ in. (53.1 × 65.2 cm.)
Artist:
Lithographer:
Printer: O. H. Bailey & Co., Boston
Publisher: O. H. Bailey & Co., Boston
Key/Vignettes/Misc: Refs. A, 2–62; 16 vignettes
Locations: BPL–R; Pettaguamseatt Historical Society, Kingston, Rhode Island
Catalogs/Checklists:

3885
Place: Warren, Rhode Island
Date: 1877
Title: View of Warren, R. I.
Size: 18⅛ × 25⅝ in. (46.1 × 65.1 cm.)
Artist: O. H. Bailey & J. C. Hazen
Lithographer: C. H. Vogt
Printer:
Publisher: O. H. Bailey and J. C. Hazen, Boston
Key/Vignettes/Misc: Refs. A–H, J–M, O
Locations: BPL–R; RIHS–P
Catalogs/Checklists:

3886
Place: Warren, Rhode Island
Date: 1890
Title: Warren, Rhode Island. 1890
Size: 20½ × 25⅛ in. (52.1 × 63.9 cm.)
Artist:
Lithographer:
Printer: O. H. Bailey & Co., Boston
Publisher: O. H. Bailey & Co., Boston
Key/Vignettes/Misc: Refs. A, 2–27; 26 vignettes
Locations: BPL–R
Catalogs/Checklists:

3887
Place: Washington, Rhode Island
Date: 1888
Title: Washington, Rhode Island. 1888
Size: 16⅛ × 25⅛ in. (41 × 63.9 cm.)
Artist:
Lithographer:
Printer: O. H. Bailey & Co., Boston
Publisher: O. H. Bailey & Co., Boston
Key/Vignettes/Misc: Refs. A, 2–17; 3 vignettes
Locations: BPL–R; RIHS–P
Catalogs/Checklists:

3888
Place: Westerly, Rhode Island
Date: 1877
Title: View of Westerly, R. I. 1877.
Size: 19⅛ × 25¼ in. (48.7 × 64.2 cm.)
Artist: O. H. Bailey & J. C. Hazen
Lithographer:
Printer:
Publisher: O. H. Bailey & J. C. Hazen, Boston

Key/Vignettes/Misc: Refs. A–H, J–P, R–V
Locations: BPL–R; LC–M; RIHS–P
Catalogs/Checklists: LC–M, 881.1

3889
Place: Westerly, Rhode Island
Date: 1911
Title: Aero View of Westerly, Rhode Island 1911.
Size: 19¼ × 35¹³⁄₁₆ in. (49 × 91 cm.)
Artist:
Lithographer:
Printer:
Publisher: Hughes & Bailey, New York
Key/Vignettes/Misc: 30 vignettes; unnumbered business directory; description
Locations: LC–M
Catalogs/Checklists: LC–M, 882

3890
Place: Wickford, Rhode Island
Date: 1888
Title: Wickford, Rhode Island. 1888
Size: 19¾ × 30 in. (50.3 × 76.3 cm.)
Artist:
Lithographer:
Printer: O. H. Bailey & Co., Boston
Publisher: O. H. Bailey & Co., Boston
Key/Vignettes/Misc: Refs. 1–56; 18 vignettes
Locations: BPL–R
Catalogs/Checklists:

3891
Place: Woonsocket, Rhode Island
Date: 1876
Title: Woonsocket, R. I.
Size: 21¼ × 32½ in. (54.1 × 82.7 cm.)
Artist: H. H. Bailey & J. C. Hazen
Lithographer: C. H. Vogt
Printer: J. Knauber & Co.
Publisher: H. H. Bailey
Key/Vignettes/Misc: Refs. 1–22
Locations: RIHS–P
Catalogs/Checklists:

3892
Place: Charleston, South Carolina
Date: [1831–33]
Title: Charleston South Carolina from Fort Pinckney
Size: 9¾ × 13⅜ in. (24.9 × 34.1 cm.)
Artist: G. Lehman
Lithographer: G. Lehman
Printer: Childs & Inman, Lithrs. Philadelphia
Publisher:
Key/Vignettes/Misc:
Locations: SCL–C; YUAG–NH
Catalogs/Checklists:

3893
Place: Charleston, South Carolina
Date: Ca. 1845
Title: Charleston in Sud Karolina
Size: 5¼ × 7 in. (13.4 × 17.8 cm.)
Artist:
Lithographer:
Printer:
Publisher:
Key/Vignettes/Misc:

Locations: Unknown. See Old Print Shop Portfolio, XIII, p. 15, No. 19
Catalogs/Checklists:

3894
Place: Charleston, South Carolina
Date: 1851
Title: Charleston, S. C.
Size: 24⅞ × 41¹³⁄₁₆ in. (63.2 × 106.1 cm.)
Artist: Smith & Smith after John William Hill
Lithographer:
Printer:
Publisher: Smith Brothers & Co., London
Key/Vignettes/Misc:
Locations: NYP–S; CAA–C; CHS–C; SCHS–C; SCL–C
Catalogs/Checklists: Bilodeau, Art in South Carolina, no. 143; Stokes Addenda P. 1850—Views–12

3895
Place: Charleston, South Carolina
Date: [1852–59]
Title: Eastern View of the City of Charleston, S. C. [front]
Size: 16 × 21½ in. (40.7 × 54.7 cm.)
Artist: William Keenan
Lithographer: W. Keenan
Printer: S. H. Mellen [Charleston]
Publisher: W. Keenan, Charleston, 250 King Cor Hasel St.
Key/Vignettes/Misc:
Locations: CAA–C; SCL–C; NYH–NY
Catalogs/Checklists: Bilodeau, Art in South Carolina, no. 145; Pyne, no. 415

3896
Place: Charleston, South Carolina
Date: [1852–59]
Title: North Eastern View of Charleston with North Eastern Railroad
Size: 13¹¹⁄₁₆ × 21⅝ in. (34.8 × 55 cm.)
Artist: Wm. Keenan
Lithographer: Wm. Keenan
Printer: [S. H. Mellen, Charleston]
Publisher: Wm. Keenan, 250 King Cor. Hasel St. [Charleston]
Key/Vignettes/Misc:
Locations: SCHS–C; LC–P; NYH–NY
Catalogs/Checklists: Bilodeau, Art in South Carolina, no. 146

3897
Place: Charleston, South Carolina
Date: [1852–59]
Title: North–western View of Charleston, So. Ca.
Size: 14½ × 22⅜ in. (36.8 × 57.1 cm.)
Artist: Wm. Keenan
Lithographer: W. Keenan
Printer: [S. H. Mellen, Charleston]
Publisher: Wm. Keenan, 250 King Cor. Hasel St. [Charleston]
Key/Vignettes/Misc:
Locations: LC–P; NYH–NY
Catalogs/Checklists:

3898
Place: Charleston, South Carolina
Date: [1852–59]
Title: Southern View of the City of Charleston, So. Ca.

Size: 15⅜ × 21¾ in. (39.1 × 55.2 cm.)
Artist: Wm. Keenan
Lithographer: Wm. Keenan
Printer: S. H. Mellen, Charleston
Publisher: Wm. Keenan, 205 King cor Hasel St. [Charleston]
Key/Vignettes/Misc:
Locations: CAA–C; SCHS–C; SCL–C; NYH–NY
Catalogs/Checklists: Bilodeau, Art in South Carolina, no. 144

3899
Place: Charleston, South Carolina
Date: 1863
Title: The Attack on Charleston by the Yankee Iron Clad Fleet, April 7th, 1863
Size: 10⅛ × 15½ in. (25.5 × 39.5 cm.)
Artist: A. Grinevald
Lithographer:
Printer: B. Duncan, Columbia, S. C.
Publisher:
Key/Vignettes/Misc: Refs. 1–23
Locations: SCHS–C
Catalogs/Checklists:

3900
Place: Charleston, South Carolina
Date: [1865?]
Title: Charleston City.
Size: 12¾ × 17¾ in. (32.4 × 45.1 cm.)
Artist:
Lithographer:
Printer: L. N. Rosenthal, Philadelphia
Publisher: J. W. Bradley, Philadelphia
Key/Vignettes/Misc:
Locations: SCL–C
Catalogs/Checklists: Bilodeau, Art in South Carolina, no. 201

3901
Place: Charleston, South Carolina
Date: 1872
Title: Bird's Eye View of the City of Charleston, South Carolina, 1872.
Size: 20¹³⁄₁₆ × 33⁷⁄₁₆ in. (53 × 85 cm.)
Artist: C. Drie
Lithographer:
Printer:
Publisher: C. Drie
Key/Vignettes/Misc: Refs. 1–90; 3 vignettes
Locations: LC–M; SCL–C; CM–C; SCHS–C
Catalogs/Checklists: LC–M, 883; Bilodeau, Art in South Carolina, no. 219

3902
Place: Columbia, South Carolina
Date: 1872
Title: Bird's Eye View of the City of Columbia South Carolina 1872.
Size: 22½ × 28 in. (57.3 × 71.3 cm.)
Artist: C. Drie
Lithographer: C. Drie
Printer:
Publisher: C. Drie
Key/Vignettes/Misc: Refs. 1–45
Locations: LC–M; SCL–C; LC–P
Catalogs/Checklists: LC–M, 884

3903
Place: Spartanburg, South Carolina
Date: 1891
Title: Bird's–Eye View of the City of Spartanburg, South Carolina. 1891
Size: 17⅞ × 28¾ in. (43.6 × 73.2 cm.)
Artist:
Lithographer:
Printer: [L. R. Burleigh, Troy, N. Y.?]
Publisher: [Ruger & Stoner, Madison, Wis?]
Key/Vignettes/Misc: Refs. 1–38; 3 vignettes
Locations: NYH–NY
Catalogs/Checklists:

3904
Place: Aberdeen, South Dakota
Date: 1883
Title: Aberdeen, Brown County, Dakota.
Size: 12 × 20 in. (30.6 × 50.9 cm.)
Artist: W. V. Herancourt
Lithographer:
Printer:
Publisher:
Key/Vignettes/Misc: 3 vignettes
Locations: SDHS–P
Catalogs/Checklists: SDH VIII–3, p. 227

3905
Place: Aberdeen, South Dakota
Date: 1883
Title: Birds Eye View of Aberdeen, Dak.
Size: 15 × 25 in. (38.2 × 63.6 cm.)
Artist: H. Wellge
Lithographer:
Printer:
Publisher: F. H. Hagerty & H. M. Marple, Aberdeen Dak. T.
Key/Vignettes/Misc: Refs. 1–6, A–F; 7 vignettes
Locations: LC–M; HEHL; LC–P
Catalogs/Checklists: LC–M, 885; Reps, Cities on Stone, p. 91; SDH VIII–3, p. 226

3906
Place: Brookings, South Dakota
Date: 1881
Title: Brookings. Brookings County Dakota 1881.
Size: 14 × 17 in. (35.6 × 43.3 cm.)
Artist: Frisbie
Lithographer:
Printer:
Publisher:
Key/Vignettes/Misc: Refs. 1–13; 6 vignettes
Locations: SDHS–P
Catalogs/Checklists: SDH VIII–3, p. 229

3907
Place: Chamberlain, South Dakota
Date: 1882
Title: Bird's–Eye View of Chamberlain, Dakota
Size:
Artist: Wm. Valentine Herancourt
Lithographer:
Printer:
Publisher:

Key/Vignettes/Misc: 2 vignettes
Locations: SDHS–P (newspaper illustration)
Catalogs/Checklists: SDH VIII–3, p. 230

3908
Place: Clark, South Dakota
Date: 1883
Title: Bird's Eye View of Clark, Dakota, County Seat Clark Co. 1883.
Size: 12 × 18 in. (30.5 × 45.8 cm.)
Artist:
Lithographer:
Printer: Beck & Pauli, Lithographers, Milwaukee, Wis.
Publisher: J. J. Stoner, Madison, Wis.
Key/Vignettes/Misc: Refs. 1–27; 7 vignettes
Locations: LC–M; SDHS–P (photo)
Catalogs/Checklists: LC–M, 886; SDH VIII–3, p. 231

3909
Place: De Smet, South Dakota
Date: 1883
Title: Bird's Eye View of De Smet, Dak. County Seat of Kingsbury County 1883.
Size: 7 × 13 in. (17.7 × 33 cm.)
Artist: H. Wellge
Lithographer:
Printer:
Publisher: J. J. Stoner, Madison, Wis.
Key/Vignettes/Misc: Refs. A–L; unnumbered business directory
Locations: SDHS–P
Catalogs/Checklists: SDH VIII–3, p. 233

3910
Place: Deadwood, South Dakota
Date: 1884
Title: Deadwood, Black Hills, Dakota.
Size: 12⁷⁄₁₆ × 20⅞ in. (31.5 × 51.9 cm.)
Artist: W. V. Herancourt
Lithographer:
Printer:
Publisher:
Key/Vignettes/Misc: 3 vignettes
Locations: ACMW–FW; SDHS–P; LC–M (facsimile)
Catalogs/Checklists: ACMW–FW 1144; Reps, Cities on Stone, p. 92; SDH VIII–3, p. 232; LC–M, 887

3911
Place: Flandreau, South Dakota
Date: 1883
Title: Bird's Eye View of Flandreau, County Seat of Moody Co., Dakota 1883.
Size: 13 × 21 in. (33 × 53.4 cm.)
Artist: H. Brosius
Lithographer:
Printer: Beck & Pauli, Milwaukee
Publisher: J. J. Stoner, Madison
Key/Vignettes/Misc: Refs. 1–40; 2 vignettes
Locations: LC–M; SDHS–P (photo)
Catalogs/Checklists: LC–M, 888; SDH VIII–3, p. 234

3912
Place: Frederick, South Dakota
Date: 1883

Title: Bird's Eye View of Frederick, Dak. 1883.
Size: 10¼ × 15 in. (26 × 38.1 cm.)
Artist:
Lithographer:
Printer:
Publisher: C. F. Campau, Frederick
Key/Vignettes/Misc: Refs. 1–22; 1 vignette; description
Locations: LC–M; SDHS–P
Catalogs/Checklists: LC–M, 889; SDH VIII–3, p. 235

3913
Place: Gary, South Dakota
Date: 1883
Title: Bird's Eye View of Gary, Dak. County Seat of Deuel County
Size: 8⁷⁄₁₆ × 14³⁄₁₆ in. (21.5 × 36.1 cm.)
Artist:
Lithographer:
Printer:
Publisher: P. A. Gatchell
Key/Vignettes/Misc: Refs. 1–10; 1 vignette
Locations: LC–P; SDHS–P (photo)
Catalogs/Checklists: SDH VIII–3, p. 236

3914
Place: Howard, South Dakota
Date: 1883
Title: Bird's–Eye View of Howard City, County Seat of Miner County, Dakota.
Size: 14 × 21 in. (35.6 × 53.4 cm.)
Artist: James McCoy
Lithographer:
Printer:
Publisher:
Key/Vignettes/Misc: Refs. A–H; 1 vignette
Locations: SDHS–P
Catalogs/Checklists: SDH VIII–3, p. 237

3915
Place: Huron, South Dakota
Date: 1883
Title: Pen Drawing of Huron in 1883
Size: 9¹³⁄₁₆ × 18¹⁄₁₆ in. (25 × 46 cm.)
Artist: Wm. Valentine Herancourt
Lithographer:
Printer: Huron Daily Times
Publisher:
Key/Vignettes/Misc: 2 vignettes
Locations: SDHS–P; LC–M (photo); WHS–M
Catalogs/Checklists: SDH VIII–3, p. 238; LC–M, 889.1

3916
Place: Lead, South Dakota
Date: 1884
Title: Lead City, Black Hills, Dakota
Size: 12 × 19¹⁄₁₆ in. (30.4 × 48.4 cm.)
Artist: W. V. Herancourt
Lithographer:
Printer:
Publisher:
Key/Vignettes/Misc: 4 vignettes
Locations: ACMW–FW; SDHS–P (photo)
Catalogs/Checklists: ACMW–FW 1145; Reps, Cities on Stone, p. 94; SDH VIII–3, p. 239

3917
Place: Madison, South Dakota
Date: 1883
Title: 1883 Bird's Eye View of Madison, County Seat of Lake Co. Dakota
Size: 13 × 20 in. (33 × 50.8 cm.)
Artist: H. Brosius
Lithographer:
Printer: Beck & Pauli, Milwaukee
Publisher: J. J. Stoner, Madison, Wis.
Key/Vignettes/Misc: Refs. 1–45; 2 vignettes
Locations: LC–M; SDHS–P (photo)
Catalogs/Checklists: LC–M, 890; SDH VIII–3, p. 240

3918
Place: Pierre, South Dakota
Date: Ca. 1883
Title: Pierre, Hughes County, Dakota
Size: 14 × 21 in. (35.6 × 53.4 cm.)
Artist: Wm. Valentine Herancourt
Lithographer:
Printer:
Publisher:
Key/Vignettes/Misc: 2 vignettes
Locations: SDHS–P
Catalogs/Checklists: SDH VIII–3, p. 241

3919
Place: Rapid City, South Dakota
Date: 1883
Title: Rapid City, Dakota, in 1883.
Size: 11¼ × 19¹³⁄₁₆ in. (28.5 × 50.3 cm.)
Artist: W. V. Herancourt
Lithographer:
Printer:
Publisher:
Key/Vignettes/Misc: 2 vignettes; advertisement
Locations: LC–M (photo); SDHS–P (photo); WHS–M
Catalogs/Checklists: Reps, Cities on Stone, p. 96; SDH VIII–3, p. 242; LC–M, 890.1

3920
Place: Redfield, South Dakota
Date: 1883
Title: 1883 Bird's Eye View of Redfield, Dak.
Size: 12 × 15½ in. (30.5 × 39.4 cm.)
Artist: H. Wellge
Lithographer:
Printer:
Publisher: Dakota Sun News Book and Job Printing House.
Key/Vignettes/Misc: Refs. A–X, 2–6; 3 vignettes
Locations: LC–M; SDHS–P (photo)
Catalogs/Checklists: LC–M, 891; SDH VIII–3, p. 243

3921
Place: Rosebud, South Dakota
Date: N.D.
Title: Rosebud Indian Agency, D. T. Established Sept. 1, 1879 by William J. Pollock, U. S. Special Indian Agent.
Size: 16 × 20 in. (40.7 × 50.8 cm.)
Artist: James McCoy
Lithographer: James McCoy

Printer:
Publisher:
Key/Vignettes/Misc:
Locations: SDHS–P
Catalogs/Checklists: SDHVIII–3, p. 244

3922
Place: Sioux Falls, South Dakota
Date: 1881
Title: Sioux Falls, Minnahaha County, Dakota.
Size: 20 × 24 in. (50.8 × 61 cm.)
Artist:
Lithographer:
Printer:
Publisher: Chas. A. Carson & Co.
Key/Vignettes/Misc: Refs. 1–20; 2 vignettes
Locations: SDHS–P
Catalogs/Checklists: SDH VIII–3, p. 245

3923
Place: Spearfish, South Dakota
Date: 1884
Title: Spearfish, "The Queen of the Valley."
Size: 12 × 19½ in. (30.6 × 49.6 cm.)
Artist: W. V. Herancourt
Lithographer:
Printer:
Publisher:
Key/Vignettes/Misc:
Locations: SDHS–P (photo); LC–M (photo); Grace Balloch Memorial Library, Spearfish, South Dakota
Catalogs/Checklists: SDH VIII–3, p. 246; LC–M, 891.1

3924
Place: Watertown, South Dakota
Date: 1883
Title: Bird's Eye View of Watertown, Dak. County–Seat of Codington Co. 1883.
Size: 12⅜ × 20½ in. (31.4 × 52.1 cm.)
Artist:
Lithographer:
Printer: Beck & Pauli, Lithographers, Milwaukee, Wis.
Publisher: J. J. Stoner, Madison, Wis.
Key/Vignettes/Misc: Refs. A–E, 1–15; 3 vignettes; unnumbered business directory
Locations: LC–M; SDHS–P
Catalogs/Checklists: LC–M, 892; SDH VIII–3, p. 247

3925
Place: Yankton, South Dakota
Date: 1875
Title: Bird's–Eye View of Yankton, Yankton County, Dakota, Territory
Size: 19¾ × 24 in. (50.3 × 61 cm.)
Artist: Augustus Koch
Lithographer:
Printer: Chas. Shober & Co., Chicago
Publisher:
Key/Vignettes/Misc: Refs. 1–20
Locations: SDHS–P (photo); Dakota Territorial Museum, Yankton, South Dakota
Catalogs/Checklists: SDH VIII–3, p. 248

3926
Place: Anderson, Tennessee
Date: N.D.
Title: View of Anderson, Tennessee
Size: 7⅜ × 10¹³⁄₁₆ in. (18.7 × 27.5 cm.)
Artist: N. B. Abbott
Lithographer:
Printer: Henry C. Eno, 37 Park Row, N. Y.
Publisher:
Key/Vignettes/Misc:
Locations: YUAG–NH
Catalogs/Checklists:

Place: Bristol, Tennessee
Date: 1912
See Bristol, Virginia, 1912.

3927
Place: Chattanooga, Tennessee
Date: 1871
Title: Birds Eye View of the City of Chattanooga, Hamilton County, Tennessee 1871.
Size: 21¼ × 30⅝ in. (54 × 78 cm.)
Artist: A. Ruger
Lithographer:
Printer:
Publisher: A. Ruger, St. Louis, Mo.
Key/Vignettes/Misc: Refs. 1–11, A–F, G–H, K–P, R
Locations: LC–M
Catalogs/Checklists: LC–M, 893

3928
Place: Chattanooga, Tennessee
Date: 1886
Title: Chattanooga, County Seat of Hamilton County, Tennessee. 1886 Population 30,000
Size: 20½ × 28⅛ in. (52 × 71.4 cm.)
Artist: H. Wellge
Lithographer:
Printer: Beck & Pauli, Milwaukee, Wis.
Publisher: Norris, Wellge & Co. No. 205 Second St. Milwaukee, Wis.
Key/Vignettes/Misc: Refs. 1–24, A–Y; 2 vignettes
Locations: LC–M; LC–P
Catalogs/Checklists: LC–M, 894

3929
Place: Chattanooga, Tennessee
Date: 1887
Title: Chattanooga, Tenn. as Seen from Bragg Hill, Missionary Ridge.
Size: 18⅝ × 25 in. (47.3 × 63.5 cm.)
Artist:
Lithographer:
Printer: [Beck & Pauli Lith. Co. Milwaukee, Wis.]
Publisher: J. C. Anderson, trustee (copyright)
Key/Vignettes/Misc:
Locations: LC–M; LC–P
Catalogs/Checklists: LC–M, 895

3930
Place: Chattanooga, Tennessee
Date: 1897
Title: Chattanooga and Lookout Mountain
Size: 14⅞ × 26¹⁵⁄₁₆ in. (37.8 × 68.5 cm.)
Artist: Henry Wellge
Lithographer:
Printer:
Publisher: American Fine Art Co. Milwaukee, Wis. (copyright)
Key/Vignettes/Misc: Refs. 1–12; 1 vignette
Locations: ACMW–FW
Catalogs/Checklists:

3931
Place: Clarksville, Tennessee
Date: 1870
Title: Bird's Eye View of the City of Clarksville, Montgomery County, Tennessee 1870.
Size: 22 × 25¹⁵⁄₁₆ in. (56 × 66 cm.)
Artist: [Albert Ruger]
Lithographer:
Printer: Merchant Lith. Co., Chicago
Publisher: Stoner & Ruger, [Madison, Wis.]
Key/Vignettes/Misc: Refs. 1–16; 2 vignettes
Locations: LC–M
Catalogs/Checklists: LC–M, 896

3932
Place: Harriman, Tennessee
Date: 1892
Title: Harriman, Tenn. 1892.
Size: 19¹¹⁄₁₆ × 28⅞ in. (50.1 × 73.6 cm.)
Artist: Geo. E. Norris
Lithographer:
Printer: Burleigh Lith. Co., Troy, New York
Publisher: Geo. E. Norris, Brockton, Mass.
Key/Vignettes/Misc: Refs. 1–60; 12 vignettes
Locations: LC–M; BPL–R; LC–P
Catalogs/Checklists: LC–M, 897

3933
Place: Jackson, Tennessee
Date: 1870
Title: Bird's Eye View of the City of Jackson, Madison County, Tennessee 1870.
Size: 22 × 26⁵⁄₁₆ in. (56 × 67 cm.)
Artist: A. Ruger
Lithographer:
Printer: Chicago Lithographing Co., Chicago
Publisher:
Key/Vignettes/Misc: Refs. 1–17, A–K; 2 vignettes
Locations: LC–M
Catalogs/Checklists: LC–M, 898

3934
Place: Knoxville, Tennessee
Date: 1871
Title: Bird's Eye View of the City of Knoxville, Knox County, Tennessee 1871.
Size: 21⅝ × 25¹⁵⁄₁₆ in. (55 × 66 cm.)
Artist: [A. Ruger]
Lithographer:
Printer: Merchants Lith Co., Chicago
Publisher:
Key/Vignettes/Misc: Refs. 1–17, A; 2 vignettes
Locations: LC–M; Knoxville–Knox County Public Library, Knoxville, Tennessee
Catalogs/Checklists: LC–M, 899

3935
Place: Knoxville, Tennessee
Date: 1886
Title: Knoxville, Tenn. County Seat of Knox County 1886. Population: 30,000.
Size: 20⅛ × 28¹⁄₁₆ in. (51.1 × 71.3 cm.)
Artist: H. Wellge
Lithographer:
Printer: Beck & Pauli, litho., Milwaukee, Wis.
Publisher: Norris, Wellge & Co. No. 205 Second St. Milwaukee, Wis.
Key/Vignettes/Misc: Refs. A–Z, 1–26; 2 vignettes
Locations: LC–M; Knoxville–Knox County Public Library, Knoxville, Tennessee; LC–P
Catalogs/Checklists: LC–M, 900

3936
Place: Memphis, Tennessee
Date: [1851]
Title: Memphis, Ten.
Size: 5¾ × 7⅞ in. (14.7 × 20 cm.)
Artist:
Lithographer: A. Forbriger
Printer: Onken's Lith. Cin. O.
Publisher: [Otto Onken, Cincinnati, Ohio]
Key/Vignettes/Misc:
Locations: CPL–R; LC–P
Catalogs/Checklists:

3937
Place: Memphis, Tennessee
Date: [1854–57]
Title: Memphis, Tennessee
Size: 6⅜ × 8⁵⁄₁₆ in. (16.2 × 21.9 cm.)
Artist: Henry Lewis
Lithographer:
Printer: C. H. Muller, Aachen
Publisher: Arnz & Co., Dusseldorf
Key/Vignettes/Misc:
Locations: MHS–SP; NYH–NY; HEHL; LC–R; NL–C; HNOC–NO
Catalogs/Checklists: Stokes 1846–47—F–77

3938
Place: Memphis, Tennessee
Date: 1870
Title: Bird's Eye View of the City of Memphis, Tennessee 1870.
Size: 22 × 34³⁄₁₆ in. (56 × 87 cm.)
Artist: [A. Ruger]
Lithographer:
Printer:
Publisher:
Key/Vignettes/Misc: Refs. 1–35, A–D
Locations: LC–M
Catalogs/Checklists: LC–M, 901

3939
Place: Memphis, Tennessee
Date: 1887
Title: Perspective Map of the City of Memphis, Tenn. 1887.
Size: 24¾ × 40¾ in. (63 × 105 cm.)

Artist:
Lithographer:
Printer:
Publisher: Henry Wellge & Co.,
Milwaukee
Key/Vignettes/Misc: Refs. 1–19, A–I,
a–g, l–r; 18 vignettes
Locations: LC–M
Catalogs/Checklists: LC–M, 902

3940
Place: Nashville, Tennessee
Date: Ca. 1855
Title: General View of the City of
Nashville, 1855
Size: 16 × 25 in. (40.7 × 63.6 cm.)
Artist:
Lithographer:
Printer: J. F. Wagner, Lithographer
[Nashville]
Publisher:
Key/Vignettes/Misc:
Locations: Elder's Book Store, Nashville,
Tennessee; Tennessee State Library,
Nashville, Tennessee (facsimile)
Catalogs/Checklists:

3941
Place: Nashville, Tennessee
Date: [1849–55]
Title: Nashville.
Size: 13¾ × 18¹¹⁄₁₆ in. (35 × 47.5 cm.)
Artist:
Lithographer:
Printer:
Publisher:
Key/Vignettes/Misc:
Locations: NYP–S
Catalogs/Checklists: Stokes 1849–55—
F–68

3942
Place: Nashville, Tennessee
Date: 1872
Title: Birdseye View of the City of
Nashville, Tennessee, 1872.
Size: 24¹¹⁄₁₆ × 34¹³⁄₁₆ in. (62.9 × 88.6 cm.)
Artist: Augustus Koch
Lithographer:
Printer: Ehrgott and Krebs, Cincinnati
Publisher:
Key/Vignettes/Misc: Refs. 1–54
Locations: Tennessee State Library,
Nashville, Tennessee
Catalogs/Checklists:

3943
Place: Nashville, Tennessee
Date: 1888
Title:
Size:
Artist: [H. Wellge?]
Lithographer:
Printer:
Publisher: [Norris, Wellge & Co.?]
Key/Vignettes/Misc:
Locations: Tennessee State Library,
Nashville, Tennessee (facsimile)
Catalogs/Checklists:

3944
Place: Alvord, Texas
Date: 1890
Title: Alvord, Texas 1890

Size: 9⅞ × 17³⁄₁₆ in. (25 × 43.6 cm.)
Artist: T. M. Fowler
Lithographer:
Printer:
Publisher: T. M. Fowler & James B. Moyer
Key/Vignettes/Misc: Refs. 1–8
Locations: ACMW–FW; LC–M
Catalogs/Checklists: LC–M, 902.1

3945
Place: Amarillo, Texas
Date: Ca. 1912
Title: Aeroplane View of Business District
Amarillo, Texas.
Size: 17 × 19½ in. (43.2 × 49.6 cm.)
Artist: E. E. Motter
Lithographer:
Printer: Panhandle Printing Co., Amarillo
Publisher: G. C. Sturdivant
Key/Vignettes/Misc:
Locations: LC–M
Catalogs/Checklists: LC–M, 903

3946
Place: Austin, Texas
Date: 1873
Title: Bird's Eye View of the City of Austin
Travis County Texas. 1873.
Size: 19¾ × 28⅛ in. (50.1 × 71.4 cm.)
Artist: Augustus Koch
Lithographer:
Printer:
Publisher: [J. J. Stoner, Madison, Wis.]
Key/Vignettes/Misc: Refs. 1–24; 2
vignettes
Locations: UTB–A
Catalogs/Checklists: Reps, Cities on Stone,
p. 91

3947
Place: Austin, Texas
Date: 1887
Title: Austin, State Capital of Texas
Size: 28¼ × 41 in. (71.7 × 104.1 cm.)
Artist: Augustus Koch
Lithographer:
Printer:
Publisher:
Key/Vignettes/Misc: Refs. 1–67; 1
vignette
Locations: Austin, Texas, Public Library
Catalogs/Checklists: Reps, Cities on Stone,
p. 91

3948
Place: Austin, Texas
Date: Ca. 1895
Title: Partial View of Austin, Texas. The
Most Beautiful and Wealthiest City of its
Size in the United States
Size: 26¼ × 38¾ in. (66.7 × 98.5 cm.)
Artist:
Lithographer:
Printer:
Publisher:
Key/Vignettes/Misc:
Locations: Texas State Archives, Austin,
Texas
Catalogs/Checklists: TSA–A, 926E

3949
Place: Bastrop, Texas
Date: 1887
Title: Birds Eye View of Bastrop Bastrop

County Texas 1887
Size: 16⅝ × 22⅞ in. (42.3 × 58.2 cm.)
Artist: Aug. Koch
Lithographer:
Printer:
Publisher:
Key/Vignettes/Misc:
Locations: Bastrop County Historical
Society Museum, Bastrop, Texas
Catalogs/Checklists:

3950
Place: Belton, Texas
Date: 1881
Title: A Bird's Eye View of the City of
Belton, Bell County Texas
Size: 17½ × 22⅞ in. (44.5 × 58.3 cm.)
Artist: Augustus Koch
Lithographer:
Printer:
Publisher:
Key/Vignettes/Misc: Refs. 1–16
Locations: Belton, Texas, City Library;
UTB–A
Catalogs/Checklists:

3951
Place: Brenham, Texas
Date: 1873
Title: Bird's Eye View of Brenham,
Washington County, Texas. 1873.
Size: 18⅝ × 24⅛ in. (47.5 × 61.5 cm.)
Artist: Augustus Koch
Lithographer:
Printer:
Publisher:
Key/Vignettes/Misc: Refs. 1–19
Locations: UTB–A; LC–M (photo)
Catalogs/Checklists:

3952
Place: Brenham, Texas
Date: 1881
Title: Bird Eye View of the City of
Brenham, Washington County, Texas.
Size:
Artist: Augustus Koch
Lithographer:
Printer:
Publisher:
Key/Vignettes/Misc: Refs. 1–18
Locations: LC–M (photo)
Catalogs/Checklists: LC–M, 904

3953
Place: Castroville, Texas
Date: N.D.
Title: Vue de Castroville et de ses Environs
Prise du Mont Gentily
Size: 8⅝ × 14¹⁵⁄₁₆ in. (22 × 38 cm.)
Artist:
Lithographer:
Printer:
Publisher:
Key/Vignettes/Misc:
Locations: UTB–A
Catalogs/Checklists:

3954
Place: Childress, Texas
Date: 1890
Title: Childress, Texas. 1890
Size: 9⅝ × 16¼ in. (24.4 × 41.2 cm.)
Artist: T. M. Fowler

Lithographer:
Printer:
Publisher: T. M. Fowler & James B. Moyer
Key/Vignettes/Misc: Refs. 1–5
Locations: ACMW–FW; LC–M
Catalogs/Checklists: ACMW–FW 1098;
LC–M, 905

3955
Place: Clarendon, Texas
Date: 1890
Title: Clarendon, Texas, Donley Co. 1890
Size: 14½ × 25 in. (36.9 × 63.5 cm.)
Artist: T. M. Fowler
Lithographer:
Printer:
Publisher: T. M. Fowler & James B. Moyer
Key/Vignettes/Misc: Refs. 1–7
Locations: LC–M
Catalogs/Checklists: LC–M, 906

3956
Place: Cuero, Texas
Date: 1881
Title: Birds Eye View of Cuero De Witt
County, Texas.
Size: 14¾ × 22 in. (37.5 × 55.9 cm.)
Artist: Augustus Koch
Lithographer:
Printer:
Publisher:
Key/Vignettes/Misc: Refs. 1–13
Locations: ACMW–FW
Catalogs/Checklists: ACMW–FW 1229

3957
Place: Dallas, Texas
Date: [1872]
Title: Bird's Eye View of the City of Dallas
Texas.
Size: 15¹³⁄₁₆ × 22⅞ in. (40.1 × 58.1 cm.)
Artist: H. Brosius
Lithographer:
Printer:
Publisher:
Key/Vignettes/Misc: Refs. 1–21
Locations: Dallas Historical Society,
Dallas, Texas
Catalogs/Checklists: Reps, Cities on Stone,
p. 92

3958
Place: Dallas, Texas
Date: 1876
Title: Gollner's Map of the City of Dallas
Texas 1876
Size: 26 × 34 in. (66.2 × 86.5 cm.)
Artist: E. G. Gollner
Lithographer:
Printer:
Publisher: S. M. Williams [and] E. G.
Gollner, Dallas, Texas
Key/Vignettes/Misc: 14 vignettes;
advertisements and directory on verso
Locations: ACMW–FW (photo)
Catalogs/Checklists:

3959
Place: Dallas, Texas
Date: 1892
Title: Dallas, Texas. With the projected
River and Navigation Improvements
Viewed from Above the Sister City of Oak
Cliff.

Size: 21 × 29 in. (53.3 × 73.7 cm.)
Artist: Paul Giraud
Lithographer: Paul Giraud
Printer: Dallas Lith. Co.
Publisher:
Key/Vignettes/Misc:
Locations: LC–M
Catalogs/Checklists: LC–M, 907

3960
Place: Denison, Texas
Date: 1886
Title: Denison, Texas, Grayson County
1886.
Size: 20 × 27 in. (50.8 × 68.6 cm.)
Artist:
Lithographer:
Printer: Beck & Pauli, Milwaukee
Publisher: Norris, Wellge & Co.
Key/Vignettes/Misc: Refs. 1–65, A–Z; 3
vignettes
Locations: LC–M; ACMW–FW
Catalogs/Checklists: LC–M, 908

3961
Place: Denison, Texas
Date: 1891
Title: Denison, Grayson County, Texas
1891
Size: 20⅞ × 33⁹⁄₁₆ in. (53 × 85.2 cm.)
Artist: T. M. Fowler
Lithographer:
Printer:
Publisher: T. M. Fowler & James B. Moyer
Key/Vignettes/Misc: Refs. 1–13, A–N; 9
vignettes
Locations: ACMW–FW; LC–M;
WMM–SA; UTB–A
Catalogs/Checklists: ACMW–FW 1099;
Reps, Cities on Stone, p. 92; LC–M,
908.1

3962
Place: Eagle Pass, Texas
Date: 1887
Title: Bird's Eye View of Eagle Pass
Maverick Co, Texas. 1887.
Size: 17⅜ × 22¾ in. (44.2 × 57.9 cm.)
Artist: A. Koch
Lithographer:
Printer:
Publisher:
Key/Vignettes/Misc: Refs. 1–16
Locations: ACMW–FW
Catalogs/Checklists:

3963
Place: El Paso, Texas
Date: 1885
Title: Bird's Eye View of El Paso
Size: ca. 20 × 30 in. (ca. 50.8 × 76.3 cm.)
Artist: Aug. Koch.
Lithographer:
Printer:
Publisher:
Key/Vignettes/Misc: Refs. 1–12, A–C
Locations: Private collection
Catalogs/Checklists:

3964
Place: Fort Worth, Texas
Date: 1876
Title: Fort Worth Tarrant Co. Texas

Size: 14⅛ × 18¹³⁄₁₆ in. (35.9 × 47.7 cm.)
Artist: D. D. Morse
Lithographer:
Printer: Chas. Shober & Co. Props.
Chicago Lith. Co. [Chicago]
Publisher:
Key/Vignettes/Misc: Refs. 1–7
Locations: ACMW–FW
Catalogs/Checklists: ACMW–FW 1459;
Reps, Cities on Stone, p. 93

3965
Place: Fort Worth, Texas
Date: 1886
Title: Fort Worth, Tex., "The Queen of the
Prairies," County Seat of Tarrant County
1886.
Size: 26½ × 34 in. (67.3 × 86.4 cm.)
Artist: H. Wellge
Lithographer:
Printer: Beck & Pauli, Milwaukee
Publisher: Norris, Wellge & Co.,
Milwaukee
Key/Vignettes/Misc: Refs. 1–87, A–Z; 14
vignettes
Locations: LC–M; ACMW–FW
Catalogs/Checklists: LC–M, 910

3966
Place: Fort Worth, Texas
Date: 1891
Title: Perspective Map of Fort Worth, Tex.
1891.
Size: 17¹⁄₁₆ × 33¼ in. (43.3 × 84.5 cm.)
Artist: H. Wellge
Lithographer:
Printer:
Publisher: The American Publishing Co.,
Milwaukee
Key/Vignettes/Misc: 1 vignette
Locations: ACMW–FW; LC–M
Catalogs/Checklists: ACMW–FW 1929;
LC–M, 911; Reps, Cities on Stone, p. 93

3967
Place: Fort Worth, Texas
Date: [1914?]
Title: Bird's–Eye View of Fort Worth,
Texas
Size:
Artist: Amos S. Harris
Lithographer:
Printer:
Publisher:
Key/Vignettes/Misc:
Locations: LC–M (photo)
Catalogs/Checklists: LC–M, 912

3968
Place: Fredericksburg, Texas
Date: Ca. 1852
Title: Friedrichsburg, Texas
Size: 11¹³⁄₁₆ × 18⅝ in. (30 × 47.4 cm.)
Artist: H. Lungkwitz
Lithographer:
Printer: Rau & Sohn, Dresden
Publisher:
Key/Vignettes/Misc:
Locations: ACMW–FW; WMM–SA;
UTB–A
Catalogs/Checklists:

3969
Place: Fredericksburg, Texas
Date: [1873–87?]
Title:
Size:
Artist: Augustus Koch
Lithographer:
Printer:
Publisher:
Key/Vignettes/Misc:
Locations: Unknown. Information from exhibit caption, Institute of Texan Cultures, San Antonio, Texas
Catalogs/Checklists:

3970
Place: Galveston, Texas
Date: [1855?]
Title: Bird's Eye View of the Eastern Portion of the City of Galveston, with the Homes Destroyed by the Great Conflagration of November 13th, 1885. . . .
Size: 18½ × 23¾ in. (47 × 60.5 cm.)
Artist:
Lithographer:
Printer: M. Strickland & Co. . .Galveston, Texas.
Publisher:
Key/Vignettes/Misc: Refs. A–V; description
Locations: UTB–A; RL–G
Catalogs/Checklists:

3971
Place: Galveston, Texas
Date: Ca. 1855
Title: Ansicht von Galveston
Size: 10¹¹⁄₁₆ × 16½ in. (27.2 × 41.9 cm.)
Artist: C. O. Bahr
Lithographer:
Printer: I. Willard, Dresden
Publisher: I. Willard, Dresden
Key/Vignettes/Misc:
Locations: NYP–S
Catalogs/Checklists: Stokes C. 1855—G–40

3972
Place: Galveston, Texas
Date: 1871
Title: Bird's Eye View of the City of Galveston Texas 1871
Size: 22⅜ × 34³⁄₁₆ in. (57 × 87 cm.)
Artist: C. N. Drie
Lithographer:
Printer: Chicago Lithographing Co. 150–54 S. Clark, Chicago, Ill.
Publisher:
Key/Vignettes/Misc: 8 vignettes
Locations: RL–G; UTB–A
Catalogs/Checklists:

3973
Place: Galveston, Texas
Date: 1885
Title: Galveston Texas.
Size: 26⁵⁄₁₆ × 40⅛ in. (66.8 × 101.9 cm.)
Artist: Aug. Koch
Lithographer:
Printer:

Publisher:
Key/Vignettes/Misc: Refs. 1–61; 18 vignettes
Locations: ACMW–FW; RL–G
Catalogs/Checklists: ACMW–FW 1234; Reps, Cities on Stone, p. 93

3974
Place: Gatesville, Texas
Date: 1884
Title: Birds Eye View of Gatesville Coryell County, Texas 1884
Size: 15 × 23½ in. (38.2 × 59.9 cm.) (facsimile)
Artist: Aug. Koch
Lithographer:
Printer:
Publisher:
Key/Vignettes/Misc: Refs. 1–8
Locations: Gatesville, Texas, Public Library (facsimile)
Catalogs/Checklists:

3975
Place: Greenville, Texas
Date: 1886
Title: Greenville, Tex., County Seat of Hunt County 1886.
Size: 18 × 25 in. (45.8 × 63.5 cm.)
Artist: H. Wellge
Lithographer:
Printer: Beck & Pauli, Milwaukee
Publisher: Norris, Wellge & Co., Milwaukee
Key/Vignettes/Misc: Refs. 1–36, A–N; unnumbered business directory
Locations: LC–M; ACMW–FW
Catalogs/Checklists: LC–M, 913

3976
Place: Greenville, Texas
Date: 1891
Title: Greenville, Hunt County Texas, 1891
Size: 13¹⁵⁄₁₆ × 29¼ in. (35.4 × 74.2 cm.)
Artist: T. M. Fowler
Lithographer:
Printer:
Publisher: T. M. Fowler & James B. Moyer
Key/Vignettes/Misc: Refs. 1–14, A–F; 5 vignettes
Locations: ACMW–FW
Catalogs/Checklists: ACMW–FW 1102

3977
Place: Honey Grove, Texas
Date: 1886
Title: Honey Grove, Tex. Fannin County. 1886.
Size: 12¹¹⁄₁₆ × 16⅞ in. (32.3 × 53 cm.)
Artist: Henry Wellge
Lithographer:
Printer: Beck & Pauli, Litho. Milwaukee, Wis.
Publisher: Norris, Wellge & Co., Milwaukee, Wis.
Key/Vignettes/Misc: Refs. 1–43
Locations: ACMW–FW; LC–M
Catalogs/Checklists: LC–M, 914; Reps, Cities on Stone, p. 93

3978
Place: Houston, Texas
Date: 1873
Title: Bird's Eye View of the City of Houston, Texas. 1873.
Size: 23⅛ × 30¹⁄₁₆ in. (59 × 76.5 cm.)
Artist: Augustus Koch
Lithographer:
Printer:
Publisher: [J. J. Stoner, Madison, Wis.]
Key/Vignettes/Misc: Refs. 1–39; 1 vignette
Locations: UTB–A; DRT–SA (photo)
Catalogs/Checklists:

3979
Place: Houston, Texas
Date: 1891
Title: Houston, Texas. (Looking South.) 1891.
Size: 23 × 42⅝ in. (58.4 × 108.2 cm.)
Artist: [A. L. Westyard]
Lithographer:
Printer:
Publisher: D. W. Ensing, Jr., [Chicago]
Key/Vignettes/Misc: Refs. A–Z; 10 vignettes; unnumbered church directory
Locations: ACMW–FW; LC–M; LC–P
Catalogs/Checklists: LC–M, 915; Reps, Cities on Stone, p. 93

3980
Place: Houston, Texas
Date: 1912
Title: Houston—A Modern City.
Size: 16½ × 21 in. (41.9 × 53.4 cm.)
Artist: Hopkins & Motter
Lithographer:
Printer:
Publisher: Hopkins & Motter
Key/Vignettes/Misc:
Locations: LC–M
Catalogs/Checklists: LC–M, 916

3981
Place: Indianola, Texas
Date: 1860
Title: View of Indianola taken from the Bay, on the Royal yard, on board the Barque Texana, Sept. 1860.
Size: 14¼ × 23¼ in. (36.3 × 59.1 cm.)
Artist: Helmuth Holtz
Lithographer:
Printer: Ed. Lang's Lithographical Establishment, Hamburg
Publisher: Helmuth Holtz
Key/Vignettes/Misc:
Locations: MM–NN; LC–P; ACMW–FW; UTB–A
Catalogs/Checklists: MM–NN, LP 934; Reps, Cities on Stone, p. 93

3982
Place: Jefferson, Texas
Date: 1872
Title: 1872 Bird's Eye View of Jefferson, Texas.
Size: 20 × 27½ in. (50.8 × 69.9 cm.) (facsimile)
Artist: H. Brosius
Lithographer:

Printer:
Publisher:
Key/Vignettes/Misc:
Locations: LC–M (facsimile)
Catalogs/Checklists: LC–M, 917

3983
Place: La Grange, Texas
Date: 1880
Title: Birds Eye View of La Grange, Fayette County, Texas
Size: 17⅞ × 22½ in. (45.5 × 57.3 cm.)
Artist: Augustus Koch
Lithographer:
Printer:
Publisher:
Key/Vignettes/Misc: Refs. 1–12; 1 vignette
Locations: WMM–SA; DRT–SA (facsimile)
Catalogs/Checklists:

3984
Place: Ladonia, Texas
Date: 1891
Title: Ladonia, Fannin County Texas. 1891.
Size: 9½ × 20³⁄₁₆ in. (24 × 51.2 cm.)
Artist: T. M. Fowler
Lithographer:
Printer:
Publisher: T. M. Fowler & James B. Moyer
Key/Vignettes/Misc: Refs. 1–4, A–D
Locations: ACMW–FW; LC–M
Catalogs/Checklists: LC–M, 917.1

3985
Place: Laredo, Texas
Date: 1892
Title: Perspective Map of the City of Laredo, Texas. The Gateway to and from Mexico.
Size: 19¹¹⁄₁₆ × 33⅛ in. (50 × 84.1 cm.)
Artist:
Lithographer:
Printer:
Publisher: American Publishing Co., Milwaukee, Wis.
Key/Vignettes/Misc: 10 vignettes; description; tables of population & imports and exports; advertisement
Locations: LC–M; ACMW–FW
Catalogs/Checklists: LC–M, 918; ACMW–FW 1823; Reps, Cities on Stone, p. 94

3986
Place: Matagorda, Texas
Date: 1860
Title: View of Matagorda (taken from the Bay, Sept. 1860).
Size: 14⅛ × 20⅞ in. (35.9 × 53.1 cm.)
Artist: Helmuth Holtz
Lithographer:
Printer: Ed. Lang, Hamburg
Publisher: Helmuth Holtz
Key/Vignettes/Misc:
Locations: MM–NN; LC–M
Catalogs/Checklists: MM–NN, LP 935

3987
Place: Mckinney, Texas
Date: 1876
Title: Bird's Eye View of Mc. Kinney

County Seat of Collin Co. Texas, 1876.
Size: 10⅜ × 13¹⁄₁₆ in. (26.4 × 33.2 cm.)
Artist: D. D. Morse
Lithographer:
Printer: Chas. Shober & Co. Prop. Chicago. Lith. Co. [Chicago]
Publisher:
Key/Vignettes/Misc:
Locations: ACMW–FW
Catalogs/Checklists:

3988
Place: New Braunfels, Texas
Date: [1850?]
Title: Panorama der Stadt New–Braunfels in Texas Aufgenommen von der Sudwestseite in Sommer 1847.
Size: 6 × 55 in. (15.2 × 139.8 cm.)
Artist:
Lithographer:
Printer:
Publisher:
Key/Vignettes/Misc:
Locations: Prince Maximillian Archives, University of Texas, Austin, Texas
Catalogs/Checklists:

3989
Place: New Braunfels, Texas
Date: Ca. 1850
Title: New–Braunfels. Deutsche Colonie in West Texas
Size: 7¼ × 17⅞ in. (18.5 × 45.5 cm.)
Artist: C. G. Iwonsky
Lithographer:
Printer: J. G. Bach, Leipzig
Publisher:
Key/Vignettes/Misc:
Locations: WMM–SA; UTB–A
Catalogs/Checklists:

3990
Place: New Braunfels, Texas
Date: 1881
Title: Bird's Eye View of New Braunfels Comal County Texas 1881.
Size: 17¹⁵⁄₁₆ × 28½ in. (45.5 × 72.3 cm.)
Artist: Augustus Koch
Lithographer:
Printer:
Publisher:
Key/Vignettes/Misc: Refs. 1–16
Locations: ACMW–FW
Catalogs/Checklists: ACMW–FW 1230; Reps, Cities on Stone, pp. 94–95

3991
Place: Paris, Texas
Date: 1885
Title: Paris, Texas. County Seat of Lamar County.
Size: 19½ × 25½ in. (49.5 × 64.7 cm.)
Artist: [Henry Wellge]
Lithographer:
Printer: Beck & Pauli, Litho. Milwaukee, Wis.
Publisher: Norris, Wellge & Co., Milwaukee, Wis.
Key/Vignettes/Misc: Refs. A–Z, 1–51; 1 vignette; advertisement
Locations: LC–M
Catalogs/Checklists: LC–M, 919; Reps, Cities on Stone, p. 95

3992
Place: Plano, Texas
Date: 1891
Title: Plano, Collin County. Texas 1891
Size: 12¾ × 22⁹⁄₁₆ in. (32.4 × 57.2 cm.)
Artist: T. M. Fowler
Lithographer:
Printer: A. E. Downs, Boston
Publisher: T. M. Fowler & James B. Moyer
Key/Vignettes/Misc: Refs. 1–8, A–E
Locations: ACMW–FW; LC–M (photo)
Catalogs/Checklists: LC–M, 919.1

3993
Place: Port Arthur, Texas
Date: Ca. 1912
Title: City and Harbor of Port Arthur, Texas Birds Eye View Looking South to the Gulf of Mexico.
Size: 16 × 36½ in. (40.7 × 92.8 cm.)
Artist: E. S. Glover
Lithographer:
Printer:
Publisher: Port Arthur Board of Trade [Port Arthur]
Key/Vignettes/Misc:
Locations: LC–M
Catalogs/Checklists: LC–M, 920

3994
Place: Quanah, Texas
Date: 1890
Title: Quanah, Texas. 1890.
Size: 10⁷⁄₁₆ × 19¼ in. (26.5 × 48.9 cm.)
Artist: T. M. Fowler
Lithographer:
Printer:
Publisher: T. M. Fowler & James B. Moyer
Key/Vignettes/Misc: Refs. 1–12
Locations: ACMW–FW; UTB–A; LC–M (photo)
Catalogs/Checklists: Reps, Cities on Stone, p. 96; LC–M, 920.1

3995
Place: San Antonio, Texas
Date: Ca. 1860
Title: San Antonio de Bexar
Size: 16¹³⁄₁₆ × 19 in. (42.7 × 48.2 cm.)
Artist: Hermann Lungkwitz
Lithographer: L. Briedrich
Printer: Rau & Son, Dresden
Publisher:
Key/Vignettes/Misc: 8 vignettes
Locations: ACMW–FW; UTB–A
Catalogs/Checklists: ACMW–FW 1379; Reps, Cities on Stone, p. 97

3996
Place: San Antonio, Texas
Date: 1873
Title: Bird's Eye View of the City of San Antonio Bexar County Texas. 1873
Size: 23⅛ × 28½ in. (59 × 72.5 cm.)
Artist: Augustus Koch
Lithographer:
Printer:
Publisher: [J. J. Stoner, Madison, Wis.]
Key/Vignettes/Misc: Refs. 1–41
Locations: WMM–SA; UTB–A; DRT–SA (photo)
Catalogs/Checklists:

3997
Place: San Antonio, Texas
Date: 1886
Title: Bird's Eye View of San Antonio Bexar Co. Texas 1886. Looking North East.
Size: 28¼ × 37 in. (71.9 × 94.2 cm.)
Artist: Augustus Koch
Lithographer:
Printer:
Publisher:
Key/Vignettes/Misc: Refs. 1–93
Locations: Office of City Clerk, San Antonio, Texas; DRT–SA (photo)
Catalogs/Checklists:

3998
Place: San Antonio, Texas
Date: N.D.
Title: San Antonio. Texas.
Size: 25⅛ × 39⅝ in. (64 × 101 cm.)
Artist:
Lithographer:
Printer:
Publisher: San Antonio Brewing Assn., San Antonio, Texas
Key/Vignettes/Misc:
Locations: UTB–A
Catalogs/Checklists:

3999
Place: San Marcos, Texas
Date: [1873–87?]
Title:
Size:
Artist: Augustus Koch
Lithographer:
Printer:
Publisher:
Key/Vignettes/Misc:
Locations: Unknown. Information from exhibit caption, Institute of Texan Cultures, San Antonio, Texas
Catalogs/Checklists:

4000
Place: Schulenburg, Texas
Date: 1881
Title: Birds Eye View of Schulenburg, Fayette County, Texas
Size: 13⅜ × 22⅝ in. (34 × 57.6 cm.)
Artist: Augustus Koch
Lithographer:
Printer:
Publisher:
Key/Vignettes/Misc: Refs. 1–8
Locations: WMM–SA
Catalogs/Checklists:

4001
Place: Seymour, Texas
Date: 1890
Title: Seymour, Baylor County Texas 1890
Size: 15½ × 28½ in. (39.3 × 72.3 cm.)
Artist: T. M. Fowler
Lithographer:
Printer:
Publisher:
Key/Vignettes/Misc: Refs. 1–12; 7 vignettes
Locations: ACMW–FW; LC–M (photo)
Catalogs/Checklists: LC–M, 920.2

4002
Place: Sunset, Texas
Date: 1890
Title: Sunset, Montague Co., Texas. 1890
Size: 8¹/₁₆ × 14⅜ in. (20.4 x 36.5 cm.)
Artist: T. M. Fowler
Lithographer:
Printer:
Publisher: T. M. Fowler & James B. Moyer
Key/Vignettes/Misc: Refs. 1–4
Locations: ACMW–FW; LC–M; UTB–A
Catalogs/Checklists: ACMW–FW 1105; LC–M, 920.3

4003
Place: Texarkana, Texas
Date: 1888
Title: Perspective Map of, Texarkana, Texas and Arkansas.
Size: 15 × 26³/₁₆ in. (38 × 66.5 cm.)
Artist:
Lithographer:
Printer: Beck & Pauli, Milwaukee
Publisher: Henry Wellge & Co., Cor. Wells & Second St. Milwaukee, Wis.
Key/Vignettes/Misc: Refs. 1–55
Locations: LC–M; LC–P
Catalogs/Checklists: LC–M, 15

4004
Place: Victoria, Texas
Date: ?
Title:
Size:
Artist: H. Brosius
Lithographer:
Printer:
Publisher:
Key/Vignettes/Misc:
Locations:
Catalogs/Checklists:

4005
Place: Waco, Texas
Date: 1873
Title: Bird's Eye View of the City of Waco, McLennan County, Texas. 1873.
Size: 17¹/₁₆ × 25¾ in. (43.5 × 65.6 cm.)
Artist: H. Brosius
Lithographer:
Printer:
Publisher:
Key/Vignettes/Misc: Refs. 1–15; 1 vignette
Locations: UTB–A; DRT–SA (photo)
Catalogs/Checklists:

4006
Place: Waco, Texas
Date: 1886
Title: Waco, Tex., County Seat of McLennan Cy. 1886. Population: 16000.
Size: 18¹¹/₁₆ × 30½ in. (47.4 × 77.5 cm.)
Artist:
Lithographer:
Printer: Beck & Pauli, Litho. Milwaukee, Wis.
Publisher: Norris, Wellge & Co.
Key/Vignettes/Misc: Refs. 1–90, A–Z; 2 vignettes
Locations: LC–M; ACMW–FW
Catalogs/Checklists: LC–M, 921; Reps, Cities on Stone, p. 99

4007
Place: Waco, Texas
Date: 1892
Title: Waco, Texas 1892
Size: 25 × 43 in. (63.5 × 109.3 cm.)
Artist: A. L. Westyard
Lithographer:
Printer: Shober & Carqueville, Chicago
Publisher: D. W. Ensign & Co.
Key/Vignettes/Misc: Refs. A–Z, a–z; church directory; unnumbered business directory
Locations: LC–M
Catalogs/Checklists: LC–M, 922

4008
Place: Waxahachie, Texas
Date: 1876
Title: Birds Eye View of Waxahachie County Seat of Ellis Co. Tex. 1876
Size: 15⅝ × 19⅝ in. (39.8 × 49.9 cm.)
Artist: D. D. Morse
Lithographer:
Printer: Chas. Shober & Co. Prop's Chicago Lith. Co. [Chicago]
Publisher:
Key/Vignettes/Misc: Refs. 1–8
Locations: Nicholas P. Sims Library, Waxahachie, Texas (facsimile)
Catalogs/Checklists:

4009
Place: Whitewright, Texas
Date: 1891
Title: Whitewright, Texas 1891
Size: 10¾ × 22⅛ in. (27.2 × 56.1 cm.)
Artist: T. M. Fowler
Lithographer:
Printer:
Publisher: T. M. Fowler & James B. Moyer
Key/Vignettes/Misc: Refs. 1–9
Locations: ACMW–FW
Catalogs/Checklists:

4010
Place: Wichita Falls, Texas
Date: 1890
Title: Wichita Falls, Texas. 1890
Size: 19³/₁₆ × 28¾ in. (48.7 × 73 cm.)
Artist: T. M. Fowler
Lithographer:
Printer:
Publisher:
Key/Vignettes/Misc: Refs. 1–16; 8 vignettes
Locations: ACMW–FW; UTB–A
Catalogs/Checklists: ACMW–FW 1106

4011
Place: Wolfe City, Texas
Date: 1891
Title: Wolfe City, Texas. 1891
Size: 14⁷/₁₆ × 20¾ in. (36.6 × 52.7 cm.)
Artist: T. M. Fowler
Lithographer:
Printer:
Publisher: T. M. Fowler & James B. Moyer
Key/Vignettes/Misc: Refs. 1–19; 6 vignettes
Locations: ACMW–FW; LC–M; WMM–SA; UTB–A
Catalogs/Checklists: ACMW–FW 1107; LC–M, 922.1

4012
Place: Brigham City, Utah
Date: 1875
Title: Bird's–Eye View of Brigham City, and Great Salt Lake, Utah Ty. 1875.
Size: 13⁵⁄₁₆ × 22³⁄₁₆ in. (34.6 × 56.3 cm.)
Artist: E. S. Glover
Lithographer:
Printer: Strobridge & Co. Lith., Cincinnati, Ohio
Publisher: E. S. Glover, Salt Lake City
Key/Vignettes/Misc: Refs. 1–17, A–M
Locations: LC–M; ACMW–FW; UHS–SL
Catalogs/Checklists: LC–M, 923; Reps, Cities on Stone, p. 91; Moffat, 135

4013
Place: Corinne, Utah
Date: 1875
Title: The City of Corrine, Utah, and the Bear River Valley, Looking North.
Size: 14⅛ × 21¼ in. (36 × 54 cm.)
Artist: [E. S. Glover]
Lithographer:
Printer: Strobridge & Co. Lith. Cincinnati, O.
Publisher:
Key/Vignettes/Misc: Refs. 1–33
Locations: UU–SL
Catalogs/Checklists: Moffat, 136

4014
Place: Logan, Utah
Date: 1875
Title: Birds Eye View of Logan City, Utah Territory, 1875.
Size: 14½ × 21¼ in. (37 × 54 cm.)
Artist: E. S. Glover
Lithographer:
Printer: A. L. Bancroft & Co. Lith. S. F.
Publisher: E. S. Glover, Salt Lake City
Key/Vignettes/Misc: Refs. 1–23, A–C; 2 vignettes
Locations: UHS–SL; UU–SL; BYU–P
Catalogs/Checklists: Moffat, 137

4015
Place: Ogden, Utah
Date: 1875
Title: Birds Eye View of Ogden City. Utah, Ty. 1875.
Size: 17 × 22½ in. (43.2 × 57.1 cm.)
Artist: E. S. Glover
Lithographer:
Printer: Strobridge & Co., Cincinnati, O.
Publisher: E. S. Glover, Salt Lake City, Utah, Ty.
Key/Vignettes/Misc: Refs. 1–26, A–I
Locations: LC–M; UHS–SL; BYU–P
Catalogs/Checklists: LC–M, 924; Reps, Cities on Stone, p. 95; Moffat, 138

4016
Place: Ogden, Utah
Date: 1889
Title: View of Ogden City, Utah Territory
Size: 17¹¹⁄₁₆ × 36⁹⁄₁₆ in. (45 × 93 cm.)
Artist: Eugene F. Darling
Lithographer:
Printer:
Publisher:

Key/Vignettes/Misc:
Locations: LC–M
Catalogs/Checklists: LC–M, 925

4017
Place: Ogden, Utah
Date: 1890
Title: Perspective Map of Ogden, Utah 1890
Size: 20 × 35½ in. (50.8 × 90.3 cm.)
Artist:
Lithographer:
Printer:
Publisher: American Publishing Company, Milwaukee
Key/Vignettes/Misc: 10 vignettes
Locations: LC–M; ACMW–FW; UHS–SL
Catalogs/Checklists: LC–M, 926; Moffat, 233

4018
Place: Salt Lake City, Utah
Date: 1852
Title: Great Salt Lake City, Utah Terry
Size: 18½ × 12 in. (47 × 30.6 cm.)
Artist: W.[illiam] W.[arner]
Lithographer:
Printer: A. McLean Lith., 15 Chestnut St., St. Louis
Publisher: Robt Williams
Key/Vignettes/Misc: Refs. 1–7
Locations: HLDS–SL
Catalogs/Checklists:

4019
Place: Salt Lake City, Utah
Date: 1867
Title: View of Great Salt Lake City
Size: 11⁹⁄₁₆ × 28½ in. (29.3 × 72.3 cm.)
Artist: C. Inger
Lithographer: H. J. Toudy & Co.
Printer: H. J. Toudy & Co. 505 Chestnut St. Phila.
Publisher: Philip Ritz, Walla Walla, W. T.
Key/Vignettes/Misc: 5 unnumbered refs. below places identified
Locations: ACMW–FW; NYP–S; UCBL–B; CHS–C; HEHL; HLDS–SL; LC–M (facsimile); LC–P
Catalogs/Checklists: ACMW–FW 1153; Stokes P. 1866—G–84; Reps, Cities on Stone, p. 97; LC–M, 927

4020
Place: Salt Lake City, Utah
Date: 1869
Title: Salt Lake City, Utah
Size: 18 × 31 in. (45.8 × 78.9 cm.)
Artist:
Lithographer:
Printer: H. J. Toudy & Co., Lith, Philadelphia
Publisher: James Dwyer
Key/Vignettes/Misc: 7 refs. on 1 line
Locations: HLDS–SL
Catalogs/Checklists:

4021
Place: Salt Lake City, Utah
Date: 1870
Title: Bird's Eye View of Salt Lake City Utah Territory 1870.

Size: 29 × 35 in. (73.6 × 88.9 cm.)
Artist: Augustus Koch
Lithographer:
Printer: Chicago Lithographing Co., Chicago
Publisher:
Key/Vignettes/Misc: Refs. 1–46, A–C; 8 vignettes
Locations: LC–M; HLDS–SL; BYU–P; UU–SL
Catalogs/Checklists: Reps, Cities on Stone, p. 97; Moffat, 102; LC–M, 928

4022
Place: Salt Lake City, Utah
Date: Ca. 1870
Title: Great Salt Lake, Utah
Size: 8⁷⁄₁₆ × 12⁷⁄₁₆ in. (21.4 × 31.6 cm.)
Artist:
Lithographer:
Printer:
Publisher: Currier & Ives, New York
Key/Vignettes/Misc:
Locations: NYP–S; UCBL–B; UHS–SL
Catalogs/Checklists: Stokes C. 1870—G–99; Peters, C & I, 4225

4023
Place: Salt Lake City, Utah
Date: 1875
Title: Birds–Eye View of Salt Lake City, From the North, Looking South–East, Utah, 1875.
Size: 24½ × 32½ in. (60.9 × 82.5 cm.)
Artist: E. S. Glover
Lithographer:
Printer: Strobridge & Co. Lith. Cincinnati, O.
Publisher: E. S. Glover, Salt Lake City
Key/Vignettes/Misc: Refs. A–H, unnumbered refs.
Locations: LC–M; UHS–SL; UCBL–B
Catalogs/Checklists: LC–M, 929; Reps, Cities on Stone, p. 97; Moffat, 139

4024
Place: Salt Lake City, Utah
Date: 1878
Title: Map of Salt Lake City. Presented to Valley House Salt Lake City U. T. U. S.
Size:
Artist:
Lithographer:
Printer:
Publisher: Bond & Chandler, Chicago
Key/Vignettes/Misc: Refs.
Locations: Utah Division of State History, Salt Lake City, Utah
Catalogs/Checklists:

4025
Place: Salt Lake City, Utah
Date: 1887
Title: Salt Lake City, 1887.
Size: 20 × 32½ in. (50.9 × 82.7 cm.)
Artist:
Lithographer:
Printer: Gast & Co., St. Louis & New York
Publisher: S. W. Darke & Co., Salt Lake City (copyr't)
Key/Vignettes/Misc: 2 vignettes

Locations: HEHL; UHS–SL; HLDS–SL; UU–SL
Catalogs/Checklists:

4026
Place: Salt Lake City, Utah
Date: 1891
Title: Salt Lake City, Utah. 1891.
Size: 24 × 44½ in. (60.9 × 113 cm.)
Artist: H. Wellge
Lithographer:
Printer:
Publisher: American Publishing Co., Milwaukee
Key/Vignettes/Misc: Refs. 1–59; 10 vignettes; advertisement
Locations: LC–M; UHS–SL; LC–P; UCBL–B; BYU–P
Catalogs/Checklists: LC–M, 930; Reps, Cities on Stone, p. 97

4027
Place: Barre, Vermont
Date: 1884
Title: Barre, Washington County Vt 1884.
Size: 17⅝ × 22⅞ in. (44.8 × 58.3 cm.)
Artist:
Lithographer:
Printer: Beck & Pauli, Milwaukee
Publisher: Geo. E. Norris, Brockton, Mass.
Key/Vignettes/Misc: Refs. 1–42; 1 vignette
Locations: BPL–R; SM–VT; VHS–M (photo)
Catalogs/Checklists:

4028
Place: Barre, Vermont
Date: 1891
Title: Barre, Vt. (The Granite City) Looking East. Population 8,000. 1891.
Size: 18¼ × 30⁷⁄₁₆ in. (46.4 × 77.5 cm.)
Artist: Geo. E. Norris
Lithographer:
Printer:
Publisher: Geo. E. Norris, Brockton, Mass.
Key/Vignettes/Misc: Refs. 1–59, A–S; 1 vignette
Locations: LC–M; VHS–M; SM–VT; LC–P
Catalogs/Checklists: LC–M, 931

4029
Place: Barton, Vermont
Date: 1889
Title: Barton, Vt.
Size: 12¾ × 22⅛ in. (32.4 × 56.3 cm.)
Artist: Geo. E. Norris
Lithographer:
Printer: The Burleigh Lith. Est. Troy, N. Y.
Publisher: Geo. E. Norris, Brockton, Mass.
Key/Vignettes/Misc:
Locations: BPL–R
Catalogs/Checklists:

4030
Place: Bellows Falls, Vermont
Date: [1845]
Title: Bellows Falls, Vermont
Size: 15½ × 26¼ in. (39.4 × 66.8 cm.)
Artist:
Lithographer:
Printer:

Publisher:
Key/Vignettes/Misc:
Locations: SM–VT
Catalogs/Checklists:

4031
Place: Bellows Falls, Vermont
Date: 1855
Title: View of Bellows Falls, Vt. From Table Rock. June. 1855
Size: 19⅜ × 27⁹⁄₁₆ in. (49.4 × 70.2 cm.)
Artist: From daguerreotypes taken by S. W. Hull
Lithographer:
Printer: L. H. Bradford & Co's Lith. [Boston]
Publisher:
Key/Vignettes/Misc:
Locations: CHS–C; VHS–M; BA; LC–M (photo); LC–P
Catalogs/Checklists: LC–M, 931.1

4032
Place: Bellows Falls, Vermont
Date: 1886
Title: Bellows Falls, Vt.
Size: 14½ × 26³⁄₁₆ in. (36.8 × 66.6 cm.)
Artist:
Lithographer:
Printer: Burleigh Lith. Co., Troy, N. Y.
Publisher: L. R. Burleigh
Key/Vignettes/Misc: Refs. 1–27
Locations: BPL–R; LC–M; SM–VT; UVT–B
Catalogs/Checklists: LC–M, 932

4033
Place: Bellows Falls, Vermont
Date: N.D.
Title: Bellows Falls, Vt.
Size: 12¾ × 26 in. (32.4 × 66.2 cm.)
Artist: Mrs. Webber
Lithographer:
Printer: Pendleton's Lithography, Boston
Publisher:
Key/Vignettes/Misc:
Locations: SM–VT; NYH–NY
Catalogs/Checklists:

4034
Place: Bennington, Vermont
Date: 1877
Title: Birds Eye View of Bennington & Bennington Centre Bennington Co. Vermont, 1877
Size: 22 × 24¼ in. (56 × 61.7 cm.)
Artist: [Albert Ruger]
Lithographer:
Printer: Shober & Carqueville Litho Co. Chicago
Publisher: J. J. Stoner, Madison, Wis.
Key/Vignettes/Misc: Refs. 1–26, A–N, P, R
Locations: VHS–M; LC–M (photo)
Catalogs/Checklists: LC–M, 932.1

4035
Place: Bennington, Vermont
Date: 1887
Title: Bennington, Vt. 1887.
Size: 17⅜ × 30½ in. (44.2 × 77.5 cm.)
Artist: L. R. Burleigh
Lithographer:

Printer: Burleigh Litho. Troy, N. Y.
Publisher: L. R. Burleigh, Troy, N. Y.
Key/Vignettes/Misc: Refs. 1–37; 2 vignettes
Locations: LC–M; VHS–M; UVT–B; BPL–R (lacking date); RCHS–T; LC–P
Catalogs/Checklists: LC–M, 933

4036
Place: Bennington, Vermont
Date: N.D.
Title: Bennington, Vt
Size: 12½ × 28⅞ in. (32 × 73 cm.)
Artist:
Lithographer:
Printer:
Publisher: Charles H. Potter [Bennington, Vermont?]
Key/Vignettes/Misc: Refs. 1–13, A–L
Locations: UVT–B; VHS–M
Catalogs/Checklists:

4037
Place: Bethel, Vermont
Date: 1886
Title: Bethel, Vt. 1886.
Size: 13⅛ × 20½ in. (33.4 × 52.1 cm.)
Artist:
Lithographer:
Printer: Burleigh Lith. Establishment, Troy, N. Y.
Publisher: L. R. Burleigh, Troy, N. Y.
Key/Vignettes/Misc: Refs. 1–17
Locations: LC–M; BPL–R
Catalogs/Checklists: LC–M, 934

4038
Place: Bradford, Vermont
Date: 1857
Title: Bradford, Vermont, 1857, From Saddle Back Hill
Size: 12 × 19½ in. (30.5 × 49.6 cm.)
Artist: H. P. Moore
Lithographer:
Printer: F. F. Oakley, Boston
Publisher: H. P. Moore, Concord, N. H.
Key/Vignettes/Misc:
Locations: SM–VT; VHS–M
Catalogs/Checklists:

4039
Place: Brandon, Vermont
Date: Ca. 1890
Title: Brandon, Vt.
Size: 15¼ × 28 in. (38.8 × 71.2 cm.)
Artist: L. R. Burleigh
Lithographer:
Printer:
Publisher: L. R. Burleigh, Troy, N. Y.
Key/Vignettes/Misc: Refs. 1–26
Locations: VHS–M; LC–M (photo)
Catalogs/Checklists: LC–M, 934.1

4040
Place: Brattleboro, Vermont
Date: 1849
Title: View of Brattleboro, Vermont, 1849
Size: 10⅞ × 16½ in. (27.7 × 42 cm.)
Artist: M. Stephen
Lithographer:
Printer: Nagel & Weingaertner, New York
Publisher:
Key/Vignettes/Misc:

Locations: SM–VT
Catalogs/Checklists:

4041

Place: Brattleboro, Vermont
Date: 1851
Title: Brattlesboro, Windham Co, Staat Vermont
Size: 7⅜ × 10½ in. (18.5 × 26.5 cm.)
Artist:
Lithographer:
Printer: F. Walther, Weimer
Publisher: Frobel, Rudolstadt
Key/Vignettes/Misc:
Locations: UVT–B
Catalogs/Checklists:

4042

Place: Brattleboro, Vermont
Date: Ca. 1855
Title: Brattleboro, Vt.
Size: 11 × 16½ in. (28 × 42 cm.)
Artist: M. Stephen
Lithographer:
Printer: Nagel & Weingartner, N. Y.
Publisher:
Key/Vignettes/Misc:
Locations: Unknown. See Old Print Shop Portfolio, XXIX, p. 74, No. 3
Catalogs/Checklists:

4043

Place: Brattleboro, Vermont
Date: 1856
Title: Brattleboro Vt.
Size: 17¾ × 27¹³⁄₁₆ in. (45.2 × 70.7 cm.)
Artist:
Lithographer:
Printer: J. H. Bufford's Lith, 313 Washington St., Boston
Publisher: John Batchelder
Key/Vignettes/Misc: 17 unnumbered refs. below places identified
Locations: NYP–S
Catalogs/Checklists: Stokes P. 1855–G–51

4044

Place: Brattleboro, Vermont
Date: 1876
Title: Brattleboro, Vt. 1876.
Size: 19½ × 25⅛ in. (49.6 × 63.9 cm.)
Artist: H. H. Bailey & J. C. Hazen
Lithographer: C. H. Vogt
Printer: J. Knauber & Co.
Publisher: H. H. Bailey & J. C. Hazen
Key/Vignettes/Misc: Refs. A–N
Locations: BPL–R; VHS–M; LC–M (photo)
Catalogs/Checklists: LC–M, 934.2

4045

Place: Brattleboro, Vermont
Date: 1886
Title: Brattleboro, Vt. 1886.
Size: 13⅞ × 26⅞ in. (35.3 × 68.3 cm.)
Artist: L. R. Burleigh
Lithographer:
Printer: Burleigh Lith. Establishment, Troy, N. Y.
Publisher:
Key/Vignettes/Misc: Refs. 1–19

Locations: LC–M; BPL–R; SM–VT; UVT–B
Catalogs/Checklists: LC–M, 935

4046

Place: Brattleboro, Vermont
Date: N.D. State I
Title: Brattleboro, Vt
Size: 17¾ × 27¾ in. (45.2 × 70.6 cm.)
Artist: [unsigned]
Lithographer:
Printer: J. H. Bufford's Lith. 313 Washington St., Boston
Publisher:
Key/Vignettes/Misc:
Locations: VHS–M; LC–M (photo)
Catalogs/Checklists: LC–M, 934.3

4047

Place: Brattleboro, Vermont
Date: N.D. State II
Title: Brattleboro, Vt
Size: 17¾ × 27¾ in. (45.2 × 70.6 cm.)
Artist: Ambrotype by J. L. Lovett
Lithographer:
Printer: J. H. Bufford's Lith. 313 Washington St., Boston
Publisher:
Key/Vignettes/Misc:
Locations: VHS–M
Catalogs/Checklists:

4048

Place: Bristol, Vermont
Date: 1889
Title: Bristol, Vt.
Size: 13¾ × 24 in. (34.9 × 61 cm.)
Artist: Geo. E. Norris
Lithographer:
Printer: Burleigh Lith. Est., Troy, N. Y.
Publisher: Geo. E. Norris, Brockton, Mass.
Key/Vignettes/Misc: Refs. 1–24
Locations: BPL–R; LC–M; VHS–M (photo)
Catalogs/Checklists: LC–M, 936

4049

Place: Burlington, Vermont
Date: 1846
Title: View of Burlington, Vermont. From the Hill
Size: 10¾ × 16 in. (27.3 × 40.7 cm.)
Artist:
Lithographer:
Printer: T. Wood
Publisher: Jos. H. Hills, Burlington, Vt.
Key/Vignettes/Misc:
Locations: MM–NN; SM–VT; VHS–M (facsimile); UVT–B
Catalogs/Checklists: MM–NN, LP 2701

4050

Place: Burlington, Vermont
Date: 1854
Title: Burlington, Vermont, 1854
Size: 27½ × 21½ in. (70 × 54.8 cm.) [includes frame]
Artist:
Lithographer:
Printer: Endicott & Co., New York
Publisher: H. P. Moore, Concord, N. H.
Key/Vignettes/Misc:

Locations: SM–VT
Catalogs/Checklists:

4051

Place: Burlington, Vermont
Date: 1858
Title: Burlington, Vt. 1858. From the Lake
Size: 14¹⁄₁₆ × 23¹⁵⁄₁₆ in. (35.8 × 60.9 cm.)
Artist:
Lithographer:
Printer: Endicott & Co., New York
Publisher: H. P. Moore, Concord, New Hampshire
Key/Vignettes/Misc:
Locations: NYP–S; MM–NN; SM–VT; VHS–M
Catalogs/Checklists: Stokes 1858—G–52; MM–NN, LP 466

4052

Place: Burlington, Vermont
Date: 1877
Title: Birds Eye View of Burlington and Winooski, Vt.
Size: 21⅛ × 28 in. (54 × 71 cm.)
Artist: E. Meilbek
Lithographer:
Printer: Shober & Carqueville Lith, Chicago
Publisher: J. J. Stoner, Madison, Wisconsin
Key/Vignettes/Misc: Refs.
Locations: SM–VT; VHS–M; UVT–B; LC–M (photo)
Catalogs/Checklists: LC–M, 936.1

4053

Place: Castleton, Vermont
Date: 1889
Title: Castleton, Vt. 1889
Size: 15¼ × 24 in. (38.8 × 61 cm.)
Artist: L. R. Burleigh
Lithographer:
Printer: The Burleigh Lith. Est. Troy, N. Y.
Publisher: L. R. Burleigh, Troy, N. Y.
Key/Vignettes/Misc: Refs. 1–18
Locations: BPL–R; LC–M; VHS–M; RCHS–T
Catalogs/Checklists: LC–M, 936.2

4054

Place: Derby Line, Vermont
Date: 1881
Title: Bird's Eye View of Derby–Line, Vt. & Rock Island, P. Q. 1881.
Size: 9½ × 18¾ in. (24.2 × 47.7 cm.)
Artist: H. Wellge
Lithographer:
Printer:
Publisher: J. J. Stoner, Madison, Wis.
Key/Vignettes/Misc: Refs. 1–5, A–H
Locations: VHS–M; LC–M (photo)
Catalogs/Checklists: deVolpi & Scowen, Eastern Townships, Plate 105; PAC (1976); LC–M, 936.3

4055

Place: Dorset, Vermont
Date: N.D.
Title: View of the East Dorset. Italian Marble Mountain & Mills.
Size: 14¾ × 20¾ in. (37.6 × 52.8 cm.)
Artist: F. Childs

Lithographer:
Printer: Ferd. Mayer & Sons, New York
Publisher: D. L. Kent & Co., East Dorset, Vt.
Key/Vignettes/Misc:
Locations: VHS–M
Catalogs/Checklists:

4056
Place: Enosburg Falls, Vermont
Date: 1892
Title: Enosburg Falls, Vt. 1892
Size: 15½ × 19⅝ in. (39.4 × 49.9 cm.)
Artist:
Lithographer:
Printer:
Publisher: Geo. E. Norris, Brockton, Mass.
Key/Vignettes/Misc: Refs. 1–31
Locations: BPL–R; VHS–M
Catalogs/Checklists:

4057
Place: Fair Haven, Vermont
Date: 1886
Title: Fair Haven, Vt.
Size: 10⁵⁄₁₆ × 23⁷⁄₁₆ in. (26.2 × 59.5 cm.)
Artist: L. R. Burleigh
Lithographer:
Printer:
Publisher: L. R. Burleigh, Troy, N. Y.
Key/Vignettes/Misc: Refs. 1–22
Locations: LC–M; BPL–R; LC–P
Catalogs/Checklists: LC–M, 937

4058
Place: Hardwick, Vermont
Date: 1892
Title: Hardwick, Vt. 1892.
Size: 12³⁄₁₆ × 17¹¹⁄₁₆ in. (31 × 45 cm.)
Artist:
Lithographer:
Printer:
Publisher: Geo. E. Norris, Brockton, Mass.
Key/Vignettes/Misc:
Locations: LC–M; LC–P
Catalogs/Checklists: LC–M, 938

4059
Place: Ludlow, Vermont
Date: 1859
Title: Ludlow, Vermont, 1859, from South Hill
Size: 15⅝ × 23⅞ in. (39.5 × 60.5 cm.)
Artist:
Lithographer:
Printer: Endicott & Co., New York
Publisher: H. P. Moore, Concord, N. H.
Key/Vignettes/Misc:
Locations: SM–VT; VHS–M; UVT–B; LC–P
Catalogs/Checklists: LC–M, 938.1

4060
Place: Ludlow, Vermont
Date: 1885
Title: Ludlow, Vt.
Size: 14 × 23 in. (35.6 × 58.5 cm.)
Artist: L. R. Burleigh
Lithographer:
Printer:
Publisher: L. R. Burleigh, Troy, N. Y.
Key/Vignettes/Misc: Refs. 1–20

Locations: LC–M; BPL–R; VHS–M; UVT–B
Catalogs/Checklists: LC–M, 939

4061
Place: Lyndonville, Vermont
Date: 1884
Title: Lyndonville, Caledonia County, Vermont. 1884
Size: 13⅝ × 16½ in. (34.7 × 41.9 cm.)
Artist: A. F. Poole
Lithographer:
Printer: Geo. H. Walker & Co., Boston
Publisher: Geo. E. Norris, Brockton, Mass.
Key/Vignettes/Misc: Refs. 1–26
Locations: BPL–R
Catalogs/Checklists:

4062
Place: Manchester, Vermont
Date: 1872
Title: View in Manchester Vt. from the Hill Northeast of the Depot.
Size: 26 × 38⅜ in. (66.2 × 97.6 cm.)
Artist: Frank Childs
Lithographer:
Printer: J. H. Buffords Lith. 490 Washn. St. Boston
Publisher: Frank Childs
Key/Vignettes/Misc:
Locations: SM–VT; LC–P
Catalogs/Checklists:

4063
Place: Middlebury, Vermont
Date: 1886
Title: Middlebury, Vt.
Size: 12¼ × 24⅞ in. (31.1 × 63.3 cm.)
Artist: L. R. Burleigh
Lithographer:
Printer: Beck & Pauli, Milwaukee
Publisher: L. R. Burleigh, Troy, N. Y.
Key/Vignettes/Misc: Refs. 1–12
Locations: LC–M; BPL–R; SM–VT; SAM–M; LC–P
Catalogs/Checklists: LC–M, 940

4064
Place: Montpelier, Vermont
Date: [1855?]
Title: Montpelier, Vt.
Size: 14½ × 20 in. (36.9 × 50.9 cm.)
Artist: From dag. by Hull
Lithographer:
Printer: Bradford [Boston]
Publisher:
Key/Vignettes/Misc:
Locations: Unknown. See Goodspeed's Catalogue No. 127 (Oct.–Nov. 1918), no. 800
Catalogs/Checklists:

4065
Place: Montpelier, Vermont
Date: 1884
Title: Montpelier, County Seat of Washington County, & Capital of Vermont. 1884
Size: 14½ × 24 in. (37 × 61.5 cm.)
Artist: A. F. Poole
Lithographer:
Printer: Geo. H. Walker & Co., Lith., Boston

Publisher: Geo. E. Norris, Brockton, Mass.
Key/Vignettes/Misc: Refs. 1–14, A–Z; 1 vignette
Locations: VHS–M; UVT–B; LC–M (photo)
Catalogs/Checklists: LC–M, 940.1

4066
Place: Montpelier, Vermont
Date: 1889
Title: Approach to Montpelier, Vt. (From the West)
Size: 12¾ × 24¾ in. (32.5 × 63 cm.)
Artist: J. F. Gilman
Lithographer:
Printer:
Publisher:
Key/Vignettes/Misc:
Locations: SM–VT
Catalogs/Checklists:

4067
Place: Morrisville, Vermont
Date: 1889
Title: Morrisville, Vt.
Size: 13 × 20⅜ in. (33 × 51.9 cm.)
Artist: Geo. E. Norris
Lithographer:
Printer: The Burleigh Lith. Est., Troy, N. Y.
Publisher: Geo. E. Norris, Brockton, Mass.
Key/Vignettes/Misc: Refs. 1–28, A–I
Locations: BPL–R; LC–M; VHS–M (facsimile)
Catalogs/Checklists: LC–M, 941

4068
Place: Newbury, Vermont
Date: Ca.1850
Title: View of Newbury, Vermont from Mt. Pulaski. Showing the great Ox Bow on the Connecticut River.
Size: 11⅝ × 18¼ in. (29.6 x 46.5 cm.)
Artist: B. F. Nutting
Lithographer: B. F. Nutting
Printer:
Publisher: B. F. Nutting, Boston
Key/Vignettes/Misc:
Locations: SM–VT; VHS–M; LC–M (photo)
Catalogs/Checklists: LC–M, 941.1

4069
Place: Newport, Vermont
Date: 1881
Title: Bird's Eye View Newport, Vermont, 1881
Size: 9⅛ × 20 in. (23.3 × 50.9 cm.)
Artist:
Lithographer:
Printer: Beck & Pauli Lith. Milwaukee, Wis.
Publisher: J. J. Stoner, Madison, Wis.
Key/Vignettes/Misc: Refs. A–D, 1–6; 2 vignettes
Locations: SM–VT
Catalogs/Checklists:

4070
Place: Northfield, Vermont
Date: N.D.
Title: Northfield, Vt.
Size:

Artist: From ambrotype by S. O. Hersey
Lithographer:
Printer: J. H. Buffords, Lith. [Boston]
Publisher:
Key/Vignettes/Misc:
Locations: VHS—M (photo); LC—M (photo)
Catalogs/Checklists: LC—M, 941.2

4071
Place: Poultney, Vermont
Date: 1886
Title: Poultney, Vt.
Size: 12⅞ × 19⅞ in. (32.7 × 55 cm.)
Artist: L. R. Burleigh
Lithographer:
Printer: C. H. Vogt & Son, lith., Cleveland
Publisher: L. R. Burleigh, Troy, N. Y.
Key/Vignettes/Misc: Refs. 1–25
Locations: BPL–R; LC–M; VHS–M
Catalogs/Checklists: LC–M, 942

4072
Place: Richford, Vermont
Date: 1881
Title: Bird's–Eye View of Richford, Vt.
Size:
Artist:
Lithographer:
Printer: Beck & Pauli, Milwaukee, Wis.
Publisher: J. J. Stoner, Madison, Wis.
Key/Vignettes/Misc: Refs. 1–18; 1 vignette
Locations: VHS–M (facsimile)
Catalogs/Checklists:

4073
Place: Rutland, Vermont
Date: 1865
Title: Rutland. From near the Junction of East and Otter Creeks.
Size: 25⁹⁄₁₆ × 37¾ in. (74.5 × 96 cm.)
Artist: Prof. F.[rank] Childs
Lithographer:
Printer: J. H. Bufford, 313 Washington St., Boston
Publisher: F. Childs
Key/Vignettes/Misc:
Locations: NYP–S; SM–VT
Catalogs/Checklists: Stokes P. 1864—G–78

4074
Place: Rutland, Vermont
Date: 1885
Title: Rutland, Vt.
Size: 16¾ × 30 in. (42.6 × 76.3 cm.)
Artist: L. R. Burleigh
Lithographer:
Printer: C. H. Vogt & Son, lith., Cleveland
Publisher: L. R. Burleigh, Troy, N. Y.
Key/Vignettes/Misc: Refs. 1–53
Locations: BPL–R; LC–M; VHS–M
Catalogs/Checklists: LC–M, 943

4075
Place: Saint Albans, Vermont
Date: 1858
Title: St. Albans, Vt. from Aldis Hill
Size: 18¼ × 26½ in. (matted) (46.4 × 67.5 cm.)

Artist:
Lithographer:
Printer: Endicott & Co., New York
Publisher: H. P. Moore, Concord, N. H.
Key/Vignettes/Misc:
Locations: SM–VT; VHS–M; YUAG–NH; LC–M (photo)
Catalogs/Checklists: LC–M, 943.1

4076
Place: Saint Johnsbury, Vermont
Date: 1884
Title: St. Johnsbury County Seat of Caledonia County Vt 1884.
Size: 20¼ × 32 in. (51.6 × 81.4 cm.)
Artist: H. W. Studley & G. E. Norris
Lithographer:
Printer: Beck & Pauli, Milwaukee
Publisher: Geo. E. Norris, Brockton, Mass.
Key/Vignettes/Misc: Refs. 1–59, A–F; 2 vignettes
Locations: BPL–R; LC–M; SM–VT; LC–P
Catalogs/Checklists: LC–M, 944

4077
Place: Springfield, Vermont
Date: 1886
Title: Springfield, Vt.
Size: 12⅞ × 25¼ in. (32.8 × 64.2 cm.)
Artist: L. R. Burleigh
Lithographer:
Printer: Beck & Pauli, Milwaukee
Publisher: L. R. Burleigh, Troy, N. Y.
Key/Vignettes/Misc: Refs. 1–30; 1 vignette
Locations: LC–M; BPL–R; UVT–B; LC–P
Catalogs/Checklists: LC–M, 945

4078
Place: Vergennes, Vermont
Date: [1890?]
Title: Vergennes, Vt.
Size: 17⅞ × 28⅝ in. (45.6 × 72.9 cm.)
Artist:
Lithographer:
Printer: The Burleigh Lith. Est., Troy, N. Y.
Publisher: The Burleigh Lith. Est., Troy, N. Y.
Key/Vignettes/Misc: Refs. 1–26; 3 vignettes; description
Locations: MM–NN; SAM–M; VHS–M (photo); LC–M
Catalogs/Checklists: MM–NN, LP 1927; LC–M, 946

4079
Place: Vergennes Falls, Vermont
Date: N.D.
Title: Vergennes Falls, Vermont
Size: 10⅞ × 17⅞ in. (27.6 × 45.5 cm.)
Artist:
Lithographer:
Printer: J. L. Giles & Co., 111 Nassau St, N. Y.
Publisher: Sidney M. Southard, Vergennes, Vt.
Key/Vignettes/Misc: Advertisements
Locations: SM–VT; MM–NN; UVT–B
Catalogs/Checklists: MM–NN, LP 1263

4080
Place: Waterbury, Vermont
Date: 1884
Title: Waterbury, Washington Cty., Vt. 1884
Size: 18 × 24 in. (45.8 × 61 cm.)
Artist:
Lithographer:
Printer: Beck & Pauli, Milwaukee, Wis.
Publisher: Geo. E. Norris, Brockton, Mass
Key/Vignettes/Misc: Refs. 1–27
Locations: Office of Town Manager, Waterbury, Vermont
Catalogs/Checklists:

4081
Place: West Randolph, Vermont
Date: 1886
Title: West Randolph, Vt. 1886.
Size: 14⅜ × 23¼ in. (36.5 × 59.1 cm.)
Artist:
Lithographer:
Printer: The Burleigh Lith. Est., Troy, N. Y.
Publisher: L. R. Burleigh, Troy, N. Y.
Key/Vignettes/Misc: Refs. 1–11; 1 vignette
Locations: LC–M; BPL–R; VHS–M; LC–P
Catalogs/Checklists: LC–M, 947

4082
Place: Westmore, Vermont
Date: N.D.
Title: Willoughby Lake House, Westmore, Vermont
Size:
Artist:
Lithographer:
Printer: J. H. Buffords Lith., Boston
Publisher:
Key/Vignettes/Misc:
Locations: SM–VT
Catalogs/Checklists:

Place: White River Junction, Vermont
Date: 1889
See West Lebanon, New Hampshire, 1889.

4083
Place: Williamstown, Vermont
Date: 1894
Title: Williamstown, Vt.
Size: 12¾ × 19¾ in. (32.4 × 50.3 cm.)
Artist:
Lithographer:
Printer: George E. Norris, Brockton, Mass.
Publisher:
Key/Vignettes/Misc:
Locations: SM–VT
Catalogs/Checklists:

4084
Place: Wilmington, Vermont
Date: 1891
Title: Wilmington, Vt.
Size: 13¾ × 25³⁄₁₆ in. (35 × 64.1 cm.)
Artist:
Lithographer:
Printer: Burleigh Lithographing Establishment, Troy, N. Y.
Publisher: L. R. Burleigh

Key/Vignettes/Misc: Refs. 1–25; 1
vignette
Locations: LC–M; SM–VT; UVT–B;
LC–P
Catalogs/Checklists: LC–M, 948

4085
Place: Windsor, Vermont
Date: 1859
Title: Windsor, Vermont, From the
Cornish Hills, 1859
Size: 16 × 23¹³⁄₁₆ in. (40.7 × 60.6 cm.)
Artist:
Lithographer:
Printer: Endicott & Co., N. Y.
Publisher: H. P. Moore, Concord, N. H.
Key/Vignettes/Misc:
Locations: SM–VT
Catalogs/Checklists:

4086
Place: Windsor, Vermont
Date: 1886
Title: Windsor, Vermont 1886.
Size: 13³⁄₈ × 21¼ in. (34 × 54 cm.)
Artist: L. R. Burleigh
Lithographer:
Printer: Burleigh Lithograph
Establishment, Troy, N. Y.
Publisher: L. R. Burleigh, Troy, N. Y.
Key/Vignettes/Misc: Refs. 1–15
Locations: LC–M; BPL–R; VHS–M;
LC–P
Catalogs/Checklists: LC–M, 949

4087
Place: Woodstock, Vermont
Date: [1854–55?]
Title: Woodstock, Vermont
Size: 14 × 22½ in. (35.7 × 57.3 cm.)
Artist: Henry P. Moore
Lithographer:
Printer: Bradford [Boston]
Publisher:
Key/Vignettes/Misc:
Locations: Woodstock Historical Society,
Woodstock, Vermont
Catalogs/Checklists:

4088
Place: Charlotte Amalie, Saint Thomas,
Virgin Islands DATE: CA. 1850
Title: [title trimmed]
Size: 14½ × 21½ in. (36.9 × 54.8 cm.)
Artist:
Lithographer:
Printer:
Publisher:
Key/Vignettes/Misc:
Locations: Unknown. See Old Print Shop
Portfolio, XXIV, p. 60, No. 18
Catalogs/Checklists:

4089
Place: Charlotte Amalie, Saint Thomas,
Virgin Islands DATE: CA. 1850
Title: St. Thomas
Size: 15 × 27 in. (38.2 × 68.7 cm.)
Artist:
Lithographer:
Printer: Em. Baerentzen &Co.
Publisher:
Key/Vignettes/Misc:

Locations: Unknown. See Old Print Shop
Portfolio, XXVI, p. 135, No. 31
Catalogs/Checklists:

4090
Place: Charlotte Amalie, Saint Thomas,
Virgin Islands DATE: [1840–50]
Title: View of the Town of St. Thomas, in
the West Indies Taken from the Residence
of P Van Vlierden Esqr
Size: 12¼ × 20½ in. (31.2 × 52.2 cm.)
Artist: Lieut W. T. Bellairs R. N.
Lithographer: W. L. Walton
Printer: Hullmandel & Walton
Publisher:
Key/Vignettes/Misc:
Locations: NYP–S
Catalogs/Checklists: Stokes P. 1840–50—
H–11A

4091
Place: Charlotte Amalie, Saint Thomas,
Virgin Islands DATE: CA. 1855
Title: Saint Thomas
Size: 14 × 22¼ in. (35.7 × 56.7 cm.)
Artist: Melby
Lithographer:
Printer: Tegner & Kittendorff
Publisher:
Key/Vignettes/Misc:
Locations:
Catalogs/Checklists:

4092
Place: Charlotte Amalie, Saint Thomas
Island, Virgin Islands
DATE: 1856 **Title:** Parti af St. Thomas
Size: 9⁵⁄₁₆ × 10¾ in. (23.7 × 27.4 cm.)
Artist: From daguerreotype by H. Hansens
Lithographer: A. Nay
Printer: Em. Barentzen & Co. lith Inst.
Publisher: Em. Barentzen & Cos.
Key/Vignettes/Misc:
Locations: Private collection
Catalogs/Checklists:

4093
Place: Charlotte Amalie, Saint Thomas
Island, Virgin Islands
DATE: 1856 **Title:** St. Thomas. (Parti af
Byen og Havnen.)
Size: 9⅛ × 11 in. (23.2 × 28 cm.)
Artist: From daguerreotype by H. Hansens
Lithographer: A. Nay
Printer: Em. Barentzen & Co. lith Inst.
Publisher: Em. Barentzen & Cos
Key/Vignettes/Misc:
Locations: Private collection
Catalogs/Checklists:

4094
Place: Christiansted, Saint Croix Island,
Virgin Islands DATE: 1839
Title: Christianstaed Paa St. Croix
Size: 11¹⁵⁄₁₆ × 20⅞ in. (30.4 × 53.2 cm.)
Artist: Th. Christ. Salroe
Lithographer:
Printer:
Publisher: J. F. Fritz, Flensborg, Denmark
Key/Vignettes/Misc:
Locations: MM–NN; NYP–S
Catalogs/Checklists: Stokes P. 1838—
H–33; MM–NN, LP 460

4095
Place: Christiansted, Saint Croix Island,
Virgin Islands DATE: 1856
Title: Christianssted. (St. Croix.)
Size: 9³⁄₁₆ × 11 in. (23.4 × 28 cm.)
Artist: Capt. P. Seidelin
Lithographer: A. Nay
Printer: Em. Barentzen & Co lith Inst.
Publisher: Em. Barentzen & Cos.
Key/Vignettes/Misc:
Locations: Private collection
Catalogs/Checklists:

4096
Place: Cruz Bay, Saint John Island, Virgin
Islands DATE: 1856
Title: Cruxbay. (St. Jan.)
Size: 9³⁄₈ × 11⅛ in. (23.8 × 28.3 cm.)
Artist: F. G. Melby
Lithographer: A. Nay
Printer: Em. Barentzen & Co lith Inst.
Publisher: Em. Barentzen & Cos.
Key/Vignettes/Misc:
Locations: Private collection
Catalogs/Checklists:

4097
Place: Frederiksted, Saint Croix Island,
Virgin Islands DATE: 1856
Title: Parti ved Frederikssted. (St. Croix.)
Size: 9 × 10⅞ in. (22.9 × 27.7 cm.)
Artist: Capt. P. Seidelin
Lithographer: A. Nay
Printer: Em. Barentzen & Co lith Inst.
Publisher: Em. Barentzen & Cos.
Key/Vignettes/Misc:
Locations: Private collection
Catalogs/Checklists:

4098
Place: Saint John, Virgin Islands
Date: 1856
Title: St. Jan. (Parti af det Indre.)
Size: 9¼ × 11 in. (23.5 × 28 cm.)
Artist: F. Melby
Lithographer: A. Nay
Printer: Em. Barentzen & Co lith Inst.
Publisher: Em. Barentzen & Cos.
Key/Vignettes/Misc:
Locations: Private collection
Catalogs/Checklists:

4099
Place: Alexandria, Virginia
Date: [1854?]
Title: View of Alexandria Va.
Size: 20 × 30⅝ in. (50.8 × 77.9 cm.)
Artist: E. Sachse & Co. [James T.
Palmatary]
Lithographer:
Printer: E. Sachse & Co., Baltimore
Publisher: J. T. Palmatary
Key/Vignettes/Misc: Refs. 1–49
Locations: Alexandria, Virginia, Public
Library; LC–P (photo)
Catalogs/Checklists:

4100
Place: Alexandria, Virginia
Date: 1863
Title: Birds Eye View of Alexandria, Va.
Size: 14³⁄₁₆ × 23³⁄₁₆ in. (36.1 × 59 cm.)
Artist:

Lithographer:
Printer:
Publisher: Chas. Magnus, 12 Frankfort St.
New York & 520 7th St. Washington, D.
C.
Key/Vignettes/Misc: Refs. 1–12
Locations: NYP–S; MM–NN; LC–P;
CHS–C; WRHS–C; YUAG–NH; LC–M
(facsimile); NYH–NY
Catalogs/Checklists: Stokes P. 1867–
G–72; MM–NN, LP 110; LC–M, 950

4101
Place: Bedford, Virginia
Date: 1891
Title: Perspective Map of Bedford City,
Va., County Seat of Bedford Co. 1891.
Size: 14⅛ × 28¼ in. (36 × 72 cm.)
Artist: H. Wellge
Lithographer:
Printer:
Publisher: American Publishing Co.,
Milwaukee
Key/Vignettes/Misc: Refs. 1–58; 5
vignettes
Locations: LC–M
Catalogs/Checklists: LC–M, 951

Place: Berkley, Virginia
Date: [1891?]
See Norfolk, Virginia, [1891?]

4102
Place: Bristol, Virginia
Date: 1912
Title: Aero View of Bristol, Va.–Tenn.
1912.
Size: 18½ × 33 in. (47 × 84 cm.)
Artist: T. M. Fowler
Lithographer:
Printer: [Charles Hart, New York, N. Y.]
Publisher: T. M. Fowler, Passaic, N. J.
Key/Vignettes/Misc: 13 vignettes;
unnumbered business directory
Locations: LC–M
Catalogs/Checklists: LC–M, 952

4103
Place: Buena Vista, Virginia
Date: 1891
Title: Perspective View of Buena Vista, Va.
1891.
Size: 23½ × 36 in. (59.8 × 91.6 cm.)
Artist:
Lithographer:
Printer:
Publisher: American Publishing Co.,
Milwaukee
Key/Vignettes/Misc: Refs. 1–9, 21–40,
A–H; 6 vignettes
Locations: LC–M
Catalogs/Checklists: LC–M, 953

4104
Place: Burner's White Sulphur Spring
Date: 1857
Title: Burner's White Sulphur Spr.
Shenandoah. Co.
Size: 12½ × 18½ in. (31.8 × 47.1 cm.)
Artist: Ed. Beyer
Lithographer:
Printer: W. Loeillot, Berlin
Publisher:

Key/Vignettes/Misc:
Locations: YUAG–NH; VHS–R
Catalogs/Checklists:

4105
Place: Charlottesville, Virginia
Date: 1856
Title: View of the University of Virginia,
Charlottesville and Monticello Taken from
Lewis Mountain
Size: 17¾ × 26⅝ in. (45.1 × 67.7 cm.)
Artist: E. Sachse & Co.
Lithographer:
Printer: E. Sachse & Co., Baltimore
Publisher: C. Bohn, Washington, D.C. and
Richmond, Va.
Key/Vignettes/Misc:
Locations: Alderman Library, University of
Virginia, Charlottesville, Virginia; VSL–R;
LC–M (facsimile)
Catalogs/Checklists: LC–M, 953.1

4106
Place: City Point, Virginia
Date: 1866
Title: City Point At the Confluence of the
Appomattox with the James River,
Headquarters of the Armies, Operating
Against Richmond.
Size: 7⅜ × 10¹¹⁄₁₆ in. (18.7 × 27.2 cm.)
Artist: F. Dielman
Lithographer:
Printer: E. Sachse & Co., Lith. Baltimore
Publisher: C. Bohn, Washington
Key/Vignettes/Misc:
Locations: LC–P
Catalogs/Checklists:

4107
Place: Danville, Virginia
Date: N.D.
Title: View of Danville, Va.
Size: 9¹⁵⁄₁₆ × 14⅛ in. (25.3 × 35.9 cm.)
Artist:
Lithographer:
Printer: Endicott & Co. Lith., N. Y.
Publisher: J. M. Thurston
Key/Vignettes/Misc:
Locations: LC–P
Catalogs/Checklists:

4108
Place: Emporia, Virginia
Date: 1907
Title: Birds Eye View of Emporia, Virginia
1907.
Size: 20 × 27½ in. (51 × 70 cm.)
Artist: T. M. Fowler
Lithographer:
Printer:
Publisher: T. M. Fowler, Morrisville, Pa.
Key/Vignettes/Misc: 25 vignettes
Locations: LC–M
Catalogs/Checklists: LC–M, 954

4109
Place: Franklin, Virginia
Date: 1907
Title: Birds Eye View of Franklin,
Southampton Co., Virginia 1907.
Size: 14⅛ × 61 in. (36 × 61 cm.)
Artist: T. M. Fowler
Lithographer:

Printer:
Publisher: T. M. Fowler, Morrisville, Pa.
Key/Vignettes/Misc: 9 vignettes
Locations: LC–M
Catalogs/Checklists: LC–M, 955

4110
Place: Fredericksburg, Virginia
Date: 1856
Title: View of Fredericksburg, Va.
Size: 20½ × 32 in. (52.1 × 81.3 cm.)
Artist: E. Sachse & Co.
Lithographer:
Printer: E. Sachse & Co.
Publisher: E. Sachse & Co. Baltimore, Md.
Key/Vignettes/Misc: 9 vignettes
Locations: VHS–R; James Monroe Law
Office–Museum and Memorial Library,
Fredericksburg, Virginia
Catalogs/Checklists:

4111
Place: Fredericksburg, Virginia
Date: 1862
Title: View of Fredericksburg, Va. Nov.
1862.
Size: 8⅝ × 16½ in. (22 × 42 cm.)
Artist:
Lithographer: E. Sachse & Co.
Printer: E. Sachse & Co., 104 S. Charles
St. Balto.
Publisher: E. Sachse & Co., 104 S. Charles
St. Balto. (copyright)
Key/Vignettes/Misc:
Locations: LC–M; LC–P
Catalogs/Checklists: LC–M, 956

4112
Place: Hot Springs, Virginia
Date: 1857
Title: Hot Springs. Bath County Va
Size: 10¼ × 15¾ in. (26.1 × 40.1 cm.)
Artist: Ed. Beyer
Lithographer:
Printer: W. Loeillot, Berlin
Publisher:
Key/Vignettes/Misc:
Locations: VHS–R; YUAG–NH
Catalogs/Checklists:

4113
Place: Lexington, Virginia
Date: 1857
Title: View of Lexington, Va. The Military
Institute and Washington College
Size: 21 × 31 in. (53.5 × 78.9 cm.)
Artist: E. Sachse & Co.
Lithographer:
Printer: E. Sachse & Co., Sun Iron
Building, Baltimore, Md.
Publisher: Casimir Bohn (copyright)
Key/Vignettes/Misc:
Locations: Washington & Lee University,
Lexington, Virginia
Catalogs/Checklists:

4114
Place: Lynchburg, Virginia
Date: N.D.
Title: Lynchburg, Va.
Size: 19½ × 37½ in. (49.6 × 95.4 cm.)
Artist: Ed. Beyer

Lithographer:
Printer: Nagel & Weingartner, New York
Publisher: Aug. Heuser, Newbern, Va.
Key/Vignettes/Misc:
Locations: MM–NN
Catalogs/Checklists: MM–NN, LP 4334

4115

Place: Newport News, Virginia
Date: 1891
Title: Perspective map of Newport News, Va. County seat of Warwick County, 1891. Populaton 8,000.
Size: 20¾ × 33¾ in. (52.8 × 85.8 cm.)
Artist:
Lithographer:
Printer:
Publisher: American Publishing Co. Cor. South Water & Ferry Sts. Milwaukee, Wis. U. S. A.
Key/Vignettes/Misc: 8 vignettes
Locations: LC–M; LC–P; MM–NN
Catalogs/Checklists: MM–NN, LP 197; LC–M, 957

4116

Place: Norfolk, Virginia
Date: 1851
Title: Views of Norfolk and Portsmouth from the Marine Hospital.
Size: 18³/₁₆ × 27⁵/₁₆ in. (46.2 × 69.5 cm.)
Artist: E. Sachse
Lithographer: E. Sachse
Printer: E. Sachse & Co. 5 N. Liberty str. Baltimore, Md.
Publisher: Casimir Bohn, Washington, D. C.
Key/Vignettes/Misc: 2 vignettes
Locations: MM–NN
Catalogs/Checklists: MM–NN, LP 1226

4117

Place: Norfolk, Virginia
Date: Ca. 1852
Title: View of Norfolk and Portsmouth From the U. S. Naval Hospital.
Size: 18½ × 27½ in. (47.1 × 70 cm.)
Artist:
Lithographer:
Printer: E. Sachse, No. 3 N Liberty St., Baltimore
Publisher:
Key/Vignettes/Misc: 2 vignettes
Locations: Unknown. See Old Print Shop Portfolio, XXXV, p. 31, No. 11
Catalogs/Checklists:

4118

Place: Norfolk, Virginia
Date: 1862
Title: Views of Norfolk & Portsmouth From the U. S. Naval Hospital
Size: 8¾ × 16½ in. (22.3 × 42 cm.)
Artist:
Lithographer:
Printer: E. Sachse & Co.
Publisher: C. Bohn
Key/Vignettes/Misc:
Locations: Unknown. See Old Print Shop Portfolio, XXXI, p. 141, No. 48
Catalogs/Checklists:

4119

Place: Norfolk, Virginia
Date: 1873
Title: Norfolk & Portsmouth, Virginia 1873.
Size: 21⅝ × 33¾ in. (55 × 86 cm.)
Artist: C. N. Drie
Lithographer:
Printer:
Publisher: C. N. Drie
Key/Vignettes/Misc: Refs. Portsmouth, 1–23, Berkeley, 1–3, Norfolk, 1–43
Locations: LC–M; LC–P
Catalogs/Checklists: LC–M, 958

4120

Place: Norfolk, Virginia
Date: [1871–74]
Title: View of Norfolk and Portsmouth from the U. S. Naval Hospital
Size: 20¼ × 28 in. (51.6 × 71.2 cm.)
Artist: E. Sachse
Lithographer: E. Sachse
Printer: E. Sachse 5 No Liberty St. Baltimore, Md.
Publisher:
Key/Vignettes/Misc: 2 vignettes
Locations: Unknown. Old Print Shop 9/21/79
Catalogs/Checklists:

4121

Place: Norfolk, Virginia
Date: 1876
Title: 1776—Virginia, 1876—City of Norfolk
Size: 8 × 10 in. (20.3 × 25.4 cm.)
Artist: W. Brotherhead
Lithographer:
Printer: H. J. Toudy & Co., Steam Lith. [Philadelphia]
Publisher:
Key/Vignettes/Misc:
Locations: MM–NN
Catalogs/Checklists: MM–NN, LP 63

4122

Place: Norfolk, Virginia
Date: [1891?]
Title: Bird's Eye View of Norfolk, Portsmouth and Berkley, Norfolk Co., Va.
Size: 29⅞ × 41¼ in. (76 × 105 cm.)
Artist: Augustus Koch
Lithographer:
Printer: Morning News Lith., Savannah, Ga.
Publisher:
Key/Vignettes/Misc: Refs. 1–67
Locations: LC–M
Catalogs/Checklists: LC–M, 959

4123

Place: Norfolk, Virginia
Date: 1892
Title: Panorama of Norfolk, Va. and Surroundings 1892.
Size: 20⅜ × 40 in. (51.9 × 102 cm.)
Artist: H. Wellge
Lithographer:
Printer:
Publisher: American Publishing Co., Milwaukee
Key/Vignettes/Misc: 10 vignettes

Locations: LC–M; CM–S
Catalogs/Checklists: LC–M, 960

4124

Place: Petersburg, Virginia
Date: 1866
Title: Petersburg, Va. From Dun's Hill
Size: 4¾ × 7¼ in. (12.1 × 18.5 cm.)
Artist: E. Dielman
Lithographer:
Printer: E. Sachse & Co. Balto.
Publisher: C. Bohn [copyright]
Key/Vignettes/Misc:
Locations: VHS–R
Catalogs/Checklists:

4125

Place: Pocahontas, Virginia
Date: 1911
Title: Aero View of Pocahontas, Va. 1911.
Size: 13¾ × 25⅛ in. (35 × 64 cm.)
Artist: T. M. Fowler
Lithographer:
Printer:
Publisher: T. M. Fowler, Flemington, N. J.
Key/Vignettes/Misc:
Locations: LC–M
Catalogs/Checklists: LC–M, 961

Place: Portsmouth, Virginia
Date: 1851
See Norfolk, Virginia, 1851.

Place: Portsmouth, Virginia
Date: Ca. 1852
See Norfolk, Virgnia, ca. 1852.

Place: Portsmouth, Virginia
Date: 1862
See Norfolk, Virginia, 1862.

Place: Portsmouth, Virginia
Date: 1873
See Norfolk, Virginia, 1873.

Place: Portsmouth, Virginia
Date: [1871–74]
See Norfolk, Virginia, [1871–74].

Place: Portsmouth, Virginia
Date: [1891?]
See Norfolk, Virginia, [1891?]

4126

Place: Richmond, Virginia
Date: 1851
Title: View of Richmond from the Church Hill
Size: 20¼ × 27¼ in. (51.6 × 69.4 cm.)
Artist: E. Sachse
Lithographer: E. Sachse
Printer: E. Sachse & Co., 3 N. Liberty St., Baltimore
Publisher: Casimir Bohn, Washington, D. C.
Key/Vignettes/Misc:
Locations: VM–R; VSL–R; VHS–R
Catalogs/Checklists: Weddell, Plate XXXIII

4127

Place: Richmond, Virginia
Date: 1853
Title: View of Richmond, Va.
Size: 20½ × 37⅞ in. (52.1 × 96.3 cm.)

Artist: J. W. Hill
Lithographer: F. Palmer
Printer: F. Michelin
Publisher: Smith Bros. & Co., New York
Key/Vignettes/Misc:
Locations: MM–NN; CHS–C; VSL–R;
NYH–NY; NYP–S
Catalogs/Checklists: MM–NN, LP 1228;
Stokes P. 1852—G–10; Weddell, Plate
XXX

4128
Place: Richmond, Virginia
Date: 1854
Title: Richmond, Virginia. From
Hollywood Cemetery
Size: 19 × 30 in. (48.4 × 76.3 cm.)
Artist: Wm. MacLeod
Lithographer: Wm MacLeod
Printer: Endicott & Co. New York
Publisher: Wm MacLeod (copyright)
Key/Vignettes/Misc:
Locations: VM–R
Catalogs/Checklists: Weddell, Plate
XXXIII

4129
Place: Richmond, Virginia
Date: 1854
Title: View of Richmond from the Union
Hill
Size: 18 × 27¼ in. (45.8 × 69.3 cm.)
Artist: E. Sachse
Lithographer: E. Sachse
Printer:
Publisher: Casimir Bohn, Washington
Key/Vignettes/Misc:
Locations: MM–NN
Catalogs/Checklists: MM–NN, LP 776

4130
Place: Richmond, Virginia
Date: Ca. 1856
Title: View of Richmond, Va. From Belle
Isle
Size: 11 × 19½ in. (28 × 49.6 cm.)
Artist:
Lithographer: E. Crehen
Printer: Lith Press of Ritchie &
Dunnavand [Dunnavant], Richmond, Va.
Publisher:
Key/Vignettes/Misc:
Locations: BECH–B; VSL–R
Catalogs/Checklists:

4131
Place: Richmond, Virginia
Date: 1857
Title: View From Gambles Hill Richmond,
Va.
Size: 10½ × 18½ in. (26.7 × 47.1 cm.)
Artist: Ed Beyer
Lithographer:
Printer: W. Loeillot, Berlin
Publisher:
Key/Vignettes/Misc:
Locations: MM–NN; VSL–R; VHS–R
Catalogs/Checklists: MM–NN, LP 5054

4132
Place: Richmond, Virginia
Date: 1865
Title: Richmond, Va., in commemoration

of the glorious Victories of the 3rd and 9th
of April, 1865.
Size: 14⅝ × 18⁵⁄₁₆ in. (37.2 × 46.6 cm.)
Artist:
Lithographer:
Printer: Charles Magnus, New York
Publisher: Charles Magnus, New York
Key/Vignettes/Misc: 5 portraits; 30 maps;
description
Locations: MM–NN; VSL–R; VHS–R;
BA; NYH–NY
Catalogs/Checklists: MM–NN, LP 539

4133
Place: Richmond, Virginia
Date: 1865
Title: The Evacuation of Richmond, Va.
Size: 12 × 18 in. (30.6 × 45.8 cm.)
Artist:
Lithographer:
Printer:
Publisher: Currier & Ives
Key/Vignettes/Misc:
Locations: VM–R; NYH–NY
Catalogs/Checklists: Weddell, Plate LXVI

4134
Place: Richmond, Virginia
Date: 1865
Title: The Fall of Richmond, Va., on the
Night of April 2d. 1865.
Size: 17⅜ × 22¼ in. (44.2 × 56.6 cm.)
Artist:
Lithographer:
Printer:
Publisher: Currier & Ives, New York
Key/Vignettes/Misc:
Locations: VM–R
Catalogs/Checklists: Weddell, Plate LXVII

4135
Place: Richmond, Virginia
Date: Ca. 1865
Title: View of Richmond, Va. From
Church Hill
Size: 7 × 12¾ in. (17.8 × 32.5 cm.)
Artist: F. Dielman
Lithographer:
Printer: E. Sachse & Co., Balto.
Publisher: C. Bohn, Washington and
Richmond
Key/Vignettes/Misc:
Locations: VM–R
Catalogs/Checklists:

4136
Place: Richmond, Virginia
Date: 1876
Title: City of Richmond, Va. From
Manchester. 1876.
Size: 22 × 32½ in. (56 × 82.7 cm.)
Artist: Packard
Lithographer:
Printer: A. Hoen & Co., Richmond
Publisher: Burgett & Co., Richmond, Va.
Key/Vignettes/Misc:
Locations: HEHL; VSL–R; LC–P
Catalogs/Checklists:

4137
Place: Richmond, Virginia
Date: N.D.
Title: Richmond, Va.

Size: 4⅛ × 7⅜ in. (10.5 × 18.7 cm.)
Artist: Ramm
Lithographer: Ramm
Printer: Ramm, Maint., 219, Richd., Va.
Publisher:
Key/Vignettes/Misc:
Locations: LC–P
Catalogs/Checklists:

4138
Place: Richmond, Virginia
Date: N.D.
Title: View of the Ruins of Richmond.
From Camble Hill.
Size: 7 × 12¾ in. (17.8 × 32.5 cm.)
Artist: F. Dielman
Lithographer:
Printer: E. Sachse & Co., Baltimore
Publisher: C. Bohn, Washington
Key/Vignettes/Misc:
Locations: VM–R; NYH–NY
Catalogs/Checklists:

4139
Place: Roanoke, Virginia
Date: 1891
Title: Perspective Map of the City of
Roanoke, Va. 1891.
Size: 17⅝ × 37¾ in. (45 × 96 cm.)
Artist:
Lithographer:
Printer:
Publisher: American Publishing Co. South
Water & Ferry Sts., Milwaukee, Wis.
Key/Vignettes/Misc: Refs. 1–57, A–N; 12
vignettes
Locations: LC–M; Roanoke Valley
Historical Society, Roanoke, Virginia
Catalogs/Checklists: LC–M, 962

4140
Place: Roanoke Red Sulphur Springs,
Virginia
Date: 1857
Title: Roanoke Red Sulphur Spr. Roanoke
Co
Size: 13 × 18½ in. (33 × 47.1 cm.)
Artist: Ed. Beyer
Lithographer:
Printer: W. Loeillot, Berlin
Publisher:
Key/Vignettes/Misc:
Locations: VHS–R; YUAG–NH
Catalogs/Checklists:

4141
Place: Rockbridge Alum Springs, Virginia
Date: 1857
Title: Rockbridge Alum Spring.
Rockbridge County Va
Size: 13⅝ × 20⅛ in. (34.7 × 51.2 cm.)
Artist: Ed. Beyer
Lithographer:
Printer: W. Loeillot, Berlin
Publisher:
Key/Vignettes/Misc:
Locations: VHS–R; YUAG–NH
Catalogs/Checklists:

4142
Place: Staunton, Virginia
Date: 1857
Title: Staunton, Va.

Size: 17⁵⁄₁₆ × 28⁷⁄₈ in. (44.1 × 73.5 cm.)
Artist: Ed. Beyer
Lithographer: W. Rau
Printer:
Publisher: Edward Beyer (copyright)
Key/Vignettes/Misc:
Locations: NYP–S; VHS–R; LC–P
Catalogs/Checklists: Stokes P. 1856—
G–50; LC–M, 926.1

4143
Place: Staunton, Virginia
Date: 1891
Title: Perspective Map of the City of
Staunton, Va. County Seat of Augusta
County, Virginia 1891.
Size: 13¾ × 32¼ in. (35 × 82 cm.)
Artist:
Lithographer:
Printer:
Publisher: American Publishing Co.,
Milwaukee
Key/Vignettes/Misc: Refs. 1–11, 13–35,
A–H, K–L, P–X; 12 vignettes;
unnumbered list of newspapers
Locations: LC–M
Catalogs/Checklists: LC–M, 963

4144
Place: Stribling Springs, Virginia
Date: 1857
Title: Stribling Springs. Central R. R.
Augusta County Va
Size: 12¾ × 18¾ in. (32.5 × 47.7 cm.)
Artist: Ed. Beyer
Lithographer:
Printer: W. Loeillot, Berlin
Publisher:
Key/Vignettes/Misc:
Locations: VHS–R; YUAG–NH
Catalogs/Checklists:

4145
Place: Suffolk, Virginia
Date: 1907
Title: Birds Eye View of Suffolk,
Nansemond Co., Va. 1907.
Size: 15 × 28¾ in. (38 × 73 cm.)
Artist: T. M. Fowler
Lithographer:
Printer:
Publisher: Fowler & Kelly, Morrisville, Pa.
Key/Vignettes/Misc: 32 vignettes
Locations: LC–M
Catalogs/Checklists: LC–M, 964

4146
Place: Warm Springs, Virginia
Date: 1857
Title: Warm Spring's. Bath County Va.
Size: 10¾ × 14⁵⁄₈ in. (27.4 × 37.2 cm.)
Artist: Ed. Beyer
Lithographer:
Printer: W. Loeillot, Berlin
Publisher: Ed. Beyer (copyright)
Key/Vignettes/Misc:
Locations: VHS–R
Catalogs/Checklists:

4147
Place: Waynesboro, Virginia
Date: [1891?]
Title: Perspective Map of the City of
Waynesboro, Va.

Size: 16⁷⁄₈ × 32¼ in. (43 × 82 cm.)
Artist:
Lithographer:
Printer:
Publisher: American Publishing Co.,
Milwaukee
Key/Vignettes/Misc: Refs. 1–25, 27–52;
6 vignettes; description
Locations: LC–M
Catalogs/Checklists: LC–M, 965

4148
Place: White Sulphur Spring, Virginia
Date: 1857
Title: White Sulphur Spring, Montgomery
Size: 12⁵⁄₈ × 16½ in. (32.1 × 42 cm.)
Artist: Ed. Beyer
Lithographer:
Printer: W. Loeillot, Berlin
Publisher:
Key/Vignettes/Misc:
Locations: VHS–R; YUAG–NH
Catalogs/Checklists:

4149
Place: White Sulphur Springs, Virginia
Date: 1857
Title: Fauquier White Sulphur Springs.
Fauquier County Va
Size: 13⅛ × 17¾ in. (33.4 × 45.2 cm.)
Artist: Ed. Beyer
Lithographer:
Printer: W. Loeillot, Berlin
Publisher:
Key/Vignettes/Misc:
Locations: VHS–R; YUAG–NH;
NYH–NY
Catalogs/Checklists:

4150
Place: Winchester, Virginia
Date: 1926
Title: Bird's Eye Map of the City of
Winchester
Size: 12 × 20 in. (38.2 × 50.8 cm.)
Artist: Woods
Lithographer:
Printer:
Publisher: W. A. Ryan
Key/Vignettes/Misc: Refs. 1–7, 9–18,
20–43, A–O; 1 vignette; unnumbered list
of garages
Locations: LC–M
Catalogs/Checklists: LC–M, 966

4151
Place: Yellow Sulphur Springs, Virginia
Date: 1857
Title: Yellow Sulphur Springs.
Montgomery County Va
Size: 11¼ × 16¾ in. (28.7 × 42.6 cm.)
Artist: Ed. Beyer
Lithographer:
Printer: W. Loeillot, Berlin
Publisher:
Key/Vignettes/Misc:
Locations: VHS–R; YUAG–NH
Catalogs/Checklists:

4152
Place: Yorktown, Virginia
Date: Ca. 1863
Title: Yorktown, Va.

Size: 10¼ × 17 in. (26.1 × 43.3 cm.)
Artist:
Lithographer:
Printer: A. Hoen & Co., Baltimore
Publisher:
Key/Vignettes/Misc:
Locations: Unknown. See Old Print Shop
Portfolio, XV, p. 183, No. 21
Catalogs/Checklists:

4153
Place: Cheney, Washington
Date: 1884
Title: Bird's Eye View of Cheney, Wash.
Ter. County Seat of Spokane County. 1884
Size: 9⁷⁄₁₆ × 19¹⁵⁄₁₆ in. (23.9 × 50.6 cm.)
Artist: H. Wellge
Lithographer:
Printer: Beck & Pauli Lith. Milwaukee,
Wis.
Publisher: J. J. Stoner, Madison, Wis.
Key/Vignettes/Misc: Refs. 1–17; 2
vignettes; unnumbered business directory
Locations: LC–M; EWHS–S; LC–P
Catalogs/Checklists: LC–M, 967

4154
Place: Dayton, Washington
Date: 1884
Title: Panoramic View of Dayton, W. T.,
County Seat of Columbia County. 1884.
Size: 10⁵⁄₈ × 24¾ in. (27 × 63 cm.)
Artist: H. Wellge
Lithographer:
Printer: Beck & Pauli, Litho. Milwaukee,
Wis.
Publisher: J. J. Stoner, Madison, Wis.
Key/Vignettes/Misc: Refs. 1–24; 1
vignette; unnumbered business directory
Locations: LC–M
Catalogs/Checklists: LC–M, 968

Place: East Olympia, Washington
Date: 1879
See Olympia, Washington, 1879.

4155
Place: Ellensburg, Washington
Date: 1890
Title: Ellensburgh, Washington—Brick
Buildings Erected Since the Great Fire of
July 4, 1889.
Size: 23³⁄₁₆ × 35⅜ in. (59 × 90 cm.)
Artist: Routledge
Lithographer:
Printer:
Publisher: The West Shore, Portland,
Oregon
Key/Vignettes/Misc: 26 vignettes
Locations: OUL–E
Catalogs/Checklists:

4156
Place: Everett, Washington
Date: 1893
Title: Birdseyeview of Everett,
Washington. 1893
Size: 26 × 37⁷⁄₈ in. (66.2 × 96.4 cm.)
Artist:
Lithographer:
Printer:
Publisher: Brown's Land and Engineering
Co. Inc.

Key/Vignettes/Misc: Refs. 1–60; 10
vignettes; description
Locations: UWL–S; Snohomish County
Museum and Historical Association,
Everett, Washington
Catalogs/Checklists:

4157
Place: Fairhaven, Washington
Date: 1891
Title: Fairhaven, Washington 1891.
Size: 23³⁄₁₆ × 38½ in. (59 × 98 cm.)
Artist: B. W. Pierce
Lithographer: R. H.
Printer: Elliot Pub Co. 120 Sutter St. S. F.
Publisher: Fairhaven Land Co.
Key/Vignettes/Misc:
Locations: NHM–LA; WHS–M; LC–M
(photo)
Catalogs/Checklists: LC–M, 968.1

4158
Place: Goldendale, Washington
Date: N.D.
Title: [Goldendale, Washington]
Size: 19½ × 25½ in. (49.6 × 64.9 cm.)
Artist:
Lithographer:
Printer: Lewis & Dryden. . .Portland, Or.
Publisher: Goldendale Sentinel
Key/Vignettes/Misc: 3 vignettes;
advertisements
Locations: Private collection; Klickitat
County Historical Society, Goldendale,
Washington (photo)
Catalogs/Checklists:

4159
Place: Montesano, Washington
Date: [1890]
Title: Bird's Eye View of Montesano,
Chehalis County, W. T.
Size: 12⅝ × 28⁵⁄₁₆ in. (32 × 72 cm.)
Artist: J. E. Calder
Lithographer:
Printer: Elliott Publishing Co. San
Francisco
Publisher: J. E. Calder, Real Estate Dealer
Key/Vignettes/Misc:
Locations: OUL–E
Catalogs/Checklists:

Place: New Tacoma, Washington
Date: 1878
See Tacoma, Washington, 1878.

4160
Place: North Yakima, Washington
Date: 1889
Title: View of the City of North Yakima,
Washington
Size: 18¹⁄₁₆ × 31 in. (46 × 79 cm.)
Artist: S.[yd] W. Arnold
Lithographer:
Printer:
Publisher: Spike & Arnold Map Publishing
Co.
Key/Vignettes/Misc: Refs. 1–51, 11–61,
and 41 unnumbered residences; 2 vignettes
Locations: LC–M; WSHS–T; Yakima
Valley Museum & Historical Association,
Yakima, Washington
Catalogs/Checklists: LC–M, 969

4161
Place: Olympia, Washington
Date: 1879
Title: Bird's–Eye View of the City of
Olympia, East Olympia and Tumwater,
Puget Sound, Washington Territory. 1879.
Size: 18⅞ × 29⅞ in. (48.1 × 76 cm.)
Artist: E. S. Glover
Lithographer:
Printer: A. L. Bancroft & Co.,
Lithographers, San Francisco
Publisher: E. S. Glover (copyright)
Key/Vignettes/Misc: Refs. 1–15, 2
unnumbered refs. below places identified
Locations: ACMW–FW; LC–M;
UCBL–B; BPL–R; UWL–S; WSHS–T;
EWHS–S; LC–P
Catalogs/Checklists: LC–M, 970; Reps,
Cities on Stone, p. 95

4162
Place: Olympia, Washington
Date: 1903
Title: Olympia the Capital on Puget
Sound, Washington the City of Refinement
and Cultivation, Manufacture and
Commerce, Educational Facilities, etc.
Size: 17½ × 20½ in. (44.5 × 52.2 cm.)
Artist: Edw. Lange
Lithographer:
Printer: Franklin Engraving &
Electrotyping Co., Chicago
Publisher: Edw. Lange, Olympia, Wash
Key/Vignettes/Misc: 17 vignettes
Locations: LC–M
Catalogs/Checklists: LC–M, 971

4163
Place: Port Gamble, Washington
Date: [1862–64] State I
Title: Puget Mill Co.'s Mills, Teekalet W.
T. M. C. Talbot & Co. San Franciso,
California
Size:
Artist: T.[rautman] Grob
Lithographer: T. Grob
Printer: Nagel, Fishbourne & Kuchel, 529
Clay St., San Francisco, Ca.
Publisher:
Key/Vignettes/Misc:
Locations: UWL–S (photo)
Catalogs/Checklists:

4164
Place: Port Gamble, Washington
Date: [1862–64] State II
Title: Puget Mills Co.'s Mills. Teekalet, W.
T. Pope and Talbot, San Francisco,
California
Size:
Artist: T.[rautman] Grob
Lithographer: T. Grob
Printer: Nagel, Fishbourne & Kuchel, 529
Clay St., San Francisco, Ca.
Publisher:
Key/Vignettes/Misc:
Locations: UWL–S (photo)
Catalogs/Checklists: Peters, COS, p. 172

4165
Place: Port Ludlow, Washington
Date: Ca. 1862
Title: Port Ludlow, Puget Sound, W. T.

Amos, Phinney & Co.'s Mills.
Size: 18¼ × 24⅝ in. (46.4 × 62.7 cm.)
Artist: C. B. Gifford
Lithographer: C. B. Gifford
Printer: T. Nagel
Publisher:
Key/Vignettes/Misc:
Locations: UWL–S
Catalogs/Checklists:

4166
Place: Port Townsend, Washington
Date: 1878
Title: Bird's Eye View of Port Townsend,
Puget Sound, Washington Territory. From
the North–East. 1878
Size: 15⅞ × 24⁷⁄₁₆ in. (40.4 × 62.2 cm.)
Artist: E. S. Glover
Lithographer:
Printer: A. L. Bancroft & Co. Lith., San
Francisco, Cal.
Publisher: E. S. Glover, Portland, Oregon
Key/Vignettes/Misc: Refs. A–T
Locations: LC–M; BPL–R; MM–NN;
UCBL–B; LC–P
Catalogs/Checklists: LC–M, 972;
MM–NN, LP 195

4167
Place: Port Townsend, Washington
Date: [before 1889]
Title: Port Townsend, W. T.
Size: 19⅛ × 25¾ in. (48.7 × 65.6 cm.)
Artist:
Lithographer:
Printer:
Publisher: Townsend Call
Key/Vignettes/Misc: 4 views surrounded
by advertisement
Locations: SHS–S
Catalogs/Checklists:

4168
Place: Roslyn, Washington
Date: [189–?]
Title: A General View of Roslyn Looking
Toward Clealum.
Size:
Artist: Edw. Lange
Lithographer:
Printer:
Publisher: Northern Pacific Coal Co.
Key/Vignettes/Misc: Refs. 1–20; 8
vignettes
Locations: SHS–S (photo)
Catalogs/Checklists:

4169
Place: Seattle, Washington
Date: 1878
Title: Bird's–Eye View of the City of
Seattle, Puget Sound, Washington
Territory, 1878.
Size: 19½ × 30½ in. (49.5 × 77.4 cm.)
Artist: E. S. Glover
Lithographer:
Printer: A. L. Bancroft & Co.,
Lithographers, San Francisco
Publisher: E. S. Glover (copyright)
Key/Vignettes/Misc: Refs. 1–20, A–B
Locations: ACMW–FW; LC–M;
UCBL–B; LC–P
Catalogs/Checklists: LC–M, 973; Reps,
Cities on Stone, p. 98

4170
Place: Seattle, Washington
Date: Ca. 1879
Title: Seattle, Washington Territory
Size: 10 × 16³/₁₆ in. (25.5 × 41.2 cm.)
Artist:
Lithographer:
Printer: The West Shore, Portland, Oregon
Publisher:
Key/Vignettes/Misc: 1 vignette
Locations: NYP–S
Catalogs/Checklists:

4171
Place: Seattle, Washington
Date: 1884
Title: Bird's Eye View of the City of
Seattle, WT. Puget Sound. County Seat of
King County. 1884.
Size: 16¼ × 32⅝ in. (41.4 × 82.8 cm.)
Artist: H. Wellge
Lithographer:
Printer: Beck & Pauli, Litho. Milwaukee,
Wis.
Publisher: J. J. Stoner, Madison, Wis.
Key/Vignettes/Misc: Refs. 2–10, 12–37,
A–H, J–M; 2 vignettes
Locations: CHS–C; NYP–S; SHS–S;
UWL–S; Seattle, Washington, Public
Library; NYH–NY; LC–M
Catalogs/Checklists: Stokes 1884–G–86;
Reps, Cities on Stone, p. 98; LC–M, 974

4172
Place: Seattle, Washington
Date: 1884
Title: Seattle, W. T. 1884
Size: 8½ × 27½ in. (21.6 × 69.9 cm.)
Artist: A. Burr
Lithographer: C. L. Smith
Printer:
Publisher: The West Shore, Portland,
Oregon
Key/Vignettes/Misc:
Locations: ACMW–FW; UWL–S; SHS–S
Catalogs/Checklists: ACMW–FW 942

4173
Place: Seattle, Washington
Date: 1889
Title: Seattle, 1889
Size: 24¹⁵/₁₆ × 37¹⁵/₁₆ in. (63.5 × 96.5 cm.)
(facsimile)
Artist:
Lithographer:
Printer:
Publisher: Llewellyn, Dodge & Co., Seattle
Key/Vignettes/Misc: Refs. 1–58; 20
vignettes
Locations: SHS–S (facsimile); UCBL–B
Catalogs/Checklists:

4174
Place: Seattle, Washington
Date: 1889
Title: Seattle, 1889.
Size: 22¼ × 35¾ in. (56.6 × 90.9 cm.)
Artist: C. L.(?) Stubbs
Lithographer:
Printer: Schmidt L. & L. Co., San
Francisco

Publisher: The Elliott Pub. Co., 120 Sutter
St. San Francisco
Key/Vignettes/Misc: Refs. 1–58; 20
vignettes
Locations: UCBL–B; SHS–S
Catalogs/Checklists:

4175
Place: Seattle, Washington
Date: 1891
Title: Birds Eye View of Seattle and
Environs. Kings County, Wash., 1891.
Eighteen Months After the Great Fire.
Size: 33¼ × 50¹/₁₆ in. (84.6 × 127.3 cm.)
Artist: Augustus Koch
Lithographer:
Printer: Hughes Litho Co. Chicago
Publisher: Augustus Koch (copyright)
Key/Vignettes/Misc: Refs. 1–120, A–I,
K–L
Locations: LC–M; ACMW–FW;
UCBL–B; UWL–S; Seattle, Washington,
Public Library; LC–P
Catalogs/Checklists: LC–M, 975; Reps,
Cities on Stone, p. 98

4176
Place: Seattle, Washington
Date: Ca. 1903
Title: Main Business District Periscopic
Seattle.
Size: 19¼ × 20¹³/₁₆ in. (49 × 53 cm.)
Artist: Ross W. Tulloch
Lithographer:
Printer:
Publisher: Periscopic Map Co., Seattle
Key/Vignettes/Misc:
Locations: LC–M
Catalogs/Checklists: LC–M, 976

4177
Place: Seattle, Washington
Date: 1904
Title: Bird's Eye View City of Seattle
Size: 25¾ × 41⅜ in. (65.5 × 105.3 cm.)
Artist:
Lithographer: FL
Printer: Tucker Hanford Co. Seattle
Publisher: Seattle . . .[missing or illegible]
Key/Vignettes/Misc:
Locations: UWL–S
Catalogs/Checklists:

4178
Place: Seattle, Washington
Date: Ca. 1925
Title: Seattle Birdseye View of Portion of
City and Vicinity.
Size: 30⅝ × 55 in. (78 × 140 cm.)
Artist: Edwin C. Poland
Lithographer:
Printer:
Publisher: Kroll Map Company, Seattle
Key/Vignettes/Misc:
Locations: LC–M (photo)
Catalogs/Checklists: LC–M, 977

4179
Place: Seattle, Washington
Date: N.D.
Title: Bird's Eye View of the Waterfront,
Seattle, W. T.

Size: 9⅜ × 15⅞ in. (23.8 × 40.4 cm.)
Artist:
Lithographer: A. G. Walling
Printer:
Publisher: The West Shore, Portland,
Oregon
Key/Vignettes/Misc:
Locations: MM–NN
Catalogs/Checklists: MM–NN, LP 859

4180
Place: Snohomish, Washington
Date: N.D.
Title: Birds–Eye View of Snohomish,
Washington
Size: 9⅞ × 16⅛ in. (25.1 × 41 cm.)
Artist:
Lithographer:
Printer: North Pacific History Company,
Portland, Oregon
Publisher:
Key/Vignettes/Misc: 3 vignettes
Locations: Snohomish, Washington, Public
Library
Catalogs/Checklists:

4181
Place: Spokane, Washington
Date: 1884
Title: Bird's Eye View of Spokane Falls, W.
T., 1884.
Size: 16¾ × 26¾ in. (42.5 × 67.8 cm.)
Artist: H. Wellge
Lithographer:
Printer: Beck & Pauli, Milwaukee
Publisher: J. J. Stoner, Madison
Key/Vignettes/Misc: Refs. 1–30; 4
vignettes; unnumbered business directory
Locations: Washington State University
Libraries, Pullman, Washington; EWHS–S
Catalogs/Checklists:

4182
Place: Spokane, Washington
Date: Ca. 1885
Title: Spokane Falls, W. T. and
Surroundings
Size: 12⁵/₁₆ × 19¾ in. (31.4 × 50.3 cm.)
Artist: W. O. Andrew
Lithographer:
Printer: Waugaman–Lith–532
Commercial St. S. F.
Publisher: The Wasp
Key/Vignettes/Misc: 7 vignettes
Locations: UCBL–B
Catalogs/Checklists:

4183
Place: Spokane, Washington
Date: [1888]
Title: Spokane Falls, W. T.
Size: 16⅞ (cropped) × 20⅜ in. (42.9 ×
51.9 cm.)
Artist: J. T. Pickett
Lithographer:
Printer: Lewis & Dryden Print Co. Lith.
Publisher:
Key/Vignettes/Misc: 10 vignettes
Locations: OHS–P
Catalogs/Checklists:

4184
Place: Spokane, Washington
Date: [before 1890]
Title: Spokane Falls and Her Natural
Resources, the Variety and Extent of which
are Not Equalled by Any City in the World
Size: 5¾ × 12¾ in. (14.7 × 32.5 cm.)
Artist:
Lithographer:
Printer: Gies & Co., Buffalo, N.Y.
Publisher:
Key/Vignettes/Misc:
Locations: UCBL–B
Catalogs/Checklists: LC–M, 978.1

4185
Place: Spokane, Washington
Date: 1905
Title: Spokane, Washington
Size: 39 × 60 in. (99.2 × 152.6 cm.)
Artist:
Lithographer:
Printer:
Publisher: John W. Graham & Co.,
Spokane, Wash.
Key/Vignettes/Misc: 1 vignette
Locations: LC–M
Catalogs/Checklists: LC–M, 978

4186
Place: Steilacoom, Washington
Date: 1862
Title: View of Steilacoom, W. T.
Size: 17½ × 26 in. (44.5 × 66.2 cm.)
Artist: T. Grob
Lithographer:
Printer: L. Nagel
Publisher:
Key/Vignettes/Misc:
Locations: WSHS–T; CHS–C
Catalogs/Checklists:

4187
Place: Tacoma, Washington
Date: 1878
Title: View of New Tacoma and Mount
Rainier, Puget Sound, Washington
Territory. Terminus of the Northern Pacific
Railroad.
Size: 16⅛ × 24⅛ in. (41 × 61.4 cm.)
Artist: E. S. Glover
Lithographer:
Printer: A. L. Bancroft & Co. Litho., San
Francisco, Cal.
Publisher: E. S. Glover, Portland, Oregon
Key/Vignettes/Misc:
Locations: NYP–S; LC–M; UCBL–B;
WSHS–T
Catalogs/Checklists: Stokes P. 1877—
G–92; Peters, COS, pp. 55, 124; LC–M,
979; Reps, Cities on Stone, p. 98

4188
Place: Tacoma, Washington
Date: 1884
Title: View of the City of Tacoma, W. T.
Puget–Sound County Seat of Pierce Cty
Pacific Terminus of the N. P. R. R. 1884.
Size: 14⅝ × 32⅜ in. (37.2 × 82.4 cm.)
Artist: H. Wellge
Lithographer:
Printer: Beck & Pauli, Litho. Milwaukee,
Wis.

Publisher: J. J. Stoner, Madison, Wis.
Key/Vignettes/Misc: Refs. 1–31; 1
vignette
Locations: ACMW–FW; LC–M; NYP–S;
WSHS–T; EWHS–S; Tacoma,
Washington, Public Library
Catalogs/Checklists: ACMW–FW 1930;
LC–M, 980; Reps, Cities on Stone, p. 98

4189
Place: Tacoma, Washington
Date: 1885
Title: City of Tacoma, W. T. Western
Terminus of N. P. R. R. Puget Sound.
1885.
Size: 15¾ × 33¼ in. (40.1 × 84.6 cm.)
Artist:
Lithographer:
Printer:
Publisher:
Key/Vignettes/Misc: Refs. 1–35
Locations: LC–M; Tacoma, Washington,
Public Library (cropped)
Catalogs/Checklists: LC–M, 981

4190
Place: Tacoma, Washington
Date: 1889
Title: Tacoma 1889.
Size:
Artist:
Lithographer:
Printer: Elliott Pub Co., 120 Sutter St. S. F.
Publisher: Geo. W. Traver
Key/Vignettes/Misc: Refs. 1–88; 19
vignettes
Locations: Tacoma, Washington, Public
Library (facsimile)
Catalogs/Checklists:

4191
Place: Tacoma, Washington
Date: 1889
Title: The City of Tacoma
Size: 18 × 36 in. (45.8 × 91.5 cm.)
Artist:
Lithographer:
Printer: Lewis & Dryden Printing Co.
Publisher: J. B. Gromwell Co. (Real Estate)
Key/Vignettes/Misc:
Locations: MM–NN
Catalogs/Checklists: MM–NN, LP 4851

4192
Place: Tacoma, Washington
Date: 1890
Title: Tacoma
Size: 21⅞ × 35¹³⁄₁₆ in. (55.7 × 91.1 cm.)
Artist:
Lithographer:
Printer: Elliott Litho Co., S. F.
Publisher: Geo. W. Traver [Tacoma]
Key/Vignettes/Misc: Refs. 1–99, A–G; 16
vignettes
Locations: LC–M (photo); WSHS–T;
CHS–C; PAC
Catalogs/Checklists: LC–M, 982.1

4193
Place: Tacoma, Washington
Date: 1890
Title: Tacoma. Western Terminus of the
Northern Pacific Railroad.

Size: 32 × 43½ in. (81.4 × 110.7 cm.)
Artist: Will Carson
Lithographer:
Printer:
Publisher: Will Carson (copyright)
Key/Vignettes/Misc: Refs. 1–45; 11
vignettes
Locations: LC–M; UCBL–B; WSHS–T
Catalogs/Checklists: LC–M, 982

4194
Place: Tacoma, Washington
Date: 1893
Title: Tacoma, Washington. 1893
Size: 26¼ × 41⅛ in. (66.8 × 105 cm.)
Artist:
Lithographer:
Printer: The Blachly Co. Lith. Tacoma
Publisher: J. R. McIntyre, Tacoma
Key/Vignettes/Misc: Refs. 1–60; 20
vignettes
Locations: WSHS–T
Catalogs/Checklists:

Place: Teekalet, Washington
Date: [1862–64]
See Port Gamble, Washington, [1862–64].

Place: Tumwater, Washington
Date: 1879
See Olympia, Washington, 1879.

4195
Place: Utsalady, Washington
Date: 1862
Title: Grennan & Cranney's Saw Mills,
Utsalady, Camano Island, Puget Sound, W.
T. 1862.
Size: 14½ × 23¾ in. (36.9 × 60.5 cm.)
Artist:
Lithographer: C. B. Gifford
Printer: I. Nagel, S. F.
Publisher:
Key/Vignettes/Misc: Description
Locations: UWL–S
Catalogs/Checklists:

4196
Place: Vancouver, Washington
Date: 1858
Title: Vancouver, Clark County, W. T.
1858.
Size: 13⅞ × 20⅛ in. (35.1 × 51 cm.)
Artist: Kuchel & Dresel
Lithographer: Kuchel & Dresel
Printer: Kuchel & Dresel, Lithographers,
176 Clay St. S. Francisco, Cal.
Publisher: Camp & Co., Vancouver
Key/Vignettes/Misc: 19 vignettes
Locations: ACMW–FW
Catalogs/Checklists: ACMW–FW 1276

4197
Place: Vancouver, Washington
Date: Ca. 1858
Title: Vancouver, Washington Territory
Size: ["medium"]
Artist: Kuchel & Dresel
Lithographer: Kuchel & Dresel
Printer: Britton & Rey
Publisher:
Key/Vignettes/Misc: [no vignettes]
Locations: Unknown
Catalogs/Checklists: Peters, COS, p. 145

4198
Place: Waitsburg, Washington
Date: 1884
Title: Panoramic View of Waitsburg, W. T. Walla–Walla County. 1884.
Size: 13 × 19 in. (33.1 × 48.3 cm.)
Artist:
Lithographer:
Printer: Beck & Pauli, Litho. Milwaukee, Wis.
Publisher: Ruger & Stoner, Madison, Wis.
Key/Vignettes/Misc: Refs. 1–23; 1 vignette
Locations: Waitsburg Historical Society, Waitsburg, Washington
Catalogs/Checklists:

4199
Place: Walla Walla, Washington
Date: 1866
Title: [Walla Walla Washington] 1866
Size: 18⅜ × 26⅞ in. (46.8 × 68.4 cm.)
Artist: From photographs by P. F. Castleman
Lithographer:
Printer: Grafton T. Brown & Co., Lith. 543 Clay St. S. F. Cal.
Publisher:
Key/Vignettes/Misc: 29 vignettes
Locations: PLW–WW
Catalogs/Checklists:

4200
Place: Walla Walla, Washington
Date: 1876
Title: Bird's Eye View of Walla Walla, Washington Territory, 1876.
Size: 19 × 28½ in. (48.2 × 71.1 cm.)
Artist: E. S. Glover
Lithographer:
Printer: A. L. Bancroft & Co., Lithographers, San Francisco, Cal.
Publisher: Everts & Able, Walla Walla
Key/Vignettes/Misc: Refs. 1–22
Locations: LC–M
Catalogs/Checklists: LC–M, 983; Reps, Cities on Stone, p. 99

4201
Place: Walla Walla, Washington
Date: Ca. 1881
Title: [Untitled]
Size: 10½ × 16¾ in. (26.7 × 42.7 cm.)
Artist: A. Burr
Lithographer:
Printer: A. G. Walling, Portland, Oregon
Publisher: [F. F. Adams, Walla Walla, Washington]
Key/Vignettes/Misc: Advertisement
Locations: PLW–WW
Catalogs/Checklists:

4202
Place: Walla Walla, Washington
Date: 1884
Title: Panoramic View of the City of Walla–Walla, W. T. County Seat of Walla–Walla Co. 1884
Size: 18 × 27½ in. (45.9 × 69.9 cm.)
Artist: H. Wellge
Lithographer:
Printer: Beck & Pauli, Milwaukee, Wisconsin

Publisher: J. J. Stoner, Madison, Wisconsin
Key/Vignettes/Misc: Refs. A–H, 2–21; unnumbered business directory
Locations: LC–M; PLW–WW
Catalogs/Checklists: LC–M, 984

4203
Place: Walla Walla, Washington
Date: 1889
Title: Walla Walla Washington (1889)
Size: 22⅜ × 35¾ in. (57 × 90.9 cm.)
Artist: B. W. Pierce
Lithographer:
Printer: Elliott Litho & Pub. Co. S. F.
Publisher: Elliott Litho & Pub. Co. S. F.
Key/Vignettes/Misc: Refs. 1–44; 28 vignettes; advertisement
Locations: PLW–WW
Catalogs/Checklists:

4204
Place: Walla Walla, Washington
Date: 1889
Title: Walla Walla Washington The Garden City 1889
Size: 22⅜ × 35¾ in. (57 × 90.9 cm.)
Artist: B. W. Pierce
Lithographer:
Printer: Elliott Litho & Pub. Co. S. F.
Publisher: Elliott Litho & Pub. Co. S. F.
Key/Vignettes/Misc: Refs. 1–44; 27 vignettes; advertisement
Locations: PLW–WW
Catalogs/Checklists:

4205
Place: Yakima, Washington
Date: 1935
Title: Early Days in Yakima, Washington Territory, Settled 1885
Size: 14 × 19³⁄₁₆ in. (35.7 × 48.8 cm.)
Artist: H. D. Guie & C. A. Badeau
Lithographer:
Printer: Republic Publishing Co., Yakima, Washington
Publisher: Republic Publishing Co., Yakima, Washington
Key/Vignettes/Misc:
Locations: Yakima Valley Museum & Historical Association, Yakima, Washington
Catalogs/Checklists:

4206
Place: Bayard, West Virginia
Date: 1898
Title: Bayard, West Virginia
Size: 14 × 17 in. (35.5 × 43.2 cm.)
Artist: T. M. Fowler
Lithographer:
Printer:
Publisher: T. M. Fowler, Morrisville, Pa.
Key/Vignettes/Misc: Refs. 1–8
Locations: LC–M (photo)
Catalogs/Checklists: LC–M, 985

4207
Place: Berkeley Springs, West Virginia
Date: Ca. 1889
Title: Berkeley Springs, a Celebrated and Fashionable Health Resort, County Seat of Morgan Co., W. Va.

Size: 16½ × 22¾ in. (42 × 58 cm.)
Artist:
Lithographer:
Printer: A. Hoen & Co., Lith. Baltimore
Publisher: John Moray
Key/Vignettes/Misc:
Locations: LC–M
Catalogs/Checklists: LC–M, 986

4208
Place: Blue Sulphur Springs, West Virginia
Date: 1857
Title: Blue Sulphur Spring. Greenbrier County Va
Size: 11½ × 18⅛ in. (29.3 × 46.1 cm.)
Artist: Ed. Beyer
Lithographer:
Printer: W. Loeillot, Berlin
Publisher:
Key/Vignettes/Misc:
Locations: VHS–R; YUAG–NH
Catalogs/Checklists:

4209
Place: Bluefield, West Virginia
Date: 1911
Title: Aero View of Bluefield, West Virginia 1911.
Size: 18½ × 38⅛ in. (47 × 97 cm.)
Artist: T. M. Fowler
Lithographer:
Printer:
Publisher: Fowler & Basham, Flemington, N. J.
Key/Vignettes/Misc: 25 vignettes; unnumbered business directory
Locations: LC–M
Catalogs/Checklists: LC–M, 987

4210
Place: Buckhannon, West Virginia
Date: 1900
Title: Buckhannon, West Virginia 1900.
Size: 12³⁄₁₆ × 23³⁄₁₆ in. (31 × 59 cm.)
Artist: T. M. Fowler
Lithographer:
Printer:
Publisher: T. M. Fowler & James B. Moyer, Morrisville
Key/Vignettes/Misc: Refs. 1–16, A–I
Locations: LC–M; WVAD–C
Catalogs/Checklists: LC–M, 988

4211
Place: Cairo, West Virginia
Date: 1899
Title: Cairo, West Virginia 1899.
Size: 11 × 20¹³⁄₁₆ in. (28 × 53 cm.)
Artist: T. M. Fowler
Lithographer:
Printer:
Publisher: T. M. Fowler & James B. Moyer, Morrisville, Pa.
Key/Vignettes/Misc: Refs. 1–12; 14 vignettes
Locations: LC–M; WVAD–C; NYH–NY
Catalogs/Checklists: LC–M, 989

4212
Place: Cameron, West Virginia
Date: 1899
Title: Cameron, West Virginia 1899.

Size: 15⁵⁄₁₆ × 21¼ in. (39 × 54 cm.)
Artist: T. M. Fowler
Lithographer:
Printer: Wheeling News Lith
Publisher: T. M. Fowler, Morrisville, Pa.
Key/Vignettes/Misc: Refs. 1–10; 7 vignettes
Locations: LC–M
Catalogs/Checklists: LC–M, 990

Place: Clark, West Virginia
Date: 1911
See North Fork, West Virginia, 1911.

4213
Place: Clarksburg, .West Virginia
Date: 1898
Title: Clarksburg, West Virginia 1898.
Size: 18¹⁄₁₆ × 26¹¹⁄₁₆ in. (46 × 68 cm.)
Artist: T. M. Fowler
Lithographer:
Printer:
Publisher: T. M. Fowler & James B. Moyer, Morrisville, Pa.
Key/Vignettes/Misc: Refs. 1–21; 15 vignettes
Locations: LC–M
Catalogs/Checklists: LC–M, 991

4214
Place: Davis, West Virginia
Date: 1898
Title: Davis, Tucker County, West Virginia 1898.
Size: 13³⁄₈ × 23⁹⁄₁₆ in. (34 × 60 cm.)
Artist: T. M. Fowler
Lithographer:
Printer:
Publisher: T. M. Fowler, Morrisville, Pa.
Key/Vignettes/Misc: Refs. 1–22; 1 vignette
Locations: LC–M
Catalogs/Checklists: LC–M, 992

4215
Place: Elkins, West Virginia
Date: 1897
Title: Elkins, Randolph County, W. Va. 1897.
Size: 14¹⁵⁄₁₆ × 24³⁄₈ in. (38 × 62 cm.)
Artist: T. M. Fowler
Lithographer:
Printer:
Publisher: T. M. Fowler & James B. Moyer, Morrisville, Pa.
Key/Vignettes/Misc: Refs. 1–19, A–G
Locations: LC–M
Catalogs/Checklists: LC–M, 993

4216
Place: Fairmont, West Virginia
Date: 1897
Title: Fairmont and Palatine, West Virginia 1897.
Size: 19⁷⁄₈ × 28¾ in. (50.6 × 73.2 cm.)
Artist: T. M. Fowler
Lithographer:
Printer:
Publisher: T. M. Fowler & James B. Moyer, Morrisville, Pa.
Key/Vignettes/Misc: Refs. 1–18, A–L
Locations: LC–M; WVAD–C
Catalogs/Checklists: LC–M, 994

4217
Place: Grafton, West Virginia
Date: 1898
Title: Grafton, West Virginia 1898
Size: 23 × 26½ in. (58.5 × 67.4 cm.)
Artist: A. E. Downs
Lithographer:
Printer:
Publisher: Fowler & Downs, Boston, Mass.
Key/Vignettes/Misc: Refs. 1–18; 12 vignettes
Locations: LC–M
Catalogs/Checklists: LC–M, 995

4218
Place: Harper's Ferry, West Virginia
Date: Ca. 1857
Title: Harper's Ferry from Jefferson Rock Jefferson Co Va
Size: 12½ × 18½ in. (31.8 × 47.1 cm.)
Artist: Ed. Beyer
Lithographer:
Printer: Rau & Son Lith. Dresden
Publisher:
Key/Vignettes/Misc:
Locations: VHS–R; WRHS–C; YUAG–NH
Catalogs/Checklists:

4219
Place: Harpers Ferry, West Virginia
Date: [1860–63]
Title: Harper's Ferry, Va.
Size: 9⅛ × 14¹³⁄₁₆ in. (23.2 × 37.7 cm.)
Artist: A. Weidenbach
Lithographer:
Printer: E. Sachse & Co. 104 S. Charles St., Balt. Md.
Publisher:
Key/Vignettes/Misc:
Locations: LC–P; NYP–S
Catalogs/Checklists: Stokes C. 1860–63—G–85

4220
Place: Harpers Ferry, West Virginia
Date: N.D.
Title: View of Harpers Ferry, Va. (From the Potomac.)
Size: 14¾ × 20¼ in. (37.6 × 51.6 cm.)
Artist:
Lithographer:
Printer:
Publisher: Currier & Ives 152 Nassau St. N. Y.
Key/Vignettes/Misc:
Locations: NYH–NY
Catalogs/Checklists:

4221
Place: Harpers Ferry, West Virginia
Date: ?
Title: Harper's Ferry, W. Va.
Size: 18¹³⁄₁₆ × 25 in. (47.9 × 63.6 cm.)
Artist:
Lithographer:
Printer:
Publisher: Kurz & Allison, Chicago
Key/Vignettes/Misc:
Locations: WRHS–C
Catalogs/Checklists:

4222
Place: Harrisville, West Virginia
Date: 1899
Title: Harrisville, Ritchie County, W. Va. 1899.
Size: 10¼ × 19⁵⁄₈ in. (26 × 50 cm.)
Artist: T. M. Fowler
Lithographer:
Printer:
Publisher: T. M. Fowler & James B. Moyer, Morrisville, Pa.
Key/Vignettes/Misc: Refs. 1–14
Locations: LC–M; WVAD–C
Catalogs/Checklists: LC–M, 996

4223
Place: Keyser, West Virginia
Date: 1905
Title: Bird's–Eye View of Keyser, West Va.
Size:
Artist: T. M. Fowler
Lithographer:
Printer:
Publisher: Fowler & Kelly [Flemington, N. J.]
Key/Vignettes/Misc: 15 vignettes
Locations: LC–M (photo)
Catalogs/Checklists: LC–M, 997

4224
Place: Keystone, West Virginia
Date: 1911
Title: Aero View of Keystone, West Virginia 1911
Size: 9⁷⁄₁₆ × 20 in. (24 × 51 cm.)
Artist: T. M. Fowler
Lithographer:
Printer:
Publisher: T. M. Fowler, Flemington, N. J.
Key/Vignettes/Misc:
Locations: LC–M
Catalogs/Checklists: LC–M, 998

4225
Place: Mannington, West Virginia
Date: 1897
Title: Mannington, West Virginia 1897.
Size: 14½ × 22 in. (37 × 56 cm.)
Artist: T. M. Fowler
Lithographer:
Printer:
Publisher: T. M. Fowler & James B. Moyer, Morrisville, Pa.
Key/Vignettes/Misc: Refs. 1–15, A–D
Locations: LC–M; WVAD–C
Catalogs/Checklists: LC–M, 999

4226
Place: Morgantown, West Virginia
Date: 1897
Title: Morgantown, West Virginia 1897.
Size: 15¾ × 27⁷⁄₈ in. (40 × 71 cm.)
Artist: T. M. Fowler
Lithographer:
Printer:
Publisher: T. M. Fowler & James B. Moyer, Morrisville, Pa.
Key/Vignettes/Misc: Refs. 1–21, A–G
Locations: LC–M
Catalogs/Checklists: LC–M, 1000

4227
Place: Moundsville, West Virginia
Date: 1899
Title: Moundsville, West Virginia 1899.
Size: 17¼ × 25⅛ in. (44 × 64 cm.)
Artist: A. E. Downs
Lithographer:
Printer:
Publisher: James B. Moyer, Myerstown, Pa.
Key/Vignettes/Misc: Refs. 1–14, A–F; 7 vignettes
Locations: LC–M
Catalogs/Checklists: LC–M, 1001

4228
Place: New Martinsville, West Virginia
Date: 1899
Title: New Martinsville, West Virginia 1899.
Size: 14½ × 23⅛ in. (37 × 59 cm.)
Artist: T. M. Fowler
Lithographer:
Printer:
Publisher: T. M. Fowler & James B. Moyer, Morrisville, Pa.
Key/Vignettes/Misc: Refs. 1–11, A–E; 8 vignettes
Locations: LC–M
Catalogs/Checklists: LC–M, 1002

4229
Place: North Fork, West Virginia
Date: 1911
Title: Aero View of North Fork and Town of Clark, West Virginia 1911.
Size: 8⅝ × 18¹⁄₁₆ in. (22 × 46 cm.)
Artist: T. M. Fowler
Lithographer:
Printer:
Publisher: T. M. Fowler, Flemington, N. J.
Key/Vignettes/Misc:
Locations: LC–M
Catalogs/Checklists: LC–M, 1003

4230
Place: Old Sweet Spring, West Virginia
Date: 1857
Title: Old Sweet Spr. Monroe County Va.
Size: 13⅜ × 20½ in. (34 × 52.2 cm.)
Artist: Ed. Beyer
Lithographer:
Printer: Rau & Son, Lith., Dresden
Publisher:
Key/Vignettes/Misc:
Locations: VHS–R; YUAG–NH
Catalogs/Checklists:

Place: Palatine, West Virginia
Date: 1897
See Fairmont, West Virginia, 1897.

4231
Place: Parkersburg, West Virginia
Date: [1861?]
Title: Parkersburg
Size: 18⅝ × 30⅜ in. (47.4 × 77.3 cm.)
Artist:
Lithographer:
Printer: A. Hoen & Co., Baltimore
Publisher:
Key/Vignettes/Misc:

Locations: LC–M; CHS–C
Catalogs/Checklists: LC–M, 1004

4232
Place: Parkersburg, West Virginia
Date: 1899
Title: Parkersburg, West Virginia 1899.
Size: 19⅝ × 32⅛ in. (50 × 81.7 cm.)
Artist: T. M. Fowler
Lithographer:
Printer:
Publisher: T. M. Fowler & James B. Moyer, Morrisville, Pa.
Key/Vignettes/Misc: Refs. 1–20, A–M; 1 vignette
Locations: LC–M; WVAD–C
Catalogs/Checklists: LC–M, 1005

4233
Place: Parsons, West Virginia
Date: 1905
Title: View of Parsons, West Virginia 1905
Size: 14½ × 21³⁄₁₆ in. (37 × 54 cm.)
Artist: Fowler & Kelly
Lithographer:
Printer:
Publisher: Fowler & Kelly, Morrisville, Pa.
Key/Vignettes/Misc: 12 vignettes
Locations: LC–M; NYH–NY
Catalogs/Checklists: LC–M, 1006

4234
Place: Pennsboro, West Virginia
Date: 1899
Title: Pennsboro, West Virginia 1899
Size: 11 × 20¹⁄₁₆ in. (28 × 51 cm.)
Artist: T. M. Fowler
Lithographer:
Printer:
Publisher: T. M. Fowler & James B. Moyer, Morrisville, Pa.
Key/Vignettes/Misc: Refs. 1–19
Locations: LC–M
Catalogs/Checklists: LC–M, 1007

4235
Place: Philippi, West Virginia
Date: [187–?]
Title: Town of Phillippi, Barbour County, West Virginia. 1861.
Size: 20⁹⁄₁₆ × 30 in. (52.4 × 76.3 cm.)
Artist: Mrs. M. D. Pool
Lithographer:
Printer: [German & Brother, Louisville, Ky.]
Publisher:
Key/Vignettes/Misc:
Locations: LC–M; LC–P
Catalogs/Checklists: LC–M, 1008

4236
Place: Philippi, West Virginia
Date: 1896
Title: Philippi, West Virginia. Scene of the First Battle of the Rebellion, Fought June 3rd, 1861.
Size: 16¹³⁄₁₆ × 26⅞ in. (42.8 × 68.5 cm.)
Artist:
Lithographer:
Printer: The Friedenwald Co. Lith. Balto.
Publisher: Lafayette Keller (copyright)
Key/Vignettes/Misc:

Locations: LC–P
Catalogs/Checklists:

4237
Place: Philippi, West Virginia
Date: 1897
Title: Bird's Eye View of Philippi, West Virginia 1897.
Size: 11 × 14⅞ in. (28 × 37.9 cm.)
Artist: T. M. Fowler
Lithographer:
Printer:
Publisher: T. M. Fowler & James B. Moyer, Morrisville, Pa.
Key/Vignettes/Misc: Refs. A–E, 1–10
Locations: LC–M; WVAD–C
Catalogs/Checklists: LC–M, 1009

4238
Place: Red Sulphur Springs, West Virginia
Date: 1857
Title: Red Sulphur Spring. Monroe County Va
Size: 12 × 15½ in. (30.6 × 39.4 cm.)
Artist: Ed. Beyer
Lithographer:
Printer: W. Loeillot, Berlin
Publisher:
Key/Vignettes/Misc:
Locations: VHS–R; YUAG–NH
Catalogs/Checklists:

4239
Place: Red Sweet Springs, West Virginia
Date: 1857
Title: Red Sweet Springs Monroe County Va
Size: ca. 12 × 15½ in. (30.6 × 39.4 cm.)
Artist: Ed. Beyer
Lithographer:
Printer: W. Loeillot, Berlin
Publisher:
Key/Vignettes/Misc:
Locations: VHS–R; YUAG–NH
Catalogs/Checklists:

4240
Place: Saint Marys, West Virginia
Date: 1899
Title: St. Mary's, West Virginia, 1899.
Size: 10¼ × 20⁷⁄₁₆ in. (26 × 52 cm.)
Artist: T. M. Fowler
Lithographer:
Printer:
Publisher: T. M. Fowler & James B. Moyer, Morrisville, Pa.
Key/Vignettes/Misc: Refs. 1–9, A–D
Locations: LC–M
Catalogs/Checklists: LC–M, 1010

4241
Place: Salem, West Virginia
Date: 1899
Title: Salem, West Virginia 1899.
Size: 11¾ × 22¾ in. (30 × 58 cm.)
Artist: T. M. Fowler
Lithographer:
Printer:
Publisher: T. M. Fowler & James B. Moyer, Morrisville, Pa.
Key/Vignettes/Misc: Refs. 1–9; 1 vignette
Locations: LC–M; WVAD–C
Catalogs/Checklists: LC–M, 1011

4242
Place: Salt Sulphur Springs, West Virginia
Date: 1857
Title: Salt Sulphur Spring. Monroe County Va
Size: 11¼ × 16⅜ in. (28.7 × 41.7 cm.)
Artist: Ed. Beyer
Lithographer:
Printer: W. Loeillot, Berlin
Publisher:
Key/Vignettes/Misc:
Locations: VHS–R; YUAG–NH
Catalogs/Checklists:

4243
Place: Sistersville, West Virginia
Date: 1896
Title: Sistersville, West Virginia 1896.
Size: 15¼ × 21⅛ in. (38.8 × 53.8 cm.)
Artist: T. M. Fowler
Lithographer:
Printer:
Publisher: T. M. Fowler & James B. Moyer, [Morrisville, Pa.]
Key/Vignettes/Misc: Refs. 1–24
Locations: LC–M; WVAD–C
Catalogs/Checklists: LC–M, 1012

4244
Place: Thomas, West Virginia
Date: 1905
Title: Thomas, West Virginia. 1905.
Size: 11⅛ × 20¹⁵⁄₁₆ in. (28.3 × 53.3 cm.)
Artist: T. M. Fowler
Lithographer:
Printer:
Publisher: Fowler & Kelly
Key/Vignettes/Misc:
Locations: NYH–NY
Catalogs/Checklists:

4245
Place: Wellsburg, West Virginia
Date: 1899
Title: Wellsburg, West Virginia.
Size:
Artist: T. M. Fowler
Lithographer:
Printer:
Publisher: T. M. Fowler, Morrisville, Pa.
Key/Vignettes/Misc: Refs. 1–17, A–F; 1 vignette
Locations: LC–M (photo)
Catalogs/Checklists: LC–M, 1013

4246
Place: West Union, West Virginia
Date: 1899
Title: West Union, West Virginia. 1899
Size: 12⅜ × 19½ in. (31.5 × 49.7 cm.)
Artist: T. M. Fowler
Lithographer:
Printer:
Publisher: T. M. Fowler & James B. Moyer, Morrisville, Pa.
Key/Vignettes/Misc: Refs. 1–12; 2 vignettes
Locations: LC–M (photo); private collection
Catalogs/Checklists: LC–M, 1015

4247
Place: Weston, West Virginia
Date: 1900
Title: Weston, West Virginia 1900.
Size: 11 × 23⅛ in. (28 × 59 cm.)
Artist: T. M. Fowler
Lithographer:
Printer:
Publisher: T. M. Fowler & James B. Moyer, Morrisville, Pa.
Key/Vignettes/Misc: Refs. 1–17, A–G
Locations: LC–M; WVAD–C
Catalogs/Checklists: LC–M, 1014

4248
Place: Wheeling, West Virginia
Date: [1854–55?]
Title: View of Wheeling. From Chapline Hill.
Size: 19⅛ × 30¹⁵⁄₁₆ in. (48.7 × 78.7 cm.)
Artist: E. Sachse & Co.
Lithographer:
Printer: E. Sachse & Co. 3 N. Liberty St., Balt. Md.
Publisher: J. T. Palmatary
Key/Vignettes/Misc: Refs. 1–26
Locations: NYP–S; MM–NN
Catalogs/Checklists: Stokes P. 1851–54—G–12; MM–NN, LP 952

4249
Place: Wheeling, West Virginia
Date: 1870
Title: Bird's Eye View of the City of Wheeling, West Virginia 1870
Size: 22½ × 34 in. (57.2 × 86.4 cm.)
Artist: [Albert Ruger]
Lithographer:
Printer: Chicago Lithographing Co. [Chicago]
Publisher: Ruger & Stoner, Madison, Wis.
Key/Vignettes/Misc:
Locations: LC–M
Catalogs/Checklists: LC–M, 1016

4250
Place: White Sulphur Springs, West Virginia
Date: 1857
Title: White Sulphur Springs. Greenbrier Co. Va.
Size: 13⅛ × 20 in. (33.4 × 50.9 cm.)
Artist: Ed. Beyer
Lithographer:
Printer: Rau & Son, Dresden
Publisher:
Key/Vignettes/Misc:
Locations: VHS–R; YUAG–NH
Catalogs/Checklists:

4251
Place: Ahnapee, Wisconsin
Date: 1880
Title: Bird's Eye View of the City of Ahnapee, Wis. Kewaunee County. 1880.
Size: 10½ × 14³⁄₁₆ in. (26.7 × 36.1 cm.)
Artist:
Lithographer:
Printer:

Publisher:
Key/Vignettes/Misc: Refs. 1–22
Locations: Algoma High School, Algoma, Wisconsin
Catalogs/Checklists: Maule

4252
Place: Alma, Wisconsin
Date: 1877
Title: Bird's Eye View of the Village of Alma, Buffalo Co., Wis.
Size: 7⅞ × 19⅝ in. (20 × 50 cm.)
Artist:
Lithographer:
Printer:
Publisher: American Oleograph Co. Milwaukee
Key/Vignettes/Misc:
Locations: WHS–M
Catalogs/Checklists: Maule

4253
Place: Alma, Wisconsin
Date: [1880]
Title: Alma County Seat of Buffalo County Wisconin
Size: 11 × 26⁵⁄₁₆ in. (28 × 67 cm.)
Artist: H. Brosius
Lithographer:
Printer: Beck & Pauli, Litho. Milwaukee, Wis.
Publisher: Ruger & Stoner, Madison, Wis.
Key/Vignettes/Misc: Refs. 1–45; 1 vignette
Locations: WHS–M; Prairie Moon Musem, Cochrane, Wisconsin; LC–M (photo)
Catalogs/Checklists: Maule; LC–M, 1016.1

4254
Place: Antigo, Wisconsin
Date: 1886
Title: A Bird's Eye View of the City of Antigo, Wis. County Seat of Langdale County. 1886. Population 2500, June, 1882
Size: 12⅝ × 22⅞ in. (32.2 × 58.3 cm.)
Artist:
Lithographer:
Printer: Beck & Pauli, Litho. Milwaukee, Wis.
Publisher: Wellge & Co. No. 205 Second St. Milwaukee, Wis.
Key/Vignettes/Misc: 4 vignettes
Locations: LC–M; WHS–M (photo); LC–P
Catalogs/Checklists: LC–M, 1017; Maule

4255
Place: Appleton, Wisconsin
Date: 1867
Title: Appleton Outagamie County, Wisconsin 1867
Size: 20⅛ × 27¹⁵⁄₁₆ in. (51.2 × 71.1 cm.)
Artist: A. Ruger
Lithographer:
Printer: Chicago Lithographing Co. [Chicago]
Publisher:

Key/Vignettes/Misc: Refs. 1–24
Locations: LC–M; CHS–C; WHS–M
Catalogs/Checklists: LC–M, 1018; Maule

4256
Place: Appleton, Wisconsin
Date: 1874
Title: Bird's Eye View of Appleton, Wis. 1874.
Size: 20¹⁵⁄₁₆ × 32⅛ in. (53.3 × 81.7 cm.)
Artist: Stoner & Vogt
Lithographer:
Printer: Am[erican] Oleograph Co. Print. [Milwaukee]
Publisher: Stoner & Vogt
Key/Vignettes/Misc: Refs. 1–16, A–P, R–X
Locations: BPL–R; WHS–M (photo); Lawrence University, Appleton, Wisconsin
Catalogs/Checklists:

4257
Place: Appleton, Wisconsin
Date: 1881
Title: Appleton, Wis.
Size: 20¼ × 32½ in. (51.6 × 82.7 cm.)
Artist:
Lithographer:
Printer: Beck & Pauli, Milwaukee, Wis.
Publisher: A. C. Damm
Key/Vignettes/Misc: 9 vignettes
Locations: Unknown. See Old Print Shop Portfolio, XXXII, p. 19, No. 30
Catalogs/Checklists:

4258
Place: Appleton, Wisconsin
Date: [1881]
Title: Birds Eye View of the City of Appleton
Size: 5⅞ × 9¹³⁄₁₆ in. (15 × 25 cm.) (photo)
Artist:
Lithographer:
Printer: Marr Richards Eng. Mil.[waukee]
Publisher: Appleton Post [Appleton]
Key/Vignettes/Misc:
Locations: LC–M (photo); WHS–M (photo)
Catalogs/Checklists: Maule; LC–M, 1018.1

4259
Place: Appleton, Wisconsin
Date: 1896
Title: Appleton, Wis., 1896
Size: 34 × 49 in. (86.5 × 124.7 cm.)
Artist:
Lithographer:
Printer:
Publisher:
Key/Vignettes/Misc: Refs. 1–48
Locations: Outagamie County Historical Society, Kaukauna, Wisconsin
Catalogs/Checklists:

4260
Place: Ashland, Wisconsin
Date: [1885?]
Title: Ashland, the Metropolis of the New Wisconsin.
Size: 12⁹⁄₁₆ × 25⅛ in. (32 × 64 cm.)
Artist:

Lithographer:
Printer: Marr. Richards. Eng. Mil, St. P.
Publisher:
Key/Vignettes/Misc:
Locations: WHS–M
Catalogs/Checklists: Maule

4261
Place: Ashland, Wisconsin
Date: 1886
Title: A Bird's Eye View of the City of Ashland, Wis. County Seat of Ashland Co. 1886.
Size: 13¾ × 32⅝ in. (35 × 83 cm.)
Artist: H. Welg [Henry Wellge]
Lithographer:
Printer: Beck & Pauli, Litho. Milwaukee, Wis.
Publisher: Norris, Wellge & Co. No. 205 Second St. Milwaukee, Wis.
Key/Vignettes/Misc: Refs. 1–64, A–H, K–P; other numbered and lettered refs.; 1 vignette
Locations: LC–M; WHS–M (photo)
Catalogs/Checklists: LC–M, 1019; Maule

4262
Place: Ashland, Wisconsin
Date: 1890
Title: Ashland, Lake Superior, Wis. 1890. Population 16,000. Increase in Ten Years, 11,000.
Size: 19¼ × 39⁵⁄₁₆ in. (49 × 100 cm.)
Artist: C. J. Pauli
Lithographer:
Printer: Marr & Richards Engraving Co., Milwaukee
Publisher: Ashland Daily Press [Ashland]
Key/Vignettes/Misc: Refs. 1–61; 2 vignettes
Locations: WHS–M; LC–M
Catalogs/Checklists: LC–M, 1020; Maule

4263
Place: Baraboo, Wisconsin
Date: 1870
Title: Bird's Eye View of Baraboo Sauk County Wisconsin, 1870.
Size: 16⅞ × 20¹⁄₁₆ in. (43 × 51 cm.)
Artist:
Lithographer:
Printer: Merchants Lithographing Co. Chicago
Publisher: Ruger & Stoner, Madison, Wis.
Key/Vignettes/Misc: Refs. 1–10; 2 vignettes
Locations: WHS–M; LC–M (photo)
Catalogs/Checklists: Maule; LC–M, 1020.1

4264
Place: Barton, Wisconsin
Date: 1878
Title: Barton, Washington Co., Wisconsin. 1878.
Size: 8¼ × 11⅜ in. (21 × 29 cm.)
Artist:
Lithographer:
Printer: [Beck & Pauli, Milwaukee, Wis.?]
Publisher:
Key/Vignettes/Misc: Refs. 1–8

Locations: WHS–M
Catalogs/Checklists: Maule

4265
Place: Bayfield, Wisconsin
Date: 1884
Title: Bird's Eye View of Bayfield, Wisconsin, Summer of 1884.
Size: 4¾ × 8 in. (12 × 20 cm.) (photo)
Artist:
Lithographer:
Printer: Marr–Richard [Milwaukee]
Publisher: Bayfield County Press [Bayfield]
Key/Vignettes/Misc: 2 vignettes
Locations: WHS–M (photo)
Catalogs/Checklists: Maule

4266
Place: Bayfield, Wisconsin
Date: 1886
Title: Birds Eye View of Bayfield, Wis. County Seat of Bayfield County, 1886.
Size: 12⅝ × 20⅛ in. (32 × 51 cm.)
Artist: H. Wellge
Lithographer:
Printer: Beck & Pauli, Litho. Milwaukee, Wis.
Publisher: Norris Wellge & Co. . . .Milwaukee, Wis.
Key/Vignettes/Misc: Refs. 2–25, A–H, K–L, N, P, R, Y; 1 vignette
Locations: LC–M; Madeline Island Historical Museum, La Pointe, Wisconsin; WHS–M (photo); LC–P
Catalogs/Checklists: LC–M, 1021; Maule

4267
Place: Bayfield, Wisconsin
Date: 1893
Title: Bird's Eye View of Bayfield and the Apostle Islands, Lake Superior
Size:
Artist:
Lithographer:
Printer: Marr–Richards, Mil. St. Paul
Publisher: Bayfield County Press [Bayfield]
Key/Vignettes/Misc:
Locations:
Catalogs/Checklists: Maule

4268
Place: Beaver Dam, Wisconsin
Date: 1867
Title: Birds Eye View of the City of Beaver Dam Dodge Co., Wisconsin, 1867
Size: 22½ × 24½ in. (57 × 62.2 cm.)
Artist: A. Ruger
Lithographer:
Printer: Chicago Lithographing Co., Chicago
Publisher:
Key/Vignettes/Misc: Refs. 1–17
Locations: LC–M; WHS–M (facsimile); Dodge County Historical Society Museum, Beaver Dam, Wisconsin (photo)
Catalogs/Checklists: LC–M, 1022; Maule

4269
Place: Beaver Dam, Wisconsin
Date: 1879
Title: Beaver Dam Dodge County, Wis. 1879

Size: 21 × 24 in. (53.5 × 61.1 cm.)
Artist:
Lithographer:
Printer: Beck & Pauli. Lith. Milwaukee, Wis.
Publisher:
Key/Vignettes/Misc: Refs. 1–26, A–R
Locations: Dodge County Historical Society Museum, Beaver Dam, Wisconsin; WHS–M (photo)
Catalogs/Checklists: Maule

4270
Place: Beloit, Wisconsin
Date: 1874
Title: Beloit. Rock County. Wis. 1874.
Size: 18⅞ × 25⁹⁄₁₆ in. (48 × 65 cm.) (facsimile)
Artist:
Lithographer:
Printer: J. Knauber & Co., Print. Milwaukee, Wis.
Publisher: J. J. Stoner, Madison, Wis.
Key/Vignettes/Misc: Refs.; 3 vignettes
Locations: WHS–M (facsimile); Beloit Historical Society, Beloit, Wisconsin
Catalogs/Checklists: Maule

4271
Place: Beloit, Wisconsin
Date: 1890
Title: Perspective Map of Beloit, Wis. 1890.
Size: 20⅛ × 27¾ in. (51.2 × 70.6 cm.)
Artist: [H. Wellge?]
Lithographer:
Printer:
Publisher: American Publishing Co. Cor. South Water & Ferry Sts. Milwaukee, Wis.
Key/Vignettes/Misc: Refs. A–Z, Aa–Am, 1–29; 3 vignettes; unnumbered business directory
Locations: LC–M; WHS–M (photo); Beloit Historical Society, Beloit, Wisconsin
Catalogs/Checklists: LC–M, 1023; Maule

4272
Place: Berlin, Wisconsin
Date: 1867
Title: Bird's Eye View of the City of Berlin Green Lake Co. Wisconsin. 1867
Size: 18⅛ × 24⅜ in. (46 × 62 cm.)
Artist: A. Ruger
Lithographer:
Printer: Chicago Lithographing Co. 152 & 154, Clark St. Chicago
Publisher:
Key/Vignettes/Misc: Refs. 1–15; 2 vignettes
Locations: LC–M; Clark School Museum, Berlin, Wisconsin; WHS–M (photo)
Catalogs/Checklists: LC–M, 1024; Maule

4273
Place: Berlin, Wisconsin
Date: 1892
Title: Berlin, Wis. 1892.
Size: 15¾ × 22 in. (40 × 56 cm.)
Artist: C. J. Pauli
Lithographer:
Printer:
Publisher: C. J. Pauli, Milwaukee, Wis.

Key/Vignettes/Misc:
Locations: Berlin, Wisconsin, Historical Society; WHS–M (photo)
Catalogs/Checklists: Maule

4274
Place: Black Earth, Wisconsin
Date: 1876
Title: Bird's Eye View of Black Earth. Looking from the North West. 1876
Size: 9⁷⁄₁₆ × 12³⁄₁₆ in. (24 × 31 cm.)
Artist:
Lithographer:
Printer: D. Bremner & Co. Lith. Milwaukee
Publisher:
Key/Vignettes/Misc: Refs. 1–14
Locations: WHS–M; LC–M (photo)
Catalogs/Checklists: Maule; LC–M, 1024.1

4275
Place: Black Earth, Wisconsin
Date: 1883
Title:
Size:
Artist:
Lithographer:
Printer:
Publisher:
Key/Vignettes/Misc:
Locations: Private collection
Catalogs/Checklists: Maule

4276
Place: Black River Falls, Wisconsin
Date: 1875
Title: Bird's Eye View of Black River Falls, Jackson County, Wis. Looking Southwest
Size: 14¹⁵⁄₁₆ × 20¹³⁄₁₆ in. (38 × 53 cm.)
Artist: H. Brosius
Lithographer:
Printer:
Publisher: J. J. Stoner, Madison, Wis.
Key/Vignettes/Misc: Refs. 1–6, A–E
Locations: LC–M (photo); WHS–M; Jackson County Historical Society, Black River Falls, Wisconsin
Catalogs/Checklists: Maule; LC–M, 1024.2

4277
Place: Boscobel, Wisconsin
Date: 1869
Title: Bird's Eye View of Boscobel Grant Co. Wisconsin. 1869
Size: 18⅛ × 22½ in. (46 × 57 cm.)
Artist: [Albert Ruger]
Lithographer:
Printer: Chicago Lithographing Co, Clark St. [Chicago]
Publisher: Ruger & Stoner Madison, Wisconsin
Key/Vignettes/Misc:
Locations: WHS–M; LC–M
Catalogs/Checklists: LC–M, 1025; Maule

4278
Place: Brodhead, Wisconsin
Date: 1871
Title: Brodhead, Wis. 1871
Size: 14½ × 19³⁄₁₆ in. (36.9 × 48.8 cm.)

Artist: H. H. Bailey
Lithographer:
Printer: Doniat & Zastrow, Milwaukee
Publisher:
Key/Vignettes/Misc: Refs. 1–8
Locations: LC–M (photo); BPL–R; WHS–M; Memorial Library, Broadhead, Wisconsin
Catalogs/Checklists: Maule; LC–M, 1025.1

4279
Place: Burlington, Wisconsin
Date: 1871
Title: Burlington, Wis., 1871
Size: 12⁹⁄₁₆ × 19⅝ in. (32 × 50 cm.) (photo)
Artist: H. H. Bailey
Lithographer:
Printer: Chicago Lithographing Co. [Chicago]
Publisher: T. M. Fowler & Co., Madison, Wis.
Key/Vignettes/Misc: Refs. 1–8, A–P, R
Locations: Burlington, Wisconsin, Historical Society; WHS–M (photo); LC–M (photo)
Catalogs/Checklists: Maule; LC–M, 1025.2

4280
Place: Burlington, Wisconsin
Date: 1876
Title: Burlington, Wis. 1896
Size: 12³⁄₁₆ × 20 in. (31 × 51 cm.)
Artist: C. J. Pauli
Lithographer:
Printer:
Publisher: C. J. Pauli, 234 22nd St. Milwaukee, Wis.
Key/Vignettes/Misc: 1 vignette
Locations: LC–M (photo); Burlington Historical Society, Burlington, Wisconsin; WHS–M (photo)
Catalogs/Checklists: Maule; LC–M, 1025.3

4281
Place: Cassville, Wisconsin
Date: [1854–57]
Title: Cassville, Wisconsin, in 1829
Size: ca. 6½ × 8¼ in. (16.5 × 21 cm.)
Artist: Henry Lewis
Lithographer:
Printer: C. H. Muller, Aachen
Publisher: Arnz & Co., Dusseldorf
Key/Vignettes/Misc:
Locations: MHS–SP; NYH–NY; HEHL; NL–C; HNOC–NO; LC–R
Catalogs/Checklists:

4282
Place: Cedarburg, Wisconsin
Date: [1879?]
Title: Cedarburg, Wisconsin
Size: 16½ × 21⁹⁄₁₆ in. (42 × 55 cm.)
Artist: H. Wellge & J. Bach
Lithographer:
Printer: Beck & Pauli, Milwaukee, Wis.
Publisher: H. Wellge & J. Bach, Milwaukee
Key/Vignettes/Misc: 1 vignette

Locations: Cedarburg, Wisconsin, Public Library
Catalogs/Checklists: Maule

4283
Place: Cedarburg, Wisconsin
Date: 1892
Title: Cedarburg, Wis. 1892
Size: 17¼ × 24¾ in. (44 × 63 cm.)
Artist:
Lithographer:
Printer:
Publisher:
Key/Vignettes/Misc: 8 vignettes
Locations: Cedarburg, Wisconsin, Public Library; WHS–M (facsimile)
Catalogs/Checklists: Maule

4284
Place: Chilton, Wisconsin
Date: 1878
Title: View of Chilton Wis. 1878 Pop. about 2,000
Size: 17¼ x 23⅛ in. (44 × 59 cm.)
Artist: H. Wellge & J. Bach.
Lithographer:
Printer:
Publisher: H. Wellge & J. Bach
Key/Vignettes/Misc: 5 vignettes
Locations: WHS–M(facsimile); private collection
Catalogs/Checklists: Maule

4285
Place: Chippewa Falls, Wisconsin
Date: 1874
Title: Bird's Eye View of the City of Chippewa Falls, Chippewa County, Wisconsin 1874
Size: 12 × 26 in. (53.4 × 66.2 cm.)
Artist:
Lithographer:
Printer:
Publisher:
Key/Vignettes/Misc: Refs. 1–37
Locations: Private collection
Catalogs/Checklists: Maule

4286
Place: Chippewa Falls, Wisconsin
Date: 1886
Title: Chippewa–Falls, Wis. County–Seat of Chippewa–County 1886. Population: 10,000.
Size: 20½ × 26½ in. (53.5 × 67.3 cm.)
Artist: H. W.[ellge?]
Lithographer:
Printer: Beck & Pauli, Litho. Milwaukee, Wis.
Publisher: Norris, Wellge & Co. No. 107 Wells St, Milwaukee, Wis.
Key/Vignettes/Misc: Refs. 1–65, A–D
Locations: LC–M; WHS–M (photo)
Catalogs/Checklists: LC–M, 1026; Maule

4287
Place: Chippewa Falls, Wisconsin
Date: 1907
Title: Chippewa–Falls, Wisconsin, County–Seat of Chippewa County. 1907. Population 12,000.
Size: 17¹¹⁄₁₆ × 30¼ in. (45 × 77 cm.)

Artist: H. W.[ellge?]
Lithographer:
Printer:
Publisher: H. Wellge, Milwaukee, Wis. (copyright)
Key/Vignettes/Misc: Refs. 1–21, A–H, J–L, O–P, R–W; 4 vignettes
Locations: LC–M; WHS–M (photo)
Catalogs/Checklists: LC–M, 1027; Maule

4288
Place: Clinton, Wisconsin
Date: 1871
Title: Clinton, Wis. 1871.
Size: 11¼ × 13³⁄₁₆ in. (28.5 × 33.5 cm.)
Artist: H. H Bailey
Lithographer:
Printer: Doniat & Zastrow, Milwaukee
Publisher:
Key/Vignettes/Misc:
Locations: CHS–C; WHS–M (photo); LC–M (photo)
Catalogs/Checklists: Maule; LC–M, 1027.1

4289
Place: Columbus, Wisconsin
Date: 1868
Title: Bird's Eye View of Columbus Columbia Co. Wisconsin 1868
Size: 16⅞ × 23¹⁵⁄₁₆ in. (43 × 61 cm.)
Artist: A. Ruger
Lithographer:
Printer: Chicago Lithographing Co. 152 & 154, Clark St., Chicago
Publisher:
Key/Vignettes/Misc: Refs. 1–12
Locations: LC–M; WHS–M (photo)
Catalogs/Checklists: LC–M, 1028; Maule

4290
Place: Columbus, Wisconsin
Date: 1893
Title: Columbus, Wis. 1893. Looking West.
Size: 12³⁄₁₆ × 19⅝ in. (31 × 50 cm.)
Artist: C. J. Pauli
Lithographer:
Printer:
Publisher: C. J. Pauli, 726 Central Avenue, Milwaukee, Wis.
Key/Vignettes/Misc: Refs. 1–39
Locations: WHS–M; Columbus, Wisconsin, City Hall
Catalogs/Checklists:

4291
Place: Darlington, Wisconsin
Date: 1871
Title: Bird's Eye View of Darlington Lafayette County Wis. 1871 Looking North West
Size: 14½ × 19⅝ in. (37 × 50 cm.)
Artist: H. Brosius
Lithographer:
Printer:
Publisher:
Key/Vignettes/Misc: Refs. 1–4, A–D; 2 vignettes
Locations: WHS–M; LC–M (photo)
Catalogs/Checklists: Maule; LC–M, 1028.1

4292
Place: Darlington, Wisconsin
Date: 1881
Title: View of Darlington, Wis. County Seat of Lafayette Co. 1881
Size: 11⅜ × 20 in. (29 × 51 cm.)
Artist:
Lithographer:
Printer: Beck & Pauli, Lith., Milwaukee, Wis.
Publisher: J. J. Stoner, Madison, Wis.
Key/Vignettes/Misc: Refs. 1–10, 12–19
Locations: WHS–M; LC–M (photo)
Catalogs/Checklists: Maule; LC–M, 1028.2

4293
Place: Darlington, Wisconsin
Date: 1896
Title: Darlington, Wis. 1896
Size: 14⅛ × 21⅝ in. (36 × 55 cm.)
Artist: C. J. Pauli
Lithographer:
Printer:
Publisher: C. J. Pauli, 234 Twenty–second Street, Milwaukee, Wis.
Key/Vignettes/Misc:
Locations: WHS–M; LC–M (photo)
Catalogs/Checklists: Maule; LC–M, 1028.3

4294
Place: De Pere, Wisconsin
Date: 1871
Title: De Pere, Wis. 1871
Size: 12 × 18 in. (30.6 × 45.9 cm.)
Artist: H. H. Bailey
Lithographer:
Printer: Chicago Lithographing Co. [Chicago]
Publisher:
Key/Vignettes/Misc: Refs. 1–8, A–F
Locations: De Pere Historical Society Museum, De Pere, Wisconsin; WHS–M (photo); LC–M (photo)
Catalogs/Checklists: Maule; LC–M, 1029.1

4295
Place: De Pere, Wisconsin
Date: 1893
Title: De Pere, Wis. 1893 Looking North
Size: 28 × 40 in. (71.3 × 101.7 cm.)
Artist: C. J. Pauli
Lithographer:
Printer:
Publisher: C. J. Pauli, 726 Central Ave. Milwaukee, Wis.
Key/Vignettes/Misc: Refs. 1–40; 2 vignettes
Locations: De Pere Historical Society Museum, De Pere, Wisconsin; WHS–M (photo); LC–M (photo)
Catalogs/Checklists: Maule; LC–M, 1029.2

4296
Place: Delavan, Wisconsin
Date: 1884
Title: Delavan, Walworth Co., Wisconsin. 1884.

Size: 17½ × 27½ in. (44.4 × 69.8 cm.)
Artist: H. Brosius
Lithographer:
Printer: Beck & Pauli, Litho. Milwaukee, Wis.
Publisher: J. J. Stoner, Madison, Wis.
Key/Vignettes/Misc: Refs. 1–19; 1 vignette
Locations: LC–M; WHS–M (photo)
Catalogs/Checklists: Maule; LC–M, 1029

4297
Place: Dodgeville, Wisconsin
Date: 1875
Title: Bird's Eye View of Dodgeville. Iowa County Wis. Looking South East
Size: 15¹¹⁄₁₆ × 20 in. (40 × 51 cm.)
Artist: H. Brosius
Lithographer:
Printer:
Publisher:
Key/Vignettes/Misc: Refs. A–F, 1–6; 2 vignettes
Locations: WHS–M; LC–M (photo)
Catalogs/Checklists: Maule; LC–M, 1029.3

4298
Place: Eau Claire, Wisconsin
Date: 1872
Title: Bird's Eye View of the City of Eau Claire, Eau Claire County, Wis. 1872 Looking North East
Size: 20 × 25½ in. (51 × 65 cm.)
Artist: H. Brosius
Lithographer:
Printer:
Publisher:
Key/Vignettes/Misc: Refs. A–F, 1–8; 2 vignettes
Locations: WHS–M; LC–M (photo); CVM–EC
Catalogs/Checklists: Maule; LC–M, 1029.4

4299
Place: Eau Claire, Wisconsin
Date: 1880
Title: Eau Claire, Wisconsin. 1880.
Size: 17¹¹⁄₁₆ × 27⅞ in. (45 × 71 cm.)
Artist:
Lithographer:
Printer: Beck & Pauli, Lith., Milwaukee, Wis.
Publisher: J. J. Stoner, Madison
Key/Vignettes/Misc: Refs. 1–38; 1 vignette
Locations: WHS–M; LC–M (photo); CVM–EC
Catalogs/Checklists: Maule; LC–M, 1029.5

4300
Place: Eau Claire, Wisconsin
Date: 1891
Title: Eau Claire, Wis. 1891. Looking West.
Size: 18⅞ × 35 in. (48 × 89 cm.)
Artist: C. J. Pauli
Lithographer:
Printer:

Publisher: C. J. Pauli, 726 Central Ave. Milwaukee.
Key/Vignettes/Misc: Refs. 1–91
Locations: WHS–M (photo); LC–M(photo); CVM–EC
Catalogs/Checklists: Maule; LC–M, 1029.6

4301
Place: Edgerton, Wisconsin
Date: 1871
Title:
Size:
Artist: H. H. Bailey
Lithographer:
Printer:
Publisher:
Key/Vignettes/Misc:
Locations: Private collection
Catalogs/Checklists: Maule

4302
Place: Elroy, Wisconsin
Date: 1879
Title: Elroy Juneau, Co. Wisconsin, 1879.
Size: 8⅝ × 15¹¹⁄₁₆ in. (22 × 40 cm.)
Artist:
Lithographer:
Printer: Beck & Pauli Lith. Milwaukee, Wis.
Publisher: J. J. Stoner, Madison, Wis.
Key/Vignettes/Misc:
Locations: WHS–M
Catalogs/Checklists: Maule

4303
Place: Evansville, Wisconsin
Date: 1871
Title: Evansville, Wis., 1871
Size: 11 × 17½ in. (28 × 44.5 cm.)
Artist: H. H. Bailey
Lithographer:
Printer: Chicago Lithographing Co. [Chicago]
Publisher:
Key/Vignettes/Misc: Refs. 1–11
Locations: Unknown. See Old Print Shop Portfolio, XXXII, p. 19, No. 29
Catalogs/Checklists:

4304
Place: Evansville, Wisconsin
Date: 1883
Title: Evansville, Wis., 1883
Size: 12 × 20 in. (30.6 × 50.8 cm.)
Artist:
Lithographer:
Printer: Beck & Pauli, Lith. Milwaukee, Wis.
Publisher: J. J. Stoner, Madison, Wis.
Key/Vignettes/Misc:
Locations: Rock County Historical Society, Janesville, Wisconsin
Catalogs/Checklists:

4305
Place: Florence, Wisconsin
Date: 1881
Title: Bird's Eye View of Florence, Wis. 1881
Size: 7½ × 16½ in. (19 × 42 cm.)
Artist:

Lithographer:
Printer:
Publisher: J. J. Stoner, Madison, Wis.
Key/Vignettes/Misc: Refs.
Locations: WHS–M; LC–M (photo)
Catalogs/Checklists: Maule; LC–M, 1029.7

4306
Place: Fond Du Lac, Wisconsin
Date: [1861–62]
Title: Fond du Lac, Wis. From Marr St. Methodist Church
Size: 14⁷⁄₁₆ × 22½ in. (36.7 × 57.2 cm.)
Artist: L. Kurz
Lithographer:
Printer: Kurz & Seifert, Milwaukee
Publisher:
Key/Vignettes/Misc:
Locations: NYP–S; YUAG–NH
Catalogs/Checklists: Stokes C. 1861–62—G–65

4307
Place: Fond Du Lac, Wisconsin
Date: 1867
Title: Fond du Lac Wisconsin 1867.
Size: 20⁷⁄₁₆ × 27⅞ in. (52 × 71 cm.)
Artist: A. Ruger
Lithographer:
Printer: Chicago Lithographing Co. 152 & 154; Clark St, Chicago
Publisher:
Key/Vignettes/Misc: Refs. 1–14
Locations: LC–M; WHS–M; Fond du Lac County Historical Society, Fond du Lac, Wisconsin
Catalogs/Checklists: LC–M, 1030; Maule

4308
Place: Fond Du Lac, Wisconsin
Date: [1866–71]
Title: Fond du Lac in 1837
Size: 9³⁄₁₆ × 14¼ in. (23.4 × 36.3 cm.)
Artist: Mark Harrison
Lithographer:
Printer: Chicago Lithographing Co. [Chicago]
Publisher:
Key/Vignettes/Misc:
Locations: CHS–C
Catalogs/Checklists:

4309
Place: Fond Du Lac, Wisconsin
Date: 1876?
Title:
Size:
Artist: C. J. Pauli
Lithographer:
Printer:
Publisher:
Key/Vignettes/Misc:
Locations: Unknown. [Beckman, Milwaukee Illustrated, note for no. 28]
Catalogs/Checklists:

4310
Place: Fond Du Lac, Wisconsin
Date: 1896
Title: Fond du Lac, Wis., 1896. Looking North–West

Size: 16⅞ × 32⅝ in. (43 × 83 cm.)
Artist: C. J. Pauli
Lithographer:
Printer:
Publisher: C. J. Pauli, 234 22nd St.
Milwaukee, Wis.
Key/Vignettes/Misc: Refs. 1–30; 2
vignettes
Locations: WHS–M (photo); Fond du
Lac, Wisconsin, Public Library; Fond du
Lac County Historical Society, Fond du
Lac, Wisconsin; LC–M (photo)
Catalogs/Checklists: Maule; LC–M,
1030.2

4311
Place: Fort Atkinson, Wisconsin
Date: 1870
Title: Bird's Eye View of Fort Atkinson
Jefferson County Wisconsin Looking
North East 1870
Size: 17½ × 20½ in. (44.5 × 52.2 cm.)
Artist: [Albert Ruger]
Lithographer:
Printer: Merchant's Lith. Co., Chicago
Publisher: Ruger & Stoner, Madison, Wis.
Key/Vignettes/Misc: Refs. 1–14
Locations: LC–M; CHS–C; HHM–FA
Catalogs/Checklists: LC–M, 1031; Maule

4312
Place: Fort Atkinson, Wisconsin
Date: 1880
Title: Bird's Eye View of the City of Fort
Atkinson Jefferson Co. Wis 1880
Size: 10½ × 19¾ in. (26.7 × 50.3 cm.)
Artist: A D
Lithographer:
Printer:
Publisher:
Key/Vignettes/Misc: Refs. 1–15
Locations: HHM–FA; WHS–M (photo)
Catalogs/Checklists: Maule

4313
Place: Fort Atkinson, Wisconsin
Date: 1893
Title: Ft. Atkinson, Wis. 1893. Looking
Northwest.
Size: 17⅞ × 20⅞ in. (45.5 × 53.2 cm.)
Artist: C. J. Pauli
Lithographer:
Printer:
Publisher: C. J. Pauli, 725 Central Avenue,
Milwaukee, Wis.
Key/Vignettes/Misc: Refs. A, 1–36
Locations: HHM–FA; WHS–M (photo)
Catalogs/Checklists: Maule

Place: Fort Howard, Wisconsin
Date: 1867
See Green Bay, Wisconsin, 1867.

Place: Fort Howard, Wisconsin
Date: 1893
See Green Bay, Wisconsin, 1893.

4314
Place: Fountain City, Wisconsin
Date: 1880
Title: Panoramic View of Fountain City
Buffalo Co. Wisconsin 1880.
Size: 7 × 17¾ in. (17.8 × 45.2 cm.)

Artist:
Lithographer:
Printer: Beck & Pauli, Milwaukee, Wis.
Publisher: J. J. Stoner, Madison, Wis.
Key/Vignettes/Misc: Refs. 1–11
Locations: CHS–C; WHS–M (photo)
Catalogs/Checklists:

Place: Geneva, Wisconsin
Date: 1871
See Lake Geneva, Wisconsin, 1871.

4315
Place: Grand Rapids, Wisconsin
Date: 1874
Title: Bird's Eye View of the City of Grand
Rapids. Wood Co. Wis. 1874
Size: 22 × 34³⁄₁₆ in. (56 × 87 cm.)
Artist: A. J. Cleveland
Lithographer:
Printer: A. M. Oleograph. Co.
Mil.[waukee]
Publisher: A. J. Cleveland
Key/Vignettes/Misc:
Locations: WHS–M; South Wood County
Historical Museum, Wisconsin Rapids,
Wisconsin; LC–M
Catalogs/Checklists: Maule; LC–M,
1031.1

4316
Place: Green Bay, Wisconsin
Date: 1867
Title: Green Bay and Fort Howard Brown
Co. Wisconsin 1867
Size: 22 × 28 in. (56 × 71.3 cm.)
Artist: A. Ruger
Lithographer:
Printer: Chicago Lith. Co. 152 & 154
Clark St., Chicago
Publisher:
Key/Vignettes/Misc: Refs. 1–22
Locations: LC–M; WHS–M (photo)
Catalogs/Checklists: LC–M, 1032; Maule

4317
Place: Green Bay, Wisconsin
Date: 1893
Title:
Size: 12½ × 19½ in. (31.8 × 49.6 cm.)
(photo)
Artist: C. J. Pauli
Lithographer:
Printer:
Publisher: C. J. Pauli, Milwaukee, Wis.
Key/Vignettes/Misc:
Locations: Neville Public Museum, Green
Bay, Wisconsin; LC–M (photo)
Catalogs/Checklists: LC–M, 1032.1

4318
Place: Hartford, Wisconsin
Date: 1879
Title: Panoramic View of Hartford,
Washington Co, Wisconsin. 1879
Size: 11 × 18¹³⁄₁₆ in. (28 × 48 cm.)
Artist:
Lithographer:
Printer: Beck & Pauli Lith., Milwaukee
Publisher: J. J. Stoner, Madison, Wis.
Key/Vignettes/Misc: Refs. 1–25, A–F
Locations: WHS–M; Hartford,

Wisconsin, Public Library; LC–M (photo)
Catalogs/Checklists: Maule; LC–M,
1032.2

4319
Place: Horicon, Wisconsin
Date: 1892
Title: Horicon, Wis. 1892. Looking
North–East
Size: 11⅜ × 18¹³⁄₁₆ in. (29 × 46.3 cm.)
Artist: C. J. Pauli
Lithographer:
Printer:
Publisher: C. J. Pauli, Milwaukee, Wis.
Key/Vignettes/Misc:
Locations: Dodge County Historical
Society, Beaver Dam, Wisconsin; WHS–M
(photo)
Catalogs/Checklists: Maule

4320
Place: Hudson, Wisconsin
Date: 1870
Title: Bird's Eye View of the City of
Hudson, St. Croix County, Wisconsin
1870.
Size: 20½ × 23 in. (52.2 × 58.6 cm.)
Artist: [Albert Ruger]
Lithographer:
Printer: Merchants Lith. Co. [Chicago]
Publisher: Ruger & Stoner, Madison,
Wisc.
Key/Vignettes/Misc: Refs. 1–15; 2
vignettes
Locations: LC–M; MHS–SP; St. Croix
Historical Society, Hudson, Wisconsin;
WHS–M (photo)
Catalogs/Checklists: LC–M, 1033; Maule

4321
Place: Hudson, Wisconsin
Date: 1879
Title: Panoramic View of the City of
Hudson St. Croix Co., Wisconsin, 1879.
Looking North West
Size: 11⅜ × 21⁹⁄₁₆ in. (29 × 55 cm.)
Artist:
Lithographer:
Printer: Beck & Pauli Lith. Milwaukee,
Wis.
Publisher: J. J. Stoner, Madison, Wis.
Key/Vignettes/Misc:
Locations: Milwaukee, Wisconsin, Public
Library; WHS–M (photo)
Catalogs/Checklists: Maule

4322
Place: Hurley, Wisconsin
Date: 1886
Title: Hurley, Wis., Ashland County. 1886.
Size: 12½ × 19 in. (31.8 × 48.4 cm.)
Artist:
Lithographer:
Printer: Beck & Pauli, Litho. Milwaukee,
Wis.
Publisher: Norris, Wellge & Co.,
Milwaukee Wis.
Key/Vignettes/Misc: Refs. 1–28, A–I, II;
3 vignettes
Locations: LC–M; WHS–M (photo)
Catalogs/Checklists: LC–M, 1034; Maule

4323
Place: Hustisford, Wisconsin
Date: 1885
Title: Hustisford, Wis. Dodge County.
1885.
Size: 9 × 18¹⁄₁₆ in. (23 × 46 cm.)
Artist:
Lithographer:
Printer: Beck & Pauli, Litho. Milwaukee
Publisher: Norris, Wellge & Co. 107 Wells
St. Milwaukee, Wis.
Key/Vignettes/Misc:
Locations: Village Hall, Hustisford,
Wisconsin; WHS−M (photo)
Catalogs/Checklists: Maule

4324
Place: Janesville, Wisconsin
Date: [1861−62?]
Title: Janesville, Wis from the High School
Size: 16½ × 23 in. (42 × 58.6 cm.)
Artist: L. Kurz
Lithographer:
Printer: Kurz & Seifert, Milwaukee
Publisher:
Key/Vignettes/Misc:
Locations: RCHS−J
Catalogs/Checklists:

4325
Place: Janesville, Wisconsin
Date: 1877
Title: Janesville, Wis. Looking down the
River, 1877
Size: 17¼ × 24⅜ in. (44 × 62 cm.)
Artist:
Lithographer: C. H. Vogt & Co.
Printer: C. H. Vogt & Co., Milwaukee
Publisher:
Key/Vignettes/Misc: Refs. 1−51
Locations: WHS−M; LC−M (photo);
RCHS−J
Catalogs/Checklists: Maule; LC−M,
1034.1

4326
Place: Janesville, Wisconsin
Date: 1896
Title: Janesville, Wis. 1896
Size: 23⅜ × 36 in. (59.5 × 91.6 cm.)
Artist: C. J. Pauli
Lithographer:
Printer:
Publisher: C. J. Pauli, 234 22nd Street,
Milwaukee, Wis.
Key/Vignettes/Misc: Refs. 1−30
Locations: RCHS−J
Catalogs/Checklists:

4327
Place: Janesville, Wisconsin
Date: ?
Title: Janesville
Size: 19 × 27 in. (48.4 × 68.7 cm.)
Artist: J. E. Dillingham
Lithographer:
Printer: Reen & Shober's Lith Estabt.
Chicago
Publisher: Jno. E. Dillingham
Key/Vignettes/Misc:
Locations: RCHS−J
Catalogs/Checklists:

4328
Place: Jefferson, Wisconsin
Date: Ca. 1862
Title: Jefferson, Wis.
Size: 15½ × 21⅞ in. (39.5 × 55.7 cm.)
Artist: L. Kurz
Lithographer:
Printer: Kurz & Siefert, Milwaukee
Publisher:
Key/Vignettes/Misc:
Locations: LC−P
Catalogs/Checklists:

4329
Place: Jefferson, Wisconsin
Date: 1870
Title: Bird's Eye View of Jefferson
Jefferson County Wisconsin 1870. Looking
North East,
Size: 18¹³⁄₁₆ × 22¾ in. (48 × 58 cm.)
Artist: [Albert Ruger]
Lithographer:
Printer: Chicago Lithographing Co.
[Chicago]
Publisher: Ruger & Stoner, Madison, Wis.
Key/Vignettes/Misc: Refs. 1−14; 2
vignettes
Locations: LC−M; WHS−M
Catalogs/Checklists: LC−M, 1035; Maule

4330
Place: Jefferson, Wisconsin
Date: 1880
Title: Bird's Eye View of the City of
Jefferson C. S. F[or] Jefferson Co. Wis.
1880.
Size: 11 × 19⅝ in. (28 × 50 cm.)
(facsimile)
Artist: H. Wellge
Lithographer:
Printer: Beck & Pauli, Lith., Milwaukee,
Wis.
Publisher: J. J. Stoner, Madison, Wis.
Key/Vignettes/Misc: Refs. 1−36
Locations: WHS−M (facsimile)
Catalogs/Checklists: Maule

4331
Place: Jefferson, Wisconsin
Date: 1893
Title: Jefferson, Wis. 1893 Looking North.
Size: 13¾ × 20⁷⁄₁₆ in. (35 × 52 cm.)
(facsimile)
Artist: C. J. Pauli
Lithographer:
Printer:
Publisher: C. J. Pauli, Milwaukee, Wis.
Key/Vignettes/Misc: Refs. 1−38
Locations: WHS−M (photo)
Catalogs/Checklists: Maule

4332
Place: Kaukauna, Wisconsin
Date: 1881
Title: Panoramic Map of Kaukauna, Wisc.
1881 Outagamie Co.
Size:
Artist:
Lithographer:
Printer: Beck & Pauli, Lith. Milwaukee,
Wis.
Publisher: A. C. Damm, Milwaukee

Key/Vignettes/Misc: 27 refs.; 4 vignettes
Locations: Charles Grignon Home,
Kaukauna, Wisconsin
Catalogs/Checklists:

4333
Place: Kaukauna, Wisconsin
Date: 1882
Title: Birds' Eye View of the Village of
Kaukauna, Wisconsin.
Size:
Artist:
Lithographer:
Printer: Marr−Richards Eng. Mil. [i.e.
Minneapolis], St. Paul
Publisher: Appleton Post
Key/Vignettes/Misc:
Locations: LC−M (photo)
Catalogs/Checklists: Maule

4334
Place: Kaukauna, Wisconsin
Date: 1886
Title: Kaukauna, Wis. Outagamie County
1886
Size: 17¹¹⁄₁₆ × 24¾ in. (45 × 63 cm.)
Artist: H. Wellge
Lithographer:
Printer: Beck & Pauli, Milwaukee
Publisher: Norris, Wellge & Co., 205
Second St., Milwaukee, Wis.
Key/Vignettes/Misc: Refs. 1−41, 60−92,
18 lettered refs.; 3 vignettes
Locations: Charles Grignon Home,
Kaukauna, Wisconsin; WHS−M; LC−M
(photo)
Catalogs/Checklists: Maule; LC−M,
1035.2

4335
Place: Kenosha, Wisconsin
Date: [before 1850]
Title: View of Southport, Wisconsin
Size: 10½ × 17¾ in. (26.7 × 45.2 cm.)
Artist: James C. Sharp
Lithographer:
Printer:
Publisher:
Key/Vignettes/Misc:
Locations: CHS−C
Catalogs/Checklists:

4336
Place: Kenosha, Wisconsin
Date: 1882
Title: Kenosha, Wis. 1882.
Size: 16 × 27 in. (40.7 × 68.7 cm.)
Artist:
Lithographer:
Printer: Beck & Pauli Lith., Milwaukee,
Wis.
Publisher: J. J. Stoner, Madison, Wis.
Key/Vignettes/Misc: Refs. A−J, 1−29
Locations: Kenosha County Historical
Museum, Kenosha, Wisconsin
Catalogs/Checklists:

4337
Place: Kewaskum, Wisconsin
Date: 1878
Title: Panoramic View of Kewaskum
Washington Co. Wis. 1878 Looking to the
North East

Size: 9 × 14¹⁵⁄₁₆ in. (23 × 38 cm.)
Artist:
Lithographer:
Printer: [Beck & Pauli, Lith., Milwaukee, Wis.?]
Publisher:
Key/Vignettes/Misc: Refs. 1–24
Locations: WHS–M; LC–M (photo)
Catalogs/Checklists: Maule; LC–M, 1035.3

4338

Place: Kewaunee, Wisconsin
Date: 1880
Title: Bird's Eye View of Kewaunee, County Seat of Kewaunee Co. Wis. 1880
Size: 11 × 15¾ in. (28 × 40 cm.) (sheet size)
Artist:
Lithographer:
Printer: Beck & Pauli, Litho. Milwaukee, Wis.
Publisher: J. J. Stoner, Madison, Wis.
Key/Vignettes/Misc:
Locations: Kewanee Co. Jail Museum, Kewanee, Wisconsin; WHS–M (photo)
Catalogs/Checklists: Maule

4339

Place: Kewaunee, Wisconsin
Date: 1893
Title: Kewaunee, Wis. 1893. Looking West.
Size: 25⅛ × 30¼ in. (64 × 77 cm.) (sheet size)
Artist: C. J. Pauli
Lithographer:
Printer:
Publisher: C. J. Pauli, 725 Central Avenue, Milwaukee, Wis.
Key/Vignettes/Misc: Refs. 1–36; 1 vignette
Locations: Kewaunee County Jail Museum, Kewaunee, Wisconsin; WHS–M (photo); LC–M (photo)
Catalogs/Checklists: Maule; LC–M, 1035.4

4340

Place: Kilbourn City, Wisconsin
Date: 1870
Title: Kilbourn City, Wis. 1870.
Size: 10⅝ × 15⁵⁄₁₆ in. (27 × 39 cm.)
Artist: H. H. Bailey
Lithographer:
Printer: Doniat & Zastrow, Milwaukee
Publisher:
Key/Vignettes/Misc:
Locations: WHS–M; LC–M (photo)
Catalogs/Checklists: Maule; LC–M, 1035.5

4341

Place: La Crosse, Wisconsin
Date: 1867
Title: Bird's Eye View of the City of La Crosse Wisconsin 1867.
Size: 20¹³⁄₁₆ × 28¼ in. (53 × 72 cm.)
Artist: A. Ruger
Lithographer:
Printer: Chicago Lithographing Co. 152 & 154 Clark St. Chicago

Publisher:
Key/Vignettes/Misc: Refs. 1–16; 9 vignettes
Locations: LC–M; WHS–M
Catalogs/Checklists: LC–M, 1036; Maule

4342

Place: La Crosse, Wisconsin
Date: 1873
Title: La Crosse, Wis. 1873
Size: 14 × 23¼ in. (35.7 × 59.2 cm.)
Artist: Geo. H. Ellsbury
Lithographer:
Printer: Milwaukee Lith. & Eng. Co. [Milwaukee]
Publisher:
Key/Vignettes/Misc:
Locations: LC–M; WHS–M
Catalogs/Checklists: LC–M, 1037; Maule

4343

Place: La Crosse, Wisconsin
Date: 1876
Title: La Crosse, Wis. 1876
Size: 17¼ × 23¹⁵⁄₁₆ in. (44 × 61 cm.)
Artist: C. J. Pauli
Lithographer:
Printer: American Oleograph Co. Lith. Milwaukee.
Publisher:
Key/Vignettes/Misc:
Locations: WHS–M; La Crosse Historical Society, La Crosse, Wisconsin
Catalogs/Checklists: Maule

4344

Place: La Crosse, Wisconsin
Date: 1887
Title: La Crosse, Wis. County Seat La Crosse, County. 1887.
Size: 19¾ × 39 in. (50.3 × 99.3 cm.)
Artist:
Lithographer:
Printer: The Beck & Pauli Lith. Co., Milwaukee
Publisher: H. Wellge 205 Second St. Milwaukee, Wis.
Key/Vignettes/Misc: Refs. 1–57, A–G, K; 6 vignettes
Locations: WHS–M; LC–M
Catalogs/Checklists: LC–M, 1038; Maule

4345

Place: Lake Geneva, Wisconsin
Date: 1871
Title: Geneva, Wis. 1871
Size: 11¹¹⁄₁₆ × 17¼ in. (29.8 × 43.8 cm.)
Artist: H. H. Bailey
Lithographer:
Printer: Chicago Lithographin[g] Co. [Chicago]
Publisher:
Key/Vignettes/Misc: Refs. 1–12
Locations: WHS–M; Lake Geneva, Wisconsin, Public Library; LC–M; BPL–R; ACMW–FW
Catalogs/Checklists: Maule; LC–M, 1038.1

4346

Place: Lake Geneva, Wisconsin
Date: 1882
Title: Bird's Eye View of Lake Geneva,

Walworth Co., Wis. 1882. Looking Southwest. Population 2000.
Size: 16½ × 30¼ in. (42 × 77 cm.)
Artist: Wellge & Poole
Lithographer:
Printer: Beck & Pauli, Lithographers, Milwaukee, Wis.
Publisher: J. J. Stoner, Madison, Wis.
Key/Vignettes/Misc: Refs. 1–39, A–B; 10 vignettes
Locations: LC–M; WHS–M; LC–P
Catalogs/Checklists: Maule; LC–M, 1038.2

4347

Place: Lake Mills, Wisconsin
Date: N.D.
Title:
Size:
Artist:
Lithographer:
Printer:
Publisher:
Key/Vignettes/Misc:
Locations: Private collection
Catalogs/Checklists: Maule

4348

Place: Lancaster, Wisconsin
Date: [1875]
Title: Bird's Eye View of Lancaster, Grant County, Wis. Looking North West.
Size: 14½ × 18¹⁄₁₆ in. (37 × 46 cm.)
Artist: H. Brosius
Lithographer:
Printer:
Publisher: J. J. Stoner, Madison, Wis.
Key/Vignettes/Misc: 1 vignette
Locations: WHS–M; LC–M (photo)
Catalogs/Checklists: Maule; LC–M, 1038.3

4349

Place: Lodi, Wisconsin
Date: 1874
Title: Lodi, Columbia County, Wisconsin. 1874
Size: 8¼ × 9¹⁄₁₆ in. (21 × 23 cm.) (photo)
Artist:
Lithographer:
Printer: J. Knauber & Co.
Publisher: J. J. Stoner, Madison, Wis.
Key/Vignettes/Misc: 1 vignette
Locations: Private collection; WHS–M (photo)
Catalogs/Checklists: Maule

4350

Place: Lone Rock, Wisconsin
Date: 1879
Title: Bird's Eye View of Lone Rock, Richland Co., Wisconsin 1879
Size: 6¹¹⁄₁₆ × 10¼ in. (17 × 26 cm.)
Artist:
Lithographer:
Printer: [Beck & Pauli, Lith., Milwaukee, Wis.]
Publisher:
Key/Vignettes/Misc: Refs. 1–7
Locations: WHS–M; Brewer Library, Richland Center, Wisconsin; LC–M (photo)

Catalogs/Checklists: Maule; LC−M, 1038.4

4351
Place: Madison, Wisconsin
Date: 1855
Title: View of Madison the Capital of Wisconsin. Taken from the Water Cure, South Side of Lake Menona, 1855.
Size: 12³⁄₁₆ × 21½ in. (31 × 54.7 cm.)
Artist: S. H. Donnel
Lithographer:
Printer: C. Curriers Lith. 33 Spruce St., New York
Publisher:
Key/Vignettes/Misc:
Locations: NYP−S; MM−NN; CHS−C; LC−M (facsimile); NYH−NY
Catalogs/Checklists: Stokes 1855—G−34; MM−NN, LP 2188; LC−M, 1038.5

4352
Place: Madison, Wisconsin
Date: 1864
Title: Madison, the Capitol of Wisconsin
Size: 21½ × 26¾ in. (54.8 × 68.1 cm.)
Artist: Louis Kurz
Lithographer:
Printer: Louis Kurz [Chicago]
Publisher:
Key/Vignettes/Misc: 12 vignettes
Locations: CHS−C
Catalogs/Checklists:

4353
Place: Madison, Wisconsin
Date: 1867
Title: Madison, Wisconsin, 1867
Size: 21¼ × 28¼ in. (54.1 × 71.9 cm.)
Artist: A. Ruger
Lithographer:
Printer: Chicago Lith. Co., Chicago
Publisher:
Key/Vignettes/Misc: Refs. 1−23; 4 vignettes
Locations: LC−M; CHS−C; WHS−M
Catalogs/Checklists: LC−M, 1039; Maule

4354
Place: Madison, Wisconsin
Date: 1885
Title: Madison. State Capital of Wisconsin. County Seat of Dane County. 1885.
Size: 24⅜ × 31¹⁄₁₆ in. (62 × 79 cm.)
Artist: H. Wellge
Lithographer:
Printer:
Publisher: Norris, Wellge & Co., Milwaukee, Wis.
Key/Vignettes/Misc: 20 vignettes; advertisements
Locations: LC−M; WHS−M
Catalogs/Checklists: Maule; LC−M, 1041

4355
Place: Madison, Wisconsin
Date: 1885
Title: Madison, State capital of Wisconsin, County Seat of Dane County 1885
Size: 21⅜ × 31⅛ in. (54.3 × 79 cm.)
Artist:
Lithographer:

Printer: Beck & Pauli, Litho. Milwaukee, Wis.
Publisher: Norris, Wellge & Co., Milwaukee, Wis.
Key/Vignettes/Misc: Refs. 1−43, A−H, J−N; 1 vignette
Locations: LC−M; WHS−M (photo); LC−P
Catalogs/Checklists: LC−M, 1040; Maule

4356
Place: Madison, Wisconsin
Date: 1908
Title: Panoramic View of Madison, Wis. State Capital of Wisconsin. University of Wisconsin.
Size: 12⁹⁄₁₆ × 24 in. (32 × 61 cm.)
Artist: H. Wellge
Lithographer:
Printer:
Publisher: H. Wellge, Milwaukee, Wis.
Key/Vignettes/Misc:
Locations: WHS−M
Catalogs/Checklists: Maule

4357
Place: Manitowoc, Wisconsin
Date: 1869
Title: Birds Eye View of Manitowoc Manitowoc Co. Wis. 1869.
Size:
Artist:
Lithographer:
Printer: Middleton, Wallace and Co. [Cincinnati, Ohio]
Publisher:
Key/Vignettes/Misc: Refs. 1−36; 4 vignettes
Locations: WHS−M (photo)
Catalogs/Checklists:

4358
Place: Manitowoc, Wisconsin
Date: 1870
Title: Manitowoc, Wisconsin, 1870 [On Verso]
Size: 9¾ × 15¾ in. (24.8 × 40.1 cm.)
Artist:
Lithographer:
Printer: J. Knauber, Milwaukee
Publisher:
Key/Vignettes/Misc:
Locations: Private collection
Catalogs/Checklists: Maule

4359
Place: Manitowoc, Wisconsin
Date: 1883
Title: Manitowoc, Wis. 1883
Size: 9¹³⁄₁₆ × 20¹⁄₁₆ in. (25 × 51 cm.) (photo)
Artist:
Lithographer:
Printer: Beck & Pauli, Lithographers, Milwaukee, Wis.
Publisher: J. J. Stoner, Madison
Key/Vignettes/Misc: Refs. 1−25, A−H, J−K
Locations: WHS−M (photo); LC−M (photo)
Catalogs/Checklists: Maule; LC−M, 1041.1

4360
Place: Manitowoc, Wisconsin
Date: [1895]
Title: Manitowoc, Wis.
Size: 12⁹⁄₁₆ × 20 in. (32 × 51 cm.) (photo)
Artist: C. J. Pauli
Lithographer:
Printer:
Publisher: C. J. Pauli, 234 22nd Street, Milwaukee, Wis.
Key/Vignettes/Misc: Refs. 1−26
Locations: WHS−M (photo); LC−M (photo)
Catalogs/Checklists: Maule; LC−M, 1041.2

4361
Place: Marinette, Wisconsin
Date: [1871]
Title: Bird's Eye View of the Towns at the Mouth of the Menominee River.
Size: 9¹⁄₁₆ × 22 in. (23 × 56 cm.)
Artist: O. H. Bailey
Lithographer:
Printer: Strobridge & Co. Lith, Cincinnati, Ohio
Publisher:
Key/Vignettes/Misc:
Locations: Marinette County Historical Society, Marinette, Wisconsin; WHS−M (photo)
Catalogs/Checklists: Maule (Menominee River)

4362
Place: Marinette, Wisconsin
Date: 1881
Title: Bird's Eye View of Marinette, Wis. 1881
Size: 13¾ × 33 in. (35 × 84 cm.)
Artist:
Lithographer:
Printer: Beck & Pauli Lith. Milwaukee, Wis.
Publisher: J. J. Stoner, Madison, Wis.
Key/Vignettes/Misc: Refs. 1−35, A; 3 vignettes
Locations: WHS−M; LC−M (photo); MCHM−M
Catalogs/Checklists: Maule; LC−M, 1041.3

4363
Place: Marshall, Wisconsin
Date: 1879
Title: Marshall Dane Co. Wis. 1879
Size: 7¹⁄₁₆ × 11¾ in. (18 × 30 cm.)
Artist:
Lithographer:
Printer: Beck & Pauli, Lith, Milwaukee, Wis.
Publisher: J. J. Stoner, Madison, Wis.
Key/Vignettes/Misc: Refs.
Locations: WHS−M; LC−M (photo)
Catalogs/Checklists: Maule; LC−M, 1041.4

4364
Place: Marshfield, Wisconsin
Date: 1883
Title: Bird's Eye View of Marshfield, Wis. 1883

Size: 14⅝ × 22¾ in. (37.2 × 57.9 cm.)
Artist:
Lithographer:
Printer: Beck & Pauli, Lithographers, Milwaukee, Wis.
Publisher: J. J. Stoner, Madison, Wis.
Key/Vignettes/Misc: 1 vignette
Locations: Mayor's office, Marshfield, Wisconsin
Catalogs/Checklists: Maule

4365
Place: Marshfield, Wisconsin
Date: 1891
Title: Marshfield, Wis 1891 Looking North
Size: 23½ × 29½ in. (59.8 × 75.1 cm.)
Artist: C. J. Pauli
Lithographer:
Printer:
Publisher: C. J. Pauli, 726 Central Ave., Milwaukee, Wis.
Key/Vignettes/Misc: 6 vignettes
Locations: Mayor's office, Marshfield, Wisconsin
Catalogs/Checklists: Maule

4366
Place: Mauston, Wisconsin
Date: 1870
Title: Mauston, Wis. 1870
Size: 10⅝ × 18⁷⁄₁₆ in. (27 × 47 cm.)
Artist: H. H. Bailey
Lithographer:
Printer: Doniat & Zastrow, Milwaukee
Publisher:
Key/Vignettes/Misc: Refs. 1–13
Locations: WHS–M; Boorman House, Mauston, Wisconsin; LC–M (photo)
Catalogs/Checklists: Maule; LC–M, 1041.5

4367
Place: Mayville, Wisconsin
Date: 1885
Title: Mayville, Wis. Dodge County. 1885.
Size: 11¾ × 20¹⁄₁₆ in. (30 × 51 cm.)
Artist:
Lithographer:
Printer: Beck & Pauli, Litho. Milwaukee, Wis.
Publisher: Norris, Wellge & Co., Milwaukee, Wis.
Key/Vignettes/Misc:
Locations: Mayville Museum, Mayville, Wisconsin; WHS–M (photo)
Catalogs/Checklists: Maule

4368
Place: Mazomanie, Wisconsin
Date: [1875]
Title: Bird's Eye View of Mazomanie Dane County, Wis.
Size: 13 × 17¼ in. (33 × 44 cm.)
Artist: H. Brosius
Lithographer:
Printer: C. Shober & Co., Prop. Chicago Lith. Co. [Chicago]
Publisher: J. J. Stoner Madison, Wis.
Key/Vignettes/Misc:
Locations: WHS–M; LC–M

Catalogs/Checklists: Maule; LC–M, 1041.6

4369
Place: Medford, Wisconsin
Date: 1885
Title: Medford, Wis. County Seat of Taylor County Before the Great Fire May 28th. 1885.
Size: 15 × 18½ in. (38.1 × 47.1 cm.)
Artist: H. W.[ellge?]
Lithographer:
Printer: Beck & Pauli, Litho. Milwaukee, Wis.
Publisher: Norris, Wellge & Co. . . .Milwaukee, Wis.
Key/Vignettes/Misc: Refs. 1–50; 1 vignette
Locations: LC–M; WHS–M (photo)
Catalogs/Checklists: LC–M, 1042; Maule

4370
Place: Menasha, Wisconsin
Date: 1870
Title: Menasha, Wis. 1870
Size: 15⁵⁄₁₆ × 19⅝ in. (39 × 50 cm.)
Artist: H. H. Bailey
Lithographer:
Printer: Doniat & Zastrow, Milwaukee
Publisher:
Key/Vignettes/Misc: Refs. 1–9, A–S; 1 vignette
Locations: WHS–M; LC–M (photo)
Catalogs/Checklists: Maule; LC–M, 1042.1

Place: Menekaune, Wisconsin
Date: [1871]
See Marinette, Wisconsin, [1871].

4371
Place: Menomonee Falls, Wisconsin
Date: 1886
Title: Menomonee Falls. Waukesha County. Wisconsin 1886
Size: 18 × 18⅜ in. (45.8 × 46.8 cm.)
Artist:
Lithographer:
Printer: Beck & Pauli, Litho. Milwaukee, Wis.
Publisher: Norris, Wellge & Co. No. 205 Second St. Milwaukee, Wis.
Key/Vignettes/Misc: Refs. 1–23, A–F
Locations: LC–M; WHS–M (photo)
Catalogs/Checklists: LC–M, 1043; Maule

4372
Place: Menomonie, Wisconsin
Date: [1875]
Title: Bird's Eye View of Menomonee Dunn County Wis.
Size: 14⅛ × 20¹⁄₁₆ in. (36 × 51 cm.)
Artist: H. Brosius
Lithographer:
Printer:
Publisher:
Key/Vignettes/Misc: Refs. A–C, 1–5; 1 vignette
Locations: WHS–M; LC–M (photo)
Catalogs/Checklists: Maule; LC–M, 1042.2

4373
Place: Merrill, Wisconsin
Date: 1883
Title: Bird's Eye View of Merrill, Wis. County Seat of Lincoln Co. 1883.
Size: 13½ × 31 in. (34.4 × 78.9 cm.)
Artist: H. Wellge
Lithographer:
Printer: Beck & Pauli, Lithographers, Milwaukee, Wis.
Publisher: J. J. Stoner, Madison, Wis.
Key/Vignettes/Misc: Refs. 1–25, A–H
Locations: LC–M; WHS–M (photo)
Catalogs/Checklists: LC–M, 1044; Maule

4374
Place: Merrillan, Wisconsin
Date: 1883
Title: Merrillan–Jackson County, Wis.
Size: 12 × 21½ in. (30.6 × 54.7 cm.)
Artist: H. Budel
Lithographer:
Printer: Beck & Pauli, Milwaukee, Wis.
Publisher: J. J. Stoner, Madison, Wis.
Key/Vignettes/Misc: Refs. 1–40
Locations: Private collection
Catalogs/Checklists: Maule

4375
Place: Middleton, Wisconsin
Date: 1876
Title: Bird's Eye View of Middleton, Dane County, Wisconsin. 1876.
Size: 9¹⁄₁₆ × 12³⁄₁₆ in. (23 × 31 cm.)
Artist:
Lithographer:
Printer:
Publisher:
Key/Vignettes/Misc: Refs. 1–9, A; 1 vignette
Locations: WHS–M; LC–M (photo)
Catalogs/Checklists: Maule; LC–M, 1044.1

4376
Place: Milton Junction, Wisconsin
Date: 1881
Title: Bird's Eye View of Milton Junction. Rock Co. Wis. 1881.
Size: 8¼ × 14¹⁵⁄₁₆ in. (21 × 38 cm.)
Artist:
Lithographer:
Printer:
Publisher:
Key/Vignettes/Misc:
Locations: WHS–M; LC–M (photo)
Catalogs/Checklists: Maule; LC–M, 1044.2

4377
Place: Milwaukee, Wisconsin
Date: 1854
Title: Milwaukee, Wisconsin.
Size: 25 × 40¼ in. (63.5 × 102.3 cm.)
Artist: Geo. J. Robertson
Lithographer: D. W. Moody
Printer: Endicott & Co., New York
Publisher: Smith Brothers & Co. 59 Beekman St. N. Y.
Key/Vignettes/Misc:

Locations: WHS–M; MM–NN; LC–P; CHS–C
Catalogs/Checklists: MM–NN, LP 4781; Maule; Beckman, no. 3; LC–M, 1044.3

4378
Place: Milwaukee, Wisconsin
Date: 1856
Title: View of the City of Milwaukee, Wisconsin
Size: 29 1/16 × 52 5/16 in. (73.8 × 132.8 cm.)
Artist: [James T. Palmatary]
Lithographer: Middleton, Wallace & Co.
Printer: Middleton, Wallace & Co. Litho. 115 Walnut St. Cincinnati, O.
Publisher: J. T. Palmatary
Key/Vignettes/Misc:
Locations: WHS–M
Catalogs/Checklists: Maule; Beckman, no. 7

4379
Place: Milwaukee, Wisconsin
Date: 1857
Title: View of Milwaukee, from Judge Smith Addition, 5th Ward.
Size: 9 5/16 × 18 1/8 in. (14.2 × 46 cm.)
Artist: Brooks and Stevenson [Samuel Marsden Brookes & Thomas H. Stevenson]
Lithographer: L. Lipmann
Printer: H. Seifert, Milwaukee
Publisher:
Key/Vignettes/Misc:
Locations: MCHS–M
Catalogs/Checklists: Beckman, no. 9

4380
Place: Milwaukee, Wisconsin
Date: 1861
Title: Milwaukee, Wis. From Wm. H. Metcalf's Res Cor. of Cass & Division Sts.
Size: 14 7/8 × 22 7/16 in. (37.8 × 56.9 cm.)
Artist: L. Kurz
Lithographer:
Printer: Kurz & Seifert, Milwaukee
Publiher: Kurz & Seifert, Milwaukee
Key/Vignettes/Misc:
Locations: CHS–C
Catalogs/Checklists: Beckman, no. 14

4381
Place: Milwaukee, Wisconsin
Date: 1866
Title: Panorama of Milwaukee
Size: 16 3/4 × 30 11/16 in. (42.5 × 77.9 cm.)
Artist: From a photograph by John P. Hawkins
Lithographer:
Printer: Louis Lipman
Publisher:
Key/Vignettes/Misc:
Locations: WHS–M (photo); MPL–M
Catalogs/Checklists: Beckman, no. 15; Maule

4382
Place: Milwaukee, Wisconsin
Date: 1872
Title: Milwaukee, Wis.
Size: 25 × 38 1/16 in. (63.6 × 96.9 cm.)

Artist: H. H. Bailey
Lithographer:
Printer: Milw. Lithographing & Engraving Co. [Milwaukee]
Publisher: Holzapfel & Eskuche, 443 E. Water St. Milw.
Key/Vignettes/Misc: Refs. 1–55
Locations: LC–M; WHS–M; LC–P; MPL–M
Catalogs/Checklists: LC–M, 1045; Maule; Beckman, no. 17

4383
Place: Milwaukee, Wisconsin
Date: 1874
Title: Milwaukee, Wis.
Size: 16 1/2 × 29 1/2 in. (41.9 × 75 cm.)
Artist: C. H. Ellsbury [George H. Ellsbury]
Lithographer:
Printer: Milwaukee Lith & Eng. Co.
Publisher: Geo. H. Ellsbury and Vernon Green (copyright)
Key/Vignettes/Misc: Refs. in 3 lines
Locations: YUAG–NH; LC–P; Milwaukee Art Center, Milwaukee, Wisconsin; MCHS–M; MPL–M
Catalogs/Checklists: Beckman, no. 25

4384
Place: Milwaukee, Wisconsin
Date: 1876
Title: Milwaukee, Wis. From the Rolling Mills. 1876
Size: 19 × 25 3/16 in. (48.3 × 64 cm.)
Artist: C. J. Pauli
Lithographer:
Printer: American Oleograph Co., Milwaukee
Publisher: C. J. Pauli, Milwaukee (copyright)
Key/Vignettes/Misc:
Locations: MPM–M
Catalogs/Checklists: Beckman, no. 28

4385
Place: Milwaukee, Wisconsin
Date: 1877
Title: Milwaukee, Wis. From the Lake
Size: 16 1/2 × 28 7/8 in. (42 × 73.3 cm.)
Artist:
Lithographer:
Printer: Milwaukee Litho. & Engr. Co. [Milwaukee]
Publisher:
Key/Vignettes/Misc:
Locations: CHS–C; University Club of Milwaukee, Milwaukee, Wisconsin
Catalogs/Checklists: Beckman, no. 29

4386
Place: Milwaukee, Wisconsin
Date: 1879
Title: Milwaukee, Wis. 1879
Size: 25 3/4 × 38 11/16 in. (65.5 × 98.4 cm.)
Artist:
Lithographer:
Printer: Beck & Pauli, Lithographers, Milwaukee, Wis.
Publisher: J. J. Stoner & Co., Madison, Wis.
Key/Vignettes/Misc: Refs. 1–83

Locations: LC–M; LC–P; WHS–M; MCHS–M; MPL–M
Catalogs/Checklists: LC–M, 1046; Maule; Beckman, no. 32

4387
Place: Milwaukee, Wisconsin
Date: 1882
Title: Milwaukee, Wis.
Size: 12 5/8 × 24 13/16 in. (32 × 63 cm.)
Artist:
Lithographer:
Printer:
Publisher: Beck & Pauli, Milwaukee, Wis. (copyright)
Key/Vignettes/Misc: 10 vignettes
Locations: LC–M; MPM–M
Catalogs/Checklists: LC–M, 1047; Maule; Beckman, no. 35

4388
Place: Milwaukee, Wisconsin
Date: 1883
Title: Milwaukee, Wis. (Im Jahre 1883.)
Size: 12 5/8 × 24 13/16 in. (32 × 63 cm.)
Artist:
Lithographer:
Printer:
Publisher: Beck & Pauli, Milwaukee, Wis. (copyright)
Key/Vignettes/Misc: 10 vignettes; description
Locations: Goethe House, Milwaukee, Wisconsin; MPM–M
Catalogs/Checklists: Beckman, no. 36

4389
Place: Milwaukee, Wisconsin
Date: 1886
Title: Milwaukee, Wis. 1886.
Size: 24 1/16 × 30 9/16 in. (61.2 × 77.8 cm.)
Artist:
Lithographer:
Printer: The Milwaukee Litho. & Engr. Co.
Publisher: Albert Mueller (copyright)
Key/Vignettes/Misc: 19 vignettes
Locations: LC–P
Catalogs/Checklists:

4390
Place: Milwaukee, Wisconsin
Date: 1892
Title: Looking East from Wauwatosa. Wauwatosa and the Western Suburbs of Milwaukee. Mean Elevation above Lake Michigan 180 Feet. 1892.
Size: 16 3/8 × 28 15/16 in. (41.8 × 73.5 cm.)
Artist:
Lithographer:
Printer: Marr & Richard Engraving Co., Milwaukee
Publisher: Marr & Richards Engraving Co., Milwaukee
Key/Vignettes/Misc: Refs. 1–10, A–L; advertisement for Richter Schubert & Dick. . .Real Estate and Insurance
Locations: LC–M (has advertisement for Warner Bros & Wambold in place of Richter, etc.); MPL–M
Catalogs/Checklists: Beckman, no. 45; LC–M, 1065

4391
Place: Milwaukee, Wisconsin
Date: 1892
Title: Milwaukee, Wis. 1892 Looking South
Size: 11 × 22⅞ in. (28 × 58 cm.)
Artist: C. J. Pauli
Lithographer:
Printer:
Publisher: C. J. Pauli, Milwaukee, Wis. (copyright)
Key/Vignettes/Misc:
Locations: MPM–M; MCHS–M
Catalogs/Checklists: Beckman, no. 43

4392
Place: Milwaukee, Wisconsin
Date: 1898
Title: Map of Electric Railway System T. M. E. R. & L. Co.
Size: 19¹⁄₁₆ × 26⅞ in. (48.4 × 67 cm.)
Artist: John I. Beggs
Lithographer:

4393
Place: Milwaukee, Wisconsin
Date: 1898
Title: Panoramic View of Milwaukee Wis. Taken From City Hall Tower
Size: 12¹¹⁄₁₆ × 47⅜ in. (44 × 125 cm.)
Artist:
Lithographer:
Printer: [The Gugler Lithographic Co., Milwaukee]
Publisher: The Gugler Lithographic Co. (copyright)
Key/Vignettes/Misc: 59 unnumbered refs. in 5 lines below places identified
Locations: ACMW–FW; CHS–C; LC–P; MPL–M; MCHS–M
Catalogs/Checklists: Maule; Beckman, no. 46; Reps, Cities on Stone, p. 94; LC–M, 1047.2

4394
Place: Milwaukee, Wisconsin
Date: [1907–08]
Title: Panoramic View of Greater Milwaukee Wis.
Size: 18¹⁄₁₆ × 37⅝ in. (46 × 95.5 cm.)
Artist: H. Wellge
Lithographer:
Printer:
Publisher: C. N. Caspar Co. (copyright)
Key/Vignettes/Misc:
Locations: MCHS–M
Catalogs/Checklists: Beckman, no. 48

4395
Place: Milwaukee, Wisconsin
Date: Ca. 1920
Title: The Milwaukee Harbor Project
Size: 9⁷⁄₁₆ × 23⁹⁄₁₆ in. (24 × 60 cm.)
Artist:
Lithographer:
Printer:
Publisher:
Key/Vignettes/Misc:
Locations: WHS–M (photo); MPL–M
Catalogs/Checklists: Maule

4396
Place: Mineral Point, Wisconsin
Date: 1872
Title: Bird's Eye View of Mineral Point, Iowa County, Wis. 1872. Looking South East
Size: 18½ × 22⅜ in. (47 × 57 cm.)
Artist: H. Brosius
Lithographer:
Printer:
Publisher:
Key/Vignettes/Misc: Refs. A–E, 1–6
Locations: WHS–M; LC–M (photo)
Catalogs/Checklists: Maule; LC–M, 1047.3

4397
Place: Monroe, Wisconsin
Date: 1871
Title: Monroe, Wis. 1871.
Size: 18¹⁄₁₆ × 24⅜ in. (46 × 62 cm.)
Artist: H. H. Bailey
Lithographer:
Printer: Doniat & Zastrow, Milwaukee
Publisher:
Key/Vignettes/Misc:
Locations: WHS–M; LC–M (photo)
Catalogs/Checklists: Maule; LC–M, 1047.5

4398
Place: Monroe, Wisconsin
Date: 1877
Title: Monroe, Green County, Wisconsin 1877
Size: 18 × 24 in. (45.8 × 61.1 cm.)
Artist: C. J. Pauli
Lithographer:
Printer: C. H. Vogt & Co. Lith. Milwaukee
Publisher:
Key/Vignettes/Misc: Refs. 1–28
Locations: Green County Historical Society, Monroe, Wisconsin
Catalogs/Checklists:

4399
Place: Monroe, Wisconsin
Date: 1895
Title: Monroe, Wis. 1895
Size: 20¼ × 33¾ in. (51.6 × 85.9 cm.)
Artist: C. J. Pauli
Lithographer:
Printer:
Publisher: C. J. Pauli, 234 22nd St., Milwaukee, Wisconsin
Key/Vignettes/Misc: Refs. 1–24
Locations: Green County Historical Society, Monroe, Wisconsin
Catalogs/Checklists:

4400
Place: Muscoda, Wisconsin
Date: 1879
Title: Muscoda Grant Co. Wis. 1879
Size: 7½ × 12³⁄₁₆ in. (19 × 31 cm.)
Artist:
Lithographer:
Printer: [Beck & Pauli, Lith., Milwaukee, Wis.?]

Publisher:
Key/Vignettes/Misc:
Locations: WHS–M; LC–M (photo)
Catalogs/Checklists: Maule; LC–M, 1047.6

4401
Place: Neenah, Wisconsin
Date: 1870
Title: Neenah, Wis. 1870.
Size: 14¹⁵⁄₁₆ × 22¾ in. (38 × 58 cm.)
Artist: H. H. Bailey
Lithographer:
Printer: Doniat & Zastrow, Milwaukee, Wis.
Publisher:
Key/Vignettes/Misc: Refs. 1–18, A–V
Locations: WHS–M; LC–M (photo)
Catalogs/Checklists: Maule; LC–M, 1047.7

4402
Place: Neenah, Wisconsin
Date: 1879
Title: Bird's Eye View of Neenah, Wis. 1879.
Size: 18⅞ × 23¼ in. (48.1 × 59.2 cm.)
Artist: H. Wellge & J. Bach
Lithographer: C. H. Vogt
Printer: [Beck & Pauli, Lith., Milwaukee, Wis.?]
Publisher: H. Wellge and J. Bach
Key/Vignettes/Misc: Refs. 1–25, A–H, a–g
Locations: BPL–R; Neenah, Wisconsin, Public Library; WHS–M (facsimile)
Catalogs/Checklists: Maule

4403
Place: Neillsville, Wisconsin
Date: 1880
Title: Bird's Eye View of Neillsville Clark Co., Wisconsin 1880.
Size: 8⅝ × 20¹³⁄₁₆ in. (22 × 53 cm.)
Artist:
Lithographer:
Printer: Beck & Pauli, Lith., Milwaukee, Wis.
Publisher: J. J. Stoner, Madison, Wis.
Key/Vignettes/Misc: Refs. 1–14; 1 vignette
Locations: WHS–M; LC–M (photo)
Catalogs/Checklists: Maule; LC–M, 1047.8

4404
Place: New Holstein, Wisconsin
Date: 1879
Title: New Holstein, Calumet Co., Wis. 1879.
Size: 8⅝ × 22 in. (22 × 56 cm.)
Artist:
Lithographer:
Printer: Beck & Pauli, Milwaukee, Wis.
Publisher: Beck & Pauli, Milwaukee, Wis.
Key/Vignettes/Misc:
Locations: New Holstein Historical Society, New Holstein, Wisconsin
Catalogs/Checklists: Maule

4405
Place: New London, Wisconsin
Date: 1871
Title: New-London, Wis. 1871.
Size: 11¾ × 18⅞ in. (30 × 48 cm.)
Artist: H. H. Bailey
Lithographer:
Printer: Chicago Lithographing Co.
[Chicago]
Publisher:
Key/Vignettes/Misc: Refs. 1–9
Locations: WHS–M; LC–M (photo)
Catalogs/Checklists: Maule; LC–M,
1047.9

4406
Place: Oconomowoc, Wisconsin
Date: 1870
Title: Oconomowoc, Wis. 1870.
Size: 13⅜ × 20¹⁄₁₆ in. (34 × 51 cm.)
Artist: H. H. Bailey
Lithographer:
Printer: Doniat & Zastrow, Milwaukee
Publisher: T. M. Fowler & Co., Box 668,
Madison, Wis.
Key/Vignettes/Misc: Refs. 1–13
Locations: WHS–M; LC–M (photo)
Catalogs/Checklists: Maule; LC–M,
1047.95

4407
Place: Oconomowoc, Wisconsin
Date: 1885
Title: View of the City of Oconomowoc,
Wis. Waukesha County. 1885.
Size: 20 × 30½ in. (50.9 × 77.6 cm.)
Artist: H. Wellge
Lithographer:
Printer: Beck & Pauli, Litho. Milwaukee,
Wis.
Publisher: Norris Wellge & Co. No. 107
Wells St. Milwaukee, Wis.
Key/Vignettes/Misc: Refs. 1–49, A–J
Locations: LC–M; Waukesha County
Museum, Waukesha, Wisconsin
Catalogs/Checklists: Maule; LC–M,
1047.96

4408
Place: Oconomowoc, Wisconsin
Date: [1890?]
Title: Oconomowoc, Waukesha and the
Lake Region of Waukesha County,
Wisconsin. . . .
Size: 15¾ × 34³⁄₁₆ in. (40 × 87 cm.)
Artist:
Lithographer:
Printer: Marr & Richard Eng. Co.,
Milwaukee
Publisher:
Key/Vignettes/Misc: Refs.
Locations: LC–M
Catalogs/Checklists: LC–M, 1048

4409
Place: Oconto, Wisconsin
Date: 1871
Title: Bird's Eye View of Oconto, Wis.
1871.
Size: 14¹⁵⁄₁₆ × 19⅝ in. (38 × 50 cm.)
Artist: T. M. Fowler & H. H. Bailey

Lithographer: C H Vogt, Lith.
Printer: Milwaukee Lith & Eng. Co.
[Milwaukee]
Publisher: T. M. Fowler & H. H. Bailey
Key/Vignettes/Misc:
Locations: Oconto County Historical
Society, Oconto, Wisconsin:; WHS–M
(photo)
Catalogs/Checklists: Maule

4410
Place: Omro, Wisconsin
Date: 1870
Title: Omro, Wis. 1870.
Size: 12–⁹⁄₁₆ × 19–⅝ in. (32 × 50 cm.)
Artist:
Lithographer:
Printer: Chicago Lithographing Co.
[Chicago]
Publisher: Th. M. Fowler & Co., box 668
Madison, Wis.
Key/Vignettes/Misc:
Locations: WHS–M; LC–M (photo)
Catalogs/Checklists: Maule; LC–M,
1048.1

4411
Place: Oshkosh, Wisconsin
Date: [1861–62]
Title: Oshkosh, Wis. From H. L. Cottrill's
Block
Size: 15⅜ × 22⁵⁄₁₆ in. (41.5 × 56.6 cm.)
Artist: L. Kurz
Lithographer:
Printer: Kurz & Seifert. Milwaukee Wis.
Publisher: Kurz & Seifert. Milwaukee,
Wis.
Key/Vignettes/Misc:
Locations: LC–P
Catalogs/Checklists: LC–M, 1048.2

4412
Place: Oshkosh, Wisconsin
Date: 1867
Title: Oshkosh. Winebago, Co. Wisconsin
1867.
Size: 22½ × 28¼ in. (57.3 × 71.9 cm.)
Artist: A. Ruger
Lithographer:
Printer: Chicago Lithographing Co.
Chicago
Publisher:
Key/Vignettes/Misc: Refs. 1–12
Locations: LC–M; WHS–M (photo);
Oshkosh, Wisconsin, Public Museum
Catalogs/Checklists: LC–M, 1049; Maule

4413
Place: Oshkosh, Wisconsin
Date: 1871
Title: Oshkosh, Wisconsin—1871.
Size: 16¼ × 26 in. (41.4 × 66.1 cm.)
Artist: August Schoen
Lithographer:
Printer: Milwaukee Lith. & Eng. Co.
[Milwaukee]
Publisher: August Schoen (copyright)
Key/Vignettes/Misc: 14 vignettes
Locations: Unknown. See Old Print Shop
Portfolio, XXI, p. 83, no. 17
Catalogs/Checklists:

4414
Place: Oshkosh, Wisconsin
Date: 1911
Title: Oshkosh, Wis.
Size:
Artist:
Lithographer:
Printer:
Publisher: Castle Pierce Pts. Co.
(copyright)
Key/Vignettes/Misc:
Locations: WHS–M (photo)
Catalogs/Checklists: Maule

4415
Place: Peshtigo, Wisconsin
Date: 1871
Title: Bird's Eye View of Peshtigo
Wisconsin Sept. 1871.
Size: 12³⁄₁₆ × 16⅛ in. (31 × 41 cm.)
Artist:
Lithographer:
Printer: Chars. Shober & Co. Proprs.
Chicago Lith Co. [Chicago]
Publisher: T. M. Fowler & Co., Madison,
Wis.
Key/Vignettes/Misc: Refs. 1–12
Locations: WHS–M; Oconto County
Historical Society, Oconto, Wisconsin;
LC–M (photo); MCHM–M
Catalogs/Checklists: Maule; LC–M,
1049.1

4416
Place: Peshtigo, Wisconsin
Date: 1881
Title: Bird's Eye View of Peshtigo, Wis,
1881.
Size: 10¼ × 18½ in. (26 × 47 cm.)
Artist:
Lithographer:
Printer: Beck & Pauli Lith., Milwaukee,
Wis.
Publisher: J. J. Stoner, Madison, Wis.
Key/Vignettes/Misc: Refs. 1–14
Locations: WHS–M; LC–M (photo);
MCHM–M
Catalogs/Checklists: Maule; LC–M,
1049.2

4417
Place: Platteville, Wisconsin
Date: [1875]
Title: Bird's Eye View of Platteville Grant
County Wis. Looking North East.
Size: 14¹⁵⁄₁₆ × 20 in. (38 × 51 cm.)
Artist: H. Brosius
Lithographer:
Printer:
Publisher:
Key/Vignettes/Misc:
Locations: WHS–M; LC–M (photo)
Catalogs/Checklists: Maule; LC–M,
1049.3

4418
Place: Plymouth, Wisconsin
Date: 1870
Title: Plymouth, Wis. Sheboygan County,
1870.
Size: 11⅜ × 16⁵⁄₁₆ in. (29 × 41.6 cm.)

Artist: H. H. Bailey
Lithographer:
Printer: Doniat & Zastrow, Milwaukee
Publisher:
Key/Vignettes/Misc: LC–M; BPL–R;
LC–M (photo); Reff. 8–18
Location: WHS–M; BPL–R; LC–M
(photo)
Catalogs/Checklists: Maule; LC–M,
1049.4

4419
Place: Plymouth, Wisconsin
Date: 1879
Title: Plymouth Sheboygan Co. Wis. 1879.
Size: 9¹⁄₁₆ × 15⁵⁄₁₆ in. (23 × 39 cm.)
(photo)
Artist:
Lithographer:
Printer: Beck & Pauli, Milwaukee, Wis.
Publisher:
Key/Vignettes/Misc:
Locations: WHS–M (photo)
Catalogs/Checklists: Maule

4420
Place: Portage, Wisconsin
Date: 1868
Title: Bird's Eye View of the City of
Portage Columbia Co. Wisconsin 1868.
Size: 22½ × 28 in. (57.3 × 71.2 cm.)
Artist: A. Ruger
Lithographer:
Printer: Chicago Lith. Co. 152 & 154,
Clark St. Chicago
Publisher:
Key/Vignettes/Misc: Ref. 1–16;
2 vignettes
Locations: LC–M; WHS–M (photo)
Catalogs/Checklists: LC–M, 1050; Maule

4421
Place: Poynette, Wisconsin
Date: 1882
Title: Poynette Columbia County.
Wisconsin 1882.
Size: 12 × 15¾ in. (30.6 × 40.1 cm.)
Artist: H. B. [Herman Brosius?]
Lithographer:
Printer: Beck & Pauli, Lith. Milwaukee,
Wis.
Publisher: J. J. Stoner, Madison, Wis.
Key/Vignettes/Misc: Refs. 1–26;
1 vignette
Locations: Poynette, Wisconsin, Public
Library
Catalogs/Checklists: Maule

4422
Place: Prairie du Chien, Wisconsin
Date: [1854–57]
Title: Prairie Du Chien, Wisconsin, in
1830
Size: ca. 6½ × 8¼ in. (16.5 × 21 cm.)
Artist: Henry Lewis
Lithographer:
Printer: C. H. Muller, Aachen
Publisher: Arnz & Co., Dusseldorf
Key/Vignettes/Misc:
Locations: MHS–SP; NYH–NY; HEHL;
LC–R; NL–C; HNOC–NO
Catalogs/Checklists:

4423
Place: Prairie du Chien, Wisconsin
Date: 1870
Title: Prairie Du Chien, Crawford County,
Wisconsin 1870
Size: 22 × 28 in. (56 × 71.3 cm.)
Artist: [Albert Ruger]
Lithographer:
Printer: Chicago Lithog. Co. No. 150 &
154 S. Clark St. Chicago
Publisher: Ruger & Stoner, Madison, Wis.
Key/Vignettes/Misc: Refs. 1–11, A–B
Locations: MHS–SP; LC–M; WHS–M
Catalogs/Checklists: LC–M, 1051; Maule

4424
Place: Prairie du Sac, Wisconsin
Date: 1870
Title: Bird's Eye View of Prairie Du Sac
Sauk County, Wisconsin 1870. Looking
South West.
Size: 16 × 17 in. (40.8 × 43.3 cm.)
Artist: [Albert Ruger]
Lithographer:
Printer: Chicago Lithographing Co.
[Chicago]
Publisher: Ruger & Stoner, Madison,
Wisc.
Key/Vignettes/Misc:
Locations: LC–M; WHS–M
Catalogs/Checklists: LC–M, 1052; Maule

4425
Place: Princeton, Wisconsin
Date: 1892
Title: Princeton, Wis. 1892. Looking
North.
Size: 11⅜ × 19⅝ in. (29 × 50 cm.)
Artist: C. J. Pauli
Lithographer:
Printer:
Publisher:
Key/Vignettes/Misc: 1 vignette
Locations: WHS–M
Catalogs/Checklists: Maule

4426
Place: Racine, Wisconsin
Date: Ca. 1862
Title: Racine, Wis.
Size: 14½ × 22 in. (36.9 × 56 cm.)
Artist: L. Kurz
Lithographer:
Printer: Kurz & Seifert, Milwaukee
Publisher: Kurz & Siefert, Milwaukee
Key/Vignettes/Misc:
Locations: WHS–M
Catalogs/Checklists:

4427
Place: Racine, Wisconsin
Date: 1874
Title: Bird's Eye View of Racine.
Wisconsin. 1874.
Size: 17¼ × 27⅞ in. (44 × 71 cm.)
Artist: H. Brosius
Lithographer:
Printer: Chas Shober & Co. Prop. Chicago
Lith. Co. [Chicago]
Publisher: J. J. Stoner, Madison, Wis.
Key/Vignettes/Misc: Refs. 1–51;
1 vignette
Locations: WHS–M; Racine, Wisconsin,

Public Library; LC–M (photo)
Catalogs/Checklists: Maule; LC–M,
1052.1

4428
Place: Racine, Wisconsin
Date: 1883
Title: Racine. Wis. County Seat of Racine
Co. 1883 Looking South West.
Size: 23 × 34 in. (58.6 × 86.5 cm.)
Artist: H. Brosius
Lithographer:
Printer:
Publisher: J. J. Stoner, Madison, Wis.
Key/Vignettes/Misc: Refs. 1–67, A–H,
J–P, R–Y; 15 vignettes
Locations: LC–M; WHS–M; Racine
County Historical Museum, Racine,
Wisconsin
Catalogs/Checklists: LC–M, 1053; Maule

4429
Place: Reedsburg, Wisconsin
Date: 1874
Title: Bird's Eye View of Reedsburg, Sauk
County, Wis. 1874.
Size: 15 × 16½ in. (38.2 × 42 cm.)
Artist: [Albert Ruger]
Lithographer:
Printer: J. Knauber & Co. Print.
Milwaukee, Wis.
Publisher: J. J. Stoner, Madison, Wis.
Key/Vignettes/Misc: Refs. 1–13
Locations: LC–M; WHS–M (photo)
Catalogs/Checklists: LC–M, 1054; Maule

4430
Place: Richland Center, Wisconsin
Date: [1875]
Title: Bird's Eye View of Richland Center.
Richland County Wis.
Size: 13 × 20¹³⁄₁₆ in. (33 × 53 cm.)
Artist: H. Brosius
Lithographer:
Printer:
Publisher: J. J. Stoner, Madison, Wis.
Key/Vignettes/Misc:
Locations: WHS–M; Brewer Library,
Richland Center, Wisconsin; LC–M
(photo)
Catalogs/Checklists: Maule; LC–M,
1054.1

4431
Place: Ripon, Wisconsin
Date: 1867
Title: Bird's Eye View of the City of Ripon
Fond Du Lac Co. Wisconsin. 1867.
Size: 21 × 24 in. (53.5 × 61.1 cm.)
Artist: A. Ruger
Lithographer:
Printer: Chicago Lithographing Co. 152 &
154 Clark St. Chicago
Publisher:
Key/Vignettes/Misc: Refs. 1–15;
5 vignettes
Locations: LC–M; Ripon, Wisconsin,
Historical Society; WHS–M (photo)
Catalogs/Checklists: LC–M, 1055; Maule

4432
Place: Ripon, Wisconsin
Date: 1892

Title: Ripon, Wis. 1892
Size: 12½ × 22⅞ in. (31.8 × 58.2 cm.)
Artist: C. J. Pauli
Lithographer:
Printer:
Publisher: C. J. Pauli
Key/Vignettes/Misc:
Locations: Ripon Historical Society,
Ripon, Wisconsin
Catalogs/Checklists: Maule

4433
Place: River Falls, Wisconsin
Date: 1880
Title: Bird's Eye View of River Falls Pierce
County Wisconsin 1880.
Size: 14½ × 20 in. (36.3 × 51 cm.)
Artist:
Lithographer:
Printer: Beck & Pauli, Lith., Milwaukee,
Wis.
Publisher: J. J. Stoner, Madison, Wis.
Key/Vignettes/Misc: Refs. 1–32
Locations: University of Wisconsin–River
Falls Area Research Center, River Falls,
Wisconsin; WHS–M (photo)
Catalogs/Checklists: Maule

4434
Place: Sauk City, Wisconsin
Date: 1870
Title: Bird's Eye View of Sauk City. Sauk
County, Wisconsin 1870. Looking North
East.
Size: 15 × 18½ in. (38.2 × 47.1 cm.)
Artist: [Albert Ruger]
Lithographer:
Printer: Chicago Lithographing Co.
[Chicago]
Publisher: Ruger & Stoner, Madison, Wis.
Key/Vignettes/Misc: Refs. 1–6
Locations: LC–M; WHS–M; CHS–C
Catalogs/Checklists: LC–M; 1056; Maule

4435
Place: Sauk City, Wisconsin
Date: 1883
Title: Bird's Eye View of Sauk City, Wis.
1883.
Size: 9⁷⁄₁₆ × 18½ in. (24 × 47 cm.)
Artist:
Lithographer:
Printer: Beck & Pauli, Lithographers,
Milwaukee. Wis.
Publisher: J. J. Stoner, Madison, Wis.
Key/Vignettes/Misc:
Locations: WHS–M
Catalogs/Checklists: Maule

4436
Place: Sheboygan, Wisconsin
Date: 1885
Title: Sheboygan, Wis. County Seat of
Sheboygan Cty. 1885.
Size: 22½ × 31 in. (57.3 × 78.9 cm.)
Artist: H. Wellge
Lithographer:
Printer: Beck & Pauli, Lith. Milwaukee,
Wis.
Publisher: Norris, Wellge & Co. No. 107
Wells St. Milwaukee, Wis.
Key/Vignettes/Misc: Refs. 1–72;

1 vignette
Locations: LC–M; WHS–M
Catalogs/Checklists: LC–M, 1057; Maule

4437
Place: Sheboygan Falls, Wisconsin
Date: 1871
Title: Sheboygan Falls, Wis. 1871.
Size: 11 × 14¹⁵⁄₁₆ in. (28 × 38 cm.)
Artist: H. H. Bailey
Lithographer:
Printer: The Calvert Lith. Co. Detroit
Mich.
Publisher: Th. M. Fowler & Co. Box 668
Madison, Wis.
Key/Vignettes/Misc:
Locations: WHS–M; LC–M (photo)
Catalogs/Checklists: Maule; LC–M,
1057.2

4438
Place: Stevens Point, Wisconsin
Date: 1874
Title: Birds Eye View of City of Stevens
Point Portage County, Wi 1874
Size: 23½ × 33⅝ in. (59.8 × 85.6 cm.)
Artist: A. J. Cleveland
Lithographer:
Printer: American Oleograph Co.,
Milwaukee, Wi
Publisher:
Key/Vignettes/Misc: Refs. 1–32
Locations: City Hall, Stevens Point,
Wisconsin
Catalogs/Checklists: Maule

4439
Place: Stevens Point, Wisconsin
Date: 1891
Title: Stevens Point, Wis. 1891. Looking
East.
Size: 17 (cropped) × 35 in.
(43.3 × 89 cm.)
Artist: C. J. Pauli
Lithographer:
Printer:
Publisher: C. J. Pauli, 726 Central Ave.,
Milwaukee, Wis.
Key/Vignettes/Misc: 1 vignette
Locations: WHS–M
Catalogs/Checklists: Maule

4440
Place: Stoughton, Wisconsin
Date: 1871
Title: Stoughton, Wis. 1871.
Size: 10⅝ × 16⅛ in. (27 × 41 cm.)
Artist: H. H. Bailey
Lithographer:
Printer: Chicago Lithographing Co.
[Chicago]
Publisher:
Key/Vignettes/Misc: Refs. 1–11
Locations: WHS–M; LC–M (photo)
Catalogs/Checklists: Maule; LC–M,
1057.3

4441
Place: Stoughton, Wisconsin
Date: 1883
Title: Bird's Eye View of Stoughton, Wis.
1883.
Size: 9⁷⁄₁₆ × 21¼ in. (24 × 54 cm.)

Artist:
Lithographer:
Printer: Beck & Pauli, Lithographers,
Milwaukee, Wis.
Publisher: J. J. Stoner, Madison, Wis.
Key/Vignettes/Misc:
Locations: WHS–M; LC–M (photo)
Catalogs/Checklists: Maule; LC–M,
1057.4

4442
Place: Sun Prairie, Wisconsin
Date: [1875]
Title: Birds Eye View of Sun Prairie Dane
County Wisconsin
Size: 10¼ × 13 in. (26 × 33 cm.)
Artist: H. Brosius
Lithographer:
Printer:
Publisher: J. J. Stoner, Madison, Wis.
Key/Vignettes/Misc:
Locations: WHS–M; LC–M (photo)
Catalogs/Checklists: Maule; LC–M,
1057.5

4443
Place: Superior, Wisconsin
Date: 1856
Title: City of Superior, Wisconsin, Novr.
1856.
Size: 17⁷⁄₁₆ × 23¹⁄₁₆ in. (44.3 × 58.6 cm.)
Artist: J. Bachmann
Lithographer:
Printer: P. S. Duval & Son, Phila.
Publisher: James S. Ritchie, Pennsylvania
(copyright)
Key/Vignettes/Misc:
Locations: MM–NN; CHS–C; LC–P
Catalogs/Checklists: MM–NN, LP 4074

4444
Place: Superior, Wisconsin
Date: 1883
Title: Bird's Eye View of Superior, Wis.
County Seat of Douglas County. 1883.
Size: 13 × 31½ in. (33.1 × 80.1 cm.)
Artist: H. Wellge
Lithographer:
Printer: Beck & Pauli, Lithographers,
Milwaukee, Wis.
Publisher: J. J. Stoner, Madison, Wis.
Key/Vignettes/Misc: Refs. 1–23, A–P,
R–Z, XX, XXX; 11 vignettes
Locations: LC–M; WHS–M (photo)
Catalogs/Checklists: LC–M, 1058; Maule

4445
Place: Superior, Wisconsin
Date: 1893
Title: Bird's Eye View of Superior 1893
Size: 8 × 10⅝ in. (20 × 27 cm.)
Artist: Charles Lagre
Lithographer:
Printer:
Publisher: Charles Lagre
Key/Vignettes/Misc:
Locations: WHS–M; LC–M (photo)
Catalogs/Checklists: Maule; LC–M,
1058.1

4446
Place: Superior, Wisconsin
Date: 1910

Title: The Twin Ports—Superior,
Wisconsin and Duluth, Minnesota
Size: 13¾ × 35⅝ in. (35 × 90.6 cm.)
Artist: H. Wellge
Lithographer:
Printer:
Publisher: C. E. Wales, Minneapolis, 1910
and Northern Scenic Publishing Co.,
Duluth-Superior
Key/Vignettes/Misc:
Locations: MM–NN
Catalogs/Checklists: MM–NN, LP 1247

4447
Place: Superior, Wisconsin
Date: 1913
Title: Bird's Eye View Superior, Wisconsin,
"The New Steel Center" 1913
Size: 21 × 27½ in. (53.5 × 70 cm.)
Artist:
Lithographer:
Printer: Bureau of Engraving, Minneapolis
Publisher: Bradley-Brink Co.
Key/Vignettes/Misc:
Locations: LC–M; WHS–M
Catalogs/Checklists: LC–M, 1059; Maule

4448
Place: Superior, Wisconsin
Date: 1915
Title: The Twin Ports
Size: 16½ × 35½ in. (42 × 90.4 cm.)
Artist: H. Wellge. Rev. 1915—Russell
Lithographer:
Printer: Freeman Eng. Co., Minneapolis
Publisher: Northern Scenic Publishing
Company (copyright)
Key/Vignettes/Misc:
Locations: LC–M
Catalogs/Checklists: LC–M, 1060; Maule

4449
Place: Tomah, Wisconsin
Date: 1870
Title: Tomah, Wis. 1870.
Size: 10¼ × 16⅛ in. (26 × 41 cm.)
Artist: H. H. Bailey
Lithographer:
Printer: Doniat & Zastrow, Milwaukee
Publisher:
Key/Vignettes/Misc:
Locations: WHS–M; LC–M (photo)
Catalogs/Checklists: Maule; LC–M,
1060.1

4450
Place: Two Rivers, Wisconsin
Date: 1879
Title: View of the City of Two Rivers, Wis.
1879.
Size: 14³⁄₁₆ × 19 in. (36.1 × 48.4 cm.)
Artist: H. Wellge & J. Bach
Lithographer:
Printer: Beck & Pauli, Milwaukee, Wis.
Publisher: H. Wellge & J. Bach,
Milwaukee
Key/Vignettes/Misc: A–F, 1–5, I–VII
Locations: WHS–M; Two Rivers
Historical Society, Two Rivers, Wisconsin
Catalogs/Checklists: Maule

4451
Place: Viroqua, Wisconsin
Date: 1879
Title: Bird's Eye View of Viroqua, C. S. of
Vernon Co. Wis. 1879
Size: 8¼ × 13⅜ in. (21 × 34 cm.)
Artist:
Lithographer:
Printer: Beck & Pauli Lith. Milwaukee,
Wis.
Publisher: J. J. Stoner, Madison, Wis.
Key/Vignettes/Misc: Refs. 1–14
Locations: WHS–M; LC–M (photo)
Catalogs/Checklists: Maule; LC–M,
1060.2

4452
Place: Washburn, Wisconsin
Date: 1886
Title: Birds Eye View of Washburn, Wis.
Bayfield, County. 1886
Size: 16 × 20½ in. (40.7 × 52.2 cm.)
Artist:
Lithographer:
Printer: Beck & Pauli, Litho. Milwaukee,
Wis.
Publisher: Norris, Wellge & Co. No. 205
Second St. Milwaukee, Wis.
Key/Vignettes/Misc: Refs. 1–25, A–G, K,
M, P; 1 vignette
Locations: LC–M; WHS–M (photo)
Catalogs/Checklists: LC–M, 1061; Maule

4453
Place: Washburn, Wisconsin
Date: 1896
Title: Washburn, Wis. 1896.
Size: 14½ × 21⅝ in. (37 × 55 cm.)
Artist: L. H. Ruggles
Lithographer:
Printer:
Publisher: L. H. Ruggles
Key/Vignettes/Misc: 20 vignettes
Locations: WHS–M (photo); Washburn,
Wisconsin, Public Library
Catalog/Checklists: Maule

4454
Place: Washburn, Wisconsin
Date: [191-]
Title: Birds-Eye View City of Washburn,
Wisconsin.
Size: 15½ × 23 in. (39.4 × 58.5 cm.)
Artist: Gene Ford
Lithographer:
Printer:
Publisher:
Key/Vignettes/Misc:
Locations: WHS–M (photo); Washburn,
Wisconsin, Public Library
Catalogs/Checklists: Maule

4455
Place: Waterloo, Wisconsin
Date: [1875]
Title: Bird's Eye View of Waterloo
Jefferson County Wisconsin.
Size: 13⅜ × 20⁷⁄₁₆ in. (34 × 52 cm.)
Artist: H. Brosius
Lithographer:
Printer:

Publisher: J. J. Stoner, Madison, Wis.
Key/Vignettes/Misc:
Locations: WHS–M; LC–M (photo)
Catalogs/Checklists: Maule; LC–M,
1061.1

4456
Place: Watertown, Wisconsin
Date: Ca. 1857
Title: Watertown, Wis From Milwaukee &
Western R. R. Bridge
Size: 16 × 22 in. (40.7 × 56 cm.)
Artist: Louis Kurz
Lithographer:
Printer: Louis Kurz & Co.
Publisher: William Wolff
Key/Vignettes/Misc:
Locations: BM–NY; YUAG–NH
Catalogs/Checklists:

4457
Place: Watertown, Wisconsin
Date: 1867
Title: Watertown, Jefferson Co.,
Wisconsin. 1867.
Size: 22½ × 28½ in. (57.3 × 72.5 cm.)
Artist: A. Ruger
Lithographer:
Printer: Chicago Lithographing Co. 152 &
154 Clark St. Chicago
Publisher:
Key/Vignettes/Misc: Refs. 1–16
Locations: LC–M; Octagon House,
Watertown, Wisconsin; WHS–M (photo)
Catalogs/Checklists: LC–M, 1062; Maule

4458
Place: Watertown, Wisconsin
Date: 1876?
Title:
Size:
Artist: C. J. Pauli
Lithographer:
Printer:
Publisher:
Key/Vignettes/Misc:
Locations: Unknown
Catalogs/Checklists: Beckman, note for
exhibit item 25

4459
Place: Watertown, Wisconsin
Date: 1885
Title: The City of Watertown, Wis. Dodge
& Jefferson Counties 1885.
Size: 23 × 31½ in. (58.6 × 80.1 cm.)
Artist:
Lithographer:
Printer: Beck & Pauli, Litho. Milwaukee,
Wis.
Publisher: Norris, Wellge & Co. 107 Wells
St. Milwaukee
Key/Vignettes/Misc: Refs. 1–58;
1 vignette
Locations: LC–M; Octagon House,
Watertown, Wisconsin; WHS–M (photo)
Catalogs/Checklists: LC–M, 1063; Maule

4460
Place: Waukesha, Wisconsin
Date: [1861–62]
Title: Waukesha, Wisconsin

Size: 16 × 22⅛ in. (40.1 × 56.2 cm.)
Artist: L. Kurz
Lithographer:
Printer: Kurz & Seifert, Milwaukee
Publisher: Kurz & Seifert, Milwaukee
Key/Vignettes/Misc:
Locations: LC–P
Catalogs/Checklists:

4461
Place: Waukesha, Wisconsin
Date: 1874
Title: Bird's Eye View of Waukesha
Waukesha County Wisconsin 1874.
Looking South West
Size: 19¹³⁄₁₆ × 24⁵⁄₁₆ in. (47.9 × 61.9 cm.)
Artist:
Lithographer:
Printer:
Publisher: J. J. Stoner, Madison, Wis.
Key/Vignettes/Misc: Refs. 1–29; A–H;
3 vignettes
Locations: BPL–R; WHS–M; WCM–W;
Waukesha, Wisconsin, Public Library;
LC–M (photo)
Catalogs/Checklists: Maule; LC–M,
1063.2

4462
Place: Waukesha, Wisconsin
Date: 1880
Title: Bird's Eye View of Waukesha, C. S.
of Waukesha Co. Wis. 1880
Size: 20 × 26 in. (50.9 × 66.2 cm.)
Artist: H. Wellge
Lithographer:
Printer: Beck & Pauli Lith. Milwaukee,
Wis.
Publisher: J. J. Stoner, Madison, Wis.
Key/Vignettes/Misc: Refs. 1–10, 12–32,
A–H, J–K
Locations: LC–M; WHS–M; WCM–W
Catalogs/Checklists: LC–M, 1064; Maule

4463
Place: Waukesha, Wisconsin
Date: 1880
Title: Waukesha, Wis. 1880
Size: 16⅞ × 21⁹⁄₁₆ in. (43 × 55 cm.)
Artist:
Lithograher:
Printer: J. Knauber & Co. Lith.
Milwaukee
Publisher:
Key/Vignettes/Misc: 1 vignette
Locations: WCM–W; WHS–M (photo)
Catalogs/Checklists: Maule

4464
Place: Waukesha, Wisconsin
Date: 1887
Title: Waukesha, Wis. County Seat of
Waukesha County, 1887.
Size: 14¹⁵⁄₁₆ × 25¹⁵⁄₁₆ in. (38 × 66 cm.)
Artist: H. Wellge
Lithographer:
Printer: J. Knauber & Co. Lith.
Milwaukee
Publisher: Henry Wellge & Co. Cor. Wells
& Second St. Milwaukee, Wis.
Key/Vignettes/Misc: 4 vignettes
Locations: WCM–W; WHS–M (photo)
Catalogs/Checklists: Maule

Place: Waukesha, Wisconsin
Date: [1890?]
See Oconomowoc, Wisconsin, [1890?]

4465
Place: Waukesha, Wisconsin
Date: [189–?]
Title: The Lake Region of Waukesha
County, Wisconsin. Looking North from
Government Hill.
Size: 11 × 27½ in. (28 × 70 cm.)
Artist:
Lithographer:
Printer:
Publisher: Marr & Richards Eng. Co.,
Milwaukee
Key/Vignettes/Misc: WHS–M
Locations: WHS–M
Catalogs/Checklists: Maule

4466
Place: Waupaca, Wisconsin
Date: 1871
Title: Waupaca, Wis. 1871.
Size: 12³⁄₁₆ × 17¼ in. (31 × 44 cm.)
Artist: H. H. Bailey
Lithographer:
Printer: Chicago Lithographing Co.
[Chicago]
Publisher: Th. M. Fowler & Co. Box 668,
Madison, Wis.
Key/Vignettes/Misc: Refs. 1–10
Locations: WHS–M; LC–M (photo)
Catalogs/Checklists: Maule; LC–M,
1064.1

4467
Place: Waupun, Wisconsin
Date: 1870
Title: Waupun, Wis. 1870
Size: 10¼ × 16⅛ in. (26 × 41 cm.)
Artist: H. H. Bailey
Lithographer:
Printer: Chicago Lithographing Co.
[Chicago]
Publisher:
Key/Vignettes/Misc: Refs. 1–12
Locations: WHS–M; LC–M (photo)
Catalogs/Checklists: Maule; LC–M,
1064.2

4468
Place: Waupun, Wisconsin
Date: 1885
Title: View of the City of Waupun, Wis.
Situated in Fond du Lac & Dodge
Counties. 1885.
Size: 15¾ × 24⅜ in. (40 × 62 cm.)
Artist: H. Wellge
Lithographer:
Printer: Beck & Pauli, Litho. Milwaukee,
Wis.
Publisher: Norris, Wellge & Co. No. 107
Wells St. Milwaukee, Wis.
Key/Vignettes/Misc: 1–36; 2 vignettes
Locations: WHS–M; LC–M
Catalogs/Checklists: Maule; LC–M,
1064.3

4469
Place: Wausau, Wisconsin
Date: 1879
Title: Bird's Eye View of the City of

Wausau, Wis. County
Seat of Marathon Co. 1879.
Size: 12³⁄₁₆ × 20 in. (31 × 51 cm.)
Artist:
Lithographer:
Printer:
Publisher:
Key/Vignettes/Misc: Refs. 1–33
Locations: WHS–M; MCHS–W
Catalogs/Checklists: Maule

4470
Place: Wausau, Wisconsin
Date: 1891
Title: Wausaw, Wis. 1891. Looking North.
Size: 20 × 35⅜ in. (51 × 90 cm.)
Artist: C. J. Pauli
Lithographer:
Printer:
Publisher: C. J. Pauli, 726 Central Ave.,
Milwaukee, Wis.
Key/Vignettes/Misc: Refs. 1–90
Locations: WHS–M; MCHS–W; LC–M
(photo)
Catalogs/Checklists: Maule; LC–M,
1064.4

4471
Place: Wauwatosa, Wisconsin
Date: 1892
Title: Looking East from Wauwatosa.
Wauwatosa and the Western Suburbs of
Milwaukee. Mean Elevation Above Lake
Michigan 180 feet. 1892.
Size: 16½ × 29¹⁄₁₆ in. (42 × 74 cm.)
Artist:
Lithographer:
Printer:
Publisher: Marr & Richards Engraving
Co.
Key/Vignettes/Misc: Refs. 1–10, A–L;
1 vignette
Locations: LC–M; Milwaukee, Wisconsin,
Public Library; WHS–M (photo)
Catalogs/Checklists: LC–M, 1065; Maule

4472
Place: West Bend, Wisconsin
Date: 1878
Title: West Bend. Washington Co. Wis.
1878. Looking to the North West.
Size: 10⅝ × 19¼ in. (27 × 49 cm.)
Artist:
Lithographer:
Printer:
Publisher:
Key/Vignettes/Misc: Refs. 1–22, A–G
Locations: WHS–M (photo); LC–M
(photo)
Catalogs/Checklists: Maule; LC–M,
1065.1

4473
Place: West Bend, Wisconsin
Date: 1892
Title: West Bend, Wis. 1892. Looking
West.
Size: 10⅝ × 19¼ in. (27 × 49 cm.)
Artist: C. J. Pauli
Lithographer:
Printer:
Publisher:
Key/Vignettes/Misc:

Locations: WHS–M (facsimile)
Catalogs/Checklists: Maule

4474
Place: West Superior, Wisconsin
Date: 1887
Title: Perspective Map of West Superior, Wis. 1887
Size: 18 × 21½ in. (45.8 × 54.7 cm.)
Artist: Henry Wellge & Co.
Lithographer:
Printer:
Publisher: A. L. Langellier (copyright)
Key/Vignettes/Misc:
Locations: LC–M; WHS–M (photo)
Catalogs/Checklists: LC–M, 1066; Maule

4475
Place: Weyauwega, Wisconsin
Date: 1870
Title: Weyauga, Wis. 1870.
Size: 10¼ × 12¹⁵⁄₁₆ in. (26 × 33 cm.)
Artist: H. H. Bailey
Lithographer:
Printer: Doniat & Zastrow, Milwaukee
Publisher:
Key/Vignettes/Misc: Refs. 1–8
Locations: WHS–M; Little Red Schoolhouse Museum, Weyauwega, Wisconsin; LC–M (photo)
Catalogs/Checklists: Maule; LC–M, 1066.1

4476
Place: Whitewater, Wisconsin
Date: 1870
Title: Bird's Eye View of the City of Whitewater Walworth County Wisconsin 1870
Size: 17¹¹⁄₁₆ × 23⁹⁄₁₆ in. (45 × 60 cm.)
Artist:

Lithographer:
Printer: Merchant's Lith. Co., Chicago
Publisher: Ruger & Stoner
Key/Vignettes/Misc:
Locations: WHS–M; BECH–B; LC–M (photo)
Catalogs/Checklists: Maule; LC–M, 1066.2

4477
Place: Whitewater, Wisconsin
Date: 1885
Title: View of the City of Whitewater, Wis. Walworth-County. 1885.
Size: 19½ × 31 in. (49.6 × 78.9 cm.)
Artist:
Lithographer:
Printer: Beck & Pauli, Litho. Milwaukee, Wis.
Publisher: Norris, Wellge & Co. No. 107 Wells St. Milwaukee, Wis.
Key/Vignettes/Misc: Refs. 1–37; 3 vignettes
Locations: LC–M; Whitewater, Wisconsin, Public Library; Whitewater Historical Society, Whitewater, Wisconsin; WHS–M (photo)
Catalogs/Checklists: LC–M, 1067; Maule

4478
Place: Cheyenne, Wyoming
Date: 1870
Title: Bird's Eye View of Cheyenne Laramie County, Wyoming Territory. Looking North West
Size: 16 × 22½ in. (40.1 × 57.1 cm.)
Artist: Augustus Koch
Lithographer:
Printer: Chicago Lithographing Co. [Chicago]
Publisher:

Key/Vignettes/Misc: Refs. 1–19
Locations: Wyoming State Archives, Museums and Historical Dept., Cheyenne, Wyoming
Catalogs/Checklists: Reps, Cities on Stone, p. 92

4479
Place: Cheyenne, Wyoming
Date: 1882
Title: Bird's Eye View of Cheyenne, Wyo. County Seat of Laramie Co. 1882.
Size: 10¹¹⁄₁₆ × 19 in. (27.2 × 48.2 cm.)
Artist:
Lithographer:
Printer: Beck & Pauli, Lithographers, Milwaukee, Wis.
Publisher: J. J. Stoner, Madison, Wis.
Key/Vignettes/Misc: Refs. A–G, 2–19; 5 vignettes; unnumbered business directory
Locations: LC–M; Wyoming State Archives, Museums and Historical Dept., Cheyenne, Wyoming; LC–P
Catalogs/Checklists: LC–M, 1068; Reps, Cities on Stone, p. 92

4480
Place: Green River, Wyoming
Date: [1875?]
Title: View of Green River, Wyoming Territory. (Looking North.)
Size: 16½ × 21 in. (42 × 53.4 cm.)
Artist: E. S. Glover
Lithographer:
Printer: Chas. Shober & Co. Props Chicago Litho Co. [Chicago]
Publisher:
Key/Vignettes/Misc:
Locations: NYP-P
Catalogs/Checklists:

Acknowledgments

A complete listing of the persons who helped me with this study and a summary of their contributions would result in a statement of enormous length. Hundreds of curators, archivists, and librarians responded to my initial questionnaires concerning their holdings of lithographic city views, and many of them provided additional information in replying to my further queries. I regret that it is impossible to name them all, for my gratitude for their assistance is profound.

Curators of many museums, libraries, and historical societies with unusually rich resources of city views were particularly helpful in allowing me to search their collections, to make photographs of some of the prints, or in providing me with full cataloging data for large numbers of lithographs. In New York State these curators include Wendy Shadwell, The New-York Historical Society; John L. Scherer, New York State Museum; James Corsaro, New York State Library; and A. K. Baragwanath and Steve Miller, Museum of The City of New York.

In California they include Lawrence Dinnean, Bancroft Library, University of California, Berkeley; Joseph A. Baird, Jr., North Point Gallery, San Francisco; June Whitesides, California Historical Society, San Francisco; William M. Mason, Los Angeles County Museum of Natural History; the staff of the Henry E. Huntington Library; and Warren Howell, San Francisco.

Curators of collections in Massachusetts who provided similar assistance include Laura V. Monti, Boston Public Library; Bettina A. Norton, Essex Institute; Georgia B. Bumgardner, American Antiquarian Society; and Sally Pierce, Library of the Boston Athenaeum. Elsewhere I was extended the same courtesies by Richard Field, Yale University Art Gallery; Larry A. Viskochil, Chicago Historical Society; John A. Mahe II, The Historic New Orleans Collection; Judith Ciampoli, Missouri Historical Society; Robert D. Monroe, University of Washington Libraries; Alan D. Frazer, New Jersey Historical Society; Elizabeth Winroth, Oregon Historical Society; and Frank L. Green, Washington State Historical Society.

Bernard Reilly, Curator of Historical Prints, Division of Prints and Photographs, Library of Congress, provided me with complete cataloging information for all of the lithographic city views under his jurisdiction. In the Division of Geography and Maps of the Library of Congress, Patrick E. Dempsey furnished valuable information on several occasions and made it possible for me to include as part of my catalog entries the reference numbers to the revised checklist of the Division's holdings. Kathy Heavey checked scores of my incomplete entries against the originals or copies in the Division of Geography and Maps. I am deeply in debt to all three for their aid.

At the Public Archives of Canada, Edward H. Dahl and Louis Cardinal in the National Map Collection and James Burant in the Picture Division offered expert assistance during my visit and continued to provide information in answer to my further queries. In addition to those many Canadians who kindly responded to questionnaires by sending me cataloging data about one or a few prints, several others provided major help that required them to spend substantial amounts of time on my behalf. They include Gary Tynski, McGill University; Conrad Graham, McCord Museum; Scott Robson, Nova Scotia Museum; John Crosthwait, Metropolitan Toronto Library Board; William R. MacKinnon, New Brunswick Provincial Archives; Geoff Castle, British Columbia Provincial Archives; Frances Woodward, University of British Columbia; Margaret Campbell, Public Archives of Nova Scotia; and Mary Allodi, Royal Ontario Museum. Peter Winkworth's help was also invaluable.

My decision not to visit and search certain collections was based in large part on the thoroughness and accuracy with which many persons reported their holdings to me, providing such detail that I was able to prepare full catalog entries in Ithaca. They include Eleanor M. Gehres, Denver Public Library; Kristin Woodbridge, Connecticut State Library; Melancthon W. Jacobus, Connecticut Historical Society; Edward F. Heite, Delaware Hall of Records; Janice Petterchak, Illinois State Historical Library; Carol Hunt, Putnam Museum; Diana Fox, Iowa State Historical Department; Jill M. Christopherson and Nancy Erickson, Minnesota Historical Society; Charles A. Isetts, Ohio Historical Society; Donna-Belle Garvin, New Hampshire Historical Society; Bonnie Gardner, South Dakota Historical Resource Center; Marsha Peters, Rhode Island Historical Society; Martin Schmitt, University of Oregon Library; Frances Rodgers, Barker Texas History Center, University of Texas, Austin; Carroll Guitar, Shelburne Museum; John Buechler, University of Vermont Library; Laura P. Abbott, Vermont Historical Society; Lawrence L. Dodd, Whitman College Library; Ellen J. Hassig, West Virginia Archives and History Division; Ronald L. Becker, Rutgers University Library; and Michael J. Fox, State Historical Society of Wisconsin.

John C. O'Connor and Ralph M. Yeager of State College, Pennsylvania, were good enough to supply information about several prints listed in the splendid catalog of their unrivaled collection of Pennsylvania town views. Kenneth Newman, proprietor of The Old Print Shop in New York City, generously allowed me to search his extensive file of negatives used for illustrations in the sales catalogs issued by his shop.

For their help in Syracuse on some of the New York viewmakers I thank Richard N. Wright of the Onondaga Historical Association and Todd S. Weseloh of the Canal Museum.

James Raymond Warren, Sr., sent me interesting material on T. M. Fowler and the Bailey brothers. I acknowledge also the aid of Ronnie C. Tyler, Amon Carter Museum; Elizabeth Roth, New York Public Library; Richard Stephenson and his colleagues in the Reference Section, Division of Geography and Maps, Library of Congress; and Barbara Berthelsen, Map Librarian, and virtually every person who occupied a seat for even a fleeting moment at the Reference Department of Olin Library, Cornell University.

Other persons carrying out research on the city views of their states have been generous in sharing their findings with me. For their cooperation in this joint enterprise I am indebted to John Cumming, Central Michigan University Library; Christine Bauer Podmaniczky, William A. Farnsworth Library and Art Museum; Robert Karrow, Newberry Library; David Ruell, Ashland, New Hampshire; Ron Rayman, Western Illinois University Library; Karen S. Pearson and Helen Brooks, formerly of Lincoln, Nebraska; and especially Thomas Beckman, Milwaukee Art Center.

Over a period of several years many students in the graduate programs of the College of Architecture, Art, and Planning at Cornell participated in one way or another in the search for and the recording of the views listed in the catalog. I owe all of them my thanks, and only the fear that my listing might omit one or more prevents me from identifying them by name.

In 1982 Catherine Bauman and Susan Jones prepared maps for about fifty viewmakers to show the locations of all places depicted by them in their lithographic views for each year the artist or publisher was active. Charles Uhl's master's thesis on the accuracy of several views proved a major contribution to my work and saved me the time and trouble that would have been required to carry out my own studies on the subject.

Dan Bartholomew modified an existing computer program to make it possible for entries to be searched, displayed, and printed in a variety of ways. His work turned out to be far more time-consuming than had been anticipated. He has my thanks for performing a task not made easier by my lack of knowledge of computer programming. I am also indebted to Paul Brandford for his help in dealing with budget problems arising from the use of more computer time than had been requested in the original grant proposal.

I am especially grateful to Mimi Bussan, who developed the computer data base from my records and who provided me with printouts when I needed them. Her contribution went far beyond these routine tasks, for she offered countless suggestions about ways in which data might be analyzed, and she called my attention to numerous inconsistencies, errors, and anomalies in my entries. No stranger to computers could have had a more cheerful, informative, and unfailingly helpful guide.

Beverly Buckley typed the manuscript with speed, skill, and unusual care. Helena Wood kept track of my expenditures from her office at the Program in Urban and Regional Studies at Cornell, and several other members of the support staff of my Department of City and Regional Planning helped in other ways. To them all I owe my thanks.

Whatever errors and shortcomings remain in this study are my own.

J. W. R.
Ithaca, N.Y.
1983

Index

association with Henry Wellge, 193–94, 213–14; 1884 view of Lebanon, N.H., 3, **96**; 1887 view of Antrim, N.H., 70; mentioned, 6, 15, 65. See also Poole & Norris

Norris, Wellge & Co., 54, 194, 215; view published by, **141**

Norris, Wellge, & Swift, 215

Northern Lith. Co., 170

Norwich, Conn.: 1849 view of, 189

Novato Rancho, Calif.: undated view of, 173

O

O. H. Bailey & Co., 163, 171. See also Bailey, Oakley Hoopes

Oberlin, Ohio: 1868 view of, 41, 68, 203

Oconomowoc, Wisc.: 1870 view of, 161, 175

Ogdensburg, N.Y.: 1860 view of, 192

Olympia, Wash.: 1879 view of, 180

Omaha, Nebr.: 1868 view of, 4, 56, **98**, 202

Omro, Wisc.: 1870 view of, 175

Oneida, N.Y.: 1874 view of, 164

Osborne, J. W.: lithographic camera developed by, **36**

Otis, Bass, 24–26; lithograph by, **25**

Otis, Fessenden Nott, 196, 198

Otto Krebs Lith.: view published by, xi

P

Painesville, Ohio: 1871 view of, 204

Painted Post, N.Y.: 1850 view of, 213

Palmatary, James T.: as business agent for Edwin Whitefield, 40, 194, 196, 215; association with Charles Parsons, 194, 196; biographical information on, 194–96; employed by E. Sachse & Co., 195–96, 204–5; 1852 view of Washington, D.C., 204; 1853 view of Baltimore, Md., 195, 204; 1854 view of Alexandria, Va., 204; 1854 view of Chillicothe, Ohio, 59, 195; 1854 views of Columbus and Dayton, Ohio, 195; 1854 view of Indianapolis, Indiana, **106**, 195; ca. 1854 view of Madison, Ind., 195, 196; 1854–1855 views of Wheeling, W.Va., and Zanesville, Ohio, 195; 1855 view of Louisville, Ky., 195; ca. 1855 view of Portsmouth, Ohio, 59, 63, **148**, 195; 1856 view of Milwaukee, Wisc., 62, 196; 1857 view of Chicago, Ill., 48, 195; 1858 view of St. Louis, Mo., 195; sketches for 1868 view of Syracuse, N.Y., 195, 208; undated views of Sandusky, Ohio, 195, 196; mentioned, 6, 206

Palmyra, N.Y.: 1880 view of, 168

Parsons & Atwater, 196–98; 1876 view of New York, N.Y., x. See also Atwater, Lyman W.; Parsons, Charles R.

Parsons, Charles: as artist and lithographer for the Smith brothers, 64, 196, 207; association with James T. Palmatary, 194, 196; as apprentice to George Endicott, 196; as lithographer of works by J. W. Hill and George Robertson, **148**, 196; as lithographer for Currier & Ives, 196; biographical information on, 196–98; 1851 view of Rome, N.Y., 196; 1853 view of Lancaster, Pa., 194, 196; 1854 view of Portsmouth, N.H., 196; mentioned, 21, 183, 184, 208

Parsons, Charles R.: biographical information on, 196–98; association with Lyman W. Atwater, 196–98; as lithographer for Currier & Ives, 196–98; 1874 view of Newark, N.J., 197; 1878 view of San Francisco, Calif., 197; 1879 view of Brooklyn, N.Y., 197; 1880 view of Baltimore, Md., 197; 1880 view of Washington, D.C., 21, **126**, 197; 1892 view of Washington, D.C., 197. See also Parsons & Atwater

Patchen, W. R.: as agent for Joseph John Stoner, 41, 52

Pauli, Clemens J.: possible association with Lucien Rinaldo Burleigh, 168, 198; possible association with Augustus Hageboeck, 181, 198; association with Adam Beck, 198; association with Joseph John Stoner, 198; association with Henry Wellge, 198; probable association with C. H. Vogt, 198; biographical information on, 198–99; 1876 view of Burlington, Wisc., 198; 1876 view of Milwaukee, Wisc., 20, 198, 199; 1890 view of Lansing, Mich., 61, 65, 68; 1891 views of Mobile, Ala., and Vicksburg, Miss., 198; 1892 view of Milwaukee, Wisc., 198; mentioned, 8, 15, 20, 167. See also Beck & Pauli

Pawtucket, R.I.: 1877 view of, **112**

Peale, Rembrandt, 212

Pease, ———, 41

Pendleton, John, 27, 28

Pendleton, William: employed Fitz Hugh Lane, 189; employed Henry Walton, 212; mentioned, 27, 213

Pendleton's Lithography: view printed by, **101**

Penn Yan, N.Y.: 1874 view of, 163, 177

Peoria, Ill.: 1872 view of, 165

Philadelphia, Pa.: 1837–1838 views of, 48–50, 51, 52, 216; 1842 view of, 186; 1850 views of, 45, 62, **108**, 160, 183, 206, 215; 1856 view of, 187; 1857 view of, 190; 1875 view of, 197

Philadelphia Publishing House, 170

Phoenix, Ariz.: 1885 view of, xvi, 167, 172; 1890 view of, 173

Photographic techniques: the development of and their effects on lithography, 23

Photolithography: development of, 35–38; types of cameras used for, 36; commercial use of, 37; extent used, 37–38

Pictou, N.S.: 1878 view of, 41, 210

Pierce, Bruce W.: association with William Wallace Elliott, 173, 174, 199; biographical information on, 199; 1886 view of Red Bluff, Calif., 199; 1888 view of Los Angeles, Calif., 199; 1890 view of Portland, Ore., 199; 1893 view of Pasadena, Calif., 199; 1893 view of San Pedro, Calif., **111**, 199; 1894 view of Los Angeles, Calif., 199; mentioned, 6

Pittsburgh, Pa.: 1849 view of, 60, 206; 1850 view of, 206, 208; 1874 view of, xi

Pittsfield, N.H.: 1884 view of, 52, **140**

Plymouth, N.H.: 1883 view of, 42, 52, 62

Pollard, C. J., 188. See also Britton & Pollard

Pomona, Calif.: 1886 view of, 173

Poole, Albert F.: methods of seeking subscribers, 42, 52; association with George E. Norris, 193, 200; biographical information on, 199–200; use of gravure process in printing views, 200; association with Henry Wellge, 200, 211, 213, 215; association with Joseph John Stoner, 211; 1880 view of Bar Harbor, Maine, 200; 1881 view of Holyoke, Mass., 3, **97**; 1882 view of Brockton, Mass., 200; 1882 view of Lake Geneva, Wisc., 200, 215; 1883 view of Plymouth, N.H., 62; mentioned, 15, 38

Port Arthur, Ont.: 1885 view of, 53

Port Arthur, Tex.: 1912 view of, 180

Port Jervis, N.Y.: 1874 view of, 163

Port Townsend, Wash.: 1878 view of, 180

Portland, Maine: 1849 view of, 206; 1855 view of, 184, 196; 1876 view of, 212

Portland, Ore.: 1855 view of, 187; 1879 view of, 51, 180; 1890 view of, 199

Portsmouth, N.H.: 1854 view of, 96, 207; 1877 view of, 52

Portsmouth, Ohio: ca. 1855 view of, 59, 63, **148**, 195

Potsdam, N.Y.: 1885 view of, **116**

Pottsville, Pa.: ca. 1855 view of, 187

Poughkeepsie, N.Y.: 1874 view of, 55, 161

Prang, Louis: 35, 160; view published by, ix

Prescott, Ariz.: 1891 view of, 167; undated view of, 172

Preston, Minn.: 1874 view of, 192

Providence, Pa.: 1892 view of, 54

Providence, R. I.: 1849 view of, 40, 51, 64

Q

Quanah, Tex.: 1890 view of, 19, 21, 22, **120**, **131**

Quartzburg, Idaho: 1880 view of, 209

Quebec, Quebec: 1832 view of, 209; 1852 view of, 194

Quincy, Mass.: 1877 view of, 18, **119**, 215

R

R. Hoe & Co.: presses manufactured by, 33, **34**. See also Hoe, Richard

Railroads: as sponsors of city views, 56

Raleigh, N.C.: 1872 view of, 20, **126**, 172

Rau & Son: view printed by, **127**

Red Bluff, Calif.: 1866 view of, 199

Redlands, Calif.: 1880s view of, 192

Redwood, Calif.: 1891 view of, 192

Rey, Joseph, 188. See also Britton & Rey

Richmond, Ind.: 1884 view of, 171

Richmond, Va.: 1851 view of, 204; 1853 view of, 183

Richmond, W. D., 35

Ritz, Philip: view published by, **127**

Robertson, George James: 1853 view of Chicago, Ill., **145**; 1854 view of Milwaukee, Wisc., **100**; mentioned, 4, 196, 207

Robinson & Snow: view published by, **129**

Robyn, Charles, 200

Robyn, Edward: biographical information on, 200–201; 1853 view of St. Louis, Mo., 200; ca. 1860 views of Hermann and Washington, Mo., 200; ca. 1860 views of Carondelet and Jefferson City, Mo., 201

Rochester, Minn.: 1868 view of, 174

Rochester, N.H.: 1877 view of, 52

Rochester, N.Y.: 1847 view of, 59, 61; 1853 view of, 183, 184; 1880 view of, 168

Rock Island, Ill.: ca. 1874 view of, 181

Rocky Bar, Idaho: 1880 view of, 209

Rogers, ———, 190

Rome, N.Y.: 1851 view of, 196

Rosenthal, L. N., 35

Rowley, H. H.: as employer of Lucien Rinaldo Burleigh, 168, 201; biographical information on, 201; as owner of H. H. Rowley Company, 201. See also H. H. Rowley & Co.

Ruger & Stoner, 210. See also Ruger, Albert; Stoner, Joseph John

Ruger, Albert: use of agents, 41; speed of production, 45, 46; pricing of views, 51; income of, 58; newspaper publicity for, 61; association with Thaddeus Mortimer Fowler, 164, 202–3, 204, 211; association with Eli Sheldon Glover, 175, 178, 202, 203, 210; association with Joseph John Stoner, 180, 202, 203, 210; possible association with Augustus Koch, 184, 202, 203; possible association with D. D. Morse, 193, 203; biographical information on, 201–4; association with Joseph Warner, 202, 210; possible association with Herman Brosius, 202, 203; possible association with Camille N. Drie, 202, 203; use of Lucien Rinaldo Burleigh as printer, 203; unsigned views attributed to, 204; 1866 views of Adrian, Ann Arbor, Battle Creek, Hillsdale, Marshall, and Monroe, Mich., and

Index to the Catalog

(All numbers refer to catalog entries rather than pages.)